The New York Times
JUMBO SUNDAY
CROSSWORD PUZZLE BOOK

The two questions most frequently asked a puzzle editor are:

1. How long should it take to solve one of those large Sunday puzzles?

2. Is it cricket to use dictionaries and other reference works in solving a puzzle?

The answers are:

1. If you take pride in speed-of-solving you are missing a lot of fun. Crosswords are for relaxation and enjoyment, not for competitive one-upmanship, so take all the time you want.

2. The crossword puzzle is each solver's own individual property, and the solver is welcome to do it any way he or she pleases. It is nobody's business how it is done.

Now with that in mind, it's time to settle down to a selection of large puzzles that originally appeared in the Sunday *New York Times*. If you must fudge once in a while, the solutions are in the back of the book.

WILL WENG

The New York Times
JUMBO SUNDAY CROSSWORD PUZZLE BOOK

400 Sunday Puzzles

From *The New York Times* *Sunday Crossword Puzzles,* VOLUMES 1-8

PORTLAND HOUSE

The New York Times
JUMBO SUNDAY CROSSWORD PUZZLE BOOK

5 Word Weaving

ACROSS

1. Let off
7. Short of
13. Italian foods
19. From office boy to boss
20. Expert teaser
22. Eastern Christian
23. Philosophic doctrines
24. Cupboard
25. Surveyor's helpers
26. Wander
27. Creator of Hans Castorp
29. Finery
31. Degrees
32. Old measure
33. Less taxing
35. Fastener
36. Eleonora
37. Condescend
39. Capek
41. Corrupts
43. Peaks
45. Wrap in waxed cloth
47. Tidy
48. Flew in a way
50. Purvey
51. Finishing touches
55. Settled up
56. Computer word
59. Girl's name
60. —— tenens (stand-in)
62. "Make thee —— of gopher wood"
63. Mother-of-pearl
64. Farewell: Lat.
66. Common effort
69. Box of a kind
70. Off center
72. With: Scot.
73. Column style
75. Associate of Phiz
76. Top men
79. Plane wing support
81. Of deserts
82. Girl's name
83. Opera heroes
84. Large birds
86. Vegetable
87. Given by word
88. Restore
92. U.S.

violinist
94. Axe mark
98. "Go Tell —— Rhody"
99. An Allen
101. Brings to mind
103. Arctic explorer
104. Man's name
105. Expressed contempt
107. Gone
108. Bean
109. Gossip, down South
111. "The —— Worker"
113. Lawless one
115. Patterns for tracing
116. Grudging
117. Interpolate
118. Gives pause

119. Deeds
120. Lost sheep

DOWN

1. Made points
2. Release, in a way
3. Wild sheep
4. 500 sheets
5. Poetic dusk
6. Tense state
7. Deceitful one
8. "Camelot" librettist
9. —— sahib
10. Repute
11. More crafty
12. Equivocation
13. Strict
14. Buffalo's cousin
15. A Caesar

16. Jewish month
17. Relaxed
18. Five ——
21. Plunder, old style
28. Questioned
30. Eye part
33. Wind
34. News summary
36. Type of computer
38. Festivity
40. Makes dull
42. Roman poet
44. French claret
46. Queen: Sp.
48. More dignified
49. Iridescent
50. Pilot's concern
52. Islands in

Bay of Bengal
53. Stheno et al.
54. Pepper effect
55. Devastate
56. Finland, to the Finns
57. Musketeers and others
58. Image
61. Form of carbon
65. In one's ——
67. Follow
68. More fussy
71. Adjusts sails
74. Church laws
77. Perspicacity
78. Having a dull finish
80. Machete

83. Japanese verse form
85. Overstuff
87. Ability
88. Poured
89. Gibraltar to Lapland
90. Getting nowhere
91. Topic
93. Appraise
95. Not so fresh
96. Steichen's eye
97. Sincere
100. Audacity
102. High perch
105. Suffix with gang or mob
106. Platform
108. Asea
110. Exist
112. Small house
114. Political winners

6 Quotations

by Hume R. Craft

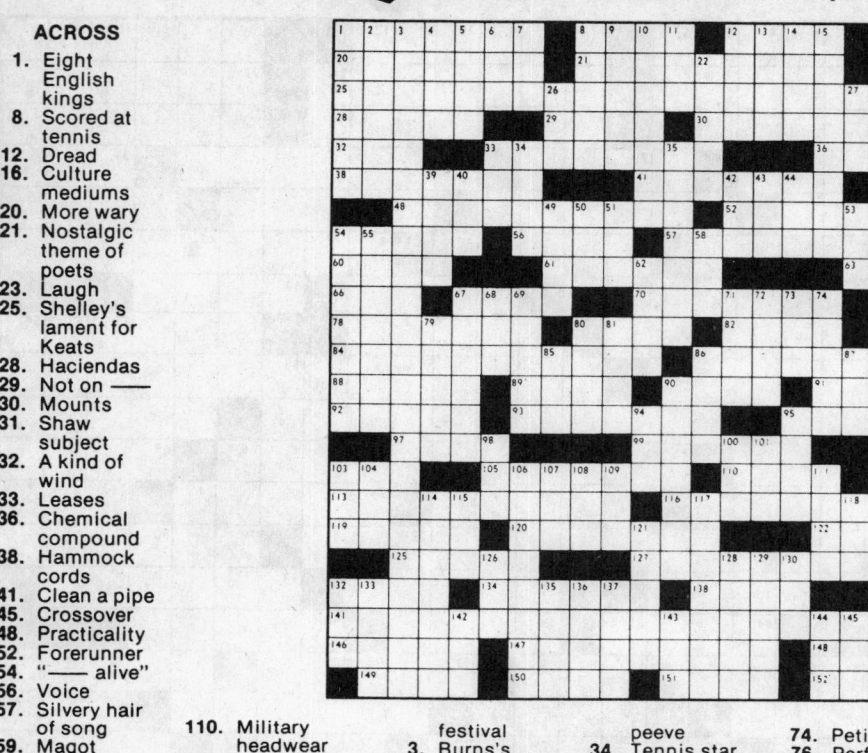

ACROSS

1. Eight English kings
8. Scored at tennis
12. Dread
16. Culture mediums
20. More wary
21. Nostalgic theme of poets
23. Laugh
25. Shelley's lament for Keats
28. Haciendas
29. Not on ——
30. Mounts
31. Shaw subject
32. A kind of wind
33. Leases
36. Chemical compound
38. Hammock cords
41. Clean a pipe
45. Crossover
48. Practicality
52. Forerunner
54. "—— alive"
56. Voice
57. Silvery hair of song
59. Magot
60. Seed coat
61. Point in an orbit
63. Biblical king
66. Rent
67. Goes to court
70. Quixote, et al.
75. Gels
78. Warning signals
80. Hipsters
82. Patsy
83. Kentucky school
84. Certain growths
86. Censured
88. Sounding made by radar
89. Medley
90. French painter
91. Bode
92. Suiting
93. Large basket
95. Lee's men
96. Indian reed
97. It —— laugh
99. Finger lake
102. Staple
103. Bristle
105. Exported
110. Military headwear
112. Famous players
113. Oedipus and others
116. Certain craving
119. Attempts
120. Legendary ivory statue
122. Lover of beauty
125. Lucifer
127. Ring men, familiarly
131. Rodent
132. Spin: Scot.
134. Command
138. Beginning golfer
139. —— as a fiddle
141. Tennyson title
146. Leads
147. Lords it over
148. Sentimental talk
149. East: Sp.
150. N.C. college
151. Or ——
152. Sioux

DOWN

1. Call forth
2. Hindu festival
3. Burns's words for a beastie
4. Field
5. Rough waters
6. Crossword clue: Abbr.
7. Broadway sign
8. Whaling man and others
9. Electronic device
10. Ham actors
11. TV room
12. Verb for Tinkerbell
13. Comfort
14. Pine
15. Double-checked mss.
16. Prepositions
17. Insects
18. Campion title
19. Coal deposit
22. Italian food
24. Sullivan and Begley
26. Beta or gamma
27. Theory
33. Kind of peeve
34. Tennis star
35. Squatters
37. Verb ending
39. Eastern weight
40. Tax bureau: Abbr.
42. Damage
43. Digit
44. Hagen
46. Droop
47. Poet's word "—— giddy as . . ."
49. Small drink
50. W. W. II area
51. Civil War initials
53. Users of cellars
54. Small spaces
55. Pronoun
58. Organizes (with up)
62. Zoroastrians
64. Spy
65. Small seal
67. —— corda (soft pedal)
68. Bar
69. Field: Lat.
71. Slangy negative
72. Road surface
73. Petiole
74. Perform again
76. Cowboy gear
77. Drags: Colloq.
79. Quarter
80. Shortly
81. Pier union: Abbr.
85. Actor Calhoun
86. Unruly group
87. Lacus Asphaltites
90. Bartender's rocks
94. Engrossed
95. Vibrate: Abbr.
98. Musical instrument
100. Horse talk
101. Baseball name
102. Quick-witted
103. Price ——
104. Climax
106. Lupino
107. Clay: Prefix
108. Biblical song: Abbr.
109. Appian Way
111. Hollywood area
112. Soaking, and no kidding
114. Adherent: Suffix
115. Ne'er-do-well
117. Wartime agency
118. Made of wood
121. Cutting: Fr.
123. Scotsman's aims
124. Word after hand or horse
126. Chars
128. Camera glass: Var.
129. Bird
130. Army man: Abbr.
132. "Winnie —— Pu"
133. Organic compound
135. Earth's envelope: Abbr.
136. Climb
137. Middle East port
139. Triple or homer
140. Noun suffix
142. Before dee
143. "—— a deal!"
144. Time period
145. Time period

Guess Who

by Betty Leary

ACROSS

1. Renounce
7. Actress Elsie
12. Egyptian goddess
16. Beak
19. Smallest ones
20. Turn outward
21. Easily done
23. Biblical name
24. Presiders.
25. Toy
27. Folios: Abbr.
28. Fuel
29. Shell
30. Place
31. Purposeful
33. Appendage
34. To the ——
36. Constructed: Abbr.
37. Nonsense!
38. Pearl Buck heroine
39. Second-rate
41. Elm fruit
43. "Come —— faithful"
44. Halo
45. Style of fiction
48. Iowa town
50. Tasted, in a way
52. Any of the Furies
53. Hair style
55. Constellation
56. Desk item
57. Pedestal parts
59. Poison tree
61. Cooked
63. Bower
65. Waterfall: Scot.
66. Packaged, in a way
68. Like Prospero and Miranda
69. Adjective suffix
70. Old Dutch measures
72. Long-legged birds
74. Pawns
75. Huckster
78. Business abbreviation
79. Cut ——
83. Glossy lacquer
84. People of rank
87. Algerian city
88. Suffix with block and brig
89. Bounce
90. Archeology finds
91. Pronoun
93. Fenced areas: Abbr.
95. Race horse
96. Vehicle
97. Sounds from the gallery
99. Turkish weights
100. Haven
101. Frenchman's roof
103. Basket material
106. Texas city
108. Garment
110. Cornbread
112. Couple
113. Informal wear
115. Canadian physician and others
116. Busybody
120. Math abbreviation
121. French adjective
123. Orchestra section: Abbr.
124. Walls in
125. Etruscan title
126. Occupied
127. Rome, to Caesar
129. Signify
130. Can. province
131. 1002
132. All
135. Opening in a game
137. Half boot
138. Staves off
139. Slow learner
140. Eliminate
141. Sign, informally
142. Shaggy dog
143. Advantage
144. Stopped over

DOWN

1. One of the Furies
2. Lament
3. Advice from Mother Goose
4. Recipient
5. Road map entry
6. Letter
7. Flat
8. Sailor's call
9. Connecting part
10. Annoy
11. Refinery worker
12. Arid wastes
13. Acid prefix
14. Lhasa's site
15. Workers' group: Abbr.
16. Part of an adage
17. Maneuvered
18. Pear
21. U.S. agency
22. Laud
26. Public officer
29. Pronoun
32. Fitzgerald
34. Splendor
35. Round
36. Bull form of Ra
40. Congo animal
41. Warning devices
42. Consequence
43. College title: Abbr.
45. Laborer
46. Campus area
47. Good times
49. Woeful
50. Biblical wife
51. German philosopher (1855-1941)
54. Disgusting
56. Not clerical
58. Price cut: Abbr.
60. 100 centavos
62. Turpentine resins
64. Harmony
66. Chits
67. Der ——
68. Eastern college
71. In ——
73. British subway
74. —— around
76. Swiss river
77. Fort in Kentucky
80. Pros
81. Just sits
82. Good queen
85. Steak garnish
86. Goldbricks
89. Palmetto State native
90. English spa
92. To be: Lat.
94. Hale's Philip ——
95. Golf term
96. Spanish uncle
97. Sits in judgment
98. First name in Dogpatch
102. Football's Simpson et al.
104. Girl of song
105. Shaggy dogs
107. Legendary king and others
109. Times of day
111. Words for a poor dresser
114. Notions in Paris
116. Trembled
117. Container
118. Indian in America
119. Boxed
121. Make oneself heard
122. In good time
124. Goal
126. Kaffir warriors
128. Abbreviation in rental ads
129. Teenage hairdo
130. Abbess
133. Certain verbs: Abbr.
134. Project
135. Weight units: Abbr.
136. Of age: Lat.

8 In the Old Sod

by A. J. Santora

ACROSS

1. Town near Salerno
6. In cipher
11. Years
15. Kneehole
19. Nikolai
20. Knowing
21. Extinguish
22. Matrimony
23. "—— look at it"
24. 1835 novel
26. ——prinz (Ger. title)
27. Feel pity
28. Zigzag
29. Knowing
31. Nobel physicist, 1925
33. —— majesty
34. Children's writer
36. Halberd and battle-ax
39. Cables
41. I hate: Lat.
42. Spells
44. Parhelion
45. Flamboy-ance
49. Journey
50. Belgian town
51. Urey, for one
53. Streaked, as wood
54. That is: Lat.
56. Iconoclast's opposite
58. Go-go dancer of myth
60. Reagan, for short
61. Item
63. With
64. Belgian shoe
66. Foxy
67. Dairy case item
70. Japanese apricot
73. ——-brac
74. Poetic start
75. Prepo-sitions
76. Easily shifted: Abbr.
79. Jitters
81. Pears' cousins
84. Crown
86. Federal group: Abbr.
87. Sets in an order

89. Warsaw for one: Abbr.
91. Kosygin's no
92. Like some satellites
94. Home: Abbr.
95. Big leagues
97. Month: Abbr.
98. Northern ——
100. Autocratic
101. Freely, in music
103. End of the loaf
105. Rule: Fr.
107. Record player
108. Nun of an order
112. Color
114. Arabian Nights' total
115. Light overcoat
117. Shore

118. Compo-sition
119. Good taste
120. —— water
121. —— curiae
122. Verse man
123. Injection, familiarly
124. Prows
125. Followings

DOWN

1. Raines
2. Nut tree
3. Ready to putt
4. Some poems
5. Like: Suffix
6. Rome's "censor"
7. Man ——
8. Beclouds
9. Clears a tape
10. Blood rels
11. Together, in music
12. Bay of song

13. Envoy's home: Abbr.
14. Burst
15. Medic of films
16. Reconcilia-tions
17. Blarney
18. U.S. artist
25. Type of watch spring
28. Bosses
30. Shoot
32. Part of Mao's name
35. Cobras
37. Extras, in music
38. Honey drink
40. Disen-tangled
42. To-do
43. Church listing
44. White clovers
46. To an

extreme
47. Restore
48. Whirlpool
51. Hint
52. Dies ——
55. Ballet move-ment
57. Church service book
59. —— of strength
62. Cultivated
65. —— ahead (lead)
68. Cliff
69. Auditors
70. E Pluribus ——
71. Arizona sight
72. Prickly
76. Medical center
77. A rabbit
78. Atlas lines: Abbr.
80. Ghoul-like
82. John's

problem, off and on
83. Newspaper pioneer
85. Rapidly
88. Settle down
90. Rory —— Irish rebel
93. Spiny lily
95. "To —— truth"
96. Corroded
99. Appears suddenly
100. Obliging
101. —— punch
102. Lake, in Ireland
104. "To —— human"
106. Put into law
107. Biblical land: Var.
109. Bismarck
110. Speck
111. Soaks
113. Pronoun
116. Myrna
117. Prosecutors

9

Fit to Be Dyed
by Mary Murdoch

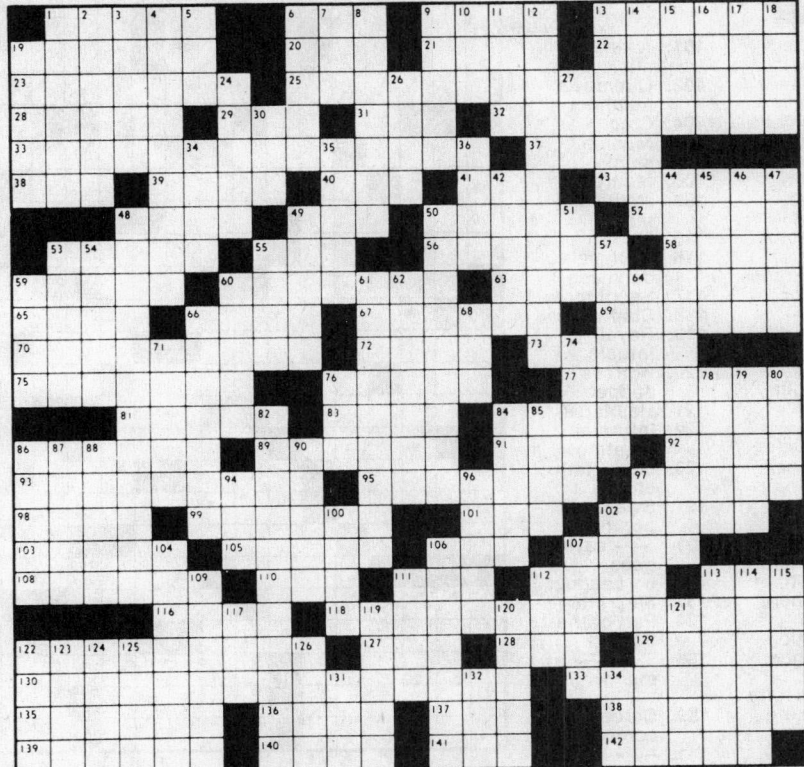

ACROSS

1. Meld
6. Variety bit
9. Black Sea arm
13. Signature of a playwright
19. Indian timber tree
20. Shout
21. Appoint
22. Record
23. Outer layer
25. Sea birds
28. Missile
29. —— de vie
31. Chemical prefix
32. Coin-tossing routine
33. Asparagus sprengeri
37. —— of dishes
38. Writings: Abbr.
39. Fare
40. Recent: Pref.
41. Adjective suffix
43. Corrupt
48. Brief biography
49. Mediter-ranée, for one
50. Coins
52. Girl's name
53. Cuts of meat
55. Witticism
56. Goodbyes in Roma
58. Droop
59. Time period
60. Mme. ——
63. Rats
65. Suffix for top or typ
66. Wine
67. Jane Fonda film
69. Mischie-vous: Sp.
70. Poet Walter et al.
72. Lozenge
73. Terry
75. Channel
76. Hairlike structure
77. Mountain passes
81. Observing
83. Landing vessels
84. Pales
86. Euryale, for instance
89. Italian man's name
91. Cassini
92. Mellow

93. Regards too highly
95. Theater tests
97. Springs
98. Cockney dwelling
99. Stew
101. Wife
102. Literary works
103. Carried on
105. Golf great
106. Ballet step
107. Sally ——
108. Trumpet call
110. Under warranty: Abbr.
111. Civic: Abbr.
112. Mass of ice
113. Sawlike: Prefix
116. Ohio city
118. English primrose
122. I.O.U. holders
127. Chemistry degree
128. Bear: Sp.
129. Moon valley
130. Smollett's spendthrift
133. Go back in
135. Indian

136. Exude
137. Be troubled
138. Sovereign's stand-in
139. Chair parts
140. Prong
141. Aves.
142. Horse sound

DOWN

1. Sayings
2. Holds forth
3. Air-tower gear
4. Drink flavoring
5. Goddess of healing
6. Debate
7. Sedan
8. Globe, for instance
9. Gun girl
10. Ibex
11. Melville novel
12. Kind of marble
13. Inhabited by gremlins
14. Salts
15. Comedian Laurel
16. Arizona

tribe
17. Aleutian island
18. —— Indies
19. "Go —— Rover!"
24. Judith Anderson role
26. Ape
27. Docs
30. Fore's partner
34. Wagons-
35. Concerning
36. Kind of instrument
42. So ——
44. Sporting place
45. Flavoring
46. Missile places
47. "...could —— lean"
48. Common
49. Obligations
50. Unfeelingly
51. French coin
53. French school
54. Florida city
55. Dumas ——
57. Kind of wax

59. Spanish hero et al.
60. Carl Van
61. Renounced
62. Sooner
64. Asserts
66. Films
68. Certain discs
71. City official
74. Household gods
76. Litigant: Abbr.
78. Melodies
79. A Yokum
80. Scottish tools
82. Demantoid
84. Takes a trip
85. Business abbrevi-ations
86. Burgess's boors
87. Immature seed
88. Varnish ingredient
90. Flower
94. Thine: Fr.
96. Some Arabians
97. Bills: Slang

100. Pilgrimage to Mecca
102. Simple's partner
104. Elation
106. Australian birds
107. Operetta composer
109. Headings: Fr.
111. Twice DCL
112. Certain noblemen: Abbr.
113. Fur worker
114. Give in
115. Passive
117. French pronoun
119. —— to eat
120. Carols
121. A Beatle
122. Accoun-tants: Abbr.
123. Corded fabric
124. Of an age
125. Ten: Prefix
126. Kind of truck, for short
131. Fasten
132. Sat down
134. Pause fillers

What's That Again
by Elmer Toro

ACROSS

1. Sufficient
6. Fabric
10. Uriah's family
15. Carpenter's tool
21. Sacred text of Islam
22. Prepare
23. Available
24. Ham actor
25. Dance
28. Ill, in France
29. Director
30. "L' ——, c'est moi"
31. Disparages
33. Cheers
36. Tranquility, for one
38. Seven: Prefix
41. High peak
42. Direction: Abbr.
43. Tumult
46. Marienbad and others
47. Miss Street and others
49. By: Sp.
50. Attraction
52. A science: Abbr.
56. Swift's forte
57. Assuming airs
60. Garden workers
61. Go over with a dry mop
63. Born
64. Pensacola, for one: Abbr.
65. Eye parts
66. Kind of novel: Abbr.
67. Jumble
72. Boxing champ of the '20s
73. Crew chiefs, for short
75. Be in the red
76. Rialto sign
77. Hitchcock movie
80. Hard wood
81. In opposition
85. Ralph
88. Two or more eras
89. Tools for cutting holes
91. Word of disgust
93. Fleming
94. Certain beans: Var.
96. Entice
97. Mischief
101. A kind of stick
102. Quemoy's neighbor
104. Crag
105. Muslim saint
106. Maltreats
109. Nautical term
110. Deceit
115. Mythical darkness
117. Set of three
118. Stadium call
119. Royal initials
120. Actress Judge
121. Hesitates
122. Informal greeting
126. Ger., Neth., etc.
127. Sweet potato
131. —— saying goes
132. Ivy Leaguer
133. Serpents
134. Part of the South
136. "... —— a man with ..."
139. Carbon compound
141. —— Fideles
142. Jumbled
149. School task
150. Like a lot informally
151. Tabriz's land
152. Cleanse
153. Heedful, old style
154. King of Judea
155. Pulls
156. Pass

DOWN

1. Egyptian spirit
2. Farm sound
3. Golf tour member
4. Strips
5. Noun suffix
6. Black widow
7. St. Pierre, for one
8. Shoe part
9. Sea speed unit
10. More piquant
11. Ref. book
12. An anesthetic: Abbr.
13. —— call on
14. German count
15. Erasure
16. Visions
17. Pivotal
18. Condition
19. Mosquito genus
20. Take by force
26. Serves a purpose
27. Part of the island state
32. Makes return
33. Roulette plays
34. Lend ——
35. Every which way
37. Xanadu's river
39. Map
40. Printing error, for short
43. Wildly
44. ——-hoo
45. Attract
46. Bristles
48. Put the ——
51. Metallic sound
52. Desire strongly
53. Willies
54. Period of history
55. Writings: Abbr.
58. Letter
59. Slangy answers
60. Confusedly
62. Biblical pronouns
68. Have
69. Army unit: Abbr.
70. Ganymede, for one
71. Female rabbit
72. Muffin
73. Plant study: Abbr.
74. Crew member
77. Uncle ——
78. Tibetan animal
79. Cricket sides
(shut)
82. Person
83. Sea eagle
84. Korean soldier
86. Yutang
87. "Mighty —— a rose ..."
90. Korean port
92. Yarn measure
95. Black Bird
97. Derisive cries
98. Curved lines
99. Godly: It.
100. " —— and Mehitabel"
102. Rug
103. Fortas
104. "Arms and ——"
107. Fancywork
108. Dawn
111. Expressions of disgust
112. Chimney dirt
113. Bean of India
114. Pump
116. Sunday talks: Abbr.
118. Tolerant
121. Creator of Shangri-La
123. Passed, as time
124. Greek district
125. Fatty acids
127. City in Florida
128. Youngest son
129. Take —— (pause)
130. Moon crater
131. In reserve
133. Exhausted
135. Exclamation of surprise
137. Do a newsroom job
138. Learner
140. Monster
143. British oath
144. 12 dozen: Abbr.
145. Handle rudely
146. A Spanish queen
147. Medal: Abbr.
148. Again

11 Variety Package
by Peter E. Price

ACROSS

1. Children's game
11. Priest's vestment
14. "Pease porridge ——..."
20. Circum-spect monkey
21. Aces
23. Washrooms of a sort: Var.
24. Anybody's guess
25. Dutch pottery
26. Shelley's elegy for Keats
28. Wire: Abbr.
29. Mustard, laughing, etc.
30. Tartu's river
31. High: Music
33. Word for bad liquor
35. —— bad example
37. Henry and Jane
39. "Mona Lisa," et al.
41. Capital of Spain under Moors
46. Certain starlets
48. —— and ahed
49. Mobile home
50. Song of French Revolution
51. Make a move
54. Red Sea land
56. Wroclaw's river
57. Champion filly, 1957-8
58. Calliope et al.
59. Indian tourist attraction
61. Pro ——
62. Repair
63. —— Douglas, novelist
65. Rebel
66. —— stand-still
67. Chaney
68. Scared out
70. Kind of poet
72. Chinese river
74. Teutonic god
75. Tried
77. Famed New York boss
79. Smallest state capital
82. Before Sept.
83. Western group: Abbr.
84. Alias the Cowardly Lion
86. Lap robe
87. Railroad network: Abbr.
88. Gullet
91. Society founded in 1776
94. Ness and others
96. Honey-combs: Lat.
97. Type size
98. Cafe
99. It —— much to ask
100. W.H. —— poet
101. Where the wise old owl sat
103. Clock sounds
105. Pension plan of the '30s
107. Prudent: It.
108. Tomb of the ——
111. N.Y. lake
112. Invitation P.S.
114. Korean city
115. Brave talk
116. Evergreen
117. Put-ons
121. Pronoun
123. Testing devices
125. Hebrew measures
127. Musical based on "Shrew"
130. Child's behavior at times
132. Yore
133. Alms: Lat.
134. Opera by Verdi
135. Music to torero's ears
136. Radio transmitter

DOWN

1. Daddy long-legs genus
2. Egg, in Paris
3. City in S. Calif.
4. Shifted: Abbr.
5. —— a time
6. Detroit name
7. Thighbones
8. Chekhov's first play
9. Formal award
10. The sign, to a Spaniard
11. Nootka Indian
12. Booty
13. Monday ail-ment
14. Somewhat: Suffix
15. Falls for a married woman
16. King of Siam's friend
17. Jet housings
18. Andaman people
19. Birthplace of Anacreon
22. Selective philosophy
23. Tom Collins
25. Fiscal problem
27. Unspecified quantity
32. Rival of Tulane
34. Closet bar
36. Jewish scriptures
38. Member of F.D.R. Cabinet
39. Medals
40. Neighbor of la.
42. Fashion name
43. Card game
44. French headgear
45. Famous mountain
47. French waters
52. Author of "The Care-takers"
53. Northern capital
55. Town in N.W. France
58. Big name in vases
59. Mock orange
60. God of the winds
62. Caress
64. At a loss, financially
67. New Guinea port
68. Missouri mountains
69. Isn't it, Shake-speare style
71. Thermo-meter abbreviation
72. Book by Sammy Davis
73. Russian composer
76. Reimburses
77. Venetian fishing boats
78. Woman, in Hawaii
80. Ptomaines found in meat
81. Adjective suffixes
85. Part of a box score
87. Scat!
88. Ogled
89. Persons exacting retribution
90. Casements
92. Injunctions
93. Aleutian isl.
95. Small beds
96. Brouhaha
99. Kind of triangle: Var.
100. Quinn and Newley
102. Scullers
104. Jewish delicacies
106. Suffix for polli
109. Onetime N.Y. greeter Grover ——
110. Voided
113. Dun-color-ed: Prefix
115. —— -les-Bains, France
117. Terrier
118. Yesterday: Fr.
119. Org.'s cousin
120. Russian river
122. Latin abbr.
124. Book by E.E. Cummings
126. Handwriting on the wall
128. Silkworm
129. Prior to
131. Slum area need: Abbr.

12 Words to the Wise
by A.J. Santora

ACROSS

1. Assemble
5. Victor's due
9. Hebrew letter
13. Dennis of tennis
20. Indigo
21. Prefix with distant
22. Stevenson's retreat
23. Factor
24. Taro
25. Discovers
27. Limits
28. Benét play, with "The"
31. Lead a horse
32. Nagy of Hungary
33. Strange
34. Alert
35. Type of ink
37. Bizarre
39. Rebozo
44. Hosp. people
45. Goad
47. Parts of ski lifts
49. Ref. book
51. Square
52. Arthur of tennis
54. Silvery salmon
56. Flabella
58. Management's concern
60. Rent
62. With 79 Across, an old "Laugh In" phrase
64. Misuses the thermostat
66. Gems
69. Hong Kong or Asian
70. Direction
71. Split
72. West Indian music
74. Spelling
75. Farm tool inventor
76. —— disant
79. See 62 Across
85. Map abbreviation
86. Hunter of the sky
87. Oahu town
88. Spiteful ones: Colloq.
89. Payment
91. —— Anne
92. College at Cedar Rapids
94. Fat
95. Dredging bucket
98. Nuclear experiments
100. Predatory fish
101. Young hare
102. Nobleman
104. Urban problem
106. —— pinch of salt
110. Sobeit
111. Symington, familiarly
113. Brisk
115. Gulpers
117. Fleming
118. Pari —— (equally)
120. Writing fluid: Fr.
122. Approaches
124. Style of painting
126. Hilum
128. Yastrzemski
129. Comedians of a sort
131. Forgotten names are left to them, said Preston
137. Alpaca's cousin
138. Flattened: Sl.
139. Without: Fr.
141. Ring-shaped
142. Eared seal
143. Prefix with plasm
144. N. Z. pine
145. Roof style
146. Dogs, for short
147. "—— in the course of . . ."
148. Italian family

DOWN

1. West
2. Ups ——
3. Lateral air-flow
4. Czech neighbor
5. Mesta
6. Zoo's counterpart
7. Sally ——
8. Flubbed
9. Chili con
10. To me: Fr.
11. Model
12. Meat dish
13. Viewpoint
14. Excuse
15. Glasses
16. Struck
17. Head, in Paris
18. Unique person
19. P.M. times
22. Beetle gem
26. Confess
29. Adherents: Abbr.
30. "If I —— king"
31. Scarlett's estate
36. Rock ——
37. Speak
38. Initials on a skivvy
40. Despised
41. Song
42. Departed
43. Falls back
46. L.A. time
48. —— of fish
50. Procession
53. Glen ——, Ill.
55. Costello
57. "—— the rose"
59. Pronoun
61. Detect
63. Sharp
65. Panorama
66. Eye: Prefix
67. Dad
68. Got down
69. Crossword puzzle standby
73. Placates
74. Savarin
75. The double helix
76. Skated
77. Fashion first name
78. Paris suburb
80. Coin of Iran
81. Kitty of novel
82. Bide ——
83. California wine area
84. Order of frogs
89. Signs
90. Guard unit: Abbr.
91. European river: Fr. sp.
92. Football player: Abbr.
93. Willow
95. Applaud
96. Late golf pro
97. Sts.
99. Lively music
100. Take form
103. Continent: Abbr.
105. Eating pal
107. Graphs
108. Chickens out
109. Termites
112. Preposition
114. Flashy: Informal
116. Call for cattle
119. College in East Orange, N.J.
121. Drive-in girl
123. Fully renovated
125. Verse
127. Movie award
128. Shades of brown
130. Undealt cards
131. Panama Indian
132. —— of Cutch
133. Burden
134. —— a turn
135. Stroller
136. Engrave
137. Group of whales
140. Prosecute

13

Point of View by William Lutwiniak

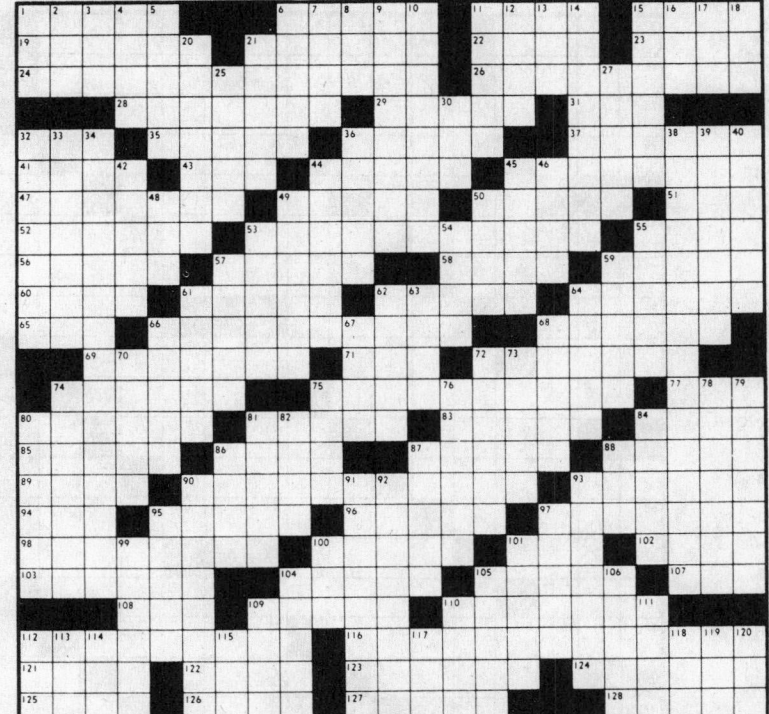

ACROSS

1. Flavorful seed
6. Turkish V.I.P.
11. Potter's adjunct
15. Hymenopteron
19. Oil color vehicle
21. Hearing defect of sorts
22. Federal org.
23. Corn lily
24. Time of the week
26. They know everything
28. Musical passages
29. Give-and-take affairs
31. Teachers' org.
32. Stomach
35. Peerage members
36. Honshu volcano
37. Layers
41. Chemical endings
43. Family members
44. Boors
45. Like some tomatoes
47. Be social
49. Halloween costume
50. Irish darling
51. Pre- ——
52. Outdoor people
53. With 24 Across, a know-it-all
55. Entr' ——
56. Proxy
57. Malayan sirs
58. Barnyard sound
59. Different
60. Football play
61. Garment
62. Eased off
64. Scuba fishing gear
65. Depressing
66. Words from a "friend"
68. Mother of Achilles
69. European bison
71. Numerical prefix
72. Wood finisher
74. Accumulating
75. Certain

remarks
77. Motorist's need
80. Fine wool
81. Name in Broadway fame
83. Embellish
84. Dream: Fr.
85. Kind of verb: Abbr.
86. By hand: Prefix
87. Irish spade
88. French painter
89. Incursion
90. Bridge-table encores
93. Go back
94. G.I. address
95. Very: Music
96. Disseminates, as tales
97. Distinct
98. Desert rodent
100. Takes five
101. Ruler: Abbr.
102. Wise
103. Early ascetic
104. Contradict
105. Hussar's gear
107. Had charge
108. Object
109. Valentine figure
110. Salty one
112. It's always 20-20
116. Unerring appraisals
121. By word
122. Cover fully
123. Cutlery
124. Young eels
125. Terrier
126. Weakens
127. Longhorn
128. Servicewomen

DOWN

1. Sand: Prefix
2. Modern: Prefix
3. Auto system: Abbr.
4. Caesar et al.
5. Lift up
6. Reels: Scot.
7. Harding et al.
8. Six in Italy
9. Distributes
10. Moot
11. Ollie's friend
12. Oxford's river
13. Place for books: Abbr.
14. Soft muslin
15. Sorceror
16. Fireman's gear
17. Title
18. Family members
20. Ill-starred lover
21. Works hard
25. Corday's victim
27. Grand ——
30. German river
32. Accidents
33. Leeward island
34. Part-timers
36. Then: Fr.
38. Fighter of a kind
39. Lacks stability
40. Math aces
42. Disbursed
44. Crude shelter
45. Mark
46. Fasten
48. Scrap for Fido
49. Protects
50. Rose's love
53. Coverlet
54. Newspaper part, for short
55. Tete- ——
57. Leather strip
59. Certain sports tourneys
61. Office help
62. Engraving tool
63. —— were
64. Leveling wedges
66. "Of thee ——"
67. Other: Sp.
68. Cup: Fr.
70. Venerably traditional
72. Skedaddles
73. French exclamation
74. Ponchos
75. Fish bait
76. Unproductive ones
78. Mean
79. Orderly
80. Delusion
81. Social class
82. Knowledgeable
84. Ecstatic reviews
86. Girl's name
87. Condition
88. Cyclotron abbreviation
90. Art of disputation
91. Certain monuments
92. Not migratory
93. Income
95. Some skirts
97. Ferber novel
99. Parish official
100. Congressman: Abbr.
101. Carnelians
104. Tag ends
105. More reasoned
106. Fishing gear
109. Fellow
110. Action
111. Initials on a card
112. Exclamations
113. Nettle
114. Vote against
115. Area of India
117. French co.
118. Multitude
119. Misdo
120. Draft initials

Passing the Word

by Cornelia Warriner

ACROSS

1. Hanger-on
5. Rascal
10. Metal beam
14. Hobo's vegetable
18. Tennis star
19. Light craft
20. Uncanny
21. Chicago name
22. TV fare of sorts
25. Noted jockey
26. Nautical chain
27. Yew
28. Roundup gear
29. Prepares to swim the Channel
30. Sea birds
31. French psychologist
32. Short
33. Baldwins
36. Dancer Pauline
37. Workmanship
41. Restrain
42. Computer workers
44. Form of Rachel
45. Lips
46. Silk, in Paris
47. River to the Seine
48. Sea-story writer
49. Elec. unit
50. Press items
54. Ship
55. Is worthwhile
57. Like a child's nose
58. Hair tints
59. Anon
60. Eye cell parts
61. Once, in a prescription
62. Slender probe
64. Emphatic words
65. Some news items
68. Shrew and others
69. Brinkley, Wallace et al.
71. Spinner
72. Solar deity
73. Prefix for an antiseptic
74. Former diva
75. Places: Lat.

76. Three-way joint
77. Without words
81. Sea off Australia
82. "—— its martyrs"
84. And —— grow on
85. Scuffle
86. Rabbit
87. Ship parts
88. Positive
89. British party
92. Add
93. Both: Prefix
94. Old French coin
97. Rig out
98. Cramped quarters
101. Sausage
102. Roman road
103. Fiber for rugs
104. Baseball team
105. Soil

106. Disorder
107. Heat, as milk
108. Stepped

DOWN

1. Tense
2. Catch sight of
3. Loafer
4. Lacrosse team
5. Mocks
6. Concerns
7. Handle: Fr.
8. Family member
9. Shedding
10. Mosaic piece
11. Animal
12. Jason's ship
13. Ham on ——
14. Biblical words
15. Criticizes: Colloq.
16. Muslim tongue
17. Ocean, to poets

21. Egyptian god
23. Infection for short
24. Sounder
29. Way out: Fr.
30. Trees
31. One kind of fan
32. A garnish
33. Catch ——
34. Some TV time
35. Publicity agent of yore
36. Name for Santa
37. Concord
38. U.N. workers
39. Indian title
40. Leap and light
42. T.V.A. output
43. A.M.'s to poets
46. Divide
48. Entertained

50. Memos
51. Notched: Bot.
52. Roman wars, 264-146 B.C.
53. Burdens: Lat.
54. Delineates
56. Certain bucket
58. Brings up
60. Punctuation mark
61. Location
62. Marine ray
63. Fire ——
64. River nymphs of Greek myth
65. Mouth: Prefix
66. Kind of train
67. Heavy stake
69. Not up
70. Roasting rods
73. The men —— life
75. Mislay

77. Intrude suddenly
78. Wavers
79. Golfing words
80. Old capital of Egypt
81. Item for a whatnot
83. Orchestra man
85. Took a bath
87. Shoe parts
88. —— a rat
89. Obscene
90. Water: Prefix
91. Famous duelist
92. Mal de ——
93. Theater org.
94. Recipe word
95. Words of disbelief
96. Kind of car
98. Dickens boy
99. Vibrate: Abbr.
100. Can. province

15 Stepquote

by Eugene T. Maleska

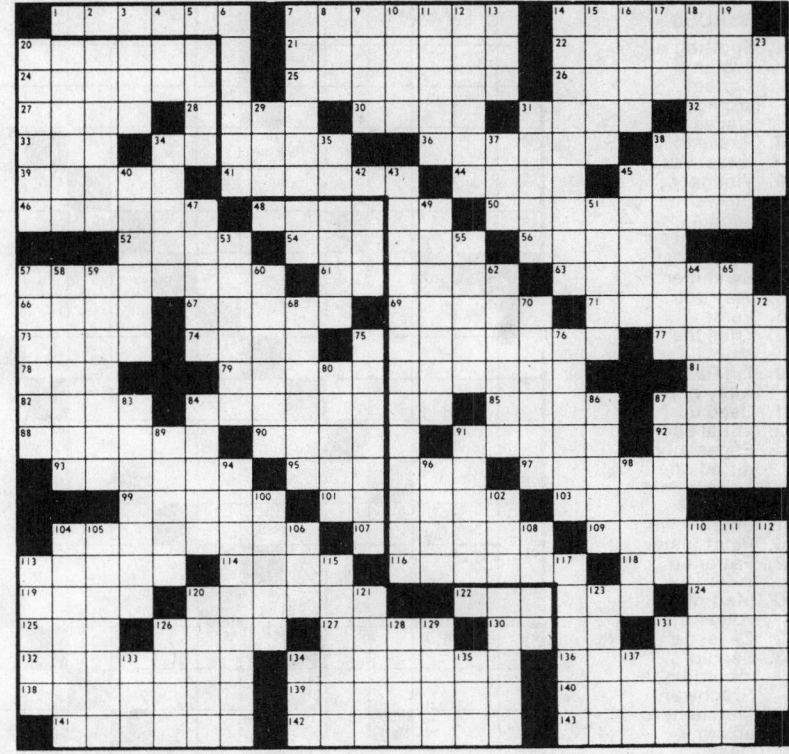

ACROSS

1. Start of an eleven-word quote descending in stairstep fashion to 143 Across
7. Misfit of W.W. II
14. Lorraine's partner
20. White's " —— from the Fortieth Floor"
21. Interstices
22. Peter made three
24. Encore for boxers
25. Argentine seaport
26. Stepquote source
27. Words of confidence
28. What debeo means
30. Indian weight
31. Tam-tam
32. Prefix for gram or logue
33. Boone
34. Type of bigot
36. False
38. Two cups
39. Sheep
41. Stepquote part
44. Style name
45. Flood and spring
46. Flee
48. Vaughan et al.
50. TV cabinets
52. Barkley
54. Write a music score
56. Paris subway
57. Lone
61. Heel over
63. Terminal
66. Cap- ——
67. Funny fellows
69. Isle of the oracle
71. Cognition
73. Tennis terms
74. Theater section
75. Scattering
77. Moist
78. Nobel product
79. Goes out on a limb
81. Indiana Indians

82. No longer new
84. Emergency care
85. Where Zeno taught
87. Hoover Dam's lake
88. Calm
90. Not for all the —— China
91. Staggers
92. Ye —— tea shoppe
93. Estimate
95. See 57 Across
97. Summoned back
99. For —— sake!
101. Mend the oxfords
103. Ruined city in Iran
104. Fish spears
107. Logomachy
109. Be frugal
113. The mating game
114. Layer
116. Stepquote part
118. Levant or Hammerstein
119. Zola's "Le ——" (1888)
120. Military lodging
122. With the result
124. —— pro nobis
125. St. Pierre
126. Buffoon
127. Yemeni
130. Sediment
131. Struck
132. Citizens of Valletta
134. Bohemian composer
136. Flaccid
138. Stepquote author
139. Baby hare
140. Expanded
141. "Thanatopsis" poet
142. Cuban province
143. End of Stepquote

DOWN

1. Novel by R.P. Warren (1959)
2. Sanguineous
3. Author Hunter
4. Mass. campus
5. Spore clusters of rust fungi
6. Stepquote part
7. Willy Loman, for one
8. Coach Parseghian
9. Gov't. branch
10. Concert rendition
11. Babylonian deity
12. —— mouse game
13. Large parrot
14. Recessed
15. Sierra ——
16. Close-fitting
17. Publicize
18. Voltaire hero
19. Malbin, Stritch, etc.
20. Camera support
23. Jalousie

parts
29. Comes in first
31. Make neat
34. Convened again
35. Old card games
37. Twitch
38. Guided
40. Blues
42. Judo exercises
43. Stepquote part
45. Body part
47. Brilliant gray
49. See 38 Down
51. Goad
53. A —— (presumptive)
55. Sniggler
57. Break of continuity
58. Bounding main
59. Scatters trash

60. Dieter's dish
62. Not at all
64. "Not so deep ——..."
65. Citrus drink
68. Makes taut
70. Carrie or Kenny
72. Dug
75. Type of glass
76. Uganda group: Var.
80. Elevator's neighbor
83. Scorn
84. Olivia's clown
86. Spore sac
87. Teeth
89. Obligations
91. Passes on
94. Opinion
96. Tennis strokes
98. Neckcloth
100. Fence stairs
102. Bleach
104. "Behold —— of God

..."
105. Convivial one
106. Salt: Fr.
108. This, in Spain
110. "—— bury Caesar..."
111. Seaman
112. Babbled
113. Malfeasant's act
115. Fruit-juice gadget
117. Stepquote part
120. Wisent
121. "Three Coins" fountain
123. Savory jelly
126. Pueblo site
128. Fit to ——
129. Bossy's home
131. Skiddoo
133. Essay
134. Road sign
135. Trampoline
137. Bantu language

Miscellany

ACROSS

1. Spotting systems
7. Certain storage places
14. Pause in verse: Var.
20. Vinegary
21. Drowsing
22. Legal claimant
23. Bee's goal
24. Swimmer
25. Way out
26. Verse
27. Tries the bait
29. Tin Pan Alley girl
31. Used up
32. Initial score
34. Especially gifted one
36. Temple, old style
37. Small town
38. Paint tester
39. Fattened steer
40. Martinique volcano
42. Causerie
43. Sacred mountain in Szechwan
45. Merchant to an army
47. Desert hazard
49. Cicero topic
53. Pushes on
54. Closes the gap
55. Rope-ladder rungs
57. Shopping centers
58. Savory
59. Sets a tempo
60. Hymenopter
61. People for
62. Clairvoyance
64. Chaser for tequila
65. Large lizard
66. Less
67. Silas Marner's golden girl
68. Worthwhile quality
69. Regions
71. Of an Eastern people
72. Capital of Albania: Var.
73. Artificial
74. Harness ring
76. Turned into
77. Name for a field dog
79. Awry
80. Sublease
81. Vilify
84. Get along well
86. —— noire
87. Sum, ——, fui
91. Newsprint plants
93. John 1:1-14 as part of a mass
95. Shooting match: Fr.
96. Tropical sunhat
97. Small-horse drivers
98. Clear
99. Draw forth
101. Iatric
103. Bring into accord
105. Opening
106. Cut off
107. Patcher
108. Wobble
109. Braced for shock
110. Virulent ones

DOWN

1. Decamped
2. Sin of sloth
3. Decree in Scotland
4. Lawyer: Abbr.
5. Laughing
6. Jots down
7. Caliber
8. Kind of computer
9. Ranked
10. Dolorous word
11. Achieve
12. Abrasives
13. Try
14. Do housework
15. Teatime at sea
16. Discourse: Abbr.
17. Discomfort
18. Seaport on the Don
19. Leblanc thief Lupin
28. Not so gay
30. Classic roué
33. Singing groups
34. Gains altitude
35. Swiss miss
38. Grilling
41. Right-angle extensions
42. Linked set
44. Religious music
45. More chic
46. Hullabaloos
47. Lukewarmness
48. Lamentable
50. Word switch
51. Real
52. Fourth ——
53. Ascribe
54. Most precise
56. Athletic aftermath
58. In stitches
59. Songbird
62. Usurp
63. Binge
64. Ventilates
66. Image of eternity
68. Cheese fanciers
70. Small civet
71. Impels
72. Signal one's punches
75. Most be-times
76. Davis
78. Jackpot starter
80. Rebounded
81. Best, as a pupil
82. Receiver of goods
83. Rebel
85. A thanedom for Macbeth
86. District in Yugoslavia
88. Neat
89. Fisherman
90. Churchmen
92. Measurer
93. Union unit
94. Port of old Rome
97. Heap
100. Small boat
102. Female hare
104. Oriental New Year

17

Literal World

by Anthony Morse

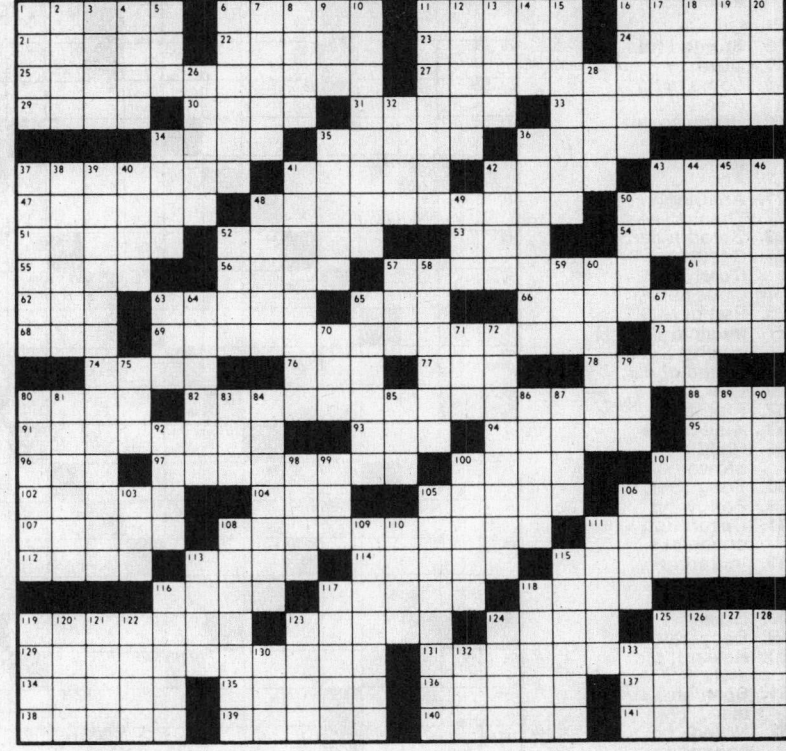

ACROSS

1. Anaconda's relative
6. Prankster
11. Spectral type in the sky
16. City near Bombay
21. Type of architecture
22. Yellowish-red color
23. High spot
24. Ration
25. Relatives in Haarlem
27. Poilus march off
29. Stub ——
30. Carol
31. Candy
33. Father of Ajax
34. Row
35. African antelopes
36. Lancelot's uncle
37. Satellites
41. Modern name for Lutetia
42. Without pity
43. Exclamation
47. Doctrinal rejection
48. Rascals in Havana
50. Court decree
51. Fads
52. Venetian feature
53. Bad
54. Buck
55. Matured
56. Suffix for some acids
57. Aquatic mammal
61. Relative of 1 Across
62. Star
63. A locale in "My Fair Lady"
65. Whole
66. Rests upon
68. "...the end is not ——"
69. Weapon for a soldado
73. World area
74. Ancient road
76. Man: Latin
77. Specially-shaped clock
78. Scottish resort
80. Compos mentis
82. Young man got mad
88. Drink
91. Invention
93. Dutch cupboard
94. Auriculate
95. Choler
96. —— Roy
97. Establishes
100. Heel over
101. Anti, out west
102. —— la Cité
104. Period
105. "To —— human"
106. Celestial fluid
107. Entreat
108. Bahians off the beam
111. Pin used in ceramics
112. Former Chief Justice
113. Prune
114. Certain paintings
115. Supports
116. Carriage
117. Doesn't exist
118. Old Brazilian money
119. Navy men
123. More depressed
124. English poet
125. Nautical word
129. Cockneys take a close look
131. Gossips in Lampang
134. Shepherd in "As You Like It"
135. Tarzan's rope
136. Talk-show host
137. Thin mortar
138. Filch: Slang
139. Joined
140. Ancient tomb
141. Islamic spirit

DOWN

1. Opera girl
2. Set-to
3. Preposition
4. Trio of rhyme
5. Berliner's alas
6. Craft
7. Result of high-pressure living
8. A kind of road
9. Japanese apricot
10. Rural poem
11. Disreputable
12. Feudal people
13. Card
14. River to the Rhone
15. College officials
16. Cloys
17. Tree genus
18. Spatial infinity
19. New: Prefix
20. Egyptian disk
26. Concord
28. Drove
32. Neat as ——
34. Heroine of 1891 novel
35. French smoker's need
36. Circus purchase
37. Full of sayings
38. Three miles
39. Squawk from Peron
40. Requirement
41. Penal
42. Tutoring
43. Charlemagne's domain: Abbr.
44. Dark periods in Riyadh
45. Lead-part players
46. Finally
48. Religious law
49. Norse goddess
50. Mime
52. Early associate of Caesar
57. Ale server
58. Arabs
59. Common contraction
60. Bristly
63. Enzyme suffix
64. Wrench
65. 1952 Pulitzer play with "The"
67. Shoe material: Abbr.
70. Bro's opposite
71. O.K.
72. Ace ——
75. Refreshment
79. River bottom
80. Director's guide
81. Swiss pine
83. Cattle genus
84. Meantime
85. Headland
86. Eastern women
87. Bits
89. Baltimore man
90. Styles
92. Even
98. Ancient Syria
99. Siberian river
100. Vial
101. Feigns
103. Grammar case: Abbr.
105. Approves
106. Notes
108. Without restraint
109. Covered in a way
110. Moon figure
111. Evaporates
113. Spanish numeral
115. Early U.S. homes
116. Penalty, in France
117. Form of Helen
118. A Montague
119. Less than mins.
120. Omar word
121. Old Roman fields
122. Radar dot
123. Bill
124. Gait
125. Israeli port
126. Capital of Aisne
127. Case
128. Italian family
130. Godly: It.
132. Rascal
133. Embryonic fowl

Music Lesson

by John Owens

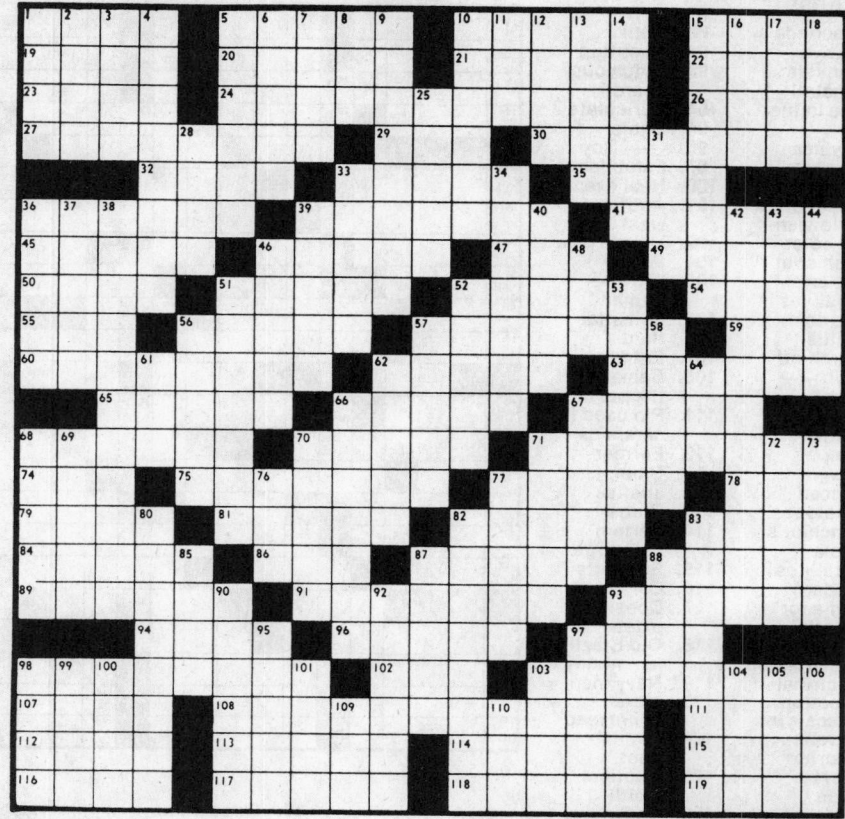

ACROSS

1. Gil ——
5. Stunted tree
10. Doze
15. Some radio men
19. Hindu scale
20. Record player: Abbr.
21. Anathema
22. Thanks ——
23. Borodin hero
24. Beethoven Quartets Opus 59
26. Part of N.B.
27. Musical quality
29. A kind of ear
30. Quadrangle
32. Prohibits
33. Kind of pie
35. Reddish brown
36. Song: Ger.
39. Following
41. Decoration on metal
45. Imitating
46. Disease germ
47. Breach
49. Dehydrated
50. Reward, old style
51. Spanish cleric
52. Noted columnist
54. Flying prefix
55. Plead
56. Passageway
57. "Turn of the Screw" composer
59. —— jour
60. Evil Jewish spirit
62. Do a grammar chore
63. Amen
65. Uneven
66. Pentateuch
67. Passengers
68. Monks
70. Indian soldier
71. Choral works
74. —— Ala- mos
75. Danish composer (1865-1931)
77. —— organ
78. Irving character
79. French opera section
81. Soot marks
82. Lowland: Scot.
83. Sheath
84. Perfume
86. Paleolithic, for one
87. French painter
88. Greenland base
89. U.S. com- poser
91. Composer of symphonic poems
93. Rang a bell
94. Lawyers: Abbr.
96. Tidal flood
97. Connery
98. Italian opera, with "La"
102. Large bird
103. One kind of partner
107. —— soit...
108. Baroque forms of compo- sition
111. College course:
Abbr.
112. Greek letters
113. U.S. emblem
114. Stale
115. Bristle
116. System: Abbr.
117. Taters
118. Misplayed
119. Waste allowance

DOWN

1. Small herring
2. Como
3. Greek contest
4. Spanish dance
5. Schumann's first sym- phony
6. Talks
7. Optimistic
8. One: It.
9. Small shop
10. Wall bracket
11. Former Broadway play
12. Formerly, old style
13. Glacial ridge
14. TV place
15. Carmen specialty
16. Shake ——
17. Prefix for gram or lith
18. British gun
25. Without
28. Eng. or Lat.
31. Police activity
33. Lehar's widow
34. Title of six Bach suites
36. Viola da
37. Swords
38. Composer of "Ozark Set"
39. Teams
40. Experience
42. Liszt opus
43. Vive ——
44. Tooth: Prefix
46. Worth
48. Kitty
51. South African composer
52. Finery
53. Heavily: Music
56. Ornament
57. Nobleman
58. Direction
61. —— pro nobis
62. Gregory et al.
64. Miss Lillie
66. Having left a will
67. Opera
68. Gordon of the comics
69. Composer of the "Dyb- buk"
70. Legatos
71. Centers
72. Passageway
73. Tempo
76. Uncle: Dialect
77. Pastor's home
80. Throw into ecstasy
82. Old French dance
83. Violin part
85. S.A. monkey
87. Myopic cartoon Mister
88. —— she blows!
90. Conditions
92. Egyptian king
93. Stopped
95. Subway fixture
97. Outpouring
98. Pronoun
99. Routine
100. Med. course
101. Pointed: Fr.
103. Recipe word
104. Cooler
105. Half or quar- ter, for in- stance
106. Pest
109. King Cole
110. Timetable abbreviation

19 Space Madness by Eileen Bush

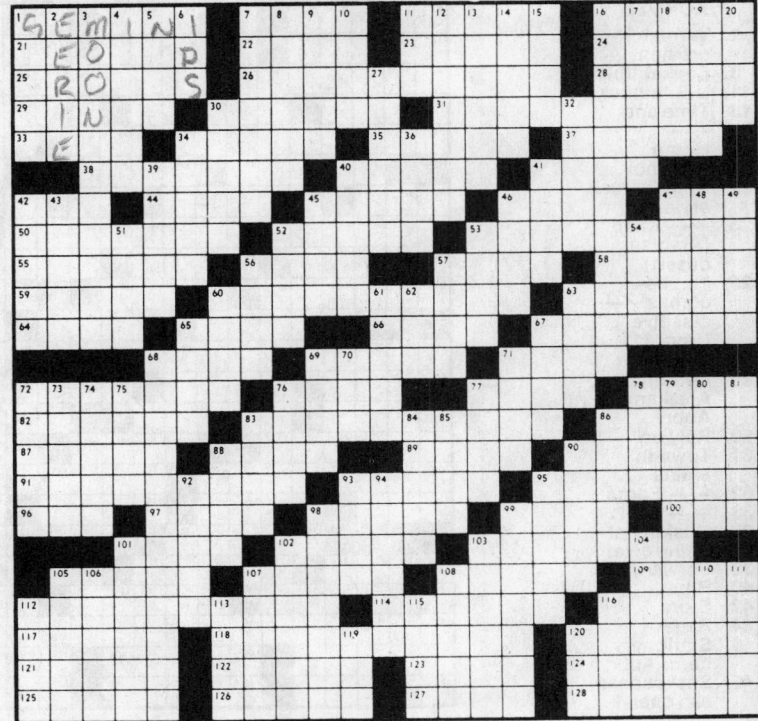

ACROSS

1. Early astronaut program
7. Particular: Abbr.
11. Truman's birthplace
16. Universe: Prefix
21. One of a meteor swarm
22. Cinema, in Europe
23. —— in arms
24. Hollywood name
25. Suffers attrition
26. Name of a planet's transit, perhaps
28. Chic
29. Forty ——
30. Rejects
31. Old and New
33. Kind of sign
34. Silly
35. Paw: Fr.
37. Like a julep
38. "The groves were God's first ——"
40. Spells
41. Numerical prefix
42. —— Magnon
44. Light ——
45. Drilled
46. Look of sorts
47. Chinese name
50. Round figure
52. Shore birds
53. Fighter planes
55. Conductor's word
56. River to the Colorado
57. Inform
58. Soviet moon rocket
59. Warm glow
60. Docking
63. Early dulcimer
64. Band, in heraldry
65. Humid
66. Art works
67. Fan
68. Seep
69. Artist's wear
71. —— d'oeuvre
72. Oct. 31 wear
76. Juncture
77. Ruth's husband
78. U.S. satellite
82. Narcotic
83. Dive, astronaut style
86. Upper space
87. Stroke on a letter
88. Twofold
89. Pronoun
90. Rise
91. Pendants on watch chains
93. Water bird
95. Absent
96. Desire
97. Reddish color
98. Employes
99. Part of N.B.
100. "To —— With Love"
101. Descended
102. Face for 72 Across
103. Organ stop
105. Kiel or Suez
107. Legal plea
108. Shopping areas
109. Color
112. Computing machine
114. Substantial
116. Overeats
117. Illinois city
118. Lunar blues, so to speak
120. Catch one's
121. Alpine peak
122. Mountain chain
123. Attracted
124. Kind of bean soup
125. A Churchill
126. Seed coating
127. Indian weights
128. Direction on a ship

DOWN

1. Early astronaut
2. Uncanny
3. Like lunar living?
4. Oily hydrocarbon
5. Deny: Fr.
6. Libidos
7. Master of a vessel
8. G.I.-locker photos
9. Access
10. Bathos: Slang
11. Wash basin: Abbr.
12. Backed in a way
13. Certain art works
14. Malign
15. Balance
16. Humor for serious astronauts
17. Former Philippine President
18. Meager
19. Borgnine role
20. Scraps
27. Ad astra per
30. Chef's creation
32. Mohammedan noble
34. Moonship's forte
36. Implements
39. Perfume ingredient
40. Greek goddesses
41. U.S. problem
42. Poke fun at
43. 100 kopecks
45. Forward
46. Maid
47. Helden-
48. Fence passage
49. Glacial ridge
51. That: Ger.
52. Retrogress
53. Under: Fr.
54. Burlap fiber
56. Part of a chromosome
57. U.S. President
60. Level
61. Goes like a spaceship
62. London's Old ——
63. French preposition
65. Type of roof
67. Fictional detective
68. Sign on astronaut's door
69. Convince: Colloq.
70. Pasture sound
71. Intimidates
72. TV star Bill
73. —— citato
74. Tempter of Ulysses
75. Part of a comet
76. Hot Springs et al.
77. Biography word
78. Do art work
79. Moon eruption, perhaps
80. Frenchman's name
81. Fraternal group
83. Fat
84. Host
85. Music pieces
86. Colorado park
88. Do housework
90. Top-notchers: Colloq.
92. Old pen
93. Half: Ger.
94. Navy man
95. Form of Helen
98. Snood
99. U.S. painter
101. Seaport of Italy
102. Inundates
103. One who sponges
104. Aid to success
105. Type of lily
106. Church area
107. In harmony
108. Watered silk
110. Type of nonsense
111. Pale
112. Hacks
113. Common Latin verb
115. Tote board listings
116. Mardi ——
119. Bible book: Abbr.
120. Win —— mile

Birth of a Nation *by Bert Beaman*

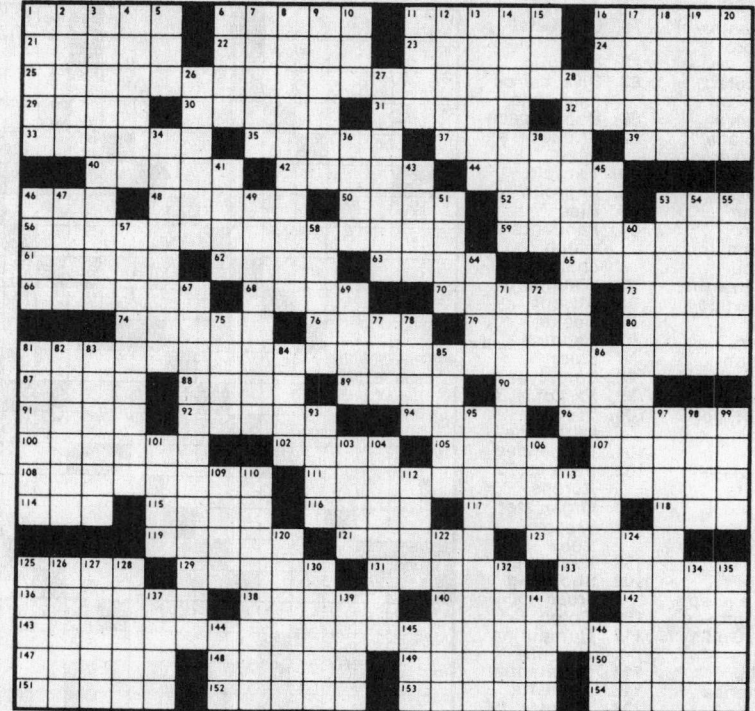

ACROSS

1. Varnish ingredient
6. Basket fiber
11. U.S. author
16. Time and ——
21. Home
22. —— Godunov
23. Architecture style
24. —— Khali (Arabian desert)
25. "...be-comes —— dissolve..." (from 111 Across)
29. Certain Alaskans: Abbr.
30. Rely on
31. Town in Maine
32. —— Forge
33. —— light
35. Oilskin hat
37. Asian civet
39. Forward
40. Rips
42. Store
44. Rage
46. Stationery item: Abbr.
48. Shakespearean character
50. Chemical suffixes
52. Bovary
53. Kind of dirt
56. With 111 Across, a document
59. "...us beyond —— tried..."
61. Networks
62. Resting
63. Asian river
65. Items on pirate flags
66. W.W. II vessels
68. Action: Suffix
70. Range
73. Golfer's concerns
74. Fat: Prefix
76. Smorgasbord items
79. Fabric finish
80. Being: Lat.
81. "—— Governments are instituted ..."
87. Make over
88. Laugh: Fr.
89. Flying prefix
90. Shorthander
91. Soon
92. Experience
94. Speed
96. Czech composer
100. Removes stitches
102. Mild oath
105. Concert offering: Abbr.
107. "—— mind in ..."
108. Boston ——
111. See 56 Across
114. Peer Gynt's mother
115. Word with drop or fall
116. French town
117. Rock shelf
118. Message: Abbr.
119. Spectral type
121. Actress Vivienne
123. Give —— (heed)
125. Men's party
129. Breaks
131. Showed gloom
133. "Life ——"
136. Hindu poet
138. Kind of ion: Suffix
140. "—— the West Wind"
142. River to the Rhine
143. "Our Lives, —— Honor"
147. Spaces
148. Alla —— in music
149. Remoulade
150. Reach
151. Layers
152. Beasts
153. —— Testament: Ger.
154. Gray

DOWN

1. Sticks
2. Portly
3. President's stratagem
4. —— Fideles
5. French article
6. Construction piece
7. Spore cluster
8. Carpenters' gauges
9. Erect
10. Inner: Prefix
11. Scent
12. Revere
13. Scenes of action
14. Counterstrokes
15. King conqueror
16. Harp: It.
17. Prepares peas
18. Poplar
19. Approach midnight
20. A signer of 56 Across
26. Spatial
27. Balkan state
28. Subdued
34. Attack
36. Came down
38. Certain
41. Stage direction
43. British cavalry force: Abbr.
45. Cover
46. Common French verb
47. Pacific islands: Abbr.
49. Union members
51. Close
53. Kosciuszko, for one
54. Most qualified
55. Words of assent
57. Phone sounds
58. Au revoir
60. Large fowl of West
64. Track event
67. One at a stadium mike
69. Antitoxins
71. Deform
72. Combine with: Suffix
75. Global area
77. Richard Henry ——
78. Rope part: Abbr.
81. Shock
82. Certain rinses
83. With one's back to: Fr.
84. Whale
85. Accumulate
86. Normans, for example
93. Psychiatrist's problems
95. Paid: Slang
97. Tracked down
98. Noun ending
99. Ship part
101. Admonish
103. Times of day: Abbr.
104. Quandary
106. —— cloth
109. Hayworth
110. Charms, in London
112. Kind of gage
113. Writer Marsh and others
120. Old capital of Brittany
122. Footless
124. Copies
125. Ermine in summer
126. Bull: Prefix
127. Coincide
128. Succeed
130. Symbol of leakiness
132. Look like the ——
134. Ridge
135. Influenced
137. Betsy
139. Employs
141. —— bien
144. Auto dealer's abbreviation
145. Shipper's group: Abbr.
146. Titled Turk

21

Up and Away

by Cornelia Warriner

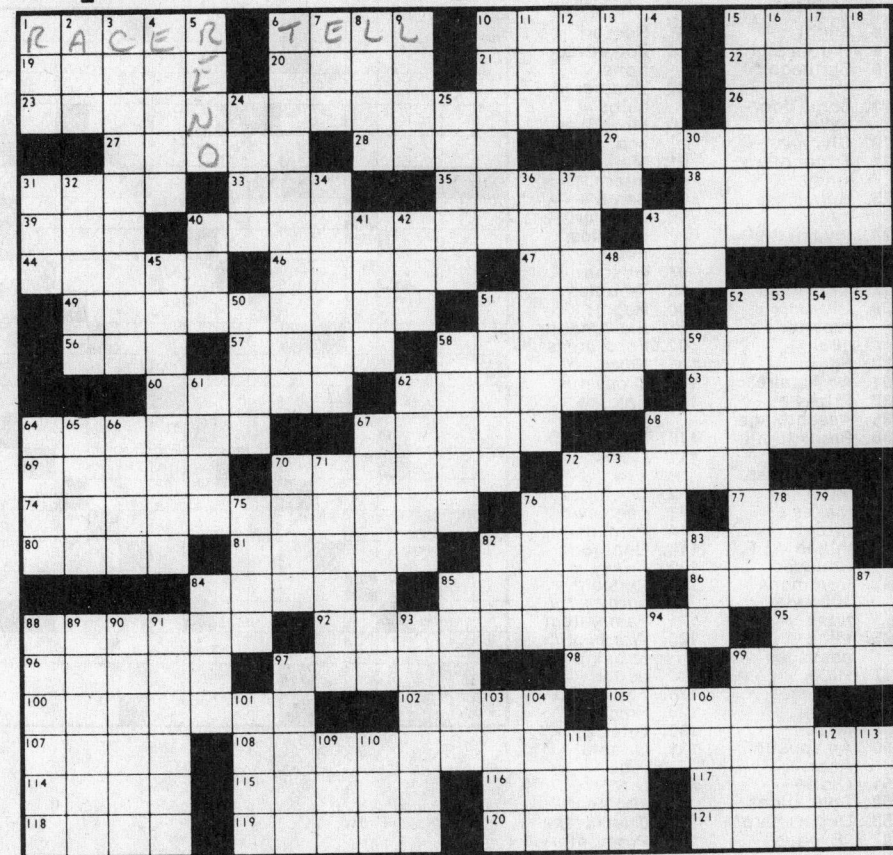

ACROSS

1. Le Mans entry
6. Tattle
10. Theda et al.
15. Down with: Fr.
19. Soap plant
20. Opera
21. Roman official
22. Bridge: Fr.
23. Subject of a Verne novel
26. Church booklet
27. Rule the ____
28. Permeate
29. Navy specialists
31. Like falling off a log
33. Article
35. Take again
38. "____ Not Alone"
39. Poetic form
40. Name for early moon-bound spider's home
43. ____ weensy
44. Billiard stroke
46. Lisa and others
47. Brazilian Indians
49. Preference
51. Month
52. Confound!
56. "____ had a million"
57. Party man
58. Ingredient of a satellite
60. Former V.I.P. at U.N.
62. Unpolished
63. Gladden
64. Taker
67. Footwear
68. Plays
69. Dog-tired
70. Leisured
72. Song
74. Mariner's job
76. Sped
77. Shoshonean
80. Soft-drink quality
81. Lariat
82. Separated
84. English dramatist
85. ____ worms
86. Pine substance
88. First baseball czar
92. Certain V.I.P.'s
95. Blaster's need
96. New York city
97. "____ twig is . . ."
98. Shrewd
99. Grasslands
100. Glass, in pharmacy
102. Saarinen
105. Did dishes
107. Increase, old style
108. Assignment for the Apollo II men
114. One in ambush
115. Missouri tributary
116. Black: It.
117. Asian sorghum: Var.
118. Porsena
119. Salamanders
120. Coffee grind
121. Successful

DOWN

1. Rule, in India
2. I love: Lat.
3. ". . . ____ the stars"
4. Man's name
5. Western city
6. ". . . be a dog and ____"
7. Eng. course
8. Flurries
9. Lessen
10. Phone sound device
11. Navy man: Abbr.
12. ____ de Oro
13. In space
14. Classman: Abbr.
15. Point in orbit
16. One of trio on first moon orbit
17. Companion of 16 Down
18. Obdurate
24. Baltic state: Abbr.
25. Assembles
30. Has an obligation
31. July 31, for example: Abbr.
32. Cotton from Bengal
34. Selfish one
36. Labor pioneer
37. Architects' patterns
40. Private eye
41. Relatives, familiarly
42. West
43. Soft mineral
45. ____ fire
48. Russian hemp
50. Flanged beam
51. Set ____ of interest
52. "Au Clair ____"
53. Paper measure
54. Movie dog
55. Pipe joints
58. Brant
59. Man of the hour
61. Whetstone
62. Australian shrub
64. Bligh: Abbr.
65. ____ breve
66. Flight ____
67. Medical assay
68. Three: Ger.
70. English painter
71. Musical syllables
72. Brown colors
73. Words for a good splashdown
75. Very: Fr.
76. State: Abbr.
78. Put through a dry run
79. Scottish city, to poets
82. ____ Paulo
83. Alternatives
84. Evergreen
85. Inch along
87. Certain times: Abbr.
88. Gemini spaceman
89. Girl's name
90. Infernal
91. Brave ones
93. College chores
94. Beginner
97. Divert
99. Fruit
101. Preposition
103. Covering
104. River to the Baltic
106. Prefix for a country
109. Shooter
110. Deputy: Abbr.
111. Silkworm
112. Gold: Sp.
113. Fuzz

22 Wherewithal

by H.L. Risteen

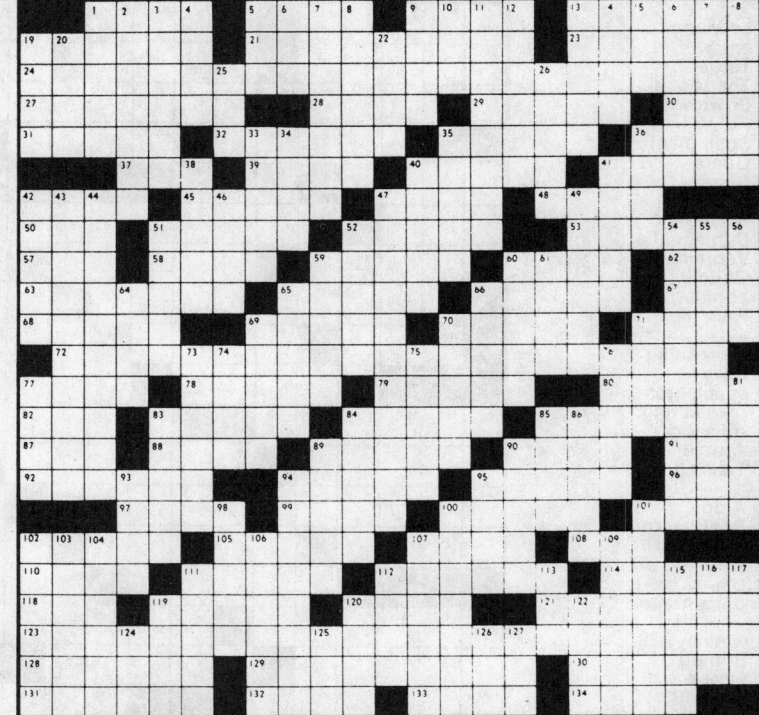

ACROSS

1. Slight
5. Harbor sight
9. Carthage foe
13. Some doorbells
19. Olympian
21. Editor of a kind
23. Burger ballad
24. Plea of the '30s
27. Trades
28. Nobleman
29. Old-time reporter's goal
30. Edge
31. An Astaire
32. Prizes
35. Assemblage
36. Prefix for fit or factor
37. Old English letter
39. Makes turbid
40. Indian V.I.P.
41. Reduced
42. Common abbreviations
45. Mine passages
47. Hitler predecessor
48. Mark
50. An apostle: Abbr.
51. Old ——
52. Solicitudes
53. Dumas hero
57. "Exodus" hero
58. Portuguese money
59. French city
60. Aaron
62. Parseghian
63. Most rigid
65. French keys
66. Artery
67. Young animal
68. Bristles
69. Paired
70. Onward
71. —— majesty
72. Inconsistent
77. Monterrey money
78. Ventilator
79. —— of thought
80. Confuse
82. Insect
83. Fishing equipment
84. Of an arm bone
85. Salutation in Soissons
87. Dessert
88. Zoo attractions
89. Undergrad clubs
90. Moved, at sea
91. Merkel
92. Infer
94. Santa ——
95. Cobbler supplies
96. Fetch
97. Obscure
99. Troubles
100. Report
101. Exclamation
102. Farm areas
105. Flirts
107. Cross out
108. Folding money
110. Water birds
111. Crosscut saw
112. Doctor's needlework
114. Palm genus
118. Unburden
119. Frisky
120. Persian sprite
121. Pastry item
123. Words prior to being parted
128. Shore bird
129. Freckle
130. Grieg girl
131. Oriental rugs
132. U.S. engineer
133. Coal layer
134. Promontory

DOWN

1. Strand
2. Annoys
3. Disregard
4. Beverage
5. Ocean: Abbr.
6. Leave —— huff
7. Groups of nine
8. Old English coins
9. Stem: Prefix
10. Siamese coins
11. Rigging
12. Person of great wisdom
13. Athenian foe of Sparta
14. Bestow, as praise
15. Neither Dem. nor Rep.
16. Drudge
17. Small animal
18. Oozed
19. Eastern church title
20. Rooted custom: Abbr.
22. Rock pinnacles
25. Army man: Abbr.
26. Urban sunbath areas
33. Eastern notables
34. Obligation
35. Throws
36. Vamp of silents
38. Summons
40. Roman goddess
41. Alaskan attire
42. French political units
43. Middlesex money
44. Mint worker
46. Dutch coin
47. Kennedy items
49. "We —— on like this"
51. Long —— (money)
52. Grow, as a vine
54. Earns, informally
55. Fabric
56. Marquis de ——
59. Fix a dress
60. Does a vaudeville turn
61. European river
64. Healthy: Sp.
65. Lawyers' staple
66. Tree
69. Gets stuck
70. Coins of India
71. Headwear: Slang
73. Noisy canine
74. Message
75. Western range
76. Byways
77. Cashier's stamp
81. Muse
83. Molten outpourings
84. Soviet range
85. Heavy knife
86. Public
89. Business gamble: Colloq.
90. Big hit
93. Roman period
94. Tropical plant
95. Pacific sea
98. Islamic text
100. Suite
101. Well-known Greek
102. Heavenly being
103. Toy
104. —— pools
106. Nondieter's friend
107. Farm animals
109. Holy Land man
111. Chicago team
112. Numerical prefix
113. Period
115. Kicks
116. Indonesian isle
117. Russian river
119. Russian whip
120. Sibilant signals
122. Asian land
124. Cells
125. State: Abbr.
126. High note
127. Vegetable

Digging into Things by Ruth Ball

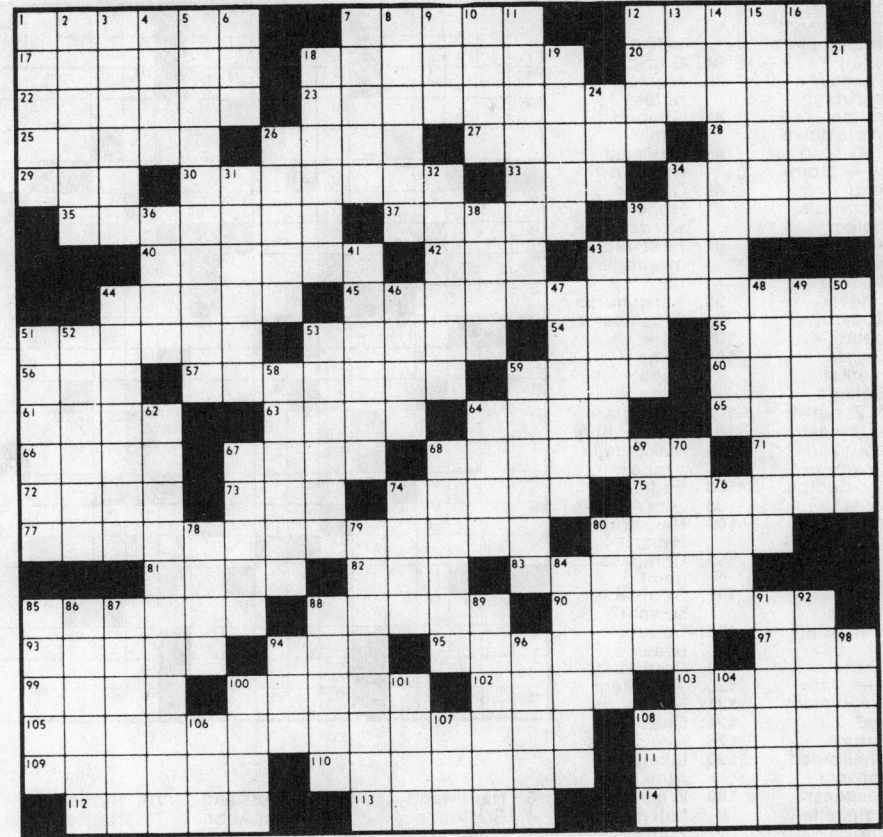

ACROSS

1. Glacial epoch
7. Quality
12. Setting for "Kate"
17. Well-excavated city of Egypt
18. —— mark
20. —— phrase
22. Paris subways
23. Experts in looking back
25. Belonging to: Suffix
26. Formerly, old style
27. Comes in last
28. Then, in France
29. Furnace man: Abbr.
30. Roistering
33. Theater area
34. Rain in Paris
35. "—— bug in . . ."
37. Up
39. Amundsen and others
40. Shrewish ones
42. Shoe width: Abbr.
43. Eject
44. Mexican coins
45. Materials for a dig
51. French revolutionary family
53. Caravansary
54. Sullivan and others
55. —— machine
56. Gums: Prefix
57. Alpine tunnel
59. Endure: Scot.
60. Stratagem
61. Marionette maker
63. Man's name
64. Denials
65. Dwellings of a kind
66. Building beam
67. Potpourri
68. Really?
71. Grasp
72. Part of N.B.
73. Settled down
74. Stared
75. Overage
77. Moraine
80. Mountain in Greece
81. Le Gallienne and others
82. Boater
83. Clog in a way
85. Lorna and family
88. Watched the late show
90. "Beneath the —— frown he stands. . ."
93. Fragrant root
94. —— de deux
95. A geological age, for short
97. Famous Giant
99. 500 sheets
100. Confused skirmish
102. Golf positions
103. Earth
105. Locale for Schliemann
108. Ancient Cretan
109. Antelope of India
110. Dessert
111. Settle
112. Blinds, as a hawk
113. Rigid
114. Imminent

DOWN

1. Betels
2. Dark rocks
3. King in "Iliad"
4. —— cadabra
5. Certain scientists
6. Feminine suffix
7. Sculptured form
8. Clergyman
9. Residue
10. Sloping type: Abbr.
11. Locale of a Marx movie
12. Directions for readers: Abbr.
13. Before Sept.
14. Excavate in a special way
15. Destroy the spirit
16. Former Belgian queen
18. Clan identity
19. Rose-red dye
21. Blockheads
24. Tennis term
26. Mitigates
31. Aegean sight: Abbr.
32. Trash item
34. Elegant: Slang
36. Eye part
38. H.H. Munro
39. Charlotte ——
41. Word form for cave
43. Most peculiar
44. Proportionately
46. Ore deposit
47. Sea nymph
48. Germs
49. Gladdens
50. Slips
51. Pondering
52. —— of love
53. Elf
58. Marine fishes
59. Russ. river
62. Idol
64. Hitler
67. Spanish jars
68. Compute
69. Improved
70. Archaeologist's work
74. Fall guy
76. Rio's beach
78. Times of day
79. End slowly
80. Lily plants ——
84. —— be (in case)
85. Mark Van ——
86. Appetite, in psychology
87. Divine revelation
88. Of a Frankish people
89. Son of Poseidon
91. Impassable
92. Layers
94. Cosset
96. Saltpeter
98. Former Chief Justice
100. But, in Paris
101. Word in Mass. motto
104. Ref. work
106. Lace
107. Post: Abbr.
108. English teachers' group: Abbr.

24

Riddles

by Frances Hansen

ACROSS

1. Moved like a snail
6. Remove a cartridge primer
11. Wets down
16. "My Lord, —— Morning!"
21. Actress's helper
22. African antelope
23. —— of the finger
24. Took to court
25. Greek market
26. Enlarge
27. N.Z. native
28. Allow as how
29. Down-in-the-dumps lama?
31. Whirlybird hitchhiker?
34. Informal greetings
35. Thos. and others
36. Malaysian sir
37. Uneasy
38. —— date
40. Small plant leaf
42. Fatty
46. Unadorned convent headgear?
50. Constellation
53. Strong ——
54. Chemical suffix
55. Italian poet: 1754-1828
56. —— Mater
58. Persian fairy
59. Aim
61. Wee one
63. Becomes winterbound
64. Footless animals
65. Cousin of a sari
66. Constant
67. Long distance, figuratively
68. Bit ——
69. Nimble
72. "Young Man of Caracas" author
74. José's aunt
76. Individual
77. Jaunty bird?
81. Tasteless

84. Corrida cry
85. Musical notes
86. Almond drink
88. City near Boys Town
89. Cup: Fr.
91. Hobo song words
93. First name in whodunits
95. Asian nurse
99. Organ parts
100. Bulk
101. Hugh Capet, for one
102. A Borgia
104. Type of billy
105. Makes fast a rope
106. Endured
108. Like Abner
109. New York Indian
111. Compass point
112. Excusable servant?
116. Certain beds
118. Dorm buddy
120. —— Mare
121. Makes tea
124. Chassé
125. —— Darya
126. Likely: Abbr.
130. Breakfast fish exporter
134. Brooding Indian
136. Jewish months
137. Lugger
138. Loup ——
141. Fragrant oil
142. Vocal style: Abbr.
143. Musical work
144. Confederate general
145. Fingerprint feature
146. Baltic people
147. She just growed
148. Hit a high fly ball
149. Roles

DOWN

1. Coarse fabric
2. Scoundrel
3. Hard wood
4. Brightens
5. Mine car
6. Petula Clark hit
7. Norse boys' names
8. El ——
9. Honest one
10. Hairnet's companion
11. Vic
12. Don't be ——!
13. Between l and r
14. Polynesian skirt
15. Flowering shrub
16. Unidentified one
17. Cheerful dad?
18. Take ——
19. Adjust
20. Mime
30. Bone: Greek
32. In the pink
33. Attacked
36. Kind of dance
39. Faucets and pipes: Abbr.
40. Zola
41. Spud grader
43. Small change in 25 Across
44. Piano mute: Sp.
45. Lived
46. Muslim title of respect
47. Don Juan's mother
48. Plateau
49. "Be —— so humble..."
51. See 2 Down
52. Red powder of India
56. Shoe, in Italy
57. Whensoever
60. Oil country: Var.
62. Chicken purchaser
63. —— man answers
64. Embarrass
66. Hard to pin down

70. Revolves
71. Native: Suffix
73. Mild rural expletives
75. Lupino
77. Saucepan ammunition?
78. Herb genus
79. Does a cobbler's job
80. Live teddy bears
82. Nymphette of fiction
83. Shoe widths
87. Scotch uncle
90. Cracked spar
92. Beauty spot
94. O'Grady
96. Bamako's country
97. "Questa o quella," for one
98. State of misery
102. Arise

103. Noble: Ger.
105. More plain
107. Ancient cast
110. Loathes
112. Yea or nay
113. Comes forth
114. Tuck's partner
115. Dry-cleaner
117. Sonnet part
119. Fish hawk
122. Snap
123. Watch the late show
125. Soap plant
127. Machine part
128. Modern paintings
129. Rolls a log
130. Poet Shapiro
131. French notion
132. Agreement
133. Jaywalkers: Abbr.
135. Bawl
139. Bird of prey, Cockney style
140. Ferdinand V

25 Capital Ideas

by Kirk Dodd

ACROSS

1. Hails
8. Cavies
13. Coin of Mid-East
20. Address loudly
21. People of Teheran
22. Plunge into a fluid
23. City in Granada
24. N.A. geological era
26. Grampus
27. Early Brazos settler
29. Moslem saint
30. Nobel physicist: 1952
32. Set a course
33. Heads
34. Middling
35. Hibernia
36. Styptic
37. Sheepfolds
38. Fountain orders
39. Children's game
41. City in West Germany
42. Satchel
43. Mean sea-level line
44. Interweave
45. Summon
46. Oddments
48. Beverages
49. One-time caller at Trinidad
53. Pea and nut
54. Erie, for one
55. Cracow people
56. Number
57. Strikes
58. Pebbles
60. Burma, Pakistan, etc.
61. Indian
62. Lemur
63. Aegean island
64. Perfume
65. Archipelago of Pacific
67. Grass genus
68. Ones at the helm
69. Elder: Fr.
70. Opted
71. American family of painters
72. Thin layer
75. Teen-agers' monopoly
76. Bewailed
79. Poplar
80. Opinions
81. Restrain
82. —— clock scholar
83. Soviet press agency
84. See eye ——
85. Productive
86. Hauls
87. High note
88. English essayist (1861-1922)
91. Agency of the 30s: Abbr.
92. Sec. of State under Wilson
94. Idle
96. Enliven: Lat.
97. Jog
98. Drain
99. Result of a salary cut
100. Rapiers
101. Encourages

DOWN

1. —— as a judge
2. Chaplin
3. Fruit
4. Inoperative
5. Cache
6. U.S. sculptor
7. Like some churches
8. Biblical treasure city
9. Court decree: Fr.
10. French city
11. Nova Scotia's —— Royal
12. Located
13. Liquid measures: Fr.
14. Kaffir fighters
15. Word of concurrence
16. Indian weight
17. Locale in Marine song
18. Peacocks
19. Emblem of 15th century
25. "Drang nach ——"
28. Rel. of sing.
31. Barley and rye
34. Oregon city
36. Vis- ——
37. Dances
38. Sorcerer
40. "——, sorry"
41. Of a space
42. Dells
44. Inclinations
45. Presidential family
46. Second-stringer
47. Tropical raccoon
48. Dyeing technique
49. Beverage
50. Dog
51. Eastern Christian
52. Torrefies
54. Siren of "Odyssey"
55. Ceremony: Fr.
58. Novel heroine
59. Poker move
60. Mollusk genus
62. Singer Frankie
64. Leeds's river
66. Postal system
67. Does an after-sports routine
68. Quince, for example
70. Indian
71. Girl's name
72. Pitchout, in football
73. Ear shell
74. Ore range
75. Famous sculpture
76. Guipure
77. Understanding
78. Prescription units
80. Kind of ball
81. Low parts of ships
84. Czech range
85. Meander
86. Western attire
88. Garment
89. Lie at anchor
90. Leaves
93. Type measures
95. Winter topic of talk

Colorful Airs

by Anne Fox

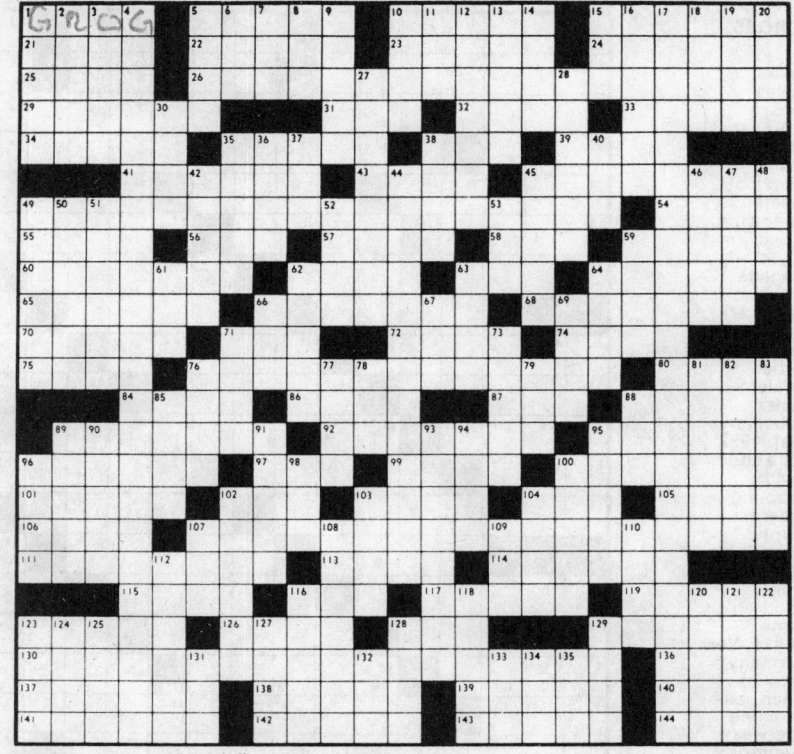

ACROSS

1. Sailors' drink
5. Monkey
10. Half of a magic formula
15. Wheedle
21. San ——
22. Oriental rug
23. Man of Meshed
24. Cut out
25. Hindu god
26. Music by Cole Porter
29. Moves furtively
31. Apiece
32. Levee
33. Up ——
34. Pacific org.
35. Bone
38. Meet
39. Piano piece
41. Card game
43. Sew up
45. Mogul
49. Music by Gershwin
54. Dance
55. Irish exclamation: Var.
56. "Conning Tower" man
57. British marshal of W.W.I.
58. Gelid
59. Barrier of physics
60. Keepsake
62. Apocrypha books: Abbr.
63. Half of a musical
64. Capers
65. Somewhat
66. Capuchins
68. Theater ticket bargains
70. Cliff dwelling
71. Clash
72. S.A. weapon
74. Runabout
75. Fur
76. Song of 1862
80. Defense group
84. Baleful
86. Old pottery pail
87. Clumsy fellow
88. U.S.A. rank
89. Nonsense!
92. Recanted, in a way
95. Gypsy: Fr.
96. Art form
97. Exclamation of disgust
99. Fall guy
100. Musical of 1933
101. Téte-à-téte
102. Musical syllable
103. White House tenant
104. Gas: Prefix
105. Family members: Abbr.
106. Dub
107. Lyrics by Mitchell Parish
111. Zinc
113. Sea birds
114. Punk
115. A Chaplin
116. Zip
117. Lowlander
119. Mediterranean ship
123. War ——
126. Cartoonist Addams
128. Gumbo
129. State of India
130. Part of "Annie Laurie"
136. An age
137. —— middle course
138. Golden
139. Manifest
140. Dare, old style
141. Residue
142. American poetess
143. Spanish port
144. Letters

DOWN

1. Shade of green
2. Rule: Fr.
3. Vincit —— veritas
4. Part of an academy song
5. Bulges
6. Kirghiz city
7. Guevara
8. Round Table knight
9. Giraffe's cousin
10. Wharf
11. Sphere
12. —— Forks (B.C. battle)
13. Dark
14. Material
15. Navy initials
16. Wild sheep
17. Music by Hoagy Carmichael
18. —— about
19. Unaspirated
20. Arctic island
27. Return partner's suit
28. Tenfold
30. Eyelid darkener
35. Allegro, for one
36. Pelvic bones
37. Containers: Abbr.
38. Dance
40. Kind of ball
42. Strapping
44. Town wear of song
45. Edging
46. Mood
47. Agalloch
48. Turns left
49. Witches
50. One of the Du Ponts
51. Italian condiment
52. Thai language
53. Offer
59. Talent
61. Scotch refusal
62. Poetic times
63. Holm
64. Fairbanks
66. Fortify
67. Pronoun
69. W.W. II initials
71. Guys
73. Under way
76. Ency. ——
77. Uh-huh
78. Swat
79. Principle
81. Incense holder of old Rome
82. Drum
83. An enzyme
85. Wild goat
88. Game shot
89. Position tracker
90. Group of Islamic savants
91. Iroquoian
93. Old Rhodes sight
94. Japanese ware
95. Not with it
96. Slam
98. Chin
100. Actress Ada
102. Wallop
103. Salon item, for short
104. Vapor: Prefix
107. Languid
108. Ease
109. Duty
110. Cunning
112. Old fogy
116. Prize
118. For this: Lat.
120. Cheap merchandise
121. Worn at the edges
122. Coins
123. Go by
124. Flower: Prefix
125. Item sometimes big
127. Piece of metal
128. Mickey and family
129. Capital of Moselle
131. Cape
132. German dessert
133. Girl's name
134. Florid
135. Son of Gad

Sizing Things Up

by Eva Pollack Taub

ACROSS

1. Skirt
7. Indian weight
11. Greatest
15. Man with a sword
16. Arithmetic device
19. Nonentity
21. Well-known Cockney
23. Bird
24. Canals on U.S. border
25. Mean abode
26. Track
27. Evergreen
28. Helper: Abbr.
30. Forbearance
32. Place for a barbecue
34. Home buyer's concern: Abbr.
35. Luster
37. Give the go-by
39. Meaning
41. Buddhist temple
42. Plumber's concern
45. "—— corny as . . ."
47. Role in "Barber of Seville"
49. On the loose
52. Planet
54. Word in a Hardy title
56. Greek letter
57. ". . . we all do fade as ——"
59. Disturb
61. Embankments
63. Recent: Prefix
64. Kingfish
65. Fastened
67. One of the Three Stooges
68. Groups: Abbr.
70. Town on the Hudson
73. Secular
74. Girl's name
76. Swelling disease of fish
77. Early age
79. English river
80. Postulate
82. Slack part of a sail
83. Minor prophet
84. Noun suffix
85. Writ against a debtor
87. Nickname for Miss Ederle
89. Fabrics
91. One who makes up
93. State: Abbr.
94. Hostess's request
95. Container
97. Flint: Prefix
99. Swedish chemist
101. Gladden
105. Word element for a country
107. Silent star
109. Plants of a region
112. Caledonian
113. Charge
115. Scratchers
117. Dunne
119. Chem. prefix
120. Bridge moves
121. Broadway play of 1953
124. Flowers
125. Design
126. Bull-like
127. Tree toad
128. Modern concern
129. People of a world area

DOWN

1. Winter footwear
2. Indolent
3. Bolivia's La ——
4. Esau's wife
5. Biblical locale
6. Treasure ——
7. Ballerina Maria
8. Sash
9. Plaster backing
10. Misbehave
11. Star in Cetus
12. A kind of den
13. Gear for hams
14. Russian cart
15. Flat-topped hills
17. Bones
18. Dog
19. Vast
20. Lease again
22. Poetic words
29. Tissue: Anat.
31. Arizona city
33. Privy to
36. Chemical liquid
38. Village in New York
40. Vain: Ger.
43. Shining
44. Wailed
46. Thick-set
48. Of snow
49. City in Illinois
50. French saint
51. Area of Queens, N.Y.
53. Scout activity
55. Strangest
58. Dye workers
60. Slow, in music
62. Chinese mediums of exchange
65. Abdomen: Prefix
66. River of Ukraine
69. Weather word
71. Ex-film star Jack
72. Taunts
75. Ancient Greek city
78. Unworldly
81. Tim's quality
83. Feature
86. End: Pref.
88. Unhearing
90. Army men: Abbr.
92. Boxing jabs
95. Headpiece
96. Not on credit
98. Sound like an old door
100. Japanese seaweed
102. Colorless liquid
103. Subway items
104. Storehouse
106. European thrush
108. Signed in a way
110. Lariat
111. Indian coins
114. Fluids
116. Bristle: Prefix
118. Small case
122. Richthofen, for one
123. Relative of Mme.

Working People by Thomas W. Schier

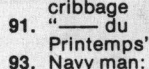

ACROSS

1. Smooth off
7. Lugosi
11. Marlowe, for one
15. Living quarters: Abbr.
19. Minnesota Fats, for one
20. Michigan's waterfront
21. Pack animal
22. Kind of hog
23. Offer a legal excuse
24. Heath genus
25. Faust
27. Memorable play of 1946
30. Brand of figs
31. Attach firmly
32. Staff officers
33. Sets ——
37. Neck wrap
38. Glacial ridges
40. Luminous circles
43. Mediocre
44. Campus building
45. Kind of jacket
48. Door-to-door lads
51. Overly bland
55. Hip bones
56. Word of mouth
57. Bristle
58. Elevation: Abbr.
59. Doing: Suffix
61. Collaborator
63. Slope, in fortification
67. Merry-andrew
69. Exclamation
70. Teachers' org.
71. African javelin
72. From —— Z
73. Makes a scene
75. Foggy
77. Danish coin
78. Bell sound
81. Well-known Russian
85. Ripened
86. Prefix with corn or form
87. Illinois first name
88. Hercules's captive and others
89. Jack in

cribbage
91. "—— du Printemps"
93. Navy man: Abbr.
96. Peas or beans: Abbr.
97. Musical composition
101. African fetish
102. Glad, to poets
103. Swedish town
104. Stake
105. Pronoun
106. Item in a bibliothèque
108. Cordelia's father
110. Onlooker
113. Cooper man
117. Find by chance
118. Raceway event
119. City in West
120. Candy
122. Lawyers: Abbr.
126. Wheel part
127. Petitions
129. Town of Asia Minor (Latin sp.)
131. This, in old Rome
132. Metal piece
134. John Gay opus
139. Hothouse workers
143. Negative contraction
144. Type of decoration
145. In —— shell
146. Bell town
147. Yes ——
148. ——-camp
149. Fabric
150. Sounds for attention
151. Kind of tube
152. Coin user of a sort

DOWN

1. Cards in a low straight
2. Garden features
3. Grayish-green
4. Mine: Fr.
5. Eastern ketch
6. Nine: Prefix
7. Stove part
8. Discoverer of Vinland
9. Part of a train, for short
10. P.I. sumac
11. —— pencil
12. Fragment
13. Offend
14. Extremely
15. Military acronym
16. Hairdo
17. Quivering motions
18. Rivulet
20. Leave port
21. English spa
26. Calm area
28. Unit of metric length
29. Word for annual winds
34. Flanders Field symbol
35. Sailing
36. Newsman
39. Helpers of Drs.
41. Excluding both
42. Piercing

tool
44. Sweet: It.
46. Pismire
47. Chauffeurs of a sort
49. Fence part
50. Domineering
51. —— Mahal
52. Be obligated
53. Cricket sides
54. Spring wild flower
60. Impossible
62. Gambler's mecca
64. Excited
65. Like Ben Jonson
66. Variegated
68. Child's game
71. Month: Abbr.
73. Electronics initials
74. Member of a Burmese people
76. Western group:

Abbr.
78. Sofian: Abbr.
79. Unique person
80. Unless: Lat.
82. Cheer
83. Copter, at times
84. "—— Three Lives"
85. Man's nickname
87. Pungent
90. Surpass
92. Metal point
94. Sourpuss
95. 4,840 square yards
98. Jutting rock
99. Clumsy boat
100. Noun suffix
102. Household plants
104. Item for a leaky boat
107. Steam
109. Consort of Shamash
111. Sheathed
112. Spanish

queen
113. Champion of the people
114. Batter's quest
115. Palliates
116. Forest group
118. Threefold
121. French historian
123. "... —— a way"
124. Harangue
125. Alpine figure
127. Soul: Fr.
128. Surprised exclamation
130. —— as a pig
133. Concerning
135. Rope fiber
136. Wyandot's cousin
137. Miscellany
138. Siliques
140. Beat the
141. Prison areas: Abbr.
142. Interweave

Taking a Position by Threba Johnson

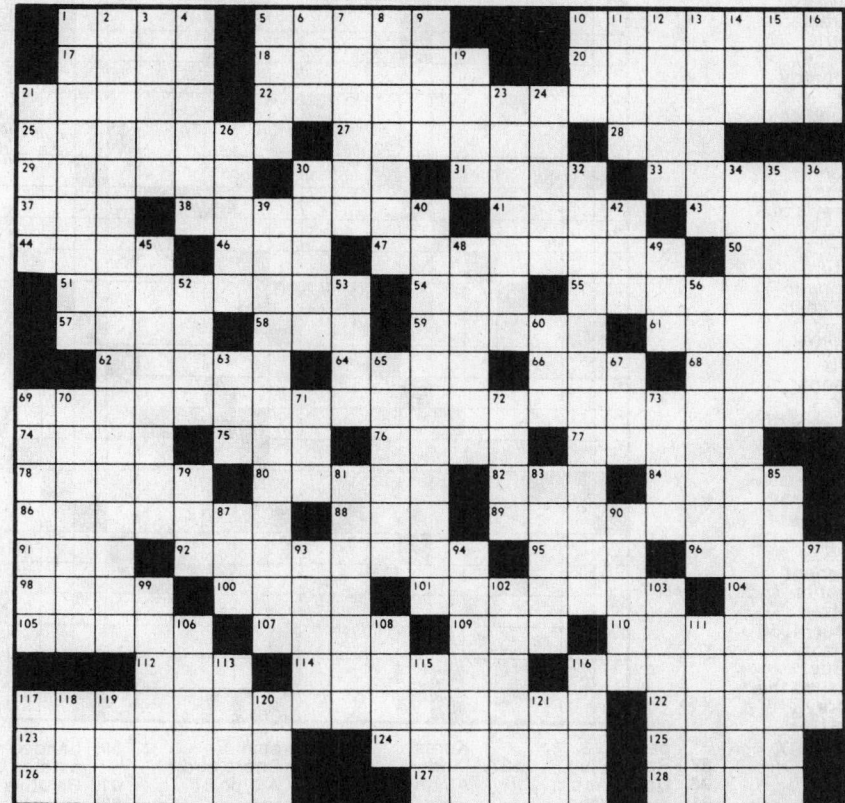

ACROSS

1. Hero of Greek legend
5. Shakespearean shepherdess
10. Himalayan animal
17. Alaskan city
18. Order: Fr.
20. Madison Ave. thinkers
21. Author O'Connor
22. Goodman book
25. Making a thrust
27. Cassia plants
28. Wrong: Prefix
29. —— cantorum
30. Like: Suffix
31. Welsh name
33. Racetrack pests
37. Negrito
38. Theologian of 16th cent.
41. Alike: Fr.
43. Old weapon
44. Choices: Abbr.
46. Conditions
47. Gounod's "—— et Baucis"
50. Army medal
51. Means of transportation
54. French season
55. Skilled interpreter
57. Marquis de
58. Initials on an airline board
59. Backed a cause
61. S.A. catfish
62. Kind of eclipse
64. 1949 treaty
66. Word of respect in India
68. Feminine suffix
69. Epitaph for a movie palace
74. Preposition
75. Divinity degree
76. Majority
77. Do a grammar chore
78. Mexican Indian
80. Hinder legally
82. Sit-down result
84. Vestments
86. On the —— a wave
88. Letter
89. Slight
91. U.S. dept.
92. Devices for catching fish
95. Pique
96. Homeless tot
98. Rat- ——
100. Nautical term
101. "No" voter
104. Road: Abbr.
105. —— the land
107. Testing places
109. Long time
110. Sell: Fr.
112. Young seal
114. Rattle on a harness
116. Subscription affair
117. On Cloud 9
122. Part of to have: Fr.
123. Without means of rowing
124. One-up word
125. Bow man
126. Circuses
127. Momentum
128. Places of refuge

DOWN

1. Ones called for service
2. Leonard Woolf book
3. Mexican friend
4. Of old age
5. Steal, in Scotland
6. 1949 peace Nobelist
7. Toast
8. Cinched
9. Have —— ear
10. Sleeper
11. Dutch cheese
12. Ledger entry
13. Singers
14. Large bird
15. Gas: Prefix
16. 3 mins. of boxing: Abbr.
19. Nine: Prefix
21. Maxwell and others
23. Called to order
24. Treatment
26. Village of East Bengal
30. Caucasus native
32. Some social climbers
34. Rostin book
35. With a will
36. One who quits
39. Miller play
40. Part of a Goldsmith title
42. Smoked salmon
45. Diligent
48. Adjective suffix
49. Composer Rorem
52. Medical prefix
53. Borge
56. Obeys a street sign
60. Compass reading
63. Sternward
65. A king of Egypt
67. "—— body meet..."
69. Madeira port
70. Inimical planet
71. Pinafore
72. French town
73. Soviet range
79. Lawyer: Abbr.
81. Darkness
83. Par ——
85. Sports areas
87. Danish money
90. Pass a rope through
93. Fruit
94. Make oneself heard
97. Senses
99. Formal wear
102. Regulate
103. Tebaldi
106. Code, in Spanish law
108. Are: Fr.
111. To no extent
113. Kind of school
115. N.M. colony
116. Marsh grass
117. Central area
118. Zoology suffix
119. Biblical prince
120. Football scores: Abbr.
121. Article

No Extra Charge
by W.E. Jones

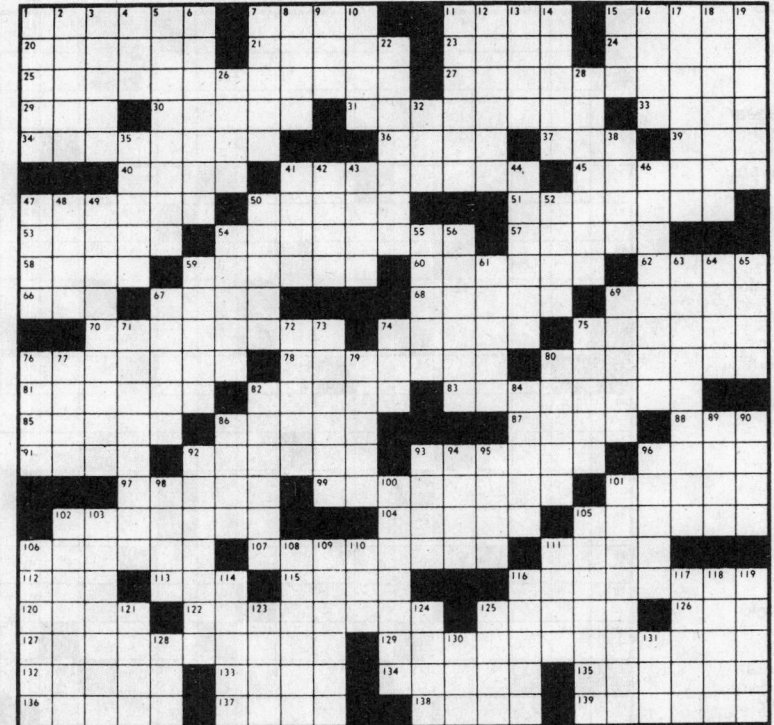

ACROSS

1. Character in "Faerie Queene"
7. Lombardy lake
11. Iceland epic
15. Concentrates
20. Layer
21. States
23. Money's offshoot
24. Yoga posture
25. Acrobatic bookkeeping
27. Wall St. prefix
29. Calendar abbr.
30. Sell —— of goods
31. The's, e.g.
33. During
34. Head areas
36. The —— of Tempe
37. Spire ornament
39. Direction
40. Pulitzer author, 1958
41. Advisory groups
45. Finished the laundry
47. Relatives
50. Of melody
51. Graduation guests
53. Hogarth men
54. Buck
57. That is: Lat.
58. Defeats at bridge
59. Moon goddess
60. 40,000- —— (big ship)
62. Genus of bees
66. —— bonne heure
67. Mailed
68. Makes a stab at
69. Belief
70. Slow as ——
74. Grants
75. Shed copiously
76. Inspire
78. Of heat
80. Costa Rica export
81. Takes a new tenant
82. Tunneled
83. Formality
85. Cooking byproducts
86. Panama port
87. Roman jug
88. Dock: Abbr.
91. —— everything
92. Flair
93. "... —— trash"
96. Relative of zool.
97. Special drink
99. Symbol of wealth
101. Cavity: Anat.
102. Stars, for Cicero
104. Port where Greeks sailed for Troy
105. Most feeble
106. Of the wrist
107. Poured
111. Town in Hungary
112. Wine vessel
113. His: Fr.
115. Chinese dynasty
116. Student's emblem
120. Wash: Lat.
122. Mozart opus
125. Contradict
126. City in Korea
127. Modern Aladdin's lamp
129. Has it made
132. Publicized
133. Batting backstop
134. Water wheel
135. Long time for poets
136. Eastern civet
137. Stettin's river
138. Tiresias was one
139. Large basket

DOWN

1. Illinois city
2. Polo
3. Leaves undone
4. Inlet
5. Blows up
6. Cats
7. Puts and ——
8. Athletic field
9. "Testimony of Two ——"
10. Killer whale
11. Chancel
12. Shore bird
13. A type of net
14. Lane: Fr.
15. Golf goal
16. Mountain in Thessaly
17. Garb
18. Jets, e.g.
19. Worked on floors
22. Sycophantic
26. Wing: Fr.
28. Ambitious one
32. Color
35. Extra jurors
38. Angers
41. —— about
42. Presently
43. Bundle
44. Quills
46. Toronto man
47. —— Major
48. A season
49. Provide a treat of sorts
50. Jousts
52. Drinks
54. That makes ——
55. Mink's relative
56. Eric, for one
59. Landed estates
61. Relative
63. Smart to a point
64. Concept
65. Fixes a lawn
67. Flaps violently
69. Boat
71. Go too far
72. Elève's school
73. Wraparound
74. Cape
75. Grand Central feature
76. Cupid
77. Mother of Castor
79. Slowly: Music
80. Pretty one, in Rome
82. Fled
84. Passages
86. —— Grande
89. Cowpoke's mount
90. Level
92. Most improbable
93. Rabbit's tail
94. Lacquered ware
95. Writer Bagnold
96. Machetes
98. Waves: Sp.
100. Comedian of silent films
101. Tiny Tim's voice
102. Biblical city of Palestine
103. Name in golf Hall of Fame
105. Extolled
106. Spur: Biol.
108. Develop
109. Live coal
110. Noun suffix
111. Friend
114. Dry: It.
116. Romero
117. Landing places
118. Goddess of peace
119. Saltpeter
121. Horace's metier
123. South African assembly
124. Son of Seth
125. Biscay, to the French
128. Chemical suffix
130. Before
131. —— publica

31 Looking Sharp

by A.J. Santora

ACROSS

1. Señor's talk
6. Throwback
13. The —— luxury
18. Bargains
19. Suite
20. Type of ether
21. Broadway name
23. Collier
24. In trouble
25. Bit of reading
27. Compass point
28. Great miler
29. Impudence
31. Slithery
32. Mineo and namesakes
33. Credibility
34. Stitch for samplers
38. Plains Indian
40. Senior member
41. Part of R.B.I.
42. Bedrock
43. Quenched
45. Kind of rug
47. Heraldic fur
48. Fearful
49. Recoil
50. Neapolitan, for one
54. Pitch pipe
55. Glances of a kind
57. Holiday time
58. Floodlights
59. Mexican mullet
60. Fit to ——
61. Entrance
62. "—— Got Rhythm"
63. Led the attack
67. Threadlike
68. Tints over
70. Paid up
71. Winner of olés
72. Siouan
73. Grand and others
75. Dissenting view
76. Book section
78. Carry: Lat.
79. Bridge seats
80. Hang fire
82. 1926 Pulitzer novel
84. Cheer
87. Cupid
88. Philippine tree

90. Suffix for gang or trick
91. Irritate: Colloq.
92. Word connector
93. Library worker
96. "—— tennis?"
99. Foolish
101. Overhead liability
103. Ground quartz
104. Reprimand
105. Commiserates
106. Delicious
107. Certifies
108. Word on a French map

DOWN

1. Out at the elbows
2. The Veep
3. Ironside of TV
4. Table extender
5. Pitched in
6. Custody
7. Ball holder
8. "Take —— from me"
9. Passport entry
10. Approximately
11. Boulevard of note
12. Decoration
13. Court marker
14. Mon ——
15. Support for edgy people
16. Pull —— (tease)
17. Anticipate
18. Chekhov

—— Uncle
21. Small town
22. Instruct
26. —— joint
30. Released: Colloq.
32. Affirm
34. Stud or draw
35. Seen
36. Weight
37. Circle or sanctum
39. Guinness et al.
40. Defies
43. Road turn
44. Army men
45. Severity
46. Disturbed the peace
47. Dog, for short
48. Step
49. River of a blues song

51. Campus girl
52. Zoo adjunct
53. Paris version of IRT
55. Active one
56. Takes aboard
59. Elks
61. Buenos ——
63. U.S. painter and illustrator
64. Inimical one
65. Don's January
66. Stocks selling —— (bear market)
67. Onward
69. Mink's cousin
71. Tryout
74. Pertaining to uprising

75. Figure in O'Neill play
76. Rubinstein
77. Cleaning aid
79. Correct
81. Dit's companion
82. Way off beam
83. Groups of aides
84. M-16's
85. Pale green
86. Possessive
89. Jai-alai gear
91. Brief novel
93. Relative of sultry
94. Gardner
95. Relatives of TV's: Abbr.
97. Skip
98. —— chance
100. Profit
102. Poetic word

32 Rhymes from Way Out · by Edward J. O'Brien

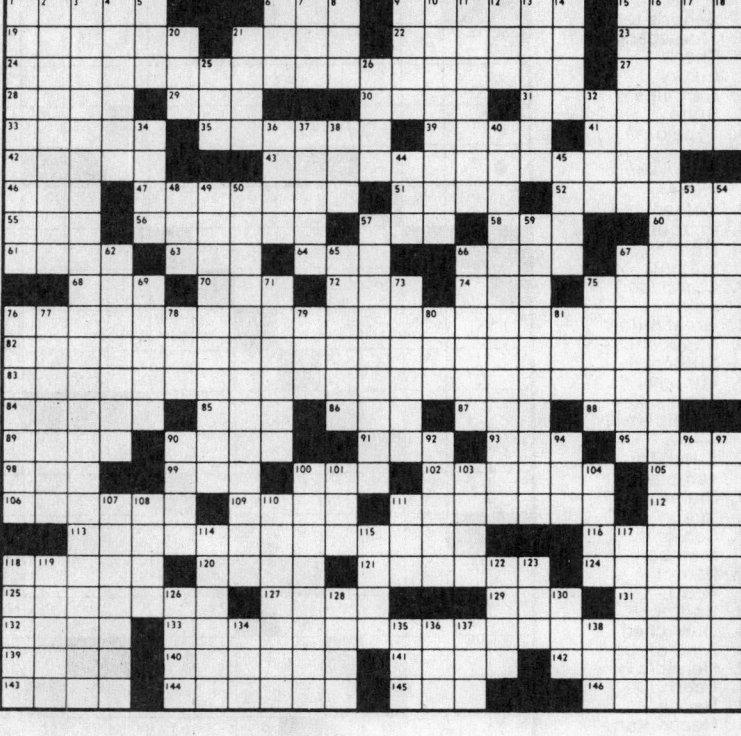

ACROSS

1. Amphibians
6. Relative: Abbr.
9. Of a Mideast nation
15. "It's —— story"
19. —— gatherum
21. Did a farm job
22. Mexican lady
23. Went on horseback
24. Refusal to a Friday hold-up man
27. Relative of a cockney 'ero
28. Exclamation of surprise
29. Grain
30. Relatives of orgs.
31. Structures of like origin
33. Rio's Açucar
35. Entertain lavishly
39. Centers
41. Dionnes' doctor
42. Part of an English county
43. Words for a cabled smoke signal
46. Possess: Scot.
47. Living-room eyes
51. Church court
52. ". . . in deepest grief ——"
55. Electrical unit
56. Party
57. Sand ridge
58. Certain words: Abbr.
60. Prevail
61. Duo
63. Word after waste and want
64. French friend
66. Chair
67. Berle, for short
68. Novel
70. Scot's denial
72. Life ins. man
74. Energy: Abbr.
75. Throat, in England
76. Clerical union's demand for a raise
82. One who keeps 64th notes
83. Words for a navigator's role
84. Now
85. Against
86. Three, in Rome
87. Fast plane: Abbr.
88. She: Ger.
89. Speeds
90. Wan
91. "A rose —— rose"
93. Fireproof material: Abbr.
95. Plant beards
98. Balaam's transport
99. Whitney
100. Droop
102. Consecrate
105. Misfortune
106. Earthquake: Prefix
109. Extracted
111. Ridicule (with "of")
112. Charlemagne domain: Abbr.
113. No. 1 airport runway
116. Do —— turn
118. Paints
120. Poetic adverbs
121. Took out
124. New Deal name
125. One more
127. Points
129. Shoe size
131. "When I was ——"
132. Aqua ——
133. Forecast for a poor shoe repair
139. Flying initials
140. Excite
141. Roman date
142. Tuneful
143. Soccer star
144. Couch
145. Receive
146. Suffered

DOWN

1. Leading mod art store
2. Laughter in Nebraska
3. Dictum of a prudish girl watcher
4. Nursery words
5. Latin possessive
6. Lad
7. Kind of pronoun: Abbr.
8. Harem room
9. "There —— answer"
10. Try to attain
11. Hearts, clubs, or whatever
12. Digits: Abbr.
13. Poker player's words
14. Coral islets
15. Have —— for (esteem)
16. Comment on how part of an audience will react
17. Bell town
18. Slow-witted
20. Muscle: Prefix
21. Despise
25. Conflict
26. French river
32. Norse god
34. Corporation levies: Abbr.
36. Earth goddess
37. Girl's name
38. Fleur-de——
40. Heroic sea rescue
44. Time period
45. Old form of be
48. Long time
49. Thrifty
50. Words for a star at liberty
53. Castor bean
54. In the earth: Fr.
57. Large steam shovel
59. "—— Wimpole Street"
62. Eye parts
65. Woodchuck
66. Chair backs: Var.
67. Fever disease
69. Like a V-shaped object
71. Flemish name of Ixelles
73. Brimless hats
75. Waters
76. Start of some riddles
77. Abelard's beloved
78. These: Fr.
79. Of age: Abbr.
80. French pronoun
81. Royal initials
90. Laborer
92. City in Turkey
94. Heat measure: Abbr.
96. Out of fish
97. eggs, too
100. Shabby feat
101. Rational
103. Reverence
104. —— out
107. Hindu grant
108. N.M. capital
110. Before mash
111. Jogged some
114. Damage
115. Region of France
117. —— majesty
118. Travel briefly
119. Slurp
122. Occupied
123. Lampreys
126. State: Abbr.
128. Food: Slang
130. Fr. miss
134. Oahu town
135. Scrap
136. Lively dance
137. Poem
138. Wager
    Conjunctions

33 Around the House by Emanuel Berg

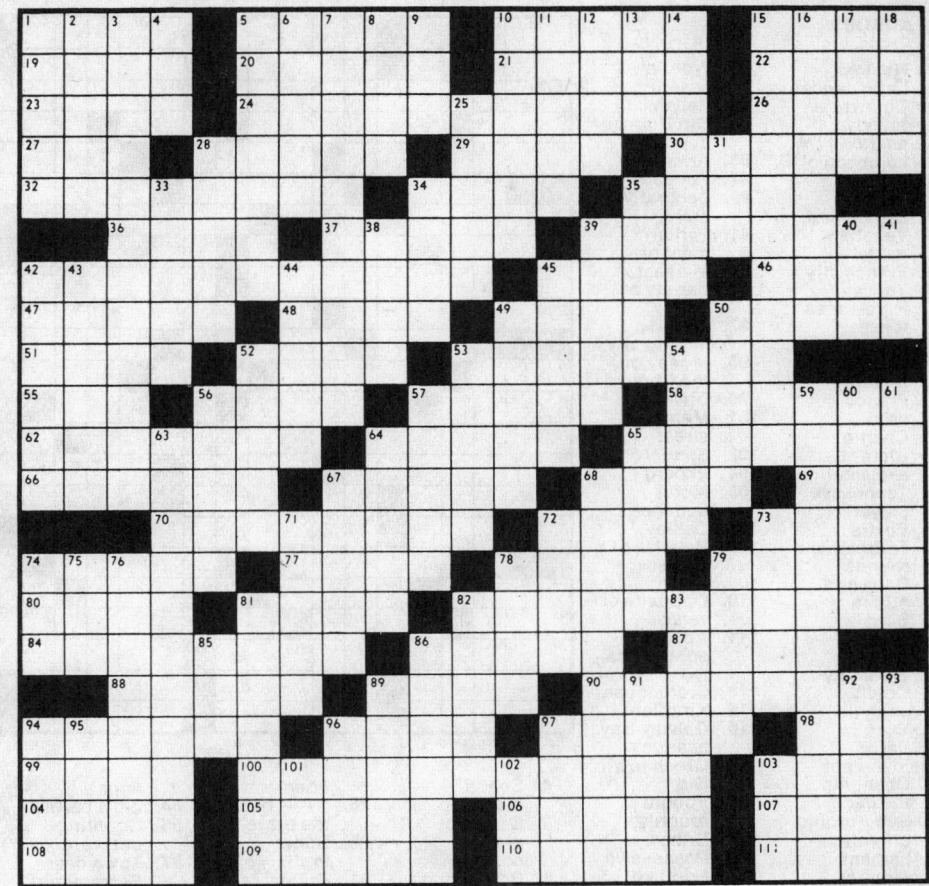

ACROSS

1. Projects
5. Went hot-rodding
10. Investment item
15. Merganser
19. Biblical giant
20. Allen
21. Lombardi
22. Greek liqueur
23. —— et orbi
24. "—— human hopes"
26. Sinn ——
27. Not any, in law
28. "—— were the days"
29. Holm oak
30. S.A. plains
32. It's yet to come
34. Tennis points
35. Matches up
36. Starchy plant
37. Beaverlike
39. Tasteful
42. Do-nothing
45. Arctic sight
46. Wine: Prefix
47. Sheol and others
48. Silver: Abbr.
49. Droplet
50. Soil science: Abbr.
51. Havens
52. Pairs
53. Nearer
55. Bishopric
56. Shofar
57. Nandus
58. Pacific isles
62. Fit to drink
64. Pass off (with "on")
65. Disappeared
66. Guarantee
67. Gay
68. European capital
69. Writer Victor, to cockneys
70. Reaction
72. Roric
73. Cinch
74. Surveyed the joint
77. Track
78. —— with (favor)
79. Wood: Prefix
80. Gluck
81. Drum staves
82. Unpopular bird
84. Lung ailment
86. Boa
87. Vex
88. Poignant
89. Clever move
90. Resembling the Acropolis
94. Artist's pad
96. Auction word
97. Field mice
98. Dirigible, for short
99. Bowfin genus
100. Pasqui-naders
103. Hand: Sp.
104. Type of etching
105. Irregular
106. Siren signal
107. African antelope
108. Nervous
109. Stormed
110. Western sights
111. June 6, 1944

DOWN

1. Brief trip
2. California's Jesse ——
3. Deipnoso-phists
4. Sports gear
5. Hurl again
6. Musketeer
7. Father Brown's creator
8. Roof part
9. Life-essen-tial acid
10. More sinister
11. Takes the hook
12. Chalcedony
13. Army grade: Abbr.
14. Collapse
15. Fine till now
16. Kind of cheese
17. Pinza
18. Tony of early radio
25. More subtle
28. Pressure units
31. First-cen-tury date
33. Keens
34. Field: Lat.
35. Search into
38. Iowa city
39. At —— for words
40. Daughter of Cadmus
41. Against
42. Dance step
43. From —— in
44. —— thing
45. Fishing bob
49. Hallowed
50. When the scholar used to come
52. Handouts
53. Animal's spine
54. Pluvial
56. Engaged
57. Dinner course
59. Parlor Romeo
60. Lake near Como
61. Visit
63. Rule of too many thumbs
64. Suomi people
65. Wooden pin
67. Covered with a cosmetic
68. Garden plot
71. Aspect
72. Fashion name
73. Seal
74. Mushroom part
75. Word with out or aboard
76. Vilifying
78. Cask part: Scot.
79. Columbia team
81. Golfer Gene
82. Italian coin
83. Churchmen
85. Herb
86. Flew, in a way
89. Small wood
91. Extreme
92. African country
93. Kind of resin
94. Stare
95. Surrounded by
96. City problem
97. Mean
101. Sky Altar
102. Business org.
103. Up-to-date

Executive Suite

by Ross L. Jamison Jr.

ACROSS

1. Nestors
6. Latin dance
11. Cut over
16. Prickly pears
21. Lambeau of football fame
22. Lag behind
23. Venetian medal
24. French city
25. Yucca
27. Hard-times token
29. Yutang
30. Throat feature
31. French drink
32. Charlie Chan exclamation
33. Tennessee player
34. Elixirs
36. Tournament rounds
38. Baba and others
39. Simple
40. Unemployed
41. Water lily
42. Coldly analytic
44. Year, in Paris
46. Five-spot
47. Changing the decor
49. San Antonio attraction
52. Lament
53. Monitor lizard
55. Prospector's find
56. Grant an extension
57. Enterprise
59. Danube tributary
60. Townsman
62. Root
63. Limestone formation
65. Complete costume
66. Windy City, for short
67. Household member
68. Scandinavian
70. Duo
71. U.S. time zone: Abbr.
74. Spider monkey
76. Precious stone
78. Bring upon
80. Word of assent
81. Italian city
83. Old Roman day
85. Answer
87. Pat gently
89. Decorative braid
91. Parliament of Mideast
93. Variety of cherry
97. Spanish mining city
98. Money on the Corso
99. Drive
101. Memphis street
102. Spatial
104. Ekberg
105. Metal fastener
106. Oakley
107. Relative of a flapjack
109. Crafty
110. Opposite of verso
111. Approached, poetically
113. Storehouse
115. Kingfish
116. Galway Bay islands
118. Czech town
119. Old
120. Fought roughly
123. Bribe
124. Possessive
125. Footlike part
126. Confederate general
128. Sea union: Abbr.
129. Woman's coverall
132. Chinese vermilion
134. Chemical compound
135. Cavity
136. Immense expanse
137. Singer Della
138. Courser
139. Kind of drum
140. One of the strings
141. Skaldic poetry

DOWN

1. Brave's trophy
2. TV section
3. Subsidy
4. Shade maker
5. Cardiologist's concern
6. British guns
7. Bellicose god
8. Huckster's milieu
9. Lodging place
10. Tankard contents
11. Cookie of baseball
12. Son of Isaac
13. Moment, for short
14. Former Detroit slugger
15. Site of Statuary Hall
16. Third word of "Aeneid"
17. Kind of lamp
18. Carriage horse
19. Quartet member
20. Cordage fiber
26. "—— but the brave"
28. Bone: Prefix
31. Outer garments
35. Similar in action
37. Graz's river
38. Set straight
39. He-devil
41. River to Gulf of Gaeta
42. Thatch grasses
43. —— diem
44. Moslem V.I.P.
45. One of the Parcae
46. Kismet
48. Spanish peso
50. Ear of corn, in Africa
51. Proprietors
53. Bravery
54. New word: Abbr.
58. Fish afflictions
61. Parthenogenetic
64. Zig's partner
65. Counting-out word
67. Town near Sacramento
69. Atlantic sea bird
71. Winter melon
72. Filched
73. "Grass Harp" author
75. Forage plant
77. Singer Torme
79. —— avis
82. Fermi's nationality
84. Sully
86. Variety of cotton
88. Superiors
90. Revoke a legacy
92. Operatic piece
93. Infested with tiny insects
94. English breed of cattle
95. Yokel
96. Aware of
98. Release
100. Mah-jongg piece
103. Sudden collapse
108. Greek letter
110. Put back
112. Eggs: Ger.
114. Region of France
115. Mutts
116. Residue
117. Resting place
119. Awareness
120. Early Haitian Indian
121. Ancient city of Syria
122. Certain ranchers
124. Flock
125. Rain hard
127. Soviet range
130. Victory sign
131. Cell constituent
132. Ad ——
133. Man's nickname

Showing the Way by Nancy Schuster

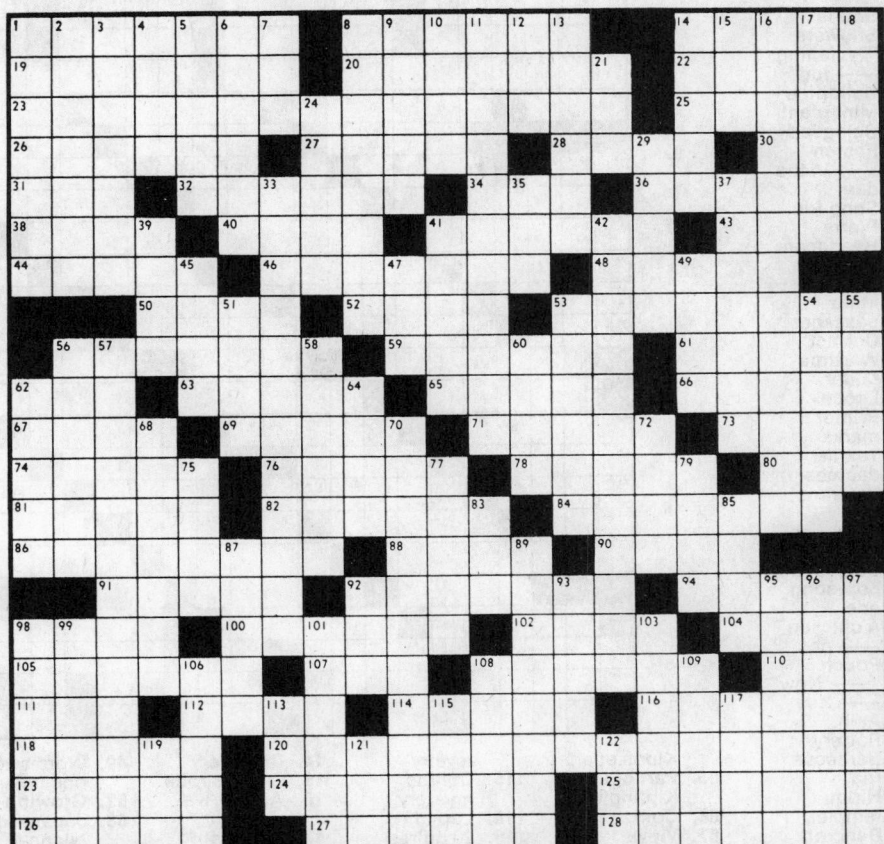

ACROSS

1. Add more stickum
8. Recital pieces
14. Ivan's villa
19. In
20. More annoyed
22. Chills
23. Prisoners of a kind
25. —— Bulba
26. Prayer form
27. Tie up
28. Brontë heroine
30. Number prefix
31. Collection of sayings
32. Beaux ——
34. —— sack
36. Substitute
38. Canasta play
40. Fine fur
41. Entree
43. Manner
44. Sandy ridge
46. Latticework
48. Of a grain
50. Wire measures
52. Paris name
53. Losing money
56. Sink fixtures
59. Nervous walking
61. Signore's land
62. Try to outdo
63. Pale
65. Part of the forest scene
66. Branch of peace
67. "—— corny as..."
69. Wire: Abbr.
71. African antelope
73. River to North Sea
74. Baseball hit
76. Long-beaked Atlantic fish
78. Passion
80. Sounds of hesitation
81. Color
82. Bears, mice and pigs
84. Elicitors
86. Skyline sights
88. Drooping
90. Pseudo-esthetic
91. Composer
92. Popular dosage

94. Radical in famed 1921 trial
98. Wings
100. Pants
102. Whale
104. Splash over
105. Briefcase item
107. Weaken
108. Some poultry
110. Cockney's distress cry
111. Tending to: Suffix
112. Lancaster
114. Waters: Sp.
116. Ethiopian town
118. "—— the West Wind"
120. Covert
123. TV fare
124. Early epoch
125. Retinue
126. Wood nymph
127. Caught

128. Frightened, hillbilly style

DOWN

1. Publicity
2. Lancelot's love et al.
3. Part of a coach's job
4. Official deeds
5. Goad
6. Zero and successors in "Fiddler"
7. Dutch commune
8. Crowned a certain way
9. 1900-mile Asian river
10. Protection
11. Polka dot on a garment, in a way
12. Article in Bonn
13. Move back

14. Office stamp
15. Moslem title
16. Animal act, usually
17. Beating items
18. Official edict
21. Alfonso, for one
24. Perfume
29. Met again
33. Prepares
35. Scientific group: Abbr.
37. Agreeably
39. John's predecessor
41. "Half ——"
42. Involved explanation
45. Baltic gulf
47. Back talk
49. Chemical prefix
51. At sea
53. —— form
54. Young eels

55. Textile workers
56. Apish
57. "Louder-and funnier" area
58. Biblical pauses
60. Kansas college
62. Early movie name
64. Prefix for a body network
68. Cut off
70. Stage cover
72. Gloomy
75. Italian painter
77. Barks
79. Enlistees: Abbr.
83. —— -disant
85. Nestling
87. Former Indian leader
89. Charged a

certain way
92. Gardner
93. Kind of potato
95. Detergent
96. University unit
97. Resisting
98. Furnish
99. More clashing
101. Nautical direction
103. "—— Krupp"
106. Popular investment
108. Soft candy
109. —— Coeur
113. Baseball data: Abbr.
115. Pesty bug
117. "—— horse!"
119. Philippine tree: Var.
121. Garden tool
122. Old Gov't. agency

36

OutYonder

by Mary M. Murdoch

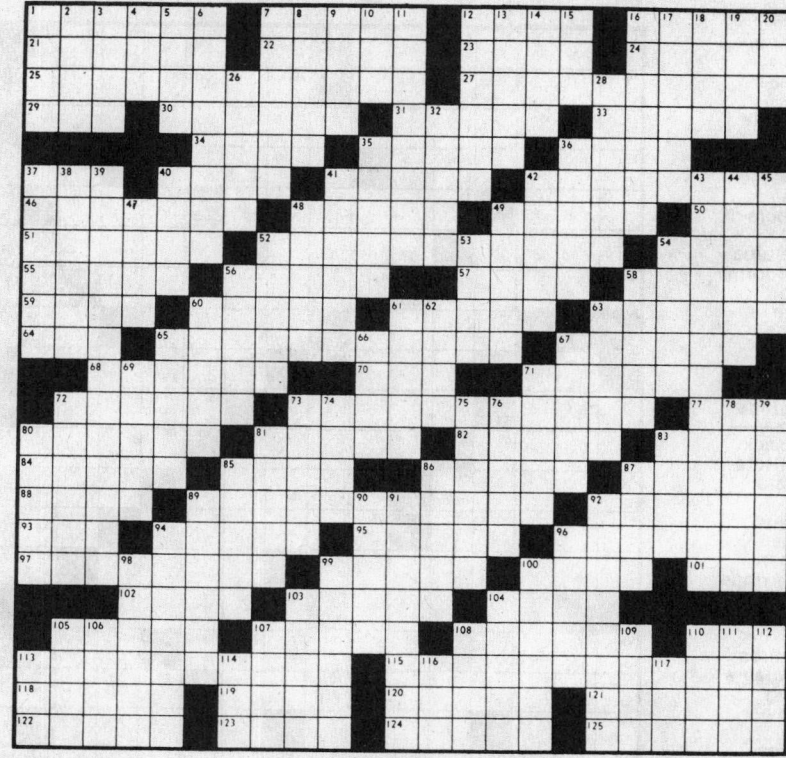

ACROSS

1. Shuns
7. Showers
12. "...falling —— log"
16. Solidifies
21. Mint plant
22. Being led
23. Fasten
24. —— in the dark
25. Song for Pierre
27. Headgear
29. Highest note
30. Mine passages
31. Correct
33. Wartime raider
34. Loose
35. Printer's marks
36. Textile degrees
37. Veterans' org.
40. Diagonal
41. Works
42. Subject of a pop-song ode
46. A chicken —— pot
48. Pouch
49. "—— Now"
50. —— tree
51. Akin
52. Pottery
54. Barbecue rod
55. Hindu temples
56. Bancroft and others
57. Top-notch
58. Pule
59. Otherwise
60. Babble
61. Goes by plane, old style
63. Go pale
64. More: Sp.
65. Large sponge
67. Common contraction
68. Plants of regions
70. Gob
71. Water tank
72. Related
73. Electrical device
77. Physics and others: Abbr.
80. City officials
81. Old-World sandpiper
82. Leaders
83. Black
84. Wells's Mr.

Kipps et al.
85. Part of a Kipling trio
86. Coin
87. View
88. Direction: Fr.
89. Rich and strong
92. Hartebeest
93. Scot's snow
94. Cleaving tools
95. News sections, for short
96. Joined in a way
97. Trellis
99. More plucky
100. Elan
101. First, etc., in football: Abbr.
102. Throw
103. Church part
104. Church season
105. Popular refrain of tots
107. Show off
108. Careened
110. Tangled mass
113. Period of revelry
115. Collins mystery
118. Lop off
119. 20 quires
120. "—— give you..."
121. Two-seated wagons
122. Like a fork
123. State: Abbr.
124. Nova Scotian cape
125. U.S. Indians

DOWN

1. Summit
2. African river
3. Other: Sp.
4. Partner of ft.
5. "—— Irae
6. Hot-tempered one
7. Moon valleys
8. "What's in ——?"
9. Obsession: Suffix
10. One, two, etc.: Abbr.
11. Like sugar
12. Attacks
13. Mythical deities
14. Discovery
15. Priest's robe
16. Auto-drive part
17. Snoops
18. Mother of Zeus
19. Peace Nobelist in 1946
20. State and Main: Abbr.
26. Southern caverns
28. Be away, as a suburb
32. Turmoil
35. Classifies
36. French drink
37. Crown
38. Writer Thirkell
39. Odd plant
40. $2-window fodder
41. Serving piece
42. Vegetables
43. Houseleek
44. Deems
45. Corroded
47. Farewell: Lat.
48. African people
49. Word after one fell
52. Growing out
53. Japanese island
54. Devon, for one
56. Hungarian hero
58. Pup
60. French dads
61. —— of potatoes
62. Color
63. Caprices
65. Roulette colors
66. Exist: Fr.
67. Sycophant
69. Harold of silents
71. Mont ——
72. Lawrence's "—— Rod"
73. Market sign
74. Therefore
75. Orator
76. S.A. tanagers
78. Swindlers
79. Sam and others
80. Parsonage
81. Planing tool
83. Behold: Lat.
85. Lily plants
86. Parent in London
87. Abel's brother
89. San Quentin
90. Jalopy
91. Fanciful
92. Give ear
94. Nonplused
96. —— -man
98. Adjust
99. Flashes
100. Early explorer of America
103. Opera parts
104. Delineates
105. French mate
106. Vingt-——
107. Entreaty
108. Scant
109. Certain medals
110. Polish measure
111. Pay up
112. Hardy girl
113. N.Y., for one
114. Chair part
116. Initials of fairy-tale author
117. Chinese pagoda

Word Assortment
by William A. Lewis Jr.

ACROSS

1. Salad plant
6. Interlock
10. Tops
15. Confine
16. Russian country house
17. Up and around
19. Office worker
21. Companionably
23. Vessel
24. Gobs
25. The past
27. Shellgamer's need
28. Leak
30. Adds up
32. Brother
33. Spoiled one
34. Council
36. Confines
38. Accessible
39. Corresponded
40. Midge
42. Out of shape
44. Prepares vichyssoise
45. Filler material
48. Certain mail
49. At will
50. State: Abbr.
51. Tease
53. Word in L.A.
54. Good word for Charlie Brown
55. Military group: Abbr.
57. Like some containers
59. Redistilled liquor
63. To the good
65. Hope and ——
66. Roast: Fr.
67. Catch
68. Very unpleasant
70. Marina sights
72. Wax
73. Actor Claude
74. Certain room
75. One's nature
77. Form of Rachel
78. Guzzles
80. Take it easy
82. Kohinoor, e.g.
84. Defend
85. Harbor sound
87. Snow vehicle
88. Car co-ops
89. Livid
90. Catty sound
92. Easy prey
95. Ill temper
96. Skillet
98. Bit of liquor
100. Blue or green
101. Bravo!
102. Academic elite, informally
104. "There —— any more"
106. Hebrew letter
107. Prosperous
109. Military to-dos
112. In a grand manner
113. Roundish
114. French relative of F.B.I.
115. Giggle
116. Indiana port
117. Gambling choice

DOWN

1. Flavor
2. Modern convenience
3. Lazy writer's abbreviation
4. Please
5. Chair part
6. Degrees: Abbr.
7. Nymph of myth
8. Place for things
9. Breadstuff
10. Tavern workers
11. Rice
12. Runners
13. Kind of ear
14. Aerial maneuver
15. Digging tools
16. Housecoat
17. Held back
18. Very
20. Support
22. Ship men
26. Reruns
29. Place to fish
31. Rebuff
33. Oral summary
35. Smear
37. Cheerful
39. Companion of deals
41. Former Russian
43. Move heavily
44. Bin
45. Biblical wife
46. Word of greeting
47. Men's-wear items
49. "Across the —— plain"
52. Variety acts
54. Early invaders
56. Light covered cart: Var.
58. Feature of an old floor
59. Informal title
60. Provincial
61. Deep sound
62. Joined, in a way
64. Factotums, old style
66. Pay, in a way
69. Uncontrollable
70. Relative of uh-huh
71. Earth fault
74. Ruthless
76. Season
78. Team that scores upsets
79. Scads
80. Car
81. —— bien
83. See 61 Down
84. Violin stroke
85. Word for a pilot
86. Not at all
89. Take offense
91. Tenuous strip
93. Quaker-ladies
94. Meaning
96. Violin item
97. Roman emperor
99. Grind, as teeth
102. Memphian deity
103. Burn
105. Straight
108. Caustic
110. Pen
111. Altar: Lat.

Punny Girls

by John Willig

ACROSS

1. Scheme
6. Gaucho gear
11. Where the Acheron flows
16. Saw
21. Raid
22. "Stop ——"
23. Grownup
24. Parlor piece
25. Gateway to U.S. wonderland?
27. Invalid, in a girlish way
29. Have status
30. Chinese weight
31. Without spirit
33. Eases
34. Seam
35. Catch-all for some
36. "—— forgive..."
37. With venom
41. Film director
42. Bird: Lat.
43. Shield knob
47. Somewhat
48. Police conveyance?
50. Scottish terrier
51. Atoll ingredient
52. Too much: Music
53. —— jacet
54. Golf nickname
55. Periods
56. —— over lightly
57. Father of Boys Town
61. Relative of a plater
62. Rude refusal
63. Entertain
65. Dessert
66. Moving back and forth
68. Just manage, with "out"
69. Going at a good clip?
73. Tax, in Dublin
74. At hand
76. Electric
77. Ring name
78. Some lotions
80. Girlish tantrums
82. Fuller explanations?
88. Kipling's O'Hara
91. Former Italian colonial
93. Bishop in "Henry V"
94. Mistreat
95. Feminine suffix
96. Drop bait lightly
97. Small covered passage
100. Annoyer
101. Formerly, of old
102. Part of long-run play title
104. Dawn goddess
105. Split ——
106. Play part
107. Illuminated
108. Settles anew?
111. Withdraw
112. "Simon ——"
113. V.I.P. place
114. Hawk leashes
115. Chiding mother, for one
116. Odd: Scot.
117. Links
118. Kind of collar
119. Basic items
123. Stale
124. Assert
125. Sumptuous
129. Tag for a hot rodder?
131. Name for an eloper?
134. "—— at last!"
135. Siouan
136. Old word of regret
137. Kind of crime
138. Smartly dressed
139. Carried
140. Retreats
141. Stage devices

DOWN

1. Distant
2. Piano hit of 1920's
3. Pluck
4. Duchesse, for one
5. Observe
6. Kind of garden
7. What Buzzards Bay is
8. Asian sea
9. Hamilton bill
10. Signifies
11. Cutting tool
12. Astaire
13. In a proper way
14. Building wing
15. Has top billing
16. Confuse
17. Low place
18. English river
19. Trot or gallop
20. Butts
26. Saragat's country
28. Tidings
32. Lauder, to cockneys
34. Certain tone
35. Paw, in Paris
36. Salad ingredient
37. Creed set up in 325 A.D.
38. Hooded jacket
39. Girl's gift
40. Start of Clement Moore poem
41. Postal device
42. Hillbilly's anti
43. Mideast initials
44. Attired like a mouse
45. Some Irishmen
46. Walk ——
48. Heartsease
49. Eureka's relative
50. Jargon
52. Barnstorm
57. Newspaper section: Abbr.
58. One kind of gift
59. Started, to poets
60. Inert gases
63. Camel's-hair cloth
64. Textile dealer, in London
65. Filch
67. Kind of train: Abbr.
70. Pasture
71. Winglike part
72. Liturgical prayers
75. Reckoned: Abbr.
79. Noun suffix
80. Awards
81. Yemen's land
83. Resinous substance
84. Lack of vigor: Var.
85. —— du Diable
86. Building beams
87. Inning units
89. Where to be on a rainy day
90. One's own thing
92. Grate upon
98. Some turkeys
99. Group of fifty
100. Revolutionary general
101. Of the church: Abbr.
103. Muscle: Suffix
105. Super's helper
106. Long time
108. Sound range
109. Polished
110. Smallest one
111. Disdain
113. Attracted
115. Swiss ——
116. Sec. of State under Cleveland
117. Swell
118. Oust
119. Thai language
120. Honduran port
121. "Thanks ——!"
122. Confined (with "up")
123. —— and potatoes
124. Macaws
125. Young salmon
126. Bone: It.
127. Organ part
128. Gossipy women
130. Inner: Prefix
132. Drink
133. Owned

Down to the Sea
by B.H. Kruse

ACROSS

1. Russian agency
5. Hawaiian shrub
10. Ship of ——
15. Like: Prefix
19. Oriental babysitter
20. Records
21. Ocean routes
22. Pal of void
23. Kind of skirt
24. First ocean steamer
26. Duck
27. Crucial time in tennis
29. Stake
30. Leather workers
32. Armadillos
33. Experience
35. Polish city
36. Reproductive cell
38. Captain's role, at his table
39. Hags
42. Jewish months
43. Famed clipper
46. —— cost
47. Kind of pronoun: Abbr.
48. Hall of ——
49. Blockhead
51. Broadway signs
52. Roof ornament
53. Constitution
55. Least in age: Abbr.
56. Flag
58. German river
59. Macaw
62. Church area
63. One kind of man
65. Auricular
66. New Havenite
67. Socrates, for one
68. Buffoon
72. Fleming
75. Liner holding Atlantic record
79. French article
80. Group
82. Emphatic word after yes or no
83. Attention-calling words
84. Building beam
85. U.S. admiral (1874-1939)
87. Some ads
89. Jewish liturgy
90. Definite period
92. Sugar source
93. Toolbox item
94. Part of a poetic foot
95. Take part in
97. Bake eggs
98. Thugs
100. Town on Thames
101. One who makes trades
104. Within: Prefix
105. Genoese admiral
109. Lion's trademark
110. Sea, to poets
111. Radioman's O.K.
112. Certain exams
113. Tritons
114. Fat
115. Famed acting family
116. Outdated
117. Printer's term

DOWN

1. Perth wear
2. Gallic companion
3. Chris craft
4. Clipper owners
5. Clothes
6. Otto and E.J.
7. In —— (peeved)
8. French article
9. King of Judah
10. Point of view
11. Owner of la plume
12. Bancroft
13. Crumpets' companion
14. Biblical valley
15. Pleads
16. Historic troopship
17. Relating to: Suffix
18. Reverses
25. Shakespeare's "—— deep"
28. Horse fare
31. U.S. bureau
33. One who lugs
34. Houston player
35. Tea
36. Stares
37. Proficient
38. Like N.Y. in summer
39. Aisle walker
40. Genesis name
41. Method: Abbr.
43. Framework
44. Pantywaist
45. Accesses
48. Roman historian
50. Chinese silk
53. Eastern vine
54. Knobby
57. Direction
60. Creeks
61. Do Hamlet
63. Procrastinator's word
64. Writer James and family
65. English impostor
67. Lorelei, for one
68. Swiss city
69. Type of lifeboat
70. Walking
71. Slangy word of derision
72. "—— I can do it"
73. Asian range
74. Ill-fated ocean
76. Palms
77. Detection device
78. A title for Macbeth
81. Fulton's Folly
84. Ancient vessels
86. Being, in philosophy
88. Colombian town
89. Came down
91. French wine
93. Group of words
95. Scatter
96. Gardeners
97. Canvas
98. Diamonds
99. Two-toed sloth
100. Keenness
101. Bikini parts
102. ——en point
103. What's left
106. Alternative
107. Afr. brandy
108. Hour: It.

(43. Framework — continued) queen

40 Thanksgiving Fare by W.W.

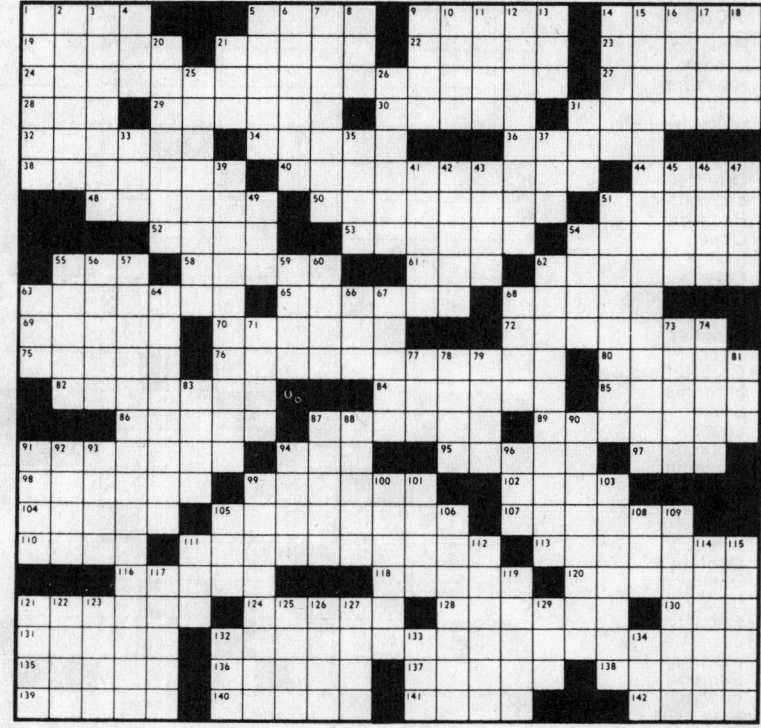

ACROSS

1. Designation: Abbr.
5. Between sum and fui
9. Tricks
14. Lion
19. Whimpers
21. —— a million
22. Creators of jams
23. Shape in a way
24. Holiday dining décor
27. Plant fiber
28. Columbus campus
29. Get the air
30. Of a body fiber: Prefix
31. Begins to work
32. Limousines
34. Ventured
36. Girl's name
38. Controversial
40. Mom's baking standby
44. Words of disavowal
48. Officer of ——
50. Keen qualities of sense
51. Supporting bar
52. Coty
53. Of a volcano
54. Frolics
55. Young one
58. Airstrips: Abbr.
61. Day times: Abbr.
62. Sandwich filler
63. Football platoon
65. Atelier items
68. C.P.A. job
69. U.S. composer
70. Yearly pay for a few
72. Foulard items
75. Derisive sound
76. Table décor
80. Roman halls
82. Western smokes
84. Social bore
85. Fawn
86. Moslem prayer
87. Dark rock
89. Late-flowering tulip
91. Soup seeds
94. Man's nickname
95. Bone: Prefix
97. Caesar's but
98. City in Picardy
99. Cubes and spheres
102. Hindu deity
104. Behaves well
105. Road menaces
107. Parallel
110. Novelist's problem
111. Sleigh for today's grandma
113. Shooting, in a way
116. Bare the head, old style
118. "It's —— thing"
120. Scourge
121. Scott hero
124. Some dogs
128. Certain Italian, to French
130. Peer Gynt's mother
131. Alert
132. Repast topper
135. Nonconformist
136. Skin: Prefix
137. Ten: Lat.
138. Obtain repairs
139. —— work
140. Tree secretion
141. Biblical tower
142. Scout groups

DOWN

1. Place in proximity
2. Heartbeat control device
3. Strong approval
4. Your: Fr.
5. Inward: Anat.
6. Ocean-research unit
7. One source of salt
8. Kind of service man: Abbr.
9. Prestige
10. Standout
11. Doer: Suffix
12. Subway workers
13. Silence!
14. Hit a high fly
15. Holiday menu item
16. 1969 champs
17. Famed island
18. Arabian Sea gulf
20. Frugal one
21. Scot's alas
25. Privileged people
26. Well-done part of a roast
31. Red or White
33. Residue
35. Verb suffix
37. Possessive
39. Vegetable for mom's table
41. Mayan month
42. News pieces
43. Spanish relatives
45. State: Abbr.
46. Slue
47. "—— deal!"
49. Evergreen
51. Drool
54. Musical ending
55. Sea birds
56. In progress
57. Crux of a holiday meal
59. Kennel sound
60. Ad subject
62. Home-cooked item
63. Metric units: Abbr.
64. Tennis scores, in a way
66. Medit. island
67. Eagles
68. Galatea's beloved
71. Kiln
73. Craft
74. Agreed with
77. Khan
78. Well-known Italian
79. Small violins
81. Scottish county
83. Misfortunes
87. City of Brazil
88. Of an acid
90. Like a moonlit night
91. Bedside item
92. Ludwig
93. Spanish lad
94. Name in movies
96. Refrain syllable
99. Like a freshly cleaned suit
100. Lower
101. Indian titles of respect
103. One who transfers property
105. Scottish precipitation
106. Slipped over
108. Girl with a headset: Abbr.
109. Veld animal
111. Short of
112. Third of a famous nine
114. Stick one's
115. Welcomes
117. Songs
119. Eastern V.I.P.
121. —— avis
122. Was beholden to
123. Cake
125. Comparative suffixes
126. Prefix for god or john
127. Oxygen prefix
129. Navy V.I.P.: Abbr.
132. New Deal man
133. Presidential initials
134. G-man

Getting the Word by Jack Luzzatto

ACROSS

1. Dog-sled driver
7. Hard feelings
13. Takes it easy
19. Bird with hanging nest
20. Watcher over me?
21. Specialized ornament
22. Site of S.M.U.
23. Wings of buildings
24. Minimal beach wear
25. Like printers' hands
26. Customarily
28. Wool fabric from Asia
30. Sholokhov's quiet river
31. You: Ger.
32. Woodworkers' aids
33. Dostoevski
34. Glacial offshoot
35. Spoiled-child specialties
37. Water-proofed, as ropes
38. Meticulous
39. Estimate
40. Furthers
41. Place for rolling stock
43. Draw from
46. Deprives of energy
48. System of beliefs
51. Adversary
52. Morose
53. Rage and elation
56. Heels
57. Seafood treat
58. Telling of tomorrow
59. Brief mornings
60. Models of cold perfection
62. Music to a matador
63. Comic's routine
65. Acclaims
66. Amused expression
67. Slipping, as of a disk
68. Slick
69. Vogue

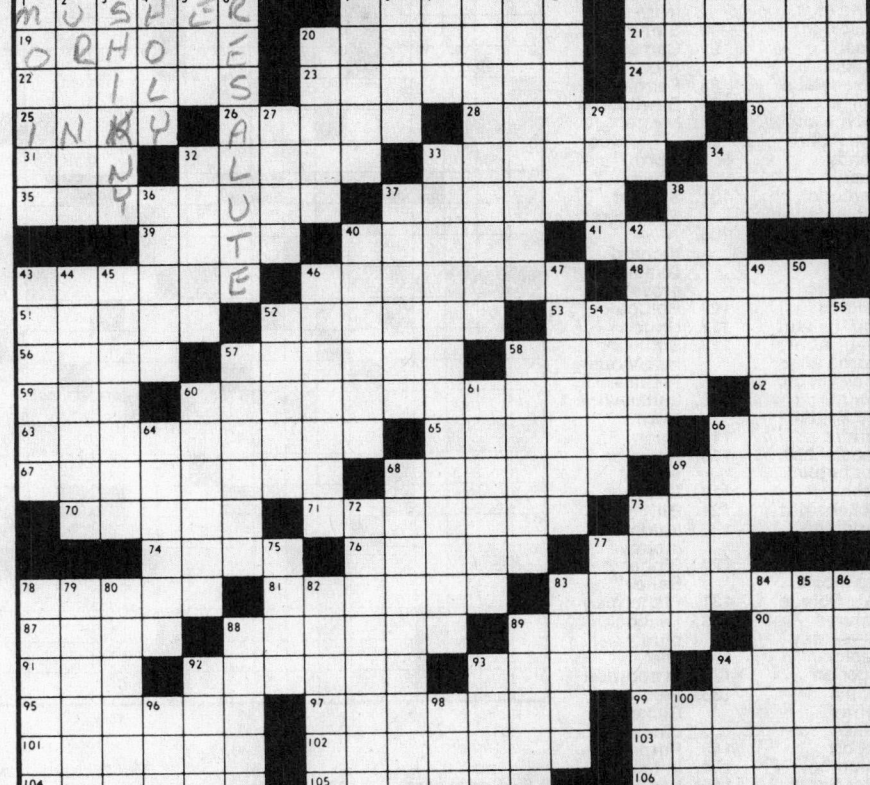

70. Circe's product
71. Movie pioneer
73. Mrs. Grundy and others
74. Hindu scriptures
76. Bungle
77. Blueprint
78. Younger son
81. Crafty qualities
83. Sudden city
87. Hebrew measure
88. Game for anyone
89. Revivers for swooning ladies
90. Tramp, for short
91. Take forcibly
92. Rouse to fury
93. Disconcert
94. Nautical place

95. Numeral system
97. Role for wide-eyed girl
99. Out of the weather
101. Undeveloped
102. Desserts
103. Snows: Fr.
104. Grooms
105. Officer to Macbeth
106. One who manages

DOWN

1. Follower of fashion
2. Muse of astronomy
3. Lustrous
4. Pious
5. High note
6. Strong of purpose
7. Characterizations
8. Encourag-

ing word
9. Trawl
10. Metal fastener
11. Adjective for Podunk
12. Live
13. Pole tossed by Scots
14. Overlook
15. Arctic diver
16. Projector inserts
17. Vocalists
18. Meager
20. Surfeits
27. Show rage
29. Physical entity
32. Slang for easy money
33. Mistaken suppositions
34. Cage bird, for short
36. Crops
37. "—— the tales..."
38. Beer heads
40. Rock salt

42. Takes as one's own
43. Vamoose
44. Charms
45. Colorful Arctic fall
46. Followed
47. Successive
49. Drove
50. Chemical dye
52. Mops of hair
54. Time period
55. Rises on a wave
57. Inclined
58. Edible South Sea worm
60. Earth
61. Berates
64. Twist
66. Wordless sound
68. Cheerfully
69. Mine vehicles
72. Height
73. Novelist's concern
75. Ripe

77. End of the earth
78. Island makers
79. Unaware of right or wrong
80. Douglas forte
82. Some wear, familiarly
83. Military centers
84. Accommodate
85. Expressionless
86. Most recent
88. Diplomatic assets
89. Reject rudely
92. Fur
93. Pearly mussel
94. Saudi Arablan area
96. Nectar collector
98. Dine
100. Born

Gift Suggestions

by Frances Hansen

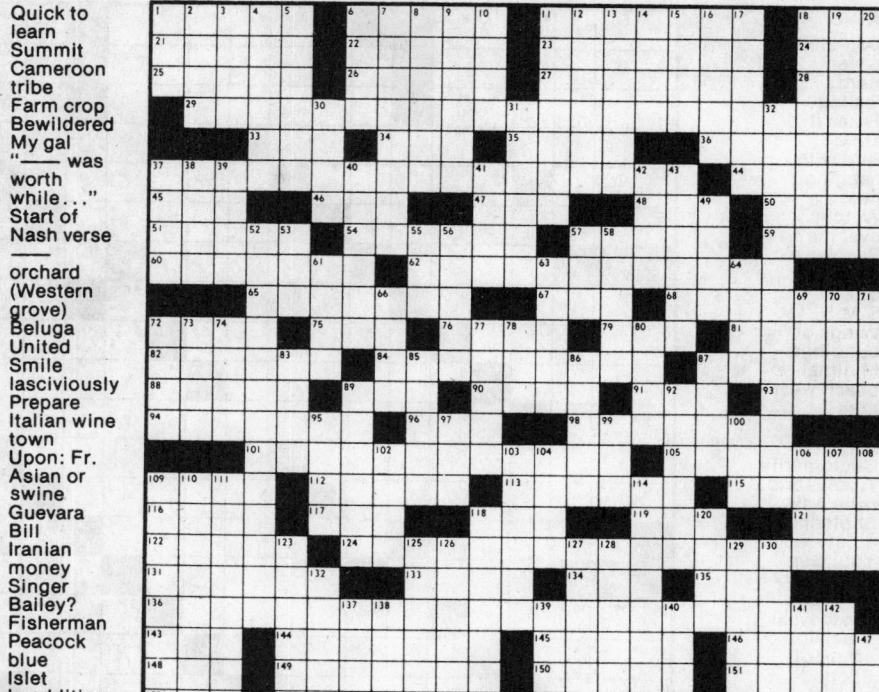

ACROSS

1. Betty of song et al.
6. Resort in West
11. Makes passes at a fly
18. Wayne and Dix: Abbr.
21. Handy
22. Nasty
23. Narcotic
24. Exclamation
25. Prisoner's castle, in fiction
26. Ice-cream holders
27. Equally taut
28. Ring: Abbr.
29. Words after "Hey" in old song
33. Old British middle class: Abbr.
34. Not public: Abbr.
35. Dickens girl
36. Reddish brown
37. Popular play and movie
44. Razor-blade features
45. "I —— gay musician"
46. Nigerian people
47. Coffee maker
48. Cut off
50. Columbo
51. After Santa
54. "Now, Jonah, he lived in ——"
57. White poplar
59. Eye: Prefix
60. Most like Daddy Warbucks
62. New York town
65. Came onstage
67. Sternward
68. Item for the press
72. In style
75. Nabokov book
76. Superlative endings
79. German spa
81. Raleigh's rival
82. Greatly
84. Something fur me?
87. Specify
88. River to Tiber
89. Quick to learn
90. Summit
91. Cameroon tribe
93. Farm crop
94. Bewildered
96. My gal
98. "—— was worth while..."
101. Start of Nash verse
105. —— orchard (Western grove)
109. Beluga
112. United
113. Smile lasciviously
115. Prepare
116. Italian wine town
117. Upon: Fr.
118. Asian or swine
119. Guevara
121. Bill
122. Iranian money
124. Singer Bailey?
131. Fisherman
133. Peacock blue
134. Islet
135. In addition
136. Familiar Dickens phrase
143. Purpose
144. In fashion
145. Lend ——
146. Mennonite
148. Vital cell acid: Abbr.
149. Ancient one
150. Hawaiian chants
151. Slow to catch on
152. "—— lords aleaping..."
153. Old and New England towns
154. Rub out
155. "King Lear" role

DOWN

1. Kissing kin, familiarly
2. Baby's shoe size
3. Lab burner
4. "—— want a brand-new car"
5. Did a garden job
6. Spore sacs
7. Part of the winter scene
8. Poilu's wine
9. Like Adam's abode
10. —— -ce pas?
11. Tint delicately
12. Felt indisposed
13. Equally high
14. Pronoun
15. Prefix for an Asian
16. Orgs.
17. "—— is cast"
18. Confronting, with "to"
19. Most like Twiggy
20. Sea N.E. of West Indies
30. Squatter's cult
31. Del Sarto
32. O'Casey
37. River to Moselle
38. All: Prefix
39. Secular
40. Emulated Webster
41. Asian tents
42. Hebrew letter
43. Ruby and emerald
49. Marquette
52. "I'll take ——" (coat choice)
53. Of bronze: Abbr.
55. "Scots Wha ——"
56. English poet
57. Landon
58. Kind of nut
61. Corset part
63. Tack
64. Swiss painter
66. Turnpike exit
69. Land mass
70. Delighted
71. Letters
72. Dickens, for short
73. Symbol of satiety
74. Place to wear furs
77. Nordic bard
78. Recipe abbreviation
80. Miserly
83. Turner
85. "—— the bag"
86. Chemical compound
87. Word with cote or tail
89. Totals
92. Wide collar
95. Namesakes of a Spanish queen
97. Ibsen role
99. Son of Odin
100. Ms. men
102. After "days of"
103. "—— summer's day"
104. Between huit and dix
106. To thee: Fr.
107. Now: Lat.
108. Graf ——
109. Widely separated
110. —— with (conforms)
111. Set arranger
114. Solvents
118. Matures
120. Diminutive suffix
123. Opening word
125. In —— position (resting)
126. Armed ship
127. Infer
128. Anglo-Indian troop
129. Hair dressing
130. Lodged
132. Take it easy
137. Tender, Scotch style
138. Fake: Abbr.
139. Specify
140. Gds.
141. Tweed's group
142. She: It.
147. Part of H.R.H.

ACROSS

1. Upstairs and downstairs
6. California wine valley
10. Drooping
14. Change lines in music
19. Map addition
20. Civil War combatants
22. U.S. textile inventor
23. Cobbler
24. Air terminal of sorts
26. Plow soles
28. Word of obligation
29. Mythical place of darkness
30. Hankering
31. Basilica area
33. Periodical, for short
34. Minuscule
35. Compass reading
36. Resign
38. Mischief-maker
40. McGuffey's output
43. Gyrated
45. Coated iron plates
47. "—— blue?"
48. Where Ybor City is
52. Look after
53. Locations
54. Business-letter abbreviation
55. Wind around
56. "...can you spare ——?"
58. Recipients
61. Bulrush
62. Went on about
63. Sunday talk: Abbr.
64. Butterfly
66. Home of the IRT
67. Weak consonants
69. Belief
71. Some jewelry
73. Expose
74. Fur animal
77. Mauna ——
80. Restraint
82. "Recessional" word
84. Nickname for Australians
86. Couple
87. Kilmer title
89. Relatives of rabbets
90. TV name
92. Precipitated, old style
93. Item in the black
94. "—— was saying"
95. Worthless
96. Gets off the track
97. Dour
99. Before
100. —— -terre
102. Dull noise
105. German article
106. High note
108. Insulative material
109. Freudian concepts
112. Hill nymphs
114. Orange oil
117. Tragus
119. Certain go-between
123. Flycatcher
124. Drew, for one
125. Palmist's reading
126. Equip for battle, old style
127. River to Hudson Bay
128. Paris airport
129. Whilom
130. Eye swellings: Var.

DOWN

1. Little girl
2. Lizard genus
3. Galaxies
4. Scout doing
5. Rill
6. Filch
7. Stein's repetition
8. Robin's pal
9. —— Domini
10. Old Greek war cry
11. Certain U.S. campus
12. Like three
13. Before omega
14. Welcomes again
15. Let up
16. Payola
17. High male voice
18. Dodger name
21. Masses
25. Urgency
27. Barbecue parts
32. Escarpments
34. Professional mourner
37. Bones et al.
38. Kind of flight
39. Hodge-podge
41. Mike man
42. In a brown study
43. Movie biggie
44. Foot keyboards
46. Kind of book
49. Funicular
50. Synthetic fiber base
51. Man's nickname
54. Arthurian lady
57. German river
59. Happening
60. Singing voice: Abbr.
65. Asian boundary river
68. Cul-de-——
70. Singer Diana
72. Got the import
73. Can. province
75. Pinkish colors
76. Oil jar
78. Soup pods: Var.
79. Slanting
81. Axes
83. Starting places
85. People of Assam
88. Certain watchmakers
91. Roman official
95. —— -hand
98. Girl
101. Storehouses
102. Famed Idaho name
103. Tropical palm
104. Thought-provoking
107. Skeptical
108. Mickey et al.
110. U.S. industrialist: 1804-1886
111. Banana bunches
113. Lily plant
115. Eye
116. Learning: Scot.
118. Let out
120. Even if, for short
121. Chalice veil
122. Asian holiday

Yuletide Thoughts

by Anne Fox

ACROSS

1. —— Flow
6. Give up
10. Erst
16. Kind of tree
20. Cry ——
21. "Render therefore —— Caesar . . ."
22. Greek goddess
23. U.S. statesman
25. Of a bone
26. Nobility: Ger.
27. Type of patch
28. Exciting edition
29. State: Abbr.
30. Give the once-over
32. Go up
34. Pourboire
36. Gen. Arnold
37. Conniption
39. A lot
40. Marrow
41. Saison
42. Fatima slept here
43. Savor
45. Panegyric
46. Gloomy one
47. Words by John Donne
53. Famous hunter
54. Egg: Prefix
55. Plain of southwest U.S.
56. Old English letter
57. Soak
58. Mudskippers
61. —— majesty
62. Categorizes
66. Aleutian island
68. Whimsical
70. One of a Latin trio
72. Spelt
73. Sub follower
75. L.B.J. in-law
77. Kind of coffee
79. Wing
80. Words by Walter de la Mare
87. —— polloi
88. Out of the way
89. Relative of esse
90. Outer: Prefix
91. Old Greek coins
93. Duration
95. Harangue
98. Foil
102. Might
104. Passport entry
106. Asian area
108. Tiergarten sight
109. A degree
110. Capricious
112. Smidgen
113. Dutch wife
115. Words by Esther S. Buckwalter
121. Widely
122. Waters: Lat.
123. Christmas
124. Writer Rand
125. Relative of st.
126. Chinese tree
127. English age: Abbr.
128. Alsatian brandy
132. Marble
133. Drink
134. Ruled out
137. Channels
138. Live
139. Yeah
141. Links
143. Approach
145. Ruy Diaz de Bivar
147. American pioneer
148. Republic created in 1948
149. System of exercises
150. Like some seals
151. Weather word
152. Hoss
153. Bustle
154. African lake

DOWN

1. Work group
2. Arum lily
3. Birdlike
4. Grass genus
5. Following "The Gospel"
6. Scruple
7. Wavy, in heraldry
8. Native: Suffix
9. See 62
10. Words from St. Luke
11. Living
12. Holy picture
13. Come to earth
14. Siouan
15. Speak of
16. Words by William Morris
17. Relative of a whammy
18. Busy
19. Corrigendum
24. Micronesian native
31. Pacific island
33. Rabbit tails
35. "It grows as ——" (N. Mex. motto)
38. Call to hunting dogs
39. Forte
40. Defendant's answer
43. French painter
44. Game piece
45. Native
47. Roman public areas
48. State: Abbr.
49. Hayworth
50. Raise
51. U.S. agency
52. Exclamation of surprise
59. Puts out
60. ". . . and they were —— afraid"
62. With 9 Down, words from Ecclesiastes
63. Pipe
64. High
65. Manche capital
67. Prefix with corn or cycle
69. Letter sign-off
71. African people
74. Friendliness
76. Impetus
78. Board member: Abbr.
80. Cut up
81. Tramp
82. Kind of act
83. Drink
84. Canadian writer
85. Sew together
86. In our time
92. Focusing medium
94. State: Abbr.
96. Persian rug
97. Literature Nobelist in 1948
99. Sea of Russia
100. Rounder
101. Go to ——
103. Each: Fr.
105. Sports gear
107. Air: Abbr.
110. Part of a taxi meter
111. Caesar, at one time
114. Bombast
115. Swift's "Tale ——"
116. Blankets
117. Samuel Butler novel
118. Kind of fringe
119. "—— child is loving . . ."
120. —— monde
128. Sheikdom of Arabia
129. Holy: Lat.
130. Blubbers
131. Gabler
134. Exceedingly
135. Son of Isaac
136. Calendar abbreviation
137. Academy Award film: 1958
140. Spanish number
142. "A rose —— . . ."
144. Dash's partner
146. Put down

45 Gadget Counter

by William Lutwiniak

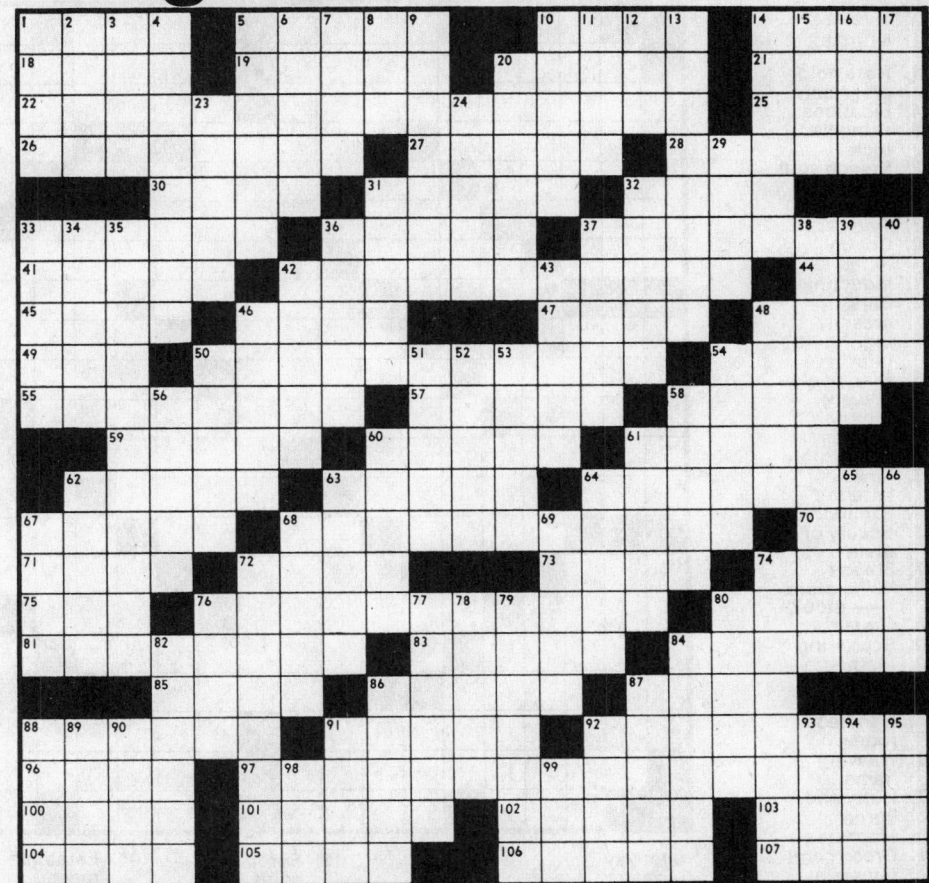

ACROSS

1. Rebuff
5. Complies
10. Ululates
14. —— song
18. Girl who wants, and gets
19. Musical piece
20. Lively dance
21. Porthos et Aramis
22. Surprise
25. Platform
26. Caprices
27. Points
28. Clefts
30. Neighbor of Ala.
31. Cocktail garnishes
32. Noun ending
33. Calling by name
36. Tonsorial service
37. Self-inflated one
41. Have —— to
42. Manicurist's concern
44. ——-disant
45. Italian numeral
46. Bearish times
47. Coffee-makers
48. Esteemed panfish
49. Numerical prefix
50. Honestly
54. Folkways
55. Guards
57. Fencing move
58. Of a cereal
59. Incites
60. Small cabaret
61. Toxophilite gear
62. Wrap
63. Land of Minos
64. Encircled, of old
67. Money of Thailand
68. Contributes
70. Galena
71. Wishes undone
72. Reward, old style
73. Have a go
74. Silk, in Paris
75. Neighbor of Oreg.
76. Approached a solution
80. Traveled, in a way
81. Combinations
83. Staff men
84. Compulsion
85. Over-eager
86. Villain's forte
87. The McCoy: Abbr.
88. New York
91. City of Peru
92. Certain writers
96. His: Fr.
97. Performs obsequies of a kind
100. Popular garnish
101. —— price
102. Kind of seal
103. Topnotch
104. Berra
105. Social group
106. Service-women
107. For fear that

DOWN

1. European
2. She-wolf: Sp.
3. Sleep like ——
4. Hill of Rome
5. Near future
6. Part of a White House name
7. Individuals
8. Sound of gusto
9. Background
10. Inexperienced ones
11. "—— well"
12. Pronoun
13. TV offerings
14. Withering
15. Straw in the wind
16. Haystack
17. Invites
20. Term in grammar
23. Vogue
24. Turning point
29. Farm animals
31. Washer cycle
32. Group of three
33. What Sam made too long
34. Con ——, in music
35. Firing
36. Sounds of dolor
37. Granite center
38. Daft
39. City on the Seine
40. Pointers
42. Atropos et al.
43. Cloud: Fr.
46. Nasty
48. Relative of tequila
50. Exams
51. Blackthorn fruit
52. S.A. capital
53. Below: Ger.
54. Corday's victim
56. Street sounds
58. One lap, for Armstrong
60. City on the Mark
61. Boundary
62. —— Arabia
63. Collegians
64. Men of Tartu: Abbr.
65. Iroquoians
66. Realty papers
67. Hat feature
68. Covered with moisture
69. Athirst
72. Musical instruments
74. Of a branch of medicine
76. Fiji's capital
77. Bert of golf
78. Mortgages
79. Conceives
80. What Jack did
82. Papeete's island
84. Wood nymphs
86. Revered one
87. Different
88. Like last week's meat
89. Melange
90. Oil used in varnish
91. Igneous rock
92. Immunologist's concerns
93. Oxford
94. Sawbucks
95. Opposite of dele
98. Shoshonean
99. Fortune

Word Collection
by Lewis C. Breaker

ACROSS

1. Note holders: Abbr.
4. Libations
8. Bring bad luck
12. French soul
15. Mortar ingredient
17. Two
20. Comminuted
21. Inducting
23. Eats greedily
24. Light-bulb filler
26. Kind of ale
27. Prevent
28. Silvery
32. Former Indian state
33. Towel lettering
34. Excursion
35. Beauty of myth
37. Shreds
38. "Wherefore —— thou?"
39. Grates
40. Scattering
42. Method: Abbr.
43. Ferment
44. Handled rudely
45. Weaving frame
47. Hetty and Lorne
50. Machetes
51. Green gem minerals
55. Take it easy
56. Spartan serf
57. Origination
58. Son of Adam
59. Surrounding spaces
61. Asiatic river
62. Donkey disciples
64. Certain stocks
65. Belief
66. Slides
67. Learns, old style
68. Propositions
69. Examine critically
70. Turns over
71. Japanese assembly
72. U.S. air group: Abbr.
75. Mean persons
77. Middle East

waterway
78. German article
81. Moslem holy man
83. —— the punch
84. Raced
85. Spanish muralist
86. Edible roots
88. Assets
90. Legal thing
91. Bouquet de Flore
93. Channel seaweed
94. Stock exchange man
95. Payment
99. Place of suffering
101. A judge, at times
102. Put in ecstasy
103. Astral sign
104. Throw
105. Bunch of bananas
106. Road curve

DOWN

1. Conduit under a road
2. New York's North and East
3. Inkling
4. —— Baba
5. Skink, gecko, et al.
6. Issue
7. Grasslike plant
8. Estate tenures for wives
9. Cheshire Cheese, for one
10. Steel town in Norway
11. Indian memorial
12. Extemporize
13. Liliom's creator
14. Posers
15. Trill
16. European coins: Abbr.
18. Shrew
19. Vitality
20. City on Vltava River
22. German author
25. Sergeant's words
28. Yorkshire river
29. Angered
30. "—— or never!"
31. Removes hair
34. L.A. team
36. Electrodes
39. Wryneck genus
40. Name for Shropshire
41. One using an exit
43. Intense ones
44. Greek state
46. Muezzin's perch
47. Alumni, for short
48. Establishment opposer
49. Varnish ingredient
50. Lahr and others
51. Locks up
52. Eras
53. Musical work
54. Aegean island
56. Warmer
57. Snoops
59. Modern home construction
60. Nobles
63. Smart
65. In the home of: Fr.
67. Post-Thanksgiving menu
68. One-all
70. Small violins
71. Union obligation
72. Hindu guitar
73. Bewilders
74. Kind of sundae
76. Menlo Park monogram
77. Apparition
78. Eastern cedars
79. M. Lupin
80. Metric measure
82. Illinois city
84. Knowing, old style
85. Private eye
87. Free-for-all
89. Fads
90. Minotaur's home
92. Greek goddess of vengeance
94. Recipe abbreviation
96. Opposite of syn.
97. Army man: Abbr.
98. French adjective
100. Actor of sorts

New Year's Party
by Frances Hansen

ACROSS

1. Order to torpedoman
6. Present
11. "—— are about to die..."
16. Architect Jones
21. Word games: Abbr.
22. Of an acid group
23. French airmail word
24. "Sing —— songs..."
25. —— bell
26. All set
27. Loud cries
28. Hartebeest
29. Broadway phrase
32. "—— fairer than the day"
33. Start of Keats poem
34. Writer Rand
35. Times of day, for short
36. Fervent plea, with "us"
38. Gray: Fr.
40. Collected writings
41. Overseas address
42. Mouth: Slang
43. Sandburg words, after "I am"
52. Sound: Prefix
53. Clement and Marianne
54. Eastern nurse
55. —— good turn
56. The Bulbul Amir
58. Chinese dynasty
59. Nevada bandit
61. Talking bird
65. Decorate again
67. Frown
69. Moves furtively
71. Unit of loudness
72. Zambales people
74. Showy perennials
76. Malay hysteria
78. Sympathy's partner
79. Poe's lament
85. Presidential nickname
86. Famous fiddler
87. Israeli dances
88. Man for introductions
89. Combine: Suffix
91. Fiber plant
94. Xmas V.I.P.
96. Poem part
99. Mustapha Kemal
101. Latecomer's penalty
103. Holiday months: Abbr.
105. Kills
106. Corrode
108. Garish sign
109. Ascended rapidly
111. Intentions
112. What "no man lives without"
118. Bread: Prefix
119. Greek letters
120. "Ain't We Got ——?"
121. Savvy remark
122. Part of winter lawn scene
124. Hair job, for short
126. Between sine and non
129. Start of Xmas carol
133. Swords
134. Biblical quotation
137. Alentejo's capital
138. Writer Jones
139. Devil
140. "—— ears," said the rabbit
141. Mortise partner
142. Voter
143. Churchill gesture
144. Titter
145. Cunning
146. Sits
147. Heaps
148. U.S. Indians

DOWN

1. Native of area of Iran
2. J.F.K. and L.B.J.: Abbr.
3. —— check (hunting term)
4. Party worker of a kind
5. Man's name
6. Mountain lake
7. Last in a series
8. Pepys' pride
9. Append
10. Toy
11. "—— with a maid"
12. Consequence
13. Rogers and others
14. One kind of smoke
15. Cricket sides
16. Signed in a way
17. Hostess's oversight
18. "No man —— to his valet"
19. Hunting code
20. Harem room
30. Dialect
31. Heavy hair
32. Shouted down
36. Unit of fuel use: Abbr.
37. Shipping term: Abbr.
39. Catch sight of
40. Pleased sounds
41. Excited
43. Ivan, for one
44. "—— Sound, Fla."
45. Tippy furniture
46. Profit's partner
47. Norse king
48. Voice parts
49. Cockney flats
50. False god
51. Funny show: Abbr.
57. Discovered by chance
59. "... —— that I know is damn'd"
60. Union general
62. Result of being trod on
63. "—— Year's gift..."
64. Cure
66. Creates
68. Accompanying
70. Flower stalks
73. Canary's cousin
75. Body fluids
77. Old ones: Abbr.
79. "—— o' kindness"
80. —— -kiri
81. Party disappointment
82. Mahatma
83. Bone: Suffix
84. "Don't ——" (plea of hostess)
90. Label for a gay party, with "Babel"
92. On the ocean
93. Uris
95. Emoting: Abbr.
97. Ferment
98. Set a value on: Abbr.
100. Indian dye
102. "The flowers ——..."
104. Wheat of India
107. Actress Louise et al.
109. Japanese coin
110. Place firmly
112. An Apostle: Abbr.
113. After "now"
114. —— dime
115. Hebrew letter
116. Demote: Colloq.
117. Descendant of Adam's son
123. Intended
124. Tree genus
125. French school
126. Seemingly
127. Up to
128. Equally old, with "of"
130. Madagascan lemur
131. Free-for-all
132. Gardner's namesakes
134. "...see my stuff"
135. Hostess initials
136. Danube tributary
137. King of Siam's word: Abbr.
138. Seat of a sort

Word Parade

by Joseph LaFauci

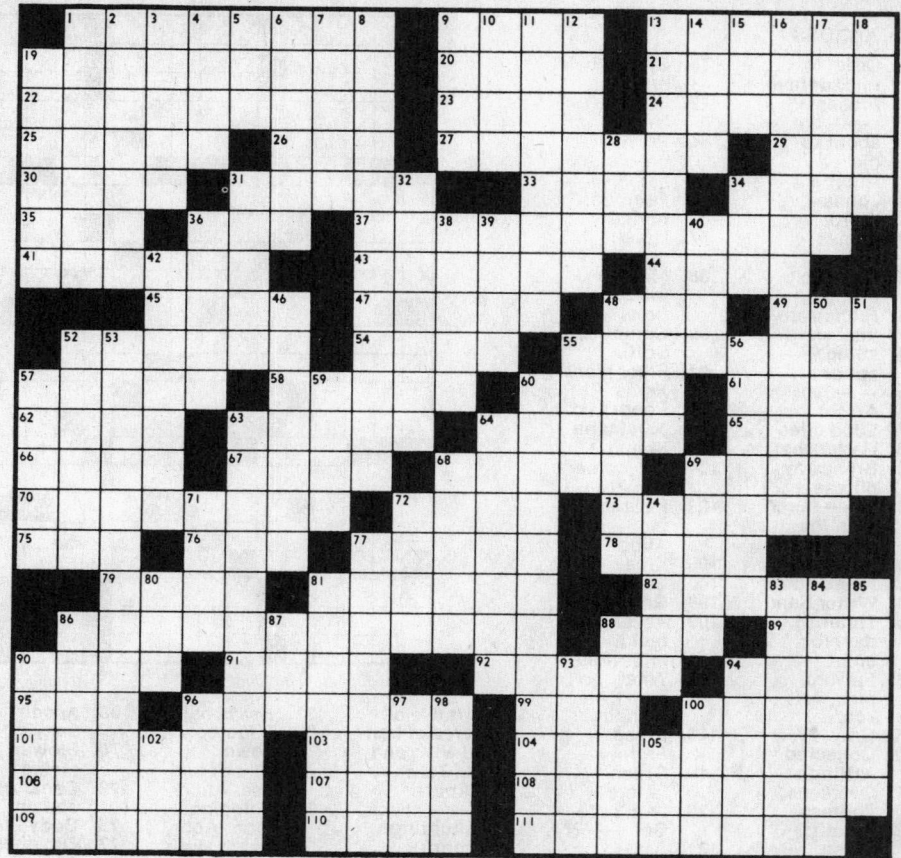

ACROSS

1. Light gray
9. Slovenly chap
13. Brown, rainbow, etc.
19. Italian cheese
20. Etna's output
21. Greet, as a villain
22. Honor
23. Caused to see red
24. Belong
25. Rhone tributary
26. Unkempt hair
27. Housewifely chore
29. Sourdough's find
30. Yard and boom support
31. Fundamental
33. Girl Friday's station
34. Biblical city
35. Generation
36. With: It.
37. Intolerantly petty
41. Pretends
43. Disapproving sounds
44. Track supports
45. Yesterday, in Rheims
47. Run on
48. Sindbad's bird
49. Never: Ger.
52. Role in "Private Lives"
54. Mechlin or Honiton
55. Serenade, for one
57. Football fields, for short
58. Blackbeard
60. Blend
61. Hollow sound
62. Buffalo of India
63. Epithet for a kettle
64. Gradual decrease
65. —— fixe
66. —— one's time
67. Origin
68. Manservant
69. Crossed out
70. Seize
72. Masonry creation
73. Shopped

75. Name for a dog
76. Hasten
77. Orchestra strings
78. Flying prefix
79. Heraldic fur
81. Big name in Pittsburgh
82. Printed matter
86. Resourceful
88. Face: Slang
89. Hindu deity
90. France's Le ——
91. Cure of a kind
92. Attempt
94. Destiny
95. Days of yore
96. TV comedy star
99. Drone
100. Novarro
101. Wild golf strokes

103. Ancient Syria
104. Working
106. Lease signer
107. Bare
108. Consigned to obscurity
109. Aspects
110. Garden
111. Lee's horse

DOWN

1. Foreshadow
2. Tennis term
3. Ward off
4. Lacerated
5. Corse, for one
6. Ungentlemanly one
7. Cooper Indian
8. Town hall, for one
9. Drifted
10. Byron poem
11. Exaggerated

12. Fast traveler
13. Mull
14. Sonority
15. Kirghiz city
16. Make a wise judgment
17. Defiled
18. Bullock
19. Original
28. Doctrine
31. Filleted
32. Galleon
34. "Fables in Slang" author
36. Numismatist's goodies
38. Freshwater fish
39. Consider
40. Pleasing
42. Like some fast deals
46. Resembling a pest
48. Egyptian city

50. Poor
51. Incited, with "on"
52. Succeed
53. Quality of some psychedelic drugs
55. Actress Velez
56. Watched jealously
57. Eva
59. Alleviate
60. Not making the grade
63. Expert advisers
64. Words for a summer drink
68. Italian actress
69. Singer Bobby
71. Pronoun
72. TV maestro
74. Kind of race

77. Concentrated
80. Feminine suffix
81. Entitle improperly
83. Human being
84. Recover from
85. Tied
86. Degraded
87. "Leave —— to Heaven"
88. Girl's name
90. D.C. hostess
93. Dandy
94. Ruinous
96. Part of N.B.
97. Counterweight
98. Govt. agents
100. Frenzy
102. Coolidge
105. Gun an engine

Centerpieces

by Thomas W. Schier

ACROSS

1. Dolmans
6. Bridge over Moslem hell
11. Climb
16. One at ——
21. Style of painting
22. Employed
23. Ambitious
24. Boo-boo
25. Statesman and author
28. Alpaca's cousin
29. Vaudeville turns
30. Long-billed bird
31. Wide-awake
32. Bullets, in France
33. French marshal
34. More reasonable
35. —— barrel
36. Small antelope
37. Arias
38. Actor
39. Boring tool
40. Orator and novelist
46. L.P., for one
49. New World capital
50. Lear's daughter
51. Greek region
52. Barton
54. Inter ——
55. Darling: It.
56. Military groups
57. Man of parts
58. Bad guy and film bad guy
63. Red
64. Carney
65. Transports
66. Man's name
67. More gentle
68. Antisocial one
69. —— polloi
70. Flower, in Berlin
71. Hallows
74. All rose —— man
76. Use one's neck
77. Houston
80. Canadian city
81. Former quarterback and novelist
84. Cay
85. Sudden reaction
86. Bowling

alley
87. River to Baltic
88. Electron tube
89. Song refrain
90. Juvenile writer Oliver
92. Doctor's allotment
94. Telepathy's relative
95. Justice and Ohio man
98. African tribe
100. Effects
101. Highest point
102. Able, Baker,
105. Like a swamp
107. —— de lune
109. Cry of contempt
112. Stassen
113. Prospector's companion
114. Dissertation
115. —— War
116. Range areas
117. Socialist and novelist
120. Wrathful
121. Endeavored
122. Kitchen implement
123. Play backer
124. Lease anew
125. Scowl
126. Bergen's Mortimer
127. Solan and gannet

DOWN

1. Broadway name
2. Swiftly
3. —— line
4. Slips
5. Augean stable, for one
6. Alluring
7. Accustom
8. Kind of monger
9. Slippery —— eel
10. Lacrosse team
11. Fur-hunting
12. Frisk
13. Athens sight
14. Baltic native
15. Poetic word
16. Excited
17. German dramatist
18. Wholly
19. Baltic port
20. Take out
26. Muse of comedy
27. Grotto
32. Purses
34. Arrange
35. O'Neill
36. Surmise
37. Old porticoes
38. French painter
39. Understanding
40. Boatman
41. Assess for a purpose
42. "Instant Replay" author
43. —— how
44. Lind or wren
45. Hostile
46. Furious
47. Uneven
48. Do a banquet job
49. —— Cali-

fornia
52. Part of a table setting
53. Greene of TV
55. Examples
56. More hostile
59. Hard rubber
60. Small ruling group
61. Collusion
62. Accompanying
63. Stuck to
67. Censure
68. Organized, with "up"
70. Tributary
71. Digression
72. Patriarchs
73. Ship's deck
74. To any degree
75. Kind of poll
76. Kind of gang
77. Type of car
78. Lay
79. Bare
81. City in Japan
82. —— ego
83. Red dye
85. Grayish

color
90. Famous trail
91. Implore
92. Legal rights
93. Repute
95. Bagnold
96. Build up
97. Sumac plant
98. "Jane Eyre" creator
99. Ready
102. Church area
103. French port
104. Of a surface
105. Mandalay's land
106. Abalone
107. Italian philosopher
108. Like some excuses
109. Harbor sight
110. 4,500-mile range
111. Games man
113. Do eggs
114. Unconvincing
115. Long hair
117. Badger
118. Corp. officers
119. Witch

The Face Is Familiar
by Eugene T. Maleska

ACROSS

1. Termagant
6. Cleft
12. Epithet for Samuel Johnson
16. Relative of hi-fi
17. Panay port
18. Papa Bear of football
20. Patti Page
22. Wards off
24. Bittern
25. Eating places
26. Bishop's headdress
28. Novelist Levin
29. Grub
30. Entanglement
31. Bremen's river
32. Connery
33. Harriman's nickname
34. Arctic base
35. —— Devi, Indian peak
36. Piece of gossip
37. Schnauzers
39. Mexican shawl
40. Hindu's fast to get justice
41. "—— Lynne"
42. Kyle or Tobin
43. "—— My Sunshine"
45. Play the siren
48. Valuable tree of N.Z.
50. Checks
53. —— Kabaivanska, soprano
54. Rathbone
55. Chilean export
57. Use a straw
58. Useless
59. Cyd Charisse
61. Color in French flag
62. Culbertson
63. Shaman
64. Sniggler
65. Blossom in Brest
66. Prof's stand
68. Wailed
70. Drinks noisily
71. Smuts's philosophy
73. Auction word
74. Korean statesman
75. Iosif V. Dzhugashvili
77. Choir voices
79. Knight fights
83. California's Santa ——
84. Pigtail
85. Cluster
86. Cargo unit
87. Grampuses
88. La ——, Honduran port
89. Fissure
90. "—— move on!"
91. Bowl call
92. Count Basie plays it
93. Cathay
94. Braid of gold or silver
95. Small-time
97. Cary Grant
100. Usher's beat
101. Jeer at
102. Emissary
103. Capitol Hill count
104. Worked on galleys
105. Wroth

DOWN

1. Track official
2. Mackerel-like fish
3. Algerian port
4. Author of "The King Ranch"
5. Ken Murray
6. Nonsense!
7. Agalloch
8. Has an oar-deal
9. Sesame
10. Krypton, for one
11. Miss von Kappelhoff
12. Trout
13. Engage in
14. Drink
15. Leila Koerber
16. "The ravel'd —— of care"
19. Tune
20. Flimflam
21. Name for a ship's carpenter
23. Kringle
27. Congou
30. Anagram for "sheet"
31. Baseball's Big or Little Poison
32. Delusion's partner
34. Royal adornment
35. Natasha Gurdin
36. Midwest airport
38. Meet, as alumni
39. Central theme
40. Indian millet
42. Bed of flowers
44. Horse opera
45. Caliban's opposite
46. Chef's spoon
47. Claudette Colbert
48. Narrative
49. Walked
51. Traffic jam
52. Rail sidetracks
54. George —— (Nathan Birnbaum)
56. "—— Three Lives"
59. City in N.W. Italy
60. Actress Gwyn and others
61. Cornflower
63. Girl in "As You Like It"
65. Hosiery color
67. Turnpike fees
69. Old port of Rome
70. Oyster shell
72. Enriching brine
74. Pope John XXIII
75. Recreation
76. Pacific battle site: 1943
78. Drudged
79. Tia ——
80. Battologize
81. Announcement
82. Grind together
84. Lillie
85. Suborned
88. Adduces
89. Reprove
90. Alexander's epithet
92. Like thick rugs
93. Voucher
94. Former queen of Greece
96. Dan Beard's org.
98. Dernier ——
99. Article in Berlin

51 Off and Running

by A. J. Santora

ACROSS

1. Child's ailment
6. Prefix for theater
11. Celebrator's sound
15. Michener book
21. Masochist of a sort
23. Inheritances of a sort
25. Advantage
26. Trifles
27. Spanish ladies
28. Cinema's Sommer
29. Pacific island group
30. Sibilant sound of derision
31. Astronaut John and family
33. One of the Joneses
35. Inspiration
37. Orb
40. Harbor boat
41. Comparative word
43. Siesta
44. Madrid wife: Abbr.
47. Emphatic negative
53. Rep.
54. Scorch
55. TV host
56. Sister Eileen's state
57. From A ___
59. Imitative
61. Indian writer
63. Turtle feature
64. "Rain" girl
66. Spools
67. Helper: Abbr.
70. Love 'em and leave 'em
73. Metrical foot
74. Desire
75. Prongs
76. Horse transport
77. "The Rain ___"
80. Spoil
81. Ice-bucket item
82. Sonoran: Abbr.
83. Add
85. Indian ape
86. Using the rink
88. Peaked
89. Wicked city
90. River areas
91. To be, in Paris
92. Just in time
96. Sky animal
97. Spore sac
98. Long times
99. Augury
100. Correlative
102. ___ one talk
104. Tennis unit
105. Turkish lake
106. Rye or corn
110. Lamented
111. "___ in the stilly night"
113. All-inclusive
118. Pronoun
119. California's Big ___
120. Bridge positions: Abbr.
121. Charged atom
122. Luau instrument
123. Like a rain forest
125. Conger
127. Yellow-green hues
130. Melville title
132. Pineapples
134. Fragrance
136. ___ fours
139. Omaha's achievement
141. Radio men
144. Controlling firmly
145. Final stage
146. Undertakes
147. Paris suburb
148. "Can't teach ___ dog . . ."
149. Prevent, in law

DOWN

1. Greek letter
2. ___ de jambe
3. Approximately
4. Taking advantage
5. Piano part
6. Height: Abbr.
7. Napoleonic battle site
8. Indian verandas
9. Mild cussword
10. Nettled
11. Elite
12. "I ___ dream"
13. Minstrel performer
14. Washington newsman
15. Biddy
16. Reaches a total
17. "___ me!"
18. Bristles
19. Some voters: Abbr.
20. Magazine number: Abbr.
22. Spanish coin
24. Sounding sheepish
32. No, in law
34. Roman emperor
36. Other shoe
37. Compass point
38. Hebrew day
39. And the like: Abbr.
42. Reach
44. Cobbler
45. Cranes' relatives
46. Floodlights
48. Accommodation
49. Assent
50. "A man may see . . . with ___"
51. Mountain passes
52. Certain Hindu
53. Mas d' ___, French town
54. Cut-rate
58. Pindar output
60. Bacon order
62. Sinclair
63. Hard blow
64. Tunisian port
65. Book man
67. Goals
68. Deploys, as police
69. Sinks the cue ball
71. Hybrid tongue, with 112 Down
72. Handicap race, for one
78. Presiding spirit
79. Space agency
81. ___ knot
82. Planet
83. Over-shadows
84. Norse god
87. Aligned
88. Attacked
89. Ornamental patterns
90. Pack animal
93. Retreat
94. Deer
95. Vagrant
97. Town in Italy
101. Musical dir.
103. Rake
105. Gaelic
107. French drink
108. Flatboat
109. Ike
112. See 71 Down
114. British explorer
115. Male hawk
116. Trough
117. Establish
119. ___ march on
120. Church councils
123. Classmen
124. ___ Gras
126. Low Hindu caste
127. Prefix for naut
128. Ink: Fr.
129. Heaven's ___!
130. Whether
131. Coin of low value
133. Piercing tools
135. Lord in "Winter's Tale"
137. Baltic native
138. Wolf: Prefix
139. Poke, in Scotland
140. Id
142. Law degree
143. Engine power: Abbr.

Word Assortment

by Nancy W. Atkinson

ACROSS

1. Put together
6. What sopranos give dogs
14. Zenana
19. Philosophy of a sort
21. Italian seasoning
22. Bijoux
23. Unspecified time
24. Timetable listing
25. Wacky
26. Enlists
28. Silent star Naldi
29. At no extra ___
31. Pianist Peter
33. Start
35. Zones
37. Ship's hoist
39. Repute
40. Backfield players: Abbr.
42. ___ team
45. Perspectives
50. Large decanters
54. Bold ones
55. Area of Europe
56. Fading politico
58. ___ packing
59. Some fishermen
60. Mindanao natives
61. Gallery sounds
63. Certain believers
65. Mineo and others
66. Color for the Baron
67. Eskimo knives
69. Bristle
70. Capuchin monkey
71. Cheese
73. Threesomes
75. Wrinkle
77. Kind of berry or bug
78. Barbarians
80. Cheerless
82. Bemoans
84. Native of Provo
85. Kind of iron
87. Most stereotyped
88. Flower parts
89. Fastens again
91. Lush
92. Greenland settlement
94. Strips
96. Installs
100. Wins recognition
106. Trophies
108. Use straws in a way
109. Russian range
110. Police weapon
112. Effrontery
114. Creek
115. Break one's word
117. Come to terms
120. Faint clues
121. Quit trying to argue
122. Water animal
123. Heraldic bearing
124. Analyze in a way

DOWN

1. Andes animal
2. Appraiser of Snow White
3. Opposed to
4. Cabinet man: Abbr.
5. Flying jib
6. Developed
7. Inferior one
8. Home: Abbr.
9. Lawyers: Abbr.
10. Like one in a monastery
11. Depend on
12. In any ___
13. U.S. composer
14. Chinese dynasty
15. Flower spike
16. Arm bones
17. Muse
18. Yucatan native
20. When the scholar comes
21. Certain Oscar winners
27. German conjunction
30. Old shields
32. Roman poet
34. Antelope
36. Booted
38. ___ much as
41. Check suddenly
43. First king of Egypt
44. More flamboyant
46. Capitol Hill men: Abbr.
47. Cherish
48. Skyways
49. Most flip
50. Flies off the handle
51. Recent time
52. Cage bird from India
53. Looks high and low
57. Low Indian caste
59. Puts on
62. Fountain order
64. Kind of poker
68. Bondmen
72. Ceylon ape
73. One-fifth of the Union
74. Havens
76. Flats: Abbr.
77. Shook up
79. Strong winds
81. Livid, old style
83. Vientiane's land
85. Name in U.S. journalism
86. Kind of power: Abbr.
90. Babe Ruth or Hank Aaron
93. French spirit
95. Few and far between
97. Overdue debt
98. Contaminates
99. Bundle up
100. An ___ the ground
101. On the job
102. Attacked
103. Relative
104. Sorrowful, in poems
105. Century plant
107. Arabian nomad
111. Japanese measures
113. Eucalyptus wax
116. Eur. language
118. Babylonian god
119. ___ culpa

53

City Landmarks

by Marjorie K. Collins

ACROSS

1. Loos
6. Christie and Magnani
11. Malay sailboat
15. ___ Nova
18. Grinding tooth
19. Had in mind
20. Civil War men
21. Voltage term in physics
22. Literary work
23. Philadelphia
26. Burdened man
27. Musical passage
28. Sheep
29. European blackbird
30. Boston
32. New York City
34. Not in vogue
35. Move with care
36. Seamen's quarters
37. Presidential initials
38. Cherish
41. Binge
42. Wound memento
45. "Dear ___"
46. Prepare for action
47. Man's name
49. Cur
51. Rhythmic tunes
52. Make an opinion
56. Style
57. Witch town
58. Steering blade: Abbr.
59. "Zhivago" character
60. Word of afterthought
61. San Francisco
64. City in Oklahoma
65. Egg on
66. Recent: Prefix
67. Insect homes
68. Wild and white
69. Gangsters' disciplinarian
71. Hair jobs
72. Handled
73. Jannings
74. Chemical suffixes
75. Diamond lady
76. Gabor and Little
78. Companion on the range
79. Woolen fabric
84. College degree: Abbr.
87. Bedaubed
89. Valley
90. Scull
91. Washington
94. Miami
97. God of Islam
98. Wire: Abbr.
99. Outer coat
100. 1964 Olympic site
101. Pittsburgh
105. Printers' frames
106. Before, to poets
107. Hymn word
108. Did business
109. Goliath, for one
110. Two: Sp.
111. Beach sight
112. Europeans
113. Kefauver

DOWN

1. Certain sportsman
2. On time
3. Of the lower back
4. Foot bone: Prefix
5. Metric measure
6. French town
7. Heckle
8. Port of Brazil
9. Reply: Abbr.
10. Farm area
11. Does squad-car duty
12. Disposes of again
13. Outmoded: Abbr.
14. ___ in the dark
15. Maligned
16. Take care of the lawn
17. Lithe
22. Peasant's shoe
24. Respond
25. Pronoun
27. Burn
31. Medical prefix
32. Copse
33. After primo, in Italy
36. Baltimore
39. Houston
40. Venue
41. Terrazzo worker
43. Bow shape
44. Detroit
46. River of Southwest
48. Subtle shading
49. Persian, for one
50. Risky
51. Cabinet post
52. U.S. Indians
53. Possessive pronoun
54. Evaporated
55. U.S. inventor
56. Plum variety
57. Pintail duck
61. Seize and hold
62. Exposed
63. Veterinary degrees
68. Downfall
70. Red or Yellow: Abbr.
71. 5-point type
75. Respirator
77. Much in love
78. Main Line town
79. Sky sights
80. Split
81. Have a ___ (give the once-over)
82. Perry Mason and others
83. Guthrie and others
84. Put on
85. Green: Prefix
86. Beauties
88. Forever, in poetry
89. Openwork barrier
92. Ill-bred person
93. ___ of steam
94. Kidney or liver
95. Spirit of a people
96. Crow
102. Seamen's group: Abbr.
103. Do sums
104. Teachers' group: Abbr.
105. Little one: Suffix

54 Phraseology

by Bert Beaman

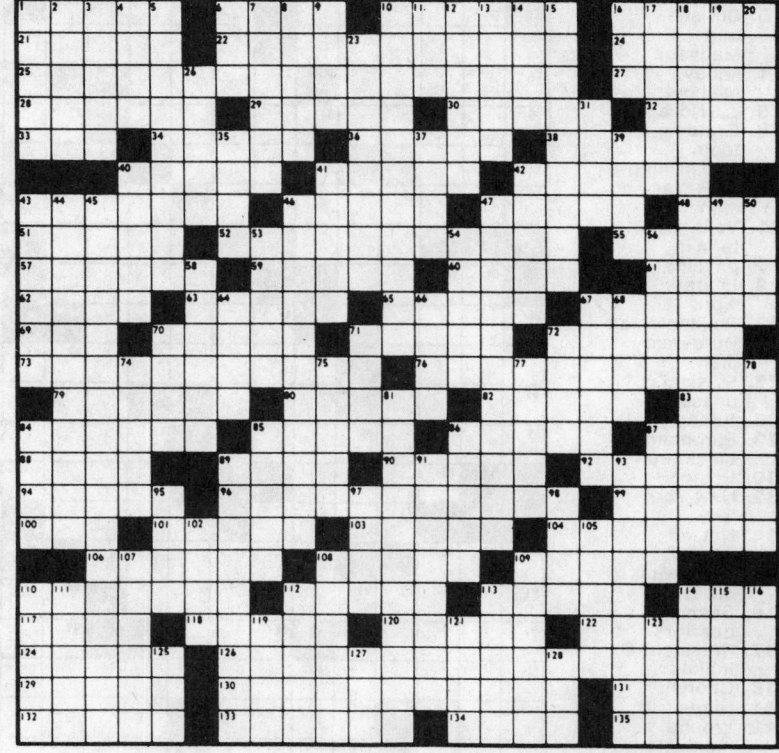

ACROSS

1. Canadian resort
6. Comprehending words
10. Make possible
16. Spanish ladies
21. Edie or John Quincy
22. Process that makes water bubbly
24. Fourflusher
25. Err
27. Fizzle
28. Famous bridge jumper
29. Dead duck
30. Rhythm, in Britain
32. Renovate
33. One kind of man
34. Morning song
36. Man: Prefix
38. Looked happy
40. Equipment for Leinsdorf
41. Math abbreviation
42. Berth
43. ___ grade (succeed)
46. Go off
47. Uses a crystal ball
48. Western alliance
51. Zola
52. Ocean salvaging equipment
55. Develop
57. Yummy
59. Exposed
60. Sped
61. Verb suffix
62. Heraldic term
63. Hersey's town
65. Images
67. Kind of vessel
69. Award: Abbr.
70. Mirthful
71. Accustom
72. Drub
73. 3-R centers
76. Victory celebrations
79. Retreats
80. Bushlands
82. Like some foods
83. N. Y. subway
84. Clasp
85. Chou ___
86. Reserves
87. River to Danube
88. College official
89. Alder or birch
90. Generate
92. Of an old Nile city
94. British Lady of note
96. Zero, to athletes
99. Blackthorns
100. Confronted
101. Make ___ of things
103. Doctor's concern
104. Escorts
106. Lawyer's problem
108. Nonpartisans: Abbr.
109. Inverted V
110. Wear ___
112. Vermont city
113. One kind of relations
114. Stupid one
117. Cape near Lisbon
118. Philippine bananas
120. Prefix for a poison
122. Execrate
124. Turkish carriage
126. Put aside and forget
129. Eastern faith
130. ___ lips (slips out)
131. Capitol features
132. Name for a pitcher
133. Derides
134. Western hill
135. European

DOWN

1. Loquacious
2. Antarctic cape
3. Bags: Sp.
4. Postal abbreviation
5. Judgments
6. Kind of cap
7. Cotton processor
8. Mistaken: Abbr.
9. Black
10. Rapt
11. Slangy retort
12. Kind of pile
13. A Duke of Courland
14. Bewildered
15. Invigorated
16. Student's objective: Abbr.
17. Brian
18. History-making move
19. Vacuum tube part
20. Church council
23. Kind of town
26. British waste land
31. Gardner
35. Touched, as a starting line
37. "___ man with seven ..."
39. Girl's name
40. Misrepresent
41. Prefix for a metal
42. Woods dwellers
43. French wines
44. Wild West talk, for one
45. Celebrate
46. Certain New Englanders
47. Food birds
49. Like some college courses
50. Pythoness, for one
53. Mexican timber tree
54. Annoyance
56. Condescend
58. Acclaimed
64. Indian timber trees
66. Fellow
67. Most undeveloped
68. Babylonian god
70. Disturb
71. Land area: Sp.
72. Line a roof
74. College town
75. Standish
77. Money in Uppsala
78. Urgency
81. Cools
84. Gouda's relative
85. Irregular
86. Limits
87. Estuary
89. Kick over
91. Side entrances
93. Small planets
95. At any ___
97. German river
98. River to Danube
102. Rotterdam's river
105. Fish in a way
107. ___ Mater
108. Resort off Florida
109. Light craft
110. Thin as ___
111. Eric, for one
112. Bench, in Spain
113. Sierra ___
114. One at ___
115. Did a blacksmith job
116. Common item
119. Bartlett's relative
121. Mouth: Prefix
123. Acknowledge
125. Poet Lowell
127. Manuscript abbreviation
128. Youth org.

55 In Good Season

by Eva Pollack Taub

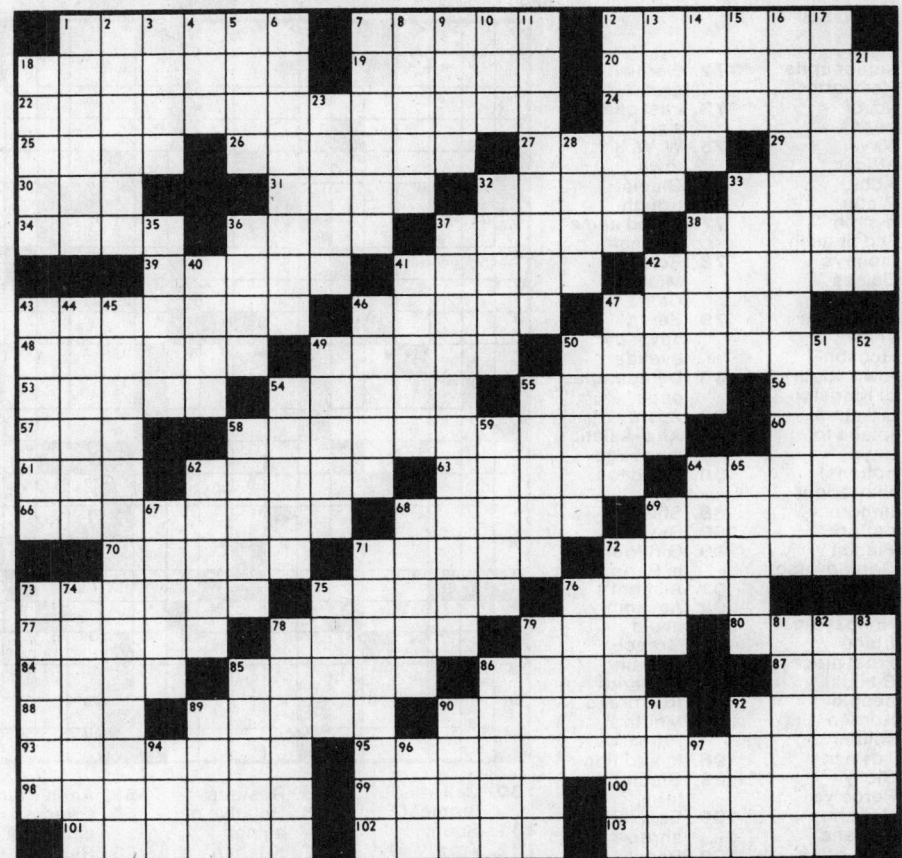

ACROSS

1. California mountain
7. Metrical accent
12. Coldest
18. Of rock debris
19. Hangman's symbol
20. Hot-dog topping
22. Eugene Field subject
24. Polish city
25. Pats, in Scotland
26. Property
27. Task
29. Tout's specialty
30. Expert
31. Plant fiber
32. Garish
33. "___ but the brave..."
34. Renovate
36. Grain
37. Film award for animals
38. Less dangerous
39. P. I. rope fiber
41. Freshwater fish
42. Butler's milieu
43. Kind of cheese
46. Profoundness
47. Place for a glider
48. Earth pigments
49. Statistician's concern
50. Postponers
53. Actor John
54. Coax
55. Takes out
56. Comic-strip cry
57. Doctrine
58. Fancy trimmings
60. Relative of st.
61. Perceive
62. Town in Iowa
63. Domestic help
64. Scatter
66. Of an early Greek doctrine
68. Pickles
69. Frenchman's four
70. One of an early rabbi group
71. ___ panky
72. Cowboy
73. Hard
75. Onward
76. Car part
77. River to the Missouri
78. Shallow boats
79. Fireplace problem
80. Russian press agency
84. Lacquer: Sp.
85. Folkways
86. Gossip
87. Navy man: Abbr.
88. Common verb
89. Item in a London parlor
90. Classes
92. Spoken
93. Ziegfeld musical
95. Sherlock Holmes of films
98. More close-fitting
99. Pupil: Fr.
100. Red colors
101. Garden flowers
102. Road curves
103. African insect

DOWN

1. Water channel
2. Kept close to
3. Gardner and others
4. Term of respect
5. Fabric strip
6. Flavoring
7. Confined person
8. Short surplice
9. Lacerated
10. Employ
11. Male seal
12. Give form to: Var.
13. Spicy dish
14. "___ what you mean"
15. Diminutive endings
16. Superior people
17. Athletes' helper
18. Be, in Spain
21. Deception
23. City in N.Y.
28. Quiet
32. Cloister courtyard
33. French city
35. Of a grain
36. Tatters
37. Candies
38. Girls' names
40. Expose
41. "___ porridge..."
42. Pushed a raft
43. Bovine
44. Writer Sean
45. Of an Old World tree
46. Argentine statesman
47. Chinese waxes
49. Suffix for photo
50. Acts
51. Well-known horseman
52. Rod for meat
54. Leg bone
55. In a deadpan manner
58. Old ___
59. Afghan town
62. Organic compound
64. Done for, familiarly
65. Be silent, in music
67. Greek letter
68. Wall game
69. Four: Abbr.
71. Insect
72. Extend
73. Sun rooms
74. Russian ruler
75. Roll up
76. Plant pest
78. Conic lines in geometry
79. Moves in a way
81. Spanning
82. Foster's river
83. Shoe parts
85. Taxi part
86. Initiative
89. Buster Brown's dog
90. Chemical sugars
91. Marie and others: Abbr.
92. News piece
94. Army org.
96. Jolson, etc,
97. Otto I's domain: Abbr.

Countdown

by Herbert Ettenson

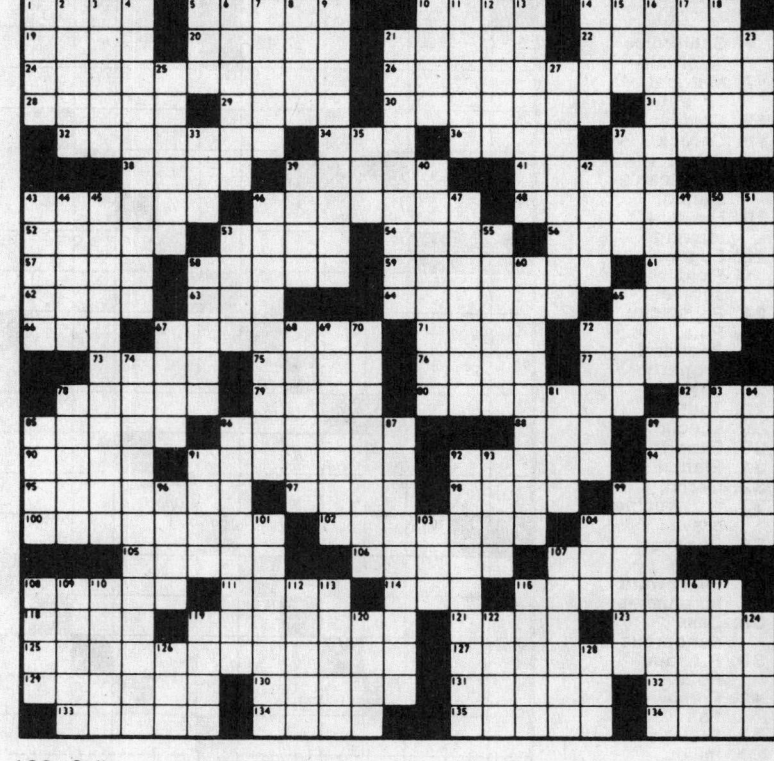

ACROSS

1. Liquor units
5. Not worth __ of beans
10. Naval officer: Abbr.
14. Water nymph
19. Old English moneys
20. Daises
21. Certain vaudeville show
22. Hudson town south of Kingston
24. __ store (place to buy notions)
26. Play about tinhorn bettors
28. Pianist Gabrilowitsch
29. Comedian Danny
30. Nonpaying friend
31. Frost piece
32. Biblical people
34. Korean soldier
36. Town in Sicily
37. Perceive
38. Uncanny
39. The end
41. Love affair
43. Presidential middle name
46. Dogcart
48. Branch of study
52. Make one
53. Title of respect
54. Computer stuff
56. Record keeper
57. Ferber
58. More judicious
59. Outdoor
61. Dwarf: Prefix
62. Shady agreement
63. Exhibitionist
64. Most favorable conditions
65. Alcohol burners
66. Subsidiary
67. Released a claim to
71. Concerning
72. Garnish green
73. Last card of a suit
75. W. W. II town
76. Glacial trough
77. Noted name in West
78. Role for Michael Caine
79. Sew a hawk's eyelids
80. Detachable page
82. Assn.
85. Afro-Asiatic language
86. Filled the bill
88. Shelter
89. Sky: Fr.
90. Girl friend in Paris
91. Ailment
92. Assembly in old Greece
94. Cruising
95. Nut-and-fruit bread
97. Mouth: Prefix
98. In addition
99. Glacial term
100. East Indian shrews
102. People fleeing a land
104. Gems
105. Sauce, in Italy
106. Tin, in Paris
107. Epithet for Clio, Erato, etc.
108. "__ will is the wind's will"
111. Speaker of baseball
114. __ for one
115. "Had a __ big as a whale"
118. Sunburns
119. Caps of a kind
121. The fat __ the fire
123. Literary villain and namesakes
125. Obscenities
127. Necessity à la Thomas Marshall
129. Water animals
130. Cell terminal
131. Spent
132. Fuzz
133. Body: Prefix
134. Gambling game
135. Rimy coatings
136. Silk: Sp.

DOWN

1. Equally
2. Junk
3. Medieval guild
4. Dreggy
5. Soldier's address
6. Game
7. Light bulbs, in the comics
8. Streaked
9. Slugabed
10. Bivouac
11. "__ a Grecian Urn"
12. Windfall
13. Graph of muscular contractions
14. Approaching
15. Residue
16. Relative of a jingo
17. Kitchen wear
18. Italian actress and family
21. Beat it!
23. Dotted, as enamelware
25. Kind of bathing suit
27. Time of the new moon
33. Attempt
35. Fuegian
37. Diamonds, for one
39. Golfer's word
40. Scouring items
42. Bouquet
43. Curfew: Sp.
44. Covered by
45. Rare case
46. Cans
47. Hat
49. Another's meat, so to speak
50. Nursemaids
51. Biblical man
53. Anna's land
55. Grieg character
58. Reporter's question
60. Without distinct form
65. Part of Q.E.D.
67. Control
68. Metric units
69. Ennoble
70. Gloomy
72. Port opposite Gibraltar
74. Method of crop rotation
78. Intend
81. Possessive
83. Singer Della
84. Product of sand
85. Kind of drum
86. Ominous
87. Dinner topper
89. Whip
91. Valley
92. Tax day
93. Singer Campbell
96. Grasslands
99. Spatial
101. Area of Borneo
103. "My __ Sal"
104. Asian sheep
107. What two fins make
108. When life begins, in a title
109. Northern Europeans
110. Only __ a customer
112. __ ear . . .
113. Curved metal bar
115. Old Greek temples
116. Farming student
117. __ so
119. Supreme
120. Taro root
122. Shadow: Prefix
124. Spanish girl: Abbr.
126. Refrain part
128. Football scores: Abbr.

Fractured Curios

by Frank Nosoff

ACROSS

1. Close watch
6. Perform
9. Certain flights
15. Covering over a throne
21. Old Italian port
22. Favoring
23. Chop's relative
24. Creature lacking color
25. Fruity tree, perhaps
27. Old man at the baccarat table, e.g.
29. Slangy negative
30. Ivy League campus
32. Cups' friends
33. Coarse sound of laughter
34. Girl's name
36. Future tulip
38. Spanish agate
39. Duck of a kind
40. Predecessor of British Airways
41. South Pacific native
43. Yo-Yo or top
44. Frame of mind
45. Living-room item
47. Costs
49. Dreadful
50. Husband of Bathsheba
51. Couple
53. Poems
54. Make a ___ case of
57. Type
58. Rural, in France
60. Wind instrument
61. St. Pierre, e.g.
62. Fraternal man
63. Culmination
65. Obligation
66. Container
67. Image
68. Uncle: Scot.
69. Cubes
70. Fixture of midtown N.Y.
72. Low cabinet
76. Large flowerpot
78. Extraordinary
79. English designer's fruit, perhaps
81. Majority
82. German number
83. Talking bird
84. Fares
85. Colleen's home
86. Childish pouts
88. Kind of dance
91. Hgt.
92. Musical passage
93. Baby carriage
95. Future roses
96. Edge of woven fabric
98. Very: Ger.
99. Bank function
100. Morse and others
101. ___ does it
102. Classman
104. Monochrome
106. Minor slip
108. Gov't. agency
109. Accounting word
111. Winged
112. Work on copy
113. Conjecture
115. Gentlemen
116. Passed over
119. Pronoun
120. Czech composer
122. Sitting
124. Attention
125. Underground artists, maybe
128. Was pertinent
130. City of N.W. Spain
131. Distracted: Fr.
132. Shrill bark
133. Actor Delon
134. Centaur of myth
135. Give more medication
136. Hindu title
137. East ___

DOWN

1. Irish woman patriot
2. Everyday
3. Verging on
4. Slower, in music: Abbr.
5. Train unit
6. Burning
7. State: Abbr.
8. Trunk façades
9. Seafood item
10. Large cask
11. Lawyers: Abbr.
12. Of old Troy
13. Avenges
14. Exterior wall coverings
15. Framework
16. Beverages
17. Knicks' league: Abbr.
18. Rich Texan of 1800s, perhaps
19. Of the lungs: Prefix
20. New ___
26. Veranda
28. Wriggly
31. Abner's partner
35. Wanderer
37. Overdecorated symbols of bad luck?
39. Entice
41. Dakota Indians
42. Insect nest
44. Skin
45. Seed covering
46. Elizabethan song
48. Letter
49. Overcame
50. Luau music maker
52. Star: Fr.
54. Ring weapons
55. Accompanying
56. Eyeglass: It.
59. S. A. Indian
60. Musical notes
63. Minor prophet
64. Teaching
66. Upright: Abbr.
67. Isfahan's land
68. Austen novel
69. Graduation awards: Abbr.
70. Market again
71. U.S. author
72. Spanish beds
73. Reichenbach's hypnotic force
74. Homers by Mickey, perhaps
75. Lyric poem
77. Arena performer
80. Shade of green
85. Set of values
86. Signified
87. Indian buffalo: Var.
88. Old English coach?
89. European river
90. Road curve
92. Instance
93. Japanese coin
94. Quoting France's XVI, perhaps
95. Gaucho weapons
97. Immense
98. Marine art
100. Popular American decor
102. Moira or Norma
103. Put out a new edition
105. Rumanian king
106. Instruction
107. Stick to
108. Stock
110. Seminary title: Abbr.
113. Pearly items
114. Basted
116. Low Greek pillars
117. Dine at home
118. Sluggard
120. Christ, in poetry
121. Incan beaker
123. Box
126. Important workers: Abbr.
127. Relatives of sts.
129. Culbertson

58 Adverbs a la Tom Swift

by Edward J. O'Brien

ACROSS

1. "Cards?" asked Tom ___
10. Mild oaths
17. ___ Swifties
20. Buy stocks in hope of a rise
21. "It will fly," said Wilbur
23. Good guys
24. Possibilities in a 3-way armature
25. "___ see"
26. "Times try men's souls," said Tom ___
28. Wept: Scot.
29. Relatives of inches: Abbr.
30. Assert
32. Reclined
33. Man's nickname
35. Patronal feast
37. Agcy. of 40's
40. Adjusts to
45. Singer Perry
48. Mend socks
49. Messy food
50. ___ error: Baseball trio
51. Incite
52. Waste allowance
53. Cow part
55. Girl's name
56. Life: Lat.
58. Once - controversial plane, the F ___
60. Of unbelievers
63. Macaw
64. "Instant coffee," said Tom ___
66. Expect: Lat.
68. "___ thing," said Midas touchingly
70. "Moo," said Elsie ___
71. "I can't," ___ philosophically
73. ___ Grande
74. "Here," said Tom
75. Fate
78. Prisoner ___
81. Hilly City
82. Korean city
84. Rel. of a xylophone
87. Men of the cloth: Abbr.
88. "___," sighed Beatrice infernally
91. Red gem
92. Ohio town
93. Wolf: Prefix
94. "Take heart," said ___ coolly
95. Onassis
96. Squirming
98. Self
100. Family man
101. Stein words
102. Droop
105. ___ - bitty
109. Words in Xmas hymn
114. Fiji pine
116. Heavyweight name
118. "It adds up," Tom said ___
120. "Be witty," ___ epigrammatically
121. Of voting
122. Cricket sides
123. "Bad music," said Milton
124. "I sang and danced," said ___

DOWN

1. "Love,"said Don ___
2. Vine-covered
3. Religious units
4. Vibrato: Abbr.
5. ___ challenge (is tested)
6. Indian word
7. Flying time?
8. She-wolf: Lat.
9. City in Michigan
10. "Martini," said Tom
11. Mature
12. Pasts
13. Ideas: Abbr.
14. "___ you it's true"
15. Of a decade
16. Toper
17. Russian ruler
18. Spanish jar
19. Agatha Christie work: Abbr.
22. City on Skye
27. Denial
31. Constitutional addition: Abbr.
34. South Bend campus
35. Communist boycott of a parley?
36. Three: Ger.
37. Aged
38. Dais
39. "___ for your thoughts"
41. "John ith," lisped ___
42. "Drop by drop," said ___
43. "Neap," said Tom ___
44. Actor Keach
45. Knight: Abbr.
46. Kimono sash
47. "I ___ ," said Simon simply
49. "I've no last name," said Hilda ___
54. Postal initials
57. Antoinette
59. Eskimo hut
61. Indisposed
62. Rio ___
65. Norse city
66. Indian lute
67. All: Prefix
68. S. A. mammal
69. "___ mark, get set . . ."
71. Salmon
72. Peaks: Abbr.
76. Took excessive medicine
77. Short skirt
79. Curved line
80. Relative of Army Q.M.
83. Where: Lat.
85. Golf duffers, so to speak
86. Locomotives: Abbr.
89. Digit
90. Glue: Sp.
96. Army woman
97. The date: Sp.
99. ___ mio (dear me)
100. Table mat
102. Bagpipe sound
103. Large halls
104. "The Beggar's Opera," wrote John ___
105. "___ sorry"
106. Sir, in Asia
107. Pronoun
108. Synagogue instrument
110. Defense offices: Abbr.
111. But, in Paris
112. Israeli airline
113. Donkey: Lat.
115. To the king, in France
117. Romans' 2,100
119. Old farmer's monogram

59

Country Air

ACROSS

1. Rural crossing
6. Italian poet
11. Attach
16. "The ___ Fellow"
21. Ataturk
22. Water animal
23. Register
24. Excessive
25. Kind of sandwich
27. Barrier
29. Verne hero
30. Trifles: Fr.
31. Con ___, in music
32. Mercury
33. Ten percenter
34. Cloth trimmings
35. Turner
36. Manolete et al.
40. Moon stage
41. Animal feet
45. Baffles
46. Hangman's tool
47. Transported in a way
48. Bum
49. Andrea ___
50. Snack-tray items
53. Sitar music
54. Signed
55. Hep
56. Buzzing
57. TV personality
58. ___ were
59. Tanker
60. Scaloppine
61. Preparing for an exam
62. Mayday's cousin
63. Antlers of Sherwood Forest deer
66. Army command
67. Native places
69. Unfashionable
70. Cud
71. Fruitcake ingredient
73. Words of bafflement
79. River, in Thailand
82. On ship
83. Clears
84. Revolted
85. Insect nests
86. Recently
87. Broadway offering
88. Arrow poison
90. Venetian bridge
91. Uno, dos, ___
92. Odd couple
94. Waters
95. Suffer
96. Wallops
97. Go for, as a pitched ball
98. Existentialist writer
99. Tennis-court limit
101. Paint filler
102. Like a courtyard
104. ___ da-fé
105. One who grieves
106. Shoe gadgets
107. Medical
110. Vogue
111. Hear of
112. "South Pacific" star
116. Congé
118. Food for Pahlavi
120. Bonne ___
121. Judge's call
122. Dine, in Bonn
123. Spirits
124. Supervises
125. Dull
126. Metric measure
127. Trail

DOWN

1. ___ deep
2. Gallic head
3. Moslem leader
4. French composer
5. Whitney
6. More classy
7. Site of U. of Georgia
8. Stretch, in Scotland
9. Indian weights
10. Pirate gold
11. Shawnee chief
12. "Who ... believed ___"
13. Sevareid and others
14. ___ avail
15. Norse name
16. Made a chess move
17. Open
18. First mate
19. ___ of thumb
20. Wrigglers
26. Odysseus's dog
28. Wall St. items
31. Debacle
33. Beat ___ horse
34. "Hamlet" role
35. Also-ran
36. In ___ res
37. "Tempest" role
38. Driers
39. Go on ___
40. Models
41. Muskets
42. Eastern times
43. Conestogas
44. Sprinkle
46. U.S. Japanese
47. Playwright Brendan
50. Gulps
51. Durant
52. Jug
53. Hindu title
57. "You've ___" (I give up)
59. Upright
60. Do a civic duty
61. Kind of hydrometer
63. Atlanta university
64. Gulps down
65. Charioteer
68. Some exams
70. Picardy output
71. Harvard man
72. Michener opus
73. Tardy
74. Mets and Yanks
75. Eye swelling: Var.
76. Cerumen
77. Snake
78. Actor Rip
80. Cling to
81. Deceived
85. Explosive, for short
87. Peter Nero's forte
88. Lined, as a roof
89. Complete
90. Pinnipeds
92. Hairpiece
93. Dense tree growth
96. Channels
98. Opera part
100. Won
101. Colanders
102. Pencil part
103. Herb genus
105. Home of many Goyas
106. Succinct
107. "___ first you don't ..."
108. English composer
109. State: Abbr.
110. Region: Abbr.
111. For fear that
112. Power Source: Abbr.
113. Novelist Grey
114. "___ love with you"
115. News item
117. Cut off
118. Footlike part
119. Explosives: Abbr.

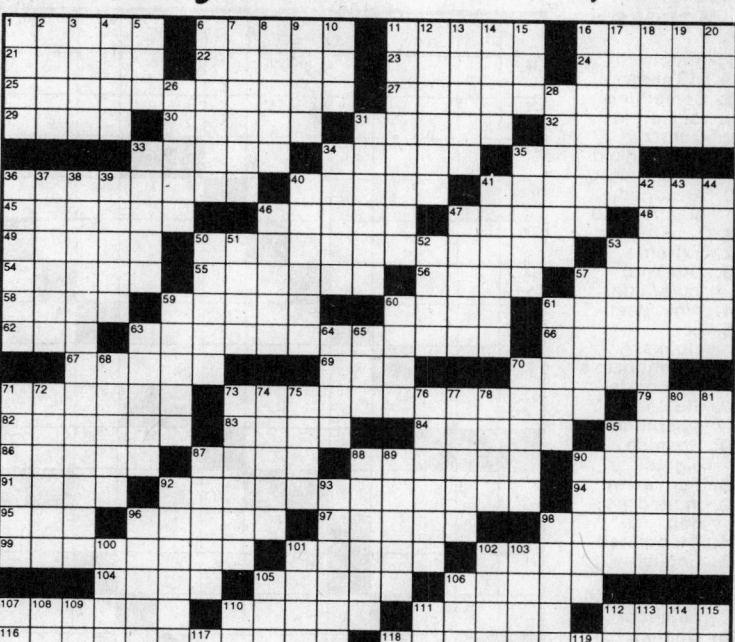

Two-Way Middles

by Joan DeRosso

ACROSS

1. Shepherd of Tekoa
5. Something for Garcia
12. Quartz
18. Familiar, old style
20. Arranged; disarranged
21. ___ Thule
22. Extreme
23. One who says "I do"
24. Whirl past
25. Long cloaks
27. D'Annunzio's inamorata
28. Flu symptoms
29. Spanish eights
30. Turn away
32. Incited, as a dog
34. Articulated
36. English county
37. Thailand's neighbor
38. Codlike fish
39. Cautious
40. Softens
41. Genetic initials
44. Golf club
45. Twisted
46. ___ order
47. Mast
48. Cassowary's cousin
49. Subdue; baton stroke
51. Telegram
52. Take off
54. Maple genus
55. Beaches
56. Beak membrane
57. Lighter
59. Bearing
61. Zeus's blood
64. Spring beer
65. Scales
69. Mastwood
70. Impend; aftermath of sorts
74. Stop ___ dime
75. Aria
76. Small change
77. Avifauna
78. Complacent
79. Poets' early days
80. Imparts
81. Places
82. Metric unit

83. German craft
85. Portions
86. Dental problem
87. Forks' tablemates
88. Did a hair job
89. Interrupt
90. Community character
91. English composer
92. Le Mans events
95. Pretty girl, familiarly
97. Arrived, with a bar
100. Reef
101. Illinois city
102. Some British students
103. Island near Zanzibar
104. Most strange

105. Thickly
106. Believe

DOWN

1. ___ of good cheer
2. Breakwater
3. View, and be careful
4. Afflicted
5. Longitude lines: Abbr.
6. W. W. II initials
7. Everything
8. Leggy
9. Encourage
10. Alluvium
11. French verb
12. Menu word
13. Andes animals
14. Troublesome
15. Fool with a bowling target
16. Plant
17. Beams

19. Minces
20. Goddess of hope
26. Offspring
30. Lend ___
31. Zodiac sign
32. Apia's area
33. "___ my heart in . . ."
34. Recoils
35. City in Italy
36. "On the Beach" author
37. Cornelia, for one
39. Fad
40. Potato
42. Ointment
43. Greek god
45. Milldam
46. Quondam
47. Proust man
49. Uncle Remus word
50. ___ straight line

53. Image: Prefix
55. Scorch
57. Brest and Boston
58. German exclamations
59. European thrush
60. St. Pierro and others
61. ___ dixit
62. Composed
63. Rob, and support
64. Divers' affliction
65. Premium
66. Enter with a paycheck
67. Accustom: Var.
68. Wise ones
70. "Neptune's ___"
71. Outlets
72. Static
73. Avarice

78. Channeled
80. Undoes
81. Hippie park events
82. Petty ruler
84. Man of odds
85. French revolutionist
86. Nasty one
87. Endured
88. Penned
89. Alley dwellers
90. Roper
91. Word on a brandy bottle
92. Pika
93. Bohemian river
94. Bridge bid
96. Inactive: Abbr.
98. Never: Ger.
99. Relative of qt.

61

Bundle of Nerves

by Frances Hansen

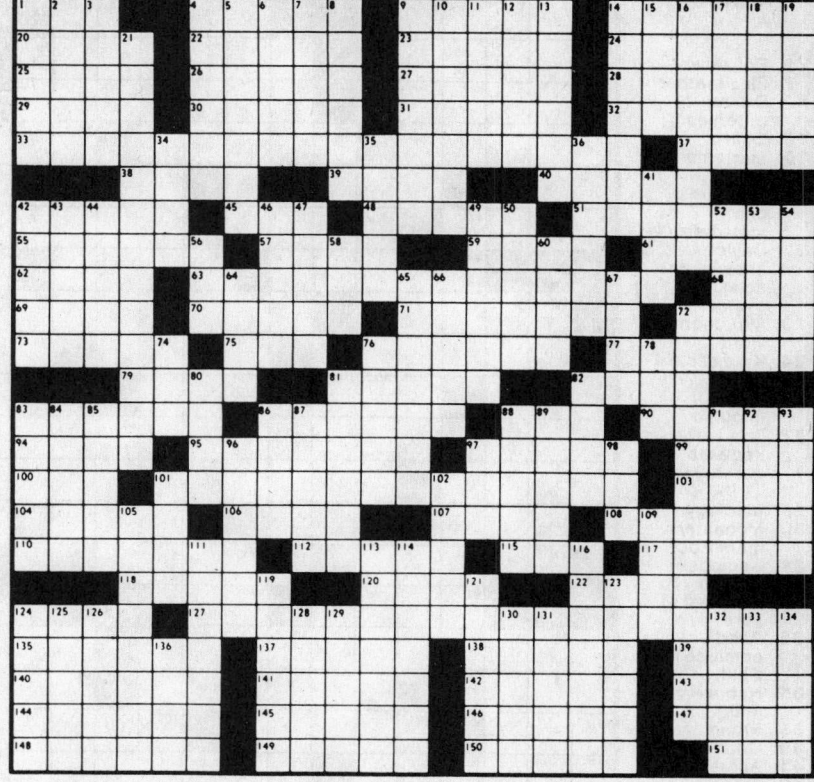

ACROSS

1. Wee: Scot.
4. Injures
9. Lincoln Center ladies
14. Dewlapped
20. Between quatre and six
22. Standish's advocate
23. Zola
24. Crown in a way
25. Moving: Lat.
26. Massey
27. Outer reaches
28. Former German republic
29. Honshu city
30. Purport
31. Attach
32. Royal fur
33. Dice maneuver
37. Packs tightly
38. "Be it ___ so . . ."
39. Hearty drink
40. Canines
42. Colette novel
45. Dixieland, for short
48. Jewish eves
51. Grand or Petit
55. After 38 Across
57. Echo of the Third Reich
59. Alas, in old Rome
61. City near Boys Town
62. Early church pulpit
63. Tree
68. Cap
69. Extend over
70. Morris's naked ape
71. Most artless
72. Adorned: Fr.
73. Loy
75. Choir member: Abbr.
76. Sappy trees
77. Played an ice game
79. Greenland base
81. Made a catty sound
82. "Oh dear"
83. Minos, for one
86. Two ___
88. Grate on
90. Make ___ at
94. Brinker
95. Shoo, early style
97. Under
99. Girl's name
100. Lupino
101. Robin Hood's backpack
103. Recess
104. Town S. W. of Saigon
106. Branches: Bot.
107. Forsaken
108. Interweave, as twigs
110. Roots
112. In ___ (befuddled)
115. What is it?
117. Heady stuff
118. Adjective suffixes
120. Island off Sumatra
122. Present
124. Ship post
127. Joe Jacobs's remark (with "I")
135. Buddhist monks
137. Suffix for flirt or visit
138. Terrain: Abbr.
139. Miffed
140. Boil inwardly
141. Date-ripening stage
142. Rouse
143. Quiz
144. Hospital worker
145. Coolers
146. Come up again
147. Senor's assent
148. "And ___ not into . . ."
149. Organ stop: Var.
150. Duel preludes
151. Lepidopterist's aid

DOWN

1. Analyzes verse
2. Biblical prophet
3. Sinuses
4. Proprietor: Fr.
5. Listening intently
6. Surprise wedding response
7. Forget ___
8. Foul-ups
9. Lose hope
10. Encroach on
11. Bit of food
12. Star near Mizar
13. "Eyes have they, but they ___"
14. Brilliant salesman
15. Oddball
16. Trinket
17. Keats poem
18. Antelope
19. Works of a French painter
21. Friends' hats
34. Kind of eye
35. Civil War general
36. Breathers
41. Noun suffix
42. Deep gap
43. Like a camel's back
44. Hinder
46. Topic
47. Virile one
49. Do a job on a lily
50. Slice thinly
52. Special kind of day
53. Midwest terminal
54. Yclept
56. Biblical suffix
58. Saud
60. Compass points
64. George Herman
65. Daunted by
66. Town in north Nebraska
67. Engrave
72. Grammarians' concerns
74. ___ loss
76. Likewise
78. Fringefoot
80. Korean apricot
81. Prado locale
82. Lined up
83. Marx brother
84. Speed-trap item
85. As a friend: Fr.
86. Hindu god
87. Fluid affliction
88. Lewis
89. Incomparable
91. Marriage pledge
92. Soap plant
93. Man in white
96. Cherry brandy
97. Relative: Abbr.
98. Compass point
101. Give up
102. Shake like ___
105. Distraught
109. Atmosphere: Prefix
111. Quonset huts' relatives
113. Pyrenees state
114. Ben-Gurion, for one
116. Unnerved
119. Penetrate fully
121. Spectral types
123. Lawn tools
124. Flavoring leaf
125. Good-night girl
126. Greek letter
128. City on the Mohawk
129. Green colors
130. Symbol of ring defeat
131. Shadowy: Lat.
132. Corner
133. Blot out
134. Resign
136. Road-routing sign

62 Phrasing It Right

by Jack Luzzatto

ACROSS

1. Boil down
7. Fine feather
12. British orderlies
18. Charm
19. Marrying in haste
21. Hard area of a strawberry
22. Device showing the solar system
23. McLuhan word
24. Kind of card
25. Busy
26. Nasty impulse
27. "He knoweth the way that ___"
29. Ideology
30. Monastery man: Abbr.
31. Composer Albeniz
33. Irish lord of yore
35. Reed common in Calif.
36. Hebrew letter
38. Prong
39. Gormandizers
41. Apart from
43. French movie
44. Sun: Prefix
45. Kind of battery
47. "Fidelio" overture
50. Windshield cleaner
53. Formal scolding
55. Old clothes
56. Flowed steadily
59. Choral work: Abbr.
60. Jargon
62. Holy Roman emperor:
63. Make over
64. In error
68. Cap ___
69. Refined guy
70. Swell
71. Pikelike fish
72. Job for the lazy
74. Garroway
75. Junior snowplows
77. Name for Shropshire

78. Old word for sailors
81. Poet
82. Seeker of the flame
84. Stringy
85. Preserves
87. Memory
91. Deadly kind of race
92. Peak
96. Irish island
97. Infallible authority
98. Fight off
100. Put the whammy on
101. Edge
102. City
103. Central parts
105. Unconnected
107. Ocean-study craft
109. Ringed, as a belle
111. Strike back for

112. Open up
113. Western ranges
114. Closet item
115. Steady
116. Cause to think twice
117. In the wake

DOWN

1. East Indian cedar
2. Dress in
3. West Indians
4. Straw in the wind
5. Welsh dog
6. The least one can do
7. Summer flounder
8. Hopeless, as a cause
9. Rendering fruitless
10. Farrow

11. Manipulate events
12. Sponsor unwisely
13. Square area
14. Article
15. McLuhan word
16. Leave on a lonely shore
17. Tennis players
19. Put on a jury list
20. Gain entry
26. Pronounced
28. Author Sholem
32. Meddling
34. Certain cartoons
35. Threefold
37. Stoppage
40. Journalist Abel
42. ___ Arabia

43. Work with
45. Ship taken by Jones
46. Music maker
48. Seize, old style
49. Word in Kansas motto
51. Appears
52. Made a new hand
53. She-wolves: Sp.
54. Like a beaver
57. U.S. missiles
58. Active people
61. Crescent-shaped article: Var.
62. Baby bird
65. Coal barge worker
66. Ambassador

67. Hollow stone
73. Unemotional
74. Amusing
76. Passport entry
79. Spider
80. Diatribes
83. German title
86. Diamond appraisers
87. Ankle
88. Express of fame
89. Condiment
90. Imprisons
91. Unpaid bill
93. Shift
94. Combination
95. Hosp. aide
99. Scoria
102. Faulty pitch
104. Monster
106. Held in
108. Tennis shot
110. Gosh!
111. So!

63 Musically Speaking
by Alfio Micci

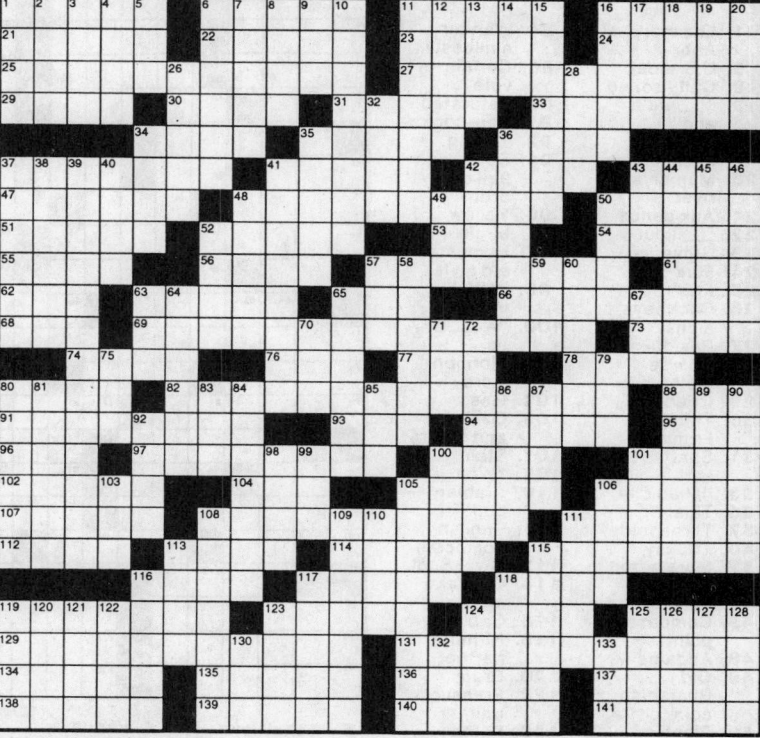

ACROSS

1. Fares
6. Provides
11. ___ days
16. Dark color
21. Strad's cousin
22. Relation
23. Indian of Peru
24. Storms
25. Telephone sound
27. Child's game
29. Marie and others: Abbr.
30. At the: It.
31. Representations
33. Claws
34. Wing: Fr.
35. Abusive person
36. ___ decamp
37. Politely
41. Lebanese port
42. Gaelic
43. Black Sea arm: Var.
47. Blackbirds
48. Untidy one
50. Vacation spot
51. Make joyful
52. Street sights
53. King of Judah
54. Gets
55. ___ wolf
56. Arachnid
57. Agenda
61. Aliped
62. Relative of ltd.
63. River into Lake Chad
65. Constellation
66. Misses a deadline
68. Inquire
69. Postal warning
73. Roman way
74. Pitcher
76. Porgy of Japan
77. Gazelle
78. Hasty
80. Old slave
82. "___ in air"
88. Uncle: Scot.
91. Go over with a brush
93. Corrode
94. Prods
95. Needlefish
96. Countrywide: Abbr.
97. Cavalry men
100. Turkish inn: Var.
101. Girl's name
102. ___ bagatelle
104. Swedish district
105. Bequeaths
106. Cheeses
107. Water worms
108. Took a match to
111. Entreaty, in France
112. Resting places
113. Shipbuilder
114. Like dirt roads
115. Farm man
116. House plant
117. Coins
118. Eur. land
119. Extended
123. Purport
124. Potpourri
125. "Je t'___"
129. Question for a vanishing lady?
131. Musical troublemaker
134. Semblance
135. Bits
136. Of a space
137. Unrefined
138. Discourage
139. "___ are my jewels"
140. Abodes of a kind
141. Three grains

DOWN

1. Locomotive areas
2. Neglect
3. Labyrinth
4. Vous ___
5. Form a lap
6. Overornamented
7. Ern
8. Burner
9. Day: Sp.
10. Entreats
11. Pundit
12. Lend ___
13. Myrna and family
14. City official: Abbr.
15. Pedantic
16. Feel for
17. Grate
18. Author James
19. Equal
20. Arctic People: Abbr.
26. Navigates
28. André
32. Zip ___
34. ___ in one's bonnet
35. Composer Erik
36. Peaceful place
37. Fielding title
38. Criminals
39. Musical creator of monster?
40. Der ___
41. Fraction
42. Comfort
43. Exclamation
44. Quinn, Norwegian style?
45. Decorative
46. Rankle
48. Scottish landowner
49. Exclamation of disgust
50. Observed
52. Govt. agent
57. Eastern title
58. Tough cord
59. Military initials
60. Architectural rib
63. Pronoun
64. Conceal
65. Be ___ man for it
67. Fleur de ___
70. On the ___ (fleeing)
71. Biblical mountain
72. In a random way
75. Sopping
79. Legal chiefs: Abbr.
80. Verdi opus
81. Tar
83. Movie initials
84. Kind of harp
85. Degrees
86. Musical syllables
87. Car parts: Abbr.
89. Ravel's "___ l'Oye"
90. Pencil part
92. Highways: Abbr.
98. Course
99. Conclude
100. Pleated skirts
101. Colleen's isle
103. Thoroughfares: Abbr.
105. Petty pier thief
106. Spoiled one
108. ___ over
109. Disease of plants
110. Smoke, in Rome
111. Monastery man
113. Want
115. Cooks in a way
116. Hen
117. Painter of dancers
118. Animal cry
119. Roman poet
120. Woman, in law
121. Campus group
122. Margin
123. Head: Fr.
124. Stove part
125. Emanation
126. River to the Danube
127. Tableland
128. Whilom
130. Indian of Northwest
132. Exist
133. At times: Abbr.

64 Merry Month

by Barbara H. Lewis

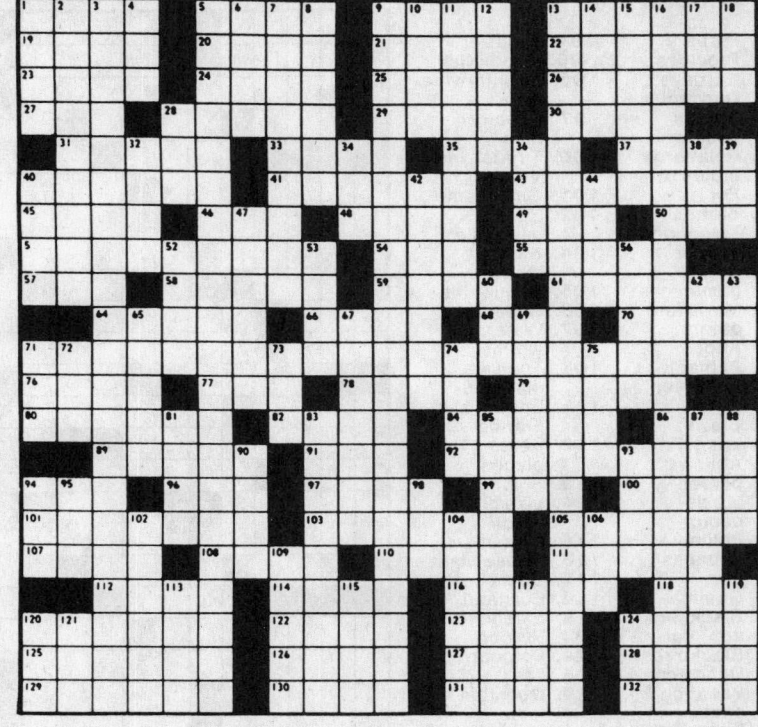

ACROSS

1. Life story: Abbr.
5. U.S. eider
9. Catty sound
13. "___ wit's end"
19. Irish exclamation
20. Munich's river
21. Auk genus
22. ___ it out
23. Glove
24. Fork part
25. Fibs: Scot.
26. Cockneys' aides
27. Residue
28. Coarse cloths
29. Cried
30. Thirst, in France
31. Spartan serf
33. Italian city
35. This: Sp.
37. Threshold
40. Tricksy
41. More adroit
43. Two
45. Food fish
46. Compass point
48. Addams
49. Old Rumanian coin
50. Plant
51. Without tines
54. Panay native
55. Late actor Robert
57. Evergreen
58. Montague
59. V.I.P.'s in Br. navy
61. Rich men
64. Ramble, old style
66. Eur. capital
68. Grain
70. "'Twas ___ oyster" (Pope)
71. "Let all thy ___" (Quarles)
76. Charity
77. ___ minute
78. Defective: Prefix
79. Seed coat
80. ___ eye dog
82. Hebrew letter
84. Wander aimlessly
86. Certain vote
89. Saturated
91. Pan-cook
92. Yelling
94. Suffix with dull or drunk
96. Yellow bugle
97. Homestead, old style
99. W.W. I initials
100. "A ___ B as..."
101. Mormon word
103. Gas
105. Oz figure and others
107. Stain
108. "Woe ___!"
110. Arabian gulf
111. English composer
112. Own: Scot.
114. Caesar's alas
116. Cabbages
118. Hither's partner
120. Drum
122. Pressure unit
123. Paton
124. Tool
125. Greek letters
126. Dominion
127. Take it easy
128. Neighbor of Thailand
129. Spring time
130. Mine yields
131. Panama: Abbr.
132. Unfledged bird

DOWN

1. Crimson Tide, for short
2. Tales of Old Sod
3. "...fairer than the day ___" (Wither)
4. Channel
5. "I shall love you in December ___" (Joyce)
6. Land mass
7. Ingredient of steel
8. Throng: Fr.
9. Springtime words of Chaucer
10. Robt. ___
11. Realm of Cyrus the Great
12. Rebecca et al.
13. "In March, July, October, May the ___ day"
14. Venus locale
15. Like a snake
16. Spring aphorism
17. Mal de ___
18. Lengths: Abbr.
28. Sea call
32. Mortgage
34. Between tic and toe
36. Related
38. Zodiac sign
39. Wallace
40. Discern
42. Dine in
44. Food fish
47. Lion slain by Hercules
52. Snatch
53. Black stuff
56. Astern
60. Descendant
62. Farm sound
63. Messy place
65. Bone: Lat.
67. Fish delicacy
69. Dress
71. Man's name: Abbr.
72. Corrida cheer
73. Utter
74. Auto man
75. Innkeeper, in Italy
81. Black: Fr.
83. Man ___
85. Order of woody plants
87. Animal parasites
88. Greek contest
90. Arab shrubs
93. Ruler
94. Classified items
95. Old car
98. Tiny one
102. Exalted
104. S.A. monkey: Var.
106. Fr. pronoun
109. Paris subway
113. Jot
115. Gardner
117. Wear
119. Cape
120. Pro ___
121. Honshu town
124. Drink

Peering In

by Mary M. Murdoch

ACROSS

1. Woolly fabric
7. Poplar
12. Blacksmith's need
17. Hindu deity
21. Vines
22. State
23. Treaty org.
24. ___ du Salut
25. Flower
27. Old railroad showpieces
29. Classmen: Abbr.
30. ___ one goes (stays solvent)
31. Small sum
32. Hawaiian emblem
33. Corbett or Braddock
34. Rulers
36. Caama
37. Beverage
40. Nymph wed to Paris
42. Gun extra
46. Burden
47. Spoil for a fight
51. British parallel of U.S.M.A.
52. Agreement
53. Destitute of water: Abbr.
54. Black
55. Comic-strip captain
56. Ness, for one
57. Revolutionary figure
58. Some temples in Japan
60. Gypsy village
61. Kind of house or boat
62. Sly look
63. Chem. suffix
64. Window part
65. Eye part
66. Graduated series: Abbr.
67. Birds
72. Appoint
73. Hot-dog places
75. "___ but you"
76. Saddle horse
77. "...ate ___ meal"
79. Compiler of certain rules
81. Girl's group: Abbr.
84. "___ midi d'un Faune"
85. Kiss
86. Land measure
87. Mil. groups
88. Sing in a way
89. Indian
90. For ___ being
94. Dash
95. Sacred bull
96. Adversaries
98. Horse
99. Girl's nickname
100. Eye cell
101. Fasten
102. Fish stocks
105. Whale
106. Pro football team
108. Access
109. Dept. store employe
110. Picnic guests
111. Flagmaker
112. Throw off balance
116. Ornamental stone
119. Rows
120. Rail rod
121. Auditor
124. Dance
126. Flowers
129. Will- ___ - wisp
130. Lake ___
131. French king
132. Gob
133. Dictator
134. Smarted
135. Plus-side item
136. Bristle

DOWN

1. "___ well"
2. Story teller
3. Tablets
4. Some
5. One of the magi
6. Shillong's land
7. Wrong
8. Capuchin monkey
9. Apple parts
10. Direction
11. Saul's uncle
12. Yearns
13. Tidies
14. Farewell: Lat.
15. Give ___ try
16. Poetic Hall
17. Make abundant
18. Soviet range
19. Blackbird
20. Holly
26. Caustic
28. Comforts
31. Counting-out word
33. Cap-and-bells fellow
34. That's ___ (not allowed)
35. Friars
36. Oaks: Scot.
37. Tree resins
38. Very soon: Slang
39. Lace
41. Summary: Abbr.
42. Urbane
43. Some people's hair
44. TV personalities
45. Shout
47. Ballet step
48. Inconvenient
49. Paraphernalia
50. Dizzy and Daffy
56. Blackmore girl
59. Ship-shaped clock
60. French stations
61. Heyward character
64. Famous Quaker
65. Murmuring sound
67. Girl's name
68. Opposites of exts.
69. Current
70. Old-time tubs
71. Implement
72. Jury member
74. Root plants
76. Wool fabric
77. Cartoonist
78. Fiend: Sp.
79. Pursuit
80. Cudgel
82. Golf term
83. Equally close
85. Fox and Rabbit
87. Get back
90. Tipsters
91. Word in an O'Neill title
92. Fr. pronoun
93. Letters
96. Hosiery-counter items
97. Baseball term
98. Type sets
102. Irish tribe
103. Dispenser at a clambake
104. Soubriquet for Clemenceau
107. Angry one
109. College post
111. Large ball: Sp.
113. Strike again
114. Truck union: Abbr.
115. Italian dish
116. Tax
117. Butter units
118. Section of Vedic writing
119. Locale of Diamond Head
120. Containers
121. Headgear
122. Guard: Abbr.
123. Movie dog
125. Angkor ___
126. Nepal native
127. Norway town
128. Numerical prefix

66 Going Places

by Bruce R. Shaw

ACROSS

1. Name in U.S. banking
5. Record: Prefix
10. Beer feature
14. Small blister
18. Dies ___
19. Beach product
20. Years: Lat.
21. Fence
22. Skin: Prefix
23. Custom-house: Sp.
24. Folding money
25. Blue: Prefix
26. Trolley center of note
29. Interest moneys
31. Organ stop
33. Counting-out word
34. Tossers, usually of mud
35. Trap
37. Brontë
39. Stand: Lat.
40. Young one
41. Dusting powder
43. Coalition
44. Immoral
48. Hagen
49. Intertwine
52. Weak
54. Egg: Prefix
55. Hair job
57. Bounces off
59. Abstruse
60. Of a Bronze Age culture
61. Chemical prefix
63. Knockout punch
65. Sequin
67. 4,000 chilly miles
72. Japanese wax trees
73. Mountain chain
74. Defendants, in law
75. Skillfully
76. Kiln
78. "Last of the Romans"
80. Choke
84. There: Lat.
85. Rasping sound
87. "___ my right arm for . . ."
89. Arts degree
90. Sky sight

92. Seaweed substance
94. Truly
95. ___ gratia
96. Catch
97. Chides
99. 8-point type
101. Qualifies
105. Fastener
108. Leaflike parts
109. Bearded
110. Train-tune town
112. Melody
113. Game fish
115. Illinois city
116. Over
119. Bell sound
120. During
121. Special
122. Advice, old style
123. Surfeit
124. Vogue
125. Finnish lake
126. North Sea tributary

DOWN

1. Eye part
2. Galena
3. Puffball-like fungus
4. Wail
5. City slicker
6. Take effect
7. Stanza
8. Tooth
9. Out ___ (insecure)
10. Lot
11. Undivided
12. Cancel
13. St. Louis sight
14. Cause
15. Old weapon
16. Duck

17. Joy
19. Nob Hill sight
27. Sound off
28. Byron heroine
30. Caper
31. Prepare
32. $100 bill
34. Old Chinese money
36. Jazz lady
38. Bi-level British bus
42. Medit. tree
45. Let pass
46. Palate part
47. Preferred
50. Pennsylvania wagon place
51. Abrasive, in France
53. Plateau

56. Virile
58. Bull: Ger.
60. Strip of gear
62. Davis domain: abbr.
64. World ___
66. Brew
67. Teach
68. Hasidic leader
69. Improvise
70. Danube tributary
71. ___ bell
77. Goes up
79. African fly
81. Surrenders
82. Precipitation
83. Poker holdings
85. List
86. Cabbage milieu

88. Before febrero
91. Specified amount
93. Backslide
98. Smooth cloth
100. Caprice
101. Old oaths
102. Water wheel
103. Spoil
104. Fluid swelling
106. Roman wear
107. Fruit gadget
110. Morse, for one
111. French resort
114. Fit out
117. Pindaric
118. Each

Step On It

by Threba Johnson

ACROSS

1. Kind of warrant
7. Bullfighter's cloak
11. Khan
14. Iowa town
18. A kiss ___
20. Junto
21. It. coins: Abbr.
22. Italian philosopher
23. Sculpture site
25. ___ draw
27. Historic island
28. Do a pitching job
29. Small passage
30. Bible book: Abbr.
31. English astronomer
32. Within: Prefix
34. Kind of mother
35. Nichols hero
36. Vital item in the West
41. 1965 movie
44. Rapid view: Fr.
45. Handbag
47. Hairpiece
48. Goose egg
49. Of Apollo's island
50. Slave
51. Bulwark
54. Part of a journey
57. Meager
59. English school
61. "Life ___ dream"
62. ___ cry
63. Impassive
65. Disburse
67. "___ the chief"
69. East Indian tree
72. Fall apple
74. Glacial stage
76. Famous poem
77. Trivial amount
80. Daily grind
82. After-drink drinks
84. Pavlova and others
85. Open a bit
87. Sister of Orestes
89. Ship's rope
90. Place for Italian drama
92. Certify
94. "Five-foot-two, ___, blue . . ."
97. Norse goddess
98. Army man: Abbr.
100. Adjust
102. Heard a court case again
105. Arabic place name
106. More thorny
108. Thin
110. Alert color
112. Hezekiah's mother
114. Nouns: Abbr.
115. Point of dispute
117. Lung part
118. Ordinary
122. Newman movie
125. Major or Minor
126. Part of a Marquand title
127. ___ Khan
129. Take for ___
130. Tumble: Scot.
131. Certain flower
133. Make wide changes
135. Aoudad
139. Control-tower data
141. Beginning of a fast trip
143. " . . . by ___ unresting sea"
144. Got: Abbr.
145. Rockfish
146. "___ Kilimanjaro"
147. Outside: Prefix
148. Chemical prefix
149. Drinks
150. Photo print

DOWN

1. Identical
2. Chemical compound
3. Rub- ___
4. Frog genus
5. Lab man: Abbr.
6. Gilden novel
7. Arrived
8. Upstairs
9. Family people
10. Drink
11. African grass
12. Midwest city
13. "Stay ___ you are"
14. Scottish alder
15. Part of the navy
16. Imitative
17. Small Asian bird
19. Folksy poet
20. Exercises
22. Bashful
24. Plod heavily
26. Blue Nile source
29. Man's nickname
31. Pour gently
33. Beat ___
35. Greek nickname
36. Hula hoop or skate board
37. Copies
38. Order to broker
39. Efforts
40. ___ Dimittis
42. Weight: Abbr.
43. Explosive
46. Fix leftovers
50. Galway's land
52. Assess a fine
53. Cheer
55. Greasy-spoon
56. ___ Pointe
58. Girl's name
60. Fast train
62. Pretensions
64. Rid of vermin
66. Relative
68. P.I. native
69. Thinker, for one
70. Hummeling machines
71. English satirist
73. French writer
75. Rocky debris
78. Course
79. Medit. land
81. Does a tailor's job
83. Harvard club
86. Part of a nursery rhyme
88. Phoenician port
91. Against: Abbr.
93. In a scary way
95. Threatening words
96. ___ mignon
99. Seine
101. Strained
103. Jewish month
104. Having gold
106. Thor's wife
107. Doctrine
109. Transports again
111. Cold ___
113. Scarf
116. Ate noisily
118. Drum sound
119. Of the Finno-Ugric language
120. Kind of dress
121. Adjective suffix
123. Wool: Prefix
124. Ant and Black
128. "When shall we two ___?"
131. Exclamations
132. Skink
134. Gil ___
135. "A one, ___"
136. New Yorker man
137. Space mysteries
138. Undecided
140. Man's name: Abbr.
141. Sky Altar
142. ___ -de-rol

68 Choice Words

by Jean Reed

ACROSS

1. Bridge call
5. Make ___
11. Heroes of W.W. I
17. Provides power
20. Make a member
21. Brush holder
22. With "not," firm disavowal
24. Roll
25. Cargo: Abbr.
26. City on the Aare
27. Human group
29. Half a fly
30. Novelist Kingsley
32. Yellow-fever pioneer
33. British plotter
35. Fr. pronoun
36. Riviera resort
38. Poetic word
40. Expense-account item
41. Expert
43. M.I.T. grad: Abbr.
44. Closet catastrophe
46. Car or steak
47. Fairway cry
49. Tills
50. Some peaches
54. Puzzles
58. Enormous
60. China city
61. Indigo
62. Part of Macbeth
64. Social reformer
66. Bosses: Abbr.
67. Escalate
68. Make Greek
70. Musical ending
71. Cleric's degree
72. "Mens ___ . . ."
73. W.W. I land
75. European airport
76. Tide's havoc
79. Does edging
81. Ropes for ship ladders
83. Buffet dishes
85. " . . . ___ your houses"
87. Injury, old style
88. Legal job
89. Candy
92. "___ can never hurt me"
96. Brine
98. Airfoils
99. U.S. dept.
100. "___, dull care!"
101. Sum: Abbr.
102. Standards
104. ' . . . or ___ Hecuba?"
106. Being: Lat.
107. Roy
108. Praying preyer
111. Landmark
113. One: Ger.
114. Medium's specialty
117. Monetary maxim
120. Slow
121. Bone-breakers of 92 Across
122. Sagacious
123. Compounds
124. Evening glory
125. Impart

DOWN

1. Sweet sorrow, to some
2. Latin case: Abbr.
3. Boor
4. Divides
5. British writer
6. Single: Abbr.
7. Cut short
8. Sharpen
9. Fat
10. Enticing trap
11. City for W.W. I doughboys
12. Pirate gold
13. Pronoun
14. Disaster of 1876
15. Depletes
16. "Union Now" author
17. Blot out
18. Thomas
19. " . . . the ___, the yellow leaf"
23. " . . . and ___ grow on"
28. Mil. officers
31. Cold sign
34. Eastern port
37. Chem. compound
39. Snow remover
40. Buffet
42. Peso in Spain
44. Kind of marine
45. "All this and ___"
46. French shouts
48. Home: Abbr.
51. Transfer property
52. Sell
53. Tries
54. Delilah, briefly
55. Grieg girl
56. Ultimatum
57. Eyed
59. Adjust sails
63. Map area: Abbr.
65. Moslem dress
69. Cosa ___
70. Invented word
72. Lyons fabric
74. Marie
77. Moon areas
78. Dramatist
80. Rudiments
82. Smooth, in phonetics
84. Dieter's goal
86. Feature of living
90. ___ quo
91. Form foam
93. Ambled
94. Badge
95. " . . . eyes, but they ___"
96. French writer
97. Cicero words
98. Angelico
100. Of the north
103. Signs
105. Ascot and Windsor
109. " . . . ___ the pumpkin"
110. Parallel words: Abbr.
112. Neck part
115. Dir.
116. About: Abbr.
118. Between bee and dee
119. Adam's original

69 Literally So

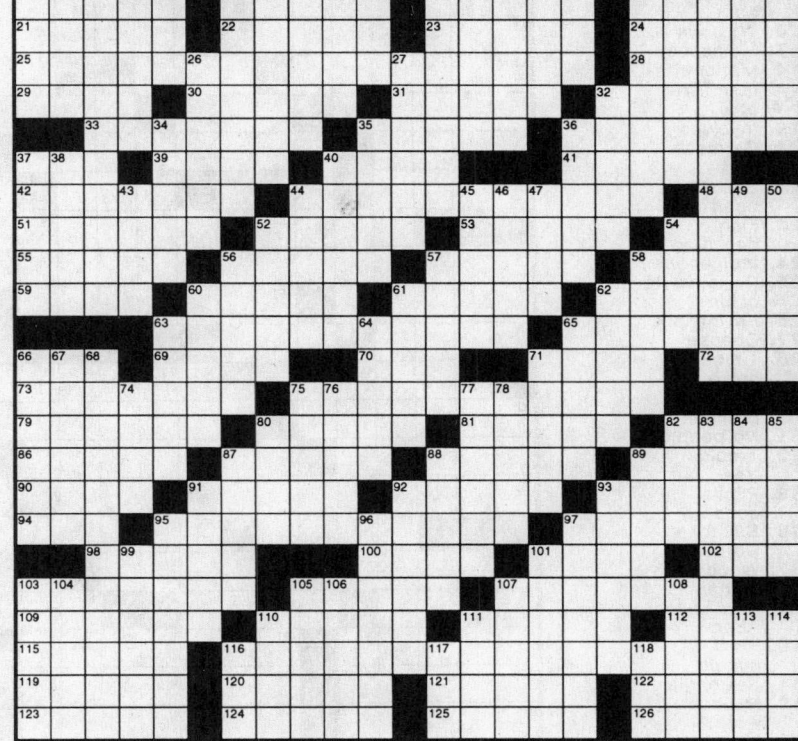

ACROSS

1. Moslem prince
6. Rulers
11. Oceanic tunicate
16. ___ as the eye can see
21. Excuse
22. O'Grady
23. Hum
24. Eli word
25. Maid forages in the pantry
28. Aoudads
29. Duck
30. Subtle qualities
31. Chore
32. 18th century English novelist
33. Dancer of a kind
35. Enclosures
36. Like a football shoe
37. Oriental temple
39. Campus queen
40. African tree
41. Rough
42. Youngsters
44. Rolling pins
48. Chemical suffix
51. Reach for
52. Blacksmith
53. Lumps
54. Sly as ___
55. Fumes
56. Guys
57. Interlude
58. Plantagenet country
59. Fictional Georgia site
60. Lace pattern
61. Beneficiary
62. Forbid to fly
63. Sailors in July and August
65. Bird sound
66. Br. fliers
69. Flag
70. Vietnam port
71. The best
72. Time periods: Abbr.
73. Flexible
75. Moynihan at a White House reception
79. Enter in a way
80. Coquette

81. Miss Lisa et al.
82. Galatea's lover
86. Alaskan native
87. In the natural state
88. Ex-dictator of Venezuela
89. Disposed
90. Cheerio
91. Set of bells
92. Brainy ones
93. Shooting affair
94. Kirghiz city
95. Bargain for Peggy Fleming
97. Iron
98. Glossy cover
100. Spanish city
101. Tops
102. High, in music
103. ___ halt (stopped)
105. Papal vestment
107. Yield
109. Blues
110. Stoop to
111. Austrian province
112. Part of a play
115. Polite refusal
116. A-one tutor
119. Type size
120. Babylonian abode of dead
121. ___ a time
122. Sideshow figure
123. Stage settings
124. Trapshooting
125. Low joints
126. Conditions

DOWN

1. Hosses
2. Moslem teacher
3. Telegrapher
4. Better prepared
5. Twice
6. Groups of thespians
7. Went bad
8. "...wagon to ___"
9. Originate
10. Wine quality

11. Nova ___
12. Okie's neighbor
13. Choice cuts
14. Frost
15. Reply: Abbr.
16. Mitigating agents
17. ___ a boil
18. Seven-plus summer days
19. Straighten
20. Tore down: Var.
26. Current author
27. Groom
32. Chunks
34. Chillers
35. River of Rumania
36. Sloping runway
37. Clever
38. Biblical prophet
40. American author
43. Little chief hare

44. Early source of oil
45. Next to nothing
46. Sleuth material
47. Come in last
49. Neighbor of 12 Down
50. Gives out
52. Wedgelike pieces
54. Wild ox
56. Risible
57. Pushed a punt
58. Court decree
60. City on the Po
61. Cow
62. Namesakes of Italian star
63. ___ out (stay to the end)
64. Divide
65. Gem

66. Stiff collar of 1600's
67. Greek war cries
68. Turn toward the orchestra
71. De Mille
74. Jaeger
75. Decline
76. Currents
77. Daughter of Cymbeline
78. Greek musical works
80. Wife of Odin
82. Greek gulf
83. Dairy farmer
84. Totally
85. Ukrainian river
87. Lobster claw
88. Canal Zone town
89. ___ Vecchio
91. Greek island

92. South Seas wear
93. Rhubarb
95. Food dispenser
96. One of the pharaohs
97. Modern composer
99. Excellence: Sp.
101. North wind
103. Thrashed
104. Chem. compound
105. Carnivora
106. Passage
107. Fruit drink
108. Abalone lining
110. Weapon
111. Ethiopian lake
113. Group
114. Bores
116. Notes
117. Go bad
118. Back

Finding a World

by Cornelia Warriner

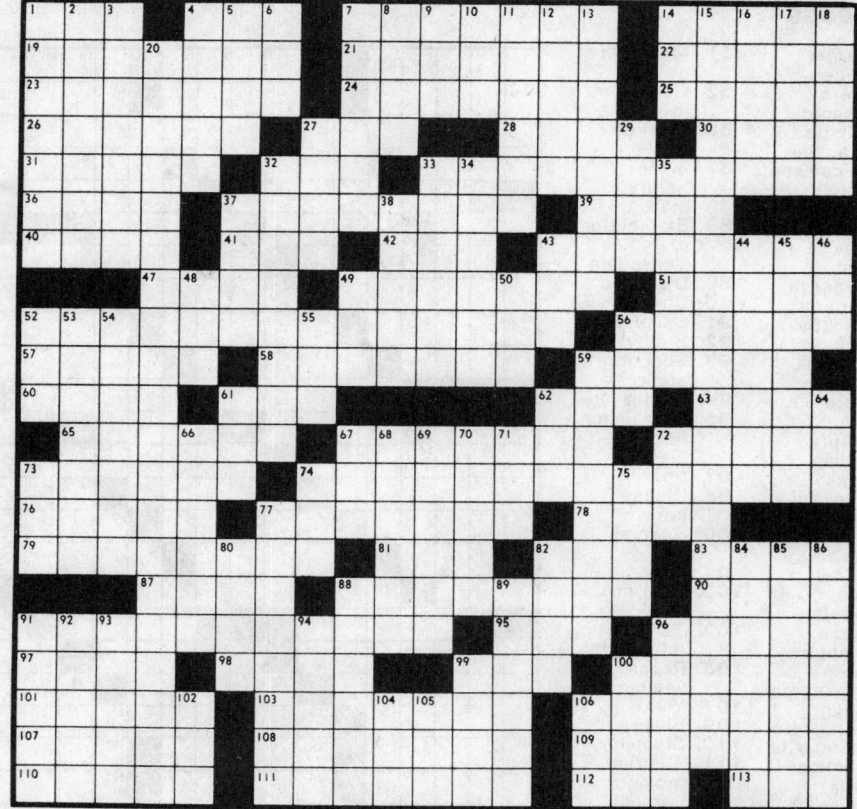

ACROSS

1. Phone book abbr.
4. Wt. units
7. Molasses
14. Marionette-man Tony et al.
19. Involves
21. Burmese port
22. Ghost's need
23. Fish delicacy
24. Indigenous
25. Certain side of life
26. Paving mix
27. Choose
28. Timber spike
30. Math branch
31. No-people
32. Tropical tree
33. Pilot's concern
36. Bakery worker
37. Wood platter
39. Print style: Abbr.
40. River nymph
41. Sea eagle
42. Nautical word
43. Medieval swords
47. Turner
49. Like a hard rain
51. As a friend: Fr.
52. Words describing 1400-1700 A.D.
56. Run in Bea Lillie's hose
57. Guile
58. Certain dives
59. Name in baseball lore
60. Queen of Hearts product
61. Hymenopteron
62. Snack-table item
63. Gloomy Dean
65. Standards of behavior
67. Shattered
72. Bay off White Sea
73. Berry nub
74. Queen Isabella's goal
76. Village in Haiti
77. Memo books
78. Flowing hair
79. Drop in on friends
81. Gas: Prefix
82. Six, in Italy
83. Weskit
87. Earth Day subject: Abbr.
88. Of the stars
90. "To ___ his own"
91. Navigator's route
95. Skill
96. Microwave device
97. Horse color
98. Tree knot
99. Times of day: Abbr.
100. Sly
101. Divert
103. Creatures
106. Easing of tensions
107. Marquis and others
108. "___ d'Arthur"
109. One joining a toast
110. Kind of preview
111. Tenants
112. Gibraltar, for one: Abbr.
113. Noises: Abbr.

DOWN

1. Add varnish
2. Magnify
3. Began
4. Turkish coins
5. Coalition
6. Compass point
7. Cutting tool
8. Declaim
9. Remnant
10. Epoch
11. Long wave
12. French river
13. Applauding for more
14. Draft org.
15. Seneca's prediction in "Medea"
16. Keep on subscribing
17. Columbus's birthplace
18. Block: Var.
20. Title conferred on Columbus
27. ___ sea
29. Moderate
32. Charges
33. Put aside
34. Wobble
35. Scalp parts
37. Care for
38. Athenian demagogue
43. Whatever
44. Aria part
45. Came out
46. Title of respect
48. Astern
49. Weight abbr.
50. Tax agency: Abbr.
52. Play part
53. Magna ___ (Gr. colonies)
54. Mundane
55. Weekday: Abbr.
56. Sass
59. Bacon
61. Tennis score
62. Agnus ___
64. Chemical suffix
66. Untouched
67. Guevara
68. Repair in a way
69. ___ camp
70. Kind of drum
71. Chiefs: Abbr.
72. Everest, for one: Abbr.
73. Elec. unit
74. Geom. lines
75. Jib
77. On the whole
80. Secure
82. Indian weights
84. Curved handrails
85. Like some love letters
86. Reading, etc.
88. Fabrics
89. Egyptian king
91. Kind of widow
92. Cato, for one
93. ___ vie
94. Princess of India
96. Taxi feature
99. Old one: Ger.
100. Fabric
102. Arctic native: Abbr.
104. Sept. and Dec.
105. Land measure
106. Refugees: Abbr.

71

Stepquote

by Eugene T. Maleska

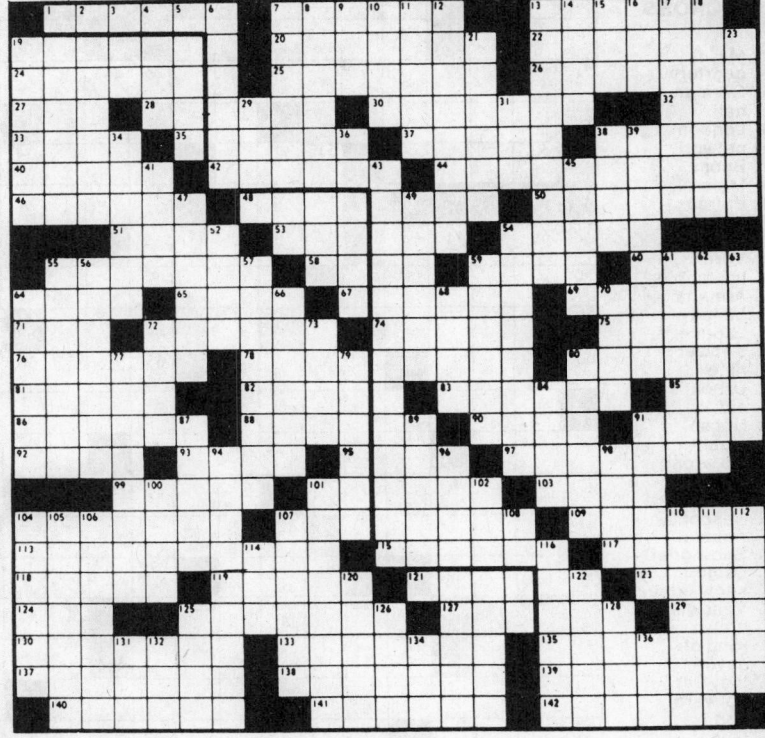

ACROSS

1. Start of a 12-word Stepquote ending at 142 Across
7. Infancy
13. "Things ___ what they seem"
19. Poet of Shakespeare's day
20. Permissive
22. Guernsey lilies
24. Greek port
25. Seminole chief
26. Miss Hard, former tennis player
27. Siouan
28. Devours
30. Toned down
32. Preacher's talk: Abbr.
33. Flower holder
35. Pan-fries
37. City in S.E. France
38. Spyri heroine
40. Castle of yesteryear
42. Part of Stepquote
44. Hears rumors about
46. Ali Baba word
48. With 13 Down, source of Stepquote
50. Unventilated
51. "___ 18," Uris novel
53. Best ___
54. Melville novel
55. Diving ducks
58. Legal paper
59. Flower
60. Gives a hand
64. Winnie the Pooh
65. Resumé
67. Dress
69. Extent
71. Follower of Mar.
72. Take off flab
74. Pardon
75. Blandly urbane
76. Visit briefly
78. Bread spread
80. Office gal
81. Companion of Paul
82. Lawyer's homework
83. Of earth: Lat.
85. Native of: Suffix
86. Diner dish
88. In the phone book
90. Judge
91. Liszt's teacher
92. Sonoran Indian
93. Second-hand
95. Port ___
97. Foreordain
99. Cremona creation
101. Hall of Fame name
103. Waste time
104. Spongelike cake
107. Bruised
109. Spread rumors
113. Item that gives confidence
115. Part of Stepquote
117. Scapegrace
118. Concur
119. Head monk
121. All
123. Voluble
124. Shaveling
125. Forceful
127. Atelier items
129. Nabokov heroine
130. City in Calif.
133. Naught
135. Misleads
137. Boxers
138. Magnify
139. Cued up
140. Italian resort
141. Faculties
142. End of Stepquote

DOWN

1. Fourth Sunday in Lent
2. Dictates
3. "Conning Tower" man
4. "___ Kleine Nachtmusik"
5. Greek vowels
6. Part of Stepquote
7. Aaron, Ruth, etc.
8. Held in esteem
9. Olden: Abbr.
10. Was left on base
11. Arrowsmith's wife
12. Photo developer's device
13. See 48 Across
14. Decipher
15. Blunder
16. Nonexistent
17. Way-clearer's words
18. Aegean island
19. Frankish king
21. Sets aside, as a motion
23. Printer's cross-strokes
29. Tree of Pacific
31. Big A action
34. Captivate
36. Surgical instrument: Var.
38. Sign on
39. Form a coalition
41. Give out
43. Part of Stepquote
45. Did dishes
47. Field-hockey team
49. Account book
52. Dry-as-dust
54. Wavered
55. Fencing position
56. Joyful singer
57. Made a slip
59. Undone
61. Man from Teheran
62. Aficionado
63. Folksinger Pete
64. Hines, Tozzi, etc.
66. Mite or tick
68. Skip
70. Town near Padua
72. Appear
73. Troublemaker of myth
77. Hudson River sight
79. Arrives
80. Strong man
84. Offshore hazard
87. City on the Po
89. Thin
91. Dam foundation
94. Author of Stepquote
96. Ending
98. Captured
100. Place for a child's house
101. Islands off New Guinea
102. Presents again
104. Graduated
105. Wild sheep
106. Green
107. Hut: Fr.
108. Place for V.I.P.'s
110. Crusaders' foe
111. Plain
112. Vitiate
114. ___ Saud
116. Part of the Stepquote
120. Tenth part
122. Former queen of Italy
125. White House monograms: 1953-61
126. Oriental Sherlock
128. Bridge bid
131. Baseball V.I.P.
132. Uncle: Scot.
134. Office holders
136. Rubber tree

On the Bounding Main

by Jorgen Rohleder

ACROSS

1. Mil. quarters
4. German hall
8. London network
11. Boom
15. Mineral
16. Entrée
19. Indian shrub
20. Yarn
21. Invincible Armada
25. Melody
26. Launce
27. Shower time
28. U-boat's aid
30. Not so much
31. Go wrong
33. Norse mariner
35. Response: Abbr.
36. Show grief
37. Esoteric knowledge
38. Yellowish brown
43. Kind of sayer
45. Ice: Ger.
46. Forward end
50. Gun attendant
52. Life jacket
54. Tentacle
56. Sea mammal
58. Do a double take
59. Strived
60. British queen
61. Penury
63. Middle East capital
65. Draft agcy.
66. Salty accounts
70. Resin
71. System of plowing
72. Submissive
73. Jurassic division
75. House of
77. ___ River in Poland
79. Chancel seats
81. Mounts
82. Kind of garden
84. Repeated
85. Model's concern
86. Biblical father
87. ___ circle
89. Concise
90. Direct
93. Bikini part
94. Gibbon
97. Never mind!
98. Old warship weapon
99. Moves in circles
103. Navigator's aid
105. Relief org.
107. Offender's concern
110. Musical-work
111. Certain travel fee
114. Get under one's skin
115. Israeli name
116. Group meeting of a kind
117. Tangle
118. Beverages
119. ___ Alte
120. Editor's word
121. Roof finial

DOWN

1. Name for Tweed
2. African village
3. French river
4. Bank items
5. Asian tree
6. Like some bridge hands
7. Shelter
8. Neck wrap
9. Utter joys
10. Lacks ability
11. Navigator's aid
12. Arctic wear
13. Foreigner
14. Old Sp. coins
17. Sea maneuver
18. Drench
19. Relaxes, nautically
22. British body: Abbr.
23. Old salt's words for novices
24. Title of respect
29. Cricket sides
32. Space
34. Censure: Abbr.
38. Code word for A
39. W. Va. town
40. Clingers
41. Defunct auto
42. Caddoan
44. Golf area
46. Born: Fr.
47. Tar
48. Prepares, as a sloop
49. Aphrodite's aide
51. Pays in a way
53. Old habitats
54. More open
55. German number
57. Sierra ___
59. Grove features
62. Triton
64. Daughter of
67. Acquired character
68. Eight: Fr.
69. Type style
70. Speak imperfectly
74. French marquis
76. Charge
78. Serai
80. Mil. group
82. River in Bolivia
83. Wax, in prescriptions
86. After Hamlet's "or"
88. Unrestrained
90. Gulf state: Abbr.
91. Like some tuxedoes
92. God of fire
94. "Ad ___ per . . ."
95. Risk
96. Drive out
99. Attack
100. Br. fliers
101. Reproach
102. Purse part
104. ___ the line
106. Privileges: Abbr.
108. Verb suffix
109. Himalaya wonder
112. Mideast initials
113. Sp. article

Away From It All

by Nancy Schuster

ACROSS

1. My Gal and others
5. Panama city
10. Argyll resort
14. Taiwan city
20. Quality
22. Well's companion
23. Diet
24. Like some beds
25. Manikin: It.
26. Mets, Muses, et al.
27. Flutter
28. Stoppage of fluid
29. Kit-bag advice
33. Purposes
34. Guthrie
35. Guide
36. Beach substitute
38. ___ la
41. Particles
43. Exclamation
45. Goes on the town
48. Galileo's crime
50. Skiing place
53. Silent
55. Harem room
56. Brit. sea unit
57. Handy
58. Proverb
60. Houston initials
62. Honshu town
64. Prepared chestnuts
66. Big deal from the boss
70. Whale
71. "Wish you were ___"
72. Admit
73. Ancestor: Ger.
74. Most important
77. Dickens heroine
79. Hebrew letter
80. Bird output
82. Roman bronze
83. Toll road
85. Kind of seer
87. Gather
89. Golf place
90. Dim
92. Ring
94. Rose of ___
96. Pie à ___
98. Research room
99. Genesis wife
101. Danish weights
102. Ten: Prefix
103. Twain book
106. Igloo dwellers
110. Name in Cuba
111. German title
112. Mug
114. Common contraction
115. "___ dien"
116. Prefix for derm or gram
119. Harness strap
121. Time spans: Abbr.
122. Travel ___
123. Ballet gear
126. Oliver's partner
128. Broadway role
130. The fair ___
131. Kneecap
133. Sea term
136. Youngsters
138. Skipper, familiarly
140. Blasé remark of tourists
146. Straightens
148. Steady
149. Abrogate
150. High nest
151. One of a Biblical tribe
152. Number for a Henry
153. Sierra ___
154. Reaches port
155. Okayed
156. Poet Wilcox
157. To the point
158. Plant part

DOWN

1. Telegram word
2. Vergil word
3. Secular
4. ___ putt
5. Grand place to visit
6. Medley
7. "Peanuts" character
8. Manifest
9. Bird
10. Soldier ___
11. Sumatra wildcat
12. Sons of Ishmael
13. ___ ultra
14. Scuffled
15. Pismire
16. Moslem leaders: Var.
17. Mug shot of a kind
18. Miss Adams
19. Rudolf or Myra
21. Accommodation to avoid
30. Shrewd move
31. Paper measure
32. Inner: Prefix
37. Woman with ___
38. Yonder, out West
39. Repeat
40. Code for callers
42. Instrument
44. Madame de ___
46. Word for parasol users
47. Playing card
49. Downs or salts
51. Printing process, for short
52. Authorities
54. Sandy ridge
58. Nabokov work
59. Folk dance
61. Aft
63. Exclamations
65. Solar event
67. Luggage man
68. Judicious
69. Smokes in a way
74. Childish fare
75. Swell
76. Jet-set delight
77. Scarcity
78. Aegean island
81. Turn right
84. English theater name
86. Compact
88. Tour offering
91. Tropical tree
93. Light beam
95. Judge's word
97. City V.I.P. in France
100. Rodents
102. Retreat
103. P. I. tree
104. Gangplank strip
105. Lady of the waves
107. Kind of store
108. Not repeatedly
109. River of myth
113. Theory
117. Crowded
118. Groundless
120. Place for a chignon
122. Eastern nurse
124. Astringent
125. Garment part
127. Describing some diets
129. Churchill's successor
132. Verdi chorus
134. Jeanmaire
135. Melchior, for one
137. Lab sample
138. Bounders
139. Jai ___
141. Eye: Fr.
142. Hebrew letters
143. River of Italy
144. Venetian resort
145. For fear that
147. After printemps

74 Wise Words

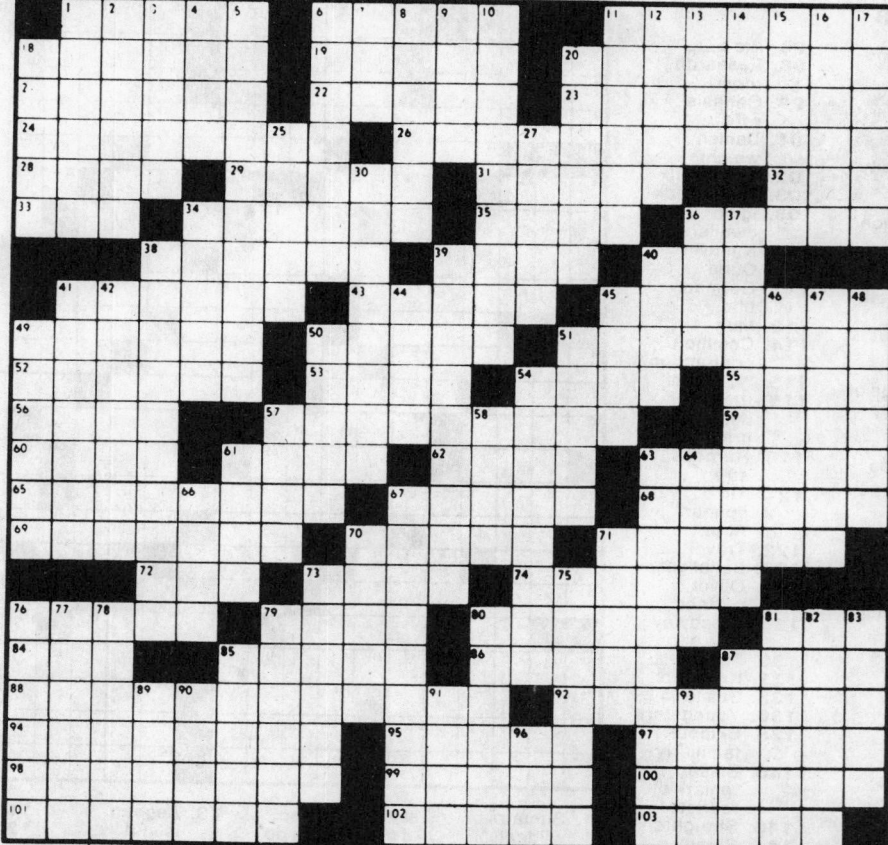

ACROSS

1. Occupation
6. Lesser Sunda island
11. Ran a spread
18. Ancestor of human race
19. Habituate
20. Smoke-eater's gear
21. Eat crow
22. Snooped
23. Friml's forte
24. Become weedy
26. Man with a ladder
28. Fountain order
29. Take out
31. Saharan hackney
32. Fish
33. Poet's word
34. Lured
35. Hateful person
36. Like some apples
38. Judgment
39. Helsinki native
40. Potato chip's friend
41. Noel Coward's spirit
43. Campaign
45. Predicament
49. ___ Hélène
50. Abundance
51. Approach
52. Made up for
53. Drink flavor
54. Beauty parlor job
55. Narrow margin
56. Ocean route
57. Breed of sheep
59. Loop in anatomy
60. "Roger and ___"
61. Fillet
62. Current
63. 1936 campaigner
65. Suspect
67. Sweetie pie
68. Space a paragraph
69. Least challenging
70. Poem division
71. Furs
72. Writings: Abbr.
73. Bona ___
74. Smoothed a pillow
76. Cash, for one
79. Tuscan city
80. Commemorative coins
81. Goddess: Lat.
84. Tangle
85. Roast slightly
86. End on ___ of sadness
87. Authenticate
88. Variety of non-clam
92. Enact again
94. Well-read
95. Hale character
97. Pitcher
98. Brightly inlaid
99. White sauce
100. Refer, with "to"
101. Not coincidental
102. Tenor role in 49 Down
103. Arctic explorer

DOWN

1. "Key Largo" Oscar winner
2. Shrink
3. Soprano Lucine
4. Mild cussword
5. Confirmed
6. Cowboys' table setting
7. Daughter of Cadmus
8. Went by dog team
9. Mountain: Prefix
10. Tending to diminish
11. Rushed headlong
12. Of a space
13. St. Philip ___
14. Snow goose genus
15. More summery
16. Regard highly
17. At great cost
18. Sometimes purple output
20. One on the other side
25. "___ est laborare"
27. French river
30. Sowing season
34. Italian seven
36. Strategem
37. Munificent
38. Gourmand's big moment
39. Flint
40. Thin coin
41. City in N.Y.
42. Queen of the beasts
44. Frolic
45. Bird
46. Ramble
47. French houses
48. Downright
49. Strauss opera
50. Viewpoint
51. "Of Human Bondage" hero
54. Up for grabs
57. Army
58. Suggestion
61. Smack
63. "Stop the World" hero
64. Ponies up
66. Support
67. Felt in one's bones
70. Kid of the West
71. Mexican grass
73. Solidified
75. Embellished
76. British novelist
77. Like seawater
78. Of any of fifty
79. Called it quits
80. Austrian composer
81. Las Vegas employe
82. Lunchroom
83. Not easily fooled
85. Famous clergyman
87. Pergolesi's "La ___ Padrona"
89. Altar area
90. Harte
91. Moved violently
93. Primitive
96. I love: Lat.

75 Sleight of Hand

by Hume R. Craft

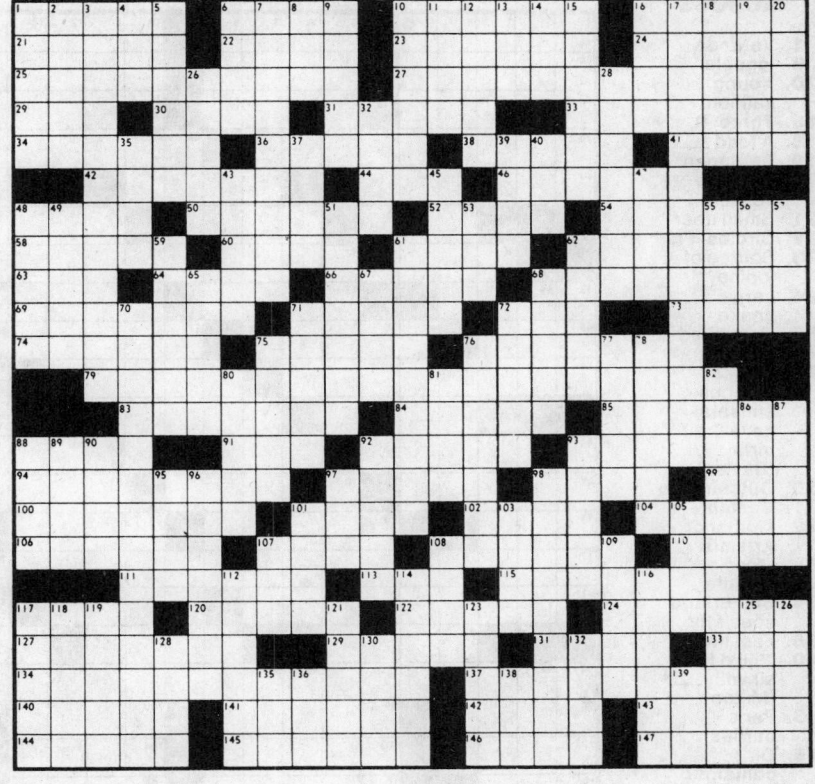

ACROSS

1. Remains
6. Ponselle
10. Corn-husk contents
16. Rio de la
21. Diagonal line
22. Mich. and 5th
23. Greek places
24. Overhangs
25. People on certain diets
27. Puzzle
29. Cabinet dept.
30. Court jester
31. Great Plains sight
33. ___ brief for
34. Triflers
36. Electrical pioneer
38. Church platform
41. Lazy times in Monte Carlo
42. Early Jewish mystics
44. Navy off.
46. Cat
48. Burma's neighbor
50. Metamere
52. Copper or gold: Abbr.
54. Sailboats
58. Fight ___
60. Callao's land
61. British gun
62. Government program
63. Grassy square
64. City near Des Moines
66. Wisconsin town
68. Mimicking bird
69. Adjusted sails
71. Fortification
72. ___ polloi
73. Exuded
74. Kind of partner
75. One with a trained eye
76. Italian resort
79. Some flutists
83. Ivan et al.
84. Of a bird part
85. No-good one

88. Ariz. Indian
91. Slav rulers
92. Hereditary factors
93. Materialistic
94. Exalted
97. Clothes or saw
98. Main idea
99. Color
100. Paul's family
101. Singer Lily
102. Scratch
104. Butler
106. Alarms
107. Amusement park feature
108. Tasks
110. Cockney abodes
111. Japanese trees
113. Relative of olé
115. Stalk
117. Hindu hero
120. Virginia willows
122. Despicable one
124. ___ Pointe
127. Neglectful one
129. Ties up
131. Br. composer
133. Opposite of ant.
134. Scavenger mollusk
137. Helps a magician
140. Radio name
141. Croquet term
142. Earl of Avon
143. Legerdemain, in France
144. Activists
145. Throws out
146. Word for Ben Jonson
147. Golfer Sam

DOWN

1. ___ as a pig
2. Irish bay
3. His contracts had escape clauses
4. Direction
5. Wool gatherers
6. Assess
7. Tie-breaking periods
8. Sun. discourse
9. Helpers: Abbr.
10. ___ Zee
11. Ailment
12. Particles
13. Biblical lion
14. Wool: Prefix
15. Biblical queen
16. Strip
17. Stairway for leather-footed conjurers
18. Sea call
19. Plating alloy
20. Old Greek vase
26. Orbital point
28. More raucous
32. Robt. ___
35. Let up
37. Arabian ruler
39. Frank
40. Radio's ___ and Abner
43. Drugged

45. Author of nature books
47. Fitzgerald
48. Endures
49. Love
51. Soup bowls
53. Man's nickname
55. Missouri River dam
56. Kind of school
57. Spanish painter
59. Pie à ___
61. Fireworks
62. Aviary sound
65. Botanical part: Suffix
67. Intention
68. Of melody
70. Hypnotist's credo
71. Takes a break
72. Fences
75. Hairnet
76. Shrill cry
77. Hot fragment

78. More sordid
80. "___ moi, le . . ."
81. Ages
82. Spirit's dispatch
86. Mexican grass
87. Certain pups
88. Linen marking
89. Guinness
90. Soviet river
92. Hopeless case
93. Planted
95. Expanse
96. More irritable
97. Scuttle
98. Overseer
101. City of Italy
103. Cuts off
105. Entire: Prefix
107. Be sorry
108. Snow-goose genus

109. Roadside scenery
112. English historian
114. White poplars
116. Some candies
117. Itinerant
118. Starch: Prefix
119. Cotton thread
121. Cachets
123. Fall flower
125. Ex-member of U.A.R.
126. Done
128. Sawbucks
130. Asian area, for short
132. Pierre's friend
135. Portion: Abbr.
136. Born: Fr.
138. Oklahoma city
139. U.S. neighbor

76 Breathing Exercise

by Adelyn Lewis

ACROSS

1. Veranda
6. Ignoble
10. Young salmon
15. Three: It.
18. A fond ___
19. Astringent
20. Wartime vessel
21. Small deer
22. Circles: Fr.
23. Source of iodine
24. Large snake
25. Unspoiled site
26. "What glorious sunsets have their birth ___" (Davies)
30. Outstanding
31. Containers
32. Mother of Artemis
33. Moon module
34. Sutherland specialty
35. Feel tired
40. "Fill'd the air with ___" (Milton)
43. Paris parties
45. Oil container
46. English village
47. Oxford tutor
48. Cassowary's relative
49. Some monsters
51. Pale
52. Fr. composer
54. April ecological event
56. Becomes taxing
57. "___ Spring"
58. Salt: Prefix
59. Adjusts
60. Fade away
61. Disprove
64. Marsh bird
65. Name for W. J. Bryan
69. Sour substances
70. Ready: Fr.
71. Preserves
72. Greek letter
73. Labor org.
74. Encourage
75. Church part
76. Laborer
77. R. L. Stevenson line
83. Solid fats
84. Suffix for Cyprus natives
85. Wine: Prefix
86. Nautilus man
87. Silver: Abbr.
88. Ready to perform
92. Hamlet's words for the air around him
98. Space
99. Zodiac sign
100. Some predictions
101. ___ Canarias
102. Stingy
103. Caretakers of a sort
104. German river
105. Uncritical
106. High, in music
107. Word for some cities
108. Summer times
109. Noun suffixes

DOWN

1. Apple-giver of myth
2. Dental prefix
3. ___ doigts: Fr. finger bowl
4. Marks under consonants
5. Shady dealer
6. Cascade peak
7. Drinks
8. Like some pollutants
9. Big store
10. Sets of bells
11. French cleric
12. Fourth of an acre
13. Keeps talking
14. Extended one's vacation
15. Confusion
16. Bad odor
17. Serf
21. Suckfish
27. Metrical foot
28. Spanish articles
29. Musial
34. Proper order
35. Places for statues
36. ___ Park
37. Clothe
38. Disdain
39. Opinion
40. Eye chart, to some
41. Stevenson
42. "Streetcar" sign
43. Relative of a social
44. Doctors' org.
49. Indian ranges
50. Fruitless
51. Inclined
52. Hazes
53. Chorus girl
55. Dull sound
56. Culture centers in Rome
57. Powdered, in heraldry
59. Golf areas
60. Van man
61. Invasions
62. Acclaim
63. Flower: It.
64. English railway town
65. Instances
66. ___ - do-well
67. W.W. II area
68. Norse sea goddess
70. Speech-sound character
71. Geometric solids
74. Yalta people
75. Listened to
76. Plant substance
78. Malaysian town
79. ___ Rabbit
80. "And ___ bed"
81. Hebrides island
82. Of wasps
87. Pantywaist
88. Parts of cricket games
89. Of a royal court
90. Serious
91. Road curves
92. Biblical miracle site
93. City on the Oka
94. Undiluted
95. Japanese race: Var.
96. Hardwood tree
97. Worry

Words of Interest

by Peter E. Price

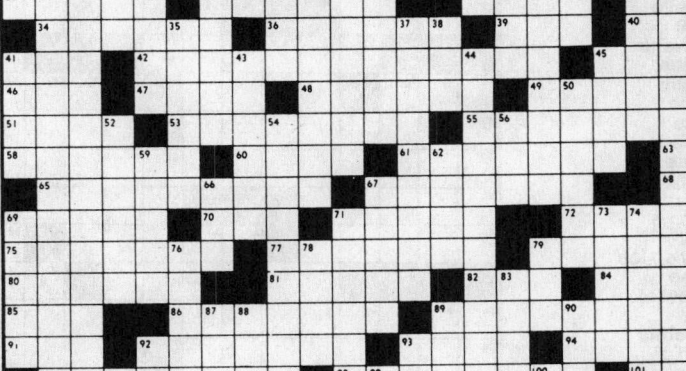

ACROSS

1. Bottom part of a record
9. Jockey Bobby ___
15. Took off in a hurry
22. Cut with the grain
23. Take shorthand
24. "How to Handle a Woman"
25. Blanch
26. Stir: Ger.
27. Whammy
28. Alcohol heaters
29. Ahead: Fr.
31. Graf ___
33. City of Ukraine
34. Injury
36. Biblical father of Obed
39. Spring month: Abbr.
40. Strip, in Scotland
41. Opp. of plaintiff
42. Will-have-been tense
45. Like delicate edging
46. Friend, in France
47. Dixmude's river
48. Dwarfishness
49. "___ to the Trees"
51. Artist Joan
53. Jivaran shrunken heads
55. V.I.P.
58. Human soul
60. Votes against
61. Academic protest
63. Monk's title
65. Encounter informally
67. Dickens family
68. Neighbor of Md.
69. Modern name of Emmaus
70. Afterthoughts: Abbr.
71. Put a label on
72. Chinese name of Dairen
75. Enzyme
77. Capable of
79. ___ a pig
80. Significant
81. Rather
82. Bee: Prefix
84. Word of surrender
85. Rural postal initials
86. French playwright Jean
89. Slang for a bungler
91. Father of Osiris: Var.
92. Blowhard of sorts
93. ___ bug in one's ear
94. Forget
96. Part of a place setting
98. Magic spore, in old lore
101. Contemporary hairdo
102. Pirandello
103. Golf tourney
105. June 6, 1944
107. Parson bird
108. Lacks, for short
110. Where the girls are
113. F.D.R.'s successor
114. City in South Korea
115. Harrogate, Tenn., campus
116. "___ Rag" of jazz fame
117. Alpine hideaway
119. "Who's that knocking ___ door?"
120. Western hero
122. "...and we shall ___ family"
124. ___ far as the end of one's nose
126. Was injured
128. Three, proverbially
131. "___ assumption" (pretty sure)
133. Prohibitive odds
134. Ballet step
135. Laid the groundwork
136. Secret
137. Informal wear
138. Elementary school class

DOWN

1. Part of f.o.b.
2. One afraid of spiders
3. Sentiment on souvenir sachets
4. Animal loin
5. Oyster plant
6. Frigate bird
7. International breathers
8. Apple country
9. Not regretted
10. Segment of Oregon Trail
11. Napoleon's retreat
12. Attention
13. Highway: Abbr.
14. Cravings
15. "Good night; ___"
16. Lid
17. Ancestors: Lat.
18. Poe's heart
19. Victim of Dorothy's landing on Oz
20. Pal of Pooh
21. U.S. poet
30. Thrice: Prefix
32. Moccasin
35. Dismissal
37. Plato's pupil
38. Baseball positions: Abbr.
41. Moist
43. Planet
44. U.S. trade laws of 1800's
45. German river
50. Variations
52. Sea: Sp.
54. Fallacy
56. Pierre's "here"
57. Advice from countess in "All's Well"
59. Attacks
62. Part of Q.E.D.
64. Parsonage
66. Disclose in verse
67. Taxes' partner
69. Stravinsky et al
71. Like Daisy's beau's bicycle
73. In ___ (angry)
74. The girl: Sp.
76. Long John Silver had one
78. Who: Lat.
79. Be indisposed
83. Plato work
87. Of coins
88. Honshu river
89. Nice aspects
90. Printer's line
92. Gad about
93. Defrosted in advance
95. "Honi ___ qui..."
97. Skating leap
99. Concession, in rhetoric
100. Teacher
104. ___ disant
106. Agreed, old style
108. Hero sandwich
109. Bent over
111. Pronoun
112. Elevations: Abbr.
115. Writer Jones
118. East wind: Sp.
121. Concordat
123. Scottish isle
125. Fence: Sp.
127. Calif. Rep.
129. Terrify
130. Regret
132. Depot: Abbr.

78 Roman Holiday

by Philip K. Youritzin

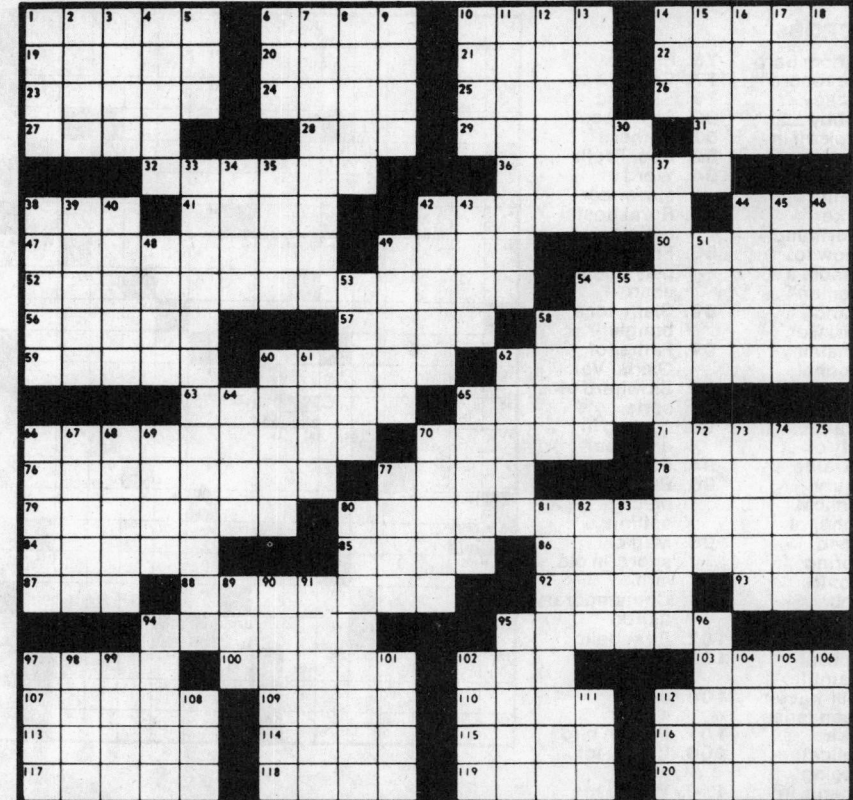

ACROSS

1. Letter-opener for some
6. African gazelle
10. Duel souvenir
14. Rustle
19. Rustic place
20. Time periods
21. White: Prefix
22. Church income
23. Zeal
24. Play an ice game
25. Eldest of the Pleiades
26. Kind of band
27. Apparatus
28. You: Ger.
29. Well-soaped
31. Quibble
32. Locust tree
36. Disengage
38. Stock-market word
41. Asian sea
42. Czech town name
44. Symbol of power
47. In ___ way (tunefully)
49. Alas, to Caesar
50. Western lake
52. Scene of old Roman war games
54. ___ churchmouse
56. Downstairs: Fr.
57. Caesar's way
58. Taken
59. Film actor Arnold
60. Church areas
62. Asians who sealed Marcus Crassus's fate
63. Moscow money
65. Traverse, as through tulips
66. Emperor who started the Colosseum
70. ___ hair (lava froth)
71. Egypt's hub
76. Like a babe
77. Role for Liz
78. Boo-boo
79. Having a wall bracket
80. Father of Latin poetry
84. Graze past
85. Western Indians
86. "Let that be a ___ you"
87. Nevertheless
88. Lacking experience
92. Mexican coin
93. Army V.I.P.
94. Loan shark
95. Beverages
97. Off-center
100. Gin's friend
102. Chinese pagoda
103. Elec. units
107. Shrew
109. Napoleonic battle site
110. Visitor to Siam
112. Ennoble
113. French year
114. Culture medium
115. Garish
116. Andrea ___
117. Max and Buddy
118. Little Helen
119. ___ majesty
120. Go onstage

DOWN

1. Ore refuse
2. Disrupted
3. Saga's relative
4. Athenian center
5. Debussy topic
6. U.S. power agency
7. Mistress of Caligula
8. Singer Callas
9. Wight
10. Uncle and Spade
11. Robert Graves's emperor
12. Remains
13. Cookouts
14. Ways: Abbr.
15. Broom user
16. Willow
17. Persian tiger
18. Hired hands
30. Ox of Tibet
33. Famous Roman reformer
34. Bows
35. Loom part
37. He wanted Carthage destroyed
38. Tempos
39. Lover, in France
40. Cuban dance
42. Recoils
43. Fear: Fr.
44. Maureen or Scarlett
45. German flowers
46. Neckwear
48. Extend over
49. Diminutive suffixes
51. African sheep
53. Up
54. Hair lines
55. Vision: Prefix
58. Cod or Horn
60. In ___ (beset)
61. Land map
62. Flier
64. One who benefits
65. Certain ages
66. City in Sweden
67. Ink: Fr.
68. Tapir's pride
69. Opera's Lily
70. Carried on
72. Pisa's river
73. Metal-drum hook
74. Way
75. Welles
77. Clever
80. Hill of Rome
81. Domitius ___, Roman jurist
82. Gardener's need
83. Sum, ___, fui
89. Zany one
90. Kind of ancient horse
91. Make an error at bridge
94. Shoe part
95. Portage item
96. Britisher
97. Famous whaler
98. Turner
99. French river
101. Psychologist Jung
102. Like some stories
104. Trade center
105. Ballet movement
106. Top banana
108. O.K.
111. Drink
112. Dutch town

Light Verse

by Frances Hansen

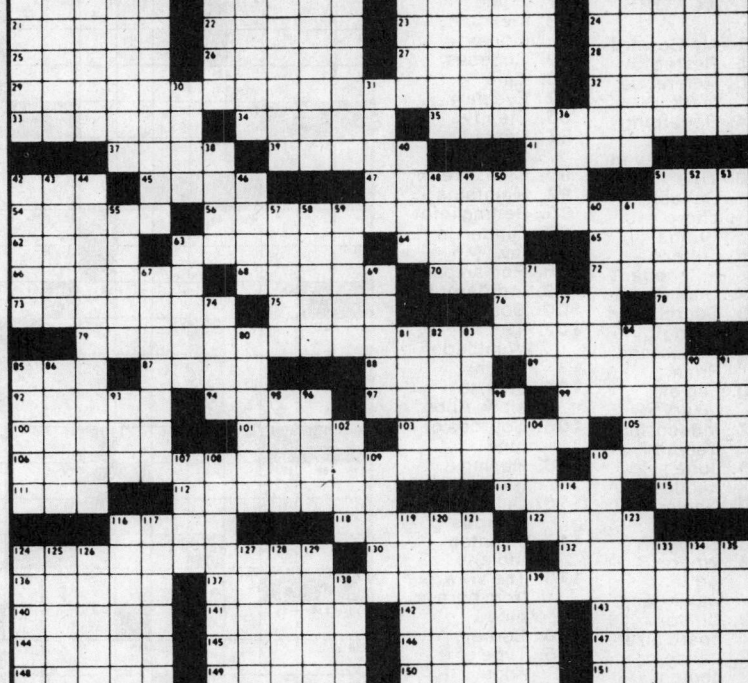

ACROSS

1. Must
6. Aye-aye
11. Biblical titles
16. Mosey along
21. New York city
22. Fatuous
23. Dull
24. Actress Leslie
25. Chaplain
26. Jot
27. Deer: Prefix
28. Stadium features
29. Start of a verse, with 56, 79, 106 and 137 Across
32. Bleak
33. Grievously
34. Metric measure
35. Speak gobble-dygook?
37. Kind of apple
39. Mature, legally
41. Bit of foolishness
42. Bags: Abbr.
45. Fraulein's refusal
47. "When I feel you ___"
51. So!
54. Stocking cap
56. More of 29 Across
62. Border on
63. Not ripped
64. Soil: Prefix
65. Goose eggs
66. Assertions
68. Buddhist saint
70. Marsh bird
72. Egg-boiling aid
73. Certain shipments
75. Body: Suffix
76. Asian priest
78. Not natural: Abbr.
79. More of 56 Across
85. Scenery chewer
87. Present
88. "And ___ is awfully rich..."
89. Thingumbobs
92. Vestment
94. Easily bruised things
97. Across: Prefix
99. Town near Sandy Hook
100. Derring-do
101. German valley
103. Verdi opus
105. Relative of "oh, dear"
106. More of 79 Across
110. Curl of the lip
111. Kind of lettuce
112. Foams
113. Facile
115. Unburden
116. Ben Adhem
118. Suffixes for young and old
122. Father
124. Civil War battle site
130. Disney's middle name
132. Soprano's warm-up
136. Welcome to Hilo!
137. End of verse
140. Stares
141. Do-nothing
142. Squelched
143. Old Greek temples
144. Turn inside out
145. Nine: Latin
146. Form of Helen
147. Queen ___ lace
148. Starts an urban renewal job
149. First name in movie lore
150. Nelson and Mary Baker
151. Sprees

DOWN

1. Indians
2. Place to remember
3. Jewish festival
4. Pâtisserie items
5. Solo
6. Bean
7. Geraint's wife, et al.
8. "...owed by so ___ so few"
9. World relief group
10. Parasite fish
11. Start of learning song
12. Sheepish remark
13. Body sac
14. Well-known chorus
15. Caramel candy, for instance
16. Misbehaves
17. ___ d'hôtel
18. Stroke of luck
19. Peter of films
20. Send upward
30. Cithara's cousin
31. Within the law
36. Gerald O'Hara's pride
38. After "tres"
40. Wagnerian goddess
42. Sharply, in music: Abbr.
43. Xanadu name
44. Standish, to hippies?
46. Naldi of silents
48. Man from M.I.T.
49. Mrs. Helmer
50. French star
51. Cyclotron
52. Nonsense!
53. "...like ___ in spring"
55. Practical
57. Defeat
58. "But when ___ I cannot tell"
59. A friend: Fr.
60. Strapped, financially
61. Thee: Fr.
63. "Give ___ tools..."
67. Kipling poem, with "Mine"
69. Unspoken
71. "Green Pastures" role
74. Withered
77. Polynesian
80. Rue
81. Zimbalist
82. Puppeteer Lewis
83. Hair rinse
84. Madison Ave. worker
85. Cry or June
86. Writer Jorge
90. Former Japanese news agency
91. Mortimer
93. Mountain pass
95. Painful sound
96. If it fits, put it on
98. Stated
102. School curriculum, once
104. Compass points
107. Blossom: Sp.
108. Intimidating
109. You, in Madrid
110. Summer theater
114. Thin cover
116. Stick to
117. Burdened ones
119. French President's home
120. Lewd
121. Fried lightly
123. Lily maid
124. $2 item
125. Caste of India
126. Bandleader Vincent
127. Witch's home
128. Puzzle out
129. Weather word
131. Impassive
133. Theater-in-the-round
134. Enticing one
135. Pile up
138. First word of "Aeneid"
139. ___ much as

Drawing the Shades

by Marjorie K. Collins

ACROSS

1. Mr. Coward
5. Rested
10. Reference mark
14. Regarding
18. Nimbus
19. Hackneyed
20. Title
21. School chore
23. Brains
25. Letter's antecedent
27. Utah range
28. Scoreboard listing
29. Daughter of Priam
30. Lap of luxury
37. Indeed, in Ireland
38. June beetles
39. Geologic time
40. Ship part
44. Where we're weightless
49. Cut to board size
52. Italian genius
54. Knocking sound
55. River to North Sea
56. Tropical fruits
57. Metric measures
59. Balance
60. For a ___ (cheaply)
61. Biblical land
63. German numeral
65. At full speed
67. Exhortation for le roi
71. Manner
72. Shallow
74. French painter
75. Mosque priest
76. Attention-getter
77. Snide
78. Mexican money
79. Chooses
80. Cure
82. Eye part
85. Steady
87. Casts ___ on
90. Chin: Prefix
92. Maintains
95. Betting info
97. Hinder, in law
98. Roman poet
99. Indifferent
100. Boat gear
102. 1956 Wimbledon champ
104. Fast, to slow: Abbr.
105. Sources of junk
113. Having a grudge
116. Dallas campus
117. Yucatan Indians
118. The view from here is nice
120. Sorcery
125. Type of edge
126. Logical
127. Tidal flow
128. Western org.
129. Counsel, old style
130. Models: Abbr.
131. Planes
132. Chinese island

DOWN

1. Plater
2. Possessive
3. Pitcher's concern: Abbr.
4. Store
5. Ladd movie
6. ___ Miles, girl in old tire ad
7. ___ run
8. Acadia's Grand ___
9. Norse god
10. Nature writer
11. Western lake
12. Small cavity
13. Literary initials
14. ___ of woe
15. Dried flower, in a way
16. Distant: Prefix
17. Sign
22. Before automne
24. Wire measure
26. Breakfast treat
30. Brace
31. Container: Sp.
32. Posse's quarry
33. Campus unit
34. More unrestrained
35. Offspring
36. Antiseptic: Prefix
41. Siamese twin
42. Far sound: Sp.
43. Heraldic flower
45. Live it up
46. Law man: Abbr.
47. North, for one
48. Enduring
50. State of India
51. Floor cleaner
53. Johnson
58. Red and others
60. Naps
61. Unusual power
62. ___ Passos
64. Certain kind of stitch
66. Ones: Scot.
68. Paper size
69. Winemaker's need
70. Type measures
73. Brontë's Jane et al.
81. Biblical judge
83. ___ pink
84. Back porch
86. Youth org.
87. Exclamations
88. ___ canals
89. Parts of gals
91. Ocean fish
93. Fix the piano
94. Plane types: Abbr.
96. Convened
101. Go after a fly again
103. Injure
106. Big name in cards
107. Edit
108. Decoys
109. Shell layer
110. Children
111. "Pants" man
112. Yoga posture
113. Fishing term
114. Finished
115. Entwined
119. W.W. II group
120. Poker word
121. Gibbon
122. Pod
123. Japanese statesman
124. Demure

81 All to the Goods

by Anne Fox

ACROSS

1. Miss Page
6. Greek letter
9. Cabal
13. U.S. dept.
16. English engineer
19. Part of the Erechtheum
24. Uninvited one
25. Killjoy
26. Radioman's room
27. Spanish relative
28. Way out
30. ___ mater
31. Effrontery
32. Fictional plantation
33. All ___ up
34. Gov't. sleuthing agency
35. Shout
37. Reprove
38. Valley of Europe
40. Spanish port
42. One of the F.F.V.
43. Wool: Sp.
44. Milk ingredient
47. Scull
48. Dean
50. Think
52. What Sam Goldwyn said to "include me in"
56. Chic
60. Viking name
61. ___ B'rith
62. Swiss canton
63. Elec. unit
65. Hep
66. Tonsorial call
67. Car part: Abbr.
68. Indian greeting
69. Inventor Howe
71. English poet
72. Dakota sight
74. City of Peru
76. Aardvark's delicacy
77. Reside
78. Fictional pair
84. "___ a little shadow..."
85. Hunter's limit
86. Sandpiper
87. British ___
88. Service
89. One's word
91. Came in first
92. Make obscure
93. Mexican sandwich
97. Chemical compound
98. ___ pro nobis
99. Honshu peak
101. ___ d'Azur
102. Scrammed
103. Western capital
105. U.S. writer
109. Type of school: Abbr.
111. Coconut fiber
112. Kayoed
113. Crying items
114. Doubles and triples
116. Somewhat: Suffix
118. Newark's county
120. Alley sound
121. Puerto Rican city
122. Portico
124. Exclamations
125. Invite
126. Arabian gulf
130. Gem stone
131. Heat standard: Abbr.
132. Well!, in Spain
134. Abner
135. "...bitten, ___ shy"
136. Congressman from Ill.
139. Firemen's training structures
142. Play by Ibsen
143. Town named for Syrian saint
144. Cooking abbr.
145. Uh-huh
146. Miss West
147. Cut the lawn

DOWN

1. Czech capital
2. Perfume
3. Perry Mason's debut
4. Fictional friar
5. Type of verb: Abbr.
6. Fix
7. Site of Berwick market
8. Réunion, for one
9. Size of type
10. Van, in London
11. Kind of world
12. Drink
13. Constellation
14. Words by Eugene Field
15. Get back
16. Not for: Abbr.
17. Drink
18. Scairt
20. Lined, as a roof
21. Gov't, agency
22. A Fitzgerald
23. First name with 3 Down
29. Eastern U.S. borough
33. Flier
34. Car part, for short
36. Nevada city
37. Queen, for short
39. Kind of line
40. Moslem judge
41. Bantu language
44. Possum's cousin
45. Wheel part
46. Tunisian port
47. ___ even keel
49. Cut of meat
51. Rulers: Abbr.
53. Railroad tool
54. Counsel, in Nice
55. Singer Frankie
57. "The Lady ___"
58. Fusty
59. According to ___
64. French sailors
68. Bad actor
70. Old cry of surprise
73. Chem. suffix
74. Harbor craft
75. Skillful
77. Postal limbo: Abbr.
78. Run-down
79. Snivel
80. Jackson's war secretary
81. Borneo native
82. Bill
83. Took in
89. Peeved
90. ___ importance
92. Pay, as the bill
94. Lily plant
95. Part of a honeycomb
96. Sees red, in a way
100. Narwhal
101. Main feature
104. Of another sort
106. Repeat
107. Farm tools
108. As well
110. Foggy
114. Chinese province
115. Miffed
117. Rugged
119. Food fish
120. Thousand: Prefix
121. Larboard
123. Irish river
125. Bosh
127. Honey: It.
128. Biting
129. State: Suffix
131. Parcel: Abbr.
133. Ansate cross
134. Money in Italy
135. "___ the mornin' to you"
137. Small drink
138. Girl of song
140. Ad ___
141. Male animal

82 Workaday World

ACROSS

1. ___ or nothing
4. "___ Three Lives"
8. Biblical word
11. Elec. unit
14. Biblical name
15. Hawaiian shark
16. Garden tool
17. Two-wheeled vehicles
20. Heating vessel
21. Fundamentals
22. Greek letter
23. Spa
24. Hear a case again
26. Oil, in old Rome
28. Response
30. ___ of Cutch
31. ___ seedling (plant)
32. Dawn goddess
33. Dark
34. Argues in favor of
36. Go back
39. Italian beach
40. "...the giftie ___ us"
41. Some G.I.'s
43. Sensed
44. False god
45. Donkey
46. Doer: Suffix
47. Certain space flights
50. ___ in a poke
52. Pub drink
53. Guarantee
55. Scoff
57. Remove
60. Prepares clams
62. Cause: Prefix
63. Six-day Biblical advice
67. Perfume: Var.
68. ___ God
69. Somewhat: Suffix
70. First-rate
71. Groom
73. Mischievous one
75. By any chance
77. Lacks truth
78. Spanish cape on Medit.
79. Stand-off
80. Maintained
84. Scottish river
85. "Arma virumque ___"
86. Go wrong
87. Concerning
88. Murderous person
92. Labor Day orator, perhaps
95. Roman emperor
96. Housewife
97. Girl's name
98. Mellowed
99. ___ in his life
102. Off the cuff
103. Writer Marsh
105. Star in Draco
106. Lie
108. Jacket
110. Asian country
111. Pours
112. Stir
113. French verb
114. Uncles, etc.: Abbr.
115. Small bird
116. Rocky peak
117. Victory margin
118. Peers: Abbr.

DOWN

1. Sky body
2. Retarding, in music
3. Advice from Longfellow
4. "___ little teapot"
5. Grant's words about toil
6. Inserts
7. A ___ one's own medicine
8. Words by L.B.J.
9. In demand
10. Indeed
11. Zoological suffix
12. Gender: Abbr.
13. A job for heaven
14. Poet's above
18. Huron or Erie
19. Endured
23. The dead may "___" (Bible)
25. Chem. suffix
27. Place of ideal perfection
28. Eggs
29. Direction
32. Sounds of hesitation
34. Roman 151
35. African spirit
37. Move shrubbery
38. Suffix for acids
42. Trick, in Italy
47. Racetracks
48. "Flow-gently" river
49. French river
51. Little, in Paris
54. Korean G.I.
55. ___ Casazza
56. Building beams
58. Start of a jazz piece
59. Dentist's degree: Abbr.
61. Ivy leaguer
63. ___ Vegas
64. Bird of prey
65. Rumanian folk song
66. One: Scot.
72. Winnie
74. All in
76. Part of speech
79. "___ the judge"
81. Made lovable
82. Landed slaves: Var.
83. Three: Prefix
85. Coins: Abbr.
88. Camper's gear
89. King Arthur's father
90. Greek letter
91. Scottish alder
93. "My Sister ___"
94. Fleming
100. Prefix with bus and present
101. Bedim
104. Cricket sides
106. Kind of cat
107. Marriage words
109. Born: Fr.

Words on Parade

by Ross L. Jamison Jr.

ACROSS

1. Purpose
7. "Gil Blas" author
13. Daisy Mae's creator
17. Fugue composer
21. Small space
22. "Cymbeline" heroine
23. Oriental nurse
24. Gingko
25. Prying
27. Hamlet's forte
29. Rumanian coin
30. Fugue part
31. P. I. natives
33. Developed
34. Nibble
36. Circle, in Germany
37. Truck compartment
38. First name in British letters
39. Aromatic seed
42. Surface measure
43. Growing in pairs
45. Roof ornament
46. Roman scholar
48. Hang fire
49. Mysterious
51. Hindu land grant
54. Hero of Norse myth
55. Consisting of 50 days
60. ___ shirt
61. In the manner of
62. Hungarian Communist
63. Charley's relative
64. City north of Genova
65. As well as
66. Moon: Prefix
68. Move with a rustle
70. Fasten anew
71. Teachers' org.
72. Moslem saint
73. Heed
74. Alley of the comics
76. Reasonable
78. ___ law
81. City on the Rio Grande
85. Lock
86. Cheated
88. Dull finish
89. Pronoun
90. ___ disant
91. Samovar
92. Lunisolar difference
95. Designated
97. Mr. ___
101. Remote-control bomb
102. Hitchhiking fish
104. Broth, to a Scot
105. Day times: Abbr.
106. Goose eggs
107. Two: Prefix
108. Astrological aspect
111. Blue, in Spain
112. Egg part
114. Yugoslav river, to Germans
115. Dwarf
116. Water-level measure
118. Bible book: Abbr.
120. Runs
122. Druggist's drops: Abbr.
124. Dealers in certain cakes
125. On ___ (aggressive)
128. Sweep
129. Weighed a container
131. Socialite
132. Off-color
133. Spore sacs
134. Byproduct of divorce
136. Possessive
139. Animal that sponges on another
141. Dropping of legal action
144. Large toad
145. Wild plum
146. Consecrate
147. Perceptible
148. Old English court
149. Sound from the sty
150. Old weapons
151. Sanction

DOWN

1. ___ Eireann
2. Sea bird
3. Consecutive
4. Chit
5. Sparkle
6. Political cartoonist
7. Educators, writers, etc.
8. Ham
9. Military mission
10. Exchange premiums
11. Region: Suffix
12. Interweaving
13. Melon
14. O.T. book
15. Buddy
16. Sorority name
17. Organisms sharing a trait
18. It was auld to Burns
19. Insect sound
20. Called attention
26. Vex
28. Burden
32. Bike
35. Indigo
38. U. S. tree
39. Jumping insects
40. Former gold coin
41. Whisky
43. Gets a hit the hard way
44. Linen fabric
47. Luminary
48. Andean wind
50. Aquarium fish
52. Trojan hero
53. Military fruit salad
56. V.I.P.
57. Senate voting concern
58. Word of respect
59. 2,240-pound units
62. Breeches
67. Grand
68. Musical piece: Abbr.
69. Garden tool
75. Examined
77. Rainbow: Prefix
78. Robust
79. Western gulch
80. Tall and gaunt
81. Water
82. Arabian tea: Var.
83. Eccentric
84. Indian bean
87. Foils
90. Saturday, in Paris
93. Feather trim for hats
94. Administrator: Abbr.
96. Sassy kid
98. African area
99. Cosmetic
100. Razor clam
103. Hollow space in birds
105. Panay native
109. Hill of Rome
110. Endeavors
111. U. S. writer
113. Citrus fruit
117. Molting
119. Hawaiian island
121. Hide and ___
122. French
123. Chemical compound
125. ___ balloon
126. Be contingent
127. Big-money racehorse
129. Claw
130. Buzzing beetle
133. At another time
135. Temporary star
137. Malayan sir
138. Sediment
140. River of Asia
142. ___ shoestring
143. Sigmoid figure

84 Tall Titles

by Eugene T. Maleska

ACROSS

1. Scopes
7. Plea
15. Ablutions
20. Sideshow man
21. ___ boom
22. Kind of committee
23. Sequel to "Dad's Awakening"
25. The ending
26. Spy name
27. Dockers' union: Abbr.
28. Math ratios
29. "Yes, ___" by Sammy Davis
30. Kittiwake
32. Town on the Hudson
34. Main force
35. Most miserly
39. Abbreviation in physics
40. More chichi
42. Ham it up
43. Buzzes
45. Ruler's epithet
46. Resin
49. Masefield heroine
50. Addison's colleague
52. "As You Like It" girl
53. Forum garb
54. Leghorn's largesse
56. Encomium
57. Bills
58. Less perilous
59. Civic center
61. Signify
63. Coat fur
64. Chits
65. Cupola-shaped
67. Oriental nurse
68. Bishop's headdress
70. Inflict
71. Benefit
75. Throbs
76. Ring champ, 1934
77. Dissuade
79. ___ Pea of Popeye strip
80. Shea occupants
81. Sesame
82. Feel by insight
84. Native of: Suffix
85. Blonde shade
86. Rails
87. Subject to
88. Poe's foster father
90. Dines at home
92. Part of U. K.
93. Musical flourishes
95. Shade of brown
97. Astaire
99. Do pruning
100. Greedy
101. Wine and dine
103. Ad ___
104. Bullring cries
108. Under legal age
110. "Portnoy's Complaint"
113. Provide with
114. Pupils, at times
115. Roman goddess
116. Takes it easy
117. Finale on Broadway
118. Tool for boring

DOWN

1. Miracle drug
2. Asian deer
3. ___ Rabbit
4. Discernment
5. Spanish uncle
6. Doddering
7. Fitzgerald
8. We: Lat.
9. Braces
10. Peals again
11. Avenging spirit
12. Lost
13. Post-picnic catsup bottles
14. It is so
15. ___ Dai of Vietnam
16. Esteem
17. Medusa's coiffure
18. Navaho lodge
19. Meager
24. Sentry's call
31. Salt Lake City team
33. German localities
34. Snippet
35. Belief
36. Mature insect
37. Orchestral variation
38. Tale of a so-so adult student
39. Heavy shoe
41. Chinese pagoda
44. Dr. Gesell's co-author
45. Ligurian port
47. Askew
48. Vikki the songstress
51. Bohea and congou
52. Granting
53. Tamerlane's people
55. Siesta sounds
58. About
60. Colors
62. Ice, in Berlin
66. Unfolds
67. Town of Italy
68. Sound from a doll
69. Sherbets
70. Michener title
72. Emotional disorder
73. Bristles
74. Part of a lifetime
78. Goal
81. Cattle genus
83. Anklebones
86. Swinery
87. Expose
89. City in Indiana
91. "Over ___" (sign-off)
92. Writ against a debtor
94. Open
95. Circus performer
96. Of birds: Var.
98. Put up
102. Stratum
103. ___ majesty
105. Pilot's maneuver
106. Sicilian spouter
107. Burmese group
109. In medias ___
110. Refrain syllable
111. Evangeline's Grand ___
112. Remote

85

Both Directions

by Keith Blake

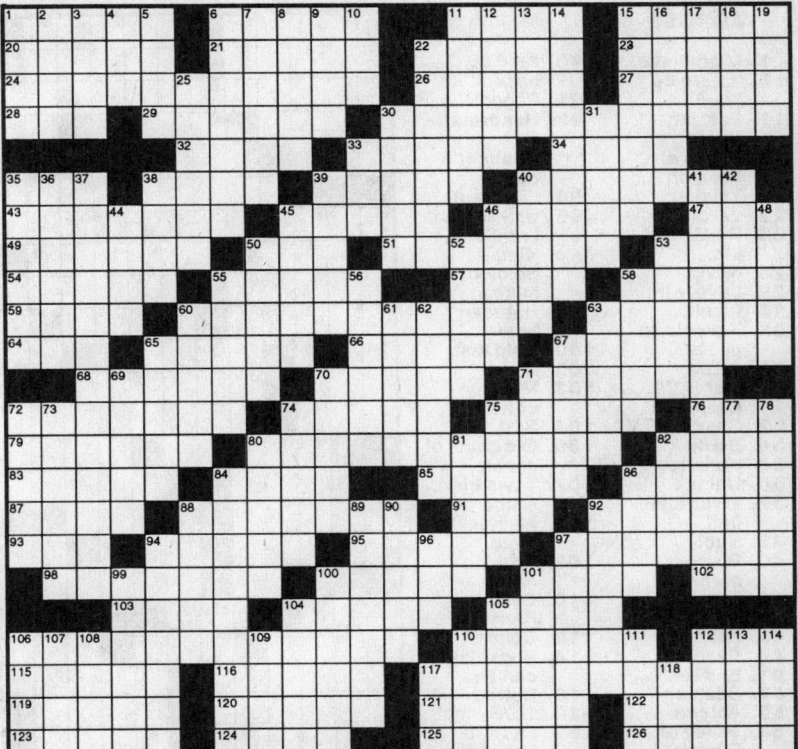

ACROSS

1. Kind of pride
6. Struck out
11. ___ homo
15. Proofreaders' marks
20. Eared seal
21. Like Humpty Dumpty
22. Old Irish writing
23. ___ firma
24. First family greeting
26. Threadbare
27. Gibson garnish
28. Wheat: Fr.
29. Theatrical devices
30. Sign in animal shelter
32. Greenbacks
33. "Looking Glass" game
34. "I did, ___?"
35. Month: Abbr.
38. Coasted
39. Carbons
40. "One ___ hope"
43. Bucket passers
45. Artist Edouard
46. Get on toward midnight
47. Plural ending
49. Gil Blas creator
50. Make lace
51. Certain muscle
53. Confess
54. Pupil, in Paris
55. Outdoor area
57. Maple genus
58. ___ de menthe
59. Glut
60. Radar, sis and arara
63. Gazed dreamily
64. "___ for the show"
65. Used up
66. British sand hills
67. Body substance
68. Philo and others
70. Following
71. Warning
72. Humdinger
74. Punjab town
75. Moves in a slinky way
76. Scrap
79. Coaches
80. Challenge to Sir Noel
82. Recognized
83. Astaire partner
84. Person
85. Lock
86. Ex-Dodger star
87. ___ en scène
88. Prudent
91. German article
92. Video set
93. Greek letter
94. It is permitted: Lat.
95. Auto-safety man
97. Exalted
98. Chemical compound
100. Scotsman's tossing-log
101. Sea bird
102. British House: Abbr.
103. Put away, old style
104. Small bell
105. Legislative body
106. Why owls shun the tropics
110. Coin game: Var.
112. "___ Sir Oracle"
115. Town in C.Z.
116. Image: Prefix
117. When a certain man was able
119. Honshu city
120. Slackening bar on a loom
121. Sierra ___
122. Arabian title
123. "Win a few, ___ few"
124. Coaster
125. Southern constellation
126. Battle of the ___

DOWN

1. Search widely
2. Type face: Abbr.
3. ___ mecum
4. George's lyricist
5. Cornice molding
6. Minister: Dialect
7. Baffled
8. Stows
9. Greek letters
10. Party man: Abbr.
11. Barnum's "This way to the ___"
12. Money substitutes
13. Elder or Younger
14. Editor
15. ___ one's rights
16. Bowling target
17. Iroquoian
18. Pony
19. ___ serif
22. Octet: It.
25. Irish princess
30. Blacksmith, at times
31. Forty - ___
33. Swindle
35. Most capable
36. Future attorney's course
37. Advice to a seated M.P.
38. Seasoning
39. Fabric
40. Delicacies
41. Advice for good people
42. Navy - clerical men
44. Conveyed
45. Early prayer
46. Shoe parts
48. Nobel
50. Wayside Inn fare
52. Circus expert
53. Bouquet
55. Writer Walter
56. Random grouping
58. Inner areas
60. Sets the tempo
61. Kind of rocket
62. Kind of play
63. Progressed
65. Between: Fr.
67. Filaments
69. Take ___ in a play
70. Call ___ to (stop)
71. Ritzy quality
72. Impress
73. Dweller in a certain colony
74. Noise abroad
75. Pledge
77. Sow again
78. Sporting wear
80. Distributed
81. Concern of Robert's Rules
82. Indian hemp: Var.
84. Groups
86. Check
88. Loop of lace
89. Type of bed
90. Boston name
92. Third: Lat.
94. Ky. racetrack
96. Retreat
97. Kind of diver
99. "Wherever I hang my hat ___"
100. Lost interest
101. Basketball scores
104. Opted
105. ___ base (be stranded)
106. Comet part
107. Hep
108. Wood sorrels
109. Eastern vine
110. Forest sight
111. "___ the night . . ."
112. Holly
113. Busy as ___
114. Spoils
117. Tree
118. Scottish uncle

ACROSS

1. Misbehave
6. "___ to be you"
11. East, in Spain
15. Draws a bead on
21. Thicket
22. ___ prayer
23. Relative of etc.
24. Novice
25. Level with
28. Picnic
29. Reveals, to poets
30. "___ a star...?"
31. Besmirch
32. Spade of TV
34. Blade
35. Kennedy
36. Unique
37. Electrical unit
38. Duct
40. Black or green
41. Esthetic doctrine
46. Pshaw!
48. Resolve
51. Endure
52. Seaman
53. Astaire
56. Valley of Europe
57. Abundantly
61. British title: Abbr.
62. Crew member
63. Foreign
65. Commando command
68. Spartan magistrate
69. Famous island
70. Land of the Peacock Throne
71. Shoot dice
72. Cat, in Rome
74. Gums: Prefix
75. Histories
77. Use a curb space
78. Similar
79. Inc., in Britain
82. Yutang
83. Like Pauline's rescuers
86. Poetic word
87. At the age of: Abbr.
88. Negatives of a sort
89. Turkish weights
90. Kind of hosen
91. Pagoda
92. Headwear, in Chaucer's day
94. Lily plant
95. U. S. Indian
96. Land of King Solomon's mines
98. Hebrew letter
100. Hold fast
102. Jerks
103. Moon crater
104. Serf
105. Old coins of Japan
107. Town in China
108. Master, in India
109. Ocean: Abbr.
110. Over, in Paris
112. Colorer
114. Buckeyes' campus
115. Hotrodding
120. ___ Simbel
122. Eastern bay: Abbr.
124. Hymenopter
125. Like, teen-age style
126. Relative of Sandy
129. Dash off
131. Farm sound
133. Virginia
135. Opulent, in Ponce
136. Game
137. Feverel's burden
139. Hoodwink
143. Restless
144. Pulitzer Prize novelist
145. Scottish slopes
146. Useful quality
147. Part of an insect's wing
148. Scepters
149. Sight, for one
150. U.S. Pioneer in mental hygiene

DOWN

1. Churchman
2. Fabric
3. Kind of TV show
4. Stringed instruments
5. Kind of rug: Abbr.
6. ___ March
7. Locarno's canton
8. Mad one
9. "___ Alone"
10. Time periods
11. Most uncanny
12. Delays
13. Color
14. Fraternal men
15. Coffee quality
16. Note
17. Particle
18. "Forget it"
19. Eldest daughter: Fr.
20. Ancient city of Greece
26. Cigarette type
27. Knox and Dix
33. Prevent
36. Suffix for dull or stand
39. Spoil
41. Clothes-drying frame
42. Fred or Steve
43. Ottoman slave
44. In any way
45. Marx
47. Choose
48. Dread Count
49. French saint
50. Invisible symbol
54. Where Regulus is
55. Goof
58. "Your ___ only peacemaker..."
59. Clyde, Forth and others
60. Take out
61. Phil Silvers role
64. Thwart
66. Pursued
67. Operates
72. Leading
73. Highest point
76. Med. subject
77. Actress Molly
78. Tread
80. Mosey
81. Opener of sorts
84. Hale character
85. Armada: Sp.
93. Point in an orbit
94. Eniwetok
95. Wont
97. Trick
98. Skill: Lat.
99. Mauna ___
100. Stiff hair
101. Ping follower
104. Casals
106. ___ David
110. Conclusions
111. Within: Prefix
113. Bartender's need
116. Used a certain utensil
117. Supreme Court justice
118. Roman magistrates
119. Playful
120. Near
121. Carried
123. Actor Williams
126. Big game
127. Tree
128. Legal expenses
130. Lions or Bears
132. Glacial ridges
134. Decays
136. Sit for
138. Enzyme
140. Self
141. Choler
142. Gift of sorts

Selected Words

by Joseph LaFaucl

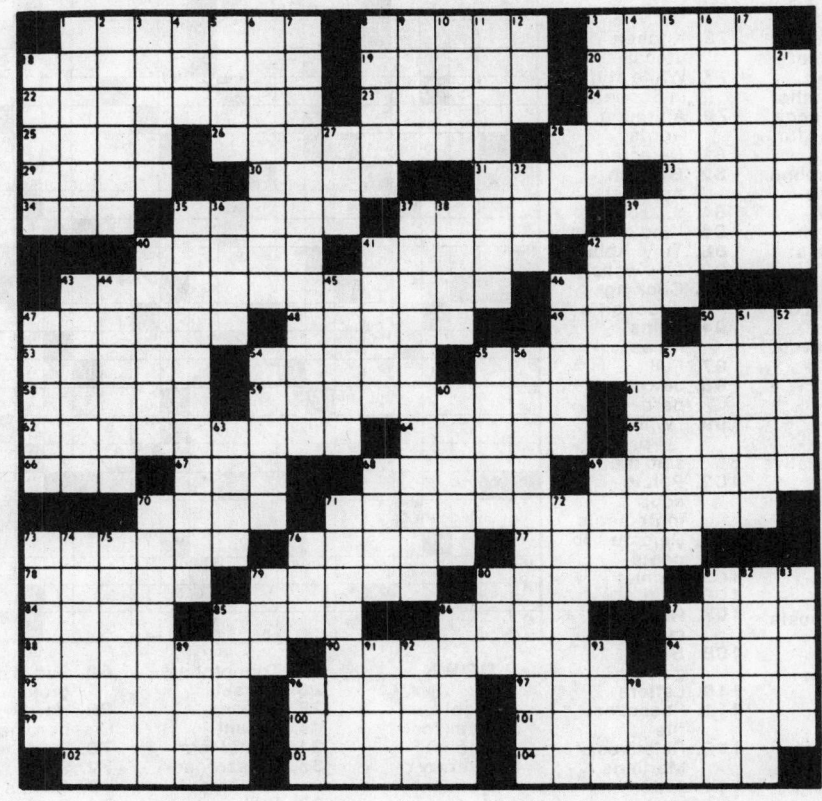

ACROSS

1. U. S. missile
8. Nile feature
13. Ignominy
18. Combative
19. Ethiopian town
20. Source
22. Elevation
23. Mansion
24. Princeton color
25. Range
26. Tactful one
28. Assail vigorously
29. Campbell
30. Ruin
31. Neighbor of Turkey
33. Modified organism
34. Attention
35. Tobacco mixture
37. Daughter of David
39. Amory, for short
40. Elmo
41. Willamette Univ. site
42. Smoker's gadget
43. Type of playhouse
46. Evening: It.
47. Golfer's wear
48. Inspire
49. Chinese dynasty
50. Discourse: Abbr.
53. Purport
54. Lively
55. Hobby hours
58. ___ acid
59. Sometime city flood source
61. Austerity
62. U. S. system of W. W. II aid
64. Florida cape
65. Spanish corn bread
66. Compass reading
67. Malay gibbon
68. Word of mouth
69. City in Conn.
70. Earthen building material
71. July 4 parade feature
73. Inhabit
76. Kind of lily
77. Lively dances
78. In company with
79. Racetrack fences
80. Gaze
81. Mil. award
84. ___ temperature
85. Nobleman
86. Stadium sounds
87. Strip of wood
88. With extra calories, so to say
90. Encounter
94. Kind of code
95. Carrying on
96. Nymph loved by Minos
97. Rapid-fire joke
99. Immediately
100. Antelope
101. In a stringent way
102. Stage direction
103. Playing marble
104. Foot lever

DOWN

1. Stuffed olive
2. Kukla's friend, formally
3. Cambric or damask
4. Used up
5. Famous fan dancer
6. Occurrence
7. Pick up speed
8. Famous friend
9. Dutch cheese
10. Large moth
11. False friend
12. Swiss river
13. Golf club
14. Injury
15. Strauss opera
16. Threatened
17. Impress deeply
18. Coalesce
21. British marshal of W. W. II
27. Part of a jar
28. Tribunal
32. Crash into
35. Financing
36. English limestone
37. Fancy vests
38. Toward shelter
39. Cozy bistro setting
40. Take a safe dueling role
41. German river
42. Find out
43. Certain pub drinkers
44. Like a frog
45. Choice segment
46. Alan Ladd film
47. Mate of a sort
50. Register
51. Hammed it up
52. Sought office again
54. Cognizant
55. Shoe
56. Aimless drifting
57. Headbands
60. "West Side Story" girl
63. Dude territory
68. Tiresome person
69. Musician Richard ___ Bennet
70. Calif. range
71. Army camp event
72. TV newsman Harry
73. Pacific island
74. Imitate
75. Geometric figure
76. Jalopy
79. Scottish explorer
80. Trifle
81. Weedy grass
82. English essayist
83. Cautious
85. Trimming device
86. Like snakes' eyes
87. Scottish landowner
89. Formerly
91. Spoken
92. Pit
93. Granular snow
96. Shell-game item
98. Grassland

Habit-Forming

by Alfio Micci

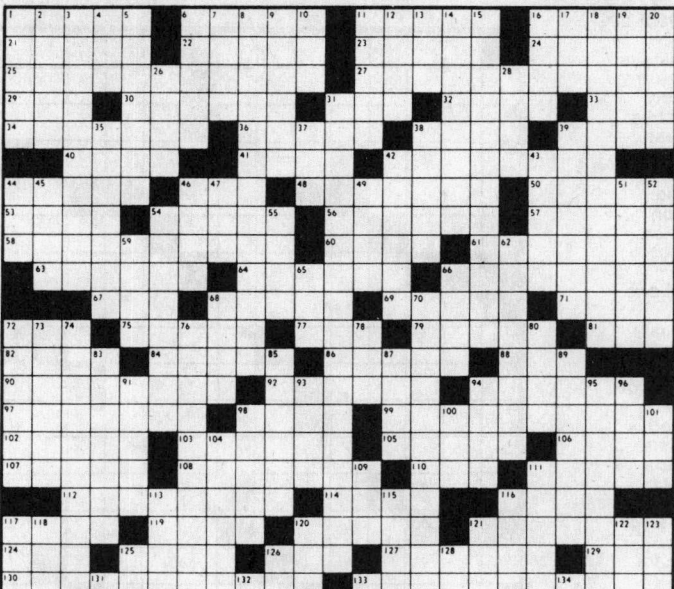

ACROSS

1. French composer
6. "Golden Boy" author
11. Off balance
16. Subway for René
21. Night sound
22. Delicate
23. Wife of Abraham
24. Put one's ___
25. Family garment of sorts
27. Track event
29. Kind
30. Fertile
31. ___ de-lance
32. ___ now
33. Comparative ending
34. Discards
36. Toys
38. Family girls: Abbr.
39. Name in motors
40. Large boats
41. Rabbit's title
42. Stadium area
44. Cuzco people
46. Prince of drama
48. Length of some plays
50. French Alp
53. Mango parts
54. ___ boredom
56. Amount ___ (insurance term)
57. French story
58. Rooted
60. Horse color
61. Changes into particles
63. Sunk without ___
64. Shaped
66. Bauble
67. German pronoun
68. Musical speeds
69. Stone
71. Earth, in Berlin
72. Summer hours: Abbr.
75. Kitchen utensil
77. White stuff, in Scotland
79. Affirming words
81. Dejected
82. German numeral
84. "___ d'arte"
86. Kind of train
88. Tiny: Abbr.
90. Low walls
92. Cooking direction
94. Ships' ropes
97. Full
98. Jewelry part
99. "Will you ___ parlor, said the ..."
102. Potato-soup ingredients
103. Rejected, to poets
105. Hamlet
106. Graf ___
107. Road curves
108. Ballet garment
110. Letters
111. Passover rite
112. Relatives of Martians
114. Arden and others
116. Have on
117. Wading bird
119. Gumbo: Var.
120. Feels poorly
121. Enzyme
124. Negation
125. Dumbarton ___
126. Romaine
127. Italian sculptor
129. Typist's abbr.
130. Weds
133. Family garment
135. Fault
136. Lasso
137. Hearth
138. Biting
139. French remainder
140. Cuts, old style
141. Winter wear
142. Misplaces

DOWN

1. Light ___
2. Sam, for one
3. Literary garment
4. Age
5. Upholsters anew
6. Teutonic hero and others
7. Uninteresting
8. Some flowers
9. A ___ two (occasionally)
10. Lawyers: Abbr.
11. Residue
12. Arabian tambourine
13. Kind of verb: Abbr.
14. Homestead and other legislation
15. Unfashionable garments
16. Majority
17. Attention
18. Hiking garments
19. Put through a sieve
20. Topnotchers
26. Morsels
28. Señor's assent
31. Postal term
35. Classroom equipment
37. Still
38. Czech city
39. Former
42. Kashmir alphabet
43. ___ charge account
44. Business abbr.
45. Okinawa city
46. Hair's partner
47. W.W. I group
49. Western Indian
51. List
52. Examined
54. Double-crosser
55. Memo-pad word
59. Foray
62. Waiting for ___ to come in
65. Certain records
66. Full of a grain
68. Hardy heroine
70. Elude
72. Spot
73. Climbs
74. Some bridge hands
76. Urban garments
78. "Exodus" man
80. Sign
83. Harbor sights
85. Composer Jacques and family
87. Helper: Abbr.
89. Hungry-one's cry
91. ___ car (overtake)
93. Genus of frogs
94. Waterers: Abbr.
95. Boxoffice stars
96. Pintail duck
98. ___ notte
100. Long time
101. Slangy pronoun
104. Rind of a kind
109. Sixth-century date
111. Sedative drug
113. Ark builder
115. Texas city
116. Decline
117. Among: Prefix
118. Drink, in Paris
120. Jots
121. Tahoe and Como
122. Miss Thompson
123. Terrapins
125. Wine-bottle, in Italy
126. Shelter
128. Spanish painter
131. Toper
132. Scottish negative
133. Hack
134. Sgt., for one

Squarely Figured

by A. J. Santora

ACROSS

1. After-midnight hours
7. Last Commandment
13. Spring date
20. Green crust on metal
21. "Give the devil ___"
22. "Peekaboo, ___"
23. Chem. compounds
24. Italian city
25. "...sleep, perchance ___"
26. Dine
27. Sharp sound
29. Defeats
31. Goddess of infatuation
32. Malay dagger: Var.
34. Hank of yarn
36. Deer
37. Court judgment
39. New York street
42. Japanese coin
44. Makes an offer
46. Not at home
47. Cornbreads
49. In ___
50. Spar on a sail
52. Shouted
54. Eases off
58. What some scouts look for
59. Vaulter's concern
61. Renew old school ties
62. Ex-Senator from Nebraska
63. Male deer
64. Provided that
66. Fairly old auto
67. Gypsy
68. Contended
70. Smother
72. Sesame
73. Jewish month
75. Room in a casa
76. Phila. team
77. Whole
79. Part of a book
81. Hitter
83. Repeats
84. Sam and J.C. of golf
86. Note declining an invitation
87. Pulverize
88. Planet
90. Glistened
91. Strange
92. Caveman of comics
96. Friend in Paris
97. What a duffer does at times
101. Small pair
102. Raffle-ticket marking
104. Ulan ___
107. Anna's land
108. Spigot
109. The ___ be counted
111. In unison
114. Numerical prefix
115. Bulldog, for one
118. Verdi opera
120. Explosive
122. Expires
123. Mews: Fr.
124. Council of 325 A.D.
125. Impost at Aqueduct
126. Annoy
127. Smarts

DOWN

1. Kind of swimsuit
2. Italian spice
3. Ear trouble
4. ___ hand
5. Over again
6. Cattle feed
7. Show gratitude
8. Door piece
9. Spanish coin: Abbr.
10. Famous London address
11. Gum tree
12. Learned
13. Stage fright
14. Service-club units
15. Little Edward
16. Always, to poets
17. Life span of a locust
18. Exactly
19. Heraldic bars
28. Pale
30. Bribe
33. Gapes
35. Mine strike
37. More likely
38. Popular song about a highway
40. Catnap
41. Rat ___
43. Prefixes for recent
45. Lubricate
47. Mine sweeps on ships
48. Underlying layer
50. U.S. Playwright
51. Peacock's pride
52. Student
53. Lao-tse's followers
55. Type of pump
56. Not ventilated
57. Mesta et al.
58. Destructive insects
60. W.W. II group
65. Pullman
69. Fordhamite
70. Douay Bible name
71. Repeat number
74. Pipe-cleaning tool
76. Brass in a musical
78. Arborvitaes
80. Phileas Fogg's travel time
82. Turkish title
85. Hit sign
89. Voiced sounds
91. River of Spain
92. Where 126 is
93. Put on cargo
94. Ida of films
95. Opposite of neg.
98. Young pet
99. Tahiti wrap
100. Fifth of the Indy 500
103. Sign of the flu
105. Aunt in Paris
106. Willow
109. Mouthy
110. Factual
112. Code letters
113. Send out
116. Initials on a crate
117. Elec. particle
119. Lawyer: Abbr.
121. Chemical prefix

Coded Phrases

by Edward J. O'Brien

ACROSS

1. Old timer
8. "On ___ of Bibles"
14. Card game
17. Concern of Congress
20. 43,560 square feet
21. By law: Fr.
22. Half a story
24. 19th century advance
27. Main et al.: Abbr.
28. Allay
29. Hospital doctor
30. Canapé spread
31. Christian symbol
33. Skill: Lat.
34. Play the shrinking violet
36. Doorway: Abbr.
38. In ___ (fearing)
40. German road
43. Numerical prefix
45. ___ dinner (entertains)
47. Cartes
48. One ___ million
50. Quiet flower
52. Leading
55. Classman: Abbr.
56. ___ of armor
57. Leaves for, in a casual way
61. Adds juices
63. Highways: Abbr.
64. Get
65. Medical drains
67. Titanic
69. People of Brazil
70. Drink
71. Northwest people
72. Constellation
76. Stellar, sportswise
78. Addicted to cigars
81. Germane
82. Rubbernecked
83. Roman 1501
84. Russian secret police
85. Cookery style
86. Of a poison: Prefix
87. Trojan et al.
91. Elephant
92. French cup
93. One more: Abbr.
94. Habitat: Prefix
95. Summer mos.
97. Vietnamese holidays
98. " . . . room to ___ cat"
100. Warrior of Japan
102. Neighbor of Den.
103. Pursued
105. Throw an apostle overboard
107. College groups
110. Wool: Prefix
111. Carries on
113. Relative of Able and Baker
114. Charm
116. Sets of boxes
118. Unsophisticated
121. Stop!: Sp.
123. Spectral
124. "___ Macabre"
125. Crimean or Boer
126. Think ___
128. Simpson and Grange: Abbr.
130. One, in Naples
131. Roman 151
133. U.S. sculptor
135. Tittle
137. Hosp. vehicle
140. Lapidarists' concern, with "Will"
145. Reemploy
146. ___ all
147. The measure: It.
148. Footlike part
149. Man's name
150. Book of Apocrypha
151. Beauties

DOWN

1. Old wooden tubs
2. Body of soldiers
3. Debating sides: Abbr.
4. Morse sound
5. Jaundice: Prefix
6. "There must be ___"
7. Peggy and Pinky
8. Suitable
9. "I___ with my own eyes"
10. Ditch outlet, in a way
11. "It's ___ much for me"
12. Gaggles
13. Large vat
14. State V.I.P.
15. Still
16. Pianist Peter
17. Bklyn. campus
18. Girl's name
19. After midnight
23. Roller or fitter
25. Undiluted
26. John Wilkes Booth performance
32. West Coast inst.
33. Mame's corsets
35. Prison breaks
37. Dundee denial
39. Floors with sunset views
40. Youth org.
41. Exclamations
42. Kind of figure
44. Milan opera wear
46. Do lacework
49. Pronoun
51. Calif. campus
53. Touches on
54. Small quantity
58. Whether going ___
59. Uncoerced
60. N. C. Cape
62. Indonesian island
66. Steady customer's bar order
67. Attacks
68. Excessive
69. In style
73. Wall St. house
74. Sublease
75. Yankees: Abbr.
77. Freshens
79. Small bird
80. Moldings: Abbr.
85. Gem wts.
87. Bantu language
88. Hitler aide
89. One ___
90. Italian arrest
96. Embellishes
99. Noun suffix
101. ___ tree
102. Falcons, Eagles et al.
103. Wins big
104. Descriptive of a lone ram
106. Jennet
108. Across: Abbr.
109. Pen
112. F.D.R. agency
115. Mundane
116. Indiana campus
117. Dry-plaster painting
119. Added items of decor
120. Judge Crater's last words
122. Norse Red
125. More discerning
127. Girl's name
129. French chemist
132. Jacob's son
134. Fraternal org.
136. Sooner
137. Aleutian island
138. Blackbird
139. Rels.
141. These: Fr.
142. Lady of Spain
143. G.I. wear
144. Ship-shaped clock

Hidden Blemishes

by Arthur Bennett

ACROSS

1. Fine violins
7. Type designs
12. Restrictions
18. Endurance
19. Originated
20. Flatbush and others
22. Certain fighters
24. Dessert
25. U.S. inventor
26. Merle
27. Guided and others
29. Harem room
30. Peer Gynt's mother
31. Corrida sounds
32. Israeli port
33. Southwest wind
34. Decades
36. Top banana
37. All: Lat.
38. Have ___
39. Disabled
41. Golf veteran
42. Like an ox
43. Secret doctrines
46. Thing done
47. France: Prefix
48. ___ - skelter
49. Canoes of Malaysia: Var.
50. Acrid-tasting
53. Zodiac sign
54. Milton
55. Devoured
56. Direction
57. Geological stage
58. Singer born in N.Y.
60. Detective of fiction
61. Channel
62. Atropos et al.
63. Neglects
64. Casino money
65. Man against the ___
67. Campus groups
68. Broadway play of 1969-70
69. Tall and lean
70. ___ of humor

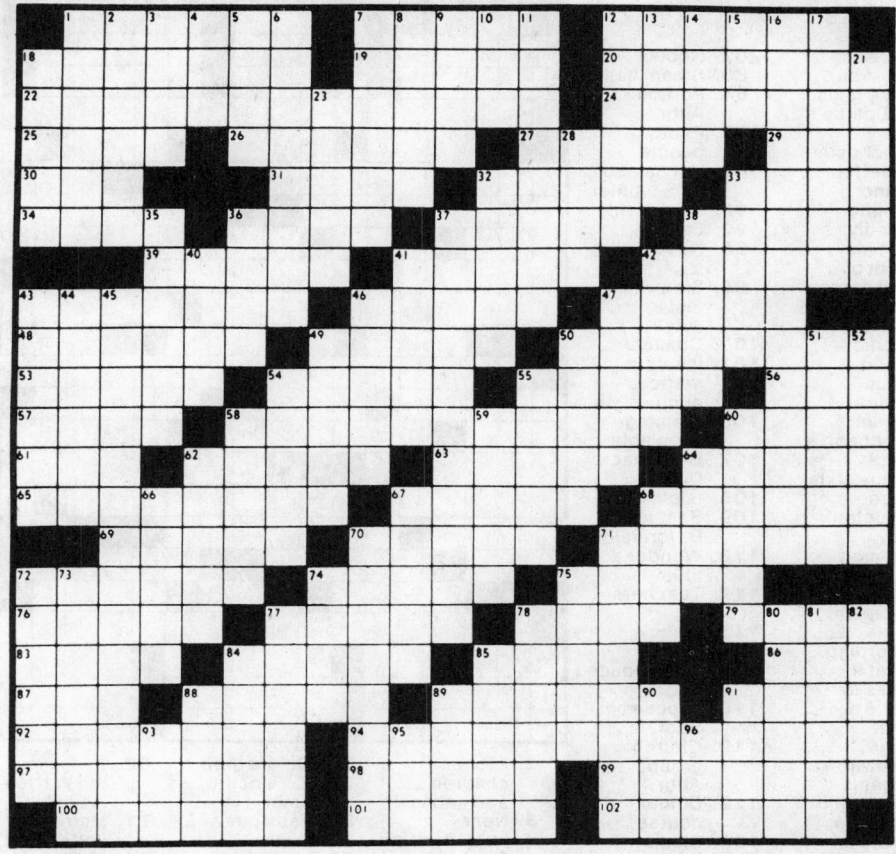

71. Exposed to risk
72. Certain animal
74. Salt trees
75. Spanish girls
76. Unkempt
77. Word with case or well
78. Partner of snick
79. Hillock, in England
83. Hurries
84. Hammer parts
85. Suffix for rheo or thermo
86. "___ a drop to drink"
87. East, in Bonn
88. Circulated
89. Shoe
91. Vehicle
92. Easily dominated
94. Babe

97. Ionosphere layer
98. Cancel
99. Meanness
100. Real ___
101. Bother
102. Horses

DOWN

1. Military command
2. Actor Karl
3. Sums: Abbr.
4. Ascot
5. Japanese box
6. Surgeon, to a gangster
7. More comely
8. Old Greek city
9. German botanist
10. Superlative ending
11. Verse forms
12. Ivory palms

13. Ward off
14. Power units
15. Fuegian
16. Way to make a mountain
17. Beer mugs
18. Churchill word
21. Peevish
23. Fished
28. Fetid
32. Big birds
33. Strong as
35. Early schoolroom needs
36. Persian name
37. Like a good pitch
38. Part of Poe's name
40. Beverages
41. Staircase, in Rome
42. Delicacies
43. Ballpark cry
44. Antenna

45. Certain insects
46. Molding edge
47. Wooden shoes
49. Marquette et al.
50. Fountain drinks
51. Blackbirds' place
52. Perfumed
54. Balmy
55. Choice group
58. Tropical fruit
59. Collect
60. Messiah
62. Boggy
64. Priest: Sp.
66. "Downstairs" people
67. Cat genus
68. Rozelle
70. Keep one's cards

71. Lays claim to
72. Stranded
73. Kind of time
74. To ___
75. Chaotic
77. Halcyon
78. Fixed
80. New
81. Drives
82. Kind of vote
84. Automatic
85. Alone
88. O. T. name
89. Moth
90. Indian peasant
91. Heavenly being: Fr.
93. Life ins. man
95. Scottish one
96. Teens

Turkey Talk

by Frances Hansen

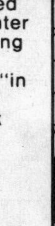

ACROSS

1. Soft shoe
4. Got: Abbr.
8. False gods
13. Dr. Dolittle's pig
19. Winchester
21. Cheerful sound
22. Smiling broadly
23. ___ time
24. Perth of New Jersey
25. Drag strip for chariots
26. Pacific island group
27. It's tutu divine
28. Pyncheon's pride, punny style
32. Deed
33. Reluctant: Var.
34. Ms. men
35. Fr. girl
36. Jabberwocky
40. Recipient
42. "This ___ recording"
45. What it takes to make a wink
46. Runs lukewarm
49. Organic compound
50. Govt. air agency
51. Armada: Abbr.
52. Wall hanging
56. Number one
58. "Waitin' on ___"
60. Map features
61. Gaelic
62. Without exception
63. Police-deploying tactic
67. Sticky stuff
68. Arctic explorer
70. "___ About the Boy"
72. Old card game
73. TV late show
75. Holmes's words for a tea party
81. Wedge-shaped: Prefix
82. Nootka
83. Steam bath
84. Portion: Abbr.
85. Panay people
86. Hat named for a painter
90. Kind of ring
92. Eager
96. No room "in ___"
98. Sidewalk test in July?
100. Comical
101. Ibsen matron, punny style
105. Framing-shop abbr.
107. Blue-black: Dialect
108. Islets
109. Samuel F. B., formally
110. Wander a little
112. Teachers' org.
113. Idaho capital
114. "...produced a ___"
118. Impose on: Scot.
119. Church group: Abbr.
122. Dinner course
123. Siouan
124. Warning in a Riley poem
131. Garden shrub
132. Kind of yell
133. Small case
134. Surprised exclamations
135. Consign to perdition
136. Sound of a knight's approach
137. Yo-ho-ho drinks
138. Old musical symbol
139. Kind of prunes
140. Nincompoops
141. Small baracuda
142. Carriers: Abbr.

DOWN

1. Copy: Prefix
2. "To tell children ___ and goblins"
3. Near
4. "___ I had the wings..."
5. Had it out
6. Eat high off ___
7. Risk
8. Ignoble
9. Century plant
10. Kind of forces
11. Daniel's arena
12. Catch
13. Ate dessert, in a way
14. Helpless
15. Starr of the West
16. Burst of laughter
17. Shoshoneans
18. Blink the eyes
19. Bowl sound
20. Order to a platoon
29. "___ me, pretty maiden..."
30. Before 'nuff
31. ___ vincit amor
36. Faux pas
37. Walk ___
38. Likewise, I'm sure
39. Ukraine city
41. Choose
42. Entire: Prefix
43. Classify
44. Girl's name
47. Coaster
48. Row
49. Letter
52. Having buds
53. "___ of God, I come!"
54. Hut of Guiana
55. Dinner course
57. Suit material
59. ___ Ashbury
62. Wire: Abbr.
64. "Words have ___ life than deeds"
65. Japanese game
66. S. F. hill
69. "...go to the Warres in ___"
71. Metric units: Abbr.
74. Moth
75. Tyrone or Arlo
76. Town in Spain
77. Gobble
78. Artist's need
79. Lead
80. W. W. II craft
81. Lion trainer
87. "And more ___ more"
88. Get an effort
89. City: Lat.
91. Urge
93. "Don't ___ dinner!"
94. Kukla's friend
95. Language: Prefix
97. Monogram for Jesus
99. "___ your pardon"
100. Loss of rank
102. Letter-shaped bar
103. Morning hrs.
104. Third Reich name
106. Gog's partner
110. Preen again
111. "I hate to be ___"
113. Puccini's "La ___"
115. Columbus campus
116. Antisocial ones
117. Fracas
118. Kind of boss
120. Rhyme schemes
121. Fully: Lat.
124. In ___ (vexed)
125. Pheasant group
126. Killer whale
127. B.P.O.E.
128. Itemize
129. Elec. units
130. Employ
131. Science degrees

93 Office Doings

by Gladys V. Miller

ACROSS

1. Open house
7. Battery terminal
12. Singer Clark
18. Alcohol
19. Defiant one
20. Desk items
22. Leroy Anderson work
24. Clerical cap
25. Ear part
26. Plasters over
27. Sky body
29. Kind of space
30. "___ Old Spanish Garden"
31. Awkward
32. Exams
34. Liven, with "up"
35. Instance: Fr.
36. John and Mark: Abbr.
37. Falling-out
39. Miserly
41. Union Pacific et al.
42. Parents' need, at times
44. Vitality
46. Pry
48. Tennis placements
50. Roof décor
52. Arena V.I.P.
55. Tammany man
59. Light color
60. "Blossom in purple ___"
61. Vapor
62. African village
63. River features
65. "How stupid ___!"
66. Letterhead abbr.
67. Suffix for acids
69. Vivid display
70. Lamb, old style
71. Standard
73. Gillette and Louise
75. Appraisals: Abbr.
77. Galatea's lover
78. Takes a rifle position
80. Depression initials
81. Galápagos sight
83. Bouts
84. Lose one's bankroll
86. Carry on
87. Flower
89. New star
90. Truman and Myerson
94. Kind of stool
96. Action
98. Verne hero
100. Air group: Abbr.
101. Jungfrau
102. Writer Seton
104. Removes dross
106. Church man
108. ___ breve
109. Zodiac sign
111. Where: Lat.
112. Entrance
113. Out of bed
114. Swizzle stick
116. Third Reich et al.
119. Muster
120. Nursemaids
121. "It makes ___ to me"
122. Voters
123. Chair piece
124. Foot in the door

DOWN

1. Acropolis city, to Greeks
2. Omega
3. Throw one's ___ the ring
4. Cameo stone
5. Mass of hair
6. Chooses
7. Unstable
8. Cosmetic implement
9. Fragments
10. Aberdeen's river
11. Baseball statistic
12. Small stones
13. Silkworm
14. Edible root
15. Finish
16. Pat
17. Highway
18. Principles
21. Shirts, in Scotland
23. Chinese dynasty
28. L.A. player
31. Broadcasts
32. Policeman
33. Anna and Clara
36. Faction
38. Inspired
40. Between A.M. and P.M.
43. Certain master
45. First
47. Church calendar
49. Attack
50. Builder's afterthought
51. Covered with clay
53. Forward
54. Danish port
55. Name in 1950 robbery
56. Greek nymph
57. African raptor
58. London borough
64. Flower oil
68. Copies
72. Baseball team
73. Resources
74. "___ qui peut"
76. ___ Mater
77. Greek god
79. Movie studios
82. Eye part
85. Eggar
88. Freshens up a perm
91. Cracker
92. Certain shape
93. Meager
94. Life raft
95. Grieg dancer
97. Alehouse
99. Russian province
100. Zero
103. Pianist Claudio
105. Tycoon
107. What to do with your boots
108. Tribe of Israel
110. Chemical group
112. Adjective suffix
113. Aide: Abbr.
115. Consume
117. Opposite of exp.
118. Swoboda or Nessen

Keeping House

by Christine Valence

ACROSS

1. Beach sight
7. British ___
12. Little terror
16. Heretofore, old style
20. Did a July 4 chore
21. Sharp-pointed
22. Greek letter
23. Slangy denial
24. Seeing eye of a sort
26. Access for Hans Brinker
28. Ox of Tibet
29. Streamlet
30. Russian city
32. So-long!
33. Weekday: Abbr.
34. Fleer
36. Certain eggs
37. River to the Elbe
39. Partner of groans
41. Somerset spa
43. Track officials
45. Certain athletes
46. Mural artist
47. Expect
49. Now: Lat.
50. Curtain material
51. Divide
54. Poured
56. Warm up
58. Certain transoms
60. Unpredict-able
62. Jumble
64. O'Casey
65. Diminutive suffixes
66. ___ Moines
67. Laugh
69. Thus: Lat.
70. Drop in for
72. Printer's mark
73. ___ of Cremona
75. Planned
77. Yokels
78. Kind of farm
80. Slides for some children
82. Organ stops
83. Decorative plants
84. Small room
85. Amen
87. Basics
88. Certain bags
89. Louis or Philip
91. Young animal
92. Reign, in India
95. Field sound
96. Marquis de
97. Godhead
100. Copious
102. Third degree, in a way
105. Because
107. Forge apparatus
108. Bases of bone tissue: Var.
109. "___ your pardon"
111. Sale condition
113. Relative of groovy
114. Spot
115. Closely-knit group
116. Poplars
118. Sisters
119. Indisputable things
121. Dartmoor, for example
122. Line, as a roof
123. English city
125. High in pitch
126. Certain shape
128. Ascend
130. Holm oak
131. Boxing units: Abbr.
134. Embryo house
137. House area
140. Forsaken
141. Mixture
142. Huntress and namesakes
143. Small cavity
144. Views
145. Cried
146. Appetizing
147. Grew more interested

DOWN

1. Imitate
2. Opera excerpt
3. Type of intrigue
4. Lawyer: Abbr.
5. Sinew: Prefix
6. Without aim
7. Here: Fr.
8. Many-windowed places
9. Luck and others
10. Jackets
11. Makes clothes
12. One club or one spade
13. Ways
14. Perfume
15. Social grace
16. Pass-catcher
17. Attic, so to speak
18. Golf club
19. Sea swallows
21. Hole puncher
25. Impish
27. Piper's milieu
31. Composer Jerome
35. Tableware
36. Extend
38. Make a boo-boo
40. Not imit.
41. Laid open
42. In the know
44. River of central Europe
45. Sneaky ___
46. Chair part
48. Ties up
50. It's out for welcome guests
51. Golfing name
52. Voices
53. Sibilant sounds
55. Personal book
57. Bring out
59. ___ rose
61. Tea
63. Singular
68. Dispute settler
71. Middles: Abbr.
72. Somewhat, with "of"
73. Spirits
74. Great ___
76. Dined in a café
77. Money deliverers
78. Prohibits
79. Building style
81. Love
82. Courage
83. North Dakota city
84. Fogies
86. Jazz form
88. Tannish
90. Resident
92. Place to play
93. Colorado resort
94. Mocks
96. Errs
98. Nothing: Fr.
99. Picture holder
101. Recovered
103. Word of caution
104. Eur. measure
106. Sesame
110. Fragrance
112. ___ bill of goods
115. Mint variety
116. Wanderer of fiction
117. Alternate
119. Tall story
120. Brass or steel
121. Trickery
122. Roman ___
124. Newspaper edition
127. Bird known for straight flying
129. Letter-signing servant: Abbr.
130. Possibilities
132. Pass out
133. Timetable, for short
135. Being, in abstract
136. Add up
138. Arthurian knight
139. Father of Abner

95 Fitting Phrases

by Bert Beaman

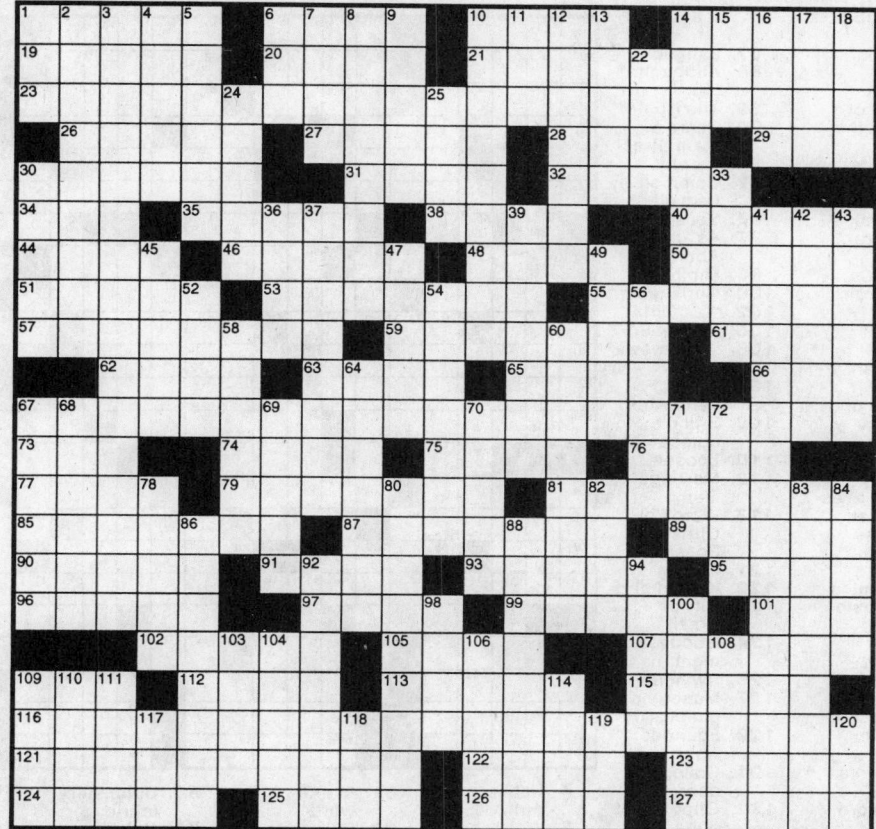

ACROSS

1. Peachy
6. ___ California
10. Wine barrel
14. Kind of comedy
19. Malaga raisin
20. Norse name
21. On the blink
23. Prepare to shave
26. Insurance problems
27. Pass off
28. Author's concern
29. Relative of Mme.
30. Opposed to
31. Calpurnia, for one
32. Paris areas
34. Publisher's abbr.
35. Some racers
38. Brood of young birds
40. Attacked
44. Beery
46. Himalayan denizens
48. Electrical units
50. Before febrero
51. Great Horde division
53. Depreciate
55. Bills
57. Glasses
59. French pince-nez
61. Drills
62. Ineffectual
63. Branches
65. Come-on
66. Wheel spoke: Fr.
67. Designate in a way
73. Suffix for drunk or cow
74. Table extender
75. Kind of case
76. Roman emperor
77. Strains: Scot.
79. Intertwines
81. Eradicated
85. Accord
87. Trouble
89. ___ administravit
90. Road to Alaska
91. Cake ingredient
93. Show rudeness
95. Snorri Sturluson creation
96. Some looks
97. Old recompense
99. Wives, informally
101. Roll of hair
102. Elapsed
105. Eggs, in Bonn
107. Cape Vert natives
109. African charm
112. Mine: Fr.
113. ___ in the right direction
115. Stone pillar
116. Done with
121. Guiding principle
122. Pinza
123. Composition
124. Riding schools: Abbr.
125. River to North Sea
126. Music sign
127. More protected

DOWN

1. Ship departure: Abbr.
2. Got rid of
3. Egg on the chin
4. Public figures
5. Large hurdy-gurdy
6. Cattle genus
7. Hebrew letter
8. Kind of window
9. Fasten
10. Scheming one
11. Same: Prefix
12. Reliable pitcher
13. Down-under attraction
14. Certain samples
15. Heavy-duty wire: Abbr.
16. Stadium sounds
17. Party equipment
18. Soup ingredient
22. Sherry mold
24. School assignment
25. "The frost ___ the . . ."
30. Hawks
33. ___ Rosa
36. Phone part: Abbr.
37. Light
39. Swings
41. Gardener's faith in his carrots
42. Debtor's situation
43. ___ the towel
45. Biblical enemy of Jews
47. Ragout of game
49. Seed: Prefix
52. Gibe
54. Significant
56. ___ the road
58. Horn
60. Mother, for one
64. Cordial
67. French mathematician
68. A.L. player
69. Boys'-book writer
70. Deeds
71. Kind of light
72. Guitar opening
78. Boa
80. Party-going dandy
82. Breath: Prefix
83. Patience
84. College officials
86. Subjugates
88. Release, as hoarded funds
92. Kind of bill
94. ___ - Japanese War
98. Region: Abbr.
100. Arrangements
103. Indication
104. Stew
106. Clear sky
108. Networks
109. Silly
110. Farm ___
111. Spanish pot
114. Greek letters
117. ___ man out
118. Caucho tree
119. In demand
120. Neighbor of Den.

Christmas Thoughts

by Anne Fox

ACROSS

1. Superior monk
6. Whack
10. Native of a city on the Arno
15. ___ juste
20. Midlothian port
21. First name in opera lore
22. ___ nous
23. Of starch
24. Tops of birds' heads
25. Siberian river
26. Genus of mites
28. That is ___
29. Govt. agency
30. Snake eyes
32. Informal address
34. Custom
35. Jackets
36. ___ vomica
37. Conclusion
40. Indian soldier
42. French poodle
44. Words from an old English carol
50. California fort
51. First word of "Marseillaise"
52. Common verbal contraction
53. Chemical prefix
54. Dance step
56. Fruit
57. Coarse wool
59. Tizzy
61. Take up
63. Preposition
65. Waylay
68. Rectory
69. Needle's partner
70. Cut off
72. Halloween vehicle
73. Biblical brother
75. August occurrence
77. Henchman
78. ___ rasae
82. Words from St. Matthew
85. Beach grass
86. With a crest.
87. Languor
88. Although: Lat.
89. The Hunter
90. Rome's Main Street
91. Trophy
92. Common field plant
95. Season
97. As above: Abbr.
98. Minimum
100. Christie
102. "___ Girls"
103. Those: Sp.
105. "So part we ___"
107. Type of verb: Abbr.
108. Shine's companion
110. Loosen
112. Marriage: Ger.
113. Words by Christina Rossetti
121. Follow
122. Kind of bird
123. City of Brazil
124. Goddess of night
125. Swindle
127. Masefield girl et al.
129. Founded: Abbr.
131. College degree
132. Opposite of nope
133. "___ of One's Own"
134. Song of gladness
136. Christiania
139. Mexican grass
141. Lady of sonnets
142. Mole
143. Exclamation of some heat
144. Type of acid
145. Handles: Fr.
146. ___ René Lesage
147. Man bites dog
148. Demand

DOWN

1. Italian mountain soldier
2. Lebanon's capital
3. Mississippi city
4. Native: Suffix
5. Words by Frederic W. Farrar
6. Have place
7. Resemble: Suffix
8. Flipper
9. Spume
10. Words by Thackeray
11. Business abbr.
12. ___ Bethlehem
13. Ravine
14. Gender: Abbr.
15. Words by Charles Wesley
16. Put on an act
17. Nursery-rhyme character
18. Buck heroine
19. Certain gifts
27. Religious groups
31. March word
33. Berkshire village
38. O.T. book
39. Convinced of
41. Times: Abbr.
43. Four inches
45. ___ brown
46. French pastry
47. Kids
48. Stolid ones
49. Olden time
54. Musical work
55. Novel of 1895
57. "Welcome ___"
58. Leatherstocking name: Var.
60. Estate in India
61. Genus of plant pest
62. Chemical compound
64. The hunted
66. Upholstery fabric
67. N.C. cape
71. Where the Acheron flows
72. Arctic bay
74. Thailand money
76. Warning
77. Mouse: Fr.
79. City of Peru
80. Black ___
81. Pharaohs' land
83. Type of cheese
84. Postal limbos: Abbr.
90. Conn. village
92. Spanker
93. ___ -Finnic
94. Causing wonder
96. Court word
97. Fuel
99. Hgt.
101. Japanese native
104. Weaver's reeds
106. Mosquito genus
109. Opera part
110. Middle East org.
111. Christmas ___
114. Again
115. Type of library
116. New Hampshire city
117. Jostles
118. African antelope
119. Purely intellectual
120. Look for
125. Offenses against law
126. Monitor lizard
128. B'way group
130. Go to ___
135. Finial
137. Pronoun
138. Wallace
140. Strain

Dress Circle

by Thomas Sheehan

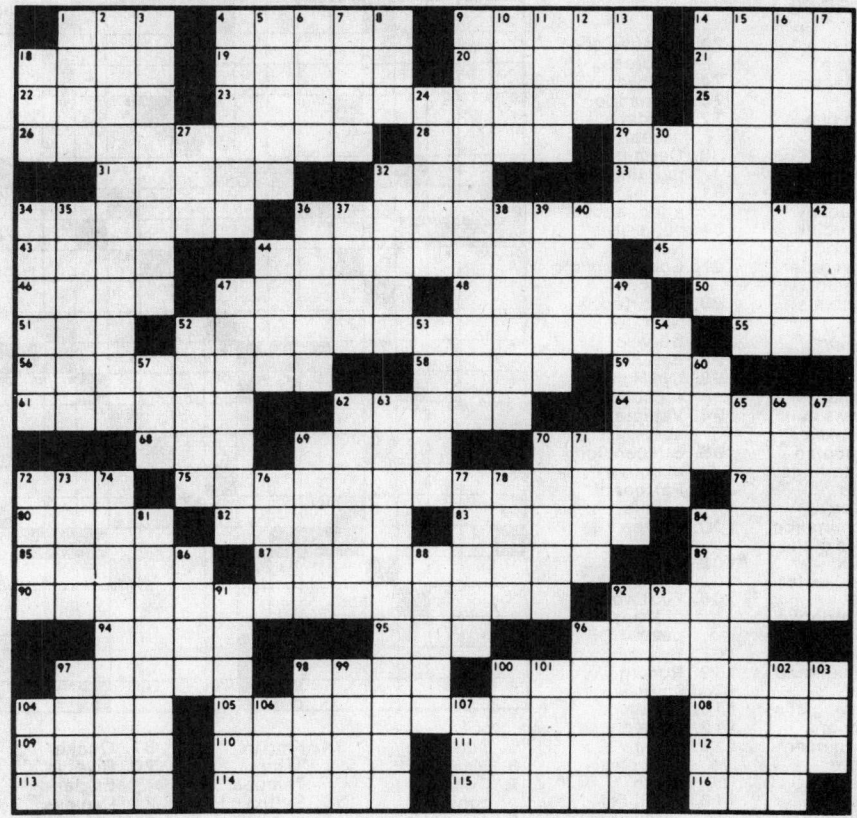

ACROSS

1. NKVD's predecessor
4. Affix
9. Wrap
14. Invasion craft
18. Victorian mouthwash
19. Cigarettes, at times
20. Impulses
21. Okla. Indian
22. Coffee containers
23. Reverses in a way
25. Asta's mistress
26. Underskirt
28. Blood: Prefix
29. Showing an emotion
31. America's Cup entry
32. Apiece
33. Brazilian plant
34. Pastry order
36. Screen fare
43. Zoological suffix
44. Bugaboo
45. Like some sheep
46. Actor Dullea
47. Song of joy
48. Chilean seaport
50. P. M.'s address
51. "___ Magic"
52. Gridiron seizure
55. Scene for bit players
56. NBC and CBS
58. Riverfront Stadium team
59. Snake charmer
61. Placed: Lat.
62. Chemical compound
64. Gushed
68. Kind of jet
69. Scottish slope
70. N. Y. street
72. Singing voice: Abbr.
75. Bar offerings
79. First-down yardage
80. Shipshape
82. Playwright Jones
83. Name in evangelism

84. Coin
85. Ethan or Fred
87. Words to a sentry
89. Bedouin
90. Cowards
92. Charles ___ Stengel
94. Rumanian coins
95. Pioneered
96. Opposite of a busy signal?
97. "___ Go Gentle into . . ."
98. S.A. monkey
100. Slows down
104. Kind of dancer
105. Capt. Corcoran's command
108. Melville romance
109. Arrow poison
110. Degrade
111. Spoken for
112. House plant
113. Look a ___
114. Roman spirits
115. Occur
116. Religious title

DOWN

1. Tennessee's Albert
2. Milquetoasts
3. Resident of Buffalo, e.g.
4. Lithographer's liquid
5. ___ water (hard put)
6. Literary pseudonym
7. Gust, in Scotland
8. Baseball great
9. Deceitfully agreeable
10. Gum or rubber
11. Irish writing
12. Celtic Neptune
13. Output of 6 Down
14. Silver
15. Holder of many records
16. Conservative one
17. Great amount
18. Higher: Abbr.
24. Luster
27. Here: Fr.
30. Slangy denials
32. Full: Prefix
34. Atoll
35. Late-show time on TV
36. Ventures upon
37. French political unit
38. Bitter words
39. Norse hero and others
40. Kings, queens, etc.
41. Small combo
42. Uppity one
44. Kind of football field
47. Examination
49. Herring
52. Dorsal
53. Indians
54. Chance's partner
57. Barrister's accessory
60. Old times
62. "Will and intellect ___ and the same . . ."
63. Certain bonds
65. Grandma Moses, for one
66. Nevertheless
67. Make a (impress)
69. Justice White
70. Math term
71. Dickens's Uriah
72. Take up quarters
73. Heraldic bearing
74. Glorified foxholes
76. Joins a union
77. Bundled
78. Whale-oil cask
81. Scarlett's in-law and others
84. Enumerates
86. Taboo, new style
88. Coil of yarn
91. Nevertheless
92. Adequate
93. Class
96. Leverets
97. Kierkegaard
98. Godunov
99. ___ dixit
100. Tunisian port
101. Norse god
102. ___ song (cheaply)
103. Dahomey native
104. Cratchit
106. Executive's degree
107. Used up

Button Up

by Herbert Ettenson

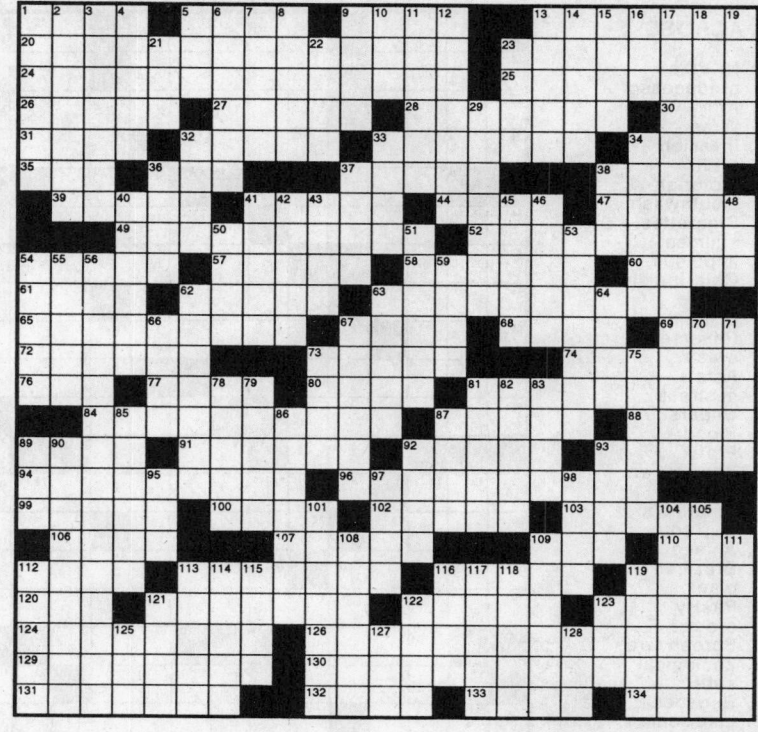

ACROSS

1. Part of a refrain
5. Tobacco kiln
9. Part of a Taiwan name
13. Roadhouse of sorts
20. Salad ingredient
23. Broiled-meat order
24. Gossip
25. Lincoln's Ann
26. Eastern state: Abbr.
27. Revoke, as a legacy
28. Offers bait
30. Asian ox
31. Iroquoian
32. Underlings: Abbr.
33. Rises to prominence
34. Wide of the mark
35. Camillo, for one
36. Superlative suffix
37. Macaw
38. Muhammad et al.
39. Nidologist's concern
41. Town near Rome
44. Boating hazard
47. He wrote "Devotions"
49. Oldtime movie actor
52. English historian
54. What Polonius hid behind
57. Hyalite and harlequin
58. "___ through the coming day!"
60. Uses thread
61. Nasty look
62. Feature
63. Civil War battle scene
65. Sandwiched
67. Colt or filly
68. In the direction of movement
69. Home-buyer's burden: Abbr.
72. Asian partridge
73. Relative of 1 Across
74. Be loyal
76. Gumshoe
77. Feudal vassal
80. Certain paintings
81. Facial annoyances
84. "Like-it-is" talk
87. Speleologist's concern
88. Imparted
89. Man ___
91. Survive
92. Eateries
93. Old Roman receptacles
94. Vehicle of a sort
96. Suspension of activity
99. Partner of snicks
100. "When I was ___"
102. Superb
103. Digs
106. First word of Xmas poem
107. Belief
109. Roman spirit
110. Hagen
112. Linden
113. "...no ___ birth and death"
116. "...bit of ___ the best of us"
119. Perfume: Var.
120. Sea bird
121. Dogcart
122. ___ boredom
123. Other: Fr.
124. Well-thought of
126. Poet
129. Sharp-tongued critics
130. President
131. Maple and Walnut
132. Fleuret
133. Affectations
134. Oregon bay

DOWN

1. Had a speech problem
2. River of Woe
3. Of jungle royalty
4. Between a rag and a hank
5. Scrap
6. Dismayed
7. Cutter and pung
8. Jewish month
9. Ancestral line
10. Cry's partner
11. Skin condition
12. Professional mourners
13. Respite
14. Observances
15. "___ well"
16. Adjectival ending
17. Certain fan
18. He wrote "Red Star Over China"
19. Olid
21. Japanese outcast
22. Word with chic or bien
23. Young, lively one
29. Enraptured
32. Holly of southern U.S.
33. Of a time
34. King in "The Tempest"
36. Suffixes for numbers
37. Bothers
38. Fruit drink
40. Gives the willies to
41. Wine pitchers
42. Beau
43. Joust
45. Brightest star
46. Nasser
48. Navy officer: Abbr.
50. Body of knowledge
51. Toasts
53. Checks for errors
54. Canting
55. Adoree of the silents
56. Du Maurier heroine
59. She: It.
62. Entice by music
63. Like anthracite
64. River bottoms
66. Snitch
67. Quaker
70. River in England
71. Exploits
73. "The Bridges at ___-Ri"
75. "___ - than-thou
78. City on the Mohawk
79. Claude ___ famous highwayman
81. Cloth of India
82. Public
83. ___ majesty
85. Harrowing experience
86. Gave a new appraisal
87. May or Horn
89. Gives approval to
90. Maxwell Anderson play
92. Sure thing, to a Britisher
93. Autocrat
95. Edition: Abbr.
97. River to the Elbe
98. Israeli name
101. French kind of tour
104. "Theirs ___ and die"
105. "The ___ down to rise upon ..."
108. Nix
109. ___ death
111. Mountain ridges
112. Youngsters
113. Long-tailed sky body
114. Customers
115. Energy units
116. Cheap cigarette of India
117. Sicilian mount
118. Pipe-organ stops
119. Like gold
121. Printing term
122. ___ Dag, Turkish mountain
123. Union group: Abbr.
125. Dutch commune
127. Wheat: Fr.
128. Aurora

Calling All Men

by Betty Leary

ACROSS

1. Le Mans sight
6. Traveled in a way
12. Norwegian saint
16. Convict's goal
17. Appropriated
19. Adriatic wind
20. Summer boon to parents
21. Fond of music
23. Kick ___
24. Card game
26. Late afternoon, usually
27. Jewish month: Var.
29. Umps' companions
30. False gods
32. Team members: Abbr.
33. Ranger's status
34. Letter
35. Whipper-snapper
39. Silver
41. Joins
43. Part of Q.E.D.
44. Sea call
45. Teeth
47. Strong emotion
49. Chinese guild
50. Old car
51. Exudes
52. Recondite
57. Eight: Ger.
58. Words of annoyance
61. Upward: Prefix
62. Silk from France
63. Other: Prefix
64. Egyptian heaven: Var.
65. Recipe abbr.
66. Cosmic cycle
67. Pink
71. News item
72. Outpourings
74. "There was ___ woman..."
75. One of an evil seven
76. Ms. people
77. Pointed instrument
79. Alarm clock for some
81. Add up
84. A thou
85. Emotion
86. Censures
88. Conform
90. Gardner
93. Pressure units: Abbr.
94. ___ Claire
96. Vehicles
97. Sibs: Abbr.
98. Nonsense!
99. Dog
103. Roman money
104. Soil
105. Imitate a jumping jack
108. Mosaic piece
110. Wife of Cuchullainn
111. Tardy
112. Fur
113. Letters for a hostess
114. Does a framer's job
115. Staggers

DOWN

1. Words for Pollyanna
2. Son of Zeus
3. Fuel
4. Tree
5. Succeeds
6. House part
7. Item for a tray
8. Night, in Paris
9. Heraldic fillet
10. Hebrew measure
11. At ___ door
12. Music maker
13. Chaney
14. Home of the Hopi
15. Garment parts
16. Leaves
18. Fragment
20. Challenge
22. Science degree
25. Trees
28. Parts of yards
30. Subside
31. Familiar symptom
33. "C'est ___"
35. Bad luck
36. Court decree
37. Do a class chore
38. W.W.II area
40. Terre ___
42. Blank: Ger.
45. Ends
46. ___ of ice cream
47. Go ___ (become seedy)
48. Iterated
49. Bunk
51. More ___
53. Part of a casa
54. Crowded quarters
55. Gunther title word
56. Eggbeater
58. Grovels
59. Cassini
60. Milton of the silents
65. Body part
67. Edge furtively
68. Duke of Hollywood
69. Entrance
70. Irish lakes
73. Lasts
75. Entrée order
78. Word with little and late
79. Old car style
80. Lord Boyd and family
81. Nicholas
82. Ale time
83. Drums
85. Widgeon
87. Percolate
88. English artist
89. Antelopes
91. Your: Fr.
92. Somali people
95. Urchin
97. Red Square name
99. Paint thinner: Abbr.
100. Move slowly
101. Cheese
102. Hurdy-gurdy
104. Girl's name
106. Girl's nickname
107. Soak
109. Before

100 Choose Your Weapons

by H. L. Risteen

ACROSS

1. Total: Abbr.
4. Remonstrances
7. Camelot notable
14. Well-known street and others
21. Beach sight
23. Clam's big brother
24. Dixie river
25. Behave stubbornly
27. Mideast land
28. Legal copy
29. Stage monarch
30. Italian philosopher
32. Normal: Abbr.
33. Water bird
34. ___ tables
36. Praying figure
37. Fare for Miss Muffet
38. Malaccan measures
41. Wallet items
42. Street urchins
44. Subjunctive and indicative
45. U.S. balloon pioneer
46. Calendar source
47. Bridled
48. Binge
49. Man's nickname
50. Wall St. purchase
51. Shetland natives
52. Demand
55. Rocks
57. Ship officer
58. Table wine
59. Odorless gas
60. Rare animals
61. Impudent
62. Bloodhound feature
63. McKuen
64. Darnay's friend
65. Like some excuses
66. Ferrer
67. Charges
69. Satire of 1894
72. Haberdashery items
73. Salutation
74. Yawn
75. Kind of biscuit
76. Fed. agency
77. Western team
79. Armadillo
80. Dour
81. Finally
84. Enlightens
86. Authors' concerns
87. Merchant of drama
88. Business deals
89. Did a job in Denver
90. Italian locale
91. Educ. group
92. Malay weapon
93. Villella, e.g.
94. Olympian
95. Periods
96. Marksmen's sport
98. Eel
99. Bloom
100. Scottish stipend
101. Excavations
102. Noted Italian
103. Vestment
104. Common abbr.
105. Brew
106. North Sea feeder
107. Book of N.T.
109. Eating place
114. Alaskan peak
116. Stabbed in a way
119. "The ___ Worker"
120. Recorded
121. Beginning
122. Musical groups
123. Beverage experts
124. Campus V.I.P.'s
125. Roman 151

DOWN

1. Church section
2. Channels
3. Pluck
4. Petitioners
5. Valhalla man
6. Las Vegas opening
7. Started, in poems
8. Poplars
9. Light beam
10. Sea growth
11. Net time of a football game
12. Mass. cape
13. Discovers
14. Arty gatherings
15. Decide upon
16. "Quién ___?"
17. Jidda garb
18. His living depends on net income
19. Was theatrical
20. Scotchmen
22. Foaming
26. Manifesto city
31. Sally or Ayn
35. Printery supply
36. Old card game
37. Bulky cloth
38. Winged
39. Heavy shoe
40. Fast-draw trio
41. Light shades
42. Wartime plenty
43. Zodiac sign
44. Shed feathers
46. Tiresome one
47. Ring of policemen
48. Make tight
50. Give way a little
51. ___ del Este
52. Railway employee
53. Beginning
54. Movie units
56. N.M. art colony
57. Sentence-analyser
58. Salty one
60. South American plains
61. Russian whips
64. Fabrics
67. Traveler
68. Escape
69. Marbles
70. Atomic expert
71. Summoned
72. Marsh: Prefix
76. "___ boy!"
78. Startles
80. Because
81. Loop in anatomy
82. Tuscany city
83. Banquet feature
85. Came to rest
86. Slight amount
87. Delicate
89. Short cape
90. Money in Madrid
93. Juan and Quixote
94. Dance
95. Performer's bonus
96. Bursts of activity
97. Highlander
98. Lost ___
99. Be reflective
100. European capital
102. Distributed
103. Dear: Fr.
104. Ardent
106. Meek ones
107. Tiny quantities
108. African weight
110. Flier's word for bombs
111. Wash. tribunal: Abbr.
112. Jib
113. Although: Lat.
115. Riga coin
117. Put ___ pedestal
118. Dental degree

101 INFLATION *Mel Rosen*

ACROSS

1. Medieval fabric
7. Earth pigment
12. Recede
15. Air-gun pellets
18. Chemical compounds
19. Papal cape
20. Gershwin
21. Exotic island
22. New name for old whip
24. Needlefish
26. Western capital
27. Apparitions
29. Convictions
30. Location
32. Words of denial
33. Jaunty
34. Make over
38. Snooped, with "about"
41. Comedian Mort
42. Curve
43. Love in Turin
45. Door sign
47. __ nibs
49. DiMaggio
52. Low-price place, updated
59. Caught, as a fish
60. Suckfish
61. Doolittle and others
62. Huntley
64. Not public: Abbr.
65. Boring tools
66. Low person
69. Social Security abbr.
70. High note
71. She, in Paris
73. French marshal
74. Ingrained
76. Festive
78. In a __ (put out)
79. Shore bird
80. Use hard-sell tactics
82. Hebrew month
87. Plays an oversize piano
91. Drink
92. River of Scotland
93. City of Yemen
94. Flash
95. Overdraft abbr.
98. Dormouse

101. Sonata movement
104. Swiss painter
105. Alaskan town
107. Volcano
108. Village, in Africa
110. Goose genus
111. San Clemente citizen
115. Dross
119. Diner's reading matter
121. Next step for fanciers of the occult
124. Sea-speed unit
125. Tree
126. Growing out
127. Equiangular figure
128. Eastern weight
129. Swindle
130. Kind of geometry
131. Abandon

DOWN

1. Neighbor of It.
2. Oriental nurse
3. Small sum
4. Matinee __
5. Heads, in Reims
6. Russian poet
7. Away, to a Scotsman
8. Crop
9. Broadway show
10. Fitzgerald
11. Pine products
12. Bliss, modern style
13. Dye pigment: Var.
14. Profession
15. Twelve, nowadays
16. Cheerless
17. Milksop
21. Waits
23. Defense pact
25. "__ down!"
28. Done __ turn
31. German donkey
34. Headland
35. Man's name
36. Part of an Eastern hymn
37. Medit. port
39. Put into action
40. Crummy joint
44. Pass-catcher
46. Metal molds
48. Furtive
50. "__ Ben Jonson!"
51. In disorder
53. Poured
54. Old letters
55. "Thin Man" wife
56. Dernier __
57. Pivot
58. Poke: Scot.
63. Slam bid, maybe
66. Rope
67. Chorus topic
68. __ your thoughts, new style
69. Soviet city
70. Otherwise
72. Tilt
75. Suffix for hill or bull
77. Sound of disgust
78. Musical sign
81. Fibber
83. Chang's companion
84. Defraud
85. Indigo
86. Filament: Suffix
88. With gravity
89. Kind of bag
90. Marie, e.g.
96. Target game
97. Minor league club
99. Hostelry
100. Bridge calls
102. Old verb
103. Flower
105. Pillages
106. Empty
109. Chaser of a sort
112. Strange: Prefix
113. Shape
114. Pacific grass
116. Old cars
117. Author of "Bus Stop"
118. Ancient lyre
120. Brain-wave record: Abbr.
122. Nickname
123. Door: Abbr.

102 WORDS IN PLACE *William Lutwiniak*

ACROSS

1. Eastern big wheel
5. Shut-eye
10. Boo-boo
15. Haul
19. Komsomolsk's river
20. Eccentric
21. "I want ___ . . ."
22. Mountain: Prefix
23. Clipper feature
25. Chaotic
27. Cockney idol
28. Person
29. Chemical compound
31. ___ Andreas
32. Means
34. Friend of Trajan and Tacitus
35. Bars
39. Accomplished
40. Footpaths, old style
41. Turnips and cabbages
42. Equity member
45. Cuckoopint, for one
46. Occult character
47. Army off.
48. Famed comedian
49. Go-between
52. Rough cloth
53. Native: Suffix
54. Pulpits
56. Ukase's cousin
57. Relative of Mauna Loa
58. Indurated
60. Today's youth
61. Study hard
62. Not a sideshow
68. Featureless
69. River areas
70. Keep
71. "___ Is Born"
73. Rustle
75. Thread
76. Neighbor of Ger.
77. Semiaquatic creature
78. Hockey area
80. ___ and now
81. Panay native
82. Oyster
84. Takes heed of
85. "Waiting for ___"
86. Companies
88. Greek city-state
89. The works
90. Employs
91. Property
92. Macule
96. Direction
97. ". . . ___ horse to . . ."
98. Hall: Ger.
99. Letter
100. Like the green traffic light
104. Unfathomable
107. Mil. acronym
108. Brilliant glass
109. Nonprofessionals
110. Fodder
111. Pond
112. Playing cards
113. Colorado park
114. Blackthorn

DOWN

1. Merited
2. Con ___
3. Knight's shirt
4. Neighbor of Uru.
5. Went it alone
6. Oners
7. Common Latin abbr.
8. Sea bird
9. Like a flower part
10. Some Americans
11. Suffering
12. Speak, with "up"
13. Elders: Abbr.
14. Blissful
15. Peerage members
16. Timetable word: Abbr.
17. Race an engine
18. Nursery item
24. Out of bed
26. Cup: Fr.
30. Place for Sunday drivers
33. Reputation
34. Exerts pressure
35. Main impact
36. Virtuous
37. Great expanse
38. African cattle
40. Electron tube
41. Bric-a- ___
42. Leaning
43. Net
44. Political group
45. Sphere of action
50. Norse epics
51. Weather word
52. Alliance
54. Erect
55. Blanc, for one
57. ___ Triomphe
59. Fanfare
60. Not quite wet
61. Poker move
63. Ballgame delayer
64. Dense areas
65. Flowers
66. Colorado county
67. Vocal group
71. Within ___ of
72. Writer Ernest Thompson ___
73. Thumbs through
74. Dampens
75. Within the law
79. Trustworthy
80. Evergreen oak
82. Musical sign
83. Appropriate
85. Flicker
87. Saddle part
88. Yaks
89. Bronze and pewter
91. Cantankerous
92. Mesa's cousin
93. Consummate
94. Sixth: It.
95. German state
97. Mislay
98. Have ___ (begin)
100. Loud sound
101. Use credit
102. High rock
103. Seagoing: Abbr.
105. Western org.
106. Spanish article

103 SOLVING MATERIAL   *Martha DeWitt*

ACROSS

1. Traffic light
6. Lieu
11. Competitor
16. By-product
21. Sight from Apollo craft
22. Do the honors at dinner
23. Hovel or house
24. Rope
25. Things within a stone's throw
27. Lucky girls
29. City on Danube
30. Piquant
31. Motors
33. Dip again
34. Junkyard, for one
36. Part of Troy's trouble
37. Kind of party
39. __ van Delft
40. Hand holder
41. Wise men
42. Hash
44. Thicket
47. Entertainments
49. Surgical instrument
53. Asian nurse
54. Yields
55. Ends' associate
56. Gossip
57. Glove-compartment item
58. Spices
59. Run
60. Swiss river
61. Bull or Olsen
62. Class of mollusks
64. Nonconformists
66. Way to cook tough meat
67. More composed
68. Euterpe
69. Home of some Alaskans
70. Asian goats
71. Rend
73. Type of TV tube
75. Julia of cookery
77. West Asian
78. Minnelli
79. Card game
82. Harridans
83. Thousand-legger
85. Transitory
86. Mike's look-alike
87. Auctioneer's last word
88. Macadamias
89. Small bays
90. Furrow
91. On the brink
93. Air outlet
94. Rock blend
95. Busy city
96. Ascetic
97. Ignored
99. Musical pieces
100. Lacking sunlight
102. Cleaves
103. Medieval tale
104. Collard's family
107. Measure
108. Parisian parents
109. Vestige
113. One with endurance
115. Fishing boot
116. Metropolitan thrush
117. Anaconda
118. Hardwear
121. Vulnerable ones
124. Old town in Asia Minor
125. Peers
126. Indian's castle
127. Force out
128. Appears
129. Schedule
130. Ship area
131. Late Chicago mayor

DOWN

1. Debate
2. Girl's nickname
3. Censure
4. Loop sights
5. Give back
6. Twenty
7. Kind of ship
8. Hesitant sounds
9. Means
10. One who wants
11. Red, white and black
12. Nile creature
13. German prefix
14. Say more
15. Regard, in a way
16. Soviet city
17. Light-bulb part
18. __ -ral
19. "__ told by an idiot"
20. Beam
26. Injure
28. Career military men
32. Movie fade-out
35. Window part
36. Surfaces
37. Pride, envy, etc.
38. April 15 items: Abbr.
41. Was partial
42. Update
43. Have it made
44. Vacation places
45. Peruvian volcano
46. Opposites of wolves in sheeps' clothing
47. Working on interiors
48. French brainstorm
50. Hallway fixture
51. Fisherman
52. Tartan trousers
54. Cavort
56. Hides
58. Unit
59. Firmly fixed
60. High point
63. Cable spools
64. Hazy condition
65. Scottish island
66. E. I. heartwood
68. Crumbly earth
70. Shades
72. Whine
73. Joshes
74. Desert animal
75. Onion's relative
76. Cods' relatives
78. Well-educated
80. Ridicule
81. Singers
83. Banker
84. Calembours
85. Broods
87. Lollobrigida
89. Spelunkers' milieu
92. Something to be done
93. Amphora
94. Spread
95. Rack's companion
97. Variety of peeve
98. Oversees
99. Marred
101. Bifocals, e.g.
103. Son of Jacob
104. N. Z. birds
105. Got up
106. Lax
108. Old hat
109. Age
110. Seething
111. Time-being
112. Savory
114. Navy facility
115. Shoe part
116. Textile worker
119. Holbrook
120. Mouths
122. Tarzan's foster parent
123. Zsa Zsa's sister

104 VALENTINES *Dan Girardi*

ACROSS

1. Bible book: Abbr.
4. Swedish island
8. Coxa
11. Angel or short
15. Whatever
16. "Lohengrin" bird
17. Sleeve card
18. Suppose
20. Memphis deity
21. Almost: Prefix
22. Corded cloth
23. Little Jack
24. Turn back
26. Miscued
28. "__ straws"
30. Bandleader Jones
31. Like some steak
32. Coal size
33. Table d'__
34. Cheat
36. Wages
39. Comedian Sahl
40. Roman money
41. Nibbles
43. Berber tribesman
44. Sailor's gear
45. Hamelin denizen
46. B.&O. et al.
47. Novelist Moravia
50. German river
52. Terminal: Abbr.
53. Picadors, in a way
55. Nap
57. Pewter coin
60. Work-heat units
62. River to Moselle
63. Feb. 14 symbols
67. Mortgage
68. Elegance
69. Earth: Prefix
70. Handle: Fr.
71. Ma Bell's concern
73. Ape
75. River crossing
77. Nice and Lido
78. Chem. suffix
79. Postage item: Abbr.
80. Army men: Abbr.
84. Building beam
85. Prefix with present
86. On __ level
87. Borders: Lat.
88. Learning time
92. Its emblem was an eagle
95. Maddened
96. Rodrigo Díaz
97. Angler's flies
98. Purse items
99. Freeloader
102. Fried, in Toledo
103. Eastern Christian
104. Hatbox toters
105. Impair
107. Pout
109. He, in Italy
110. Soft-__
111. Pirate gold
112. Doorways: Abbr.
113. Asian holiday
114. Robert Burns word
115. Glen Canyon, e.g.
116. Noted "racketeer"
117. Call on

DOWN

1. TV fare
2. Word repetition
3. Cole Porter sentiment
4. Serpent
5. Sub-rosa deals
6. Cook a certain way
7. Homer, with none on
8. "__ Savannah"
9. Kind of cap
10. Willie of ring fame
11. Eccentric one
12. Months: Abbr.
13. Film of 1950
14. Spanish months
19. Clio's sister
20. Optical devices
23. Miss., Ala., Ga., etc.
25. Zonal clocking: Abbr.
27. Moths
28. Yarn measure
29. Cyst
32. Portions: Abbr.
35. Relief org.
37. Do a transplant job
38. "Henry VI" character
42. Defunct rulers
47. Set right
48. Niobe's output
49. Declaim
51. Morning moisture
54. Campus people: Abbr.
55. Monastic officer
56. Dancing Castle
58. Holds sway
59. Nepal peak
61. Stifle
63. Completely
64. Kind of football pass
65. Religion
66. Head feature
72. Timber wolf
74. Actor Carl or Rob
76. Poker term
79. Rich cheeses
81. I.O.U. recipient
82. Tear into
83. Takes care of
85. Ref. book
88. Sample
89. Charley horse
90. Exalted ones
91. "... the giftie __ us"
93. Where the 600 rode
94. Southwest campus
100. O'Casey
101. That, to Ovid
105. Up-to-date
106. Macaw
108. Compass point

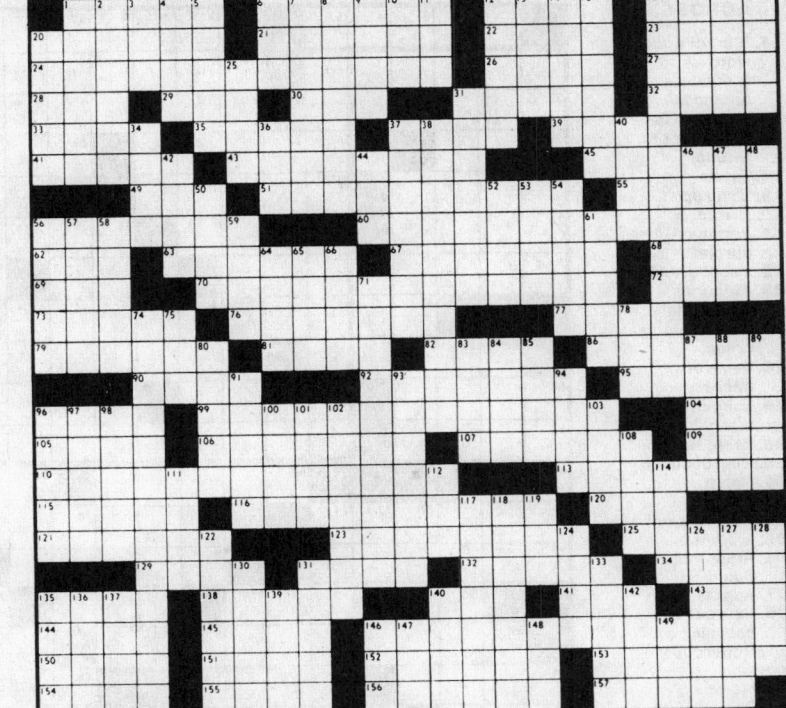

ACROSS

1. Anna or Maria
6. Finally
12. Island near Corsica
16. Knob
20. Binges
21. Certain clock
22. Cadence
23. Israeli name
24. French singer and Chinese V.I.P.
26. Bradley
27. Dog's name
28. Metric measure
29. Slovenly woman
30. Oahu neckpiece
31. Moon goddess
32. French seasons
33. Ancient Briton
35. Louisiana feature
37. British gun
39. Naval officer: Abbr.
41. Steel city
43. Wartime concern
45. Explosive device
49. Lincoln Center tenant
51. Forms a mosaic
55. McPherson of evangelism
56. Bulwark
60. Leander's milieu and high priest
62. Expend
63. Peep shows
67. Liner of tragedy
68. Arrow poison
69. Clear of
70. Muse and wall writing
72. Remedied: Abbr.
73. U.S. President
76. Capital of Honan
77. Teasdale
79. Hayward or Stanford
81. Improvise in jazz
82. Track concern
86. Ambrosia's companion
90. Blue-green hue
92. Chorus
95. __ a tune
96. Shangri-La V.I.P.
99. Arty district and actress
104. Tropical tree
105. Upper: Ger.
106. Emote
107. Swarmed
109. Adjective suffix
110. Winter Olympics site of 1956 and movie star
113. Commissions
115. Stock-market listings
116. Of a 19th-cent. essayist
120. Make edging
121. Detective
123. Expresses again
125. Drives and putts
129. Highway
131. Immovable
132. Soviet chain
134. Masculine
135. Site
138. Money boxes
140. Hindu title
141. English town
143. Words in ode titles
144. Coagulates
145. Malay boat
146. Thieves' nemesis and French cake
150. Foolhardy
151. Stravinsky
152. Abuse
153. Winter hazards
154. Away from weather
155. Hawaiian goose
156. Like a lawn
157. Observes

DOWN

1. Extra tires
2. Soviet cooperatives
3. Educ. group
4. Carnegie or Cal.
5. Mohammed's associates
6. Needle: Prefix
7. Certain Ranger
8. Scorecard data
9. Tree of India
10. Expanse
11. Numerical prefix
12. Conceal, old style
13. Bean
14. Famous Mont
15. "The Lady Is __"
16. Egyptian queen and S. A. lake
17. News item
18. Florida county
19. Son of Seth
20. __ capsule
25. Irish script
31. Name for Adenauer
34. Weather-ear abbr.
36. Nickname of ex-Giant QB
37. Add chips to the pot
38. Scolding
40. Martin
42. Imminent
44. Soviet city
46. Kind of acid
47. What asterisks do
48. Postpone
50. Mine car
52. Cardinals or Orioles
53. Early menial
54. Prolongs, with "out"
56. Bucolic
57. Stage remark
58. Hero's reward
59. Migrate
61. Blue area on map
64. Greek org. of W. W. II
65. Homeric
66. Living-room piece
71. Does a math job, in Britain
74. U.S. general and tennis ace
75. Ship's plank curve
78. Cook's guide: Abbr.
80. Apply lightly
83. Mild oath
84. "I __ you!"
85. Beget
87. Metroliner, for one
88. Hungarian hero
89. Old Scottish coins
91. Flaring stars
93. Goes to a restaurant
94. Alaskan port
96. Ness and neighbors
97. Seething
98. Unite
100. Pilot's place
101. Leading man, in Italy
102. French political writer
103. "Bird thou never __"
108. Haul
111. Math ratio words
112. Insect study: Abbr.
114. Particle
117. Family of pianist José
118. Football passes
119. Depression agency
122. Old feminine weapon
124. English river
126. Shaped with a machine
127. Mocks
128. Joinings
130. Funeral song
131. Signal light
133. Abridge
135. Taj Mahal site
136. Sincere
137. Other
139. Diving bird
140. Hindu deity
142. Kind of log
146. S. A. country
147. Irish god
148. Turkish title
149. Female ruff

106 STEPQUOTE *Eugene T. Maleska*

ACROSS

1. Start of a six-word Stepquote ending at 115 Across
6. Recorder of events
14. Estate
19. Gone up
20. ___ roof
21. Perkins purple
22. Yacht's home
23. Author of Stepquote
24. Pyromaniac's crime
25. Items of interest
26. London artery
28. Even: Brit.
30. Ring decision
31. Notch
33. Jots
34. Sailors' saint
35. ___ Rabbit
36. Artist from Spain
37. Augury
38. Source of cameline oil
41. Buttercups' kin
43. Marsh
44. Shows disdain
45. Gallimaufry
46. Ten, for Cicero
48. Lingers
51. Beaches
53. Calms a patient
55. Prepares to drive
56. TV camera screen
57. School subject
59. Road stopover
61. Refrain syllable
62. Teases
63. Part of Stepquote
66. Loser to Braddock
67. Hockey star
68. Name for Rayburn
69. "___ a man with . . ."
70. Writing fluids
71. Garden tool
75. "On ___" (Source of Stepquote)
77. Seed covering
79. More rigorous
81. Feudal domestics
82. Ruler in Teheran
83. Harmoniously
85. Native: Suffix
86. Places to eat
90. Chews
92. South of Ky.
93. Indonesian boat
94. Snack spread
95. Gnawed: It.
96. City in Pripet Marshes
97. Yemen capital
98. Caliph's name
99. Clobber
101. Priscilla's in-laws
103. Hebrew letter
104. Small papal coin
106. Gregarious
108. Kind of rock
110. Successor to H. H. H.
111. Tiptoer's opposite
112. Sausage
113. Stands the gaff
114. Kennedy and Baker
115. End of Stepquote

DOWN

1. Man from Tabriz
2. Wondrous event
3. "___ was saying . . ."
4. Clan
5. Part of Stepquote
6. Invents
7. Island off China
8. Cocktail garnishes
9. Wild Bill Donovan's org.
10. Trawler equipment
11. Noted, as a detail
12. Escutcheons
13. Inner-city sight
14. Oriental nurse
15. Edsel
16. Like certain paints
17. Called forth
18. Madrileño
19. "Private Lives" heroine
27. Man's slipper
29. Tried to claw
32. Dressing gowns
35. ___ l'Etang (French port)
38. Bivouac break-ups
39. "Had ___ many"
40. Withered
42. Glory or maid
43. Nourished
46. Gape
47. Part of prosody
49. Calif. motto
50. Bowsprits
51. Evening party
52. Inc., co., etc.
53. Suffixes with mob and gang
54. "___ as a seal . . ."
56. Develops
58. Inlet
60. New Guinea port
64. Henry James heroine
65. Part of Stepquote
66. Chess pieces
72. Stupid
73. Whilom
74. Join the pensioners
76. Born: Fr.
78. Concha
80. Glides downhill again
82. Import
84. Former R. I. Senator
86. Proffers
87. Ciceronian activity
88. Marine mammal
89. More polished
90. White wine
91. Fruit-eating bird
92. Steering device
94. Of Paul or Pius
96. Picasso
99. Yields
100. Cotton
102. Silk: Fr.
105. Court call
107. Suitable
109. Conducted

FRAGMENTS
Frances Hansen

ACROSS

1. Wheresoever: Lat.
7. Burdens
12. Arab name for Acre
16. Book jacket info
21. Discompose
22. Coypu's cousin
23. Biblical kingdom
24. Demolished: Var.
25. Finally!
26. Before Unis
27. Ives
28. Lab solutions: Abbr.
29. Bellow
30. Beauty spots
31. Ascent
32. Part of a magic word
33. Lone Ranger's friend
35. Jabberwocky word
36. Kind of jacket
38. Between iota and lambda
40. Fur
41. Belay's partner
43. Dutch painter
44. Haunt the mind
45. Thought for Omar's "Sorry Scheme"
48. Balsam
49. Rosé
50. Menu entry
51. Porter
52. Rubbing
57. Needle: Prefix
58. Charon's crossing
60. Church part
64. Stamp on
65. June 14 sights
67. __ on parle français
68. Met patron Otto et al.
70. People in a Sheridan play
71. Yale
72. Major of comics

74. Character-actor Eric
75. Violin
76. House wrecker's big brother
78. Kind of leather
79. Ait
80. Show up
81. The: Sp.
82. Greeting for the Mets
83. Beauts
84. Snooze
85. Wickiup's cousin
87. More lecherous
88. Pueblo Indian
89. Chemical prefix
91. Bern's river
92. Literary backing, of a kind
93. Casa dweller
95. Club men
97. Nettle
98. Between epsilon and theta
102. Bookbindery equipment
110. Girl's name
111. "__ fan tutte"
112. Curaçao's neighbor
113. Hook, in biology
114. Active ones
115. 1956 wedding locale
117. Sign
118. Hebrew months
119. Eyelash: Prefix
120. Nurse of India
121. Not so zany
123. "Let __ as it may . . ."
124. Wan
125. Roast: Fr.
126. Leftward, at sea
127. Effect
129. Make up for
130. Wild guess
131. Rebel against Moses
132. Exactly
133. Czech leader
134. Dame Myra
135. Writer St. Johns

136. Spuds

DOWN

1. Page sizes
2. Defang
3. Peachtree St. locale
4. "Rigoletto" feature
5. Us, in Essen
6. Of age: Abbr.
7. "__ finger writes . . ."
8. Eatery
9. Least newsworthy
10. Bird
11. Right pert
12. Walks about
13. Pairs
14. Boat loads
15. Waving in the breeze
16. Tennyson's advice to sea
17. Tear into
18. Throne seizer

19. Backslide
20. Wall St. purchases: Abbr.
34. Morsel
35. Word with aqua or sub
37. Jannings
39. Ibsen role
42. Puccini girl
44. Export of 112 Across
46. Deplorable deeds
47. "When the __ the cradle . . ."
48. Not so easily duped
51. Rings
52. Blaze __
53. Wells to the surface
54. Montana county
55. Part of A.A.U.
56. Breaks up, in a way
57. Shade of blue

59. Proceed warily
61. Artist's colors
62. __ the arm (boosters)
63. Fit to be tied
65. Like a basset's ears
66. Small amount
69. Segovia and friends
71. Texas city
73. Famed physician
76. Kind of split
77. Krazy __
82. __ gift horse in . . .
86. Kemal
87. Central Texas city
90. Ladies in India
92. Krupp product
94. Native: Suffix
96. Nonclerical
98. British letter

99. Declaim
100. Ski part
101. Kennedy tenant
102. Beethoven's forte
103. Pittsburgh intake
104. Digit
105. Tea
106. Natural __
107. Ape
108. Having more fibers
109. Secreters of Dead Sea Scrolls
111. Prairie wolf
115. Fen
116. City of 1970 fair
122. Like peas in __
124. Movie monster's birthplace
127. Mel
128. Stole

FANCIFUL TOUR
Edward J. O'Brien

ACROSS

1. Kennedy wear
5. Prepaid: Abbr.
8. Alphonse's pal
14. Silent sister
18. Fraud
19. Hawaiian island
20. Arbiter
21. Preposition
22. B'way hero
23. Liberal or fine
24. Part of Rushmore
26. Southern facade
28. Whole
29. Scottish alder
30. Rolling or bowling
31. Mass. rhythm
34. Goals: Abbr.
36. Hunt cries
39. Tom, Dick and Harry
40. Principle
42. Possess: Fr.
43. Transit to Fisherman's Wharf
46. Inferior imitator
50. And not: Lat.
51. Cousins of 4 F's
53. B. & O., etc.
54. __ one side (swerve)
55. Houston's Astrodome, in a way
61. French opinions
62. Misty
63. Year Richard I died
64. Difficult, to a cockney
65. Ibsen figure
66. D. C. summers, to some
72. Sgt.
74. Annex
75. Alley
76. Organic compounds
78. Tea varieties
80. Conquers the Grand Canyon
84. Invest with
85. Haut or low
86. Shoshonean
87. Melanesian
88. Formidable one
89. Excavation in Chicago
94. Yesterdays: Fr.
96. Result
98. Sole
99. Animal awards
100. Got wind of
103. Autumns in part of N.Y.
107. Harvest goddess
108. Lyric poem
110. Mr. Fawkes
111. Relative of iron duke
115. Dusky divestiture
118. Number of nights
119. Sight of St. Louis gateway
120. Cupid
121. No place __
122. Explosive inventor
123. Handicap or stake
124. Tartan pattern
125. Keep __ mind
126. Diminutive suffixes
127. Honduran port

DOWN

1. Wear for Ann or May
2. New Hebrides island
3. Match
4. Part of e.g.
5. Glance off
6. "__ penny for tribute"
7. Roil
8. Dick
9. Affaire de coeur
10. Foam up: Lat.
11. Can
12. Give __ a few
13. Closely akin
14. Card game
15. Bumbling
16. Discolor
17. Brasses
19. Martin and Tyler Moore
25. Phila. divorce court
27. Miami touch
32. Sesame
33. Hubs: Abbr.
35. Unkempt abodes
36. __ fire (pend)
37. Conjugate __
38. Painted Desert quality
41. "We may __ again"
43. Davis's union: Abbr.
44. __ Magnon
45. Branch
47. Arthur and Veronica, to admirers
48. Natives: Suffix
49. Plane part
52. Workers on a digest
56. Educ. group
57. Initials of "Little Women" author
58. Type of train: Abbr.
59. Kind of tide
60. Eyes: Lat.
61. Cry of disdain
67. Aims of a Q B
68. Pile
69. Units of length: Abbr.
70. Bridge loss
71. Eur. land
72. Night: Prefix
73. African tree
77. Timid
79. Water animal
80. Court
81. Swine: Prefix
82. Outcry
83. Collide gently
85. Lead: Ger.
90. Nursery item
91. Prone: Abbr.
92. Showing favoritism
93. Omitted
95. Has __ (fits in)
97. Harmony
99. __ air (daylight)
100. Tubes
101. Tracing pattern
102. Like __ (probably)
104. Get __ on yourself
105. Cicerone
106. Long times
109. "__ boy!"
112. Dies __
113. Clerical: Abbr.
114. Zeus's mother
116. Concorde, for one
117. Even if, for short

SHAPING UP *Arnold Moss*

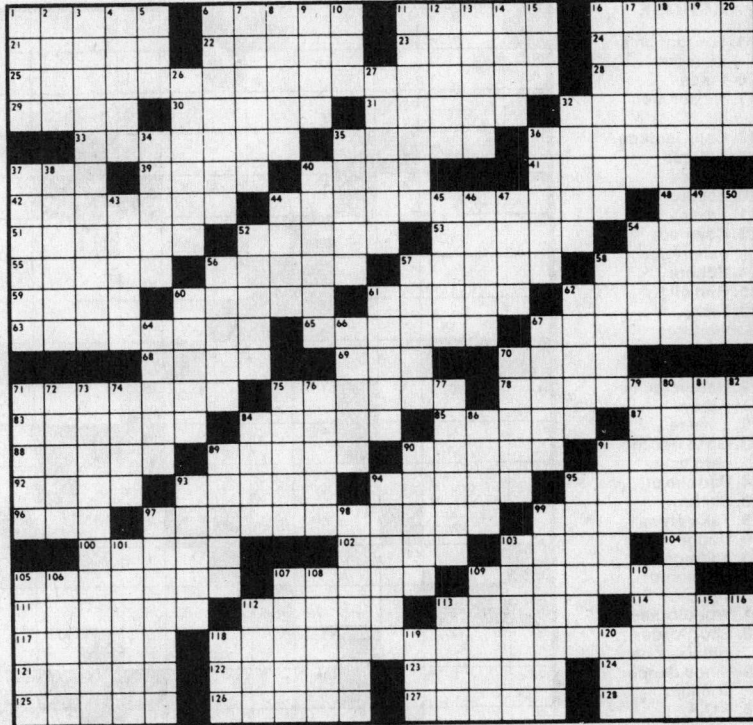

ACROSS

1. Marsh plant
6. Word of disgust
11. Comes in third
16. Ways
21. Written: Fr.
22. In harmony
23. Realty sign
24. Moral code
25. Pirates' milieu
28. "Hi, __!"
29. Passable
30. Italian river
31. Kind of thief
32. Dig further
33. Flower parts
35. Certain maid
36. Section of Alps
37. Telly network
39. Certain shop
40. Lollapalooza
41. On __ diet
42. Stirring up
44. Khufu's milieu
48. Conway or Holt
51. Disquiet
52. Footnote's place
53. Belgrade people
54. Loosen
55. Quechuas
56. "All __, all dead"
57. Stuffed roast
58. Idiom
59. Norse name
60. To one side
61. Yucatan people
62. Baltimore player
63. Where jacks hang out
65. Utter delight
67. Limits
68. Izmir money
69. Honshu town
70. Et __
71. Verdi opus
75. Classify
78. "__ the Sea"
83. What "sumer is"
84. Gray
85. Like a sumo wrestler
87. Same: Prefix
88. Tent parts
89. Rope fiber
90. Nerve-cell part
91. Row

92. Hula hoops et al.
93. __ Rapids
94. City of Spain
95. Xmas in Pisa
96. Bering or Messina: Abbr.
97. Poor man's Riviera
99. Pre-school artist
100. Stomach woes
102. Sale-tag words
103. Musical lines
104. Road curve
105. "Much Ado" role
107. Lithium, for one
109. "... thou, __, art far more fair ..."
111. Moths
112. Legacy law
113. City near Cleveland
114. __ Eireann
117. __ once
118. Crystal ball, to some
121. Pee Wee
122. Irene's concern
123. One of the media
124. Musical "ssh!"
125. Peace Nobelist, 1911
126. Saracen quarters
127. Willow
128. Watchful

DOWN

1. Wanes
2. Nymph of fable
3. Skirt hoop, in a way
4. Leg of mutton
5. W. W. II area
6. Amateur Santa's need
7. Mugs
8. Chesapeake Bay arm
9. Pony up
10. Who, in Bonn
11. Kind of comedian
12. Before moon and dew

13. Prince Igor's wife et al.
14. "One-and-a-two" man
15. Anne, for one: Abbr.
16. Faded slowly, with "out"
17. Olympian
18. Large brass container
19. Takes on
20. Vista
26. Complaint
27. "That which __ today ..."
32. Food shops
34. Equal to a mile
35. Where Manila is
36. Disney film
37. Men from U.C.L.A.
38. Auto hood in Leeds
40. Adam's mythical first wife

43. Let
44. Equipment
45. Violinist
46. Showed an old movie
47. Certain lights
49. Arthurian lover
50. Boundaries
52. Like a man-about-town
54. U.S. Indian
56. Kind of whale
57. Party gift
58. Shaw
60. Outsider
61. Dixon's friend
62. Chemical compound
64. Ballet movements
66. Painter's gear
67. Girl's name
70. Field of activity
71. Berbers
72. Brilliance

73. Student milieus
74. Sports men
75. Analyze ore
76. Puppeteer Lewis
77. Poisons
79. Page facing a verso
80. Conformist's fun
81. Light fabrics
82. Raincoats
84. __ -mémoire
86. Forward
89. Horse quality
90. Purpose
91. Sauce for pasta
93. Students
94. Strasbourg's region
95. Standard
97. Flight of a kind
98. Juvenal works
99. Tend
101. Wrinkle

103. "Yowzah" band-leader of yore
105. Brazilian state
106. Eyes
107. Writer on seapower
108. Choose
109. Children's book
110. Perfect
112. German count
113. College degrees
115. Cake decorator
116. Man from Riga
118. Ostend or Brest: Abbr.
119. Peruvian gold
120. Lizard

ACROSS

1. Sourdough's concern
6. Place
11. ". . . for man or —"
16. Calif. Indians
18. Actress Wendy
20. Zodiac sign
21. So-so
23. Covered gallery
24. Sphere
25. Run off
26. Risky ventures
28. Prosecutors, for short
29. Harem rooms
31. Affront
32. — were
33. Goes out, in a card game
34. Partake of
36. Ski turn
38. Take place
39. Nudge
40. Endings for major and cigar
41. Workhorses
43. Short-order initials
45. Hindu dance dramas
46. P.G.A. veteran
47. No. 49
50. Deadly snake
54. Faucet
55. Chinese dynasty
56. Bother
58. Epiphany figures
61. Troubles
63. Purpose
67. As to
68. Flock of mallards
69. Paris area
70. Tower
71. Artistic feat
75. Arctic command
76. Org.
77. Conway of TV
78. Ring arbiter
79. Genève, for one
81. Watery abysses
83. Airport areas
85. Pentateuch
87. Iron: Prefix
91. Favorable times
92. Indelibly impressed
94. Garson
95. Hot pants, etc.
98. Con man
100. Allgood
102. Mud volcano
103. French friend
104. Relative of etc.
105. Czarist state council
107. A-one
108. Encyc. unit
109. Tangles
111. Colorado resort
112. Small island
113. Soothsayer
115. TV bleep material
119. Sines and cosines
120. Shoot up
121. Navy specialists
122. Glaze
123. Cheeses
124. African villages

DOWN

1. Vertebrates
2. Pounds
3. Military weapon: Abbr.
4. Native of: Suffix
5. Clubs
6. Mall visitors
7. Occasion
8. Tree
9. Hebrew letter
10. Manifested
11. Prisoners' see-throughs
12. Business-letter abbr.
13. Longfellow locale
14. Some cars
15. French bit of hair
16. Iceboat
17. Horizontal timbers
19. Lexia, for one
20. Blank check
22. Raccoon's cousin
27. Ice: Ger.
30. More like some summers
33. Understands
35. She: It.
37. Blanc or Tremblant
38. Brazilian area
42. Tight
44. Catch
47. "My kingdom for —"
48. Small hawks
49. Tapestry
51. Stage settings
52. Bets big with a small pair
53. Kind of horn
57. U. S. composer
58. Glove
59. Idiocy
60. Crosspatch
62. Homily: Abbr.
64. Lunchtime hr.
65. Arabian king
66. Conjugation words after eram
72. Bead
73. Veil
74. Merit
80. Heels
82. German coins
84. Trick
85. English novelist
86. Phone operators' gear
88. Prepared to refire
89. Breathes
90. Brother of Electra
92. Gets on the plane
93. Peach or plum
95. Prefers
96. Without ethical precepts
97. Widen
99. GATT treaty: Abbr.
101. Last words
106. Certain entrance fees
109. Deer track
110. Unsounded consonant
111. Dyeing agent
114. French co.
116. Wrap
117. Ingest
118. Knicks' league

ALONG THE GRAIN

H. Hastings Reddall

ACROSS

1. Peak
4. Dr. Rhine's field
7. Jeff Davis, for one
14. Home for some
17. Mat. time
20. Sayings
21. W. W. II area
22. Wilmot, for one
23. Chem. suffix
24. Golfer's problem
25. John Adams's party
27. Lovers of cruelty
28. Certain pitches
30. Work hard
31. Tang
33. Order to a broker
34. Actual being
36. School course
37. Quartet for a world traveler
42. Scheduled
43. Exposes
44. Reactor part
45. One of a Poe pair
46. Grimaces
49. Sweetsop
50. Worried about
51. Birthplace of Mohammed
55. Bible book
56. Persian tiger
57. Boot, in Paris
58. "Money is ___ of . . ."
60. Eur. country
61. Evian and Vichy
62. Entices
63. Gunsight
64. Reine's spouse
65. Attire, in old Rome
67. September times
68. Capricorn
69. Digits: Abbr.
70. Steering brace
71. Stop
72. Uneven
73. Chew of tobacco
74. Ship's complement
75. Handy shopping spot
77. Places
78. Blockhead
79. Embers
80. Greek letters
81. Casabas
83. Insect study: Abbr.
84. Parts of innings
85. Dress up
86. Like Buster Keaton
87. One of a Latin trio
88. Pitcher parts
89. Hoof sounds
90. Exploit
91. Japanese statesman
92. Feelings of malice
94. Disorder
95. Fishing maneuver
96. Max or Buddy
97. Scoff
98. Edge
99. Arrange
100. Antiquated
101. Smidgen
103. Relative
104. Point of land
105. Corrode
106. Land's End, Falmouth, etc.
113. Garment seen at U.N.
114. S. A. monkey
115. Stratum
116. Scandinavian country
117. Flying prefix
119. Deceived
121. Drop ___ (write briefly)
124. Sextant scale
126. Salutation
127. Western state: Abbr.
128. Soup ingredients
129. French season
130. Channel
131. Babylonian god
132. Draft initials
133. People with hunches
134. Naval craft: Abbr.
135. Relatives of mins.

DOWN

1. White House name
2. ___ a kind
3. Transistor
4. Poetic word
5. Posture
6. Salk's conquest
7. Navy guards: Abbr.
8. Stenos' needs
9. Black Chamber workers
10. Three monkey's taboos
11. Inconveniences
12. Superlative suffix
13. Grafted flower unit
14. Chaser of a sort
15. Not alert
16. ___ gratia
17. Put on guard
18. Forth or Clyde
19. Storm Country girl
26. Dodges
29. Snakebird
32. Babbles
35. Outbuilding
38. European land: Abbr.
39. U.S. physicist
40. Defense positions
41. Pointed
46. Bundle of sticks
47. Certain citizen
48. Basic element
49. Exclamations
50. Town in Newfoundland
52. Endless supplies
53. Harmonizes
54. Panay people
56. Tater
57. Case for church cloth
58. Comb, in a way
59. Emotion
61. Put away
62. Bank deals
63. Yokels
66. Greek god
67. Blackbirds
68. Despairing sound
71. Covers
72. Diminutive suffixes
73. Faucet reading
75. Bridge ploys
76. Permeates
77. Tire fault
79. Rope fiber
81. Soften
82. Certain noise
83. Hearing devices
85. Tara, for instance
86. Columbia, for one: Abbr.
88. Navigation aid
89. Tough cloth
90. Fur animal
93. Hardwicke of stage
94. European carp
95. Hairdo
96. P. I. peninsula
98. Thai money
99. Show-off
100. Friend
102. Some dogs
104. English essayist
105. Wading birds
106. Do the honors at dinner
107. Bay window
108. Record parts
109. Rinses out, in Scotland
110. Unusual
111. Stable sound
112. Doleful, to poets
113. Attempt
118. Scraps
120. Ring outcomes
122. Affection, in Scotland
123. W. W. II org.
125. On Social Security: Abbr.

SPRING IS SPRUNG   *Cornelia Warriner*

ACROSS

1. Dog-paddled
5. Abie's Rose
10. Basic fact
13. Confer upon
19. Pueblo Indian
20. Jason's wife
21. Devout, in Spain
22. Unimpaired
23. Strays
24. Heraldic stripe: Var.
25. Greek letter
26. Cossack chief
27. React to spring stimuli
31. Nantes's river
32. "Please step to the __"
33. Wither
37. Dredge
39. Goes on the cuff
42. "... in corpore __"
43. Culture: Prefix
44. Nicene and others
45. Crumb: Fr.
46. Green or split
47. Greek letter
48. Water or musk
50. Live bait
53. Chapters of auto union
55. Seasonal yen
59. Saarinen and others
60. Villains at times
62. Precious ones
63. Glove units: Abbr.
64. Brats
65. Islamic spirit
66. Biblical coins
70. Certain words: Abbr.
71. David's daughter
72. He-man's strong point
73. In a quandary
76. Walton tools
78. Pakistani town
79. Goofs off
81. Nymph
83. Lower-Niger people
84. Capek play
85. Wee, in Scotland
86. Go for flies
89. Queen's spread
91. Cupid
93. Shower curtain, of a sort
95. Fund-drive V.I.P.'s
96. Lost
98. Fling
99. Early fiddle
100. Nature lovers
105. Someday
108. Carpenter __
109. English shrub
110. Standoffs
112. Neckwear
113. Perry Mason's concern
114. Poet who mused on April
115. Avon, for one
116. Tatler man
117. Odin's son
118. Lorna
119. Gambol

DOWN

1. Pronoun
2. Production
3. Spring do for a fiancée
4. Mint improperly
5. Meaning
6. Tear apart
7. Kind of thoughts
8. Sibyl
9. Hall item
10. Has attraction
11. Night spot
12. Coconut fiber
13. Seaside crowd
14. Word on a door
15. State of inertia
16. Cratchit heir
17. Old English money
18. Cyst
28. Metric meas.
29. Note
30. As cheap __
34. Fog
35. January in Peru
36. Soils
37. Scrape off metal
38. Flammable gas
39. Caesar's forehead
40. Split
41. Collect
44. Woodwinds: Abbr.
49. Pitchers
50. French river
51. Start of a toast
52. Lady's vest
54. Put the tennis ball in play
56. Swelling
57. French historian
58. Scottish landowner
61. Steal: Sp.
63. Branches of animal kingdom
65. Table-hops
66. October wear
67. Seasonal storm
68. Move clumsily
69. Former Indian soldiers
71. Portuguese city
72. Yearly: Abbr.
73. Pertinent: Lat.
74. Bull: Prefix
75. Cyclades island
76. Euphrates town
77. French menu item
80. Spend the summer
82. Low Hindu
86. Stroll
87. River of Bavaria
88. Asserted
90. Dance
92. Silk filament
94. Sham
95. Take out
97. Record, old style
99. Cleric's gown
101. George of films
102. Refuse: Lat.
103. Recital group
104. Antitoxins
105. Sens. and Reps.
106. Carney
107. Scot's denial
111. Devious

113

ROUNDUP *William Lutwiniak*

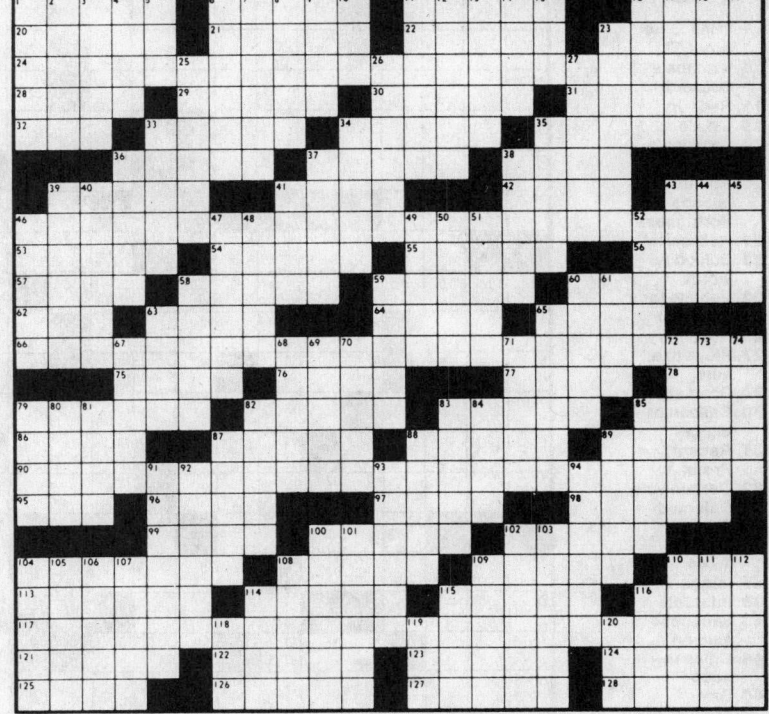

ACROSS

1. Then: Fr.
6. Tallow ingredients
11. Smash, in show biz
16. Small armadillo
20. Scuba user
21. "__ Gloaming..."
22. Arabian demon
23. Residents of Aarhus
24. Intercepting, Western style
28. Girl-watch
29. Stew ingredient
30. __ to high heaven
31. Card game
32. These, in Paris
33. Bird cries
34. Clerical headgear
35. Most leisurely
36. I.O.U.'s
37. Young kangaroos
38. Timetable, for short
39. Area of Asia Minor
41. Beg: Scot.
42. Fork feature
43. Diminutive ending
46. Answer to a Matt Dillon query
53. Greek city
54. Literary device
55. Hangs laxly
56. __ Alto
57. Seamstress's angle
58. Ducks
59. Favorite song
60. Continues
62. The works
63. Patisserie item
64. Lyrical creation
65. Bern's river
66. Familiar ultimatum
75. Shutter's companion
76. Well-known Camino
77. Common Latin verb
78. Ace
79. Scram, to Hamlet
82. Rubbish
83. Reputations
85. Uncluttered
86. Height: Prefix
87. Be eminent
88. Short-haired dog
89. Merchant guild
90. Champion survivor of frontier days
95. Indian greeting
96. ". . . __ won fair lady"
97. Palm leaves: Var.
98. Cognizant
99. Small bit
100. Nursery kind of ache
102. Hebrew leader
104. Cold wind of France
108. Adorn
109. Ghastly
110. Brace
113. Dormant
114. Suspect's defense
115. Undergo chemical change
116. Popular garnish
117. Relative of "Came the dawn"
121. "Aux __!"
122. Thermoplastic
123. C'est __
124. Point of view
125. Snug place
126. Championship
127. Ulan __
128. Vestibule

DOWN

1. Kind of committee
2. City of Belgium
3. Roundish shapes
4. Counsel, of yore
5. Hindu title
6. Document seal
7. Frees
8. Mores
9. "__ there were none"
10. Educational inst.
11. Football score
12. Bids
13. Marsh bird
14. Carson et al.
15. Cooperstown name
16. Custard apple
17. Lake of Finland
18. Outplays
19. Resource
23. Cryptography man
25. Not at all
26. Prized pearl
27. Last Chance Gulch, today
33. Defrosts
34. Eel
35. Removes cream
36. Mexican avocados
37. __ Hopkins
38. Fashion
39. Cause quivers
40. Wine and dine
41. Put away
43. Addams
44. French composer
45. N. C. college
46. Cigares et cigarettes
47. Rain cloud
48. Pick up the tab
49. Concede
50. Name-giver of a weekday
51. Out on __
52. Expedite
58. French river
59. City on the Odra
60. Unit of magnetism
61. Caen's river
63. Kind of gun
65. Allege
67. Withdrawn
68. European iris
69. Stratagem
70. Not live
71. Red Sea country
72. Kitchen must
73. Warm-sea fish
74. __ home (out)
79. City of England
80. Little Sir __
81. Flourished
82. Heat unit
83. "There's __" (impossible)
84. W. W. II coalition
85. V.I.P. of India
87. Baseball ploy
88. Daft
89. Conformed, with "to"
91. Merry ones
92. Angel
93. Of modern Greece
94. Native salt
100. Of an allied group
101. Polished
102. Spanish numeral
103. Toxophilite
104. French family member
105. River of France
106. Door sounds
107. Doctrine
108. Ready
109. Part of what stet means
110. Drab
111. Sam or Tom
112. Additional
114. Turkish regiment
115. Russian council
116. Hand, in Rome
118. Adherent
119. Hebrew measure: Var.
120. Queen's pilots

114 WORDS IN A ROW
Jordan S. Lasher

ACROSS

1. "Hell __ no fury..."
5. Ivanhoe's beloved
11. Red: Sp.
15. Oh, dear
19. Jamaica's __ Rios
20. Atlantic islands, to Portuguese
21. Hebrew letter
22. Soliloquy words
23. Vehicle for a gardener
25. Rosemary
27. Ploys of a sort
28. Road sign
30. Balloon or blimp
31. Recent: Prefix
32. Certain vote
33. Dejected
34. Tied
35. Event of 1944
37. Image: Prefix
38. Infatuate
43. Japanese salmon
44. Chinese soup
46. Day brightener
48. Certain review
49. All smiles
51. Spanish queen
52. Poor rating
54. Copenhagen, in song
58. Spring mo.
59. Certain reply
60. Audience
61. Ararat visitor
62. Girl's name
63. People of Brazil
65. Predatory bird
69. Door sign
70. Uneven
72. Timetable abbr.
73. Court
74. Portal: Abbr.
76. Marseilles season
77. Time, Times, etc.
79. Toaster
81. __ Locks
82. Jane and namesakes
83. After Harry
84. Get rid of a hangover
86. Game stick
89. Tim
91. __ to (ignores)
92. Wine prefixes
93. Insincere talk
94. Argo or Titanic
97. Map abbr.
98. Durocher
100. German name part
102. Do séance work
106. TV personality
110. Astronomer's field
111. Maine county
112. Tip of Alaska
114. "__ horse!"
115. Action: Suffix
116. Victim of a political shake-up
117. Alaskan port
118. Paradise
119. Mango parts
120. Chemical compounds
121. __ Pea, Popeye's friend

DOWN

1. Words of commiseration
2. More pained
3. Comic-book cousin of Superman
4. Square dances
5. Moroccan port
6. Florida city
7. Defeat
8. Be human, in a way
9. Broadway gas
10. Nile dam
11. Firearm devices
12. Hodgepodge
13. St. Lawrence, e.g.
14. Go __ oneself
15. Italian town
16. __ over (domineers)
17. Lawyer of Madrid
18. Attached, in a way
24. "__ Sylphides"
26. Common verb
29. Fortified work
36. Borealis's predecessor
37. Menu item
39. Bridge call
40. Gets ore
41. Bridge call
42. In medias __
43. Spoonerism
44. Bankroll
45. "A __ lama is a priest..."
46. Gobs
47. Tainted
48. Carson's predecessor
50. Old school-desk items
53. Firma or cotta
54. Game fish
55. Yerby novel, with "The"
56. __ length (inch or meter)
57. Most recently from
64. Evaluate
66. Awn
67. Roused
68. Struck, in a way
71. Tortoise genus
75. Shoe holder
78. Poetic word
80. "__ was saying..."
83. Being hauled
85. Horses' foot parts
86. Ropes
87. Weighed a container again
88. Citizen's right
90. Conjures
93. Celestial halo
95. Give __ thought
96. Ex-Dodger Reese
98. Football positions: Abbr.
99. Devoured
101. Section of a cone
102. Thrust
103. Join
104. Jazz instrument, for short
105. Herb genus
107. Of the dawn
108. Move back and forth
109. Pronouns
113. N.Y. subway

FIRST READER   *Nancy W Atkinson*

ACROSS

1. Advance sampling
8. In proximity
14. Certain readers
21. Swiss lake
22. Did a tailoring job
23. Count
24. Miracles
25. Popular English novelist
27. Hemingway novel
29. Cassette
30. Scottish now
31. Faction
32. Beneficiary in a suit
33. Scottish weather
34. Relative
35. __ war
38. Present times
40. Verne captain and others
42. Unhappy states
43. Designed
45. Minor college sport
48. Good friends
50. Small duck
52. Frankie
53. Braised meat dish
56. Arabic letters
59. Uppity one
61. Pacific porgy
62. Author of "Wall Street Jungle"
66. Scottish resort
68. Gardner and others
70. Patrol vehicle
72. Compiègne's river
73. Valley of fame
75. Number ending
76. Blew up photos
78. Youth org.
79. Popular nonfiction book of a decade ago
83. Hitler aide and writer of memoirs
85. Missive: Abbr.
86. Starlike
88. Dutch commune
89. Preserves
90. Paris seasons
92. Ready to go onstage
94. "Uneasy __ the head that . . ."
96. Steady fare
97. Fragrant herbs
99. __ capita
101. Explosives
103. Honshu town
104. Voice source
105. Dreams: Fr.
107. Heart and __
109. Orchid tubers
111. Small fish
114. Word in Miller title
118. Norms: Abbr.
119. Fun's partner
121. Bristle
123. __ reason at all
124. Reception
125. Prattle
126. P. I. native
129. Room, in Madrid
131. Gabor
132. "Do you __ car?"
134. Writers Leon, Charles and Antonia
139. Writers Shirley and Irwin
141. Impetuous lovers
142. Introduction
143. Oddballs
144. "It makes __ to me"
145. Picket-line member
146. Out-and-out
147. Fly's nemesis

DOWN

1. Laments
2. Terminates
3. Popular science
4. Musical subject
5. Joyce's land
6. Prunes, in Scotland
7. Swiss canton
8. Gift for a man
9. Root or Yale
10. Appraises, with up
11. To some extent
12. Creditors
13. River to the Fulda
14. Allen and Frome
15. Belief
16. Japanese statesman
17. Strained
18. Unredeemed man
19. Backings on floors
20. Races
22. Subscriber's encore
26. Uganda people
28. Admired one
36. Danube tributary
37. Charges
39. Out!
41. Archy's friend
42. "__ you really know?"
44. Andrews
46. Inlets
47. In reserve
48. Red wine
49. Pronoun
51. Erich Segal's tear-jerker
54. Authorize
55. Rawhides
56. Author of 79 Across
57. On the verge of
58. "No Exit" author et al.
60. Uses to the utmost
62. Trundle, as ore
63. Home of Lagos
64. Early mystics
65. Add __ one's life
67. Annamese measure
69. Mini-test
71. __ cruise
74. Epoch
77. Award
80. Steep slope
81. Edible herb
82. Kipling hero
84. Vessel of a kind
87. Orator Chauncey
91. Betrays, with out
93. Wife of Siva
95. Bounce, in Scotland
98. Miss West
100. Accelerates
102. Beach sight
105. One making a new try for grass
106. Vacillates
108. Card game
109. Writer Donald Ogden __
110. As graceful as __
112. Pupil
113. Musial
115. Offer
116. Direct opposite
117. Less fine
118. Noisy dances
119. James or John Nance
120. Nichols hero
122. Early New Englanders
125. Safari V.I.P.
127. Danube tributary
128. Geologic stage
130. Running
133. "__ want for Xmas is . . ."
135. Forsyte, for one
136. Writer Moss
137. Ponselle
138. In __ (peeved)
140. Diving bird

116 FOR A MAY QUEEN
Alfio Micci

ACROSS

1. Mountain ash
6. Medicine unit
10. London policeman
16. Taxpayer's hope
17. "__ is Paris!"
19. "... maids __ row"
20. Ancient Urfa
21. Economy
22. __ pin
24. Present for Mother
27. Geometrical solids
28. Mad one
29. Partitions
30. Prepared to propose
31. To be: Lat.
34. __ left field
36. Andes animals
38. Kind of whale
40. Dernier __
41. Follow
42. Warplane crewman: Abbr.
45. "__ of All Flesh"
47. Posse's critters
50. Wisconsin city
52. Seeks to attain
54. Spad
55. Arabian cloak
57. Oodles
58. Kind of dive
59. Heathen
61. Remoras
62. Madrid attraction
65. Honor card
67. Galena
68. Grating
69. Burr
70. Gluttonous
74. Collar
76. Chowder
77. Donkey
78. Noun suffix
79. Fill the plates
83. Saves
85. Like some night skies
87. Garçon's name
88. Direction
89. Convene anew
92. Wonder
93. Partner of trick
94. Loos and others
96. Pacific island group
99. Porter
100. Acquired characters
104. __ hand
106. Kind of cord
108. Singers
109. Present for Mother
114. Outdoor area
116. Aloft, in France
117. Shut again
118. More like Snow White
119. Finishes furniture
120. Builds
121. Does garden work
122. Army man: Abbr.
123. Feminine suffixes

DOWN

1. Italian naturalist
2. Brain matter
3. Present for Mother
4. Confused
5. Draw __ (approach)
6. Present for Mother
7. Other: Sp.
8. Turkomen
9. Big name in towers
10. Certain boxers
11. Bull
12. Russia's Riviera
13. Gnawed
14. Silly
15. Stand
16. Kind of book: Abbr.
17. Time in the jug
18. Flour and sugar
23. One connected with: Suffix
25. Heating abbr.
26. Williams hero
31. This: Sp.
32. Globes: Abbr.
33. Ooze
35. Jewish month
37. Atmosphere
39. Get rid of, in a way
42. Life stories, for short
43. Ready
44. Untidy
46. Assent
48. Thor's wife
49. Whitney
51. Present for Mother
53. Adam's son and others
55. Gas: Prefix
56. Suffer
60. Present for Mother
61. Toast
62. Old-hat
63. Has it made
64. Sharp ridge
66. Aurora
71. Understand
72. __ fog
73. Discard
75. Pourboire
77. Have __ for (desire)
80. Mountain: Prefix
81. U.S.S.R. range
82. French head
84. Arm badge
85. Positions
86. Some dogs
90. Pirate John and others
91. Willow
95. Arrests
97. Express
98. In bondage
100. Corrode
101. Bass and treble
102. Set __ for (ambush)
103. Andrea __
105. Large rooms
107. Warn
110. Additional: Scot.
111. Fairy-tale word
112. Charlie Brown expletive
113. Navy police: Abbr.
115. Letter

ONLY HUMAN *Marian Pearce*

ACROSS

1. Bank features
6. Fills
11. Deceived
16. Sometime money
21. Follow
22. Pick up the tab
23. Hole __
24. Stage
25. Pastoral district
27. Inlet
29. Western pact
30. Viewpoint
31. Hari et al.
32. Farm machine
33. Fretful
34. Relatives of oaters
35. Chicago landmark
36. Dominate
40. Conserve, in a way
41. Dispossessed
45. Hebrew god
46. False
47. Mosquito genus
48. Scottish name
49. Band instruments
50. Strenuously
53. Bondman
54. Musical group
55. Whales
56. Comparative endings
57. Relied: Var.
58. Glaciation stage
59. Gatsby, for one
60. Catkin
62. Bit
63. Numerical suffix
64. Sieve
66. Divination
67. West Indian sorcery
69. "__ the land of . . ."
70. Emotion
71. Visible
73. Give the once-over
79. Fail
82. Expunge
83. O. T. book
84. Family member
85. Seventh-century date
86. "__ a Man"
87. Indian of Sonora
88. Miss Toklas
89. Irish writer
90. Printing direction
91. Spare, plus
94. Actor Walter and family
95. Sabbath talk: Abbr.
96. Cowboys' wear
97. Shield bands
98. "Chanson __"
99. Magazines
101. Outdoorsy cloth
102. Overlappings in music
104. Central or Estes
105. Church part
106. River to the Amazon
107. Hans's shoes
110. Strips of rock
111. Crazed
112. Snappish person
116. Like an English king
118. Jams
120. Part of a certain even trade
121. French beast
122. Of hearing
123. Restrict
124. Beginnings
125. Stair part
126. Controls
127. Guitar parts

DOWN

1. Laurel of comedy
2. Old Irish oath
3. Matter-of- __
4. Vestige
5. But, to Cicero
6. Impassive
7. Mysterious
8. __ -bopper
9. Direction
10. French church abbr.
11. Pipe-organ stop
12. Green
13. Fleshy fruits
14. Son of Seth
15. Court case figure: Abbr.
16. Milieus
17. Two-times
18. Grate upon
19. Response to "Get it?"
20. Bosc
26. Soviet river
28. Kind of agent
31. Band man
33. Kind of wrestling
34. Thomas and others
35. Noontimes in Provence
36. "Two Years __ the Mast"
37. Evoke
38. Highway hazards
39. Old pronouns
40. Take turns
41. Scarcity
42. Place for doubloons
43. Worker
44. With skill
46. After-theater snag
47. Concerning
50. Pentateuch
51. Gideon's victim
52. "Mon __!"
53. Twilled fabric
57. Dubliner's lake
59. Brightness
60. Protozoan: Var.
61. Sahl
62. Squalid
64. Rhythms
65. Variety of apple
68. Meadow sound
70. N. Z. trees
71. "Potemkin" locale
72. Axis
73. Pronoun
74. Rhino features
75. Wash. agency
76. Like the moon at times
77. Greek tourist sights
78. Story start
80. Broadway district
81. Laundry cycles
85. Bookkeeper's entry
87. Lie in hiding
88. More qualified
89. Strips
91. Scant
92. Reply to the expected
93. German numbers
96. Scythe handles
98. Hiatus in war
100. Name giver
101. Steal
102. Summer covering
103. Singing gymnastics
105. Sky Whale
106. Writer Angelo
107. Scoria
108. Elder: Fr.
109. Smuts, for one
110. True, in Tours
111. Grimace
112. Dam
113. Height
114. Burlesque number
115. Whispering sounds
117. Continent: Abbr.
118. Candy shape
119. Vietnam-war initials

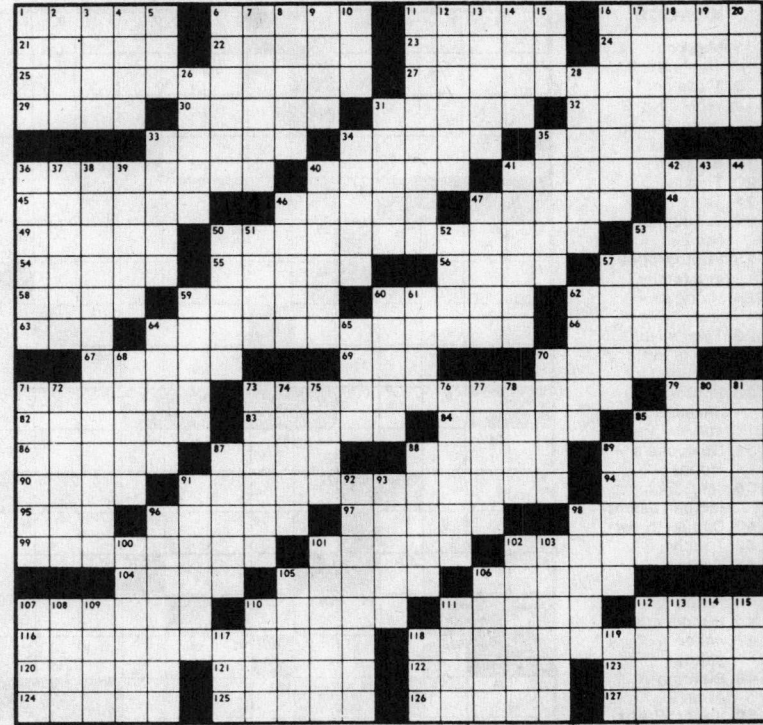

ACROSS

1. Masked man's No. 2
6. Made neat
12. Where No. 2 is No. 1
18. Noisy
19. Stassen
20. Tied to
21. Terra __
22. Jacqueline's No. 2
23. Photographer and family
24. Hairy, as a leaf
26. Tyler's No. 1
28. Pea of India
29. Acquaint
30. Photo-developing abbr.
31. Cowpoke's mount
35. "My __" (embarrassed)
40. Casual throw
42. Touch
43. Boston fixture
44. "Jane __"
45. Bundle again
47. Italian painter
48. Slanting: Abbr.
50. Vapor: Prefix
54. Trimmed
55. Vents frustration
58. Between holier and thou
59. TV logo
60. Take __ garbage
61. Infinite: Abbr.
62. No. 2 in 1968
71. Cuckoo
72. Eclipse sight
73. Old Dutch measure
74. Fibber
76. Readies a fishing line
80. Chemical sugar
83. Bone: Prefix
84. Service initials
85. Ontario river
86. Adjusts
87. Between ifs and buts
90. Does cobbling
92. Initials of a No. 1 and others
93. Endure, in Scotland
94. Pirates
96. Salinger character
97. Willie Winkie
99. Finally
101. Adjust
103. Corps member, to Nixon's No. 2
105. Kind of nabobs, to Nixon's No. 2
111. Most valorous
112. Homely one
115. Pass the buck
116. Fogs
117. Declared
118. Mediterranean union
119. Small fish
120. St. Lawrence, for one
121. Stealthily

DOWN

1. G.O.P. No. 2 in 1952
2. Spanish town
3. Standard
4. Vapid
5. Praying figure
6. Key Biscayne products
7. Dies __
8. No. 2 in Madrid
9. French pronoun
10. Letter addressees
11. Covet
12. The Spirit of __ -six
13. Political collegian
14. Spanish nothing
15. Repents
16. Dovetail part
17. Ford
19. Shout
20. Grape residue
25. Like a bird with a crest
27. Circumference formula
31. Dwell on
32. Higher, in Bonn
33. Split-level places
34. Posture
36. Coupon: Abbr.
37. Sword
38. N. Y. college
39. Nixon's No. 2
41. County hub
44. Root or Yale
46. No. 1 in Shakespeare drama
48. "__ be in England . . ."
49. English spa
51. Strom's family
52. Long hair
53. Just
56. __ generis
57. Radiation unit
62. Moon sight
63. Etats __
64. Southwest campus
65. Wagner of baseball
66. Scraps
67. Horse
68. Rutledge
69. Revere
70. Chemical compound
75. "Step to the __"
77. Chinese poet
78. Relative of etc.
79. Switchblade
80. Ortega y __
81. Appear
82. Being, in Rome
88. Most groovy
89. Abhors
90. Slum hazard
91. Took five
93. Slander
94. Pedro or Fernando
95. Town on Hudson
97. Fabian Society pioneers
98. Zimbalist
100. W. W. II craft
102. Political tenures
104. Pernicious
105. City in Japan
106. Deucey's No. 1
107. Sincere
108. Problematical
109. Armstrong
110. Neutral
113. Greek letter
114. Handful

IN OTHER WORDS
Herbert Ettenson

ACROSS

1. Flowers of Whitman poem
7. Goldish
11. Papal name
15. Indian's word with big
19. Obsession for repeating certain words
22. Relative of abracadabra
24. High-level argot
25. Baby talk spoken by adults
26. Dollar bills
27. Hayworth or Gam
28. Radio or TV remote
30. Tahoe or Louise
31. Moon vehicle
32. Pig genus
33. British blackjack
34. Goriot
35. Tent fixtures
36. Plant stem
37. Hector
38. Cobwebby things
40. Decrees
41. Wavy, as a leaf edge
44. Business title abbr.
45. Store event
46. Yellow ocher
47. Like neon
48. Fervor
49. Pick out
50. Sweet wines
54. "Complected," for one
56. African antelope
57. Bob Feller specialty
58. Hesitant sounds
59. Predilections
60. Putting on guard
62. Certain bones
63. Like Irish eyes of song
65. Barbara __ Geddes
66. Eccentricity
67. Nonprofessionals
68. "Do not __, spindle or . . ."
69. Voters
72. Equanimous
73. Antwerp man, to French
75. Festive
76. Nineties, for one
77. Throb
80. Hawaiian thrush
81. Florid language
83. South Pacific sight
85. Pagoda
86. Headache
88. Cordon
89. Mispronunciation of "r"
91. Patagonian trees
92. Addition word
93. Laundry item
94. Ruffle, as hair
95. Gourmand
96. Spanish aunts
97. ". . . are __ forgotten"
98. Snaky sounds
99. Town __
102. Vitamin source
104. Chimney output
105. Rockfish
106. Engendered
107. Latin verb
108. Social science: Abbr.
109. Young doe
112. German cry
113. Hebrew letter
114. Jerk's cousin
115. Western state: Abbr.
116. Toots
117. Relative of gibberish
120. "All well stop send money stop"
123. Chelly tree, for example
124. Speech that runs like sixty
125. French seasons
126. New York's way
127. River to North Sea
128. Sitting, as a statue

DOWN

1. Reason, in philosophy
2. Turkish statesman
3. Places for earrings
4. Envoys: Abbr.
5. Coolidge
6. Kind of hormone
7. Cuckoo
8. Daughter of Cadmus
9. Elsa, for one
10. Certain bettors
11. Volcanic hill of France
12. Entreat
13. Prowlers of W. W. II
14. Hose
15. Ben __
16. Wife of Iago
17. Away
18. French apples
20. Horace, for one
21. Story of gods
22. Unit of conductance
23. Fellow
29. Size up
33. Melodious
34. Swimming or car
35. Hoosegow unit
36. Letters such as b and m
37. Snide remark
38. Metric weights
39. Relative of soft soap
40. Dossier
41. Currant genus
42. Equip for war, old style
43. Frivolous talk
44. Actress Edna
46. Marionette man
48. Enthusiasm
49. Speaks to privately
50. Fur
51. Meaningless talk
52. Came down
53. Murder
55. Rip
56. Chinese weight
57. Skin-diving gear
61. Rifle range: Fr.
64. Nonstop talkativeness
65. Hokum
67. Relative of 123 Across
69. Bundle
70. Every
71. Interdiction
72. Secret group
73. Village barrier in Africa
74. Ludwig
75. Cotton and sloe
77. Ship deck
78. Armor plate
79. Soprano Emma
81. Victory: Ger.
82. Talk noisily
83. "__ with a view"
84. ". . . thicker __ water"
87. Acidity
90. __ à dire
92. Like some pipers
93. Quality
96. What the brave deserve
97. Shore plants
98. Water-cooled pipes of East
99. Hold protectively
100. Paint over
101. Deposit in the earth
102. Miserable one
103. Nitty- __
104. Steep slope
106. Baa
108. High-strung
109. "One of __ days"
110. Red dye
111. Super
113. City official: Abbr.
114. Metric length: Abbr.
115. Very: Ger.
116. Fish delicacy
118. Air-rifle fodder
119. Baton Rouge campus
121. Spear: Abbr.
122. Before: Prefix

120 EXTRA VALUES Keith Blake

ACROSS

1. Baseball throw
4. Ten: Lat.
9. Egyptian god
12. Word with air or way
15. Forebear, in Berlin
16. Fault
18. Singing voice
20. Princess of G. & S.
21. "Guys and Dolls" guy
23. "__, thou winter wind"
25. Collection
26. Miss Page
27. Work unit
29. Hit the hay
30. Cover again
32. Optical beams
35. Checks one's arithmetic
36. Spigots
37. Off balance
39. Mother's plea
41. __ Dai
42. Dry
43. Faulkner title
47. Scottish port
49. Kahn et al.
50. English school
51. Deal in hot tips
52. Inscribed
53. Dress up
54. Kind of talk
57. Hepburn role
60. Jezebel's king
61. Service initials
62. Kelp, for one
63. Frost line
68. Heavy cart
69. Direction
70. Mountain snow
71. Spanish zither
72. Skelton or Holzman
73. Evangeline's Grand __
74. Upstate N. Y. county
76. Word of disgust
77. "Umble" person
78. __ avis
79. Sines, e.g.
81. Round words
84. Way: Abbr.
86. Men's org.
87. King Cole
88. Half a Jules Verne number
89. Plain in Spain
91. Ones with low IQ's
94. Large, in Italy
96. "But there's __ in your eyes"
98. __ régime
99. Brynner
100. Like raisins
103. Someone, in Seville
104. Son of J.F.K.
107. Reproof for the angry
110. Wolframite
111. Extinct bird
112. Calm expanses
113. Essence
114. Cape
115. Greek letter
116. Fourth-down maneuvers
117. Political victors

DOWN

1. Barnum
2. Bivouacked
3. Before whiz
4. Depression
5. Give out
6. Roman saint
7. Before
8. See 63 Across
9. "__ Ballads"
10. Wing
11. German theologian
12. Water barrier
13. Broadway show
14. Grows light
15. What Bismarck called politics
16. Indonesian
17. Wheel part, in London
19. "__ is me!"
22. Discs: Abbr.
24. Tattle about
28. Kind of monkey
31. Vermont mountain
33. Like a Mid-east alliance
34. Day of worship: Abbr.
37. Aid's partner
38. Mao __ -tung
40. Fly
43. Commandment breaker
44. Type mold
45. Lack of accent
46. Record
48. Certain votes
52. Reporter's question
54. Entreaty
55. "Rome of Hungary"
56. Hemingway
57. Naval off.
58. Rent
59. "When I was __"
60. Mellow
61. Samovar
62. Brass instruments
64. Admission fee to child's show
65. Operatic barber et al.
66. Mouths
67. Mexican's assent
73. Through
74. "... succeed __ again"
75. "__ a Camera"
76. __ Alto
77. Narcotic
79. Cruise port
80. Remain mounted
81. Jo, Meg et al.
82. Hang back
83. Map-making device
85. Textile devices
86. Mexican state
90. Be __ loser
91. Serious
92. Province of Saudi Arabia
93. Pry
95. Inning units
96. Conjunctions
97. Dutch town
101. Tenant's concern
102. Annoys
105. Chiefs: Abbr.
106. We, in Italy
108. Burmese people
109. Roman 1,101

ACROSS

1. Motionless
7. Racing site
12. Word of regret
16. Penults, sportswise
21. Mexican fare
22. One who snoops
23. Frank's wrap
24. Some writing
25. Popular line for printers
27. Kind of press
29. Tennis term
30. Of the ear
31. Baby talk
33. Severn tributary
34. Poetic word
35. Solo
37. Do a farm chore
39. Movie dog
40. Railing support
42. Log
45. Drudgery
47. Vegetable
48. Soothe
51. Zodiac sign
53. French titles
55. Wheys
59. Worship
60. Where to learn the score
63. Suez peninsula
64. Filch, old style
65. Tipplers
67. Begins, poetically
68. Davis or Ryder
71. Come upon
72. Blanc, etc.
74. Slicker
77. Roman dictator
79. Even up
80. November sky sight
82. Kilns
83. Do galley labor
85. Term of respect
86. Golfer's goal
87. Common verb
88. Got ready to drive
89. Kind of "we"
92. Triple Crown horse
95. Vast plains
98. River of France
99. Approximates
100. Trifling

102. Light carriage
103. Stub __
105. Intersperse
106. "__ deal"
107. __ avis
109. Le Gallienne
110. Earth, to Plautus
112. Peanuts' showcase
116. Kind of beam
118. Synthetic
120. Photog's solution
121. Sandy's to
122. Decline, in Arles
123. Wearing brogans
125. Time periods
127. Surprise
130. Won back
134. Oafs
136. Old wheat measure
137. India, China, etc.
141. Red Baron, e.g.
142. Building beam
143. Ardor
144. Applications
146. Direction
147. Help Wanted, for one
150. Vehicles for debs
154. Gold unit: Var.
155. Distant: Prefix
156. Dewy
157. Aerie tenant
158. Eye swellings
159. Port of Algeria
160. Seed: Prefix
161. Inhibits

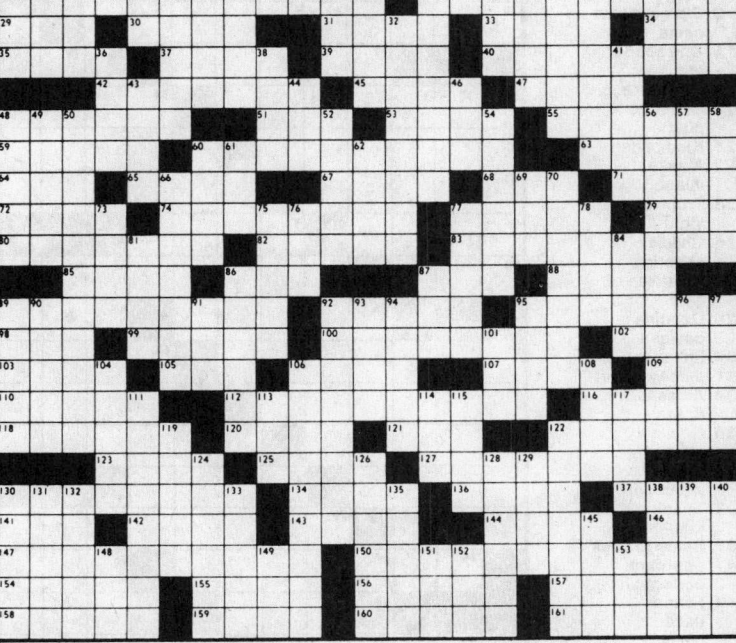

DOWN

1. Inscribed pillar
2. Yam's relative
3. Violin maker
4. Oriental morality
5. Pelvis: Prefix
6. Middle
7. Sidewalk sight
8. Lawn waterer: Abbr.
9. Spanish hero
10. Maryland town

11. Obvious fact
12. Fish of Brazil
13. Spanish article
14. Preakness winner in 1942
15. Eastern European
16. Thistle parts
17. Period
18. Choral piece
19. French river
20. Passover feast
26. Southern fish
28. Soft drinks
32. Certain dancers
36. Discordant
38. __ Alto
41. Letter stroke
43. Cheers
44. Irish sea god
46. Relay-race unit
48. Twice-told
49. Roman official
50. Typesetters
52. Indians

54. Established
56. International precedent
57. Violent desire
58. Word with lop or one
60. Terminals: Abbr.
61. Greek letter
62. Tiff
66. Sent for
69. Gums: Prefix
70. Guy Fawkes, for one
73. In a __ (excited)
75. Short fibers
76. Peaked
77. Flower arrangement
78. For __ (not free)
81. Mashie, e.g.
84. Accounting: Abbr.
86. Virgil of cartoons
87. Cry of triumph
89. Gladden

90. Fond grandparent
91. Samoan bird
92. Like auto-seller's extras
93. Varied: Abbr.
94. "With __ of thousands" (movie ad)
95. Cookie
96. Overhangs
97. Kind of tire
101. Swiss canton
104. Remove
106. Used unduly
108. Shepard
111. Nonbelievers
113. Grandchild, in Dundee
114. Pagoda
115. Take it easy
117. Batman
119. Snake deity
122. Showing surprise
124. Unheeding
126. Fits of energy
128. Faithful
129. Dismiss

130. Draws off wine
131. Applause
132. Relative of darling
133. Laundry unit
135. Nose
138. Phase
139. Scoff
140. Dry runs
145. Prophesy: Scot.
148. Auto group: Abbr.
149. High note
151. Labor initials
152. Mideast land: Abbr.
153. Govt. sleuth

122 MAN'S WORLD — Thomas W. Schier

ACROSS

1. Beats it
5. Footnote words
10. Old newsreel name
15. One spade, etc.
19. Sleep like —
20. Under, to poets
21. Kind of den
22. Alaskan island
23. Tropical sight
25. Childish shooting
27. Relatives of cols.
28. Gelatine devices
30. Emissary
31. Jersey resort
34. Aides to Santa
35. Goalie's specialty
36. Chemical compound
37. Shankar's instrument
38. Came to pass
41. Approach perfection
42. Former Italian domain
44. — Cruces
46. Eve's eldest
47. Twist
48. Nail part
49. Confined
50. N. E. cape
51. Offerings of some museums
55. Transition in music
56. Thorn, in old Rome
57. — even keel
58. Newsman
59. Child's swing, at times
62. Fabric finish
63. Place for a pea
64. San —
65. Behold, à la Cassius
66. Oak's beginning
67. Roman official
68. Chesterton creation
71. Dance step
74. Fund-raiser's word
75. Tarry
76. Old French coins
77. Rumor personified
78. "Fables in Slang" writer
79. Prayer
83. Mehta's need
84. Chronic loser
86. Sweetened the pot
87. Bull Run, for one
88. Jungle denizens
89. Oklahoma Indians
90. Dismiss summarily
91. Forearm bone
94. Blazing
95. York or Devon
96. Russian physiologist
98. Promote, in a way
103. Sahl
104. Queen for Louis
105. Be stationary, as a ship
106. Cut of meat
107. Beards of grass
108. Well-worn pants areas
109. Berry tree
110. Exercise cult

DOWN

1. Circuit
2. — loss
3. Janitor's need
4. Moon walkers
5. Equal in value
6. Kind of cash
7. Sedans
8. Native: Suffix
9. Topics
10. Trees
11. Footless creatures
12. Hot info
13. Squeeze
14. Rivaled
15. Slammed
16. Light-bulb lighter
17. Game item
18. Terrier
24. Mandarin's quarters
26. Leeward island
29. Cacholong
31. Approximately
32. Kind of flu
33. Enter informally
34. Did a job in Hamelin
35. Attack
37. Health-resort feature
38. Ex-champ
39. Legal writ
40. Blue river
42. Kind of geometry
43. Title for Macbeth
45. Bullock
47. Coiled: Prefix
49. Juan or Eva
51. Think
52. Dog
53. Reserved
54. Chef's implement
55. Disdain
56. Steps
58. Evinces
59. Ending
60. Pretentious
61. Twaddle
62. Poet's concern
63. Work on pans
66. Formed a bow
68. — a fiddle
69. Arabian gulf
70. Animals, in France
71. Page
72. Soap plant
73. Less wacky
75. Warrior in Norse lore
77. Kind of advice
79. Infield fly
80. Hometowners
81. — about
82. Village sight
83. Mideast port
85. N.O. players
87. Legal deliverer
89. "A Majority — "
90. Paratrooper's need
91. Fissure
92. Declare
93. Embroider
94. "I cannot tell — "
95. Raced
97. Worthy of honor: Abbr.
99. Unctuous speech
100. Ripe old age
101. Sharp movement
102. Spanish queen

123

SEA FARE *Frances Hansen*

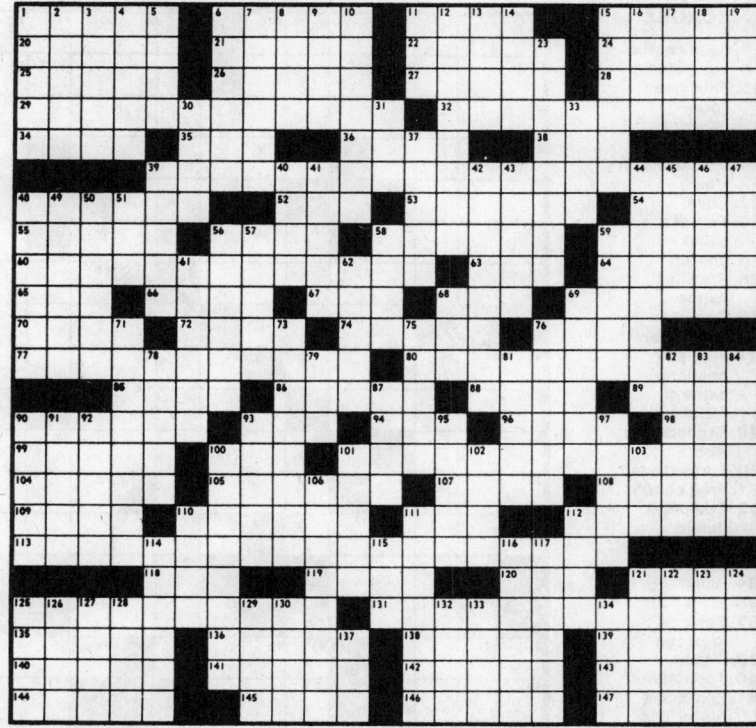

ACROSS

1. Half an operatic name
6. Court of equity: Abbr.
11. Where Luang Prabang is
15. Beanie wearer
20. Believer: Suffix
21. Hoople, for one
22. Titan
24. Where Ephesus was
25. Boojum
26. In embryo: Lat.
27. Lobster claw
28. Fish
29. Folk-opera names, fishy style
32. Unscrupulous ones
34. Latin infinitive
35. Office-seeker: Abbr.
36. Take the hook
38. Lost-mail dept.
39. Attractive paella
48. "The __ the Pussycat"
52. Words of inquiry
53. Rolled a log
54. __ time (pronto)
55. Flower: It.
56. Between a and f
58. Fuel again
59. Celestial spectral type
60. Proceed clumsily
63. Us, in Berlin
64. Yugoslavian town
65. Kind
66. Dravidian
67. Derisive sound
68. Pou __ (base)
69. Fig-bird
70. Stadium
72. Desensitized
74. Kaffir village
76. Weapon: Fr.
77. Ski-trail pattern
80. Exclamation, menu style
85. Kind of code
86. Comic-strip girl
88. "__ the morning to you"
89. Stamped on
90. Fish dish
93. Writer Josephine
94. W. W. II craft
96. African river
98. French pronoun
99. Of __ to (inclined)
100. Hurok
101. Warning to the undecided
104. Sorrowing figure
105. Medicine-cabinet item
107. Bridge hand
108. Where Wiesbaden is
109. European capital
110. Popular salad
111. Army unit: Abbr.
112. Group of five
113. What Pistol said to Falstaff
118. Purchase
119. Moore work
120. Noun suffix
121. Delays
125. Treat for 29 Across, maybe
131. Relative of yipes
135. Mature
136. Letter
138. Turnpike features
139. Ruth's mother-in-law
140. Earl Carroll specialty
141. Like an old sweater
142. Spry
143. Steel city
144. Dominion
145. Lear's Pobble hasn't any
146. Stendhal character
147. Shellfish

DOWN

1. Canadian peninsula
2. Peter et al.
3. Some fishermen
4. At __ (on the lam)
5. Like a squid's weapon
6. Musical key
7. Treat
8. Do __ on (trick)
9. Resurging star
10. Bob and Bing
11. Wax ingredient
12. Muscular
13. Kitchen staple
14. Senora's room
15. "... __ the sea" (Genesis)
16. City on the Tevere
17. Corker
18. Worm product
19. Sailors
23. Launces
30. Endorsed: Abbr.
31. Dr. Ota __, Czech reformer
33. Slipped, old style
37. Jewish month
39. Concerning
40. African people: Var.
41. By __ (incidentally)
42. Baby steelhead
43. Grassy plain
44. Most dubious
45. Musical vamp
46. French delicacy
47. Vast number
48. Distant in manner
49. "How __ marry ... ?"
50. Pretty gal
51. Islands off New Guinea
56. Source of 90 Across
57. Prepare, as fish
58. German river
59. "One __ master ..."
61. Bill collector
62. Like a certain bucket
68. My gal
69. Furniture decoration
71. "There's __ in the sky"
73. Filleted
75. Deep gulf
76. Appearance
78. Decree
79. Certain vote
81. Bar orders
82. First __
83. Alcott
84. Revised
87. Jewel piece
90. Boat: Fr.
91. Mennonite
92. __ d'orchestre
93. Trifled
95. On __ (active)
97. Upper space
100. Terrier
101. Madden: Lat.
102. Like a grain
103. Big or Gentle
106. Mexican state
110. French vineyards
111. Shark suckers
112. Orchestra part: Abbr.
114. __ dictum
115. O. T. book
116. Like Simon
117. Prickly herb
121. Restrain
122. Came up
123. Paired
124. Walk like Theda Bara
125. Fish
126. To that point: Lat.
127. Between s and x
128. Chimney part
129. Vivid display
130. German king
132. Como or Nemi
133. Norse giant
134. Experienced
137. Rickover et al., to friends

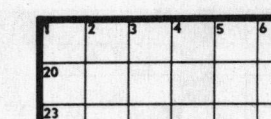 **LITERARY LICENSE** *Eugene T. Maleska*

ACROSS

1. Sells or tells
8. Vacillated
15. They need good memories
20. Armpits
21. Restlessly, in music
22. Cove
23. Tale of a colicky cherub
25. Brazilian dance
26. Con __ (vigorously)
27. Five-star headline name of 1934
28. Granada girl: Abbr.
30. Formed a lap
31. Fruit punch
32. Complete defeat
33. Teachers' org.
34. Allied org.
35. Main point
37. Early Mexican
39. No bid
40. Topnotcher
41. Like some butterflies
43. Coin for Plato
45. Class
47. Mots of a sort
48. Emulates Petruchio
50. Inviting word
52. Revivalist's advice
55. Least ruffled
57. Vashti's successor
59. Tilled land in Texas
60. Swedish port
61. Viscount's superior
63. Antitoxins
64. Calendar abbr.
65. Monstrous hot-dog with beer
69. Hebrew letter
70. Pielet
72. Seed for a plot
73. Homes, in Ponce
74. Where a belle might dwell
76. Packed
78. Pittsburgh pro
80. Triplets
81. Yemen's neighbor
82. Used a whetstone
83. Control

84. Business-letter abbr.
86. Price
87. Discusses at length
91. Savoir-faire
93. Bald __ eagle
95. Accent
98. Third Reich salute
99. Nobel chemist
100. Waikiki wreath
101. Where to find an M.D.
102. Sky Altar
103. Hodges or Blas
104. Line of cliffs
106. Beldams
108. Mardi __
109. Quink or brant
111. Tale of a scale
114. Big Bertha's birthplace

115. Saint-Exupéry
116. Oeufs à __ (menu item)
117. Loved too fondly
118. Man with a yen
119. Insecticide, sort of

DOWN

1. Collections of trivia
2. Introductions
3. Most neat
4. Further
5. Inauspicious
6. "The best __ schemes . . ."
7. Bars used in shipbuilding
8. Graceful tree
9. Italian broker
10. Roman streets
11. Catch-all abbr.

12. Bowl calls
13. Ceaseless
14. Fishing boats
15. "David and __"
16. __ rut
17. Sequel to "The Beggar's Opera"
18. Discount
19. Machine part
24. County in Montana
29. Assignment
34. Music works
36. Did a stenog's job
37. Add color
38. Treatise on economy
39. Mad or had
42. __ the mill
44. Nectar expert
46. French pronoun
48. Filibuster

49. City in Michigan
51. Part of H.S.H.
52. Catamarans
53. Printing mistakes
54. Tale of missing cubes
55. Malaccas
56. Tamerlane
57. Wallach
58. Kind of gin fizz
60. Frantic
62. In medias __
66. Disencumber
67. Valley
68. Of the nostrils
71. Score
75. Shore
77. U.S.N.A. grad
79. Aurora
80. Hardy girl
83. Orthographizes again

85. Aftershave item
86. One of Sadat's people
87. U.S.S.R. river
88. Next
89. Organ-pedal coupler
90. Swordsman, at times
91. Pulled hard
92. Melodious
94. St. Lawrence
96. Sovereignty
97. His work is on the house
104. Mail
105. Fiber plant
106. Chew the fat
107. Side dish
108. Surfeit
110. Grasp
112. Cockney's oath
113. Lippo Lippi

INDEPENDENCE DAY
Sylvia Baumgarten

ACROSS

1. Five, for Cicero
8. En __
13. Shade of green
20. Rare-earth metals
21. Of a mouth part
23. Withstood
24. Toothed, as a leaf
25. Enliven
26. The Magi, e.g.
27. Methods: Abbr.
28. Overall fabric
29. Serve tea
30. Crucial signal choice from North Church
37. Rate of interest: Abbr.
40. Foreign
41. Opposite of a magnum
42. Scottish county
43. Jumping
45. Common French verb
46. Juilliard degree
49. Porridge choice
50. Kadiddlehopper
51. Batters anew
53. Yr. Obdt. __
55. __ Mater
57. Casino game
58. Seven: Prefix
59. Sounds of inquiry
61. Mrs. Priest and others
62. Blitzen's buddy
63. Word for Rome
66. Shorten sail
68. French season
69. Ties
70. Element in uranium series
71. Mascara recipient
73. Prefix for derm or plasm
74. Grow rapidly
75. Capable of an answer
76. Hymn tune
80. Hardy girl
81. More out of practice
82. Woman's accessory
83. "__ Again"
86. Writer Anais
87. Isaac's son
88. Go Marcel Marceau one better
89. Worn away
90. "The Razor's __"
92. Religious degree
93. Impatient
94. Shensi city
95. British country wear
97. Gumshoe
99. Igneous rock
100. Brace
101. Quiet!
102. Disastrous defeat
104. Scottish hillside
106. Missile platform
107. Style
108. Prop for a stage extra
110. Matured, as fruit
112. Wool: Prefix
113. Date of a famous warning
119. Certain word
120. Part of a phono record
121. "...upon so __ subject as myself"
125. Leeward island
128. Damaging, as a fender
129. Color of embarrassment
131. __ (Beetle) Smith
132. Pastoral scene, to French
133. Angels' home
134. Type of pass
135. Combatants in a certain battle
136. Mortarboard adornments

DOWN

1. Math abbreviations
2. Nobel chemist
3. Saud and others
4. Capone lieutenant
5. Apparently
6. Draft program: Abbr.
7. Mariner's direction
8. Windfalls
9. Adjusted
10. Organizer of 57 Down
11. __ Zagora, Bulgaria
12. Consumed
13. Helmsman
14. Make an __ (finish)
15. Without __ (certainly)
16. Like some winter coats
17. Wash. neighbor
18. Atmosphere: Prefix
19. Kildare and Welby
21. Follower of 30 Across
22. Yorkshire city
28. Textile workers
31. Enemies
32. Honorary mil. commission
33. Having twin A.C. circuits
34. Spanish greeting
35. Small hole
36. Weapons suppliers
37. Doers of a grammar chore
38. Spotted cat
39. Sub's weapon
44. April 19 in New England
47. Latin adverb
48. Emulates the grasshopper
50. Battle town
52. Troops at 50 Down
54. Junior Pliny
56. Embattled farmers' place
57. Significant party of 1773
60. Blinds, as a falcon
62. Nazi camp near Munich
64. Entertained
65. Circuits
67. Groove in a pillar
72. Chasm: Var.
73. Imitate
77. Mrs. John Adams
78. Thin layer
79. Family name of dukes of Bridgewater
83. "Seven __ Baldpate"
84. Cromwell's son-in-law
85. Having sound
86. Wifely pick-me-up
91. Nigerian
95. Behind __ (in trouble)
96. Colonial grievance
98. Cleveland Clinic founder
99. Snake charmer's clarinet
101. Mollusk genus
103. Up on deck
105. Bee: Prefix
108. Poet Alan or singer Pete
109. Girl's name
111. Lopez et al.
114. Historic Danish family
115. Cricket term
116. Hot-goods handler
117. Pirates' domain
118. Twice 100ths
122. "Born __"
123. Linden tree
124. Nimitz and Halsey: Abbr.
125. Shoemaker's tool
126. Basketball org.
127. Asian holiday
129. Vampire
130. Spanish queen

126 REVERSALS *Paul R. Barnes*

ACROSS

1. Backward spring month
6. Simpleton
10. Trick
14. Anser or brant
15. Occupy
16. Wheys
17. Sherman or Reynolds
18. Cartoonist Hype __
19. First man
20. Aides of drs.
21. Writer Carson
23. Lucrezia
24. Occult doctrine
26. Asian sea and town
27. "I __ to a suggestion"
29. Island off Naples
32. Heavy blow
33. Piles
34. Of age: Abbr.
37. Imagine
40. Mold anew
42. Part of E.S.T.: Abbr.
43. Person
45. Fish sauce
46. Begin a meal
47. Buckingham, for one
49. Towaway __
52. Dutch city
54. Pepper's partner
55. Houston eleven
57. Peer Gynt's mother
60. Head: Fr.
61. Tiny thing
62. More accurate
64. Got off
65. Within: Prefix
66. Big artery: Fr.
67. Deteriorates
68. Bonded laborer
69. Hebrew prophet

DOWN

1. Sew a falcon's eyes
2. Unless, in old Rome
3. Bright room
4. Cut off
5. Kind of grape
6. In __ of a mess
7. Small flute
8. Exchange premium
9. Berber
10. Decisive point
11. Macaw
12. Riding contest
13. Disconcert
22. Burrows or Lincoln
25. Implement
26. Exclamations
27. Mild oath: Var.
28. Deodar or baobab
30. Listen
31. Ginger
33. Little devils
34. Most heartless
35. Sheltered
36. Rubber
38. Metal
39. Happy: Fr.
41. Every
44. Bien __ (of course)
46. Turns informer
47. Freshwater fish
48. Brave
49. Printing marks
50. Name
51. Upstate N.Y. city
53. Norman Vincent __
55. French names
56. Repute
58. Endings with sen and jun
59. Hari
63. Consumed

AFTER YOU ALPHONSE

Frances Hansen

ACROSS

1. Milquetoast
7. Teen-age party wear
14. Goose variety
20. Grounded
21. In fashion
22. Small simian
23. Impassive
24. Separate
25. Cesar of films
26. Certain employee
28. Prisoner's remark to judge
30. Ridge
31. Indians
32. Big birds
33. Cheese
35. Autocrat
39. Daunt
42. Legal claim
45. Motto of Oxford unit
51. Parser's concern
53. Refrigerator bin
54. Gay
55. __ out (evade)
56. Western org.
57. Seine areas
59. Among: Prefix
60. File
62. Falcon's source
63. Antimacassar
64. Apology to Clementine
70. Catface
74. Daub
75. Intensifies
80. Defeat
82. S.A. Monkey
83. Boxer's move
86. Potter's tool
87. Superior
88. East or West
90. "It takes __ livin' . . ."
91. Cleveland Amory people
95. Handle: Lat.
96. Browne
97. Lafayette College town
98. Lawyers: Abbr.
100. Gallup item
102. Fashion name
105. Mosquito genus
109. "Oops, sorry"
113. Bump in a road
116. __ mind
117. Singer
119. Right away
120. Not seemly
121. Illusion
122. Handgun
123. Cowboys
124. Regrets
125. Navigator's aid

DOWN

1. Roman conspirator
2. About
3. Thrust
4. Social asset
5. Coated, as a seed
6. Magenta, etc.
7. Churchman
8. Vibrant
9. Breeds of fowl
10. Sun god
11. Sahl
12. Military asst.
13. Ooze
14. To Bugs Bunny's taste
15. Footless class
16. Remote TV broadcasts
17. Danish measure
18. Skin: Prefix
19. Stub __
27. Girl's name
29. Running wild
34. Writer Eric
35. M.D.'s
36. Discovery
37. Sniffs
38. "Mind and Society" author
39. Violin
40. Declined
41. Ledger item
42. "Green Pastures" role
43. Prefix for logy
44. Girls' names
46. Sgt., e.g.
47. Initials of the 30's
48. Ice: Ger.
49. Color or corn
50. Cue
52. Whitelaw or Ogden
58. Chalcedony
61. Take five
62. Wall: Fr.
65. José's friends
66. Loathe
67. __ middling
68. High tea
69. Uh-huh
70. Horse of 1955
71. Lethal snake
72. "__ With a View"
73. Invitation initials
76. Satisfy fully
77. Esprit
78. Fiber knots
79. Portico
81. Golf word
83. Peerce
84. Cuckoo
85. __ nose
89. After "hoot"
92. Lets up
93. Tea and sympathy
94. Not any
99. Bovine
100. Baby food
101. Willow
102. 1912 Nobel physicist
103. Unmoving
104. Vegetables
106. Tapir
107. Early colonist
108. Young fish
109. Ivory: Lat.
110. A kind of phobia
111. David, for one
112. O. T. book
113. Spruce
114. Unique place
115. Sweetheart, British style
118. So!

128 THE GANG'S ALL HERE
Nancy Schuster

ACROSS

1. Voracious S.A. fish
7. Gave support
12. A Davis
17. Having wings
18. Disregards
20. City of the Prater
22. ___ one's own
23. Historic do
25. Curl
26. Miss Merrill
27. Purloin
28. Remorseful one
29. Pronoun
30. Pain reliever
33. Preceding month: Abbr.
34. ___ facias
35. Flimsy pretense
37. News edition
39. Group having a common culture
40. Mark of disgrace
42. Sky item?
43. Fail, familiarly
44. Stendhal
45. Name coined in 1880
51. Scold
53. Form of Greek language
54. Flour base
55. Ne'er-do-well
56. Swiss canton
57. Arranged
59. Fashion name
60. O'Hara home
61. Play about
63. Islands off Galway
64. Christ: Poetic
65. River to North Sea
66. S. A. capital
67. Female swans
68. Part of the street scene
71. Decimal base
72. Maple genus
73. Swedish river
74. Dostoevski heroine
75. Eats greedily
77. Game some people play
80. Sick's partner
81. Lamb
82. ___ de mer
83. Fortune-telling cards
85. Sugar or salt
88. Brown pigment
90. Pond sight
93. Flynn
94. Common verb
95. Tag again
97. Ginger or pepper
99. Italian lake
100. Like neon
102. Father
103. Words on a valentine
105. Fundamental of democracy
108. With "all," a smarty
109. Tranquil
110. Discourses
111. Move back
112. Old instruments
113. Campus V.I.P.'s
114. Stage remarks

DOWN

1. Snag
2. Sacker of Rome
3. Dashing
4. News article
5. Aid and abet
6. Sullivan and Begley
7. Pain
8. Mad
9. Morse signal
10. Olympian
11. Fitted with teeth
12. Race track
13. Use a straw
14. Emergency group
15. Moldering
16. Intestine: Prefix
18. Footnote word
19. Engraved pillar
21. Actor Lew
24. Mother's plea
26. Sidestep
31. Pinner
32. Spread out
34. End
36. Cruising
38. Spike
39. Churchman
41. Marketplaces
43. Baseball term
44. A full glass
46. Nothing, in Paris
47. Indian state
48. Cooked
49. Serving dish
50. Aches for
51. Coarse cloth
52. Beethoven's Third
53. Central part
58. Devil: Var.
59. Stop
62. Killjoy
64. Crossroads: Abbr.
67. Cocoon dwellers
68. Janitor's concern
69. Bird
70. Busybodies' delights
74. Thrust
76. Evening, on a prescription
78. Whoop
79. Absorbed in
80. Seneca, e.g.
84. Some clocks
85. Factions
86. Implement
87. The art of heraldry
88. Noted chemist and family
89. ___ one's laurels
91. Declared
92. Conquer's partner
94. Amazon or soldier
96. Legal claims
98. Distributes
100. Angers
101. Ancient port
104. Places
106. Chemical suffix
107. Scottish wee
108. Ape of India

129 STIR CRAZY *Edward J. O'Brien*

ACROSS

1. Postal items: Abbr.
5. Decline
8. Filipinos
15. Balcony: Abbr.
18. Shout for attention
19. Teachers' org.
20. Glossy paints
21. Santa's sounds
22. 63481, 71120, 52893, etc.
24. Plucky penologists
26. Possess
27. Bound
28. Steal: Slang
29. More pleasant
31. "Life __ an empty dream!"
33. Tuscaloosa inmate's song
38. Wrong
39. Roman god
40. Jannings
41. Whales
42. Ventilate anew
43. Ziegfeld
44. Sarcastic telegram
47. Riboflavin: Abbr.
48. Western state: Abbr.
49. Dine
50. In itself: Lat.
51. Wing
53. __-cat
54. Rice-field vehicle
57. Golf's Palmer
59. Mil. medal
61. "I'm doing well, __?"
62. Red gurnards
64. "Master, __?" (Judas's question)
66. Lemon color: Abbr.
67. Independence monogram
69. "... as lovely as __"
70. __ fit (clothier's offer)
72. Ancient flint
74. Pronoun
75. Stare, in England
76. Inmate's side of the story?
79. Recipe units: Abbr.
83. Spanish uncle
84. "... could __ horse!"
86. Conclude
87. Eur. nation
88. Gas: Prefix
89. Black Maria?
92. Grid scores
93. Las Vegas area
94. Corded fabric: Var.
95. Chem. compound
96. Wander
97. Allen and Lawrence
98. Convicted bigamist
102. Pretenses
103. __-missabib (Jer. 20:3)
104. Day: Abbr.
105. Growl
107. Printing devices: Abbr.
109. Value of yeast
113. Stack of mod records
115. Master: Var.
116. Gush back
117. Miss Arden
118. Closing word
119. Tokyo coins: Abbr.
120. Lies atop
121. Attention
122. Old rulers

DOWN

1. Toadfish
2. "__ heart shall be called prudent"
3. Keystone prison conditions
4. Opp. of antonym
5. Antagonism
6. Lager
7. 24 hours in a Paris jail
8. Mendicant
9. As a whole
10. Where Pago Pago is
11. "I am __ of the rabble"
12. Evergreen
13. Carte or mode
14. Eurasian union
15. "__ Nights"
16. They power cells?
17. "His glassy __ an angry ape"
23. Dilute: Sp.
25. Book of lives: Abbr.
30. Boxing units: Abbr.
32. Incarcerate Bambi?
34. Peking name
35. I go round: Lat.
36. Mine: Fr.
37. Harvests: Abbr.
38. Afternoon, in Australia
43. Angelico
44. Cattle fold
45. "__ off"(sale ad)
46. Affluence
48. Thesis abbr.
49. Optometrist's cherished alma mater?
52. The, in Nice
55. Deplete: Dialect
56. Piths
58. Spins again
60. Last night: Scot.
63. Front yards
64. In a small-minded way
65. Birdman of Alcatraz
68. Ph. D., for some
70. Deputy: Abbr.
71. Hydrocarbon
73. Eye part
77. "... an __ a sail"
78. Suffix with joy
80. Moment for a tennis player
81. Brit. writer
82. Bribes
85. Arabian gulf
90. Climbs skyward
91. Eclipse
92. Hebrew letter
93. Wading bird
94. Phono-record abbr.
96. N. Y. village
97. Typewriter bar
99. A Wright, for short
100. Brit. ridges
101. Release
106. Flaring star
108. Wash. men
110. Misjudge
111. Born: Fr.
112. Plane parts: Abbr.
114. Bed, to some

ACROSS

1. Jewish feast
6. Kind of tow or boot
9. Uses a scythe
14. "_ steals my purse..."
17. Nerve conductor
18. Charged atom
19. Transfer permit
20. Sumptuous
22. Cain's home
24. Call up
25. "Be Prepared," for one
26. Museum offering
27. Activate a cradle
28. Linden tree
29. Sweetened the kitty
31. Roman 650
32. Chuck-a-luck unit
33. Old anthology
35. Biblical coin
37. Warning
38. Other
39. Succinct
41. Kind of storm
42. Gloomy man
44. Serling
47. Diminutive ending
49. _ publica
51. What lilies don't do
53. Asserts
55. Moslem mascaras
57. Sound of despair
60. Glowing
62. Rumanian composer
64. Saunter
66. Disengaged
67. Society gal
68. Condensed: Abbr.
70. Relating to eight
71. March or Holbrook
72. Decrepit boat
75. Spooky
77. _ the track
79. Membrane
81. Like Sherlock's methods
84. Used an ax
86. French city
87. French tree
88. Musical ending
90. Oriental principle
91. Greetings for Orphan Annie
92. Antelope
93. After upsilon
94. Scottish river
97. Server
100. Ball
103. Trade combine
105. Gypsy
108. Comment of Henry Ford
111. Gain
112. West
113. Take in
114. Relatives
115. Computer fare
116. Certain records
117. Emulated Mata Hari
118. Halt abruptly
120. Toasts to Morpheus
122. Bridge reverses
123. Lena
124. Drink
125. Pyle
126. Lease
127. Filled
128. Thor or Zeus
129. Teams

DOWN

1. Vegetable dishes
2. Eastern church title
3. Retiring child's wisecrack
4. Pass-catcher
5. Stock up
6. Because
7. Nutty one
8. Neither Dem. nor Rep.
9. Some TV fare
10. Salon events
11. Group of Greek dialects
12. Man of pipes
13. U.S. violinist
14. Maligns
15. Song of 1942
16. Singing group
21. Scuttles
23. Rapiers
25. Jouster's wear
28. Hole: Fr.
30. Chemical suffixes
33. Famous last words
34. Sea god
36. Boat parts
40. Work unit
43. Jesse of Calif.
45. Admit
46. Time abbr.
47. Squeezed out
48. Kind of poem
50. Speech pauses
52. Rock Hudson movie
53. Confounds
54. Henry or Edward
56. Hard to get
58. Old chest
59. Mountain gap
61. Duck genus
63. News piece
65. Geneva, for one
69. German state
73. Fliers' org.
74. Prohibits
76. Continent: Abbr.
78. Educ. group
80. Kingdom
81. Hammarskjold
82. Sea eagle
83. Behold: Fr.
85. U.S. money: Abbr.
89. Flying
93. Paris area
95. Flew with a flourish
96. Camera part
98. Math branch
99. Is charitable
101. Relaxing
102. Burden
104. Classify
106. Serving dish: Var.
107. Certain replies
108. Famed W. W. II internee
109. Urge
110. Slangy affirmatives
111. Carried on
115. Queen of Carthage
119. Neckpiece
120. Plater
121. Dernier _

WILD FLOWERS

Mary M. Murdoch

ACROSS

1. High and reverse, e.g.
6. You love: Lat.
10. Bureau: Abbr.
14. Levels
19. Rent again
20. Parcel of land
21. Seaweed
23. Sherry
24. Flower's parting words
26. Elite of flowerdom
28. Flowery proposal in old song
30. Broadway signs
31. Paris airport
32. Some cats and dogs
33. Shoe parts
36. Run __ in the paper
37. Italian pot
38. Waldorf, for one
41. Ocean: Abbr.
43. Estimate
47. Word with way and sea
48. Danish measures
49. __ -Magnon
50. Remnant
51. Flowery put-off
54. Aspen gear
55. Cloth strainer
56. Kind of alcohol
57. Boxing outcomes: Abbr.
58. Scabbard part
59. Alike: Fr.
60. Gem weight
61. Weekday: Abbr.
62. Gay ones
63. Kind of room, for short
64. Very wealthy flower
67. Arbor
68. Frog sound
70. Up to __
71. Opera voices
72. Make even
74. Flowery animal groups
80. Rested
83. Four-baggers
84. Long time
85. Dances
86. Pianist Hess
87. Fuses
88. Buses and trains: Abbr.
89. Guardian of sailors
91. Aspect
92. Rehan et al.
93. Transgress in a flowery way
95. Lasso
96. Peleg's son
97. Girl, in Paris
98. Old big-game guns
99. Shout
100. Spread hay
101. Scolded
102. Bits
103. Fraternal org.
105. Fortification
107. Pub offerings
108. Perry's creator
109. Italian island
113. "Aster no questions __"
119. Halt, in a flowery way
122. Stein words
123. Of birds
124. Swift descent
125. Open
126. Paint worker
127. Furious
128. Early slave
129. TV's Parker
130. Methods: Abbr.

DOWN

1. Luggage pieces
2. Fisherman
3. __ the good
4. Puzzle
5. British gun
6. Benedict or Hap
7. Virile
8. Sharp
9. Bachelors' dinner, e.g.
10. Fliers
11. Cooper et al.
12. Baby's bed
13. Gypsum
14. Surpasses
15. Green, in Paris
16. Time period
17. Seine
18. Draft system: Abbr.
20. Headpiece
22. Cardboard box: Abbr.
25. Utopias
27. Available
29. Close again
34. Listless, gardenwise
35. Kind of bass
36. Snakes
37. Wife of Ahasuerus
38. One who pillages
39. Slack, old style
40. Camera part
42. __ bet (wagers badly)
43. Flower
44. Actors' milieu
45. Shrubby kind of degree
46. Ludwig
47. Deadly
51. Scoundrel: Scot.
52. Artificial fly
53. Small case
54. Put-ons
58. Brooch
60. Dice game
61. Edible root
62. Scottish hillsides
64. City on the Loire
65. Preposition
66. Eastman
69. Orchestra section
71. On earth
72. Frustrate
73. European buck
74. Convict's goal
75. Cured
76. Kind of wolf
77. Emancipators
78. Vends
79. Blood: Prefix
81. Mountain ridge
82. Soviet republic
86. Certain delivery
88. Pinball flash
89. Put up
90. __ Russia (title of Ivan IV)
91. Cleaving tool
93. Food
94. Author of "Phineas Finn"
97. Kukla, __ Ollie
99. E. Indies weights
103. Prickly plants
104. Braid
106. __ Lama
107. Illinois city
108. It's nobody __ business
109. Ex-pitcher Face
110. Civic club
111. Assail
112. Son of Jacob et al.
114. Wall and State: Abbr.
115. U. S. inventor
116. Some poetry
117. Moved, as a ship
118. Cereal
119. Smoking __
120. Gardner
121. Women's __

132 OBSERVATIONS *Henry V. Straka*

ACROSS

1. Syrian city, to French
5. Vehicle
9. Pair up
14. Fighter planes of W. W. I
19. Greek dais
20. Roofing piece
21. Zola
22. Paine product
23. Indians
24. Indian plum
25. Mass. port
26. Nest
27. Playboy's version of a right
31. Harem
32. Force: Lat.
33. Newspaper section: Abbr.
34. Radical
35. Roman writer
38. Restrain
42. "I wasn't there"
46. Flaunted
47. Bright bird
48. Tabula __
49. Laws: Abbr.
51. W. W. II vessel
53. Blue glass
54. Coal dust
55. Ankles
56. Troupers
59. Reno leavers
60. Horse
62. Yokel
64. Formality
66. Possible query of a zoo ape
72. Sir Robert
73. Indian of West
74. The Met forbids these
76. __ cry
80. Depletes
82. Salinger girl
84. Louvre name
85. Pacific island group
87. Guinness, e.g.
88. Kind of breath
89. Coins in Riga
90. Three in one
92. Plane-engine housing
95. Units of force
96. Reparation
97. Nail décor
98. Keresan Indian
100. Kind of bunt
102. Saratoga, for one

103. City near L. A.
108. Millionaire's pad
114. Cottontails
115. Lag behind
116. __ over lightly
117. Binge
118. Small ones: Suffix
119. French year
120. River to Elbe
121. Instrument
122. Germs
123. Rises high
124. Time periods in Wild West
125. Goes down

DOWN

1. Borders on
2. River of Hades
3. Eastern prince
4. Kemal __
5. Basic item
6. Serene
7. Tucson suburb
8. College figure
9. Scylla's strait
10. Gathered
11. Spanish linden
12. Musical symbol
13. Rope fibers
14. Track officials
15. H-hour at a newspaper
16. Egyptian abode of dead
17. Roman 602
18. Word on a proof
28. Fields: Lat.
29. Baseball great
30. Capable of
35. Swift output
36. Ancient Briton
37. Gather on a surface
39. Deception
40. She, in Paris
41. Soaks flax
42. Alms box
43. Girl's name
44. Moslem faith
45. Well-known deer
46. Buddy
49. Restrained
50. Oilers
52. Old galley
56. Eggs on
57. Game fish
58. Removed pits
61. Mischief-maker
63. "Once __ a . . ."
65. Common abbr.
67. Lily maid
68. What crystal gazers do
69. Xmas plant
70. Of a lake area
71. Trace: Fr.
75. Lip
76. Movie dog
77. MacDonald's asset
78. French friend
79. Early English Puritan
81. Mideast land
83. Marie, for one
86. "Days of Wine __"
88. Pasture sound
91. Genesis name
93. Drum out of office
94. Pierces: Var.
95. Lulu
98. Pele's game
99. Annoying ones
101. Spectral type
103. Old Asian coin
104. Sedans
105. Weeper of myth
106. Hoof: Scot.
107. Diminutive suffixes
108. "Now hear __!"
109. Sound
110. Gardner
111. Sea bird
112. Blue Nile source
113. O'Hara Pal

133 URBAN RENEWAL A. J. Santora

ACROSS

1. Becomes clogged
6. Beyond
10. Steeple
15. L.A. time
18. Stroller
19. Lover
20. Breadwinner
21. "__ Gang"
22. Earhart
23. "...fetch __ of water"
24. Box-office bargain
25. Sky object
26. Theatrical lament
29. Provisory
30. Hawaiian tree
31. Old come-on in book ads
33. Blood prefix
35. Strong point
36. Medley
37. Doing a bar job
41. Nuclear pact
43. Hockey star
45. Gust of wind
47. War vessel
48. Natives of Cagliari
50. Wine: Prefix
52. Come __ halt
54. Asian antelope
55. Splash
58. Metal sheets
62. S. A. city
64. Average
65. __ debt to society
66. Air-booking problem
67. Place for the moon
70. Nasal bones
73. Weird
74. Portland product: Abbr.
75. Snake
76. With dispatch
82. Three, in Naples
83. Noun suffix
84. Units of fluidity
85. Missile charge
87. Unique birds
90. On the canvas
92. That: Lat.
93. Snare
94. Wire: Abbr.
95. Remainder
97. Storm
99. Partner of older
101. Auto of yore
103. Writer Levin
104. Boron's table listing: Abbr.
106. Barnstorming
108. Drain
110. Flying group: Abbr.
113. Put __ (halt)
117. O. Henry output
119. A-one
121. Moon goddess
123. Norwegian name
124. Where a heart is
127. State: Abbr.
128. Arizona city
131. Legal eagle
135. Metric unit
136. Spinets
137. Sierra __
138. Former U.N. name
139. Athens letter
140. Directionals
141. Type of beam
142. Works in concert
143. Diego or Remo
144. Resources
145. Printing word
146. St. __, Leeward island

DOWN

1. Person
2. Morning-after items
3. French composer
4. Svelte
5. Attempt
6. __ the picture
7. In __ of speaking
8. French river
9. "Holy" city
10. Looked into
11. City in Utah
12. Overrun
13. Stage direction
14. Make a bevue
15. Backless couch
16. Word addition: Abbr.
17. Kind of weight
18. Gape
19. Speed-trap item
20. Of a people
27. Savings item
28. Presidential name
29. Racing classic
32. Fuegians
34. Phrase for baseball busts
35. Diet
38. Dialect
39. Vamp of silents
40. Suffix for ana or epi
42. Dance, in Paris
44. Answer in kind
46. Slang for money
49. Traffic sign
51. Magazine
53. Tune
55. Medic
56. Truant
57. River of Bolivia
59. In __ (so to speak)
60. Put to __
61. Salmon
63. Triple Crown winner
66. Biblical name
68. Left-hand pages
69. "This __ treat"
71. Present
72. Spy
77. __ -Bains, French spa
78. Scarlett et al.
79. Kind of interest: Abbr.
80. Lopez theme
81. Salvador
86. Eastern state: Abbr.
87. News or fine
88. Must
89. Doer: Suffix
91. Airline-board abbr.
93. Deuces
96. Footballer's protection
97. Handle: Lat.
98. Drinker
100. Mar
102. Streams
105. Samoan bowl
107. Breathe
109. Swamp
111. Fatty
112. Angler's need
114. Make believe
115. Gifts
116. Bachelor __
118. Wasteland
120. Fishing leaders
122. Gray drab
125. Curtain fabric
126. Part of a golf shoe
128. Chatters
129. Sky bear
130. "Meet __ St. Louis"
132. Breaks
133. To you: Fr.
134. Querying word
136. Miss Mason

SURNAMES

Elaine D. Schorr

ACROSS

1. Porridge
5. Covenant
9. Abbr. on a map
13. Kind of shoe or suit
17. Operatic prince
18. Covering: Ger.
19. Mitigates
21. Foot: Prefix
22. Slum-clearance problem
24. Lookout for some
26. Fictional hero's larder
28. Deprives, in a way
31. Slant
32. Author Victor
33. Stradivari's teacher
34. Italian poet
35. Honest name
37. Grafted, in heraldry
40. Appoints
41. Cooper
42. Lord's demesne
44. Neighbor of Neth.
45. Ratite birds
46. Leaf division
47. Russian saint and others
48. Schurz
49. Compass point
50. "Blithe Spirit" author
52. Roulette choice
53. Delibes opera
54. Singer Frankie
56. Result
58. Kind of girl
59. Lobby décor
61. Epic poem
62. Words of apology
63. Tenant
64. Valentino locale
65. Balances
66. Latin abbrs.
67. Nontalker
68. Harrow
71. Graduate degree
74. Air: Prefix
75. Cowpoke's need
76. Macaws
77. French coins
78. Family member
79. Inscribe
80. Perdition
81. Georges of opera
82. Poets' words
84. __ through
85. General at Gettysburg
87. Gland: Prefix
88. Bridge seat
90. Back talk
91. Property conveyer
93. Certain actress's tonic
99. Where not to go from
100. Helplessly
104. Latin that
105. Uses a mop
106. Adams and others
107. Precious
108. Campus figure
109. Young oyster
110. Loss of value: Abbr.
111. Rodin subject

DOWN

1. Echo's title
2. Bronze or Iron
3. Tiny mass: Abbr.
4. Divides in balance
5. Certain golf strokes
6. Came to rest
7. Shoemaker, in London
8. Rarefied condition
9. Game for a playwright
10. Wash
11. Hebrew lyre
12. Land areas: Abbr.
13. Kind of cake or rubber
14. Wilson aide's largesse
15. Stettin's river
16. Lean and strong
18. Blood: Prefix
20. Does ship carpentry
23. Columbus, to friends
25. Greek letter
27. Use a shuttle
28. Some are great
29. Moslem leaders
30. Boston patriot's plant
34. Ali
35. Miss Dickinson
36. Wild beast
38. One serving a sentence
39. A Queen
41. A Champion
43. Vocally
46. An isolate
48. Leslie of films
50. Commends
51. English writer's hideaway
53. Certain beam
55. __ -Saxon
57. Penpoint
58. British chaps
59. Polite word
60. Girl's nickname
61. Choleric
62. City on the Meuse
64. Winged
67. Movie, in Europe
69. Revered event of 1775
70. Seed cover
72. Former tennis star Maria
73. Mary or John
75. Cooks further
77. Ally
80. Stitched anew
81. Scottish child
83. Used a cellar
86. Angkor __
89. Road sign
91. More qualified
92. Ballads
93. Commerce group: Abbr.
94. Aureole
95. Cries of pain
96. Swaddle
97. Log hut in Minsk
98. Blunder
101. Fr. pronoun
102. Mil. officers
103. "Of course"

135 PROMISSORY NOTES

John Willig

ACROSS

1. Kind of child
6. Baht spender
10. "... gang aft ___"
15. City of Greece
21. River of France
22. "It ___!"
23. "___ evil"
24. Imbibed freely
25. Dentist's promise
28. Style, in Madrid
29. Greek letters
30. River to North Sea
31. Start of a June promise
33. Fishy road sign
36. Parrot of N.Z.
38. Deserves
41. Laborious
42. Manpower program: Abbr.
43. Parting promise
46. U.S. journalist
47. Find
49. Ring verdict
50. Effect
52. Portico
56. Loudly vulgar
57. Promise to a hounded postman
60. Operetta man
61. Crate
63. Krone part
64. "___ Sylphides"
65. Turn away
66. Clod
67. What Florida promises
72. Verdon
73. Town in China
75. Light shade
76. ___-disant
77. Safari help
80. P. R., for one
81. Most intimate
85. Picture on a fiver
88. Crosses out
89. Refrigerants
91. Sky Altar
93. Hawks of Hawaii
94. Get rid of
96. Toothy look
97. Politician's promise

101. W. W. II org.
102. Crow over
104. "The ___ Seed"
105. Haul
106. ___-the-board
109. Petulant
110. Police chief's promise
115. Deft
117. Spear-carrier
118. Starlike object
119. Last month: Abbr.
120. Relative of itsy-bitsy
121. Confident
122. Boss's promise to son
126. Plan
127. Cutting weapon
131. Unanimous
132. ___ de mer
133. Proof mark
134. What money doesn't promise
136. Pot or bag
139. Mystery-title word
141. Famed express-no-more
142. Tout's promise
149. Forward: It.
150. ___ space
151. Stimulus
152. Tin: Fr.
153. Loser to F.D.R.
154. Primp
155. Sound unit
156. Partners

DOWN

1. N.Y.C. subway
2. Encouraging cry
3. Onassis
4. Map feature
5. Salamander
6. Glitter
7. Pres. initials
8. Pallid
9. Paper promises
10. Off base
11. Perfect thing
12. Rumanian coin
13. Pens: Abbr.
14. Attention-getter
15. ___ off (get over a jag)
16. Gets on a crowded bus
17. J. J. or Vincent
18. Zoo favorite
19. Ultimate end
20. Be fond of
26. Annie et al.
27. Fishing gear
32. Alto and tenor
33. Corm
34. Con ___
35. Broker's stock promise
37. Hormone initials
39. Unruly one, in Scotland
40. Unfeeling
43. Lindsay's remark about N.Y.C.
44. N. Z. tree
45. Running out of
46. Holds esteem
48. Songwriters' org.

51. Rug feature
52. Cut apart
53. Freeloader's promise
54. Thames sight
55. Skill
58. Relating to: Suffix
59. Headland
60. Politician's promise
62. These: Sp.
68. Mideast org.
69. Compass point
70. Bengal native
71. Clock reading
72. Harden
73. Cover
74. Mideast land: Abbr.
77. ___ nova
78. Play period: Abbr.
79. Quiet!
82. Poetic word
83. Tool
84. Three, in Asti
86. "No soap!"
87. Iowa college
90. Angered

92. Affected
95. "And ___ a big red rose"
97. Wools: Lat.
98. 5-2, for one
99. Besides
100. "The ___ Truth"
102. Some drs.
103. Costello
104. Butter at Maxim's
107. Of a Spanish area
108. Hemp fiber
111. Remunerates
112. Irish cry
113. Interior cover: Abbr.
114. Mouth: Prefix
116. Kind
118. A Roosevelt
121. Ancestral religion
123. Not yet existing
124. Grin in a way
125. Semblance
127. Boating hazard
128. Grub
129. Of bees

130. ___ time
131. Assyrian god
133. Greek letter
135. "___ on red"
137. Cobras
138. Wolfe
140. Hold back
143. Paris season
144. Before haw
145. Hoodwink
146. Word with cake or meal
147. She, in Bonn
148. U. S. N. A. grad

136 MIXED PAIRS *Gladys V. Miller*

ACROSS

1. Devastation
6. "As __ you can"
12. Past events: Abbr.
16. Fellini's milieu
17. Chestnut clam
19. Bread spread
20. Movie-set area
21. Smasher
23. Stained
24. Guevara
26. Sinful man
27. Female ruff
29. French or Dutch
30. Scorches
32. Ineffective
33. Skin: Prefix
34. Poetic word
35. High-hat
39. Praise
40. De Carlo of films
42. Mystical poem
43. Broadcast
44. Hasty, for one
46. Twilight
48. Scowl
52. Met highlights
53. Walk daintily
54. Wine jug
56. Piquant
57. Jumble
59. Antiquity, to poets
60. Fraternal men
61. Major- __
62. Slant
63. Control
64. Uncle: Sp.
65. Tied
69. Voice
70. Stiff fabric
73. Miss Evert
74. Endorsements
75. Familiar name in tennis
76. Earthy: It.
78. Slander
80. Polite word
81. Twig
82. Ate less
83. Grand, for one
86. Gobbledygook
88. Plant part
91. Armadillo
92. Cretan sight
94. Better's partner
95. Nobel physicist
96. Photo, for short

97. Over __ (helpless)
101. Slangy denial
102. Lock part
103. Willy-nilly, to Caesar
106. Ship's nemesis
108. Arab prince
109. Greek: Prefix
110. Carriage
111. ". . . in corpore __"
112. Reduce
113. Gives a party

DOWN

1. Nursery-rhyme start
2. English river
3. African landscape
4. Shoulder: Prefix
5. Contagious
6. Deception
7. "__ was saying"
8. French town
9. Incredible
10. "Pluck __ rose"
11. Thatched
12. Holly tree
13. State: Abbr.
14. Lose one's cool
15. Bullring man
16. Boat
18. Sturluson work
20. Tarry
22. Fleming
25. Be unwilling
28. Letters
30. State: Abbr.
31. Stretched out
33. Hog breed
35. Hawaiian yams
36. Asian leopard
37. Indivisible: Abbr.
38. Curling target
39. Metric measure
41. May 8 and Aug. 15, 1945
43. De Mille or Moorehead
44. Pebbly surfaced
45. Of a Russian range
46. Phoenician city
47. West Indian birds
49. Influence peddlers
50. Primitive implements
51. Rudolph feature
53. Consequence
55. Actor Richard
57. Madagascar native
58. Evident: Sp.
61. Check
63. Turkish liquor
66. Stage curtain
67. Vibrate
68. Previously, old style
71. Weeper, in adage
72. Deep blue
74. Vision: Prefix
77. French coin
78. Aspires
79. Direction: Abbr.
82. __ mater
83. Gen. Arnold
84. Believes
85. Western port
86. Wonder
87. "O rare" poet
89. Terminate a mission
90. Circus unit
92. Saud
93. Track event
95. Moroccan port
97. Flying prefix
98. Function
99. Wings
100. Radziwill, etc.
102. Whodunit V.I.P.'s
104. Rubbing fluid: Abbr.
105. Compass point
107. Cote sound

TIME PIECE

Guido N. Scarato

ACROSS

1. Catfish
6. Sample TV film
11. Latch again
16. Like some eyes
21. Spanish month
22. "__ Mio"
23. Remove
24. Proportion
25. Steel, in Paris
26. Clear
27. Squalls
28. Old Times Sq. hotel
29. St. Peter's and Farnese, e.g.
33. Drop __ (suggest)
34. Waste allowance
35. Height: Abbr.
36. Does math work
40. Furnish
42. "__ deal!"
44. Kind of relief
45. Roll-call note: Abbr.
48. Closet items
50. Here, to Caesar
52. Café additive
54. Salad
55. Antique-buyer's choice
62. Chemical prefixes
63. Chemical compound
64. Sea bird
65. Sierra __
66. Colony near Hong Kong
67. Beaks
68. Explorer
69. "I can't __!"
71. Chisholm, for one
73. Italian family
75. Like a grain
77. Miss Claire
78. Sphinxes, etc.
85. Recent: Prefix
86. Mediocre
87. City officials: Abbr.
88. Eastern title
89. More daft
92. Word with shoppe
94. One opposed
96. Latin nine
100. Maple and box elder
101. Rose lover
102. Toxic protein
103. Empty
104. Certain tapestries
109. Shortly
110. Bakery worker
111. U. S. storyteller
112. Sea off Greece
113. Biblical name
114. Decree
115. Cleaner's concern
118. Salutation
122. Actual being
123. After pi
124. Lively: Abbr.
126. Struck
128. Space station, maybe
139. Color over
140. Grind, as teeth
141. Room, in Paris
142. P. I. island
143. Judge's call
144. "My cup __"
145. Shade of gray
146. Works on copy
147. Like some moss
148. Performs, old style
149. Former L. A. mayor
150. Bristles

DOWN

1. Costly
2. Fairy-tale word
3. Guide
4. Kind of code
5. Genoese admiral
6. Visits casually
7. Safety zone
8. Make a __ (finance)
9. Acid suffix
10. Dogma
11. Compunction
12. Ejects
13. Wild party
14. Italian city
15. Take five
16. Plant parts
17. Bridge seat
18. Pacific island
19. Fashion name
20. Poetic time
30. "__ jewel" (words for a new maid)
31. Chilean port
32. Puff up
36. Nautical word
37. Shaw product
38. Column style
39. Italian army men
41. Caprice
43. Fine lace
45. Lamp rubber
46. Blocking
47. As __ sugar
49. Indian state
51. Diamonds
53. Reverence
54. Cygnus
56. Civil War ship
57. Banishes
58. Tease
59. Sea nymph
60. Sawlike: Prefix
61. Woolwich initials
68. Attempt: Scot.
69. Miler's need
70. Sidon's neighbor
72. Handle: Fr.
74. Gardener
76. Liquid ester
78. Islands in Bay of Bengal
79. Geologic era
80. Area of France
81. Peanuts
82. As red __
83. Jury panel
84. Early period
90. Triplet
91. Noun suffix
93. Brooklyn campus
95. Agency of 1930's
97. Lobby pieces
98. Vergil hero: Var.
99. Middle, in law
101. Drink
102. Army address: Abbr.
105. French capital in W. W. II
106. Inevitable accident
107. Of sight
108. Shabby
114. Through street
116. Goes by
117. "I wouldn't bet __!"
119. Early stable man
120. Talisman
121. Extremely
125. Disordered
127. Slackens
128. Too much: Fr.
129. "As you __"
130. Norse myth
131. Russian vote
132. Lowdown
133. Have it made
134. Western alliance
135. Commanded
136. Leave out
137. Statistics
138. Gaelic

INNER MEANINGS

Anthony Morse

ACROSS

1. Traffic maneuver
6. Swizzle stick
11. Heat milk, in a way
16. Black entry
21. Cold
22. Doddery
23. P. I. island
24. Author of children's books
25. Dostoevsky subject
26. Like a parade
29. English capital: Abbr.
30. Bowl
32. Got the word
33. African banana
34. High notes
36. Stretch out
37. Like S. F. or Rome
38. Pathetic
39. Cushion
40. Constellation
42. Punishment, in law
44. Elec. unit
45. Ooze
46. Capital of Eritrea
47. Object of playing postoffice
50. Quebec, etc.: Abbr.
51. Middle, in law
52. Guides
53. Moss Hart book
54. Jargon
57. Metal
58. Stream
59. Zodiac sign
60. Christian symbol
63. Part of a scarecrow
67. Documents
68. Cover
69. Troubles
70. Korean family
71. Mountaineer's parent
73. Draw a bead on
74. Fat: Prefix
75. Bring up
76. Hammer parts
77. Make out
78. Spenser lady
79. Bow
80. Wing
81. Takes on fuel
82. Channing
83. Sawbuck
84. Linen braid
86. Garibaldis take to the alleys
88. Agreeable word
89. Pine product
90. Russian range
91. Weather prediction
92. Hesse or Ohio
93. Trait of bigotry
94. Timid
96. Italian fare
101. Man's nickname
102. Fibbing before snoozing
104. Pool addict
105. Star in Cygnus
107. College degrees
108. Route to north
109. Land measure
110. Jujube
111. Glove shade
112. Swiss city
114. Jet housing
115. Abbot's counterpart
116. Daughter of Cyrus
118. Canadian peninsula
119. Lighthouses
122. Realm: Suffix
123. University
126. Air: Prefix
128. Witch's home
129. Clown
130. Talk: Fr.
131. Group of ten tones
132. Stingers
133. French river
134. Do a sheep job
135. Joint

DOWN

1. Friend of John Bull
2. Alpine natives
3. Where a baby often is
4. Engine rate: Abbr.
5. U. N. word
6. N. Z. people
7. __ simple
8. Aztec god of sowing
9. Dash
10. Home: Abbr.
11. Sideshow man
12. Place for locks
13. Boiling
14. Put down
15. Power: Prefix
16. Modify
17. Titles
18. Miss America at night
19. Stud with gems
20. __ -pont (bridgehead)
27. Stands out
28. Rams or Cubs
31. Bone
35. Pair of horses
37. Sound for attention
38. Valentino role
41. "... __ I saw Elba"
42. Rice dishes
43. Lyric poem
44. Musical group
45. Dressler
47. More willing, old style
48. Changes
49. Bakery workers
50. Taylor or Erskine
52. Denoting more than one
55. One invested in ministry
56. Dutch explorer and family
58. Sinkiang town
60. Damages
61. It rules the waves
62. Puritan penal equipment
63. Sorted out
64. Asian weight
65. Phobias
66. Ledge
71. Takeoff
72. In line
76. Allergy source
77. Fictitious
81. Raccoonlike animal
82. Picked
85. Measure
86. __ "Elegy"
87. Form of diving
90. Prussian lancer
94. Cereal grass
95. This is usually enough
96. Footwear
97. Tropical tree
98. Imitation diamond
99. End
100. Part of a phone number
103. Fuel line
104. George Eliot character
105. Gull
106. Town in Westphalia
107. False god
109. One of the Jacks
111. Tyrants
112. Sew
113. Macaulay's chieftain
114. Italian town
117. Traffic sign
118. African antelopes
119. God of Egypt
120. Take on
121. Bar item
124. Here, in France
125. Downs' partner
127. Buddhist sect

139 WORD EXPERTISE *Diana Sessions*

ACROSS

1. Good and plenty
7. Egyptian symbol
13. Shade of red
19. Emote
21. Mosaic gold
22. Ormandy
23. Oscar winner of 1953
24. Force
25. Fits
26. Calendar abbr.
27. Writing flourish
29. Sauterne
31. Undergoes
32. Setter or potato
34. Army officer: Abbr.
35. Various
36. Van __
37. Writer Ernie
38. Light-bulb units
39. __ horse
40. Mrs. Ponti's maiden name
41. Indifference
43. Darkness
44. Tarboosh
45. Whistlelike instruments
48. Small boats
49. Diamond surfaces
52. Be a coward, with "out"
53. Sheepskin
55. Zodiac beast
57. Church taxes
58. Baby bird
59. Prefix for tasse
60. Arab prince
61. Jewelry item
62. Living-room items
63. Girl's nickname
64. Corral helper
65. Gewgaw
66. Title in India
67. Toward Polaris
68. Sociable one
69. Wood-burning kiln
71. Threadbare
72. Place for certain birds
73. Kind of stare
74. Study carefully
75. Disregard
76. Peculiarity
79. Waggish one
80. "__ d'Arthur"
81. Energy units
85. Impel
86. Listen
87. Ornamental tree
88. Go slowly
89. Bear: Sp.
90. Ali __
91. Seeking to get even
93. Letter
94. Serving vessel
96. City on the Moldau
98. Turn to good account
100. Went to Gretna Green
101. "__ said than done"
102. Spoke candidly
103. Lustrous
104. Score
105. Disconnects

DOWN

1. Chat
2. Birdhouse
3. Kind of soup
4. Old Danish money
5. Notched bar
6. Tan color
7. Mrs. Astor's realm
8. Spring harbinger
9. Creature of Egyptian myth
10. Cordage item
11. Beverage
12. Protection
13. Skullcap: Var.
14. Barbarous
15. Turkish title
16. Gentle breeze
17. Part of a jet engine
18. Shrink
20. Costume material
28. Currier & Ives prints: Abbr.
30. Squid's output
33. Examines
35. Swamp
36. Nap
38. Diminishes
39. Hay shelter in England
40. Discourse: Abbr.
42. Cheap operator
43. Alice's tea companion
44. Snake equipment
45. Singing groups
46. Monster of myth
47. Eastern Church litany
48. Sloganlike expression
49. Ward off
50. Quake
51. Piece of needlework
53. Hodgepodge
54. Intellect
56. Distress
58. Do a spooky job, in dialect
59. Relative
61. Guarded
62. Old weapon
64. Calhoun
65. Carousal
67. Isthmus
68. Gay
70. Engage
72. Air __
74. Bridge barrier
75. Art bargain, at times
76. States a price
77. Miss Andress
78. Luzon native
79. Truck area
80. Mozart piece
82. Rail at
83. Odd chap
84. Makes haste
86. Convenient
87. Initiate
88. British pioneer in India
90. Has- __
91. China-shop item
92. All-purpose trucks
95. Roof piece
97. Chilly
99. Coin in Bulgaria

WET STRENGTH

Virginia W. Schneider

ACROSS

1. Fourth or real
7. Day of prayer
12. Badger
16. Source of some cigars
21. Tool
22. Watered silk
23. Blame
24. Of Mars
25. Fabled fritterers
27. "South Pacific"role
29. Wash. title
30. Best __
31. Beings: Fr.
33. Kenya's neighbor
34. July-August people
35. "Some like __"
36. Prune, in Scotland
37. Stir
40. City on the Hudson
41. "All we can do __"
42. Some lenses
46. Troop actions
48. Lizard
49. Guilty, for one
50. Map abbr.
51. Went up and away
52. "__ Me?"
55. Suet: Prefix
56. O'Neill heroine et al.
57. Words of disgust
58. Seagoing initials
59. Play for time
60. Safecracker
61. Smell __
62. Gloves and hose: Abbr.
63. Red
64. Direction
65. Like bustles
70. Plane's route
71. __ fire (hot shot)
73. U. S. writer and editor
74. Vedic god
76. Refer to
78. Tools
81. Thine: Fr.
84. Mickey or Annie
85. Young one
86. Mr. Martini
87. Interlock
88. Peace Nobelist, 1911
89. Beat-up auto

91. Certain room
93. Creator of Ah Sin
94. Good Queen __
95. People who produce corn
98. Water sportsman
99. World aid org.
100. Overdo the toast
101. "Two hearts that beat __"
102. Ghost story
103. __ milk (bland)
105. Commoners
106. Police problem
107. Lowell
108. Dashes about
109. Centers of activity
110. Layer
111. Fixed standard
114. Rejuvenate
115. Scout and eye
117. Espouse
120. "Old __ Sky"
122. Stolen sweet
125. __ -propre
126. Auk genus
127. Expect
128. Heavily favored
129. Boxes
130. Trudge
131. Lab jobs
132. Singer Bobby and family

DOWN

1. Nog ingredients
2. Father
3. Fed
4. Kaline and Capp
5. Hardy heroine
6. The Unready
7. Occupy
8. Sulks
9. German drink
10. Blunder
11. Find a new home
12. Highland brigand
13. Cove
14. Small combos
15. That: Sp.
16. Star in Pleiades

17. Spanish export of 1588
18. Ignoble
19. Sidekick
20. Writer Seton
26. Spreads
28. Persistent creditor
32. Pigs or R's
35. "The good men do __ interred ..."
36. Music pieces
37. Analyzes
38. Lorna and family
39. Florida's flower
40. Gets even
41. Dope
42. Some tax men
43. Gulf Coast city
44. __ motion (set aside)
45. Pompous
47. Certain drama: Abbr.
48. Arterial trunk
52. Banters

53. English painter
54. In __ (actual)
55. Open-eyed
57. Church list
59. Partly-closed eyes
61. Playing marble
62. Thoreau milieu
63. H. Q. for Sadat
65. Senior
66. Subway supports
67. Dug
68. Labor org.
69. Balfour and Harum
72. Old French measures
75. Gainsay
76. Largest peninsula
77. Certain bridge cards
79. Highland unit
80. Take effect
82. Respect
83. Port's counterpart

87. Crumbly earth
89. Israeli dances
90. Kalpas
91. Insufferable ones
92. Sawbucks
93. Après sept
95. Wet-track runner
96. Bisect
97. "__ you mean"
98. Type of food fish
100. Sports jackets
102. Taxco's sky
104. Therefore: Lat.
105. Edged with scallops
106. Bill of __
109. Telephone call
110. Agreement, of a kind
111. Coarse fabrics
112. __ pump
113. Portico

114. Moon valley
115. Greek letters
116. Drink additive
117. "Able __ ere ..."
118. Jacket
119. Retreats
121. Mug
123. Have creditors
124. Guide: Abbr.

ACROSS

1. Cay
6. Moral nature
11. Play parts: Abbr.
14. Alaskan port
18. Ascribe
19. Tai people
20. Emoter
21. Decorator of a kind
22. Mermaid
23. Rings: Abbr.
24. Train mail abbr.
25. Tiber tributary
26. 4
28. Sanction
29. Yale men
30. Weasels
31. 12
33. Aleutian island
37. Tokay, for one
38. Japanese port
39. Preminger
40. Dessert
42. Serpents
43. Ordinal suffix
44. African region
45. Meddles
47. Appears
51. 14
55. Conrail units: Abbr.
56. "To __ His Own"
57. Engage in a sport
60. Goldilocks words
61. Village in Norway
62. Mesta
63. "__ my word!"
64. Locomotive
65. Pontius __
67. Protuberance
68. Car of a kind
70. Partner of haw
71. Aquatic bird
72. Marie, for one
73. Jai __
74. Kind of book: Abbr.
75. 0
78. Enmeshed
80. Cat of Africa
81. Manifest
85. Fedora
86. French pronoun
87. Certain Manhattanite
91. Makes lace
93. Blue colors
94. Plenty, poetically
95. Arnaz
96. ½
98. Not traversed
100. Ericson
101. Dies __
102. 52
107. Eur. capital
108. Raleigh, for one
109. Recognition
110. __ quality (shoddy)
111. Dravidian Indian
112. Fastener
113. Silly
114. Snores and snorts
115. Box
116. Direction
117. Brawl
118. Fisherman

DOWN

1. Hungary's Nagy
2. Slacker: Brit.
3. Stringed instrument
4. Jackets
5. 8
6. Delight
7. 14
8. Leporids
9. __ -over-lightly
10. Titles for Thant and Lie: Abbr.
11. Whodunit sounds
12. Tapioca root
13. Struck
14. 12
15. Leopardlike cat
16. Sheep
17. Blot out
18. "__ all in the game"
27. French roof
28. Dithers
31. Elizabeth's friend
32. Distinction
33. Speed-up: Abbr.
34. While, for short
35. Color
36. Yen
38. Insurance abbr.
41. Dawdle
43. German spa
46. Bone: Prefix
47. Synthetic
48. Paris stations
49. Brilliance
50. __ khan (tiger)
52. Railway car, for short
53. Took more than one's share
54. Larcenist
55. Take it easy
57. No-fat man
58. Bear of Down Under
59. Quechua
61. 19
62. Five-spots in card games
65. Do road work
66. Draw
69. 2
74. Inactive: Abbr.
75. French lass
76. U. S. composer
77. Roman poet
79. Endure
80. Critic Barnes
82. Dutch town
83. Home: Abbr.
84. Numerical prefix
86. Dilate
88. S. A. woody perennial
89. Black earth
90. 1
91. Binds
92. Armpit
93. Nests
96. Openings
97. Bits of hay
98. Mayan month
99. Crusoe creator
102. Unit of loudness
103. P. I. tree
104. Japanese town
105. Garden worker
106. Corp. officials
109. Pronoun

BRIGHTWORK *Hume R. Craft*

ACROSS

1. U.S. suffragist
5. In short supply
10. Took a break
16. Old plaster source
21. Suffix for cell or pop
22. Less vivid
23. Symbol of rank
24. Nest
25. Bright ones
27. Weapon
29. Certain husbands
30. Uber __
32. Kind of cluster for a medal
33. Biblical twelve: Abbr.
34. Norse god
35. __ fixe
36. Riled
39. Misfortunes
40. Part of F.O.B.
42. Sleeve card
44. Slugger Roger
46. Gay-nineties novelties
51. __-a-Dale
56. Car groups
57. Indonesian island
58. Ottoman title
59. Area around hockey goal
60. Irish expletive
61. Commercials
62. Reactor areas
65. Togetherness symbol
67. Symington
68. Miss the __
69. Baseball thrill
70. Feel for
71. Rodin work: Abbr.
72. Hero-Leander locale
74. Greek city-state
75. Painter Rockwell
76. Holy one: Abbr.
77. Radiation detectors
82. Raggedy doll
83. Gallery
84. Golf club
85. Merited
87. Mat. days
89. Colonizers
90. Menu items
91. Deface
92. Whimsical
93. Carnival men
95. Sheriff's men
96. Drinking man
97. Zoo exhibit
98. Fitted out
99. Abner or Diamond
100. Musketeers, e.g.
102. Revive a court case
103. Objects of perception
104. Pole vault
109. Day
111. Saul's uncle
112. Items in the black
113. Event in Madrid
117. Pommel accessory
119. Select
121. Exclamation
122. City trains
125. Flappers' hats
127. Songbird
129. Detailed
131. Go for
134. Cartoon family
136. Wild sheep
137. Makes happy
138. Complete: Prefix
139. Advantage
140. Menials
141. Relics found in North Africa
142. Clairvoyants
143. Look in a way

DOWN

1. Brazilian rhythm-maker
2. Finished
3. Powders
4. Caroline group
5. Blabbed
6. Items once eaten as toasts
7. "Woe is me"
8. Tennis gear
9. Common chord
10. Mirror
11. Perry's creator
12. Fruit drink
13. Comedian Conway
14. Direction
15. Runarounds, of a sort
16. Garage sign
17. __ fruit: African berry
18. Spur part
19. Word for Miss America
20. Feudal slaves
26. Laments
28. Nile, as a god
31. Mr. Sprat's fare
35. Peruvian
37. TV award
38. Kind of dance
40. Famous dog
41. Condition: Suffix
43. One of the Plinys
45. Chalcedony
46. Bridge call
47. Spanish directions
48. Flash of wit
49. Warm-water fish
50. Copper money
52. Fishing spear
53. Deep-sea denizen
54. On the briny
55. Fit together
59. Far or battle
61. Neighbor of Hung.
63. Leave undone
64. Weathers
65. Trojan Horse figure
66. Northern island
68. Eur. capital
69. Green features
70. River to Rio Grande
73. Decorations
74. Carries on
75. Biblical verb
76. Celebrity
78. Road for Cato
79. Poet's relative of 'gins
80. Straight
81. Take to the door
86. Units of force
87. Fast planes
88. Edgar __
89. Oyster's home
90. Lawgiver
91. T-man's concern
94. Start a hand
95. Bowler's target
96. Gentlemen
97. Props
99. Inferior
101. Kind of number
102. English streams
104. Strips sugarcane
105. Linen marking
106. Go back abroad
107. Kind of blue
108. Sheds
110. Arena sounds
113. Behave badly
114. Mrs. Luce
115. Japanese city: Var.
116. One of five
118. Hobby
120. Barn features
122. Literary work
123. Fencing move
124. Villain's trademark
126. Dutch painter
128. News piece
129. Partner of forget
130. Ladder rung
132. __ de France
133. Form of Anna
135. Author Harper

143 CHOICE WORDS — Jordan S. Lasher

ACROSS

1. Utter
6. To the sunrise
15. Fasteners
20. Mr. America et al.
21. Mr. Wickfield's clerk
22. Barely ahead
23. Cordial flavor
24. Something for good measure
25. City on the Mohawk
26. Skater Sonja
27. Earth pigment
28. Macaw
29. Detecting device
30. Red signals
32. Antipathy
34. Hides
35. Israeli group
36. Do a takeoff
40. Dorado browns
41. Speakers' platforms
46. "Rose __ . . ."
47. Conversations
48. In bloom
49. Twists, in Scotland
50. Lobster claw
51. Morally offensive, old style
52. Stem's counterpart
53. Part of the biota
54. Reply to "Are too!"
55. Pacific neckwear
56. Hockeypuck's destination
57. Anthology
59. Batters' concerns: Abbr.
60. Arab cloak
61. System of manual training
62. Of a fertilizer chemical
63. Track-shoe adjunct
64. Mouth-watering
66. Simper
67. Inundates
68. Franklin's wife
69. Gary Cooper's negatives
70. Apprentice
71. Giver of lip
72. Spore cluster
73. Hive
74. Defeatist
76. Listens
77. Certain survey
81. Some cigars
86. Triple Crown winner
87. Period
88. Argentine measure
89. Young hooter
90. Famous empire
91. Secured an anchor
93. New York county
94. "You __ right!"
95. Period of great prosperity
96. Former buddy
97. Auto style
98. Of course!
99. Plant-stem part

DOWN

1. Eastern rulers
2. Principle
3. Kind of acid
4. Taste again
5. Prepares to be dubbed
6. Extol
7. Girl turned into a spider
8. Vacation objectives
9. Sound qualities, in Scotland
10. Buzzing sound
11. Exclamation
12. Road workers
13. Cheapen
14. Props for extras
15. Realty sign
16. Chekhov
17. Paris divider
18. Goblins: Var.
19. Coast Guard girls
31. "__ your hand . . ."
32. Loos
33. Feudal slavery
35. Malaysian capital
36. Oak-tree afflictions
37. City on Lake Erie
38. Krypton, xenon, etc.
39. Pray: Lat.
40. Darling, in Nice
42. Part of S.P.C.A.: Abbr.
43. Lunch-hour time span
44. Turncoats
45. Today's painters, mod style
47. Line in a circle
48. Void
50. Satiates
51. Eskimo craft
53. Baking staple
54. Ripeners
57. Work from the ground __
58. U. S. Indians
59. Lily plant extract
61. Absolute necessity
63. Exam-cramming material
65. Instance, in Paris
66. French historian
67. "__ Jacques"
69. __ than (time-limit words)
70. Place for oolong
72. Safekeeping
73. Singer Mimi
75. Medicinal plant
76. Kind of collision
77. African reed instruments
78. Love, in Venice
79. Crippled
80. Forbidden City
81. Ear projections
82. In the middle
83. Run off
84. Kingly
85. Passé
88. Derision: Sp.
92. Spicy

FARE GAME   *Joseph LaFauci*

ACROSS

1. Prepare clams
6. Firefighting needs
11. Wash. agent
15. Roman field
19. Yearn for
20. States or Nations
22. Movie western
24. Old instrument
25. Deserved
26. Nullify
27. Prince Valiant's wife
28. Rawboned
29. Worship
30. "It is to laugh,"etc.
32. Magician's word
34. Kind of house
35. Arizona city
36. Apollo's mother
37. Top bananas
38. Nigerian city
39. Grand old name of song
40. Morning sound
42. Bullet
43. Arabic letter
46. Gems
48. __ cry
49. Raiment
51. Color
52. Iris expert
54. Feminine suffix
55. "__ on you!"
56. London flophouse
57. Coupled
58. Peep show
60. Cubic meter
61. Thrash
62. Celebes beast
63. Strictness
64. Open-eyed
65. Villella, e.g.
66. Ship-shaped clock
67. Encrust
68. Well-known streetcar
70. Englishman
71. Panted
73. Annoying
74. Not permanent
75. Henry Cabot, etc.
76. Inflame
77. Fish
78. Peruvian city
81. Took a break
82. Spoke at length
83. Brazilian city
85. Handle
86. Stratagems
87. Hunks
88. Took out
89. Splendid
90. Russian city
91. Fido's friend
92. S. A. rubber
93. In an expert way
95. Veneto, for one
96. Guest and Hers
97. Jewish month
98. Great, teen-age style
99. Word in poems
100. Encourage
101. Kind of servitude
103. Bede or Smith
104. Dit's partner
107. Old-hat
109. Wax, in prescriptions
110. Cut
111. Call to mind
112. Facing stone
114. La Scala fare
117. Maria or Cruz
118. Machination
119. Eurasian sandpiper
121. Biblical landfall
122. Eye pencil
123. A bit
124. Playing marble
125. Where R.F.K. served
126. "__ You Glad You're You?"
127. Pitcher
128. European river
129. Taxi feature
130. Verbose

DOWN

1. Bow's partner
2. Shopped
3. Sponge
4. Ward off
5. Iranian's ancestor
6. Certain protests
7. __ Street (well off)
8. Ancient monograms
9. Common abbr.
10. Egyptian king
11. George Jessel sobriquet
12. Swedish port
13. Early film stutterer
14. Tennis gear
15. German river
16. Poser for Spencer Tracy
17. State: Fr.
18. Italian river
21. Promulgate
23. Ecstasy
31. Comparative suffix
33. Frenetic state
35. De mer and de tête
37. Viscous mud
39. Domestic
40. Chaser, of a sort
41. Kind of news
42. Sudden reaction
44. "Emma" novelist
45. German river
47. Trial action
48. Prefix for naut
50. "I told you so!"
52. Arabian land
53. Chaplin prop
56. "Inferno" man
59. Like fine cheese
60. Broken-arm décor
61. Enticements
63. Went wild over
64. Irani or Yemeni
65. Laughable
67. Hockey goals
69. Boo-boo
70. Certain diet
72. Ford
74. Rose of baseball
75. Annie of song
76. Atelier item
79. Anthracite
80. With competence
81. Verify
82. Buttonhead, for one
84. Winglike
85. Maintained
87. Did lawn work
88. Art style
89. Countersink
91. Kern musical
92. Bread-crumb sauces
94. Campus figure
96. "So long!"
102. Suffix for north or east
103. Make effervescent
105. Take charge
106. Comrade, sea style
108. Do over
109. Minotaur's home
110. Afghan city
111. Illinois city
112. Church part
113. Like some racehorses
114. Alumnus
115. Utah town
116. Bread, to Miss Loren
117. Cabbage dish
120. Swellhead's hang-up

HALLOWEEN THOUGHT

Threba Johnson

ACROSS

1. English dramatist
6. New-shoe tragedy
11. Drift
16. High style
17. Every 60 minutes
18. Drink for a cold day
20. Start of a quote from "Hamlet"
24. Quantity: Abbr.
25. Dress again
26. Speeds
27. Egg __ yong
28. About: Abbr.
30. Sp. Amer. plain
32. Kinds
33. Use Rotten Row
34. Harden
36. __ -Saud
37. Goblin
39. "Now you __ ..."
40. More of quote
44. Inner: Prefix
45. Part of Mao's name
46. Inc., in Britain
47. Urge
48. Breathe
52. Certain records
54. Cargo
58. High note
59. Artless
62. Bother
64. Pentateuch
65. Eyelashes: Prefix
67. More of quote
70. River
71. Throat-clearings
73. Psyche parts
74. Feature of boxer shorts
76. Wallach
77. October décor
79. Jackie's spouse
80. Mocking one
82. U. S. fliers of W. W. II
83. Month: Abbr.
85. Barn area
88. Inflation concern: Abbr.
89. More of quote
98. Strayed
99. U. S. fur trader
100. "__ the ghost of . . ."
101. Consume
102. Son of Hera
103. Blackbirds
104. Short poem
107. Term of address
108. Go down swinging
109. Breathless
110. Relatives of prelims
112. Reagan, for short
113. End of quote
118. Continent
119. Writer Ramée
120. Approached
121. Candle
122. Prepare to play marbles
123. Inhibit

DOWN

1. Quack dosage
2. Mass. cape
3. Warehouse charge: Abbr.
4. Julia and Elias
5. Use Amtrak
6. The whole works, and more
7. Group of witches: Scot.
8. Process: Suffix
9. __ and wide
10. Routing for a broomstick rider
11. What the plot may do
12. Routines
13. Catch-all abbrs.
14. Kind of degree
15. One who exalts
16. Bahama resort
19. Of a battery pole
20. Implied
21. Tolkien creation
22. Like Troy
23. "Pride __ before . . ."
29. Crawl
31. Concerning: Abbr.
33. Event for old grads
35. Red dye
38. Spooky birds
39. Oct. 31 wear
41. Raid
42. Alas, in Paris
43. France's Saint-__
48. Summarize
49. Root or Yale
50. Witch city
51. Shade of blue
53. One who keeps busy
54. Kind of shoe
55. Charlie Brown's good word
56. Market: Fr.
57. "... lost __ mittens"
60. Bean of India
61. Three-min. units
62. Fish of Hawaii
63. Outs' partner
66. Pierces
68. Out on __
69. __ wahr?
72. Bard of old Scandinavia
75. S. A. tongue
78. "__ Were King"
79. Guthrie
81. Insects
83. Italian town
84. Favorite ghost
86. Fine rug
87. Riches
89. Current
90. Roman poet
91. Adjust
92. Colorful bird
93. Partner of to
94. New World native
95. Bar gadget
96. "Let's toast __ comrades"
97. Turn over
103. Brotherly love
105. Vacuum tube
106. "We're off __ the wizard . . ."
109. Resting on
111. Do in a fly
114. Org. of the 30's
115. Sister
116. Connection
117. Mine yield

IN GOOD FORM   *Bruce R. Shaw*

ACROSS

1. Queen's baked goods
6. Wastes
11. Shatter
16. Indonesian island
21. Love, in Italy
22. "... upon __ of violets"
23. Hoist
24. Tie score
25. Memento
26. Auto mechanic's ward
29. Street game
31. Relieve
32. Logarithm word
33. Pismires
34. Waiter's worry
36. __ souci
38. Prison camp
40. Author Erica
43. Hebrew measure
45. View
47. Paradise
48. Outdo
51. Flightless bird
52. Gymnast's props
55. Ethiopian lake
57. __ Ste. Marie
59. Tease
60. Lets
61. Big or Little
62. Implied
64. French writer
66. Society-page word
67. Indian chiefs
68. Mountains
70. River of Italy
72. Carries on
74. Author Wiesel
75. Fundamental
77. Orbit
79. Paulo or Luiz
80. Songs
81. Round landmark of N.Y.C.
85. In harmony
87. Traffic warning
88. Word for the rich
89. Gal Friday
90. Booted
91. Items for Astor
93. Inventor of diving bell
95. Manned
99. Vessels

101. Headache compound
103. Aspect of personality
105. "__ nacht..."
106. Old catapult
107. Fatty acid: Prefix
109. Shamrock land
111. As a friend: Fr.
112. Berlin area
113. Soda jerk's offering
116. Angelico et al.
117. Compass point
118. Wool: Prefix
120. Drunkards
121. Tech grad: Abbr.
122. Spring period
123. French mathematician
125. Near or Ole
127. Wien's river
129. Italian town
132. Voices
134. Trim
136. Gear
140. Incoming pilot's concern
144. Charged atom
145. Town officer
146. Anglo-Saxon coin
147. Spasm
148. Disdain
149. Soprano Emma
150. Deserves
151. Sources
152. French heads

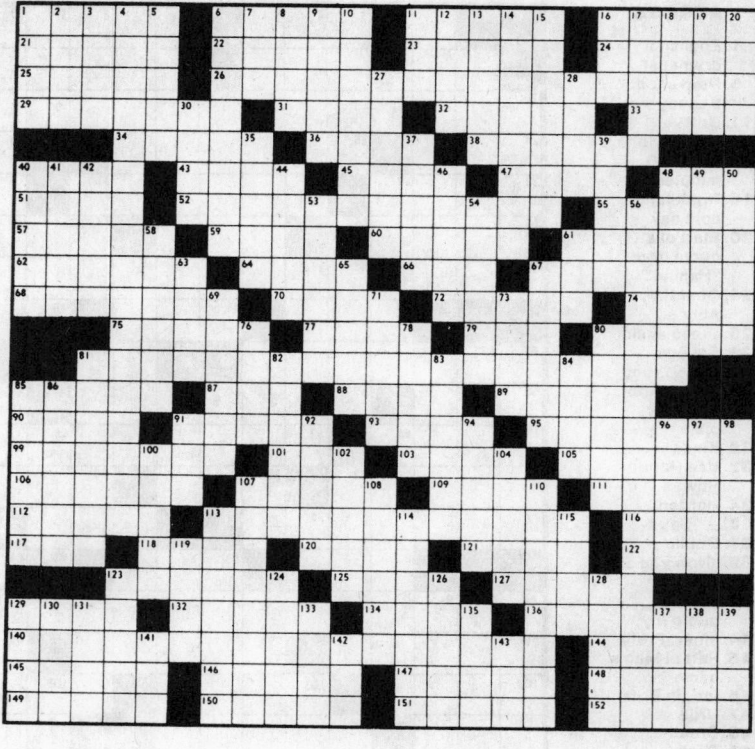

DOWN

1. Pacific root
2. Theban deity
3. Function
4. First-aid gear
5. Plaster painting
6. Hurt: Sp.
7. Sash
8. __-Coburg
9. Reserve item, in France
10. Ship rigging
11. Bahamas, etc.: Abbr.
12. Scottish pool
13. Lake Titicaca's range
14. Royal symbols
15. Screw parts
16. Heir
17. Free from censorship
18. Chow or lo
19. Baseball strategy
20. Copies
27. Pawnbroker
28. Gardner
30. On
35. Risk
37. Moon: Prefix
39. Prank
40. Alou of baseball
41. Arabian
42. N. C. river
44. Gaseous element
46. Doubleday
48. Northern sea fish

49. Lack of vigor
50. Breaks down a sentence
53. Pauses
54. Resting
56. Politician's concern
58. Harangue
61. German article
63. Hindu slave
65. Baghdad native
67. Ermines
69. Talks back
71. Chopin piece
73. Annoys
76. Take it easy
78. Papa Bear of Chicago
80. Grown together
81. Anchoring
82. Record
83. Turn in coupons
84. Soaks
85. Ties

86. Macbeth and others
91. __ annum
92. Glasses, for short
94. Golfing flaw
96. Blaze
97. Violinist Mischa
98. Certain believer
100. "Most Happy" guy
102. Cue-ball shot
104. Fern leaf
107. Hip pain
108. Eye part
110. Gluts
113. __ quarters (crowded)
114. Approvals
115. Sea bird
119. Quickly: Abbr.
123. Annoy
124. Aloof one
126. Hebrew letter

128. Sea call
129. Raison d'__
130. Met home
131. Vibrating, in music: Abbr.
133. Laurel
135. Item of inflation
137. Disorder
138. Distressing
139. Austrian river
141. Recipients: Suffix
142. Officers: Abbr.
143. Biblical land

147 REVERSE ENGLISH · Thomas Sheehan

ACROSS

1. Defensive barricade
7. Doghouse dweller
11. Hayseeds
16. Hercules, e.g.
18. Santa's standbys
19. Pale
20. Edward Bellamy title, taken literally
24. Dance
25. Ms. people
26. Bar items
27. Arrived
29. Time period out West
30. Carol
32. _ anchor (be moored)
33. Nitwit
34. Earthy clay
35. Retaliate
38. Certain movie scenes
40. Mask
41. Irritate
42. Sports: Abbr.
43. Weapon for Aaron
46. Badminton need
47. Malay sailboat
48. Angora fabrics
52. Briefly
54. Be found wanting
56. Screening
57. Theodore and family
58. Answers a phone memo
59. Well-known Benedict
60. Canasta term
61. Retraces one's steps
62. Hindu gentleman
63. Luxuriate
64. Flinches
65. Middleman's specialty
67. _ glance
68. Reverts to
69. Char's millinery
70. Vagrancy
72. Support
73. "_ Mable"
74. Mode of Biblical reading
75. Berne's river
76. Dearth
77. Corday's victim et al.
79. Ready for a duel
83. Holder of the last straw
87. Places of refuge
88. Young _
89. Kind of snake
90. "_ in the Money"
91. Rival of NBC
92. Arctic sight
93. On the _ of (chummy)
96. Dakota Indian
97. N. H. city
99. Emulate John Osborne?
102. Charlie Chan portrayer
103. Exchange places
104. ". . . toil and _"
105. Weird Sisters
106. Musicians' stints
107. Words for a certain friend

DOWN

1. In-laws of the Mullenses
2. Brigitte of films
3. One who degrades
4. Haul
5. Annoys
6. Faction
7. Wishful winker
8. Albanian coins
9. Nigerian people
10. Self-centered
11. Attention
12. Baton Rouge campus
13. Epitaph for Atlas
14. Land
15. Barber's headaches
17. Racing fan
18. Kind of preview
21. Kellogg-_ Pact
22. Dancer José
23. Beats it
28. Speedometer initials
31. Operculum
33. Returns on the q.t.
34. Miss Hari
36. German sprite
37. Eastern rulers
38. Hits a ball out of play
39. Thai money
41. Reduces, as prices
43. Lobster-eater's wear
44. Lively, in music
45. Emulates a shrinking violet
47. Gets sassy
48. Sham
49. Grampus: Var.
50. Gas-pump word
51. Wall, etc.: Abbr
53. Bandleader
54. Joins the also-rans
55. Bad writer
58. Cleat's relative
59. Area of the wise men
61. Bavarian river
62. Hems in
63. Scrooge word
64. _ de Calais
65. Part of R.F.D
66. Roof ornament
68. Trumpeter A
69. Abandoned ship
71. Dumbarton, for one
73. Napery fabric
76. Liberal giving
77. After lundi
78. Direction at sea: Abbr.
79. Supporting
80. Old Assyrian city
81. Suffix of origin
82. Tillstrom
83. _ age
84. Organism needing oxygen
85. Cookery style
86. Tipped over
89. Covers
92. River areas
93. Insect
94. Grain sorghum: Var.
95. Dark
98. Compass point
100. Whillikins' partner
101. Hungary's Bela

148 OBSERVATIONS *Bert Beaman*

ACROSS

1. Whittier's boy
9. "I saw __ asailing..."
14. Trouble spots of 1960's
22. Show who's boss
23. Puppeteer Lewis
24. Be equivalent
25. Humbles
26. Athapascan abode
27. Memorable lion
28. Astrologer's sign
29. Kind of mine
31. Mary __, fictional ship
33. Dill
34. "Waiting for Lefty" author
37. Sham
38. Blanch: Fr.
39. Navy officers: Abbr.
40. Color: Abbr.
42. Kind of scholar
44. Indian otter
46. Surrenders
48. Burma or open
50. Ancient Asian kingdom
51. Vex
53. Hot pants, for one
56. He, in Rome
57. Horse-breeder's purchase
58. Story opener
59. Vipers
60. Salutation
61. Arising within one
63. Rings
65. Observation
67. Give it a go
68. Chair part
70. Of the kind of: Suffix
72. Guthrie
73. German river
75. Eagle: Prefix
76. Salmon
77. "Try __ for size"
78. Will Rogers words, with 117 Across and 11 Down
84. Greek commune
85. Greeting
86. Cockney steed
87. Biblical son
88. __ instant
89. River to Danube
90. Honey drinks
92. Went through papers
96. __ ear (listened)
98. Hidden
101. Part of Greece
103. Common Market: Abbr.
104. Opposed: Abbr.
106. Bindle stiff
107. Indian maid
108. Threshold
109. Indian title
110. See 35 Down
112. Swing around
113. Silkworm
114. Rice dish
116. City of Rumania
117. See 78 Across
119. Hamilton's bill
120. Mayan god
122. Effect of past experience
124. Long ago
126. To be, in Spain
128. Heart, in Egyptian religion
129. Church sections
130. Emulates Greeley
132. River to the Missouri
135. Suggestive of
137. S. A. shelter
139. Thrusts out
142. "There's no __ an old..."
143. Waters
144. Logical
145. Bridge plays
146. Before febrero
147. Biased

DOWN

1. Madrid marriage
2. Affirm
3. How some tourneys are run
4. Misjudged
5. Canadian river
6. Like: Suffix
7. Pindar output
8. Hardy girl
9. Houston players
10. Valentino role
11. See 78 Across
12. Choler
13. Storied exterminator
14. Intrigue
15. __ Cup
16. See 35 Down
17. __ off (defer)
18. Loosen
19. Has a chance
20. Clear sky
21. Out of __
30. Motif
32. Noble
35. Shaw quote, with 110 Across and 141 and 16 Down
36. Kind of plexus
40. French port
41. Radio O.K.
43. Repairs, in a way
45. Spore sacs
47. Ledge, in Britain
49. Dissimilar
51. Italian astronomer
52. Lafayette College's home
54. Legendary island
55. U. S. arctic explorer
62. Substance
63. Gray poem
64. Extremely
66. Straw mattress
69. Film producer Berman
71. Ehrenburg
74. Greek letters
76. Lazy __
78. Roman officials
79. Coating
80. Lincoln's cause
81. "__ girl just like..."
82. Clear
83. Visits
91. Needles
93. Like some store items
94. Girl's nickname
95. Singer Bob
97. U. S. culture group: Abbr.
99. "Ay, __ rub"
100. Kind of cracker
102. Terre __
105. Alternate non-toll road
107. Charm, for one
111. Lansbury role
115. Winter sight
117. Melodic passage
118. Supplies
120. Grain husks
121. Vietnam capital
123. Verb suffixes
125. More curious
127. Dialect of India
131. Brazilian heron
133. Sarazen of golf
134. Founded: Abbr.
136. Viscous liquids: Abbr.
138. Oven, in Britain
140. Tunisian cape
141. See 35 Down

SEASONAL TIDINGS
Anne Fox

ACROSS

1. Letter
4. Disdain
9. Jabbed
14. Poet Chartier
19. Evidence
20. Minced, in cookery
21. __ Gay (W.W. II plane)
22. Cape Cod Indian
24. Handle
25. To be, in Spain
26. Tiny thing
27. City on the Liffey
28. Selected passage
30. Pig, in Paris
32. Girl's nickname
33. A.W.O.L.
34. Kind of pocket
35. Jezebel's husband
37. "Hasta __!"
39. Not the same
41. Words from an 18th cent. carol
48. Italian glass
49. Part of a mountain
50. Bye-bye
51. Gypsy horse
52. Where roses bloomed in song
55. Highway man
58. Magnify
61. Floors: Fr.
62. Extinct bird
63. Eastern U. S. capital
65. __ chance
66. Vegetable
67. Neighbor of Mont.
69. Dick Tracy's trademark
71. Card
72. Be
73. Priest of Shiloh
74. "Mon __ ami"
75. Zestful
77. Lincoln's V. P.
79. Words from a 17th cent. carol
86. Vietnam town
87. Disney character
88. Shakespearean dog
89. Resin
90. Junk
92. Irish rebels: Abbr.
94. Star
95. Egg: Prefix
96. Tom Sawyer's Polly
97. Chinese province
98. Snap
100. Defile
102. Twelve: Prefix
104. Binge lover
106. Termagants
108. Instructed
109. Deplore
110. Gibe
112. Spanish wave
113. Large watch
115. Words from a 13th cent. plainsong
123. Patrician
124. Up __ (cornered)
125. N. M. resort
126. State: Abbr.
127. Moola
130. __ ton
132. Tackles' neighbors
134. Printing process
136. Certain spirits
137. Japanese in U. S.
139. Slangy affirmative
141. __ homo
142. Separate
143. On the way
144. Orleans' river
145. Downfall
146. Badger
147. Substantive
148. Revoke, as a legacy
149. Choose

DOWN

1. Heady drink
2. Supports
3. Entertain
4. Words from a Cornish carol
5. Alexander Selkirk, for one
6. Before Nov.
7. Liszt specialty: Abbr.
8. Orange oil
9. Words by Frederic W. Farrar
10. Can. province
11. African antelope
12. Sailor's saint
13. Florida beach
14. "__ : Fear not . . ."
15. Symbol of victory
16. Brown hair color
17. __ de Pinos
18. German denial
19. Tawdry
23. Explosive
29. Obliteration
31. Approach on the double
36. Jonson
38. Logging operator
40. Lug
42. Semblance
43. Explorer De
44. Netherlands city
45. Monsters
46. Rye fungus
47. Willing, old style
52. Dogs, for short
53. Balbo
54. State: Abbr.
56. Indian prince
57. Little __
59. Looseness
60. "La Sonnambula"
62. Dull
64. Man of property
68. Tibetan creature
70. "__ plaisir"
74. Yacht-race category
76. God: Fr.
78. Griffin of TV
80. ". . . the use of him is more __ can see"
81. Flourishes
82. Lone Ranger's friend
83. More forlorn
84. Weapon
85. Outward: Anat.
90. Monotonous sound
91. "__ angelorum"
93. Blackbird
96. Take up
97. "And they were __ afraid"
99. Slav
101. Concerning
103. Futile
105. Chinese weight
107. Greek physician
108. Think much of
111. Commonplace: Var.
114. Mil. service initials
116. Emptiness
117. Wanderers
118. Cab
119. Spanish permit
120. Barfly's sound
121. Cause
122. Glasgow
127. Pop
128. "Step __!"
129. Sever
131. European capital
133. Booted
135. Son of Agrippina
138. Compass point
140. Speed

Eugene T. Maleska

ACROSS

1. Cager's target
5. Intimidated
10. Banter
14. Sticker
19. Code word for A
20. Macaw
21. Ubangi tributary
22. Residence
23. Everywhere
25. Marooned
27. Saw-toothed
28. Refusal
30. Hairy
31. Loom bar
32. Biblical verb
34. Legendary Irish beauty
35. Old hand
37. Former comedy team
41. Have hard going
42. Marine plant
43. Quiet and __
45. Suffix with unit and budget
46. Ibis's relative
48. Coop sounds
51. Coffee type
52. Harper Valley group
53. Pang
54. Scottish port
55. College in Iowa
56. Eraser users
58. Splendid
61. "Vissi __" (Tosca aria)
62. Ref. book
63. Utter confusion
64. Transaction policy
68. Singer in a group
70. Tolstoy
71. __ and Addison
72. Toy with
73. Scene of Tell legend
75. Swift's "The Tale of __"
77. British film maker
78. Good soil
79. Bask
80. Mister of cartoons
82. Dept. store area
85. Cabdriver
86. Symbols of drudgery
89. __ and sticks
91. Mal de __
92. Flash
93. "How __ you!"
94. Ubiquitous G.I.
96. Ten tens: Abbr.
97. Cross-country team
100. Bar order
103. Academic wear
105. Upright
106. German article
107. Buoyantly
108. Alas
109. A sight __
110. Caroler's word
111. Compact
112. Eddie of baseball

DOWN

1. __ and hems
2. Off-Broadway award
3. Taylor, Zachary
4. Burke's subject
5. Lope
6. __ and law
7. U.A.R. political group
8. Time division
9. Weedy grasses
10. Kind of puppet show
11. "__ the land of the free . . ."
12. Like Reynard
13. Stacked
14. Serve the soup
15. Loathed
16. Parisians' park
17. Sharpen
18. Kashmir town
24. Soprano Loeveberg
26. Halo
29. Pulitzer novelist: 1958
32. Mystical poet
33. Last part
35. Exchange
36. Estonian port
37. Planes, for short
38. Indigent
39. Mythical pair
40. Child
42. Resort near Naples
44. Inventor of a sign language
46. Account
47. Cowper poem
49. Better than 58 Across
50. Men from Brazil
54. __ macabre
57. __ es Salaam
58. What con artists do
59. Pub game
60. Faith: Fr.
64. Littleneck
65. P. I. natives
66. Beef casing
67. Debt assignor
68. Dagger and __
69. Cease-fire
72. Dapple
74. Signs a contract
76. Overshoe cord
81. Glutted
83. Start a roulette game
84. Aeolus
85. Time for a good time
87. Boy's collar
88. Rembrandt's birthplace
89. "What is __ as . . .?"
90. __ and toss
93. Sky animal
94. One of the Fijis
95. Caesar's fatal day
97. Money in Seoul
98. Fordham team
99. Small barracuda
100. Put into type
101. S. A. port
102. Chemical suffix
104. All and __

ACROSS

1. Fastenings
6. Krishna __
11. Trouble
14. Dickens name
17. Traffic ploy
18. Tree genus: Var.
19. Theater group
20. __-en-scène
21. Famous lover
22. Cleric's abbr.
23. Ups
25. Helen Hayes play
28. Painted, for one
29. Go in: Fr.
30. Mother of Ares
32. Bewildered
33. Month: Abbr.
35. "__ say more?"
38. Lab vessel
39. Inlet
40. "__ Stranger"
43. Shift to new quarters
45. Fracas
48. __ poke
50. Opera by Cherubini
51. Film Dolly
52. Former
54. Anarchist
55. Pitcher's concern: Abbr.
57. Roman money
58. Inner: Prefix
59. Land of the ghats
61. Adored one
62. Editor's mark
63. Play about Hollywood
67. Peeve
70. Tree of Brazil
71. Stain
72. Banking abbr.
74. Critic Huxtable
75. Curve
76. Kind of train: Abbr.
77. Do a network job
81. Grande dame
84. Shanks, in heraldry
86. Finds a new title
87. Pale
88. __ presence (use ESP)
91. Take umbrage
92. Mag men
93. Rotterdam's river
94. Blue Grotto locale
96. Civil War abbr.
97. "I would not __ pin . . ."
99. U.S. holly
100. Arch part
103. Russian groups
105. Walrus's observation
111. T V evenings
113. Close, to poets
114. Added liquor
115. N.F.L. team
116. Kind of bed or hog
117. Raccoon's relative
118. Blackened
119. Enzyme: Suffix
120. Day for ch.
121. Hide away
122. Italian specialty

DOWN

1. Offended
2. Thine: Fr.
3. EDT, for instance
4. Fix one's feathers
5. Explosive sound
6. Mrs. March
7. Ledger keeper
8. Standard
9. What beer has
10. Church part
11. Soothing agent
12. Japanese admiral
13. "Shane" star
14. Baseball statistics
15. River of France
16. Famous hostess
19. "Love Is __ Thing"
20. More foggy
24. __ hole in (rips)
26. Verdi opera
27. Swayed
31. Kind of meal
33. Mallard genus
34. Wyoming's __ Agie River
36. Party man: Abbr.
37. Area of Europe
41. Seven __ man
42. Squelch
44. Perfect moment
46. Ash, e.g.
47. Kiln
49. French city
51. Island near Java
53. Bagnold et al.
55. Anthony's family
56. Blackguard
60. Genetic abbr.
61. "__ had the wings of . . ."
62. Namesakes of Wagner heroine
64. Normandy city
65. Kind of pentameter
66. Pooh man
67. Parent
68. G. & S. princess et al.
69. Old man
73. Targets of punches
76. Dog star
78. Spanish city
79. __ store
80. This: Sp.
82. Frees
83. Shop sign
84. Ground
85. Depot: Abbr.
88. Wee: Scot.
89. Rochester name
90. Butter, etc.
95. Cheer words
97. Film director Frank
98. Tapestry
101. L.I.R.R. stop
102. Caribbean tree
104. Ships: Abbr.
106. Bugle call
107. __ the finish
108. City in Ark.
109. Encounter
110. Norse work
112. Certain note

ON THE SHADY SIDE
Arnold Moss

ACROSS

1. Psalm word
6. Senator Birch
10. Tempo
14. Saunter
19. Camera pole
21. __ animo (calmly)
22. Roman wife
23. Casaba
24. Fall back
25. Sailor's sounding lead
27. ". . . nothing like __"
28. Plant of arum family
30. TV's Calmer
31. Plays the vamp
33. Dawn goddess
34. Photo, for short
35. Insect
36. A carrot and __
37. Flour pot
39. Red: Sp.
41. Convenes
42. __ cadabra
45. What Gelett Burgess never did
49. Tax org.
50. Music groups
51. Winged
52. Certain party people: Abbr.
53. Draws a bead on
55. Pieces of flinty rock
56. Snoop
57. Eye: Prefix
59. Of a body fluid
61. In __ time
62. Burn out
63. Former believer
65. Praise, old style
66. Fish
67. Kind of floss
69. Kids
71. Poet's word
72. Others: Sp.
73. Anti-union ploy
78. Fads
81. Miquelon, e.g.
82. Jerusalem hill: Var.
83. Cornell's home
86. Libido
87. Over
89. Center-pieces
92. He, in Paris
94. Gal of song
95. Yorick's predecessor
97. Buckler of old
98. Williams et al.
99. Turkish sultans
101. V.I.P. in Belgrade
102. Hess, for one
103. Weizmann
104. Sky scales
105. Ziegler or Nessen
106. Barfly's fancies
110. Tense
111. N.C.O.
112. Winner at Brandywine
113. Father of Oedipus
114. Prayer
116. Dictionary entry: Abbr.
117. Indian weight
118. Degree for a space engineer
121. Kind of mat
123. Old hand
124. Features of whodunits
129. Believer: Suffix
130. Canadian capital
133. Hair tints
134. Onward
135. Stutz, for one
136. Bean
137. Put up with
138. Time periods: Abbr.
139. Kind of diet
140. Logwood and catechu
141. "Whither __ thou?"

DOWN

1. Billow
2. Spanish month
3. Rock suffixes
4. Cap-__
5. Salty dance
6. Neighbor of Neth.
7. Water: Prefix
8. Chinese river
9. Short trip
10. Sound of West Coast
11. Fired
12. Dove talk
13. Borgnine, etc.
14. Cremonan
15. Health program
16. Pacific slave ship
17. Capital of Togo
18. Chemical suffixes
20. Of God: Fr.
21. Arab robe
26. Not at all
29. Phone part: Abbr.
32. Theater ad abbr.
35. Garlic, in Lima
36. Ventilator
37. Stuff
38. Report-card entry
39. Get back on
40. Mil. school
41. Famed Alpine tunnel
43. Kneecap
44. Evaluate
45. __-troid
46. Orally
47. Fritter
48. Swing
50. Cleric's degree
54. Prankish one
55. Spanish hero
57. October stone
58. Hill, in Italy
59. Longer-limbed
60. Make a louder sound
63. Sweetsop
64. N.M. resort
66. Girl's name
68. Humorist Bill et al.
70. Old English poet
72. U.S. publisher
74. The same
75. Like a willow
76. Words for a movie sequence
77. To __ (exactly)
78. Add more seasoning
79. Law-rence's place
80. High-priced bars
84. Not radio-active
85. C.P.A. job
87. City lines
88. Speck
90. Demolish
91. Cook-out unit
93. Doctrines
95. State: Abbr.
96. Botanical cycle
98. Arabic letters
100. Stinging
102. Compass reading
103. Insect sound
105. Urban task
107. Euripides title
108. At __ (resting)
109. State capital
111. "Play it again, __"
115. Eastern societies
116. Nature writer
118. Follow
119. Textile workers
120. Entry in black
121. W.W.II girl
122. __ Gardner
123. ". . . __ brevis"
124. Movies' Calhoun
125. Gaelic
126. Brit. medals
127. Brooder
128. Blue: Prefix
131. Vietnam port
132. Trough

153 STRAINED RELATIONS — Edward J. O'Brien

ACROSS

1. Hersey town
6. Like a cupola
11. Iraqi port
16. Gives the slip
17. Oil alcohol
19. Card games
21. Mrs. Bailey
23. "__ crowd"
24. Former film director
25. Adjective suffix
26. Phobia about relatives?
28. Play or bull
29. Glass oven
30. Old Korean
32. Exodus locale
34. Isle off New Caledonia
36. Cupid
37. Hair: Prefix
39. Succors
40. Five: Prefix
42. Height: Abbr.
43. "A breath reeking __"
46. Famous racetrack
47. Broke fast
48. Hesitate
49. Beret
52. __ soda
53. "Let him save himself __ Christ"
56. Panay native
57. Type of film
59. Petition
60. Fine lace
61. Literary monogram
63. First Chinese dynasty
65. Rainbow
66. Bella Abzug for several years
70. Hindu music
73. Wagering words
74. Mideast initials
75. Compass point
76. Little mo.
79. Ethically neutral
81. Chess piece: Abbr.
83. Lawful, in León
85. Eureka!
86. Not C.O.D.
87. French evergreen
89. Profane, in Hawaii
90. Repeatedly
92. Foreseen uses, in patent law
94. Level tract: Abbr.
95. Hawaiian anchovies
96. Castle crossing
98. Turkish hat: Var.
99. Indies or River
101. Geneviève, for one
102. Dr. King had one
104. Clarinet material
109. Cholers
112. Befuddled: Scot.
113. Boxer Max's dad
115. South Bend campus
116. Battle site of '44
117. Satisfied
119. Young Weld
122. Confines
123. Place for red-eye
124. Blood disease
125. Block-heads
126. "A House __ a Home"
127. Pries

DOWN

1. Friendless
2. Rembrandt, to some
3. Go by, as rules
4. Society-page word
5. Courtier in "Hamlet"
6. Rob of beauty
7. Bullfinch: Var.
8. Most submissive
9. With full force
10. Greene
11. Larded, in cooking
12. Common verb
13. Adele Astaire
14. Sow again
15. Yoga postures
16. Ludwig
18. Jurists' degrees
19. Summer, in Strasbourg
20. DeGaulle relative
22. Missouri River dam
27. Do a new wax job
31. Lone male sibling
33. Topping or Cupid
35. Home-grown, in Havana
38. Bank abbr.
40. Bridge call
41. Son of Isaac
43. Two __ kind
44. Ex-Justice Tom Clark, to Ramsey, in a way
45. Mouth: Prefix
47. Biblical town near Tyre
50. Cuckoo
51. Rainier et al.: Abbr.
54. Horace's folks
55. Sprite
58. Palter
62. Symington, to friends
64. Part of ancient Greece
66. Cold or price
67. Cornhusker's home
68. March
69. Takes a ladylike dive
70. Type of session
71. Elec. unit
72. Zeus and Hera
76. Years in the priesthood
77. Alas, for Caesar
78. Anathemas
80. Chemical prefix
82. L.A. time zone
84. In accord
88. Before, before
91. Prepossessions
93. Map abbr.
94. Drew
96. Davenport
97. Greek halls
100. West Indian bird
103. Mimics
105. Abbreviations for "he died"
106. Island of 50th state
107. Sways
108. North Bornean
110. Havelock
111. Drink mix
114. Liquid units: Abbr.
118. Word with total or off
120. Type of dad
121. __-Magnon

ACROSS

1. Greek letter
6. Related group
10. Court decree
11. French composer
12. Insect bides its time
15. Building beam
16. Spanish article
19. __ you go
20. Letter
21. Ore pit
22. Scrap
23. Gas bag
24. Fluids
25. Headgear
28. Ham
30. River to Seine
31. Offer
32. Victor __
33. Helsinki bath
34. __ standstill
35. Adjective ending
36. Spud
37. Amount due for some foreign pottery
44. Quaking
45. Kind of pole
46. Press for payment
47. Well-known
48. Whale-oil cask
49. Rested
50. First part of a drama
51. Fuel depot
55. Peace: Lat.
56. Principal
58. Little figures in art
59. Fish
60. Lobster feature
61. Common verb
62. Post of etiquette
63. King, in Spain
64. Old one: Ger.
65. Mislaid rope
67. Mop's companion
68. Mongol
69. Fired
70. Babylonian abode of dead

DOWN

1. Indians of Kansas
2. Constellation
3. Valued
4. Apostle
5. Uncertain
6. Scale
7. Lip: Lat.
8. Finnish islands
9. "This train will run neither Christmas __"
12. Words for an upstaged blonde
13. Old __, Conn.
14. Bark
16. Forgetfulness flower
17. Town near Bangor
18. Scarecrow
19. Planet
23. Like snakes' eyes
24. Gun attachment
25. Garb for Fonteyn
26. Dyeing apparatus
27. Time of day
29. Early fratricide
31. Saloon fixture
32. Easily available bottle tops
35. __ fatuus
36. Oriental weight
37. Twist
38. Chinese dynasty
39. Summit
40. Feed
41. Cowboy actor
42. Australian cry
43. Land of the pasta
49. Short nap
50. Eastern V.I.P.
52. Islamic deity
53. Proportion
54. Lived
56. Medit. island
57. Howling
58. Latin-beginner's word
62. Beige
66. Indian cymbals

SEASONAL ART *Robert Roop*

ACROSS

1. Kind of log
5. Newborn
9. Seasonal visitor
14. Defeat
19. River of Hungary
20. Russian city
21. Primp
22. Betel palm
23. Massys work in Met. Museum
27. Present time
28. Señor's farewell
29. Arthurian lady
30. Deprive of office
33. Independent
34. Winter sportsman
35. Adjective suffix
36. Gun maker
39. Young fowl
41. Chess ending
43. Gather
44. "They _ serve who . . ."
45. LSD word
49. Seven-year item
50. British gun
51. Spanish aunts
52. Israeli dance
53. Van der Weyden subject
58. Exclude
59. Vale of _
60. Tartan-wearing groups
61. Kick downstairs
62. Cornmeal patty
65. Eyelashes
66. Overdue
67. Card game
68. Doyle's middle name
69. Urchin
70. Three: Fr.
71. Gerard David painting
76. Kind of billy
77. Reading, for one
78. Wee ones
79. Weird
80. Offspring
81. React to yeast
82. "What's in _?"
84. Prop for Lincoln
85. Read closely
86. Jackets
89. Compass reading
90. Army mule et al.
94. Name in U.S. theater
95. Disorderly one
97. Stress
98. Dough
100. Partitions
102. Hieronymus Bosch work
108. Present or perfect
109. Adjust
110. Information
111. _ regni
112. Chemical compound
113. Beau _
114. Bovines
115. Certain word

DOWN

1. Besides
2. Word of disgust
3. Lila or Peggy
4. Muse
5. Frontier
6. Musical offering
7. Group
8. High note
9. Certain weavers
10. Palmer of golf
11. Pisgah summit
12. English river
13. Aardvark tidbit
14. Bill holder
15. Hill nymph
16. Cached in a new place
17. Postcard décor
18. Lion's mentor
24. Miss Dartle
25. Household gods
26. Greetings
30. "You _ on purpose"
31. Planet
32. Kind of card
33. Money in Rouen
34. Writer Glaspell
37. Adult
38. Signs
39. Feature of old bronze
40. Mixtures
42. "_ is this?"
45. Part of the Nativity scene
46. Capek creation
47. Wrathful
48. Cut
50. Eden denizen
54. Approaches
55. Hockey infraction
56. Islamic god
57. Opposite of 'tis
58. Slender: Fr.
61. Populace
62. Hebrew letters
63. Dingy, in Scotland
64. French school
65. Like some rattlers
66. Cake-to-be
68. Shut
69. Troll
71. Exhibitions
72. Medit. land
73. Beer ingredient
74. Lever: Var.
75. Before Polk
77. Capri feature
82. Calif. seafood
83. Hale character
85. Cogitate
87. Annie, for one
88. Location
90. Dull finish
91. Tooth woes
92. Inkling
93. _ fire
94. Parisian's finger
96. Ottoman founder
98. Bull or ram
99. Patriot of 1700's
100. Tunisian port
101. Feminine suffix
103. Kind of doll
104. Early French king
105. Upward: Prefix
106. African beast
107. Charged atom

156 ALWAYS BELITTLING
William Lutwiniak

ACROSS

1. Correctly
7. Factotum
12. Florists' items
17. Helmsman's course
20. Go headlong
21. Prankish spirit
22. Bonehead
23. Chase flies
24. Ham it up
28. Mss. men
29. Schnozzles
30. ___ prosequi
31. Logger's hook
32. Got to
33. Be worthy of
34. Grand Ol'
35. Family members
38. Front on
39. Copland
40. Don Juan's mother
41. Helmsman's course
44. Like a $10 bid for "Mona Lisa"
49. P.M. affair
50. Saucers, maybe
51. Gil ___
52. Lacerate
53. Gloomy Dean, to cockneys
54. Huge one
56. Caucasian
58. Biting insect: Var.
59. M.I.T. grads
60. Writer Bergson
61. Eastern V.I.P.
62. Had a 67 Across
63. Unclean place
64. Worthless thing
66. Oriented
67. Social affair
68. German article
69. Put out
70. Piscine features
72. Worthless thing
76. Ferryboat
79. Called
80. Disgusting ones
81. Map feature
82. Ride ___ fall
83. Dalai et al.
84. Gun parts
85. Features of certain hogs
86. Like Angora cats
87. Bede
88. ___ d'oeuvres
89. Incorrect: Prefix
90. French bird
91. Flop
97. Farm animal
98. Serpents
99. Chatter
100. Boorish ones
101. Marie, for one
102. Vedic dawn goddess
103. ___ Grosso
104. Superior
105. Striking phrase
108. Promising one
109. Privation
111. Musical syllable
114. Trivial accomplishment
118. Kimono adjuncts
119. Place of action
120. Rice dish
121. Quake aftermath
122. Cattle genus
123. Genial, in Britain
124. Sudden increase
125. Anger

DOWN

1. Culmination
2. Thunderfish
3. Peeves
4. Thou, or ten C's
5. Skirt features
6. Lop off
7. Where Porto Novo is
8. Speechify
9. Gives a leg up
10. Durocher
11. Argentine cowboys
12. Orchestra section
13. Grown up
14. Locate
15. Long time
16. Corks
17. Knife: Slang
18. Source of harm
19. Like chins at breakfast
23. Two-wheeler
25. Plane section
26. Element
27. ___ rima
33. City of France
34. ___ a time
35. Presses forward
36. Consecrate
37. Like some music
38. Kind of sample
39. Lothario's specialty
40. Do-nothing
41. Dolce far ___
42. Rang the bell
43. Over
45. Outfits: Abbr.
46. Bizarre
47. Father of Nora and Peer
48. Valse ___
54. Bivouac features
55. Black
56. Man of Muscat
57. Theol. center
58. City on the Tigris
60. Took on
61. Mine features
62. Tackles
64. Wayside Inn fare
65. Forwards
66. ___ Park, Colo.
67. Straw hat
69. This month: Abbr.
70. Tail
71. Shaggy
72. Free-wheel
73. Crewman
74. B-vitamin
75. Sign up
76. North wind
77. Confirmed
78. Oater critter
79. Jet
80. Sea birds
82. Blow a ___
84. ___ up (increases power)
85. Basswood
86. Dissembles
88. Cries of adoration
89. Spells: Scot.
90. Parties in a bribe
92. Kenya people
93. Mine rail passage
94. One of the Mongolias
95. Film-studio player deal
96. Caulking material
102. Exclamations of disgust
103. Months, to Hiawatha
104. Hungarian composer
105. Snooty one
106. Timber wolf
107. Elevator man
108. Comb: Prefix
109. N.Z. timber tree
110. Bawl
111. ". . . or not ___"
112. Bylaw
113. Solar disk
115. Twelve doz.
116. Pourboire
117. Cooperage abbr.

157 TIME REMEMBERED   *Keith Blake*

ACROSS

1. French soldier
6. Month: Abbr.
9. Western lake
13. Stupid one
16. Baseball statistic
17. Frosted
19. "__ assisted by . . ."
20. Gay __
22. Swarms
23. What leap-year dates are
26. Cleft in parts
28. Like heads on schooners
29. Actress Landi
30. "Crabbed __ youth cannot . . ."
33. Unfold, to poets
34. Triangular inserts
35. Overtime for 1980
42. Sheep flocks
43. Merits
44. Archeologists' milieu
45. French beverage
48. Peculiar: Prefix
49. Aspen gear
50. Ten percenter: Abbr.
51. Reagan, for short
52. Crosses out
53. "Ring out the __" (Tennyson)
61. Brief
62. Gulls
63. Poplars
64. Laconic words of defeat
66. "When constabulary __ to be done"
67. In a keen way
68. Esprit de corps
69. __ comic drama
70. Shares: Fr.
71. 1800, 1900, 2000
74. Wee, in Scotland
77. Wrong: Prefix
78. Roulette bet
79. Linkletter
80. All-night cafe sign
81. Doer: Suffix
82. Younger son
84. Singer Callas
86. Campaign lineup
87. Ecclesiastical time reckoners
90. Liszt or Lehar
92. Bow
93. Tasket's mate
94. Words for a black sheep
95. Chesterton's middle name
97. Nautical term
99. What 35 Across makes 1980
102. Novices
106. Nag
107. Ponder
108. Miffed
109. Leave out
110. Roget specialty: Abbr.
111. Cut
112. Good as __
113. Old fiddle

DOWN

1. Favorite
2. Swedish coin
3. Fury
4. New Year band name
5. College in Collegeville
6. Area of France
7. Kind of test
8. Race an engine
9. Kind of voyage
10. Declines
11. Associate
12. Hair job
13. Originated
14. Dr. of cartoon books
15. Evening, in Eboli
18. Repudiate
20. Air-race markers
21. Burning
24. Movie extras, for short
25. Set out
27. Govt. agency
30. Attach
31. Hollow rock
32. Satan
36. Tahoe, e.g.
37. Siberian
38. Speaker of baseball
39. Nets
40. Hindu ages
41. Chem. prefix
45. Fish, in a way
46. Like old socks
47. Concludes
53. Oar pin
54. Pants: Ger.
55. Rolled up
56. Out
57. "__ see what I see?"
58. Relish
59. News items
60. G-men, e.g.
61. Blind strip
64. "__ me!"
65. Painter Max
66. __ the world (asleep)
67. Chem. liquid
68. Year McKinley was shot
69. Factions
70. Drunk: Sp.
72. Knobs
73. Connelly
74. Belgian premier
75. Fr. measure
76. "__ of robins in . . ."
80. Kind of type
82. Ship line
83. Aussie
84. Borgnine film
85. Mehitabel's friend et al.
86. Short snort
87. Tag
88. Hid away, as an animal
89. Greek letter
90. Caprice
91. Boca __
94. Bite: Ger.
95. Part of K.K.K.
96. Naturalness
97. Swiss river
98. Prepare tea
100. M.D.'s org.
101. Long time
103. Kid
104. Poem
105. Short time

158 NEW YEAR LIMERICK
Frances Hansen

ACROSS

1. Asian peninsula
6. Small bottle
11. Kind of sergeant
16. Pipe parts
21. Soap plant
22. Madrid museum
23. Massacre scene in Vietnam
24. Drip-dry fabric
25. __ bell
26. Wanders
27. Sinclair
28. Kind of trope
29. Limerick, with 58, 82, 109 and 138 Across
33. Boredom
34. TV's Antoine
35. Red or Dead
36. Britisher's exclamation
37. Easter fare
40. Aleutian island
42. Artemis
46. Sent back: Abbr.
48. Polite interruptions
51. Compass point
53. __-eyed (gaping)
54. Between avril and juin
55. Franciscan order: Abbr.
58. See 29 Across
64. Nonplus
65. India, e.g.
66. Streisand film, with "Day"
67. __ uproar
68. Certain wagons
73. Deer of Asia
74. Hoop: Sp.
77. Suffix for halit or neur
79. Stops, as a missile flight
81. Pitch
82. See 29 Across
89. Cream puffs at six paces
90. Furs
91. Tie
92. MS. men
93. Fabrics with lines
96. Lunch hour
100. Fed. agents
102. Goes astray
104. Scoundrel
105. Choir screen
109. See 29 Across
115. Ark man: Var.
116. "__ Were a Rich Man"
117. Melville book
118. Golfer's pou sto
119. Evergreen genus
120. Calmer of TV
121. Late March, to head-cold victim
123. Comedian Bert
126. Albanian coin
127. Overseas addresses
131. British colonial rulers: Abbr.
133. __ disant
135. Provoke
138. See 29 Across
147. Shaw
148. Relative of adieu
149. Refuge
150. Babylonian abode of dead
151. "__ ev'ry little star . . ."
152. Billiard shot
153. Ward off
154. Verse cadences
155. Snide
156. Hostile one
157. Bloody and Queen
158. Cousins of oenochoes

DOWN

1. French spouse
2. Oriental nurse
3. Like Tonto's friend
4. Pond scum
5. Aspire
6. Shoot
7. Gained
8. Pompeii's ruin
9. That is: Lat.
10. Go __ (decay)
11. Complacent
12. Printing boo-boo
13. Prefix for tude or meter
14. Young deer: Fr.
15. Mob member
16. Limey locale
17. Famous fountain
18. French pronoun
19. Ballerina Shearer
20. Like Kilimanjaro's peaks
30. Double helix
31. Principle
32. Knocking sound
37. Triumphant cries
38. "There'll be __ time . . ."
39. Desert sight
41. Not suitable
43. Branch
44. Teachers' org.
45. Writer Rand
47. Last resort, sometimes
49. Christmas trio
50. Italian Mr.
52. Sea bird
55. "__ and you're dead!"
56. Like church windows
57. A nose __
59. Rein
60. Pyle and Ford
61. Trappist cheese
62. Threw a party
63. Winged
69. Biblical verb
70. Honest one
71. Fracas
72. Test
74. Freshens a martini
75. Give road directions
76. __ hill (washed up)
78. Tilts
80. Novelist Jean-Paul
83. Form of Elizabeth
84. African people: Var.
85. Ziegfeld
86. Sum of little Indians
87. Ouida
88. Veer
94. Puckish
95. Singing exercise
97. Here: Fr.
98. Detroit dud
101. Kind of do-well
103. Prayed before dinner
106. __ Eireann
107. Start of a fairy tale
108. Badlands state: Abbr.
110. Some punches
111. Diamond man
112. For: Sp.
113. Lift
114. Tough
122. New York
124. Does ghosting
125. Operate
127. Over
128. Gate: It.
129. German kings
130. Word for ex-cager Wilt
132. Car style
134. Caste of India
136. Author Marsh
137. Of a flower part
139. Lamarr
140. Kind of dale
141. Weaver's need
142. "__ slip showing?"
143. Continually
144. Musical intro
145. Exlie island
146. Ploy

159 UNDERHAND STROKES James V. Shannon

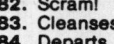

ACROSS

1. Hectic existence
8. Excludes
14. Drink mixer
21. Palm civets
23. Miss May
24. Leafstalk
25. Provider of enchantment
26. __ hand (helps)
27. Launched, poetically
28. Gambler's insurance
30. Pea-shuffler's medium
32. Magpie
33. Sovereign concession
36. Madison Ave. concerns
37. One-up tactic
38. "The wings of __ black and white"
41. Street game
43. Thread
44. Sleeve lining, at times
45. River in Italy
47. Miss Dahl
48. Mideast country
50. What birds do
52. Grammatical case: Abbr.
53. __ and chain
54. In a lax way
58. Ultimate goal
60. Partner of dark and handsome
62. Ending for psych or laryng
64. Attention
66. Landscape
68. Veal specialties
69. Saratoga
70. Up and about
73. Old English money
74. Golf club
75. Beginning
78. Re-sounded
80. Words for a duet
82. Scram!
83. Cleanses
84. Departs
85. Bar need
87. Trims
88. Miss Rehan
89. Like some drains
91. Crystalline rocks
93. Writer Deighton
94. Full of sandbanks
95. Money in Mexico
96. Snake
100. Calif. city
102. One kind of consent: Abbr.
104. Sweatshirt size: Abbr.
106. Burmese rice
107. Encircle
108. Gum-yielding tree
110. Killer whale
112. Race an engine
113. Of the cheek
116. Mineral named for Pa. city
119. Cry of encouragement
121. "__ love with . . ."
122. Blip expert: Abbr.
123. Void states
124. Treaty group
125. Golf club used in traps
128. Sharper's standbys
132. People living under the same meridian
133. Positioned: Lat.
136. Separations
138. Same
139. Rye grass
140. Nose openings
141. English resort
142. Indolent
143. Perfume

DOWN

1. Pensioned off: Abbr.
2. Onassis et al.
3. Assay
4. Record again
5. Early church follower
6. Spitefully
7. Refrain from "The King and I"
8. Highly pleasing
9. One kind of college
10. Sugar daddy's lure
11. Help
12. Hosp. workers
13. Black and Red
14. Turnpike posting
15. Writer H.G.
16. Sloping type: Abbr.
17. Label holders
18. Certain trains
19. Crystalline alcohol
20. Saloon offering
22. But, to Caesar
29. Two, in Toledo
31. Holbrook
34. Louisiana city
35. __-Saud
38. Subdue
39. Image
40. Pinochle play
42. Meteor science
43. Wear well
46. Flower oil
49. Snail genus
51. Basketball maneuvers
55. L'__ (Aegean Sea): Fr.
56. Grantor
57. Native of a Caroline island
59. At __ (on the loose)
61. Material for marbles
63. Shoe material: Abbr.
65. Deserves
67. Earth
68. Did a matador's maneuver
70. Of peripheral body parts
71. Some photos
72. Alaskan people
74. Took action
76. Indefinite quantity
77. Honors
79. Lesion
81. Carry on, as war
82. Liberian people
84. Bank deal
86. New World Indian
90. Crap-shooter's insurance
91. Cloture, for one
92. DeMille specialties
94. Mix
95. Acquires a green coating
97. Rosemary, e.g.
98. Spread
99. Shade of blue
101. Prehistoric man
103. Outside a chemical group
105. Evangeline's home
109. P.I. people
111. Achieves
113. Make a faulty sight
114. Miss Blake of "Gunsmoke"
115. Cotton machine
117. In the midst of: Abbr.
118. Igloo resident: Abbr.
120. Arterial trunks
122. Talking style, in music: Abbr.
126. N.Z. insect
127. Image: Prefix
129. Telepathy, for short
130. Cowpoke's oath
131. Not regular: Abbr.
134. Baseball league: Abbr.
135. Hindu title
137. Compass reading

VARIETY PACKAGE *Jack Luzzatto*

ACROSS

1. Solemn promise
7. Sentimental fools
12. Multitudes
18. Of direct descent
19. Spooks
21. Wind-borne
22. Set free
23. Mini-people country: Var.
24. Near-homer
25. Paltry
26. Polite word
28. Nit-pick
30. __ mater
31. Don't miss it
32. Serape
33. In a photo finish
36. Store-ad features
38. Taro roots
39. Takes on cargo
40. Cartoonist Peter
41. Kind of remark
42. Taunt
44. Lease again
46. Third-rank univ. student
47. From the same mother
51. Small valleys
52. Criteria
53. Rival of long standing
55. Old French coins
56. Christmas toe
57. Hot-rod site
58. Titanic message
59. Worst of friends
61. Engine: Abbr.
62. Displays
64. Fond fools
65. Geste, e.g.
66. Hurt in return
67. Country quaffs
68. Beer bases
69. Thirty, in Paris
70. U.S. beasts
71. Code man
72. Tangy
74. Nautical cry
75. Girl in "La Bohème"
76. Horrify
79. Port of Brazil
81. Wisdom
85. Relative of a kind
87. Reject
88. Speak of love
89. Big __ of Calif.
90. Limber
91. European region
93. Cut
94. Poplars
96. African land
98. Words of sympathy
100. "Merchant of __" (movie ad villain)
101. Nearing a culmination
102. Infuriate
103. Oodles
104. Chain of hills
105. Word on a thin-ice sign

DOWN

1. Sounds the depth
2. Form a queue
3. Put in a box
4. College V.I.P.
5. Silencer
6. Peanut fancier
7. Mata Hari job, old style
8. Art medium
9. From "A" to "indeed"
10. Capsize
11. Worker on house sides
12. Begin to function
13. Urbanity
14. Clay, today
15. Tore
16. Evil intent
17. Quarterback ploys
19. Great numbers
20. Wager
27. French composer
29. Like the ocean
32. Begets
34. Norse sagas
35. Swimming
37. Summons
38. Sign up for
41. Wagner heroine et al.
43. Golf clubs
44. Make a comeback
45. Baffling
46. Sampled
48. Prison inmates
49. Flatter, in a way
50. Medit. island
51. Forsake
52. Pigwoman of "Odyssey"
53. Abalones
54. Beastly holes
56. Dealer in fish or gossip
57. Watch lever
59. Barrier of a sort
60. Knotty
63. Kind of floss
65. Eyewash acid
67. Non-soldier: Slang
68. Certain voter
70. Footloose fellow
71. Resettled
73. Sulky race
75. Hawaiian island
76. Teas of India
77. Love letter: Fr.
78. Old legend of India
80. Allen or Frome
81. Timber prop
82. Morning-after millinery
83. Haul-away cost
84. Wild blue __
86. Ascends
87. Net
92. Seagoing stockade
93. Egotist's instrument
95. Sweet apple, for short
97. Honshu town
99. Turn __ dime

ACROSS

1. Added liquor
6. Pub fare
10. Electric catfish
15. Make another curve
21. Of Florentine or Roman style
23. __ in the face
24. Kill __
25. Song title
27. Conveyor of property
28. Old beater for clothes
29. Author Wister
30. Rush the passer
32. Small shark
33. Spanish wave
34. __ -disant
36. Adverse or Wayne
38. Star in Leo
40. Former Indiana legislator
43. Econo-mizes
44. Eaglestone
45. Stone or Iron
46. Tilted
47. Consumer's woe: Abbr.
49. Easter items
52. Lubricant devices
55. Miss Massey
56. Grand-father: Lat.
57. Trims a photo
59. Con's quarters
60. Like Kansas land
61. Certain diets
63. Exists, old style
65. Mancini song
68. Rogues: Fr.
69. Silly actions
71. Disen-gaged
72. Marsh gas
74. Thrice: Prefix
75. Cobbling word
77. P.I. peasant
78. Costly
79. Initials of 1930s
82. Like some coffee-table books
85. Others: Sp.
88. __ stay (nautical rope)
90. "__ choose to run"
92. U.S. author
95. Irish heir-appar-ent
96. Canaries' cousins
97. Chemical suffixes
98. Pitcher's slip
100. Canonical hour
101. Mil. official
102. Did rowing
104. Baseball's Walter and family
107. Hebrides island
108. Place to fly down to
109. Succeeding
110. French vineyard
111. Captured again
113. French neurologist
115. Famed alias
121. Lathe accessory
122. Symbol of industry
123. Green or black
124. Work gang: Sp.
125. Tamarisk tree
126. Avignon feature
128. __ account
130. David's works
132. Canadian name
134. Farewell words to Ophelia
137. Covetous one
138. Prisons, to cons
139. City of Northwest
140. F.H.A., for one
141. French weight
142. Meeting: Abbr.
143. Church council

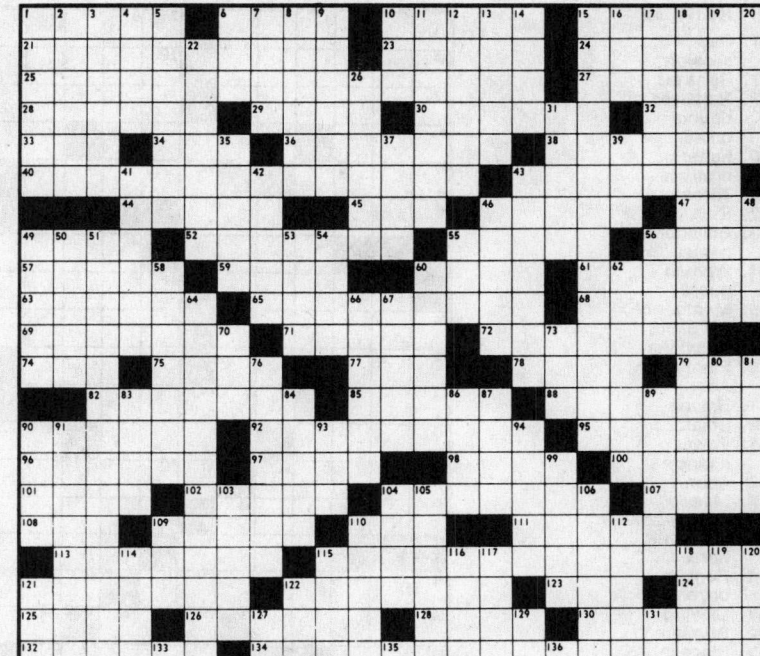

DOWN

1. Places of oblivion
2. Buckley's "God and Man __"
3. Middle-East garment
4. Hebrew month
5. __ home (eats in)
6. At all
7. Wash: Lat.
8. Indian city near Agra
9. Actress Royle
10. Fled
11. "With __ of the pen"
12. Deranged: Fr.
13. First-rate
14. Expedited
15. Writers of 25 Across
16. Cockney cry
17. Vinegar
18. Sheik personified
19. Twilight
20. Toasting word
22. Merchant of Venice
26. Catch, in a way
31. Chemical solid
35. Of metrical stress
37. Thermal actions: Abbr.
39. Begone, cowboy style
41. Evening star
42. Squirmed along
43. Like a mailbox
46. Type of clock
48. W.W.II craft
49. Great success
50. Grumble
51. Former Colorado V.I.P.
53. Bass or treble
54. Suffix for sec or pop
55. Pier union: Abbr.
56. "You're gaining __"
58. English cheese
60. Hat
62. Of a coast
64. Table tidbits
66. Adds up again
67. Wasteland
70. Wind direction
73. Asian holiday
76. Backless seat
80. Up and about
81. __ part (performs)
83. "You can bet __"
84. Beauty-parlor item
86. Globes
87. Photocopy, for short
89. Rub with oil
90. River to the Danube
91. Conse-crating
93. Objective
94. Town in Ontario
99. Prepared to be knighted
103. Corn gruel
104. Coxey's for one
105. Prefixes meaning loin
106. Anti-mine ship
109. Timetable abbr.
110. Water tank
112. Follower of Aristotle
114. Tea alkaloid: Var.
115. "It's __ January"
116. Yiddish gossips
117. Streaky, as an insect's wing
118. Keep an engine running slowly
119. Uno or dos, in Spanish
120. Sailed into the sunrise
121. __ hole-in-one
122. Nod
127. Attention-getting sound
129. Mel and family
131. "And __ we go"
133. And not: Lat.
135. Part of Mao's name
136. Santa sounds

IN GOOD SPIRITS
Elizabeth A. Yaro

ACROSS

1. Rap session
7. Runs off
13. Relatives of double takes
20. Funeral orations
21. Threaten
22. Rich
23. Belladonna genus
24. Woman guard
25. Member of the same class: Var.
26. Plant study: Abbr.
27. Bravos
29. Smart __
31. Power agency: Abbr.
32. Mesa's state: Abbr.
34. "__ of wild horses. . ."
36. Roman dozen
37. Cloying
39. Strollers
42. Places: Abbr.
44. Peak of Nepal
46. Upright: Abbr.
47. Ready, in France
49. Scottish hoop
50. Costa __
52. Divide an angle
54. Pioneer in the occult
58. English resort
59. Registered again
61. Source words
62. Of a Soviet range
63. Continent
64. Mine yields
66. Compass points
67. Flying org.
68. Confutes
70. Little ghost
72. One of the zones: Abbr.
73. This, in Spain
75. Japanese wrestling
76. "Damn Yankees" girl
77. Assert
79. Vamooses
81. Cyrano's family
83. Did sight-seeing
84. Be unsteady
86. Veined, as a leaf
87. Wasted time
88. Word in U.S. motto
90. Earthquake
91. Grey of stage
92. Dreamy states
96. Season in Nice
97. Blood ail-ment: Var.
101. Tanker
102. Road material
104. Yoga posture
107. Diana of movies
108. __ tree
109. Rumored
111. Medit. island
114. Nonsense!
115. Clam genus
118. V.I.P. at 1 Across
120. Gas-rating word
122. Phantom
123. Beethoven symphony
124. Fish-clean-ing gadget
125. Sonnet parts
126. Light shoe
127. Fencing pieces

DOWN

1. Sailor's luggage
2. Corrida star
3. Of a blood trunk
4. __ Dinh Diem
5. Mushroom
6. Biblical brother
7. Ant
8. Charter
9. Can. province
10. Distortion of memory
11. Earth science: Abbr.
12. Old: Lat.
13. Deducting, as from pay
14. Body of poetry
15. Moonshine container
16. Drink
17. One airing grievances
18. Varying
19. Layers
28. Show surprise
30. U.S. agency
33. "Viva __" (Brando film)
35. "__ the cruelest month"
37. Binge
38. Wiener and knack
40. See again: Fr.
41. Medium states
43. Jeanne and Therese
45. Draw a bead on
47. Sets aside for future use
48. Medium's output
50. U.S. stage name
51. Drum sound
52. Dream: Ger.
53. Balcony
55. Enigma: Fr.
56. Came forth
57. Grated
58. Most lucid
60. Agnus __
65. Kind of wagon
69. Relative of Mac or pal
70. Women's clubs
71. Waterweed
74. Adjust
76. Medium's forte
78. Quieted
80. Mr., in Ponce
82. Favor, old style
85. European country: Abbr.
89. Shea people
91. Kind of African goat
92. White and Blair
93. Mod youth of earlier days
94. Tartans
95. Gal of song
98. Esprit de corps
99. Mangle
100. Flowers
103. Wars of the __
105. Latin girlfriend
106. Port of Brazil
109. "Thanks __"
110. Port of Guam
112. Fling
113. Old Syrian fabric
116. Toper
117. Rubber tree
119. Purge
121. Unpaid bill

THE NAMES OF THE GAMES

Ward W. Smith

ACROSS

1. Social position
6. Height: Prefix
10. Resist
16. Gem stone
20. In progress
21. German area
22. Double-__
23. Persian coin
25. Prefix for wave or scope
26. Wife of Henry VIII
28. Straighten
29. Curving
31. Famous archer
32. Little Theresa
33. Eye shape
34. Observed
35. Woodwind
37. Golf score
39. Ohio River feeder
41. Combers
43. By way of: Var.
45. Measures: Abbr.
46. Diminutive suffixes
47. Coal size
49. Salamanders
50. Atlantic bay
54. Book sizes
56. Before: Abbr.
57. Templeton
58. Hard and soft
62. Arab prince
63. Court worker
64. Whole and half
66. Life, to Longfellow
67. Multitude
68. Cat call
70. Showman
72. Each
74. Fleet
76. Gets nosy
77. Scoffed
78. Brut
81. Chassis part
82. Wets down
83. Particle
84. Draft initials
85. Church body
87. Takes shape
88. One of 13
90. Bucolic
91. Whatnot item
92. Noah's concern
93. Church part
97. Concept: Fr.
98. Earthy pigment
100. Derring-do
102. Greasier
104. Ride a bike
106. Donnybrook
107. During
108. Quantities
109. Frontiersman
112. Sinn __
113. Channel
114. Law expert: Abbr.
117. Fabric
118. Coconut fiber
119. Big wind
121. Miss Bardot
125. Liberian
126. Slangy suffix
127. Body of poetry
130. Somewhat
131. Split
133. Gatling, etc.
135. Stay to the end
137. Singing voices
138. Powhatan's girl
141. Income: Fr.
142. Sports events
143. Orbit point
144. Take out
145. Wrath
146. Canal
147. Tenfold
148. Baltic feeder
149. Mall component

DOWN

1. Town in Washington
2. Burning
3. Athenian teacher
4. City of Italia
5. Boy's collar
6. Botanist Gray
7. Eddie and Ida
8. Indian queens
9. Russian city
10. Exclamation
11. Alloys
12. Fence stake
13. Pindar, for one
14. Meaning
15. Work unit
16. Harem women
17. Date and coconut
18. Melodic
19. Songbird
24. Surrenders
27. Foolish talk
30. Atlantic arm
33. Dancer Pavlova
36. Uses the mutuels
38. European country
40. Relative
42. Son of Jacob
44. Benefit incomes
47. Elegant
48. Repeat
50. Men in a shell
51. Bitter drug
52. Sneaky __
53. Weird
55. Study field
56. One-up tactic
59. Some looks
60. Shoe parts
61. Cutters
63. Herring keg
65. Ciudad Trujillo today
69. Congers
71. Van der Rohe
73. Hammerhead
75. Low-caste Hindu
76. Manchurian town
77. Aria
78. Paper token
79. Dodge
80. Packaged
82. Dissenter
83. Peaty tract
86. Word with home or bed
87. Certain decision-maker
88. Lump
89. Korean border river
91. Stylish
92. Dart
94. Samoan port
95. Bristle
96. Formerly, old style
99. Vault
101. Vespucci
103. Scottish island
105. Gifts
108. Word with space
110. Turn
111. One backing a bet
112. Realty sign
114. Genesis name
115. Capital of Kerry
116. Giggle
119. Bivouacked
120. Watch lever
122. Hindu loincloth
123. Figure of speech
124. Image: Var.
128. Kind of space
129. Cubic meter
132. Star in Lyra
134. Open
136. Gershwin et al.
138. Floating leaf
139. Attention-getter
140. Sun. talk

164 UNDER THE COUNTER
Walter McSherry

ACROSS

1. Innocent one
5. __ march on
11. Marquand's Mr. et al.
16. Watering spot
19. Drug plant
20. Tawdry
21. Type of mail
23. Church court
24. Ancient: Prefix
25. Wall St. and poker items
26. Briefs of a sort
28. Curve
29. Church area
30. Salvation, e.g.
31. Irish county
34. Topography
37. Analyzes a sentence
39. Diamond gal
40. Chem. suffix
41. Compass point
42. Luzon native
44. Certain marbles
47. Millay and Best
49. Paperback
51. Hair color
53. In working order
57. Beauty spot
58. Physicist Bruno
60. Gate fee
62. Wall St. saying with 70 Across
66. City near Moscow
67. Opposite of bid
70. See 62 Across
72. Religious school: Abbr.
73. Dispirit
75. Minding the business
77. Caused trouble
79. Weird
80. San __
84. Make certain
85. Duke of Windsor
88. Receives
90. One who quotes
92. Eggs à la __
94. Maid of Astolat
95. Old exclamation
98. Formal wear, for short
99. Seize
100. Ledger items
102. Intact fossil specimen
104. Junkyard, for one
107. Arthritis drug
109. Regarding
110. Greek letter
112. Manhattan address
115. Favorites of cool investors
118. Freedom of a sort
119. Shot and shell
120. Starts
121. Academy men
122. Coal bed
123. Part of a genus: Abbr.
124. Stone slab
125. Passover events
126. Truman monograms

DOWN

1. Porsena
2. Hilo hello
3. Military car setup
4. Downbeat of sorts
5. Depots: Abbr.
6. Harangue
7. Surround
8. Pale
9. Rent
10. Drink
11. Name for phone company
12. Some stocks
13. Extended credit to
14. Shout
15. Regulatory agcy.
16. Grass genuses
17. Wasp genus
18. M. Lupin
22. "__ she blows!"
27. Alpine area
32. Smooth-talking
33. Japanese aborigine
35. Weariness
36. Transfer
38. Metric measures
42. Ticker-tape symbol
43. Gunk
45. Amen, for one
46. Combo instrument
47. Long-suffering one
48. Back talk
50. From first __
52. Pollen carriers
54. Drill parts
55. Learning
56. Hindu land grant
59. More muddy
61. Lack of foresight
63. Merriment
64. Lixivium
65. Glacial ridges
67. Peak
68. Asian people
69. Teases
71. Relatives
74. White: Prefix
76. 1929 event
78. Arrange
81. Knowledges
82. Alp: Abbr.
83. Chemical suffix
86. Fay of "King Kong"
87. French river
89. Sports-shoe part
91. Put into effect
93. Place for jewelry
95. Algerian soldiers
96. Welles and Bean
97. Buying info
99. Czech river
101. Market man
103. French roof
105. Marsh
106. Rowed
108. Blood: Prefix
111. Cad
113. Meeting: Abbr.
114. Ewell and Jones
116. Family member
117. Rested
118. Letter abbr.

MEANINGFUL *Anthony Morse*

ACROSS

1. Finnish lake
6. Wheel part
11. Chose
16. Lunch
20. Ohio city
21. Barred
22. Establish
23. Like some peanuts
24. Small members of a panel
26. Admission of debt to a grange man
28. Verses
29. Water holes
30. Symbols of authority
31. Indolent
32. Telegrams
33. Carpentry joint
34. Odd, in Perth
35. Ordains
39. Beneficiary
40. Jaeger
41. Jazz
44. Gives cues
45. The staff departs
47. Number
48. Flycatchers
49. Drain
50. Routes
51. Blend
52. Correct
53. Does knightly work
54. Hitchcock's 39
56. Grown-up ditch
57. Pretenses
58. River of Italy
59. Loser of a race
60. Cover with spots
61. French article
62. What Calumet Farm has done
66. Stalled
67. Teach
69. Baptism et al.
70. Notre Dame's team
71. Wandered off
73. What Amazons were doing at times
76. Initials on a vessel
79. They're often stewed
80. Florida county
81. Oléron et al.
82. French author
83. Had a tantrum
84. General drift
85. Measured amounts
87. Goal for some girls
88. Advantage
89. Island in S.F. Bay
90. Take possession, in law
91. Low form of life
92. Fish
93. Actors' club members go to Las Vegas
96. Scoffed
97. Compass point
98. See
99. Skips
100. What queens are often used for
101. Eastern title
102. Insects
103. Detection device
104. Hebrew word for God
107. Edible part of fruit
108. Asian palm
109. Sloth
113. What wine connoisseurs have
115. Phyllis Diller does burlesque
117. Quiet
118. High spot
119. Soul
120. Farming student
121. Plum
122. High-landers
123. Mongol
124. Operetta man

DOWN

1. Montreal event of '67
2. Requisite
3. Stake
4. Late philanthropist
5. Lunch
6. Scotland's Mary et al.
7. Analyzes
8. Part of an orchestra
9. Hebrew measures
10. Greek goddess
11. Narcotics
12. Go on
13. Forest ranger's post
14. Preliminary times
15. Roman goddess
16. Black or Santa
17. Sea saint
18. Tropical tree
19. Homer's instrument
23. Petty official
25. Dives
27. Debating sites
30. Dug
32. Dried
33. Styles
34. Approvals
35. Take to a higher court
36. Incubator baby
37. Wrestling match
38. Signs
39. Special food
40. Scenic view
41. Scouts for Bligh's ship
42. In the showcase
43. Skinned
45. Concede
46. Jugs
49. Tie up
51. ___ a pig
53. Drift
54. Sail rope
55. Low joints
56. Game bird
58. Constellation
60. Pools
62. Howled
63. Of an eye part: Prefix
64. River to Gulf of Guinea
65. Utmost degree
66. Coins
68. Indian V.I.P.
71. Binges
72. Barters
73. Temples
74. Friendly goblin
75. Part song
77. Navy man
78. Valuable instruments
80. Triple Crown unit
82. Lily plants
84. Florida city
85. Unpaid bills
86. Paintings
87. Moslem prince
89. Club for Palmer
90. Al or Kate
91. Records
93. Bequest
94. Cordelia's relative
95. Piles up
96. Brandy drink
100. Mohammed's daughter
101. Pilasters
102. Mean look
103. Word on a bill
104. Arab garments
105. Valley
106. European capital
107. Circus performer
108. Property in old Rome
109. Impel
110. Close
111. Samoan port
112. Addict
114. Fall behind
115. Boat
116. Indian fiber

166 AIRS APPARENT *Herb Risteen*

ACROSS

1. Kind of stone
5. Gloomy
9. Run together, in music
13. King-queen at times
17. Like an armadillo
19. Observe
22. Dismisses in disgrace
23. Large tuba
24. Harding
25. Headpieces
26. Ends, tackles, etc.
27. Hollow
28. Some votes
30. Concert numbers
33. Isère tributary
35. Tear down
36. Dismiss
38. Paris relative
39. Part
40. Tiresome one
41. Unaccented
43. Igneous rock
45. __ the altar
47. Kind of fir
49. Monaco name
50. Band instruments
51. Cupid
52. Periods
54. Direction in Bonn
55. Raise __
56. Order to a dog
57. Do sums
58. Masks
60. Card game
61. Compass point
62. Victor Herbert hit
64. Debating side: Abbr.
67. White poplar
68. Spangles
70. Hindu saint
73. Rex's relative
74. Cry of disgust
75. Grass genus
76. End in __ (draw)
77. Biblical name
78. Thick sticks
80. Wolves' fortes
82. Musical direction
84. Trial
85. P.O. notation
87. Flours
88. Troubles
89. Thinkers' place
90. Ross et al.
92. Esau's wife
93. Chemical suffixes
94. Blues pioneer
95. Old Turkish coin
97. Like some cheese
99. Chinese tea
100. Hayworth
101. __ fixe
103. __ loss
104. Old-World bird
108. Gear for Galahad
111. Rattlers of a sort
112. Popular song of 1940s
113. Geological period
114. Without
115. U.S. reformer
116. Head: Fr.

DOWN

1. Plains lizard
2. Get __ (be avoided)
3. Doctrine
4. Tilt
5. Solicit
6. Cereal spore
7. Jap. herb
8. Kind of book: Abbr.
9. Peter and Paul: Abbr.
10. Thai people
11. Hula accompaniment
12. Stay
13. Brood
14. Biblical verb ending
15. Jungle beast
16. Italian composer and family
17. W.W.II time
18. Prod
20. Zola novel
21. Entertain
29. Berlin's forte
31. Math branch
32. Space to navigate
33. Leaf
34. "Only a __"
35. Horse color
37. Stacked
40. Swiss city
41. Egyptian skink
42. Billiard-cue objective
44. Music makers
45. Police-blotter entry
46. Bone: Prefix
48. Young chinooks
50. Choral piece
53. Singer Beverly
55. __ Rica
59. Born: Fr.
60. Common prefix
63. Most costly
64. Bow, in Italy
65. Tie
66. Waste
67. Regions
69. Pentateuch part
70. Does the scale
71. Use a pitch pipe
72. Islands: Fr.
75. Annoying
79. Congeals
80. Barnum's singer
81. Snick and __
83. Verdi work
85. Central Am. city
86. Dixie trail
89. Siberians
91. Moves, in a way
93. Deeds
94. Sped
96. __-do-well
98. Virginia
100. Farm crops
102. Direction
105. F.D.R. agency
106. Wire repairer: Abbr.
107. Letter
108. Weight of India
109. Roman 151
110. Way: Abbr.

GETTING WITH IT   *Gladys V. Miller*

ACROSS

1. Soviet agency
5. Conniptions
9. Horse for busting
14. Popular savants
19. Civilian dress
20. Molding
21. "_ cock horse . . ."
22. Sneezeweed
23. Popular pad
25. Below, to poets
26. Chaliapin et al.
28. Cheap cigars
29. Teachers' degrees
31. Claw
33. Explosive
34. Mend
35. Mosque features
36. Drunkard
37. Algonquian
38. Discover
40. Beef cut
41. U.S. penologist
42. Bank name
43. Cuckoos
44. Of a disciple
45. Farm units
46. _-a-brac
47. User of the mails: Abbr.
48. Resembling: Suffix
49. Suppresses
51. Recipient
54. Concubines, in Turkey
57. Cousins of 14 Across
58. Problem pupils
59. Popular rhythm
61. Cain's land
62. Large amounts
63. Fixed course
64. From, in Paris
65. Alder: Scot.
67. Begins to like
69. Advise, old style
70. Harness pieces
73. Norwegian composer
75. Kansas river, with Creek
76. Gives up

77. Basque city
78. Reneges, new style
80. _ generis
81. Olympic skater Schenk
82. Le Sage's Blas
83. Snack items
84. Women's thing
86. Certain escapes
90. Mod costume
92. Kiel or Welland
94. Tense
95. "_ be neat . . ." (Jonson)
96. Bible book
97. Fr. preposition
98. Man's name
100. Necklines
101. Poisons
102. Smoking material of today
105. After I, J, K, L
106. Finger painting, often
108. Tree enemy
109. Certain dogs
110. Korean port
111. Plant
112. Quartz gems
113. Novelist Alan
114. Parcel's associate
115. Hirt and Kaline
116. Mass. town
117. Organization: Abbr.
118. Cassock
121. River to Oder
123. Certain record
126. Stagy events, 1960s style
128. Assert
129. _ cit.
130. Russian police
131. Greek jar
132. Austrian area
133. Under, to poets
134. Fuse
135. Meeting: Abbr.

DOWN

1. Clump
2. Mod coiffure
3. Old hands
4. Ape
5. Cries of disgust
6. ". . . but _ on forever!" on forever!"
7. "O _! O mores!"
8. Initial funds
9. Generals, etc.
10. Free of
11. Early French king
12. Specially planned urban areas
13. Appetizers
14. Eva of films
15. _ Bator
16. Headland
17. Loose, in today's world
18. Sticks' colleagues
19. Gender: Abbr.
24. Lamprey
27. Printer's mark
30. Franklin
32. French article

35. N. or S. state
36. Vetches
37. Fiber: It.
38. Vegas or Palmas
39. _ the line (last stop)
40. Swindle
41. Airs of gentility
42. Skeet devices
44. Hideouts
45. Intolerant one
46. Headache dose
48. Sommer and namesakes
50. Chaney
51. Persona non _
52. Music work
53. Kefauver
55. Famous John
56. Heraldic bends
58. French sculptor
60. Mr. Kringle
62. Party member: Abbr.
66. Recent: Prefix

68. Neighbor of Neb.
69. Spaded again
70. Stock listings
71. Running wild
72. Big campus, today
73. Reached
74. Actor Clu _
76. _ de Guerre
78. Jargons
79. Bell sounds
81. Oklahoma city
83. More faint
85. Meadow sound
87. Bridge-game remark
88. Places for modern Platos
89. Barber's utensil
91. Fold
92. Brake plants
93. Rock-festival background
96. Firm foreign policy

99. Mil. address
101. Russian composer
103. Origin
104. Plant beard
105. Tenon's partner
106. Kind of dive
107. Bother
108. Cry of contempt
109. Islet
110. Kea and Loa
112. Trinidad band material
113. _ out (lose one's nerve)
114. U.S. writer
116. Regarding
118. Potato
119. Dinh Diem et al.
120. Feminine suffix
122. Medit. island: Abbr.
124. Carte or mode
125. Nonsense!
127. Verbal adjective: Abbr.

THE KING'S ENGLISH
Bert Kruse

ACROSS

1. Troop quarters
7. Redshank
11. Mouths
14. Hebrides isle
18. A.L. player
19. In front
20. Wheels
22. Highway ad sign
24. Raised, as a car axle
25. Spoke
26. Word with sorry
27. Glacial ridges
29. Prior to
30. Lukewarmness
33. Natives: Suffix
34. Appliance
35. _ California
38. Lone: Scot
39. Act like a tide
41. Stadium sound
43. Historic time
44. Mr. Domino
45. Apple parts
47. Lacks
50. Famed N.Y. hall
52. Kind of car
54. Breaks
56. Moslem noble
57. Swing about
58. Pastry item
60. Satanic
61. Kind of child
63. Smooth
64. Rocky peak
65. Asian prefix
66. Spoiled
68. Dickens name
70. Worldwide
72. Grass moisture
73. Part of Q.E.D.
75. German denial
76. Ball of yarn
77. Gram. connector
79. Italian river
80. Boner
81. Young ones
82. Stone with crystals
85. Communications medium
87. Beach sportsmen
89. More tanned
91. Model-type girl
93. Tennis start
94. High bond ratings
95. Prefix for logy and nomics
96. French seasons
98. Engineers' org.
99. Cut
100. Greek letters
101. Endure
104. Powder
106. Auto style
109. Org. for servicemen
110. Strange guy
112. Graf _
113. Compelled
116. Emcees' gear
118. Small feathered creatures
122. Coconut source
123. Forcefully
124. Medic's prescription
125. Chemical suffixes
126. Stupid one
127. Horse
128. N.H. prep school

DOWN

1. Stern's opposite
2. Spring flower
3. Miss Lee
4. Nabokov girl
5. Slur over
6. Asian export
7. Composer of 55 mazurkas
8. Fewest
9. Hearing device
10. Icelandic work
11. _ d'art
12. Mob member
13. Dean of F.D.R. cabinet
14. Variety of skate
15. Senior
16. Kind of surgeon: Prefix
17. Poplar
19. Domiciles
21. Japanese coins: Abbr.
23. Half
28. Winter-sports items
31. Map
32. Some sailors
31. Map
32. Some sailors
34. Castle et al.
35. Kind of ray
36. Saroyan character
37. Excellent
40. One Karamazov: Abbr.
42. Roman money
44. Experienced
45. Table vessel
46. Dugongs
48. Locker attendant
49. Book back
51. N.Y. player
52. In the open air
53. Uninteresting
55. Road warning
57. Weighty
59. Farm machine: Abbr.
62. Ringing sound
66. Kodiak
67. Wall hanging
69. Old autos
70. Bright light
71. Cosmic principle
74. Grooming process
76. Artful
78. Fresh
83. Tenth: Prefix
84. Cupid
86. Select
88. Monk's title
89. Kiss: Fr.
90. Transported
92. Ancient Greek mistress
94. Of a mountain range
97. French rooms
99. African charm
100. Compliment
101. Like some mattresses
102. Kind of flu
103. Column base
105. Becomes an also-ran
107. Hammerstein
108. Put in a container
110. Channel
111. Mine car
114. Gentle oath
115. Border
117. Pinafore, e.g.
119. "_ rambling wreck . . ."
120. White House initials
121. Indian weight

PONYING UP
Jean J. Davison

ACROSS

1. Amatory
7. Flog
12. Math abbr.
15. Predicament
21. Diego of murals
22. Aura
23. Prefix for corn
24. Second-rate horse
25. U.S. and others
26. What some taxpayers hope to get
28. Rock
29. Ego
30. Kicked
32. Hollywood girl
34. Black Panther name
35. Frank
37. Gather in: Var.
38. Last item
40. Color
41. Gaze
44. Pet lamb
48. Gold or tin: Abbr.
50. French river
52. Traces
53. French islands
54. Virgin or Aegean
56. Nog ingredients
60. Pi, for one
61. Kettledrum
63. Track pest
64. Mother of Ares
65. Perry locale
66. Words of surprise
67. Kind of puncture
68. Fume
70. Arizona peak
71. Festive cup
73. Gait
74. Stamped
76. Little: Scot.
77. Assam native
78. Hokum: Var.
79. Maidens' river
80. With 31 Down a C.D. Warner cynicism
87. One who rants
88. Destiny
89. Tim
90. Wire measure
91. Turmoil
93. Pool frame
94. I.R.S. quarry
99. Unknown: Abbr.
100. Bulk
101. Devon river
102. Ice-cream holder
104. "L'__, c'est moi"
105. Intertwine
107. Thing
109. Cancel
111. Elicit
112. Pintado
113. Expose
115. Take __ of (be unimpressed)
116. More boorish
117. Great ruler, for short
119. Mr. Foxx
120. Indian measure
121. Picnic equipment
122. N.Y. player
125. Roman date
127. Relatives
129. Spoke sharply
131. Byzantine art items
133. Village in Italy
135. Household members
137. __jure
141. Explosive
143. Tax man
145. Nearby
147. Ignores
148. Morgue, for one
149. Kind of squash
150. Thirsted
151. New
152. Billboard matter
153. Screwballs
154. Muffet and America

DOWN

1. Work units
2. Laugh, in Paris
3. Face shape
4. Certain form numbers
5. N.Y. subway
6. Brahman, e.g.
7. Identical
8. Walked
9. Man's nickname
10. __ of pottage
11. "__ your heart upon't" (E.B. Browning lament)
12. Argument
13. Secretary's abbr.
14. Netherlands features
15. Gateway city: Abbr.
16. More stingy
17. Tax __
18. Essential oil
19. English dramatist
20. Goofed
27. Hits the silk
31. See 80 Across
33. "...the days of __ come" (N.W. Bible)
36. Cuban coin
39. Eviction
41. Katharina
42. Coronet
43. Those against
45. Moslem scholar
46. Paper size
47. Sixth-sense initials
49. Gym gear
51. Shoe width
55. Not unusual
57. Spiritual knowledge
58. Name for a marine
59. Added turf
62. Burr
66. Benzell
69. Indian state
72. Hindu retreat
73. Pronoun
74. Badly
75. Weight of Japan
77. Greek contest
78. Deposit
80. Hikers' areas
81. O.T. book
82. Reveal
83. Asian holiday
84. Nervous
85. Kitchen item
86. Rend
92. Shadowed
93. Corrective
95. Holmes specialties
96. Musical piece
97. A.J. Foyt, e.g.
98. Doers: Suffix
102. Musical ending
103. Affirmatives, in Lyon
106. Age
108. Fine leather: Abbr.
110. Krazy __
111. Silkworm
114. Mortars' partners
118. Take advice
122. Carpentry joint
123. School: Fr.
124. Gin additive
126. Spinal bones
128. Controversial anarchist
130. Hymn
132. Pheasant nest
134. Garish
135. Meat order
136. Sea birds
138. Boxers
139. Word with snick
140. Bookie's quote
142. N.Y. time
144. Excessively
146. Fern rootstock

170 MEASURING UP *A. J. Santora*

ACROSS

1. Campus halls
6. Humane org.
10. Luxurious
14. Behind the __
19. Grant of clerical leave
20. Miseries
21. Eastern title
22. Fran's dragon
23. Majors
25. Forthright
27. Rehan
28. French drink
29. Defense arm
31. Pop
32. Like some tuxedos
34. __ many words
35. "Do unto __..."
37. Unfeeling
40. Heartened
44. Jesters
47. Wall decor
49. Hawaii's plus
50. P.I. native
51. Type of therm.
52. Stay on
54. Operated
55. Driver, e.g.
58. Dishes
60. Lazily
61. Lamb's "Essays __"
62. Complain
64. Ogden residents
66. "The wages __..."
67. Smarties
69. Reached
72. Boring tools
74. Tiger, in India
75. Beethoven symphony
76. Highlander
78. Lasagna filling
80. Kings
82. Basin
83. "Hillbillies" role
84. Fondant, e.g.
85. Outfit
86. No help
88. Clover
91. Spot
92. Network
93. Burlesquing
96. Deepest
100. Poker pair
101. Poodle's world
105. Guess
108. Bubbles over
110. Dear one of letters
111. Single
112. Today's Jehus
114. Immeasurable
117. Dine at home
118. Burl
119. Mean one
120. Buenos __
121. Bouquet
122. Golfer, at times
123. Study
124. Vigorous

DOWN

1. Exclude
2. Rust
3. Lear's daughter
4. Bad: Prefix
5. Connie or Risë
6. Contract for
7. Not sing.
8. Soap
9. St. Francis, for one
10. Coarse person
11. Labrador sight
12. Map
13. Compartment
14. Year of Charlemagne's coronation
15. Evolve
16. Chorister
17. Fibbed
18. Helen's mother
24. Furthers
26. Rather weak
30. French entree
33. Stalemate
34. Slowly
36. Destroy
38. Biblical twin
39. Beige
41. Criteria
42. Common Latin abbr.
43. Gainsay
44. Mr. __ of cartoons
45. Hit __ (get along)
46. High spots
48. Tie down
49. S.A. Indians
51. So. state
53. Collectors of a kind
56. Coquette
57. Movie: Sp.
58. Seek damages
59. Woman with __
60. Koh-__ (diamond)
63. Classify
65. Find __ hair
67. Delays
68. Chinese tea
70. __ off the old block
71. Savory
73. Supposed
75. Close
76. Griffe
77. Instance
79. Sub weapon: Abbr.
81. Except
83. Harlow
84. Long time
87. Irish county
89. Corrodes
90. __-all (fracas)
91. Aerial bomb, to fliers
94. Type of graph
95. Regular
97. Gossip
98. Canyon
99. Playing card
102. Workers
103. Assault
104. Untidy
105. Mets' home
106. White frost
107. Preminger
109. European land
110. Diffuse
113. Put __ show
115. __-la
116. Brooklyn campus

STEPQUOTE
Eugene T. Maleska

ACROSS

1. Start of Stepquote
8. Trapeze artist
15. Chocks of wood
21. Bravery
22. Showgirl
23. Polished
25. Used up in part
26. Oberon's wife
27. Decorative disks
28. Open a barrel
29. Republic since 1949
31. Seaways
32. Malacca
33. U.K. lawmakers
34. See 67 Down
36. Strings group
38. Teacher's milestone
40. Clan
41. Running wild
43. Stepquote part
46. White Nile tributary
47. United: Fr.
48. Birth-control pioneer
50. State firmly
52. One on the run
54. Copycat
56. Longhorns
58. It crosses the bar
59. Univ. students
60. Clergymen's terms
64. Magic number for 9 Down
66. Believe
68. Book reviewer
69. Accustomed: Var.
71. Neckpieces
75. Son of Gad
76. Numerical suffixes
77. Hesitated
79. Start a golf game
80. Brace
81. Razzle-dazzle has four
82. Ring-shaped island
83. Headland
85. _ Elum, city in Washington
86. Bald flier
88. Mitigates
90. Hole-in-one
91. Roofing item
92. Beauty-shop process
94. Dickens heroine
95. Passed through
97. Pub order
99. Berg's "Der _"
100. Amulet
101. Bellwether
104. Hunter's call
106. Put on a feast
108. Thrust
109. Discomfiture
112. Lightning flash
114. Blue-penciled
118. Dam
119. Less recent
121. Stepquote part
123. Cubic meter
124. Water plant
125. Secular
127. Gives it a whirl
129. Ferry's berth
130. June beetle
131. Tapehole plug
132. Hector
135. Tooth or spike
137. Since
138. Mystical interpretation
140. Rank
142. Of home-landers: Sp.
144. "There _ a cab when you want one"
145. Income
146. Altar shelf
147. Assails
148. Sandy
149. End of Stepquote

DOWN

1. "_ no lady . . ."
2. Greek courtesan
3. Enzyme
4. "Vive le _!"
5. "_ Kleine Nacht-musik"
6. Suffix with real and ideal
7. Stepquote part
8. Function
9. Believers in the millenium
10. Roster
11. Algerian port
12. Developer of I.Q. tests
13. Cordial flavorings
14. Bohea or jasmine
15. Apart
16. Button-woods
17. Network
18. Golden or dog's
19. Coats, etc.
20. More pungent
24. Bed canopies
30. Fitzgerald
32. Kind of cigarette
35. Dignified
37. _ Antilles
39. Hide _ hair
40. Latin pronoun
42. Gentle heat
44. Episcopacy
45. Stepquote part
49. Appraise anew
51. Fingerling
53. Puts up
55. Yes, indeed
57. Third-year deer: Brit.
60. Like some silverware
61. Jet route
62. Straight man
63. Kind of salad
65. "Slowly _ the lea"
67. Life jacket, with 34 Across
69. Lunch joints
70. Tenfold
72. Read aloud
73. Stepquote author
74. Quick
77. A cut above Truman's Deal
78. Transfer designs
81. Acme
84. Congress unit
87. Backtalk
89. Moo
91. Choice morsels: Var.
93. Stepquote source
95. Castles in _
96. Oodles
98. What's new
100. In rich supply
101. Islamic fasting period
102. Ear shells
103. German nobleman
105. Piece of gossip
107. Sky Altar
110. Poseidon's realm
111. Gumshoe
113. Do cable stitching
115. City of Israel
116. Daughter of Icarius
117. Testified
120. Special kind of dog
122. Stepquote part
126. Part of A.W.O.L.
128. Delusion's partner
131. Round Table knight
133. Solar deity
134. _-Japanese War
136. Relative of etc.
139. Understand
140. Mrs. in Madrid
141. Born: Fr.
143. Ceremonial words

ACROSS

1. Fall fete
4. Do lawn work
7. Chair part
12. Some animals
19. Fan
21. Winged
22. Attracts
23. "__ I didn't like"
25. Art piece
26. Paint tester
27. Belief
28. Family members
29. Save
32. Certain legal action
36. Clerical title
39. Miss. River straddler
44. Bone: Prefix
45. Chico, Groucho, etc., for short
47. Upright
48. Fries lightly
50. Vast plains
51. State: Abbr.
52. Fungus cores
53. Come down on
54. Agitates
55. Old cabs
57. Compass reading
58. "Zhivago" girl
59. Reduce
60. Ignited
61. Area unit
63. Outlanders
66. Tops
67. Symbol for Jesus
68. African lake
70. Wine: Prefix
71. Siamese twin
72. Barracks area
74. Ad man's concerns: Abbr.
76. Sacred: Prefix
78. Streisand hit
79. Sediment
80. Little __
82. Mudlike
83. Radiations
84. Replace
85. Tuscan city
86. "Take __" (B'way play)
88. Deer trail
89. Predatory insects

92. "__ Spain"
94. Crow
95. Dutch painter
98. Lemur
102. Do a balloon job
105. North, for example
108. More plump
109. Onward
110. Sapped completely
111. Occupations
112. Shore
113. Sales pitches
114. Male or female

DOWN

1. Entrance
2. Fabric
3. Uniform
4. Metric unit
5. Poetic word
6. Party: Abbr.

7. Shiny fabric
8. Scheme
9. Certain duck
10. Rat-__
11. Playing card
12. Common people
13. Voice ranges
14. Viewpoint
15. Some boys
16. Mouth: Prefix
17. Part of I.T.T.: Abbr.
18. Ship direction
20. Make a camera boo-boo
24. Small cases
30. Kind of sore throat
31. Top non-coms: Abbr.
32. Spread hay

33. Of a pseudo-science
34. Arrive hastily
35. Shoe widths
36. Times of day: Abbr.
37. Vampires
38. Beer base
40. One kind of band
41. Sri Lanka's waterfront
42. Kind of drop
43. India and indelible
46. Fraternal org.
48. Scorch
49. Hathaway
52. Addams
54. Medit. island: Abbr.
56. Holy one: Abbr.
58. Inc., in England

59. Snead, e.g.
61. Help
62. King of the two-reelers
63. Ditto
64. Words to a starting racer
65. Type measures
66. Kind of cake
68. Long mantle
69. "__ smoke!"
71. Wyatt
73. Color
74. His, in Paris
75. Wax: Lat.
76. Big around the middle
77. Words of disbelief
80. Took to court
81. Baseball's Mel
82. Audit man: Abbr.

83. Legal officials: Abbr.
84. Tin: Prefix
86. Vexes
87. Winter vehicle.
90. Furious
91. Horse opera
93. Wine vessels
95. Brine: Prefix
96. Suffix for cyclo
97. Millay
99. Frees of
100. Concerning
101. River of myth
102. Service medal
103. Greek letter
104. Pro
105. Heel
106. Arab garment
107. Law degree

ACROSS

1. Emulated a flag
6. Chessmen
11. Anklebone
16. Tendency
21. Wind: Prefix
22. "Darling, Where __?"
24. Baffle
25. Scatter
26. Start of a McCullers title
27. He shrugged, said Miss Rand
28. Ralph of U.N. fame, politely
30. "E'en __ it be a cross . . ."
31. Cousin of okay
33. See 31 Across
34. Seed or wire
35. Porker's home
37. Journalist's degree
40. Province of Iraq
41. Dawn goddess
42. Outdoor area: Abbr.
43. Kind of deal
44. Court
46. Between phi and psi
48. Lament
51. Running wild
53. Prague poet
54. Village on Hudson
58. Start of a French toast
59. Hancock or Doe
60. Cries caused by a mouse
61. "He who __ tiger . . ."
62. Singer Frank
64. Gives the appearance of
66. Scribe
67. Crew's plea to Columbus
69. God of Islam
70. Certain dwarf's weakness
71. "__ a drink!"
72. Shaw's "House" et al.
75. Fracas
76. Relative of ain't
77. Italian town
78. Vichy name
83. "The way to a __ through . . ."
87. Part of Hispaniola
92. Dirges
94. Burdened one
95. G. Washington slept here
97. Like a fat cat
98. Gang weapons
100. Beach material
101. Aits
102. Cook quickly
103. Miss Lane of "Superman"
105. Sandpiper genus
106. Prepares clams
107. Dillon
108. Old slave
109. Of a certain volcano
110. Grass or whisky
111. "Exodus" hero
112. Smorgasbord item
113. Fish eggs
114. Collection
117. Relatives of mins.
119. Explosive
121. Compass point
122. U.S. flying branch: Abbr.
123. Cleopatra's nemesis
126. Vied
129. Louis XIV, e.g.
131. Palpably
133. Beetle family
134. Certain chat, with "heart"
139. Happen
140. Kind of clam
141. "There __" (song)
142. Shelf
143. That is: Lat.
144. Ship deck
145. Pile up
146. Rebuke, with "down"

DOWN

1. "__ face red!"
2. Cave: Fr.
3. Some words
4. Flightless bird
5. Blue
6. Concise
7. Tennis star
8. Letter
9. Japanese drama: Var.
10. Full of fat
11. What hearts do
12. Of age: Abbr.
13. Medieval poem
14. Major or Minor
15. Stairway for Jack
16. Homey places
17. Height: Prefix
18. Potbelly
19. State
20. Student's bugaboos
23. Cheer
29. Primo
32. Swiss lake
35. Temple of Hera site
36. Start of a waltz song
38. Two flowers going steady
39. Monkey
42. Entire: It.
43. Reign, in India
45. Exclamations
47. Treat, as salt
48. Met singers
49. Spa on Lake Geneva
50. Many, to Burns
52. Prepared to propose
53. Romero
55. Kind of point
56. Didn't, in olden days
57. Silvery grunt
63. Fearing disgrace
65. Sea-union agency: Abbr.
66. Stands firm on
68. Short melodies
70. Skirmish: Scot.
73. Miss Rutledge
74. Law man: Abbr.
78. Sinclair
79. Make __ of oneself
80. Town: Fr.
81. "On __ Day"
82. What I did in S.F.
84. Kind of burn
85. Warmth, in Soho
86. Village in Sweden
87. Transplant for Midas
88. Poisonous gas
89. Silly
90. Pacific islands
91. Hydrindene
93. Napoleon, e.g.
96. Old-timer
98. "Cross my __"
99. Strength
102. Wee, in Glasgow
104. Musical piece: Abbr.
114. Mites
115. Wanderer
116. Confound
118. Starting words, after "Ready"
120. Marching boys' step
121. "__ Song In My Heart"
122. Musical beats
123. Start of learning songs
124. Hits hard
125. Burning heaps
127. Those in favor
128. A jar, sometimes?
130. Suffix for reformat
131. Bank workers: Abbr.
132. Bakery worker
135. Loki's daughter
136. Inner: Prefix
137. Pro __
138. Motorist's org.

ACROSS

1. Worth __ ransom
7. Diffracted bands of color
14. Fable
18. Custard: Sp.
20. Intuitions
21. Aureoles
22. Joy
23. Glazes
24. Scented
25. Early films
26. Headlight switch
27. Pallid
28. Meet
29. "Home __" (resort's seasonal sign)
32. Put on record
33. Torpid
34. Cries of dismay
35. Witty remark
36. Think tank?
42. Fair Deal initials
43. Impulse-sending devices
47. Dislodges
48. U.N. agency: Abbr.
50. Musical group
52. Morse code unit
53. Fall asleep, as a foot
54. Noah's eldest
55. Small yard
56. Pair
57. Siouan
58. Verse: Fr.
59. Plump
60. Embroider
61. Army surplus Quonset hut?
65. Vestment
68. Slices: It.
69. "Young man with __"
70. Alan and Robert
74. Deer
75. Discuss
76. Kipling hero and others
77. Schulz dog
78. N.C.O.
79. Strident
80. Compass point
81. Rangoon sights
82. Firmament
84. Word with mark or ring
86. Domestic wine?
87. Nigerian
88. Querying sounds
89. God: Lat.
91. Mail
94. Where an enlisted man is quartered?
101. Miss Prentiss
102. Round: Abbr.
103. Horace's hello
104. Plane-wing controls
106. Single: Abbr.
107. "This seat __"
109. Montalban
110. Left-Bank lapper
111. Oligarch
112. More smartly dressed
113. Poultry
114. Opposes
115. Java's island group: Var.

DOWN

1. Donkeys, in Paris
2. Moslem leader: Var.
3. Balbo
4. Explosive ingredient
5. Sparkle
6. Indolence
7. Lassie, for one
8. In a weak way
9. As a friend: Fr.
10. Metric measures: Abbr.
11. Baseball's "show-me" attitude
12. Passes on
13. Orgs.
14. Natural gifts
15. Vigilant
16. Horse-training rope
17. Glyceride, for one
19. Namesakes of English saint
21. Short-order cook's theme song?
30. Type of down
31. Notes
35. __ deadline (gets out on time)
36. Quasi-modo's creator
37. Body of poetry
38. Wild buffalo
39. Batter
40. Atlanta stadium
41. N.Y.C. wagering
42. Suburban developer, in a way
43. Dissemi-nated
44. Ends' partner
45. Profligate
46. Store
48. Where the doe's home is
49. Blood: Prefix
51. Poles tossed by Scots
54. As __ silk
58. Sellers and Lorre
62. City near Adige R.
63. Spare
64. Sailboat
65. Washington Sq. feature
66. Canter
67. Lugosi
71. Extinct bird
72. On __ with
73. Method: Abbr.
77. Avuncular name
81. Back door
83. Strings
85. Viper
86. Snail genus
88. Set apart
89. Strip
90. Contests
91. Imitative
92. Rajah's wife
93. "Here's __ your eye"
94. More slippery
95. Turkish liqueurs
96. Howe
97. Hundred: Prefix
98. Egg-shaped
99. Yellow pigment
100. Over
105. Rail
108. P.I. people

GREGORIAN TOUR *Diana Sessions*

ACROSS

1. Chevron stripes
5. Accessory for Al Hirt
9. Sell at a quick profit
14. Near
21. Invectives
23. Pointed sayings
24. More loose-jointed
25. Patron saint of Naples
26. Arab prince
27. Studied Form 1041
28. Business-letter abbr.
29. Confront
30. Purple shrub of Europe
32. Garment for Cornelia
34. Home garden favorite
36. Sediment
37. That: Sp.
38. Girl's nickname
39. Church bodies
40. Soft
42. October stone
44. Siesta
46. Adherent: Suffix
47. Kind of bowl
48. Furtive
49. Alcott girl
52. Song of a city
56. Wind
57. Lining fabric
59. Showy bramble
61. Stirs up
62. __ bug
63. Freeway sections
64. Canadian isthmus
65. Eyelid ailment
66. Goliath
68. Anti-sub device
69. "__ la guerre"
70. Con Ed et al.: Abbr.
71. Herd
72. Building boards
73. Hanging shred
74. Pronoun
76. Sphere of action
77. What Sgt. Friday wanted
78. Develop
81. Dolphins' state: Abbr.
82. Dueling weapons
83. __ hound
84. Tamer
85. Roman era
87. Fishermen
89. Rival
90. Autumn-flowering tree
92. British brews
94. German article
95. Grating
96. __ Manuel river, Brazil
97. Diversion, for short
98. Noxious weeds
101. Clenches
102. Western good guy
104. A league: Abbr.
108. Plaster and leather dye
109. Toward shelter
110. California city
111. Ovation word
112. Leonid
117. Sandwich filler
119. __ volente
120. Colorful sea creature
121. Deletes, with "out"
122. Emily Brontë's "fifteen wild __"
124. One who mocks
125. Golf-course halves
126. Inge or Williams
127. Stablemen
128. Annoying
129. Feudal slave
130. Spanish numbers

DOWN

1. Resolve
2. Theater area
3. Uri or Bern
4. Movies' Erwin
5. Swamp
6. Whereness
7. Germanic
8. Letter
9. Glazes
10. Jazz group
11. Field, to Cicero
12. Place
13. Counterpart
14. Bolar
15. Praises
16. Electrical wave: Prefix
17. Ricochet
18. Any one
19. Itsy-bitsy
20. Trying experience
22. Indian of Nicaragua
30. Dwindle
31. Censures
33. Certain U.N. workers
35. Closet intruders
39. Rushes
40. Blender specialty
41. __ arms
42. Spills all
43. Jane of fiction
45. Craftsmen of Cremona
47. Exhausted
48. Snooper
49. Vast sum
50. Foster
51. Phone-book abbr.
52. In harmony
53. Governesses
54. Imperfect piece of goods
55. Ladies of Spain: Abbr.
56. Small draft
58. Oil-yielding fruit: Var.
60. So far
63. Yokel
66. Smilax
67. Charged atoms
68. French military town
69. Transit for steers
71. Vision
72. Mass. port
73. Strauss waltz area
74. Three __ kind
75. Diminutive suffix
76. More likely
77. Thoroughly
78. __ bank
79. Exposes to moisture
80. Before
82. Eater: Suffix
83. Army cars
84. Secure
86. Hair style
87. Poetic once
88. Flatters
91. Relief
93. Shelves
96. Prophet
98. Woolly: Sp.
99. Drafts of fresh air
100. Underlying
101. Fugitives
102. Worthless
103. Colorful bird
105. "__ Japan"
106. "Be it __ humble . . ."
107. Perches
109. Doubleday
110. Honors
111. Crimson Tide, for short
113. Jannings
114. Custom
115. Miss Adams
116. Miss Louise
118. Thread: Suffix
122. Presidential monogram
123. Heat measure: Abbr.

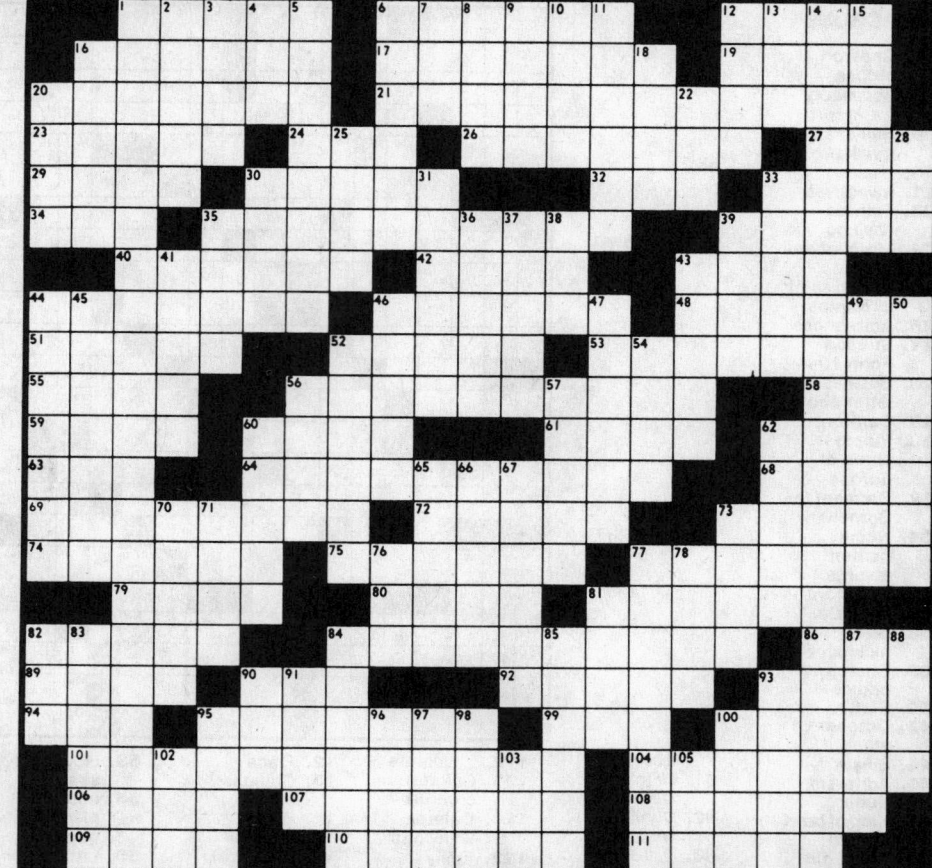

ACROSS

1. "__ and Variations"
6. Texas river
12. __ Major
16. Balakirev tone poem
17. Composer's first effort
19. Lampblack
20. Enjoy to __
21. Certain Chopiniana
23. __ de basque (leaps)
24. Indian ape
26. One joining a toast
27. Krypton or neon
29. Miller and Sheridan
30. Plunders
32. Medit. land
33. W.W.II craft
34. Brit. fliers
35. Tebaldi, e.g.
39. Sieve, in England
40. Napoli's land
42. Sand, in Capri
43. Having a spice flavor
44. Fireplace fodder
46. Bygone: Sp.
48. Certain student
51. Releases
52. British parent
53. Play a sidewalk game
55. Tear down: Var.
56. "Eine kleine __"
58. Mus. voice
59. Indian replies
60. "Rheingold" role
61. Aida's river
62. Past, old style
63. She, in Bonn
64. "__ in Paris"
68. Mil. force
69. "Fiddle-Faddle" man
72. Opera heroine
73. W.W.I river
74. Tenant
75. Decent
77. Not performed
79. French river
80. Melon
81. Garden shrub
82. Desert ship
84. "Firebird" composer
86. __ tree
89. Elec. units
90. Fort Collins campus
92. What some divas do
93. Turkish titles
94. Cheer
95. Dutch philosopher
99. Police org.
100. Glass ovens
101. Composer's direction
104. Like memoirs of stars
106. Author Seton
107. Annapolis men
108. Respect: Fr.
109. U.N. vote
110. Examiner's object
111. Gawk

DOWN

1. Masterpiece, almost
2. Knife handles
3. Big birds
4. Bad: Prefix
5. Lied subject
6. Recital piece
7. G.I. address
8. Tome: Ger.
9. That __ say
10. Certain word
11. "La Vie __"
12. Neighbor of Pol.
13. Louis or Philippe
14. Hand-me-downs of sorts
15. Box-score entries
16. Higher __ kite
18. 'iggins of "Fair Lady"
20. Ruler
22. Doer: Suffix
25. Church court
28. Compass point
30. French composer
31. Valley, in Scotland
33. French cubist
35. Coolidge and others
36. Adjust
37. Arm __
38. Heel's relative
39. Shea accessory, for short
41. French heads
43. Bandman Jones
44. Scrutiny
45. Conjecture
46. "__ in Terris"
47. Gaelic hero
49. Table piece
50. Indicated
52. Heathens
54. Oven
56. Nanette words
57. Not shy
60. Light beam
62. Copy
65. Arab prince
66. Madrid airport item
67. Smitten
70. Road curves
71. Dance
73. Miss Garden
76. I.R.S. concern: Abbr.
77. Steals a scene
78. U.S. missile
81. Highbrow
82. Vehicle
83. "Today I __"
84. Like some skies
85. Prevail on
87. Gay city
88. Fixed a tax base: Abbr.
90. U.S.N. rank
91. China Sea gulf
93. Chief Norse gods
95. Photocopy
96. Ye __ shoppe
97. British letters
98. Shake, in pharmacy
100. Burbot genus
102. Caustic
103. Western Indian
105. Follower of F.D.R.

OPEN WATER *Arnold Moss*

ACROSS

1. Kind of town
6. Sales term: Abbr.
10. Fish-landing hook
14. Utter
19. Meet again, in Paris
21. Director Carlo
22. Actor Walter
23. ". . . nothing like __"
24. Have __ on (be tipsy)
25. Depression singer
27. Brands
28. "I'll eat in port," says she
30. "__ it isn't so"
31. "__ in Gaza"
33. Kind of man
34. Beverage
35. Approves
36. Longfellow setting
37. Omar's sales
39. Mutilate
41. Mulligan
42. Hose run
45. Seats for Crusoe and Friday
49. Days of yore
50. "Bottoms up!"
51. Wraps
52. State: Abbr.
53. West Point
55. Egyptian rattles
56. Lode contents
57. Fear
59. Did six fur-longs at Belmont
61. Symbol for Jesus
62. Miss Sumac
63. Timorous
65. Bar sign
66. "Apres __"
67. Partook
69. U.S. engineer
71. ". . . from Ghent to __"
72. Ophelia's thought flower
73. Passage-way of a sort
78. Hit hard
81. Time period: Abbr.

82. Nature science: Abbr.
83. Scantiest
86. Anklebones
87. South African leader
89. Term in embryology
92. Work on hide
94. "Knock on __ Door"
95. Spiral
97. Confusion
98. Withered
99. Woods-man's cry
101. Farm unit
102. Fonda
103. Ultimate gambling loss
104. French range
105. Prose-cutors: Abbr.
106. Fishy inlet for a ruler
110. Secular
111. Ship post
112. Girl's name
113. Trap-shooting
114. Auto-body trim
116. Pinafore, e.g.
117. Inlet
118. Flow's partner
121. Lair: Fr.
123. Fly of a kind
124. Senior citizens' stream
128. Images
129. Consecra-ted marine view
133. Table, in Naples
134. Word with full
135. Hence
136. Felt pain
137. Bet
138. Flaws
139. Greek letters
140. Son of Seth
141. "An __ of the People"

DOWN

1. Sweet Rosie O'__
2. Skater Sonja
3. Range areas
4. Chaser
5. Tenses
6. Sullen

7. Blue shade
8. Eye sore
9. Trajan year
10. Parties
11. Adroitly
12. __ simple
13. Gypped
14. Subdued
15. Matisse subjects
16. Decide to seize a sea
17. Skunk River city
18. Fewer
20. Forwarded
21. Expert
26. Plea to Mae West
29. Biblical word
32. Veer, as a boat
35. Well yield
36. Ponce's time zone
37. Places for some bells
38. "Les Mise-rables" setting
39. Felon
40. Tree
41. Study group

43. Jutland port
44. Like a calm lake
45. New York city
46. Diet of fame
47. Caribbean sorcery
48. Narrow shoes
50. Caesar
54. Theater sign
55. Month: Abbr.
57. Consider
58. Extremist
59. Led astray
60. __ income
63. Lavish
64. Spice
66. Ave's partner
68. Piedmont city
70. Splash
72. Paris rec. area
74. Priest or monk
75. Where a skier's leg often is
76. Nemesis of certain thieves

77. "For want of a __"
78. Of a political unit
79. Brown paper
80. Athena's dive
84. Writer Gertrude
85. Algerian measure
87. Debussy topic
88. Neighbor of Den.
90. Curse
91. Complies
93. Tennis items
95. "For __ a jolly . . ."
96. With the beat
98. __ out (exclude)
100. Happen, to Shake-speare
102. Kind of set
103. Chemical salt
105. Verse of two feet

107. Elevations: Abbr.
108. Gumbo
109. Mock passes
111. N.Y.C. unit: Abbr.
115. Ventures
116. Santa sounds
118. Elicit
119. Port of Brazil
120. Civil War lensman
121. Affluent
122. Loud-speaker nuisance
123. "__ My Heart"
124. European capital
125. R. E. and Peggy
126. Health field: Abbr.
127. John, in Kiev
130. Royal initials
131. New Guinea port
132. Yang's kin

AFTER EVE *Alexander Black*

ACROSS

1. Little shots
4. Four qts.
7. Demonstrates again
14. Shoddy
19. Fact, in Rouen
21. Embassy staffer
22. Swiss girl's name
23. Male chauvinist cheer
24. British mystic poet
25. Mountain chain
26. Kind of name or voyage
27. Of age: Abbr.
28. Miss Kett of comics
30. Confined
31. Navy brass
32. Possess
33. Outdoor affair
36. Kind of TV show
37. Share the limelight
39. Walking __
40. Ogles
41. Doctrine
42. Rio de __
43. Brilliant, in Biarritz
47. Racket
49. Some Vietnamese
52. Resident of an Arno city
53. Flubbed golf stroke
56. Border river
57. Common contraction
58. Cafeteria items
59. Moon feature
60. Girl of song
62. Wild West time period
63. "N'est-ce __?"
64. N.Y.C. betting initials
65. Atlas abbr.
67. Uncut gem
71. Half-shell items
74. Employ for a purpose
76. Aspen visitors
77. Miss. town
79. Coats' milieu
80. Actress Berger
81. Baking instruction
82. Johnny __
83. In a pleasing way
85. Anger
86. Court
88. Port of Fiji
92. Missouri town
93. Scamp
95. Claire et al.
96. Mixed thoroughly
100. "__ baby makes three"
101. Writing by David
102. Pnom __
103. Did blacksmith work
104. Suffix with claim or cool
105. Serve a sentence
106. Let loose
108. Greek letter
111. Common check-signer
112. Short fibers
113. Speed equaling sound
114. Lease in advance
115. Bag paper
116. Lures
117. Possessive in Paris
118. Drinker's disease

DOWN

1. Prickly shrub
2. Atomic discharge
3. Fill up
4. Taunted
5. Sun god
6. Science writer Willy
7. Plunders
8. Coup d' __
9. Actor Erwin
10. Witch
11. Earth color
12. Question that Freud couldn't answer
13. Life, for one
14. Half a dance
15. Certain gatherings
16. Type of statesman
17. Hollywood figure
18. Meat pie
20. Ballpark event
27. Kipling observation
29. Kind of geometry; Abbr.
32. Mil. school
33. Off-street parking
34. Perfume
35. Sask. village
38. Having sound
41. Verb form: Abbr.
44. Puts on
45. Broadway girl
46. Explosive
48. Conditions
50. Nothing
51. Sounds of hesitation
53. Pen
54. Kind of barrel
55. Leo's ex-wife
57. Society girl
59. Cheer
61. Ands, in Avignon
63. Portions: Abbr.
66. Tosspot
68. Marriage partner
69. Cicero, for one
70. Recent: Prefix
71. Of a singing group
72. Holds dear
73. Mary Todd's husband
74. Rubber tree
75. Kind of reporter
76. Biology: Abbr.
78. Eddy
79. __-Magnon
81. Scored the hard way
84. Guadeloupe et Martinique
87. Chronic
89. Alone
90. Town near Le Havre
91. "__ the eye"
94. Riviera resort
96. Spirit
97. Quartet member
98. Kind of chintz
99. Proclamation
101. Corn breads
104. Tops
105. Virginia __
107. Denver clock reading
109. Greek letter
110. Legendary bird
111. Local officials: Abbr.

179 ADVISORY *Bert Beaman*

ACROSS

1. Dictators of a sort
12. Trifle
21. Italian waterfront
22. Wolf music
23. Be precise
25. Palm of Brazil
26. U.N. name
27. Radame's love
28. Obstacles
32. Dried
33. But, in Madrid
35. Kind of blood
38. Aunt in "Oklahoma!"
40. Edges
42. Kisser
46. Exaggerates
49. Music pieces
50. Peruvian native
51. Distant: Prefix
52. School, in Paris
53. Torrent
54. A guy and —
55. Cheat
56. Errs at bridge: Var.
58. Places for hocks
60. "Cry __"
62. Serfs
64. Bait, in Naples
65. Golf area
66. Be active
71. Jujube
72. Dispatched
73. Biblical word
74. __ Tagh range, China
76. Water
78. Spot
81. Spartan: Lat.
82. Unit of loudness
83. Watches one's waistline
86. Intensity
87. Construction piece
88. Sugar: Prefix
89. "Where __ boy . . .?"
90. Sara and T.R.
92. Brain passage
93. Allen et al.

95. Signs: Lat.
96. Native: Suffix
97. Suffixes for cloth and cash
99. Strained
101. Rosters
103. Pungency
105. European tax
107. City in Tuscany
111. Conform to custom
117. __ roof (complains)
118. Menu term
119. Chicago suburb
120. Dining places

DOWN

1. "I __ little pony . . ."
2. Nigerian natives
3. Crafts' partners
4. Asian trees
5. Hawaiian misses
6. Had a bite
7. Three, on a clock
8. Certain campuses: Abbr.
9. Biblical brother
10. Schisms
11. Hebrew letters
12. Peeved
13. "Thanks __"
14. Spaceman Grissom
15. Jolson et al.
16. Turkic language
17. Kenyan's neighbor
18. German song
19. Burbot genus
20. Navy rank: Abbr.
24. Shrimps
29. Modify
30. Candied
31. Be determined
33. Fretful
34. Gist
35. Gum up
36. Determined a mean figure
37. Liberation
39. Enjoy
41. __ open (give access)
43. Hard to reach
44. Timid ones
45. Mud volcano
47. Capek creation
48. Musical symbols
57. __ up (in the bag)
59. Irish village
61. Peeress: Abbr.
63. Take the sun, in Acapulco
67. More shrewd
68. Joins a cause
69. Hydrous salt
70. Friend of Fran
71. Singers
75. Scandinavian
77. Gaiety
79. Rib: Prefix
80. Pick up the tab
84. Like some roofs
85. U.S. body of 100
91. More immature
94. Expert on a certain board
95.
98. Snowy bird
100. Ten __ odds
102. Brahman precept
103. Ski lift
104. Large land mass: Fr.
105. Holy Roman emperor
106. Certain carriers: Abbr.
108. Plant shoot
109. Gael or Breton
110. Enzyme suffixes
111. Whale
112. Kind of radio: Abbr.
113. W.W.II command
114. Welcome item
115. __ rule
116. Southern campus

WORD PLAY *Herbert Ettenson*

ACROSS

1. Water, in Sonora
5. Ad __ per aspera
10. Actor Robert
14. Rhubarb's relative
20. Notation on a laundry slip
22. Wings
23. Damage
24. Jesse Owens forte
26. Theater district
27. Dog breed
28. Wailed
29. Greek communes
31. Apennines or Vosges: Abbr.
32. East: Ger.
33. Passage, in anatomy
35. Give assent
37. Do lawn work
38. Money of Peru
39. "Woe __!"
41. Confines
44. Like corsets
46. Where ocelots save money
51. Provided that
52. Stuff for la plume
53. Manuscript symbol
54. "The King __"
55. Fish-cleaning gadgets
57. Entire: Prefix
58. Made a fuss
59. Algebra problem, in a way
61. Take back
63. Indian title
64. Margaret Mead's study area
66. Paint thinners, for short
67. River of Quebec
68. Ar's neighbor
69. P.I. canoe
71. Sublease
73. Fish
74. Climbing vine
76. Rajah's consort
78. Pluvian
80. Boil, old style
81. Shield: It.
83. Garden tool
85. Erupting mount: Abbr.
88. Hard rubber
91. Sans __
93. __ Oro
95. Wedding words
96. Ararat's region
97. Circular cloth, of a kind
99. Medium
101. Gal's leg
102. Williams et al.
104. M
105. Take a certain elevator
106. Outbreaks
108. Game fish
109. Quartet without strings
111. Town in County Clare
112. Vibrate
114. Greek peak
115. Part of Mao's name
116. Up-to-date
117. Infant
118. Et __
120. "__ walks in beauty . . ."
123. Grand __
124. Grant of amnesty, in India
126. Within one's abilities
129. Decorator
132. Summer acquisition
134. Time spent at a spa
137. Published
138. Venial and original
139. Hell's Angels, for example
140. Tristram Shandy's creator
141. Scottish terrier
142. Confused
143. Like a quidnunc

DOWN

1. Tapestry
2. "Whither thou __ . . ."
3. Merkel and others
4. Deed: Fr.
5. Metric measure
6. Item in a vampire movie
7. Candle
8. Prevalent
9. Presently
10. Macbeth title
11. Gums
12. Intersperse
13. Statue base
14. Took on
15. Left-Bank chums
16. Evian, e.g.
17. Fish hunt of a sort
18. Relative of a pebble
19. Love
20. Nigerian people: Var.
21. Last syllables
25. Gashes
30. Certain plant nursery
34. Asian holiday
36. Adherents
38. Boy
39. Out of work
40. Runs before the wind
41. Tree of Brazil
42. Light boat: Var.
43. Crude
44. Wedding V.I.P.
45. Triangle shape
46. __ for the wear
47. Certain rods
48. Rock-festival wear
49. Kind of blade
50. Soldier from down under
55. Hindu wear
56. Prepared
59. Postal checker
60. Gary sight
62. Piquant
65. Defense made of trees
70. Cooky flavor
72. __ thought (mental process)
74. Solitary
75. Aloof quality
77. Feverish conditions
79. "But if a man bites __ . . ."
80. Paine-in-the-neck to British
82. Flowers
84. Monastery official
85. Part of TV
86. Condemnation
87. Air-show thrills
88. Tidal flow
89. Faith in one's smartness
90. Dine, in a way
92. Mental midget
94. Indians
98. Debauchee
100. Lizard of Egypt
103. Rash
105. Tenant
107. Ascot
109. Live off the __ the land
110. Louis, par exemple
113. Knotty
116. Pierre's world
118. Baseball's Matty, etc.
119. Place for a flower box
120. Snoopers
121. Name of many kings
122. Work units
123. Greek letters
124. French city
125. Norwegian name
127. Indian city
128. Kind of camp
130. Check
131. Actor Ray
133. Caucasian goat
135. One or another
136. Govt. agency

181 FOURTH DIMENSION *Anne Fox*

ACROSS

1. Thin mortars
7. __ as a pig
12. Take the bait
17. Apex
21. Mame
22. Offshoot
23. Asian range
24. Solo
25. Key words
28. Works
29. Gaelic
30. News prints, for short
31. For shame!
32. Irish saint
34. TV star
36. Grand __
38. Polyhedron
40. Japanese herb
41. This __
44. Polish
46. Father of Farouk
47. Robin
49. Words of June 17, 1775
53. Girl of song
54. Mobster's knife
55. Certain dogs
56. Racket
57. Crown of Osiris
59. Tara's locale: Abbr.
60. Miss Taylor
61. Light
64. Infinite
68. "Thy torch __"
74. Oil country: Var.
75. Do sums
76. Rumanian city
77. Use a mirror
78. Islands of Denmark
81. Close
83. False front
84. Utah city
85. Kind of cat
87. U.S. writer
88. Cui __
89. Words of May 1, 1898
96. Composer Edouard
97. Honore d'__
98. Mass. cape
99. Mouths
100. Like an egg
102. Seagoing initials
104. Roman poet
106. Spoon's partner in flight
108. Highest note
109. Former President's in-law
118. Rock, in Paris
119. Pres., e.g.
120. Seasonal songs
121. Kitchen gadget
122. Spirit of Saint Louis
123. Arbor
125. Rabbit's tail
126. Greek letter
127. Comedienne Kaye
129. G.I.
130. Waited
133. Coarse cloth
137. __ B'rith
138. Words by David T. Shaw
143. Do an inside job
144. Officer, familiarly
145. Capital of Ghana
146. Synthesis
147. Linemen
148. Catches sight of
149. Teamed
150. Calif. city

DOWN

1. Entrance
2. Rhine tributary
3. Some bills
4. Treaty city
5. Spanish uncle
6. Hides
7. Back up
8. "And __ bed"
9. Fuddy-duddy
10. U.S. dept.
11. U.S. milestone
12. Fury
13. Wing
14. __ standstill
15. Hard material
16. Rows
17. Piece of mail
18. Where Montevideo is
19. Indefinitely
20. Clergymen
26. Old Hebrew measure
27. N.J. fort
33. Japanese ware
35. Exclamation
37. Wish undone
38. Stows
39. Cheer
41. Greek peak
42. Strong rope
43. Wire: Abbr.
44. Stuffed __
45. African cat
46. Abbr. in a letter sign-off
48. Western U.S. address
50. Small broom
51. Mud
52. Bucolic poem
58. Okay!
60. Covers
62. Powers that be
63. Box-score initials
65. Offshore
66. Timetable, for short
67. New-castle's river
69. Dissimulation
70. Scotch refusal
71. Selassie
72. Kind of paper or silk
73. "__ at 'em!"
78. Bird
79. Turkish chief: Var.
80. Noble: Ger.
81. Besides
82. Horse
83. "Ma __!"
85. Low person
86. Boob
88. Foolhardy
90. Put out
91. Foray
92. Sing to a Saint Bernard
93. Beams
94. Overthrow
95. Collegian
101. Hideaway
103. Biblical country
105. Old __
107. Cleaned, as a walk
109. Fish in a certain way
110. "The __ White"
111. Edda country
112. Morning phenomenon
113. Tool
114. Chit
115. Reverse
116. Wilde, for one
117. Melanesian people
124. Exams
125. Scion
126. U.K. troops Abbr.
128. Extends
129. Birds
131. Tipsy: Fr.
132. Pair
134. Rara __
135. Laborer
136. Florence's river
139. Barn sound
140. Still
141. Mil. man
142. Drama of 1920

ACROSS

1. Niagara feature
7. Impulsive one
13. Bottle attachments
19. Speaks freely
21. Verdi opera
22. "__ parade"
23. Dessert
24. Disavowal
25. Proverb
26. Park of West
27. Game with men
29. Go to court
31. Very: Ger.
32. Wild
35. Slaughter of baseball
36. Turns away
38. Elaine's home town
41. African capital
43. Art piece
46. Longtime Dodger manager
50. Certain newspaper
52. Maine town
53. N.Y. campus
54. From __ Z
55. Struts about
57. Rocks and rockets
58. French marshal
59. Crunch and crackle foods
60. Acted
61. Lock
62. Cow genus
63. Bridge play
65. Buddy
66. Wedding place
69. U.S. dept.
70. General rank
72. Degrees
75. Golf group
77. Wit of a sort
78. Squeak cure
79. "__ I dwelt in . . ."
80. Crafts: Sp.
81. How to ride a horse
84. British lunch
85. Too, too proper
86. Rented
87. A.L. team
89. Skin a whale
91. Money in Sonora
94. Jabberwock slayer
98. To the __ (fully)
101. Asian Turkey
104. Way up
105. Sacred cows' home
106. Chew words
107. Cowboys' home
110. Humbles
112. Thinks darkly
113. Person who knows
114. Cuts
115. "But there's __ in your eyes"
116. Certain repeat rider
117. Indian state

DOWN

1. Surf noises
2. Strike __
3. N.J. port
4. Gap
5. British awards: Abbr.
6. Shine giver
7. Fashions
8. Nuclear event
9. Thick
10. Early date
11. According to
12. Befoul
13. Shopper's memo
14. Jai __
15. Happy ending
16. __-les-Bains
17. Slow, in music
18. Wise men
20. Lace loop
28. Towel word
30. Equal: Prefix
32. Fries and simmers
33. Monsoon products
34. European capital
37. Cockney's brave man
39. Vietnam's neighbor
40. Special ball-game
41. __ impasse
42. Fill
43. Angora fabric
44. Exams
45. Good-turn group
47. Fib
48. Natives: Suffix
49. Cape
51. Tree of India
53. Spanish hero
56. Grassy plant
57. Interior
59. Pirate
60. Ornate
62. Suntanned lad
64. Two wives of Henry VIII
65. Garnish
66. In __ of temper
67. Calif. wine city
68. Divot ingredient
69. Sum: Abbr.
71. Repast
72. U.S. capital
73. __-memoire
74. Citizen Kane's Rosebud
76. Prefix for potent
77. Optical device
80. Space
82. Decimal base
83. Impetuosity
85. Begged
88. Sash
89. G-men's org.
90. Acts arrogantly
91. Namby-__
92. Harden: Var.
93. Eye in the sky
95. Cay
96. Jane Addams's partner
97. Kind of pudding
99. Batter's product
100. Cup, in France
102. Tea shoppe word
103. Minus
105. "__ be wrong, but . . ."
108. Hewer
109. Records: Abbr.
111. Tree

WONDERING *C. McInerney*

ACROSS

1. Latin friends
6. Exclamations
9. Queens stadium
13. Onstage phone, e.g.
17. Arabic letter
20. Seventh _ a seventh . . .
21. Garland
22. Grave spot for a Carian king
24. Keep close to
25. Takes it easy
26. Income outgo
27. Capital city
28. French one
29. Mars: Prefix
30. Dream, in Lyon
31. Dunce, in England
32. Newts
33. Places to buy pups
35. Of a Western tribe
36. W.W. I soldier
39. Razor clam
40. "_ are called . . ."
41. What souffles often do
44. Ripened
47. European country: Abbr.
48. Vague threat
50. No partner
51. Kimono parts
52. Track stubbornly
53. Pro
54. Thin Jack
56. Hair: Prefix
57. Visual flash
59. City on the Meuse
62. Holbrook
63. _ esteem
64. Site of 22 Across
66. Common Latin word
68. Checked
70. DeLuise of TV
71. Empress
73. Redeemed, as a check
76. Certain morn
81. Ate away
82. Western port
84. Hold one's _
85. "As _ a compass needle"
87. Food fish
88. Women's-lib H.Q. in Ephesus
93. Speech flaw
97. Eris's relative
98. Struck
99. Takes more second helpings
100. Peruvian
101. Please
103. _ de mer
104. Garish
105. Gramp's spouse
106. Half a giggle
107. Salad item
110. Bulges
111. "_ no justice?"
114. Espousal
116. Swiss river
117. "It's _ point" (debatable)
118. Clipping, holding, etc.
119. Frozen dessert
121. Friend of a small seven
125. Extent
127. Saturated
128. Margin
129. Some bills
130. Dutch town
131. Commandment words
135. Dander
136. Dances
137. Not beaucoup
138. Golf club
139. Cult of Orient
140. Expo city in 1970
141. Flying abbr.
142. Seckel
143. _ de jambe
144. Ram's dam
145. Like some letters

DOWN

1. _ in the face
2. Marianne
3. Sea passage
4. Chares's harbor job
5. Maybes
6. Doctored
7. Seventh _
8. Hockey teams
9. Wee, in Dundee
10. Outcome of a suspense story
11. Civil well-being
12. Yoga squat
13. One-up job
14. Kind of pronoun: Abbr.
15. Non's opposite
16. Day times: Abbr.
17. Cover for Cheops
18. Nimrod forte
19. Seven _ of man
23. Sesame order
30. Casting lure
32. High note
34. Rocky peak
35. Dove, in Cádiz
36. Kind of science: Abbr.
37. Chemical suffixes
38. _ du Salut
40. French wine
41. Demeter
42. Ship pilot's concern
43. N.Y. time
44. "Seven maids with seven _"
45. Rose fancier
46. Cashbox
47. Woe follower
48. Roast leg _
49. Reines' mates
52. Tree trunks
55. Ptolemy's bright idea
57. Creator of 75 Down
58. Chinese dynasty
60. Tennis-racket material
61. Early monastics
65. _ de guerre
67. Little fellow
69. Poetic word
72. Macaw
73. Instance: Fr.
74. Red-faced
75. Gold-and-ivory Olympian
77. Grapefruit
78. Double: Prefix
79. Gantry and Davis
80. Settle a debt
83. Escort's offer
86. Height: Abbr.
89. Coin of Persia
90. Coup d'_
91. City near Fresno
92. French floor
94. Concerning
95. Capone feature
96. Window part
101. _ glance
102. Brute salute
108. Midnight fuel
109. Jan. and Feb.
111. Coca
112. "And _ bid farewell to . . ."
113. Ski _
115. Dupin's creator
116. Blue shade
117. Merry one
119. Petty officer
120. Port for gold and apes
121. "_ the day"
122. Wedding byproduct
123. Hard woods
124. Literary piece
125. Clan
126. Light bulb, in cartoons
127. Litigant
131. Recipe abbr.
131. Recipe abbr.
132. See 106 Across
133. Gametes
134. Coated with a metal: Abbr.
136. Sweetie

184 OBTUSE ANGLES *Arthur Bennett*

ACROSS

1. Goya subject
5. Hebrew letter
10. Meets one's Waterloo
15. Danish town
19. Mecca resident
20. Dismay
21. Stage line
22. But, in Spain
23. Earnings: Abbr.
24. Certain awards
26. Rials are used here
27. Pay back
29. Playwright James
30. Burdened
32. Negative particle
33. Stranger
35. Antelope of Asia
36. Sews
38. Sorry one
39. Inquisition decree
42. Buddy of TV
43. Early school headwear
46. Indonesian island
47. Long ago
48. Opera girl
49. Tapestry
51. Bridge defeats
52. Mouth: Prefix
53. Small power unit
55. U.S. Indian
56. Exposes to attack
58. Essence
59. Hack
62. Frankish peasants
63. Appraises
65. Absolute
66. Buckeyes' campus
67. Theft: Sp.
68. Fliers' award
72. Norm: Abbr.
75. Certain bumps
79. __ Miss
80. Praise
82. Russian society
83. Slangy negatives
84. Relate, in a way
85. Peaks
87. Pyrite
89. Chemical prefix
90. Burley, etc.
92. Sharpen
93. Turning points
94. Danish astronomer
95. Dalmatian features
97. Hebrew letter
98. Program
100. Brand
101. Elver
104. Miss Evans
105. Certain fairgoer
109. __ noire
110. Extensions
111. Type size
112. Zoo creature
113. Other: Sp.
114. Loch __
115. Networks
116. Heavy grasses
117. Belgian river

DOWN

1. Cripple
2. Buffalo of India
3. Nautical apparatus
4. Hooky player
5. Prohibitions
6. Masters' river
7. Footless
8. Smidgen
9. British isle
10. Slipper size
11. Willow
12. Dimensions
13. Dutch town
14. Sonnet part
15. Cliffhanger divisions
16. Piddling
17. Hillside, to Burns
18. "__ Cassius..."
25. Chaplain
28. Given: Scot.
31. Lined up
33. Prevention unit
34. Caries
35. Suffragist Anthony
36. "It had to __"
37. "__ loser"
38. Biscuits
39. Month
40. Lot
41. Gaelic
43. Comic-strip boy
44. Outrigger
45. Guardian
48. Pirate island off Haiti
50. Fastens
53. M.C.'s place
54. Prohibit
57. Gums: Prefix
60. "... and empty __"
61. Gathering
63. Red: Prefix
64. "__ for Adano"
65. Heaped
67. Newspaper sections
68. Mom's pie need
69. Big A reading
70. Array
71. Fabrics
72. Blind part
73. Tortilla
74. Gym gear
76. Part of a sentry's call
77. Mold of metal
78. Dawdles
81. Lovable quality
84. Cabin worker
86. Warm-sea fish
88. Holiday spot
89. Certain exec.
91. Bar offering
93. Street sounds
95. Seven: Prefix
96. Plant scale
97. Unique
98. Arabian gulf
99. Writer Zona
100. Struck
101. U.S. agent
102. To be: Fr.
103. King of drama
106. __ du Diable
107. Relative of an org.
108. Man's name

OUT OF PRINT *Keith Blake*

ACROSS

1. Noon-hour's end
6. D.D.E.
9. Jib or lantern
13. Scotsman's so
16. Missouri initials
19. Go to court again
20. News piece
21. Held of stage
22. Carmer book locale
24. Teen readers' old favorite
27. Disparages
28. Webster
29. Printed over the edge
30. Old juvenile favorite
32. Debs' former reading
34. Plan of action
35. _ of eight
36. Small pond
37. Bridge bids
38. Victim
39. Paris subway
40. Free of
41. Chats
43. "Don Juan" poet
44. Scouts' Beard
45. Mornings: Abbr.
46. Raises
47. Miss Lombard
48. French writer
52. Seashell pink
55. Kind act
56. Draws quickly, as a gun
57. Addison-Steele issues
59. Father of basketball
62. Big bird
63. Have pain
64. Slower, in music: Abbr.
65. Amtrak items
66. Football field
67. Condemns
70. Nether-world
72. "... could _ fat"
73. Nomadic group
74. _ du Salut
75. Tawny: Sp.
76. Young sheep
77. Mild reproof
78. Honest one
79. Brash magazine of 1930s
81. Old family fare, with 87 Down
86. Words of interruption
88. Champion-ship
90. Loser
91. Cracker seeds
92. Scarlett's love
94. Danish coin
95. Farm animal
96. Veterans' org.
97. Worthless one
98. Yankee reading
101. Auto pedal
102. Of an arm bone
103. "I cannot tell _"
104. Father's Day toast
105. Baum's Land _
107. Ubiquitous man
109. Aptitude
110. Kind of furnace
111. Old slick magazine
113. Volga tributary
114. British dessert
115. Of a one-seeded fruit: Var.
116. Style-setter of 1800s
122. Roman author
123. Flee, in Spain
125. At a distance
125. Iron, in Bonn
126. Begley et al.
127. Make out
128. Sovereign
129. Road material
130. Small drink

DOWN

1. Ending for hick or chic
2. Recent: Prefix
3. Physics abbr.
4. Magazine of 1800s
5. "... call _" (Falstaff)
6. Japanese statesman
7. Actress Fanny and family
8. Use
9. Spinach annoyance
10. Black cuckoo
11. Vitamin B component
12. French street lamp
13. "Rain" gal
14. Smart ones
15. Apiece
16. Saluted
17. Dirty-politics ploy
18. Armor plate
20. German pronoun
23. Dye compounds
25. Houston
26. Aged: Abbr.
31. Army man: Abbr.
32. Button one's lip
33. Boom: Ger.
34. Co. executive
35. Speak at length
37. Improvises in jazz
38. Lab tube
39. Sculptor of Discobolus
40. Rackstraw
42. Part of R.F.D.
43. Munich native: Abbr.
44. Bits
47. "Perfect love _out fear"
48. Uniform cloth
49. "_ is human"
50. Bombastic
51. Old music magazine
53. Scrutinizes
54. U.S. inventor
55. Crusoe's man
56. "Picnic" author's signature
58. By voice
60. In an angry way
61. Post time, for short
66. _ far (overdo)
67. Phones
68. "Tiny Alice" author
69. Encounters
70. Dances
71. Foretell
73. Central parts
75. Radiation device
77. President
79. Basilica areas
80. Certain ship
82. Peep show
83. Worries about
84. Show boredom
85. Sam of golf
87. See 81 Across
89. Wire: Abbr.
92. O.K.
93. Resonant
94. Neglect
98. Treat for dobbin
99. "_ in translation"
100. Fuel container
101. Luckless ones
102. Gums
103. Draws a bead on
105. Leaf shape
106. Pretended
107. Saddle sack
108. "Whither shall _ from ...?"
109. Kind of blade
110. Young one
112. Antler part
113. Jean or Walter
114. Presiden-tial initials
117. Across: Prefix
118. Swiss river
119. Spanish bear
120. Poet's word
121. Chess piece: Abbr.

ACROSS

1. Baby word
5. Smith et al.
8. N.C.O.
12. Decks
17. Army addresses
18. Type of opera
19. Expect
21. Sound from a lily pad
22. Pegasus, in a way
24. Mailer, of a sort
26. Spanish article
27. Like a top seller
29. To be: Fr.
30. TV annoyance
31. Bus-rider's purchase: Abbr.
33. Alan or Robert
34. Coty
35. Recipe units: Abbr.
36. Exam
38. Looks
40. Damage
43. Melodic
45. Military units
48. Fixes leftovers
51. They're often just
54. Israeli natives
56. Biblical crossing
57. Part of R.F.D.
59. Standish
61. Error's partner
62. Prefix with light
65. Marquand's Mr.
66. Like mosaic
68. __ Benedict
69. Port: Abbr.
70. Recently delivered
74. Society-page word
75. Skinner of stage
77. Polytheists
78. Raines
79. Grads-to-be: Abbr.
80. Western or country fare
82. Designer Emilio
83. Cherished ones
85. Moslem elite
87. Cover

90. Subsidiary news piece
94. Where reds turn blue
96. Tightened
98. Baffle
99. Repairs Venus de Milo
101. Flocks of mallards
103. Arab scholar
104. Former Peking name
106. Letters for Old Mac-Donald
108. Composer Thomas
109. Neighbor of Md.
110. Debates: Abbr.
112. One __ (ball game)
113. Banana plant
115. Depot: Abbr.
118. Zero, literally

121. Bread-end, in Havana
123. Snide attack
124. Onetime Black Panther Bobby
125. Card
126. Some votes
127. Catches
128. Over-from-Dover time
129. Holy __
130. Thread: Prefix

DOWN

1. Actress Arlene
2. Upolu port
3. Pluto and Lassie
4. Light color
5. Arteries
6. Finish of a relay
7. Certain drivers
8. Mil. title
9. W.W.II agency
10. Hot-rod man

11. Fixed dates
12. Portion: Abbr.
13. Black and fine
14. "This window closed," etc.
15. Skewered meat cubes
16. Swerves
18. __ Canals
20. Spatula
23. Relative of 128 Across: Abbr.
25. Jacket
28. Tropical isle
32. Handbill
36. Experienced
37. Bread
39. Some underwater trips
41. "Mad as __ hen"
42. Nucleus
44. Bit
46. Type of dress fabric

47. Pierre's parlor
49. Scanty
50. Mud volcanoes
52. Scout unit
53. Henchman
55. Shriveled
58. Roman garment size
60. Edges
62. Wolfe or à Kempis
63. It came after the twist
64. Paddy's slippers
67. __ Lama
71. Regatta entry
72. French ink
73. Scotland, etc.
76. "Yes, __!"
81. Face, in Spain
84. Stiff hairs
86. Bombard
88. Familiar

89. Takes away
91. What Elsie might catch
92. French friend
93. Turns, for short
95. __ curiae
97. Service plate
100. Furrowed
102. U.S.S. Hornet, in a way
104. Wet place
105. Smell
107. "I've got __ and that . . ."
109. Put on
111. Breeze
113. Victim
114. Con vote
116. Abound
117. As well
119. A.M.A. members
120. High note
122. Dynasty of China

ACROSS

1. Certain award
6. Perry of fiction
11. Impecu- nious
17. Bella Abzug feature
20. Paltry
21. Antarctic cape
22. Incite
23. Bedouin tribesman
25. Popular reading
29. Rulers: Abbr.
30. TV tuners
31. Sablefish
32. Character in 25 Across
33. Direction
34. Like whitecaps
35. Fastens
36. Creator of Nick Charles
38. Play- grounds in Lyon
39. Anesthetic
41. Molding
42. County north of S.F.
44. Form of Hosea
45. Some tigers
50. U.S. author and playwright
55. Field of 6 Across
56. Actress Sommer
57. Ladies of Paris
58. Indiana rail town
?. Coconut fiber
61. Pens
62. __-bitsy
63. Ill at ease
65. Process: Suffix
66. Planes
67. Maori spirit
68. Sturm __ drang
69. See 25 Across
79. Poetic word
80. Nigerian tribesmen
81. Spread
82. Outer: Abbr.
83. With 63 Down, author
86. Large bird
87. Arrive
89. Hebrew measure

90. Time of day
91. French port
92. Jazz form
93. Semitic deity
94. Month: Abbr.
95. British author
100. See 25 Across
102. Goddess of victory
103. Humiliate
104. "__ ne va plus"
105. Forbidden
107. Storehouse
109. Prolific British author
112. S.A. rubber
113. Killer whales
114. Blue- pencil-men: Abbr.
117. Lapses
118. Burdens
119. "I want __ just . . ."
120. Skip
121. Subversive group of sorts
126. French fabric
127. Rec-room item
128. Encircles
129. Stubborn
130. Rorem
131. Sam and J.C.
132. Item for café or the
133. Sanctify

DOWN

1. Verb suffixes
2. College units
3. Bellyache
4. Prepares for war
5. Kind of bread
6. Wild one
7. Famous Jane
8. Without joy
9. Cinnabar, etc.
10. Kind of weight
11. Cab-driver
12. More affected
13. Disturbs
14. Groups of two
15. Seagoing initials
16. Play or fountain

17. "We __ the enemy . . ."
18. White poplar
19. Letter- shaped opening
24. Common contraction
26. Relief ornament
27. Miss Williams
28. Choice cut __
34. Name used by E.S. Gardner
36. Chinese province
37. Roman field
38. Nosy one: Var.
39. Billy Sol __
40. Hardy girl
42. Compiler of "Morte d'Arthur"
43. Some migrant workers
44. Heraldic band

45. Tables, in old Rome
46. Sea call
47. Kazan
48. N.F.L. team
49. Influence
50. Vade __ (manual)
51. Friedan
52. Girl's name
53. Copies: Abbr.
54. Still abed
59. Mother of Pollux
61. Crowd
63. See 83 Across
64. "Do __ others . . ."
66. Deride
67. European nation
70. Age group
71. Finger- pointers
72. Clad, old style
73. Confeder- acy
74. "__ your life!"

75. __ cog (err)
76. The country: Fr.
77. Breathe
78. Flat
83. Plenty, for Omar
84. Lomond or Ness
85. Indian pot: Var.
86. Common Latin word
87. Lizard
88. Tropical tree
89. Small German war craft
91. Poet's sea
92. Vivacity
95. Bern's land, to French
96. Arrow poison
97. Not ignoble
98. Fire-bomb material
99. Stage darkenings: Abbr.

101. Mild oath-word
105. Moved to the runway
106. Sharp crests
107. Moves aimlessly
108. Crushed, as leather
109. Chess endings: Abbr.
110. Fabric
111. Miss Venner
112. Little; Lat.
113. Turkic persons
114. Author Gaboriau
115. Tecs
116. Restrains
118. Bird sound
119. Continent
120. Test
122. Linemen: Abbr.
123. Craving
124. Mil. unit
125. Slacken

ASSORTED WORDS   *Manuel Canyes*

ACROSS

1. Rhythms
6. Suffers, in a way
12. Music passage
16. Part of an atoll
17. Seed coats
18. Rectify
20. Certain family men
22. Caged
24. Water passage
25. Strange
26. Physician
28. Island land: Abbr.
29. Bagnold
30. Kills time
31. Eastern church areas
32. Voucher
33. Thy, in Paris
34. Inter__
35. Nature writer
36. Preceding
37. Solon, for one
39. Opera voices
40. Calif. city
41. P.I. natives
42. Shoe part
43. Most boring
45. Panicky
48. Spars
50. Insect molting stages
53. Yarns
54. Germ cell
55. Bamboo and rattan
57. Miss Murray
58. Jejune
59. Actors' output
61. Play a loggers' game
62. Columbia, in anthem
63. Kind of fence
64. Legal wrongs
65. Skirt strip
66. Kind of triangle
68. Boys' hockey game
70. Adoree et al.
71. In an orderly way
73. Takes back, as one's words
74. Direction
75. Surgeon's finale

77. Gets as due
79. Amazes
83. Obliterate
84. Inkles
85. Church areas
86. Alley of comics
87. Fruit-cake filler
88. Ord and Knox
89. Snooped
90. Texas flag feature
91. Black bird
92. "Home, Sweet Home" author
93. Heathen
94. Boy, in Bonn
95. Of a metallic element
97. Poles apart
100. Fragrant seed
101. Pearly shells

102. Allow
103. Law: Abbr.
104. Viscid
105. Word in a Jane Austen title

DOWN

1. Somewhat like Jabbar
2. Urged on
3. Sahl
4. Hawaiian dish
5. __res
6. Gawks
7. Wife of Zeus
8. Tennis star
9. Map abbr.
10. Archery items
11. Seed-shaped cartilage
12. May and Ann
13. Augury

14. Haunt
15. Winter dosage
16. Songbird
19. Asian tree
20. Vatican treasure
21. Criminal
23. Stone: Prefix
27. Swedish district
30. 24-book poem
31. Harass
32. Whitecap
34. Pays up
35. Frogs, toads, etc.
36. One of the media
38. Like some owls
39. Canton of Norway
40. Court impositions
42. Rungs

44. Melon features
45. Type of coach
46. Printing mark
47. Sustaining processes
48. Blemish
49. "... the whips and __ of time"
51. Peep show
52. Betrays
54. Mishandle, as beans
56. Pretentious
59. Outpouring
60. Habits
61. African native
63. Kind of drum
65. Mexican money
67. Economize, in a way
69. First word of a toast

70. Scolded
72. Desire
74. Perfumes
75. City on the Meuse
76. Muse
78. Wingless
79. Of bees
80. V.I.P.
81. Feasible
82. Berlin's river
84. Trifle
85. Fleet of ships
88. Bezel
89. Racehorse
90. Scottish hill areas
92. Tuscany city
93. Prefix for scope or meter
94. Secret group
96. Harness part
98. Big Board initials
99. Fem. suffix

ACROSS

1. Bragg and Ord: Abbr.
4. City in Shinar
9. Miss Farrow
12. Get lost!
17. Food staple on the Corso
19. Kind of theater
20. Up
23. Fanon
24. Kind of clock
25. Sensational
26. Cremona name
27. Hood of note
28. Handel work
31. Meyerbeer work, at La Scala
33. Crave
34. Formosa Strait island
35. Instrument
36. Mark on a proof
37. Spanish relatives
39. "__ in the Crowd"
41. Pines of Hawaii
42. Gen. Arnold
45. Mayan god of rain
47. Hasty
49. Cordage fiber
53. Shrub genus
55. Incurred, as debts
58. Curb
59. Concurred
61. Highway to Fairbanks
62. Small missile
64. Greek letters
66. Fortification
67. Crop anew
69. Denizens
71. Scruff
73. __ pet
74. Weight units: Abbr.
75. Writer Shute
77. Ball team
78. Inter__
79. Fool
80. Turned out to be
82. Oblique
84. Eastern name
87. Nazimova
88. On one's toes
92. Getting on
93. Miss Hogg
96. Horse color
97. Dance
98. Louvre name
100. Showed boredom
102. Play part
104. Toper
106. Holdings
108. Well-known Indian
109. Spanish news medium
111. Partner of stew
113. Spanish month
114. Jugs
115. Sea bird
116. Highway areas
119. Farm sight
121. Deer
122. Full of: Suffix
123. Numskull
125. Choir's place
127. Rain check
131. Hair job
133. Makes: Abbr.
135. Bent outward, as arms
139. Sibelius score
141. Berlioz work
144. Aquatic animal
145. Lands
147. Egg-shaped
148. Dinsmore
149. Wagner's river
150. Strange
151. Rhythm, in Soho
152. Garments
153. Mrs. Fitzgerald
154. Reply: Abbr.
155. Letters
156. Understand

DOWN

1. Disloyal
2. Ivan and Peter
3. Kind of jacket
4. Indonesian island
5. __ for one's money
6. Kentucky college
7. Elgar's variations
8. Evans and Reaves favorite
9. Egyptian goddess
10. Doctrine
11. Part of a Dickens title
12. Plant clusters
13. Nile critters
14. Clerical collar
15. Straighten
16. Egyptian amulet
17. Receipt word
18. Gershwin favorite
21. Rossini work, at Covent Garden
22. Pillages
29. Jacob's wife
30. Indian veranda
32. Asian grass
35. Mushroom
38. Puppeteer
40. Lurch
42. Celery tidbit
43. Author Michael
44. Early Britons
46. Popular cornet solo
48. Party fare
49. Anger
50. Radio and TV
51. Limas
52. Ferber and Millay
54. Vehicle
56. English hymn translator
57. European mole
60. Mussorgski "Picture"
63. 6th-century date
65. East Indian tree
68. Blackbird
70. Black or Red
72. Matted together
76. Rodents
81. Family member
83. "Le __ du Printemps"
84. Conform
85. Money
86. Bury
89. Made lace
90. "__ Got a Secret"
91. Respighi opus
93. __ sanctum
94. Paris subway
95. Like __ of salts
99. Niger River mouth
101. Cry of surprise
103. Mermaid, for one
105. Numerical prefix
107. Mar
110. Bedeck
112. Miss Adams
117. Coral family
118. Terza __
120. Bank deal
124. Collections
126. Baron and duke, e.g.
127. Accented, in music: Abbr.
128. Church tax
129. Before
130. Cooking direction
132. Grief, old style
134. Coin receivers
136. En __
137. Goosefoot herb
138. Court cry: Var.
140. Tract
141. Dwellings: Abbr.
142. Extreme
143. Roman date
146. German article

FIRST AND TEN *Jack Rosenthal*

ACROSS

1. Soviet agency
5. Those: Sp.
9. Study intently
13. Agreed!
16. Lend __
18. Stubborn as
19. Post-W.W.II spy
20. Ocean: Abbr.
21. Prelim
22. Notre Dame name
24. Samples
25. Rogers
26. Battering units of West
29. Kind of lease
31. More trying
32. Famed sculpture
34. Old slave
37. To-do
40. Griese or Hope
43. Cart
44. Espy
45. Indian
46. Florida beach
49. Arctic native: Abbr.
50. Irish hill
51. Chicagoan
53. Hand tool
54. Sevilla wives
57. June campus fringe
59. Members of a big union
63. Conrad
66. Poor maker of matches
67. French region
70. Mrs. Ram
71. Inter-mezzos, of a sort
75. Conjunc-tion
76. Initials of affection
77. Hirohito's son et al.
78. BB launcher
80. "Write your Congress-man __"
82. Stadium sound
85. Columbus, e.g.
87. Hardened
89. Linemen
93. Nelson
94. City of Brazil
97. Masculine
99. First __
100. Handle: Lat.
101. Starts, to poets
102. Last mo.
103. Greek god
105. Part of N.F.L.: Abbr.
106. "The time __"
108. Flight
111. "Camino __"
113. Wisconsin moving man
119. French friend
121. Castor's mother
123. Move away
124. Free
125. Meredith
126. Exam
127. Camptown events
128. Numskulls
129. Spitz, e.g.
130. Greek letters
131. Trees
132. Cartoonist

DOWN

1. Kind of back
2. Part of A.D.
3. Net units
4. Bernhardt et al.
5. Zola
6. Giant tureen
7. Peaks
8. Jeane Dixon
9. Unitas, Luckman, etc.
10. Sash
11. Instant __
12. Otherwise
13. Suburban sights from a car
14. W.W.II area
15. Artful
17. Actor Colman
18. Matured
23. Kind of session
27. So-so, with "no"
28. Ojibwa sect
30. Wise one
33. Likes
35. Miss Bayes
36. Greek letters
37. Boston
38. Used up
39. Red or Black
41. Pronoun
42. Colts' home
47. Times: Abbr.
48. Kicking unit
52. Way: Abbr.
55. Manage-ment
56. Iran
58. Go through __ (progress)
60. Suffixes of origin
61. Mornings: Abbr.
62. __-jongg
63. Shea player
64. Hooter
65. Bench
66. Thread: Prefix
68. Groza
69. Ocean eagle
72. Front fours, etc.
73. U.S. agency
74. Small bird
79. Whisky
81. Casino or Rue
82. Notre Dame name
83. Vase
84. Friend of David
85. Sweet cherry
86. Ferber
88. Scot's denial
90. Business org.
91. Sine __
92. Ocean inlets: Abbr.
95. Ohio tigers
96. Old zither
98. Proclaim
101. Well men in Texas
104. Football fur: Var.
107. Conjoin
109. Singer Emma
110. Cons
112. Off center
114. Saarinen
115. Campus sports org.
116. Beverage nut
117. Suffixes
118. Time-out
119. Tot up
120. Jersey sound
122. Bao__

COMPOUNDS *Thomas W. Schier*

ACROSS

1. Yemen's capital
5. Conducted oneself
10. Orange Bowl site
15. Sitting Bull, e.g.
20. D.C. agent
21. Tennyson heroine
22. 1,523-mile highway
23. Prison of fiction
24. Compassion
25. Politician and actor
28. __ for trouble
29. Safe, to a yegg
30. Ashy residue
31. Fruit
32. Cockney pad
33. Skating hazard
35. City of Georgia
36. Renown
38. Kind of sapphire
39. Barber's call
40. Subjoin
41. __ Abner
42. Audit man
44. Muddled
46. Variety of 31 Across
47. Humiliate
49. Sudanese people
53. Circle parts
54. Family member
55. Writer Seton
57. Math systems
58. Spanish uncle
59. Proof mark
61. Keats works
62. Cheese for pasta
63. Rooms with many windows
65. Equality seekers
67. Word for Santa
68. Soul, in Sèvres
69. Truck weight
70. Widow's income
71. Back of a book
72. Author of "The Affair"
73. Early Briton
74. Area of a ship
76. Kind of appeal
78. On the summit
80. Two-faced deity
82. Words of surprise
83. Auto-racing city
86. Roman spirit
87. Famous friend
88. Stage lights
89. N.Y. lake group
90. Discontinue
92. British P.M.
93. Oleoresin
95. __ Juana
96. Place for an easel
97. Lathered
99. Sphere
100. Brook trout
101. October event
102. Majorcan port
103. Basilica part
105. Allen
106. British medal
107. Spanish queen
108. "Lead __ into . . ."
110. Valueless item
111. Italian family
114. Certain teacher
116. Game score
117. U.S. writer
120. In statu __
121. Native of Japan
122. 1,007.
123. Scarce
124. Self-esteem
125. Writer and novelist
130. River to Baltic
131. Muse
132. Ebb and neap
133. Queen
134. Vt., N.H., etc.
135. Arty gathering
136. Indian wear
137. Fisherman
138. Chip in

DOWN

1. March man, for short
2. Mennonite sect
3. Singer and songwriter
4. Some
5. Having wings
6. Happened, with "about"
7. Deuce, e.g.
8. Settle snugly
9. Slander
10. Karl or Zeppo
11. State: Abbr.
12. Card
13. Prop for a spring dance
14. Miss Stevens
15. Ruler
16. Kind of party
17. Metal mold
18. Plant disease
19. Traveler
21. Throw out
26. Poet and late spiritual leader
27. Singer and essayist
29. Impish one
34. Certain films: Abbr.
35. Hosp. aides
36. Cut __
37. Type of price
38. Béchamel
40. Top-rated
43. Flourishing
44. Word for a chubby one
45. Sky sight near Taurus
46. Adriatic wind
48. Has-__
50. Suffragist and statesman
51. Texas shrine
52. Strength
54. Apostle and statesman
56. Montague's son
57. Coolidge et al.
59. Reptile, for short
60. Words for a homer with one on
62. Obese
64. On one's toes
66. Raptorial birds
67. Humorous
70. "__ disturb"
71. National concern
72. Animal body
75. Wild dog of India
77. Italian saint
78. False name
79. Oncle's wife
81. Moslem lord
84. River nymph
85. Timid
87. Uses a towel
88. Coal bed
89. Withered
91. Abridge
92. Pivotal
94. Found's partner
97. ". . . in corpore __"
98. City in Virginia
100. Perry of song
102. Deep purple
104. Mystery writer
105. Give notice to
109. Evening party
110. Field flower
111. Horseman: Lat.
112. Above
113. Adding-machine reading
115. Troop bodies
117. Draw together
118. Spy
119. Oslo's land
121. Ever and __
122. Kind of media
123. Piping sound
126. Plains tribe
127. Navy officer: Abbr.
128. Neckwear
129. Building wing
130. Go __ binge

ACROSS

1. Worries
6. In __ by itself
12. Clover yield
18. Creator
20. Plot anew
21. Strong flow
22. Plan
23. Awns
24. Clay houses
25. Bogdano- vich film about a Texas town
28. Antitoxins
29. Exclama- tions
30. Proprietors
31. Untamed
35. Certain
37. Pronoun
38. Like a mad hen
40. Tokyo's old name
41. Camel's nemesis
46. Condition: Suffix
49. Islamic month
51. Edgar and C.P.
52. Of the ear
54. __ con- tinuum
56. Novice: Var.
57. Crichton novel
59. Group in Bond movie
62. Mars: Prefix
63. Plains home: Var.
64. Heel-__
66. "Grecian Urn" man
68. Wise counselor
72. O'Neill
74. River to the Caspian
75. Depilate
77. Beckett play
83. Son of Isaac
84. Cruel
85. Virile one
86. Scottish dance
87. Lace collar
88. Auditory
90. Cobblers' gear
92. Chem. suffix
93. Telepathy
95. __-jongg
97. Merkel et al.
98. __ novarum
100. Arouse
103. Place for a car key: Abbr.
104. Man of Indochina
108. Go whole hog
112. African fly
115. Irish port and bay
116. Kind of speech sound
117. Jargon
118. Baltic land
119. Modest
120. Position
121. Onslaughts
122. Mae and Rebecca

DOWN

1. Goes without food
2. Pleated trim
3. Anesthetic
4. Reigning fad
5. Immortality potion
6. Atmosphere: Prefix
7. A Marx and others
8. Stewart Brand compilation
9. Adjusts
10. Kind of crow
11. Utter
12. Webster
13. Place to get off
14. Poet John __ Ransom
15. Bathing place
16. Ibsen character
17. Backfield men: Abbr.
19. Last __
20. Medium sounds
26. "__ that ate the malt"
27. Compass point
32. Measure of Algeria
33. Doesn't give __
34. Sole
36. Ship initials
39. Got away
41. War craft of 40s
42. Soul
43. Kierke- gaard
44. Cry of disgust
45. Inflict
47. Doctrine
48. Barbecue part
50. Vapor: Prefix
53. Father of Menelaus
55. Lively, in music: Abbr.
58. Turn
60. Onetime radio show
61. To-dos
65. Else, in Scotland
67. Bridge scores
69. Start of a song about Paris
70. Water hole
71. Laughing
73. Besides
76. Kirmans
77. N.H. city
78. More unusual
79. Sculpture, etc.
80. Time zone east of N.Y.
81. Cry of contempt
82. Sufficient
84. Flanged beam
86. State: Abbr.
89. Copy
91. Group of nine
94. Hair: Prefix
96. Girl's name
99. Sinclair
101. Short letters
102. Vulgar: Sp.
103. "__ shame!"
105. Cheat
106. Divergent
107. British __
109. __ majesty
110. Garlands
111. Gush
112. Scout groups: Abbr.
113. Posed
114. Greek letter

ACROSS

1. S.A. city
6. Black bands
12. Cleric
16. Product of a schism
20. With reverent dread
21. Sound of gunfire
22. Gather
23. Sprite
24. Tiger
26. Cow
28. May 15, in old Rome
29. Be ready for
30. Pleasant refuges
32. Cheered
33. Spread
34. Words of approval
35. Spar
36. Early helmets
37. Variety of wheat
38. Fur
39. Howe
40. Thwarts
43. Gorilla
45. Old song title
48. Distributive word
49. South, at one time
50. Like a piper
51. Unbend
52. Pomme de —
53. Wear for head of family
54. Families
56. _ Selassie
57. Miss Durbeyfield
58. Wolf
59. Certain scores
60. Lineman
61. Bone: Suffix
62. Kitty
66. Old footwear
67. Archery accessory
69. Dropsy
70. Grieve
71. Tavern employee
73. Lions
75. Elec. unit
78. One who shirks
79. Rider
80. Small person
81. On the blue
82. Tandems
83. Flower
84. Fastening strip
86. Pigment ore
87. Unique object
88. Block of stamps
89. Common contraction
90. France's F.B.I.
91. Word with cent or capita
92. Wolf
95. Post-impres-sionist
96. Church recesses
97. Form of address
98. Having a trunk
99. Cranes
101. 30 days
102. Keep out
103. Punch
106. Hydrangea pink
107. Quid pro quo for a mile
108. Obscure
109. Own
110. Bear
112. Bull
115. Points
116. First two notes
117. "But _ cent for tribute"
118. Ready to diet
119. Med. subject
120. Decides to
121. Virginia and others
122. Outdoes

DOWN

1. Permitted
2. Terminal
3. Lost color
4. Tools
5. Zuider, for one
6. Worsted yarns
7. Disavow
8. Fruit-pest genus
9. Burns, e.g.
10. Prior to
11. Sharpened a razor
12. Rebellious
13. Pulitzer poet, 1929
14. Sprees
15. Roof piece
16. Moves furtively
17. Intensify
18. Calls into court
19. Prepared to drive
23. Vendor of rhyme
25. Germ cell
27. 10,000
31. Gobi-like
34. With dispatch
35. Asian garments
36. Dancing girls
37. Vaticinators
38. Catchy tempo
39. Grape pigments
40. Malay chief
41. Dueling weapons
42. Fox
43. High trump
44. _ about (stirring)
45. Skunks
46. More robust
47. Those in bankruptcy
49. Weapon
51. So much: Mus.
53. Hard question
54. Tiny bit
55. Crescent-shaped
56. They're often apparent
58. Pry
60. Inverted V
62. Grains
63. Diverges
64. Boy's name
65. Retainer
66. Auction word
68. _ the gun
70. Barn-storming flier's forte
71. Jazz form
72. Sheeplike
73. Chair worker
74. Gentle sarcasm
76. Runs into
77. Gay _
79. Teeth
81. Stinging
83. Cocktail spreads
84. Experi-mental use
85. Pilot's place
86. _ Mongolia
88. Soft color
89. Eng. essayist and others
90. Delicates-sen item
92. Greek region
93. Realms
94. Corn crop
95. Certain art pieces
96. Shore bird
98. "Thy will _ . . ."
99. Poe's detective
100. Playing field
101. Spiritless, old style
102. Storehouse
103. U.S. outlaw
104. Seaman's shout
105. Czech patriot
106. Movie dog
107. On the roof
108. Greek letter
109. Goddess of youth
111. Flurry
113. "_ a chance"
114. Thickset horse

UNLIKELY PEOPLE
Eugene T. Maleska

ACROSS

1. Terre Haute's river
7. Profane
14. He's tied up in show biz
20. Graceful dance
21. Gymnast
22. Airport reneger
23. Call Edwin or Shirley
25. Young Athenian
26. Sommer
27. Break __
28. Hang loosely
30. Law degree
31. Inlet
32. Tire
33. Make into new coins
34. Fuel material
35. Sicilian city
37. Strike out
39. City in Peru
40. "Nun's Story" author
41. Loses hope
43. Capitol Hill product
45. Baby carriage
47. Shade trees
48. Promenades
50. Dictum
51. Cajuns' early home
54. Asian herb
56. Crosiers
59. Drama about robots
60. Type of type
62. Draft
64. Account
65. Modify
67. Tyrone's untemptable relative
69. Climbing pepper
70. Judge
71. Kind of soup
72. Alpine ridge
74. Kinsman: Abbr.
75. Lake in N.Y.
77. Defensible
79. Monks' garments
81. Mideasterner
83. King of flush
84. Reiner or sbad

85. Unite
88. Fatty: Prefix
89. __ box
93. Town in S.E. Illinois
94. Kompong __, Cambodian bay
96. Dislodge
98. Find fault
99. Intelligence
100. Excludes
102. Drink
103. Wrath
104. Cry of disgust
105. Naval reply
106. Italian town
108. Group of relatives
109. Loose
111. Hugh's British cousin
114. Bank employee
115. Ionic-style grooves

116. Ferocious
117. Emerson products
118. Least protected
119. Compliant one

DOWN

1. Like some silks
2. Quartet gal
3. Bulgaria, Greece, etc.
4. Askew
5. Use a straw
6. Dec. 24 sounds
7. Sackers of Rome
8. Glacial epoch
9. By hook crook
10. Old card game
11. Dwelling
12. Japanese straw rug

13. Names of races, tribes, etc
14. Used a prie-dieu
15. Slangy refusal
16. U.S.S.R. silk city
17. Alexander G.'s Italian relative
18. At fault
19. Feel the heat
24. Bids
29. Midge and punkie
33. Gary's musical kin
34. Beat
36. Mimicked
37. Joltin' Joe
38. French actor
40. Hall-of-Famer Waite
42. "__ needs a good memory

44. Spanish jar
46. Coarse file
48. Scurry
49. Breakwater
51. Farmland in Southwest
52. Diamond facet
53. H.G.'s earthy relatives
54. Be frugal
55. "__ well it were done quickly"
57. Argosy
58. Is bearish
61. Wonder
63. River in Yorkshire
66. Comes forth
68. Type machines, for short
69. Imperial or Vandyke
71. Isolated
73. Scot. title
76. Like old meat

78. Bunyan's ox
80. Political unit
82. Grasp intuitively
84. Famed nurse
85. Prove false
86. Liquid fats
87. Havana, e.g.
89. One of the horsey set
90. Amtrak's concern
91. Classify
92. "Faerie Queene" poet
95. Possibly
97. Cattle feeds
100. Colorers
101. What old grads do
105. __-deucey
106. Asian tree
107. Further
108. Inlet
110. State: Abbr.
112. Skedaddled
113. Little bit

HEARSAY — *Elaine D. Schorr*

ACROSS

1. Dresser décor
6. W.W.II craft
9. Met again
14. Family-store abbr.
18. "Zoo Story" author
19. Bahamas island
21. Spear carrier
22. Short: Prefix
23. Outlandish lamp, for one
26. On the level
27. Tints
28. Host, in Rome
29. Spanish pots
30. Fare for a swinger
31. Ship: Abbr.
32. Boundary
33. Kicked
34. Unpopular pupil
35. Ducks the issue
39. Twaddle
40. English author
42. French king
43. River to Seine
44. Jungfrau, etc.: Abbr.
47. Like translators at the U.N.
51. Words to a business contact
54. Sea passage
55. Field deities
56. Converse, in Paris
57. More logical
58. Compass reading
59. Careens
60. Hackie's hope
61. Movie-set light
62. Bard's word
63. Weaverbird
64. Legal right
65. Football field
67. Advice to a traffic violator
76. Was beholden
77. "My _ is Legion"
78. Yorkshire river
79. Yeast acid: Abbr.
80. Actor Richard
83. Sister of Ares
84. Thing to champion
86. _ crow
87. Close to, in poems
88. Chair strip
90. Hoods' honeys
91. _ Flow
93. Doris Day film
95. Janus, in a way
97. Pipe curve
98. Decree
99. Sleeper of note
100. Live
101. Legal degrees
102. Head operator
107. Parlor-game subject
111. Czech city, to Germans
112. Pants part
113. Hiatus
116. Bacterial organism
117. Time word
118. Baltic land: Abbr.
119. Kind of coat
120. French composer
121. Doorbell answerer
125. Vibrate
126. Faction: Fr.
127. Band man
128. Teen talk
129. Drinks
130. Kind of william
131. Tenn. athlete
132. Intervals

DOWN

1. Meister-singer Hans
2. Political muscle
3. Doubleday
4. Speeds the engine
5. Emolument
6. Medit. vessel
7. Univ. course
8. Moreover
9. Dig new furrows
10. Napoleon and Peron
11. Stand in good _
12. Bows
13. Scottish preposition
14. George of films
15. Splendid
16. Sheeplike
17. Hindu guitar
19. Simpletons
20. Exchange rate in India
22. Talkative one
24. Desert Fox of W.W.II
25. Manx cat's feature
30. Opera voice
34. Linen fabric
35. Execrate
36. Revise
37. Gypsy roads
38. Shouting sounds
39. Cotton pod
40. Smuggler
41. A Queen
44. Skirt length
45. Hammock anchor
46. N.C.O.
47. North Dakota city
48. "_ a million"
49. Like some speech
50. Violin-string base
51. English poet Thomas
52. Ring
53. Essayist's middle name
56. Span
59. George Apley, for one
60. Chimney parts
63. Shinar's dud
65. Pod, in Paris
66. Artifice
68. Kind of eclipse
69. ". . . the _ of parting day"
70. Falconry word
71. Leave out
72. "_ be sorry!"
73. Side show stars
74. Sulking
75. Siberian
80. Cod or May
81. Town of Spain
82. Dickens girl
84. Bridge feats
85. Greece's neighbor: Abbr.
88. Passe
89. Hingle et al.
90. Drudge
91. Historian _ Grammaticus
92. Bed: Prefix
94. Famous wit
95. Sugar-coated nut
96. What babies do
102. Flossy
103. Squash gear
104. Advanta-geous
105. Musical signs
106. Persian hymn group
107. _ ballot (vote)
108. Gave attention to
109. Shaw
110. Ruffles
111. Chessman
113. Chisel
114. Joseph or Stewart
115. Men of words
117. Gush
119. Arthur or Chester
121. Draft initials
122. Bible edition: Abbr.
123. Scoreboard reading
124. Enjoys

ACROSS

1. Beer, ale, etc.
6. Multitude
10. Dies __
14. Blockhead
17. Musical Count
18. Lily plant
19. Bow tip
20. Vanzetti's friend
22. Warble
23. Who
26. Playing card
28. Kind of pan
29. Mall units
30. Refractors
33. Portuguese coin: Abbr.
34. Like a fork
35. What
42. Encroach on
43. Possess, in Ayr
44. Harvests
45. Records, for short
48. Board men: Abbr.
49. Defense weapons: Abbr.
52. Corporation initials
53. __ de France
54. Compass point
55. When
61. "What __ boy am I!"
62. Graf __
63. Embroidery décor
64. Fountain items
66. Ways: Abbr.
67. Vied in a log game
68. Burden, in Spain
69. Footwear
70. Crude tartar
71. Where
75. Dental degree
78. Fleur-de__
79. W.W.II zone
80. Mine cars
81. Science: Abbr.
82. Passé: Abbr.
83. Kiel or Erie
85. Varnish base
86. Ball star
87. Why
92. Child: Prefix
94. Lupino
95. Coercion
96. See 87 Across
97. British composer et al.
99. "Without __"
101. How
104. English novelist
108. Like Maine's coast
109. Network
110. Sea eagle
111. Upset
112. Letter addenda
113. Bills
114. Donna
115. Oak or Blue

DOWN

1. British TV
2. Cheer
3. That, in Toledo
4. Certain ties or chairs
5. Words to a bartender
6. Between hic and hoc
7. Kind of shoppe
8. Do farm work
9. Bridal gift
10. Prevail upon
11. Military group: Abbr.
12. Yearn
13. Squeeze out
14. Earth pigment
15. Feigned
16. Exclamations
20. Certain protests
21. Past, in the past
24. Devil-may-care
25. Prohibit
27. Seagoing initials
30. Stuffy one
31. Pine substance
32. Harden
36. Sports slacks
37. Kind of seal
38. I.O.U. matter
39. Banal
40. Hebrew letter
41. Hindu weight
45. Hosiery fabric
46. Carried on
47. Canonical hour
50. A __ fish
51. Between Aug. and Nov.
55. Writer Marsh
56. Midwest campus, for short
57. Wise counselor
58. Dominion
59. Neophytes
60. Shout
61. Principal
64. Hindu title
65. Plait
67. German historian
68. Normandy town
69. British math pioneer
70. City of Jordan
72. Conveyed
73. Indian district
74. Evils, in law
75. Do research
76. Parcels out
77. Winter transports
81. Bertie
83. Systematize
84. Swiss resort
86. Mistake
87. Criminal
88. Shrinks
89. Concert halls
90. Part of M.A.
91. Old Tokyo
92. Agreements
93. Voices
96. Kind of waist
97. Arabian gulf
98. Latin or Anglican
99. First-class
100. Prune: Scot.
102. Family member: Abbr.
103. Wrath
105. G-man
106. Relative of an assn.
107. Summer, in Nice

ACROSS

1. Defensive device
7. Snake
10. Russian dancer Serge
15. Asian hardwood
19. Did housework
21. Mauna __
22. P.I. spirit
23. Biblical treasure port
24. Dancers from an exotic island
26. Royal Russian ballerina
28. Foxtrot on a Russian plain
29. Closes
31. Lawyer: Abbr.
32. "__ Girls"
33. Small pies
34. Dance enthusiast's ailment
37. Shoelace tips
40. Gaunt
41. Entrance protectors
42. Horn sound
43. Agnew
45. Platform
46. Hat
50. "The __ of Summer"
51. Boss in Africa
52. Species
53. Make coat repairs
54. Not present: Abbr.
55. Trolley sound
56. Candy drop
57. Road covers
58. Annoy
59. Sauce source
61. Pass over
63. Pronoun
64. Sessions: Abbr.
65. English naturalist
66. __ de jambe
67. Wail
68. Telegram
69. Father of French twins
71. Theater offering
73. German river
74. Parliament man
75. Withered
76. Indefinite tense
78. Black cuckoos
79. Exhausts
80. Becky
81. Kind of flight
83. Mood, in Scotland
84. Fuel
85. Decree
86. Second-raters
88. Greek letter
89. Ballet footwear
91. Mild cussword
92. Opera locations
93. Detailed study: Abbr.
94. Overthrow
95. Store event
96. Whetstones
97. Hosiery material
98. Prepares for burial
100. Morse or zip
101. Most singular
102. Ballet for a clumsy girl
106. Pitiless
108. One: Scot.
109. Japanese statesman
110. Unique people
111. Prado items
115. Saloon stance
118. Hot-sofa ballet, in a way
120. Tie __ (carouse)
121. Homecoming: Prefix
122. Egg: Prefix
123. Heraldic bird
124. Vapid
125. Relative of twixt
126. Pipe joint
127. Certain votes

DOWN

1. Audit man: Abbr.
2. Play a tuba
3. Atmosphere: Prefix
4. Bartenders
5. Put in office
6. Passover events
7. Wings
8. Hurok
9. Native, in Southwest
10. Vichy premier
11. Graceless
12. Red Cross program
13. __ standstill
14. Take turns
15. Month: Abbr.
16. __ con carne
17. Bridal gift
18. Rub out
20. Bureau: Abbr.
23. Breakfast cereals
25. Chess pieces: Abbr.
27. Jazz dancers
30. Large deer
34. Siren of silents
35. Parts of qts.
36. Years: Lat.
37. Eban et al.
38. Spheres: Sp.
39. Nonclergy dancers in a ballet
40. Those who wait
43. Ballet of the Old South
44. Forest god
45. Sup
47. Grieg heroine is nervous
48. Unite
49. Requests
51. Insipid
52. Big name in piracy
53. Ballets on the reservation
55. __ fire
56. Flirtatious girl
57. Variant of Ted
60. Wild hogs
62. Garish
63. Menotti opera, with "The"
64. Singer's warmup notes
67. Writer Jean
68. Admonishes
70. Venetian V.I.P.
71. Dinner course
72. Chess pieces
73. Bermuda, for one
75. Chase, as fly balls
77. Adds up
78. Aleutian island
79. Show-biz dance routines
80. Trig word
82. Quoit: Fr.
84. Marge or Gower
85. Singer's boo-boo
87. Tool for Paul Bunyan
90. Flow through
91. Jacques of ballet
92. Soul's partner
93. Relief operations
95. On the seas: Abbr.
96. Nightclub
97. Fourth Sunday in Lent
99. Consecrate
100. Mongrel
101. Burlesque promenade
102. Wooden shoe
103. Climbing vine
104. Legal term
105. Locale of John the Baptist
106. Neighbor of Ore.
107. French trial scene
111. Ballet movement
112. Actor Asther
113. Prize: Scot.
114. Places
116. "Raven" man
117. Haul
119. "__ got you . . ."

ACROSS

1. Famous twin
7. Stage ash-tray, e.g.
11. Type of brick
16. Marshes of central Italy
17. Sweet liqueur
18. Send back
20. Busy
21. Shays, for one
22. Staved off
24. Biblical setting
25. Soft job
27. Roman goddess
28. Tennessean
29. Mobster's pad
30. Wire measure
31. __ accompli
32. Worn
34. Within: Prefix
35. Bee genus
37. __ macabre
38. Eminence
39. Sea east of Caspian
40. Andy Capp's sport
41. __ the cup (just missed)
43. Church reading
47. Grecian theater
48. Suit
49. Kowtower
50. Swiss city
51. Winged
52. Antarctic explorer
54. Nickname for a princess
57. Bootstring
59. Ness or Lomond
60. Preeminent
61. Composer Montemezzi
63. England's Isle of __
64. Show thespian zeal
66. Tippler
67. Related
68. Mine car
69. Made up for
70. Minotaur's home
71. Some F.B.I. men
75. Pitchman's forte

76. Ready, as an audience
77. Tiny bit
78. Colleen's cry
79. Court decree
80. U.N. plaza décor
81. Manhandle
84. Kind of highness
87. Iris layer
88. "Mamma __!"
89. Faculties
91. Crown component
92. PX
94. How dreadful!
96. Cheerless
97. __ cordiale
98. Cordial flavor
99. Surfeit
101. Become ragged
102. Spiritual
103. Set right
104. Distrustful
105. Kind of TV show
106. Tarry

DOWN

1. American vulture
2. Doer of good deeds
3. Baseball's Man
4. Tamper: Scot.
5. Prejudiced
6. Made over
7. Ready for use, as lumber
8. Disprove
9. Hebrew measure
10. Ex-star in 40 Across
11. Musketeer
12. Harass
13. Augury
14. Shameless
15. Spellbind
16. Annoyance
17. King of Thebes
19. Formulated
23. Stamping device
26. Maiden-name word
29. Two-fisted fellows
30. The last __
33. Popular singer
35. Tosca's "Vissi d'__"
36. Biblical land: Abbr.
37. Conductor Antal
39. African fox
40. Haggis fancier
41. Calif. oak
42. Miss America, to Bert Parks
43. Set apart
44. Nobel Prize category
45. Pledge
46. Deposited
48. "La __"
52. Air-show feature
53. Instances
54. Succeed
55. Top-drawer
56. Lost soul
58. Sonnet part
60. Any minute
62. Tooth nuisance
65. Marian, for one
66. Check
68. Causerie
69. Excited
70. Anxieties
71. Instrument
72. "__ guidance suggested"
73. Kind of palooza
74. P.I. tribesman
75. Deli purchase
76. Hollandaise or marinara
80. Sunday best
81. Zoroastrian
82. Birch-family tree
83. Undersized
85. Less messy
86. Set firmly
88. Poet's concern
89. Stigmatize
90. Twangy
93. Being: It.
94. Eire legislature
95. Sicilian city
96. Bell sound
100. Two fins

ACROSS

1. Hiding place
6. Fire extinguisher
10. Yokum's creator
14. Calls
20. Frome or Allen
21. Places of wealth
23. Unit for My Son John
25. Start of a familiar poem
28. Nobleman
29. Scottish mushes
30. Salt deposit
31. Rates of speed
32. Church land
34. Sickle users
38. Pitched high
39. Sports gear
41. Headache source
45. Packs
48. Bess et al.
50. Try to convince
54. Lummox
55. Crime statistics
57. Fuel
58. Gathers
61. Weekday: Abbr.
64. News-agency founder
66. Kukla's friend
67. Tuna, in France
68. Jeweler's sales
72. Dear ones
76. British medal
77. Brants
78. Odor: Prefix
79. Antitoxins
82. __ wear
84. Easing
87. Upset
89. Aircraft
90. Ted's relative
92. House plant
93. Dominiques
94. Carriage
95. Cape Cod sights
97. Humorist Ward
99. French numbers
100. Glass oven
102. Winter wear
105. Tavern sales
106. Bar, in law
108. Maple genus
109. Greetings for a rajah
114. Sauce
117. Songbird
120. Atmospheric halo
123. Mrs. King
125. Word with warm or hard
127. Shrew
128. German measure
129. Most quiet
133. Intended
135. Burmese natives
138. Sambar
139. Deck hand
143. Comfort
146. English lit-course reading
151. "And so the poor dog __"
152. Relative of once more
153. G-man
154. Furniture piece
155. Cape
156. Sacred chests
157. Beau __

DOWN

1. Do a plaster job
2. Sundered, old style
3. Poem inspired by London Times account
4. Directed
5. Terminate
6. Persistent sleuth
7. Table spread
8. Totals
9. Pier
11. Half a dance
11. "Flower of my heart"
12. Greek city-state
13. Bridge ploy, for short
14. Yours: Fr.
15. Miss Claire
16. Suffix for inter or bi
17. Map listing
18. Victorian short stories
19. Degummed silk
22. Comedian Steve
24. Red-pencils
26. Reflux
27. Mayan ruins in Mexico
33. Henry Esmond or H.M. Pulham
35. Deteriorates
36. Monthly bill
37. Wintry cover: Abbr.
39. Self-esteem
40. Blue grass
42. Poet's word
43. Compass point
44. Draft initials
46. About: Abbr.
47. Osiris's crown
49. Mideast initials
51. Likely
52. Call, in poker
53. Men in a shell
56. Prefix with pod
59. Soft shades
60. Hairnets
62. Wet down
63. Ragged
65. Second-hand
67. BBC receivers
68. Banquet feature
69. Adherent: Suffix
70. Give off
71. Robin's pal
73. One-to-nine items
74. Radiation dosage
75. Like sugar maples
77. Goosy group
80. Wide-spread
81. Ancient alloy
83. Blackmore heroine
85. Agitated state
86. Adroit
88. French vineyard
91. Tragic Greek
96. "__ crust!"
98. Refrain syllable
101. Actor's quest
103. Sea god
104. Sign of a hit
105. Quadruped
107. Throw the shot
108. Rat-__
110. Home god
111. Insect
112. Had a bite
113. Poetic times of day
115. Billfold item
116. Longing
118. French connectives
119. Actor Brian and family
121. Le Gallienne
122. Ancestry
123. Sure thing
124. U.S. Indians
126. Bewildered
130. Psyche parts
131. Ecole exercise
132. Furlough
134. Business: Suffix
136. Family member
137. Highlander
140. River in Spain
141. Building beam
142. Liege, on Flemish maps
144. Remitted
145. Punta del __
147. Sailor's direction
148. Female ruff
149. Soldiers: Abbr.
150. Child's game

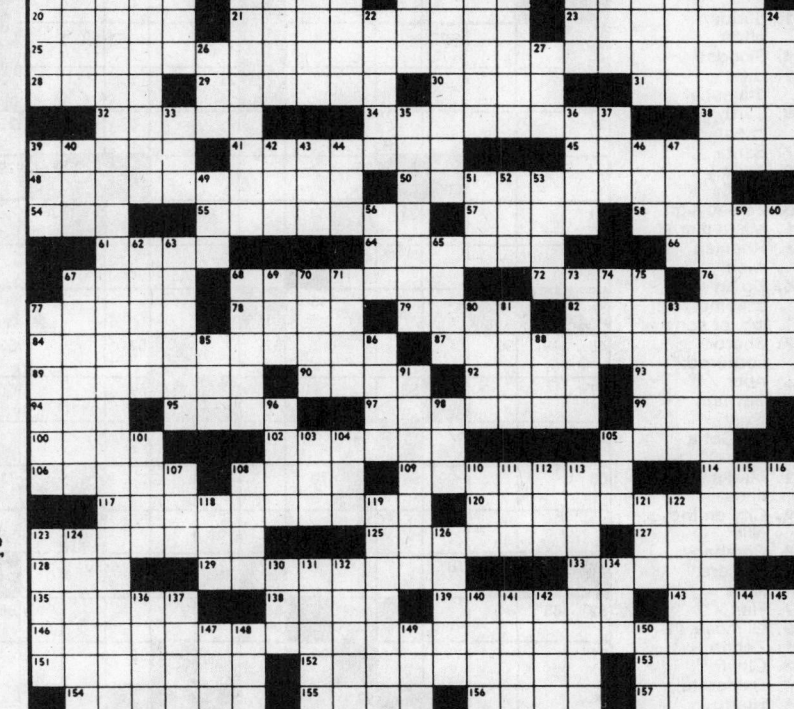

OUTDOOR EXERCISE

Sara V. Tuckerman

ACROSS

1. Sudden effort
6. Flooded
11. U.S. dramatist
16. Card cheat
17. Santa __
18. "__, my love"
20. Zodiac sign
21. Make dim
22. Rhenish wine
24. Do an assembly job, of sorts
27. Sharp-cornered: Abbr.
28. Sayings
29. Exist
30. "__ Got a Secret"
31. Marks with lines
34. City on the Nile
36. Company officers: Abbr.
37. Hail
39. Glimpse: Fr.
41. Zenith
43. City in California
44. Hindu savant
46. Kind of pitching game
47. Fashion name
48. East Coast pair
52. Menu entries
57. Tennis coup
58. Former actor Alan
59. __ Oro
60. Above: Lat.
61. Midianite king
63. Fabric pattern
67. Chinese dynasty: Var.
68. Spenser's name for an island
70. Harden
71. False god
73. Suffix for pat or port
74. Diner's choice
76. Napkin
78. Food fish
79. Dashing
81. Kennel sound
82. Apartment V.I.P.'s, for short
85. Fuel
87. Vast plain
91. Chemical compound
92. Stories: Abbr.
93. Islamic scriptures
95. Closes
96. Rubbing fluid: Abbr.
97. Golfer's aid
98. Musical chord
100. Hair pad
101. Tackle, in a way
109. Went rapidly over
110. Silks: Fr.
111. Locust tree
112. Dignified
113. Take __ at
114. Pater __
115. Philippine island
116. Irish county
117. Printing errors, for short

DOWN

1. Doctor's sign
2. Days of yore
3. Coy
4. Sprinter's forte
5. Occult
6. Desires
7. Marsupial
8. Mars: Prefix
9. City of China
10. Red deer
11. Abalones
12. Vacuum tube
13. He: It.
14. School age
15. Two-wheel carriages
16. Plane wheel rotation
19. Historic city in Bulgaria
23. With an __ (expecting)
24. Arm of the Amazon
25. __ of corn
26. "__ János," Kodály opera
32. Hence
33. Oar
35. Mounted
36. Picture of a sort
37. Flagrant
38. Drive out again
40. Mr. Heep
42. Ipse __
43. Thread: Fr.
45. Downfall
47. Of food
48. S.A. Indian
49. Sidewalk, in Seville
50. Early violin
51. Curving inward
53. Building material
54. Defeat
55. Foulard
56. Health: Fr.
62. Went by shanks' mare
64. Hospital aides
65. TV offering
66. Those who are not poor
69. Burning
72. Gay songs
75. Elected ones
76. Night sight
77. Blade
80. Beverage
82. Seasons
83. Eskimo boats
84. Certain fingers
85. Commoner, for short
86. Café au __
88. Dodges
89. Flat
90. Appraisals: Abbr.
92. Branch line
94. Mass. town
97. Greek letter
99. Blind
102. Wagnerian role
103. Mine car
104. Turkish town
105. Easy gait
106. One waiting in ambush
107. Fastener
108. Prefix for pus

201 SERVICE STATION
By Emanuel Berg

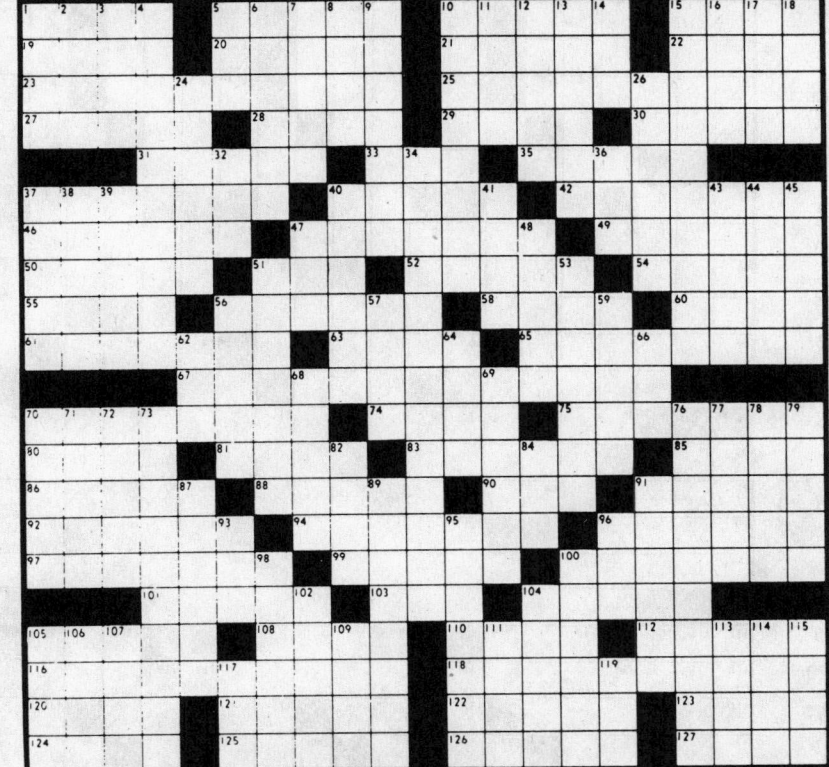

ACROSS

1. Comedian Wilson
5. Point on a compass card
10. Forecaster's aid
15. Diplomacy
19. Chaplin
20. Old Greek colony
21. Lycee-goer
22. She loved Narcissus
23. Home of North Dakota U.
25. Diamond areas
27. Almanach city
28. True, in Paris
29. Heroic work
30. Armadillos
31. __ mediocritas (golden mean)
33. Initials of the '30s
35. Office gal
37. Take __ at (look)
40. __ advantage (find handy)
42. "__ Dance"
46. Afternoons, in Spain
47. Wall trophy
49. Like a Lebanon grove
50. Coverlet
51. Silent one
52. Incensed
54. TV comedian Dan
55. Wavy, in heraldry
56. Briny
58. Roosevelt name
60. Kind of drama
61. Kind of triangle
63. Dutch vessel
65. Served the food
67. Server for the lazy
70. Liking
74. Style name
75. Particular
80. Emanation
81. Narrow fillet
83. Enlaced
85. __ Rios, Jamaica
86. South African name
88. Ice pinnacle
90. Indian of N.M.
91. Las Vegas area
92. Miss Glyn
94. Formal wear
96. Small pipe
97. Plodded
99. Soap or horse
100. Cell division
101. Urged, with "on"
103. Pitching stats
104. Miss Page
105. Synagogue V.I.P.
108. Pitcher Blue
110. Diving bird
112. Israeli port
116. Masters' place
118. Orphan Annie features
120. Opinion
121. Within __ of (near)
122. Old Japanese province
123. Hindu queen
124. Brit. House
125. Bacchante: Var.
126. Assyrian god
127. N.Y. stadium

DOWN

1. World traveler
2. Parrot fish
3. __ the finish
4. Bowery figure
5. Moroccan range
6. Western dam
7. Former world relief org.
8. Writer Waltari
9. Noted blues
10. Compound engine device
11. Unbalanced
12. Populace
13. Sacred writings
14. Good name, for short
15. It made Fall fall
16. Official moves
17. Sonny's ex-partner
18. Fling
24. French writer
26. Poet Sidney
32. Thing, in law
34. Bullpen resident
36. Ref. book
37. Ave __ vale
38. Haggard
39. Take for __
40. Dissimilar
41. Old English money
43. Made sore
44. Babylonian Hades
45. Summary: Abbr.
47. Red dye
48. City: Ger.
51. Visitors
53. Its capital is Asmara
56. Japanese admiral
57. French dept.
59. "I cast to earth __"
62. Bounced-check initials
64. Circulate
66. Relatives of mins.
68. Man's man
69. Awn
70. Arrives
71. Ex-Secretary of Interior
72. Disease
73. Southern arena
76. Cheap novels
77. Tan colors
78. Hot sauce
79. Small sharks
82. Slangy suffix
84. Kobold
87. Noodle
89. Showed up
91. Calif. gold rush name
93. Not spec.
95. Caspian's neighbor
96. Small bird
98. Actor Andy
100. Fu __
102. Couch
104. Pony-express item
105. Invitation reminder
106. Samoan port
107. Smuts, e.g.
109. Ten: Prefix
111. Grain
113. Indian maid
114. Shoe size
115. Chinese dynasty
117. L.A. player
119. Continent: Abbr.

202 DREAM WORLD By Dorothea E. Shipp

ACROSS

1. Sets off
7. Moslem coat
12. ___ of Gilead
16. "Per ardua ad ___"
21. Fox or hyena
22. "___ over one's head"
23. Hassan or ben Adhem
24. Moluccan island
25. Finger sore
26. Rushmore, for one
27. Ointment
28. Italian statesman
29. Essence
30. Indian leader of W.W. I
31. ___ homo
32. Visit
33. Tipsy
37. Ole's relative
40. Haul
41. Durrell novel
42. Kind of dog
43. These: Fr.
44. Type of arch
46. Do a head linesman's job
49. Drift shoreward
53. Supports
55. Gathering of yore
59. Without a sou
60. Sample
61. Met, as alumni
63. Attires
64. ___ hurry (grab a bite)
66. Undertake
68. Appear
71. Poppaea's husband
72. Singer Johnny
74. Durocher
75. Type of molding
77. Gem cup
78. Early Carol Burnett hit
83. Tree resin
86. Wordsworth's forte
87. Pacific fish
88. Lacking principle
92. Hera's son
94. Kind of egg
95. Mints' relatives
98. French side dish
99. Homes up north: Var.
101. Gully of Southwest
103. Goddess: Lat.
105. Arrested
106. Aspirin, for some
109. Washline item
111. Johnson and Adams
112. Asian body of water
114. Dissolute woman
115. Sulfur: Prefix
118. ___ little Indians
119. Declare
120. Roman 56
122. Inner: Prefix
123. "Poverty ___"
131. Brings forth
132. Scottish alders
133. France's saint
134. Mission building
138. Small drum: Var.
139. Gabor and Braun
140. Veal and ham
141. Made certain sounds
142. Shallow
143. Café adjunct
144. Map piece
145. Fixed peaches
146. Attended to
147. This: Sp.
148. N.L. player
149. Diminishes

DOWN

1. Child's knee décor
2. Wedding aide
3. Years: Lat.
4. Cheerful
5. Lancelot, e.g.
6. Salt, in Paris
7. Boy's nickname
8. Golf clubs
9. Cornered the market
10. "Horse Fair" name
11. Fore's companion
12. Judges' seats
13. Calculators
14. Mrs. Ponti
15. Slinger's material
16. Growing together
17. Antelope of Asia
18. Cancer or Capricorn
19. Wisconsin city
20. Improves
30. Parts of the city underground
31. Common abbr.
32. Hindu cloth
34. Eur. capital
35. Compass pt.
36. "Is ___ so?"
37. Cheated
38. Marketplaces
39. Serfs
45. Nose rubber
47. Land mass
48. Eats
49. ___ City (N.Y.)
50. ___ anchor (is moored)
51. Most passé
52. Siamese timber
54. Timber projections
55. Neighbor of Ont.
56. Sired
57. Saragossa's river
58. Fable man: Var.
61. Rack's companion
62. Identification with another
65. Elbow
67. Kind of machine
69. Light color
70. Airs
73. British beach hill
75. Hunger: Fr.
76. Ethiopian city
79. Treacherous
80. Lorry fuel
81. Famed Midwest surgeon
82. Large geese
83. Secular
84. Jason's ship
85. Dry or padded item
89. Fester
90. Farewells
91. Imparted
93. Beer
95. Add up
96. Noble: Ger.
97. Puts in type
100. Dispersed
102. Certain carriers: Abbr.
104. Foe of Henry VIII et al.
107. Parts of ephahs
108. Island off Celebes
109. Indian victory
event
110. Wash: Lat.
112. Farewell!
113. Shows anger
115. Dogmatic
116. Cigar
117. Weather-map line
119. College degrees
121. "___ girl just like . . ."
124. Greek theater area
125. Hubs
126. Concede
127. Result
128. Share in
129. Ready, in Spain
130. Vessel
135. English composer
136. Mare: Scot.
137. Ends' companions
139. Scottish uncle
140. Miss Farrow
141. Fast plane

203 CALORIE CHART By Christine Valence

ACROSS

1. Belshazzar event
6. Sun circles
11. Kind of dragon
15. Add water
16. Division of time
17. Wall plug
20. Little-girl makeup
22. Discomfort
23. Network
24. Chemical sugar
25. Suffix for reg and pop
27. "Oliver Twist" villain
29. Collections of quotes
31. Sayings of Jesus
32. Commoners
34. Queen of Carthage
35. Selling places
37. Close
39. Weather condition
41. Kind of pie
42. Pre-election concerns
44. Loop, in anatomy
45. Good ship et al.
47. Gem workers
49. Opposite of taboo
51. Places
52. McHenry and Raleigh, e.g.
55. N.Z. natives
57. Of the blood
61. "__ than a barrel of . . ."
62. Submit, as a bill
63. Mexican onyx
64. Committed perjury
65. Fare for an Aleut
68. Outside: Prefix
69. Plowed fields: Sp.
71. Badly placed
72. Bunting
74. Virile one
75. Inches along
76. Hoaxers
77. Arabian tambourine
79. Engine part: Abbr.
80. Countrified
81. Delicacy
85. Adored one
87. Go after a mosquito
91. Contract abbr.
92. Restore
93. Certain suit sizes
95. Use the rink
96. Ruin
98. __-Hawley Act of 1930
100. Candied
102. Chemical compound
103. Indian timber tree
105. French relative
106. Goose variety
108. Cloth measure
109. Cake, in France
111. Child's treat, rug's nemesis
114. Actor Omar
115. Harden
116. Headpieces
117. Type of cake
118. Booty of a certain knave
119. Male and female

DOWN

1. Cookies
2. High note
3. Emanation
4. Kill the clock
5. Sinew
6. Merce- naries
7. Seems
8. Law: Fr.
9. Take over
10. Regatta sight
11. Sweets
12. Type of buoy
13. Sweetsop
14. Scotsman's choice
15. Spanish landladies
18. Nanook, e.g.
19. Ready to drive
20. Hindu teacher
21. Turns down a leaf
26. Flying prefix
28. Puts in a lawn
30. Overfed escort
33. Grain container
36. __ Galilee
38. Fountain order
40. Suitable place
43. Cancels, as a space shot
45. Cattle catcher
46. Easy sort of job
48. Heating vessel
50. Lots
52. Indian court staff
53. River of France
54. Create air castles
55. Jumble
56. Elected ones
58. Twin crystal
59. Ara of the sky
60. African game
62. Choose
63. Seers' cards
66. Stronghold of Moab
67. Hills in South Africa
70. Semitic goddess of war
73. Works
75. Namby- pamby one
76. Raisin
78. Ed or Nancy
80. Vocal flourishes
81. Drink mix
82. Maligns
83. Biblical prophet
84. Lily plant
86. Sporty carriage
88. Brown sugars
89. Pacific sights
90. Idiot box, in England
93. Breast- bones
94. Short- changes
97. Port of Brazil
99. Jupiter's path
101. Actor Bracken
104. Roman emperor
107. Runner-up to Achilles
110. Building planners' org.
112. Continent: Abbr.
113. Before

204 WILD LIFE *By Elmer Toro*

ACROSS

1. Alas, to Caesar
4. Kingdom of old
8. Feigns
12. Building part
15. Alligator, for one
19. Stopover place
20. Heraldic band
21. Saguaros
23. Old car
24. Celestial handle
25. Blake's vision
30. Afghan or Thai
31. Employs
32. Old Dutch measure
33. Kind of puss
34. Eye part
35. Genesis name
37. Skirt
38. Pays, as the bill
42. Start of a certain recipe
49. Dallas campus
50. Towel mark
51. "... over all the universe in __"
52. Banking abbr.
53. Letter
56. Thy: Fr.
57. Church vessel
58. Devoured
59. Ship ropes
60. "Cry 'Havoc!' __"
65. Rake
66. Psyche parts
67. Fluids
68. Theater sign
69. Behold: Lat.
70. Wind device
72. __ glance
73. Inlet
74. Boone
77. Wrens' preying place
84. Draft initials
85. Before la
86. Head sign
87. "__, gentlemen"
88. Gambling pieces
89. Bellow's "Seize the __"
90. Stage item
92. Fine, to astronauts
93. Cupid
94. Bye-bye, blackbird?
102. Jargon
103. "... dreary ev'rywhere __"
104. Is in debt
105. Hero of "Exodus"
106. Noises: Abbr.
107. Ocean: Abbr.
108. Reaches
109. Solar deity
110. Shipping abbr.
111. Parlor-based line
119. Shaw
120. Chemical suffixes
121. Near, in France
122. O'Neill daughter
125. Ranges: Abbr.
128. Electrical unit
129. Wings
131. Small cases
132. Words of an oyster fancier
139. Napoleonic victory site
140. Former Chinese leader
141. Waldheim's predecessor
142. Tennyson poem
143. Right turn
144. Before, once
145. Assn.
146. Wife of Osiris
147. "Leda and the __"
148. Not jrs.

DOWN

1. Essential
2. Cordial flavor
3. Fire or jet
4. September time
5. Crumb
6. Miss MacGraw
7. Infatuation
8. Land measure
9. Conveyances
10. Rival of 49 Across
11. Tests to the limit
12. Sea bird
13. Body movers
14. Wolf
15. __ gloves
16. Part of G.B.
17. Tree
18. Kind of race
22. __ out
26. Facile
27. Early slave
28. Copier
29. Bridge word
35. Cupid's mate
36. Make __ about (complain)
37. Moon crater
39. Indic language
40. Pigment
41. N.C.O.'s
43. Villa name
44. Forcible blows
45. Bedouin home
46. Ending
47. Claire and Pleine
48. Contrary
53. English poet and family
54. Arden et al.
55. Elicits
57. Castro
58. "Be __ and ..."
59. Brace
61. Ogle
62. Food fish
63. This, in Ponce
64. Bind with ropes
70. Like Mount Everest
71. Auto org.
72. Total
73. Gypsy man
74. Carnera et al.
75. Harmony
76. "__ a small hotel ..."
78. French state
79. Vast, in poems
80. Soup: Sp.
81. Jackets
82. Winged Victory
83. Dutch town
89. Morse unit
90. Light units
91. Look for a new goal
92. Concerning
94. Arabian peninsula
95. Dark
96. Ule or banyan
97. Ayes and nays
98. Pitcher
99. Pierre's cow
100. N.Y. Indians
101. Moroccan
102. Home, in Toledo
109. Garden City college
112. Stupid one
113. Hebrew letter
114. Word for krypton
115. Bright fish
116. Walks on
117. Writer Pierre
118. Gig and Brigham
123. Niamey's river
124. Longears
126. Sub captn.
127. Alioth, e.g.
129. Fire god
130. Vessels of W.W. II
131. John, in Wales
132. Stout cousin
133. Neighbor of Den.
134. Dental degree
135. Whole __
136. Plane pilots' abt.
137. Oath
138. Epoch

205 TWISTED THOUGHTS *By Anthony Morse*

ACROSS

1. Bernhardt
6. River areas
12. Kitchen staple
17. Put in the oven
21. Planet
22. Miss Stritch
23. Peter of films
24. Hebrew ancestor
25. Zero
26. Give cash for political support
28. With 25 Across, cars, maybe
29. Inlet
30. Madrid museum
32. Doll up
33. Three in one
35. Typewriter part
36. Fruit
37. Colored
38. Jerked with a twist
40. Casks
41. Dead end
45. More concise
46. Pullman sections
49. Egg cells
50. Clobbered
51. Habits
52. Landlord's concerns
53. Intimidates
54. Everything: Ger.
55. Trainee
56. Japanese natives
57. Allotted amount
58. Covers
59. Kind of pusher
61. __ mecum
62. Absorbent
63. Chinese pagoda
64. Shah takes French leave
66. Takes a risk
67. Kind of bête
69. Gang weapon
70. Zenana
71. Made music in Dundee
73. Legatee who has children
78. Doctors' org.
81. Stars of Wash. Zoo
82. Eve's opposite
83. Encore
84. Highlander
85. Zeal
86. Old Egyptian city
87. Kind of story
88. Hungarian musician
89. Orator's spot
90. Biblical weeds
91. Dazzling
93. Sea painting
94. Greek letter
95. Cats, dogs, etc.
97. Show time
98. Rational
100. Fix
101. Ally
102. Miseries
103. Plums
105. Auks
106. Lissome
109. Aberdeen lad
110. Beam
111. Tokyo's old name
114. Cover
115. Latest hit tune
119. Côte __
121. Israeli port
122. Part of a meet
123. Chilean arborvitae
124. Consent to
125. Look after
126. Heredity units
127. Revenue agents
128. Irish poet

DOWN

1. Boom
2. His: Fr.
3. Wrinkle
4. Sports: Abbr.
5. Portable cooking units
6. Pro or con man
7. Kept out of the way
8. "__, Macduff"
9. Suggestion
10. Collection of notes
11. Boas
12. Fast train
13. Comes in second
14. African city
15. Receptacle
16. Updates a fashion
17. "Woe __ me"
18. Arab father
19. Perceptive
20. Gaelic
27. Debris
31. Gathered leaves
34. Colors
35. Capsules
36. Clean
37. Conduits
38. Poetic Muse
39. Might Geronimo?
40. Third, to Caesar
41. Craft
42. Seeder
43. Requite
44. Social divisions
45. Blue glass
46. First volume
47. Trojan V.I.P.
48. Accommodates
51. Farm sounds
53. Together
55. Drilled
56. Incarnation
57. Extra effort
59. Earth goddess
60. Wankel, e.g.
62. View
64. Hairy
65. Gibbon
66. Jackal's cry
68. Church lists
71. Suit
72. Black-belt sport
73. Biblical mount
74. Irregular
75. Firecracker
76. Armadillos
77. Put faith in
79. Pessimist
80. Up __
82. Blackbird
84. Finches
86. Posts
88. __ Saint
90. Furniture support
91. Arlen opus
92. Glass
93. __ Antoinette
95. Awning
96. Lifeless
97. Yorkshire area
99. Like a river bottom
101. Skip about
103. French river
104. Elevators
105. Firehouse sound
106. Beat it!
107. __ di petto
108. Work for
109. Good, in Vichy
111. Bible book
112. Musical pair
113. Malachite, etc.
116. Blvd.
117. High note
118. Roman statute
120. Stone or iron

206 RACKET-BUSTING By A.J. Santora

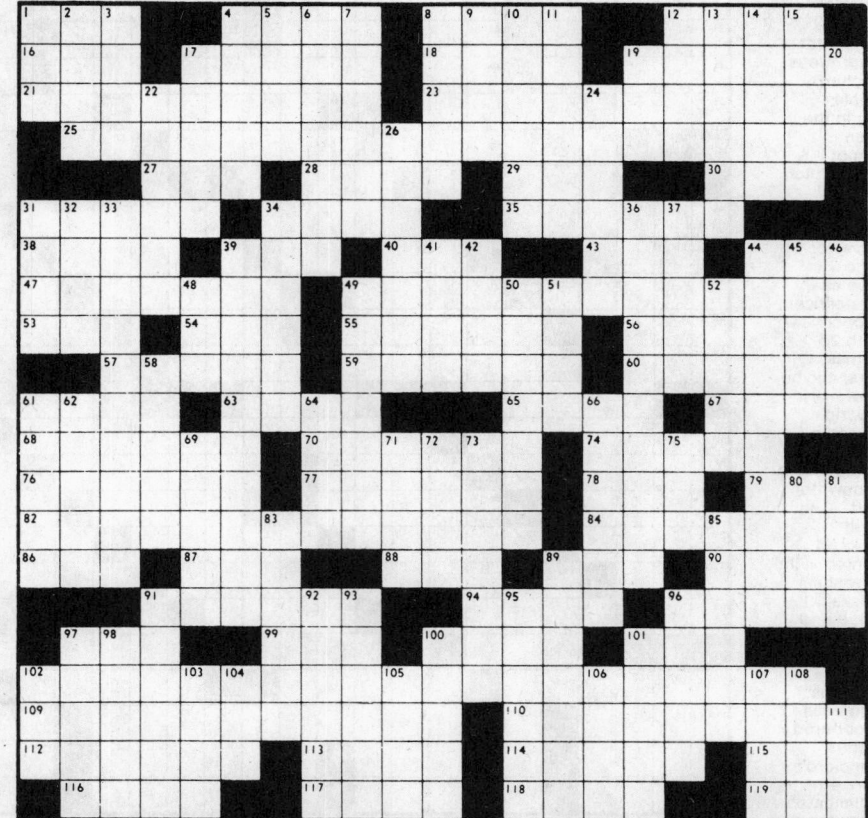

ACROSS

1. West Coast Indian
4. Loose cloak
8. Intros to holidays
12. Kimono
16. High note
17. "She's only a dream"
18. Ironwood
19. "The Iceman __"
21. Concerning a sports pairing
23. Plaudits for Arthur
25. Certain senior citizen
27. Pipe joint
28. Red and Black
29. Ending for hero
30. Ocean: Abbr.
31. Blueprints
34. Civil wrong
35. Creme de __
38. Hearing __
39. Cupid
40. Faucet
43. Musical syllables
44. New Deal letters
47. Brutes
49. Smelling victory
53. Time period
54. U.S.A., to the French
55. Do a brake job
56. Capri allure
57. Village on the Hudson
59. Threatening words
60. Gimpy one
61. "__ Smile Be Your . . ."
63. Bridge position
65. Butternut
67. Gaelic
68. Up __ (aroused)
70. __ deadline
74. Dome player
76. Relief pitcher Tug
77. Showed one's heels to
78. Batter's stat.
79. Overweight
82. Last straw
84. Port of Mexico
86. "__, Virginia, there is . . ."
87. Elected, in Paris
88. Show drowsiness
89. Her, in Berlin
90. __ impasse
91. Depress
94. Roman historian
96. Methods: Abbr.
97. Hiatus
99. Altar words
100. Actress Rowlands
101. Egg __ yong
102. Tennis player's protection
109. Tennis match of sorts
110. Certain strokes
112. Removed
113. Chemical endings
114. Running tracks
115. Make lace
116. Parties
117. __ of guns
118. Spanish artist
119. Limit, to some

DOWN

1. "Rings on __ fingers . . ."
2. Margarine
3. Onetime San Diego quarterback
4. Plot
5. __ lang syne
6. Victimizes
7. Less demanding
8. Part of 54 Across
9. Holding device
10. Kind of humor
11. Pigment
12. Kanga and friends
13. U.S. Indians
14. Stupefy
15. Merman
17. Slow periods
19. Coins: Abbr.
20. "__ my man"
22. City in Denmark
24. Pancho's nap
26. More dapper
31. Yonkers event
32. Fibber
33. In and out points
34. Japanese leader
36. Where matches develop
37. Douay Bible name
39. Dealer's choice
41. Salt tree
42. Silvers
44. Tennis earnings
45. Memory routines
46. Preceding, old style
48. __ culpa
49. Did a profile on
50. Kind of coffee
51. __-do-well
52. Promising one
58. Australian river
61. Full of branches
62. Ink for la plume
64. Air pollution
66. Uninhibited
69. "Let's __ Deal"
71. English town
72. Music group
73. __ and Young
75. Tiny one
80. Skin __
81. Weights
83. X-rated film feature
85. Promotional bribe
89. Russian city
91. Home for Leonidas
92. Roman officials
93. Emphatic refusal
95. Bewildered
96. Class men
97. Recede
98. Blow __
100. Conjecture
101. "I __ song coming on"
102. Sgt.
103. U.S. Indians
104. Law degree
105. Writer Hedin
106. Spiny lobster
107. Insects
108. Neighbor of Mont.
111. Messy place

207 CHRISTMAS LINES By Anne Fox

ACROSS

1. Roaring, for one
5. Former members
11. Barring
15. Stinger
19. Russian city
20. Love dosage
21. Last word of the Bible
22. Outside: Prefix
23. Pool
24. Actor Omar
25. Intellect
26. Beam
27. Wisconsin city
29. Monk
31. Ornate description
33. O.T. book
34. Existed
37. Kind of flight
39. Words from a Polish carol
47. Kind of glass
48. Composer of "Salome"
49. Fervor
50. Desserts
51. Advance
53. Lettuce
54. In the direction of
56. Word with in or out
57. Nahuatl
59. Florida city, familiarly
61. Capitol feature
63. Word with in or out
64. Province of Italy
66. Antiquity, in poems
68. French city
70. "Sleep __"
73. Foster
76. Type of job
77. Throat soother
78. "Exodus" hero
79. Paint thinner, for short
81. German city
83. N.M. flower
87. Lombardi of football
89. Full of prickles
91. Chicago time
93. Chase flies
94. Othello's ensign
95. King or Alda
96. Was a deputy for
99. Cruise port
100. Words by Charles Wesley
104. Magniloquent
105. __ Paul
106. Govt. agency
107. Theatrical goal
111. Note
113. Secretly
117. Vague
118. City on the Arno
120. Big Ten team
123. Sully
124. S.A. country
125. With it
126. "__ not into . . ."
127. Yaks
128. Sunrise
129. Chill
130. Moola
131. Son of Isaac

DOWN

1. Item with teeth
2. Space
3. Wassail spirit
4. Polite word
5. Lhasa __
6. German carol
7. Miss Hagen
8. Indian chief
9. Short fiber
10. Words from "Silent Night"
11. Miss Eggar
12. Cher __
13. Words by J.F. Wade
14. Farthest
15. Dickens' Silas
16. Measure
17. Bustle
18. Trot
28. French social affairs
30. Low
32. Prone
35. "__ per aspera"
36. Dallas campus
38. Fragment: Var.
39. That: Fr.
40. "Hear ye!"
41. Catchall abbr.
42. This: Sp.
43. Military address
44. Flora and fauna
45. "Vive __!"
46. N.J. county
52. Resign
55. Place for a wish
56. Acey-__
58. Patron saint of Denmark
60. Sky Peacock
62. Trench
65. Dewey's way
67. Tints
69. Steadies
71. Norse writing
72. Pill for hypochondriacs
73. Ship science: Abbr.
74. Asian sheep
75. Beatle
80. Brooklyn institute
82. Indian groom
84. Certain tree
85. Raise
86. Eager
88. Heart
90. Cruel
92. Pitch
95. Belladonna extract
97. Brace
98. Cut
101. Hebrew letter
102. Direction
103. Large U.S. foundation
107. Noah's eldest
108. Mexican sandwich
109. Côte d'__
110. Actor Robert
112. Spread
114. Not final, in law
115. Instrument
116. Japanese village
119. Trifle
121. Roman god
122. Cyprinoid fish

208 LAMENT ON JAN. 1, 1973

By Frances Hansen

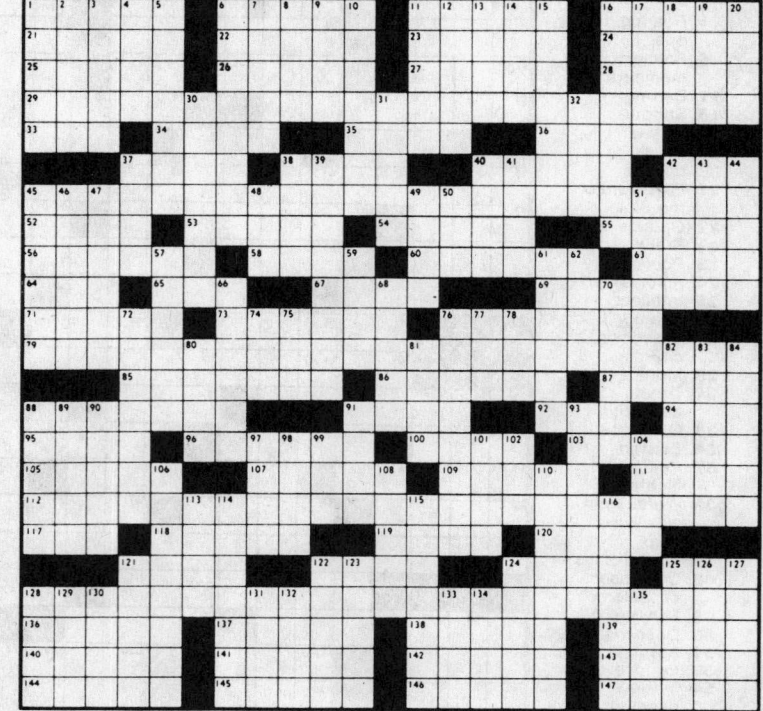

ACROSS

1. Driver or ball
6. Chaplin role
11. Cause to blush
16. Weapon for Junior
21. Victorian shade
22. Where Thales taught
23. __ Minh
24. Run off
25. Move in the best circles
26. Sturdy cloth
27. Squelch
28. All even
29. Verse, with 45, 79, 112 and 128 Across
33. See 4 Down
34. Yoked beasts
35. French department
36. Fat
37. Kind of seaman: Abbr.
38. Code word for A
40. Betting choice
42. Intention
45. More of verse
52. Jewish month
53. "__ a Nightingale"
54. Elevate
55. Popular wrap
56. Delay
58. Prate, in India
60. Of a mountain range
63. Normandy town
64. "Now I __ me down . . ."
65. Poetic contraction
67. Frosh's home
69. Hide __ (vestige of)
71. States: Fr.
73. Melodic
76. Benefited
79. More of verse
85. ". . . a large __ his stew"
86. Jack the Ripper, e.g.
87. "__ and a day"
88. Encroach
91. Small amount
92. Nicely put
94. Dutch coin: Abbr.
95. Mrs. Helmer
96. Five-legged calf, e.g.
100. Master or force
103. Second try on a movie shot
105. Horner's pie filling
107. "__ a drink!"
109. After "Over"
111. Polynesian deity
112. More of verse
117. Ship rope
118. Separated
119. Antimacassar
120. Adjust the radio
121. Aid in crime
122. Tubs
124. "Darling, je vous __ beaucoup . . ."
125. Crackerjack
128. End of verse
136. Commonplace
137. Image: Prefix
138. Porous coral
139. Sully
140. Minoan island
141. Kitchen tool
142. Small finch
143. Kind of beaver
144. Knocks for a loop
145. Well-known Kat
146. What-do-you-call-it
147. Tedious

DOWN

1. Whopped
2. Mother of chickens
3. 100 kopecks
4. With 33 Across, whammy
5. Deck swabbers
6. Giggled
7. Stubble field
8. Indigo
9. Join the crowd
10. Dispose of by fraud
11. Bret Harte character
12. Western capital
13. Play part
14. Ammo
15. Intimates
16. Will items
17. Cornflower
18. Enter
19. Capable of
20. __-ce pas?
30. Blow one's top
31. Clean the slate
32. Vallee
37. Taj Mahal site
38. Aleutian isle
39. Start of "Lonesome Road"
40. Maintained
41. Heraldry word
42. Artery
43. Early dwellers south of Rome
44. Asia or Ursa
45. Globetrotters' base
46. Think on
47. Temple dances of India
48. After Jan.
49. Oral
50. Heflin
51. Monday, to housewives
57. __ one's laurels
59. Stockings
61. Grieg girl
62. __ contendere
66. Like some eyebrows
68. Moore's Lalla
70. Kickback
72. Southern tourist trail
74. Arikara
75. "__ had my way. . ."
76. In a dither
77. Radio-wave rating: Abbr.
78. Had a bite
80. Writer Victor
81. One
82. Nullify
83. Kind of apartment
84. Trial
88. Computer data
89. Miss Malone
90. Nice Nelly
91. Letters
93. Stanley's word
97. Fashion name
98. Sign in a way: Abbr.
99. Before Aviv
101. One-hoss vehicle
102. London Gardens
104. Vapid
106. Metallic art pieces
108. Pixilated
110. Shy
113. Cast forth, as lava
114. St. or Henry
115. Wrong for the part
116. Dance
121. "__ worse than death"
122. Lupe of the flicks
123. Critic-writer Cleveland
124. Beaming broadly
125. Friend on the rancho
126. Candy shapes
127. Foyer
128. Start of a learning song
129. Honshu city
130. Don Juan's mother
131. Fragrance
132. Hartebeest
133. Slangy assent
134. "Neither you __ "
135. Basin of Germany

209 NOMENCLATURE By Edward J. O'Brien

ACROSS

1. Prefix for plasm
5. Pundit
10. Adjective endings
14. Guevara
17. Fright: Fr.
20. In front
21. Campus sports org.
22. Type of lift or mail
23. Fix
24. Chevalier song subject
25. Intaglios
27. German coin
29. Great deal
30. "_ lifeboats!"
31. Map abbrs.
32. Desuetude
34. Campers
35. Epithet for a Cardinal star
38. Hwys.
42. Big _
45. ". . . met a _"
46. Mischa or Leopold
47. Hatchery sounds
49. Mistake
50. Law degrees
51. By, in Spain
52. Register
54. Suffix with Jud and And
55. Small pin
57. Goddess of plenty
58. Renaissance composer
59. Math abbr.
60. Instance, in Paris
61. School org.
64. Traffic warning
65. B'way letters
66. Physics ratio
68. Bird of prey
69. Comparative suffixes
70. Poet's word
71. All: Prefix
72. Friend: Scot.
73. Ford or Kovacs
75. Dew: Lat.
76. Caen's river
78. For each
79. Relative of a wino
80. Seek damages
81. U.S. inventor
83. Poetry
85. Shore fare
87. Toward the mouth
88. "Away in a _"
90. Glass sections
91. Jaunty
92. N.H. city
94. "I'd rather see _ than hear one"
96. Hit _ note
97. Lateral measure: Abbr.
100. The Caped Crusader
103. Laughing or natural
105. More vexatious
107. Sanctuary fixture
108. Out of _
110. Kind of soup
111. Salad item
112. In _
113. Colonel's bird
114. Upstages
115. Gnaw
116. Timid, to some Britons
117. Surfeits
118. Dec. 24 word

DOWN

1. Wyatt et al.
2. Riven
3. Finish lines
4. Medit. port
5. Decline
6. "Seek ye the Lord _ may . . ."
7. Gas: Prefix
8. Ale base
9. Psyche parts
10. Inciter, old style
11. _ of cigarettes
12. Perfect-game pitcher
13. Relish
14. List
15. Kind of brow
16. Gaelic
18. ICBM
19. Variant of Helen
26. Set up
28. Bonnie or Clyde
30. Byron poem
33. Ornate desks
34. Deck
35. Political party: Abbr.
36. Dutch town
37. Humorist S.J.
39. R.R. car
40. Sheep tic
41. Grads-to-be
42. Place next to
43. They, e.g.
44. Samuel D. Riddle's pride
48. Huge: Fr.
53. Center, for one
55. "The _ ass" (Mr. Bumble)
56. Irish Sea body
60. Swindler
62. _-loup
63. Levy
67. Essayist Ralph Waldo
74. Laughing-stocks: Fr.
77. Bureaucracy
81. Plane ride
82. Erie cargo
83. Aperitif
84. Ref. work
86. Row
88. Medusa's slayer
89. Terrifying
92. Die, in Rome
93. Malay sirs
95. Detroit product
97. Golf _
98. River-mouth area
99. Braid
100. Fraternal soc.
101. "Casta Diva," e.g.
102. Joust
103. Score
104. Famed ship
106. Short blast
108. Time unit: Abbr.
109. French possessive

210 SPOT ANNOUNCEMENTS

By William Lutwiniak

ACROSS

1. Almanach name
6. Delineate
10. Advertise
14. I know: Lat.
18. Golf-match standing
19. Wield anew
20. Leave off
21. Pay out
22. EL
25. Calico
26. Dudgeons
27. Winged
28. Wrinkles
29. Beyond: Prefix
30. Gossamer
31. Haciendas
32. U.S. writer
33. Superfluity
36. Helm position
37. Of pitch
38. Express
39. Feeling guilty
41. OA
46. In __ (owing)
47. Fonda and Eyre
48. Diminutive endings
49. Douglas, for one
50. Zeroed in
51. Kinswomen
52. Locality
54. Exempt
56. Olympian
57. __ account
58. Spar
59. Scheduled
60. Cincinnati player
61. NE
64. Informs
65. Geodesic __
67. Sensory stimuli
68. Knock down
69. Sizing liquid
70. HE
74. Nabokov novel
77. Culminations
78. Songbirds
79. Lots
80. Man of Dundee
81. Cheers for
82. Cargoes
83. Says is so
85. Sales try
86. Amiss
87. Noun ending
88. Word with said or thought
89. Civil
90. AVI
95. Puff up
96. Fabric
97. Have __ (worry)
98. Glockenspiel unit
99. Integers: Abbr.
100. Cleans up
101. Capelet
102. Confronts
103. Perform
104. Explosive, for short
105. Paddock papas
106. Place for a Met
110. See 3 Down
111. EN
114. Martin Van __
115. Exeunt __
116. Rare family member
117. __ con pollo
118. Did the same
119. Rude one
120. N.C.O.'s
121. Twice-told

DOWN

1. Mongolian expanse
2. __ about
3. Cozy twosome, with 110 Across
4. Nissens
5. G.I. mail drop
6. Malign
7. Like a country lane
8. Arthur of tennis
9. Word for morning hours
10. Sheeting
11. Frolics
12. Operates
13. Colloid
14. Pitchman
15. AC
16. __ alia
17. Predominant quality
19. Like some oats
20. Not random
21. Elfish one
23. Sent off
24. Makes
29. Courses
30. Eminent
31. Prepares punch cards
32. Muffles
33. Family member
34. On land
35. WHE
37. Color
40. Olympian
41. __ letters
42. __ left field
43. Orchestra member
44. Buenos __
45. Scott
47. Roman goddess
51. Connectives
52. Chair feature
53. Kind of stew
54. One-master
55. El __
57. Unusual blokes
58. Bondmen
59. Expand
61. Voices
62. Recorded
63. Tasmanian pines
66. Kiln
68. Marshes
69. U.S. composer
70. __ a kind
71. Zoo denizen, for short
72. Abrasive
73. Rapid rodent
75. Zhivago, e.g.
76. European capital
77. Gator's cousin
80. Window feature
82. Detroit players
83. Blazing
84. Political clout
85. Place for 84 Down
87. Figure of speech
88. Arthurian island
89. Least colorful
91. Gave the party
92. Giants or Jets
93. More unkempt
94. Squirrel fare
95. Dispossessed
98. Peerage members
100. Erect
101. In hoc __ vinces
102. Figure
103. __ au rhum
104. Verne's skipper
105. Well ensconced
106. Spanish painter
107. Olympian
108. Chemical compound
109. Cooper's tool
111. Crop
112. Certain test results
113. Owns

ACROSS

1. __ Bill
6. African gazelle
10. Alfresco site
15. Girl's name
19. Ecstatic feeling
21. One way to get a degree
23. Brain passage of a sort
25. Mouth: Prefix
26. Riches
27. Mort
28. Full of fat
29. Bag, in Madrid
31. Approve
34. Earth pigment: Fr.
37. Kind of verb: Abbr.
38. Baby-sitters
40. Cash in Capetown
41. Marshmallow event
43. River of Congo Republic
45. Keep from
46. Relinquish
47. Heavens: Prefix
48. Curtains for Cleo
49. Ubiquitous quartet
55. Major, in music
56. Nile denizen, for short
57. Spasm
58. Rachmaninoff
59. Mao __-tung
60. Reeds
62. Kind of test
63. Prunes, in Scotland
64. Org.
65. Porter in Mideast
67. Disgorge: Var.
69. Artery: Fr.
72. Chinese wax
73. Ball: Prefix
75. Stipulations
78. Neighbor of Albania
80. Poker move
82. Scottish poet
83. Pile
84. With Street, it's a bank
88. "__ a jolly..."
89. Famous loch
90. French river
91. Keats, for one
92. Symbol of durability
93. Pines and elms
95. Land mass, to French
96. Assured
97. Neighbor of Col.
99. North: Prefix
100. Man of the cloth
102. U.S. sculptor
104. Cat: Prefix
106. Yen
108. Island off Alaska
110. Numerical prefix
111. Extreme accuracy
117. Have __ (know by heart)
118. Survivor of Field's dog-cat fight
119. Early slave
120. Examples
121. Mardi __
122. Makes fruit wine

DOWN

1. Coins of Sonora
2. Unrelated
3. Burlesque
4. Corrida cry
5. Stave, in Scotland
6. Cooked cornmeal
7. "Vive la __"
8. Shoe, for short
9. Daughter of Cadmus
10. Italian tourist city
11. Secure
12. Like some bridegrooms
13. Nigerian
14. Big Ten initials
15. Boredom
16. Guide a ship loosely
17. Was skeptical
18. "__ does it"
20. In __ (confused)
22. Letter
24. Fitted compactly: Abbr.
30. Unusual person
32. Cover, in dice
33. Sluggish
35. Indiscreet
36. __ Park
39. Math term
42. Nursery doctor
44. Plant pest
45. Modern insecticide
46. "Learn to __"
50. Globes
51. Babylonian sun god
52. Whale
53. Thwarts
54. English composer
61. Bundle
64. Defective: Prefix
66. Touched down
67. Nuance
68. Famous Quaker
69. Horsetail tree
70. Certain Southerners
71. TV-movie comic
72. Does D.A. duty
74. Hayden and Adler
75. Sign
76. Pretense
77. Barracuda
79. Ivy, in Italy
81. Irregular
85. French river
86. Author Ambler
87. Revise
94. Minute grooves
95. Kind of code
96. Edible plant
98. Stage, in Berlin
101. U.S. playwright
103. Points
104. French friend
105. Arikara
107. Math units: Abbr.
109. City on the Dnieper
112. College degree
113. Exclamation
114. Coat part: Abbr.
115. __ se
116. Indian title

212 NAMING NAMES By Tanaquil Le Clercq

ACROSS

1. Called in a way
6. Loom heddles
10. Waist wear
14. Balzac's Cousin
19. Harangued
21. "Un __ in Maschera"
22. Capable of
23. Son of Jacob
24. Hot fare
25. Umbrage
27. British guns
28. Babe Ruth
30. Of otters
32. Draft agency
33. So, to Scots
34. Twitching
35. In a straight course
36. Actor Sal
38. Field: Lat.
40. Hunt and peck
41. Swedish river
44. Ann Sheridan
47. April initials
48. Boo-boo
49. Lament
50. Inlets
51. Italian family
53. Himalayan animals
54. Small case
55. Long poem
57. Concert halls
58. Fairy queen
59. Service org.
60. U.S. Indian
61. Late rock star et al.
63. Curl one's lip
65. Squint, in England
66. "In __ and out . . ."
68. Give the __ (oust)
70. Gershwin
71. Timetables, for short
72. Jack Armstrong
77. Father: Prefix
80. Mauna __
81. Tizzy
82. Conductor Ansermet
85. Tennis star
86. Place for Miss Hellman's toys
88. Loathes
91. Frigate bird
93. French lady
94. Blackbirds' milieu
95. Stoneware: Fr.
97. Hues
98. Stage billing
99. Broke down a sentence
101. Icelandic measure
102. N.Z. pine
103. Lizard
104. Raise
105. __-Magnon
106. Sousa
110. Ukraine body
111. Critic Downes
112. House part
113. Remove, in law: Var.
114. __ wreath
116. Scottish alder
117. French painter
118. Tub
121. Handbill
123. John Barrymore
129. Tapestry
130. Ways to nowhere
132. Musk ox
133. Philosopher Benedetto
134. Deserve
135. "Tiny __"
136. Soften
137. Helen and Citizen
138. Tear
139. Verne skipper
140. Flowers

DOWN

1. Paper sizes
2. Irish cries
3. Old Maid and charades, e.g.
4. Greek letters
5. Snare's partner
6. City of France
7. Besides
8. Hebrew letter
9. Minotaur or dragon, e.g.
10. Common shrub
11. Egyptian goddess
12. Depot: Abbr.
13. Trumpeter Oran Page
14. Cover the turkey
15. Tarragon
16. Wellington
17. Vols' state
18. Gaelic
20. Roosevelt name
21. Undergarment
26. Did a baton routine
29. Abound
31. French article
35. Instrument for Orpheus
36. Warm-sea fish
37. Grand Ole events
38. Indian Ocean island
39. Soldiers
40. Ill-starred ship
42. Pestered
43. Certain crimes
44. Lone Ranger's sidekick
45. Lake Indian
46. Ant home
48. "__ Ballads"
49. My, in Milan
52. French possessive
53. Golf score
55. Dies __
56. Adenauer
57. Reveals, old style
58. Most sordid
61. N.Z. bird
62. Southern fare
64. Epoch
65. Kind of terrier
67. Be, in France
69. Penna. city
71. "__ and Lovers"
73. Realty unit
74. Napoleon II
75. "__ for a change"
76. Legendary Irish king
77. Spoil
78. Eritrean city
79. Von __ to Snoopy
83. Kind of protest
84. Nasal speech
86. Abet's partner
87. Dernier __
89. Cotton cloth
90. Harden
92. Refuge
94. Kind of peeve
96. Recorded
98. Kind of flint
100. Capone
101. Seed cover
102. Gun the motor
103. Omit
105. Dish sound
107. Word game
108. Loud sound
109. Type of movie
111. Grecian-urn tribute
115. German girls' names
116. Lend __ (help)
118. Music makers, for short
119. "I want to be __"
120. Exams
121. Want
122. __ Pater, old astrologer
123. Sea bird
124. Anger
125. Biblical oasis
126. Small dog
127. Lao-__
128. Silk thread
131. Scottish explorer

213 BRAVING THE ELEMENTS By Keith Blake

ACROSS

1. Poplar
6. Astrologers' readings
13. Leave off
18. Kind of academy
19. Going in one direction
20. Irish savant
22. American bible
25. Biddy
26. Age
27. Urge
28. Garden
29. Polite word: Abbr.
31. Son of Gad
32. Embellish
33. Athirst
35. Cry of disgust
36. Encountered
38. Start of a letter
41. Florida Key
42. Elegy man
43. Word for the Eddie Cantors
44. Greencastle campus
45. Adjust, as a watch
47. Supply
48. Heir
49. Leaving
50. F.D.R. cabinet member
51. Gluey mud
53. Curve
54. Reducing
57. Southern hero
58. Turn over
60. Man with a barometer
62. Northern climate listings
67. Oblivion
68. P.G.A. man
69. Cooler
70. Stir
73. Violin opening
75. Movable feast
77. Same: Lat. abbr.
78. Mosque tower
80. "When it __ pours"
82. Adams and Q. Public
84. Publisher
85. Tipsy
86. Jujitsu form
87. Oak, in France
88. Lowell or Dickinson
89. Pampered
92. Latin-text

word
93. Ruin, old style
94. Miffed
95. U.N. agency
96. Angeles or Gatos
97. Gray: Prefix
98. New Guinea port
101. Greek cross
102. Leo's place
103. Source of homey wisdom
109. Fanny Brice role
110. Envelop
111. P.I. island
112. Hide away
113. Endowed with land
114. Barnyard name

DOWN

1. Flower part
2. Eastern tree
3. Venus, for one
4. Thai language
5. Building wing
9. Flageolet
7. __ off (intermittent)
8. Movie V.I.P.
9. "__ memory serves"
10. Sheltered
11. Trapped
12. Cloth samples: Abbr.
13. Weather word
14. Mr. Gantry
15. Bates or Arkin
16. Blas or Diego
17. Vanish
21. Bucolic poems
23. Revered one
24. Shield
30. "Uncle Tom" author et al.
32. Insect
34. Beasts of burden
35. Family man
37. Anger
38. Phone-booth art
39. Resentful one
40. Straighten
41. Photo captions
43. Theater sign
44. Earth goddess
45. Mouth part
46. Conductor Rapee
47. Random criticism
48. "When I ope my __ no dogs bark!"
50. Conversation staple
52. Nile people
55. Neighbor of Md.
56. Like some northern ports
59. "__ Rheingold"
61. Wire: Abbr.
62. Mail privileges
63. Betsy and family
64. Home for __
65. Of the dawn
66. Norms: Abbr.
68. Sorrow, in Paris
70. Friendly
71. Kitchen aids
72. "... praise depends __"
74. Made a boo-boo
76. Container
79. Relative
81. Concerns of traffic police
82. Hardy

character
83. Kind of number
85. Column style
86. Large vessel
88. Do a shoe job
89. Took on fuel
90. Chooses
91. Party animal
93. Branches
94. Like some bread
97. Malaysian canoe
99. Smell __
100. Old Norse work
104. Away, in Scotland
105. Home: Abbr.
106. Ballistics abbr.
107. Vestment
108. Recent: Prefix

214 PLAYING GAMES
By John C. Laflin

ACROSS

1. Stadium vendor's item
6. Turkish monkeys
11. Likely
16. In present condition
20. Soleil
21. Relative of moola
22. Composer Franz
23. Italian boy's name
24. Reconcile
25. Engages in
26. Notions
27. Aware of
28. Controversial issue
31. Right's partner
32. Singer Siepi
33. Hawaiian port
34. Regatta place
35. Once-a-week menace
40. Devastate
42. Capital of Tarn
43. Roof worker
45. Actor Dullea
46. Monk's title
49. Dalmatian
54. Scorecard listing
56. Thwarted
58. Bristle
59. Insect part
61. Aug. 1 fete
63. Contour: Fr.
64. Baseball throw
65. Non compos __
67. Curves
69. One of a global five
70. Exerts leverage: Var.
72. Enoch or Elizabeth
75. Barren area
77. Leaves home and hearth
82. Phone
83. Soviet marshal of W.W. II
84. Italian composer
87. Like a solid
90. Hillside
92. Lament
95. Number in a minyan
96. Some golf tourneys
97. Of deserts
100. Like some fans
101. Half an African group
102. Like old roofs
105. Lawrence's milieu
107. July opponents
109. Thus: Sp.
110. Barn sounds
112. Items on a Paris menu
114. __ fixe
115. Foul smelling
118. Like some typed mss.
123. Famous Yankee
125. Bone: Prefix
127. Of the past month
128. "And Phoebus 'gins __"
129. Maneuver
136. Ball club
137. River in Hades
138. Horse color
139. Aforesaid
140. Safecracker
141. Giggle
142. Tail __ (also-rans)
143. Harsh
144. Too
145. Boxing decisions
146. Tobacco and Burma
147. Israeli dances

DOWN

1. To-do
2. Make over
3. Soviet sea
4. Words for a tough task
5. Equipped, in England
6. French table wine
7. Stag's pride
8. Offshore hazard
9. Irish cry
10. Middling
11. Excuse
12. Bike parts
13. Pope's "The Rape of __"
14. Afrikaans
15. __ concern
16. Marching formation
17. __ doghouse
18. Like a chimney flue
21. Dental problem
29. Bible book: Abbr.
30. "__ a Horse"
31. Social whirls
34. Eight, in Tours
35. Hare, vis-à-vis tortoise
36. African women
37. Evil
38. Let sink
39. Heater
41. Faroe winds
42. Signature of Li'l Abner's creator
44. Jamaica and bay
47. Hebrew weight
48. Arabian gulf
50. Poetic figure of speech
51. Ruins
52. Surgeon's forte: Abbr.
53. Received
55. Jewish festival
57. Parrots
60. Body of expatriate Jews
62. O'Casey
66. Rialto sign
68. Pronoun
71. Bean feature
73. Bogart role
74. W.W. II theater
76. Put up money __ (post bond)
78. Metric weights: Abbr.
79. Owl, in Berlin
80. Beak
81. Like a bed at times
85. Approached
86. Not idle
87. __ Nostra
88. Asian tree
89. Early stages
91. Private: Abbr.
93. Lamb's lament
94. Debt: Abbr.
98. Steel beam
99. Roman 103
103. Durante asset
104. Slimy stuff
106. Mountain
108. Familiar Latin song
111. __ path for
113. Mumbled one's words
116. Lake near Utica
117. Avoid
119. Cockney's aides
120. Small-runway planes
121. Greek letters
122. Jewish benediction
123. "There is __ slip . . ."
124. Arabian gazelle
126. Snow gear: Var.
129. Mock
130. French river
131. Samoan council
132. Village of Russia
133. Roman road
134. Other, in Spain
135. Cribbage jacks
137. Inc., in England

215 VARIABLES By Jack Luzzatto

ACROSS

1. Served secretly
6. Card games
13. Forcing house
19. Dark-room activity
20. Part of TNT
21. Reluctant
22. Pregame practice
23. Device that measures current
24. Mental image
25. Island near Quemoy
26. Trimming implement
28. Speed-trap device
30. Exist
31. Torme
32. Sun: Prefix
33. Redeemer
35. Whirring sound: Var.
36. High-level brat
39. Chutzpah
40. Becomes
41. Any new hot seller
43. South American
45. Wine glasses
48. Jail
50. Ice grabbers
52. Throbbing
53. Card game
54. Like Wagner's output
57. Pert cap
58. Dutch specialty
59. Humiliate
60. Daughter of Loki
61. Caen's river
62. Poor solace
64. Beautiful girl
65. Headland
66. Digging animals
67. Mass. campus
68. French river
69. In a thick-headed way
71. Kind of tax
72. Garage-shelf item
73. Lyric poem
74. Not sterilized
76. Weakest
77. Occupation
79. Arctic dangers
81. Old flames
83. Upholstered piece
85. Gets ready to sound off
89. Schoolgirl
90. Swaggers
92. Horse opera
93. Charge
94. Heart
95. Followers of dogs
96. Aircraft shed
98. Pole or Serb
99. Star, in Paris
101. Interval of delay
103. New Orleans campus
105. Unit of doubt
106. Gormandized
107. Slick paint
108. Passover feasts
109. Released claim to
110. Widow's legacy

DOWN

1. Maker of joints
2. Parlay betting system
3. "I'll See You __ Dreams"
4. Old French coin
5. Pillage
6. Cotton fabric
7. Run-of-the-mill viragos
8. Egyptian dancing girl
9. Sorry fellows
10. New Year in Viet Nam
11. Drain of pep
12. Harem
13. Ethiopian city
14. Finished
15. Private eye
16. Getting the party rolling
17. Vivacity
18. Checks
19. Overwhelm
27. Land areas: Var.
29. Cute girl
32. Healthiest
34. Spry
35. Hog family
37. Australian thicket
38. Unaccented
40. Hold supplies
42. Buck-passing item
44. Nuclear trial
45. Hollywood film family
46. Work
47. Makes time
49. Science-fiction figures
51. Jagged range
53. Hornless cows
55. Golf scores
56. Customer
58. Charge at the bridge
59. Loving
62. Marked for Identification
63. Stubborn
64. Suavity
66. The original Goldfinger?
68. Long and narrow
70. Pondered
71. No-fat man
72. Added an external section
75. Gushing
76. Famed sculpture
78. East, in Spain
80. Puffed oneself up
81. Approach
82. Calm down
84. Speaker with panache
86. On fire
87. Thinner
88. Without a slant
90. Scads
91. Body of Islamic law: Var.
95. Wine fermenting agent
97. Sorry cry
98. Side dish
100. Carplike fish
102. Hebrew letter
104. One, in Spain

DAFFY EDIBLES By Arnold Moss

ACROSS

1. Sydney soldier
6. Apples
11. Some Scouts
15. Fabric
20. Cheese
21. Vigilant
22. Ali's faith
24. Ara of the sky
25. Songwriter Harold
26. Shakespearean role
27. Met diva Lucine
28. "__ man put asunder"
29. Give Rose a buzz
31. Icy stares
33. Basic nature
34. Hawaiian hawks
35. Soho thankyous
38. "Right you __!"
39. Speech part: Abbr.
40. Gold standard
49. Wax ointment
53. Popular book
54. Eastern nurse
55. Ancient Mariner's cry
56. Ladies of Spain: Abbr.
58. Type of theater
59. In abeyance
60. Tell an old joke
64. Relatives of rtes.
65. Indian craft
66. River area
67. Fish
68. Corrode
69. Ill. city
70. Citizen's __
71. Vicinity
73. Toward the mouth
75. U.S. electrical pioneer
77. Cop a __
78. Victory on the Charles River
81. Prestidigitator's request
86. Whitney and Wallach
87. Possibly
89. Actress Louise
90. Robert __
91. Actor Hardwicke
94. Debussy theme
95. Clerical garment
97. Story word
99. G. and S. princess
100. Texas landmark
101. __ ton
102. Yankee city on March 17
105. Splits
106. Surpass
108. Yellow-fever man
109. U.S. missile
110. Norse god
111. Shaw has trouble breathing
114. Fronton game
115. Cease-fire bid
117. Neighbor of Aust.
118. Teachers' org.
119. Singer Johnny
120. Girl of song
121. Preserves
125. Lower take-home pay
132. Do-it-yourselfer's concern
136. Home
137. Concur
139. __ marbles
140. Indian lute
141. Pig and cast
142. Ballet bends
143. Pacific group
144. Plautus' stage
145. __ home (out)
146. Famed football coach
147. Sounder
148. San Juan Hill name

DOWN

1. On edge: Fr.
2. Bayes and Helmer
3. Bantus
4. Astaire
5. "__ see another's woes?"
6. Russian dog man
7. Potpourris
8. Alley sound
9. Gardner
10. Set in motion
11. Govt. agency
12. Defense branch: Abbr.
13. Washed-out
14. New Delhi garb
15. Mutt, to Jeff
16. Spread
17. "Tell __ the ..."
18. Gaunt
19. Libido
23. Certain canes
30. Bona __
32. Where Mosul is: Var.
36. French artist
37. Fat: Prefix
39. Man of the world
40. Columnist Adams et al.
41. West: Sp.
42. Deviate
43. U.S. poet
44. Fiji's airport
45. Imitated Atalanta
46. "Mother __"
47. Tortillas
48. Kind of metal
49. Charles Boyer milieu
50. Waiting, in Madrid
51. Nader man
52. Biblical well
56. Cracked pots
57. Touch up
59. Botanical sheath
61. Of a singing group
62. Spiffy
63. Shoshonean
69. Rights org.
70. Llama's cousin
72. Affirmation
74. Madness
76. Stone slab
77. Held immobile
79. Inter __
80. "In one __ ..."
82. "Like __, all tears"
83. Former S.F. Mayor
84. Bloody, in Scotland
85. Miss Durbin
88. __ sinister
91. Channing
92. Omit
93. Boat device
94. Orate
96. College in Ky.
98. Inscribe
101. Dressed like a nurse
102. "Let her __ way . . ."
103. Monster's lake
104. Sesame
107. Dark Ages date
111. __-deucy
112. W.W. II agency
113. With no opener
114. Riches
116. Disquiet
117. Mitzi or Janet
120. Prank, in Scotland
121. Electricity
122. Behaved
123. "__ My Shadow"
124. Kind of dog
125. Killer
126. River in Spain
127. Plunder
128. Ferber
129. "The __ American"
130. The Magi
131. Discerns
133. Ancient Greek city
134. Former Alaskan governor
135. Kind of prof.
138. Approximate: Abbr.

ACROSS

1. Bowsprit
5. Sassafras drink
10. Levantine wind
15. Did the trudgen
19. Argentan's river
20. Eastern bigwig
21. Not a soul
22. Combustible heap
23. Greek units of length
24. Julie joins Hugh
26. Cuzco Indian
27. Dabbles in
29. French pronoun
30. Adjective for Rome
32. Richard III's need
33. Slowly, to Cicero
34. Malefic
35. Schary
36. "Little __"
38. Sell or tell
41. Romeo and Juliet
42. B'way turkey
43. Wahine's dance
45. What old grads do
46. Leftovers
47. Finicky grammarian
49. Berliner's refusal
51. Sturdy cart
52. Compass point
53. Weight unit
54. Flues
57. A.F.B. in Colorado
58. Signals for Revere
60. Lorne takes on crooner
62. Pindar's output
63. Cooperstown name
64. Blue or White
65. Two actors
69. Skin discoloration
73. Supplement, with "out"
74. Less svelte
75. "__ We Dance?"
76. Bern's river
77. He came after Bacon
79. Variety
80. Swift's forte
82. Embog
83. Pippin
85. Sweepings
87. Shed feathers
89. P.I. canoe
89. "Dooryard" bloomers
91. Like Dali's style
93. Norse Fate
94. Noun suffix
95. Pamphleteer of '76
96. Singer Geraldine
98. Barber takes on Ali
101. Actress Merrill
102. At the fringe
104. Baal or Mammon
105. Fred gets Justice
108. Foreign trade discount
109. Pure and simple
110. Equally
111. Milk: Prefix
112. Clan
113. Handle: Fr.
114. More exposed
115. Uneven
116. Or follower

DOWN

1. Placebos
2. Band leader gets a Reed
3. Singer and actor moored together
4. Touches up old masters
5. Ad subjects
6. Dino's song topic
7. Glass
8. Ref. book
9. O.T. book
10. On the carpet
11. Two no-hit pitchers: 1968-69
12. Clara of films
13. Bancroft
14. Bed canopy
15. Full of life
16. Two late comedians
17. Alms box
18. Kind of ticket
25. What one little pig had
28. __ bien
31. Invariably
33. Last straw
36. Marsh birds
37. City in N.Y.
39. Fatuous
40. Where Tacloban is
41. Rod's partner
42. George smokes with Natalie
44. Two ex-Senators (Vt.-Mich.)
47. Mom and Dad
48. Lana, Jim and Nat
50. Britain's Chamberlain
53. Relinquishes
55. Gynt
56. Coating for pills
59. Sandboxer
60. Handed out
61. Grassland
63. Writers Isaac and John
65. __ Bayar of Turkey
66. Giraffe's cousin
67. Shirley and Diana
68. Southeast wind
69. Discourage
70. Eva Marie and Heather
71. Fredric and Claude
72. Precinct
75. Agora sights
78. Two singers
81. Responsive
82. Event for Figaro
84. Churchly: Abbr.
86. Athlete's mentor
88. Ham follower
90. Wampum
92. Arena
96. Data
97. Okie's relative
98. "Green Mansions" girl
99. Actress Barbara
100. Asian border river
102. Egyptian cotton
103. Mislay
106. Free of
107. Small ape

218 ANSWERING SERVICE

By J.A. Felker

ACROSS

1. City in Iraq
6. Medit. island, to French
11. Shaggy beast
16. Poker item
20. Come to pass
21. Pasty
22. Plump
23. English architect
24. Forget-me-not
28. Elusive one
29. Pompous
30. Lithuanian river
31. Botfly
32. Phooey!
34. Med. course
35. Ore vein, in England
36. French documents
37. Engine-room worker
39. Tibet's capital
40. Backward ones
41. Catch
43. Hammer
44. Trousers, in Bonn
45. Actor Erwin
48. Snails, for one
54. Takes on
55. Dam's mate
56. Irish river
57. German king
58. About
59. Chemical compound
60. Navigation aid
61. Palmer et al.
63. Musical work: Abbr.
64. Pottage dealer
65. Smart guy
66. Olive genus
67. Two
76. Birds' class
77. "Honi __ ..."
78. Radios
79. "__, team!"
80. Des __
83. Spinal and vocal
84. Blackjack player's words
86. O'Casey
87. Lo, in Italy
88. Miss Mater
89. Wild ox
90. Play
91. Tipperary
98. Desperate trio
99. Consumers
100. Mottled
101. Does gardening
102. Doubly
103. Plant shoot
105. German poet
107. Retards
110. Place for art
111. Time of day
112. Red quartz
116. "__ last!"
117. Georgia city
118. Cheer up
120. Music group
121. Rome
125. City near Arles
126. Hitherto
127. Server
128. Certain cone
129. Warm-sea fish
130. Poker Flat author
131. U.S. chemist and family
132. Ponies up

DOWN

1. Yielded
2. Belly __ (grouch)
3. La __
4. Dirt-road feature
5. Onassis et al.
6. Red wood
7. Squared stone
8. Butler
9. Challenge
10. Photo-lab abbr.
11. Retreats
12. Michener locale
13. Finch
14. Spanish bears
15. Old clock
16. Raccoons' relatives
17. Dispatch
18. Printing-press part
19. Boscs
23. __ banana peel
25. More corny
26. Available
27. Wreath
33. Perfectly
35. __-eye
36. Grammar case: Abbr.
38. Cleo's servant
39. Newer
40. Dean
41. Religion of the East
42. Kind of mind
43. Entangle
44. Roman epistle writer
45. Bristle: Prefix
46. Kind of bag
47. Certain saucers
48. Pronoun
49. Certain writings
50. Prepared to smoke
51. __ Gay (W.W. II plane)
52. Auger
53. Blue river, to Germans
59. Slaves of old
60. Endures
61. Winged
62. Order forms: Abbr.
64. House part
66. Kind of show
68. Estate house
69. Tristram's lady et al.
70. Bellini lady
71. Kind of wave
72. "That __ much for me"
73. Nautical response
74. Responds
75. Musical direction
80. London back streets
81. Spanish eight
82. Desserts
83. Memorial pile
84. Uta of stage
85. Thoroughly
86. Adders, etc.
90. Welsh John
92. O'Neill and McCarthy
93. Congo town
94. Six, in Ponce
95. __ Hound (Canis Major)
96. Time of day
97. Dr. Seuss character
102. Esteemed
103. Chest item
104. South African author
105. In a pious way
106. Takes out
107. Times of day
108. Character
109. Biblical town
110. Butterfly
111. Haut __
113. Expert
114. Sixteen annas
115. Units, as of salts
117. Arizona sight
118. Eur. river
119. This: Sp.
122. Stadium sound
123. Not sing.
124. __-to-one odds

219 APPLICATION By Jean J. Davison

ACROSS

1. Disperse
6. Links place
10. Top
14. Space group
18. Like a $3 bill
20. Hair style
21. Carol
22. Author Hunter
23. Casino game
25. Walrus feature
26. Trick
27. Analogy words
28. Bushy clump
29. Certain solvents
31. Rule
32. Actor Will
33. Articles
35. Ahead
37. Singer MacKenzie
39. Biddy
40. Water, in Sonora
41. German region
44. Site south of Eye, England
49. World service agency
51. "Vesti La Giubba," e.g.
52. Commoner
53. New Deal org.
55. Bldg. debt
56. Mata
59. Prefix for dox or pedic
61. Fan
63. Anna's destination
65. Pitch
67. Bert and Harry of old TV ads
69. Spanish others
70. Basis for one's thing
74. Coconut meat
75. Forest of W.W. II massacre
76. Travel-ad offering
77. Jewish month
79. Goals
81. Sahl et al.
83. Town, in Africa
85. Conceit
86. Women's org.
87. Jacob's son
89. Aspect
91. Barber-shelf item
93. Items in "These Foolish Things"
98. Poet Hermann
99. Diving bird
100. One, in Bonn
101. Laud
103. Equals
106. Texas player
107. Missy
111. Astir
112. Like some music
114. Margin
115. Italian hatred
116. Liquid sound
117. Actor Richard
118. Decamp
121. Hebrew letter
122. Limit
123. O'Flaherty
124. Rest, in Santiago
125. Greek god
126. Exploits
127. Being: Lat.
128. __ fixes

DOWN

1. Parsley unit
2. Pronoun
3. Way
4. Stuffs
5. Word for a bairn
6. Light-intensity unit
7. Vehicle for green men
8. Fish outings
9. Worth, for one
10. TV accessory
11. Place for serving
12. Eating place
13. Leather __
14. "Happy __!"
15. City near Madrid
16. Caesar or tossed
17. Over
19. Snowmen of Tibet
24. Clan symbol
30. Priestly
31. Baedeker for the 400
34. Western sight
36. Moth
38. Kind of worm
39. Mountain-road hazard
41. Cadges
42. Opposite
43. Postwar Italian leader
45. __-Magnon
46. Handsome ones
47. Buttinskis
48. High tribunal
50. "Drat!" or "Darn!"
54. "__ longa . . ."
57. Chess piece
58. Moslem
60. Feature of Truman's kitchen
62. Great Barrier island
64. Old Medit. port
66. "And __ bed"
68. Pornography
71. Shouts
72. Spiral motion
73. Mideasterner
74. Spanish hero
78. City near Utica
80. Attack
82. Mrs., in Spain
84. Botanist who gave name to a flower
88. Wine crops
90. Golf feats
92. Showed age, as paper
94. Does farm work
95. Organic compounds
96. Drastic
97. Narrow groove
102. Sex appeal
103. More qualified
104. Timid one
105. Condition
106. Turkish army units
108. Confuse
109. Long period
110. Wading birds
111. Indian region
113. Salt tree
117. Large bird
119. Dutch cupboard
120. Yes, in Caen

ACROSS

1. Have __ loose
7. Laugh
11. Embrace, as ideas
16. Scolded
20. Fragrant oil
21. Electrical unit
22. Mexican man
23. Prefix for sphere
24. Jet-setter
26. Dispatch boat
27. "Yes, __ fatal man . . ."
28. Bad in Germany
29. Coin of Korea
30. Purse item
33. Eye or back
35. Styled, as hair
38. Food for Don Ho
39. Nigerian tribe: Var.
40. G-men's place
41. Where above: Lat.
44. Added
47. Sweetbread: Fr.
48. Most drenched
51. Merchandise
53. Ref. book
54. Frisky as __
56. After jay
57. Mimic
58. Clue of a sort
62. July game
64. __ lard
65. Arabian gulf
66. Lynne or Orange
67. Bear Bryant's team
68. Fiends
71. Being: Fr.
75. Simplified English
77. Protozoan
79. Siamese twin
80. Newspaper, to some,
81. December line
88. __ hunch
89. Greek letters
90. Change
91. Excuses

92. Force down
94. Outpourings
97. Pluck
98. River of Korea
99. Stravinsky
101. Go by again
103. Make __ about
106. Old grapevine
111. __ tide
112. D.D.E. locale
113. To the back
114. Raleigh or Scott
115. Barfront light
117. Harmful flies
119. Headland
120. Subjugate
124. Fly catchers
126. __ 1 (tie score)
127. "__ as a Stranger"
128. Daughter of Cadmus
130. Word with way or case
131. Smooth
135. Old-World reptile
140. Son of Jacob
142. __ daze
143. Cereal
144. "You __ mouthful"
145. Olympic runners' goals
149. "That __ hay"
150. Sea duck
151. Joyous
152. Cheap liquor
153. Fernando de __
154. Hairnet
155. German king
156. Curious

DOWN

1. Show backer
2. Southern city
3. Charing or double
4. Thieve
5. Tesla's field: Abbr.
6. Quickly

7. Cloche
8. Carney
9. After hic
10. Old alchemy stone
11. Neat __
12. Hindu deity
13. Chem. suffix
14. G.I. store
15. Organ stops
16. Variety of pine
17. Get a report
18. Like a stranded ship
19. Pepys et al.
21. Blended, as colors
25. Carouse
31. Extinct bird
32. Treat a cut
34. Quonset
36. Raises
37. Brash one
42. Scrams
43. Sesame man
45. Old clock

46. Way in: Abbr.
48. State: Abbr.
49. Fish
50. Singing item
52. Linemen: Abbr.
55. Movies, in Spain
59. Some votes
60. Two __ kind
61. Ames et al.
63. Kind of vaccine
64. Least challenging
67. State of Brazil
69. Goolagong's game
70. Dread
72. Roman officials
73. Hindu queen
74. Incites, with "on"
75. Get __ tip
76. Nursemaid
78. Antifreeze: Abbr.

82. Amtrak unit
83. Baboons
84. Flying circuses
85. Certain church watchdogs
86. Drivel
87. Farm unit
93. Arno city
94. Tippler
95. Work unit
96. Pulpit offering: Abbr.
100. Manager
102. Criticize
103. More filmy
104. French season
105. Sea call
106. Xylophones
107. Handel work
108. Vibrant
109. Diamond name
110. Eventful period
116. Actor Pendleton
118. Lao follower

121. Neck ties
122. Disguise
123. Spanish queen
125. Prolix
129. Prefix for dox
132. Zodiac sign
133. Finish
134. Unpleasant
136. Go __ a huddle
137. Beach resort
138. Thought: Prefix
139. Mild oath
141. Sacred image
146. Quick to learn
147. Navy man: Abbr.
148. Sioux Indian

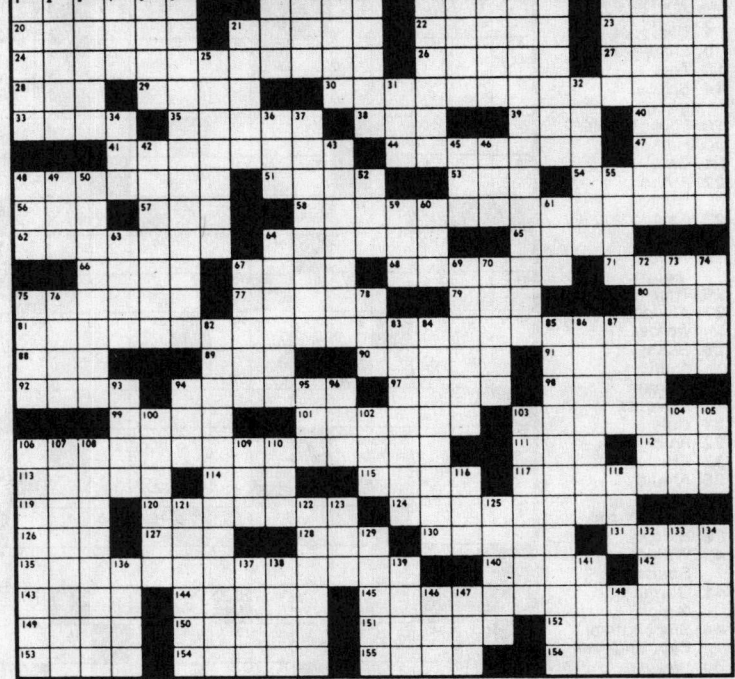

221 ON THE BALL By Anthony Morse

ACROSS

1. Concerns of sentries
5. Early French king
10. Grouchy ones
15. Get lost!
19. Tule
20. Place for Xanthippe
21. Early viol
22. Part of Northwest Territory
23. "And what __ rare . . .?"
24. Low-down thief
26. Shrill bark
27. "From Here to __"
29. Sordid
30. Wipes out
32. Tooth part
33. Bog material
34. Toscanini, etc.
35. Villa __
36. Emulated a virtuous girl
39. Jet housing
40. Toddler
41. Goddess of plenty
42. Pretenses
43. Sea flier
44. French soap
47. Candlenut tree
48. Put aside
50. Favoring
51. Kind of joint
52. What some girls do
54. Regular courses
57. Headland
58. Bearing
59. Measure
60. Squirrel, e.g.
61. Pearl Harbor shrine
63. Early guitars
64. Du Maurier character
65. Climbers' spikes
66. More sensible
67. Helper
68. Dress, with "out"
69. Come home
70. Coffee leavings
72. Links cry
73. Aldo
74. Constellation
75. Compass reading
76. French artist and family
77. Jam down
79. Greek letters
80. French goose
81. Kind of deal
82. Connective
83. Trainers spar
86. God of Islam
89. Early TV comedy show
91. Streak
92. Strings of horses
94. Texas A. & M. team
95. Armadillos
97. Friendly
98. Nitwit
99. Confidential slant
102. Garden pest
103. Chill
104. Color of ebene
105. "Swan Lake" character
106. Kind of drive
107. Soaks
108. Imposing
109. River of the Ukraine
110. Asterisk

DOWN

1. Sautéed
2. Gave the thumb to
3. Ascetic
4. Brief visit
5. White House furniture
6. Small type
7. Nosegay
8. Prior to
9. Corn features
10. Invent
11. Bevel out
12. With competence
13. Get-together
14. Roller coaster sounds
15. Beans
16. Cashbox guardian
17. Plane wing part
18. On deck
25. Hard wood
28. Inert gas
31. Dakota Indian
33. Tropical fruit
34. Habits
36. Eve
37. Places for politicos
38. French winter
43. Wear away
44. Odds and ends
45. Visigoth king
46. Guests' canoe
47. Playing field
48. On-deck men
49. Star: Prefix
50. Investigation
52. Rackets
53. Dive
55. Bonus of a sort
56. Puts on
58. Cash
60. N.L. players
62. Samson's birthplace
63. Somewhat tardy
64. Take a train
66. Silken
67. Wing
70. "There __ old . . ."
71. U.A W., for one
72. Goose wails
76. __ Lama
77. Region of India
78. Mystical use of words
79. Getting on the ready
80. Spanish bishops
81. Pawl
83. That: It.
84. Stepped around
85. Withered
87. Even if
88. State capital
90. Scoffs
92. Column part
93. Passover event
95. Land of the Pamirs
96. Spool
97. To-do
100. Connective
101. Fish

222 WHEN IN ROME · By Ronald Hirschfeld

ACROSS

1. Mr. __ (squatty one)
5. Greek city
11. Pago Pago's location
16. Central Am. Indians
21. African sheep
22. Trojan hero
23. Canine young
24. Run off
25. Husband: Fr.
26. Lox's partners
27. Menu user
28. Bewildered
29. Teacakes
31. Maxim for the middle-aged
34. __-Simon test
35. Stravinsky
36. Name of 13 Popes
37. Lon of films
39. Volcano
40. Ad __
43. Arden and namesakes
48. Fissile rocks
49. Kennedy
50. Greek god
52. Hebrew measure
53. "I __ a tale unfold . . ."
54. Sedate
55. Beldam
56. ". . . they who never __ newspaper"
57. Paintings
58. Potok or Weizmann
59. Biblical sufferer
60. N.J. fort
62. Velocity initials
63. Company officials: Abbr.
64. Brag
65. The word, at times
66. Clayey earth
67. Bluish color
68. Cuckoopint
69. Double-crossed
71. Paid __
73. Roman dressing place
78. Whip
80. Parcels out
81. Garden clock
83. Very: Ger.
84. Boxer Max
85. Cologne waters
87. Building addition
88. Suffixes for pun or road
90. Spigot
93. Rudiments
94. Study
95. "All for __ . . ."
96. Insults
97. "Road" film star
98. Evaluator
101. U.S. playwright
103. Marie Antoinette, for one
104. __ leaguer
105. Overact
106. Box-office word
107. Hajj objective
108. Picasso, e.g.
109. Fortune cards
111. Old auto
112. __ Royale
113. Knowing, old style
114. I, in Essen
116. Aleutian island
117. Heavens
118. Navigate widely
125. Gross
129. "__ by Jury"
130. Cautions
131. Y.A. of football
133. Stupid one
134. Chemical compound
135. Omit
136. Turns outward
137. Critic Downes
138. Adam et al.
139. Do a printing job
140. Strip down a sailboat
141. Bridge holding

DOWN

1. Theda Bara, e.g.
2. Scottish hill
3. Mongol tent
4. Pool-table hazards
5. Women in famous painting
6. Lumber hook
7. Anxiety
8. Female ruff
9. Prayer shawls
10. Allocated
11. Slow, in Scotland
12. Famous whaler
13. Dole
14. Cassini
15. Kind of fool
16. Newscaster Harry
17. Can. province
18. Greatest amount
19. Summit
20. Harbor or eared
30. Having prongs
32. Young horse
33. Born: Fr.
37. Singing group
38. Transports
39. Was: Fr.
40. Thyme or rue
41. Spanish gold
42. San Juan beach
44. Unlock, to poets
45. Jerked beef
46. Was influential
47. Mideast winds
48. Burns, for one
49. Greek letters
51. Biblical range
54. Hoaxes
55. Droll
58. Ran
59. Kind of jaw
61. S.F. footballers
64. Nasty tot
65. Refuse heaps
66. Shea player
67. At a distance
68. Old zither
69. Fleming
70. __ de mer
72. Some degrees
73. Minnelli film
74. Where stars fell
75. College man of sorts
76. ". . . let no man put __"
77. Light: Lat.
79. Rhone tributary
82. __ du Diable
86. Geological time
88. Golf error
89. Salad base
90. Poison
91. Woman with
92. Nuisance
95. German king
96. Disposed to solitude
97. Unconventional
99. W.W. II area
100. Changes a heading
102. English river
103. Phrased again
104. Had a go at
107. Widow's gift
108. Most painful
110. Austrian coin: Abbr.
113. Marsh birds
115. Lumberjack, at times
116. Property
117. Newspaper edition
118. Brief try
119. Weapon: Fr.
120. Stereoscopic
121. Sea route
122. Glen
123. Miss Murdoch
124. Thence: Lat.
126. Author of "J'Accuse"
127. "Illiad," for one
128. Hawaiian goose
132. Pro __

223 HIGH-LEVEL ACTION — By Herb Risteen

ACROSS

1. Sirens of silents
6. October stone
10. Asian weights: Abbr.
13. Munchhausen
18. Habituate
19. Teasdale
20. Captive of Hercules
22. Desert plant
23. Craze
24. Styptic base
25. Tour players
26. Letter line
27. Chess move
31. One who strives
32. Resting on
33. Give a sign of
34. Divine or Human
37. Defended
39. Name for a field dog
43. Not right
44. Cell walls
46. Old English coin
47. U.S. Indian
48. "__ and Lovers"
49. Brawl
50. Former Australian leader
52. W.W. II naval bastion
53. Road animal
54. Kitchen gadgets
55. Cut off
56. Erode
58. Before, in law
59. Phone-book abbr.
60. Swindled
61. Buffalo
66. Clergymen
67. Noah's son
68. Declares
69. Hair follower
70. Wallace
71. Coercion
73. Vegetable
76. Dies __
77. Asks for
79. Prevent
80. Welles role
81. Biblical ending
82. Sixty years before Hastings
83. Pentagon feature
84. Did roofing
85. Big name in flags
87. Axle parts
89. Danish king
90. Jack of TV
92. Drive on
93. Directly
95. St. Peter
101. Kind of account
102. Stage offering
103. Music maker
104. High abode
106. Asian range
107. Ornamental wear
108. Favorite
109. Goes on about
110. Mush bases
111. Haggard's queen
112. Telescope part
113. Regions

DOWN

1. Energy
2. Biblical race of giants
3. Stage great
4. Non-match for a pea
5. Neptune et al.
6. River to the Missouri
7. Like a stake
8. Calla lily
9. Thrashes
10. Pussyfoot
11. Scottish title
12. Liqueur base
13. Blues street
14. Insurance men
15. Thin
16. Roman poet
17. Clock shaped like a ship
21. Confiscate
28. Northern, for one
29. "__ shame!"
30. Cap
34. Johnny
35. Melville opus
36. Fine china
37. Unoriginal one
38. Skeet device
40. Early odist
41. Compositions
42. Dawdled
44. Ice pinnacles
45. Oleoresin
49. Silas et al.
50. Hebrew letter: Var.
51. Most exaggerated
52. Journeys
54. Bard, in Rheims
57. Zoo attractions
58. __-fire
59. Gypsy
60. Scarlet and hay
61. Book size
62. Dickens clerk et al.
63. Early radio character
64. Swerves
65. Gnawing animals
66. Colonial newscaster
70. Son of Leah
71. Evel Knievel, for one
72. Pulpy fruits
73. Asian river
74. Dill
75. Ancient Asian
78. Eugenie, for one
80. Stage classic
83. Nonsense
84. Horn blare
86. Kind of column or cord
87. U.S. Indian
88. "__ i's"
89. Instance: Fr.
91. Uncooperative ones
93. Golf club
94. Counts noses
95. Native of Lodz
96. Gam
97. Turkish weights
98. Sidekick
99. Water bird
100. Rama's wife
101. Bread spread
105. Letter

224 WIRE SERVICE *By Mel Rosen*

ACROSS

1. Siamese or alley
4. Repute
8. Uses a gavel
12. Watt or ohm, e.g.
16. Scanty, in London
19. _ of thumb
20. Courtier in "Hamlet"
22. Johnnycake
23. Police-blotter entry
26. Summoned
28. Lobster trap
29. Garden
30. Some baldies
31. Name on a sample form
33. W.W. II locale
34. Poet Stephen
36. Movie dog
37. Civil War soldier
39. Decisive times
41. School topic
45. _ santé
45. Quarrel
48. Total
49. Kind of mother
50. Belgian town
52. Name for Athena
53. Russian plane
54. _ process
57. London suburb
60. Chinese dynasty
61. Con Ed problem, in a way
67. Bull: Prefix
69. Cocktail ingredient
71. Egyptian god
72. Sullen
73. Boleyn et al.
74. Earth parts, figuratively
76. Fashionable avenue
77. After waste or want
79. _ Plaines
80. Military utility bill
89. Gibbon
90. White House monogram
91. Zeno's home
92. Cork's isle
93. Greek letter
96. King or Arkin
99. Steep
100. More recent
103. Strong fabric
104. Political infight
108. Kind of code
110. Ancient poetess
112. Card game
113. "_, we have no . . ."
114. Very: Fr.
115. Chick noises
117. Kitchen meas.
120. River of Venezuela
121. Resort city
122. Rochester specialty
125. Rubber baby buggy bumper, e.g.
130. "Citizen _"
131. Possesses
132. Drinks
133. Motors or Mills
137. Unit of work
138. Enzyme
140. Outlooks
142. Spear or pepper
143. Nitrogen: Prefix
144. _ horseback (leader)
146. Name for an early discotheque
150. Care for
151. Petain
152. Time periods
153. Tour-guide listings
154. French seasons
155. Helper: Abbr.
156. Sultan of _
157. Rorem

DOWN

1. Social system
2. Eastern title
3. Set straight
4. Algerian port
5. Horse color
6. Most trite
7. Gave a refund
8. Moslem weight
9. Aft
10. Fix in advance
11. Galahad or Bors
12. African region
13. Profane, on Oahu
14. Swallow
15. Vacillate
16. Charts
17. Fabulist: Var.
18. Presbyter
21. Charisse
24. Topography
25. Century plant
27. Two aspirins, e.g.
32. Florida city
35. Campus sports org.
36. Connective
38. Youth-group initials
40. Sea off Greece
42. Advantage
43. Within: Prefix
45. Prison-cake ingredient
46. Role for Liz
47. Check
51. Look into again
53. Fixed
55. Sturm – Drang
56. Kind of maniac
58. Upstate N.Y. town
59. Cupidity
61. Chinese stage prop
62. Transported
63. Eastern servant
64. Disrupted
65. Like a spent squid
66. "Charley's _"
68. Bone: Prefix
70. Suffix for cash
75. Soft drink
78. Musical flourishes
80. Oaf
81. Harness parts
82. Stadium
83. _-de-se (suicide)
84. Island: Var.
85. Reverse, for one
86. Kingfish
87. Dies _
88. Obtain
94. "Win one for the _"
95. Parts of firm titles
97. Punching tool
98. Prefix for phyte
101. Pound
102. African thong
105. Campus mil. group
106. Rotating wheel, for short
107. Rural poem
109. Greek letter
111. Track trials
114. Exhaust
116. Quiet!
118. Hockey need
119. Posh abodes
120. Ninny
121. Honorable _
122. Coll. course
123. Charge with gas
124. Drawer of a sort
126. Refuges
127. Willows
128. Give
129. The reserves
134. Competed at Le Mans
135. Blue: Sp.
136. Another's gain
139. Old letter
141. Narrow opening
142. Fog
145. Anybody
147. Babylonian god
148. Cellular initials
149. Way: Abbr.

225 GETTING THROUGH

By Joseph La Fauci

ACROSS

1. Summit
5. Like some sopranos
9. Winery refuse
13. Festive
17. Eat like Li'l Abner
19. River of Italy
20. Inter __
21. Corroded
22. Trade observations
25. Viewpoint
26. "__ Tu?" (aria)
27. Do ushering
28. Menu listing
29. Pronunciation mark
30. Come-on ad
32. French cheese
33. Italian Paul
35. Del __, Calif.
36. Prod
37. D'Annunzio's "__ da Rimini"
41. Expectant
43. For fear that
44. Tuscan city
45. Sandy ridges
46. Labored in vain
49. Ziegfeld
50. Cornfield sound
51. Cartoonist Gardner
52. Contemptible one
53. Easy winner
56. Litmus-paper ritual
59. Indeed, of old
60. Spree
61. Election-night data
62. "Paris Bound" playwright
63. Partial
66. Observe
67. Rigatoni
68. Winter facial woe
69. Fur garments
71. Voice
72. Macaw
73. Inlet
74. Brooklyn campus
75. Polite words for "Shut up!"
80. Wall pier
82. Meaning
83. River to the Channel
84. Well-known loch
85. Big Sur locale
87. Parisian friend
88. Japanese coin
89. German river
90. Of a chemical compound
91. Certify
94. Cottonmouths' milieu
96. Like Satan's hoof
99. Asian range
100. Peach part
102. Greek poet of legend
103. Equipped for indiscretion
106. Bitter herb
107. Corrupt
108. Shower décor
109. U.S. inventor
110. Advantage
111. Ukrainian body
112. Presage
113. Patella, etc.

DOWN

1. Be distressed
2. Pie or fever
3. Film
4. Uncle, in Scotland
5. Tuck, for one
6. Riga native
7. Formic-acid source
8. Put up with
9. Dull finish
10. Winglike
11. Ruffle
12. Baking needs
13. Famous Pisan
14. In need of a dictionary
15. Word with an ear
16. Poker term
18. Northwest, for one
21. Early sword
23. Goatish look
24. Arthurian lady
31. Berserk
32. Twaddle!
34. Santa __
36. Influence
37. Sunday best
38. With flaming color
39. Colombian city
40. Schonberg's "Moses und __"
41. Speedily
42. Exit mum
43. Loamy deposit
44. Madre or Nevada
46. Blemish
47. Tendencies
48. Writer Edith
53. German prison camp
54. Clutched
55. Clods
57. Dawn affair
58. Corner
59. Ibsen's builder
62. Vote
63. __ around
64. Ram of the sky
65. Lamb
67. Great care
68. "Alfie" star
69. Cabbage dish
70. Prong
75. Customs man, at times
76. Awakening
77. Swedish saint
78. Quondam
79. Unaspirated
81. __ ends
82. Shoe part
86. French lace
87. Egyptian deity
88. Party single
90. St. Theresa's birthplace
91. Immigrant
92. Reject
93. Championship
94. Moderate
95. Rumanian city
97. Etna's output
98. Augustan Age poet
99. Up to
101. Quaker's pronoun
104. Sharpshooter's forte
105. Encina

MASTER KEYS
By Frances Hansen

ACROSS

1. Tentative efforts
6. African lake
10. Upright
15. Enigmatic one
21. Ancient: Prefix
22. Flute: Prefix
23. Pit man
24. Taiwan city
25. "If I were __ man . . ."
26. Writer C.P.
27. "__ far, far better . . ."
28. Bedecks, as Solomon
29. Start of old hymn
33. Ox yoke bar
34. Maltreater
35. Washroom: Abbr.
36. Bring into harmony
40. Sudden burst of thunder
42. Adjective suffix
45. Guinness
47. Pacific god
48. Play a fiddle, in a way
51. Literary monogram
52. Bordered
55. Scottish particle: Var.
56. __ than a pancake
57. Slightly off-key
59. Gets bawled out
62. __ love (flighty one)
63. Harem room
64. "Dwelt a miner, forty-__"
65. Dazes
66. Hidden
67. Bach or Bacharach
69. "When __ a word, it means . . ."
70. Like some cheddar
71. Pirates' gold
73. Skp
74. "Don't __" (no sure thing)
77. Sea birds
78. Night: Prefix
80. Relative of Mr.
82. Put out the wash
83. River of Spain
87. Hillbilly party
90. Gracious, in Peru
92. Penn Station builder
93. Per __
94. Soothing sounds
95. Jewelry items
98. Kind of switch
100. Parody
101. Italian poet Ugo
102. Water: Fr.
103. Mexican historian
104. "How __ tooth . . ."
107. Kind of keel
108. Together, in music
109. Elevator cage
110. Appear
111. Depot, for short
112. Little Edward
113. Holy: Prefix
114. Millay
116. Perceptible: Abbr.
117. In a piggery
119. "__ of robins . . ."
121. Freud's concerns
122. Church reader
125. Oral, for one
129. What song doctors do
135. Mount in a way
138. Half an old refrain word
139. Roman 1,003
140. Burdened
141. Away from home
142. Fad
143. "Rule Britannia" composer
144. Cat-__-tails
145. Java's neighbor
146. Mr. Kelly
147. Egg drinks
148. Confused

DOWN

1. Boxes
2. Old card game
3. Toklas or blue
4. "Vanity Fair" girl
5. Dryden's address, once
6. Melons
7. Ended a phone call
8. Lily plants
9. Probe for water
10. Ludwig
11. Stravinsky's spring thing
12. Star in Pegasus
13. "__ vie"
14. Well-known square
15. Kind of dust
16. City for Correggios and cheese
17. Employed a penniless lady
18. Vilela people
19. French marshal
20. Greek letters
30. Take a spill
31. Arson, e.g.
32. Excessively tart
37. Bring into harmony
38. Cheats at solitaire
39. Sped
41. Minoan island
43. What an adult has to listen to
44. Blue jeans
46. What avails a motorist naught
48. Twenty-one-gun affair
49. Musical key
50. __ the green (fracas)
52. Fix over
53. What veni means
54. Star in Cygnus
58. Contest for riflemen, maybe
59. Baroque music
60. Citronella grass
61. Needle case
68. Grand __
72. Baton
75. Anklebone
76. Washington bill
79. Piping notes
81. On the __ vive
84. Narcotic-ring V.I.P.
85. Tell
86. Presaged
88. Words of surprise
89. Hale et al., to friends
91. Concerning
94. Trim
96. Cleric's title: Abbr.
97. Cat, in Spain
99. Greek pitchers
100. Car style
101. Country gala
104. __ tack
105. Rock-bottom
106. Eve, in Norse myth
111. Thin cigars
115. "Any port in __"
117. Kind of quartet
118. Pour, as wine
120. Cousin of an I-beam
123. Mischa
124. Where "Aida" debuted
126. Abscissa line
127. Coeur d'__
128. Judith Anderson role
130. Inner: Prefix
131. Hindu land grant
132. Eleven: Fr.
133. Certain U.N. vote
134. Portico
135. Poke
136. Myst. aircraft
137. Russian village

227 ON THE MAIN LINE By Robert Roop

ACROSS

1. Discernment
6. Loiters
11. Doc or Sneezy
16. Kitchen utensil
17. Fasten a ship's rope
18. Competitors
20. Cap'n Andy's boat
22. Nasal in tone
24. __ carte
25. Noun suffix
26. Captain
28. Fuss
29. Spoiler
31. Zen art work
33. Stage direction
34. Salary: Abbr.
35. Cake feature
37. Parrot
39. Swiss river
40. Lorelei's home
41. Olympus drink
43. Saint's namesakes
45. Goings-on
46. Red gem, in Spain
48. Leapin' ladies
49. Move up __
50. News-dispatch feature
54. Insecticide
55. Bon Homme Richard, e.g.
58. Trees
59. Kennedy
61. Haitian port
63. Horace work
64. Certain votes
65. Tramp, for one
67. Natives: Suffix
68. Harbor boat
69. __ wage
70. __ deck
71. T-bone
72. Stretch out
74. Metric units: Abbr.
76. Meanly tricky
78. Loam deposit
79. Tuscany city
81. Ruhr yield
82. Beckett name et al.
84. Spanish clover varieties
86. Took pot shots at

90. Playing area
91. Costello
92. Boiler plates
94. Vista
95. Weathercock
96. Steamboat pioneer
98. Teen talk
100. To-do
101. Biblical verb ending
102. Kind of oil
104. Moor
106. Arctic explorer
107. One of the classes
109. Mobile boardwalk of sorts
112. One with a trap
113. Moslem prince
114. Stick-ons
115. Apparel
116. Snide
117. S.A. monkeys

DOWN

1. Headline name of 1912
2. Toward the stern
3. Portico
4. Shelters
5. Metallic element
6. Sarcastic
7. __ Plaines
8. Lacking: Suffix
9. Call up
10. Study groups
11. Dry-goods man
12. More extensive
13. Declare
14. Published
15. Cruise ship, in ads
16. Console

19. Short rail track
20. Stateroom
21. U.S. folklorist
23. Stupid ones
27. School orgs.
30. Main courses
32. Having overhangs
34. Leg parts
36. Caesar's subjects
38. Talkative people
40. Cosmetic
42. Batter's abbr.
44. Consumed
45. Sink part
47. Purposes' partners
49. Catchall book
50. Beatrice's friend

51. "I won't tell __"
52. Drake's ship
53. Uncanny
55. Leg bone
56. Goal
57. Annoying
60. British medal
62. Stock offerings: Abbr.
65. Russian city
66. Sultry
67. Kind of type
69. Tanzanian town
71. Looks over
73. "__ but you"
75. Sassy ones
77. Desperate letters
79. Cooking utensil
80. Commandment topic

82. Chairman's need
83. Declaims
84. Witty remarks
85. Necktie woe
87. Stormy birds
88. Computers
89. Actor John
91. Sea queens
93. Sam and J.C. of golf
96. Gives the gate
97. Greek image
99. Sumerian ruler
102. Decoy
103. Performs
105. Hen's forte
108. Men's org.
110. N.Y. athlete
111. Bao __

228 ODD COUPLES
By Peter T. Thornton

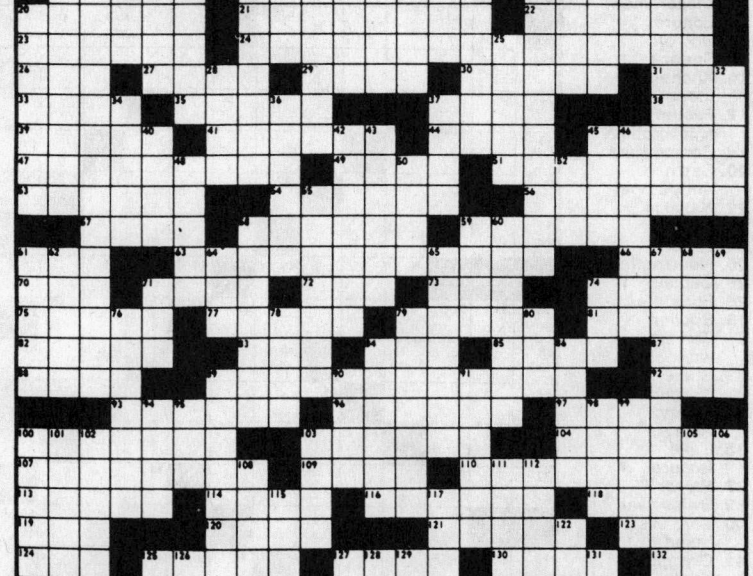

ACROSS

1. Animal trail
6. Result of a busy stock market
14. McGuffey's work
20. Ecuadorian city
21. Sarcastic
22. Ixelles, to Flemish
23. Reciprocal, to poets
24. Red and Major
26. Caucho tree
27. River to the Ouse
29. __ quam videri
30. Sidney of films
31. Stock privileges: Abbr.
33. C'est a __
35. Hawthorne's home
37. Stiff hair
38. Large tank
39. Before, in Paris
41. U.S. painter
44. Waste allowance
45. Mature insect
47. Places for skin treatment
49. Low
51. Acts
53. Tolerate
54. Polar sight
56. Without rancor
57. Eat
58. Trumpeted
59. Wild dog
61. Sooner than
63. Blanche and Edmund
66. Beam
70. Writer Wallace
71. Kind of ray
72. Mum
73. Greek letter
74. Raccoon's relative
75. Mine excavation
77. Play fpr time
79. Port of Iraq
81. Like krypton
82. Troubled
83. Marquee sign
84. Blue or Franklin
85. "Three Faces __"
87. Tappan __
88. Umpire's call
89. Arline and Victor
92. Roman alloy
93. Some tires
96. __ events
97. Nine: Ger.
100. Of a heavenly body
103. Shoal boaters
104. Iron and zinc compounds
107. Catch up with
109. Unique person
110. Befalls
113. Perfume
114. Farm unit
116. Glacial ridges
118. Baseball ploy
119. Monterey fort
120. Catherine's husband
121. Molding edge
123. Egyptian dancing girl
124. Lumber tool
125. __ seal
127. Table spread
130. Serpents
132. Jar part
133. Cornel and Monty
137. City on Lake Huron
139. Hitherto
140. By that name: Lat.
141. Fair-__ boy
142. Cars
143. Applied logic
144. Bridge player's words

DOWN

1. Boston Strong Boy of the ring
2. Nero and Hopper
3. Kind of way
4. Gumbo: Var.
5. Hindu queens
6. Defendant in a law case
7. Islands off New Guinea
8. Clan emblems
9. Ingresses: Abbr.
10. Spanish uncles
11. Teen-age woe
12. Dance step
13. Snapping beetle
14. Old-time alehouse
15. River to the North Sea
16. Old zither
17. __ point
18. Tire
19. Puts on again
20. Having a tail
25. Semiquavers
28. Nobel physicist
32. On the glacial side
34. Tedium
36. Store feed
37. Lock __
40. Noddy
42. In toto
43. __ Creed
45. Willow genus
46. Vertical window bar
48. Dodger great
50. Alan of "Shane"
52. Neighbor of Mo.
55. Bulk-mail item
58. Clobbers
59. Tittles
60. On to
61. Maxwell et al.
62. Networks
64. Lbs. et al.
65. Hellespont swimmer
67. Joan and Peter
68. Up __
69. Services
71. Board's relative
74. Townsman
76. Curious people
78. Suffixes for drunk and dull
79. Sprees
80. River to the Rhine
84. Receiver of goods in trust
86. Abstract: Abbr.
89. Game for steady hands
90. Jacket type
91. One who teases
94. Diminutive suffix
95. U.S. agency
98. Former spouses
99. Utah range
100. Indian Ocean islands
101. Impresses deeply
102. What linemen do
103. Richard or boy
105. Dress fabrics
106. Calif. pine
108. Iron, in Bonn
111. Marshaled
112. Greek letters
115. Elopers' need
117. White clay
122. Old Turkish soldier
125. Ferber
126. Long time
127. Mrs. Chaplin
128. Anita
129. Sailors' saint
131. Rebuke
134. Showed the way
135. "__ is me"
136. Chemical suffix
138. Pacific herb

229 DOING THE SCALES By Nancy W. Atkinson

ACROSS

1. Comics' goals
7. Polish patriot
14. Water gear
19. Spreads on
21. Having an advantage
22. Something to know
23. Of inferior quality
25. Beer-bar sign
26. "Thanks __!"
27. __ dawn
28. More dreadful
29. Tend a fire
30. U.N. org.
31. Relative of tortoni
33. Scottish physicist
35. Cyst
36. Aboard
38. By the bottle __
40. Overturns
43. Thames town
44. Backfield men: Abbr.
46. Light switches
47. Kind of room
48. Major and Minor
50. __-Magnon
51. __ poetica
52. Impatient
56. Noblemen
57. Delay
59. Overtook
60. Common Latin word
61. Ella
62. V.I.P.'s of states
63. Headland
64. Connectives
65. Circular: Abbr.
66. Radiation unit
67. Malachite
68. Classify
69. M.D.'s
70. Debts
71. Roosevelt name
73. Behindhand
74. Exhausting
76. Songbird
77. Column molding
78. Some syllables
79. Arrowroot
80. Tax org.
81. Cords, old style
82. Hiss' partner
83. Relative of a jiff
84. Good times
85. N.M. Indian
86. Concord
89. Performed
91. Word for a wife
93. "Thyme on my hands," e.g.
94. Teasdale
96. Phenomena for St. Joan
99. Resort
101. __ und Drang
104. Alighieri
106. "Pillow __"
107. Child's play
108. Baseball statistic
109. Berths
112. Paralyze
113. Fish spear
114. North African
115. Marquis et al.
116. Flies
117. Egyptian king

DOWN

1. Veranda
2. Moon craft
3. Deeply committed
4. Flood the market
5. Having savvy
6. __ business (give a start)
7. African lemur
8. Miss Merkel
9. Banker, at times
10. __ alteram partem
11. Austere people
12. Seoul natives
13. Madagascar lemur
14. Sell-out signs
15. Abbr. at a page bottom
16. Bus direction
17. Having a neb
18. Poplars
20. Get the last bit of gravy
24. Spade
31. Loafers
32. Certain votes
34. Personnel concern
37. Gets going
39. Army medics
41. Fuel blocks
42. Beige
44. Palm leaves
45. Daring
48. Aboveboard
49. Self-reproach
50. Exercises
51. Jellyfish
52. P.I. tribesmen
53. High jinks
54. Begin
55. Entertainer
58. Abandoned
61. Salad adornments
62. Dead ducks
68. Works of a U.S. painter
70. Home, to Nanook
72. Have __ (drink)
75. Gists
77. Volcanic rock
79. Rich dessert
83. Mexican shawls
84. Caucasic language
85. British pot fixer: Var.
86. Distresses
87. Coat fur
88. Habituated
90. Turns outward
91. Shapes
92. Meager
95. Patron of X-rated films
97. Deneb and Vega
98. Fleming
100. Orbital point
102. Debauchee
103. Area developers: Abbr.
105. Audition
107. What Mark Spitz has done
110. Comprehend
111. Miss Munson

230 MENU OFFERINGS
By Herbert Ettenson

ACROSS

1. Bridge tragedy
4. Japanned metal
8. Wandering
14. Bird
19. Popeye's sweetheart
21. Large cat
23. Sports places
25. Late Supreme Court Justice
27. Miss Dee
28. Moron
29. Hilo hellos
30. Pintail ducks
32. Hockey's Bobby et al.
33. Partisan positions
34. __ alone
35. Alan __, British actor
37. Cartoon scream
38. Classify
41. Italian coin
43. Actress Goldie
45. The Admirable Doctor
50. John Paul or Spike
51. Tiny bit
52. Begun
53. On the wagon
54. Pot-__
55. City in Penna.
56. Garden pest
57. Park lurker
59. Superman's suit size: Abbr.
61. Spitchcock
62. Forward
64. Try to find
65. Russian saint
66. Old __
67. Nonsense
68. Pitchers
69. Frost, e.g.
70. High points
73. Co-author of "Tales from Shakespeare"
76. Saki
77. Cole's follower
78. Glides high
79. Branches
80. Variety of lettuce
81. Hussy
82. Offended
83. Actor and TV personality
86. Roman 102
89. Unconscious
90. Act droopy
91. Kind of cheese
92. Caution
94. Poet Thomas
96. Like some serge
97. Pinball
98. Puff up
99. Overcharge
100. Barrymore biographer
101. Calumet
102. Chinese weight
103. Singer Siepi
104. Author's encore: Abbr.
105. Con-man's helper
107. Pretty
108. Forest people of India
113. Genus of swifts
115. Gems
117. French girl's name
120. Young eel
121. Word with out or soft
123. Composer of "The Huguenots"
126. Contract word
127. Tolerates
128. Pirate pitcher in the 60s
129. Attachment to a bill
130. Manager
131. U.S. Indian
132. W.W. II craft

DOWN

1. Furniture pieces
2. Perfume resin
3. Mosaicked
4. Schoolbag items
5. Impatient cry
6. Sky harp
7. Israeli airline
8. City in Wisconsin
9. Drawn game at Monte Carlo
10. Wake up forcefully
11. Neighbor of Mar.
12. King Cole and others
13. Aspen, at times
14. Billiard shot
15. Parseghian
16. Recent: Prefix
17. Pittsburgh name
18. Chief Justice
20. Hollywood and __
22. Is afraid of
24. Canadian prov.
26. Worthless
31. W.W. II command
36. Shoulder gesture
38. Calmed down
39. Squelched
40. Rise with the waves
41. Ferber novel
42. Consolidated
44. Word with wiedersehen
45. Emerge
46. Merely
47. Friday, for one
48. Timetable abbr.
49. Hair jobs
50. English painter
51. Secures by a tenon
53. Bobbin
56. Then, in Paris
57. Swarm
58. Thyme, e.g.
60. Cat, in Madrid
63. Unreconciled
64. Beau
65. Work
66. Triton
68. Roper and others
70. Concerning
71. Ex-Senator from Florida
72. Miler of note
73. Successful stratagem
74. Race
75. Impertinent
76. Warning: It.
78. Was outstanding
80. Beverage bottle
83. Due
84. Master, in Africa
85. Rarin' to go
86. Compartment
87. Pines or Man
88. Bohemian river
90. Couple
91. Leg part
93. York or Deal
95. Child's place
96. Playing for time
97. Be suitable, in old days
99. Fodder
100. "Beat it!"
102. Backtalk
103. Billiardists
104. Obi
106. King or queen
107. Task
108. Start tennis or dinner
109. Register, in old Rome
110. Of an eye part
111. Movie segments
112. Court decree
114. Timetable, for short
116. Marquis de __
118. Biblical mountain
119. Island: Var.
122. Saison
124. Scoundrel
125. People of Africa

231 PHYSICAL CULTURE *By Alfio Micci*

ACROSS

1. P.I. fiber
6. Golf stroke
10. Book-jacket item
15. Kettledrum
16. Small case
17. Wind-propelled vessels
19. Beauty procedures
22. Kind of desk
24. Kind
25. Casino game
26. Provinces
28. Military abbr.
29. Noted physicist
31. Eastern ketch
33. Kismet
34. Rudiments
35. Sign up
37. Menu item
39. Roman road
40. Extend a hand
41. Miss Bagnold
43. Items in Santa's barn
45. Elephant and namesakes
46. __ thought
49. Papier-__
50. Resigns
51. Scottish hardwood
52. Seth's son
54. Convened
55. Lease anew
56. Caucasian language
58. Garden tool
60. Do a tough job
64. Kind of code
66. Actor Walter
67. Flag or May
68. Blot out
69. Like a good lookout
71. Certain Louvre pieces
73. Spanish ladies: Abbr.
74. Rod of tennis
75. "__ the season . . ."
76. Consider
78. Undergrads: Abbr.
79. Went for
81. Hangers-on
83. Backslide
85. Site of Temple of Karnak
86. Bach specialty
88. Herb

89. Coins of Iran
90. Jousting wear
91. Easy walk
93. Epic of note
96. Wavy, in heraldry
97. Storied teacher
98. Handles roughly
100. Gudrun's husband
101. Ensuing: Abbr.
102. Get __ (reach)
106. San __
108. Kind of horn
109. Asterisk material
111. Pitiful
114. Tangled
115. Gaelic
116. __ beck and call
117. New
118. Certain cities: Abbr.
119. Sikkim natives

DOWN

1. Language of Ecuador
2. Strenuous
3. Honest __
4. Leather
5. Word on a "Wanted" poster
6. At, in Bonn
7. __ time (never)
8. Fish of Japan
9. Saloon event
10. Big headline
11. Told a fib
12. Rubber trees
13. Indian salts
14. Give a hard time to
15. Blazing
17. Winter foot gear
18. Golfers, at times
20. Brothers
21. Works
23. Bridge positions
27. Shop machine
30. Caddoan tribe
32. Zero on Beaufort scale
34. Judges
36. Football-team unit
38. Evade, with "out"
40. Egg cell
42. Mother's word
44. Adjective ending
45. Diving or dumb
46. Brownish gray
47. "__ cock horse . . ."
48. Pillaged
50. Editor, at times
53. Grave
55. Like some paper
57. Like some company bonds
59. Day: Abbr.
60. "__ my word!"
61. Loud
62. Ivan et al.
63. German state
65. Charters
67. Kind of card
70. Holiday times
71. Light rain
72. Replenish a lawn
75. Penalty of yore
77. 11th-century date
79. Salmon
80. Impetuous
81. Careful efforts
82. Road sign
84. __ breve
85. Bull trout
86. Went boating
87. Separated
90. Fur animal
92. Vessel
94. Adjusts
95. Bell sounds
99. Mess up
102. Word with bellum
103. Dove's home
104. Ancient mound
105. Kiln
107. Hep
11C. Rocky peak
112. Scale notes
113. Uncle of radio days

232 BEASTLY WORLD By Anne Fox

ACROSS

1. Game
6. Charles' dog
10. Johnny
14. As much again
19. Movie studio site in England
21. Arrogant
24. Din
25. Nursery name
26. Musical Bull
27. Prosperity, old style
28. Mature
30. S.A. country
31. Sister
32. Resin
34. Gas
36. City on the Tagus
39. Map feature
41. Want __
43. Ancient Greek
45. Endless: Sp.
47. Words by Septimus Winner
55. Oboe
56. Boiled __
57. Stocks
58. Business abbr.
59. __ lamb
60. Japanese writing
62. Chic
65. Vitality
66. Rock layers
68. Durability
71. Servicewoman
72. Wood
74. Betrothed
76. N.Y. city
77. Dictionary entry: Abbr.
79. Dependent
81. Novel by Hendrick Conscience
85. N.Y. lake resort
87. Elec. complex
88. Present: Fr.
89. Infuses
93. Egyptian leader
94. Hoi polloi
96. Introduces
99. Come up
100. Dock group
101. Buster
104. Haul
105. Law, in Lyon
107. __ Claire
108. Like some prose
110. Kind of maid
112. Malice
114. Words by Beaumont and Fletcher
120. Addison's friend
121. Hawaiian porches
122. Burrows
123. Kind of shell
126. Out-and-out
128. Spellbound
130. Portray
134. Memorabilia
135. Covered up
137. Sew: Sp.
139. Headlong
141. Greek letter
142. Opening words for a math trick
146. Flowers
149. Phone-book listing for a former V.P.
150. Poem by Coleridge
151. Finnish port
152. Plate call
153. Work units
154. Gardens

DOWN

1. Factotum
2. Water buffalo
3. Buttons
4. Words by Dos Passos
5. "__ here"
6. Small bristles
7. __-disant
8. Contest
9. African gazelle
10. Inherit
11. English and Welsh rivers
12. Clique
13. Initials of rank
14. Land area: Abbr.
15. "__ them" (words from Bo-Peep)
16. U.S. tax man: Abbr.
17. Descendants: Var.
18. Come after
19. Fraternal org.
20. Bewail
22. Conked
23. Bloke
29. Book by John Beecroft
33. Shopping place
35. German physicist
37. Bull sound
38. Native: Suffix
40. "Forget it!"
42. Come in third
44. Filled pancakes
46. Seamstress Betsy
47. Go down swinging
48. Asian capital
49. Australian town
50. Certain votes
51. Dickens character
52. Bean
53. Naught: Fr.
54. Catch sight of
60. Boxer's goal
61. Catkin
63. Mild oath
64. Type of tea
67. Kind of mural
69. Worsted fabric
70. W.W. I group
73. Lower
75. Poet's word
78. Handbill
80. Bandleader Brown
82. Monk
83. Egg: Prefix
84. C.P.A.
85. Priests of Mars
86. With 102 Down, an entertainer
90. Old MacDonald refrain
91. Song of David
92. Alone: Fr.
93. Kind of hat
95. Unruly horse
97. Medea's beloved
98. Spare
102. See 86 Down
103. Slangy denial
106. Olive tree genus
109. Attention-getter
111. Colorado town
113. "Say __"
115. __ to (pave the way)
116. Path of a blast: Abbr.
117. Brave
118. U.S. agency
119. Fish hawks
123. Family member
124. Close, to poets
125. City of Peru
127. __ hearts
129. Aroid
131. Believer: Suffix
132. Board game
133. Flip
136. __ many words
138. Suffix with din or luncheon
140. Veer
143. Murray.
144. Badly: Prefix
145. Swimsuit part
147. Joke
148. Big: Abbr.

233 PEOPLE IN HIDING By Eugene T. Maleska

ACROSS

1. Pioneers' route
6. Reactions to onions
11. Joins the Sherpas
17. Jeff, for one
18. Port for Rose and Peggy
19. Paid tribute
21. Writer Laurence is buried here
23. Motivate
24. Salutation
25. Aspects
26. Parseghian mans a rampart
28. Bolivian export
29. Glove for Gehrig
31. Slyly spiteful
33. Popeye's creator
34. Decree
35. "For __ sake!"
37. Prepare to drive
39. Crow's cousin
40. Cause of many errors
41. Pralines
43. Populace
45. Plundered
47. Lateen
49. Shropshire
51. "Fiddler" character
52. Verse forms
56. Swedish shale
58. Called
61. Feathered six-footer
62. Statement takes a Bow
66. Photo paper
67. Sulkies
69. Cousin of NATO
70. Start of 109 Down
72. Kind of pickle
73. Sail sounds
75. Had supicions about Torme and Helen's mother
78. Little Rachel
79. Oversentimental
81. Region of Greece
82. Memos
84. Of space
86. Querulous weakling
89. Humdinger
90. "__ My Business" (J.D. Craig)
93. Decorticated
95. Had a 3 on short hole
99. Over
100. Tree
102. Court matters involving Ibsen woman
104. Marie Antoinette, e.g.
105. Navy meal
106. Insurgent
108. Lawful
110. Take off
111. Unruly tot
112. Largest of the flatfishes
114. Damages, in Durango
116. Greek letter
117. Grassy feed for cattle
119. Ferber ties up world group
122. Hides in a grotto
123. Al of Detroit fame
124. Greet
125. Angling group
126. On end
127. Lock

DOWN

1. "__ from Pompey's Head"
2. Abie's wife gets an ornament
3. Pastime for Carney
4. Particular
5. Keats product
6. College board
7. Nubbin
8. Asymmetrical
9. Meal, in Paris
10. Get into a dither viewing Skelton
11. Remove by bits with Dogpatch man
12. He thinks two's a crowd
13. Part of M.I.T.
14. Sailor's swab
15. Noah's son keeps a realm together
16. Arranged in succession
17. Overwhelms
18. Lodged afield
20. Like many a jalopy
22. Uncluttered
27. Gelling agent
30. Small anvil
32. City on the Colorado
34. Speedy Buttons runs down acid dye
36. Far from frivolous
38. Kind of dot
40. Basso Jerome
42. Geometers' terms
44. Placate
46. Old hand
48. Nottingham products
50. Worked at
52. Victims of feudalism
53. Dickinson
54. Girls surround rifle man
55. Bridge thrills
57. Mack's vaudeville partner
59. Israeli port
60. Valleys
63. Devoured greedily
64. Furl
65. Perfume ingredient
68. Crowns of thorns
71. Showed sudden interest
74. Cruiser's asset
76. Diamond gal is in bloom
77. Of bodily tissue
80. Sourdough's time period
83. Attracted
85. Inanimate
87. Of an epoch
88. Dweller gives space to Caesar
90. End of existence
91. Sea polyp traps a captain
92. District in Pakistan
94. Time period
96. Turbulent
97. Children, in Cannes
98. Neutralize a bomb
101. Scold
103. __ Fein
106. Wrathful one
107. Kind of probe
109. Emcee's proposal
112. Experience
113. Roofing item
115. Vega or nova
118. Indian poet
120. Twitching
121. Yeu or Corse

ACROSS

1. "Who, what?" said Tom __
7. Youth org.
10. Total
13. Cotton knot
16. Ledger men
20. As gentle __
21. One, in Bonn
22. Shade
23. Set of sayings
24. Eagle: Prefix
25. "Young M.D." said Tom __
27. Sprite
28. Passed below
30. Smith or Fleming
31. Miss West
32. Methods
33. "Gold leaf," said Tom __
34. Miss Flanders
35. Rouge __
37. Not worth __ of beans
38. Wave: Sp.
39. "John," said Tomas __
40. That kept in mind
41. Singer Boone
42. Praise
44. "Do as __ !"
45. P.O. limbos
46. Israeli port
48. Warble
51. Series of notes: Abbr.
52. "Elec. unit," said Tom __
55. Ivy campus nostalgically
58. Style
59. "Go easy, Mr. Roper," said Tom __
61. French girlfriends
62. Chatters
64. Greek name
65. Foam plastic
66. "Behold, __ in thine own eye"
68. B. & O., etc.
69. Herbert of TV
70. "__ goes walking . . ."
72. Sky, in Cadiz
74. Sudan river
75. Fun sound
78. Wandering
79. Billfold
80. "Well, well!"
81. Marker
82. Sides: Sp.
83. Unreal
85. Small bribe
86. Level land: Abbr.
87. "Coda," said Tom __
90. Child's vehicle
94. Old English letter
95. Fable
97. Calflike
98. "Shirtwaist," said Tom __
99. Plunders
101. Rhine siren
103. "Wray," said Tom __
104. Incensed
105. Days of __
106. Antiseptic
107. Neithers' partners
109. Pistol man
110. German girl's name
112. Bauble
113. Herons
115. Roof worker
116. Mil. staff man
118. Written: Fr.
120. Even if
121. Garden tools
122. Like a grassland
124. Optimistic
126. Girl's name
127. Eur. country
128. Constance or Norma
129. Baba
130. "Maid's night off," said Tom __
134. Certain trains: Abbr.
135. Lamprey
136. Torme
137. Trouble
138. Bank worker
139. Stringed knob
140. Suffix with diction or function
141. Salty sauce
142. Hull curve
143. Consent to

DOWN

1. Water, on Oahu
2. Dogtag info.
3. "K-," said Tom __
4. "Pass the cards," said Tom __
5. "Greene," said Tom __
6. Craving
7. "Don't come on time," said Tom __
8. "Quiet meadow," said Tom __
9. Some
10. Have __ (be generous)
11. "Come on down," said Tom __
12. Dict. entries
13. "Zero," said Tom __
14. Boredom
15. Mexican statesman
16. Wagon
17. "Magazine," said Tom __
18. In any way
19. Girl's name
26. U.S.
29. Miss Raines
32. ". . . and lose a few," said Tom __
34. Team pet
36. Govt. agency
37. Narrow shoe size
39. Tufts
41. "Army exam," said Tom __
43. Employ
47. "Drei . . . fünf," said Tom __
49. "__ in the inn"
50. "Brothers," said Tom __
52. Nonbeliever, in Milano
53. "Intended," said Tom __
54. "Oriental gift," said Tom __
56. Jacob's wife: Var.
57. Pol. party
58. Soc. degree
60. Base metal, old usage
61. "One pair," said Tom __
63. Diplomat's concern
66. Have an __ mystery
67. Foolish
71. Under warranty: Abbr.
73. Chosen: Fr.
75. "X's and," said Tom __
76. Jinx
77. "In favor?" said Tom __
79. "I bequeath," said Tom __
80. Prefixes meaning muscle
84. Streaked
86. Timetable times
88. In the: It.
89. Engineers' org.
91. "Just Newsweek," said Tom __
92. Puffs up
93. Golfing cup
96. "Youth," said Tom __
98. "Is Elizabeth cold?" said Tom __
100. __ Aviv
102. Carrot or beet
103. Full liberty
106. Lichen genus
108. Globe
109. "Pope," said Tom __
111. Fluids
113. "Tripod," said Tom __
114. Rung
115. __-cat
116. In a fitting way
117. Severe lawmaker
119. Furious one
123. "__ glad to meet you"
124. Butts
125. Margarine
130. Possesses
131. Mil. officers
132. Shelter
133. Many mos.

235 OUTLANDISH OUTLANDS

By Thomas Sheehan

ACROSS

1. Place for a sand wedge
5. _ girls (Seoul libbers)
10. Satchels
15. Balloon need
18. Biblical tongue: Abbr.
19. Entomb
20. Incurred, as debts
21. Unmask
22. What William Tell did
24. Pepys' remark in Lhasa
26. "_ Love You?"
27. Shankar
29. Frying pan
30. Kind of verb: Abbr.
32. Kind of grit
33. Rome's Castel Sant' _
34. George Cohan, Chinese style
41. Superman, e.g.
42. Like the fox's grapes
43. Eur. capital
44. Swimsuit part
47. German port
48. Big-business monogram
49. Igneous rock
50. Baby carriage
51. L.A. campus
52. "South Pacific" words, in Africa
56. Belief
57. Something to remember
59. Descendant of Judah
60. _ on (get drunk with Chiang)
61. Art medium
62. Beans
63. Measures: Abbr.
64. French writer
67. Glacial ridges
68. German quips
73. Sluggish
74. Campaign in Tripoli
77. Large tank
78. Kind of goose
79. Chem. suffixes
80. Approves
81. Nice, in Nice
82. Insect
83. Money premium
84. Foxy, in Scotland
85. Pink or rose
86. Sir Thomas More, in Jordan
91. Amelia Earhart _
94. Tears
95. Cruelty personified
96. Western gullies
98. Opera girl
99. A-one
103. TV fare in Ohio
105. Sherman dictum, south of the border
109. Adenauer word
110. "_ the bag"
111. Statuette
112. Spread
113. _ Canals
114. Tact, for one
115. Accord
116. Word with gab or slug

DOWN

1. Melt
2. Hebrew letter
3. With finesse
4. Biblical son
5. Chime in
6. Wallet item
7. Capek drama
8. Marine bird
9. Make _ (misplay)
10. Driveway décor
11. Indian queen
12. State: Abbr.
13. Sock in the _
14. Expressed, out West
15. "G.W.T.W." star
16. Spinning
17. Brawl
21. Like sea water
23. Habits
25. Ignite, in England
28. Ledger man: Abbr.
31. Yield, à la Spassky
32. _ fait (entirely)
34. Siberian native
35. Like a malt drink
36. Relative
37. _ honors (treat)
38. Certain lake dwellers
39. Monks' titles
40. Asian nurse
44. Prepare tea
45. Ukranian body
46. Egyptian deity
49. Promises
50. Light refractor
52. "_ Got Nobody"
53. Track event
54. Ropes
55. Indo-European
56. Garden plant
58. Watery silk
60. Albee's Alice
62. "_ These Days"
64. _ mortis, Latvian style
65. Familiar sig.
66. Lincoln showcase
68. Actor Theodore
69. Haunt
70. Molding
71. Stock, in cards
72. To-dos
74. Star in Lyra: Var.
75. Getting _ years
76. Takes it easy
81. _ Arimathea
83. Cleanser ingredient
84. S.A. monkey
85. Spanish port
86. Send _ (write)
87. Famous surgeon
88. World area
89. Get _ of
90. Mulligan joint
91. River of Borneo
92. Word form for a Soviet area
93. Make an effort
97. York et al.: Abbr.
98. Friend: Fr.
100. Distant: Prefix
101. Cheers
102. Novelist's concern
104. Sancho Panza's steed
106. Sea initials
107. Chem. prefix
108. Hole or race

236 TITLE SEARCHES By George Rose Smith

ACROSS

1. Kind of cloth or hopping
6. __ pectoris
12. Cockney cavities
16. Narrow shoal
20. British __
21. Jack Horner's place
22. "A Star is Born"
23. Exercise
24. "The Vision of Sir Launfal"
26. "Gone with the Wind"
28. Round of applause
29. Ram
30. One of Sheridan's "Rivals"
32. Persian wheels
33. Cease
34. Flood stage
35. Hairnet
36. Commands
37. __ macabre
38. Pyramids' neighbor
39. Slav
40. Brides' portions
43. "My Fair Lady"
45. One-liner
48. "It's __ night for . . ."
49. Darken
50. Chose
51. Kittiwake
52. Heavy shoes
53. Physician
54. Casts forth
56. Raccoon's cousin
57. Gossips
58. Role in "Julius Caesar"
59. Pool
60. Mockeries
61. Energy unit
62. "A Midsummer Night's Dream"
66. Office copies
67. Make tidy
69. Of the kidneys
70. Kit or Johnny
71. Nonplussed
73. "The Count of Monte Cristo"
75. Football scores: Abbr.

78. French troops
79. Scott
80. Disencumbers
81. Trim a photo
82. Ear parts
83. Out of sorts
84. Delays
86. U.S. pioneer
87. Kind of glades
88. Biggers' sleuth
89. Solos
90. Shore bird
91. By
92. "Magnificent Obsession"
95. Baggage pieces
96. Courage
97. Tides
98. Rule
99. Go on a crash diet
101. Dizzy et al.
102. Perfume
103. I love: Lat.
106. Scanty
107. Meals
108. Assume as true
109. "The Third Man"
110. "The Doctor's Dilemma"
112. "Hamlet"
115. Old measure: Var.
116. Range
117. Cash-register key
118. New Orleans sight
119. Interpret
120. Jane Grey, e.g.
121. __ up for
122. Shabby

DOWN

1. Give a tenth
2. Nile dam
3. Mix
4. Do a bank job
5. N.Y. time
6. Bernhardt or Duse
7. Strong denial
8. Accost
9. Wayside and Tabard
10. Clear
11. Nazi doctrine
12. Kind of old schoolhouse
13. Cherished

14. Gabor et al.
15. Weaken
16. Stuffiness
17. "__ in writing"
18. Concepts
19. Scatters
23. Beethoven's third
25. Told tall tales
27. In readiness
31. Persian gazelle
34. Murderers
35. Black buck
36. Pinza and others
37. Protracts, with "out"
38. Killer: Suffix
39. What Jack broke
40. Hat designer
41. Flirt
42. "Conversation at Midnight"
43. Casaba
44. Fore'er

45. "A Farewell to Arms"
46. Stand-in for Standish
47. Certain menagerie
49. Conductor's need
51. Greta
53. Like most fences
54. Hat
55. Sao __
56. Dissect in a way
58. Shelters
60. Passengers
62. Scruffs
63. Sea birds
64. Orchestra section
65. Doorway: Abbr.
66. "Games People Play"
68. Arab ruler
70. I.O.U.'s
71. Orchid tubers

72. Hidden valuables
73. Maine campus site
74. Error's partner
76. Recipient
77. Barracudas
79. Open-window annoyance
81. Bobwhite
83. Tedious task
84. Stoles, etc.
85. Is unwell
86. Foolish talk
88. Abjectly afraid
89. Gives up
90. Blouses
92. Human being
93. Apple prescription
94. Binge
95. Jury panels
96. Hurt

98. Transferred again
99. Germ cell
100. Cigar-making center
101. Gave guardedly
102. Composer of "Over There"
103. Kind of board
104. Cried, as a cat
105. Sec. of State, 1895-97
106. Purple Heart memento
107. Adriatic wind
108. Old African coin
109. To __ (precisely)
111. Wolframite
113. __ bad
114. City lines

237 BIT OF HISTORY *By David A. Murray*

ACROSS

1. Pair
5. "__ horse!"
9. __ tale
13. Lady's man
17. Grapevine disease
18. Galway islands
19. Agony
20. Bone: Prefix
21. Receipt, in Paris
22. Who
25. Barnum's "bird"
27. Prior months: Abbr.
28. Slip by
29. Irish playwright
31. House, in Toledo
32. Old kind of skirt
33. What
38. Holiday times
42. Heavenly Ram
43. Long time
44. Does in
45. Food fish
46. Prince of opera
47. Showy thing
48. Part of I.T.T.: Abbr.
49. Eurasian tree
51. Functioned
52. Tamper with
54. Kind of rash
55. Soft-shells
56. Where
59. Molars, etc.
61. T.V. org.
62. Got up
63. When
70. Show of intention
71. Troubles
72. More slippery
73. Common abbr.
76. Huskies' burdens
77. Insurance abbr.
78. Actor Alfred
79. Chemical prefix
80. "__ transit . . ."
81. Fight site
83. Outfield men: Abbr.
84. Swiss lass of fiction
85. This: Sp.
87. Why
91. Ships of W.W. II

93. Stanford White's killer
94. Marriage settings
95. Piece of bread, at times
98. Accommodate
99. Smear
101. How
105. Angling gear
108. Goose: Sp.
109. Combats
110. City in Russia
111. Miss Kett
112. Wee ones
113. Closes, with "up"
114. __ the joint
115. Arabian vessel

DOWN

1. "__ Rosenkavalier"
2. Employ
3. Attaining of the throne
4. Elizabeth, to Henry VIII
5. "It's only a __ are playing"
6. Times
7. Sailors
8. Somewhat
9. "__ of the town"
10. Greek god
11. Chaney
12. Zodiac sign
13. Houdini specialty
14. On the roof
15. Soaks
16. Forfeit
19. City on the Arkansas
20. Eur. capital
23. Wharf
24. Vassals' lands: Var.
26. Cheers
29. Egg white
30. City in Finland
31. Vulture
32. Comet man
34. Attain
35. Course
36. Half, clove or rolling
37. Miss Hayes, to Roman friends
39. French hurrahs
40. Nonpoisonous
41. Perception
47. __ distance (last)
49. Halloween participant
50. Crime
52. Overfond ones
53. Bathtub leavings
54. Marble
56. Payed honor to
57. Utmost degree
58. Latin form of beware
59. Georgian capital's old name
60. Cause's partner
63. Moat
64. Explosives
65. Aunt in "Oklahoma!"
66. Miss Massey
67. River or sea
68. Discard
69. Once: Ger.
73. Bergner of films
74. Henry's house
75. Nickels and dimes
79. Gave high billing
81. Broadcast org.
82. Realities
84. Daughter of Loki: Var.
86. Greek letters
88. Adds liquid
89. Mat. days
90. Interweave
92. Prophet
95. Copy, for short
96. Cry of dismay
97. Fly, for one
98. Merganser
99. Theda
100. Carbon suffixes
102. Dental degree
103. Sioux City name
104. Ad __
106. W.W. II area
107. Gresham's, for one

238 PAINTBOX CHOICES By Elmer Toro

ACROSS

1. Indian state
6. Opera girl et al.
11. Old French coin
14. Old festival of Aug. 1
20. Solomon Islands bay
21. Decrepit
22. Number
23. Classify
24. White
28. Everybody
29. Eggs __ yong
30. Hebrew month
31. __ fixe
32. Naught
33. Yellow
37. "__ happens..."
38. Bagnold
39. Newcastle's river
40. Curve
41. W.W. II plane
43. Take pot shots at
45. Bede and Smith
49. Place
51. Clamor
54. Ruler
55. Slept
58. Champion
59. Dumas hero
61. Black
65. Social
66. Council city
67. Woes
68. Snake eyes
69. Red, in Italy
71. Country follower
72. Confederate
73. Once more
74. Hingle
75. "The __ have it"
78. Roman needle
80. Gold
83. Site of Frogner Park
84. Split
85. Slowing, in music: Abbr.
86. Give it __
87. Continent, to French
88. Columbus campus
89. Glossy cloth
91. Enjoys Chamonix
92. Old chest
93. Do burlesque work
95. Chem. suffix
97. Pink
100. Tatter's products
101. Science course
103. Thicket
104. Land parcels
105. Meat cuts
106. Partner of order
107. Dinner course
110. Jerk
112. Peewee
114. Former Mideast initials
117. Anklebones
119. Dirk
121. Tennis shots
123. Purple
129. Gardner
130. Snapshots, for short
131. Put in a hopeless spot
132. Scented plant
133. Honshu city
134. Blue
139. Give __ approval
140. Cumberland, for one
141. Burton role
142. Blackmore girl
143. Kind of box
144. Self
145. British guns
146. Moon crater

DOWN

1. "...heart that laughs __"
2. Furrows: Fr.
3. Red
4. Sandy's bark
5. Singer Anna
6. W.W. I force
7. Like most reference books
8. Old amphora
9. Edison name et al.
10. "__ evil"
11. Jazz pieces
12. Word in poems
13. Remove a toupee
14. Most recent
15. Tennis pro
16. Ecological degree
17. Green
18. Column ridge
19. Pillar: Prefix
21. Like a chimney
25. Easier
26. Laugh, in Paris
27. Common Latin phrase
34. Menlo Park name
35. Spanish queen
36. Quivery trees
37. Image
42. Single things
44. One of the tenses
46. Onassis et al.
47. Garage man: Abbr.
48. Silver
50. Caucasian tongue
52. Note
53. Prior to
56. Cantankerous
57. Swerves
58. "__ devil do you think you are?"
59. Rose oil
60. Instant
61. Advertising rate base
62. Prorate
63. Sweet: Prefix
64. Roman emperor
70. Saint, in Brazil
72. In a light manner
73. Raise __ about
74. Fish: Prefix
76. Miss Venner
77. Heavy fogs
79. Depot: Abbr.
81. N.Z. parrots
82. Border, for short
90. Taut
91. Appear
92. __ code
93. Not busy
94. Writer Gay
95. Basics
96. Tokyo drama
98. Police org.
99. Space initials
102. Imitates
104. Agitate
106. Parasite
108. Family hand-me-down
109. Feather's pal
111. __ non grata
113. Smart
115. Syrian city
116. Italian painter
118. Truck, in London
120. Compositions
121. Over there: Fr.
122. Sheeplike
124. Siouan Indian
125. Lab vessels
126. Common contraction
127. Kind of bud
128. Listens to
130. Straitened
135. Insecticide
136. __ and Cav (opera double-bill)
137. Switch readings
138. French monarch

239 MERCURY LEVELS
By Barbara Gillis

ACROSS

1. Nut
7. Participant
12. Doctrines
16. Recessed area
17. Party of a sort
19. Promoters
20. Plundered
21. As hot as hell, e.g.
22. Pacific pact
23. Recognized
24. Sweeper, for short
25. Stall sound
27. Stock-table listings
29. Bristle
30. Greet
31. Pledge
32. Long hits
34. Dishevel
36. Like some TV pictures
38. "_ is the hour . . ."
39. City on the Missouri
41. Religious belief
44. Genetic abbr.
45. Jose or Mel
46. U.S. agency
47. Arab peasants
49. Gershwin
50. Taste
52. Part of stet
54. Inattentive ones
55. British resort
57. Choice food
59. Kadiddlehopper
61. Free of taboo, in Hawaii
62. Beware
68. English river
69. Attract
70. Campus military org.
71. Uppity one
73. Lurch
76. Adult insect
78. Marmara, e.g.
80. Kick
81. Like rumble seat hair
83. Sourdough's 12 months
84. Enzyme
86. Direction: Abbr.
87. Cruelty
89. Refer to
90. Company abbr.
91. Hindu orders
92. Meal
94. Porter
97. Like Luke's hand
99. Unique thing
100. Kiln
104. London area
105. Part of Greenland
106. Height: Prefix
107. Anoint
108. Pithy
110. Elm fruit
112. Honeymooners
113. Moth, often
114. Studies
115. Understand
116. Young oyster
117. Undermine
118. Containers

DOWN

1. Horseshoe parts
2. Incomparable
3. Dart
4. Trouble
5. Equal
6. Unite
7. Attack
8. Gum
9. Thumb or Swift
10. Due
11. Statement for the press
12. Fish of Europe
13. Unimportant
14. Ditto
15. Overwhelm
18. Period in French history
19. Residue
24. Ming item
26. Rock cavity
28. Rolling and gall
30. Light
32. Shelter
33. Kind of song
35. Minerals
37. Roses or oats
39. State in Malaya
40. Incensed
41. Stalemate
42. Ship passages
43. River in Miss.
45. Mendacity
46. Banks' go-between
48. Lots
51. Handle rudely
53. _ de France
56. Learned
58. Spread to dry
60. Asian native
63. Commoners
64. Beret
65. Earth metals: Abbr.
66. Inward
67. Hangman's gear
72. Gathering
73. River of Chile
74. Yarns
75. Type of star
77. Actress Rita
79. Suffers
81. Dam
82. Swiss purchase
85. Postpone
88. Quarantine
89. Imitative one
92. Reacted to a joke
93. Place inside
95. Shoddy
96. Artery
98. Tree animal
101. Mosquito genus
102. Snoozed
103. Rorschach. etc.
105. Three: Prefix
107. Kind of duke or angel
109. Between ready and go
111. Bustle
112. Part of A.B.: Abbr.

ACROSS

1. Famous friend
6. Prove, as a will
13. Drink
16. Trophy
19. Kind of acid
20. Grid guards
21. Negligent
22. Promising one
24. Famous main street
26. Famous bell
28. Urges on, in Scotland
29. Quiets
30. Certain paintings
33. Red and Salmon
34. Utter
35. He struck out
36. Titled man
37. Certain tests
38. Boils or ulcers
39. Brew
40. Undo one's knitting
41. Sneeze inducer
44. Cooked-fruit dessert
46. Relative of mdse.
49. Shuns
50. O'Toole
51. Incite
52. Russian city
53. Plant shoots: Var.
54. Silica product
55. "... and the slithy __ did gyre"
57. Italian city
58. Berlin conclusion
59. Night sound
60. Untreated metals
61. Finally
62. Society gal
63. Ball club
67. French decrees
68. Longs
70. Japanese garment
71. Steep slope
72. Tranquilizes
74. Famous New England poet
76. Estonian river
79. Cuts short
80. Article of contention
81. To __ (exactly)
82. Auditors: Abbr.
83. British oath
84. Malign in print
85. Wall St. phrase
87. School hds.
88. Merely
89. Kind of stick
90. Beiges
91. "Les Misérables" lawman
92. Yo-Yo or kite
93. Kind of cake
96. Sui __
97. Kind of jury
98. Weld
99. Certain jewels
100. Satirical
102. Fight
103. Artery
104. Fuel
107. Card game
108. Drama section
109. Verona's river
110. Tepee
111. Ravel's "Daphnis and __"
113. Famous city
116. Alone, on stage
117. U.S. Indian
118. Red, white __
119. Off one's rockers
120. Metal rtes.
121. Pull
122. Properties
123. Regions

DOWN

1. Valleys
2. Ancient rabbi
3. Indistinct
4. Units
5. Conjunction
6. Contented
7. Moon features
8. Set of names: Suffix
9. Myerson
10. Soul, in St. Lo
11. Youth
12. Guarantor
13. Woody
14. Speaker's place
15. Certain phone: Abbr.
16. Contemporary
17. Inflorescence
18. Equals
22. Biological changes
23. Hosp. employees
25. Frightens
27. Hot-dish support
32. Hamlet
35. Students
36. People in the woods
37. Poetic temples
38. Porkers
39. Scads
40. Hicks
41. Sped
42. Birdlike
43. Hit musical
44. Asian alliance
45. Some reviews
46. Utah lake
47. Slow-witted
48. Blind parts
50. One-up tactics
52. Cargo ship
54. Dresses
55. What's human
56. Space path
57. Camel's burden
59. Toaster's word
61. Alms boxes
63. Spruce
64. Lake Geneva feeder
65. Type face
66. Caviar
67. Son of Jacob
69. "The good die __ ..."
71. Girls' names
72. Footwear
73. Ebony, in Madrid
74. Manufactured man
75. Enjoy fully
77. Mother: Prefix
78. Staff members: Abbr.
80. Bay
82. Wine vintage
84. Reason
85. Vinegar: Prefix
86. Certain test answer
87. Claus
89. Commiserates
90. Bulldog and final
91. Wit
93. French stocks
94. Bird-feeder item
95. Artery linings
96. Uses a mouthwash
97. Like a sponge
99. Shaggy: Fr.
100. Gods' blood
101. Come from behind
102. Ship propeller
103. Grownup
104. Adventure
105. Miss Loos
106. Remains
107. Prefixes for outside
108. Kind of suggestion
109. Eastern church title
110. Ex-resident of 113 Across
112. Not at work
114. Tracer bullet: Abbr.
115. City of Brazil

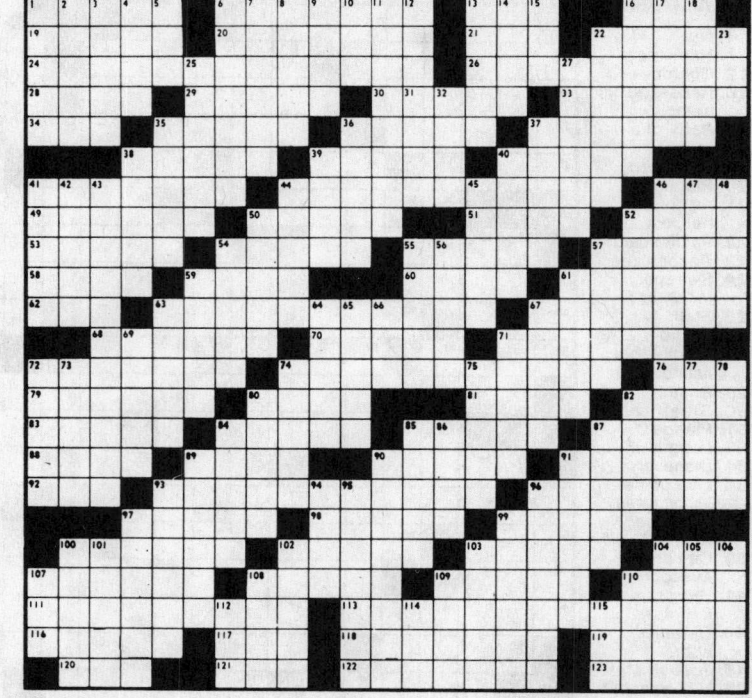

241 HOOKUPS By Elaine D. Schorr

ACROSS

1. "South Pacific" song locale
5. Metric measures: Abbr.
8. Do art work
12. Kind of note
17. Old Greek coin
18. BB, for one
19. Bride, in Bonn
21. Venetian coin
22. Pacific explorer's activity
24. Mania for cutting hair
26. Arctic bird
27. Newts
29. Unaspirated
30. _ bene
31. Outmoded: Abbr.
33. Comet's head
34. Scraps
35. Tenth of a sen
36. Rake
38. Represent
40. Aquarium fish
43. Do a tailoring job
45. Las Vegas area
47. Kind of poker, with 5 Down
50. Golf tourney
53. Big name in Troy
56. Baby wear
57. Hitchcock's 39
59. Pueblo people
61. Intimidate
62. John or Salic
65. Louis XV word
67. Left out
69. Spanish child
70. Go amiss
71. Mild oath by a compositor
74. Certain scholar's hour
75. Kind of hammer
77. Those not present
78. Flynn
79. Time periods: Abbr.
80. _-miss
82. Kind of geometry
83. Meuse city
85. Symmetrized
87. Eat humble pie
90. Descendants of Shem
94. Quick attacks
96. Lifeless
98. Roman rooms
99. Entertain in a way
101. Webster and Beery
103. Grate
104. First 3 of 26.
106. Causes soreness
108. Pintail duck
109. Month: Abbr.
110. Dear ones
112. Sea bird
113. Brimful
115. Thai isthmus
118. Star in dog-training class
121. Hugh Hefner, e.g.
123. Tilter's suit
124. Nutcracker, for one
125. Anthony
126. Immanuel
127. Statements: Abbr.
128. Boot liners
129. _ Darya (Soviet river)
130. "Picnic" author

DOWN

1. Chica or Raton
2. Eastern name
3. People in high places
4. Genre
5. See 47 Across
6. Fake furs
7. Organic frameworks
8. Falls off
9. _-la
10. Italian director, with 76 Down
11. Part of H.H.H.
12. Mdse.
13. Downfall
14. Antidote for upstaging
15. Saguaros
16. Allen
18. Ship: Abbr.
20. Bivouacked
23. Map abbrs.
25. Residues: Fr.
28. Button base
32. Symbols of redness
36. Zodiac sign
37. Spanish wave
39. Symbol of nothingness
41. Catfish
42. Link of Northwest
44. Repeat a bugging job
46. Rinds
48. Wall St. menial
49. Sutures
51. Glossy proof
52. Mast poles
54. Take for _
55. Ceremonial feasts
58. Man of Brazil
60. French porcelain
62. States of oblivion
63. Coming, in Italy
64. Stomach ache for Poe
66. Stone slab
68. Electron tube
72. Heath plant
73. S.A. beast
76. See 10 Down
81. Curb
84. Saltpeter
86. M.S. or D.D.
88. Snare
89. Stamps on
91. Rail worker
92. Ice, in Bonn
93. Weaken
95. Belle and Bart
97. The Tiger's neighbor
100. Admits
102. Gardener's gear
104. Spectral type
105. French café order
107. Brown color
109. Sandra or Ruby
111. Burns, for one
113. Ways: Abbr.
114. Can or type
116. Pealed
117. Stake
119. Aaron clouts: Abbr.
120. Common abbr.
122. Aspen sight

TRICKS OF THE TRADE

By Maura B. Jacobson

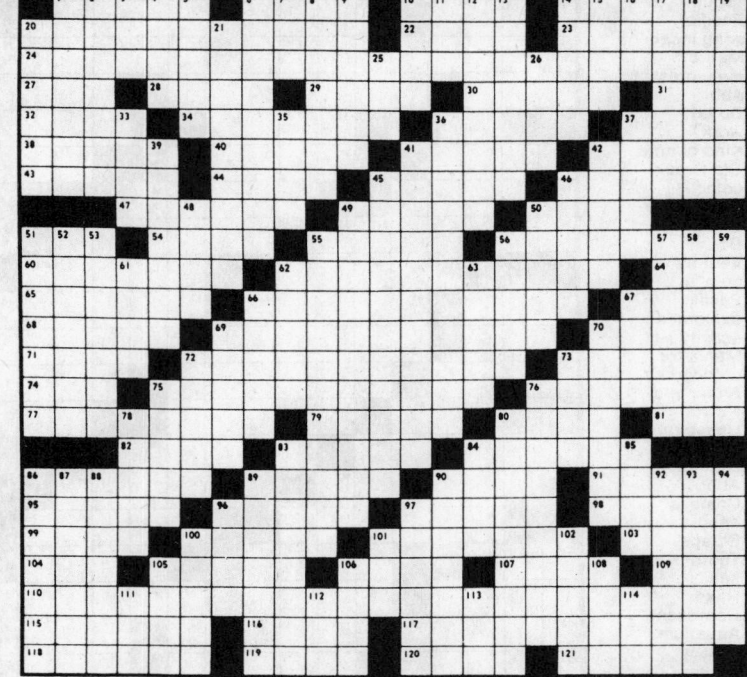

ACROSS

1. Sandman's home, perhaps
6. Suffer, in Scotland
10. European apple
14. Xmas-tree decor
20. Vision specialist
22. U.S.S.R. city
23. Chant
24. Weekender's lot, paraphrased
27. Fold: Fr.
28. Otologist's domain
29. Stable staple
30. Expect
31. Carper
32. Paddy product
34. Street sign
36. Tie up
37. Keenness
38. Accustom: Var.
40. Carries on
41. Dryad
42. Loom bar
43. _ no
44. U.S. inventor
45. Slangy vetoes
46. Fallen idols
47. "As Maine goes, _ . . ."
49. Coiffed like Simba
50. Son of Joktan
51. French monarch
54. Soldiers' groups: Abbr.
55. Living-room pieces
56. Rain gauge
60. Small sea coves
62. What students do
64. Gabor
65. Athens man and others
66. Dessert chef's specialties
67. "What's _ for me?"
68. Regarding
69. Big safari men
70. Cary or U.S.
71. Shredded
72. Plumbing workers
73. Actress Nuyen
74. Area measures: Abbr.
75. "Pride and Prejudice" girls, e.g.
76. Cursory viewer
77. Podiatrists' concerns
79. Conflicts, old style
80. Time period
81. Football measures: Abbr.
82. Pitchers' aims
83. Loudness units
84. Of the bones
86. Deodars
89. Barkers' bailiwicks
90. Sounds from Sandy
91. Works by Salvador
95. Court hearings
96. Fronded
97. Bow or Barton
98. F.B.I. man
99. What book reviewers do
100. Ferber opus
101. Temperature
103. Preminger
104. Home of the Knesset: Abbr.
105. Granite city
106. Tokyo sport
107. Bird fare
109. Wax: Prefix
110. What Edison said there is
115. Singer's exercises
116. Delayed
117. Lung exercises
118. Witchhunter's target
119. Biblical land
120. Pueblo Indians
121. Basket fiber

DOWN

1. Iridescent
2. Roman historian
3. Old French coin
4. Hungary's Nagy
5. Auto worker's product
6. All 48, in 1920
7. Sweetbread: Fr.
8. Ushers
9. Frome and Allen
10. Hurok et al.
11. City law, for short
12. Heated over
13. Photo-lab jobs
14. Polynesian symbols
15. Current month: Abbr.
16. Kind of degree
17. What's-his-name
18. Mad
19. Accountants' items
20. Fish hawk
21. Cooks' ingredients in Maui
25. "_ about time!"
26. Allergist's concern
33. Brave cockneys
35. Etats _
36. Printers
37. See 61 Down
39. Causing wear
41. Some subsidized farmers
42. Tests
45. Lapel wear at reunions
46. Dark colors, to poets
48. Catches on
49. What great events do
50. Aromas
51. Woodpecker sound
52. S.A. river
53. Dip
55. Inland pastime
56. Consumers
57. Leasehold
58. Manifested
59. Betrayers
61. Lindbergh, with 37 Down
62. Subdues
63. Endings for young and old
66. Garbs for Superman
67. Mideast land
69. Yields
70. Site of the Alhambra
72. Ale units
73. Ice field
75. Quartets
76. Obtains an official O.K.
78. Cribbage gear
80. _ a daisy
83. Of a head bone
84. Algerian port
85. Italian lake
86. Old Greek city
87. Offensive sight
88. Companion of "Yours truly"
89. Running a temperature
90. Penna. city
92. Recipe direction
93. Hospital worker
94. Heron's relatives
96. McHenry, e.g.
97. Confection
100. Smart-alecky
101. Cry's partner
102. Caravan stop
105. Cooper's products: Abbr.
106. Pipe part
108. Insecticides
111. Rubber tree
112. Actress Hagen
113. After pi
114. Comedian's forte

243 GOING PLACES *By Marie West*

ACROSS

1. Whaleboat helmsman
6. Cheers
10. Pops
14. Rope base
19. Moon crater
20. Cruising
21. Combat
22. Kind of venous
23. Moslem lords
24. Quarrel
25. Shoppers' transit
27. Tot's transit
29. Fourth word
30. Cupid
31. Daisy's transit
35. Obvious
37. Employee's concern
38. Greek letter
39. Fortas
40. __ mater
42. Part of a step
45. Ups anchor
49. Barrel of sorts
51. Perceived
54. Inactivate
56. Benefit
58. Short distance
59. Lips
61. Spanish drink
62. Pipe worker
64. Atlas item
66. Nonsense
67. Prying
68. Transit to nowhere
73. Bears or Cubs
77. Chinese money
78. Kind of too
79. Clodhopper
84. Sandwich
85. Woodwinds
87. Hebrew weight
90. Adams
91. Together
93. Northwest, for one
96. Wide smile
97. Council
98. Diva's spoken passage: Abbr.
100. Straight
102. "__ a chance!"
103. Vegetable
105. Nearby
108. Marshmallow events
110. S.F. transit
116. City in India
117. Up a __
118. Work-sheet entry
121. Lowly transit
124. Jason's ship
125. Hay machine
126. Port
127. Ferber
128. Weirdo
129. Toward the back
130. "__ of robins . . ."
131. Color expert
132. Orbs, old style
133. Takes a breather

DOWN

1. Ruthenian
2. Rickey fruit
3. Kind of decision
4. Attire
5. Abrogate
6. Grating
7. Facing, in heraldry
8. Part of a loom: Var.
9. Shiny fabric
10. W.W. II monogram
11. Sydneyites
12. Design for transferral
13. Viewpoint
14. N.M. Indian
15. Onetime transit
16. English river
17. Pointer on a map
18. Rope
26. Decamped
28. Metrical stress
32. Bacharach
33. Archangel
34. Vow
35. Fruit
36. Overhead
41. Legal matter
43. Start a certain trip
44. Begone, to Shakespeare
46. Othello's friend
47. Extra bit
48. Destroy
50. Jackie Coogan role
52. Mother of Dionysus
53. Armadillo
55. Bet participant
57. Sea god
60. Diminishes
63. Newspaper sections
65. Bank abbr.
69. Day or of love
70. Sierra __
71. Propellers
72. Spirit for a zombie
73. "__ little pig . . ."
74. Counting-out word
75. __ for one's money
76. Transit for Lindy et al.
80. Droop
81. Transit accesses
82. Dostoevsky's "The __"
83. Small change
86. Agnew
88. Political transit
89. Iron or Stone
92. __ fixe
94. Egyptian god
95. U.S. inventor
99. Barracks
101. Turnpike gate
104. Performs
106. Mental grasp
107. King-of-arms
109. Looking fixedly
110. Woolen fabric
111. Hindu month
112. Courageous
113. Fortified
114. Willing's partner
115. Summon
119. H.C.L. item
120. Goofs
122. Chessman: Abbr.
123. Attention

244 PAR FOR THE COURSE By Gladys V. Miller

ACROSS

1. Sew loosely
6. Tire
9. Wife of Mohammed
15. Patch
21. Nile city
22. Deer
23. "No morn, __" (Hood)
24. "To __ better than sacrifice"
25. Wedge products
27. Traffic hazards
29. Time period, Abbr.
30. "Rhinoceros" author
32. Orly or Kennedy
33. Tech. school degree
34. Socks
36. One, in Bonn
38. Aromas
39. French city
40. Kind of hug or market
41. Threshers
43. Halting sounds
44. Brants
45. Little Caesar, e.g.
47. Bandman Herb
49. Search widely
40. Agreement, in Paris
51. "Exodus" author
53. Seven or high
54. Design on metal
57. Miss Chase
58. Human resources
60. Burma or Tobacco
61. Aussie animal
62. Neon, e.g.
63. Things said during a physical
65. Eva or Magda
66. Hindu goddess
67. Wife of Bragi
68. High note
69. Thrice: Prefix
70. Exaggerating

72. Quarterback's repertoire
76. Productive
79. Fox's forte
80. Prerogative
82. __ polloi
83. Letters
84. Impost
85. Woods near S.F.
86. More skilled
88. __ of discretion
89. Suited
92. Feminine suffix
93. Decorative piece
94. Hunting dog
96. Trampled
97. Restraints
99. Grove: Ger.
100. River to Baltic
101. Dupes
102. Arabian garment
103. "I'd like __ question."
105. Irritated
107. Game or shock
109. Drop or lap
110. Bridge holding
112. __ for one's money
113. Bulrush
114. Suppose
116. N.Z. tree
117. Traffic-ticket candidate
120. Greek nickname
121. Mollifies
123. Warblers
125. Otto's realm: Abbr.
126. Manicurists of a sort
129. Agalloch
131. __ home (dines in)
132. Discreet: Fr.
133. Lip
134. Girl's name, for short
135. Blacksmiths
136. Thin
137. Snow, in Scotland
138. Dutch painter

DOWN

1. Berry, in botany
2. Biblical tribe
3. Reversions
4. Do a phone job
5. Fodder
6. Putters, etc.
7. Fixed course
8. German marshal
9. Conn. city
10. "No one but __"
11. Sicilian city
12. Chemical prefix
13. People who save
14. Traditional storm haven
15. Reporters: Abbr.
16. News item
17. Energy unit in physics
18. Broadway musical
19. Lilies, in Spain
20. Old ascetic
26. Garden workers
28. Actress Diana
31. U.S. agency

35. Yiddish gossip
37. U.S. diplomat
39. Moon vehicles
41. Wild: Lat.
42. Nazi organizer
44. Incite
45. Festive
46. Cards wool
48. Head part
49. Furniture part
50. Iron mold
52. Outpouring
54. Inlets
55. Certain words
56. Joss-house items
59. Higher: Ger.
60. Accelerate, for short
63. Soviet range
64. Identifying feature
66. John or Jane
67. Charged atoms
68. Begrudge

71. Unit of force
72. Word with level or second
73. Vernon's dancing partner
74. Contradict
75. Dr. __, humorist
76. Chemin de __
77. Captive of Hercules
78. Remain still, as a ship
81. Bestow, in Glasgow
86. Heeling
87. Ones who scoff
88. Gold Coast tribe
89. Place for a square peg
90. Word with ax or vault
91. Football scores: Abbr.
93. One of a dancer's seven

94. Sheep's cry
95. Geologic suffix
96. Brimless hat
98. Robust
99. "__ the brave . . ."
101. Tongs, pokers, etc.
103. Rocks
104. Raise __ (contend)
106. __ States
107. Phases
108. Cry of triumph
109. Soften a doughnut
111. March girl
114. Exploits
115. Plant walls
117. Greek letter
118. Impair
119. Fortification
121. Growl
122. Tea-leaf expert
124. Fruitless
127. Direction: Abbr.
128. Hosp. workers
130. Cleverness

245 STAGING AREA By Nancy S. Ross

ACROSS

1. Assn.
4. Matured
8. French storefront word
13. "Rheingold" role
17. Part of S.S.T.
19. Florida city
20. Actress Valli
21. Verdi heroine
22. City landmark
24. Absorbed one
25. Fret
26. Stark quality
27. Counting devices
29. Indian of Peru
30. Namesakes of Wagner heroine
33. Boundary: Abbr.
34. Tangled
36. Decline
37. Kidney-shaped
42. Linen's place
43. Depot: Abbr.
44. Agents
46. Vehicle
47. TV fare
50. Pocket site
51. Irish luck
53. Good name, for short
54. Mining damp
57. Silkworm
58. Before
61. Few: Fr.
62. Stop __ dime
64. Neighbor of Syr.
65. Some dwellings
72. African land: Initials
73. Black's partner
74. Sleuth, for short
75. Surprised sounds
76. Shinto temples
78. Bride: Fr.
80. Resin
81. Dressy chap
85. __ das Cruzes, Brazil
86. Western
90. Hair: Prefix
91. Monologue subjects
95. Metric unit
96. Colorless gas
98. Assemblies
99. O.T. book: Abbr.
100. Indian fast
101. French noble
102. Customer
105. Town of Japan
106. Teamwork
111. Union target
115. Role in Mascagni opera
116. "Just do __"
117. Lorgnette's relative
119. Do __ thing
120. Roman goddess
121. Persian elf
122. Heads: Fr.
123. Soviet agency
124. Scent, in Italy
125. Weedy plant
126. W.W. II group

DOWN

1. Shrewdies
2. Lets anew
3. Spanish V.I.P.'s
4. Fusses
5. Magnetic unit
6. Sullivan et al.
7. Sandra or Ruby
8. Mulberry bark: Var.
9. Drug plants
10. Whirring sound
11. "__ in magic and spells"
12. Orff's "__ Burana"
13. Writer Howard
14. Ceremony
15. Eur. river
16. Turns left
17. Show grief
18. __ tree
23. Give __ (consider)
27. Baseball great
28. Exude
31. Prohibit
32. Tide
34. Roman 1300
35. Side petals
37. Take it easy
38. Knicks or Lakers
39. "__ Killarney . . ."
40. Withstand
41. Spectral types
43. Wheat
44. "Coffee __?"
45. Settle a debt
48. Girl's name
49. Sorts: Fr.
52. Have a bite
55. Roman satirist
56. Noun endings
59. Tennis need
60. Vehicle
63. Elec. unit
65. Universe
66. "Time __" (Snow)
67. Indians or oranges
68. Suffix for aud or trans
69. Turns
70. All eyes
71. Part of i.e.
77. Falstaff et al.
79. Greek letters
80. Navigation aid
82. Collapsible items
83. Sibelius, e.g.
84. __ market
87. Loosen
88. Arabia's neighbor
89. "I haven't __ wear"
92. Staff man
93. African bird
94. Boxed
97. To-dos
99. Frat-man's wear
102. Beverage
103. Like some ends
104. "__ is human"
106. Coagulate
107. Mrs. Chaplin
108. Cheers for Escamillo
109. Football play
110. Neophyte: Var.
112. __-dieu
113. Bold, in France
114. Afterthoughts: Abbr.
117. Choose
118. Princess's tormentor

246 GETTING THE CLUES By William Lutwiniak

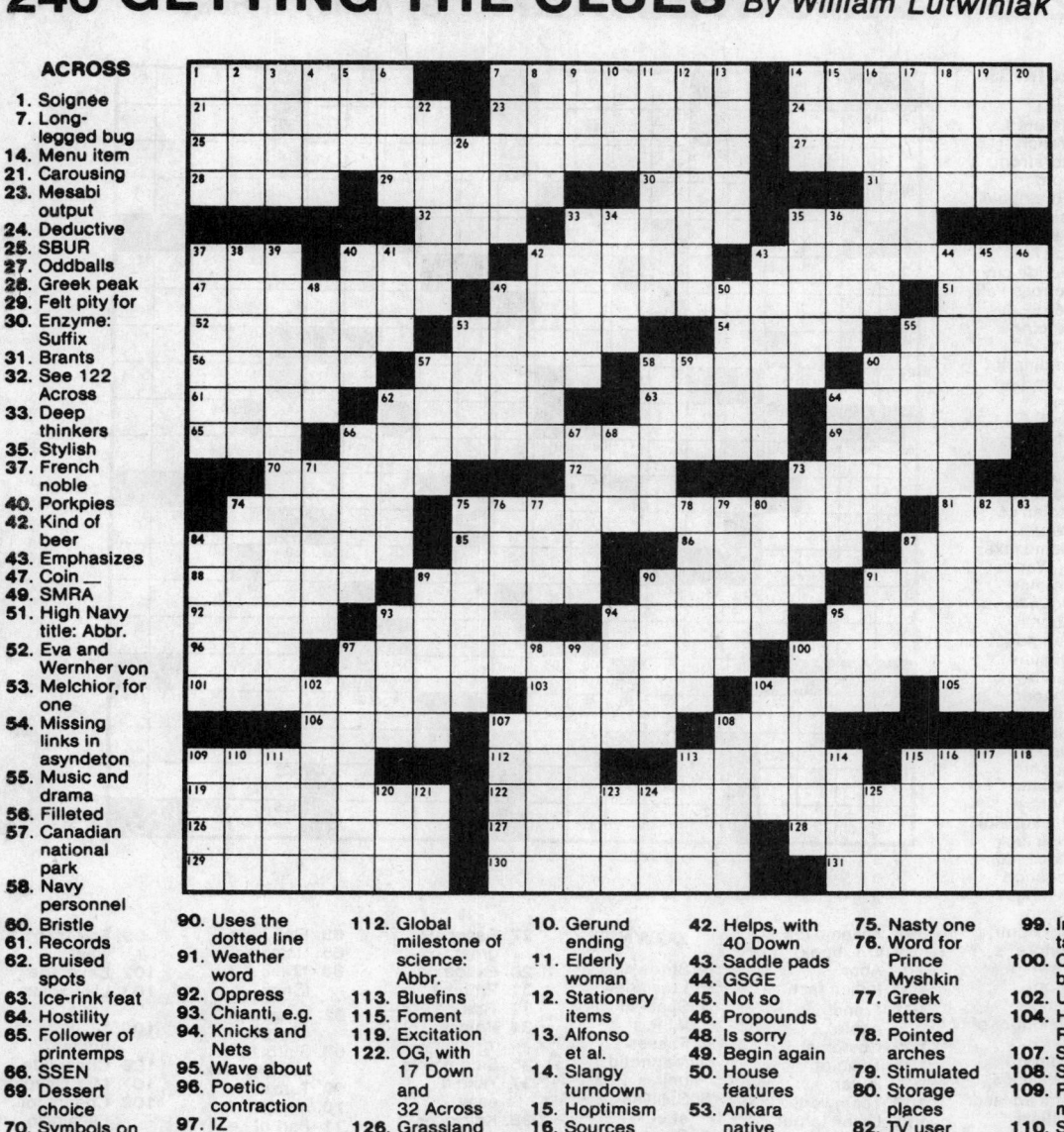

ACROSS

1. Soignee
7. Long-legged bug
14. Menu item
21. Carousing
23. Mesabi output
24. Deductive
25. SBUR
27. Oddballs
28. Greek peak
29. Felt pity for
30. Enzyme: Suffix
31. Brants
32. See 122 Across
33. Deep thinkers
35. Stylish
37. French noble
40. Porkpies
42. Kind of beer
43. Emphasizes
47. Coin __
49. SMRA
51. High Navy title: Abbr.
52. Eva and Wernher von
53. Melchior, for one
54. Missing links in asyndeton
55. Music and drama
56. Filleted
57. Canadian national park
58. Navy personnel
60. Bristle
61. Records
62. Bruised spots
63. Ice-rink feat
64. Hostility
65. Follower of printemps
66. SSEN
69. Dessert choice
70. Symbols on old manuscripts
72. Speed
73. Defamation
74. Musical key
75. BLUE SOD
81. Begley and Sullivan
84. Starlike
85. Do copydesk work
86. Networks
87. Mine passage
88. Bring to __
89. Dress feature
90. Uses the dotted line
91. Weather word
92. Oppress
93. Chianti, e.g.
94. Knicks and Nets
95. Wave about
96. Poetic contraction
97. IZ
100. Primitive people
101. Inventor, at times
103. Hawaiian geese
104. Undiminished
105. Certain citizens: Abbr.
106. Bryophyte
107. Book-jacket blurbs
108. Speedboater Wood
109. Sets the tempo
112. Global milestone of science: Abbr.
113. Bluefins
115. Foment
119. Excitation
122. OG, with 17 Down and 32 Across
126. Grassland
127. Pays no heed
128. Frequenter
129. Witnesses
130. Academic goals
131. Begins

DOWN

1. P.I. native
2. Stigma
3. Little bits
4. "__ deal!"
5. Assigned
6. Merry sound
7. Signaling device
8. Set foot on
9. Cuban rum
10. Gerund ending
11. Elderly woman
12. Stationery items
13. Alfonso et al.
14. Slangy turndown
15. Hoptimism
16. Sources
17. See 122 Across
18. Miner's find
19. Greek god
20. Dice throw
22. Tell
26. "__ on first?"
33. Cabbage
34. Field: Lat.
35. Stacks wood
36. Men
37. Do in a small way
38. Destroy
39. EARTH
40. See 42 Down
41. Onager
42. Helps, with 40 Down
43. Saddle pads
44. GSGE
45. Not so
46. Propounds
48. Is sorry
49. Begin again
50. House features
53. Ankara native
55. "Once upon __"
57. Central points
58. Declined
59. Feller
60. Social pests
62. Brackish
64. Rose's love et al.
66. Confront boldly
67. Scarlett's husband
68. Treated with
71. Coalesce
73. Graduate degrees
74. Cessation of breath
75. Nasty one
76. Word for Prince Myshkin
77. Greek letters
78. Pointed arches
79. Stimulated
80. Storage places
82. TV user
83. Make emphatic
84. Shropshire
87. Pond scum
89. Rubs off
90. Dresses lumber
91. Beware!
93. Industrial vessels
94. Kind of print or fettle
95. World or Boer
97. Minoan capital
98. Mystical interpretation
99. Imposing taxes
100. Celestial being
102. Uprising: R
104. Hand, in Rome
107. Stringent
108. Suppose
109. P.T.A. member
110. Smell __
111. Outlay
113. Pronoun o yore
114. Evian and Baden
115. __ were
116. Pincers' nippers
117. Sewing-room adjunct
118. Certain ag
120. Carney
121. French article
123. Correlative
124. Italian numeral
125. U.K. decoration

247 CHANNEL CROSSING *By Jack Luzzatto*

ACROSS

1. CBC country
7. Soaper shows
13. TV eye
19. Of deserts
20. Sweet pepper
22. Highest points
23. Newscasts, sportscasts, etc.
25. Certain TV films
26. Shoe parts
27. Drift
28. Suzette and de Chine
30. Ruby or Sandra
31. Mideast land: Abbr.
32. French impressionist
33. Skimpy
34. Rumple
35. Proved wrong
37. Latin dances
38. Vexing company
39. Relieves
40. Knotlike
41. Glacial ridges
43. Guinea pigs
45. Northern Italian city
46. Creek and Choctaw, e.g.
50. Modify
51. Marsh birds
53. Runway
55. Minor British noble: Abbr.
56. TV-ad activity
58. Cheese
59. Late-late show time
60. Ocean: Abbr.
61. Times to bunch commercials
63. N.Z. vine
64. Meadow
65. Little dog
66. Artist's colors
67. Repute
68. Business-day break
70. Dance, in Paris
71. Money
72. Destine
73. Michelangelo work
75. __ heavy (vehement)
76. __ many words
78. Subsidiary building
79. Othello's kin
80. Signature of Groucho's brother
83. Athletic throwaway
85. Faces rivals
88. Win by effort
89. Man's home
90. Canned TV
91. Twitch
92. Give __ whirl
93. Ancient: Comb. form
94. Yields
95. Joyce locale
96. Rerun time
98. Fast-pitch experts
101. English jury examiners
102. Billiard item
103. Convincing
104. Street of learning
105. Investigates
106. TV-guest greetings

DOWN

1. Boston cager
2. Like an opera song
3. TV world at times
4. Iowa city
5. Morse signal
6. Synthetic fabrics
7. Started
8. Swivel around
9. Desert ruler
10. Thing, in law
11. Good guy or cool chap
12. Fit for keeping
13. Dido
14. Sacred bull
15. Ferrer
16. Mass flight
17. Try again
18. Evaluate
21. Europe's 2nd largest lake
24. Weak consonants
29. Mexican money
32. Pondered
33. Where plugs are sparked
34. Kind of scout badge
36. Black out
37. Juvenile TV ad subject
38. Analyzes critically
40. The Flying Finn
42. Ore discovery
43. Vaquero's horse
44. Talent on trial
47. Certain zero hours
48. One-grained wheat
49. Caught fish in a way
51. Military cap
52. Made of a grain
53. Seconds
54. Vexed
56. Lines a well wall
57. Monastic people
61. Unfathomable person
62. Ease tension
67. Bizarre
69. Stone heap
71. Air stunts
73. Put a layout together
74. Enjoying success
75. Like some dorm freshmen
77. Asian vine
79. Broods morosely
80. Does a job on a bank
81. Adult
82. Friend of D'Artagnan
84. Violinist Stern
85. Nitpicks
86. One of the Horae
87. Perfumes
89. River land in Scotland
90. Book-cover entry
93. Hair wave
94. Snatch
95. __ Benedict
97. Extinct bird
99. Biafran
100. Top-rated

248 LUNCHEON LIMERICK *By Frances Hansen*

ACROSS

1. Dialect
6. Ship parts
11. School subject: Abbr.
15. Fatuous
20. "It's __!" (agreed)
21. Compete
22. Novelist Ouida
23. Pitcher's dream game
24. Undefined
25. Where Greeks met
26. Straighten
27. Arden
28. Limerick with 54, 79, 110 and 136 Across
32. Kind of cause
33. Prefix for dynamics
34. Start of a nursery song
35. British gun
36. Spring mths.
37. Eh?
39. Conquer
41. Gardens of Copenhagen
45. "Honi __ . . ."
46. Kind of dance or room
49. Don, Dame, Sir, etc.
54. See 28 Across
59. Grass genus
60. Rake with gunfire
61. Muse of poetry
62. Buddhist scripture
63. Weights of Mideast
65. Snub
66. Stagnant-pond topping
68. Veer, in space
70. Vassal: Var.
71. Hot bargains
73. Andy Capp's hangout
75. Parched
77. Breast-beatings
79. See 28 Across
83. "O __" (Neapolitan song)
87. This: Sp.
88. "Scram, lamb! Shoo, __!"
89. Lumber output
94. Tourist, for short
95. Throw or shag
97. Mosaic piece
99. Order's partner
101. Disposed to
102. Perfume oil
104. Out
106. Humbles
109. "Winnie __ Pu"
110. See 28 Across
114. "__, and yet so far"
115. Nothing
116. Tennessee players
117. Popular thesaurus
118. Andrea __ Sarto
120. Rawboned
121. Hirsute, to a cockney
123. He, in Italy
127. Last words of K.O. count
131. Pisa's river
132. Govt. agencies
136. See 28 Across
141. Pope's cape
142. Tenet
143. Poker move
144. Flaubert's birthplace
145. De Mille
146. Blues man W.C.
147. First name in light verse
148. Atmospheres
149. Auditions
150. "Now __ me down . . ."
151. Phenomenon of a circle
152. Four times a year: Abbr.

DOWN

1. Vichy name
2. Potato state
3. Hot toddy
4. Haggard
5. Cassini
6. Not a __ (no chance)
7. Severities
8. Convex molding
9. Humorist Artemus
10. Bridge bid
11. Of the cheek
12. Concord
13. Low kind of rate
14. Ass-inine remark
15. Don Juan's mother
16. Don'ts
17. Not give __
18. Statue's place
19. Allen or Frome
22. Attacked
29. Grand or Cedar
30. Violin
31. Wharton
36. Heavyweight name
37. Arf!
38. Takes cover
40. Insects
41. Rulers
42. Dolt
43. Green: Fr.
44. Florida city
45. Prestige
46. Wood-chewer
47. Not home, in Glasgow
48. "What a __ (too bad)
50. Ultima __
51. Admitted
52. White heron
53. Hosiery woes
55. Cousin of et al.
56. Peach or plum, e.g.
57. Kind of surgeon
58. ". . . and __ a goodnight!"
64. Urban problem
67. Suez or Welland
69. Ululate
72. Buzz
74. Animal-like
76. Jowl adjuncts
78. Between l and q
80. Baskervilles' beast
81. Task
82. Minimum
83. Certain men at eve
84. Correct: Prefix
85. Get on into night
86. Urn-shaped
90. "Anitra's Dance" composer
91. He married Pocahontas
92. Not rented
93. Crying things
96. Cap's partner
98. De Valera
100. Kind of blanket
103. Boer council
105. Weather info
107. Pitching infraction
108. ". . . more in __ than in . . ."
111. Bluebird genus
112. Early Muscovite
113. Kind of cott or hood
119. Chinese nut
120. Baby of Fields films
121. On high
122. Propose
123. German W.W. II craft
124. Sea swell
125. Netman Smith et al.
126. Small hooter
128. Lemon-oil base
129. __ score (retaliate)
130. Bear or boy
131. Stage whisper
132. It makes a lot of dough
133. Utter impulsively
134. Excellent
135. Genial, in Britain
137. Myra or Rudolf
138. Suffix for cyclo or iso
139. Villainous one
140. Where the Tigris flows

249 QUESTIONNAIRE By Jay Spry

ACROSS

1. Frustrate
5. Type of hat or house
10. Halfhearted
15. "I could write _ ..."
18. Sometimes a trois
20. Flowers
22. Surprised question
24. Disconcert
25. _ deep (over-involved)
26. Year: Fr.
27. Votes
29. Single, for one
30. Monopolize
31. Old term of address
34. Swelling ailment
36. Root word
39. Spanish title
41. Hair pads
43. Miss Claire
45. Gardner
46. Eatery
47. Cpls. et al.
49. "Do not _, spindle or ..."
51. Amusing fellows
54. Pastures
55. Club
56. God of Islam
58. Dormouse
60. Blanket remedies
62. Gun, as a motor
64. Arab garments
66. Alter and super
67. Skit
68. Puzzled question
74. Japanese land measure
75. Quarry
76. Fresh
77. Poetic word
78. Headlight settings
80. Tracks
83. Natural gift
87. French ash trees
88. Vapor: Prefix
91. Places for some belts
93. Feign
94. Gunpowder, for one
95. Does palmistry
97. Work-method initials
98. W.W. II agency
99. Eur. country
101. Misprints
103. Trumpets
106. Inkstains
108. Custody
110. Early followers of Mohammed
113. Russian village
115. Scottish inventor
117. Laughs: Fr.
119. Wharton man
120. Worships
122. Selfish question
126. Crown _
127. Charm
128. Drapery fixture
129. Win by _
130. Note-takers: Abbr.
131. Russian poet

DOWN

1. Sympathetic question
2. Question during an inning
3. Prying
4. Caesar's alas
5. Muscat native
6. Jean or Roberta
7. Penetrated
8. Cheer
9. Turkish title
10. Hackneyed
11. Useful tip
12. Pendulum's partner
13. Teacher's question
14. Place to buy snacks
15. Lover of Galatea
16. Rational
17. Service-station line: Abbr.
19. Greek letter
21. Sink
23. Catch
28. "... and seven _ our ..."
32. Indigo
33. Whet
35. Frenzied
37. Raincoat, for short
38. Arena
40. Grim one
42. Consolation
43. "_ body ..."
44. Lon _ of Cambodia
48. Orderly method: Abbr.
50. Venture
52. Pull out
53. Grave
55. Clouted
57. Virus infection
59. Touch base
61. Far-north city
63. Miss Miles
65. Fountain features
68. Penmanship patterns
69. Start of a drama-class question
70. Town in N.J.
71. Type of fork
72. Honor
73. Greek deity
74. Hoof sound
79. Asian palm
81. Ex of a sort
82. Airfield initials
84. Start of a song
85. Beat the _
86. Miss Sumac
89. Chagall
90. Harem room
92. Resort
96. Catch unaware
100. Carpentry pins
102. Up
104. Drawing of a sort
105. Muster
107. Word with demi
109. Southern dish
111. Shot and shell
112. Symbol of thinness
113. Mil. rank
114. Fancy
116. Scottish numeral
118. Taste
121. Antique auto
123. Pinafore, for one
124. Self: Prefix
125. Bath or wash

ACROSS

1. Partner of desist
6. Bath dusting
10. Manhattan
16. Deceive
20. Primrose
21. Matty of baseball
22. Illinois city
23. Salk's target
24. Five-and-ten special
27. New Hebrides island
28. Old swords
29. Etiquette girl
30. Peat or cranberry
31. Kind of gas
33. From __ Z
34. Pusher's quarry
36. Raises the ante
38. Cadillac model
42. Places for funds
45. Designate
46. Bare
48. Postmark ads
51. Niño's coin
53. Urge
54. X and beta
55. Pain
56. Advantage
58. Magnetic and ticker
60. Touch all the __
61. Skin swelling
63. Sea bird
64. Poor boy's champion
67. African tongue: Var.
68. Transistor
70. Comebacks
71. An __ music
74. Arm bones
77. Smell: Prefix
78. Hole, in France
82. Rare birth phenomenon
88. Shalt-not word
89. Back talk
90. Common typeface
91. The __ Sandwich
92. Spring from
96. Hebrew letter
99. Pastry
100. Mammonist
104. Thai tongue
105. Reconnoiter
108. __-percha
109. Swedish coin
110. Moslem spirits
112. French author
113. Sorrowful cry
114. Piercing tool
116. __ corn
118. "__ horse" (old poem)
120. Mostel
121. Pilaster
123. Well-off
125. Rock Hunter et al.
128. Coin for Sato
129. Attila's men
130. Mornings
133. __ dixit
134. Kind of whiz
136. Wild ox
138. Alley V.I.P.
140. "Not my cup __"
143. Mamma's advice
147. "__ up, Doc?"
148. Late-news hour
149. "Rome of Hungary"
150. Miss Dunne
151. Kind of bug or killer
152. Dinner club
153. Satisfy
154. Restored

DOWN

1. __ cropper
2. Live
3. __ the good
4. Farm building
5. Gourmet
6. Beach color
7. Mountain shrubs
8. Swag
9. Like some pearls
10. Argentine native
11. Belgrade native
12. Timber wolves
13. Catherine of __
14. Point
15. Kind of television
16. Make it the hard way
17. In the style of
18. Healthy
19. Adversary
23. Indian money
25. Caucasus people
26. __ lazuli
32. Paradise
35. Parade or bunny
37. Take care of
39. Exaggerates
40. Rental paper
41. Appliance
42. Galbraith book
43. On the __
44. Play the lead
47. Letter
48. Crow's call
49. German word of woe
50. So-long in Soho
52. On __ with
57. Time period
59. Summer, in Nice
60. Sandwich initials
62. Tenth-century Pope
64. Bridge card
65. Seep through
66. Originated
69. Labor org.
71. Dine
72. Hardwood
73. Track event
75. Upward: Prefix
76. Renaissance robe
79. Eliminate
80. Sioux Indian
81. T.V. dial initials
83. Phone
84. Glistens
85. Giant reed
86. Nathan Hale's sacrifice
87. Plans
93. __ culpa
94. Pigeon pea
95. Tropical tree
97. Dead or hard
98. Kobe's island
100. Slippers
101. Japanese city
102. __ B'rith
103. Works for
106. Yucky sound
107. Hold or dance
108. Ref. book
110. Hospital garments
111. Japanese religion
14. Mimics
115. Magi
117. James Watt's field
119. Of a blood process
122. Feel sorrow
124. Alpine home
126. Auditors
127. Put in play
130. Quaker gray
131. River of France
132. Horse
135. One who ogles
137. Gymnast Korbut
139. Japanese ship name
140. Hooter
141. Home-loan org.
142. Kind of pole
144. Cassius Clay
145. At all
146. Anger

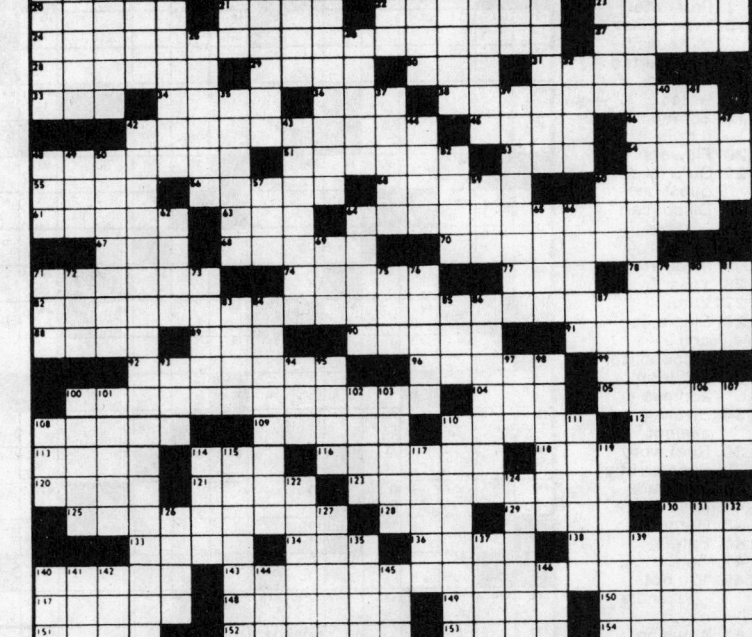

251 DECISIONS, DECISIONS   By Alfio Micci

ACROSS

1 One way to stand
4 Roman halls
9 Fool
12 Southern campus
15 Bach's "— Fugue"
17 Elevate
19 Thinks
21 Option
23 Gold-watch recipient
24 Loses one's cool
25 Malay
26 Won a card game
27 Letters
28 Wildcat
31 Furnace adjunct
34 Flower
36 Option
38 "— bitten . . ."
42 "— Rheingold"
44 Horn: Prefix
45 Estuary
46 Money, vis-a-vis evil
47 Hire
50 Alternative, in music
52 "Rose — rose . . ."
54 Struck
55 Paper quantity
57 New Deal initials
59 Wreathe
61 Composer Rorem
62 Greek letters
65 Response to a pinprick
67 Beam
68 Execrate
70 Option
73 Caliph
75 Deck officer
77 Diamond of gang era
78 Impassive
80 Head covering
82 Cut short
85 Word of disdain
86 Delete
88 Loyal
89 Dickens
91 Fabled king
95 Pepos
96 In —
97 S.F. hill
99 Underseas man
100 Part of I.R.O.: Abbr.
101 U.N. member
102 Option
105 Succinct

109 Wyoming city
111 Plunderer: Var.
113 — loss
114 Stick
117 This: Sp.
119 Queen of Henry II
121 Augury
123 Option
126 Place to stay in Europe
127 Irish and English
128 Like forks
129 Poetic word
130 Coat part: Abbr.
131 Like eyes at a Gish film
132 — Moines

DOWN

1 Introductions
2 Maximally
3 Kicks
4 Upward: Prefix
5 Explosive
6 Certain muscles
7 Niger natives
8 Napoleon's symbol of perfidy
9 Schedule abbr.
10 Stogie
11 Fabric
12 Desolate
13 Partner of snick
14 Exercised
15 Confused
16 Option
17 Finish: Ger.
18 More slippery
20 Option
22 Kind of room

29 Off one's rocker
30 Runs up bills
32 Year in Nero's reign
33 Torment
35 Cheese
37 Option
39 Convention figure
40 Do phrase-making
41 Feminine suffix
43 Utah flower
47 Sea bird
48 Want
49 Restless ones
51 Root starch
53 Sharp-cornered: Abbr.
56 Biblical word ending
58 Galatea's beloved
60 Option

63 Trouble
64 Grade
66 Missouri monogram
69 Option
71 Old Irish writing
72 Drunkard
74 Miss Muller
76 State: Abbr.
79 Villain of note
81 Matterhorn et al.: Abbr.
82 Aleutian island
83 Family business abbr.
84 Miss Reed
87 Bravo
90 Kind of TV lens
92 Does a refrigerator job
93 Mine: Fr.

94 Kind of head
98 Lawyers' concerns
102 Famous trail
103 Befit
104 Double-play name
106 Of frogs
107 Lucy and Rolling
108 Some owls
110 As thin as —
112 Sprite
114 Date: Abbr.
115 Three, in Munich
116 Gossips
118 Actor Jacques
120 During
122 Eur. country
124 Asian holiday
125 Place: Suffix

WORD SAFARI *By Richard Camp*

ACROSS

1 __ fours
6 Spur
10 __ Morgana
14 Kind of market
18 Fresh team
19 Walking __
20 Exhausted
21 French evenings
22 It first sat in 1245
25 Swiss resort
26 Groups of nine
27 Bones, in England
28 "... nothing's __ for me"
29 Hindu cymbals
32 __-foot oil
33 Gluts
34 Musketeer
35 Pasha
36 Swiss river
37 Avoid
38 "__ is an island ..."
39 Red-carpet treatment
41 Henry II, dramawise
46 "Don't __" (words to a snoop)
47 Taxes
48 Bucks
49 Hurry
50 Ham __ (sandwich order)
51 Boxer's maneuver
52 Shopping and go
54 Belief
56 Sesame: Var.
57 Joseph's pride
58 Dispatch
59 Royal families of Kenya
60 Wine quality
61 "Pickwick Papers" lady
64 Truman's birthplace
65 Blunted swords
67 Tallchief
68 Josh of theater
69 King of Tyre
70 Jungle title
74 World Bible group: Abbr.
77 London Row
78 Producer: Suffix
79 Ten-percenters: Abbr.
80 Wife of Jacob
81 Old gold alloys
82 Franciscan
83 Fabrics
85 French city
86 "__ about time!"
87 Days, in Madrid
88 Delaware resort
89 Prejudiced
90 Alhambra feature
95 Made __ (custom job)
96 Kind of pitching rarity
97 Signs
98 Writer Thomas
99 Compass reading
100 Stable quality
101 Does poetry work
102 Ex __
103 Sydney's state: Abbr.
104 Praline items
105 Macbeth title
106 Goal
108 "... devil
109 Annoy John Bull
114 Doctors' achievements
115 Brief role
116 First U.S. earth orbiter
117 "... could __ lean"
118 Sea birds
119 Customs
120 Proceed slowly
121 Driving hazard

DOWN

1 Scrap
2 O.T. book
3 Beverage
4 Kind of curtain
5 Kind of potatoes for simba
6 Hooked
7 Police jobs
8 Blas et al.
9 Leander's love, in Soho
10 "__ the __ he'd be"
11 Drug plants
12 Cans
13 Reply: Abbr.
14 Jury V.I.P.
15 Unlikely pet for Margaret's rec room
16 Old adverbs
17 Have __ in the matter
19 Kind of bandit
20 Town in Latium
21 Deli staple
23 Like a crowned head
24 Fruit baskets
28 Ship parts
29 English noble family
30 Receiver of property
31 Possible London headline in 1603
33 Trapshooting
34 Jackson and Bancroft
37 Leg part
40 Fiber knot: Var.
41 Shopworn
42 Spanish direction
43 Bury
44 Source of down
45 Defunct cars
47 River duck
51 Castle moat
52 "You __ you try"
53 Make __ at
54 Steep rocks
55 P.I. breadfruit
57 Thick liqueur
58 Port or Lake
59 Cabals
61 Cook's concerns
62 "__ vincit amor"
63 Mother of Ishmael
66 Decorous
68 W.W. II craft
69 Must
70 Gold word
71 Sea or stew
72 Singer Emma
73 Dark and teen
75 Whalebones
76 "__ an angel down"
77 Eastern ketch
80 Story teller
82 Grant's bill
83 Errol et al.
84 Bristles
85 Elsa et al.
87 Dutch coins
88 Certain whelp
89 High society
91 Cyrano's beloved et al.
92 Believes
93 Puts in a box
94 Shed
95 Game fish
98 Seascape
100 Leg bone
101 Kyushu town
102 Whimpered
104 Tempo
105 "__ the night before ..."
106 Chinese wax
107 Common Latin abbr.
109 Fort Worth campus
110 Literary initials
111 Used up
112 Feminine suffix
113 Great deal

253 SAYING CHEESE By Diana Sessions

ACROSS

1 Does petty cheating
8 Way
14 Danny or doubting
20 Feted one
21 Stir
22 Become less dense
23 Subjugate
24 Theme words for a winter eve
26 Status, for short
27 __ forth
28 Canticles
29 P.O.W. data item
30 Conducted
31 "__ my turn?"
33 Blustered
35 Narrow part of a river
36 Old __, Conn.
37 Causes hardship
39 Servicemen
40 Suffer a disk mishap
41 Motherless calf: Var.
42 Carrion-eating animal
43 Decay
44 Disagreement
45 Good guy
46 Newcomer
48 Delay
49 Sees the light
52 Marked with spots
54 Railings
56 Cereal grass
57 Goof
58 Crustaceans of a creeping suborder
59 Creative spirit
60 Grown-up
61 Politicos' specialties
63 Sun __
64 __ days' wonder
65 Pert
66 Powerful bird
67 Word of disapproval
68 Part of an aerial view
69 Church member
71 Very many
73 Pharmacy abbr.
74 Aspirin unit
75 "__ we forget"
76 Dilettantish
77 Rental ad abbr.
78 House of __
82 Power of detection
84 Generations
85 Constructed: Abbr.
86 Actor Finney
87 Amphibian
88 One in charge
89 __ Union
91 Nautical word
92 Hawaiian birds
93 Convex moldings
94 Broad expanse
95 Sounds of delight
97 Child's game
98 Traveling cases
101 Late afternoon
103 Domestic
104 Derivative lease
105 Make known
106 Principal
107 Ghent's claim to fame
108 Tile workers

DOWN

1 Recall fondly
2 Best policy
3 Motivate
4 Man's nickname
5 Geologic time divisions
6 Slot-machine features
7 Take care of
8 Kind of rule
9 Deteriorates
10 Trifled
11 Quonsets
12 Bear: Sp.
13 City of great recall
14 Leaning
15 Peddle
16 Rio de __
17 Playground equipment
18 Blazing
19 City on the Pacific
25 Part of a lamp
32 Material
34 Distress
35 Glaringly evident
36 Parrot fish
38 Imitate
40 Courageous ones
41 Ones accused: Abbr.
43 Deer: Ger.
44 Punch-drunk
45 Pronoun
47 Household: Prefix
49 Soaks
50 Army mule
51 Control
52 Street-light vapor
53 City in Michigan
54 Canopy supports
55 State: Abbr.
57 African people
58 Filled with joy
59 Canadian lake
61 Valley
62 __ low
63 Relative of "You don't say"
65 Embroider with gold
66 Noncom: Abbr.
68 Trial
69 Disney movie
70 College degrees
72 Mind the bar
74 Mockery
76 Seven __
79 Fractious
80 Visionary
81 Experienced ones
82 Mark of shame
83 Picnic equipment
84 Atmosphere: Prefix
85 Overlook
86 Greek goddess
88 With vehemence
89 Shell prized by collectors
90 Exhaust
93 Ruler
94 French cleric
96 U.S. Indians
99 __ down (abate)
100 Common Market area: Abbr.
102 Small quantity

Thebes

254 SOME OF THE PEOPLE
By Betty Leary

ACROSS

1 Barge owner, for short
5 Lazy one
10 Doe et al.
15 More livid
17 Forage grass
19 Multiple road accident
20 Pretexts
21 Goodness!
23 Contrary one
24 Music halls
26 Women's Lib goal in Paris
27 I stand: Lat.
28 Threshold
29 Iniquities
31 Insect
32 Hitler's Kampf
33 Word with "vive le"
34 Eye-pupil dilater
38 Gossips
39 Rec-room fixtures
41 Unexpressed
42 Board man: Abbr.
43 Highway spots
45 Stunted ones
46 Secular, in Paris
50 Brundage of Olympic note
51 Town in Portugal
52 Camera shots
54 Balzac's Goriot
55 Victorian quality
58 Aurora
59 Carplike fish: Var.
60 Norwegian king
61 __ signum
62 Valets
63 Beast
64 Milksops
68 Poker word
70 In the cards
72 French storm
73 Libyan measures
74 Resting
75 Embodiment
76 Kind of ring
77 Parts of qts.
78 Form of Alice
79 Tot's weapon
81 Honest ones
83 Police conveyance
85 Shoe width
87 Rex or Walter
88 Haw's partner
89 E. Indian plant
90 Invitation initials
92 Go amiss
93 Spanish ladies
97 Turtle genus
99 Seine areas
100 Fireworks piece
103 Suddenly
105 Child of Zeus
106 "__ over spilt . . ."
107 Sets up
108 Lively
109 Noncoms
110 Flower

DOWN

1 Dessert
2 Cowardly
3 Electric item
4 Approximately
5 Miss nothing
6 Miss Hagen
7 Preserve
8 Desert regions
9 Famous ship
10 Agree
11 Brew
12 Tennis crowd, so to speak
13 Florida city
14 Observe furtively
15 Missiles: Abbr.
16 Flight part
17 Henley entries
18 Obliquely
19 Paper size
22 Miss Louise
25 Weighty action
30 Roman god of agriculture
32 Ike's spouse
34 Egyptian
35 Italian poet
36 Of the number eight
37 Serbian city
38 Ausable, for one
40 Roguish
42 Ends
43 Plan
44 Unwelcome bonus for editors
45 Abounding in rocks
47 Common field plant
48 "I fall __ thorns of life!"
49 Curve
51 Cooking word
52 Series of changes
53 Contemptible ones
55 Not anybody's
56 Cicero's that
57 Mountain climber's haven
62 Cookies
63 Critic Huxtable
64 Hazes
65 Droll
66 "Either do it alone __ for help"
67 Vasco __
69 N.Y. time
71 Kind of TV show
73 Unearth
75 Pier union: Abbr.
76 Drinking place
78 Chocolate-bar additive
79 In a proper way
80 Like sardines
81 Ventilate
82 Kind of collar
83 Nigerian people
84 Moslem princes
86 Chris of tennis
87 Tire
88 "__ today . . ."
91 Attention-getting sounds
93 Enraptured
94 Old cars
95 Plant bristles
96 Deficiency: Abbr.
98 Early Irish tenant
101 Pronoun
102 Outside: Prefix
104 Sign of a crowd

TO THE MIDDLE
By Eugene T. Maleska

ACROSS

1 Scuttle
4 Loathed
9 Make fun of
14 Israeli port
19 Macaw
21 Take the stump
22 Young beauty
23 Water wheel
24 Fuel for the wealthy
26 Heron
27 Friend of Snow White
28 Outworn
29 Indonesian shop
30 Ad infinitum
32 Attack
34 __ to (arrive)
35 Dig in
38 Give out
40 Pepys words
42 Made to __
43 Pleases
46 On one's toes
47 Of a branch
49 Indigo, for one
50 Hidden
52 Lights
55 Light sarcasm
56 City in Utah
58 Handel opera
59 Small penguin
60 Vendetta
61 Bring to court
62 African people
64 Pecos man
66 Numbers game
67 Shell filling
68 Recovers
70 Go to __
72 Poetry: Abbr.
73 Tuaregs' region
75 Assassin
77 Riviera set
79 Money in Bangkok
81 Polished
83 Kind of chamber
84 Hunt, as boar
88 Mete
90 Adjusts
94 Ethiopian river
95 Jejune
96 Splits hairs
98 __ to lunch
99 Squawk
101 Impertinent one
103 Key location
104 Part of Italy
105 "As you __"
106 Akin paternally
108 Señor's assent
110 Clog
112 Piece of armor
113 Home-style bingo
114 Voices
116 Wine cask
117 Jumble
118 Successful
120 Suffer in July
122 Area in Nigeria
123 __ the punch (starts fast)
125 Isolated rock
126 Is ruined
130 Pastoral plaint
131 Choirboys' collars
133 Taunt
135 Gambling city
136 Campus in Troy, N.Y.
137 Fluff
139 Borge plays it
141 Use pressure
144 Book-cover info
145 Boards man
146 Condor's home
147 English satirist
148 Longed
149 Like an oboe's tones
150 Contract
151 Forage plant

DOWN

1 Precarious
2 Pay dirt
3 Impermanent
4 By __ crook
5 Shady retreat
6 Greek letter
7 Raison d'__
8 Mint site
9 Ann and Richard Brinsley
10 Gear tooth
11 Pronoun
12 Manumits
13 Suit perfectly
14 Domino placement
15 Sweet's partner
16 O'Hara novel
17 Worn out
18 Sword handle
19 Book after Joel
20 Function
25 His, hers, or guest
31 Jannings
33 Ocean: Abbr.
36 Drift
37 Land a haymaker
39 Head: Fr.
41 Variety
44 Certain Broadway show
45 Titoite
47 Schisms
48 Plaza de toros
49 Garb
51 Dissonance
53 More pleasant
54 Forward-looking ones
56 "__ 'er there!"
57 Tractable child
59 Pole used as a pub sign
61 Nereid's steed
63 Seasoning
65 Swards
68 Persona __
69 Cassini
71 Channel changers
74 Burrows
76 Proportions
77 Kind of watch
78 Bacheller hero
80 Slight
82 Chilean product
84 Part of R.A.F.
85 Insect stage
86 Realistic
87 Pindar, e.g.
89 Gaseous element
91 Starts rolling
92 Cavell, for one
93 Bum __
97 Bunk
100 City in India
102 Sumps
103 Phone book
105 Emerson name
107 Wavered
109 Bastes
111 Town
112 Good odds
114 In good health
115 Side dish
117 "Little man who __ there"
119 East: Ger.
121 Like some rites
122 Nag
123 Of a whitish element
124 In reserve
127 Bird life
128 Large fish
129 Item of inflation
130 Letter on a key
132 Surfeit
134 Buckeye or hornbeam
138 Bravo
140 Make a slip
142 Gershwin
143 Tavern

HAVING A BALL *By Hume R. Craft*

ACROSS

1 Lodge name
6 Extinct birds
10 Mid-Manhattan
13 French soldier of W.W. I
18 Hersey setting
19 Bright flower
20 Angry
21 Viols' relatives
22 Swings
24 Marathon scene of the '30s
26 Barrie character
27 Political housecleaning
28 Hamlet et al.
29 Shore features
30 Birchbark
31 He says "arf"
32 Seeger
33 Certain sack
36 Agreement
38 Stroked
42 Ornate chair decor
44 "_ homo"
45 Gideon Fell's creator
46 Pilot's test
47 Rajahs' spouses
48 Apache et al.
51 Replete: Suffix
52 Mississippi four
53 Rose country
55 Diggings
56 Cash-register listing
58 Squeezed out
59 Chinese port
60 Lady's Book man
62 Like some dough
63 Family member
64 Sailor's call
65 Fund held in trust
67 Shows anger
68 Most like the duckling
71 Exclamation
72 Blankety-blank's kin
74 Primitives
76 Still _ (nevertheless)
79 Decorative fur of old
80 Backflow
83 Anoints
84 Sing à la Crosby
85 Mexican pots
87 River to the Fulda
88 Sanctum or tube
89 Eagle: Prefix
90 Motives
92 Barton
93 Butterfly or drag
94 Butch Cassidy's sidekick
97 Ella
98 Late, in Dijon
100 Poet's word
101 Bullfighter's encouragement
102 Stages anew
104 Unheralded hits
106 Preside over the do-si-dos
108 Compass reading
109 Rob and Rogers
110 Greek threshing festival
111 Natives of old Cuzco
112 Prima ballerina
115 TV's Pyle
116 Sponsorship
117 Carriage power
121 Seasonal worker
123 Block-party event
125 Not _ (mum's the word)
126 Large shark
127 Moslem rulers
128 Honeysuckle feature
129 Cooking needs
130 "_ Superman!"
131 Caber play
132 Brought down the house

DOWN

1 Bounders
2 Old _
3 Scourge
4 Fairy-tale word
5 Kind of hold
6 Morning-glory
7 Wild donkey
8 China, etc., to French
9 Medit. land
10 Mead makings
11 Welder's creations
12 Links starter
13 Storage battery inventor
14 Squeaky
15 Dies _
16 Milk: Prefix
17 Applications
19 Eagle's claw
20 Three-time Derby winner
23 Parking-lot offerings
24 Maxixe and saraband
25 City on the Missouri
28 Christopher Hatton's sobriquet
30 Sidewalk sights
31 Prefix for iliac
32 Paris's Monceau, etc.
33 Informal writing
34 Seward's purchase
35 Belly action, Paris style
37 Relative of honey
38 City in Kansas
39 Bill Robinson forte
40 Chemical washings
41 Hello-girl et al.
43 Garden pest
45 Poet Thomas and family
48 Step, in France
49 Former Mauritius Islander
50 Dobbin's betters
53 Farrier's needs
54 Former film czar
57 Feedbag staples
59 Jumps aside
61 Exam
62 S.A. tanagers
64 Horatio's books
66 Javanese carriage
67 Teasdale and namesakes
69 Unit of laughter
70 Violent one
73 Make eyes at
74 John and James
75 Toughen
77 "Darkness at _"
78 Miss Alcott
81 Headpieces
82 Fathom: Fr.
84 Grants
86 Drug
87 Essay name
89 Male ants
91 Cub scout leader
92 Rattans
95 Not observed
96 Supply ship
97 Change actors
99 Ridiculed
102 N.Y. team
103 Suffixes of quality
105 Subjects of Benchley's sex study
106 Brief stage part
107 Australian natives
110 Pawns
112 Equal, in France
113 Pacific cloth
114 Unique thing
115 "Strain at a _"
116 Air: Prefix
117 Poi ingredient
118 Word with paradise
119 Summit
120 Hoover Dam's lake
122 "_ Blue"
123 Hollywood stage
124 Margery of the seesaw

257 COUNTERPARTS By Keith Blake

ACROSS

1 Capsize
6 Delve again
11 Greek porticos
16 Wife of Balder
17 Medit. wind
18 Robs
21 Rig the cards
22 Hoi __
23 Ten cents
24 Mel et al.
25 Public school
27 Hereditary
29 Vestments
30 French liking
31 Holey, in Hamburg
32 Kind of jaw
34 Old card game
35 Skip
37 __ as possible
40 Scottish cup
42 Flues
43 Production
44 Piper
45 Prefix for plop or choo
46 Extinguish
47 Area of Ethiopia
51 Caustics
53 Bore from __
54 Garment
55 River to Irish Sea
56 Hilaire
57 Red Skelton role
58 Eight: Prefix
59 Concerning
61 Aunt in "Oklahoma!"
62 Shoe job
63 Eye pullover
64 Greetings
65 French political unit
66 Crushed in
67 __-de-sac
68 Glaze
70 Young person
71 Loch Ness man
73 Suffer a canoe mishap
74 Do better on the stage
75 S.A. people
76 Footlike part
77 Fingernail mark
78 Act the big shot in a way
82 Theater group
84 Abatements
85 Turnpike crossing
86 Progeny
87 Didn't give __

89 Puppeteer Bil
90 Pacific people
91 Pained cry
93 "Let him first cast __ . . ."
96 Formerly, of old
97 Planes
98 Backs
100 Binary compound
102 Originated
104 Powerful
105 Exposed, as a lie
106 African antelopes
107 Landlord's concerns
108 Indian butters
109 Little __ (fair lady)

DOWN

1 Loosen, as a harness
2 Most glib
3 Snows of Scotland
4 Business-letter abbr.
5 Assume control
6 Irish darlings
7 Extension
8 Surrealist
9 Party to
10 Socializing
11 "I __ arrow . . ."
12 Color qualities
13 Violinist Bull
14 Skink
15 Vinegars of old
17 Animal track
19 Shield bosses
20 Mexican coin
24 Old Kremlin police
26 Very, in Nice
28 "Thanks __"
31 Proceeds slowly
33 Word with case or well
36 Ginza drink
37 Opening-night call
38 Seneca, for one
39 Gyrated
41 Certain aphid
43 Wall plug, e.g.
44 College course
46 __ of society
47 Textile-machine part
48 Ornate art style
49 Dine al fresco
50 Reef
51 Kipling poem

52 "And when the harvest . . ."
53 Jumble
54 Michigan college
55 Sponge spicule: Var.
56 Steers
57 Opportunity
60 Bars legally
62 Pirates
66 Assemble
69 Mrs. Hobby
70 Tropical tree: Var.
71 Edgar's Mortimer
72 Complain
74 Extroverted
75 Catch up with
77 Time of penitence
78 Sheep genus
79 Assumes
80 "This __" (Conelrad words)
81 Greek letters
82 Auto type
83 Item to drop or weigh
84 Girls
85 Rowed
86 Essence
88 Didn't own
89 Adam et al.
92 Sharpen
94 Webster
95 Adams
97 "Yearling" boy
99 Yutang
101 Corse, for one
103 Runner

258 NOELS A LA BERLITZ   *By Anne Fox*

ACROSS

1 Queens battleground
5 Ex-frosh
9 __ and Kashmir
14 Sky Way
19 Famous also-ran
20 African plant
21 Sky Hunter
22 Papal cape
23 Hebrew measure
24 Festive
25 __ juste
26 Star in 21 Across
27 Words from a Spanish carol
31 Roman officials
32 "__ prayer for me"
33 Kafka character
34 Old Roman province
35 Houston player
37 Southern constellation
40 Hitting stats
43 A Roosevelt
45 Recoverable sea goods
47 Burdened
49 Words by Isaac Watts
55 Like a 10-cent tip
56 Bridge work
57 Having a handle
58 Suffix with boy or girl
59 Dance
60 This: Sp.
61 Words from a French carol
71 Nightingale trademark
72 Female sprite
73 Cereal grass
74 Craving
77 Lay low
80 Sensitive plant
83 Words from a German carol
86 Cleaving tools
87 Part of Hispaniola
88 Do C.P.A. work
89 Tree
90 Some prizes
91 Red or Charing
94 __ Ferry
98 One of the Joneses
101 Comedian Silvers
102 Outdoor stairway
103 Words from an Italian carol
110 Lamblike
111 Korean city
112 Willing
113 One's own: Prefix
114 Large bill
115 Miss Bryant
116 Roman date
117 Medical Nobelist, 1970
118 Absolute
119 Parts
120 Gotham postal initials
121 Arizona town

DOWN

1 Pushed
2 Honshu port
3 Of deserts
4 Stony
5 Long tales
6 Norwegian saint
7 May fixture
8 San Simeon name
9 U.S. carol
10 Place of action
11 Opera role
12 Word with light or shine
13 "Render therefore __ . . ."
14 Principled
15 Irritating
16 Little Flower of N.Y.C.
17 Swiss painter
18 Tiger, e.g.
28 Marine conger
29 Swiss river
30 Pasture sound
35 Speech part: Abbr.
36 Sentence structure
37 Arab head cord
38 Grade
39 Wildebeest
41 Penchant
42 Dean of St. Paul's
44 U.S. author
46 Kind of hill
47 Slow, in music
48 Indian state
49 French girl friend
50 Hencoop feature
51 Actress Arlene
52 Up in __ (furious)
53 Biblical mount
54 Allergy
59 Slight taste
60 English river
62 Equally
63 Juliet's betrothed
64 Sobeit
65 S.A. monkey
66 Battle and pole
67 Utah mountains
68 Heath
69 Let up
70 The Man
74 Face
75 Green land
76 Winter pileup
77 To-do
78 Floral greetings
79 River isle
80 Not sm. or lge.
81 In the same place: Lat.
82 Vehicle
84 Roderick __
85 Edwards of vaudeville days
90 Charisse
92 Tease
93 Alkene
95 Type of veil
96 Food fish
97 Ready for sleep
99 Mother of Lavinia
100 Plastic for flooring
101 Shoshonean: Var.
102 Garden plant
103 Adroit
104 Hodgepodge
105 Eskers
106 Divorce spot
107 Drudgery
108 Astor or Jane Grey
109 Très __

259

VACANCIES *By Frances Hansen*

ACROSS

1 Caesar's enemy
6 Red, in Samoa
10 "... as ugly, ay, __"
15 Charon's river
19 Wilde
20 "Without __"
22 "Close, __ cigar"
23 Plea to tea hostess
24 Flemish artist Peter Paul
25 Beautiful young woman
26 Eastern faith
27 Ms. Mater
28 Tristan's lady
29 Broadway play of 1964
30 Attention-getting call
31 June 6, 1944
32 Crossword-puzzle activity
39 Over
40 Egg: Prefix
41 Fire bomb: Abbr.
42 News squib
43 Banjo's relative, for short
46 Ammo for TV Westerns
50 Writer's start
52 "Pain has an Element __"
55 Abba
56 Girl of song
57 One in the social whirl
58 Nonclerical
60 Andes grass
61 Coconut cookies
63 Take __ (care)
64 Sumatran raft
65 Vault or cat
66 Writer Leon and family
67 French measures
68 Bobbins
70 Drop bait lightly
73 Friction: Sp.
74 Bank concerns
77 Trieste wine measure
78 Grampus: Var.
79 Mr. Waugh
80 Gray's churchyard opus
81 Muscular strength
82 Florida beach
83 Jazz frills
84 Peruke
86 Recondite matters
91 Food fish
92 Spaghetti spice

93 Contrition
94 Unproductive
96 Discover
97 Sheet-metal cutter
98 Nod
99 What I did with my puzzle
101 Turku, in Sweden
102 __-day (vaudeville stint)
104 "Iz __ so!"
105 Second phone: Abbr.
106 Give a leg up
111 Apology for 99 Across
116 Flapper's song
119 That: Lat.
120 In a vacant way
121 __ shrdlu
122 __ for one's money
123 Florida cigar city
125 Red dye
128 Like the barefoot boy
129 __ oxide
130 Daughter of Anius
131 __ line (conformed)
132 Two of Henry VIII's wives
133 Harpo Marx, for one
134 Ayn and Sally
135 Part of K.K.K.
136 "That's the __ I can do"

DOWN

1 Kissing kin
2 __ as a lion (brave)
3 Official seal: Fr.
4 Frank
5 Prefix for a poison
6 __-jongg
7 Service org.
8 Shed feathers: Var.
9 Reagan's opponent, 1970
10 __-Diz, river of Iran
11 Dance step
12 Cards' home

13 Where raffle tickets belong
14 Upshot of a muralist's work
15 Mining nails
16 "I __ you so"
17 Arizona city
18 Candid camera shot
21 How to soothe Linus
24 Prevalent
33 Pram
34 "Terrible" one
35 Neither's partner
36 Faded away
37 Omen
38 Realms
43 Ascent
44 Acute
45 Slips
46 Legal stop
47 Grand or Petit
48 Poolhall worker
49 Greek group of W.W. II
51 Upward: Prefix
52 Faeroe island
53 Dostoevsky
54 Carte blanche
55 High notes

57 Vamoose!
59 Congo river
62 "Riding on __"
64 Mr. Vallee
67 South Vietnam town
68 "Bartered Bride" composer
69 Cribbage pieces
70 Come up with nothing
71 "__ is truth" (In vino veritas)
72 Maine port
74 Shakespeare, notably
75 Spooky
76 Old World kite
77 Not a copy: Abbr.
79 "Tinker to __ Chance"
81 Begot
83 Flow steadily
84 Right on target
85 Sea bird
86 Earth goddess
87 Slav
88 Melville book

89 Kind of truck or head
90 Sheik's garment
95 Carpenter's tool
96 Like Reynard
99 He's letter-perfect
100 Kind of insurance
103 Dakota tribe
106 Flammable gas
107 Antelope genus
108 Oxygens
109 Most tricky
110 See to
111 Dan or work
112 Empty-headed
113 Empty stare
114 Vinegar, in old England
115 Flower part
116 Paul Whiteman's kingdom
117 Solo
118 Fomer actor James
124 Dolt
126 Miss Lupino
127 Miss Tucket

260 ACCOUNTING *By Herb Risteen*

ACROSS

1 Kind of old story
5 Popular poem
10 Kind of hand or berth
15 Merle of films
17 Lease again
18 Washington bill
20 Very early Amati product
22 Shifty one
24 Peevish
25 Sword
26 Certain songs
28 Chemical suffix
29 Lacy queen
30 Of tissue
31 Good Queen
32 Indian of Cuzco
33 Carpet or Baron
34 Garment-area figure
35 "Over __"
37 __ down (belittled)
38 Tidied up, old style
40 Syngman and family
41 Gypsy
42 Boxer
44 Main idea
45 Ex-Harvard head
46 Alpinists' aids
47 Bridge teams
48 Spanish greeting
49 Critical
50 Bogged down
51 Kind of big truck
55 Grain sorghum: Var.
56 Cibola's claim to fame
58 Blackbirds
60 Did a duel chore
62 Manifest
63 Office worker
64 Shift
65 Clubs, etc.
66 Lose freshness
67 Asian tribesmen
70 Biblical patriarch
71 "Scram!"
72 Knight's need
73 Black-fin snappers
74 Contrary one
75 Wall hanging
76 Preyed

77 Spaghetti
78 Family member
81 Predicament
82 Fiji port
83 Grainger of music
84 Lab job
85 Poker move
86 Atelier equipment
88 Apollo's mother
89 __ meal (cooks)
90 Musical-show figure
92 Nick Carter's favorite time
95 Sweet time
96 Capacity unit
97 Small person
98 Equals
99 English city
100 "Now I've __ everything"

DOWN

1 Ingrained habits
2 Appeared
3 Belgian town
4 One of eleven
5 Made a big hit
6 Encore at the card table
7 Churchman
8 Electric __
9 Check
10 Foolish
11 Laborers
12 Sibilant sounds
13 Roof piece
14 European
15 Waldorf name
16 City on the Aare

18 Fur animals
19 __ store
21 Tributary
23 Prompt
27 Red as __
30 Handbags
32 "__ la Douce"
34 French river
35 Family reunion guest
36 Scratch-makers
37 Literary middle name
39 Arousing lust
40 Seine city
41 Parts
42 Mining nail
43 Printers' units
44 Meditated
45 Commandment word
47 Wallet item

48 Legatees
50 Ancient people
51 Proof notations
52 Blab
53 Whistle-stop
54 Cubs and Tigers
56 Bergen puppet
57 Plants
59 __ of (in a way)
61 Tracks
63 Alaskan port
65 Mediocre
66 Southern novelist
67 Fundamentals of education
68 O'Hare area
69 Social affairs
70 Hero's reward

71 Boastful person
72 Dance
73 English river
74 Trades
76 Friction matches
77 Annoyed
79 Campaigner's standby
80 Gaze
82 More prudent
83 Russian whip
84 Titter
86 Grafted, in heraldry
87 Be bearish
89 Indian butter
91 Tool
93 Be situated
94 County units: Abbr.

261 TEMPUS FUGIT *By Alex Black*

ACROSS

1 "__ boy!"
5 Pointed tool
8 "I would if I __"
13 Brawls
18 Flightless bird
19 Luau fare
20 Farm machine
21 East or West
23 Relative of a coon's age
27 Chatter
29 Diminutive suffix
30 "My country __ ..."
31 Island of a sort
33 Sack
34 Sash
35 Kindle anew
38 Constellation
39 Within: Prefix
40 Apple-pie maker
41 Old water clocks
45 Terminated
48 Cockney abode
49 Ingest
50 March King
51 Sultan of __
52 Kind of deal
55 Book, in Barcelona
57 Month: Abbr.
60 O'Casey and O'Kelly
62 Miss Claire
63 Chemical suffix
64 Ripe
67 Drink
68 Activist of the 1770's
71 Dancing miss of song
75 Ending for bull or hill
76 Discretion
77 Flag
78 Uses binoculars
79 Dexterity
81 Celebes ox
82 "Brother __"
83 Plaines or Moines
85 U.S.N.A. grad's rank
86 Formerly called
87 Long time
89 Compass point
90 Japanese case
92 Roebuck's partner
94 Tournament drawings
96 __ question (asked)
98 Neighbor of Minn.
99 Rolled tea
100 Zanuck film
102 End of a K.O. count
105 Ending for ster

or rhomb
106 Boggy
107 Urge, in Scotland
108 Vessel
109 Town near Emden
111 Self
112 Hindu music pattern
116 Graduate degree
117 Kind of over-65 care
119 Ink, in Iberia
121 Furniture wood: Abbr.
124 Turkish moneys: Abbr.
125 Incites
126 Indefinite hour
129 Bandleader Brown
130 Spheres
133 Pearl Buck heroine
135 Score a market coup
136 Companion of wt.
137 Watery defense
138 What son John had on

141 Jackie's late mate
142 Four scoreless quarters
144 Famous Moor
146 Lillian Russell feature
151 Stretch
152 Snooped
153 Kind of toe
154 Genus of sand snakes
155 Nasty
156 Growing out
157 Period
158 Actual being

DOWN

1 N.Z. vine
2 Delayed shocker
3 Unfaithful one
4 Common contraction
5 Off: Suffix
6 Court
7 Elevate
8 Old highways in Britain
9 Possess
10 Wavy, in heraldry
11 Spare
12 Instruction to a tailor
13 Time traveler
14 Concerning
15 Harem room
16 Like a lord
17 Attack
22 Kind of machine
24 Canonical hour
25 W.W. I admiral
26 Furtive
28 W.W. II area
32 Greek god
34 Melville work
36 High note
37 Divulge
42 Amounts of medicine
43 Wheels, in Seville
44 Aprocrypha name
46 Celtic goddess
47 State, in France
52 Staffed again
53 Montana range
54 Departed
56 Church corner
58 Malay dagger: Var.

59 Restrained
61 Fireplace part
65 Footless animal
66 English and Scottish rivers
69 "__ on parle ..."
70 Greek letter
71 Dashed
72 Hero's lover and others
73 Contestants
74 One, in Munich
79 Blind, in falconry
80 Easy gaits
84 Unexcelled
86 Must
88 Delicatessen snack
91 Orel's river
93 Asian gazelle
94 Schoolboy game
95 Obstacle
97 Soviet river
100 Auto-wheel adjustment
101 "The grass will __ the streets"
103 Unfeeling
104 Suffer, in Scotland

110 Light carriage
113 Round-the-clock
114 Calendar reformer and others
115 Aide: Abbr.
118 Man or Pines
120 Mayor, in Spain
122 French soul
123 "Vive __!"
125 Nautical direction
127 Dumb __
128 Sad
130 Shoulder: Prefix
131 Goes bad
132 Thai money
134 Residue
138 Smelly
139 Hillbilly possessive
140 Silkworm
143 Molding
145 Mongoloid tribesman
147 Comprehend
148 Gawain, for short
149 Humorist's initials
150 Devon river

262 OBSERVATIONS *By Adelyn Lewis*

ACROSS

1 Criticizes
5 Part of Vietnam
10 College degrees
14 Metrical accent
19 "Thanks __"
20 Tropical vine
21 Waterfall, in Scotland
22 Hard as __
23 Cynical quote, with 32 and 110 Across
25 Italian city
26 Suffix for hippo
27 Kind of highway
28 __ Binh, Vietnam
30 Cleaving tool
32 See 23 Across
39 Alas, in Bonn
42 N.L. player
43 Fencer, at times
44 Charged atom
45 Silvers or Harris
47 Suffix in zoology
49 Obtain
50 African fox
51 Idealistic quote, with 94 Across
57 Turns right
58 Log chute
59 Whim
60 Physics or chemistry: Abbr.
62 Theory
63 Part of a yard
65 Hard-core films, for short
67 Did cowboy work
71 Great amount
72 Here-I-come state: Abbr.
74 Kind of drum
76 Go wrong
77 Ford
79 Water birds
83 R.R. stops
84 Chemical suffix
85 Once around
87 Actor Jack and writer Alex
89 Callers of strikes
91 Swing around
94 See 51 Across
97 Northern constellation
98 Dakota Indian
99 Letters
100 Italian family
101 Swiss canton
102 Hen marking
105 Blow one's

horn
109 Papal title: Abbr.
110 See 23 Across
114 Between hic and hoc
115 Lighten
116 Of a belief
120 Every 60 minutes
123 Certain type: Abbr.
125 Politics, to Will Rogers
128 Dwelling
129 __ after (look like)
130 Bird sound
131 Solar or leap
132 Bar fruits
133 Fielding of football
134 Glad and Learned
135 Old slave

DOWN

1 Absorbed

2 Nautical word
3 Noted tourist
4 Wader
5 Adjusts
6 Most fussy
7 Pensacola, for one: Abbr.
8 Cuckoo
9 Middle, in law
10 White, in Spain
11 Author of 51 Across
12 Insect
13 More uppity
14 Like Astrodome events
15 English poet
16 Uncle, in Madrid
17 Danube city
18 Compass point
24 Weaverbird
29 Secretly
31 Butler et al.
33 Shouts, in France

34 Antiseptic: Var.
35 Instruments of knowledge
36 Kind of crack
37 Lawn gear
38 On __ uppers
39 Inform
40 Beggar's non-role
41 Author of 23 Across
46 __ Abner
48 Dripping
50 Exchange premium
52 __ day (pill dosage)
53 Suffix for a collection
54 Orbit
55 Old pronoun
56 Long periods
61 Italian painter
64 Cooking temperature

66 Showed interest
68 Noblewoman
69 Borgnine and Poole
70 Worked on mannequins
73 German lady
75 Boarding __
78 Holm oak
80 Shade tree
81 Gives lessons
82 Word in New Year song
86 Veranda, in France
88 Queen of __
90 Feminine suffix
91 Turnstile intruder
92 Harp's relative
93 Military group
95 Fruitfulness
96 ". . . and shall bring forth __"
102 Marshes

103 Nips gently
104 Alpine home
106 Confused
107 Candies
108 "__ above all . . ."
111 Ghost
112 Below, to poets
113 Belgian violinist
117 Day: Abbr.
118 Words of confidence
119 Bird membrane
120 Prince __
121 Sash
122 Male gypsy
124 Chinese truth
126 New Deal org.
127 Play or pig

MIXED DOUBLES
By Edward J. O'Brien

ACROSS

1 Words after dese
8 Catchall abbr.
11 It, in Italy
15 Curial bodies
20 Encircles, old style
21 Architect I.M.
22 Forgo a story hour
25 Spooner, e.g.
27 Shift the balance of power
28 Audubon, for one
30 In __ (mired)
31 After Lev.
32 "As sure __"
35 "__ in is a rotten egg"
37 Make, in France
39 Encounters, with "with"
41 Thing, in law
42 Diminished
44 Statement: Abbr.
45 Sky Peacock
48 Nimble
50 Ointment
51 Person
52 Safety or tie
53 Mystery man
54 Bucket
55 Cronkite's employer
58 Compass point
59 Noisy person
61 Initials on invitations
64 "I'll look __"
66 Annex
67 Playing card
70 To be: Lat.
71 Baseball positions: Abbr.
72 Too many helpers
73 Lively, as a horse
75 Clock numeral
76 Owns
77 Turkish title
78 Shelter
79 Shoe width
80 Marbles
82 Strong sales pitch
88 Pupils' trio
89 Sounds for silence
90 Prop for Miss Mullens
92 Library items: Abbr.
93 Feminine suffixes
95 Unchaff again
96 Rowing gear, old style
97 __ Dee River, N.C.
98 Draft initials
99 Truth, in Confucianism
101 Wander
103 Suffix with journal
104 Austrian statesman
106 Impend
107 World power
109 Bangla __
111 Holy Roman emperor
112 Puppet: It.
116 Baba
119 Lay one's __ the line
121 Standing
122 Imported timepiece
126 Kind of knot
127 Dixie: Abbr.
128 "Maybe it was something __"
130 Not spare the rod
132 Refuses a fish delicacy
135 Not spare the child
139 Does emcee work
140 Open or hot
141 Modern tires
142 Misses, in Madrid
143 Time periods
144 Fast plane
145 Caches

DOWN

1 Moisture
2 Wine: Prefix
3 Stengel or McGraw: Abbr.
4 Entered into conflict
5 Round trips
6 Amass
7 Founded: Abbr.
8 Hebrew bushel
9 Seesaw
10 Ring
11 Kefauver
12 One who avoids
13 Small draft
14 Chooser
15 In a relaxed manner
16 Certain stock market: Abbr.
17 __ Esther (Biblical fast)
18 Entice
19 Appeared
23 Outfield hit
24 Hay, in Hamburg
26 Hundred-weight: Abbr.
29 Signe of films
32 You love: Lat.
33 Rematches for boxers
34 Matchless vistas, as of grain
36 Sharp: Prefix
38 Missile: Abbr.
40 Melonlike fruits: Var.
43 Hindu caste
46 Twenty: Fr.
47 Words before make or level
49 Ahura-Mazda, for one
53 Desecrations
54 Delivery abbreviations
55 June, 1876, headline
56 Silent headliner
57 U.S. banking family
59 Go by again
60 W.W. II area
62 Velocity, for short
63 Caesar's alas
65 Govt. agency
66 Wanted-poster listings
68 Artful Dodger's mentor
69 Addison's partner
72 Pronoun
74 Faith: Abbr.
78 Most loyal
81 British verb ending
82 Vienna, to natives
83 __ jiffy
84 Direction
85 Burmese village
86 Tatter
87 Type of porridge
91 __ pump (stimulates)
94 Marksmen
97 Slippage, as of a disc
100 Heir
102 Maori people
105 Like some fish
106 Certificate: Abbr.
107 Use, in prescriptions
108 English writer
110 Snobbish
112 Mates of mmes.
113 Twenty-first President
114 Seek again
115 Instrument case, old style
117 "In thy green __ Nature's Darling laid"
118 "Look at __ way"
120 __ new tack (changed strategy)
123 Winter falls, old style
124 Diagram
125 With it
129 Sportlike: Abbr.
131 Restaurant workers: Abbr.
133 U.S. scholastic org.
134 Before sigma
136 Slangy negative
137 Seine body
138 Afterthoughts: Abbr.

BELONGINGS *By Bert Beaman*

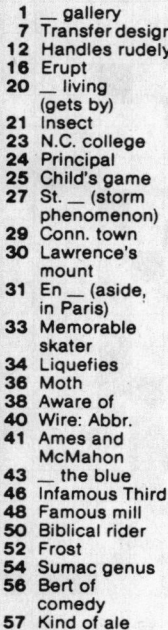

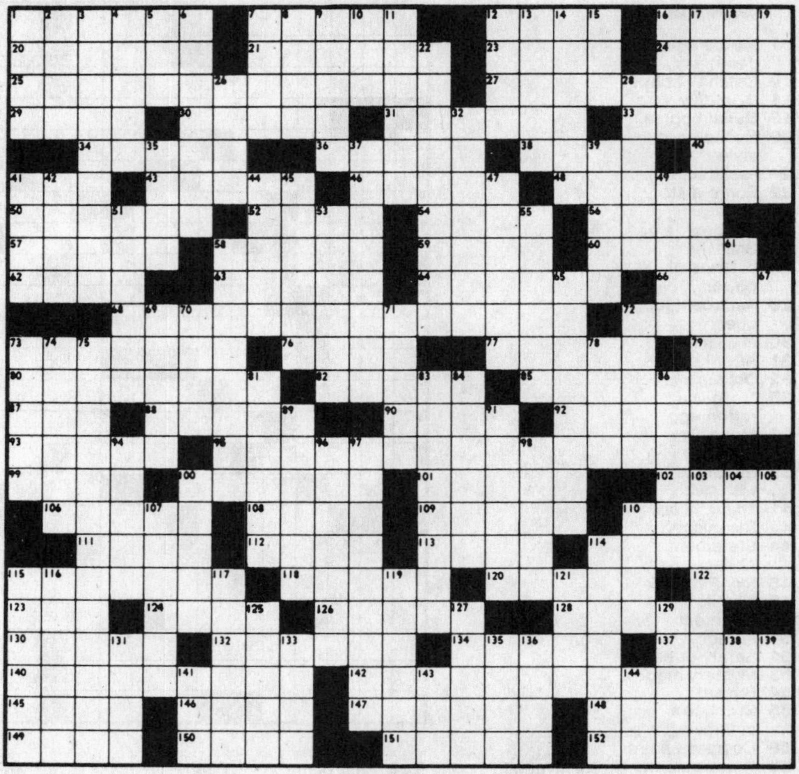

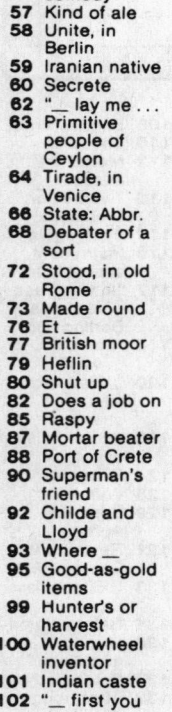

ACROSS

1 _ gallery
7 Transfer design
12 Handles rudely
16 Erupt
20 _ living (gets by)
21 Insect
23 N.C. college
24 Principal
25 Child's game
27 St. _ (storm phenomenon)
29 Conn. town
30 Lawrence's mount
31 En _ (aside, in Paris)
33 Memorable skater
34 Liquefies
36 Moth
38 Aware of
40 Wire: Abbr.
41 Ames and McMahon
43 _ the blue
46 Infamous Third
48 Famous mill
50 Biblical rider
52 Frost
54 Sumac genus
56 Bert of comedy
57 Kind of ale
58 Unite, in Berlin
59 Iranian native
60 Secrete
62 "_ lay me . . ."
63 Primitive people of Ceylon
64 Tirade, in Venice
66 State: Abbr.
68 Debater of a sort
72 Stood, in old Rome
73 Made round
76 Et _
77 British moor
79 Heflin
80 Shut up
82 Does a job on
85 Raspy
87 Mortar beater
88 Port of Crete
90 Superman's friend
92 Childe and Lloyd
93 Where _
95 Good-as-gold items
99 Hunter's or harvest
100 Waterwheel inventor
101 Indian caste
102 "_ first you don't . . ."
106 Taper a timber
108 Formerly, once
109 Mudpuddles, in England
110 General or department
111 Hill in Jerusalem: Var.
112 Have it made
113 She, in Milan
114 Hallmarks of early divas
115 Very near
118 W.C. Fields's Baby
120 U.S. violinist
122 Dissolution: Prefix
123 Slangy negative
124 Oodles
126 Hard: Prefix
128 Long times
130 Revolted
132 _ neck
134 Shadow
137 Today, in Naples
140 _ buff
142 Early swimming lesson
145 Queen Anne's _
146 _ Domini
147 _ law

DOWN

1 Substitute: Abbr.
2 Widely outspread
3 Theory of linguistics
4 Fail to spot
5 Inner: Prefix
6 Private place
7 Suffix for pachy
8 Or _
9 S.F. car
10 _ glance
11 French novelist
12 Noble
13 _ the good
14 _ Lib
15 Navy ranking abbr.
16 Vault
17 Apprentice of a sort
18 Cry out: Fr.
19 Big shots
22 Visits
26 U.S. biologist
28 Fired on
32 Antiquated
35 Haitian voodoo gods
37 French meat dish
39 City in Oklahoma
41 Abba
42 Pedestal part
44 Projecting window
45 _ way (gets oriented)
47 "The Last _"
49 Ex-U.N. name
51 Chemical compounds
53 Purple Heart, etc.
55 Kind of rights or man
58 Prosecutor's need
61 _ coat
65 Certain pet
67 _ English
69 Vertical
70 Mountain sickness
71 _ d'orchestre (organ stop)
72 Hammerhead
73 Fabric
74 _ "Republic"
75 Non-option
78 Farm machine: Abbr.
81 Card player, at times
83 View of a sort
84 Rope fibers
86 Assumes as fact
89 Starlike
91 Skier's forte
94 "For want of _ . . ."
96 Kind of gown
97 Go between
98 Attacked
100 Consider, to Cicero
103 Pyrite
104 Coxey's _
105 Literary heroine
107 Joined in a common effort
110 Sound: Prefix
114 Confronts
115 Helpless
116 Racetrack bet
117 Flammable gas
119 Comedian Ole and family
121 Merit
125 Cher's ex-husband
127 More impudent
129 _ prosequi
131 Prune, in Scotland
133 Army men: Abbr.
135 Roman 2,051
136 Smallmouth, for one
138 Waiting _
139 Roman road
141 Lady's _
143 Dog's _
144 Lawyer's _

148 "O _, pretty maiden . . ."
149 Word after pop or bug
150 French marshal and family
151 Mexican Indians
152 Farm equipment

265 PROPER NAMES By Bert Kruse

ACROSS

1 Vehicle
5 Hard-hearted girl
11 Claire of films
16 Prefix for barbital
17 Come out
18 Wall plug
20 Popular toys
22 Famous naval firer
24 Streams, in Spain
25 Decorated again
26 French silk
28 Secrete
29 Attention
30 Stephen and William
31 Penalized
32 Brazilian tree
33 More foxy
35 Numerical prefix
36 Families
37 Neatness
38 Meadow
40 Singing voice
42 Film-studio floodlights
43 City of Italia
46 Approaches
47 Old vegetable matter
48 Newlywed
50 Hole-in-one
51 Most stable
55 Unusual people
56 Bridge unit
58 Nasal sound
59 Thai language
60 Negative word
61 Make a commotion
63 Pitcher Johnny
64 Outside: Prefix
65 Item for Rosie
66 Disturbances
67 Mocking
68 Done over by a modiste
70 Advanced law degree
71 Navigation aids
73 Dutch painter
74 Signs of night
76 Saltpeters
77 Clothing protectors
80 Did lookout duty
82 Tennis unit
83 Scads
84 Françoise
85 Between sine and non
87 Orange variety
91 Vishnu incarnation
92 Steel, in Essen
93 Geometry pioneer
95 Storm center
96 Matterhorn milieu
97 Whole constituent
98 Actress Ada
99 Gait
100 Sturdy vessel
102 Beef cuts
106 Right, in France
107 Special idioms
108 Colorado park
109 U.S. President
110 Lighthouse
111 Western lake

DOWN

1 Hypothesis
2 Old autos
3 Conjunction
4 Melba or Garry
5 Those who listen
6 Alger hero's trademark
7 Requires
8 New Deal initials
9 Farming: Abbr.
10 Mercenaries
11 Golf scores
12 Attracted
13 Early Brazilian
14 Satan
15 Girl's name
16 Small bottle
19 Spread hay
20 _ bien
21 Torn
23 Time divisions
27 _ account (never)
30 White and rye
31 Burning signal
34 Queen of mysteries
36 A-one
37 Primate
39 Blackbird
41 _ Corps
42 Move like a wallaby
43 Threat
44 Certain gases
45 Eight-note musical spans
47 Make crude
48 Boo-boo
49 Had a go at
51 Dispatches, as a fly
52 Arthurian maid
53 Agnes and Elmo
54 Ice-bucket item
57 Suffix for art or humor
61 Rivulets
62 Failed to
63 Greek city
65 Actor O'Neal et al.
67 Give ear to
69 Hoyden
70 "Love Story" author
72 Greek letters
74 Finale of a sort
75 Words for a book following
77 Wall hanging
78 Rang
79 Bulwark
80 Area of Europe
81 _ of Windsor
84 Old Greek coin
86 "What a pity!"
88 Knowledgeable
89 Isles
90 Admits
92 Outpouring
93 Baseball statistic
94 Against a thing, in law
99 "So long!"
101 Kuwait asset
103 Royal abbr.
104 Turkish officer
105 Full of: Suffix

266 FINISH LINES By Elaine D. Schorr

ACROSS

1 Springs
5 French name for Morocco
10 Cenotaph
14 Short spells
16 Chemical compounds
18 "Butterfield 8" creator
20 Atwitter
21 Laughing, old style
22 Dawdling
24 A meteorologist is a __
27 Sidle
28 Safeholds
29 Give the glad hand
30 Nix!
31 Molding
32 Starboard, to a horse
33 Munchhausen
34 Vestige
35 Between Tinker and Chance
36 Hockey star
37 Fresh air
38 "Anything __"
39 Braid for Bardot
40 Rafts
41 Vivant or ton
42 Symbol of total loss
43 Freighter
46 Ayes and nays
48 German article
49 Elevations: Abbr.
52 Large groupings
53 Paintings
54 Norse god
56 Alley call
57 Mug
58 Chaucer and Hawthorne __
60 Hobgoblin: Var.
61 Sensitive leg part
62 Ives
63 Hebrew universe
64 Curtains
65 Long time
66 Shapeless lump
67 Edward of TV
69 Huffy
70 Bridge framework
72 Sleuth, for short
73 Famed instrument, for short
75 Plato's place
77 Roe source
79 Erupt

80 German coins: Abbr.
83 Certain schools, for short
84 Lake or dive
85 Emulate a demagogue
86 Indonesian islands
87 Type size
88 __ Sisters of "Macbeth"
89 Win at rummy
90 Move like Gray's plowman
91 Bert or John
92 Eskimos
95 __ princeps (first printing)
97 Tennyson maid
98 Vicarious feeling

99 Kind of whale
100 Antiseptic pioneer
101 Land
102 Ooze
103 Prefixes for wings
104 Dotted, in heraldry

DOWN

1 Fore-and-aft sail
2 Cream and powder
3 Guthrie
4 Autograph hounds are __
5 Dietrich
6 Love-in-__
7 __ to the hounds

8 Two
9 Expurgator, in Italy
10 "Uncle Tom" character
11 Exclamation
12 Refurbish
13 An orthodontist
14 Trapper
15 Bird
17 Harriet B. and family
19 Stirs up
20 Adult insect
23 Gaggle units
25 Uris and Trotsky
26 Carp at
33 Anne __
35 Behan's land
38 Goliath __
39 Flimsy
40 Done in
41 Plant pod
42 After cinco

43 Wine disorder
44 Upright: Prefix
45 Croupiers __
46 Residence of a sort
47 Kind of year or eclipse
50 Sheer fabric
51 __ tooth or pea
53 Bard's word
55 Party man: Abbr.
56 Simple organism
58 Baths
59 Templeton
60 Double, as a leaf
62 Top man
64 Tom, Dick and Harry are __
66 Bren and Sten

68 Persevere
71 Persiflage
73 Sudden rise
74 Racing-stable V.I.P.
75 Snow White's downfall
76 Groups of three
77 Kind of chair
78 Facial deformity
79 Bottle babies
80 Artist's gear
81 Insubstantial
82 Like beer
84 Marmara, for one
88 Trounce
89 Lost soul
90 "__ of Life"
93 Formality
94 Foretell, in Scotland
96 Pique

267 CREATURES IN HIDING *By John Willig*

ACROSS

1 Vast
7 Scratched
12 Auditors: Abbr.
16 Of the kidneys
21 Relaxed
22 Grenoble's river
23 "__ Make a Deal!"
24 Put forth effort
25 Partisan leader
27 Havoc
29 Shoe size
30 One or another
31 "__ the Lord..."
33 Run off
34 Oom Paul, e.g.
35 Sluggish one
36 Obscure
37 Total
40 Kitchen gear
41 Distresses
42 Pastime for Lucullus
46 Zoo category
48 "Et tu, __!"
49 "A votre __!"
50 Farm agency: Abbr.
51 Give consent
52 Induce to join
54 Stuff into
55 Flightless birds
56 Talk nonsense
57 Prefix with gram or meter
58 Ready: Fr.
59 Eartha
60 Color for the 1890's
61 Turkish titles
63 Fisherman, at times
64 Chemical suffix
65 Unrestrained uproar
67 Sculptor, e.g.
68 Do a coat job
70 Before H.S.T.
71 __ to (be capable of)
72 Suppose
73 Disguises
77 Pronoun
80 Eye inflammation
81 Bonding agents
82 Small amounts
83 __ fever
84 Hindu title
85 Open to question
86 Essence
87 Hundred: Prefix
88 "Picnic" playwright
89 Resolute
92 Caribbean export
93 Holy __
94 Eats
95 Capers
96 Sets on
97 Callous
99 Modify
100 Athletic rewards: Abbr.
101 Still
102 Wait __
103 Importune
104 Amateur: Var.
105 Apply oneself
107 Gandhi, for one
108 Appalachian range
110 Blue
113 Lively exchange
115 Forbidding
118 Winsor heroine
119 Bar drinks
120 Old name for a Soviet region
121 Sharp-edged
122 Exploits
123 Uncle of Lancelot
124 "Highwayman" author
125 Modish

DOWN

1 Modern U.S. composer
2 U.S. Indian
3 Browned
4 Zetterling
5 Belle __, Nfld.
6 Monk, for one
7 Abundance
8 Son of Jacob
9 Dullea
10 Poetic word
11 Clear-cut
12 Actress Leachman
13 Flower part
14 Part of D.A.: Abbr.
15 Compass point
16 Solitary one
17 Urge strongly
18 Tide
19 Indonesian island group
20 Military ranks: Abbr.
26 Expiate
28 Have reference to
32 Comic-strip part
35 Gander's due
36 Chemical prefix
37 Pitcher Lyle
38 Gamin
39 "Die __"
40 Some diggings
41 For the time being
42 State and trade
43 Non-pertinence
44 Trimmer
45 More daring
47 Essential part
48 Cape Verde island
49 Arouse, with "up"
52 Bluenose
53 Pearl Harbor site
54 Woolly: Fr.
56 Velvety cloth
58 Resounds
60 Disables
61 Where Mt. Aconcagua is
62 "__ Crazy"
63 Korea's Syngman et al.
65 Rain: Fr.
66 "Why not take all __?"
67 Popeye's creator
69 Lauder of cosmetics
71 Ruinous
72 Spider: Lat.
73 Former street sounds
74 Self: Prefix
75 "__ a king"
76 Water lily
78 Earnings
79 Where the locals gather
80 Part of I.R.A.
81 Did a job on the matador
83 Calif. fish
85 French impressionist
86 Yellow-fever carrier
87 Skips, as classes
89 Shackle
90 Lazed
91 Squelches
92 Honed
94 Early kind of prison
96 Like a rat in __
98 Den piece
99 "Gunsmoke" lawman
100 Restricts
103 Cheapskate
104 Western lake
105 Key-pie ingredient
106 French cleric
107 Aura
108 Actor Calhoun
109 Mrs. Chaplin
110 __ opera
111 Commedia dell'
112 Colorist
113 Mild oath
114 Stage drop
116 Dolores Del __
117 Recipe abbr.

268 BLUE NOTES · By Jim Page

ACROSS

1 Locust tree
7 Vex
11 Kind of onion
16 Pompous in speech
17 Bob 'Cratchit, e.g.
18 Word on a dollar bill
20 Spanish drama
21 Crystal set
22 Films' Buster et al.
24 Colors
25 Blues
27 Balm for sore feet
28 Curve
29 Did a sea job of a sort
30 Oxford shoe
31 To be: Fr.
32 Powder anew
34 Sorensen, to friends
35 Mutts
37 Group of three
38 __-cat (ball game)
39 Talking bird
40 Point __, Fire Island
41 Bridge high-low play
43 S.J. Perelman book
47 Shanks' and old gray
48 Command
49 Wrest
50 Blood state: Suffix
51 Moldings
52 ". . . __ but a whimper"
54 Doctrine
57 Actor Walter et al.
59 O'Flaherty
60 Merganser
61 Wagnerian maiden
63 Clinch breaker
64 Alpinist's goal
66 Moonshine gear
67 River to North Sea
68 Hindu caste
69 Places for key plays
70 Break out
71 "The busy bee has no __" (Blake)
75 Montgomery and family
76 "Jack, be __"
77 Tops
78 Willing, of old
79 Fencing move
80 Kind of needle
81 Fabled bird
84 Do a mortgage job
87 Agent: Suffix
88 Long time
89 Noisemaker in Dundee
91 Soak
92 Mather and Bowl
94 Egregious
96 Item in Beaufort's scale
97 Burke's output
98 Napoleon's lot
99 Quake
101 Mortimer et al.
102 Minnelli and Doolittle
103 Like Shakespeare's sleave
104 Girl's nickname
105 Legal right
106 One with a thought

DOWN

1 Stimulate
2 Fails
3 Noun suffixes
4 Rechewable item
5 Adverse
6 Bay in Gulf of Calif.
7 Like some slacks
8 Decorated again
9 Canal
10 Ring decisions
11 Turkish titles: Var.
12 Sign up
13 Pre-med course
14 Resembling latex
15 Drink, to W.C. Fields
16 Earth pigment
17 Minoan's home
19 Groups of four
23 Casts off
26 Stayed put
29 Pretexts
30 Grain by-product
33 Toughen
35 Vesicle
36 Miss Merkel
37 Nasal sounds
39 Hodgepodge
40 Start the bidding
41 Vilify
42 Metrical foot: Fr.
43 Shield
44 Flimflam
45 Biblical unicorn
46 Sounds from Dixieland
48 Ravel favorite
52 Kind of acid
53 On earth
54 Word for a bore
55 Trod, to poets
56 Trading places
58 Actor Maximilian
60 Vega or Polaris
62 High nests: Var.
65 Abundant
66 Beget
68 Shrub of Africa
69 Corn __
70 Girl's name
71 Moves quietly
72 Powerless
73 "Don't __ on My Parade"
74 Trinity
75 Bunkum
76 Civil-rights org.
80 __ question (raises doubt)
81 Loose coat
82 Monsters
83 Auditor: Abbr.
85 Wall St. bear
86 Horse
88 Graduate degrees
89 Billiard-ball's footing
90 Prelim's relative
93 They fit in locks
94 Cut down
95 Roman 62
96 Govt. agents
100 Midianite king
member

269 CEILING UNLIMITED

By Jean Davison

ACROSS

1 King and Cranston
6 Frenzied
11 N.T. book
15 These: Fr.
18 Rascals
20 Battery part
21 Encourage the team
22 Brubeck
23 Band instruments
25 Determine
26 Con
27 Dare, in Caen
28 Miser
31 Widespread
33 Flower
34 Pond enthusiast
36 Recount
37 __ diem
40 Period
42 Suffix for tonsil
43 Footnote term
44 Form of Helen
47 Squirt
50 Black-fin snapper
51 German article
52 Glamour man, in Spain
54 Letters
56 __ Alamos
58 Old verb
62 Pipe up
69 Subjugate
70 Shades
71 Prize giver
72 Greek god
74 "Bye-Bye"
76 Supple
77 Coarse fiber
81 Egg on
82 Carson
83 Soothe
85 Gaelic
86 Retribution
88 Snare or kettle
90 Person
91 Green shade
92 Perfect
94 Asks for a raincheck
100 Reason to see one's doctor in these times
104 Window part
105 Snoop
106 Capture
107 Engine type
109 Word of disgust
112 Johnson of TV
115 Goal
118 Hopscotch
119 Merchant's event
120 Menotti
121 Sesame
122 Haggard book
123 Safari assistant
125 Most adamant
129 Forbidden acts
133 Abscissa's partner
135 Deli item, nowadays
139 Old-fashioned person
140 Wood strip
142 Lariat
143 French encyclopedist
145 Paradise
146 __ processing
147 Former Harvard president
148 Imposts
149 Cambodian money
150 Cut
151 Medicinal plant
152 Pee Wee of baseball

DOWN

1 Triomphe, for one
2 Diving bird
3 Fields: Lat.
4 Never, in Spain
5 Aims at
6 Wise men
7 Concerning
8 Outlaw's rifle décor
9 Western state
10 __ paribus
11 Macaw
12 Disorder
13 Grivet monkey
14 Completed the martini
15 Offhand
16 Happening
17 Twilled fabric
19 Word on a proof
22 Breed developed for sprinting
24 Weather forecast
29 Bow
30 Network
32 Regale
35 Two on the __
37 Favorite
38 Run off
39 Stale TV show
41 Granular snow
45 Aerialists' needs
46 Seed cover
48 Takes five
49 Wahoo
53 "__ slow boat to . . ."
55 Feeling
57 Caged for fattening, as steers
59 Enthusiasm
60 Originates
61 Quorum for a crowd
63 Abroad
64 Wolfe
65 Undiluted
66 U.S. time zone
67 Join Leander
68 Existed
73 Roulette bet
75 Expert
77 Oxen of East
78 Indian city
79 Swiss poet
80 Currency maneuver
81 Pub order
82 African antelope
84 Morning song
87 Knight's title
89 __ Bravo
90 Assuage
93 Seth's father
95 Ares or Mars
96 Error
97 Spread
98 Eats little
99 Fruitstand sign
101 Meatball's partner
102 Mideast country
103 Religious faction
108 Soap ingredient
110 Campbell
111 Proclaims
113 Canvas cover
114 Bears
116 French number
117 Audibly
119 Depress
123 Presages
124 Deteriorate
126 Zola
127 Basque homeland
128 Western range
130 Word with hob or hang
131 Directive
132 McQueen
134 Afrikaans
136 Pro-
137 Famous canal
138 Hinds
141 Checkroom item
144 Poet's monogram

MILESTONES By. A.J. Santora

ACROSS

1 Locust
7 Nicholas, for one
11 Of grandparents
15 Horses
20 Took turns
21 "Pay __ mind"
22 Cab or dancer
23 Suffering
24 Cactus flower
25 Len Deighton novel
28 Rude beginning
30 Kind of lab
31 In addition
32 Stiff or side
33 Russian city
34 Beaver or Hoover
37 __ tree
39 Antiquity, old style
40 Condition
43 Can. province
44 Certain fashion displays
48 "My Heart Belongs __"
50 Married woman
51 Railroad span
52 Sky Altar
53 Wrath
55 Generally
57 __ combat
61 James Joyce work
65 Defeat
67 Pronoun
68 __ loan (get financing)
69 Young salmon
70 Not one __ questions
73 Court plea, for short
74 Kind of ulcer
76 Loud cries
78 "__ Born"
81 Gist of a Jolson line
84 Reddish purple
86 French tin
87 Miss Andress
88 Teen-__
89 "A horse designed by a committee"
91 Grapevine disease
93 Additional trial
97 Wrongdoing
98 Whip
100 Childhood milestone
103 __ the truth
105 Crosby alma mater
108 Gear for Killy
109 Swindle
110 Resort area
112 Mop cloth
113 Lift
116 Ruth Stuart tale
120 Prosecutors, for short
122 Weather satellite
123 Common verb
124 Coming-out party
125 Latvia, for one: Abbr.
126 Of great size
128 Shinto temple
129 Confirm in a way
131 Carrier lines: Abbr.
133 Former fall observances
139 Autumn girl
143 Teachers' goals
144 Buoy up
145 Charles Lamb
146 Grafted, in heraldry
147 Kind of paint job
148 Feel
149 Opinion
150 Restrain
151 Man of wisdom

DOWN

1 __ plea
2 Live __ (have fun)
3 Choral work
4 Dressed
5 Belief in God
6 Bede
7 Luncheon
8 Step, in Berlin
9 Jerome Chodorov comedy
10 Big game gun
11 One __ time
12 Fine lace
13 Alliance of W.W. II
14 Space dockings
15 Miss West
16 Tourist spot of India
17 Did the honors at dice
18 Isolate
19 Church councils
20 Thieve
26 Rose and cherry
27 Hiking areas
29 Trappist
cheese
35 Aleutian island
36 Blackbird
38 Guthrie and namesakes
40 Kind of sergeant
41 Bullring area
42 Bell town
43 Pianist Hess
45 Asian flower tree
46 Spools
47 Chalice veil
49 Set a trap for
50 Bryn __
54 De mal __ (from bad to worse)
56 Theatrical booking
58 Patrol or leave
59 Salami spot
60 Cupid
62 Siestaed
63 Long time, in poems
64 Indian chief
66 Sanctions
71 Harvest goddess
72 The same
73 Broadway Joe
74 Asian flower
75 Mexican coin
77 Start of a vowel recital
79 Abusive, Var.
80 Rental sign
81 Hollywood figure
82 Native of: Suffix
83 Oil suppliers
84 Spar
85 Money changing
90 Texas A. and M. student
92 Groom's party
94 Mystery award
95 "What Do You __ a Naked Lady?"
96 Does pool work
98 Well-known London street
99 Cowboy of Southwest
101 Merit
102 Alibi people
104 Aprocrypha book: Abbr.
106 Gambling
figures
107 Calmer and Rorem
111 Congregated
114 Flammable gases
115 Railroad span
116 Deep cuts
117 Bright bird
118 Reporter
119 Asian land
120 Land or cartoon
121 Perform
127 Michelangelo work
128 Temper display
130 Profits
132 Farm structure
134 De Rivoli, etc.
135 Take __ the chin
136 Irish indeed
137 Time division
138 Super plane
140 After jay or em
141 "Nothing doing!"
142 Enola or Paree

READING LETTERS

By William Lutwiniak

ACROSS

1 Paterfamilias
5 Pundit
10 Social group
14 Nut to crack
19 Land of Tralee
20 Table fowl
21 Trumpeter Al
22 Poplar
23 H
26 Sum up
27 Animal with a limited diet
28 Tones down
29 Peerage members
30 Wants for food
31 Bigot
32 Displayed
33 Noun ending
34 Do dying work
35 Safeguards
37 River of song
40 AF
42 White House nickname
44 "Cowardly Lion" actor
45 Impartial
47 Cobbling gear
48 Child's play
49 Tennis coup
50 Of of of of of of of of of of
54 Right-hand page
55 Backflows
58 Cafe patron
59 Fuddy-duddies
60 External
61 S.A. rodents
62 Basis for calculating
63 Drew out
65 Jeopardy
66 Predicaments
69 English county, for short
70 A
72 Fearful veneration
73 Morsels
74 Historic times
75 Unctuous
76 Use the teeth
77 "Quiet!"
78 C C C C C C C
82 Kind of maid or slipper
83 Schiaparelli, e.g.
86 In good time
87 White House nickname
88 Court judgments

89 Band members
90 Retort
94 Indian V.I.P.s
96 Baby animals
97 Postal chore
98 Get away
99 H
101 Go, in France
102 Ruin
103 Writer Godden
104 She was born free
105 "Now I __ . . ."
106 Org.
107 Mopsus et al.
108 Bridge outcomes

DOWN

1 Armadillos
2 Common contraction
3 Mourning figure
4 Preceding
5 Large duck
6 Navy personnel
7 Imitative one
8 French possessive
9 Set up for use
10 Monster
11 Three-time loser
12 College study
13 Utmost
14 Show off
15 Fairy king
16 O
17 Animated style
18 Congressmen: Abbr.
24 Safe place
25 __ the land
29 Golf strokes
31 Viscount Templewood
32 Remedies
34 Short notes
35 Widow's due
36 Ray
37 Winglike
38 Oppose
39 Y
41 Metallic fabrics
43 Heroic work
45 Outwitted
46 Southwest wind
48 Stonecrop
51 Comes close
52 Implicit
53 Aviator Balbo
54 Surf sound
56 __ out (comes off well)
57 All-purpose trucks, for short
59 Linger
61 As such
62 Pickle
63 Declines
64 Religious belief
65 River to the Adriatic
66 Oxeye
67 "And __ we go!"
68 Runs up
70 Gets vexed
71 Paddock sights
74 Curves
76 Footgear
79 Atomic component
80 Footgear
81 Means of expunction
82 Popular fur
84 Royal perquisite
85 Belong
87 Props for Groucho
89 Hop and tree
90 Have connection
91 Did a second-story job
92 Monopoly
93 Wildcats
94 The McCoy
95 Nazimova
96 Wine barrels
97 Apple variety
99 Between sine and non
100 Wish one hadn't

WORD DOINGS   By Charles Baron

ACROSS

1 Danube city
9 __cadabra
13 Taken, in France
17 Gallup specialty
21 Glitter
22 Made a baseball move
23 Asian nomad
24 Fencing foil
25 Drivers' needs
26 Delivers
28 Annals: Abbr.
29 Compass reading
30 Like Omar after a busy day
32 Bar staple
33 Dogtags, for short
35 Rational
36 Rough
38 Poet Countee
39 Decorative band
41 Created
42 Beverages
43 Look up to
44 Pack animals
45 Wind: Prefix
46 Hindu sacred books
48 Eastern fibers: Var.
49 Famed violinist
50 Related by blood
52 Abner's friend
54 Promontory
55 Form of Elizabeth
57 Relative of drat
60 Shopping or grab
62 Snail genus
64 Unit
66 Dalmatian island
68 "Gil Blas" author
73 N.Y.C., Rye, Hoboken, etc.
81 Thrill at Shea
82 Summer-stock figure
83 Manush of baseball
84 U.S. media org.
85 Harvest goddess
86 Miss Sumac
87 __ es Salaam
89 Arizona city
91 Musical notes
97 Medieval brocade
101 Apple, for short
103 Inflames
108 Hatred
109 Verbal contraction
111 __ of life
114 Organic compound
115 Shows warmth
116 Toot
118 Bullish word in Spain
119 Lose interest
120 Pan or Nero
121 Bequest source
122 Casual talk
124 Tunisian rulers
125 Excels
126 Haw's partner
127 Twine fiber
129 Western Indian
132 Color lightly
133 Be excessively touchy
136 Words for a birdie or eagle
138 Early English moneys
139 Terrible
140 Fuel
141 Popular entertainments
142 Meeting: Abbr.
143 Cheek
144 Fixed a tax: Abbr.
145 Dramatis __

DOWN

1 Ill temper
2 U.S. author
3 Las Vegas game
4 Summer cooler
5 Music scale of five notes
6 Early monastics
7 Make the __
8 Lab chore
9 Maugham story
10 Embryo cell group
11 Wash cycle
12 Write a p.s.
13 Advance
14 Setback
15 Alibi man
16 Watergate judge
17 U.S. humorist
18 Phone-user's quest
19 Readers' desks
20 Inferiority
27 Edge along
31 __ Prabang
34 Flops
35 Handbag part
37 "... Ruler of the Queen's __"
39 Haul
40 Morpheus's offering
41 Chinese leader
44 Get-together
47 Bench occupant
50 Navaho sheep
51 Words for Taft
53 Mottled canes
56 Bettelheim's "Children of __"
58 Sings softly
59 Oven-baked, in Hawaii
61 Civet's relative
63 In __ (having a mad on)
64 Rumanian composer
65 Ship weights: Abbr.
67 With wide scope
69 Trade-term initials
70 Commedia dell' __
71 Turns right
72 Dog and tin
73 Deep cut
74 Virginia signature
75 E.E. Cummings title
76 Have __ (know somebody)
77 Lukewarm
78 __ bit (completely)
79 Stage phone, e.g
80 River to North Sea
88 Brit. fliers
90 Nuclear particle
92 Cozy quality
93 Mine approaches
94 Irritate
95 Boy, to Caesar
96 Sweater sizes: Abbr.
97 Firemen's glove material
98 Cat seen by Alice
99 Saddle bags
100 Musical movements
102 Berra and Bench, e.g.
104 Verifies one's figures
105 Consecrated
106 __ better (outdo)
107 Building wing
110 French head
112 Agrees
113 Judge, e.g.
115 Road menace
117 Does garden work
123 Confusion
124 Kind of cap
128 Witty remark
129 "__ my word"
130 N.Z. tree
131 Gaelic
134 Routing word
135 U.S. aid agency: Abbr.
137 Greek letter

273 GREENSKEEPING
By Eugene T. Maleska

ACROSS

1 Steam baths
7 Give out
11 "Hyperion" poet
16 "Erin __!"
17 Losers to Brian Boru in 1014
19 Patrick's partner
21 Spouse of 16 Down
22 Parade month
23 By turns: Prefix
24 Of space
25 Architect's draft
27 Composer Satie
29 Hari
30 Opposite of trans-
31 Wampum
33 Gretna Green bride
35 Comedian Conway
36 Wife of Geraint
38 O.S.S. chief in W.W. II
42 "Songs of Killarney" author
44 Backbone of S.A.
45 We, in Italy
46 Bird dog
49 Botanical ripening
53 Hollies
55 Poe house
56 Glacial divide
57 Like Dixie: Abbr.
58 Day before the rebellion of 1916
62 Actress MacGraw
63 Famed puppeteer
64 McGuire Sisters
65 Certain negative: Var.
66 Dennis the Menace, for one
67 Modernizer of Japan
68 Workers in Ireland's pastures
72 Actor Ray
73 "O __ is she!" (Jonson)
75 Greenish blue
76 Aft
77 Molasses
78 Items to eat with Irish stew
81 Ten: Prefix
82 Vandyke or imperial
83 Rudiment
85 Old-time baseball cry
90 avis
92 Irish
93 Group of nine
94 Profoundly, to poets
96 Kind of time
97 Other: Sp.
99 Hatching post
100 Lanchester et al.
102 Arrested
104 Zealot
106 Irish patriot
108 Geological period
110 Irish legislators
111 Farm-machine pioneer
112 Stores grain
113 Sordid
114 Walked on
115 Acupuncture item

DOWN

1 On the wing
2 Mrs. Levy
3 Spanish vase
4 Brad and spad
5 Vital statistic
6 Ill-tempered
7 Orator Burke
8 Volcanic crater
9 Legal phrase
10 Gumshoe
11 Fabulous fighters
12 Outside: Prefix
13 Warning
14 N.Z. tree
15 Submitted, as mss.
16 Famous Kelly
18 Clam-bar worker
19 Chilean river
20 Author O'Flaherty
26 O'Hara's Joey
28 McKuen et al.
32 Rams' mates
33 Graybeards
34 Mickey of films
37 Adventurous
39 Enjoy a lough
40 Prefix with loper or cede
41 Passages
43 Power
47 Girl in a song
48 Bar legally
49 Partisan
50 Irish statesman
51 Sugary
52 Newsroom worker
53 Lend a hand
54 Part of a turbine
58 Well-known widow
59 Alpine crest
60 Brought to naught
61 Physicist Bohr
66 Sideshow worker
68 Leave a group
69 Harbinger
70 Abrasive
71 Electric catfish
74 Gully
76 C.P.A.'s record: Abbr.
78 Passé
79 Customs inspectors at docks
80 Arrow poison
82 Friendly contests
84 Apprentice
85 Medit. vessels: Var.
86 Grubs
87 Joints
88 Stood the gaff
89 Mrs. McKinley
91 Saint of Jan. 21
92 The old country, etc.
95 Joyce's forte
98 An O'Neill
100 Legendary Irish beauty
101 Dodecanese island: It.
103 Kind of test
105 O'Shanter
107 Shea player
109 Adjective suffix

BY NO MEANS
By Maura B. Jacobson

ACROSS

1 Hannibal's hurdle
5 Partner of gown
8 Cribbage gear
11 Moscow agency
15 Second courses
20 Old capital of Japan
21 France of fiction
23 Swing around
24 Bone of contention
25 No musical
29 Sprayed
30 No book
31 Son of Gad
32 Struck
34 Hagen
35 Mute consonants
36 Early Iranian
38 "_ of robins . . ."
40 Dodecuple group
43 Golfbag item
47 Below: Fr.
49 Early ascetic
52 Rainier place
54 Place for a home
56 No author
60 Aardvark's quarry
61 Give the Maine its due
64 Yours and mine
65 British inc.
66 Give off highlights
67 Retired
71 Rare beauty
74 Sly glance
76 No body of water
79 Go
81 "First _, first . . ."
83 Parent of N.B.C.
84 Impair
85 Furrow
86 Hostile one
87 No bridge bid
93 O.T.B. concern
94 Doris or Clarence
95 Demitasse contents
97 Macaw
99 Slithery one
100 Mother of Hermes
101 Changes the wording
104 Compass reading
105 No hero
112 Shor
114 Timon's home

115 Goofs
116 Shoplifter
118 Wilde locale
119 Bayou dialect
121 Native Israeli
124 Tear down
127 Choir members
130 Wallach
133 Shotgun caliber
135 Cowboy's sobriquet
136 No coeds
142 _ home (out)
144 No opera
146 Signs on
147 Long period
148 Toyed with
149 Quick drink
150 Nasal noise
151 Summer-time listings
152 Gender
153 Grid gains: Abbr.
154 Etta _

DOWN

1 Key opus
2 Punjab city
3 No electee
4 Yegg's target
5 Unchivalrous one
6 Pros _ (both sides)
7 Gourmet's sense zone
8 French swine
9 Yale
10 Sartre contemporary
11 Sudanic language
12 Danish measure
13 Devious
14 Auk's relative
15 Panning gear
16 Diffusing by absorption
17 Secondhand
18 Touchwood
19 _ precedent
22 Pates, in Rouen
26 Freud's concerns
27 Stock-market habitué
28 Ginza change
33 Bleat
37 Part of Britain: Abbr.

39 Shoebox notation
41 Light-switch positions
42 Relative of omega
44 Relative of ole
45 Roman goose
46 _ de plume
48 Arctic island of a sort
50 Abbr. for Jeanne d'Arc
51 Letter line
52 Man's nickname
53 Thrushes: Var.
54 Bounced back
55 Reception aid
56 Kind of sister
57 Plunge into a fluid
58 Dorothy's dog
59 Alaskan glacier
62 Draper's measure
63 _ culpa
68 Verne hero
69 Smell _
70 Having tendrils
71 No paradise
72 In plain view
73 Child's disease

75 Aries
77 Ruhr pronouns
78 Cole et al.
80 W.W. II command
82 No Highlanders
87 Larger than life
88 Dies _
89 Oslo people
90 U.S.S.R. river
91 Wrestlers' need
92 Prior to: Prefix
96 Remo and Diego
98 Piedmont city
102 Misdo
103 Backtalk
105 Hang back
106 One _ time
107 Sentry's pronoun
108 Shampoo direction
109 Grammar case: Abbr.
110 Mad, in Paris
111 American landscapist
113 "_ the ramparts we . . ."

116 Tied up
117 Beldam
119 "Typhoon" author
120 Stage whispers
122 Words with Aquarius or Reason
123 Tippler
125 Enthusiast
126 Dimensions
128 Minimum
129 Before ad or pod
131 Shopping aids
132 Grenoble's river
134 Diplomat: Abbr.
136 Depth measures: Abbr.
137 Nose: Prefix
138 Aviation prefix
139 Gait
140 Urges
141 Feminine suffix
143 Sty cry
145 Sullivan and Ames

275 GENERATION GAP By Louis C. Mandes Jr.

ACROSS

1 Humiliated
7 Place for a quad
13 Wild animal
17 Strain
21 Darrow, e.g.
22 Take to the skies
23 Federal org.
24 Auto part
25 Source of Lincoln's indebtedness
27 Man or ape
29 Reserved
30 "If I've __ once . . ."
31 Viscous
33 Yielding
34 Scout's daily bit
35 Oppressive
37 Peacock blue
38 Hoover or beaver
41 Zodiac unit
42 Treaty, in Tours
43 Works on proofs
47 Fancy
49 Mints
51 Royal initials
52 Kind of call
53 Page number
54 Fills with wonder
55 Peach or beech
56 Certain freshman
57 One of the Americas
58 Like some prices
60 "Now I __ . . ."
61 Money in Milan
62 Wearies
63 Not so undecided
64 Friend of Shakespeare
65 Desire
66 Slogan for the discreet
68 Magyars' land
69 Vacuous
71 Varnish base
72 Gaseous element
73 Wades into
75 Obscure utterings
80 Pewter coin
83 Seasonings
84 Some dogs, for short
85 Walking __
86 "__ scepter'd isle"
87 Julia Ward and Elias
88 Cargo ship
89 Lighter part
90 Singer Cesare

91 Time periods
92 Old instrument
93 Spiteful
94 Like rush-hour buses
95 Opposite of sou.
96 Certain veins
99 Employ, with "of"
100 Sci-fi creatures
102 Initiated in a way
103 Scruff
104 Washington and McKinley: Abbr.
105 Concerning
106 Kind of oak
107 Casserole ingredient
108 Denounce fiercely
111 Fireplace part
112 Antiseptic
114 Adjective suffix
117 Common sense
119 Nefertiti
123 Grafted, in heraldry
124 Roof part

125 Ruffles hair
126 More slippery
127 Last
128 Tie-__
129 Abe or John
130 Chaperon

DOWN

1 Charity
2 Birch of Indiana
3 On vacation
4 Matching word: Abbr.
5 Med. tests
6 In fear of
7 Whitman's last home
8 Bypass
9 Gear for a catcher
10 Cry of disdain
11 U.S. Indian
12 Toothed
13 Like back roads
14 Key opening
15 Direct
16 Defensive

walls
17 Like sea water
18 Corn lily
19 Pastry
20 Pup or circus
26 Belgian city
28 Then, in France
32 Through
35 Throw one's __ the ring
36 Answer in kind
37 Studied with care
38 Like young Shirley Temple
39 Charlotte __
40 Area for arrivals
41 Trig word
42 __ off (finish)
43 Shrink away
44 Flower
45 Vibration
46 Lustrous
48 Deride
49 Sacred song
50 Did floor work
53 Hula hoops, etc.
55 Certain Paris

finale
57 Metallic materials
58 Fire, in Italy
59 Kind of verb: Abbr.
60 Coat sizes
62 Shanghai sights
63 Doctors' devices
64 Certain decision maker
66 Staffs
67 Gantry
68 Practice
70 Designates
73 Wise goddess
74 Heavy gas
75 Fracas
76 Musical instr.
77 Shook up
78 Military groups
79 Divers
81 At the peak of maturity
82 Digressions
84 Essential parts
86 Kind of clock
88 Exceed
89 Dull

90 Purpose
92 Hung around
93 Friendly talk
94 Varnished in black
96 Dayan
97 Baba au __
98 London palace
99 High enthusiasm
101 Newscaster Dan
103 Colony dweller
106 Inevitable
107 Beach bags
108 Merganser
109 Volcano peak
110 Sweetsop
111 Swing
112 __ dixit
113 Large bird
114 "__ love with a . . ."
115 Hymn word
116 Constellation
118 Appian or right-of
120 Earth: Prefix
121 Penn __, N.Y.
122 Rubber tree

ACROSS

1 Board a vehicle
6 Route to Fairbanks
11 "Ad __ per aspera"
16 Houston player
21 Kind of luck
22 Marx
23 Sewing-kit item
24 Costly fiddle
25 Pitches
26 Amounts in excess
27 Bret
28 Thrice-told
29 __-bitsy
30 Bills perused by shoppers, perhaps
33 Oft-bounced items
35 Belittle
36 __ juste
37 Napoleon's forces
38 "Do __ others . . ."
40 Former times, in Scotland
42 Trireme necessity
44 Ones with feet: Suffix
45 Yieldings
49 Miss Korbut
50 Shrink
52 Singer John
53 It's often painted red
55 Latin form of this
57 Popular cocktail
61 Height: Prefix
62 Salk's field
63 Then, in Paris
65 Writer Ortega y __
66 Lincoln Center unit
68 Yawning state
70 One-sided
72 Native of: Suffix
73 Orals
75 Port near Tijuana
77 Tennis org.
79 Sexton
82 Religious degree
83 Depot: Abbr.
84 Shows respect
86 Gather
87 Florist's supplier
90 Sum up
91 Small particle: Abbr.
92 Seed coats
94 Persian wheel
96 Peaceful
100 Up
102 Band or umbrella
104 Group of eight
106 __ Ridge ('72 Belmont winner)
107 Taxpayers' boons
109 __ fixe
110 Places for mules
111 P.I. trees
112 Kind of warfare
114 German count
116 Least polished
118 Like some iron: Abbr.
121 Aegir's wife
122 Frozen dessert
123 Malaysian craft
124 French tins
126 "Friend or __?"
128 Family members
131 Encroachment
135 Barnum offerings, perhaps
139 Plum variety
140 Aladdin's helper
141 British painter
142 Basketball play
143 Gold or zinc
144 Meet __ (satisfy)
145 Anoint, old style
146 Outcome
147 Rugged ridge
148 French town
149 Ernie and Edsel
150 Escritoires
151 Letters

DOWN

1 Moral principle
2 Talk pompously
3 Religious case
4 Karloff, Chaney et al. at Macy's
5 Pleas for quiet
6 Sea call
7 Washed
8 Cheshire borough
9 Hat tag that didn't get removed
10 Facial feature
11 County in N.C.
12 Bursts of energy
13 Mr. America's pride
14 Muscle
15 Waugh
16 John Jacob
17 Loose ladies
18 Sled, in Spain
19 Squealed
20 Port for the Potemkin
30 This, in Madrid
31 Indian antelopes: Var.
32 Great destruction
34 Work on a sweater
39 Wised-up
41 __ Eireann
43 Between ready and fire
45 Suffix for pluto or auto
46 Apiece
47 Term of address
48 Does cobbling
50 Apollo 10 astronaut
51 Like some snow
54 Come out on top
56 Bargain-shopper's maneuver
58 Tennyson lady
59 Clear, in France
60 Willows
62 School org. units
64 But, to Cicero
67 In being
69 Destroy
71 Decorative unit
74 Parts of yrs.
76 He, in Naples
78 Shoppers with big tabs
79 Neighbor of Luzon
80 Con __ (tenderly)
81 Neighbor of Nev.
82 Radio nuisance
85 Kind of test
88 Army training place: Abbr.
89 Subordinate one
90 Second-__ (also-ran)
93 Approve
95 Finish off a cake
97 Blue or White
98 Burl or St.
99 Fishing move
101 Urbane qualities
103 Deny: Lat.
105 Sleep like __
108 Wee, in Scotland
111 Literary conflict
113 Dante locale
115 Bordered on
117 U.S. author
118 Bauble
119 Greek goddess
120 Frankie and family
122 Observed
125 In want
127 U.S. cartoonist
129 Records
130 Move in a way
132 English plotter
133 Type size
134 Removes
136 Goldbrick
137 Donkeys: Fr.
138 Noun endings
143 Miss Murray

277 STEAMED UP By Threba Johnson

ACROSS

1 Mouth of a feeder stream
7 Id __
10 German river
14 Malice
19 Sandwich fare
20 Cote sound
21 Whine
22 "__-by, baby . . ."
23 Incarnation
24 High-minded drives
26 Turkish regiments
27 Early TV's kiddy shocker
30 Varieties of a fuel
31 Military cap
32 Soap acid
33 Indian otter
35 Part of N.C.A.A.: Abbr.
37 Ruler: Abbr.
38 Suffix for thought
39 "__ brillig . . ."
42 Gardner
43 Orbit point
45 Lung membranes
48 Arab garment
49 Shore indentations
51 Wander
53 Maximum: Abbr.
54 Kind of electricity
56 Spreads
57 Road-sign word
58 Joint ailment
60 Kind of naut
61 Manhattan area
64 German number
66 Hallucinogens
67 Rodeo item
68 Barn denizen
70 Chou __
72 Spore sacs
75 Promises
77 Theater features
82 "Once __ . . ."
84 Adroit
86 German number
87 Asian capital
88 Use the radio dial
90 Paris street
91 Ziegfeld
92 Group of four
93 Fort in Calif.
94 Mardi gras doing
97 Thing done: Lat.
99 Acadians' Grand __
100 Cozy
102 Bankroll
103 Torme
105 Greek spirit
106 Good queen
107 Solid
109 Partial one
111 Rage
113 Octavio Paz book
117 Poet Marianne
118 Island of fiction
119 Senility
123 English lawyers: Abbr.
124 Biggers
125 Sibling
126 Spanish, for one
127 Start
128 Colors
129 Explosive
130 Lie close

DOWN

1 "There __ tavern in . . ."
2 Of warships: Abbr.
3 Neighbor of Ga.
4 Subsequent
5 W.W. II beach
6 Certain bugs
7 Bible book: Abbr.
8 Tender parts
9 "You got me!"
10 Comic-strip horse
11 __-visual
12 Templeton
13 Scrub again
14 Dishonor
15 Place for a certain Jack
16 "Joy to the World" composer
17 Hammett's man
18 Word with come and go
25 __ Act
28 Superlative endings
29 Spanish pots
30 Swiss pyschologist
33 Bigwig
34 Mexico's __ Camacho
36 Dynamic
38 Toffler book
40 __ in the hand
41 River and city in Maine
43 Confused
44 Teasdale
46 Electric force
47 Greek letter
50 Moscow link
52 Peso
55 __ as a feather
57 Actress Cicely
59 Doctrine
62 Bible edition: Abbr.
63 Unit of energy Abbr.
65 Inferior
69 Sugar or meat
71 Wings: Fr.
72 Compacts
73 Scorn
74 Opera-house live wires
76 Author Bellow
78 Western campus
79 Ferry man
80 Peter and Ivan
81 Marquis and others
83 Mien
85 Grand Central, etc.
89 Burmese leader
92 Excited
95 Gave up occupancy
96 Safecrackers
98 __ drop
101 Nom de __
104 Tree
106 Davis and Midler
108 French port
109 French drink
110 City on the Po
112 Troll
113 Early pulpit
114 Bank deal
115 Place for ashes
116 Part of R. and R.
120 Height: Abbr.
121 Colloid
122 Season in 108 Down

278 PAGING POLLYANNA *By Joseph LaFauci*

ACROSS

1 Digressions
7 Humbled
13 Sinews
18 Evening song
19 Prepare a page layout
21 Lowly worker
22 Try a quid-pro-quo policy
25 Anti-sub gear
26 Bitter drug
27 Checked
28 Reduces
30 Sine, e.g.
32 Hardy heroine
33 New World org.
36 Law man: Abbr.
37 "Twelfth Night" clown
38 Continuous transit facility
41 Sentiment on the Main Line
49 Authorize
50 Uncanny
51 Naval petty officer
52 Recipe direction
53 "_ boy!"
54 Least sullied
56 Miss Harding
57 Banana unit
58 Shinto temple
59 Born: Fr.
60 Beneficial drink
67 Convened
68 Libertine
69 Reveille call
70 Gypsy
71 Pulling force
75 Coloration
76 Guessing-game category
80 Thorough-going
81 "A sight _"
82 "_ Lindo"
83 What Frost's fences make
86 Undertake
87 Get in shape
88 Evangeline's Grand _
89 Poetic word
90 African lake
94 Do atelier work
95 Highway menace
99 "Indian _"
101 Roman dictator
102 V.I.P. at a durbar
106 Refrain for a trio
110 City near Milan
111 Arranged in order
112 Conceive
113 Bridge declarer's concern
114 Attraction
115 Coated with an alloy

DOWN

1 Snakes
2 Fluid: Prefix
3 Mideast land
4 Stick-on picture
5 _ nous
6 Capuchin monkey
7 Tarzan's playmate
8 Conductor's need
9 Remains
10 Marie, etc.: Abbr.
11 Brain exam: Abbr.
12 Pair
13 Resiliency
14 Actor Buchholz
15 Cleanse chemically
16 Artifices
17 Sunflower features
20 Nebraska river
21 Game fish
23 Furniture wheel
24 Paint ingredient
29 Battle port of W.W. II
30 Plexuses
31 Tennis pro
33 Dare, in France
34 Words of futility
35 Dines
37 Iowa city
39 Find the sum
40 Sparkle
41 Thrash
42 Biblical juniper
43 Caustic substance
44 Certain vote
45 Cambodia's _ Nol
46 Divinations
47 Florists' needs
48 Being, in Spain
54 Andy Gump's lack
55 Swedish county
57 Climb in a way
58 Roller and ice
60 Miss Thomas
61 _ Balbo
62 To's partner
63 Forty-_
64 Used up
65 Music group
66 Rousseau work
67 Party for the boys
72 Bay State fish
73 Wine cask
74 Resident: Suffix
75 Aprocrypha book
77 Spanish painter
78 On
79 Star State or wolf
81 Word of comparison
84 Early scripture
85 Gives the third degree
88 BB-gun fodder
90 Bit of garlic
91 Chinese province
92 Stave off
93 Lay over
94 Prune
95 Region of Africa
96 Home or armor
97 Deteriorate
98 Not as common
100 Snug: Var.
101 Eel, in England
103 Sutherland
104 Stud fee
105 Consider
107 Moon-landing vehicle
108 Macaw
109 Conniption

279 DOWNWARD LOOK By Jack Luzzatto

ACROSS

1 Rumple
7 Five of trumps, in cinch
12 Piddling
21 Eskimo group
22 Registers
24 Arrived at a sum
25 Trifle
27 Building-wall demolishers
28 Hebrew ancestor
29 Song thrush
30 Spanish poppy or pop song
32 Of an organic compound
33 Wild sowing
34 Malady
36 Miss Dunne
37 Darken
38 Wheat porridge
40 Coat fur
42 Stayed put
43 Dressing-room aides
44 Tovarich
46 Giver of a tenth
50 Duluth address, from abroad
52 Wrinkles
53 World need in Bacharach-David song
55 Nuclear trial
56 Actor's poise
59 Mount __, Australia
60 Dutch town
61 Napoleonic battle site
62 German sigh
63 Radames, for example
66 Savings-book entry: Abbr.
67 Records of lineage
69 Brightened up
70 Seething
71 Home of the Brave
73 Big deal!
77 Oasis for drinkers
79 Picture puzzle
80 Persuasive copy
81 Mark
84 High, in music
85 No prize specimen
87 Past
88 Selves
89 Dormouse
91 Sight, in France
92 Vexing people
95 Unsuitable
96 Vat for curds
99 Oath giver

100 Mules' relatives
102 Fresh one
103 Old hairpiece
105 Patriarch of Alexandria
106 Dads
107 Inclines
108 Deadlocks
111 Gilbert island
114 Flash
116 Insignificant
119 Kind of cycle
120 Isle: Var.
121 Diet essential
123 Africa's Idi et al.
124 African lake
125 Casey's box-score entry
127 "... __ but their chains"
130 Monkey's warning
131 Writer Graham
132 Running mate
133 Dialect of Spain
134 Persians'

friends
135 Gives pause to

DOWN

1 "The __ your life"
2 Lieutenant's wear
3 Part of the roadside litter
4 Litigant
5 Women's __
6 Cotton fabrics
7 Lumber hooks
8 Abstract beings
9 Go formal
10 Fol-de- __
11 Spanish jar
12 Salaries
13 Lackwit
14 Mexican gruel
15 Miss Turner
16 Law degree
17 Whistler in the kitchen
18 Killed time
19 Kind of millionaire
20 Certain salts
23 Not like a girl's best friend
26 Part of a drain
31 Met solo
34 First appearance
35 Praise for the dead
37 Heckle
39 Chaplin's Verdoux
41 Busy bon vivant
42 Burglar's forte
44 Corn-meal dish
45 Jug
47 Nursing a lost cause
48 Happening
49 __ car
50 Brew ingredient
51 Take __

52 Campus officials
54 German craft of W.W. II
57 Police function
58 Prepare copy
64 Old English cloth inspector
65 New Haven people
68 Old English bard
69 Leave town fast
70 Reducing
72 Wave trappers
74 White House family
75 Ageless time
76 Repute
77 Powders
78 Island welcome
82 Sulk
83 Hissed signals
86 Enlist anew
87 Shake __
90 Granting a

delay
93 Dickens boy
94 Humiliating
95 Of a skull part
97 O'Casey or Connery
98 Disparage
101 Painted thickly
104 Descartes
105 Prophesies
109 Mistake remover
110 Partisans
111 __ solemnis
112 Convert
113 Split country
114 Orange locale
115 Royal name
117 Gave a cheer
118 Ammonia compound
121 Hammer part
122 Standard
124 Thicken
126 Wellington or kitchy
128 Golf start
129 Bullring cheer

280 BAROMETRIC DROP By Olga Kowals

ACROSS

1 Lantern __
4 Trout
8 Crossbreeds
13 Festive time
17 Lincoln and Beame
19 Pilots' prefix
20 Way of walking
21 In a merry way
22 Harvest
23 Bulb unit
24 Snowy crusts
25 Elbow
26 Type of fabric
28 Model
29 Trumpet sounds
30 Spree
31 Yoko __
32 Plica
33 Comment at a "Stella Dallas" showing
42 Literary credit
43 Military org.
44 Plunder
45 Prefix for cycle
47 Foxx
48 Cardigan or Pembroke
50 Article
51 Make fast
52 Butterfingers
54 Stress
57 King Mark's wife
59 Kilns
61 Soviet range
62 ". . . poem lovely as __"
63 Roguish
64 Does lawn work
68 Mass. cape
69 Healthy: Fr
71 Solothurn's river
72 Seven: Prefix
74 Beauty-parlor solutions
75 Certain ships
78 Illusion
82 Creep
83 Kind of blue
85 __-a-Dale
87 Baseball or tennis
88 Kind of peeve
89 Wheeler's concerns
90 Campbell's dog
91 Betelgeuse
92 Words of frustration
98 Woolly females
99 State V.I.P.
100 M

101 Necessitate
104 Saunter
106 Truman opponent
109 Warm thoroughly
110 Unstable
111 Bradley or Patton: Abbr.
112 __ steven
114 Window placard
115 Saltpeter
116 Tear down
117 Plexus
118 Small guitars, for short
119 Appetizing
120 African ruler
121 Kind of cage

DOWN

1 Sudden shake
2 Not yet up
3 Precursor of tear
4 Macbeth's thanage
5 Like some appetites
6 Chichi
7 Nonsense
8 Not very bright
9 Chorus's distinction
10 Non-feral
11 Rank
12 Certain students: Abbr.
13 Where the Alph ran
14 Minute: Prefix
15 Succulent plant
16 Dict. definitions
18 Neat couple
21 Gas measure
27 Jet housing
28 Like e'en or e'er
29 Far-out

32 French bean
33 Ointment
34 Standout
35 Bustle
36 Slip
37 System of exercises
38 Threefold
39 Carnegie et al.
40 Hot
41 Diminish slowly
46 Wrath
48 These: Fr.
49 Fragments
51 Common home ritual
53 "Home, Sweet Home" man
55 Cave __
56 Fraternal man
58 __ Uniti (U.S., to Italians)
60 Spreader

community
63 Hallowed places
65 Most distinctive
66 Gershwin
67 Fluids
69 Power
70 French Alpine range
73 Maneuver a camera
74 "Let 'er __
76 Word in Jewish cookery
77 Russian or Pole
79 Moderate
80 "Paradise enow" poet
81 "__ in the Money"
84 Sore places
86 Soap ingredient

89 Clinton
90 Toonerville transport
93 Harasses
94 Saxon king
95 Wagner opera
96 Warbler: Var.
97 "__ is me"
101 Last words
102 Corner
103 Canterbury offering
104 Ambitious melody
105 Queens group
106 Jets or Giants
107 Kind of green
108 Abominable one
110 Insect
111 Irish lover
113 Bill

281 PLAYING WITH TOPS By Stanley Glass

ACROSS

1 Asia Minor landmark
7 Claim
14 Denmark's Victor
19 Rio Grande city
20 French explorer
21 "_ short, the art long"
22 Western, e.g.
23 Attorney Gen. under Grant
24 Printing process
25 Do or fa
26 Adjust the pitch
28 Insect eggs
29 Type of opera
30 New Testament, to Oursler
36 Peeved
37 Period
38 U.S.S.R. unit
39 Pool
40 Nonpareil
42 Weights: Abbr.
44 Utter
45 Pre-dawn phenomenon
49 Extends
52 Poetic word
53 European fish
54 Undergarment
55 Early car
56 Fire basket
60 Kind of humor
61 Beetle Bailey's boss
64 Ethel Merman in Washington
70 Desolate
71 Medit. port
72 Cordiale, for one
73 "Now _ seen everything"
74 Grande or de Oro
75 Lure
78 Room
79 V.P. under F.D.R.
82 Tops in cops
87 U.S. Indian
88 Mideast land: Abbr.
89 Stake
90 River of Europe
91 "_ in the Sun"
95 Brew
96 Kind of haircut
97 "Et tu, Brute," expanded

105 Elephant boy
106 Dear, in Bonn
107 Angora feature
108 Instrument
109 "_ Only" (marquee sign)
111 To such extent
113 Horse
115 Islands off Japan
116 Diamond center of Europe
117 Split
118 Anglo-French battle site
119 Lacking coloring
120 Passover meals

DOWN

1 During
2 Irish lake

3 Sharp ridge
4 Freed
5 Drink
6 Unsteady one
7 Factory
8 Garden tools
9 Chemical suffix
10 Nanook's milieu
11 City on the Chemung
12 Grayish
13 Awareness
14 Like a mermaid or centaur
15 Churchill's "Hinge"
16 Choir function
17 Bestow, to Burns
18 Time initials
21 Sore
27 Exploit

31 Pentateuch
32 Lab functions
33 Duct
34 False witness
35 Clarence and Doris
39 Least significant
40 Hot or flower
41 Compass point
42 Spot to be left in
43 Decelerate
45 Carnegie, e.g.
46 Sandwiches
47 Carson et al.
48 News item
49 Bean
50 Belshazzar doing
51 Specialty
57 Corrupt
58 One of a

tennis pair
59 Glacial ridge
60 Pronoun
62 Neuter, e.g.
63 Kefauver
65 Cautions
66 Less friendly
67 Believe, old style
68 Queens players
69 Fair unit
75 Minstrel Mr.
76 Study field
77 Man of alibis
79 Weight
80 Prefix for drome
81 Restore confidence
83 New Haven sports place
84 England a la "Richard II"

85 Thought: Prefix
86 Kind of land
88 Squid's output
92 Kind of type
93 With delicacy
94 Functioning
95 "_ Fideles"
96 _ bono (of what good?)
98 Series of woes
99 Simpleton
100 "_ gold in . . ."
101 Finds fault
102 Endure
103 Solitary one
104 Ogles
109 Dog-owners' org.
110 Major, in music
112 Charge
114 What, in France

COLOR-CODED By Bert Beaman

ACROSS

1 Gets mired down
5 Bara
10 Eats sparingly
15 Tom or Sam
20 European iris
22 Like a cereal
23 Merry
25 Indian, for one
26 Late-spring cold spells
28 Having a topic
30 Shrinking one
31 News bits
32 Sandra or fiddle-de
33 Kind of party
34 "__ blue, dilly, dilly . . ."
36 Where Greeks met
37 Org.
38 Mosaic glass
40 Poet Guest
42 Groom's party
44 __ blue
45 Vestments
48 Hitches
51 Large plums
55 Orange __ (drink)
57 Give __ (help)
60 English author
62 Leave in a way
63 Hawaiian island
64 Undo
66 Fran's friend
68 W.W. II craft
69 D.A., for one
70 City near Sacramento
72 River to the Severn
73 __ Yam, Israel
74 Certain ad
76 African people
77 __ off (measures)
78 Blood: Prefix
79 Mood shade
81 European fish
83 Bring under control
85 Topflight
87 Wrong-number word
89 Needles
91 Respond to a mail plea
94 Kind of root
95 Cloy
96 Brezhnev missive
98 Initials of '30s
99 Luzon group
100 Health resorts
101 Interstices
102 Shocks of hair
104 __ blue
106 __ odds (antagonize)
108 Hit
109 Make off with
110 Come after
111 Archeologist's find
113 Cliques
115 Roman poet
116 Gists
119 Dirty and second
122 Did arctic hunting
124 White __
127 Acknowledgment
130 Decorous affairs
133 Brit. fliers
135 Uris hero
136 Linen fabric
137 Crime
138 Cascade peak
140 Bit of labor hanky-panky
144 Bluish green
145 Like many feuds
146 Like some fingers
147 Aegean gulf
148 French cup
149 Apollo's mother et al.
150 Sand ridge
151 River to the North Sea

DOWN

1 Stall
2 Do a music job
3 N.Y. foes of 1775
4 South China Sea gulf
5 African garment: Var.
6 Tie a golf hole
7 French pewter
8 Unscramble
9 Walked
10 Stew
11 Kind of brake
12 Shoot
13 Have a go at
14 Farmers, at times
15 Pottery pieces
16 Kind of picker
17 Certain
18 Inveigles
19 Ruhr city
21 Fishing leader
24 Draw a bead on
27 Arctic sights
29 Computer food
35 Constellation near Argo
36 Sea of Asia
37 Part of an Arab's garb
39 Handle, to Cicero
41 Keep __ on (watch)
43 U.S. author
44 Brilliance
46 Cold wind of Southwest
47 Trees of a region
49 Crow
50 Nevada
52 Certain milestone
53 British racetrack
54 Argument
56 Kind of hand
58 Obdurate
59 Mark used in "señor"
61 Skier's spot
65 One who tosses
67 Kind of job
71 Indian state
73 Clamber up a tree
75 Dirk
77 Israeli greeting
80 Laughingstocks
82 Morse et al.
84 Standards
85 Have __ (take pains)
86 __ a limb
88 Remainder, in Paris
90 Greek island
92 Alarm
93 Slackened
96 Sine or secant
97 African fly
100 Cordon __
103 Army acronym
105 Measure, in Marseille
107 Join forces
112 Blue shade
114 Red and Coral
117 Study color
118 Rathskeller item
120 Certain Highlander
121 Quick drinks
123 Remains
124 "__ isn't so"
125 Ring
126 Sprightly airs
128 Emphatic repetition
129 On the up-and-up
131 Talent
132 Goddess of fortune
134 Bear __ witness
136 Ripped
137 Rivals
139 Latin-lesson word
141 Bandleader Brown
142 Naval V.I.P.
143 Son of Odin

18 students

283 MALEFACTORS
By Mel Rosen

ACROSS

1 Latin-primer word
4 Thinly diffused
10 Clears the windshield
15 _ fatuus
17 Bird's wing
18 Good dice throw
20 Quemoy's neighbor
21 Which TV game to watch, e.g.
23 Cay: Var.
24 Word for a sideshow member
25 Chemical ending
26 Shell man, for short
27 Pitch
28 Copy
29 Uncertain
31 Distant
33 Christmas Past and others
35 "_ damn!"
38 Angelico, e.g.
39 Kind of sayer
40 English composer
41 Dance, music, painting, etc.
45 Pinky or Lila
46 Garroway
47 Be ghostly: Var.
48 Holbrook
50 "We have nothing _ but . . ."
53 Standout
54 O.T. book
55 Gabor et al.
57 Tie down again
58 Kind of ice
59 Like helium
60 Have it made
61 Old Irish garment
62 Not suitable
65 Join
66 Molding
67 High home
68 Gaucho's weapon
69 Chemical prefix
70 Insult
72 Certain fees
73 Porkpie feature
74 Miss Naldi
76 Full of spunk
77 Bench warmer
78 Nuclear abbr.
79 Jewish month
80 Neat thing
81 Indian

turbans
83 Maryland athlete
84 Diplomat
87 Shropshire inhabitant
88 Eat away
90 Football pass
92 Hooters
94 Passable
96 Golf target
97 Alaskan port
98 Alas, in Bonn
99 Continent: Abbr.
100 Soap ingredient
104 Sundial offering
105 Absent parent
109 Bill addendum
110 Most slippery
111 Long-legged birds
112 Dutch colonists
113 French income
114 Islands off Scotland
115 Elected ones

DOWN

1 Shakespeare's merchant
2 Innocent Chicagoan
3 Columbus initials
4 Freshet
5 Pub quantity
6 Handle: Fr.
7 Tidal flows
8 Combat mission
9 Compass heading
10 Carry on
11 Call _ day
12 Stockmarket

maneuver
13 Heath genus
14 Enjoy
15 Reproductions: Abbr.
16 Lively dances
18 Old (Wellington)
19 Caesar's statute
21 Glove-compartment items
22 British mil. unit
24 Poor provider
30 A man for all seasons
31 Timetable notation
32 Necessity's mate
34 Willows
35 Anna Mary Robertson's husband
36 Turn over
37 Thrush

38 Old man Bailey
40 Stir
42 Attacks
43 _ nous
44 Wild ones
49 Potential
50 Musical chord
51 Althaea's husband
52 Sudden outbreak
56 Run-down
63 Compass heading in Cadiz
64 Set straight
65 Separated from home
69 _ a customer
71 Boxing ploy
75 Matterhorn
82 Natural resource
85 Alloys for cheap jewelry

86 Grumble
89 Tile worker
90 Hideaway
91 Naughty glances
92 Earth color
93 Although
94 Tallow ingredient
95 Hockey star
96 Odes, sonnets, etc.
98 Veneration
99 Alternative word
101 Frolic
102 Collar
103 Without, in Baden
106 Pride, for one
107 Asian holiday
108 _ nuff!
109 Relative of E.R.A.

WORD SEMINAR *By Raymond F. Eisner*

ACROSS

1 Gardened
6 Exhaust
11 Deft
16 Formula of belief
21 Miss Toklas
22 Rosalind's cousin
23 Parisian parent
24 Strictness
25 Calculus, etc.
27 Work on library cards
29 Mars: Prefix
30 Lecture
31 Case or well
32 Della and Pee Wee
33 Fred's sister
34 Auden and Frost
35 Rodin subject
36 Braggadocio
40 Dispute
41 Ontario Indian
42 Certain records: Abbr.
45 Multiplication or pool
46 Poor spellers
49 Period of time
50 Advancement
51 Heavy wood
52 Tennis strokes
53 Convertiplane
54 __-wee
55 Soft velvet
56 Coins of Iran
58 Sampler sentiment
59 Consumed
60 Seine tributary
61 Finnish architect Alvar __
62 Whalebone
63 U.S. flying unit: Abbr.
64 Secant, for one
67 Clock parts
68 Hems in
70 "West Side Story" girl
71 Mont __
72 Ready for callers
74 Waterglass painting
78 U.S. author
81 Daddies: Sp.
82 Relates
83 Paddles
84 Milland
85 Gum trees
86 Hollows
87 Vestment
89 German basin, to French
91 Fraternal men
92 Men's titles
93 Emanate
94 Bowling woes
95 Hurok
96 People who use tho and thru
99 Richardson novel
100 Rail station: Abbr.
101 Covers
102 Pays up
103 Istanbul sight
104 Window part
105 Before
106 Trolley sound
108 Green Wave
111 Dvorak
112 Miss MacMahon
113 Seeks information
117 Elementary
119 Memory-improving art
121 Collier
122 Love, Italian style
123 Robin __
124 Hen's concern
125 Quays
126 Some are leaping
127 Aptitudes
128 Clay plugs

DOWN

1 Hindu deity
2 Winglike
3 Item for Franklin
4 Reverberate
5 Ruby or Frances
6 "Boo!" shouter
7 Flower part
8 Aristocracy
9 Medit. resort
10 German article
11 Bobby Jones, e.g.
12 Pygmalion's statue
13 Kaffir warrior groups
14 Bert of comedy
15 Spanish queen
16 Short swords
17 Formalities
18 Auspices
19 Nod
20 Iron containers
26 Demure
28 Pipes
31 Damp
33 Rocket stage
34 Flat
35 1953 Nobelist for medicine
36 __ Mater
37 "__ cat I saw?" (palindrome)
38 Part of a speller's repertoire
39 Hilarity
40 Seine boat
41 City near Saigon
42 Alphabet man of a sort
43 For the time being
44 Drawing rooms
46 Desist's partner
47 Li'l one
48 Socrates's friend
53 Gannet
55 Fruit stones
56 Odds
57 Of the pelvis
58 Asian peninsula
60 Waves: Fr.
61 Lands
62 Ointments
64 La Douce et al.
65 Refine
66 Noblemen
69 Bits
71 Tiresome one
72 Maximally
73 Adapt to a need
74 Ship parts
75 Jittery
76 Elevate
77 Track events
79 Dickens's Rosa
80 Make __ (ogle)
86 Electronic tube
87 Arabian gazelle
88 Muffet or America
89 Directly
90 Gluck
92 Worked on shoes
93 Muscle protein
94 Small piano
96 Woodworking machines
97 Trumpet blast
98 Chants
103 Certain houses
104 Yonkers entry
105 Gompers' concern
106 Kind of sweep
107 Restrict
108 Pack down
109 Ancient Teutons
110 Unaspirated
111 Weapon: Fr.
112 Peruvian Indian
113 Height: Prefix
114 Photo
115 Small group
116 Chaplin et al.
118 Indian mulberry
119 Fairy queen
120 Recede

ACROSS

1 First sound of work
5 Asian mongoose
9 Outer: Prefix
12 Western resort
17 German president
19 Seethe
20 Papal name
22 Butterfingered
23 Porch
24 Mountain of Thessaly
25 Whit
26 Ezra Pound unit
27 Timely song
31 Reagan, to friends
32 Mehta's stick
33 Hindu festival
34 __-bitty
36 Rathbone
39 Eros, French style
41 Get lost!
44 More sounds
46 World aid org.
48 Benedetto of Italy
49 Atelier lady
50 African hornbill
51 Town near Ghent
53 Talk in a way
54 Gear: Abbr.
57 Hog the camera
58 "The __ the limit"
59 Greek source of name words
61 Rubber trees
63 Lets up
65 Time served by 27 Across
73 Live's partner
74 After STUV
75 Concise
76 Marquand sleuth
80 Two-up, in Sydney
81 Chimney output
83 Rita et al.
84 Cub Scout's cookie
86 __-tack-toe
89 Musical transposition
92 Large: Prefix
93 Tiomkin or Shostakovich
95 One more time
96 Kind of hat
98 "Not __!" (nothing doing)
100 Disturbances
101 Copycat
102 D.D.E. et al.
103 Madison Ave. workers
105 Jester
107 Date of work stoppage
114 Balbo
116 "__ am in Arcadia"
117 Secular
118 Growing out
119 More foxy
120 Receipt, in Reims
121 Told a whopper
122 Toomey
123 City on the Pina
124 Hindu language: Abbr.
125 U.S. holly
126 Last sound of work

DOWN

1 Wire: Abbr.
2 Cousin of a T-beam
3 Last Supper picture
4 Persian coin
5 Sub
6 German Baltic port
7 Supreme Hindu deity
8 Wings
9 Like a serial story
10 Late news time, on some dials
11 Silhouette
12 Sounds of work
13 Collection
14 Composer of 27 Across
15 Vision: Prefix
16 The "playing fields"
18 Offerings on toothpicks
21 __ Paulo
28 Poilu's lantern
29 Horned animal
30 Smoke, for short
35 Biblical weeds
36 Central African town
37 Takes steps
38 Drink-refuser's words
40 Nicklaus's stick
42 __-deucy
43 Urges
44 Claw
45 Between bee and dee
47 Poker holding
52 Molding curve
55 Interrogate
56 Master or Morris
57 Passover wafer
60 Ocean: Abbr.
62 Compass point
63 Greek war goddess
64 Not hard: Abbr.
66 Sammy Davis's "__ Can"
67 Veered, as a spacecraft
68 Tough hide
69 Smooth, in music
70 A little __ (choice)
71 Science of odors
72 Malaysian wood
76 Board measures: Abbr.
77 Mr. Roberts
78 "... stopp'd short never __"
79 Come clean
82 Corn or angle
85 Words to 14 Down
86 Play it again, Sam
87 "Thou the day and __"
88 China flaw, in England
90 Botanical sheath
91 Actor Otis
94 __ fois (many a time): Fr.
95 Chemises
97 Royal monogram
99 French port
104 Roman 2,401
105 Small handful
106 Monarch of Norse myth
108 Goddess of healing
109 Large jar
110 Plankton seine
111 Villain
112 Suffix for gen or fren
113 Editor's habitat
115 Bandleader Brown

286 IMPORTANT PEOPLE By Nancy W. Atkinson

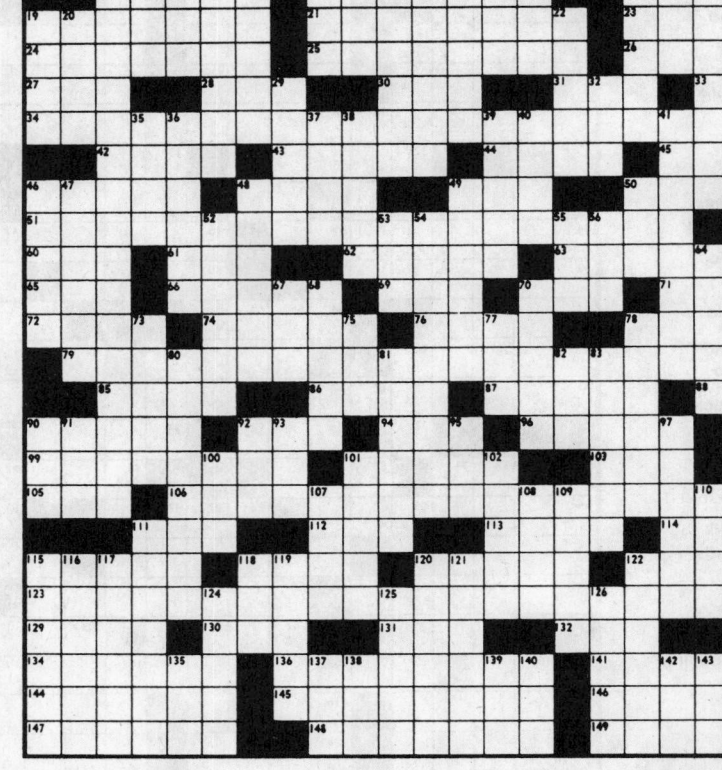

ACROSS

1 Novelist Alan
6 Ex-Prime Minister
13 Combustible mixture
19 Shah of Iran until 1979
21 Daggers
23 Record cover
24 Friendships
25 Late Emperor
26 More suspicious
27 __ Abner
28 Brit. fliers
30 Donkey: Fr.
31 __ la
33 __ other (unparalleled)
34 Premiers during 1974
42 Anguish
43 Fuel products
44 __ Kong
45 Brings up
46 Rascal
48 Congo river
49 Kind of jaw
50 Sloths
51 Kings
57 Art style
60 German conjunction
61 Simple sugar
62 Miss Adams et al.
63 Foreign-trade zone
65 Women's org.
66 Lanchester et al.
69 Royal initials
70 Greek letter
71 Puts on cargo
72 Fuegians
74 Botanical sheath
76 Outrigger
78 Arctic hazard
79 Presidents during 1974
85 Relative of nix
86 Of an ego source
87 Ermine
88 Son of Zeus
90 Sheer fabric
92 Literary bits
94 N.Z. vine
96 Ecological divisions
98 Depression letters
99 Arab ruler's domain
101 Templeton et al.
103 Puppy sound
104 Safecracker: Var.
105 Crag
106 Queens

111 French season
112 Lake bottom
113 Pacific root
114 Writer Michael
115 Willow spike
118 Religious image
120 Kind of acid
122 African village
123 Kings
129 This, in Spain
130 Type of drum
131 Certain words: Abbr.
132 Shoe width
133 Upward: Prefix
134 Less remote
136 Makes public, as a statement
141 Ex-Chancellor and family
144 Importers' concerns
145 Popular song of the '30's
146 Propitiate
147 Sun god
148 Certifies
149 Moroccan city

DOWN

1 Princes
2 High in pitch
3 Pacific porgy
4 Cook __ open fire
5 Jewish month
6 County divisions: Abbr.
7 Fish delicacy
8 Loosen
9 Ross and Dors
10 Shifts carefully
11 __ poetica
12 Caucasian language
13 Nile dam
14 Pier union: Abbr.
15 Competes again
16 Ginza entertainer
17 Stable officer
18 Thin and watery
19 Often-potted tree
20 Friend in Sète
22 Attack
29 Aspect
32 Dustcloth
35 L.A. team
36 Sneak about
37 Low-caste Indian
38 One-seeded fruit
39 Dull knocks
40 Word with gravure
41 One speaking nonsense
46 Old Italian coin
47 Harvard name
48 World culture agency
49 Associate of M. Gandhi
50 Greeting
52 Slanting
53 Old English letter
54 Sharp downdraft
55 Baseball positions: Abbr.
56 Onassis
57 Presidents
58 Natural

product
59 Parts of qts.
64 Roman Fate
67 Pitching ability
68 Photo color
70 Slacks
73 Fur piece
75 Lend a hand
77 Western org.
78 Flat-bottomed craft
80 Lehar specialty
81 Rang up
82 John __
83 Girl's name
84 Composed
89 Heroic tales
90 S.P.C.A. worker
91 Shoulder: Prefix
92 P.I. native
93 Pince-__
95 Alas, in Bonn
97 __ cord of wood
100 Pub offering
101 Berlin evening
102 Glossy fabric
107 Ben Adhem

108 Zola title
109 Idler
110 __ much as
111 Participate
115 Program
116 Locale for oils
117 Social rank
118 P.I. tree
119 Singer Vikki et al.
120 Sunrise song
121 Word for a wife
122 Everest expert
124 Vice __
125 Manifest
126 Exclude
127 Insects
128 Cyrano feature
135 Poetic word
137 After zeta
138 Coin of Riga
139 Boston time
140 Ways: Abbr.
142 Police-call initials
143 Educ. group

287 NURSERY DOINGS *By Alfio Micci*

ACROSS

1 Kind of peach
6 Living-room item
11 Gen. Arnold
14 Saarinen
18 Lover
19 Kind of acid
20 Encomium
23 Loom heddles
24 Pindar or Keats
25 Bonuses: Abbr.
26 Tamiami and Oregon
27 Indian flour
28 Viewer of X-rated films
30 _ Mahal
31 Do a nursery rhyme bit
33 Spanish uncle
35 Manly
37 Attached
38 See 31 Across
44 Greek island
47 Stone: Fr.
48 Opinion men
49 Subscribe
50 Meat garnish
51 Brynner
52 According to: Fr.
55 P.I. native
56 Hector's old status
58 Illuminators
62 _ plaisir
64 Conjunction
65 _ Joe
68 French assents
70 Capital of Guam
71 Melon
72 See 31 Across
77 Adult insect
78 Ages, as tobacco
80 "_ Ben Jonson!"
81 Volcanic discharges
83 See 31 Across
86 "_ and the River"
87 Old English coins
88 Egyptian heart
89 Think
90 Soak
93 Make a fuss over
94 Slaves of old
97 Hit sign
98 Arena cheer
99 Oates
102 Greek letters
104 "_ things!"
108 Papal agent
111 Kind of wall
116 Finished, in England
117 For all to hear
118 See 31 Across
121 Beliefs
123 Dishevel
124 Family member
125 See 31 Across
128 Bomb ingredient
130 Skiing mishaps
135 Drug plant
136 Motherless calves
137 Wagnerian god
139 Moron
140 Grow: Abbr.
141 Derisive sound
142 Richard or Michael
143 Kind of ante
144 Mango points
145 Wall and Broad: Abbr.
146 Manner
147 N.J. county

DOWN

1 Gator's cousin
2 Vein
3 "_ no hurry"
4 Promontory
5 See 31 Across
6 Family man
7 Unoriginal: Abbr.
8 1934 Beery film
9 Jack _
10 Denials
11 "Like summer tempest came _"
12 Russian range
13 Grosse _, Mich.
14 Card games
15 See 31 Across
16 Evaluate
17 Sharif
21 Sizing liquid
22 Verb ending
26 "_ meet again!" (poetic adieu)
29 Inlet
31 Work on flour
32 Bettor's concern
34 Chance, in
36 Artificial languages
38 Angelico
39 Dawn goddess
40 Auto-flow center: Abbr.
41 Wood wasted in chopping
42 Abyssinian gazelle
43 Part of Mao's name
45 Hep
46 Cooking direction
49 Regarding
53 Beer
54 Egg-shaped
57 Burmese coin
59 Grimaces
60 Coup d'état
61 Meet
63 See 31 Across
65 School subj.
66 March animal
67 Gravel ridges
69 _ the works (goes all out)
70 Ivory Coast
72 Company V.I.P.
73 Actor Stu
74 See 31 Across
75 Roman poet
76 Select
78 Raccoon's relative
79 Lacking a renter
82 Sunday speech: Abbr.
84 Honshu city
85 Scottish explorer
86 Saturn's wife
90 Writer Jaffee
91 Jewish month
92 Time for a scholar
95 In a critical way
96 Hyperbolic math function
100 Container
101 Colonists
103 Army men: Abbr.
105 Army address
106 Depressed
107 Chaney
109 Breakfast hair décor
110 Thought: Prefix
112 Large numbers, for short
113 Cuckoopint
114 Hawaiian hawks
115 Legal denial
118 Energy quantum
119 Customs
120 Pronoun
122 Flops
125 Ache
126 Arm bone
127 Magpie
129 Asian weight
131 Forum date
132 City of Brazil
133 Isolated
134 Mythical river
137 Common verb
138 Compass reading

[36 classified ads] language

288 ANNIVERSARY PIECE
By Barbara Gillis

ACROSS

1 Harm
7 Khyber or Donner
11 Western campus
14 Antiquity
17 French chestnut
18 Region of Pakistan
19 Bors or Gawain
20 Acclaim
22 Ones who prod
23 Pointless
24 Some
25 Actor Paul
26 Wood nymph
27 More closely fitting
29 Dolt
31 Ring outcome
32 Fiftieth chance
35 Clear off
36 Season in Dijon
37 Peak in Crete
38 Retreats
39 Electrical unit
41 Safety zone
44 Football runners
46 Desire
49 Symbol of crowdedness
53 Bard of old
54 Chemical action
55 Inclined
56 French pronoun
58 Reveres
60 Rawboned
61 Anger
62 Bonheur
65 Versatile
67 Calif. poppies
69 Agitation
70 Rumanian coin
71 _ far (overdo)
74 Spirited, as a collegian
75 Unravel
77 British alfalfa
78 Bengal native
79 Show sorrow
80 Amphibians
82 Until now
83 Stadium area
87 Wolfish
89 City in Granada
90 Perfect
94 Flowed
95 German article
98 Women's __
99 Sixtieth golf lie
104 Upward: Prefix
105 Miss Sheridan
106 Keats' urn
107 Brussels suburb
108 Beehive state
110 Bar staple
112 Tree of Hawaii
113 Black eye
114 "So long!"
115 __ de plume
116 Climbing spike
117 Style
118 Recipe abbr.
119 Antelope
120 Green and black
121 Restless

DOWN

1 Anti-mosquito fire
2 Bugs Bunny fare
3 Knitting pattern
4 Walk on
5 Crowd
6 Letters
7 Betty Grable photo
8 Region of Spain
9 _ de Cristo Mts.
10 Bedding
11 Dos Passos work
12 Biblical mount
13 Fifteenth plain
14 Wood
15 Toulouse-_
16 Evacuation site of 1940
18 Tenth street
21 Electron tubes
27 Fountain items
28 Like dirt roads
30 Sign
33 Nothing
34 Transportation org.
40 First trail
41 Fourteenth fortress
42 Male and female
43 Fear
45 River in France
46 Stuffs
47 Fortification
48 Favorite of Aphrodite
50 Cupid or Patch
51 Red or black
52 French marshal
57 In a peevish way
59 Twenty-fifth bonus
61 Sixth shade
63 Rush
64 __ in the dark
66 "And in the lowest __ lower . . ."
67 Thirty-fifth hue
68 French parent
71 Botch, with "up"
72 Month: Abbr.
73 Area: Abbr.
76 Province in Spain
77 Small pet
81 Pitcher
Warren
83 Diacritical mark
84 Indicate with a finger
85 Naval craft
86 Copy machine: Abbr.
88 Feminine suffix
91 Delighted
92 Small penguin
93 Port of Sicily
95 Chaperon
96 Corresponds
97 Wine
100 Cornice bracket
101 Children: Sp.
102 Ada of stage
103 Sheeplike
109 Occur, to poets
111 Large bird
113 Dallas campus

TEAM PLAY *By Tanaquil Le Clercq*

ACROSS

1 Ex-teammate of Lerner
6 Danish moneys
10 Gravy dish
14 Attention-getters
18 With 119 Across, comedy team
19 Scene of activity
20 Ragout
21 __ Coeur
22 Reporting team
25 __ one's beer
26 Candlenut trees
27 Gasoline or Tin Pan
28 Logging sleds
29 City of Vietnam
30 Tackle an Alp
31 With Martin, comedy team
32 Ship frames
33 Droop
36 Alice or Tim
37 Indonesian weight
38 Kind of code
39 Poseidon's prop
41 Keyboard and cookery team
47 Miss Dahl
48 Monk, in France
50 Ephraim's grandson
51 Formerly named
52 Currant genus
53 Evans or Kennedy
54 Shrewd
56 __-pushers
58 With 97 Across, lithography team
59 Name in spy annals
60 Rises high
61 Links wear
62 Biblical father
63 French literary team of 1800's
66 Overly sentimental
67 Pacific roots
69 Kind of surgeon
70 Devilfish
71 Added liquor
72 Vaudeville team
76 Russian coins: Abbr.
79 Festival city
80 Moslem scholars
81 Yarn unit
82 Magpie: Var.
83 Poet W.H.
84 Cowboy wear
85 Cremona name
87 Speech, in Seville
88 B. & O., etc.
89 Horse team
90 City in Turkey
91 Pantry
92 Movie team
97 See 58 Across
98 Eagle or Ranger
99 North Sea feeder
100 Grate
101 Ship-plank's curve
102 Schedule
103 Cotton worker
104 Hebrew letters
105 Seance visitor
106 Kind of recall
107 Mohammed's birthplace
108 Movie unit
112 Be indecisive
113 Marquis team
116 Have __ (look out)
117 Faults
118 Unsteady
119 See 18 Across
120 Fountain and bull
121 Former Alaskan governor
122 Makes haste
123 Penn or ship of

DOWN

1 Lhasa V.I.P.
2 Spatial infinity
3 Lanchester
4 21st-amendment backers
5 Chemical ending
6 Way of taking medicine
7 Miss Adoree
8 With 12 Down, radio team
9 Teak tree
10 Large handkerchief: Var.
11 With Johnson, stage team
12 See 8 Down
13 Kind of soldier
14 Freed in a way
15 Rock-and-roll team
16 Music combos
17 Swiss herdsman
19 Oblique
20 Exhibited
21 German-U.S. general
23 French dramatist
24 Peter of films
29 Kind of reaction
30 British guns
31 French river
33 Have the lead role
34 Reach
35 Operetta team
40 Frances and Sandra
41 Mr. Young
42 River to the Amazon
43 Opera circle
44 Miss Wray
45 Like some faucets
46 Some are electric
48 Grape residue
49 Hatred: It.
53 Le __, auto-race city
54 Basket performer
55 Homer king
56 Squarely
57 Lynne's direction
59 Gangsters
60 Amazes
61 __-dab (right on)
63 Inexperienced
64 Tear open
65 Scads
68 Skin woe
70 "The __ Love"
71 With Petrarch, a team
72 Sea-power writer
73 Charlie Chan portrayer
74 Wealth, in India
75 See 59 Across
77 Whalebone
78 Like some nights
79 Reiner or Hubbell
82 Henry VIII's last
84 Auditor: Abbr.
85 Puff __
86 With Nichols, a team
87 Persists, with "on"
89 Winter coating
90 Ancient battle town
91 Asian language
93 Lions, e.g.
94 Undivided
95 Bret Harte's "__ Chinee"
96 Mitigates
97 Like some tunes
100 Niche
102 Modern age
103 Mouth, in Milan
104 Greece's Vale of
105 Trade
106 Math course
107 16th-century date
108 High-strung
109 Canyon mouth
110 Ohio campus
111 Otherwise
113 Mad. or 5th
114 Degree
115 Recipe abbr.

HOUSING PROJECT

By Ruth N. Schultz

ACROSS

1 Sinister or B Q
4 Cavil
8 Maori canoe
12 Literary initials
15 Conceit
16 O.K.
17 Burden
18 Stage front
20 Carrier of a sort
22 Milk: Prefix
23 Safari man
25 Recipe for heat-allergy
28 Dickens pickpocket
30 Suffix in biology
31 Sea bird
32 Crystal gazers
33 Metric measure
34 Withered
35 State: Abbr.
37 Pre-grads
38 Major or Santa
42 Miss West et al.
46 Followers of sols
48 Biblical rebel
49 Boer War commander
55 Salvador
56 Scholar: Fr.
57 Bedclothes, to old grandma
58 Asian coin
60 Want __
61 Confront
62 Climaxes to jokes
66 Photography pioneer
68 Sanitaire or bleu
69 Signal
71 Kind of ego
72 Tea
73 Sandstone
75 Change for five
78 Lincoln-Douglas attire
80 Trusting
84 Japanese coin
85 Dickens girl
86 Burlesque artist
87 Brazilian tree
90 Zero
92 London gallery
95 "O sole __"
96 Spoiled kids
98 Pensacola sight: Abbr.

100 English sieve
101 Like sea water
103 Where "I'll be waiting"
108 Lourdes, e.g.
109 Saarinen
110 Habituation
113 Utah range
114 Paper measure
115 Come up again
116 Stadium sound
117 Bag or time
118 "Mind the music and the __"
119 Math branch
120 Understand

DOWN

1 Hot or trundle
2 Farming: Abbr.
3 Friars Club
4 Reader or cat
5 Money premium
6 Distinction
7 Beyond: Prefix
8 Writer Thomas
9 Med. course
10 Place for a German chef
11 At the rear
12 Beauty trio
13 Annoy
14 Villain's sounds
16 Yeast acids: Abbr.
18 Hezekiah's mother
19 Caresses
21 Follower: Suffix
24 Hosp. people
26 "__ I miss'd

men, at times
27 Prepared to be knighted
28 __ au rhum
29 Ali Baba, for one
34 Greek islander
36 Place for deferred plans
39 Nauheim, for one
40 Wing
41 Jiggs' bête noire
43 Islands off New Guinea
44 Norse saga
45 Bowling game
47 English county
49 Having idle time
50 "That's where __"

him . . ." (Gray)
51 Always
52 Kind of miss
53 Gaelic
54 After OPQ
59 Sum up
62 Toy-train sound
63 Guthrie
64 Russian city
65 Solitary one
67 Writer Eliot
68 __ Cob
70 Yodeler's accompaniment
71 Not stable
74 Scull
76 Wallach
77 One of seven
79 "Fill it out __"
81 Fans
82 German denial
83 City on the Hudson

87 Ashe
88 Native land, to Cicero
89 "__ of beauty is . . ."
91 L.A. team
93 Trumpet man
94 Adolescent
96 __ relief
97 Mailed
99 Shooting sport
100 Jazz dance
101 Smuts, e.g.
102 Gypsy man
104 N.Z. parrot
105 Dies __
106 Nut: Prefix
107 Kind of store
111 Scottish denial
112 Word with Hague or Mrs. Astor

SWINGER'S DIARY *By Tap Osborn*

ACROSS

1 Jazz style
6 Tourney round, for short
11 Iranian coin
15 Hurt
21 Mrs. Hobby
22 Baseball deal
23 Sicilian city
24 Turkish inn
25 Measure
26 Gourmet, for one
27 __ pickings
28 Advice from the antis
29 "Saturday, 9 A.M.: __"
33 Miss McPherson
34 Chaplin name
35 Scrap
36 Pull
39 Myra Hess, e.g.
43 Color
44 "Sat., 1 P.M."
47 Stowe character
48 Britain's Laurence
50 Shoe parts
51 Van der Rohe
52 Chalice veil
53 Senior
54 "Beat it!"
55 One of the ages
57 Funny one
58 "Sat., 7 P.M."
63 Uptight
64 Island décor
65 Roman official
66 Components
67 Bridge player with a good hand
68 Work unit
69 Belt, at the bar
70 Fair or trooper
71 Hates
72 Czech coins
74 Daily phenomenon
75 Woman of fashion
76 Bulb mark
78 Hindu title
79 Score a base-runner
80 Title
83 Niche
84 Bag man
85 Corny
86 "To Helen" author
87 Irving or Lucy
88 "Sat., 2 P.M."
92 Suffragist name
93 Author Bret
95 "Mila 18" author
96 Singer Page
97 Kind of scene
98 House, in Madrid
99 Code for the lawless
101 House-call need
103 Upward: Prefix
104 "Sat., 10 A.M."
107 Category: Abbr.
108 Bronte's Jane
109 Certain vote
110 Harem room
111 Tavern items
112 Weather word
114 "Sunday, 2 A.M."
122 Golfer's concern
125 Gardner
126 Vast quantities
127 Cliff nest
128 Kind of steak or sauce
129 Roman field
130 Fielder's need
131 Dors or Ross
132 Underdog's goals
133 Tennis calls
134 Building V.I.P.
135 Glasgow

DOWN

1 Rialto turkey
2 Kind of glades or green
3 Cheval or tigre
4 Great Barrier Island
5 Coat for Nanook
6 Ship
7 Obliterated
8 Dull finish
9 Thought: Prefix
10 Toiler of old
11 Does a blacksmith's job
12 Kind of waterway
13 Yak or springbok
14 Tiffany piece
15 Unmarried one
16 Pay __ rent
17 Tablecloth savers
18 "__ you sure?"
19 Brig. or Lt.
20 W.W. II area
30 Prometheus's loot
31 Fuel
32 Kind of column
36 "Sat., 5 P.M."
37 Typographical excess
38 Guards
39 Board-meeting art
40 Unite, in France
41 "Sat., late"
42 Abreast
44 "__ but you"
45 "Thanks __"
46 Amherst campus, in headlines
49 Anger
50 Biblical word
54 Coolers
55 Tizzies
56 Fountain name
57 Gave up
59 Bridge gaffe
60 Love
61 Last longer, as a garment
62 Silly
63 Giant
67 Faith
69 Bracelet or ant
70 French toast word
71 Me-too
73 In harmony
74 Alighieri
75 Water carriers
76 Laundry worker
77 Penn. city
78 Huck's transport
79 Cook on a grill
81 Durable racehorse
82 Doddering
84 Miss Miles
85 Jewish scripture
89 Now: Lat.
90 Fitting
91 Saving of a sort
93 Ringside men
94 Movie dog and namesakes
98 Hep one
99 Westbrook and family
100 Direction
101 "Faerie Queene" author
102 Mimed
105 Come forth
106 Kind of pass
107 Garment part
112 Razor __
113 Hebrew letter
114 Start the pot
115 Well-being
116 Crones
117 Rights org.
118 Because: Ger.
119 Of a period
120 Salesman's need
121 Incline
122 Actor Erwin
123 Do a phone job
124 __ poetica

K RATIONS By Jack Wherry

ACROSS

1 Jawed
7 Harbor or mitzvah
10 Eden and Heath: Abbr.
13 __ play for
18 Adorns, old style
20 Et __
21 European canal
22 Kind of verb: Abbr.
23 Chopsticks' cousins
25 Bomber pilot's concern
27 Pillage
28 Retreats
29 City near Chicago
31 Sodom specialty
32 State: Abbr.
34 Newsstand
36 Seven, to Cicero
37 Employed
38 Arctic bird
40 Squeeze out
42 "Whither thou __ ..."
44 Ref. book
45 Ghana's capital: Var.
46 Like the blacksmith's hands
48 System of measures
50 Wharf
51 Hiker's gear
54 Secretary under F.D.R.
57 "__ were king"
60 Do art work
61 Stealing: Prefix
64 Made changes
65 Heal
66 Maori canoes
68 On
70 Kind of poker
71 Fish
72 Either way
75 More passé
76 Showing sass
80 Triple-header double-letter word
85 Songlike
86 Organ-console gadgets
88 Hindu sect
89 Child's speech, often
93 Signal at a séance, maybe
94 Brimless hat
99 On an even __
100 Small-time
102 Magi, e.g.
104 Sandwich staple
105 Quiet!

106 One of New York's Fingers
108 "Show-me" men
110 Straightforward
112 Kozy __ (highway sign)
114 Deliverance
115 Certain protest
117 French wheat
119 Bumbling
121 It's mad when wet
122 Round-Table men: Abbr.
123 Pawn
124 Metal grating
126 Shade of gray
128 Impatient sound
130 Girl's name
131 Most unseaworthy
133 Caesar words
135 Tower city
138 __-tavi
140 After five, six
143 Work on dough
144 __ all, knows all
145 Scottish daws
146 __ out (persist)

147 Sixth, in Italy
148 Time period
149 Noise: Abbr.
150 Insists

DOWN

1 Belly laughs
2 Wild buffalo
3 Item for a whatnot
4 Novelist Franz
5 Paris season
6 "Big __!"
7 Develop suddenly
8 Broadcast
9 Egyptian tambourine
10 Light-fingered one
11 "Kiss __"
12 Quenched
13 Emcee's need
14 What Sandy says
15 Santa
16 Stranger
17 Docket
19 Black or coral
20 Have __ in one's throat
21 Famous

Citizen
24 502, to Brutus
26 Paving material: Abbr.
30 Stellar
33 With "no," this is good
35 Hemp product
37 Music maker
38 Out of line
39 Utah range
41 Eskimo craft: Var.
43 Violins, for short
45 __-les-Bains
47 Hebrew measure
49 Bankbook entries: Abbr.
50 Herd of seals
52 Trolley sound
53 Skewer dish: Var.
55 Liberian tribe
56 Composer Rorem
58 Office worker
59 Passages
62 Having openings: Suffix
63 Soft mineral

65 Hilltop
67 Cheese or movement
69 Korean soldiers
71 Explosive experiment
73 Feminine suffix
74 Black
75 Fatty: Prefix
76 Duties
77 The Ram
78 How bestsellers go
79 Eastern cosmetic
81 Uncovers, in poems
82 Creole cook's staple
83 Wooden pegs of old days
84 Russian coin
87 China Sea gulf
89 Brooklyn campus
90 Red or black
91 __ leaf
92 Miss Negri
95 Mel et al.
96 Football maneuvers
97 Not abridged

98 Lets up
100 Little Indian number
101 Hydrophobia
103 Dry
106 Range of view
107 Chemical suffixes
109 Kind of house
111 Turkish measure
113 Joined, as ropes
115 Makos, e.g.
116 Antiseptic
117 Prepare short ribs
118 Moonshine
120 Courses
121 Rope fibers
124 __-well card
125 Wreaths
127 Greek letter
129 Slightly risqué
131 Italian resort
132 Highways: Abbr.
134 Superlative endings
136 Sports gear
137 Concerning
139 Krazy __
141 Fleming
142 Spanish aunt

293 SHORE PATROL By Gladys V. Miller

ACROSS

1 Loses concentration
5 Heat, as milk
10 Cake or fish
15 Brahmin name
16 Sun hat
17 Chipping or song
19 Bungles a rowing stroke
21 Church figure
23 Old English moneys
24 Sri __ (Ceylon)
25 Puny one
27 Broadway sign
28 Rep. or Dem. worker
29 Earth goddess
30 Hindu cigarette
31 Worry
32 Miss Dickinson
35 Small islands
37 Chins
38 Butter trees
39 Some regions
41 Uncertain
43 Bandy words
44 Paired
46 Killer whales
47 Invited
50 Chesterfields
52 __ crow
53 Avery of Olympic note
54 Church box
57 Summery dress design
59 Soviet city
60 Term of address
61 Ferrer
62 Pilgrim's head covering
64 Moon-landing vehicle
65 Life stories, for short
67 Item for Bill Dickey
68 Like a desert spot
70 Fast planes
71 Utter folly
73 British V.I.P.s
74 Nosey one
76 Youthful
77 Famous sculpture
79 Save's partner
82 Fusses
83 Neuter, etc.
85 Amounts to
87 Robert or Grandma
89 True, in Paris
90 Inlets
92 Eastern inn
93 Jewish month
94 Iranian coin
95 Girl of comics
97 Scalpers' items, to Variety
98 Kind of room
99 Tidbit for Charles Atlas
101 Willows
102 Kind of drive or squall
103 Shirley's ship
105 Salsifies
108 Carpenters, at times
109 __ example
110 Kind of droppers
111 Parcels out
112 Facing a glacier
113 Straight

DOWN

1 Birthrate
2 Basics
3 Cry of disgust
4 Stone pillar
5 Substitute
6 Cage bird
7 Guam port
8 Yarn measure
9 Society girls
10 Garden pests
11 Ruth's mother-in-law
12 Wrestler's forte
13 Miscalculate
14 Jointed armor pieces
15 Rebounded
17 Writer
18 "When you __ tulip . . ."
19 Shade of blue
20 Teasdale
22 Shouts of joy
26 Metal beams
31 Fragments
33 Sacred city
34 Former name of Tokyo
36 Blue or winning
37 Neighbor of Mex.
38 Glass or sugar
40 Moroccan
42 Did fancy needlework
43 Food or music
45 Common mineral
47 Minos et al.
48 Plumed bird
49 Considers
51 Begrimed
53 River Afton's scenery
54 Circuit
55 French queen
56 Mean
58 New soldier: Abbr.
59 Cries of surprise
63 Egg-roll time
66 Floor smoother
67 Marbles
69 Night: Prefix
70 Malice
72 Old temple
73 Word with skirt or bike
75 Mountain, to Greeks
77 U.S. painting family
78 Little solos
80 Petty tyrant
81 Laments
83 Comprehends
84 Fabrics
86 Hockey teams
87 Earthy deposit
88 Keats's "__ Indolence"
89 Windshield flaps
91 Rigel or Adib
94 Pakistani coin
96 Western resort
99 Kamen of TV
100 Red figure
101 Words of comparison
102 Pelee product
104 Imposture
106 Besides
107 New Guinea port

294 PHYSICAL EXAM By A. J. Santora

ACROSS

1 Pollster Roper
5 Kind of garage
11 Spanish homes
16 Farrow
19 Container
20 Stripped-down sentence
21 Kind of conservative
22 "Hansel __ Gretel"
23 Eager
24 Completely
26 Rwy. depot
27 Stupid
29 Whole
30 Belgium or Norway, e.g.
32 Time period
33 Accountant's need
35 Girl's name
37 Proof mark
38 Took on Gorgeous George
40 Football's Starr, et al.
41 Dict. entry
42 "No ifs, ands or __"
43 "__ my man"
44 Mess up
45 Ineffective
48 Demolished
50 Drugstore cowboys
51 British title
52 Acre's land
53 Martin and Pickford
54 Part of a doorway
55 Sort
56 Bolivian capital
57 Gemstone
58 Madame __ of Vietnam
59 Computer
64 Igloo dweller: Abbr.
67 Suffrage
68 Growls
69 Inducts a knight
72 Slope wear
75 Biological group
76 Makes spangly
78 Type of wager
79 Obscure
80 Vegas features
81 Records
82 __ macabre
83 __ Ribbentrop
84 Sown, in heraldry
85 Nourished
86 Having polish
87 Blood feud
89 Pitcher Sparky
91 Fire god
92 Beatle name
93 Month: Abbr.
95 Laterally
97 In proximity
99 Porous rocks
101 Golf feat
102 Intensive
105 Biography
106 Athenians: Abbr.
107 Fragrant
108 Get angry
109 Old French coins
110 Inquire
111 Frolics in a pool
112 Old chariots
113 Tulsa, __

DOWN

1 Sidestep
2 Sandwich meat
3 Beaten path
4 Early auto man
5 Industrial abbr.
6 Cajoled
7 Colors
8 Hauled
9 Up and about
10 Bring up
11 Cow chew
12 Happy Warrior
13 Footrests
14 Make __ for it
15 Place for greens
16 Intrude in a way
17 Actual
18 Forever and __
25 Cancels out
28 City lines
31 Lawn grass
34 Merman
36 Rainbows
39 Break out
40 Wishful maneuver
42 Windwards, etc.: Abbr.
44 Miner's animal
45 Rinka __ (Irish dance)
46 Actress Mary
47 Words to Brutus
49 Capsize, with "over"
50 Heraldic knot
51 Whirring
53 Some dogs
54 Heavy sword
56 Sir Walter
57 Meager
60 Bacchanalian cries
61 __ ear and . . .
62 Time of 47 Down
63 Certain camper
64 She, in Italy
65 X-rated movies
66 Furniture piece
70 What a griper has
71 One's limit
73 Church officer
74 Geometric shape: Abbr.
75 Tequila bar
76 Infielder Sal
77 Opp. of NNW
79 Man-goat figure
80 Signified
82 Darn!
83 Take a flier
86 Enjoyed a camp activity
87 Borders on
88 Ending for differ
90 Jostle
92 Puts on cargo
94 __ record (equals)
95 Galsworthy output
96 Spanish pot
98 First word of Mass. motto
100 Margarine
103 Drinker's problem: Abbr.
104 Noises: Abbr.

EDITED FOR TELEVISION

By Frances Hansen

ACROSS

1 Initials of a famed novel
5 Mountain ash
10 Sorry ones
15 Eniwetok first
20 Hindu dances
22 "__ Little Nut Tree"
23 Chou __
24 Cousin of a birch
25 Burden: Lat.
26 Stevenson
27 Kind of heel
28 Arrowsmith's wife
29 Long time to wait
33 Tax man, of yore
34 Finesse
35 Millay
36 Links hazard
37 Jewish eve
38 Old Mideast initials
40 Where Gordon died
42 Kind of sack
43 Barks
47 Miss Lane of The Planet
49 Depots: Abbr.
50 Id __
52 Dense
54 Farragut's decision
60 Order of frogs
61 "See you __"
62 Swiss river
63 Dawn goddess
64 Drafty dress feature
66 "__ and away!"
67 Sacrifices by fire
70 Zodiac sign
71 Midi seasons
72 Buttons or Mill
73 Employ
74 Toppers
75 Gardner
77 Pronoun
79 Broadway show
82 "Out, __! out, I say!"
87 Like Abner
88 Rural org.
89 Unsmiling
90 Slippery fish
91 Hockey's Bobby
92 Feminine suffix
95 __ es Salaam
97 Palace adjunct
100 Movies, to Fellini
101 U.N. name
104 Mouths
105 Word on a towel
106 Bushed
107 Dike, Eunomia and Irene
108 Berlioz cantata
112 Goolagong
114 Business-letter abbr.
115 Shapeless dress
116 Standard
117 "__ we forget!"
118 Dirt or roll
120 Martini additive
122 River to the Vistula
123 Persian tiger
127 Leopold's partner
129 London locale
130 High note
132 Indulge in casually
134 Sign-off from 1 Across
138 Giraffe's cousin
140 Lawrence's steed
141 "Green Hat" author
142 Permission
143 Invalidate
144 "It's __!"
145 Swedish port
146 Sana's land
147 Welfare or ship of
148 One side of life
149 Ballet kneebends
150 Attention-getting sound

DOWN

1 Game bird
2 More pallid
3 Fly of Africa
4 Sherman's remark
5 Iranian coin
6 "Ah, me!"
7 Australian horse
8 Conforms
9 Artless
10 Shade of green
11 Set free
12 "Uncle Tom" girl
13 Croupier's tool
14 Nap
15 Turkish sweet: Var.
16 Broadway show
17 Repute
18 Debussy's "La __"
19 Half a bikini
21 Musical piece
30 Rumor about
31 Herald of measles
32 Church calendar
39 Mortified
41 Like Ethelred
42 Stars, to Virgil
44 Last words to the boss
45 __ maw (roseate tern)
46 Laps, at times
48 Switchboard wkr.
49 Ambles
51 Help!
53 __ de deux
54 Book-jacket info
55 Place for a boutonniere
56 Chopin specialty
57 Greek group of W.W. II
58 Compass point
59 German pronoun
65 Go __ (deteriorate)
67 Tristan's lady
68 Whitman's bloomer
69 Salvation, in France
73 Rival of A.P.
76 100 in the shade
78 Newspaper banner: Abbr.
80 Nicely said
81 Lead the life __
82 Acid salts
83 Non-grata one
84 French G.I.
85 Avifauna
86 "Last Case" sleuth
89 Measured time
92 Miss Waters
93 Treasure __
94 Rookies
96 Vestment
98 Alley __ of comics
99 Bourg's department
101 Bivalve protection
102 Bede's title: Abbr.
103 Poetic word
106 Kind of violet: Abbr.
109 Outer germ layer
110 Branch of calculus
111 "Mr. Roberts"
113 Sword
119 Manila hemps
121 Completely
122 Help!
124 Structural bars
125 Ecole attenders
126 Advice to sinners
128 "Swan Lake" role
129 Ape: Lat.
131 Actress Palmer
133 With skill
134 "Give a __ horse he . . ."
135 Carry on
136 Pack down
137 Space monkey
138 Western org.
139 Chess piece: Abbr.

296 SOLVING MATERIAL

By Martha DeWitt

ACROSS

1 Traffic light
6 Lieu
11 Competitor
16 By-product
21 Sight from Apollo craft
22 Do the honors at dinner
23 Hovel or house
24 Rope
25 Things within a stone's throw
27 Lucky girls
29 City on Danube
30 Piquant
31 Motors
33 Dip again
34 Junkyard, for one
36 Part of Troy's trouble
37 Kind of party
39 _ van Delft
40 Hand holder
41 Wise men
42 Hash
44 Thicket
47 Entertainments
49 Surgical instrument
53 Asian nurse
54 Yields
55 Ends' associate
56 Gossip
57 Glove-compartment item
58 Spices
59 Run
60 Swiss river
61 Bull or Olsen
62 Class of mollusks
64 Nonconformists
66 Way to cook tough meat
67 More composed
68 Euterpe
69 Home of some Alaskans
70 Asian goats
71 Rend
73 TV picture tube
75 TV cook
77 West Asian
78 Minnelli
79 Card game
82 Harridans
83 Thousand-legger
85 Transitory
86 Mike's look-alike
87 Auctioneer's last word
88 Macadamias
89 Small bays
90 Furrow
91 On the brink
93 Air outlet
94 Rock blend
95 Busy city
96 Ascetic
97 Ignored
99 Musical pieces
100 Lacking sunlight
102 Cleaves
103 Medieval tale
104 Collard's family
107 Measure
108 Parisian parents
109 Vestige
113 Tough customer
115 Fishing boot
116 Metropolitan thrush
117 Anaconda
118 Hardwear
121 Vulnerable ones
124 Old town in Asia Minor
125 Peers
126 Indian's castle
127 Force out
128 Appears
129 Schedule
130 Ship area
131 Longtime Chicago mayor

DOWN

1 Debate
2 Girl's nickname
3 Censure
4 Loop sights
5 Give back
6 Twenty
7 Kind of ship
8 Hesitant sounds
9 Means
10 One who wants
11 Red, white and black
12 Nile creature
13 German prefix
14 Say more
15 Regard in a way
16 Soviet city
17 Light-bulb part
18 _-ral
19 "_ told by an idiot"
20 Beam
26 Injure
28 Career military men
32 Movie fade-out
35 Window part
36 Surfaces
37 Pride, envy, etc.
38 April 15 items: Abbr.
41 Was partial
42 Update
43 Have it made
44 Vacation places
45 Peruvian volcano
46 Opposites of wolves in sheep's clothing
47 Working on interiors
48 French brainstorm
50 Hallway fixture
51 Fisherman
52 Tartan trousers
54 Cavort
56 Hides
58 Unit
59 Firmly fixed
60 High point
63 Cable spools
64 Hazy condition
65 Scottish island
66 E.I. heartwood
68 Loose earth
70 Shades
72 Whine
73 Joshes
74 Sarwan's animal
75 Onion's relative
76 Cods' relatives
78 Well-educated
80 Ridicule
81 Singers
83 Banker
84 Calembours
85 Brocds
87 Lollobrigida
89 Spelunkers' milieu
92 Something to be done
93 Amphora
94 Spread
95 Rack's companion
97 Variety of peeve
98 Oversees
99 Marred
101 Bifocals, e.g.
103 Son of Jacob
104 N.Z. birds
105 Got up
106 Lax
108 Old hat
109 Age
110 Seething
111 Time-being
112 Savory
114 Navy facility
115 Shoe part
116 Textile worker
119 Holbrook
120 Mouths
122 Tarzan's foster parent
123 Zsa Zsa's sister

FITTING PHRASES
By Bert Beaman

ACROSS

1 "Great!"
6 __ California
10 Wine barrel
14 Kind of comedy
19 Malaga raisin
20 Norse name
21 On the blink
23 Prepare to shave
26 Fender dimples
27 Pass off
28 Novelist's concern
29 Relative of Mme.
30 Opposed to
31 Calpurnia, for one
32 Paris areas
34 Book-printing unit: Abbr.
35 Some horses
38 Brood of young birds
40 Attacked
44 Beery
46 Himalayan denizens
48 Electrical units
50 Before febrero
51 Great Horde division
53 Depreciate
55 Ads on fences
57 Glasses
59 French pince-nez
61 Simians
62 Ineffectual
63 Branches
65 Come-on
66 Wheel spoke: Fr.
67 Ridicule
73 Suffix for drunk or cow
74 Table extender
75 Kind of case
76 Roman emperor
77 Strains: Scot.
79 Intertwines
81 Eradicated
85 Accord
87 Troubling development
89 __ administravit
90 Road to Alaska
91 Egg part
93 Show rudeness
95 Old Norse work
96 Some looks
97 Old recompense
99 Wives, informally
101 Hair style
102 Elapsed
105 Eggs, in Bonn

107 Cape Vert natives
109 African charm
112 Mine: Fr.
113 __ in the right direction
115 Stone pillar
116 Done with
121 Guiding principle
122 Pinza
123 Composition
124 Riding schools: Abbr.
125 River to North Sea
126 Music sign
127 More protected

DOWN

1 Ship departure: Abbr.
2 Got rid of
3 Egg on the chin, e.g.
4 Public figures
5 Large hurdy-gurdy
6 Cattle genus
7 Hebrew letter
8 Kind of window
9 Fasten
10 Scheming one
11 Same: Prefix
12 Reliable pitcher
13 Down-under attraction
14 Certain samples
15 Heavy-duty wire: Abbr.
16 Stadium sounds
17 Party equipment
18 Soup ingredient
22 Sherry mold
24 School assignment
25 "The frost __ the . . ."
30 Hawks
33 __ Rosa
36 Phone part: Abbr.
37 Light
39 Swings
41 Gardener's faith in his carrots
42 Debtor's situation
43 __ the towel
45 Biblical enemy of Jews
47 Ragout of game
49 Seed: Prefix
52 Gibe
54 Significant
56 __ the road
58 Hunter's wall decor
60 One who fosters
64 Cordial
67 French mathematician
68 A.L. player
69 Boys'-book writer
70 Deeds
71 Kind of light
72 Guitar opening
78 Boa
80 Party-going dandy
82 Breath: Suffix
83 Patience
84 College officials
86 Subjugates
88 Release, as hoarded funds
92 Kind of bill
94 __ -Japanese War
98 Region: Abbr.
100 Arrangements
103 Indication
104 Stew
106 Clear sky
108 Networks
109 Silly
110 Political group
111 Spanish pot
114 Greek letters
117 __ man out
118 Caucho tree
119 In demand
120 Neighbor of Den.

298 SHOWING THE WAY *By Nancy Shuster*

ACROSS

1 Add more stickum
8 Recital pieces
14 Ivan's villa
19 In
20 More annoyed
22 Chills
23 Prisoners of a kind
25 __ Bulba
26 Prayer form
27 Tie up
28 Brontë heroine
30 Number prefix
31 Collection of sayings
32 Beaux __
34 __ sack
36 Substitute
38 Canasta play
40 Fine fur
41 Entree
43 Sagacious
44 Sandy ridge
46 Latticework
48 Of a grain
50 Wire measures
52 Paris name
53 Losing money
56 Sink fixtures
59 Nervous walking
61 Signore's land
62 Try to outdo
63 Pale
65 Part of the forest scene
66 Branch of peace
67 "__ corny as . . ."
69 Wire: Abbr.
71 African antelope
73 River to North Sea
74 Baseball hit
76 Long-beaked Atlantic fish
78 Passion
80 Sounds of hesitation
81 Color
82 Bears, mice and pigs
84 Elicitors
86 Skyline sights
88 Drooping
90 Pseudo-esthetic
91 Composer
92 Popular dosage
94 Radical in famed 1921 trial
98 Wings
100 Pants
102 Whale
104 Splash over
105 Briefcase item
107 Weaken
108 Some poultry
110 Cockney's distress cry
111 Tending to: Suffix
112 Lancaster
114 Waters: Sp.
116 Ethiopian town
118 "__ the West Wind"
120 Covert
123 TV fare
124 Early epoch
125 Retinue
126 Wood nymph
127 Caught
128 Frightened, hillbilly style

DOWN

1 Publicity
2 Launcelot's loves
3 Part of a coach's job
4 Official deeds
5 Goad
6 Zero and successors in "Fiddler"
7 Dutch commune
8 Crowned in a certain way
9 1900-mile Asian river
10 Protection
11 Polka dot on a garment, in a way
12 Article in Bonn
13 Move back
14 Office stamp
15 Moslem title
16 Animal act, usually
17 Beating items
18 Official edict
21 Alfonso, for one
24 Perfume
29 Met again
33 Prepares
35 Scientific group: Abbr.
37 Agreeably
39 John's predecessor
41 "Half __"
42 Involved explanation
45 Baltic gulf
47 Backtalk
49 Chemical prefix
51 At sea
53 __ form
54 Young eels
55 Textile workers
56 Apish
57 "Louder and funnier" area
58 Biblical pauses
60 Kansas college
62 Miss Banky of the silents
64 Prefix for a body network
68 Cut off
70 Stage cover
72 Gloomy
75 Italian painter
77 Barks
79 Enlistees: Abbr.
83 __-disant
85 Nestling
87 Famed Gandhi disciple
89 Charged a certain way
92 Gardner
93 Kind of potato
95 Detergent
96 University unit
97 Resisting
98 Furnish
99 More clashing
101 Nautical direction
103 "__ Krupp"
106 Popular investment
108 Soft candy
109 __ Coeur
113 Baseball data: Abbr.
115 Pesty bug
117 __ horse!
119 Philippine tree: Var.
121 Garden tool
122 Old Gov't. agency

POTPOURRI *By Roberta Morse*

ACROSS

1 Hemingway character
6 Roman 1205
10 Riffraff
14 At ease
18 Happen
19 Nazimova
20 French river
21 Offensive
22 Transportation
24 Use of "honey," e.g.
26 Ordinal suffix
27 Fact
28 Skill: Sp.
29 Scottish V.I.P.
30 Item: Abbr.
31 Rommel
33 Road places
34 Grand, for one
37 View
38 Name for 69 Down
41 Assumed name
43 Man with a noose
48 French composer
49 Woman in a corrida
50 Go back
51 Looks at
52 Cafe holder
53 Selassie
57 A Curie
58 Onto
59 Picnic's cousin
60 Biblical plant
62 Baseball team
64 Hasta __
67 Get in touch with
70 Girl's name
71 Medal: Abbr.
74 Doctor's org.
75 Huey Long
80 Pastime
82 Carried away
84 Lab vessels
85 Mate
86 Words of surprise
87 Colosseum et al.
88 Former movie actor Lyle
89 Whalebone
92 Garment size: Abbr.
94 More fitting
95 Feminine ending
96 Party name
100 Herb genus
103 Fabric
104 Olympian
105 Malice
107 Geometry initials
108 Cooky
110 Lab worker of a sort
112 Indian
113 Blackmore girl
114 Italian painter
115 Famed sculpture
116 Golda of Israel note
117 A Hapsburg
118 Chemical endings
119 Of a bristle

DOWN

1 Mauled
2 Ruffled
3 A Harry
4 Honshu town
5 Tear
6 The Hammer
7 December name
8 Regions, in poesy
9 Road monster
10 __ Domingo
11 Classic text
12 French pronoun
13 Corn, in Africa
14 Blend
15 Natty Bumppo
16 Region
17 Adjective ending
20 Feudal man
23 Alma __, painter
25 __ mile
28 Polite: Sp.
32 Gets huffy
35 Ace
36 Lebanese seaport
39 Etudiant
40 "__ the Queen"
41 Law man: Abbr.
42 Famous mariner
44 Dog sound in comics
45 Rule in India
46 Old coin
47 Channel bass
50 A Kennedy
53 Pillagers
54 Adjective suffix
55 Comfort: Fr.
56 Altitude: Abbr.
59 High in calories
61 Pond creature
63 Hairpiece
64 Body part
65 Muhammad et al.
66 Strength: Lat.
67 Mediterranean tree
68 Indian
69 The Emperor's son
72 Nickname: Var.
73 Words of approximation
76 Siberian people
77 Eskimo
78 Cork off
79 Gets the steak ready
80 Passe footwear
81 Vietnam holiday
83 Clemenceau
85 Florida city, for short
90 To be, in France
91 __-well
93 Land of plenty
94 Without change
96 "__ afraid"
97 Sky: Prefix
98 Gait
99 Think, old style
101 Hearth goddess
102 Make __
103 Mud
106 Rulers: Abbr.
108 Perfect thing
109 Barfly
110 Askew
111 Goose: Fr.

300 BREAKING WITH HABIT

By Eugene T. Maleska

301 THIRD DEGREE By Elmer Toro

ACROSS

1 Nephew, to Cicero
6 "__ way to the Forum?"
11 Luxury spot
14 Football scores
17 Anglican: Abbr.
18 Farm implement
20 "__ Camera"
21 Counts calories
23 Words of a penny-offerer
27 Light color
28 Italian star
29 Noun suffix
30 Strike __ (hit a sore spot)
31 Contrary question
37 Inquire
38 Half a fly
39 Moray
40 Sharp tool
42 College degrees
45 Waiter's question
49 Grain beards
53 Have __ of tobacco
55 __ Paul Kruger
57 Atop, to poets
58 Bind
59 Get out!
60 Before la
61 Third-party query
66 Sea bird
67 Supreme homages
69 Monsterish state
70 Gets up
72 "... mercy on such __"
73 Call __ day
75 Shell-game unit
76 Roman bronze
79 Help
80 Query of a debater
88 __ Lanka
89 Actress Joanne
90 Mass of ivy
91 Actor Young
92 Sheep
93 Kind of chip
96 Tailors: Sp.
100 Reduces
102 Town in Utah
103 Concerned one's query
107 Shoe width
108 Son of Judah
109 Cul-de-__
110 Skylab initials
111 "What's __ score?"
112 Installs
114 Umlaut features

115 Famous last words
119 Classifieds
121 Furnace tender: Abbr.
122 Peak
123 Campanella
124 Pagoda
126 Famous first words
138 Pakistan city
139 Word science: Abbr.
140 Baltic island
141 Miss Gardner
143 Three-time poser
149 "Call Me __"
150 Oz dog
151 In times __
152 Vernon's partner
153 Word with plop or choo
154 Past
155 Slatterns
156 Aides: Abbr.

DOWN

1 Salamander
2 Hebrew bushel
3 Dame Myra's need
4 Hops kiln
5 Heats milk
6 "__ in the world?"
7 Helen of stage
8 Ridicule
9 Vineyard: Fr.
10 __ off the press
11 Shannon River area
12 French friend
13 Sylvan god
14 Rome's river
15 Rio __
16 After N, O, P, Q, R
19 384-year-old query
20 Peruvian
21 Relative of drat
22 Holy one: Abbr.
24 Swindles
25 Verb ending
26 Started, to poets
32 Whip mark
33 Certain stock mart: Abbr.
34 Club for G.I.'s
35 Italian's tooth
36 Conceal, in law: Var.
40 Go down with __(fall heavily)
41 Streaky query
43 Promoted
44 Sea signal
46 Before fo fum
47 Goes wrong
48 Joins
49 Fred and Adele
50 Greedy query
51 Gare du __
52 "All My __"
53 Attorney's
54 A.E.F.'s conflict
56 Muscle: Prefix
62 Long-run musical
63 Former U.S.S.R. police
64 Chemical suffix
65 "__ old cowhand . . ."
68 Gets ready again
71 Spigot
74 Scottish county
77 Kind of plant or head
78 Formal
81 River isle
82 Throw out
83 Olden times
84 The same
85 Curved arch
86 Popular Via of Rome
87 Curves
93 Move like Gray's plowman
94 Wine: Prefix
95 Ox, in Scotland
97 "A moan, a sigh, __"
98 Deneb or North
99 Convened
101 Undergrads: Abbr.
104 Hittite land
105 City near London
106 Arabic letter
113 Son of Isaac
116 __ action (impels)
117 Short or long
118 Watch
120 Isaac of music
125 Psychiatric speech loss
126 Persian serpent king
127 Part of R.I.
128 Tile: Sp.
129 U.S. missile
130 Neckline shape
131 Manche town
132 Yard chain
133 "So what else __?"
134 Called for
135 Forays
136 Cultured pearls
137 Incident
138 Tide level: Abbr.
142 Drinks
144 Greek letter
145 Egg drink
146 Kind of stock: Abbr.
147 Daughter of Cadmus
148 Relatives of mos.

302 MENU SUGGESTIONS By George Rose Smith

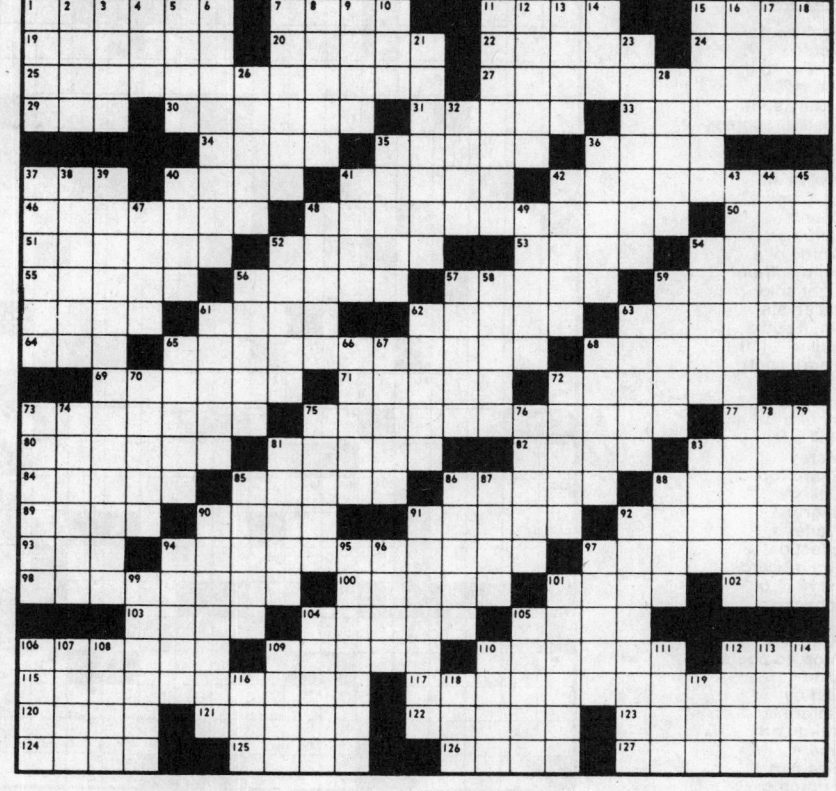

ACROSS

1 Hears
7 Chooses
11 Derby or Belmont
15 Ballet step
19 Heavily committed
20 Water wheel
22 Growing out
24 Jot
25 Muttonchops
27 Turnips
29 Six-pointers
30 Antimacassars
31 Cliché-ridden
33 Where to conform
34 Drowses
35 Macaw
36 Peter I
37 Sea eagle
40 Chassis part
41 Sea water
42 Bathed
46 Godheads
48 Pineapple
50 Line of rotation: Prefix
51 Expresses
52 Kayak
53 Film star Edmund
54 After Shebat
55 Gists
56 Goes out with
57 Split __
59 Umbrella of song
60 Greek god
61 One: Ger.
62 Uptight
63 Peasant footwear
64 Collegiate goal: Abbr.
65 French toast
68 Scram!
69 Héloïse and Abélard, e.g.
71 Charmer's prop
72 Loser of a flock
73 Designers
75 Pound cakes
77 Airport-board abbr.
80 Certain horses
81 Like Major Hoople
82 Danish moneys
83 Western Indian
84 Catkin
85 Brooklyn island
86 Streetcar sheds
88 Relative of won't
89 Two-wheeler
90 Enameled metalware
91 Musical closings
92 Phidias piece
93 Wallach
94 Rice
97 Fixed machine parts
98 Tooth parts
100 Town maps
101 City near Chicago
102 Soak
103 Peter Duchin's father
104 New and Fair
105 Computer input
106 Equal to
109 Fabric
110 Mellow film
112 Pile up bills
115 Bread and butter
117 Cabbage
120 Bitter juice
121 Farewell
122 More positive
123 Slanted
124 Swamps
125 Begged
126 Smack
127 Prohibits, in law

DOWN

1 Shopper's aid
2 Geraint's wife
3 Tots
4 Dakota Indian
5 Salamander
6 Inscrutable ones
7 Strategic football kick
8 Jabs
9 __ bien
10 Knightly title
11 One going on a pension
12 Loos
13 Appeared
14 French season
15 City on the Missouri
16 Nutty
17 Detail
18 Leisure
21 Jockey's position
23 Unit for Pearl White
26 Favorites
28 Be __ of (fear)
32 Phoned
35 Cartoonist and family
36 Prepares certain food
37 Developed
38 Ripped again
39 Soup
40 Tunes
41 Destruction
42 Breathe noisily
43 Ham
44 Glorifies
45 Most terrible
47 Pipe joints
48 One with a grudge
49 Girl's name
52 Platitudes
54 Stroll
56 Designer Christian et al.
57 Pétain
58 Wall piers
59 Fills
61 One of a baseball trio
62 House cat
63 Irish clans
65 Prevent
66 School: Fr.
67 Like underbaked bread
68 Brazilian state
70 Scented
72 Robert or George
73 Set at intervals
74 Mexican dish
75 Beach sights
76 Florida's Gables
78 Teachers' security
79 Abominate
81 Gaucho weapons
83 Songbird
85 Man with an army in 1894
86 Makes an error
87 Fusses
88 Brace
90 Grapevine shoot
91 Alpine retreats
92 Garrote
94 Kind of basin or wave
95 Wasted gasoline
96 Sound of thunder
97 Fabric
99 Hogans' relatives
101 Crocs' cousins
104 Herd
105 Valleys
106 Norse saint
107 Aswan's river
108 Bard's river
109 Fuel
110 City on the Wabash
111 Ripens
112 Wine: Prefix
113 Exude water
114 Book __
116 Wise to
118 Name for Boston
119 Squeal

303 FRENCH LEAVE By Eugene T. Maleska

ACROSS

1 Big casino, for one
8 Righteous
13 Sets with gems
19 Dilettante
20 State of lawlessness
22 Frost
23 Fun and games
25 Like Van Gogh, at times
26 Source of bifteck
27 Noted hostess
28 State capital
30 Prefix with gram or tribe
32 Babbitt's creator
34 Austere
35 Ballerina's solo
39 _ about
41 Rochester name
45 Parseghian
46 Mock
49 Medicine man
51 Rainbow Falls site
52 Zola's "Le _"
54 City south of Moscow
55 Girasol
56 Broom made of twigs
57 Sacred image
58 Except
61 Animated hound
63 Finis
64 Ketch or yawl
66 Swamp tree
68 Patron's pet
70 _ avis
71 Grapevine product
72 O'Neill character
73 Refractory
76 Purports
78 Exhausts
81 Wave, in Spain
82 Declare
84 Uses a teapot
86 Bruins' campus
87 French city official
89 Game at St. Andrews
91 Extinct wild ox
92 Jazzman Fountain
93 Raison d'_
94 Outcast
96 Ouida's real name
98 F.D.R. measure
99 Cloistered life
101 High-hat
103 Of a Greek god
105 Faux pas
107 Treasurer's wall décor
110 Spenser heroine
111 Banters
115 "Dieu et mon _"
117 _ Methuselah
121 Short order
122 Duty of the mighty
125 Words of warning
126 Most dreadful
127 One who narrates
128 Certain Louvre hangings
129 French pastry
130 Kind of tense

DOWN

1 Moppets
2 Utter
3 Part of Notre Dame
4 Bayard and Grani
5 British fruit drinks
6 Passé
7 Soigné
8 En _ (in a body)
9 Kind of punch
10 French novelist
11 Soul, in Sedan
12 Swedish Nightingale
13 Of the "Russian Riviera"
14 Bridge cards
15 Liqueur
16 O'Casey
17 Lake in Ireland
18 Agathe, Jeanne, etc.: Abbr.
21 Seine seasons
24 Condiment in Caen
29 Approach furtively
31 Up-to-date
33 Where Dryden lived
35 Lutetia, today
36 Betel palm
37 Tact
38 Forsaken
40 Account-making official
42 Stage setting
43 "Take Me _"
44 _ plume
47 Fedora material
48 Iris
50 _ de mer
53 Chou _
56 Yokels
59 Mountain ridge
60 Trucking rigs
62 Result of some showers
65 Cancel
67 Place for an atelier
69 Traffic jam
73 Cotton flannel
74 Israeli port
75 Luzon group
77 Antitoxins
79 Follower of ne plus
80 Hymn of praise
83 Stark peak
85 Water hoist
88 Signal at sunrise
90 Cobra's pride
94 Lafitte's crew
95 Olympics contestant
97 Elevate
100 Renan
102 Least furnished
104 Cowboys' home
106 Sunder
108 Word on a French mailbox
109 Linen marking
111 TV studio device
112 Hog plum of India
113 Done, in Dundee
114 "Honi _ . . ."
116 Old mound in Friesland
118 Called: Fr.
119 Chariot race
120 Famed muralist
123 Lingerie item
124 Finished, in poetry

304 FLUID DRIVE By Threba Johnson

ACROSS

1 __ tears (tire)
7 Eye parts
13 Mites
18 Like barn floors
19 Colleen's home
21 Man who says
22 Place to swim with Joyce
26 Day: Abbr.
27 Black
28 Landseer
29 Profit
30 Forwards
32 Writer Ambler et al.
35 Solemn period
36 "Tell __ the . . ."
37 Electric units
39 Live peacefully with
41 Large artery
42 Place for a troubled swim
46 Start a compulsory dive
48 Verges
49 Take the other side
51 City transits
52 French revolutionary
53 __ the iceberg
54 Body of doctrine
59 Clean again
61 Coat parts: Abbr.
63 S.A. country
64 __ code
65 Kind of dish or show
66 Flytrap of a sort
68 Time period
69 French poem
70 Flintstones' pet
71 Adz or ax
72 State: Abbr.
73 Wind or Argyle
75 Words of recognition
77 Not ornate
79 Man's name
81 Humpback salmon
83 Doctor's wall hanging: Abbr.
84 Customs
86 Protect
87 Niagara barrel route
92 Confused
94 Girl in "As You Like It"
95 Fonteyn vehicles
97 Baltic land: Abbr.
98 Bunker
99 Bunker game
100 Irish dramatist
102 Of the blood
106 __ bodikins
107 Got the card game going
108 Cry of pain
110 Bee elements
111 Swimming advice
117 U.S. Indians
118 Pistol time
119 Vietnam river
120 Brief novel
121 Brewing needs
122 Sound system

DOWN

1 Hall of Fame units
2 __ run
3 TV encore
4 "If you're __, ring my bell"
5 Drink
6 "The joke's __"
7 Treat for ants
8 Bolivian Indian
9 Pal of a sort
10 __ sont
11 Webby
12 Most nasty
13 Org.
14 Ohio city: Abbr.
15 Lack of intellectual growth
16 Red-yellow shade
17 Available for sale
20 Lost for good
23 Portly
24 In favor of
25 Not in, to the Dutch
31 Hindu worshiper
33 Ranch riders
34 Place to swim with Shakespeare
36 Adverse
38 Alps: Abbr.
40 Garment sizes: Abbr.
41 __ facto
42 Title for Elizabeth: Abbr.
43 Deacon's stole
44 Fed up with
45 French king
47 Legal writ
50 Very soft, in music
53 "Man __!" (last call at sea)
54 Adjective suffix
55 Scott's swimming companion
56 A.L. team
57 Sincere
58 Emperor in Chinese legend
60 Turf: Var.
62 Church room
65 Actor Erwin
67 German swim spot
74 Carson
76 Kind of dress
78 Eight: Prefix
80 __ rule
82 Nabokov title
84 News-photo print
85 __ wet
86 Library degree: Abbr.
87 Ale time
88 Greenery
89 Resilient
90 Tear
91 Scapegoat
93 Hanger-on
96 Certain sounds
99 Army off.
101 Kind of reaction
103 Kind of pool
104 B'way musical
105 Freight
107 Biblical word
109 Haws' partners
112 Gods: Lat.
113 F.D.R. agency
114 German cooler
115 Doer: Suffix
116 Kind of wash or hen

305 DOING THE SCALES By Jordan S. Lasher

ACROSS

1 Florida city
6 It was stormed
14 Adherences to perfection
21 Track star of note
23 Left: Prefix
24 Duchamp's nude, in a way
25 Quickly
26 Poetic word
27 Dawn goddess
28 Once around the track
29 Prototype
31 Wattlebird
32 Battering item
33 Building annex
34 Sea duck
35 Formerly, once
36 Reciprocal action
40 Diminutive endings
41 Salamander
42 London area
43 Real estate unit
44 Exits, in Scottish law
45 Biblical land
47 Native: Suffix
48 Gender
49 Dice numbers
50 Cut off
51 Counterpart of Yang
52 Typecasting mold
54 Sandbank
55 Betty __
56 After uno and due
57 Christian __
58 Part of the bar scene
59 What Farragut damned
61 Leash
62 Ore slag
63 Small flag
64 Transmitters: Abbr.
65 Bus-driver's advice
67 Get rid of
70 Old Italian coins
72 Horse operas
73 Almost: Prefix
74 Covered, as with quartz
76 Hayworth and Gam
77 Brava or Rica
78 Term of endearment
79 Luau instruments
80 Runs in neutral
81 Line to sign
82 Bee: Prefix
83 Desk-set unit
84 Blacksmith
85 Follow-up book: Abbr.
86 Common verb
87 Tarkington boy
89 Panoramas
90 Quiet-flowing river
91 Frazzle
92 Monarch of tragedy
93 Loft occupant
94 Tact
96 Fastener
97 Kind of new or name
98 Energy unit
99 Reagan, to friends
100 N.Y. time
101 Get more fondue
102 Literary collection
103 Tuck's partner
104 Hundredth: Abbr.
107 Down-under city
110 Slowly
115 Scoop seeker
116 Wentletrap
117 Poisonous gases
118 __ match
119 Asian land

DOWN

1 About, in conversation
2 D'Azur, for one
3 Culture medium
4 Hilo wear
5 Overdue debt
6 Meadow sounds
7 Reply: Abbr.
8 Chilly, in Scotland
9 Old Thai coin
10 "Your time __"
11 Alphabet member: Abbr.
12 "My Name Is Asher __"
13 Recluses
14 Yearning one
15 Single
16 Serbian measure
17 Aruba or Cuba: Abbr.
18 Musical space program
19 Fred's wife
20 Not (mediocre)
22 Vitamin group
23 Factions
30 Pindar output
32 Model T's relative
33 Sup
34 Merman
35 Poetic word
36 Variants of a compound
37 Put into symbols
38 Hitchcock opus
39 Bagel's companion
40 Department-store sign
41 Inattentive one
44 Twice 55,005
45 "High Noon" star
46 Compass points
48 "__ transit . . ."
49 Bermudas
50 Doone and Luft
53 Henna jobs
54 Mined by layers
55 Faux pas
58 Locales
59 Tasks: Sp.
60 Tyrant
62 Hot, as goods
63 Go one up
65 Risked
66 Selassie's namesakes
68 "__ your own risk"
69 Pinafore's Dick
71 Numbness
74 Bloke
75 Climbing device
77 __ au vin
80 Type of gasoline engine
81 Marking on a stone
84 Road marker
85 Locks or Canals
88 Bum __
89 True, in St. Lo.
90 Saluki, for one
91 Sally Rand's prop
93 Directive
94 Hellenic: Prefix
95 Come __ (occur)
96 "Do I __ Waltz?"
97 Adam et al.
98 __ nous
101 Formality
102 Continent, to French
103 Astronauts' agency
104 Waterfront protrusion
105 Roman 951
106 Tissue
108 French statute
109 Scottish alder
111 High degree
112 Cup handle
113 Goat god
114 Shakespearean pronoun

306 ZEROING IN *By Elaine D. Schorr*

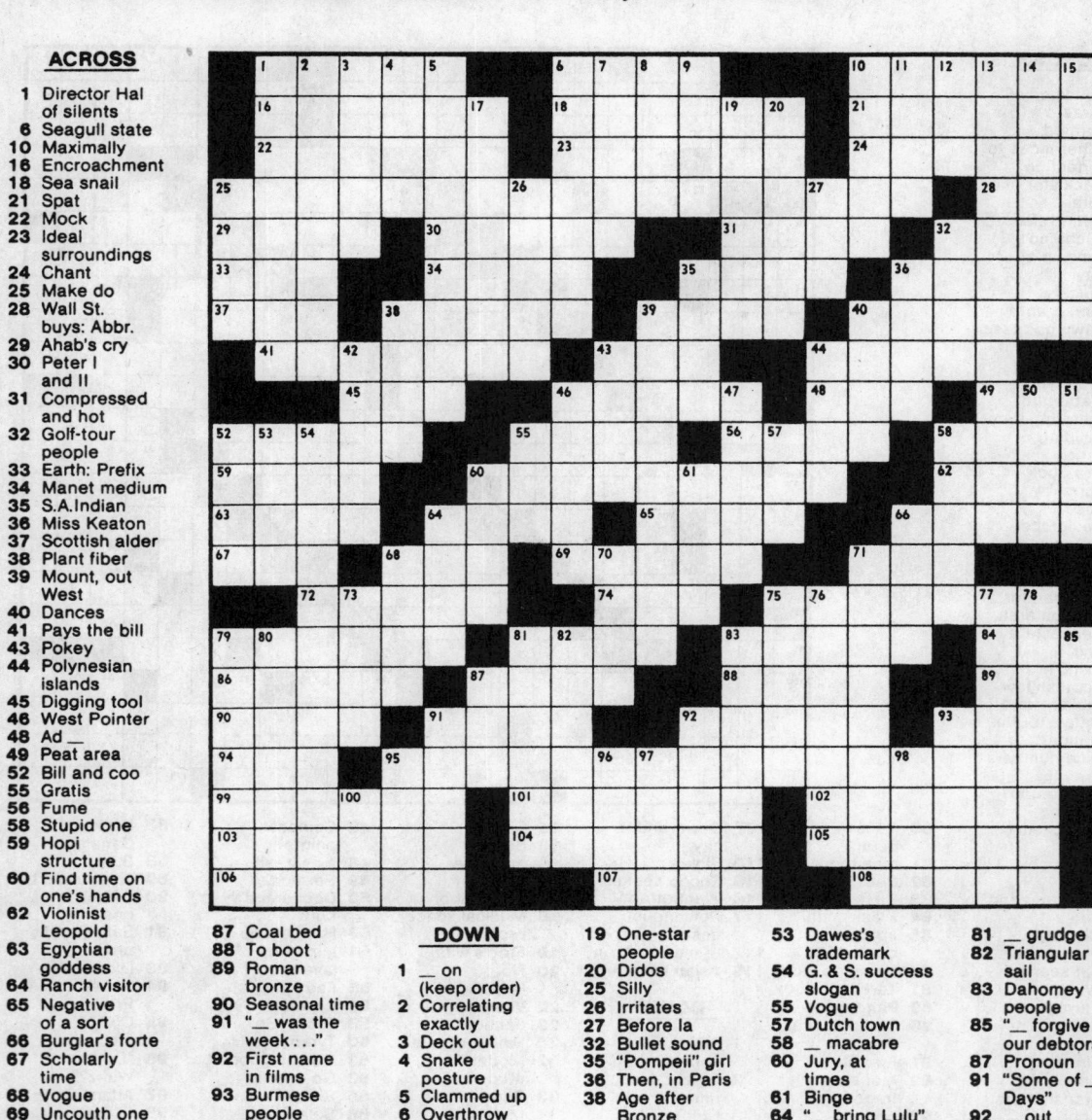

ACROSS

1 Director Hal of silents
6 Seagull state
10 Maximally
16 Encroachment
18 Sea snail
21 Spat
22 Mock
23 Ideal surroundings
24 Chant
25 Make do
28 Wall St. buys: Abbr.
29 Ahab's cry
30 Peter I and II
31 Compressed and hot
32 Golf-tour people
33 Earth: Prefix
34 Manet medium
35 S.A. Indian
36 Miss Keaton
37 Scottish alder
38 Plant fiber
39 Mount, out West
40 Dances
41 Pays the bill
43 Pokey
44 Polynesian islands
45 Digging tool
46 West Pointer
48 Ad __
49 Peat area
52 Bill and coo
55 Gratis
56 Fume
58 Stupid one
59 Hopi structure
60 Find time on one's hands
62 Violinist Leopold
63 Egyptian goddess
64 Ranch visitor
65 Negative of a sort
66 Burglar's forte
67 Scholarly time
68 Vogue
69 Uncouth one
71 They, in France
72 Sandal strip
74 Belles-lettres: Abbr.
75 Without wiles
79 British royal house
81 French Premier
83 Word on a sampler
84 Air-board listing: Abbr.
86 Serve __ on (enjoin)
87 Coal bed
88 To boot
89 Roman bronze
90 Seasonal time
91 "__ was the week..."
92 First name in films
93 Burmese people
94 Brit. award
95 Cynical words of an opportunist
99 Tuxedo wear
101 Ocean study ship
102 Rudy
103 French city
104 Miss Lansbury
105 One who gives the go-by
106 Make a bridge slip
107 Barn and screech
108 Errol et al.

DOWN

1 __ on (keep order)
2 Correlating exactly
3 Deck out
4 Snake posture
5 Clammed up
6 Overthrow
7 Period after 12
8 Galway islands
9 Center of activity
10 Money premiums
11 N.M. Indian
12 Cambridge campus
13 Just so-so
14 __ mission (dispatch)
15 Damsels' glories
17 Obtuseness
19 One-star people
20 Didos
25 Silly
26 Irritates
27 Before la
32 Bullet sound
35 "Pompeii" girl
36 Then, in Paris
38 Age after Bronze
39 Words about the new-clothes emperor
40 __ up (contrive)
42 Fountain order
43 Solicitude
44 God: Prefix
46 Bird group
47 Turning: Prefix
50 River to the Baltic
51 Kind of details
52 Card game
53 Dawes's trademark
54 G. & S. success slogan
55 Vogue
57 Dutch town
58 __ macabre
60 Jury, at times
61 Binge
64 "__ bring Lulu"
66 Building wings
68 Civil wrong
70 Styptic base
71 Relative of "You're welcome"
73 "__ to the Chief"
75 Ethan or Fred
76 Impatient
77 Water color
78 Soft-shell clams
79 Marine hazard
80 Links players
81 __ grudge
82 Triangular sail
83 Dahomey people
85 "__ forgive our debtors"
87 Pronoun
91 "Some of __ Days"
92 __ out (spare nothing)
93 Old Italian coin
95 Glassy sound
96 Scoundrel of drama
97 Great number
98 Passage
100 Partner of hee

307 WORD FRACTURES
By William Lutwiniak

ACROSS

1 Eastern nurse
5 Location
9 These, in France
12 Barker's forte
17 __ avis
18 Bollixed up
19 Wellaway!
20 Must
21 Simple arguments
23 Auto loans
25 Unselfish one
26 Bridge card
28 H'way sign
29 Corso cash
30 Appears
31 Permanent
35 Receives
38 Crowd
39 __ a dream
40 Society-page word
41 Relies on
42 Little chessmen
44 Road-litter item
45 River of France
46 Contemptible one
48 Letters
49 Sunnite Moslem
50 Times of day: Abbr.
51 Y chromosomes
55 More reasonable
56 Loser
58 Uses a certain box
59 Inferior
60 Kind of squash
61 Mooring posts
62 Alan Ladd role
63 Semifluid mixture
65 Medit. capital
66 Poetic foot
68 Scores at hockey
69 Change the indigene
71 Jazzhound
73 Back woe
74 His: Fr.
75 Delayed
76 __-clock scholar
77 Channel
78 Replenishes the cash drawer
82 Dot, in Spain
83 Chemical ending
84 Sty sound
85 Group of TV experts
86 Hungarian composer
87 Forbid
89 Suffice
90 Feel the sun
91 Compass point
92 Public storehouse
93 It's slowest in January
97 Loaded watercourse
101 Coddles wine
103 Romantic interludes
104 Lionized ones
105 Savalas
106 Words of ken
107 Italian poet
108 Railroad structures
109 Beer
110 Sleep fitfully

DOWN

1 Italian harp
2 Shopping area
3 Smell __
4 Aging Romeo's concern
5 Liqueur flavor
6 Large collection
7 In force: Abbr.
8 Unadorned
9 Seafood items
10 Wild West lawman
11 Concorde, e.g.
12 Confined people
13 Led
14 Sort of: Suffix
15 Midi season
16 Spanish article
18 Does martinis
19 Discernment
22 Parisian nights
24 NASA achievements
27 Strong odor
30 Parking space in the home
31 Incinerator contents
32 Of Quechuan extraction
33 Got close
34 Folks
35 Drooping
36 Skin layer
37 Ho ho ho, maybe
38 Twixt
39 Teen-__
43 Adored ones
46 Torment
47 Verve
49 Rhone feeder
51 Spanish invaders
52 Chemical compound
53 Fill a need, with "to"
54 Gigantic one
55 Form
57 Rocky debris
59 Cut closely
61 Hand-dyed fabric
62 Tizzy
63 Egyptian talisman
64 Gap
65 Henhouse sound
66 Whatever
67 So much, in music
69 Unaided
70 Berlin avenue
72 Had effect
74 Have __ by the tail
76 Rotates stone
78 What's-his-name
79 Weapons for extras
80 Covering, for short
81 Puts into
82 Turkish coins
86 Browbeater
88 Staggers
89 Stile
90 Becomes agitated
92 Injurious
93 Source of penicillin
94 Average
95 Start of a Soho toast
96 Marie et al.: Abbr.
97 Oppose
98 Miss Lupino
99 Scheldt feeder
100 "__ had it!"
102 Little: Fr.

308 ONE-UPMANSHIP By Bert Kruse

ACROSS

1 Veranda
6 Massenet opera
11 Propelled a dory
16 Bric-a-__
20 G-man
21 Like a toad
22 Growing out
23 Ness and Lomond
25 Late comedian of note
27 Bluffer
29 Window part
30 Fall bloom
31 Elmer and Grantland
32 Chemical compounds
33 Scoff
34 External
35 Behind time
36 N.Y. subway
39 Olive yield
40 America's Cup entry
42 Extra sense
45 Rewritten speech
48 Disloyal one
51 Tiny
53 Throw dice
54 Schoolboy of baseball
56 Ohio city
57 Install
58 Scottish moods
59 Snouty animals
61 Narrow valley
62 Beethoven's last
63 God of love
64 Twangy
65 Parlor-game pieces
67 Liquor bottles
68 Through
69 Luxuriant
70 Pretty girl
72 Parents of Pius XI
73 Market-crash year
75 Early: Prefix
76 Make a bomb harmless
77 Take a side
78 Laminated rock
81 French numbers
82 Arabic letters
85 Brian of films
86 French historian
87 Surfaces
89 Indian title: Var.
90 High lakes
91 Leg part
92 Works hard
94 Comedian Bert et al.
95 Weight system
96 Reconnoiters
98 Gaelic
99 Seething
100 Depot: Abbr.
101 __ to the wind
103 Jets, for one
106 Put more in
108 Judged
110 German article
111 Poetic word
112 Riverfront nine
113 Gives off
115 Blue dyes
117 Walked confidently
120 Melodies
121 Old Sicilian coin
122 English spa
126 Hard-luck sphere
128 Giant boot size
130 Split
131 Gold or copper
132 __ of hands
133 Climbing vine
134 N.C.O.
135 Unyielding
136 Proportion
137 Kind of throat

DOWN

1 Gooseneck, e.g.
2 Indian city
3 Bar-front sign
4 Miss Hathaway
5 Native: Suffix
6 Highly personal pronoun
7 Rush
8 Main road
9 Roman road
10 Word part: Abbr.
11 Restored, as a ship
12 In abeyance
13 Vacillate
14 Paris seasons
15 Meaning: Abbr.
16 Swagger
17 Hyman Kaplan's creator
18 Hurt
19 Sonny's ex-mate
24 Father of jrs.
26 Craze
28 Yeast
31 European area
33 Varieties
34 Yellow pigment
35 Dud
36 Foot part
37 Take on again
38 Special libation
41 As one pleases
42 Locations
43 Sports oasis
44 Wastelands
46 Dashes' partners
47 Like much pulp fiction
49 Scout of many badges
50 U.S. President
52 Ordinal-number suffixes
55 W.W. II agency
57 Canonical hours
59 Certain bud
60 O. Henry offerings
62 "__ Andronicus"
64 Hospital employee
66 Alibi people
67 Strongboxes
69 Detroit team
71 Unwrap
72 Descartes and others
74 Having calluses
76 Art connoisseur Joseph
77 Magna __
78 One of Caesar's names
79 Next to the last inning
80 Thin
83 Appear
84 Hall-of-Famer George
85 Lawmen: Abbr.
86 Complete: Var.
88 Sts.
89 Lone Ranger word
91 Rabbit tails
93 North Europeans
94 Grassy areas
96 Soaked
97 In installments
101 Infant's demand
102 Consumes
104 Earliest time
105 Kind of basin
107 Monotonous talker
109 Part of D.D.E.
113 Muse
114 Italian city
116 Holy Roman emperor
117 Ship: Abbr.
118 __ and that
119 Dream, in Dijon
120 Support
121 Miss Kirk
122 Lure
123 Gelling agent
124 Correct a piano
125 Jalopy
127 German spa
128 Projection
129 City lines

309   LINGUAL LAPSES   *By Bert Rosenfield*

ACROSS

1 Wrong: Prefix
4 Lively dances
9 Open-__ shoes
13 Mock at
18 Jewish month
20 Paris month
21 Nashville landmark
22 Former inmate
25 Ceremony
26 Words about a lion with a toothache
29 City near Milan
31 Saarinen
32 Rabbit-__
33 Decorate
34 Land and water transport
39 Scowl: Var.
41 Direction: Abbr.
42 Upstate N.Y. village
43 River bank
45 Throw a baseball
47 "__ Free"
50 Eastern Christian
53 West Indies sorcery
55 Unit of energy
59 Eels and leeches
61 Master of 26 Across
64 Fraud
66 Joins the party
67 French pronoun
68 Golly!
69 Seance visitors
72 __-cat
73 Sea urchins
75 From head to foot: Var.
77 Prefix meaning woman
81 Red dye
82 Korean G.I.
84 Sensible work periods
88 Showed the way
89 Like a windmill
91 Describing the Edwardian era
92 Harangue
94 Caves, to poets
96 "__ corny as Kansas..."
98 Young lady, old style
101 Sgt. or cpl.
102 Doctrine
104 Prefixes for dreams
107 German P.O.W. camp
109 Warning to a captain
114 Nasty
115 Court decree
116 Mexico's Pancho
117 Name of three sultans
118 Consider
119 Card spot
121 East Indian tree
122 Prepares a pizza
125 Instance: Fr.
128 1946 Louis opponent
130 Advice to gardeners
136 Cinema dog
138 Greek letter
140 French composer
141 Sioux tribesmen
143 Fedora emporium
149 "Zhivago" character
150 Ship borers
151 Tel __
152 Motif
153 Do pier work
154 Put an __ (stop)
155 Chide
156 __ Park, Colo.
157 Actual being

DOWN

1 Griffin of TV
2 Relating to Troy
3 Hindu precept
4 Most frontierlike
5 N.T. book
6 "__ I saw Elba"
7 Single or double, often
8 More vulpine
9 __ the morning
10 W.W. II agency
11 "__ tu" (Verdi aria)
12 Unit of force
13 Ex-V.P. Agnew
14 French-fries adjunct
15 Bobby of hockey
16 Dactyle, for one
17 Trouser feature
19 Look and talk in a nasty way
23 Goddess of discord
24 Girl's name
27 __-la
28 Salutation of a sort
30 Initials on a Cardinal cap
35 Asian river
36 "__, they say, hae I"
37 Buses' antecedents
38 Snakish-sounding
40 Jubilate
44 Proverbial look-alikes
46 Baby word
47 Pooh-__ of "Mikado"
48 Work
49 Win easily
51 Grain bristle
52 Rookie: Var.
54 White House initials
56 Lacking judgment
57 Brezhnev
58 Actor Stuart
60 Emanation
62 Pathway of song
63 "Ulalume" author
65 Notre Dame name
70 Covering, for short
71 Goad
74 Openings and closings
76 Netherlands town
78 River isle
79 Actress Markey
80 Another: Sp.
82 Malignity
83 Barnstorming
85 Signature of a Plymouth founder
86 Efrem Zimbalist Jr., for one
87 Ervin and Snead
89 Checkhov's Uncle
90 Of a belief
93 Dowries
95 Quiet!
97 Hit signs
99 Author Wiesel
100 Put on cargo
103 Roman 1004
104 Paintings
105 Have debts
106 Spinners
108 Muffin
110 Fabric
111 Weeping: It.
112 One of three
113 U.S. agents
120 Sleuth Hercule
123 Loves
124 Med. people
125 Suffragist
126 Tennis pro
127 Cubic meter
129 Untrue
131 Ecole attender
132 Dit's partner
133 Flush with success
134 Small type
135 Buenos Aires name
137 Thebes deity
139 From a distance
142 Buck and rip
144 Do sums
145 Tennessee initials
146 Baseball statistic
147 Asian holiday
148 Glasgow uncle

SHADY DOINGS

By Thomas Sheehan

ACROSS

1 Lox's friend
6 Foliage-tour time
10 __ odds (alienate)
15 Watchdogs' watchdog: Abbr.
19 H.R.E. emperor, 962-973
20 Singer Anita
21 "__ far, far better . . ."
22 Baseball's Mule
23 Do a behind-the-scenes job
25 Homes for closet skeletons
27 Aegean island
28 Blackjack call
29 Slapstick basics
30 Warning sound
31 Baltic land: Abbr.
33 "__ of the Yukon"
35 Honky-__
36 Tennis tie
38 Holiday in Hue
39 "Not a __ chance"
43 Spectral figure
45 Holbein portrait
48 Wishes undone
49 Hard-hearted gal et al.
51 Took it on the lam
52 Parlor game
53 Common abbr.
54 Time of day
56 Sinn __
57 Worse off than the Cratchits
58 Late-hours word
59 Dwarf: Prefix
60 Noun suffix
61 Drenched
62 React to Oct. 31 doings
66 Actor __ Robertson
68 Sheep tick
69 Like a bowstring
70 Neighbor of Can.
73 Have __ (relax)
74 Ill-gotten money
75 Fearsome ones
77 Initials on a parcel
78 Mouth or house
79 Boris of the chillers
81 Did an Oct. 31 duty
83 "__ Rhythm"
84 Sail rope
85 Cuts
86 McCarthy-era obsession
88 Norse goddess
90 Lamp dweller
91 Proverbial payee
92 "Cav" man
95 Man's seven
98 Bake anew
101 Cartoonist Walker
102 "__ Were the Days"
104 Underworld goddess
105 Mahalia Jackson forte
107 "Turn of the Screw," e.g.
109 Caesarean remark
110 Muse
111 Black-fin snapper
112 "If you knew __ like . . ."
113 Annoyer
114 Punishment lover
115 Carney et al.
116 Tax-form instruction

DOWN

1 Scary one
2 Dumas duelist
3 Oct. 31 social event
4 Dawn goddess
5 Neighbor of 31 Across
6 "A Moon __ Misbegotten"
7 "Can you spare __?"
8 Current
9 Drainpipe cleaner
10 Occult sign
11 Kennedy
12 Hombres' uncles
13 Balaam's mount
14 Features of Groucho's Lydia
15 Trick-or-treat army
16 Grabs wildly
17 "How __ repay you?"
18 Group: Abbr.
24 Oz's Dorothy, for a while
26 Scads
29 Sherwood's terror firma
32 Mel of football
34 Alternative to a finesse
35 Dull sound
37 Hagen et al.
39 U.S. agents
40 Bizarre
41 Entertained
42 Ancient lyre
43 Cry of relief
44 Value
46 "Not __ out of them" (no word)
47 __ St. Louis
50 Obstacles
51 Theme of 107 Across
52 Easy gait
55 Numero __
57 Mischievous spirit
61 Short spell of action
62 Sitting Bull's deity
63 Israeli name
64 Chair for Cicero
65 Periodical, for short
66 Smithy
67 Lamb __
70 Give __
71 German admiral
72 Gets the total
73 Black: Fr.
74 Like 94 Down
76 O'Casey
79 Doenitz
80 Bank watchdog: Abbr.
82 World area
84 Like some houses
87 Colombian city
89 TV news name
90 Mystical knowledge
92 Very, in music
93 Certain crime
94 Oct. 31 walker
96 Oct. 31 canal?
97 More subtle
98 Hostess's initials
99 Sword
100 Old Chinese zithers
101 Address for a queen
103 They, in Italy
106 Process: Suffix
107 Youth org.
108 Cask

311 HANG-UPS By Jack Luzzatto

ACROSS

1 Tentative start
8 Leading singers of groups
14 Looped rug fabrics
20 Patient one
21 Pine exudation
22 Italian cheese
23 Offshoot of Dream Street
25 Attack as false
26 Edible tubers
27 Noxious influence
28 Pale color
30 Mountain pass
31 Father of Abner
32 She had a plume
33 Nativity gift
34 Word to a certain squad
35 Chemical prefix
37 Washington fixture
40 Seances
42 Plant world
44 Tot's gait
46 Revolves, old style
47 "__ Bergere"
48 Unable to resist
49 What "this gun" was for
50 Knowing the answers
52 Giant-killer
54 Mild expletives
58 Car starter: Abbr.
59 Calif. Indians
61 Follow
63 Hide the loot
64 Sass
65 Mischievous spirit
68 Indian of West
69 Summon things past
72 Italian city
73 Dignified
75 Point of a mango
76 Intensify
78 Cavils
80 Small delivery cycle
82 Last drop
84 More depressed
86 Start the tapes
87 Halevy opera
90 Tasting of fat
91 Scares for drivers
92 Canines for Dracula
94 __ knowledge
97 Plane formation: Abbr.
98 Like a grain
99 __ la Paix
101 Knowledge: Suffix
103 Blockhead
106 Explosive
107 Sufficient
108 Pop-concert favorite
110 Fish
111 With hand on hip
113 Banquo et al.
116 Painter of bathers
117 French schools
118 Extra printed supplement
119 Third or master's
120 Settles a debt
121 Joyce subject

DOWN

1 Mortise's partner
2 In reserve
3 Master of the macabre
4 Querying grunts
5 Leftover
6 Secondary theorem
7 Exhausts
8 Self-assurance
9 Pack of paper
10 Island: Sp.
11 Wire measure
12 __ one (singly)
13 Dorothy of mysteries
14 Hair-raising hair
15 "When in __ . . ."
16 Devil's aide
17 Adding flavor
18 Dine like Henry VIII
19 Like Eddie Cantor
24 Value
29 Isle of Man's sea
32 Shredded, as documents
33 Whimpering
34 Churchillian hour
36 Of animal life
38 Mars
39 Séance V.I.P.
41 Novices: Var.
42 Pardon
43 Spilling over
45 Contacts, e.g.
47 Thwarted
48 Romp
51 Book after Joel
53 Rock instrument
55 Points of quick return
56 Worldly goods
57 Ancient coin
60 Grows hot
62 Biblical salesman
66 On the way
67 Mr. Oates
70 Mess-hall chore
71 Hackle-raising
74 Balky person
77 Croak of the raven
79 Location
81 Norse hero
83 Costume
85 Monocle
87 Gymnast's body suit
88 "I'm __ Doodle Dandy"
89 Flying swiftly
93 Cutup
95 Singular person
96 "I'd do anything __"
100 Unfreeze the wings
102 Powerful person
104 Cave
105 Goes hungry
107 Log-run Broadway man
108 Mr. Dracula
109 __-eyed (staring wildly)
110 Handle a caber
112 African kingdom: Abbr.
114 Goal at Everest
115 Former abbr. for 50th state

312   MIXED SEA FARE   *By Arnold Moss*

ACROSS

1 Kind of domo
6 Moabite king
11 Summit
15 French smoke
20 "There __ books like a dame"
21 Confirmation ritual
22 Soldier at Verdun
24 Balbo
25 Hangouts
26 Actress-writer Taylor
27 Accessory for Stern
28 Kind of pneumonia
29 Bowery-bound
31 Roman chef's pride
33 Demolish: Var.
34 Self: Prefix
35 Navy initials
38 Adjective suffix
39 Cochineal, e.g.
40 "Am I my __?"
48 Trochees and iambs
52 Give an engagement ring
53 Fitzgerald
54 Russian lake
55 To __ his own
57 Belgian violinist
58 "Now you __, now you . . ."
59 Source of "Summertime"
63 Sack of a kind
64 Romanov edict
65 April 15 org.
66 Barrie pirate
67 Fiber knot
58 Silent one of 1920's
69 Mother's kin
70 Merganser
72 Guthrie
74 Bigwig
76 Smear
77 Eardrums
80 __ detergent
85 500 city, for short
86 Yorkshire city
88 Jazzman Hines
89 Aces
90 Kind of electric switch
93 Copies for eds.
94 Mesabi matter
96 Wool units
98 Graduate degrees
99 End
100 Tin-roof dweller
101 U.S. Chief Justice
104 Correspond

105 Socrate's place
108 Bring a vessel into the wind
109 __ the town
110 Smooth, in France
111 Rocking-chair locale
114 U. of Ore. site
115 Condition after 40 or so
117 York, e.g.
118 Power org.
119 __ Lanka
120 Claire
121 Dies __
125 People with forks
132 State of some weightlifters
136 Idiom
137 Kind of eclipse
139 Solzhenitsyn, e.g.
140 Source of strength
141 Indira's robes
142 Feed a fire
143 Observant one
144 Actress Christian
145 Delusion's kin
146 Minx

147 Long bit of hair
148 Fundamentals

DOWN

1 "A __ a fish?" (The Tempest)
2 Field of conflict
3 "He __ at scars, that . . ."
4 Kind of bearing
5 Flower
6 Sailing vessel
7 Alaskan
8 Wool: Prefix
9 Mimicked
10 Verse pause
11 Month: Abbr.
12 Bills' partner
13 Odds and ends: Abbr.
14 Kazan
15 Copenhagen park
16 "Take __ from me"
17 Apulian port
18 Actor Alda
19 Old king
23 Like some phone numbers

30 Simon __
32 Indian money unit
36 Hurok
37 Match a poker raise
39 Carts
40 "Hostage" author
41 Elevations: Abbr.
42 Like blackboards
43 Shade of purple
44 Type of blouse
45 Fold
46 "Für __" (Beethoven piece)
47 Deserves
48 Listless
49 Gigantic: Fr.
50 More pithy
51 Word with plant or roll
52 College degree
55 Crisis source
56 Novelist St. Johns
58 Lula Vollmer hit of 1920's
60 French nut
61 Horse __

62 Marienbad, e.g.
68 High pass
69 Winter-cap device
71 Squirmed
73 Whetting device
75 Iraqi port
76 Girl's name
78 Filling
79 From, in Paris
81 Columbus's port
82 Prisoner
83 Spice
84 Ancient ascetic
87 __ Passos
90 Small top
91 Muscat native
92 Icy
93 Biblical people
95 Exclusive group
97 Kit Carson, e.g.
100 Lamb furs
102 __-jongg
103 Bunny __
106 Wall St. term: Abbr.
107 Book supplements: Abbr.

111 Prosody units
112 Deviate
113 Attire
114 Same, in France
116 Founder of Taoism
117 Curls the lip
120 Wight and Man
121 Aegean region
122 Persepolis sight
123 Electrode
124 Best and Millay
125 Base on balls
126 Where Tabriz is
127 Taj Mahal site
128 Roulette color
129 Bastogne word
130 Presently
131 H.H. Munro
133 Roman wife
134 Location
135 Tulip's start
138 Pol. party

313 TALL TIMBER By Herb Risteen

ACROSS

1 Hardwoods
6 Storage structure
10 P.I. trees
14 Part of T.L.
19 Fraternal order
20 Texture
21 Naldi of silents
22 Intimate
23 Predecessor of a pine
27 Kind of throat or loser
28 U.S. Indian
29 Word with today
30 Obliterated
31 Business abbr.
32 Maple genus
34 Zoo beast
35 Hardy novel
46 Patriot of '76
47 Born: Fr.
48 Water birds
49 Split
50 Ed or Nancy
51 Berlin street sight
55 Icelandic opus
56 Penrod's friend
57 Tatting
58 Where Sligo is
59 Sultan's concern
60 Brown hue
61 Ollie's partner
62 Annoying problems
64 Juvenile classic
68 City near Chicago
69 Asther of screen
70 Buddy of TV
71 Moss and Lorenz
72 Mane area
73 Dam
74 Krazy __
77 Or __
78 Ranger's concern
81 Gaucho gear
82 One who lurks
83 Pacific sea
84 __ fours
85 Bulb product
86 Winter haven
92 Place: Suffix
93 Full of trees
94 Scrap
95 Silken thread
99 Berlin's forte
101 Rehan
102 __ of the earth
106 What "they" did
111 Furry beast
112 Roulette bet
113 Asian land
114 Shark's business
115 Very small
116 Heroic work
117 Simon-__
118 Corday's victim

DOWN

1 Quantities: Abbr.
2 London locale
3 Farm worker
4 Italian family
5 Indian weight
6 Bait-and-__ ads
7 Hercules's captive
8 Card game
9 Kind of white or beat
10 Belong
11 Brauhaus offering
12 Salt tree
13 __ Paulo
14 Eric __
15 Dartle or Raisa
16 Biblical book
17 Greek township
18 Watched
24 Relative
25 Pronoun for Hamlet
26 Roman historian
31 Exacerbate
32 Ripened
33 Canadian redman
34 Topnotch
35 Tree of Java
36 Hottentot
37 Per __
38 Navy man: Abbr.
39 Group of nine
40 Herb genus
41 St. Paul's architect
42 Certain crime
43 Drafted over
44 Nobelist in medicine, 1954
45 Dairy products
51 Kind of fur
52 Cover for a cake
53 Vexes
54 Malay coins
57 U.S. novelist
59 More robust
60 Fixed period
61 Bog bird
62 Horatius's river
63 Dinsmore
64 Muse of comedy
65 Scottish herd
66 Drive __ (get an R.B.I.)
67 Words of consent
68 Pup
72 __ me tangere
74 German city, to Germans
75 Et __
76 Pacific bark
78 Sound's partner
79 Stitch lightly
80 Scold
81 __ oak
83 Starling of Africa
85 Kindergartner
87 Pleasing
88 Sure losers
89 Palm tree
90 Germ killer
91 Tarkenton
95 Harbor craft
96 Music maker
97 Feminine suffix
98 Arabian gulf
99 Organ part
100 Louisville's river
101 Armadillo
102 Portico
103 Sandarac tree
104 Russian river
105 Campus ordeal
107 Direction
108 Kind of reader
109 Actress Joanne
110 Hardwood

CONSUMER GOODS

By George Madrid

ACROSS

1 Out-and-out
6 German pronoun
9 Port in Iraq
14 Eateries
20 Play by Sartre
22 Mass. cape
23 Movie dog et al.
24 __ be (was)
25 The works
27 Butter-maker
28 Kind of voyage
29 Feminine suffix
30 Prepare to dine
33 Meal times, for some
35 Thermos's inventor
36 Brawl
37 Hourly sound
41 Clerical haircuts
43 Things to know
46 Asian holiday
48 Yokel
49 Coin for Louis IX
50 Baltic people
51 Eating place
53 Eat
58 Roman emperor and others
60 "__ Town"
61 Shot-glass measure
62 Poetic word
63 Look
64 Depart
68 Begat
71 Electric unit
73 Angel's Islamic kin
74 Santa __
75 Ancient Nile kingdom
77 Mouths
79 U.S. Indian
80 Big bird
81 Portable cafeterias
86 Before J.F.K.
87 Solar god
88 Go quickly
89 Age group
90 Kind of stick
92 Stupid ones
94 Set forth
97 Kind of potatoes
102 Subjugate
104 Chinese gelatin
105 Go amiss
106 Hair tint
107 French article
108 Dry lake of West
109 Of an early era of man

111 Eating places
115 Good exam grade
117 Some transit lines
118 Templeton
119 Type of light
120 Lanchester and Maxwell
121 Self-defense, for one
126 Houseboat's rich relative
128 Philosopher Immanuel
130 Objective
132 Old Roman port
133 Roadside come-on sign
138 Yorick's skull, e.g.
139 Flowering tree
142 Recycling material
143 Arctic air short-cut
145 Main and current
146 Like some gases
147 State: Abbr.

148 Certain retailer
149 Bothers
150 Moves carefully
151 Son of Odin
152 Prunes, in Scotland

DOWN

1 Like some letters
2 La-di-da
3 Berliner, for one
4 Places for pitches
5 Abbr. in music
6 Pan-fries
7 Trailing
8 Caught
9 Composer of fugues
10 Tennis name
11 Prepares a roaster
12 Thinner
13 __ a pin
14 Type of waiter
15 Newton or Stern

16 Place for a bite
17 Actor Byrnes
18 Way: Abbr.
19 Native __
21 Hard or big
26 Subject for Duchamp
31 Fox or turkey
32 Colorings
34 Texas Guinan's clientele
38 Marker
39 Jan. and Dec.
40 Before, to Byron
42 __ it in (needle)
44 Cynical words for cafes
45 Gauge
47 Old pronoun
50 Not manifest
51 Make sharper
52 Kind of puppy
53 Style of jazz
54 Capek play
55 Prodigious
56 Spanish town
57 Newt
59 Wise to
64 Make java, for short
65 Excelling

66 Cleaving tool
67 Pooh!
69 __ other
70 Owing
72 Sindbad's bird
76 Sellout
78 Snakes
80 Old-tie school
82 Staff person
83 Born: Fr.
84 M.D.'s helpers: Abbr.
85 Shows to a seat
87 "... no more cakes and __?"
91 Role for Paul Robeson
93 Healthy
95 Buddies
96 Turkish title
98 Gold, in Mexico
99 Sea eagle
100 Compass reading
101 Kind of about
103 Miss Vague
108 Dessert
109 Travelers' place
110 Oriental sect

111 Window or rum
112 Highest note
113 Power group: Abbr.
114 Bothers
116 Rested
120 Warehouses
121 Writer Norman
122 __ breve
123 Sign __ (end hostilities)
124 Brawled
125 Romantic table lights
127 Bit
129 Disease spread by tsetse flies
131 Atlanta campus
134 Russian agency
135 Dry
136 Leftovers
137 Work unit
139 Home for "Aida," etc.
140 "__ got sixpence"
141 __ culpa
144 Carriers: Abbr.

ROUGH STUFF
By Jim Page

ACROSS

1 Ridicule
6 Miss Claire et al.
10 Fast jets
14 One of a nonwaiting pair
18 Sphere of activity
19 Saw logs
20 __ on (defer)
21 Firebrand: Fr.
22 Movie-about baseball
25 Singer Mary
26 G.B.S. admirer
27 Dump
28 Prefix for maniac
29 Dallas time: Abbr.
32 Pound and namesakes
33 Existed
34 Sharp ridges
35 German cry
36 Word after can or ump
37 Sofa
38 Gentle as __
39 Tennis players, at times
41 Blubbers
46 Asks, in Glasgow
47 Breaks of a habit
48 Faculty member
49 Boozehound
50 Brain passages
51 Rhythmic qualities
52 Hydrocarbon
54 Lake of West
56 Biblical mount
57 Coin of Cuba
58 Farmer, in the spring
59 Deprive of
60 Mouths
61 Guerrillas
64 Pointed arch
65 Like some basses' mouths
67 Walking __
68 Atomic pioneer
69 Water plants
70 Embryonic unit
74 Pillow type: Abbr.
77 __ oneself (skip)
78 Old Finnish poems
79 Does a lube job
80 River of France
81 Minstrel-show Mister
82 Bell sounds
83 Canvas support
85 Idaho city
86 Purchase: Lat.
87 Secular
88 Baseball's Del
89 Sty sounds
90 "Big Knockover" author
95 Malenkov et al.
96 "La Plume de Ma __"
97 Appears
98 Baby or chalk
99 Xmas time
100 Believes
101 Kind of raid or waist
102 Miss Adams
103 Neck color
104 W.W. I French soldiers
105 Golden __
106 __ contents
108 Yearn, Cockney style
109 U.N.-area site
114 Cubic meter
115 Dublin theater
116 Marianne or Victor
117 Red dye
118 Kind of pot or up
119 Honey drink
120 Eastern Eur. units
121 French snow

DOWN

1 Fairy queen
2 Gershwin
3 Haberdashery customers
4 Noun suffixes
5 Medical devices
6 In __ file (queued)
7 Mrs. Charles et al.
8 __ for one's money
9 Religious school: Abbr.
10 Untidy people
11 __ up (in the bag)
12 "Do __!"
13 J.F. Cooper character
14 Overtime situation
15 Nobel author
16 Gun gals
17 Mother of Ares
19 Fine china
20 Native of Bratislava
21 ". . . cat that killed __"
23 Upperclassmen at times
24 Hindu god et al.
28 Dividend fruit
29 Italian town of W.W. II siege
30 Symbol of authority
31 Crucial pitching situation
33 Legal rights
34 Archenemy
37 Mild oath
40 __ Beach, Fla.
41 Where 34 Down reigns
42 Sluggard
43 Approaches
44 Praise, in Scotland
45 Keep in, in printing
47 Thought's father
51 __ majesty
52 Yedo today: Var.
53 Those garnisheed
54 Word for Clemenceau
55 Biblical town
57 Sound in Washington
58 Exits hastily
59 Go-getters
61 Cereal grains
62 __ Ho (Yellow River)
63 French handles
66 U.S. author
68 __ due (matured)
69 Snake
70 Cook
71 One of a daily trio
72 Lay down
73 Scoots
75 Merry
76 Having braids
77 Napping
80 "It's __ move"
82 Valleys
83 Public or bitter
84 Insects
85 Jimmied
87 Baltic natives
88 Intense actor
89 Weakened
91 Trucking companies
92 Take out a policy
93 Disturbed
94 Grundy's birth day
95 France's de __
98 Drums
100 TV Indian
101 Brazil's Rio __
102 Barbara or Hoople
104 Certain Christmas
105 African native
106 Ring decisions
107 Shipping hazard
109 See 88 Down
110 Slipper sizes: Abbr.
111 "__ live and breathe"
112 Sharp turn
113 One, in Perth

316 CHRISTMAS GLEANINGS By Anne Fox

ACROSS

1 Satisfy, as thirst
6 Perry or Lake
10 Asian ox
14 Mop: Var.
18 Not so hot
19 African antelope
20 Corday's prey
21 Certain guy
22 Old coin of Japan
23 Western brick, for short
24 "Vincit __ veritas"
25 Kett
26 Part of U.S.S.R.
27 "Let us now go __"
31 Arthur Train's lawyer
33 O.T. book
34 Realm of 66 Down: Abbr.
35 Musketeer
36 Oarsmen
38 Billing word
40 Bronx feature
43 Compete
44 Words from St. Matthew
51 Join
52 French eyes
53 Upward: Prefix
54 "__ was going to..."
55 Statute: Fr.
56 Dean of gloom
58 Potato-chip breakers
60 Gloomy __
62 Atomic-age element
65 Outer: Prefix
67 Grassland
68 Fraternal order
70 King in "The Tempest"
71 Words from a 1639 carol
76 Mean
77 Belgrade name
78 Current
79 Present, in Paris
80 Correspondence
82 Force of 44 Down
83 René's thirst
85 Noun suffix
88 Tang
89 Ruler: Abbr.
91 Gibbon
93 Be sullen
95 Type of caller
96 Words from a Spanish carol

102 Use a gunsight
103 Vessel
104 Prefix for puncture
105 Rule the __
106 Gone: Fr.
108 British holiday
110 Unshared
113 Ridicule
115 English carol words to wise old men
121 Feminine suffix
122 Author Carmer
123 Kind of branch
124 Harass
125 Take over
127 Baltic port
128 Ex-Giant Grier
129 Back up
130 Dominions
131 Loom reed
132 Work on a sweater
133 Eire president, 1938-45
134 Some homes

DOWN

1 Kind of fellow
2 Christmas cookie
3 Hardy favorite of Xmas singers
4 Diminutive suffix
5 Sharpness
6 Ancient book
7 Home of the "Stein Song"
8 Song of 1922
9 Beasts of burden
10 Victoria Falls's river
11 Sea bird
12 Heckle
13 State
14 __ pie
15 Words by Charles Wesley
16 Bone: Prefix
17 Sun sheddings
20 Wasteland
28 Certain interests
29 Words by Frederic Farrar
30 Wash
32 Dick
37 Child's question
39 Neighbor of Mex.
41 __ shoestring
42 Honshu town
44 1914-18 event: Abbr.
45 Oil: Fr.
46 Look for
47 __-be
48 King of Tyre
49 Toper
50 Malayan island
57 Eulogize
59 Hindu title
61 Goes over lightly
63 Jai __
64 For the __ (now)
66 __ the Great of Europe
69 Charlie Brown's dog
71 Bell town
72 Soviet premier
73 French cubist
74 Willows
75 Hasta la vista
81 Youth org.
84 German leader
86 One of a world seven
87 Kind of roll
90 Apiece
92 Common abbr.
94 Relative in Spain
97 In an important way
98 Arabian noble
99 Scandinavian drink: Var.
100 Soothing word
101 Negative
106 Prepares to travel
107 Ancient Mariner's cry
109 U.S. author
111 Exuded
112 Gladly: Lat.
114 Second largest of 50
116 Sergeant or New
117 N.C. college
118 Relative of oui, oui
119 Mideast king
120 Sampler ingredient
126 Formerly named

LIVING IT UP By Frances Hansen

ACROSS

1 Soprano Lucine
6 African gazelles
11 Young pig
16 Son of Zeus
21 Reception rooms
22 Rider on a pale horse
23 Circular painting
24 Like some TV operas
25 Loose dress
26 Loire Valley area
27 Sheik of Araby
28 Kaifeng's province
29 Start of a limerick
33 Skimpy skirt
34 Othello, for one
35 Therefore: Fr.
36 Pro-__
37 Ballet leap
38 B'way sign
40 Bobby Riggs's racket
42 P.I. shrub: Var.
44 More of limerick
54 Ten decades, for short
55 Dr. Dolittle's duck
56 Of bronze: Lat.
57 Krupp locale
58 Trek to Mecca
60 "It's like a __ the door"
62 East Indian sailor
65 British heroes of W.W. II
66 Wild plums
68 Dam site
71 "I love thy rocks and __"
72 "__ was saying"
73 Hair-raising place
77 Eyelashes: Prefix
78 Egyptian month
79 Equal
80 More of limerick
86 "Odyssey" beggar
87 10 C's or 1 G
88 Yodeler's counterpoint
89 East Indian gum tree
90 Merry, in Marseille
91 Chestnuts or feathers
92 __ precedent
94 Heavenly blue
98 Barley beard
99 Put __ (act la-di-da)
101 Flighty conveniences
105 Like a bump on __
106 Speed skate
108 Joseph C. Lincoln's Cap'n
109 Natural
111 Aviation org.
112 More of limerick
119 Char
120 "I never hope to __"
121 Stout or Harrison
122 Haggis-eater
125 Make a Knight of it?
127 Last Supper picture
128 Anna's new home
131 Early Briton
135 End of limerick
140 Bandleader Shaw
141 Marianne or Mary Tyler
142 Sleuth Vance
143 "Once upon __"
144 __ terre (second home)
145 Noun suffixes
146 Verb mood: Abbr.
147 Moon plain
148 Stendhal's Julien
149 Believer
150 In want
151 Use a certain iron

DOWN

1 Where Shillong is
2 Moslem title
3 Dramatic corn
4 Disreputable
5 Italian wine city
6 Bell town
7 Tooth: Prefix
8 Domo or Hoople
9 Chemical suffix
10 Quake
11 __ de Beaupré, Quebec shrine
12 Like Bluebeard
13 United
14 Skilled
15 Wild flood
16 Wan
17 Shingle repairs
18 Tyler's craft, maybe
19 Separated
20 Irish dramatist
30 Not knowing right or wrong
31 Jazzman Thelonious
32 Eastern nurse
39 Mr. Buttons
40 Mexican state
41 Curse
43 Max and Buddy of boxing
44 German pronouns
45 Popular cutlet
46 Within: Prefix
47 Baseball hitting stat
48 Tokyo's old name
49 "Give a __ horse . . ."
50 Vapid
51 Land of the Knesset
52 Taunts
53 __ ground (solid)
59 "__ loves me, this I know"
61 Curls around
63 Lock horns
64 Opposite of omega
67 Biol. or ecol.
69 Dinah's owner
70 Scheherazade counted them
74 Word on a French letter
75 Arrowsmith's wife
76 More commonplace
79 Public square
80 Barber of Seville
81 S.A. Indian
82 Jelly fruit
83 "__ human, to forgive . . ."
84 Unfriendly
85 Gardner
91 Singer Lena
93 Dog-headed ape
95 Arm bone
96 Horse color
97 Zounds!
100 Cushy positions
102 Cousin of amal.
103 Cheer
104 Weather for 91 Down
107 "Sidewalks of New York" start
110 Make do
113 Lower wall part
114 Played a tattoo
115 Most acute
116 Chinese group
117 Revolving giddily
118 Auxiliary generator
122 Cookies
123 Objet d'art
124 Water animal
126 One __ (singly)
128 Take potshots at
129 Killed time
130 Critic Cleveland
132 Perón
133 Slot-machine showing
134 Pollsters' concern
136 River duck
137 Places
138 Oh, dear!
139 Elia

318 BACK TO SCHOOL By Diana Sessions

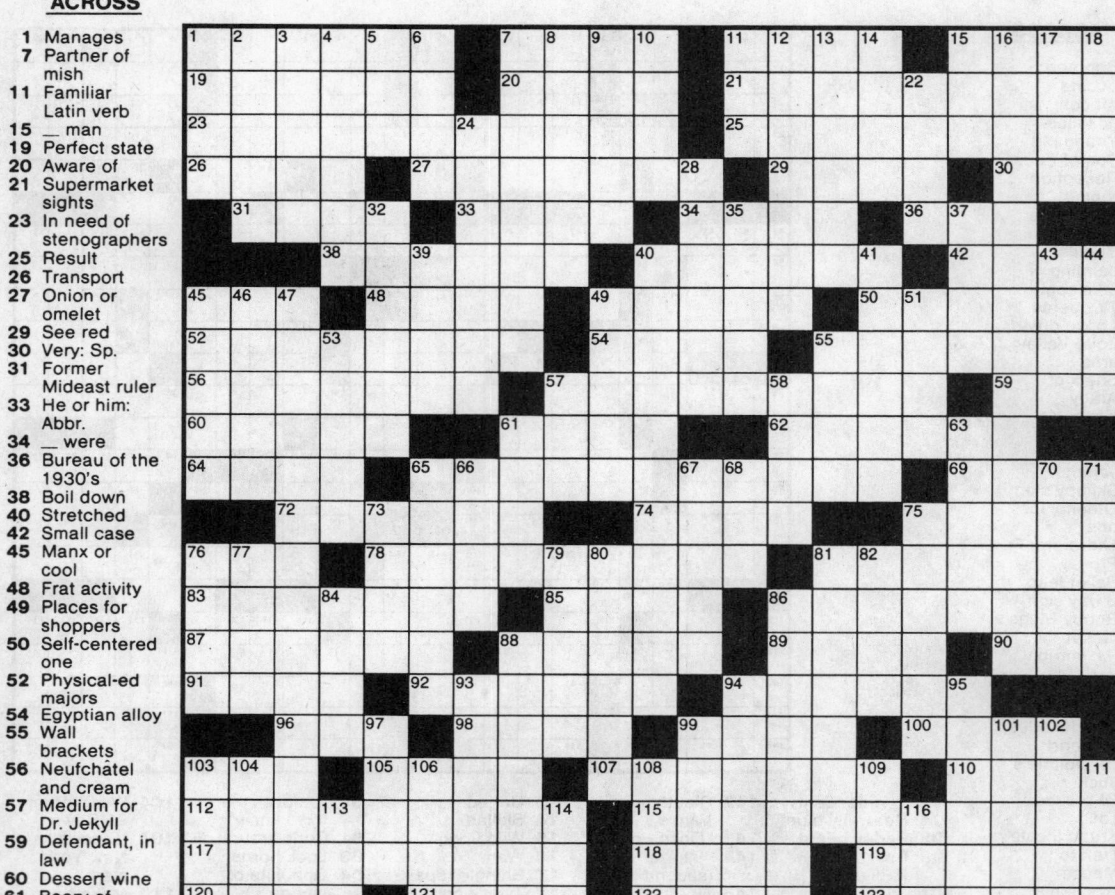

ACROSS

1 Manages
7 Partner of mish
11 Familiar Latin verb
15 __ man
19 Perfect state
20 Aware of
21 Supermarket sights
23 In need of stenographers
25 Result
26 Transport
27 Onion or omelet
29 See red
30 Very: Sp.
31 Former Mideast ruler
33 He or him: Abbr.
34 __ were
36 Bureau of the 1930's
38 Boil down
40 Stretched
42 Small case
45 Manx or cool
48 Frat activity
49 Places for shoppers
50 Self-centered one
52 Physical-ed majors
54 Egyptian alloy
55 Wall brackets
56 Neufchâtel and cream
57 Medium for Dr. Jekyll
59 Defendant, in law
60 Dessert wine
61 Beery of films
62 Nautical response
64 Egyptian goddess
65 Relative of a talking horse
69 __ of office
72 Middling: Prefix
74 Staple bean
75 Sound system
76 High-school course: Abbr.
78 Bookbinding guard
81 Great __ Reef
83 Roped
85 Marsupials, for short
86 Spicy substances
87 Relaxed
88 Sugar sand
89 Johnson of TV
90 Seized
91 Shipped
92 Outdoorsy
94 Smoothly polite
96 Earth: Prefix
98 __ facto
99 Tropical ant
100 Nilotic language
103 Hurok
105 Alter the aspect of
107 Hartz Mountains' locale
110 Brain or duck
112 Composing, as a report
115 Forte of certain borrowers
117 Persevering
118 Bone: Prefix
119 Lack of vital energy
120 Hawaiian bird
121 Works by Keats
122 Yields
123 Wickerwork material

DOWN

1 Surge
2 Moral nature
3 Eye or sweet
4 Jam or butter
5 Walk-on role
6 Cries of derision
7 Rulers
8 "... to find, __ to yield"
9 Mug
10 Mortar trays
11 Tree of Brazil
12 Bran and raga
13 Cunning
14 Pronoun
15 "__ the captain of my soul"
16 Soliloquy, e.g.
17 Famous Latin words
18 Pale
22 Assemblage
24 Places next to
28 N.Y.C. river
32 Dissenting belief
35 Game ragout
37 Laborer
39 Attractive
40 Typical example
41 Law
43 Beneficiary in a suit
44 "__ Mad, Mad ..."
45 Plants of the West
46 Greek peak
47 Non-American tongue
49 Taj __
51 Bullfight artist
53 Contract
55 Eye problem: Var.
57 Army officer: Abbr.
58 P.I. banana
61 Gas for signs
63 "__ the cream in ..."
65 Easy or one-way
66 Part of a sentence: Abbr.
67 Uproar
68 Cheat
70 Depend on
71 "__ Wessel"
73 Sky sightings
75 Silvery
76 Too bad!
77 __ Latin
79 Proclaims
80 Stadium standby
81 Well-known grafter
82 Tapir
84 Surfeit
86 Shares
88 God with a trident
93 Like the Louvre's Nike
94 One of the degrees
95 Fish trap
97 Samuel Adams's colleague
99 Came about
101 Bernard, for one
102 "__ vincit amor"
103 Thick of society
104 Whether __
106 Division word
108 Dark
109 New __
111 Actor Richard
113 Uncle: Sp.
114 Parts of qts.
116 Greek letter

319

FANCY FOODS By John Willig

320 IGNITION KEYS *By J.A. Felker*

ACROSS

1 Fuel
5 Converse
9 Nonplus
14 Month: Abbr.
18 Dance
19 French river
20 Hank Aaron's forte
21 King Arthur's father
23 Alice T. Hobart's fuel of 1930's
27 Entertain
28 Network initials
29 Rhine attraction
30 Topper
33 Take five
35 W.W. II girl
37 Spotted cats
38 _ of tea
40 Speed up
43 Look well on
45 Biblical wells
46 Grandfather: Lat.
47 Religious degrees
51 Overwhelmed
52 Naked or hairy
53 Delight
54 Dickens clerk
55 Modern-day activity
59 _ rat (suspect)
61 Hoosier poet
62 Blessings
63 Tramps
64 Slight trace
67 Overwhelms
68 Calms
69 Lose
70 Kind of plaster
71 _ hairs
72 Trojans
73 Tires
78 Stage award
79 Parry
80 Butterfly gear
81 Pluperfect, e.g.
82 Asian trees
83 Port of Egypt
84 Symbol of cruelty
86 Miss Kitt
87 Zippy
90 Give birth, as to a lamb
91 Schooner feature
95 _ fault
96 Husky's tow
98 Hosp. people
99 Resins
100 Musical notes
101 Kind of car lot
103 Abetting
111 Avocet's kin
112 Fran's friend
113 Mostel
114 Night or shanks'
115 Minerals
116 Controls
117 Eur. power
118 Fuel

DOWN

1 Japanese measure
2 "_, monsieur"
3 One and _
4 Kind of riot, in comedy ads
5 Polite, in Rome
6 Gas-pump listing
7 Kind of tray
8 Golfer's need
9 Moslem months
10 Fence sitter
11 Arbiter, for short
12 Mine, in France
13 Literary kickoff
14 French sugars
15 Kennedy
16 Vance
17 Belief
22 Moslem ruler
24 Poetic word
25 Get the _ (call the police)
26 Spanish seals
30 Lips: Prefix
31 Ancient tribe of England
32 Of a nobleman
34 Three-legged stand
36 _-sur-Marne, France
39 Muscular coups
41 Harbor unit
42 Smooths out
44 Kind of jumping bean
47 Gotham park
48 Slave
49 Brawl
50 German joke
52 Danish measure
53 Florentine painter
56 Strategic moves
57 Be rich in
58 Vacation activities
59 Closet catchall
60 Spanish dressmaker
64 Hit
65 _ troubled waters
66 Consuming
67 Buy a _ drinks
68 Kind of check
70 Town near Paris
71 Takes the wheel
74 Wavy, in heraldry
75 Share in
76 Biblical town
77 Wealth
79 Becomes a hoax victim
83 Going to court
84 Governing bodies
85 _ on (etc.)
86 "I only have _ you"
87 Passes out
88 Provide details
89 Workers in adhesives
91 Beverages
92 "When I grow too _ dream"
93 Ask, in Spain
94 Umbrella, in song
97 State: Abbr.
102 Mine gas
104 Rubber tree
105 Whitney
106 _ chou (Chinese pottery)
107 Males
108 West
109 Time
110 Determine

321 SIMPLE ARITHMETIC

By A.J. Santora

ACROSS

1 Misbehave
6 Hebrew measure
10 Locale
15 Corner fit
20 Add horsepower
22 Garbage
23 Old manuscript
24 House that fell
25 Rococo
26 "__ a nerve!"
27 Thesaurus name
28 "...would __ clock"
29 Product-yielding plants
31 "Boot" land
33 Accumulate
35 Bowwows
36 Disgusted
38 Newborns
39 Phase
42 Uncles, in Spain
44 Buzzer
46 Ballgame delayer
47 "Much" stir
50 Heckelphone
51 Slackenings
53 Tobacco chew
55 Blue dye
56 Radiation unit
57 Grief
58 Congress, at times
63 Benbow, for one
65 S.A. Indians
67 Lets off
68 Muscat people
70 Disastrous
71 Mine entrance
72 Newt
73 Finger sound
74 Nanny and billy
76 Hereditary
78 Cleaving tool
79 Half a jumble
80 Bravo!
81 Piquancy
82 Atmosphere
83 Bread spread
84 Impound
86 Bus stop
87 Outstanding
88 Lizzie or soldier
89 Twelfth part
90 Kind of pool
92 Verified
94 Warehousing
96 Art movement
98 Tipped off
101 Personal math problem
103 Peruvians
105 Brother's title
106 Norse god
107 Cry of disgust
108 Wealth
110 Irritate
111 Number
112 Road sign
114 Stupid one
117 Against
118 "... __ on such as we"
119 Prevents
121 African tongue
123 Poetic works
125 And others: Lat.
126 Lickspittle
128 Tote-board tragedy
133 Problems for M.P.'s
134 Happening
136 Well-known Dick
138 Sister Kate's dance
139 Brazen
140 Relative
141 Pretext
142 Unpopped corn
143 Krupp's city
144 Domesticated
145 Mr. in Berlin
146 French river

DOWN

1 __ now (currently)
2 Gazelle
3 Of time: Lat.
4 Cornered
5 Inconvenienced
6 In __ (existing)
7 Early golfing wear
8 Ad __ committee
9 Garden pest
10 Predicament
11 Not tense
12 Tense
13 Formerly named
14 Words on a movie marquee
15 Cotton fabric
16 Cordage fiber
17 Supporting, in a mathematically impossible way
18 Corded fabric
19 Pitching record: Abbr.
21 Pretty girl
30 Yardstick of a sort
32 Bath or wash
34 Tokyo sash
37 Mine-reading initials
38 Soft cheese
39 "Queen __ Day"
40 Taken sick
41 Mutual ties
43 Japanese statesman
45 Pistols, to small hoods
48 Yogurt, e.g.
49 Senior citizen
51 Savings and __
52 Casa rooms
54 Navy ship abbr.
55 Intention
57 Curtain
59 Success
60 Running track
61 Mayan tongue
62 Legionnaire
64 Insect stage
66 Consequences
69 Seas or Pacific
71 Sour-grapes man
73 Seclusion
75 Years
77 Fiber knot
78 Less
79 Flashy player
82 Turtle and mourning
84 "Picnic" author
85 Complications
86 Rumanian folk song
89 Actor Hunter
91 Chinese truth
93 Spanish waves
95 Pallid
96 Bounce
97 970
99 Author Linklater
100 Colorado peak
102 Arbiters, for short
104 Trapeze gear
109 Day: Abbr.
110 Breathe
112 Motor-current system
113 Kind of cycle
115 Decreased
116 Cushion
118 Harmonizes
120 Safety outlet
122 Graceful beauty
124 Dawn's opposite
125 Sheep
126 Swarm
127 Formerly
129 Hebrew month
130 Prefix for present or bus
131 Sign
132 Pitcher Sparky
133 Chem. suffix
135 Veneto, e.g.
137 "Blood and Sand" cheer

ACROSS

1 Love or hornet's
5 Andes survivors' story
10 Book about a V.P.
14 Dragon or pop
17 Cargo ship
19 European songbird
20 Winglike parts
21 Undulate
22 Dostoevsky subject
23 French port
24 L.A. athletes
25 Lined up
26 Inveigles
28 Remains
30 Red cocktail
32 Stringed instrument
34 Fiber knot
35 Traditional news spotter
36 H.W. Beecher comment, with 96 Across
45 Gift for a man
46 Nobody: Sp.
47 Mulligan, for one
48 Betelgeuse
49 Single
51 Queens athletes
52 These: Sp.
55 Sharpen
56 Group spirit
58 Pressure
61 Jogs the memory
63 Jewish festival
64 Sinn __
65 Snafu
66 Manhattan ingredient
67 Author of 10 Across
70 After H.S.T.
72 Smoking pipe
74 Old English moneys
75 Zagreb native
77 U.S. essayist
80 Horses, at times
82 Mooring rope
84 Piano theme classic
85 Grass genus
87 Common French verb
89 O'Neill heroine Leeds
90 Of a poem
91 Thomas or Condé
93 Essays
95 Vane direction
96 See 36 Across

102 Tennis gear
103 High note
104 Ship, to poets
105 Record players
108 Sawfish snout
111 Travel-lecture standbys
115 Arlene
116 Heart of fiction
118 Additional
120 Dodge
121 Jewish month
122 Turkish chamber
123 Take care of
124 Transmits
125 Weekday: Abbr.
126 Sleuth Wolfe
127 Handle
128 Literary doings

DOWN

1 Night: Prefix
2 Cork's place
3 Svelte
4 University in Phila.
5 Envoy: Abbr.
6 Pasternak heroine
7 Currier's partner
8 Hindu deity
9 Respects
10 Sinister or Mitzvah
11 Son of Eshek
12 H.H. Jackson novel
13 Put in a new category
14 Casino game
15 Ukrainian city
16 Archer's wood
18 Come back to
21 Former best-seller about rabbits
27 Kind of trunk
29 Freshets
31 Columbus campus
33 Plato's thinkings
36 Skid-row figures
37 Disciple
38 Acts as a model
39 She rated an "A"
40 Cape
41 Canadian area: Abbr.
42 Thames town
43 Kind of paper or trap
44 Minerals
45 Card wool
50 Wilde woman
53 Seed coat
54 Film-rater's concern
57 Sly looks
59 Meadow barley
60 Diplomat
62 Hindu dance gesture
65 Toscanini, for one
67 Thomas Wolfe's Eugene __
68 Wrath
69 Venture
71 Less taxing
73 Hawaiian hawks
75 Gruyère, etc.
76 Preterit or present
77 Word with paradise
78 Fashion
79 Lamb's cover-up
80 Short gaiter
81 Botches up
83 Scottish sailyard
86 "Jamaica __"
88 Egyptian tambourine
92 Bony fish
94 Stone pillars
97 Chalice veil
98 __ the gas
99 Tristram's beloved
100 Trade
101 Ridge near Jerusalem
105 Store-ad word
106 Dull sound
107 Fly high
109 Korean name
110 P.I. native
112 Copenhagen native
113 Literature of Iceland
114 Meeting: Abbr.
115 Moisture
117 Even if, for short
119 Bosh

323 NFL COMPANIONS By William Lutwiniak

ACROSS

1 Dandruff zone
6 Nitpick
10 Yakked
15 Travel
19 Rhyme scheme
20 River of Spain
21 Put straight
22 U.S.M.A. man
23 Bears
27 White House nickname
28 Dunne or Rich
29 Strains one's brains
30 Kind of show
31 Understand
32 Battery part
33 Spitz et al.
34 Abrupt
35 Kind of corner
36 Supermarket adjunct
37 Nylons
38 Eagles
49 Makes tracks
50 Having a smell
51 Assistants
52 __ on (enjoy)
53 Cricket units
54 __ over (subsides)
55 Clio et al.
56 Buenos __
57 Deprived of
58 Numskulls
59 Money of Mexico
60 Soho coves
61 __ de vie
62 Con __
63 Mouselike creature
64 Mideast ketch
65 Cards
73 Despicable
74 Show frugality
75 Bothers
76 Word with whiz
77 W.W. II viceroy of India
80 French writer
81 Shapes
83 Fuddy-duddy
84 __ in the hand
85 Number
86 Slow-witted ones
87 "__ Bulba"
88 Willis or Donna
89 Nickel beast
90 Golfing debris
91 Ham it up
92 Saints
97 Boxscore data
98 Olympus dweller
99 Crocus, for one

100 Porthos's friend
103 Comes to grips with grips
105 Chilly
107 Stamp or Mann
110 "Peace at any price," e.g.
111 German poet
112 Panegyric
113 Culture medium
114 Patriots
118 __ fixes (hangups)
119 Chips in
120 French income
121 Wherewithal
122 Jet housings
123 Lone and lode
124 Meeting: Abbr.
125 Goes after flies

DOWN

1 Heroic tales
2 Chili con __
3 Endure
4 Not energetic
5 La __
6 Crusted
7 "I'm __ goose"
8 Uncouth
9 Greek letter
10 Port of Java
11 Ah, me
12 Eye come-ons
13 Linemen
14 Calendar abbr.
15 Turned up, as a card
16 "There's nothing like __"
17 Lear's daughter
18 Harrow's rival
20 Omagh's county
22 Dross
24 __ up (arranged)
25 Turkish peak
26 Tudor and York, e.g.
32 Bring together
33 Bounding and Spanish
34 Bodies: Suffix
35 Sitting up
36 __ out (scolds)
37 Cerberus's domain
38 Carriers: Suffix
39 Attack
40 In a dudgeon
41 Bound along
42 Author's concern
43 Extreme disgust
44 Repudiate
45 Stupidity
46 Stopper
47 To __ (right on)
48 Noun ending
54 Western capital
55 Oberon
56 At another time
58 Practice
59 Aspect
60 Festive affairs
62 Erect
63 Air-show offering
64 Secret seekers
66 Exaggerate
67 Coos Bay's state
68 Finches
69 Indian of West
70 Luzon native
71 Make void
72 Yellowstone sight
77 Admonish
78 Busy as
79 Opinion
80 Passport entries
81 Chess turns
82 Fusses
83 Widely known
85 Takes off weight
86 Small change
87 Halfhearted
89 Laundry additive
90 Obscure
93 Shoppers on the Corso
94 Fool
95 Find fault
96 Laundry adjunct
100 City in Illinois
101 Went boating
102 Writer James et al.
103 Nina's companion
104 Tree
105 Alda and others
106 Bumptious ones
107 U.S. rocket stage
108 Galley-proof symbol
109 Playing cards
110 Impertinent one
111 Carry on
112 Fencer's blade
113 Acknowledge
115 Spanish article
116 Med. men
117 Letters

324 POWER PLOYS By Stanley Glass

ACROSS

1 Sheep cries
5 Diffuse by absorption
11 Eastern porters
17 Open the wine
20 Contribute
21 Boer statesman
22 Whale or platypus
23 Track officials
24 Comes forth
25 Unswerving
26 Corn bread
27 Skin blemish
28 " 'Tis the __ of summer"
31 Paint solvent
33 Start of austerity
36 Sailor
38 Durocher et al.
40 Marine peril
41 Vols' state
42 Asian tree
43 Vessel
44 Plant study: Abbr.
45 Speaks
48 Groups of sayings
49 Aeriform zoo
52 Fertilizer
55 Part of a flight
56 Buoyancy, in ballet
57 Continued
58 Drillings marked by success
64 Small harps
65 Indo-European
66 Condescend
68 Early Italians
71 Volatile fuel
73 Nerve-cell process
74 Calif. city
76 Fish
77 Brit. medal
78 Clamp
79 Stupid one
80 Dr. Seuss's jungle
82 Syrian city, to French
83 Dawn goddess
84 Relatives' assets
88 Huge
91 Mod people
92 Town near Newark
93 Decorate over
94 Type of toboggan
98 Shelley's elegy to Keats
100 Surviving mates

102 Violent speech
103 Small stream
104 Voltaire's real name
105 Wild ass
106 McCormick's moneymaker
107 Aristocracy
108 Spanish child

DOWN

1 Cadges
2 Med. course
3 Peak
4 East Africans
5 Ale month: Abbr.
6 Oil tanker
7 Southern shrub
8 Poker player, at times
9 Beget
10 Naval rank: Abbr.
11 Of a rope fiber
12 Alaskan native
13 Miss Thomas
14 Peron's land
15 Strasberg of theater
16 Part of C.B.S.
18 Electronic spotter
19 UHF tube
21 One-hoss shay man
27 Distresses

29 Turn __ on (reverse)
30 Preacher of baseball
32 __ home (dine in)
33 Dwarfed potted tree
34 Suit to __
35 Thrice: Prefix
37 Flower
38 Pulls
39 Muse
42 Vince of earlier films
44 Chicago suburb
46 Easy gait
47 Protective helmets
50 Ad-copy unit
51 Guys' friends
52 Domestic animal

53 Certain voter: Abbr.
54 Name for a large dog
57 Bevel out
59 Prior to
60 __ Kodesh (Holy Ark)
61 Irish energy
62 Haughty
63 __ ends
67 Fall heavily
68 Deliberate bridge overbid
69 Obvious fact
70 Relative of the samba
71 Beheld
72 S.C. state tree
74 Irish sculptor
75 Troy, N.Y., campus

79 Deprive of
81 Province of South Africa: Abbr.
82 Trailer
84 More unctuous
85 "And Quiet Flows __"
86 Went under cover
87 Writer Shaw
89 Dawn
90 Overfamiliar
93 Laugh, in Lyon
95 Early priests
96 Arabian port
97 Pianist Peter
98 Timetable abbr.
99 "The __ is cast"
100 Droll one
101 Farm place

325 CLANK *By Bert Beaman*

ACROSS

1 Golden and teddy
6 Nom de plume
11 Kind of line
16 Bitter
21 Person's level best
23 Willing
25 Early movie
26 Ukulele's relative
27 Mil. decoration
28 Paint the __
29 Aquatic plant genus
31 Bed part
32 Popular street name
33 Jack's need
34 Vibrant sound
35 Attacks
37 Units of measure: Abbr.
39 Western resort
41 Pro athlete's escape hatch
44 Morays
47 Peculiar, in Glasgow
48 Bosom, in Madrid
49 Contort
50 Imaginary
52 Disagreeable one
54 Item for the Red Baron
57 __ march on
58 Bargain area
60 Kind of days
61 Insecticides
63 Calendar abbr.
64 Stones: Abbr.
65 Buffalo's relative
66 Start of a Yuletide poem
67 Region: Abbr.
68 Vaulted recess
69 Nanook et al.
71 Scout's daily do
72 Links cries
73 Obscures
74 Explosives
75 Emergency allotments
78 Hemingway
79 __ up (imprison)
80 Got the word
81 Show or flower
82 Flower parts
85 Mexican people
86 Punta del __
87 Kind of silver
88 Indian weights
89 Kind of nap
90 Not discovered: Abbr.
91 Hors d'oeuvre

92 Looks closely
93 Eminence
95 Like some garments
97 Grade-B era of good times
100 Nucleus
101 ... by (believes in)
102 Blood: Prefix
103 Early TV hero
105 Medit. port
106 Concorde, etc.
107 __ d'
109 Guaranteed
110 U.S. publisher
111 Flower parts
113 Present times
115 Palindrome start
117 Miss Hogg
120 Archeologist's find
121 Part of 74 Across
123 Cutter
124 Dan McGrew's love
127 Symbol of opulence
130 Certain Civil War figures

133 Defensive back, at times
134 Tryst
135 Ray
136 Lorna
137 Climbs in a way
138 __ incognita

DOWN

1 Brass __
2 Region of Greece
3 Tropical dog
4 Asian soldier
5 Fish-line parts
6 Altar boy
7 Kind of killer
8 Like: Suffix
9 Handsome one
10 Destroyer equipment
11 "Edie __ lady"
12 G-men: Abbr.
13 Choler
14 Looks after
15 Snitch
16 Arch supports

17 Second-century date
18 Network
19 Eur. country
20 Living quarters
22 Familiar pen name
24 Seaweed product
30 Firm contract
33 Carpentry tool
34 Churlish one
35 Yellow ochers
36 Dried
37 Divulges
38 Persuaders of a sort
40 Miss Loos
42 Turkish coins
43 Stepped on
45 Sure thing
46 Business executives
47 Gambling game
48 "__ evil"
49 Beaver, for one
50 Addicts
51 Val et al.
53 Moslem priests

55 North Sea port
56 Unyielding
59 Most curious
62 Bureau
67 Chisel or file
68 Cain's father
70 "Tell __ the . . ."
71 French painter
72 __ salute (greets, in a way)
76 Innkeepers' postings
77 __ del Fuego
78 Gone out
79 Checkbook leftovers
80 "Two __ are better . . ."
83 Pilgrimages
84 Stone slab
87 Scarlet or spring
88 Albert __, Nazi architect
91 Carry on
92 City map
94 Vestige
96 Works on edging

98 Stitchbirds
99 Zoo attractions
104 Good sailor's asset
107 Assembled
108 Mideast city
109 Rushing sound
110 Hackneyed
112 Paris area
114 Killer whales
116 European capital
117 Egyptian goddess
118 Fine fur
119 Can. province
121 High __
122 Concerning
123 Ride
124 Retreat
125 Redolence
126 Annapolis campus
128 Animal expert
129 Western Indian
131 Greek letter
132 After printemps

EYE-SQUINTING

By Maura B. Jacobson

ACROSS

1 With an __ (considering)
4 Revenge
11 Makeup item
18 Marble
21 __ and then
22 Does a cobbling job
23 Actuality: Fr.
24 Arab's toga
25 Scans
27 Daddy's girl
29 Toilet cases
30 Kuwait V.I.P.
31 Candid shots
32 Storehouses
33 Kind of store: Abbr.
34 Architect of St. Paul's
35 Post or Brontë
36 Hunting clue
37 South African
38 Insects
39 Vale's opposite
42 Carson et al.
43 "A tall __ a star to steer . . ."
47 Unfamiliar
48 Home and French
50 Partner of hemming
51 Kind of up or pot
52 Machinists' supports
56 "On __ and a prayer"
57 After-bath items
59 Baseballer Hank
60 Giggle
62 Stock and Common: Abbr.
63 Fastener
65 Daytime doings
67 Trespass
68 Oahu staple
69 Adult acorns
71 "Georgie Porgie, pudding __"
72 Delhi weight
74 Is on target
79 Kind of dance or lamp
80 Cooperstown's lake
82 Silkworm
83 Literacy conflict
84 Sacks: Abbr.
86 Scientist Louis and heirs
89 Oculist's item
92 Radar signal
93 Violinist Isaac
94 Dumfound
96 Slip back
97 Calif. Indian

98 In-group's secrets
100 Not taped
101 Spite
102 Stone slab
103 Skin or pearl
104 Well-deserved
105 Like a bump on __
109 "All men __ created . . ."
110 Arizona Indians
111 Constellation
112 Euterpe's realm
114 Sponsorship
115 Shoelace hole
116 Floe
120 Postscript: Var.
122 Icy downpour
123 Parseghian et al.
124 Of hearing
125 Panoramas
127 Words for a captive Samson
129 Keep __ on (watch)
130 Striking device

131 Say yes
132 Ivy clump
133 Sigma
134 Mascara targets
135 Agree
136 "What immortal hand __ . . ."

DOWN

1 "The Lady __"
2 All: Fr.
3 Confess
4 Cleo's maid
5 Bog
6 Covered with willows
7 Hotel guest
8 Choreographer __ Ailey
9 __-do-well
10 Dayan's state: Abbr.
11 Teheran native
12 Calyx leaves
13 Greeting-card word
14 Cockney foyers
15 Become defunct

16 U.S. Indian
17 Threads
18 Formosan capital
19 Away
20 Belt sites
26 Command to Fido
28 Banal writer
31 Pintail ducks
34 Anna May of films
35 Dido's alias
37 Whiz-__
38 Pastor's people
39 "All I want is __ somewhere"
40 Baltic capital
41 Poetic word
43 Counterfeits
44 Iowa
45 Spectators
46 Rolling and bowling
47 __ ends (uncertain)
48 Pro
49 Begin
52 City on a Korean map
53 Uses the mail
54 In __ (well-known)

55 Aid for Samson, perhaps
57 Bangkok native
58 Main artery: Prefix
59 Apply __ of paint (touch up)
61 Compass reading
64 Van Gogh complaint
66 Mirror foil
68 Decalogue word
70 Back nuisance
73 Rocket prefix
75 Fragment: Sp.
76 Go undercover
77 Robe sizes: Abbr.
78 Miffed
80 Harvest goddess
81 Refined guys
85 Reject rudely
87 Not as dense
88 Photog's request
90 Papa Dionne et al.
91 Overlays

92 Brass or rubber
95 Service point
97 __ best friend
99 After zeta
100 Restrict
101 Put to flight
103 Synopses
104 Torch container
105 Protozoa: Var.
106 Arsène et al.
107 Mate of Isis
108 Adorn
110 Reese
111 Prosthetic item
113 Rib: Prefix
114 Hebrew letter
115 Miss Bordoni
116 Hidden mike
117 Clio's sister
118 Barber's gear
119 Flirty look
121 Certain Scout
122 Drinks slowly
123 Lily plant
124 Con
126 Roman way
127 Suffix for polit or tact
128 Daughter of Cadmus

327 BRAINCHILDREN By James Barrick

ACROSS

1 Extreme
4 Dimensions
8 Volcanic rock
13 Bar fly
18 Early English coin
19 Bit of news
20 Grin and __
21 Arm bones
22 Invention of 1885
25 Root and ginger
26 Stage phone, e.g.
27 Entreat
28 Invention of 1620
30 Accelerates, with "up"
31 Tenebrae candle frame
33 Playing cards
34 Shea player
35 Mass: Suffix
36 Takes it easy
37 Grasslands
39 Diamond Lil's measurements
42 Sea bass
44 Borscht ingredients
45 Witticisms
46 Word of approval
47 Twin crystal
48 Engravers' tools
50 Wheel parts
53 Like juleps
54 Miscellanea
57 Old German coin
58 Of a hand part
59 Crockett's last stand
60 Truk island
61 Chemical suffixes
62 Invention of 1887
64 Miss Moreno
65 Tokyo, formerly
66 Environs
67 "__ the pity"
68 Corday's victim
69 Gill parts
71 Green stones
72 In a brusque way
73 Be of service
74 French painter
75 Motto, in Oviedo
76 Weight allowance
77 Bearings
78 Invention of 1868
82 Croatian city
84 River to the Rhine
85 Agree: Lat.
86 Vessel
87 Pier union: Abbr.
88 Spry, in Baza
90 Betrayed
92 City of Rumania
93 Invention of 1785
96 Part of a blucher
97 Kind of gravure
98 Leontyne
99 Invention of 200's B.C.
104 Unit: Ger.
105 Prohibits
106 River of England
107 Metric unit
108 Carriage for Cicero
109 Nineveh native: Abbr.
110 Neighbor of Ariz.
111 Chemical find of 1943

DOWN

1 Drop a lawsuit
2 Ancient galley
3 Dartmouth's home
4 Perch
5 Degree: Suffix
6 Invention of 1900
7 Beryl
8 Gumshoe
9 Cheer
10 Having bristles
11 Like the first stonecaster
12 Beer mug
13 Inner or test
14 Smell, in Toledo
15 Invention of 1888
16 Small plant parts
17 Adjusts
20 Ormoc and Moreton
23 Harvest goddess
24 Roman god
29 Army medal
31 Sharpens
32 Invention of 1824
36 More feeble
38 Wriggling
40 Starch: Prefix
41 Function
43 Does a garden job
44 Region of east Europe
47 Standish
48 Photos
49 Insipid
50 Invention of 1856
51 Zoo animal
52 Invention of 1868
53 Casino game
54 Bitter drug
55 Kind of recall
56 Of a grayish hue
58 Like some infections
59 Estate
62 Hindu goddess
63 Sal and chocolate
64 Invention of 1922
66 Blue or home
68 Half a ritual
70 Glades or more
71 Deride
72 Second showing
74 Language deviations
75 Invention of 1860
76 Mercury's shoes
77 Headwaiters, for short
78 Annexed
79 Of the dawn
80 Ancient vases
81 Set up a fund
82 Invention of 1891
83 "Rats!"
85 Sheltered
89 Jelly fruit
91 Electrical units
92 Curve
94 Made a hole-in-one
95 Spanish wax
100 Warning cry
101 Suffix for cash or cloth
102 Compass point
103 "The Second __"

328 TALE-BEARING
By Ruth N. Schultz

ACROSS

1 Sermon topic
4 Half a bullet
7 Jackie's former spouse
10 Certain carriers: Abbr.
13 Indian flour
14 Oslo girl's name
16 Alloy base
18 Radio time signal
19 Study for an exam
20 Pendant of a sort
24 Oil source
25 Welsh dog
26 Silver-tongued
27 Iceberg part
28 Profit margins
30 Antiquity
31 Cpl. or sgt.
32 Mid-season ballplayers
35 "Truth is the __ of time"
38 Scoffed at
39 Carney
40 Card game
41 Cleft, in Italy
42 Eur. country
43 State V.I.P.'s
49 Old draft org.
50 Dinner or strait
54 Boxer's need
55 Friend of Snow White
56 Cool
57 Hay machine
58 Fit to be tied
59 Regeneration
65 Down to __
66 Islamic devil
67 Pacific islands
68 Pocatello's state
69 Brynner et al.
70 Scottish county
71 Society girl
74 Swift and Voltaire
76 Least bit
77 Chutzpah
79 Topeka time
80 Scottish alder
81 Like Never-Never Land
83 Nearly-extinct animals
88 Candidate for a cleanup
91 Upward: Prefix
92 Brooklyn campus
93 Mary, Charles, etc.
94 However

95 Actress Russell
98 __-lirra
99 Marner
101 Upset a can or worms
104 Aid's partner
105 Sea birds
106 Vaccines
107 Hamlet words
108 Word to Gridley
109 Bevan's nickname
110 Bedford or Orleans
111 Egg or blood
112 Mss. men

DOWN

1 Kind of gown
2 Kind of type: Abbr.
3 Phone-book entry
4 Throw away
5 Original
6 Russian novelist's signature
7 Kind of dye
8 Layoff notice: Abbr.
9 Really!
10 Received, in Paris
11 Soften one's stand
12 English pantry
13 Not well-heeled man
15 Forty-niner
17 Lily
18 Initials on a barracks door
21 Fast-food places
22 Lem, for one
23 Warehousing: Abbr.
24 Advisory groups
28 Miss West
29 Fast plane
33 Its, in France
34 Mount for Hector
36 Shoelace job, in Phrygia
37 Certain cards
42 Cocktail-party offerings
43 Snead's burden
44 Merle
45 Two gentlemen's home
46 Bright fish
47 Network
48 Sinks, old style
51 Boxing name
52 __ Army of 1894
53 Gymnast Olga
54 Fled
57 Egyptian god
59 Architect I.M. and family
60 "Mary __ little . . ."
61 Handel work: Abbr.
62 Moral principles
63 Family member
64 Russian community
70 Certain U.N. worker
71 Hoopsters, at times
72 Size up
73 Poets Stephen and William
75 Venezia's land
76 Fruit, in Naples
78 Conservation org.
80 Hawaiian lavas
81 Free of any levy
82 Type of ship: Abbr.
83 Card game
84 Closed
85 Flower-bed area: Var.
86 Pools, in Scotland
87 Abrupt
89 Jewelry piece
90 Brazilian weight
96 Miss Bancroft
97 Certain records
99 Yegg's goal
100 Bridge-player's words
102 Pay dirt
103 Deal or hide

MANGLED MUSIC   *By Tom Mixon*

ACROSS

1 Red or per
5 Checkroom leavings
10 One monitoring a joint
15 What to put on Mame
20 Oriental nurse
21 Opera-going attire
22 Confirm
23 Spring singer
24 Hawser
25 Hollywood star in a Verdi opera
28 Indian of West
29 Russian city
30 Son of Ares
31 Poverty
32 Butterfly's beverage
33 Dwell on to excess
35 Chemical prefix
36 Right-hand page
38 Fairy
39 Discharge
40 Sing, but not operatically
41 Poetic time
42 Nothing
44 Legal right
46 Highlander
47 Blockheads
49 Rumanian city
53 _ de jambe
54 Covered
55 One counting calories
57 Patrick Henry, etc.
58 Quantity: Abbr.
59 Kind of training
61 Porn
62 "... so rare _ June?"
63 "No down _" (sales come-on)
65 Moon circles
67 Golfing woe
68 Actor Carrillo
69 Group of nine
70 Star, à la Variety
71 Mennonites
72 Christie story: Abbr.
73 Sea eagle
74 Admitting
76 Of a chemical
78 Relative of nix
80 Fibbers
82 Lehmann
83 Record again
86 Cauliflower or tin
87 Trumpeters
88 Succinct
89 Changed
90 _ wet (soaked)

92 Barnyard sounds
93 Binge
95 Numerical prefix
96 Frauds
97 N.Y.C. river
99 "_ a deal!"
100 In case
101 Part of an Agee title
102 Main artery
103 Trees
105 Bumpkins
106 _ room
107 On the _
108 Admiral's boat
110 Convoke
111 Heroic poem
114 Moslem princes
116 Declare
117 Bow-shaped
120 Writer Deighton
121 Range
122 Friends, in Tours
123 Like Alice's gown
124 "_ any drop to drink"
125 Donizetti opera introduced by stage star

130 Outside: Prefix
131 Eagle's nest
132 Clothe
133 River mouth
134 Food fish
135 Musical symbols
136 Frivolous years
137 Run-down
138 Prefix with cast or type

DOWN

1 Medit. tree
2 Wax operatic
3 French-pastry diva
4 Article
5 Promising one
6 Gem
7 Sounds of surprise
8 Grasp
9 Sound system
10 Army men: Abbr.
11 Pacific atoll
12 Newspaper section: Abbr.
13 Proves
14 Get a new tenant

15 Born's companion
16 Tennis stroke
17 Lessen
18 Certain racer
19 Chou _
21 Card for a seer
26 Aria popular in South, with "La"
27 Verdi heroine linked with Nick's wife
29 News item
34 Surrounded by
35 Common prefix
36 Transplant
37 Anon's partner
38 Silver, in Spain
40 Moslem judge
43 Turkish decree
44 Curtain
45 Nose or holiday
46 Essence
48 Erwin et al.
50 Opera company with muscle
51 U.S. Indians
52 Like _ (probably)
54 Warning to piano movers

56 Haven for a castaway
57 Condition: Suffix
59 Calabar or lima
60 Toasting word
62 True up
64 Only
66 Heights: Abbr.
67 Strikes hard
70 Bell sound
71 Go-betweens: Abbr.
72 Small bit
75 Oslo people
77 Boundary
78 Wife of Canio
79 Rowed
81 Hunter et al.
84 By itself
85 Does copy-reading
87 Ill will
88 Sharp
89 Beaux-_
91 Fruit-salad items
92 Farm units
94 Walleyed or turn
97 Clock hand
98 Alhambra's style

100 "But don't bring _"
102 Strauss heroine
104 Farming: Abbr.
105 Human or rat
109 Dispatch boats
110 Salad-oil bottle
111 Composer Edward
112 Small bird
113 Standouts
115 Basis for a scout badge
117 Gasoline or Allen's
118 Complete
119 Wear away
121 City ways: Abbr.
122 Imitates
123 Undisguised
126 Insect egg
127 Reading matter on an urn
128 Channel buoy
129 Western Indian
130 Time initials

330 I.D. CARDS By Eugene T. Maleska

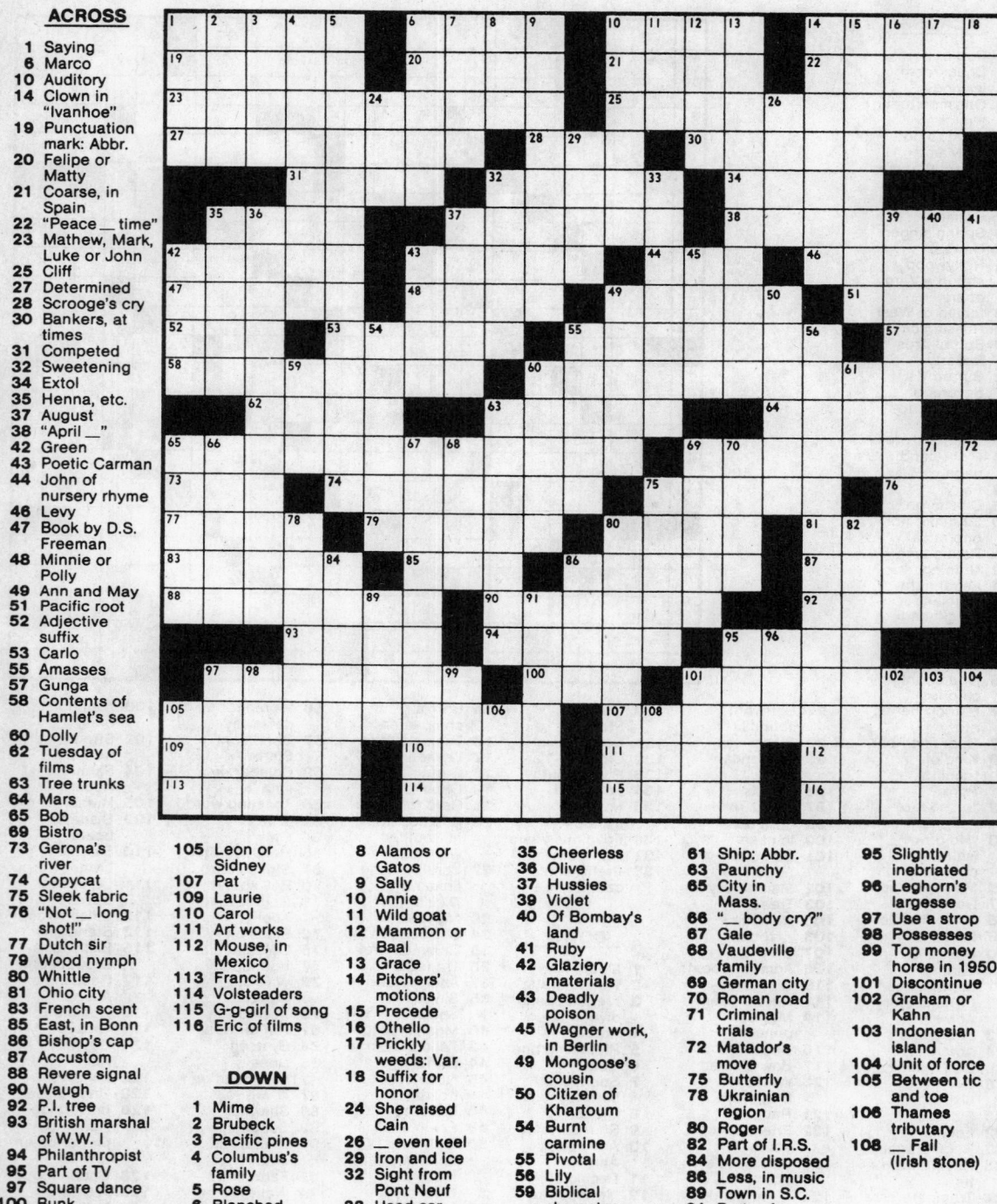

ACROSS

1 Saying
6 Marco
10 Auditory
14 Clown in "Ivanhoe"
19 Punctuation mark: Abbr.
20 Felipe or Matty
21 Coarse, in Spain
22 "Peace __ time"
23 Mathew, Mark, Luke or John
25 Cliff
27 Determined
28 Scrooge's cry
30 Bankers, at times
31 Competed
32 Sweetening
34 Extol
35 Henna, etc.
37 August
38 "April __"
42 Green
43 Poetic Carman
44 John of nursery rhyme
46 Levy
47 Book by D.S. Freeman
48 Minnie or Polly
49 Ann and May
51 Pacific root
52 Adjective suffix
53 Carlo
55 Amasses
57 Gunga
58 Contents of Hamlet's sea
60 Dolly
62 Tuesday of films
63 Tree trunks
64 Mars
65 Bob
69 Bistro
73 Gerona's river
74 Copycat
75 Sleek fabric
76 "Not __ long shot!"
77 Dutch sir
79 Wood nymph
80 Whittle
81 Ohio city
83 French scent
85 East, in Bonn
86 Bishop's cap
87 Accustom
88 Revere signal
90 Waugh
92 P.I. tree
93 British marshal of W.W. I
94 Philanthropist
95 Part of TV
97 Square dance
100 Bunk
101 Best approach

105 Leon or Sidney
107 Pat
109 Laurie
110 Carol
111 Art works
112 Mouse, in Mexico
113 Franck
114 Volsteaders
115 G-g-girl of song
116 Eric of films

DOWN

1 Mime
2 Brubeck
3 Pacific pines
4 Columbus's family
5 Rose
6 Blanched
7 Reeking
8 Alamos or Gatos
9 Sally
10 Annie
11 Wild goat
12 Mammon or Baal
13 Grace
14 Pitchers' motions
15 Precede
16 Othello
17 Prickly weeds: Var.
18 Suffix for honor
24 She raised Cain
26 __ even keel
29 Iron and ice
32 Sight from Pont Neuf
33 Used-car deals

35 Cheerless
36 Olive
37 Hussies
39 Violet
40 Of Bombay's land
41 Ruby
42 Glaziery materials
43 Deadly poison
45 Wagner work, in Berlin
49 Mongoose's cousin
50 Citizen of Khartoum
54 Burnt carmine
55 Pivotal
56 Lily
59 Biblical character
60 Lowed

61 Ship: Abbr.
63 Paunchy
65 City in Mass.
66 "__ body cry?"
67 Gale
68 Vaudeville family
69 German city
70 Roman road
71 Criminal trials
72 Matador's move
75 Butterfly
78 Ukrainian region
80 Roger
82 Part of I.R.S.
84 More disposed
86 Less, in music
89 Town in S.C.
91 Parts of records

95 Slightly inebriated
96 Leghorn's largesse
97 Use a strop
98 Possesses
99 Top money horse in 1950
101 Discontinue
102 Graham or Kahn
103 Indonesian island
104 Unit of force
105 Between tic and toe
106 Thames tributary
108 __ Fail (Irish stone)

331 CAPITAL PUNISHMENT · By Bob Lubbers

ACROSS

1 Writer Waugh
5 Binges
9 Made possible, old style
14 Marker
18 Hindu giant
19 Willow
20 Appear
22 African antelope
23 __ B'rith
24 Oversupply
25 Venezuelan noisemakers
27 Like a highwire act in Ghana
30 Golfing aid
31 Ruling system
32 __ cap for
33 Central points
35 Thing chosen up
36 French bridge
37 Square pegs, often
40 Scoria
44 Scottish terrier
47 Indian food treat
49 Much's partner
50 Dawn, in Italy
51 Boat hoist
54 Church giving
55 Stalag occupant
56 Latin-class word
57 Implement
60 Game warden
62 Barber's refrain
63 Bjorn of tennis
64 Approval sign
66 More harsh
67 Norwegian freighter
71 Like a clear night
74 Jeanne or Marie: Abbr.
75 Scottish negatives
76 Clothing
80 Choice fellow
81 Rapid __
83 Above, in Berlin
84 Employ a cockney
85 Moves slowly
89 Smells
90 Ocean bird
91 Greek letter
92 R.O.K.
95 Hunter of sky
96 Half: Prefix
98 Japanese port
99 African fox
101 Force
103 Askew
105 Ice, at times
109 Fighting Urbanans
112 Cook's meas.
114 Albanian fossil
116 Certain Formosan bank deposit
119 Fireplace fodder
120 __-bitsy
121 Common suffix
122 Dieter's standby
123 Toward shelter
124 Old hands
125 Petitions
126 African land
127 Parker of TV
128 Formerly, of old

DOWN

1 Mr. Eban et al.
2 Tilting weapon
3 Put into law
4 Nerve-minded Egyptians
5 Parliamentary toller
6 Finally
7 German: Abbr.
8 Shiny cloth
9 Big Board initials
10 Certain Isles
11 Learning
12 Fencing foil
13 French noble
14 Buses' ancestors
15 Places
16 Khatchaturian
17 Ignoble
21 French leapers of a sort
26 River known for its valley
28 Shortly
29 Space travelers
34 Make thinner: Abbr.
35 Copy, for short
38 Able
39 Here, in France
41 Rabbit fur
42 Love
43 Champion of dance
44 Songwriter Sammy
45 Winglike parts
46 Mountain goat
47 Wild dogs
48 Red Sea land
51 Irish accident coverage
52 On __ (carousing)
53 Certain word
58 Bury
59 Film studio
61 Certain Czech liberal
65 Lake near Tahoe
66 Araby V.I.P.
68 Blackthorns
69 Old coin of Siam
70 Six-pack's big brother
71 Recoiled
72 Pastry
73 Nautical term
77 Dugout
78 "Biggest little city"
79 Machine gun
82 "And things __ what . . ."
86 Comic-strip ailment
87 Continent: Abbr.
88 Traffic sign
93 Hangings
94 Suffix for fil or aer
95 Greek peak
97 Fools
99 Saws
100 Famous five
102 Neighbor of Ill.
104 Rice dish
106 Cockney rod
107 Deteriorates
108 Rendezvous
109 Long-range missiles
110 Celtic deity
111 __ wolf
112 Buster's dog
113 Reeled
115 Part
117 Affirmative
118 Call __ day

332 TIME PIECE *By Mary M. Murdoch*

ACROSS

1 Throat clearings
6 Prank
11 Vamoosed
15 U.S. President
20 Moroccan port
21 Military vacation
22 Union general
23 Signature of a general
24 River to the Rhone
25 City on the Rhone
26 Ex-Senator Sam
27 Blake's bright animal
28 Heinrich Heine's seasonal greeting
32 This, in Spain
33 Chooses
34 "... what she __ do or say ..."
35 Headland
36 __ en scene
37 Secular
39 Eggs
41 Native of Florence
45 Parlor plant
46 Chair part
49 Main course
54 Bishop Heber's greeting
59 "Long as there's __ that sets ..."
60 Coat part
61 Social group
62 Draw a bead on
63 Start over at golf
65 Roman 2010
66 German hall
68 Period
70 London gallery
71 Fence crossings
73 Lend a hand
75 Broth in Glasgow
77 John Jacob, formally
79 Music by Christian Sinding
83 Debase
87 Pottage receiver
88 Understand
89 Ship decks
94 In the know
95 __ Canals
97 Places
99 Opposite of pos.
101 Hank of baseball
102 Go off the path
104 Hen's charge
106 Puzzle
109 Auk genus
110 Christina Rossetti's greeting
114 Playground piece
115 Dawn goddess
116 Winglike
117 Honors in a way
118 Kind of doll
120 Burrows et al.
121 Blind as __
123 Fox of Africa
127 Preservationist's word
131 Get out of focus
132 Sheltered
136 Longfellow's greeting
141 Plenty, for short
142 Prickly plant
143 Secure again
144 __ the good
145 Court decree
146 "__ want to get well ..."
147 One who quotes
148 Harbor or White
149 O'Casey and Connery
150 Ringing sound
151 Vehicles
152 Noun suffixes

DOWN

1 Revolutionist's cry
2 Fasteners
3 German president
4 Callas
5 Machine gun
6 Necklace parts
7 Use a room freshener
8 Becomes wearisome
9 Continuously
10 Rage, old style
11 Gem mineral
12 Vichy premier
13 Does news work
14 __ pot (deteriorated)
15 Johnson of TV
16 Condescend
17 Seaweeds
18 Becomes acquainted
19 Dry periods
22 Doc
29 Comings and __
30 Quick as __
31 Mean dwelling
36 Prefix for hood or handle
37 Tenth-century Pope
38 Ancient citadels
40 Small wild ox
41 Rulers
42 Defeat
43 Hindu scripture
44 Irish tribe
45 Pliant
46 __ for words
47 Blood factors: Abbr.
48 Apportion
50 Gibes
51 Do over a framing job
52 Muse of poetry
53 Chemical compound
55 Danube city
56 Thread: Prefix
57 Isadora Duncan's curse
58 Physicist Enrico
64 Doers: Suffix
67 Word with roust and run
69 Italian river
72 Takes to court
74 Autocrats
76 Flea-market setting
78 Taj Mahal locale
80 Uppish folks
81 __ Arabia
82 Scottish moor grass
83 Outlays
84 __ house (free)
85 Up __
86 Loud outbursts
90 Petrarch's love
91 Gold braid
92 Use one's index finger
93 Hitches
96 French river
98 Stone pillar
100 __ whiz
103 Time period
105 Goose eggs
107 High notes
108 Members of a spectral type
111 "When __ lad"
112 Normand of silents
113 Florist's need
119 Chess ploy
120 Warn
121 Related
122 Marketgoers
123 Ref. book
124 Holiday locale
125 Buddhist scripture
126 Ruhr city
128 Giuseppe
129 Noun suffix
130 Indian hemp
131 Davis
132 "Green Hat" author
133 N.H. flower
134 __ nous
135 Antiseptics
137 Persians, etc.
138 Whales
139 Conceal
140 Hemingway

333 BEYOND THE LAW By Joseph La Fauci

ACROSS

1 Court's Evert
6 Zoroastrian
12 Stone pillar
17 In the __ (up to date)
18 Kind of energy
19 Do a sleuthing job
20 Case cracked by Mr. Dupin
23 Actual being
24 Word with de mer
25 Hawk parrot
26 Silas and family
27 Maiden-name word
28 Bonnie, to Clyde
29 Shrewmouse
30 Vetch seed
31 Besides
33 Word with silver or table
35 Cloth remnant
36 Sinatra's "Tony __"
40 Pasty
42 Perches
43 Welsh resort
44 Canary's kin
45 Excite
47 __ Ste. Marie
48 Large antelope
49 ". . . and bells on her __"
50 Come-on at bridge
51 Pyle
52 Anitra's forte
53 Blockhead
54 Venice's saint
55 Diamond standard
56 Finked
57 Isaac's mother: Var.
58 Pub drink
59 Like old jokes
61 Actor James
64 Everest's locale
66 English river
67 Add up
70 Before, in France
71 Write a p.s.
72 Salt tree
73 Dewey's way
74 Word for a girl
75 Confederate
76 Filmdom
78 Door sign
79 Chateaubriand novel
80 College girl
81 Delibes opera
82 Old English court
83 Miss Raisa
84 Asian grass
85 Branches
86 Indian weights
87 Francisco or Remo
88 "Once __ a . . ."
90 Thrash
93 Subject of Newton's law
97 Wrath
98 Sports tyro
99 Seaweed
100 Burst in rudely
105 Isolate
106 Ardent fan
107 Stock holdings
108 Greek letter
109 Harangued
110 Epigrammatic

DOWN

1 Small vessel
2 Necktie-party candidate
3 Teased
4 "__ had it!"
5 Billy Sunday offering
6 Ornament
7 Stamen parts
8 Take on again
9 Advantage
10 Norse goddess
11 Old shield
12 Where she sells sea shells
13 Small lake
14 On __ (tense)
15 Frown: Var.
16 Sheep
17 Agents
18 Do in, in a way
19 Fashionable
21 __ volatile
22 Issue
28 Reading for a gourmand
30 Traffic cop's advice
32 Partners of haws
34 Polynesian god
35 Flora's partner
36 Describe
37 Praying figure
38 Kind of pie or meat
39 Over
40 Concerning
41 Portico
42 Pelvic bones
43 Go at a fast clip
44 Dignified
46 Discover
47 Ship pilot's concern
54 Savonarola, e.g.
55 Writer Truman
56 Reacts to yeast
57 "__ and evening star . . ."
60 Like some paper
61 Caravan member
62 Sheeplike
63 Moisten the roast
65 Suburb of Minneapolis
67 Hemingway story
68 Utah town
69 Adjust
71 Of the dawn
72 Solar deity
73 Mine car
77 Closely-knit group
80 Narrowly triangular
83 French ruler
84 Fonteyn
85 Hardy
86 Robe for a femina
87 Southern bean
89 London oasis
91 Concur
92 Kind of production
93 Finished off a cake
94 "__ of your business"
95 Ludwig
96 Part of R and R
99 Perfume: Var.
101 Swearing-in words
102 Prefix for plop
103 Man's nickname
104 Novel about Ayesha

334 IMPORTANT PEOPLE By Marjorie Pedersen

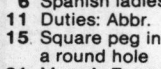

ACROSS

1 Tartan patterns
6 Spanish ladies
11 Duties: Abbr.
15 Square peg in a round hole
21 Mary A. Evans
22 Boot land
23 Mideast country
24 Moroccan port
25 Stephen Foster line
28 Holed up, as an animal
29 Taj Mahal site
30 Bolivian river
31 Cabinet member: Abbr.
32 Most-recent styles
33 Member of a family pride
35 Captivate
38 Campus figure
40 Insect often told to fly home
42 Eve's second
43 "_ hands make light . . ."
44 Clique
47 Play parts: Abbr.
48 Govt. news agency
50 A White House hostess
53 Pipe or officer
54 Ready-built
56 Lorelei, for one
58 Joanne of films
59 Part of a play
62 Attracts
64 Tough wood
65 _ the valley
67 Street hockey
69 Nobel physicist
72 Dispatch boat
74 Bell-like sounds
75 "_ or the Tiger?"
78 Arthurian wife
79 Roman 57
83 Words for a famed bank
87 Bonheur
88 Ethiopian weight
89 Holy terror
90 Laundry cycle
91 Blots
93 Opposed, in old West
94 Plant wall
95 Broadway chronicler
98 "_ a Camera"
101 Trinket
104 Simple sugars
105 Miss Claire
106 Saint _ (Jan. 20)
111 Hamburger sauce
113 Senegal port
115 Scheherazade, for one
117 Aim
118 Kiln
121 Plaintiff
122 Shape
123 Virginia _
125 Nasal twang
127 "Never had a _ nice"
129 Clam's relative
131 Queasiness
132 Polish patriot of U.S. Revolution
134 Minn. athlete
136 Miss Bayes
138 Summers, in Paris
139 Forward, in Rome
140 Merlin's mistress
144 Book for Bob Cratchit
145 Fume
146 _ blanche
147 Norse sea god
148 Cake parts
149 Boats
150 Game
151 Waste allowances

DOWN

1 Salem witch judge and family
2 Plaintive verse
3 Auto steering bars
4 _ bet (take on the field)
5 R.R. depot
6 Old novel price
7 Expiate
8 Home base for a yacht
9 Brew
10 Orchestra: Abbr.
11 Tanker
12 Bric-a-_
13 Natal city
14 Ship-plank's curve
15 Ailment
16 Incensed
17 Kind of fiction
18 Eve, e.g.
19 Small island: Var.
20 Young ones
26 Bluntly
27 Tristan's love: Var.
32 Norway canton
34 Ivory, in old Rome
36 Grammar case: Abbr.
37 Lamb or ham
39 Popular 1918 novel
41 Honshu city
45 Height: Prefix
46 Paris's Pont-_
49 Swiss river
51 Miss Sumac
52 Chess pieces: Abbr.
53 Greek letters
54 Bar order
55 Deprived
57 Maneuver for Kelly
59 Mary of films
60 Moth genus
61 Ignites, in England
63 Seawater ingredient
66 Good ship
68 Sea-trade org.
70 Thai money
71 Calif. town
72 Raggedy and Cape
73 Strives
75 Small child
76 Does weeding
77 Safecracker
78 Ideal
80 Coat slits
81 Publish
82 Particulars
84 Action
85 What Adam gave up for Eve
86 Church degree
92 Loud laugh
94 Foster girl
95 Relieves of
96 Two-toed sloth
97 Meadow saffron
98 "What _ to do?" (parent's lament)
99 Fire retarder: Abbr.
100 Singer Torme
102 Spree
103 Siouans
107 Ruth's mother-in-law
108 Strays
109 Hindu god
110 Greek group of W.W. II
112 Hawaiian fish
114 Prepare
116 Kind of man
118 Stars _ and screen
119 Crafty: Scot.
120 Ones who nag
122 Dervishes
124 Miss Ulric
126 Fire tender
128 Chem. unit
129 Does a farm chore
130 Author Norah
132 _ Mall
133 Eye part
135 Year segment
137 Ways: Abbr.
140 Pewter coin
141 Roman 700
142 Cry of contempt
143 Dine

335 BAR EXAM By Anne Fox

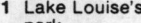

336 ECOLOGY SEMINAR *By Tap Osborn*

ACROSS

1 Looks over
6 Short jacket
12 Actress Jean
18 Let
19 Trail of note
20 One who declaims
21 9 A.M.: Ecology talk on winged life
24 Numerical ending
25 Excursion
26 Bar order
27 Hindu land grant
30 Calif. peak
32 In concert
35 Atomic form
38 10 A.M.: "Was it DDT?"
42 Expand
45 Site for vows
46 Reformer Jacob
47 Pathet __
48 Poker holding
49 Sound of despair
50 Proust's man with a way
52 Tendency
53 11 A.M.: "Debt to Winged Life"
57 Not pos.
58 Roster
59 Relative
60 Baker's need
64 Field missile
66 Verbose
68 Hobo, for one
70 Ruhr city
71 French river
72 Galway isles
73 Chinese pagoda
74 2 P.M.: "Heinous Crime"
80 Fugue composer
83 Unlucky one
84 Rome fountain
85 Gardner
86 Kind of verb: Abbr.
87 Precious
88 Old-hat
89 Strain
90 3 P.M.: "Age-old Problem"
95 Tacos' relatives
96 "Uhuru" author
97 God of fire
101 Copy, for short
102 Army member
103 Van der Rohe
105 Edible tuber
106 4 P.M.: "The Real Culprits"

114 Corroding
115 Eastern Christian
116 Grain disease
117 Like most fabrics
118 Took forty
119 Timid

DOWN

1 Fills up
2 Broad or wash
3 Hawaiian greeting
4 Lon __
5 Dark-colored
6 Student
7 TV's Johnson
8 Indian salt mixture
9 Golden or teen
10 __ a plea
11 Present
12 Food fish
13 Period
14 __ Harbor
15 W.W. II area
16 "... enough hang"
17 French ski city
22 Old Chinese unit of value
23 Templeton
28 Of bees
29 Forget-__
31 Turf
32 Asian range
33 Medium for Ade's fables
34 Poetic word
35 Cake feature
36 __ flint (go to any lengths)
37 Gold colors
39 Kind of chop
40 Massey
41 Praying figure
42 Free-load
43 Horses, at times
44 Feudal lords
49 Term-paper notation
50 Dress-shirt accessory
51 Flavorful, as a grape
52 Complain
54 Swim across: Lat.
55 Sultan's accumulation
56 Recumbent
61 Outfit
62 Jackie, boy actor of '30s
63 Made a swap
65 Eur. land
66 Ploy
67 Sand ridges
68 Like snow for the pure
69 Hindu title
71 Comedian Ole
72 Cub-scout leader
75 Jane Fonda film
76 Jots
77 Water animal
78 Down or pot
79 Gem
80 Deck posts
81 Buddhist monk
82 Burned up
87 Coolidge
88 Asian sheep
89 Tooth and hair
91 Marco Polo's China
92 Mild oath
93 Chinese warlord
94 With, in Paris
98 Latin dance
99 Cast member
100 Unpleasant
102 Carry on
103 Parcel out
104 In a pet
107 Greek letter
108 Tale
109 Photo abbr.
110 Spanish queen
111 "As ye sew so shall ye __"
112 Tourist's help
113 Curve

337 WHERE OH WHERE By Eleanor Tyler

ACROSS

1 Mme. de __
6 Recipe abbr.
10 "__ be!" (golly)
15 Milquetoast
21 Man, in Lille
22 Where de Valera governed
23 Ms. O'Grady
24 Room recess
25 Where a treasure hunt began
28 Gypped
29 Noisy bird
30 Halite source
31 Tree worker
32 Bonds
33 Machine part
34 Schubert specialties
35 Both: Prefix
38 Where Nicholas Nickleby rebelled
41 Watchdog org.
44 "State Fair" author
46 F.D.R. agency
47 Common verb
48 Courtly
50 Butt
52 Irritates
55 Samoan port
57 Medicinal drink
58 U.N. agency
59 Where an eagle dropped Gulliver
62 Recital pieces
63 Fuss
65 Word with step or way
66 Age group
67 William S. or Moss
68 Man or ape
70 Dwindle
71 Low sound
72 Indian badger
77 Dinghy, in France
78 Where Frodo destroyed the ring
82 Hard wood
83 Foot or toad
84 Classifieds
85 "Ave atque __"
86 Pain easers
88 Pisa's river
90 Colette novel
92 Winter woe
93 Old Tokyo
94 Sends back
98 Where Lorna was rescued
101 Time divs.
103 Demands
104 Shock
105 Art __ (1920's style)
106 Impair
108 1492 name
109 Goat-god
110 100 lbs.
112 Free-for-all
113 Criterion: Abbr.
114 Where Moll Flanders was born
121 Legal degrees
122 Whodunit awards
125 Gas-pump sign
126 Terza
128 Clergyman
129 French astronomer
130 Resounded
134 Big airport
135 Where Earnshaw gambled away his patrimony
137 Words of threat
138 Church area
139 Suit to __
140 Buy new guns
141 Yellowstone sight
142 Las Vegas openings
143 W.W. II craft
144 Kefauver

DOWN

1 Onetime V.I.P. in Iran
2 Fuss
3 Shot, shell, etc.
4 Discharging
5 "Vive __!"
6 Does a snitching job
7 Kinsman
8 Make a strong effort
9 Capitol unit
10 Capri's is blue
11 Squatty chest
12 Willows
13 Melon part
14 Osaka money
15 Library study space
16 Audibly
17 Tea cake
18 Where four undesirables were expelled
19 Declare
20 Herring color
26 Overwhelmed
27 Tell tales
31 Rug surface
34 "Zhivago" girl
35 Italian city
36 Ark's resting place
37 Where Tolstoy's prince was wounded
39 Choctaws, e.g.
40 British marshal
42 Miss Merrill
43 Some serves
45 Isis's father
48 Where Velvet won a race
49 Dos Passos trilogy
51 Turkey or fox
53 Tampered with a check
54 Fishline part
55 __ Arbor
56 Ballet step
57 Craggy hill
60 "__ meat is . . ."
61 Be revenged
62 Hell, in a mild oath
64 Melville book
67 Humble home
68 Parts: Abbr.
69 Where Scarlett led a reel
70 Some drs.
71 Otto's realm: Abbr.
73 French cleric
74 Where four animals won right to peace
75 Glutted
76 French river
79 Wedding words
80 Like a grown cornstalk
81 Teeming
87 Prompted
89 Country rtes.
90 Mountain pass
91 Seat or shot
92 What the Don does quiet
94 Corded fabrics
95 Depart
96 Where Rebecca was killed
97 Function
98 Artist Kingman
99 Spills, falls, trips, etc.
100 Sweet potato
102 Escorts
104 Talks on and on
107 Hodgepodges
109 Saucy
111 Flambeaux
114 Sadat's predecessor
115 Cheese dye: Var.
116 Man's opera wear
117 "Oklahoma" aunt et al.
118 Juicy fruit
119 __ equality
120 Green hue
123 Some pickles
124 Silly people
127 French city official
128 Word with simon
129 Soothe
131 Mountain pass
132 To be, in Nice
133 Milit. awards
134 Follow
135 Existed
136 "__ lost!"

338 ARRIVING AT 3.1416 By Elizabeth A. Yaro

ACROSS

1 Man at the helm
5 Holdup-man's need
10 Like a pinto
15 Town in Spain
16 Bête __
17 Relating to love
19 Old U.S. saying, with 88 Down
21 Marco Polo, for one
23 Fiber plant
24 Area under a fire grate
25 Thirty, in Paris
27 Certain athlete
28 Architect I.M.
29 Baltic people
30 Crafts' partner
31 Gyrates
32 Synthetic fiber
34 Sigh, in England
36 Laugh, in Rome
37 Pastor's home
38 __ hand (helps)
40 Part of TNT
42 Secret group
43 Hereditary ruler
45 Niagara Falls feature
46 Holy Land sight
49 Old zithers
51 Compass reading
52 Certain fruit stones
53 Notices
56 Words of unreadiness
58 Do ushering
59 Army units: Abbr.
60 Navy V.I.P.
61 Unattainable dream
63 Cheer
64 Arsène of crime tales
66 Teen problem
67 Embodiment
69 Sweetsop
70 Quilter's catchall
72 Hindu cymbals
73 Kind of seal
75 Ageless
76 "Iliad" king
78 Observers
81 Spanish ladies: Abbr.
82 Blew out a fuse

84 Candy, etc.
86 Sedans
88 "Ship __!"
89 Son of Seth
91 Certain crime
92 Cabbage dish
93 Bridge
94 Porticoes
96 __ the line
97 Former British P.M.
98 __ up (livened)
100 Of rhythmical beat
101 Zane Grey's was purple
102 Believable
104 One voicing contempt
107 __ in (get prompting)
108 Longhorn
109 Arab head cords
110 Shrimp dish
111 Genghis et al.
112 Dopes

DOWN

1 Arsenal in N.J.
2 Tibetan priest
3 All for __
4 "__ Bulba"
5 Do a clutch batting job
6 Washing is what __
7 Hue
8 __ pro nobis
9 "__ we forget"
10 Allspice
11 Practices a diet
12 To __ (exactly)
13 Fate
14 Plumbing problem
15 Abounding in willows
17 Unwilling
18 Tall tales
19 Horrify
20 Adherents: Suffix
22 Win by a __

26 Actor Claude
29 Lanchester et al.
31 Floor-smoothing machine
33 Millay and Ferber
35 Small kite
36 Counsel, old style
37 Woeful sound
39 ". . . unto us __ is given"
41 Unsettled
42 German: Abbr.
44 Of the warm regions
46 Carter
47 Intend, in Scotland
48 Stupid ones
50 "The __" (Oscar film)
52 Tea type
53 Mud volcano
54 Inference
55 New Yorkers
57 Chemical suffix

58 Fast plane
62 Remove hair
65 Kind of escape
66 Arab garments
68 Greek god
69 "Doe, __, a female . . ."
71 Nucleic acids: Abbr.
72 "Iliad" locale
74 Something, in Berlin
76 Call
77 Mankind: Ger.
79 Conks out again
80 Curly, Larry and Moe
82 Formed
83 People writing the letter "i"
85 Villainous look
86 Salad gelatin
87 Extreme
88 See 19 Across
90 "Honi __ qui . . ."
93 Fatty secretion
95 Old brocades

98 Type size
99 Office unit
100 Virginia willow
101 Happy or stick
103 Month: Abbr.
105 Essence
106 Turkish title

339 RAPID TRANSIT *By Frances Hansen*

ACROSS

1 Nom de plume
6 Eared seal
11 Heat standard of sorts
16 Clean or chimney
21 Jargon
22 Aspic: Fr.
23 Eat away
24 Wash. zoo star
25 Viper
26 Urges along
27 Electron tube
28 Famous marbles
29 Western sight
32 High as __
33 __ many (that last drink)
34 Degree for a NASA worker
35 Pip-pip
36 Stretched one's neck
37 Farragut's advice
42 Conducted
43 Clean a pipe
47 Writer Talese
48 Certain notebooks: Abbr.
49 Composer Vittorio
51 Breathed out
53 Start of the vowels
54 Shapeless dress
56 Siouans
60 Nile-source explorer
61 Decline
63 Relatives of T-bars
66 Minor official
67 Heavy books
68 Order to a marching group
71 "Zhivago" girl
72 "__ was saying"
74 Actor Erwin
75 Article
76 Cockney coin
78 Observation by Davidson
83 N.Y. lake group
85 Iowa college
86 Owned
87 Teachers' org.
88 "Exodus" author
89 Processes food in a way
94 Rulers
98 Colosseum walkways
100 "... in __ ob cotton"
101 Culbertson
102 Nero's courtyards
103 Summer months
104 __ possum
105 "And __ take the low ..."
107 Famed Egyptian stone
109 Small bird
111 At all
112 Kind of ear
113 Admiral or guard
114 Asian gift to U.S.
116 Military credo
122 Crusoe's man
124 Broad bean
125 __-Magon
126 Australian sorcerer
131 Actress Elissa
132 Snail's reply to whiting, perhaps
136 Loosened
137 Bullshot ingredient
138 Don Juan's forte
139 Miss by __
140 Part of an act
141 As red as __
142 __ Cerberus (bribe)
143 Miss Thompson
144 Chinese factories
145 Ploys
146 Bottomless pit
147 Work on a pie crust

DOWN

1 Place to remember
2 Put the __ (suppress)
3 __ course
4 Secret or press
5 In a way
6 Old Russian police
7 Concisely
8 Hilo greetings
9 Colorful tree
10 Gypsum
11 "O is __ then? My duty all ended"
12 Awn
13 "Camptown Races" refrain
14 Iceland epic
15 Look for
16 Piece of asparagus
17 Whiting's plea to snail
18 Diesel, e.g.
19 Worked on copy
20 Like most windows
30 Moulin color
31 Ways: Abbr.
36 Between B and F
38 Took on cargo
39 Root or Yale
40 Lubitsch
41 River isle
43 Take five
44 Montreal player
45 Polite interruption
46 Order to a short-order cook
50 Ode words
52 Diminish
53 Subside
54 "__ 'A' Train"
55 Bad German place
57 Praying figure
58 Deserve
59 Red deer
62 Autumn pear
64 Brown heron
65 Little Sir
66 Give rise to
69 Mistress Nell
70 Querying sounds
73 Baghdad native
77 Religious art pieces
78 Warble
79 Kind of puncture
80 Parlor piece
81 Variety of nut
82 Writer Leon
83 Topic: Abbr.
84 New Guinea people
90 Lazy one
91 Economic org.
92 Minneapolis suburb
93 Aleppo's land
95 Johnson of TV
96 Rio girl
97 German basin
99 Opposite of WNW
104 Few, in Paris
106 Lawless avenging group
108 In reserve
110 Child's word
111 __ on the back
112 Inning situation
114 Spanish dictator
115 TV actor Hal
117 Scholars' benefactor
118 Doodle-Dandy one
119 German subs
120 Sagging
121 Take __ (scold)
122 Mrs. Browning's dog
123 Assistants
127 Candle or holiday
128 Take for __
129 Chef Child
130 "__ a drink!"
132 Match-king Kreuger
133 Papuan isle
134 Senor's house
135 B'way signs

340 COARSE CODE By Alfio Micci

ACROSS

1 Actuality
5 "__ crowd of ... daffodils"
10 Separated
15 Baba
18 "__ with a View"
20 Kind of boom
21 Taste
22 Gypsy
23 Rirosyng
26 Hair quantity
27 Words to a French sweetheart
28 Spanish relative
29 Family member
30 Assess
31 Compass point
32 Sup
33 Ho Use
36 Actor Hudson
38 Norse goddess
40 New Deal initials
41 Finnish lake
42 Celebrity
44 Entertain
46 Ustinov and Falk
50 Gymnastic sport
53 Wagnerian role
54 Large deer
57 "Of and the River"
61 Single
62 Glacial ridges
65 __ colony
66 Protuberance
68 Star in Cetus
70 Chemical suffixes
72 Play part
73 Weary
74 Book-jacket item
76 Logarithmic unit
78 Scottish sundowns
80 French soul
81 "Upon a time ..."
84 Followed
87 "L'__ d'Amore"
88 Excess
91 East Indian tree
92 Graf __
93 Brusque
96 Town near Salerno
99 Wane
102 Inside dope
104 Eucalyptus secretion
106 Roo Ms

111 Land mass: Abbr.
113 Title
114 Certain pistol fodder
115 Org.
116 Hereditary factor
117 Armed-forces newcomer
119 Fuss
120 Pocposyket
123 Footlike part
124 Instrument for Casals
125 Greased
126 French bakery item
127 Dutch town
128 Our, in Munich
129 Smith and Greenaway
130 Germ

DOWN

1 Dell denizen
2 Musical passages
3 Join
4 Roman wear
5 Buness
6 Aesop's grapes
7 Ms. Dvorak
8 Amplitude
9 "Lights! Camera! __!
10 Peer Gynt's mother
11 Do a grammar stint
12 Skirt
13 Physicist Bruno
14 Attempt
15 Fleet
16 One who pillages
17 Obstruct
19 Famed aunt
24 Horse color
25 Time span
30 Remove soap
33 Against
34 Wisdom
35 Green shade
37 Kafir people
39 Electrical unit
43 __ the wrong way
45 Insect study: Abbr.
47 Possessions
48 Fietoillds
49 Shade tree
51 Barnyard sound
52 Generation, for one
54 Dressing-table item
55 Bast-fiber tree
56 Late Show, often
58 N.Z. parrot
59 Eskimo boat
60 Singer Mel
63 Lack of vigor
64 Newsroom worker
67 Woodwind
69 Fresh-water protozoans
71 More than one: Abbr.
75 Section of L.A.
77 One's image, for short
79 Hit initials
82 __-Tin-Tin
83 Metric units: Abbr.
85 Kind of welding
86 Covering network
89 Roof ornaments
90 Honor card
94 Freshen up
95 Adriatic port
96 Fire or narrow
97 Like some handbags
98 Resist
100 Portend
101 Luzon people
103 Olaf's capital
105 __ on (victimized)
107 Tree
108 Saw, file, etc.
109 English woodpecker
110 Underworld group
112 Remaining
117 Cunning, in Britain
118 Auditors: Abbr.
120 Needle: Prefix
121 Hebrew measure
122 Last: Prefix

341 DO-IT-YOURSELF By William Lutwiniak

ACROSS

1 Communicates in a way
7 Clever
12 Circus member
16 Celtic searobber
21 Grain bristle
22 Of hair
23 Come into view
24 Invierno month
25 *
29 Card game
30 Produces
32 A.L. player
33 Dairy animals
37 Famous last words
38 Footloose one
39 Sesame
40 _ dictum
42 Diminutive ending
43 Reservoir outlet
48 Passover ceremony
49
55 Inhabitant: Suffix
56 Elms and oaks
57 Word for a weak infield
58 Make happy
59 Black: Lat.
60 Solitary
61 Is footloose
62 Miss Bow
63 Greek letters
64 Cafe-table leavings
65 _ nuit
66 Word with full
67 Reconnoiter
68 Chemical ending
69
71 Large vessels
72 Cacophony
74 Holbrook
75 Port of Morocco
76 Windsor or Vernon
78
83 Cartographic item
86 Wine pitchers
87 Badgers
88 Mecca people
89 Tijuana money
90 Catface
91 Crabby
92 Tête-_
93 Life and gravy
94 S.A. toucan
95 Reporter's query
96 Interference
97 Whether _
98 Night before
99

101 Rustic crossover
102 Abandons hope
104 Gardner
105 Part of the hand
106 Hill-dweller
107 Chair panel
109 Wild goat
112 N.C.O.'s
113 Coiffure
116 Luster
117 Resident of Apia
119
121
127 Dye
128 Tropical tree
129 Plane, in France
130 Eden
131 Wails
132 Recuperate
133 Made tracks
134 Alphabetized

DOWN

1 Untrained
2 "Exodus" man
3 Morse symbol
4 Somewhat: Suffix
5 Indian of West
6 Dinnerware item
7 Estranged
8 Mirabile _
9 French pronoun
10 French winter resort
11 Organ effects
12 Outlandish bit of luck
13 Recluse
14 Ages and ages
15 _ Darya
16 Running a temperature
17 U.S. dramatist
18 Warm-sea fish
19 U.S.S.R. city
20 Took a cab
26 Do handwork
28 Reason
31 Swear
33 Having ribs
34 First coed college in U.S.
35

36 Dutch masterpieces
38 Red, to Caesar
41 Gaelic
43 Desolate
44 Plant fiber
45
46 Roman hall
47 Fermenting agents
49 Ascended
50 Times of day
51 Native of Qishm
52 Caesar's was Julius
53 Casaba, e.g.
54 "Ah, me!"
59 Port of Ghana
62 Carne's partner
65 Alpine wind
66 Social units
67 Is mournful
69 Wire measures
70 Mountain passes
71 Swiss card game
73 Alamogordo's county
75 Old stringed instrument

76 Figured expenses
77 Niche
78 N.Z. native
79 Iron, in Bonn
80 Port of Brazil
81 Garbo
82 South American
84 Arthurian locale
85 Circus harbingers
87 Beer and ale
89 Doors, in Lyon
91 Soho domestic
92 Up, in baseball
93 Piffle
95 _ prohibition
96 City of Georgia
99 Fits of temper
100 Noisy outburst
103 "_ my glove"
105 Ear part
107 Queen of _
108 Bicycle part
109 Western resort

110 Have _ of one's own
111 Sweetie
113 Bumpkin
114 Lily plant
115 Winnie _ Pu
116 Snick and _
117 To-do
118 Atlantic pact
120 German pronoun
122 Egg cells
123 Rocky height
124 Liable
125 Whopper
126 Shaver

342 HONK HONK *By Jack Luzzatto*

ACROSS

1 Stubble or Vandyke
6 Swine of a special breed
13 Gearshift-car pedal
19 Hard feelings
20 Large cupboard
21 Balzac
22 Excessive road toll, in a way
24 Observer of rules
25 Amos of baseball
26 Draws closer, in a race
27 Vertical pipes
29 Wheel to impart motion
30 Chess pieces
31 Fried, in Spain
32 Go __ (worsen)
33 Instance
34 Prayer book
36 Hardships
37 Merchandise
38 Powders
39 Lake in Egypt
40 The bill
41 Best part of life
42 Feudal underling
43 Kind of look or places
47 Jacks and jimmies
48 Hymn of praise
49 Posh area of Phila.
50 Eskimo knives
51 Stood the gaff
52 Army drill directors
53 Johnny Secesh
54 Commit turnpike arson
56 __ de guerre
57 Tightrope hazard
59 Vimy and Oak
60 Highway marking
61 Carries out
62 Shooting fields
63 Quarrel
64 Hankerings
65 Woven
66 Wells's friend
67 Go wrong
68 Riffled the pages
69 Cat for scent
70 Word with key or corner
73 Ashy
74 Penalizes
77 Brusque
78 Like monsoons
79 Composer Berg
80 Right angle
81 Miss Blyth
82 Medit. trees
83 Elusive chalice
84 District
85 Sanity
87 Hell on wheels
90 Yield of some tea leaves
91 Fire-truck team
92 Betel palms
93 Makes time
94 In cipher
95 Trims

DOWN

1 One who heckles
2 Knock, knock!
3 German exclamations
4 Rumpus
5 Acceleration contest
6 Good used car, e.g.
7 Maine college town
8 Foreign reps.
9 Smear: Var.
10 Sacred symbol
11 Iris perfume extract
12 Yellowstone sights
13 Notes in harmony
14 Tennis shots
15 French one
16 Model for junior
17 Fold
18 Mercury
19 Parallelogram
23 Scottish salmon traps
28 Letters
31 Takes pictures
32 Thickens the jam
33 Mystic system
35 Lets fall
36 Rebelled
37 Admonished
39 Invented
40 Forests of Siberia
41 Old battle weapon
42 Pioneer sci-fi man et al.
43 Danish islands
44 Ahead at the tape
45 Merchant of Venice
46 Boss backers
47 Having a sod cover
48 Rich cakes
49 Combined
51 Rodeo rider
52 Full of grassy herbage
54 Butter, in France
55 Suggested obliquely
58 Knowing
60 Decoys
62 Not kidding oneself
63 Act of preying
65 Of good lineage
66 Auto-race climax
68 French opera composer
69 Three-dimensional
70 Neckpieces
71 Adjust for peak performance
72 Fancy
73 Fire: Prefix
74 Put a bet on
75 Spanish Helens
76 Smeltery remains
78 Sugar and walking
79 __ Triomphe
82 Old U.S. car
83 Alumnus
84 Land: Lat.
86 Take to court
88 Sky observatory: Abbr.
89 Pitcher's concern: Abbr.

343 RATE SETTING By A.J. Santora

ACROSS

1 Resembling the seals
7 Actor Cronyn
11 Mme. __ of Vietnam
14 Secured
18 Mesabi yield
19 The end of __
21 Last Supper painting
23 Pot for stew
24 Hit show of 1955
27 School or collar
28 Kiddy's former TV fare
30 Irritate
31 Florida Indians
32 Kind of ego
33 Spoon River state
35 TV network
36 Short-tempered
38 Sun. talk
40 Insecticide
41 Compass point
42 Calls a number
45 "__ was saying"
46 Come __ decision
48 Shaping tool
50 In __ (quickly)
52 As __ a beet
57 Vibration
60 Elite group with Southern accents
66 One-seeded fruits
68 Aussie call
69 Be troubled
70 "__ it to me!"
72 Overseas airline
73 Cage birds
75 Cowboy's PX
78 Words from Caesar
80 Snake
83 Lao-__
84 Prohibit, in law
85 Yankee or Cub, e.g.
90 Glossary entry
94 N.Y. time
95 Detect
96 Kind of phone
97 Requires
100 Ones who overcharge
102 Nero Wolfe, for one
106 Skilled
107 Founded: Abbr.
108 Public notices
112 Ranting one
115 Zodiac animal
117 Waters: Abbr.
120 Kind of headline
121 Greek letter

122 Knicks' league
125 Invite
127 Foundry worker
130 Fabulous bird
131 Ferret's cousin
134 Sample
136 Kind of metrics
137 Calif. wine district
138 John Fowles's lady
142 Soon
143 Spanking, e.g.
144 Suffix for fore or ut
145 Cupid
146 __-ease
147 Hypodermics
148 Piles up bills
149 Kind of ball
150 French composer
151 "Gunsmoke" star

DOWN

1 Ban
2 Luxurious train unit of old
3 Refrigerated
4 Unconscious state
5 Pancakes, in Southwest
6 __ huff (went away mad)
7 Mata, the spy
8 Loosen a fastener
9 In a timid way
10 Go wrong in the process
11 Coll. athletic group
12 Matisse
13 Vast
14 Mountain wind
15 City in Pa.
16 Retarding
17 Light color
18 Old musical prelude
20 Miss Moorehead
22 __ as the hills
25 Desert rest
26 Audubon symbol
29 Squelches
34 Recognize

37 Reel, in Scotland
39 Campus military org.
43 S.S.R. country
44 Shifty one
47 Cheering, as a crowd
49 Usurps, as power
51 Counting-out word
53 Common abbr.
54 Batman and Robin
55 Slip __ (err)
56 Trapshooting
58 Kazan
59 Gun girl
61 Venturi of golf
62 That, in Spain
63 Hankerings
64 Certain thief
65 Boston fish dishes
66 Dogpatch creator
67 Musical key
71 Retained
72 Hunter and Novak
74 Droop

76 Nine-eyes
77 Neptune et al.
79 Inducement
81 Indian hemp
82 Annoy
86 King or Norman
87 Consumes
88 Staggering
89 U.S. Indians
91 Nest or goose
92 Extinct bird
93 Silent
98 Summer time
99 R.R. depot
101 Writer Ambler
103 Jackie or Mt.
104 Thought
105 Steel beam
109 Chewy candies
110 Alkaloid compounds
111 Relatives of tangents
112 Speed initials
113 Words of immediacy
114 Table wine
116 Bone: Prefix
118 Actor Anthony

119 Lyrical verse
123 Italian bowling
124 On land
126 Resin tree
127 Miss Dallas
128 Friend, of note
129 Log worker
132 Nice guys
133 Crazylegs Hirsch
135 Conk out
137 __ plume
139 __ dixit
140 Reo or Saxon
141 Querying word
142 I love: Lat.

LOCKING IN
By Diana Sessions

ACROSS

1 Furniture style
5 Resort
8 Neglects
13 Fender dent, e.g.
19 Bunkum
21 Page number
22 Lacking effect
23 Miami divider
24 Key for a certain song
26 Service org.
27 Wash or blanket
28 Approve
29 Concept
30 Carson
31 Dear people of letters
33 Sycophants
35 Sicknesses
36 Greek commune
37 Preliminary races
39 Pigeon material
40 Big blow
41 Trifled
42 Ginger or dress
43 Propelling pole
44 Two-handed game
45 Plague constantly
46 At __ (anyway)
48 Orion's pride
49 Mexican state
53 Cuba's neighbor
56 Globetrotter of basketball, e.g.
58 Opposite of vert.
59 Trespass
60 Finch's order
61 Journey
62 Short or second
63 __ around (fooling)
64 Agitate
65 Great amount
66 Switch-engine operators
67 Marmalade fruit
68 White-tailed eagle
69 Prolonged feuds
70 Jailer
71 Plains dwellings
73 Ditch, in England
74 Painful sound
75 See __
76 "__ yellow ribbon . . ."
77 Chou's associate
78 "If I were a __ man"
81 French composer and family
84 Upper-classman: Abbr.
85 Hard resin
86 Leavings
88 Like Burn's syne
89 Kind of rug
90 Compulsion
92 Indian word with "big"
93 __-Magnon
94 Orangutan
95 Feed
96 Erwin of films
98 Saint of films
99 Mayor's stock offering
102 Kickoff speaker
104 Salad plant
105 Greek letter
106 Place for Cohan's keys
107 Words of assent
108 Hold deliberations
109 Petition
110 Declaration signer Stone

DOWN

1 Sniper's spot
2 Michaelmas and upsy
3 Bottom-line horse
4 Fellow
5 Ethereal, to poets
6 Post-Easter fete
7 Certainly
8 How poor singers sing
9 Teton peak
10 "Now __ me down . . ."
11 Lizzie or hat
12 Gatherings
13 "Power Broker" subject
14 "__ lovely day today"
15 "__ 'em!"
16 Absenteeism of a sort
17 "__ Goes By"
18 Marked by sulkiness
20 Like tartar steak
25 Slothful
28 Sharif
32 Valiant
34 Louver
35 Displays of skill
36 Rio matron
38 Quick
40 Ship utility worker
41 Rail tunnel
44 Revolutionary War beverage
45 Up-to-__
47 Enzyme: Suffix
48 Celtic or Knick
49 Bell sound
50 Dwindled
51 Bring about by force
52 Islands off Scotland
53 Fate
54 Undiminished
55 Quintuplet Dionne
56 Strong desire
57 Neighbor of Wisc.
60 Body of water
61 Resembling Twiggy
63 Belgian city
64 Arrow poison: Var.
66 Scout's good work
67 Warranto or Vadis
69 Churchill symbols
70 June nest egg
72 Incite
74 Give the __ (dismiss)
76 Hope-chest items
77 Adult filly
79 Swift animal
80 Keep motionless, as a ship
81 Hanger-on
82 Iridescent glassware
83 Famous London name
84 Former Irania ruler
85 John or Paul
87 Flats' stand-in
89 Locations
90 Duplicate
91 Technique
94 "I __ we adjourn"
95 Tokyo body
97 German conjunction
100 Poets' word
101 Ill. city
102 Br. titles
103 Make a choic

ACROSS

1 Sound of sorrow
5 Prefix for medic or graph
9 Monastery head
14 Colorless
18 N.Z. native
19 __ Ike
21 Show of temper
22 Ham or Shakespearean
23 Moa or dodo
25 Orts
27 Hero for Hero
28 Brine feature
30 Tourney drawing
31 Bakery workers
32 Military body
34 Kind of wave
36 Doer: Suffix
38 Hamlet
41 N.B.C. parent
43 Paris play area
46 Draws nigh, to poets
50 Rage
51 Early-bird's victim
52 "Rats!" et al.
55 African antelope
56 Explanatory bit of Latin
58 Babylonian hero
59 Noted violinist
60 Sleekened
62 Old-time blades
64 __ of tears
66 Contemporary of O. Henry
67 Antonio or Juan
68 Mediocre mark
69 __-destruct
70 Lodge doorkeeper
71 __ in the bud
72 Oriental weights
74 Kind of charity
75 Old car
76 Visualizations
79 Lip
80 Carnegie, for one
83 N.E.A. and N.C.A.A.
85 Musical prince
86 Ostentatious success
88 Deli loaf
89 Elec. measure
91 Like a fork
93 Charged particle
94 Camel's bane
96 Impair
98 Summer drink
99 Edible root
102 Entre __
104 Suffix for cyclo

105 City in Spain
106 Is successful
108 Hendricks of baseball
110 Strike out
112 Relative of a rectory
114 Of late
115 Utah
118 Schubert opus
119 Common refrain
120 Nero or Ivan
121 Eastern ruler
122 Devotee
123 __ avis
124 Indians of West
126 Axis supporter
128 Art movement
131 Muse
134 Mao __-tung
137 Bathes
139 Venice taxi
144 Ers
147 Etuis
149 Regions
150 Shade of blue
151 Castle
152 Smooths
153 Pause
154 Earth goddess
155 Squabble
156 Arrangement: Abbr.

DOWN

1 __-Coburg
2 Greek letter
3 Cheshire cat's residue
4 Rani
5 Father: Prefix
6 Vestment
7 Reformer Jacob
8 Lot
9 Fore's follower
10 Spill the beans
11 "... and __ makes three"
12 Heraldic borders
13 Links location
14 Farm unit
15 Gold or shooting
16 Toad moves
17 Time periods: Abbr.
18 Allen or Brooks
20 Run in neutral
22 Grow together
24 Near the middle: Abbr.
26 Tuscany city
29 Recorder input
33 Walked on
35 Nuisance and sales
37 Hot __
38 Guinea corn
39 Amah
40 "The __" (Douglas book)
42 Salad green
44 Army newcomer: Abbr.
45 Well-tempered instrument
47 "What __ you?"
48 Mars
49 More treacherous
50 Dandies
51 Of greatest extent
54 Brats
57 Prefix for vision

61 Slippery one
63 Newt
65 Silkworm
70 Sisal and istle
73 __ rule
77 Adits
78 __ of consent
79 Wound, as thread
81 Box-score items
82 Ester of an acid
84 Put on
86 Tendon
87 After F.D.R.
89 Common Latin word
90 School __
92 June words
95 Thirty: Fr.
97 Craze
100 Lily
101 Indo-European: Var.
103 Barflies
105 Admit
107 Evening: It.
109 Appoints as an agent
111 Spade or Hill
113 Transport
116 Turbine part

117 Part of Q.E.D.
125 Stone marker
127 Pueblo Indian
129 Metal tag
130 Name on a sample form
131 Cobh's land
132 Ways: Abbr.
133 Rat __
135 Cooking direction
136 "__ homo"
138 Ooze
140 Crockett
141 Suffixes for sugar
142 Religious period
143 Dolt
144 Popular car for commuters
145 Holiday, for short
146 "For __ a jolly ..."
148 Genetic initials

346 CHANGING DIRECTIONS
By Emanuel Berg

ACROSS

1 Swindle
6 Actor Luther
11 Hindu music
15 Sweetsop
19 P.I. arrowroot
20 Sierra __
21 Ovines
22 Dividend period: Abbr.
23 Nightclub billing
26 Coffee makers
27 Hurricane center
28 Ball team
29 Germs
30 French seraph
31 Power org.
32 Stabilizing agent
34 Color
36 Belles-__
40 Dutch painting family
41 Source: Abbr.
42 "When __ out to sea"
43 Defense org.
45 Short stalk
47 Asian weights
50 North Carolinians
53 Manifest
55 Beat the __
56 Skin woes
57 Deadly snake
59 Israeli airline
60 Biblical judge
61 Heads: Fr.
63 Cadmus's daughter et al.
65 Weather forecasting: Var.
67 Part of a nostalgic plea
71 Of an earthy pigment
73 Kind of glance or stroke
74 Oodles
76 Part of K.K.K.
77 Roberts
79 Italian sculptor
82 Capri and Bali
84 Type of recruit
85 Thorny
87 __ ear (ignores)
89 Hersey's town
91 Brazilian port
93 Carry on
94 "I could __ horse"
95 Time periods
97 Made of wood
99 "To __ to keep the geese"
101 "Ivanhoe" lady
103 Extra hairwash
105 Chaney

106 Kind of sauce or luck
107 Most meager
109 Celtic corn god
111 Curie
114 Of an age
115 Words between one and another
118 Allot
119 Maori demon
120 Martha and family
121 Diving birds
122 Anglo-Saxon letters
123 Depend
124 Design for a fresco
125 Native of Lund

DOWN

1 Gray or night
2 Famous chemist
3 Recent
4 French vineyard
5 Lana or Nat
6 Danish measure
7 Star in Cygnus
8 Cabin material
9 Make possible
10 Entertains
11 Moderating
12 Raise __ (cause swelling)
13 Mil. title
14 "__ goes by"
15 Fish tanks
16 Reform
17 Brando's dance
18 Prefix for a poison
24 __ Creed
25 Card game
31 __ of the century
33 Of a group of Jewish scholars
35 Comedian Johnson
36 __ Grey Chaplin
37 Lunar-year word
38 What a certain answer does
39 Dr. Jonas
41 Old coin of Europe
44 Thrice: Prefix
46 Heaped
48 Secular
49 Agile
51 Chemical alkaloid
52 Makes, as a putt
54 Coagulates
58 Namely
60 Late film idol
62 Nose about
64 Mideast V.I.P.
66 Nodules
68 Engravers' tools
69 Yoga position
70 Election-night data
71 Gumbo
72 Attired
75 Asian pact
78 Red __
80 Predecessor of la
81 Hospices
83 Tunisian port
85 Punjab river
86 Maison __ (French jail)
88 Stone pillars
90 Acupuncture gear
92 Sunday-paper section
96 Tear: Sp.
98 Snare
100 Surrender symbols
101 Semantic unit
102 Like biremes or galleys
103 Director Walsh
104 Type of berry
108 Nudge
110 __ majesty
111 Reveling cry
112 Peddle
113 Actual being
116 Wash. Sq. campus
117 Fuss

BITS AND TRACES *By Fletcher Ingalls*

ACROSS

1 French marshal
5 Blood fluids
9 Detent
13 Faucet piece
19 Hebrew measure
20 Morris or high
21 Agent or jumper
23 On land
24 What you can do to water
26 Arion, for one
28 Kind of verb: Abbr.
29 Brass alloys
31 Stone markers
32 French wit
33 Judge Sewall's city
35 Prepare leftovers
36 Lick or mines
37 Poetic work
39 Early ascetic
42 Palm starch
45 Egyptian deity
46 Moistures
48 Settles
50 Russian river
52 Protective helmet
54 Time period
56 Irish cry
57 _ d' Oléron
58 Biped's claim to fame
60 Glanced off
62 Reconnoitered
64 Graham or Raye
65 Tennessee player
66 Without
67 Pirouettes
68 Up-to-date
69 One out of his element
72 Word in N.C. motto
73 Tallahassee campus
75 European ant
76 Scottish river
77 Inaugural parade unit
80 Audit entries: Abbr.
83 Motive power of yore
84 Abstract being
85 Watery sound
86 Special period of extra study
88 Fort in Calif.
90 N.Y. county
91 Swan genus
92 Full of: Suffix
93 Decrepit
95 Hymn
97 Forgives
99 Slightly inferior wares
100 Aardvark food
101 Hesitant sound
102 Goose genus
103 Fieldworks
104 Elephant's ear
106 Dame Myra
107 City near Leipzig
108 Benedictine title
109 Drive out
111 Hair tints
113 _ carrier
114 French eight
116 Bert or John
118 Assyrian god
121 Kind of old
123 Bar or horseshoe
125 Got into condition
128 "_ to a customer"
129 U.S. sprinter
133 Hippo
135 Opens
136 Dispatched
137 French pewter
138 _ up (finished)
139 Size up
140 Serf of old
141 Pickle
142 Soaks

DOWN

1 Cat family
2 Glasses or hat
3 Athletic woe
4 Experienced
5 Kaput
6 Kind of pot
7 Laughter, in Arras
8 Sports places
9 Banking abbr.
10 Dear me!
11 Whitman and Disney
12 "_ out of hell"
13 Comic ones
14 Mountain or prickly
15 Japanese measure
16 Dale Evans, e.g.
17 Gaelic
18 Virginia _
20 Chinese tea
22 Barbizon artist
25 Charity
27 Tennis and hair
30 Rotor pivot
34 Curve
37 Baltic feeder
38 Down payment
40 She: Fr.
41 Exigency
43 Mouth study, e.g.
44 Minor
47 Locale
48 Informed
49 Zola's verb
51 Air: Prefix
53 Tenebrae frame
55 Body parts: Abbr.
57 "_ a long way ..."
59 Bankroll
60 Paine's sense
61 Cottonwoods
63 French article
65 Swerved
68 Many, in Jalapa
70 Radio or matched
71 Ribbed fabric
73 _ one's back (supine)
74 Purse, to Caesar
75 Disneyland ride
77 N.Y.C. unit: Abbr.
78 Egyptian soul
79 _ around (cavorted)
80 Fanatic dresser
81 Kind of gallery
82 Sudden efforts
83 Lamb, in Vigo
85 Photo, for short
86 "Fall guy" or "gent," e.g.
87 N.Y. town
88 _ hat
89 Kind of cure
90 Shell filling
91 Ration-book agency
94 Rude action
95 Eastern garment
96 In a while
98 Toward the mouth
99 Florida settler
103 _ it (camps out)
105 Air-board listing
106 "For _ a jolly good ..."
108 Town in India
110 Defiled
112 Hindu holy man
115 Buddhist churches
117 Neighbor of Cuba
119 Like some gems
120 Willis and Walter
121 Pale color
122 Weapons
123 _ of pottage
124 Chinese river
126 Simon
127 Water bird
130 Streaks in wood
131 Thy: Fr.
132 Chemical ending
134 "_ Town"

348 WET STRENGTH By Cornelia Warriner

ACROSS

1 Health, to Cicero
6 S.A. rubber
10 Publishes
16 Cape of note
19 Dispatch boat
20 Give backing to
21 Nicety
22 Mouths
23 Trip for a politician
26 Gym piece
27 Hash houses
28 Top groups
29 Generous
31 Sound systems
32 Fry lightly
33 Type style: Abbr.
34 More strained
35 Lot measure
36 Accumulate
39 Depot: Abbr.
41 Tidal standstill
44 Macaw
45 Make fast, as a ship
49 Gods: Lat.
51 "Ah me!"
52 Kind of chamber
53 Fiery, in France
54 Row awkwardly
58 Custer's effort
59 Hazard for ships
61 Swiss physicist
62 Bearing
63 Side trips
64 Some birds' homes
65 Indulge in trickery
68 Engage
69 Princewood
70 Like some library walls
71 Die, as an engine
73 Noted retreat
75 Deliver
76 Islets
77 Valley
78 Fuss
79 Dilettantish
80 Little Woman
81 Become an ex-crewman
85 Doze
88 Shield
90 Kiln
91 Fight
96 Ship timber
97 Simple song
98 Of a geologic age
99 Utah's salt __
101 One who hesitates
103 Most sinuous
104 John __
105 Angling gear
108 Miscellany
109 Lure
110 Bitter drug
111 Cubic meter
112 Day or pole
113 Net handler
114 Gulls
115 Fool around

DOWN

1 Most reliable
2 Fly
3 "__, my children, and ..."
4 Guides of a sort
5 Socials
6 Senate runners
7 Lincoln et al.
8 Harrison
9 In a tranquil state
10 Wrote
11 Nutcracker, e.g.
12 Gorge
13 Etats __
14 Habitat: Pretix
15 Legislator
16 Sportsman to the hilt
17 Roberts
18 Palm yield
24 Town in France
25 Relic site in India
30 Impair
32 Cruel
33 Residents: Suffix
36 Take a __ at (attempt)
37 Monitor lizard
38 Friend, out West
40 Jewish months
42 Goods
43 Winglike
45 Moderate
46 S-curve
47 Biggest fish
48 Puts in new sod
50 French season
52 __ march on
54 Apple or hard
55 Learned
56 Saul Bellow's __ March
57 Like a G-rated movie
58 Math ratio
60 Fling
62 Superior of matter
64 House lily
65 Maniple
66 Imparted
67 Current
69 Hay unit
70 Whale unit
71 Hominy
72 Stratum
73 Rebecca or Mae
74 Kind of line or pooper
77 Wharf
81 Restraints
82 More vociferous
83 Made of a grain
84 Flowing
86 Behind, in Spain
87 Whimsical
89 Hebrew letter
92 Religion of Japan
93 Office __ (candidate)
94 Strong beams
95 Access
97 Sweet: Lat.
98 Cuzco's vista
99 Hoodwink
100 Miss Turner
101 River of Brazil
102 Related
103 Kind of storm or job
106 Number
107 Drink

349 COUPLETS By Norton Rhoades

ACROSS

1 Maid dropping a tray, with 32 Down
8 Legerdemain, in Italy
14 Beggars' horses
20 Joins the service
21 Lover, in Spain
22 French city
23 Find with effort
24 Kind of scout
25 Girl with an A
26 Little ones
27 Summer time
29 Shipboard sequence, with 47 Across
31 Rubber tree
33 To-do
35 Seascapes
39 Poetic Muse
42 Half a dance
43 South of Va.
45 Cousin of a mesa
46 Keep subscribing
47 See 29 Across
51 Paradise
52 Grasshopper's opposite
53 __ Magnon
55 Sinn Fein land
56 Helmsman: Abbr.
57 Army unit: Abbr.
58 __ Jeanne
59 Kiln
61 Feline teaser
63 Cubic meter
65 I order: Lat.
67 Have a strong wish for
68 Roan or Arab
69 Crop letdown for Dickens, with 30 Down
72 Elec. unit
74 __ a time
75 Like a night sky
76 Sardonic writing
77 Gazed at
79 "L' __, c'est . . ."
80 Clamor
83 Deal or moon
84 W.W. II area
85 Ivan, e.g.
87 Donovan's org.
88 Fuss
89 Lee Elder's game
91 Infielder's talent, with 63 Down
94 Roof worker
96 Zeno's town
97 Gaelic
98 Greek letters
99 Russian-dome shape

100 Plant of South
102 Walked fast
106 Choose
107 Impending dunk, with 120 Across
109 Set a dog on
111 Norwegian king
115 Sirens' calls
118 Like much modern music
120 See 107 Across
122 Nice or San Remo
123 Colorful jacket part
124 Sent for
125 Cow, to a tot
126 Kind of football kick
127 Farm machines

DOWN

1 Command, old style
2 Indian of Peru
3 Kind of rags
4 Shaggy
5 Half a fly
6 Chopin work
7 Snakes
8 Gym piece
9 Asian nurses
10 High winds
11 Perfect
12 Meet
13 Chichi
14 Signature of a publisher
15 "Do __ a Waltz?"
16 Attached, in botany
17 Double or triple
18 Scottish uncle
19 Ukraine or Latvia: Abbr.
28 Bangkok native
30 See 69 Across
32 See 1 Across
34 Seraph: Fr.

36 Sermon listeners, at times
37 Arab princes
38 River of S.C.
39 Time periods
40 Monthly bill
41 Feed the pot
42 Realty ad come-on
44 Forming a head
48 __, haec, hoc
49 Technical school exam
50 Old Greek settler
54 Turnip, in Pisa
60 Cities in N.J. and Mo.
62 Tennis needs
63 See 91 Across
64 B'way award
65 Shah's land
66 Pointed sponge
69 Complained
70 Roles
71 Gershwin et al.

72 N.Y. lakes
73 Interstice
78 Women's org.
80 Wet-watch painter
81 Thought: Prefix
82 Scandinavian goddess
84 Makes a decision
86 Frost
90 "__ the Madding Crowd"
92 Dessert base
93 Washouts
95 Chanted
101 Healing: Prefix
103 Jackets
104 Attendant spirits
105 Canyon or opera
106 Earth color
108 Hawaiian taro

110 Japanese statesman et al.
112 Italian money
113 Maple genus
114 G-men
115 __ of the sea
116 Zodiac sign
117 Inner: Prefix
119 Robe size: Abbr.
121 Eur. fish

350 WRITERS' GATHERING By Maura B. Jacobson

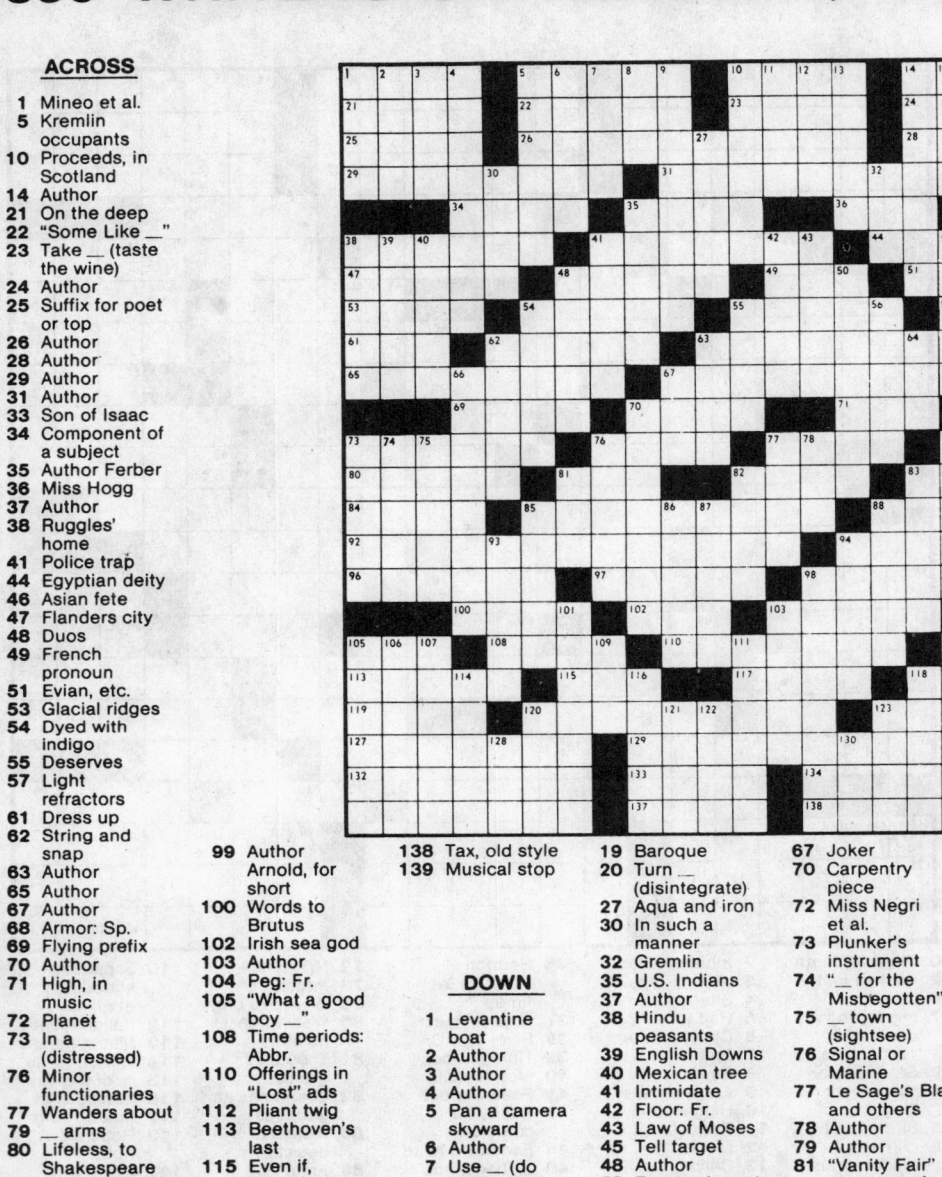

ACROSS

1 Mineo et al.
5 Kremlin occupants
10 Proceeds, in Scotland
14 Author
21 On the deep
22 "Some Like __"
23 Take __ (taste the wine)
24 Author
25 Suffix for poet or top
26 Author
28 Author
29 Author
31 Author
33 Son of Isaac
34 Component of a subject
35 Author Ferber
36 Miss Hogg
37 Author
38 Ruggles' home
41 Police trap
44 Egyptian deity
46 Asian fete
47 Flanders city
48 Duos
49 French pronoun
51 Evian, etc.
53 Glacial ridges
54 Dyed with indigo
55 Deserves
57 Light refractors
61 Dress up
62 String and snap
63 Author
65 Author
67 Author
68 Armor: Sp.
69 Flying prefix
70 Author
71 High, in music
72 Planet
73 In a __ (distressed)
76 Minor functionaries
77 Wanders about
79 __ arms
80 Lifeless, to Shakespeare
81 Do an exercise
82 Nautical bars
83 Java's neighbor
84 Foot or grace
85 Author
88 Author
92 Author
94 Two-faced god
95 Elevator buttons
96 Recipe words
97 Dickens character
98 Baptismal bowls
99 Author Arnold, for short
100 Words to Brutus
102 Irish sea god
103 Author
104 Peg: Fr.
105 "What a good boy __"
108 Time periods: Abbr.
110 Offerings in "Lost" ads
112 Pliant twig
113 Beethoven's last
115 Even if, simplified
117 Beggar's cry
118 Viet __
119 Descended: Fr.
120 Author
123 Author
127 Author
129 Author
131 Winged Victory
132 Author
133 Part of Q.E.D.
134 Four: Prefix
135 Jack London's Martin
136 Author
137 Author
138 Tax, old style
139 Musical stop

DOWN

1 Levantine boat
2 Author
3 Author
4 Author
5 Pan a camera skyward
6 Author
7 Use __ (do gardening)
8 Bosh
9 Author
10 Meter reader
11 Hammett pet
12 Vowels after "A"
13 Author
14 Menaces
15 Restaurateur Toots
16 German river
17 Strummed, as a minstrel
18 __ manner (conventionally)
19 Baroque
20 Turn __ (disintegrate)
27 Aqua and iron
30 In such a manner
32 Gremlin
35 U.S. Indians
37 Author
38 Hindu peasants
39 English Downs
40 Mexican tree
41 Intimidate
42 Floor: Fr.
43 Law of Moses
45 Tell target
48 Author
50 Encroachment
52 Author
54 Dressler's co-star
55 Norse saga
56 Author Bellow et al.
58 Moby Dick feature
59 Byword
60 __ Galilee
62 Baa
63 Ages
64 D-Day vessel: Abbr.
66 Author
67 Joker
70 Carpentry piece
72 Miss Negri et al.
73 Plunker's instrument
74 "__ for the Misbegotten"
75 __ town (sightsee)
76 Signal or Marine
77 Le Sage's Blas and others
78 Author
79 Author
81 "Vanity Fair" character, for short
82 Ziegfeld et al.
83 Tendencies
85 Egyptian sect member: Fr.
86 Sandy ridge
87 Grenoble's department
88 Rails
89 Mountebank
90 "__ Down Staircase"
91 Organic compound
93 Kind of treat
94 Steinbeck family
98 Agitated states
99 Author
101 More disloyal
103 Crimean port
104 Twain hero
105 Author Loos et al.
106 Accident
107 "__ secluded rendezvous"
109 Haggard title
111 Geniality
112 Pretend not to see
114 Piedmont city
116 Different
118 Lament
120 Destructive agent
121 Protagonist
122 Smell __
123 Suffrage
124 Author
125 Oahu guitars
126 Khayyam product
128 Letters
130 Rainy

351 APPROPRIATE PEOPLE

By George Rose Smith

ACROSS

1 Frostings
7 Understands
11 As strong as ____
15 Spinnaker
19 "Weep ____, my lady"
20 Ship deck
22 Column style
24 Actor Alan
25 "Give Me Five Minutes More"
27 "Home on the Range"
29 City ways
30 Lighters
31 Sierra ____
33 Like old castles
34 Containers
35 Large pill
36 Playwright Jean
37 ____ Mahal
40 Be fatuous
41 Wimsey
42 Bowed low
46 Spellbinders
48 "Don't Sit Under the Apple Tree"
50 Santa ____
51 Lion
52 To-dos
53 Prepare a hook
54 Dutch town
55 Gardens
56 Soil deposit
57 Small type
59 Inge's field
60 Hog food
61 Make movies
62 Islands in Galway Bay
63 Able people
64 Compass point
65 "A Farewell to Arms"
68 Ones often in distress
69 Devil's feet
71 Poker move
72 Went boating
73 In love
75 "Of Time and the River"
77 Prior to
80 Antiseptic pioneer
81 Request to the harvest moon
82 Addict
83 Remote
84 Voices

85 Pairs of horses
86 Vetch seeds
88 Spilled-ink woe
89 Asther of movies
90 Leg part
91 Coin of Near East
92 English novelist
93 Golf locale
94 "State of the Union"
97 Freeloaders
98 Vestment
100 Our, in France
101 Brief try
102 N. Y. time
103 Kind of outsider
104 Athens sight
105 Homeric
106 Nap
109 Miss Loos
110 Super-onion
112 However, for short
115 "The Bridge of San Luis Rey"
117 "Drink to Me Only With Thine Eyes": Var.
120 Sea position
121 Glove fabric
122 Bird sound
123 Writer Graham
124 Gil ____
125 Denials in Dundee
126 Rorem et al.
127 Gazes

DOWN

1 Concerning
2 Spring shape
3 Mischief makers
4 Month: Abbr.
5 ____ bag
6 Capitol people
7 Well-groomed
8 Sea birds
9 Fraternal people
10 Musical note
11 Take a recess
12 Substantives
13 Heraldic chaplet
14 Clock numeral
15 Desert
16 Came down
17 Pointless
18 Actor Alan
21 Basque games
23 Round Table site
26 Legal orders
28 Islamic text: Var.
32 Kind of power: Abbr.
35 Kodiak and bug
36 Girl's nickname
37 Certain poles
38 Tilled lands
39 "Mamma mia!"
40 June bugs
41 Greek letters
42 Goes after flies
43 "Knit two, purl two"
44 Paint

45 Biblical conies
47 Big top
48 Agenda units
49 Hard wood, in Spain
52 Alone, stage-wise
54 Rub out
56 Fine paper
57 Start the day
58 Physician
59 Populace
61 Kind of blister
62 Chemical compound
63 More logical
65 Yeas and nays, e.g.
66 Down the ____ (gone)
67 Makes money
68 Coolidge V.P.

70 Preminger et al.
72 Joint watcher
73 Angles
74 Environment
75 Noisy sound
76 Caverns in Virginia
78 Poured
79 Hemingway
81 Part of a village skyline
83 Solar disk
85 Kind of troops or therapy
86 Headdress
87 Green Gables girl
88 Short stake
90 Fishermen
91 Belittle
92 Intervals

94 Icy coating
95 Diesel and steam
96 Unsettled
97 Rural crossing
99 Investigates
101 Ship poles
104 Battery part
105 Auriculate
106 Scrape aftermath
107 Invalid
108 Olive genus
109 At a loss
110 Favor, in Scotland
111 Haul
112 Layer
113 Put an edge on
114 Persons
116 Cask
118 Wheat spike
119 Repast

352 STEPQUOTE By Eugene T. Maleska

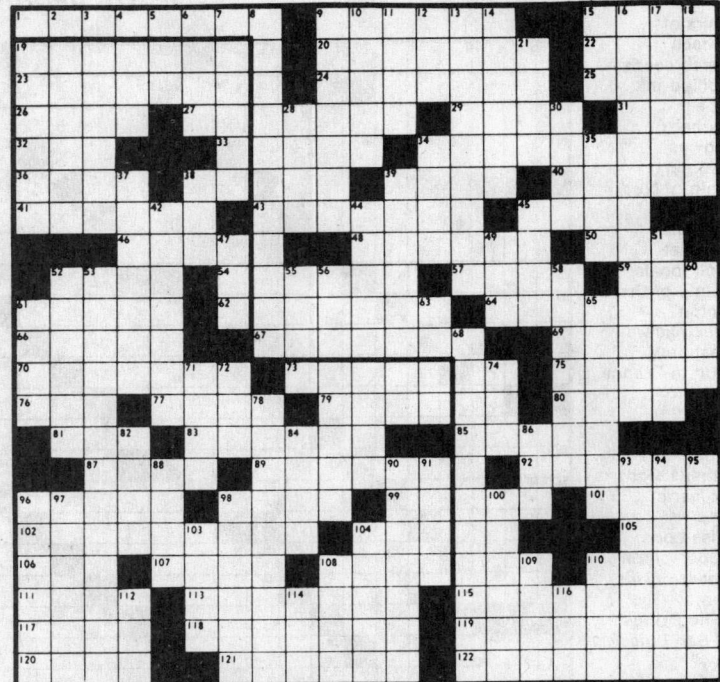

ACROSS

1 Start of the Stepquote, (along heavy line from top left to bottom right)
9 Senor's Saturday
15 Jazzman Fountain
19 Ethiopian emperor
20 Field hands
22 Effluvium
23 Belmont gate officials
24 Poem of 1847
25 Chariot race
26 Feudal domestic
27 Madre and Leone
29 Actor James
31 N.Z. woody vine
32 Fish dish
33 Below, in poesy
34 Vacuum tube
36 Revolution
38 Tempo, in Greek music
39 Big butte
40 Citizen of Kerman
41 Condescends
43 Edible seaweed
45 Jewish month
46 S.A. monkeys
48 Sweet alcohol
50 Guidonian note
52 "You Know ____"
54 Word after "woe"
57 Certain songs
59 "I ____ Camera"
61 Soft, in Siena
62 Recency
64 Of a fraternal order
66 Medieval helmet
67 Stepquote part
69 Noted pollster

70 British forest officer
73 Steering-gear units
75 Matchless
76 Capek play
77 French saint: Dec. 1
79 "Once upon a midnight ____"
80 Cries from Hamlet
81 Erode
83 Poetic form
85 Ant
87 Descartes
89 "____ jolly good fellow"
92 Emulates Brünnhilde
96 Seed
98 Road and wart
99 Nitwits
101 Office copy, for short
102 K.O. punches
104 Vermont ski resort
105 Pig ____ poke
106 They, in Tours

107 Gypsy's reading matter
108 Tapeworms
110 Topic in the tropics
111 Pro ____
113 Container for pekoe
115 Verse tragedy by Shelley
117 Made a hole in one
118 "____ Lee": 1849
119 Leading players
120 Zilch
121 River to the Aegean
122 End of Stepquote

DOWN

1 Maintains
2 Divulges
3 Mexican herdsman
4 Darnel
5 Successor to F.D.R.
6 "____ Death": Grieg
7 Wearisome

8 Stepquote part
9 Gushed
10 Deity of Islam
11 Ethnologist Franz
12 Leather-puncher
13 Prolonged tennis units
14 Port west of Karachi
15 Wire grass
16 Stepquote author
17 Hired
18 Verdi opera
21 Coal bed
28 Vogue
30 Hang or hob
34 Persian fairy
35 Kind of blue
37 Cash-register recordings
38 Inquire
39 Took no chances
42 Artist's board
44 Give a ____ to (shun)
45 Fitzgerald

47 ____ Saud
49 ____ Paul Kruger
51 Somme capital
52 Rue in a story
53 Boyhood love of 16 down
55 Ridicule
56 Those in the know
58 Poem of 1831
60 Port near Haifa
61 Volcanic crater
63 Attic promenade
65 Egglike stones
68 Stepquote part
71 In addition
72 Marsupial, for short
74 Beethoven work: Abbr.
78 Stool pigeon
82 Period
84 Wooden pegs

86 Pub. company pile-up
88 Tide
90 Henry Aaron's mother
91 Swiss town
93 Stephen, in France
94 Cure-all
95 Totalitarian policy
96 Persian rug
97 "The Haunted ____," poem of 1839
98 Miss Reddy et al.
100 ____ Pheasant
103 Judo work-out
104 Hawthorne's birthplace
108 Verboten
109 Wheys
110 Fortune's child
112 Stir
114 Mixologist's milieu
116 Boston fish

ACROSS

1 "The Story ___ Boy"
7 Furniture piece: Abbr.
10 As desired: Abbr.
13 City of Brazil
18 Embroiders, in Italy
19 Malt drink
20 Gums
21 Literal direction
22 Opposite
23 "___ child is fair of . . ."
25 Literal direction
26 Czech river
27 In ___ (kenneled)
29 Jars, in Spain
31 Brit. fliers
32 Madhouse
33 "The ___ Nights"
35 Russian ruler
39 One, in Naples
40 French phone response
41 ___ Santo
43 ___ man about a dog
44 Bewail
46 Brief glimpse
48 Drinker's woe: Abbr.
49 What to do with a hatchet
50 Energy unit
51 Bridge call
52 Congo river
54 Drinking place
55 Sup
56 Almanach de ___
58 Subordinate one
60 Self-generation
62 German's alas
63 English explorer
65 Be in session longer
67 Also ___
68 Divides, Biblically
70 Really backward punch
72 Ellice island
73 Caspian or Red
74 Normandy town
77 Sight: Fr.
78 Relatives
80 Basic time initials
82 Querying sounds
84 Retirement incomes
87 Spinning-mule part
90 Portico
91 Disordered
92 Golfer's words
95 Miss Merkel
96 Bathroom fixture
98 Second self
100 ___ as a fruitcake
102 Cockney's idol
103 Alcott girl
104 Waterfall: Var.
105 Boxing-bout unit: Abbr.
106 Go ___ the deep end
107 Old English games
109 G.I. address
111 ". . . hurt the ___ love"
113 Finger parts
116 Montana town
117 Film's Johnny et al.
119 Stylish, old style
121 Tree resin
122 Struck with reverence
123 "Flat Foot Floogie" word
124 Baste
126 Missive: Abbr.
127 London suburb
129 Landlords' collections
131 Essay name
132 Kind of comedian
135 "Hurry up ___" (G.I. cynicism)
137 Honking
139 Literal direction
140 Debt chit
141 Ship: Abbr.
142 Canadian capital
143 Moslem prince
144 Compass point
145 That, in Spain
146 Towel with "Hers," e.g.

DOWN

1 Cooking spice
2 Literal countdown
3 Maple genus
4 Grill's partner
5 Amsterdam's river
6 Children's advice to Elisha, literally
7 Indian of Peru
8 "___ Girl"
9 Kept, in Paris
10 Four: Prefix
11 Work at
12 "Eat every ___ of it!"
13 Hair style
14 Master, in Bonn
15 Math branch
16 Word of contempt
17 Hollywood figure: Abbr.
21 Ripped
22 ___ novarum
24 Literally, "___ see me sometime?"
25 Writer Shirley Ann ___
28 Running off
30 River isles
32 Gauze covering
34 Fervent: It.
36 Psalm words, literally
37 Thais and Chinese, e.g.
38 Shabby
42 Horn tissue
43 Bribe, in law
45 Cheer
47 Norse epic
49 Conjunction
53 Miss Bacall
54 Browning's advice, with "Look"
56 "Ruggles of Red ___"
57 Wood sorrels
59 Noun suffix
60 S.A. cassava
61 Tire device
64 Stock offerings: Abbr.
66 Navy police: Abbr.
69 Western lake
71 Moistly, old style
75 ___ an ear
76 Can. province
79 Tub: Var.
81 Camping unit
83 Chinook, e.g.
85 Like saliva
86 "Dear ___"
88 Roget offering
89 Writer Talese
90 Grief
93 Having parts: Suffix
94 Nickname
96 Tropical fish
97 Thing, in law
99 City of Sicily
101 Soviet city
108 Rhythm
109 Long period
110 Welsh songfest
112 Feelings of vivacity
114 Province and town near Rome
115 Scrawny animal
117 Radar spot
118 Still in abeyance
120 Florida explorer
123 Bungle, as a golf drive
125 Kind of rocket
128 Jewish month
130 Facility
131 Greenland settlement
132 Resort
133 Card wool
134 Maoris' forever
136 Negative prefix
138 Baseball's Mel

354 TROUBLE SPOTS *By Robert Roop*

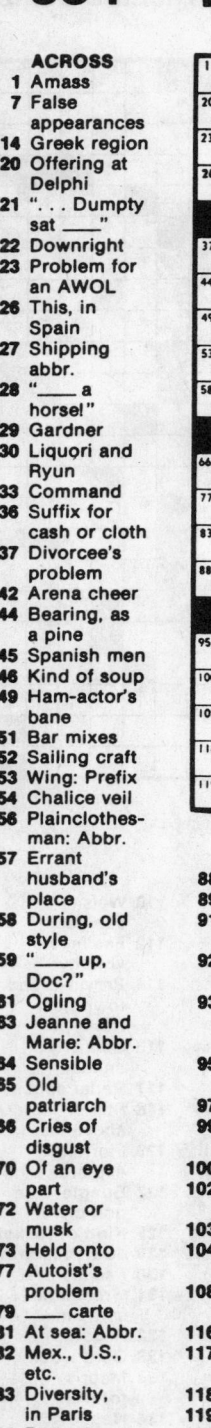

ACROSS

1 Amass
7 False appearances
14 Greek region
20 Offering at Delphi
21 ". . . Dumpty sat ____"
22 Downright
23 Problem for an AWOL
26 This, in Spain
27 Shipping abbr.
28 "____ a horse!"
29 Gardner
30 Liquori and Ryun
33 Command
36 Suffix for cash or cloth
37 Divorcee's problem
42 Arena cheer
44 Bearing, as a pine
45 Spanish men
46 Kind of soup
49 Ham-actor's bane
51 Bar mixes
52 Sailing craft
53 Wing: Prefix
54 Chalice veil
56 Plainclothes- man: Abbr.
57 Errant husband's place
58 During, old style
59 "____ up, Doc?"
61 Ogling
63 Jeanne and Marie: Abbr.
64 Sensible
65 Old patriarch
66 Cries of disgust
70 Of an eye part
72 Water or musk
73 Held onto
77 Autoist's problem
79 ____ carte
81 At sea: Abbr.
82 Mex., U.S., etc.
83 Diversity, in Paris
84 Portents
86 State of decline
88 Tangles
89 Encircle
91 Blood trunks: Fr.
92 Naval title: Abbr.
93 Rash- people's pursuits
95 Math. branch
97 Lamp parts
99 Goes stealthily
100 Beat soundly
102 Org. for G.I.'s
103 Pasture
104 Rate, in Madrid
108 Spenders' problems
116 Slightest
117 Charm, in London
118 Bret et al.
119 Valuables
120 One on a pension
121 Worn out

DOWN

1 Foot: Suffix
2 Spring bloom
3 Word for Uncas
4 Little Sir ____
5 Eskimo knife
6 Bankrupt's problems
7 Surgical tongs
8 Santa ____
9 Taxi
10 Sharp tool
11 Perform, in Scotland
12 Relative of yore
13 Snubs
14 Agreements
15 Royal initials
16 Old English moneys
17 Put into execution
18 Fireplace
19 Pilot
24 Like a certain bird
25 Receives
30 ____ Lisa
31 Explorer and family
32 Church councils
33 Scold
34 Chem. suffixes
35 Sweet or wisdom
37 Musical background: Abbr.
38 Unwilling
39 ____ alia
40 Small: Prefix
41 Form
43 Composer Villa ____
46 Target of TV pill ads
47 Serve as an optical beam
48 French seasons
50 French port
52 Comfort
55 Eastern queen
57 Phones
60 Repast
62 Carbon: Suffix
66 R. E. Lees et al.: Abbr.
67 Pearl Buck heroine
68 Bombastic talkers
69 Excites
71 Hebrew letters
72 Shawls
73 Town of India
74 Issues
75 Carolina river
76 Lock of hair
78 Ultimate end
80 Kelp
84 Heraldic border
85 Kaput
87 Jeering sounds
89 Certain man
90 Exhale: It.
93 "When I ____ lad"
94 Power source: Abbr.
95 Fragrance
96 Adores
98 Offends
101 Ginkgo or ash
104 Gang territory
105 Stake
106 Proof mark
107 African fox
109 Summer time: Abbr.
110 Compass point
111 Belfry problem
112 "What ____ doing?"
113 Conjunction
114 Letter
115 Dumbbell

PAGING MR. TELL

By Frances Hansen

ACROSS

1 Lewis's partner
6 Words for some stocks
11 Seemingly
16 "Stop!"
20 Four-bagger
21 Florida city
22 Witch's home
23 Hand or ribs
24 Writer Jong
25 Bank citadel
26 Lorna
27 Lofty perch
28 Uneasy
30 Swiss river
32 "Absolutely not!"
34 Start of an old poem
39 Before "we forget"
40 Efforts
41 Without ____ (penniless)
42 Plea to ye faithful
44 Gives the old one-two
48 "Who killed Cock Robin?"
52 Trenchant
56 Like the Dragon Lady
58 Army V.I.P.
59 Closed, old style
60 Literary alter ego
61 Norman Mailer's town
63 Teutonic: Abbr.
66 Wedding response
67 They no longer "cometh"
68 Middle, in law
69 Adored one
70 "What care I ____ she be?"
72 "____ a fine lady . . ."
74 Propriety
77 Ship-like clock
78 Do a Christmas chore
82 Single thing
83 More of 48 across
86 Sherman's word for war
87 Porgy's woman
88 Photography abbr.
89 Lively musical piece
90 Laid aside
91 Stewart film, 1950
95 Narrow shoe size
96 Less refined
98 Start of a round
101 ____ Moines
102 Schooldays initials
103 Triteness
106 Invitation words
107 Salamanders
109 U. S.-Ont. canals
111 Shelters, as a fleet
112 Greek porticos
113 Barbs of "outrageous fortune"
117 Small shaft
118 Well-known major
121 Layer of tissue
122 Adds spice to
124 Egyptian skink
127 Query re your bones
135 Subway entrance feature
137 Elevator cage
138 Out ____ (unattainable)
139 Eat away
140 Sevens' partners
143 French sculptor
146 Murre
147 Ages and ages
148 Range of central U.S.
149 Muse of song
150 Vergil's shepherdess
151 "Monkey Trial" lawyer
152 Kind of goat
153 Facing a glacier
154 Moslem title

DOWN

1 Colette novel
2 Bodies of knowledge
3 Friendly folk
4 Opposite of verso
5 Snakes
6 Prayers
7 Wood sorrel
8 French resort
9 Poe's foster father
10 Sharp knocks
11 Math proof
12 Numero ____
13 Hacienda material
14 Dostoevsky girl
15 Peaceful
16 What Molly Malone did
17 Dike, Eunomia and Irene
18 O'Neill character et al.
19 Bomb trial
23 Houston or Hill
29 Pauline Chapel locale
31 ____ ha-Shanah
33 Pirates' gold
35 Chair style
36 Cow-headed goddess
37 On one's ____
38 Chinese diplomat
43 Parisian's thanks
44 Last letter, in London
45 Tree-feller
46 ". . . how a book of ____ made"
47 Ways for 16 Down
49 Canine world
50 Foot: Prefix
51 South Pacific address
53 Prom locale, often
54 Dutch town
55 Mark or mother
57 ____ dixit
60 Onetime Mrs. Sinatra
62 Deficit
64 Whiffenpoofs' pub
65 Commuters' oasis
69 German pronoun
71 Gangster's hat
72 Place for three men
73 Single
75 Part of "Alouette" refrain
76 Coin of Nepal
79 Second court hearing
80 Vestment
81 Kind of wood
83 ". . . which ____ to our Creator"
84 ". . . head that ____ crown"
85 Sky Altar
90 Emulated Spitz
92 Man's slipper
93 Mistress Quickly
94 Pulitzer Prize book, 1926
97 "____ robins . . ."
98 Headland
99 Mel
100 Hit song from "Sunny"
103 Presaged
104 Ship rope
105 Least old: Abbr.
108 Snick's partner
110 Between dix and douze
114 Sugar: Prefix
115 Arid wastes
116 Conical fossils
119 Door or place
120 Prayer
123 Fine violins
124 ". . . ____ of snow-white horses"
125 German engraver
126 Dickens' Edwin
128 Miss Doolittle
129 Man from El Paso
130 Cookie flavor
131 "____ little, there a. . ."
132 Betimes
133 Roman 1103
134 Digger's find
136 French possessive
141 Sea bird
142 Place for pie
144 "In excelsis ____!"
145 Freud's concerns

356 LITERAL APPROACH
By Bill Hartman

ACROSS

1 Loiter
5 It's usually four
8 Jack of clubs
11 Quick
14 Soft drink
17 Bullets, etc.
18 Eastern V.I.P.
19 Bean, to Vergil
20 ____ the piper
21 Musical passage
22 Disapproved
23 Parrot, e.g.
25 Undo one's sewing
26 Chick and fire
27 Portions
29 Inbred entry
32 Prefix for naut
33 Pitching stat
34 Sharp blow
35 Dull surface
36 Climb in a way
37 Ring champ
38 Insult, in England
39 Takes in
44 Rock-vein angle
45 Bulrush
46 Coat part: Abbr.
47 Miss ____ Rio of films
48 Chem. prefix
49 Out-of-date one
50 Myra or Rudolf
51 Colors
52 Signal
53 Smart sayings
54 Gaylord Ravenal's milieu
56 Letters
57 Mount, out West
58 Drinks
59 Things often cut
60 Dove or cotton
61 Function
62 Blazing
63 "Guys and Dolls" doll
65 Large bird
66 ____ Fein
67 McLuhan words on the ad era
73 Oil plant
74 Thai isthmus
75 Singer's lapse
76 Prepared fruit
77 Berlin number
78 Sea birds
79 Rhine menace
84 Impolite
85 Barnyard sounds
86 Boating hazard
87 Most sullied
88 Banking abbrs.
89 Stupid one
90 English city
91 Ship wood
92 Gang weapons
93 Environment: Prefix
94 While, for short
95 Scottish county
96 Parlor plant
97 Graduate degrees
98 Sinner-no-more
101 Bashful
102 Branch
103 Can. province
104 ____ pros
105 Kind of collar
107 Taconite, e.g.
108 Dictum
110 Literal entry
116 "____ band played on"
118 Incas' home
119 Physicist of note
120 Nullifying law
122 Mr. Roberts
123 Beer foam
124 Dine
125 Writer George et al.
126 Eskimo knife
127 Friendly
128 Solicit
129 German spa
130 D.C. title
131 Tire part
132 Humorist Bill and others

DOWN

1 Old Baltic coins
2 U.S. city
3 High-level agent
4 Last chance for the Jets
5 Weems or bird
6 Stone, e.g.
7 Enthralled
8 Ganges city
9 Give backing to
10 Girls' shoes
11 Kind of fool
12 Totem pole, e.g.
13 Roman or italic
14 Sport
15 Keats works
16 Soldier's want
19 Spenser's Queen
21 Magna ____
24 Actor Tom et al.
26 Blemish
28 Niagara Falls feeder
30 Egg drinks: Var.
31 Saunters
37 Eur. country
38 (Sic)
40 French river
41 Like an iced drink
42 Nonresident hospital worker
43 Bailer: Fr.
44 Jolly sound
45 Annoyed
49 Mil. award
50 Tatar group
51 Girl of fiction
53 "Godfather" group
55 Showed joy
56 Alligator
57 Round-trippers
60 Zodiac sign
61 Moved, as a painting
62 Declare
64 Conspicuous
67 Defeat solidly
68 Type of auto
69 Fencing pieces
70 Pentateuch
71 Windborne
72 Baby bird
76 Town herald of old
77 English satirist
80 Inbred entry
81 Influence badly
82 Superlative endings
83 "____ your move"
85 Bull Run or Hastings
86 Certain good-byes
87 Skin: Suffix
90 Essayist Francis
91 Spanish saint
96 Danish islands
97 Design
99 "The song is ____"
100 Connectives
103 Wild ginger
106 Time, in France
107 British painter
109 Midwest airport
110 Sunk fence
111 French numbers
112 State: Abbr.
113 Measure
114 Grant
115 Insult
117 Trees
121 Whitney

357 WAY OUT

By Threba Johnson

ACROSS

1 Constructs
7 Half a continuum
12 Other half of continuum
16 American ship initials
20 Eur. capital
21 Rural areas: Sp.
22 "____ a man with seven . . ."
23 Changes, in music
25 Orderly view of cosmos
28 Mettle
29 Dress part
30 "____ homo"
31 French thoughts
32 Little devil
34 Icelandic tale
35 Seed cover
37 Detective of fiction
39 German song
41 Rabbit ears
43 Bulldozer, for one
45 Two fathers of 25 Across
47 "____ no questions . . ."
49 Diamond ____
50 Pick or wit
51 U.S. Japanese
52 E. Indian birds
53 "____ last!" (finally)
55 Avesta translation
56 ____ pamby
60 Flightless bird
61 Color
62 Dip the boat out again
64 Be sociable
65 Scythe handle
67 College course: Abbr.
69 Snake
70 Part of an atom
72 British auto parts
73 Scrooge et al., for short
75 Heavenly unit
76 Ways: Abbr.
77 Heaven on the go
83 Mouths
86 Tonic plant
87 Swagger
88 Kind of potato
91 Spectral move by Cornell eleven
94 Word of surprise
95 Bird of legend
97 Musical alley
99 Release, as a boat
100 Takes the helm
102 Choose
104 Bristle
105 French soldier
106 Dimensions: Abbr.
108 Black Sea city
110 Restless
111 ____ fideles
113 Pausing sounds
114 Times of day: Abbr.
115 Certain rays
116 Heavenly twist
120 Cooke of TV
122 Circus people
123 Lease
124 Class: Prefix
125 Night, in Norse myth
128 Rhodes, to Italians
129 Teaching degree
131 Word form for a Mideast land
133 Spanish lady
135 Fish
136 Adlai ____ Stevenson
138 Restless heaven
142 Peter's friend
143 Bone: Prefix
144 Farewell
145 Gem weights
146 Defendant: Abbr.
147 Norms: Abbr.
148 Harvested, to poets
149 Oozes

DOWN

1 Turkish title
2 Absolute
3 Heavenly route
4 Baltic or North
5 Wavy, in heraldry
6 Soul
7 Heavenly slaves
8 Nicklaus's org.
9 More la-di-da
10 Betty and others
11 Town in Italy
12 Makes a connection
13 Nigerian river
14 Heavenly circle
15 Word study: Abbr.
16 Hesitant sounds
17 Heavenly monster
18 Movie lot
19 Shoe
24 Norse bard
26 Boston square
27 Spartan serf
33 Gets gold in a way
36 Father of 45 Down
38 Pell ____
40 Ford
42 Heavenly
44 Ship: Abbr.
45 Violent view of the cosmos
46 Conjunction
47 Boats
48 ____ Saens
50 Compass point
54 Antelope
55 Kind of code
57 Baseball V.I.P.'s
58 Ink spot
59 Desires
61 Lose hope
63 Assyrian god
64 Island near Canaveral
66 Whammy
68 Yield
70 Educ. broadcasting
71 New Guinea port
74 Follow
75 Food: Prefix
78 Landon
79 Negative
80 Part of R.N.
81 ____ Lanka
82 Name linked with 7 and 12 Across
83 Down ____
84 Western city
85 Gazelle
89 Heavenly photo
90 Kind of yoga
92 Heavenly blows
93 Town near Paris
94 Peaks: Abbr.
96 Heavenly litter
98 Certain votes
100 Upright stone
101 Ways: Abbr.
103 Fondness
106 Telegram contents: Abbr.
107 Heavenly song
109 Store event
110 P.I. tree
112 Miss Lanchester
113 Mob-scene player
116 Cork or thumb
117 Farmer, at times
118 Antiseptic
119 Flavorings
120 Freedom from pain
121 Gins' companions
124 Nasty
126 Judgment
127 Lock
130 Heroic poem
132 Perfume: Var.
134 Of grandparents
137 Cheat
139 Inc., in Britain
140 Pol. party
141 Much: Prefix

358 WORKING PEOPLE
By Herb Risteen

ACROSS

1 ____ up (recap)
4 Krazy ____
7 Hawthorne locale
12 Tumbrel
16 Fuss
17 "____ or cut bait"
18 Slope: Suffix
19 Water buffalo
20 Specific
22 Grocery items
23 Roundup targets
25 Well-known clergyman
28 Asian snake
30 Comply with
31 Skill
32 Dombey relative
33 Africa's Smith
34 "____ Grit"
36 Lower part: Prefix
39 Heater
40 Well-known pressman
47 Nobel poet
48 Fold again
49 Small amount
50 Arnold hero
53 Put back
55 Friend of Athos
59 Mixtures
60 Talking birds
61 L.A. players
63 Wallet item
64 Ever and ____
65 Quarry in a child's game
66 Yields
68 Imogene
69 Family member: Abbr.
70 Marco or water
71 French city
72 "David ____"
73 Caretaker
75 Of the skull
78 Yards' relatives
79 Grid lineman
80 Metal rod
81 Doenitz's concern
83 Well-known official

89 Wood sorrels
91 Mountain: Prefix
92 S.A. Indians
93 Time period
94 Kind of roast or luck
95 Heave the shot
97 Lowdown
99 Beans
101 Well-known tradesman
108 Collection
109 Eastern Christian
110 Recluses
113 Hoosier poet
114 Edge along
115 Speak imperfectly
116 Little girl
117 Young ones
118 Weavers' reeds
119 ____ on (rebuked)
120 Spanish king

DOWN

1 Indian tribe
2 Japanese herb
3 Alberta's neighbor
4 Ukraine city
5 Italian city
6 Well-known healer
7 Kind of board
8 Mixture
9 Willing, of old
10 ". . . were Paradise ____"
11 Arizona sight
12 Slyness
13 No-voter
14 Does lab work
15 Blab
17 Mandolin part
19 Maple genus
21 Greek letter
24 Ferber
26 Support
27 African chief
28 Carson
29 Stadium sound
34 Defeat
35 Spanish stream
36 Heavy knife
37 Remote
38 Ad words for bargain paperbacks
39 Medit. island
41 Western range
42 Extra
43 Turkoman tribesman
44 Soaks
45 Cheeses
46 Gibbons
50 They all go to Rome
51 Arm bones
52 Custer foes
54 Compass point
56 Grace or Archie
57 Become liable to
58 Mining strikes
60 Wire measure
62 Roman bronze
65 City near San Antonio
66 Shows pleasure
67 David's officer
68 Germanic people
70 Cordial glass
71 Small ox
72 Regard
74 Social affairs
76 Abundant
77 Bow, in Italy
78 Crowds into
82 Apparel item
83 ____ medica
84 Campus mil. group
85 Dandy, in Soho
86 Harvest goddess
87 Asian gazelle
88 Print measures
89 Chooses
90 Follower
95 "For ____ sake!"
96 Nobel chemist
97 Tuscany, Latium, etc.
98 Grace and mash
99 Flabby
100 Here, in Paris
102 Bland
103 Bohemian martyr
104 Indigo source
105 Pheasant group
106 Silkworm
107 Love ____
111 "All About ____"
112 Authority

359 CLASSIC DOINGS By Elaine D. Schorr

ACROSS

1 Paper amount
5 Thunder unit
9 Retiree's gift
14 Acclaim
18 ____ Ata
19 Plain plinth
20 Miser, in Milan
21 Church calendar
22 Greek who knew his numbers
24 Nonsensical talk
26 Inspirations for Tennyson
28 Right items for 22 Across
31 Fashion
32 Sources
34 Edible fungus
35 Kind of bridge suit
36 South Seas island group
38 Roman Empire invader
40 Fun and games
43 "____ the house!"
45 Chinese truth
46 Jet ____
47 ____ Amboy
49 Zodiac sign
50 Quaker leader
51 Wine: Prefix
52 Puckered cloth
53 Gets sleepy
54 Medit. island
55 Showed an old movie
57 River of France
59 Swamp Fox of 1700's
60 Protest ploys
61 Kind of grace
62 Drink server
63 "____ Sympathy"
64 Author Nevil
65 Bach instrument
66 Peewees
67 Footnote abbr.
68 Cheese variety

71 ____ off steam
74 Circle parts
75 Jacques of song
76 Prudent, in Nantes
77 Egg: Prefix
78 Cote cry
79 "You can ____ horse to . . ."
80 On the outs with
83 W.W. II town
85 Fort ____
86 Gains upon
89 Gleam: Fr.
90 Miss Berger
92 Knightly sport
93 Shelley et al.
94 Apple-inspired science
100 Some gallery hang-ups
102 Peace of mind
106 Narrow shoe width
107 What to do with the news
108 Tapestry
109 Syngman ____
110 Snagged
111 Raconteurs' output
112 Gets the point
113 Cousin to the ketch

DOWN

1 Spirit sound
2 Culbertson
3 Quantity: Abbr.
4 Singer Jackson
5 ____ bah
6 Light shade
7 Chicken Little et al.
8 Injury
9 Marathon at the Met
10 Of grand-parents
11 Account

12 Blow, in Ireland
13 Diamond feats
14 Small-fry favorite
15 Fare for Plato's pupil
16 Mount of Crete
17 ____ Alamos
19 Noncoms
23 Zones
25 Upward: Prefix
27 Bother
28 Turnover item
29 Pitcher Ryan
30 Bank gift at New Year's
33 Lincoln's War Secretary
35 Map lines: Abbr.
36 Stage comment
37 Richard et al.
39 Pongee fabric

41 Plateau
42 Restrains
44 Seat for Louis XIV
48 Difficult projects
50 Ohio city
52 School heads: Abbr.
54 Mrs. Eddie Albert
56 ____ Unis
58 Porkpie
59 George Eliot character
60 Works by a French artist
61 Pottery piece
62 Brag
63 Mine cars
64 Advantage
67 Former, old style
69 W.W. I song
70 Hit's opposite
72 "____ inch a king"
73 Neap and rip
75 Is wafted on the breeze

81 Guinness et al.
82 Kind of rhyme
84 As ____ (in unison)
87 German one
88 Beginnings
91 Airline initials
93 Peach discards
95 Other: Sp.
96 Poetic word
97 Oil land
98 Maneuver-able, as a ship
99 Ladies of Spain
100 Grain
101 Buddhist people
103 Cry of triumph
104 Baste
105 Moray

360 PROPER NAMES By Bert Kruse

ACROSS

1 Family man
5 Ties securely
11 Greek promenades
16 Strange
17 Relative of "Here's how"
18 Western cactus
20 Popular musical
22 Results of applying certain sticks
24 Insects
25 Ten-point type
26 Row
28 Resembling: Suffix
29 Food fish
30 Uses a press
31 Put through a sieve
32 Stadium in N.Y.
33 Girl of Groucho's song
35 Ancient Brazilian
36 Destined
37 Throw out
38 Writings: Abbr.
40 Went very slowly
42 Looks
43 Roof worker
46 Chromosome parts
47 Specialized group
48 Light color
50 Legal matter
51 Stoop
55 Nettle
56 Old Roman province
58 Soil
59 Kind of china
60 Laver of tennis
61 Edible greens
63 Get the base-runner
64 Louder, in music: Abbr.
66 Old instrument
67 Complete
68 Grudge

70 Produced an heir
72 Greek letter
73 Home of Noah Webster
75 Small one
76 Awaken
78 Gitche Gumee features
79 Idiotic
82 Flood
84 Sioux
85 Trellis units
86 "___ Along the Mohawk"
87 Twitch
89 Calm
93 Star in Pegasus
94 Embodiments
95 Rodeo gear
97 High note
98 Black: Prefix
99 Bright ___
100 Mortgages

101 Hymn word
102 Secreted: Sp.
104 Russian entertainer
108 Decide
109 Tooth part
110 Lights
111 Korean family
112 Unswerving
113 Antony-requested loan

DOWN

1 Beat down, as hail
2 Bothers
3 Nicklaus, e.g.
4 Snake
5 Track events
6 Type of horse race
7 Surf sounds
8 Lighted-cigar tip
9 Occasional finger location

10 Enactments
11 Diatribe
12 "Over ___"
13 Shipboard title: Abbr.
14 Relative of hunky-dory
15 Move like a serpent
16 Barrie girl
19 Get ___ of the action
20 Greet
21 Hodgepodge
23 Hurries off
27 Upset
30 Eclairs, etc.
31 Blanches
34 Insect stage
36 Painting, music, etc.
37 Playing-fields school
39 Bishop's domain
41 Eagle's pad
42 Bridge bids
43 Spanish woman
44 Arrived at Kennedy

45 Fortification
47 Ringo Starr's former group
48 Dry up
49 Spruce
51 Navigation system
52 Expressing a pledge
53 Mother's relatives
54 Rain in Bonn
57 Fidel's friend
58 Tennis call
61 Tool-rack item
62 Western capital
65 Venture out
68 Fired on
69 Oral
71 Rolls
72 Plant bulbs
74 Man on first
76 Vocal arpeggios
77 Involved
79 Of the intestine

80 Loire city
81 Swizzle stick
82 Factual
83 In a weary manner
86 Square ones
88 Presidential title: Abbr.
90 French racing center
91 Smart ones
92 Doughboy
94 Edge along
95 Fleecy animal
96 Together
101 Old zither
103 Corroded
105 Can. province
106 Edinburgh negative
107 Alfred Noyes subject

361 FLOATERS *By Hume R. Craft*

ACROSS

1 First-born
7 Kind of driver
12 Oceans
17 Chaliapin, e.g.
21 Andrew Johnson, at first
22 Make ____ in one
23 Strange
24 Curtain raiser
25 Flimsy boats for crewmen
27 Boat with close ties
29 Presidential initials
30 San Simeon or Biltmore
31 Old card game
33 Judges
34 Mac's predecessor
35 Venetian medal
37 Flu variety
39 Runner
42 Jimmy Valentine, e.g.
44 Cards
46 Sawbuck
50 Dog-show figure
52 Worthless boat
55 Neighbor of Arg.
56 Bars, in law
57 Steers clear of
58 Litter member
59 Something strained at
60 Cookout leftovers
61 "____ came a spider . . ."
62 Waters down
64 Fracas
65 Nobleman
66 October figure
67 Frontier name
68 Swap notes
69 Overhead lines
70 Like Nero Wolfe
71 Coat parts
72 Game segments
73 Actress MacMahon et al.
75 Nether lands expert
77 In full ____ (speeding)
78 Early Egyptians
80 Null's partner
81 Lifting devices
83 Garage worker, for short
86 Puts up
87 Badminton equipment
88 Landlords' due
89 Big hammer
90 French infants
91 Calhoun and namesakes
92 Wiggin and Greenaway
93 Tropical fish
94 Follow the cheerleader
95 Lansbury role
96 Bistros
97 Art-store purchases
98 High note
99 Boats for Heyerdahl
102 Bounds along
103 River of S.C.
105 Wading bird
106 Boat pin
108 Educ. group
109 Mold core
111 ____ aves
113 Lineman
114 Broadway theater of note
117 Eagle rider of myth
119 "____ thing you know"
122 Humorist George
125 Devours noisily
127 Boat in a library
130 Sooty matter
131 Carthaginian goddess
132 Knock and bended
133 Roman cloak
134 Scottish foxes
135 Office-pool member
136 Impertinent
137 Small birds

DOWN

1 Do art work
2 Landlocked country
3 Ref. book
4 Lodge member
5 Dover ____
6 Crossovers
7 Tuaregs' home
8 Huntley
9 Lumberjack contest
10 Pipe joint
11 Saturday TV fare
12 Bears expenses
13 Saarinen
14 Thomas Mann's daughter
15 Sky quest
16 Perceptive
17 Yacht homes
18 Common woe
19 Cooking direction
20 Wine-tasters' routines
26 Case or well
28 Quaffed
32 Toward shelter
36 Oscar winner of 1973
38 Dumfounds
39 Tarzan's "mother," for one
40 German city
41 Sharing by chance
42 Hannibal's detour
43 Sheridan's scandal spot
45 Finches
47 Boat on a gridiron
48 Sounded off
49 Coaches
51 Active one
53 Boat in fine condition
54 "____ is bustin' out . . ."
57 One-armed bandits
59 Aladdin's friend
61 After, in Paris
62 Civil wrong
63 Boat for sewing and cooking
64 Tender spots
66 Units of loudness
67 Big names of the 1930's
68 Largest asteroid
70 Zasu of films
72 Unisex wear
74 It is allowed: Lat.
76 Lends a hand
77 Props for W. C. Fields
78 Mideast language
79 Narrow space
80 Songbirds
82 Try out again
84 Popular tour area
85 Top-drawer
87 Relative of a turkey
89 Blackbird
91 Ouida
92 Austrian writer
93 Bulrush
95 Life preservers
96 Medit. galleons
97 Fall occurrence
99 Base-stealer Lou
100 Strait off Albania
101 Horse color
102 Antisocial one
104 Puts into force
107 Jan Hus's supposed crime
110 Sierra ____
112 Park of West
114 Attention seeker
115 Bullets and peas
116 Praise
118 Minn. athlete
120 Indians of West
121 Inner or boob
122 Baker's predecessor
123 Expunge
124 Time periods
126 Grammar case: Abbr.
128 Miss Merkel
129 Hayloft

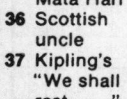

ACROSS
1 Elevations: Abbr.
4 Armadillo
8 Flag fanatics
14 Sky animal
18 Screw pines
20 Entertain
21 Biblical mount
22 Tusked animal
23 Observation by Gibran
27 Serious
28 Ekberg
29 Roof piece
30 Hit noisily
31 Loch ____
33 Sea bird
34 Helped Mata Hari
36 Scottish uncle
37 Kipling's "We shall rest ____"
43 Armstrong
44 Meadow
45 Approach an end
46 Insecticide
47 Prefix for monde
48 Scraps
50 Olive genus
51 "Dear me!"
55 Barbara of TV
56 Openers, often
58 Injurious
62 Methods: Abbr.
64 Russian city
65 Bollix a copy job
66 Conrad words in "Heart of Darkness"
71 Put on the cuff
75 Jewish fete
76 Hair treatment
81 Put on again
83 Nursemaid
84 Italian finger game
85 Angered
86 African fox
89 Rara ____
92 "____ my wits' end"
93 Common abbr.
96 Roman 604
97 Insect study: Abbr.
98 Kind of measure
99 "Come unto me, all ye that ____"
106 Pitching stat
107 Close to, poetically
108 Strain, in Scotland
109 Way out
110 Poetic word
111 Theological degree
112 Doleful
114 Passageway
118 Part of a Voltaire comment
124 Lily plant
125 Ruth McKenney's sister
126 Journey
127 "I'm all ____"
128 Show boredom
129 Lie close
130 Mixer
131 Letter

DOWN
1 Pausing sounds
2 Gait
3 Teasdale
4 Come-ons
5 Column
6 Shortly
7 Book-page offering
8 Pre-Lib wheeze
9 ____ carte
10 See: Abbr.
11 "All About ____"
12 Conceal anew
13 Scholarly wage
14 Where, to Caesar
15 "We wuz ____!"
16 Deli purchase
17 ". . . ____ in thee tonight'
19 Miser
24 Thought
25 Exist, in Paris
26 Expressed a preference
32 Farm unit
34 In one's senses
35 Make a court move
37 Incas' milieu
38 In want
39 Coins
40 Outdated weapon
41 Holbrook
42 French elevator stop
49 Old card game
52 Jar-opener's target
53 Blackbird
54 N.C.O.
57 Malta or Bali: Abbr.
59 Cupid
60 Chief, in India
61 Invites
63 Zodiac unit
64 Style
67 Room
68 Large parrot
69 Millay
70 "____ circle round him thrice"
71 Dernier ____
72 Pronoun
73 Drink
74 Roundup
77 Unoriginal
78 Restless one
79 Arbor product
80 Consumed
82 Parent: Var.
87 Lasting effect
88 Gallahad, e.g.
90 Turned upside down: Var.
91 Charon's crossing
94 Junky prose
95 U.S.O. unit
99 Room for choice
100 Interstice
101 Alaskan outpost
102 ". . . 'til the sun shines, ____"
103 Dwell on
104 Uses energy
105 Fibber
113 Prefix for dynamics
115 Love or county
116 Play the siren
117 Actual being
119 Maynard of Westerns
120 Word with remit: Abbr.
121 Bridge reverse
122 Wire: Abbr.
123 Chem. prefix

363 STACKED DECK

By Tom Sheehan

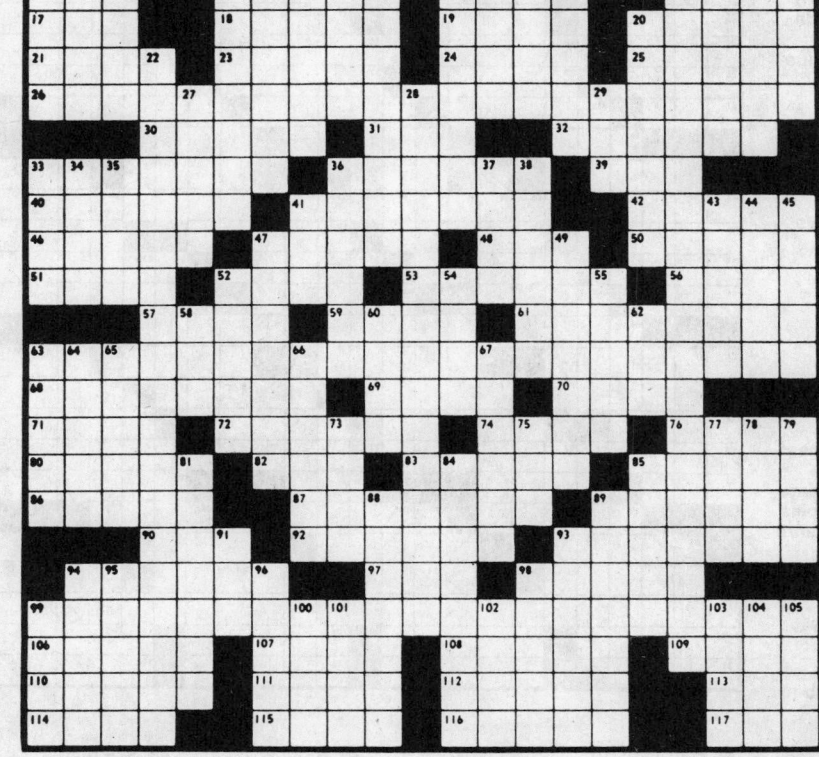

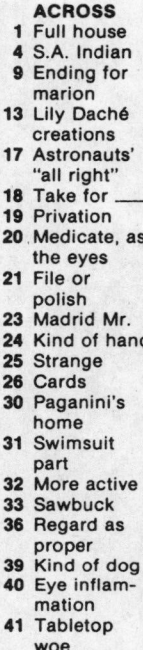

ACROSS

1 Full house
4 S.A. Indian
9 Ending for marion
13 Lily Daché creations
17 Astronauts' "all right"
18 Take for ____
19 Privation
20 Medicate, as the eyes
21 File or polish
23 Madrid Mr.
24 Kind of hand
25 Strange
26 Cards
30 Paganini's home
31 Swimsuit part
32 More active
33 Sawbuck
36 Regard as proper
39 Kind of dog
40 Eye inflammation
41 Tabletop woe
42 Fish-landing hooks
46 Pigeonholed
47 Column type
48 U.S. power org.
50 "Romola" author
51 Grope
52 Spanish evergreen
53 Relay
56 To ____
57 Song, in Bonn
59 Rosten and McCarey
61 "My cards ____ table"
63 Hands
68 "She's got ____ gold"
69 Self: Lat.
70 Raison d' ____
71 Swiss hero
72 Mugger's partner
74 Knuckles or feet
76 Pop's relative
80 Czech coin
82 Brown kiwi
83 Suppose
85 Divided, as a leaf
86 Hacienda material
87 Head near Honolulu
89 Word to a gun crew
90 Harem room
92 ____ it rich
93 Antique and double
94 He had a full house
97 Noun suffix
98 Our: Fr.
99 Pair of aces
106 Quarterback's motto
107 Work, in Spain
108 Made of a grain
109 Not difficult
110 Turk. coins
111 Roulette bet
112 Milan's river
113 Queen ____
114 Goblet support
115 Tuba player of song
116 Like a new driver
117 Jet ____

DOWN

1 Froid's predecessor
2 Crowd noise
3 Dust Bowl refugee
4 Housing for full houses
5 "We ____ amused"
6 ____ bell (get across)
7 Baal, e.g.
8 Disease
9 Insert in a plant
10 Tissue
11 ____ sheet
12 Nelson et al.
13 Jacks, and Kings or Queens
14 "There is ____ in the affairs . . ."
15 Possessive
16 Posted
20 Massive fire
22 Diamond, Heart, club, Spade
27 Like a baby's bathwater
28 Suit
29 N.C.O.
33 Spat
34 Buffalo's vista
35 Rosetta's river
36 Dead Sea find
37 Positive thinker's motto
38 Bara et al.
41 Nepotic candidate
43 ____ be tied (incensed)
44 Mountain wind
45 Mount
47 "Who ____ hair?"
49 Retinue
52 Australian city
54 In statu quo
55 Retreats
58 Comparative suffix
60 Miss Adams
62 "____ the fields we go . . ."
63 Earl Hines
64 In the foreground
65 String-quartet unit
66 ". . . abusing ____ patience"
67 Complain
73 Equestrian's concern
75 Neither Dem. nor Rep.
77 Mitch Miller purchase
78 Shakespearean king
79 Puts with
81 Hot-poker quality
84 Coarse herb
85 Ascertain
88 Dakota Indians
89 Eye parts
91 Sally ____ Howes
93 Deans of diplomacy
94 Take a ____ the beach
95 "What do ____ ?"
96 Piano-key material
98 Off
99 Turbulent waters
100 ____ ben Adhem
101 Crèche item
102 Hay unit
103 Keep ____ on
104 Hosea, in Douay Bible
105 Russian rebuff

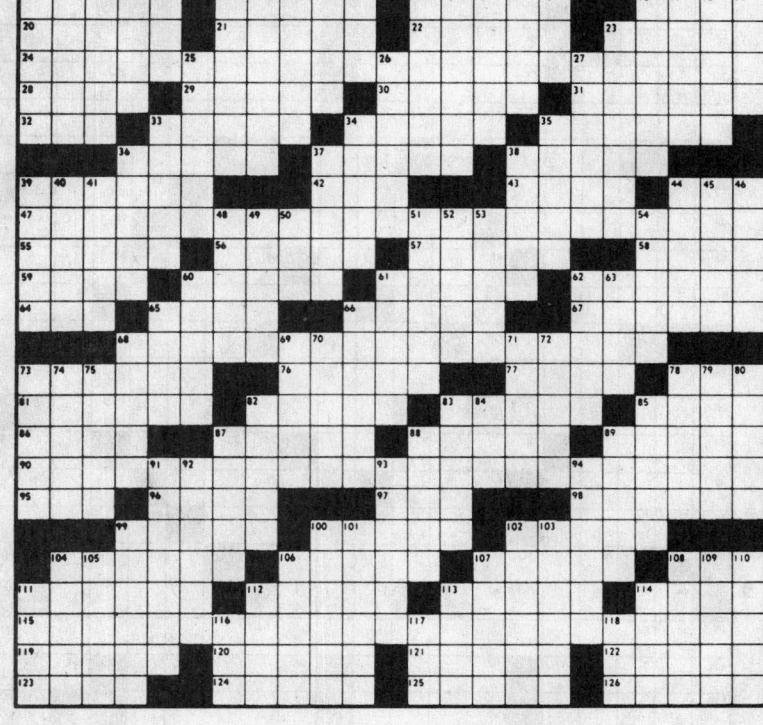

ACROSS

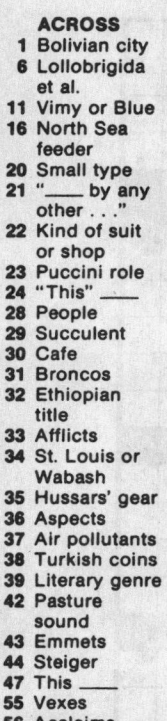

1 Bolivian city
6 Lollobrigida et al.
11 Vimy or Blue
16 North Sea feeder
20 Small type
21 "____ by any other . . ."
22 Kind of suit or shop
23 Puccini role
24 "This" ____
28 People
29 Succulent
30 Cafe
31 Broncos
32 Ethiopian title
33 Afflicts
34 St. Louis or Wabash
35 Hussars' gear
36 Aspects
37 Air pollutants
38 Turkish coins
39 Literary genre
42 Pasture sound
43 Emmets
44 Steiger
47 This ____
55 Vexes
56 Acclaims
57 Derring-do
58 "Thanks ____"
59 "QB VII" author
60 Stadium feature
61 Intimate
62 Juniper
64 Gumshoe
65 Connive with
66 Discharges
67 Go to ____ (lose one's poise)
68 "This" ____
73 District near London
76 Equals
77 See 23 Down
78 Month: Abbr.
81 Reluctant
82 Reels off
83 Fiascos
85 Unfailing
86 Cough-syrup ingredient
87 Saint- ____
88 Sierra ____
89 River of Tasmania
90 This is a ____
95 Compass heading
96 Actual

97 Harriman, to friends
98 Springs
99 Crew members
100 Goering and Goebbels, e.g.
102 Gorges
104 Cotton fabrics
106 Alone, to Caesar
107 French composer
108 Berne's river
111 Esprit de corps
112 Eniwetok, e.g.
113 Squelch
114 To boot
115 This is ____
119 White House name
120 Aviator Balbo
121 Mississippi sight
122 Go along with
123 Religious schs.
124 White House name
125 Put right
126 Advertises

DOWN

1 September day
2 U.S. rocket
3 Capitol Hill aides
4 Panay natives
5 Oriental cult
6 King Arthur's nephew
7 Blue flags
8 English county
9 Pallid
10 Implant
11 Exhaust
12 East or West
13 Watches calories
14 Left
15 Pass-catcher
16 Des ____
17 On the prowl
18 Hikers' mementos
19 Talk back
23 Doubles, with 77 Across
25 Public way
26 Flourishing
27 Helot's home

33 Weather satellite
34 Social pariahs
35 ____ of time
36 Standish
37 Snapshot expression
38 Game pie
39 Swagger
40 Flaming
41 Purposive
44 Museum piece
45 Two ____ (pass defense)
46 Is indulgent
48 Peculator
49 Must
50 Lesage's Blas
51 Master ____
52 Subleased
53 Phoney
54 Carried on
60 Decrease
61 Harbor features
62 Brief TV ads
63 Makes known
65 Enzyme suffixes
66 Strip a whale-

68 Ski-jump feature
69 ____ Volta
70 Marie Antoinette, e.g.
71 River of France
72 Windshield ____
73 Felt-hat materials
74 Acknowledges
75 Confederate hero
78 French writer
79 Wipe clean
80 Harvest goddess
82 Comedian Mort et al.
83 Throws a party for
84 Parking or odd
85 Delhi garb
87 Musial et al.
88 Denim pants
89 Crowd number
91 Son of Priam

92 Sycophants
93 Lapis ____
94 Bronze film
99 German composer
100 Pasta form
101 "____ one and one . . ."
102 Lustrous fabric
103 Made up for
104 Weather device
105 Off-white
106 Take second base in a way
107 Colander
108 Then, in Orly
109 Black-ink entry
110 Certain wines
111 Flightless birds
112 Bohemian
113 Goblet feature
114 Jason's craft
116 Morse symbol
117 Neighbor of Ga.
118 Headgear

PLAYPEN   *By Jack Luzzatto*

ACROSS

1 Walk shakily: Var.
7 Terra ____
12 Fortune
16 Thicket
21 Actress Merle
22 Specialist: Suffix
23 Bedouin head cord
24 Harshly bitter
25 "Stella Dallas" and "One Man's Family"
27 Execute a rock blast
29 Kind of hanger
30 River to the Baltic
31 Moving a bit
32 Certain people
33 Eastern tree
34 Stage chores
36 Gadgets
38 Sign of success
39 Badger
40 Liquid measure
42 Unplanted plant
43 Certain Chinese
45 One making adjustments
47 Libretto's partner
50 Presents
52 Like a certain tortoise
54 Marriage bond
55 Panic buyer
57 Neon and oxygen
58 Fear to
60 ____ pensée (hidden motive)
61 Cellar or lick
62 Police concern
64 Reward for the swift
65 Language of Christ's day
68 Items for Rosie
69 Vote for
70 "Sunny" and "Sally"
73 G.I.
76 Lease giver
77 Darted, in Scotland
78 Wiggly dance
79 It opens for a successful fall
82 American Indian
83 Runaway
86 Collector
87 Time for speed
89 Like a tiger or candy cane
90 Heaters
91 Sanatorium
94 Cowboy films
95 Chamber groups
97 Struggled
98 Sight in Appalachia
101 Mount where Hercules died
103 Prepared potatoes
104 Finagles with checks
105 Before
108 Minnie ____ Fiske
111 Multiple-marriage customs
113 Villainous look
114 Gold: Abbr.
115 Deviation from the norm
117 Of certain mountains
118 About
119 Wagner's bag
121 Mabel Normand vehicles
123 Mrs. Ike
124 Body structure: Abbr.
125 On guard
126 ____ honorable (apology)
127 Finnish island group
128 Stratagem
129 Units of force
130 Radio loner

DOWN

1 Defeats
2 Stopper of a nuisance
3 Import from Paree
4 Royal Irish name
5 Chicago district
6 Naval off.
7 Ed Wynn gear
8 Stand-offish quality
9 Cowboy gear
10 Of the cheek
11 Partner of ques.
12 Natural powers
13 "____ . . . a benefit received" (Lamb)
14 Tingly taste
15 Spanish hero
16 Loads
17 Month: Abbr.
18 Top banana of sorts
19 ____ up (appraised)
20 Realms of innocence
26 ". . . ____ to Chance"
28 Aplenty, in Paradise
31 Receiver of security goods
34 Curtain opener
35 Mack Sennett offering
37 Double ____ (big sandwiches)
39 Swarm
41 Defendants, at law
44 High nest
46 Partitions again
48 Cheer
49 Feminine suffix
50 Creator of Pal Joey
51 Raid
52 Western shrubs
54 Fiber plant: Var.
56 Heartens
57 Vasco da ____
59 Soaks
61 "Le ____ du Printemps"
62 Greek island
63 Fairground fun
66 Go wild
67 Force compliance
70 Auto-race aides, for short
71 Theater guide
72 Inheritors of the earth
73 Playing with dolls
74 Scared runner
75 Funny ones
76 Roped
78 Caribbean land
79 Work for an actor
80 Cupid
81 Welles on Mars, e.g.
84 Fur scarfs
85 Shooting game
87 Oscar Straus's soldier
88 Beautiful
92 Ship: Abbr.
93 Women who have had three children
96 Availed of
98 Emcee, in England
99 Gets one's bearings
100 Actor's dealer
102 Florence's river
104 Cliff the high place
106 Draw back
107 Blank maker
108 Molten rock
109 Of hearing
110 Words for some stocks
112 In a blithe way
113 Pep up
116 Waiter's offering
118 Stupor
120 Author Anais
121 Blue
122 Flaw

366 EQUAL RIGHTS

By Barbara Gillis

ACROSS

1 Partners
8 Difficulty
11 Bors or Gawain
14 Bridge
18 U.S. painter
19 Indonesian islands
20 Tire
21 Village in Ireland
22 Kind of case
23 Halloween props
26 Ericson
27 Pelvic bones
29 Helpless
30 Vermont resort
31 Life force: Abbr.
32 Liquor personified
35 Dawdled
36 Swallow hard
37 Claims
39 Iranian faith
42 Image
44 Israeli dance
46 Partner of a will
49 Leaf angles
50 Author Roger
51 Fluff
52 Miss Rich
53 Shell game of a sort
55 Obliquely
57 Math-sum unit
58 Pale
59 World power: Abbr.
61 Perfectly
63 Excessively
64 Ted Shawn's dance center
68 Baba or Pasha
70 Corona
71 Food fish
72 Haze
75 City in Illinois
77 Workroom
79 Famous Moor
81 English writer
82 Channels
83 First N.T. book
85 Furniture wood
86 Bills
87 Cinema's James Wong
88 Furry fliers
89 Baffles
90 Quarrel
92 Snood's burden
94 Boundary
97 Buck-passing words
100 Prepared
103 Kind of jacket
106 Bit of sediment
107 Tax, in Britain
108 Pool
109 Durable Brandon Thomas farce
112 Arrays
114 Sea in Russia
115 Descartes
116 Recent: Prefix
117 Writer of satire
118 Gemstone
119 French possessive
120 Ship: Abbr.
121 Timidity

DOWN

1 Burn
2 Church plate
3 Town near Rome
4 Mil. branch
5 Pouch
6 Native of Addis Ababa
7 Pillars
8 Moslem month
9 Swiss canton
10 Civil War creek
11 Piquant
12 Peak in Crete
13 Pacific island
14 Aft
15 Plays good golf
16 English composer
17 U.S. cartoonist
20 Many-colored plant
24 Droop
25 Spanish ring figure
28 Ink or rubber
32 Support beam
33 Contests
34 Vehicle
35 Asian peninsula
38 Showy perennial
39 Theda
40 Tools
41 Dangerous plane rider
43 Stiffness
45 Recorded
47 ___ Domini
48 Tokyo, once
50 Punjab city
51 Do a pier job
52 Pastoral poem
54 Stocking cap
56 Like steno-pad paper
57 Consign
60 Alternate
62 Israeli money
65 Malacca or sugar
66 Son of Tros
67 Breakfast food
68 Bombs, bullets, etc.
69 Kind of cloth
73 Las Vegas machine
74 "Sixteen ___"
76 In a narrow way
78 Japanese ware
80 Custom
82 Fight-timer's need
84 Hebrew letter
87 Ballplayers at times
89 V.I.P's
91 Armstrong
93 Vicinity
95 Decorative work
96 Cabaret
98 Pleasurable spots
99 Character or ham
100 Nest
101 Kind of pass or release
102 Orals
103 Cliff
104 Finished, for short
105 Austrian statesman
108 Twin's state: Abbr.
110 Born: Fr.
111 Fishing gear
113 Bauble

367 HOLIDAY THOUGHTS *By Anne Fox*

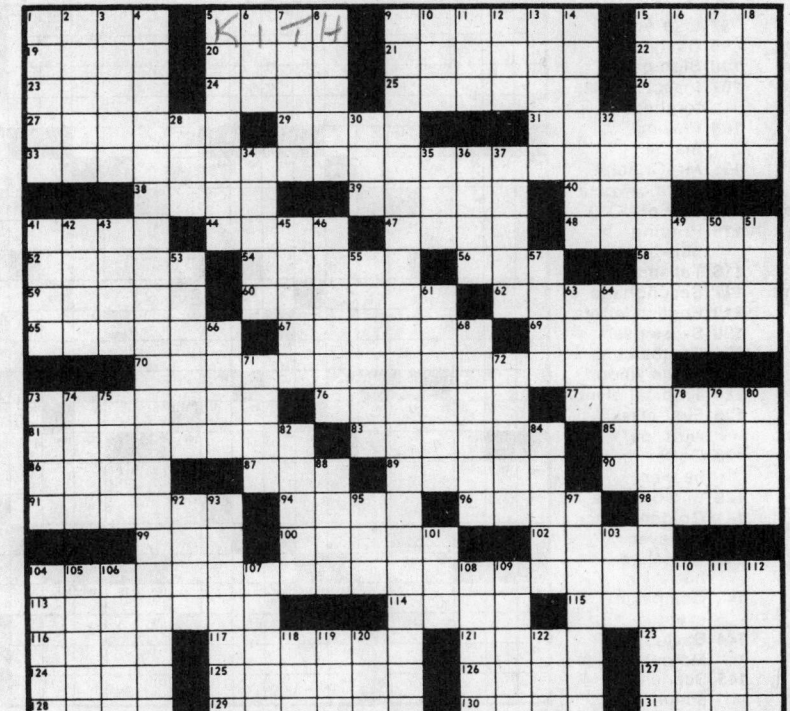

ACROSS

1 Chase, as fly balls
5 Kin's partner
9 A life ___
15 She-bears: Sp.
19 Prefix with naut or sol
20 Zhivago's beloved
21 Sweeteners: Var.
22 Void
23 Roman historian
24 Biblical giant
25 Deplorable
26 Sailors' saint
27 Farewells
29 River to the Colorado
31 Military hair décor
33 Carol of 1588
38 Eugene's daughter
39 Critic Cleveland
40 Casper's state: Abbr.
41 Castle barrier
44 Slumps
47 Fiscal or solar
48 Place for a light bulb
52 Flynn
54 Santa ___
56 Small drink
58 Yorkshire river
59 Kind of diver
60 Antiaircraft cannon
62 Peace pipes
65 Food banned during Passover
67 Prizes
69 Avengers
70 Harbingers
73 Cane-cutter
76 Of an S.A. range
77 Bantu tribesman
81 Field where Judas died
83 Cub scout's friend
85 Heaven: Prefix
86 Vain
87 Cult
89 At ___ (on the loose)
90 Decorated pillar
91 Shrimp dish
94 Miss Tennille
96 State
98 Perplexity
99 ___ Kippur
100 Indelicate
102 Rave over
104 ". . . because there was ___"
113 Kenneth Roberts novel
114 "___ the night . . ."
115 Nasty one
116 Hoover Dam's lake
117 City of India
121 Ruckus
123 Hollywood and ___
124 Glass piece
125 Crow, or Osage
126 Kind of hopper
127 Old oath
128 Jewish month
129 Going astray
130 Pet ___
131 Snoopy

DOWN

1 Fruit ___
2 Girl who preempted the Jets
3 Calif. town
4 Polish carol
5 Loud auto horns
6 Sean's relative
7 Perry Mason's opponent
8 Moslem governor
9 Words from a Latin carol
10 Evergreen
11 Period
12 Calendar abbr.
13 Piquant
14 Funds held by a third party
15 Words from a French carol
16 Grooves, in anatomy
17 Biblical tree
18 Laziness
28 Japanese herb
30 Meadow
32 Greek war goddess
34 Civil-rights org.
35 Shad product
36 Abadan's land
37 Melodic
41 Interlock
42 Whale
43 Calla lily, e.g.
45 Kid or boxing
46 Key fruit
49 Letters
50 Town of Italy
51 Miss Durbeyfield
53 Covered with wood strips
55 Plateau
57 Anguish
61 Site of Mohammed's tomb
63 Symbol of Wales
64 German vowel mark
66 Greek letter
68 Italian form of Alexander
71 Half: Prefix
72 Lake of Ireland
73 "___ oui!"
74 Elec. current initials
75 That: Fr.
78 ___ Morgana
79 Form of Agnes
80 European capital
82 Houston athlete
84 Condescend
88 Wuthering Heights vista
92 Russian weight
93 Dip
95 Kook
97 Make obsolete
101 Cut down
103 Pronoun
104 Idaho city
105 Mountain nymph
106 Colombian poncho
107 Natural ability
108 Equal
109 Island: It.
110 Architect Jones
111 Spanish girls
112 Wanting
118 Conjunction
119 ___ bono
120 Chinese dynasty
122 Cover for an i

368   ASPIRIN TIME   By Frances Hansen

ACROSS

1 Oafish
6 Annul, in law
11 Confirmation slap
16 Wagon prop
21 Trace of the past
22 Marx's advice to workers
23 Honeysuckle and clinging
24 Irish county
25 Duck
26 Curiouser and curiouser
27 Theater awards
28 Jack of Hollywood
29 Start of a cynical verse
33 Insects
34 Algerian port
35 Fold: Fr.
36 Swiss banking city
39 Biblical dancer
43 Blackbird
45 N.C.O.
49 Abba
50 Deep bow
51 Most competent
54 Between sine and non
55 More of verse
60 Kind of corn or angle
61 McCartney and Pry
62 Arrowsmith's wife
63 "Ta-ra-ra-boom ____!"
64 Laughing sounds
65 Knucklehead
68 Namely
69 Having a will
72 Feather in Yankee Doodle's hat
76 S.A. monkey
78 Exclamation of delight
80 Gymnastic feat
81 More of verse
87 Aries
88 Dawn goddess
89 Shade of black
90 Magnetite and turgite
91 Slight
95 Luau offering

97 Like Abner
99 Badly
100 Sign gas
101 Insect's forehead
103 Playing marble
105 Mr. Cratchit
108 More of verse
114 Part of I.O.U.
115 Printing boo-boos
116 Talisman
117 Secondhand
118 English letters
120 Swiss river
121 Football unit
122 Battle whoop
124 Tropical plant
126 First-class, with "de"
128 Coffee, in a beanery
129 End of verse
141 Golden Fleece retriever
142 Wretched hut
143 Campaign event
144 Baal and Moloch
145 Scene of action
146 Concerning
147 T.S.
148 Hamlets
149 Super-candid photos
150 Fuses with heat
151 Fracas
152 Tournedos on the hoof

DOWN

1 Oarsmen
2 Dream, in Dijon
3 "There ought to be ____"
4 Take out of the game
5 Like most postcards
6 Cite
7 Ruin
8 Radamès's beloved
9 Kind of ladder
10 Wife of Zeus
11 "____ santé!"
12 Tripoli's land
13 Negative atom
14 Hammer end
15 Cousin of an org.
16 Black look

17 "____ again, Sam"
18 Roué
19 "M'appari", for one
20 Actor Will
30 Tut!
31 Desert Fox of W.W. II
32 Soap-opera unit
36 Enthusiasm
37 Over: Ger.
38 Shankar
39 Writer Bellow
40 "Amo, amas, I love ____"
41 Gibbon
42 Grain
43 ____ Vista
44 One of the Yorks
46 Close game
47 Zernial or Edwards
48 Greek letter
50 Waste
51 Thine: Fr.
52 Russian wolfhound

53 Ship ropes
56 Separated
57 Western resort
58 Billy Graham meeting
59 Table scrap
64 Owns
66 Ocean: Abbr.
67 Working on a crazy quilt
69 "Stay on ____ side, sister . . .'"
70 Time's partner
71 Finial tops
72 Office V.I.P.'s
73 Arab head cord
74 Firmly attached
75 ____ Jima
77 Confucian truth
79 Mouth: Prefix
82 ____ de corps
83 Whitney
84 Rock layers
85 Not leased
86 Bean or sauce

92 Society-page word
93 Trio, with dese and dem
94 Shuffle off to Buffalo
96 Mrs. Chaplin
98 Dipper-outer
101 Fright
102 Less fresh
104 Miss Verdon
105 Autumn pear
106 Eur. river
107 Futile kind of English
108 Twelve, for short
109 Farm animal
110 Bikini part
111 Cockney's residence
112 B'way hit of 1964
113 Puccini opera
119 Old Ger. state
121 Elevates
122 Museum or paper
123 Shuns
125 Dr. Salk

126 Uniform
127 Turn topsy-turvy
128 "____ the world!"
129 "Iliad" hero
130 Young salmon
131 "On thy cold gray stones, ____!"
132 Defrost
133 Sharpen
134 ____ gai
135 Eastern campus
136 Came to roost
137 Cabal
138 Days of ____
139 Greek flask
140 Vodka-land initials

369 REINING IN

By Nancy W. Atkinson

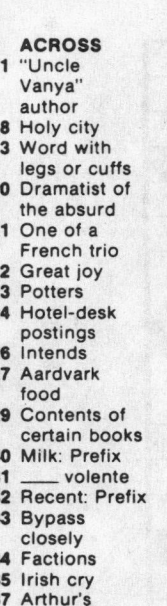

ACROSS

1 "Uncle Vanya" author
8 Holy city
13 Word with legs or cuffs
20 Dramatist of the absurd
21 One of a French trio
22 Great joy
23 Potters
24 Hotel-desk postings
26 Intends
27 Aardvark food
29 Contents of certain books
30 Milk: Prefix
31 ___ volente
32 Recent: Prefix
33 Bypass closely
34 Factions
35 Irish cry
37 Arthur's nephew
39 Great Barrier Island
42 Geste or Nash
45 Sea flier
46 Sing loudly, with "out"
47 Palm leaf: Var.
50 English game pebble
54 Makes inquiries
57 Humperdinck boy
58 Base runner, at times
60 Treatment
61 Common abbr.
62 ___ code
64 Ground defense: Abbr.
65 African native
67 Stopovers for game pieces
72 Small town
73 Gold tinctures
74 Plaster item
75 Regular: Abbr.
77 Miss Adoree
78 Contract's predecessor
80 Coin
83 Realists
86 Full go-ahead
88 Estes and Menlo: Abbr.
89 Bird plumage
90 Owned
91 Creil's river

92 Elbe tributary
93 Object of perception
95 "What ___ God wrought!"
99 Samantha
103 Miss Kett et al.
105 Roman way
107 Relative: Abbr.
108 Skin
109 Sleigh puller
111 Show surprise
112 Small herring
113 Accurate one
116 Most trim
118 Harmonizers' girl
119 Type of song
120 Set apart
121 Picks
122 As good ___
123 Early stringed instrument

DOWN

1 Large insect
2 "___ than thou"
3 Charm
4 Florida sights
5 Royal initials
6 Kind of ography
7 Author Kurt
8 Raincoats, for short
9 Moral: Abbr.
10 Begin a hotel visit
11 Chinese fowl
12 Inquiring one
13 Japanese bastion of W.W. II
14 "Zounds!"
15 Decide
16 Practical
17 Common field plant
18 Establish
19 Shelters or hostels
25 1905 manifesto
28 ___ tee
33 Hindu garment

34 Japanese orange
36 Fundamentals
38 Traveled widely
40 Flatfoot's relative
41 Social-club member
43 Squeeze out
44 Abate, old style
47 Give out iridescence
48 Of a military science
49 Carbon: Suffix
50 Guevara
51 Kind of girl
52 Delights
53 Dare: Fr.
54 Goodman's instr.
55 Sniffles
56 Asian grass
59 As ___ resort
63 Soak
65 Trafalgar and Times: Abbr.

66 Excel in the slalom
68 Tall bird
69 Less smoggy
70 Grampuses
71 Arabian capital
76 Ten: Prefix
77 Door sound
78 ___ as a daisy
79 Borneo natives
81 Portions: Abbr.
82 Querying sounds
84 Haul
85 Bowstring hemp
87 Based on moral law
90 Listen carefully
93 Crams, in Scotland
94 Grape
96 Take ___ (rest)
97 Sad, in Dijon

98 More torrid
99 Norse tales
100 Hollow stone
101 Thin cereal
102 Stroll along
104 Greek letter
106 Clownlike
109 Parking-lot hazard
110 Honor cards
111 Expanded
112 Swindle
114 Auto plate: Abbr.
115 Uncle, in Perth
117 Deer

370 SPIRIT OF '76 *By Stanley Glass*

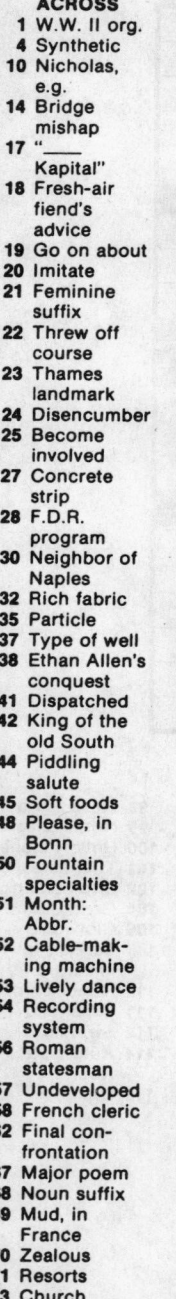

ACROSS
1 W.W. II org.
4 Synthetic
10 Nicholas, e.g.
14 Bridge mishap
17 "____ Kapital"
18 Fresh-air fiend's advice
19 Go on about
20 Imitate
21 Feminine suffix
22 Threw off course
23 Thames landmark
24 Disencumber
25 Become involved
27 Concrete strip
28 F.D.R. program
30 Neighbor of Naples
32 Rich fabric
35 Particle
37 Type of well
38 Ethan Allen's conquest
41 Dispatched
42 King of the old South
44 Piddling salute
45 Soft foods
48 Please, in Bonn
50 Fountain specialties
51 Month: Abbr.
52 Cable-making machine
53 Lively dance
54 Recording system
56 Roman statesman
57 Undeveloped
58 French cleric
62 Final confrontation
67 Major poem
68 Noun suffix
69 Mud, in France
70 Zealous
71 Resorts
73 Church musical rite
75 Long
76 Spotted cat
80 Swiss town
81 At the peak
82 Fly

83 Sore
84 Aunts, in Spain
86 The low point
88 New Jersey battle
92 Stake
93 Confine
95 Site of U.S. base in Canada
96 Adirondack river
99 Times or tack
101 Wobble
102 Packing unit: Abbr.
103 Batty
104 ____ contempt (accused in court)
106 Period
107 Korean soldier
108 Region: Abbr.
109 Football-team unit

110 British medical org.
111 Office holders
112 Vehicle
113 Aver
114 Its, in Paris

DOWN
1 Black Sea port
2 Pulpit occupant
3 Declare
4 Goof
5 Subject of Kant critique
6 Move easily
7 Titan with a burden
8 Early confrontation
9 British letter
10 Hessians' Waterloo
11 Shiny fabric
12 Swear
13 Tear

14 Site of the turning point
15 Postscript to a play
16 Kennedy
18 Vermont battle
22 This: Ger.
26 Journalism
29 Like an otary
31 Spud
33 Clerical headwear
34 Religious picture
36 France's Le ____
39 Unsmiling
40 Sicilian city
42 Atlantic islands
43 ". . . grow too ____ dream"
45 Nemesis of bad guys
46 Misbehave
47 Feather: Prefix

49 Sharp setbacks
50 Disseminated
52 Holy ____
53 Sultans' collections
55 B. & O., etc.
57 Redden, in Paris
58 City official: Abbr.
59 Goat's cry
60 Church fund-raiser
61 Bar legally
63 ____ Sea scrolls
64 Vogue's Nast
65 The C.I.C.
66 ____ gratia artis
71 Glut
72 Victim
73 Scorch
74 Expert on lines
76 Footing at Mauna Loa

77 Northwestern's home
78 Bayonne, N.J., sights
79 More feeble
80 Kind of hog
81 In unison
83 Site of a widely-heard shot
85 Eastern ruler
87 Small coach
88 Midday-sun sharer
89 Says
90 Wine measure
91 Torment
94 Port of Brazil
97 Heights: Abbr.
98 Mr. Coward
100 Network
102 Dernier ____
104 Auditor: Abbr.
105 Adversary

MEMORY LANE

By Virginia Schneider

ACROSS

1 Misrepresent
6 Cry of disgust
10 ____ majesty
14 Swanson, Crawford and Hayworth
20 Wedding words
21 Exchange premium
22 Con
23 Monogram unit
25 J. Barrymore, March and Tracy
28 Conn. city
29 Wood nymph: Sp.
30 DeMille specialty
31 "Two hearts that beat ____"
32 Raincoat, for short
33 Chang's partner
34 Service initials
35 Gilbert, Donat and Jourdan
39 Choose
40 Drug plants
41 Tribe of Israel
42 Plant liquid
47 Celtic god
48 At once
52 "____ pass this way again"
54 Vivacity
56 Emphatic pronoun
57 Gushed out
58 Part of N.B.
61 Howard, Harvey and Whiting
63 Elec. unit
64 Metric units: Abbr.
65 Dietrich and Britt
67 Loom part
70 H.M. Pulham, e.g.
71 Prospero's slave
72 Irritable, in Soho
73 Chaney, Laughton and Quinn
81 Shed ____
82 N.Z. sedges
83 City rtes.
85 "Home ____ the heart is"

87 Bara, Colbert, Leigh or Taylor
90 Taste
91 May honoree
92 Rue de ____
94 Gait
95 Pickford, Del Rio or Young
98 Quick: Fr.
101 E-flat sax
102 Big-top act
104 Guard's hut
106 Rubber tree
109 Gift for a blue lady
110 Vinegar, old style
111 Lord's house
113 ____ culpa
114 J. Barrymore & Wolfit; Marsh & Neff
120 Protection for 102 Across
123 Triumph
124 Exclamation
125 Waves, in Mexico
126 French silk
127 Wash
128 TV hook-in
130 Lincoln & Weissmuller; Markey & O'Sullivan
133 Licenses
134 Molding
135 Moon goddess
136 ____garde
137 Meal
138 Licentious
139 Plant plots
140 Snide

DOWN

1 Wheezy film-house name
2 Jugs
3 Compare
4 Writer Ehrenburg
5 Annex
6 L. Barrymore or Purdom
7 One more time
8 Coloring
9 Turf
10 Waits in ambush
11 Top a cathedral
12 Dictators' helpers
13 Iron, in Essen
14 Twin or cat
15 Sweet and Garbo

16 Circumspect
17 Japanese premier
18 Chemical suffixes
19 Louis or Paul
24 ____ Maggiore
26 Stokowski
27 Non-Hawaiian
35 "The Friends of Eddie ____"
36 Mineo
37 Resort lake
38 "Odyssey" beggar
42 Actress Minnie Maddern
43 Venomous in nature
44 Farnum, Holt and Baxter
45 Marble
46 African dowry

48 "Tiny" actors Kilburn & Beaumont
49 Warren William & Ricardo Cortez
50 Bread spread
51 Neighbor of Que.
53 Purposive
54 Container: Abbr.
55 Brown kiwi
59 Christ's-thorn
60 High notes
62 Oyster genus
65 Tar-pit site in L.A.
66 Venezuelan Indian tribe
68 Hat or Faithful
69 Harper Valley group

71 Ruggles, Benny and Bolger
74 Extreme
75 Letter
76 Dandies
77 Orderly
78 Brown fur
79 Lethargy
80 Exhibit
84 Prophesies, in Glasgow
85 Little terrors
86 Peeved
87 Metal residue
88 Ignited
89 Outer: Prefix
93 Phila. suburb
95 Like a vireo
96 Neighborhoods: Sp.
97 Chinese leader
99 British gun
100 Mollusk genus

103 Manitoba range
105 Northern Irish city
106 Not confused
107 "____ luck!"
108 Slip
111 Make do
112 Merry one
114 Trade
115 Mechanical pea picker
116 ____ nous
117 Mexican liquor
118 Progeny
119 "____ behold"
120 Anna Sten and Martine Carol
121 Happening
122 Irascible
127 Etna output
129 Ruler: Abbr.
131 U.S. agency
132 Month: Abbr.

372 ENTOMOLOGICAL FORMS

By A. J. Santora

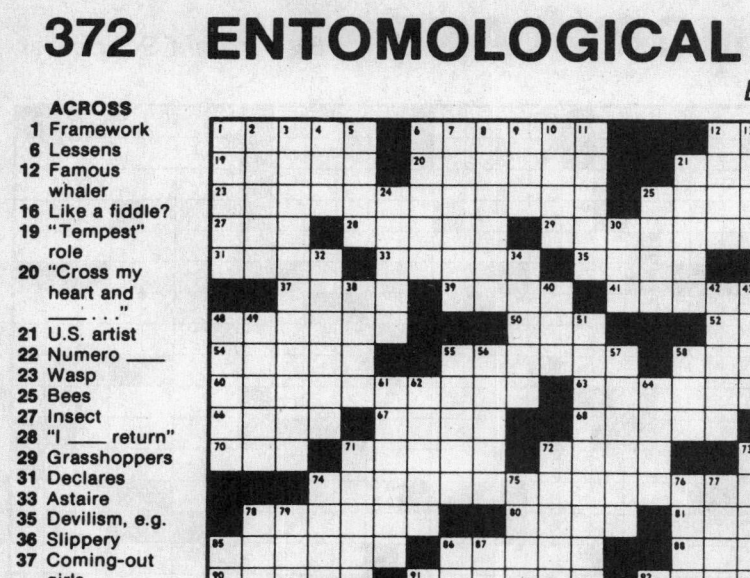

ACROSS

1 Framework
6 Lessens
12 Famous whaler
16 Like a fiddle?
19 "Tempest" role
20 "Cross my heart and ___ . . ."
21 U.S. artist
22 Numero ___
23 Wasp
25 Bees
27 Insect
28 "I ___ return"
29 Grasshoppers
31 Declares
33 Astaire
35 Devilism, e.g.
36 Slippery
37 Coming-out girls
39 Wander
41 ___ the wrist (reprimands)
45 Siesta
48 Scarab
50 Outfit
52 Over there
53 African nut
54 Get ___ start
55 Trotting-track no-no
58 Medicinal plant
59 Of the ear
60 Caterpillars
63 Portland's state
65 Portland's state
66 To ___
67 ___-Japanese
68 Name with Mason
69 Flew alone
70 Sun. talk
71 Lead-off on a tax form
72 ___ time (never)
73 Couches
74 Bugs
78 Military drill hall
80 Rage
81 Disguises
82 T.C.U. rival
85 As soft as ___ skin
86 Sleep sound
88 Formerly
89 Sign
90 Thrashed
91 Kind of stitch
92 Spiders
94 Kind of test

95 Offenses
96 City of Japan
98 ___ prosequi
99 Bull and home
100 Road or ground
101 Author Deighton
102 Beauty room
103 Telegram contents: Abbr.
104 Forgetful bridge player
108 Campus mil. unit
111 "___ boy!"
112 Sheep sound
114 Exile island
116 Overcharges
118 Leave out
121 Cricket
127 Bank robbery
129 A feast ___ famine
130 Earwigs
131 Fly
134 Small island
135 ___ pittance
136 Armenian city
137 Dye
138 Crosses out

139 Neat
140 Dead winds
141 Memory routines

DOWN

1 Madrid homes
2 Hockey rink
3 Louse
4 Part of R.P.M.
5 Yalies
6 In the lead
7 Alley frequenter
8 Moon mission
9 Pro ___
10 Common Latin abbr.
11 Kind of boom
12 Eagle: Prefix
13 China-writer Emily
14 Syrian city, to French
15 Walled city
16 Maggot
17 U.S. playwright
18 Throw
21 Italian food
24 Pursue
25 Nature's aqualung
26 Debriefing: Abbr.
30 Eur. country
32 Pay up
34 Noblemen
38 Extracted
40 Thickness unit
42 Tower
43 In no time
44 Single
46 Straightens
47 Walked the floor
48 Rum cakes
49 Wash out
51 Butterfly
53 Wombats' relatives
55 France's Citizen
56 Cheering
57 Charming, for one
58 In the past
61 Willows
62 Like a metal: Var.

64 O.T. book
65 Chess plays
69 Nauseate
71 Bridges or Nolan
72 Froglike
73 Saucerlike pieces
74 Places into
75 "The Wizard ___"
76 Campus in Atlanta
77 Chekhov's Uncle
78 Calculator
79 Moths
82 Mite
83 "The Wizard of ___ Park".
84 Auto-racer Al or Bobby
85 Clock part
86 Scorch
87 Flunking initials
89 City in Portugal
91 Jerusalem hill
92 Samoan councils

93 Insect
95 Pronoun
97 Teut. language
102 Outmoded
104 Knocking sound
105 Sort
106 Wings
107 Batter's stat.
109 "___ and to hold . . ."
110 Julius
113 Kind of deco
115 Records: Ger.
117 Ovens
119 Bordoni
120 ___ Bulba
121 Tunisian port
122 Ballet bend
123 Kind of finals
124 Early TV horse
125 Ethereal
126 Saarinen
128 Wild goat
132 Greek letters
133 Kind of physicist

373 ENCORES *By John Vezendy*

ACROSS

1 Dental degree
4 T.E. Lawrence et al.
12 Parts of acts: Abbr.
15 Nabokov novel
18 Do rodeo work
20 Philip Nolan, for one
21 Asian dye shrub
22 Hurok
23 Ancient Mariner's plaint
27 Funeral song
28 Early laborer
29 Swindlers
30 Dispute
31 Clod
33 Leitmotifs
34 Portion: Abbr.
35 Wicked one
37 Rang
38 Truth evasion
41 Kind of talk
44 Art subject
45 Tedious
48 Moss and Lorenz
49 Mrs. Kowalski of "Streetcar"
51 In ____ (untidy)
52 A ____ (deductive)
55 Wailed
56 French writer
57 Behavioral comment
61 Shock
62 Alike, in France
63 Berra
64 Gem
67 Invitation
72 Director Clair
73 Cider time
75 Successful, in Paris
76 Old Greek theater area
77 Produces
78 Elegance
80 Vulture
81 Window part
82 Stein logic
86 Article
87 Evaluate
89 Explorer of 1400's
90 Haggard
93 African fly
94 Butterfly ____
95 Actor Lew
97 "Vincit omnia ____"
99 Stepped on
102 "He's ____ yokel"
103 Willful cultivator
107 Onassis
108 Can. province
109 Conceal
110 Hole or cap
111 Color
112 "____ victis"
113 Ones who testify
114 Go amiss

DOWN

1 Arts branch
2 Feelings of anguish
3 Moocher
4 Call it ____
5 Electric unit
6 Mil. address
7 Grease base
8 Irritates
9 Musial or Kenton
10 Distant: Prefix
11 Salt, at Maxim's
12 Conspicuous
13 "____ Ishmael"
14 Quenched
15 Hebrew lyre
16 Oxford tutors
17 Brew
19 "I've had it!"
24 Dutch town
25 Detests
26 "Sous ____ Toits de Paris"
31 Shell adjunct
32 Siamese coin
33 "____ was no lady . . ."
35 Sink
36 Emphatic refusal
37 Jeopardy
38 What Farragut ordered ahead
39 Leisured
40 Draw a ____ on
42 Print measures
43 Mata ____
44 B'way show tune
45 Under-eye woes
46 Overlook
47 Catalyzing enzyme
49 Thorndike of stage
50 Extremely
52 Kind of stick
53 O'Neal
54 Wight, for one
57 Snake-charmers' clarinets
58 Caustics
59 Scarves
60 He, in Italy
65 Part of A.D.
66 Oblique look
68 Defarge
69 Stupid
70 Platinum wire loop
71 "Food of love"
73 Aide: Abbr.
74 State
76 Help!
78 Full of a salad green
79 Trail the field
80 Camper's need
82 Semitic goddess
83 One of Zsa Zsa's husbands
84 Beame
85 Go bad
87 Isaac of sci-fi
88 Hokkaido town
91 Esoteric
92 More convenient
93 Afflict
95 Height: Abbr.
96 More sneaky
97 Change
98 Lake
99 Change one's ____
100 Stem. in England
101 German king
102 Conjunctions
103 Dog or Hatter
104 Math initials
105 Iowa college
106 "____ Town"

374 DOUBLE TAKES By Tap Osborn

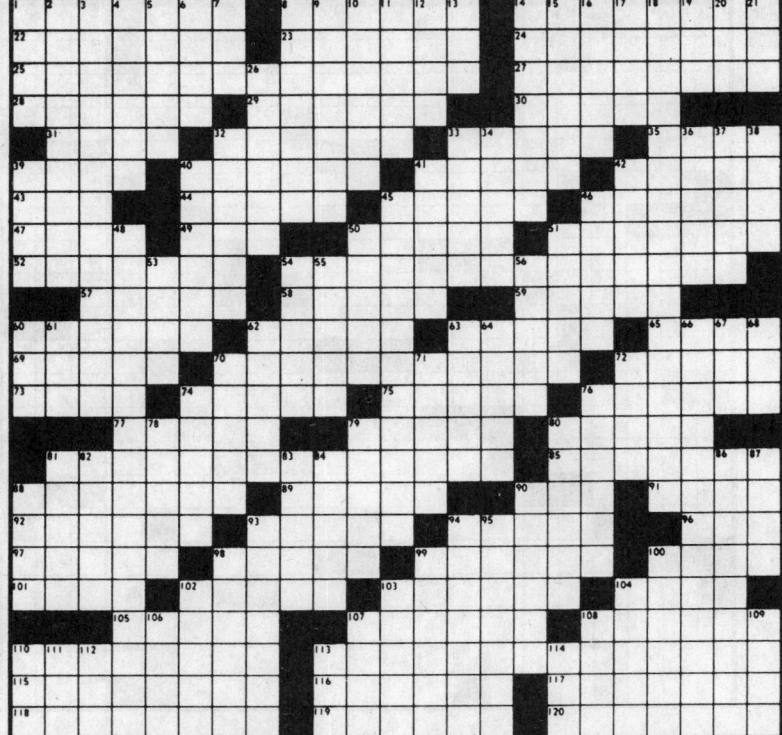

ACROSS

1 Bullock cart
8 Urban ___
14 Sanatorium
22 K. Roberts novel
23 Remit in advance
24 Treeless
25 "Flight time has been delayed"
27 Strategists
28 Receive
29 Downstairs wear
30 Dance
31 "___ a cockhorse . . ."
32 "Phèdre" author
33 Hauler
35 Scum
39 Wine casks
40 Most arid
41 "Wreck of the Mary ___"
42 House lily
43 Trig's relative
44 Repeat: Lat.
45 "Beau ___"
46 October specter
47 Eucalyptus secretion
49 Burning
50 Declaim
51 Fashion variable
52 Fabric line-marker
54 "Nuts!"
57 Pooh creator
58 "___ Irish Rose"
59 ". . . dreary, everywhere ___"
60 Venus, for one
62 ". . . when ___ at you"
63 Jack's fish
65 God of love
69 Like a jug
70 "Out, damned spot!"
72 Rockne
73 Answered: Abbr.
74 Meaning
75 Canonical hour
76 Lemon's cousin
77 "What a way to ___ living"
79 City of Italy
80 Russian girl's name

81 "Soak the rich!"
85 "___ vita"
88 Indian way
89 Court quieter
90 Cloche
91 Neighbor of Minn.
92 Come forth
93 Carries on
94 Treat, as ham
96 Before
97 Miss Adoree
98 Bibulous one
99 Pit remover
100 Fusing materials: Abbr.
101 Time periods
102 Like Monsarrat's sea
103 Like cutlery
104 Irish festival
105 Kind of tax
107 Duplicates of a sort
108 Drool
110 Shy
113 "A fat paunch never breeds fine thoughts"
115 Weaken

116 Red stone
117 Put the hex on again
118 Polite
119 Disdainful
120 Printing chemicals

DOWN

1 Nimbus
2 Faisal, for one
3 "Et, tu, Brute"
4 Makes dough
5 Cantor or Bracken
6 Hold back
7 Primary colors: Abbr.
8 Film mender
9 Condition
10 Dislike
11 Venezuelan river
12 Cautious
13 Soap base
14 Break
15 Interweave
16 Posh

17 Chinese group
18 "Here comes the judge"
19 Poem
20 Sea: Fr.
21 Begley et al.
26 Red wine
32 Withdraw
33 Seed casing
34 Asian badger
36 Exhausted
37 Lighter part
38 Temple
39 Powder
40 Taciturn
41 Loved ones
42 Colon's cousin
45 "If I am Sophocles, I am not mad"
46 Old English council
48 "How sharper than a serpent's tooth . . ."
50 Tear inducer
51 Acre dance: Var.
53 Bob at Lake Placid

54 Ancient medic
55 Small German craft
56 Enchantress
60 Hen or nut
61 Tree resin
62 Of a pelvic bone
63 Auto-da-fé
64 Pie nut
66 ". . . folks, all politics is applesauce"
67 Siouan
68 Tokyo money
70 Seashell
71 Danger
72 Type
74 Ready, in Paris
76 Film-paper worker
78 Proverb
79 Road worker
80 Satisfied
81 Circus star
82 Scene
83 Slack-jawed
84 Snarl
86 Plus for a bridge player

87 Makes do, with "out"
88 Common verb
90 Abe or Injun
93 Shook awake
94 Actor Lionel
95 Humility
98 Juin's total of days
99 Brit. Museum benefactor
100 Slimy shore deposit
102 Intelligible
103 Movies' Eric
104 Particle
106 Asian tree
107 Scottish swift
108 British gun
109 Ways: Abbr.
110 Ad ___
111 Greek letter
112 Pewter's base
113 One-star men: Abbr.
114 Onassis

375 TOUJOURS L'AMOUR
By Jack L. Steinhardt

ACROSS
1 Talkative one
7 Rio de la ____
12 Youth org.
15 Place within
21 Hit the big time
22 Loom bar
23 Fleming
24 Widened a hole
25 Rolling and birth
26 "You used to come ____ . . .
27 Electric abbr.
28 Warm-water fishes
29 Love: Crabbe
33 Liabilities
35 New World: Abbr.
36 "I ____ tell a . . ."
37 Quartzes
40 Out of line
41 Novello et al.
42 Take retribution
43 Swift
44 Mauna ____
45 Mother or silly
46 German name for 92 Across
47 Self-assured
48 Love: Johnson
55 Bradley
56 ____ lazuli
57 Without columns
61 Rumanian coins
63 One who welds
65 Container: Abbr.
67 Suffix of action
68 Miss Verdugo
70 Stimulate
71 Leading ____
73 Snooty one
74 Love: Shakespeare
79 Commotions
80 Western lawman
81 In reserve
82 Royal sight in Colorado
83 Roman 551
84 Vote against
85 Girls
86 Sediment
87 Seraglios
91 Fabric ribs
92 Belgrade's river

94 Love: Congreve
102 "____ Mucho"
105 Cousin or aunt: Abbr.
106 Extort
107 Correlative
108 Use a pencil end
109 Las Vegas employee
112 "Orphans of the ____"
113 Town near Caen
114 Old German coin
115 Hat for Al Capone
116 Herring measure
117 Boot or razor
118 Love: Dryden
122 Totaled
124 Have bills
125 Afternoon, in Madrid
126 Roman general
129 Acid prefixes
130 Russian village
131 Mideast title
132 Plant found in dry places

133 Glitter
134 Wall and Main: Abbr.
135 Ointments
136 Farm implement

DOWN
1 Balloon filler
2 Cultural field
3 Bully
4 Double
5 Tinker to ____ to . . .
6 Defendant: Abbr.
7 Soil improver
8 Frothed, as a horse
9 Garden flowers
10 Abound
11 Rubbing fluid
12 Oriental soup staples
13 Dixie port
14 Parallel thing
15 ____ while
16 Type of oil
17 Katharine Hepburn's flower

18 Electrical units
19 ". . . ____ of troubles"
20 Desk workers: Abbr.
30 ____ faire
31 Seagoing: Abbr.
32 Native: Suffix
33 Contemporary painter
34 Assertive tendencies
38 Scottish river
39 Theology degree
41 Big Ten team
45 Castor and Pollux
47 Opposite of neg.
49 Oilstone users
50 Tony of baseball
51 Stabat or Alma
52 Not restricted
53 Tree
54 Manuel de ____
58 Amount of printed matter
59 Atlantic islands

60 Johnny ____
61 Parish officer
62 Lombard king
63 Violet or modern
64 Like fall air
65 Liberator of Scotland
66 Tree trunks
69 Stone or coon's
72 Work unit
73 Flow
75 Medieval guild
76 Double-boiler part
77 Form of Cecilia
78 Worked out
79 Cutting tool
85 Medieval poem
88 Humiliation
89 Part of a fraction
90 Corroded
91 Hogs, at times
92 Breastbones
93 Interrupter's word
95 F.D.R.'s Four ____
96 Spontaneous humor
97 Pushed out

98 Vagrants
99 Dauntless
100 Lopez theme
101 Kick or leaf
102 "You ____!" (surely)
103 Victorian
104 Deli purchases
109 Graduate degree
110 Silkworm
111 Cane
112 Game official
113 Rank designation
117 Coin of Ecuador
119 Fail to keep
120 Syrian city
121 Army comm. officers
122 Silent ____
123 ____ Darya
127 Chemical suffix
128 Atop, to poets

376 FULLER EXPLANATIONS

By Elaine D. Schorr

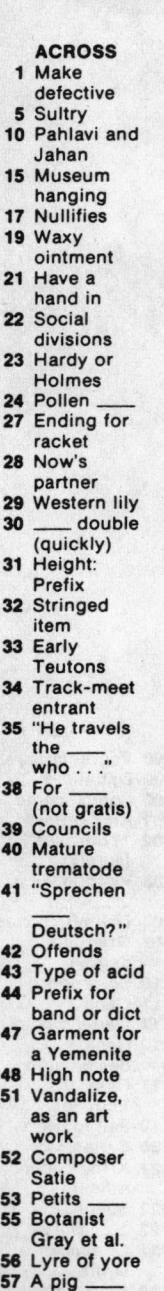

377 SPELLING IT OUT
By Alfio Micci

ACROSS

1 Western capital
6 Metric units: Abbr.
9 ____ bleu
12 Plateaus
17 African country
18 Actor Linden
19 Newts
21 Funeral oration
22 Like a wasteland
23 Cretan mount
24 Brünnhilde
26 Lucy Ashton
29 Spread hay
30 Desires
31 Paparazzo's need
32 Wonder
33 Wahoo
34 Attention-getting word
35 Previously
37 Hairy and Barbary
38 Miss Earhart
42 Baseball stat
43 Likely
45 Lunar-solar year gap
50 Sicilian port
52 Gets a flag ready
55 Cupid
56 Wager
58 Swiss canton
59 Compete with
62 Color
63 Barber's cry
64 Scale notes
65 Lolita, for one
66 Kind of pass or door
67 Tropical tree
70 Marx
74 Bro. or sis, e.g.
76 Japanese city
77 ____ out (scold)
81 Man from Riga
82 Retainer
83 Uniform fabric
85 Solo
86 Straus's was chocolate
89 Height
90 Ten: Lat.
92 Ghent river
93 Digits: Abbr.
95 Imagined
96 Understanding words
99 Omitted
101 Period
104 Road sign
105 Hind
107 Of animals
108 Turn
112 Silkworm
113 Uncas
117 Violetta Valery
119 Spanish queen
120 Oleoresins
121 Chou ____
122 Coward or Harrison
123 Staff man: Abbr.
124 Kreutzer, for one
125 Horse
126 Young plant: Abbr.
127 Cry of disgust
128 Cubic meter

DOWN

1 Wile
2 Smiling
3 Conrad's Jim et al.
4 Robt. ____
5 Don Quixote
6 Horror flick
7 Pinkerton's spouse
8 Word with bang
9 Moisten
10 Flaming
11 Halt
12 Village on the Tweed
13 ____ Rapids, Mich.
14 Bridge hand
15 Concur
16 Unkempt
17 "Dear ____"
20 At one fell ____
25 Topnotch
27 Tree
28 One of the poles
35 English river
36 Hubbub
37 Ocean: Abbr.
38 Date: Abbr.
39 African land
40 Dash
41 Talk: Abbr.
43 Of gold
44 Ruritania's Rudolf
46 Feeler
47 Oriental nurse
48 D'Azur or d'Or
49 Weight allowance
51 Fairy king and namesakes
53 Fee-faw-____
54 Spanish ladies
57 Devon river
60 Ferrara's spouse
61 Fringefoot
66 Physics, for one: Abbr.
67 Is obligated
69 French dance
70 Hand or rags
71 Unusual
72 Of the ear
73 Grapes
75 Garland
77 Be an unwitting joke victim
78 Bluish color
79 Glaciation stage
80 Court district
84 Target of Jack of Hearts
87 Bull of Norway
88 Compass reading
91 Lost
94 Have no ____ for (dislike)
97 Belgrade native
98 Dye
99 Allow
100 Scoreboard trio
101 Crosses out
102 Praying figure
103 Kind of page or role
105 Lavished love on
106 "____ things!"
108 Play part
109 Truman's birthplace
110 Consolidate
111 Italian pronoun
114 N.M. resort
115 Guest's amount o' livin'
116 Alt
118 Scottish explorer

378 IMPERTINENT QUESTIONS

By Maura B. Jacobson

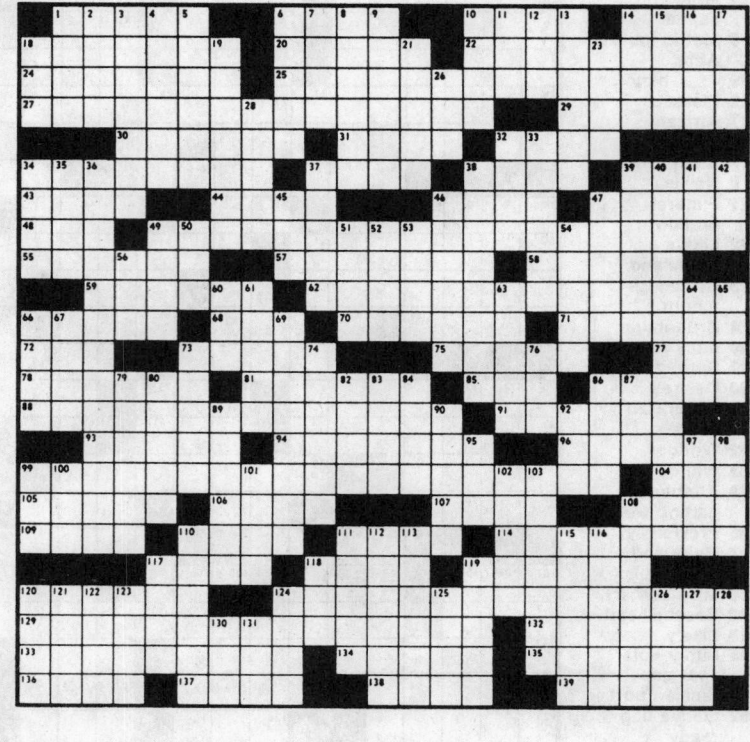

ACROSS

1 Use an index
6 Instance: Sp.
10 Fusses
14 Ancient kingdom
18 Customary
20 Kingly names in Oslo
22 Kind of pay
24 Spirited, old style
25 Where did George get tipsy?
27 Who belong to Stalin's frat?
29 Does penance
30 "As ___ the ocean"
31 Lagoon sight
32 Tiny one
34 Edna Ferber territory
37 Give ear to
38 Penalty
39 Small duck
43 Part of Q.E.D.
44 Verne captain
46 "I ___ Got Nobody"
47 Gently, in music
48 N.Y.C. div.
49 What does Grange do at dusk?
55 Disclose
57 ___ the hills
58 Thread: Prefix
59 A Gandhi
62 How did problems affect Ethel?
66 Lab items
68 Phone co.
70 Salle ___ (Aix bathroom)
71 Card game
72 Barrister's wear
73 Girl of song
75 Norse bard
77 Portion: Abbr.
78 Pass by
81 At sea
85 Environment: Prefix
86 "___ to bed"
88 What does Johann do at Roseland?
91 Walk softly
93 Garbed
94 Fairy queen
96 Ruggles's home

99 What is "la liaison"?
104 West Point of Brit.
105 Cartoonist Peter et al.
106 Long, wide shoe size
107 Requisite
108 Acheson
109 Kremlin initials
110 Maple genus
111 Tailless rodent
114 Uninformed
117 Boats of old
118 City of Russia
119 Bad-luck bringers
120 Counsel
124 Who are Dinah's Libyan kin?
129 Where is Ludwig in the batting order?
132 Disregarded
133 Catalonian city
134 Lucifer
135 Aunt's brood
136 Wife of Esau
137 Syrian city, to French
138 W.W. II craft
139 Fatigued

DOWN

1 Gambling city
2 Protection
3 Raged against
4 Client of a J.P.
5 Bacon strip
6 Public officials: Abbr.
7 Wings
8 French existentialist
9 "___ I Sing"
10 Club: Abbr.
11 Eamon's nickname
12 Egg: Prefix
13 Locale of Caesar's murder
14 Actress Virginia
15 ___ even keel
16 Land unit
17 Four posters
18 Rule, in India
19 Answer
21 Prepare slaw
23 Network
26 Pershing's gp.
28 Afflictions
32 Ho Chi ___
33 Have in mind
34 Leyte's neighbor
35 Do a Tuesday chore
36 What does Lee do outdoors?
37 Lift weights
38 ___ a glove
39 Haydn opus
40 What hangs next to Johnson's credentials?
41 First lady
42 Paint sign
45 Bleat
46 Asian perch
47 Singer Yma
49 Frees
50 Yale
51 British M.P.
52 Wild plum
53 "___ thee knight"
54 Darned
56 Queen of Spain
60 Bravo
61 Counselor-
64 Map abbrs.
65 Utah's lily
66 Ram's mates
67 Pinball gaffe
69 Words on a June greeting
73 Respite: Fr.
74 Pacific island group
76 Law, in Lyon
79 ___ the course
80 Plaintiffs
82 Preminger
83 Minaret call
84 Vol. state
86 Solar disk
87 Signify yes
89 Santa
90 Tuscan city
92 For
95 Crackerjack
97 "I met ___ with . . ."
98 React to a fast run
99 After sigma
100 After secs. and mins.
101 Mine shacks, in Britain
102 ___ diamonds (big casino)
103 Same
108 Discard with "of"
110 Small space
111 Academics
112 TV adjunct
113 Fissures
115 West-Coast fish
116 Encouraging words
117 Netman Arthur
118 Sounds of surprise
119 Elton's family
120 Eastern church title
121 Defunct
122 Cruz or Vague
123 Scratcher's concern
124 Easy job
125 Box-score info
126 ". . . in the heart ___ the head"
127 Austere time
128 Libido hubs
130 Tome: Abbr.
131 Vane reading

379 POETIC THOUGHT

By Bert Beaman

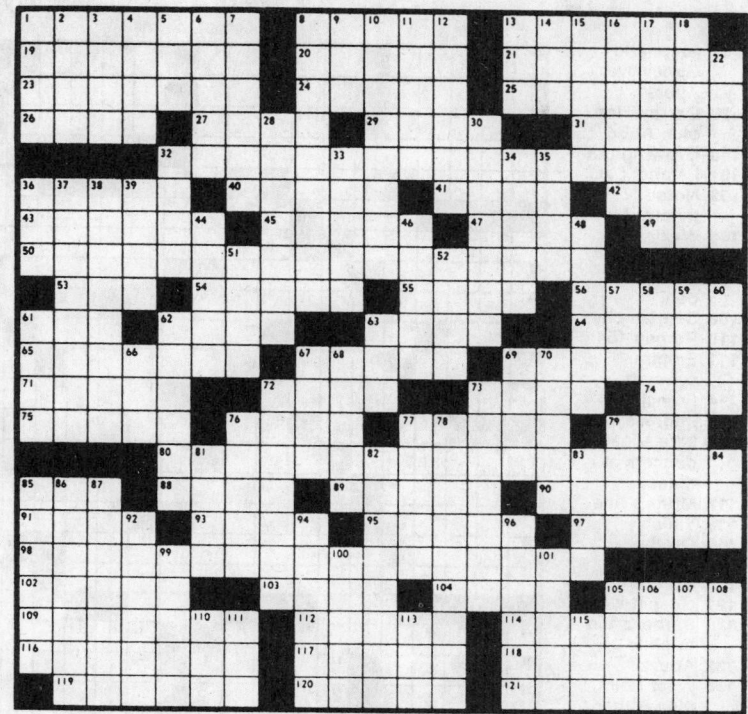

ACROSS

1 Hair creams for Valentino
8 Intrigue
13 Complained
19 ". . . shores of ___"
20 Miss St. Johns
21 Star in Scorpio
23 Legendary English town
24 Full
25 Like Paton's phalarope
26 Mind
27 Hindu mendicant
29 Yardstick
31 Vertical pipe
32 Start of an Edna Millay verse
36 Pamela or Perry
40 Kind of broke
41 Farm building
42 Formicary residents
43 Its capital is Athens
45 French spa
47 Table item
49 Understand
50 More of verse
53 Science-writer Willy
54 Compacter fodder
55 Singer Abbe
56 Suspicious
61 Smorgas-bord item
62 ___ on (torment)
63 Kind of house
64 Adjusts the radio
65 TV game-show prizes
67 More of verse
69 Kind of pool
71 Glacial ice form
72 Like some marshes
73 Title for the Pres.
74 Suffix for cash
75 Brains or beauty, e.g.
76 Sun or bridge
77 Minister under Mussolini
79 Asian sheep
80 More of verse
85 Like a garrison: Abbr.
88 Scruff
89 Cooling-off period
90 Certain drums
91 Mars: Prefix
93 Mouth part
95 Out of place
97 English potter
98 End of verse
102 Observes
103 Legal wrong
104 ___ cat
105 Fugue master
109 Letter
112 Mexican friend
114 To the right, in Paris
116 Most compact
117 Belief
118 Proposition
119 Paucity
120 Pine parts
121 Do ___ service (be of help)

DOWN

1 Egyptian god
2 Differently: Abbr.
3 Bit
4 Footless
5 U.S. money unit
6 Zoo resident
7 Hindu guitars
8 Lotharios
9 Oklahoma city
10 Sellout
11 Alaskan native
12 Dishes out
13 Like Roscoe Arbuckle
14 Italian article
15 Sometimes tall item
16 No-no for pitched baseballs
17 Getting rid of
18 U.S.-Russia topic
22 Most arid
28 Major port, e.g.
30 Manifest
32 S.A. native
33 Jewish deli offering
34 Top-drawer
35 ___ ha-Shanah
36 Welcome item
37 Olympic V.I.P.'s
38 Pittsburgh team
39 Suave
44 N.L. player
46 Ohio city
48 Seething
51 ___ bien
52 Noted philosopher
57 Quonset
58 Literary nonachiever
59 Made public
60 River to North Sea
61 She: It.
62 Fruit-jelly base
63 Snoop
66 Arctic explorer
67 Recognition
68 Computer programmer's concern
69 Word form for an Asian land
70 Is certain
72 Starred at a deb party
73 Fine leather
76 ___ luxury
77 Matter
78 Conniving together
79 Kind of judgment
81 Vicki
82 Unspoiled
83 Technical coll.
84 Full of: Suffix
85 Truckled
86 Walked en masse
87 Tooth part
92 "Potemkin" locale
94 Annual sights in Pasadena
96 Part of NATO
99 Organic compound
100 Medieval helmet
101 Hebrew letter
105 Bust's partner
106 Grass genus
107 Comb: Prefix
108 Makes hesitant sounds
110 W.W. II craft
111 Afr. land
113 Treasure
115 Collector's car

NON COMPOSER MENTIS

By Arnold Moss

ACROSS

1 Noted whaler and family
6 "Bell Song" singer
11 _____ Raton
15 White poplar
20 Ward off
21 Skull part
22 Kind of cake or cut
24 Consumers' spearhead
25 World aid org.
26 Hangs fire
27 Sadat
28 Yields
29 Witch's ride
31 Carved walrus teeth, etc.
33 Senior, in Paris
34 Adherent
35 M.D.'s org.
38 Cob's mate
39 G.I.'s rating
40 ". . . knits up the _____ care"
49 Dodges
53 Lost too much weight
54 Edison name
55 African river
56 "_____ Camera"
58 Israeli port
59 Eskimo boat
60 Suburbia site
64 April 15 org.
65 Outpouring
66 Sports org.
67 Animal for March
68 Coal product
69 Beverage
70 Costumed
71 Mlle., in Spain
73 Developed
75 Jai alai item
77 John Dickson _____
78 Child's game
81 Yiddish theater star
86 Blockhead
87 Nigerian town
89 _____ Fein
90 Singing group, in Spain
91 Swift's forte
94 Mustangs' campus
95 "_____ no use!"

97 Anne and Geneviève: Abbr.
99 Darrow, for one: Abbr.
100 Growing out
101 I stand: Lat.
102 Noted N. Y. theater byway
105 Waxy acid
106 "_____ luck!"
108 Minotaur's den
109 Belgian city
110 Roman 154
111 Empire symbols
114 French Impressionist
115 Like square dancers at times
117 Monk's title
118 Yalie
119 On the _____ (hiding)
120 Turf
121 Gospel writer
125 Barber's bid to child
132 Abuzz
136 West Point, etc.: Abbr.
137 "Prufrock" author
139 Mirror _____
140 Nerve-cell process
141 Miss. river
142 Echo was one
143 Venice street
144 Writer Gore
145 Isaac
146 Church part
147 ". . . would _____ as sweet"
148 Divinations

DOWN

1 Oil island
2 Matisse
3 _____ strings
4 Semele's nurse
5 Grand or little
6 Enzyme
7 Concerning
8 Ilk
9 Music scale
10 Subjugate
11 Dan Beard org.
12 Without: Ger.
13 Homecoming animals
14 Mideast drink
15 Adriatic port
16 Singer Joan
17 Norse epic
18 Sly look
19 Formerly, of old
23 Donald Duck's nephews
30 Producers' goals
32 Reward
36 Debussy's "La _____"
37 Birch's relative
39 Risk
40 Focus of all roads
41 _____ garde
42 Roman 52
43 Haircutters
44 Gaze
45 Dracula-like
46 Inventor Howe
47 Egg-shaped
48 Phonied

49 Turn into money
50 Buddhist temple
51 S. A. rodent: Var.
52 Airline abbr.
56 Luzon native
57 Teen-agers' woes
59 Seize illegally
61 Trifle with
62 Thumb and carpet
63 "Able was I _____ . . ."
69 One _____ time
70 January stone
72 F.D.A.'s concern
74 Mass. town
76 Friend of Pocahontas
77 Middle, to British
79 Ex-Yankee Irv

80 _____ de-vie
82 Read: Fr.
83 Cargo ship
84 _____ y Gasset
85 "Hold it!"
88 _____, haec, hoc
91 Dry-plaster painting
92 Mischievous as _____
93 Price list: Fr.
94 Zeno follower
96 Poison _____
98 Witches' town
101 Confine
102 Underworld
103 Carousal
104 N. Y. campus
107 Drops, in pharmacy
111 Containers: Abbr.
112 Knicks' org.
113 Poetic beats
114 Bar item

116 Half or Ozzie
117 "You don't say!"
120 Actor George
121 Proverb
122 Habitation
123 French historian
124 Ship bottoms
125 Doris and Dennis
126 One _____ (street game)
127 Mist
128 In bad _____
129 Novelist Ehrenburg
130 Flaccid
131 Cuts off
133 Moslem priest
134 Grey
135 Late comedian Jimmy
138 Social event in Rouen

GETTING FAMILIAR

By Ruth N. Schultz

ACROSS

1 Bede or Smith
5 Loki's son
9 B'way sign
12 Léman et al.
16 Stock the pantry
17 Threw an errant pass
19 Malay laws
21 Edward H. Harriman
23 On earth
24 _____ even keel
25 Historic council site
26 Casting _____ eyes
28 Blackbird
29 ". . . a woman be more like a _____?"
30 Mecca pilgrimage
31 Metric units: Abbr.
32 N. or S. _____
33 Girl's nickname
35 "You can fool _____ of . . ."
38 Dorothy Lamour
41 Superdome athletes
43 George Herman Ruth
45 River isles
46 Maximilian
48 Like river deltas
49 Having stains
51 Russian co-op
53 _____ Palmas
54 U.S. fighter plane
57 Comedian Mort
60 Of an element
62 Kind of processing
63 Gardner
64 Wings
65 Will Rogers
67 Indigo
68 Luxury's offering
69 Possessive
70 Hidden spoiler
71 Congo river
72 Touts
75 Dance, in Paris
76 Porkfish
79 Irish poet
80 Clear
82 Form of Cecilia
85 Kind of song
86 Area of Europe
88 Pinch pennies
90 Mae West
93 Defense org.
95 Like a Ziegfeld girl
96 Mr. 'iggins
97 Scottish denial
98 Like Lowell's June day
100 Compass point
101 Poetic word
102 Do street repair
105 Outburst
107 Not the same: Abbr.
108 Voting bellwether of yore
110 P.T. Barnum
113 Pry
114 Syrian's neighbor
115 Man or pitch
116 Convey, as a hint
117 News workers: Abbr.
118 Raced
119 Cast-off spouses

DOWN

1 Ocean or City
2 ". . . braes o' bonny _____"
3 "_____ longa . . ."
4 Perle
5 Certain plastic surgery
6 Bard's river
7 Broken
8 Wander
9 Sultan's relative
10 Town in Denmark
11 Cooperstown's lake
12 Places for retorts
13 Drink
14 Martha J. (Canary) Burke
15 Lucy _____ (reformers)
16 Moonlight et al.
18 Sea signal
20 Eddy
21 "Here _____ the Showboat"
22 Indian beans
27 Place: Abbr.
30 Other: Prefix
32 Sprightly
34 Breathe
36 Family members
37 P.I.'s Aguinaldo
38 Convenes
39 "_____ port in a storm"
40 Keen, in Scotland
42 Snow's relative: Abbr.
44 John J. Pershing
47 Lascivious ones
49 Like "Gulliver's Travels"
50 O.T. book
52 Side looks
54 "_____ alive!"
55 Unfortunate
56 Yarn
57 Shaker contents
58 Jai _____
59 Alfred E. Smith
61 Chessie et al.: Abbr.
62 Ten: Prefix
65 Huntley
66 Wind-borne
67 One from down under
73 One side of life
74 Pueblo Indian
75 Run or market
77 Spanish yeses
78 Basket fiber
80 Medieval verse
81 Genetic initials
83 Relatives of soubrettes
84 Holiday potions
85 _____ cosine
86 Like watery eyes
87 Raked with bullets
89 Observers
90 Composer Taylor
91 Compass point
92 Sancho Panza's mule
94 Vow
99 Conserve
102 Upholstery cloth: Var.
103 Pulsations: Abbr.
104 Spanish queen
105 Ooze
106 Say cheese
107 _____ bodied
109 Mind: Prefix
111 Laws: Abbr.
112 Beerbohm

382 HEADLINES By J.A. Felker

ACROSS

1 Athlete's woe
6 Fishing hooks
11 Broadway org.
16 Electrical unit
21 Vietnam capital
22 Scottish river
23 Town of Brazil
24 Not sotto voce
25 Brewing
26 Vine
27 Poetic times
28 Roman dress
29 July 10, 1925
33 "— kick out of . . ."
34 Crate section
35 Certain payments
36 Form of address
40 Blot out
42 Word study: Abbr.
44 Word with front or rear
45 Put-on
48 Room in Livia's house
50 Navy off.
52 New Rochelle college
54 Southern Indian
55 July 17, 1936
62 Carplike fish
63 U.S. Indians
64 Perry's creator
65 River's mouthpiece
66 Hand out
67 Heart and ___
68 Opposed
69 Fix a pencil
71 Miss Drew
73 Tobacco kiln
75 Bone: Prefix
77 Half a bray
78 July 17,1945
85 Gershwin
86 Like Loch Ness
87 Youthful age
88 Before febrero
89 "Tale of ___," old poem
92 Set up a golf ball
94 Vols' state
96 Moon or Spoon
100 Helot

101 Cloud type: Prefix
102 Issei's child
103 Take pot-shots at
104 July 27, 1953
109 Spy for Moses
110 Star in Serpens
111 Poetic word
112 Like British highballs
113 Big Apple: Abbr.
114 Cattle genus
115 "___ for Life"
118 Less risky
122 Inquisitive
123 Japanese wrestling
124 School org. branches
126 Actress Louise et al.
128 July 20, 1969
138 Letter stroke
139 Miss by ___
140 Kind of tube
141 Indian dwelling
142 Decree
143 Opposite of sud
144 Artful Dodger
145 Stunt fliers' feats
146 Worked on brogans
147 After frosh
148 Witness, in law
149 Swagger

DOWN

1 Son of Eliz.
2 Slew
3 Buffalo's kin
4 Spanish invader
5 Palace in Florence
6 Trevino or Palmer
7 Plant bristle
8 Brawl
9 Pure, in Madrid
10 Cold and ginger
11 Sets a goal
12 Death Valley name
13 Mystery writer
14 Roman years

15 Annual parade ground
16 Went hungry
17 Voices
18 Cross
19 German hall
20 June 6, 1944
30 Minn. village
31 Varnish ingredient
32 Kind of mission for Armstrong
36 Maternal prefix
37 One of a French trio
38 Places
39 Makes a billiard fluff
41 Plane formation
43 One in a ___
45 Garden City campus
46 Place for G.I.'s

47 Medicinal beverages
49 Stood by
51 Mil. school
53 Part of I.O.U.
54 Copycat
56 Certain plastic surgeons
57 "If I've said ___, I've . . ."
58 Trifle
59 Belly, in France
60 N.Y.C. subway
61 Harem room
68 Plant ___
69 Miss. Senator
70 Goddess of youth
72 Macbeth or Astor
74 Desserts, in England
76 Part of a play
78 Football

79 Mouth-healing science
80 American larch: Var.
81 Best
82 Inveigles
83 ___ judgment (misthinks)
84 Entering
90 Knievel
91 Pasture
93 Silkworm
95 Compass reading
97 Conquer: Lat.
98 Fencing pieces
99 Singer Helen
101 Call out
102 ___ in the bud
105 In-law of Ruth
106 Losers
107 Absolute
108 Silk fabric

114 Polished
116 Caught ___ (overtook)
117 Gawks
119 Makes up for
120 "Their ___ Hour"
121 Beef or veal, at times
123 Kind of remark
125 Avoid
127 ___ short
128 Sale sign
129 Warm-sea fish
130 Russian sea
131 Scat!
132 Camping item
133 Old weapon
134 Doubtful
135 Smell
136 Former Russian police
137 Certain egg

383 EASTERTIDE *By Robert Roop*

ACROSS

1 Part of B.C.
7 Roman pounds
13 Daytime TV offerings
20 One who takes note
21 Road pointers
22 Aggravated
23 Julia Ward Howe line
26 R.R. stops
27 Located: Abbr.
28 Mango part
29 White-rose house
30 Incapacitated
31 Game pieces
32 Churchyard
34 Neighbor of Scot.
35 Unicorn fish
36 Future grads
37 Mountain
38 "Looking Glass" game
40 Pontius et al.
42 Nerve tissue
43 Romaine
44 Hoists, in Scotland
46 High priest who condemned Jesus
48 Like the Biblical calf
49 Obtained: Abbr.
52 Protects
53 Raillery
54 Beloved, in Italy
55 Pacific tuna
56 Poetic words
57 Partner of funnier
58 ____ Noster
59 Place of no balm
61 Easter ____
62 Easter ____
63 Miss Terry
64 Game ragouts
66 On ____ toes
68 "That he is mad, ____ true"
69 Mr. Coward
70 Rajahs' spouses
71 Certain church location
73 By way of: Abbr.
74 Easter ____
75 ____ of (gets too big for)
76 Moslem doctrine
77 Traffic sign
78 Hindu deity
79 Famous Easter-egg maker
82 Biblical name
84 "____ got a secret"
85 Brit. award
88 New World: Abbr.
89 Top people: Abbr.
91 Earthquake or flood, e.g.
93 O'Hara's Joey
94 ____ tree
95 Suffixes for doers
96 Abbr. in a rental ad
97 Cyst
98 Auctioneer's word
99 Julia Ward Howe line
104 Auto buyer's offering
105 Having pillars
106 Usher, at times
107 Sonnet parts
108 Rivulet, in Scotland
109 Autos of yore

DOWN

1 Gorges
2 Miss Prynne
3 Actress Ada et al.
4 Roman date
5 But, to Pliny
6 Having three leaves
7 Actor Alan and family
8 N.Y. subway
9 Bucking horses: Var.
10 Artist Bearden et al.
11 Starts the day
12 Certain Alaskan: Abbr.
13 Disciple of 1 Across
14 Action-imparting agent
15 Standing
16 Somewhat: Suffix
17 Consecrate
18 Comedienne Bea
19 Fashions
24 Book-cover sheet
25 Hurricane center
32 Native of Jesus' land
33 Brocades
35 Insurance abbrs.
39 Tristram ____
41 Showed the way
42 Go, to Burns
45 Feminine suffix
46 Horror movie, e.g.
47 Relatives of mins.
48 Field deities
49 Drum sound
50 Favorable balance
51 Faces
52 Civil War battle
53 ____ avibus (good auspices)
54 Box or side
55 G-man
57 Director Sidney
58 Jewish festival
60 Moray
61 Extorts
62 Dreamy quality
64 Jewish tribunals
65 Years: Lat.
66 Shoulder: Prefix
67 Bit of daily reading
70 Camped in the wilds
71 Scent
72 U.S., to French
74 Snack ____
75 Junior dictionary
76 Region: Abbr.
77 More svelte
79 San Andreas and foot
80 Electrical unit
81 Female saints
83 Dexterous
85 Iberian port
86 Whalebone
87 Church officials
90 Compass point
92 Native of Malmö
95 Palm-reader's words
98 Tunisian port
100 Frogmen's unit: Abbr.
101 County units: Abbr.
102 Catch, in England
103 Teachers' org.

384 FINISHING LINES
By Alexander F. Black

ACROSS

1 Reverence
4 Aerie dweller
9 Cupid
13 Tense up
20 Nessen or Ziegler
21 Coxswain's command
23 Alaskan city
24 Box and free
25 Like Field's toy dog
28 Like Tyre or Nineveh
29 Inter ____
30 Dict. entry
31 Calif. motto
32 Teachers' org.
33 Chairman of note
34 Bambi, e.g.
35 Solomon island
37 Signs
39 Anti: Abbr.
40 Like Whitman's cradle
45 Washes
47 Compass point
48 Laugh, in Lausanne
49 Vichy seasons
50 Beauty of myth
51 Hudson's Zee
54 Through
55 Seven, vis à vis Thebes
58 Lets go
62 Actor Dullea
64 Youth org.
65 N.C.O.'s
66 Extraordinary item
67 Gains
70 Ginger
71 Friday's creator
72 Auto part
75 Expected, in Soho
76 Minuscule
77 Violin-case item
78 Sea eagle
79 Like Sandburg's fog
83 Sparks or Rorem
85 ____ Park, Col.
87 ____ Plaines
88 Prefix with meter or tude
89 Bouquet
91 Incites
92 Smith and Pacino
93 U.S. botanist
95 Bright star
96 Pueblo dweller
97 Humorist George
98 Colombian money
99 Annoyed
102 Unaccented words
104 U.S.A.F. member
105 Electronic energy condition
107 Church area
108 Eileen's state
109 Hole maker
110 Cakes' partner
112 Grass genus
114 Carroll's toves ____
121 Cuckoo
122 Civilian A.D.C.
124 Sindbad locale
125 Skittles' partner
126 Jekyll et al.
127 Prefix with angle or pod
128 Captivate
131 Time in Eng.
133 Another, in Andalusia
134 Put back to work
136 Like Dowson's Cynara
139 Withdrawn
140 English river
141 Later
142 Scottish river
143 Jack or chase
144 Lacking, in Le Havre
145 Man and Pines
146 Conversational pauses

DOWN

1 Place for slot machines
2 Like some mittens
3 Coveted
4 Continent: Abbr.
5 Imitated
6 Skirt insets
7 Legitimate
8 Son of Gad
9 Yugoslavian poet
10 Pout
11 Russian city
12 Perry Mason's lifeblood
13 Like some checks
14 Ancient writings
15 Cuzco native
16 School subj.
17 Omar's writer
18 Eastern Indian
19 Bars legally
22 Candle ingredient
26 Nobles
27 Victor and family
36 Constellation of 95 Across
38 Initials of failure
41 This, in Juarez
42 High and seven
43 Military headgear
44 Roman road
45 Meadow
46 Becomes rebellious
50 Palmer's org.
52 Singer Bailey
53 Attention getter
55 Snake
56 Prehistoric period
57 Half a fly
58 Water or Bowl
59 Warehouse
60 Markham's farmer ____
61 Misjudge
62 German canal
63 Charms
64 Gripe
68 Small bags
69 Classified-ad abbr.
70 Four or larceny
71 Morse-code units
73 On one's ____
74 Annapolis grad.
76 Power unit
77 Vintage car
80 Groundless
81 Muse
82 Nine: Prefix
84 Pair
86 Threefold
90 Cain raiser
91 Wild sheep
92 Tennis points
93 Obscure
94 Pick
97 Server's point
98 Settled up
100 Kind of party
101 Low-caste Hindu
103 Wall climber
104 Unleaded fuel
105 Induct
106 Generous portion
108 ____ bodikins
109 Cock Robin's undoing
111 Form an arch
112 Shirt cloth
113 Disquiet
115 Chinese offices
116 Arabian and silent
117 Metrical foot
118 Happen
119 Broadway lyricist
120 Eats away
122 Of a space
123 Move furtively
127 Step lightly
129 Variable star
130 Presently
132 Friend's pronoun
135 Box or bag
137 French thou
138 French connections

385 AIRS APPARENT By Herb Risteen

ACROSS

1 Garden occupant
5 Met performer
10 Fish and musical
16 Witticism
19 Honey: Prefix
20 Excuse
21 Hair application
22 Arab robe
23 Hammer part
24 Look at one's piano score
26 London swell
27 Told, as a yarn
28 Railroad and neck
29 Cordoba cheers
30 Musical works
32 Suffix for gang
34 Compass point
35 Golfer Lee
37 B'way sign
38 Madras garment
40 Peak of Crete
41 Talk harshly
44 Worcester, e.g.
46 Great: Fr.
50 Vague discomfort
53 Gazed idly
54 Antics
55 Sunwear for Sue
56 Italian river
57 Dutch exports
58 Town near Udine
60 Men's org.
61 Despicable
62 Check
63 Capacity units
65 Shows accuracy at the piano
70 Postcard offerings
71 Linear measures
72 Calif. valley
74 Ninny
77 Doorways: Abbr.
78 Legal plea
79 Concur
80 Testify
82 German city
83 Turn ____ evidence
84 Throwback
86 Harder to find
87 Adjusts, as a violin
88 Laugh, in Paris
89 Niger native
91 Suave
93 Hesitant sounds
95 Adagio or allegro, e.g.
98 Area of Italy
99 Cheese
102 Hercules, to Iole
105 Assam native
106 Off line
108 Like the Gobi
110 Khan
111 Play in a band
114 Early ocean crosser
115 Through
116 Get near at hand
117 Carried
118 French city
119 Part of i.e.
120 Actress Laura et al.
121 Interprets
122 Actual being

DOWN

1 Elec. units
2 Ocean chasms
3 Alaskan native
4 Small German bards
5 White House name
6 Astolat name
7 ____ Creed
8 Portly
9 Slowing, in music: Abbr.
10 Charm
11 Divine and Human
12 Gave pleasure to
13 ____ Vegas
14 Miss Adams
15 Groups
16 Lutes' relatives
17 Instrument
18 Filers' aids
25 Do farm work
31 ____ renewal
33 Peep show
36 Farm animal
39 One of a flag trio
42 Confused
43 Four: Prefix
44 Fountain items
45 ____ by one's own petard
46 Jeeves and Bunter, e.g.
47 Silly
48 Walter Huston's song
49 Co. officials
51 Cuts off prematurely
52 Italian film name
53 Fairy queen
54 Word with "foiled again"
57 English river
58 Paris zoo animals
59 Anesthetic
62 One-seeded fruits: Var.
63 Fail to use a trash basket
64 Musical cop-out
66 Boadicea's tribe
67 Plunder, old style
68 French pastry item
69 Fencing weapons
73 Roman bronze
74 Jewish month
75 Bristle: Prefix
76 Opera bit-role, in a way
78 Constellation
79 In harmony
81 Public
82 One of Willson's 76
83 Post: Abbr.
85 Cambridge campus
90 Vanquished
91 S.A. capital
92 Cast an evil glance
94 African tribesman
96 Places for Thoreau
97 Neighbor of Wash.
98 Resort lake
100 Divas' renderings
101 Strip and land
102 Cod or To
103 Stone and teen
104 Via del Corso's city
107 Two of eleven
109 Great or Clemence
112 Unclose, in poems
113 Vessel: Abbr.

VIEWPOINTS
By Hume R. Craft

ACROSS

1 Drays
6 Director Frank
11 Epsom items
16 Young horses
21 "Cookery is become ____"
22 Revoke
23 Love: It.
24 Kind of tube
25 Words for some stocks
26 Oil source
27 French town
28 Port of Italy
29 Woman, to Sir Walter Scott
33 ____ anchor
34 Literary monogram
35 Bookie's quote
36 River discharge
39 Puppeteer Tony
40 ". . . that ____ the malt"
42 Underworld
44 Triumph
45 Cab
46 Old thicket
48 Ordinal suffix
49 Needle part
51 Scott's Lucy
53 Old Marley, to Dickens
60 Schumann____
61 Minimal
62 Greek letter
63 Certain cats
64 Seething
65 Raggedy ones
66 "The Just"
68 Drinker's woes: Abbr.
70 Story beginning
71 Turner
72 Fuss
73 Articles
74 Chinese guild
76 Take-home item
78 Miss Dallas
80 Corporate V.I.P.
81 Dandy's partner
82 Elianic efforts
86 Word to a firing squad
87 Disgruntled sound
88 Word for St. John: Abbr.
89 Insect
90 "Cannery ____"

91 Graduate degrees
94 Dallas campus
96 Like old summer trolleys
99 H.H. Munro
100 Plunders
102 Damnable
104 Hammarskjold
105 Greek physician
106 Oil island
107 Francis Bacon, to Izaak Walton
110 Like some fenders
112 Cheer
113 Meadow grass
114 Like mechanics' hands
115 Convention-eers: Abbr.
116 Muscovite: Abbr.
118 Units of fitness
120 ____ Magnon
121 Auditor: Abbr.
125 Felt hat
127 Give ____ of approval to
128 Overly
130 Limonite
132 Books, to Jonathan Swift
136 TV card or box
138 Separately
139 Lecture
140 ". . . Sprat could ____ fat"
141 Cigar city
142 Yes ____! (natch!)
143 Utah lilies
144 More bashful
145 Like Sue
146 Trudges
147 Gardens
148 Bridge positions

DOWN

1 Welland and Kiel
2 Mollusk genus
3 Sword
4 Infringe
5 Narrow ridge
6 Playbill listing
7 Stick to
8 Harbor or Bailey
9 Enjoyed
10 Closing word
11 Cuisinier's speciality
12 Belgica, Gjoa, and Fram, to Roald
13 Yearns
14 Kilmer's love
15 Greek-oracle aides
16 Ring event
17 Popular fellow, to his peers
18 Ring formation
19 Durocher
20 Spanish Mrs.
30 Custer's or news
31 Divinities
32 Food fish
37 Type of crystalline acid
38 Marine snail
41 Playhouse, in Italy
43 Tiny particles
44 Dracula-like one
47 Cereal grain
50 Scottish one
52 Sheep of India
53 Lerner and Ladd
54 France's upper house
55 He wrote "All hope abandon . . ."
56 Capuchin monkey
57 ____ Hungarian
58 Poe's Morgue
59 Beachhead craft: Abbr.
66 Author Samuel Hopkins
67 Exclusive set, to Ward McAllister
69 Kind of limit
72 Boxing name
75 Slovenly
77 Ibsen role
79 The Union, to Lincoln
80 Early bishops' thumbstalls
81 Jutting stern of a ship
83 Babylonian abode of dead
84 Fitter of ox frames
85 Pearl-caster's targets
88 Tower over
89 ____ mercy (plead)
91 Highland fabrics
92 Stinger
93 Premium wage
95 P.T.A. people
97 Before: Prefix
98 P.I. tree
99 Passive resistance, to Gandhi
101 ____ Antonio
103 Certain tribunal: Abbr
105 Sal, e.g.
108 Saved, as a painting
109 Teary queen
111 Barter: Fr.
117 Release a fastener
119 Rich cakes
120 Fabric
122 Raccoons' relatives
123 Medieval armor
124 Choir singers
126 Attack
127 Majorca town
129 Adult
131 Corpulent
133 Pacific tree
134 Face part
135 Dame Myra
136 "____ in the bag"
137 Margery of rhyme

387 ENCIRCLED WISDOM

By Eugene T. Maleska

The circled letters from left to right, starting at the top, contain a fool's wise advice.

ACROSS

1 Boy
7 Tidbit
13 One of Macbeth's titles
18 "Walden" writer
19 Idle
20 Actor Leslie
22 Famous ferry
23 Very ornate
24 Farrell's "A World ___ Made"
25 High note
26 Bowling button
28 Over
30 G.P.'s group
31 Utah ski resort
33 Old Scratch
35 Shadow-box
36 Anchor position
38 Purse items
40 Scottish uncle
41 Adjective suffix
43 Johnson of TV
44 Veronese duo
49 Straw boss
51 Kazan
52 Romeo and Juliet, e.g.
54 Mine entrance
55 Adjusts anew
59 Initials for a 1933 act
60 Portia's maid
64 Lodge member
65 Costume
67 Chalcedony
69 Stage direction
70 Yalies
72 One of Macbeth's victims
76 Safari quarry
77 French upper house
79 Cheerless
80 Homeric work
82 Italian's "Yes!"
83 Muffin variety
86 Jewish eve
88 Ten-o'clock scholar's problem
90 Feedback of a sort
91 Composer Erik
93 "___ shanter"
94 Activating
98 Nobleman in "Henry VIII"
103 Mrs., in Poland
104 Alpaca's habitat
106 "We'll ___ a cup . . ." (Burns)
107 Suffix with Indo and Poly
108 Tagging along
110 Mailed
112 Old-womanish
115 "King ___," quotation source
116 Wine: Prefix
117 Greek courtesan
120 "Lend ___"
122 Disencumber
123 Tarry
125 "You ___!"
127 Basis of argument
129 Fishing gear
130 Will subject
131 Duchess in "Henry VI, Part II"
132 Awaken
133 Judged
134 Blush

DOWN

1 Lacking depth
2 Hamlet's friend
3 Dadaism founder
4 Shift
5 Dog ___ (shabby)
6 Charlotte ___
7 Puppet Snerd
8 Siouan
9 Costa ___
10 Smudges
11 Fire or narrow
12 Governor in "Much Ado"
13 Hammett's man
14 Lariat part
15 Disciple's emotion
16 Scene of "Love's Labour's Lost"
17 Holy hermit
18 Caught in ___
21 Dry-goods merchant
27 Knievel
29 Armenian capital
32 Play backer
34 Dud
37 Sampling
39 Blissful: Ger.
42 Relinquish
45 Actor Bruce
46 City in Egypt
47 Actress Bergner
48 French town
50 Laugh: Fr.
53 Famed N.Y. restaurateur
55 Singer Della
56 Miss Terry
57 "Every inch ___"
58 Nile growth
61 The world, to Jaques
62 Trucking rigs
63 Realms
66 Combustible heaps
68 Uninteresting
71 Messenger in "Merchant"
73 Danton's colleague
74 Ukases
75 Deadly
78 Check mark
81 Word for rum
84 Vessel
85 Like John
87 Flora and fauna
89 Unusual
92 Sprang from
94 Barkers' come-ons
95 Basket
96 Shylock's adversary
97 Lubricated
99 Related
100 Alkaloid
101 Relationship
102 Pantry
105 Misgiving
109 Merry cries
111 Overdone
113 Shunned one
114 Inventor Pliny ___
118 Irish Gaelic
119 Mr. Bede
121 Donna or Rex
124 Zoo animal
126 Native: Suff.
128 Like Ophelia, in Act IV

388 JEWEL CACHE *By William Lutwiniak*

389 TROUBLE SPOTS By Jack Luzzatto

ACROSS

1 Woman guard
7 Dinner course
12 Gossamer fabrics
18 Williams's lizard
19 Green shade
22 Prison V.I.P.
23 Room with a rack
25 ". . . ___ me death!"
26 Slip away
27 Zealous follower
28 Breughel's painting style
30 Vagabond, for short
31 On
33 Toots of Broadway
34 Passages to nowhere
36 Certain prisoner
38 By word
40 Undecided
41 Clockmaker Thomas
42 Swaps
44 Dail's land
46 Big hair-do
48 Was rude in a crowd
49 Notes
50 Clammy
52 Public tantrums
53 Boat covers
54 Slackening agents
57 Girl
58 Skipper's pursuer
60 Loud and demanding
62 Grampus
63 Prelude to murder, often
65 Naval noncom
66 Wiretap aids
68 Aramaic tongue
69 Waterless
70 Fastened a ship's rope
71 Pills at parties
72 Blank spot
74 "Able ___ ere . . ."
75 Pineapples, in Spain
76 Surrender by deed
77 Hawaiian goose
79 Fellowship: Abbr.
80 Low hound dog
81 Alpaca
84 Hooded coat
86 Taunt
88 Tire pattern
91 Her charm is fatal
93 Sponsorship
95 Sodium soap
96 Small shield
97 Big Russian lake
98 Guided
101 ___ pros (drop a suit)
102 Application of birch
104 Brat
107 Access
108 More robust
109 Untwists
110 Dispose of a purchase
111 Old or vain
112 Town Leander swam from

DOWN

1 Like a bishop's headdress
2 S. A. rodent
3 Jamesian hair-raiser
4 Start of a drum sound
5 Burden
6 Nostrils
7 Military areas
8 Ethiopian
9 Troubled king
10 Salvation, for one
11 Little bit
12 Warning with a point
13 Turkish delight?
14 Unit of work
15 Safe, as mushrooms
16 Mutiny
17 Snuff, in Britain
20 Simon ___ (cruel ones)
21 Endures, in Scotland
24 Agreed with
29 Nursemaid
32 Juan, Eva and Isabel
34 Beginners
35 Compound resembling another
37 Be delirious
39 Looked like a villain
43 Mushroom with a wallop
45 Claps in jail
47 Boca ___
48 Beetle talisman
49 Sprays for muggers
51 Dangerous bunk
52 Wild plum
53 Under control
54 Grove of old Olympics site
55 Resort near Naples
56 Flat on one's back
59 Descartes
60 Gray-hair promoters
61 Cracker or jerk
63 Stage of progress
64 Despot
67 Look ahead to
69 Quaker grays
71 Animal for a nickel
73 Dutch city: Abbr.
75 Mardi gras event
76 Ostrich or emu
78 Cleveland's waters
80 Intolerance
81 Textile worker
82 Mysterious
83 Parts of an indictment
85 Moves gradually
87 Wallow
89 Space program
90 Lacking ambition
92 ___ metal (nickel alloy)
94 Sawlike part
98 Bunyan
99 Involved with
100 Colorless
103 Resentment
105 Holmesian ambience
106 Campus clinger

390 GETTING ACROSS

By Maria G. Rice

ACROSS

1 Deputy: Abbr.
5 _____ in the hole
8 Looks after
13 Old car
16 Soak
19 Sand bar
21 Elders: Abbr.
22 Pray, in old Rome
23 Relative of the rhea
24 High note
25 Legendary crossing
29 _____ Moines
30 Insult
31 Fluids
32 "_____ Is Born"
33 Western hills
35 Long poems
37 U.S. agency
39 Miffed
40 Mountain ridge
41 Place for late movie-goers
43 Feels compassion
45 All-America crossing of 1869
47 British P.M.
48 Scoreboard trio
49 Abhor
51 _____ Canals
52 College degree
53 Initials for a Cardinal cap
54 Gershwin et al.
56 Innocent
58 Revelry
60 Features of needles
64 Warehouse
66 Baltic port
69 "We're _____ tonight on the . . ."
70 Atomic reactor
72 De _____ (too much)
73 Half a U.S. line
74 _____ age
75 Last
76 Used the long route
78 French month
80 Decisive crossing of old
85 "_____ longa . . ."

86 Palace near Madrid
88 Time periods
89 Scarce
91 Cuba _____
92 Kind of torch or hard
95 Part of A.M.
96 Secondary deals
99 Doris and Clarence
100 Catfish _____, Dogpatch delicacy
102 Run on two party tickets
104 Price
106 Rope fiber
107 Suez port
108 Can material
109 From _____ Z
111 Opposite of syn.
113 Extremely
115 Latin goddess
117 Collections
118 Crossing by 94 Down
121 French river
122 Confine
124 Stupefies
125 Algerian port
127 Plant
128 Holy Roman emperor
129 Irish hero
130 Food fishes
132 One of the five W's
134 River of Spain
136 Bird beak
137 Solo crossing
143 Actress Joanne
144 Richard or shad
145 Ancient region of Asia Minor
146 Ecol. or econ.
147 Tibetan creatures
148 Dunce
149 But, to Caesar
150 Bitter or tail
151 Fish
152 Delivered

DOWN

1 Mountain or cigar
2 Haggard novel
3 Hurok et al.
4 Most farfetched
5 Snake
6 Puzzle type
7 Early laborer
8 Road of stage fame
9 Noun suffix
10 Hero of Hindu epic
11 Tuxedo accessory
12 Old Pacific alliance
13 Reparation
14 Scottish uncle
15 Intro for a city V.I.P.
16 Biblical crossing
17 Of Zeno's school
18 Cord ornaments
20 Jumped
26 Ex-V.P. Agnew
27 Afflictions
28 Island off Japan
34 Blunder

36 Billing's partner
38 W.W. II. crossing
41 Supple
42 Admiral's crossing
44 Condition, in Arles
46 To _____ (also)
47 Attention-getting sound
50 Green or glades
55 Fish garnish
57 Lyric poems
59 Writer Shirley Ann
61 Map abbr.
62 Writer Loti
63 Weariness
64 Dash
65 Unfolds, poetically
67 One on the move
68 Relatives of ifs and buts

71 Daughter of Cadmus
73 Swamp
75 French girls
77 Biblical weeds
78 Card combination
79 Continent
81 Indulge
82 Desires
83 Lynx, for one
84 Betel palm
87 Words of approximation
90 Brit. fliers
93 News notice
94 Dollar thrower
96 Beaver or vole
97 Crème de la crème
98 Wash. people
100 Small stove
101 Gibbons
103 Sleigh across a pond

105 Reacted sharply
107 Get the reason
109 Book supplements
110 First _____ (prison newcomers)
112 Fished
114 Jimmy
116 Pretended
117 Parties
119 Mature
120 Silkworm
123 Pressure group
126 Miss Laurie
131 Province of Pakistan
133 Otherwise
135 Town of Italy
138 _____ the line
139 French co.
140 Nothing
141 Martini base
142 Missouri initials

391 THE GLAD GAME
By Bert Kruse

ACROSS

1 Bestow
7 ____ Squad
10 Biblical song: Abbr.
13 Luau food
16 Extreme disgust
17 Supplying food
21 Senegal bay
22 Hervey Allen best-seller
24 Smell ____
25 ____ relief
26 Yarn quantity
27 Flower parts
28 Push, old style
29 Cadmus's daughter et al.
31 Carriage of Java
33 Egyptian god
34 Appeal
35 Fit of temper
38 Work hard
41 What Jan. 1 ushers in
43 Of the kidneys
45 Stravinsky et al.
47 Auto racers Al and Bobby
48 Famous daredevil
51 Race, in Rome
53 William ____ Williams
54 Leg part
55 Dress insert
56 Kind of steak or sandwich
60 Roman official
61 Writers Jean and Walter
62 Pakistan language
63 Military cap
64 Ripen
65 Off. worker
67 Pope less than a month
69 Piercing tool
70 Wash. people
72 German salute
73 Bric-a-____

75 Having melody
77 "____, Brute"
78 Service addresses
79 Bonheur
80 Yellow colors
81 Synonym for "on the house"
83 Almanack man
85 Big wine bottle
88 Period of time
90 Overly-fond one
91 Mechanic's cloth, eventually
93 Garden tools
95 Cash-register keys
99 TV horse
100 Heavy cart
102 Bangkok native
104 Yemen's capital
105 Sea eagle
106 Merited
109 Early people of India
112 Force unit: Abbr.
113 Nothing: Sp.
114 Historic czar
117 Thing knotted, to Scots
118 Video programs
119 Guarantee
120 Student org.
121 Do seating, for short
122 Wooden tub
123 Neck wraps

DOWN

1 Shortly
2 Tomorrow
3 Dons
4 Hard wood
5 Extinct autos
6 Think center
7 Criminal group
8 Chan portrayer and family
9 Roman 504
10 Marquette
11 Turtle or fish
12 Up
13 Certain ex-prisoner
14 Rampaging
15 Weeping
18 Parts of yrs.
19 Poe name
20 Victor Hugo classic
21 Military misfit
23 Sycophant
30 Saunter
32 Twist or Hardy
36 Fixes over
37 Certain factors: Abbr.
39 Writer James et al.
40 Tenn. athlete
42 Ship hoists: Abbr.
44 "____," all smiles
46 Game-watcher's aid
48 Device

49 Familiarize
50 Enlists
52 Church calendars
53 Partner of desist
55 Hungarian dish: Var.
57 Horseshoe pitch
58 Onward's partner
59 Nye and Tilden
61 "____ civil tongue in your head!"
66 Kipling's "The Light ____"
68 Irritates
71 Unethical act
73 Good egg
74 Bishop's vestment
76 Writer John et al.
80 Eight: Prefix
82 "____ Town"
83 Spanish village
84 Sea off Greece

85 Brief times
86 London ordeal of W.W. II
87 Actress Farrell et al.
89 Hester and family
92 Solemn
94 Demonstrate
96 Young twins, to a sitter
97 Tolerate
98 Rooms: Fr.
101 Babylonian abode of dead
103 Left one's bed
107 Delineate
108 Rangoon measure
110 Harem rooms
111 Snug home
115 Before tee
116 Postal unit: Abbr.

392 PHRASEMAKING By Tom Sheehan

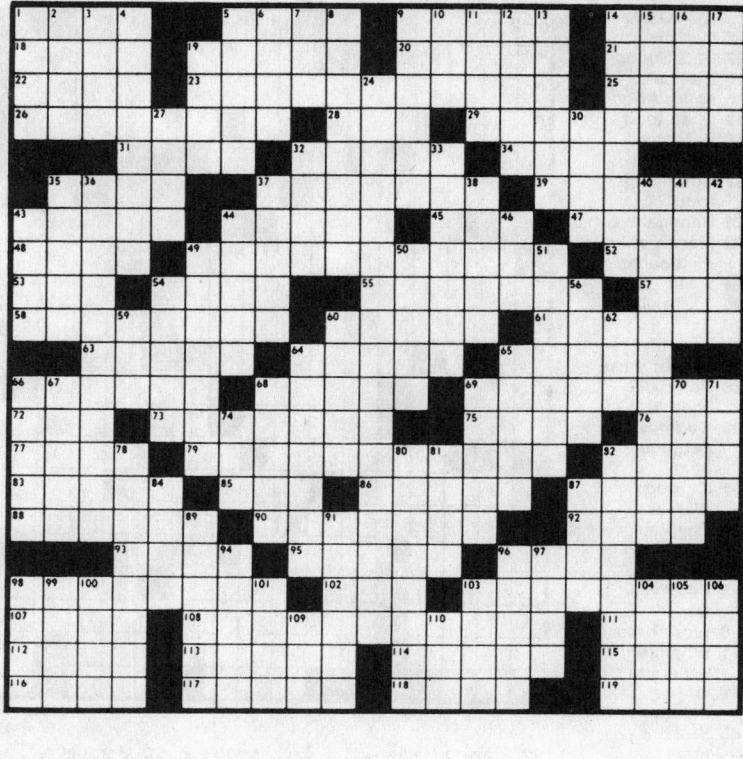

ACROSS

1 Charles or roast
5 "What ____ say?"
9 "Life ____ short"
14 Barrelhead need
18 Gazetteer data
19 Old Zionist activist group
20 Workout
21 Table spread
22 Current
23 Motto of St. Crispin
25 Humorist Rogers
26 Cockfighting
28 Plural ending
29 Alimony, so to speak
31 Vile odor
32 Farewell
34 Bats' H.Q.
35 Artist Schiele
37 Like a grieving usher
39 "The Taking of ____ One . . ." (1974 film)
43 He owned a rod
44 "____ disturb"
45 Kind of player
47 Clean ____
48 Cup part
49 Optician's place, with 71 Down
52 Sins
53 Vereen
54 Auk genus
55 Chinese island and strait
57 One, in Bonn
58 Eve, so to speak
60 Turkoman people
61 U.S. athlete Jim
63 Brash
64 Snivel
65 Macaw
66 He's left holding the bag
68 ____ khan (tiger)
69 Mafia outing
72 Globe
73 Theory of government
75 Galatea's beloved
76 What Confucius do
77 First of a Kipling trio
79 "Death ____" (maritime story)
82 Unaspirate
83 "Vive ____!"
85 A Kennedy monogram
86 Underworld figure
87 Beaverbrook and Jim
88 Dallas or Stevens
90 Crystalline mineral: Var.
92 Chair or mark
93 A Dumas
95 Coins of Iran
96 Kind of pole
98 Tavern maid
102 Neighbor of Ga.
103 Site for Icarus
107 Great Barrier Island
108 What a blacksmith has
111 Bacteriologist's wire
112 Freshly
113 Mississippi has four
114 Fiat
115 ____ robbery (flirt's forte)
116 Drum ____
117 Greek letter
118 Thomas of the clocks
119 Winged god

DOWN

1 Tehee, Variety style
2 Guthrie
3 Cat sound
4 Nursery
5 Frog sound
6 "____ Named Joe"
7 Not any, in law
8 Within
9 ____ March
10 Spanish Mrs.
11 Knight work
12 Of an acid
13 Treasure-hunter's aid
14 Rodeo rider
15 Inter ____
16 Kind of salesman's block?
17 Actress Celeste
19 Two on the ____ (Crusoe and Friday)
24 Old family prayer books
27 Robert ____ Warren
30 Holiday times
32 Senior: Fr.
33 Ebb
35 Dog ____
36 ____ it (stripper's motto)
37 Clan symbol
38 ____ share
40 Rabbit fanciers
41 Anchor position
42 Middle, in law
43 Bishop's title
44 Pip
46 Music syllable
49 Be a ____ habit
50 Creator of Tugboat Annie
51 Board a Metroliner
54 Shelters
56 Rebellion leader
59 Robe size: Abbr.
60 "____ Latin from . . ."
62 Hockey star
64 Cat feature
65 Thruway to Fairbanks
66 Embers
67 Court decree
68 Kind of sergeant
69 Leyte's neighbor
70 Candy, to Nash
71 See 49 Across
74 Continent: Abbr.
78 "Fore!"
80 French astronomer and family
81 Depots: Abbr.
82 Like a spurned pawnbroker
84 Nastase
87 "Nonsense" author
89 ____ up (excited)
91 "____ pleasant institution . . ."
94 Liquid sound
96 Louse up
97 Bridge seat
98 Wild hog
99 ____ time (never)
100 Stagger
101 Gaelic
103 Angry fit
104 Fruit
105 Eur. capital
106 Pipe joints
109 Agreed upon
110 Dutch town

393 LITERARY OUTING *By Tap Osborn*

ACROSS

1 Fix over
5 Cloak
11 Suffix for hippo
16 Ruggles's was red
19 Norway's king
20 Pack closely
21 Eton, to Harrow
22 W.W. II agency
23 Noon: Ready for a picnic
26 Demure
27 Color for an isle
28 Gullet
29 Do a bellhop job
30 12:15 P.M.: Spot picked out
37 Voice
40 Northern auk
41 Most of N.Y. outside N.Y.C.
42 12:30 P.M.: Gourmet lunch
47 Spanish aunt
48 Of grand-parents
49 Ready and willing
50 Follow
53 Mountain
54 Detect
55 Cloth sieve
56 Jettison
58 Put to oath again
60 Gas element
61 Suit sizes
62 12:45 P.M.: Thunder
66 Fly
68 Wood for wicker: Var.
69 Sun hats
72 Milk: Prefix
73 Bills of fare
74 Unite
76 Wing
77 Sign
78 H.S.T.'s birthplace
79 Like Pindar's output
80 Goddess: Lat.
81 1 P.M.: Lightning
87 Pry into someone's life
89 Robt. ____
90 Divisions: Abbr.
91 1:15 P.M.: Taking cover
96 Restrain
97 Canal
98 Blue pencil
102 Spanish wave
103 1:20 P.M.: No escape
109 Ott
110 Israeli port
111 Easygoing
112 Therefore
113 Grieg woman
114 Doctrine
115 Bed canopy
116 Grasses

DOWN

1 Beach wear
2 Biblical kingdom
3 Kind of devil
4 Triteness
5 Critical one
6 Wear down
7 Hairpiece
8 Friend, in Paris
9 Put on a tight shoe
10 Implore
11 Madison, N.J., campus
12 "Let 'er ____!"
13 Egg cells
14 Deface
15 Lodge member
16 Stroller
17 Highest point
18 Check casher
24 Maniple
25 Ride or fever
29 School-org. units
31 Part of R.F.D.
32 Warble
33 Modern park hazard
34 Belgian war town
35 Indian salt
36 Rockies or Alps: Abbr.
37 Spectral body
38 Make ____ (get rich)
39 Pie-thrower's genre
43 Impair
44 ____ barrel
45 Turn for home
46 De Valera
50 Solicited
51 Kind of meal
52 Certain drs.
54 Take care of
55 "____ Bulba"
56 Unfeeling
57 Miss Witherspoon
59 Kind of not
60 Come back
61 Laundry item
63 Well-known Boston street
64 City near Frankfurt
65 Boat spar
66 Muhammad
67 Forefront
70 Wide awake
71 Does in
73 James or Perry
74 ____ metal (nickel alloy)
75 Extra
78 Husk: Prefix
81 Decorated metal
82 African pen
83 English explorer
84 Title receiver
85 Albert or Bracken
86 1,100 ____ second (speed of sound)
87 Wetlands
88 Christmas, in Italy
91 Large snake
92 Writer Ben
93 Silkworm
94 Marsh growth
95 Indolent one
99 Widely outspread
100 Prod
101 Ring victories
103 Tizzy
104 "Cakes and ____"
105 Thai river
106 Adherent: Suffix
107 Latin abbrs.
108 Consume

394 GOOD NEWS

By Barbara Gillis

395 SPACE-SAVING
By George Rose Smith

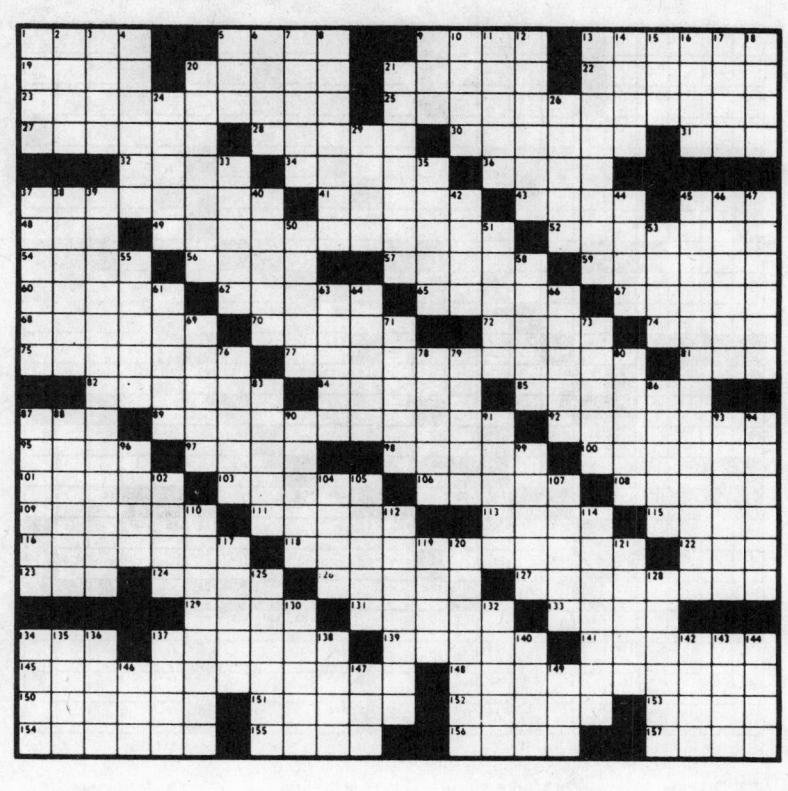

396 AQUA-MARINE By Bill Hartman

ACROSS

1 Mountain dweller
6 Juno's counterpart
10 Tree or Sunday
14 Weather abbr.
17 ____ Magnon
20 Of hearing
21 Flower
22 Et ____
23 Also
24 Barnyard dweller
25 Small land body
26 Rochester output
27 Iranian coin
28 Hard wood
29 Beverage
30 What Helen's beauty was like, to Poe
35 Effort
36 Asian land
37 Earth
38 Miss Korbut et al.
40 Consents
43 High: Prefix
44 Balsam
45 Arnaz
46 Temple vessel
49 Takes on
50 Light color
51 Duck, in Bonn
52 Print measures
53 Manner
54 Ships or clams
58 Church area
61 Meddler of a sort
64 Act
65 Moves furtively
67 Salutation
68 Adroit
71 Legal thing
72 Bridge setback
73 Area of Morocco
75 Wise one
76 Java's neighbor
79 Stevenson's craft
83 Oil land
84 Guinness
85 Missing, in a way
86 Fur animal
87 Energy unit
89 Art movement
90 Gardner
91 Give a sly glance
93 Divides
97 Reply
99 Strong drink
100 Zoo of a sort
101 What!, in Spain
102 Across: Prefix
104 Teases
106 Sauce source
107 Misbehave
110 Famous deal
117 Thames area
118 Periods
119 Pike's discovery
120 Miss Thomas et al.
121 More correct
123 Denials
124 Beset
125 Marble
126 New World explorers
135 Poetic word
136 Solidify
137 Desire
138 Yesterday: Fr.
139 Legislate
140 Edge
141 Pitching stat
142 Atlantic cape
143 Like some rumors
144 More developed
145 Bitter vetch
146 Wall and Main: Abbr.
147 Admirers
148 Colorless
149 Impertinent

DOWN

1 Café au ____
2 Drunk
3 Guthrie
4 Conductor
5 Changed
6 Record player
7 Norse mariner
8 Anger
9 T. Fuller wisdom, with 66 Down
10 Precook
11 Nom de plume
12 Untruthful one
13 Mollycoddles
14 Arose
15 Kill time
16 Ginza locale
17 Kind of horse
18 Discharge
19 Pronoun
31 Humorist Bill et al.
32 Western alliance
33 Kind of flight
34 Veteran of 1812
39 Family member
40 Small type
41 Dead duck
42 Man's nickname
43 Quick
44 Bob's son
47 Political winners
48 Pungent herb
49 Towel word
50 Recipe meas.
53 Chemical suffix
55 Cleopatra, or Bogart's boat
56 One of the Stooges
57 Once, old style
59 Jokesters' standbys
60 Glass or lady's
61 Clergyman
62 Kind of eye
63 Kind of guard
65 London area
66 See 9 Down
69 Turkish title
70 Indians or pins
72 Scottish chemist
74 Decree
76 Kind of luck or egg
77 State: Abbr.
78 Swan lady
80 Experience
81 Aviation prefix
82 Melody
88 Cigar yield
90 Wonder
92 Alike, in Paris
93 Kind of buddy
94 Maine bay
95 Horse races
96 Kind of scraper
98 Dine
100 Part of R.C.A.
102 Coloring base
103 Qualifying words
105 Bother
107 Insect
108 More trite
109 Platitudes
110 Brown envelopes
111 Greek conflict
112 Certain poker players
113 Fuse
114 Family member
115 School books
116 Tirana's land
122 Shows fury
124 Heathen
127 Lively
128 Vicinity
129 Opera girl
130 Little girl
131 Clothes or Christmas
132 Knocks
133 Desserts
134 "It's worth ____"
135 Article

397 OFF THE LEASH *By DeWitt Anderson*

ACROSS

1 Walt Kelly's possum
5 Confine
11 Friend, in Bari
16 Action words
17 Snares
18 Split or cream pie
20 Hunts in style
22 Board workers
24 Annul
25 Images
26 Raison d' ____
28 Chemical suffix
29 Word part: Abbr.
30 Adult
31 Nasty
32 Igneous rock
33 Resin
35 Thus, in Spain
36 Bets on
37 Capital of Jordan
38 Neighbor of Que.
40 Fugitive
42 Most wily
43 Share
46 Wyatt and family
47 "Give ____ a horse he . . ."
48 English prison of note
50 Occasional limit
51 Secondary benefits
55 Collegiate vines
56 Chinese province
58 Fireside ____
59 Vex
60 Pensacola sight: Abbr.
61 Symbol of cleanliness
63 Anais ____
64 Hoary
66 Areas in the Seine
67 "____ Grow Too Old . . ."
68 Roulette bets
70 Echoes
72 Hawaiian staple
73 Bleach
75 Lawns, etc.: Abbr.
76 Concerns
78 Marx associate
79 Stage fare
82 Hamburger spreads
84 Turkish title
85 Bucolic
86 Foible's opposite
87 Murphy's or Salic
89 Map part
93 Slightly
94 Blouse
95 French artist
97 Headpiece
98 "____ fan Tutte"
99 Eve's grandson
100 Caper
101 ____ Morgana
102 Dominate vocally
104 Conscience, to Francis Thompson
108 Type of tale
109 Cicero, e.g.
110 Western
111 Flight: Fr.
112 Nations
113 Bitter herbs

DOWN

1 Vend
2 Mountain: Prefix
3 Literary monogram
4 Rome's old port
5 Limited to an organization
6 Sky sight
7 Black eye
8 Mil. branch
9 Radical
10 Perfumes
11 Have ____ eye view of
12 Tide, in Calais
13 Cadmus's daughter
14 Orion's neighbor
15 Former
16 Durable plastic
19 Scents
20 Stratagem
21 Eight: Prefix
23 Point of view
27 Small child: Var.
30 Tiny portions
31 Foolish
34 Tree grove
36 "His ____ than . . ."
37 Arkin
39 Overly
41 Looked over carefully
42 Bessie or Kate
43 Sack
44 Originates
45 ____ barred
47 Phosphate mineral
48 Coin of Iran
49 Dissolute ones
51 Was eminent
52 Crowning ornament
53 Plays at love
54 Common or non
57 Locations: Abbr.
58 Iowa college
61 Female deer
62 Former Saigon name
65 Opinionated ones
68 Head
69 N.Y. city
71 River to the Caspian
72 Miss Duke
74 Miss Balin
76 Pre-Xmas beehive
77 Eclat
79 Athenian lawgiver
80 Erase
81 Grain awns
82 Elbow, in Spain
83 Tailors, to Carlyle
86 N.Y. lakes
88 Urchin
90 Poem parts
91 Trencherman
92 Govt. agent
94 Certain wizard's park
95 Alighieri
96 Ethereal fluid
101 Karma
103 "____ six of one . . ."
105 Gold, to Cortés
106 Detroit-based org.
107 ____ Claire

398 YOKING MATTER
By Joseph La Fauci

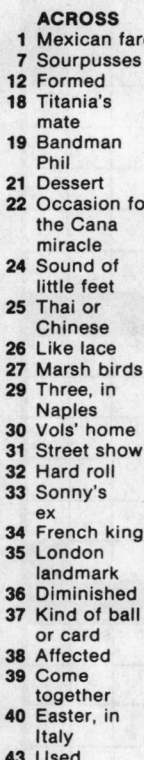

ACROSS

1 Mexican fare
7 Sourpusses
12 Formed
18 Titania's mate
19 Bandman Phil
21 Dessert
22 Occasion for the Cana miracle
24 Sound of little feet
25 Thai or Chinese
26 Like lace
27 Marsh birds
29 Three, in Naples
30 Vols' home
31 Street show
32 Hard roll
33 Sonny's ex
34 French king
35 London landmark
36 Diminished
37 Kind of ball or card
38 Affected
39 Come together
40 Easter, in Italy
43 Used the rink
45 Sidestep
46 Mountie's action
47 Would-be thin man
48 Afternoon, in Madrid
49 Yemen's capital
50 Tokyo, once
51 Revoke a legacy
52 Hair-care product
53 Seal
54 Bask
55 Fiber knots
56 Preceded
58 Salt tree
59 Asian river
60 Pickling solution
62 "____ Devil" (old 3-D film)
63 Laurence or Tuck
64 Kind of horn
65 Informal
66 Miss Bow
67 Prospective TV shows

68 Impress deeply
70 Stimulating
71 Offenbach's "La Belle ____"
72 Make fast
73 Potato or whiskey
74 Iranians' ancestors
75 Glory or gold
76 Salad green
77 Jewelry term
78 Scientist's place
81 What the dawn did
83 Arrange a loan
84 Talk group
85 Syrian city
86 Elec. unit
87 James Dean film
88 Italian cheese city
89 Kind of holiday
90 More sordid

92 Long-term merger
95 Glorify
96 Balanced
97 Order of the day
98 Designed
99 White poplar
100 Kilt ingredient

DOWN

1 Marinara base
2 Brought low
3 Sheep breed
4 Scottish island
5 Beef cut
6 Spanish queen
7 Gladdened
8 Feature of an A-frame home
9 Mountain crest
10 Barnyard sound

11 Little lady
12 Blab
13 Humble homes
14 Candlenut tree
15 Move for a new way of life
16 Finnish lake, to Swedes
17 Inhibit
20 Unaccountable
21 Worked with Mata Hari
23 Plagued
28 U.S. writer
31 Friend of Fido
32 ____ in (intrude)
33 Son of Ham
35 Carved emblem
36 Domestic goal
37 De Lesseps achievement
38 Companions
39 Robert or Samuel

40 Polish Mrs.
41 Billow
42 Former sinners
43 Source of added income
44 Preparing for 36 Down
45 Famous Florentine
46 Mme. Lupescu
47 Samson and others
48 Like saloon pianos
49 Italian city
52 Welcome bid by partner
53 Downright
57 Flooded
58 French city
60 Face up to
61 Critic's acclaim
63 Word with mignon
66 Critic Judith
67 Soft ____ (muffle)
69 Slide or as a

70 Whisper
71 Now
73 Unyielding
74 Synthetic
76 Irish county
77 Calif. city
78 Banker Thomas
79 Peregrine Pickle's wife
80 East Indian tree
81 Instances
82 Flower spike
83 U.S. poet
84 Home-song writer
85 Painter Winslow
87 Verbal thrust
88 Common person
89 Northern capital
91 Particle: Abbr.
93 Egg cells
94 Coiffure piece

399   LIGHTS OUT   By Alfio Micci

ACROSS

1 Point of land
5 People of Anatolia
10 Opening moves
17 Raccoon's relatives
19 African lemur
21 Title-transfer receiver
22 Burning
23 Peeks
24 Sprouts or lace
25 Chat for Doris Day
27 Tenant's concern
29 Groove
30 ___ de deux
31 Thrice: Pref.
32 Greek god
34 Freshwater fish
36 Sweet grass
40 Feeling no pain
45 Flower arrangement
48 Upward: Prefix
49 Small barracuda
50 One on the other side
51 Boy
52 Stunt-flier's maneuver
53 Arise
55 Schedule abbr.
57 Map additions
60 Mideasterner
62 Ransack
63 ___ Paulo
64 Jane or John
65 Mine entrance
66 Surgeon's handiwork
72 Sea bird
74 Way to stand
76 Pancakes
77 Stopping-place
78 Tipplers
80 Kind of down
82 Pale
84 U.S. Indian
86 Irish, for one
87 It's often crazy
89 "Two ___"
91 Unrefined
93 Time span: Abbr.
94 Certain safeguards
100 TV show
102 ___ amis
103 Labor initials
104 Warm-sea fish
105 Ace

108 Bit
111 Spanish bear
112 Prohibition
114 Mavourneen's place
115 Gums
116 ___ crow
118 Glut
120 Car of old
121 Author Seton et al.
122 Broadcasts
128 Bewails
129 More, in Milan
130 Caddoan tribe
131 Neighbor of Ga.
132 Part: Abbr.
135 Coins: Abbr.
137 Bottom
139 Spirit raisers
143 One of the classes
147 Repeat
149 U.S. Indians
150 Stuffed oneself
151 ___ the aisle (choice spots)
152 Asian mountaineer
153 Worked on walls
154 Concede
155 Day before: Abbr.

DOWN

1 Balkan city
2 Cloys
3 Kind of type: Abbr.
4 Horse food
5 Pipe for Xaviera Hollander?
6 Inquire
7 Words from Hamlet
8 Italian port
9 Hebrides island
10 Needlefish
11 Lake Albert people
12 Do harm to
13 Give
14 Chemical suffix
15 ___ Aviv
16 Its, in France
17 Li'l Abner creator
18 Betsy Ross, e.g.
19 In the manner of

20 Office seeker: Abbr.
24 Carefree situation
26 Oct. 31 alternative
28 Meet
33 Ensue
35 W.W. II area
37 Disturb
38 Insect
39 Bettor's concern
40 Not live
41 Provide with weapons
42 Russian girl's name
43 Politician Harold
44 Spyri heroine
45 Cunning
46 He felled an Usher
47 Like Bali

53 Shankar's instrument
54 Court figure: Abbr.
56 Grate
58 Musical symbol
59 Social groups
61 Fall-air quality
67 Prior to
68 Ivan or Peter
69 Breeding place
70 Sword
71 Basted
72 Abbrs. on letters
73 Rake
75 Clump
79 Blighted areas
81 Not buying
82 ___ends
83 Expanse
85 Bit part

88 Corner
90 Hitting stats
92 Purchase for Mme. Tussaud
95 Stranded
96 Picture-taker, in Bonn
97 Wane
98 Headpiece
99 More peeved
101 Disburse
106 Inlet
107 Weights: Abbr.
108 Ox or rat
109 Oil flask
110 Steak order
113 Depart
117 Viper
119 Was in store for
121 Emma Goldman's goal

123 Concert cry
124 Starry
125 Snail genus
126 Athenian judge
127 Slightly: Suffix
132 Equals
133 Moved slowly
134 She, in Italy
136 Place
138 Orchid genus
140 Siouan
141 Crew
142 "Of ___ I Sing"
143 Cut off
144 Gardner
145 Big___
146 Composer Rorem
148 U.S. highway

400 CONGLOMERATES

By A.J. Santora

ACROSS

1 Part of a double chin
5 Shows grief
9 Seasonal beer
13 Selected
19 Throb
20 Get lucky, Mr. Mimic
24 Barfront light
25 Fake out an old Celtic star
26 Fight-game name
27 Of a layer
28 Kind of gin
29 Danger
30 Stations
33 Counter-weights
34 Went fast
35 Some birds' homes
36 On a cruise
37 Young hawk
38 Caraway offering
39 Kind of plane
40 Short rifle
42 Rip
43 Island of charm
44 That, in Paris
47 Batter's wear
49 Make cloth
52 Numerical prefix
53 Dracula, for one
55 Roof border
56 Salute the creator of the mini
61 Approach
62 Networks
64 Senor's coin
65 Full-scale drawing
66 Argument
68 Greek letter
69 Selassie
71 ____ in the bucket
72 Miss Leigh
73 Unsym-metrical
75 Old instrument
76 Armament
79 ____ up (confessed)
80 Anchor ring
81 Green hat
82 Gold, in Mexico
83 Sullen
85 Send payment
86 Elder nine tails?
87 In ____ (irritated)
89 ____ 'acte
90 Prepares to pay Paul Anka
94 U.S., Can., etc.
95 Rest
97 Took the bait
98 Willow
99 Kind of femme
101 Mideast land: Abbr.
102 Rita and Grande
104 Relative
106 Relish
107 Fairway cry
108 "Too bad!"
109 Judge's seat
112 What a spat covers
115 Cut the bird
117 Gelatin
118 Trooper's beam
119 Engineer's beam
120 Recipient
121 Coaster
122 Circlets
124 Normal
125 Dig ex-Governor's no-change stance
128 Hindu god
129 Incites a general
130 Printing word
131 Baby's foot
132 Insects
133 Invites
134 Poet Pound

DOWN

1 Hemp fiber
2 Spotted cat
3 Pooh-poohs an economist
4 Deighton
5 Stammer
6 Gold embroidery
7 Organ stop
8 Joins an ice show
9 School subj.
10 Betting in N.Y.C.
11 Refrigerator unit
12 Slew
13 U.S. rights org.
14 Latin American
15 New York lake
16 Cubic meter
17 Havelock ____
18 Dickens girl
20 Nouns: Abbr.
21 High notes
22 Oaf
23 Otto's realm: Abbr.
31 Yoked
32 Dressing flavor
34 Kind of sick
35 Mountain pass
38 Burn up watching a comic
39 Utility duct
41 Ordinal suffix
42 Muscle Shoals project: Abbr.
43 Slope, in Scotland
44 Interview a swimmer?
45 Single
46 To be: Fr.
47 German philosopher
48 Have an ____ the ground
49 Control
50 Before where
51 Before amas
52 Paint thinner, for short
54 Beginning
57 On foot, in Paris
58 War town in Flanders
59 ____ngu (Vietnamese writing)
60 Scottish title
63 Climbs a rope
67 Miss Gillette
70 Run like ____
71 High nest
72 Panel member
74 ____ off (kicked a habit)
75 Win easily
76 Parking-place fixture
77 Bay window
78 ____ Dame
80 Exam
81 Spoiler
83 Disorder
84 Kind of child
85 Hitting stats
86 Dernier ____
88 "____ tuffet"
91 Instrument
92 Id follower
93 Two ____ kind
96 Ben Franklin offerings
100 Of grand-parents
103 Anger
104 Lamp rubber
105 Former Cairo initials
106 Scribbles
107 Least con-strained
108 Program
109 Streisand
110 Decorates
111 "____ of the North"
113 Dropout
114 Printing slips
115 Stanley's river
116 Touch ____ (risky)
117 Wings
118 Roster
120 Recital offering
121 R.R. depot
122 Alley and cool
123 Terminate
126 Beef cut, in Scotland
127 Fraction: Abbr.
128 Compass point

1

```
COILS   DARKS   ABASH
PICNIC  INANE   FORGOT
SEVENTHHEAVEN   FRITTER
ALIAS   OUT  EASTEND  LEE
KILN  COMES  DEICE  CITE
EOS  SALUTES  OFT  PANED
SNEAKS  SIGNOFF  PINERY
RAISE   COACH   SOLI
TOVARICH  SITUATIONISM
ABA  RUSES  LEMMA  TEMPO
BONA  STACK  TOOLS  SPAR
ULTRA  ARRAY  RULED  ORE
SISTERSTATES  RECESSES
WRAY   TILLS   DUMAS
UPTOIT  ICELAND  REGINA
SHARE  ASH  SNOOZES  BAR
HANK  CLIPS  TOROS  FIVE
EST  PULSATE  PIU  ALLIN
REROUTE  PEACEANDQUIET
DUBLIN  ENTER  DAUNTS
MILES   ROSES   SHAKY
```

2

```
NOTHIN   BUSHER   BARDS
TARRING  SALTINE  PARTIES
ORIENTS  CLAUDIA  ATACAMA
PRO  CHORAL  BEGGARED  GAR
HALT  ENOLA  SMALL  ALONG
ATEUP  EEDSRE  ANTA  ANTE
TESTED  SETOFF  SAY  TWAIN
ONES  DETOUR  REAR  LCT
TURNUPS  DARTED  DIET
MARS  TACT  SMITES  MARAUD
AGA  HAHA  ILONA  EDIRNE
NONE  UNREGENERATED  MIDI
ORISON  PRONG  TREE  SIS
FEASTS  SONTAG  YELL  SENT
ATES  DIESES  NEOCENE
ICE  EWES  CRONES  DOUR
TAMAR  GPS  STRAIT  TROPES
ALEM  MEAD  HERPEO  BURNT
LENIS  EAGER  CHIPS  SEGO
IND  TINKERER  HOLLOS  CIA
ADAMANT  NINETEN  ELEMENT
NATIVES  EVADERS  STRIPES
RENEE   SENSES   HABITS
```

3

```
BOGS   COLOR   WRAP   ASST
EXAM  ARISE  HALO  ATETE
AUTUMNALEQUINOX  STEED
USE  ONLY  UNTIE  STUMPS
NOES   MECHS   CAEN
KAFIRS  BASLE  ALFRESCO
ADAMS  WINTERGREEN  ULM
BULB  LAGO  AGAS  SMEE
OWL  OUTOFSEASON  TOMAN
BASSINET  LAMPS  FAMERS
BONER   WAGES   BOXER
CHALKS  TOKEN  DANISHES
RACES  SOMERSAULTS  ONA
INKS  SAXE  BEES  BUTS
MOO  SPRINGFIELD  RISES
PINDARIC  RENTS  CELERY
ALAS   SALAS   SOCK
BOUNTY  SETON  AQUA  FAN
OUNCE  SPRINGASURPRISE
ACTED  TURF  EXEAT  AXIS
THOS   ADAY   READS   JEST
```

4

```
METAL  COSTA  DELAY  STAEL
OZONE  OPTED  EROSE  PORTE
BRONXCHEERS  CROSSBOWMAN
YALE  LENIN  PLANT  LIESTO
BARON   MEANY   SALA
FASTENER  LEAST  ANDERSON
AMIENS  LIARS  ACIER  ENA
MALAE  WHISTLESTOPS  ACES
IDEST  OASTS  ERRS  TROIS
NINE  TOILE  PATEN  BRENDA
EST  FALLENARCHES  LANDAU
BLIP   LEE   IDAS
EQUINE  RUBBERBRIDGE  TAA
SUTTER  ASIAN  LURCH  MONT
POLES  AGAS  FOCAL  SARTO
ITER  STAGECOACHES  COIRS
EER  MESNE  ALIKE  PAREUS
DESPISED  STIRS  CHARISMA
ASTA   TAHOE   DROSS
MALICE  CHIOS  LOATH  XRAY
INANUTSHELL  DUMBWAITERS
LAVIE  AIMEE  ARUBA  BRICE
EMEND  GRADS  WESER  NADIR
```

5

```
SPARED   ALMOST   PASTAS
CAREER  NEEDLER  UNIATE
ORGANA  ARMOIRE  RODMEN
ROAM  MANN  REGALIA  MAS
ELL  EASIER  RIVET  DUSE
DEIGN  KAREL  VENALIZES
ACMES   CERE   SNUG
SOLOED  CATER  ICINGS
REPAID  SOPHISTICATION
ADA  LOCUM  ANARK  NACRE
VALE  COOPERATION  LOGE
ATILT  AMANG  IONIC  BOZ
GENERALISSIMOS  CABANE
EREMIC   SUZAN   TENORS
EMUS   BEET   PAROL
REINSTATE  STERN  NOTCH
AUNT  ETHAN  EVOKES  RAE
IRA  SNEERED  AWAY  LIMA
NORATE  MIRACLE  RIOTER
EPURES  ENVIOUS  INSERT
DETERS   GESTES   ESTRAY
```

6

```
EDWARDS  ACED  FEAR  ARTS
LEERIER  HOMEPLACE  TEHEE
IWEEPFORADONAISHEISDEAD
CASAS  ABET  STEEDS  ARMS
ILL  PAYSRENT  IMINE
TIETIES  REAMOUT  STILE
EARTHINESS  ANTECESSOR
SAKES  EMIT  THREADS  APE
ARIL  APOGEE  AGAG
LET  SUES  ERRANTS  AGARS
TOCSINS  CATS  GOAT  BEREA
ELONGATIONS  REPRIMANDED
RAWIN  OLIO  DORE  PORTEND
SERGE  PANNIER  REBS  NAL
ISTO   CAYUGA   RICE
AWN  SHIPPED  KEPI  LUNTS
PATRICIDES  SWEETTOOTH
TRIES  GALATEA  ESTHETE
MATCH  RASSLERS  RAT
PIRL  ATEASE  TEER  ASFIT
FLOWERINTHECRANNIEDWALL
CLUES  DOMINEERS  TREACLE
ESTE  ELON  ELSE  SANTEES
```

7

```
ABJURE JANIS   SATI  NEB
LEASTS EVERT  FACILE ONO
EMCEES JACKINTHEBOX  PGS
COKE  HUSK  LOCATE  TELIC
TAB POINT BLT  ROT  OLAN
ONEHORSE  SAMARA   ALLYE
 NIMB  PICARESQUE  AMES
SIPPED ERINYS  UPDO  ARA
LAMP  DADOES  UPAS  BAKED
ARBOR LINN  BALED  ISLED
IAL AAMS STILTS  HOCKS
CHEAPJACK ULT OFONESJIB
 JAPAN NOBLES  ORAN  ADE
CAROM  BONES  HERS  ENCLS
PACER TAXI  HISSES  OKES
ARK TOIT  OSIERS  DALLAS
ROBE JOHNNYCAKE   DUAD
LEVIS  OSLERS  QUIDNUNC
IQED SES VLS MURES  LAR
INUSE PATRIA  MEAN  ALTA
MII EVERYMANJACK  GAMBIT
PAC STALLS  DUNCE REMOVE
INK SKYE  STEAD STAYED
```

8

```
EBOLI  CODED  AGES  DESK
LENIN  AWARE  DAMP  RITE
LETME TARASBULBA  KRON
ACHE CORKSCREW  SCIENT
HERTZ  LESE  AAMILNE
 GISARMES GUYS  ODI
SORCERIES  SUN  PANACHE
TREK SPA CHEMIST  ROED
IDEST IDOLATER  MAENAD
RON ONE CUM SABOT  SLY
  MUNSTERCHEESE
UME BRICA OPE  ATS  MBL
NERVES  AVOCADOS  TIARA
USIA ENRANKS  CTO  NYET
MANMADE RES THEMAJORS
 APL SPYS  DESPOTIC
SCIOLTO  HEEL  REGLE
STEREO POORCLARE  TINT
IOOI ULSTERETTE  DINAH
OPUS GOUT INHOT  AMICI
NASH HYPO STEMS  SECTS
```

9

```
MERGE  ACT AZOV  GBSHAW
GAMARI RAH NAME  NOTATE
EXODERM GREENCORMORANTS
TITAN EAU ACI ODDMANOUT
EMERALDFEATHER   ASET
MSS DIET NEO EAN DEBASE
VITA MER CENTS  SONIA
LOINS  PUN ADDIOS  WILT
CYCLE DESTAEL SQUEALSON
ICAL PORT BALLOU AVIESO
DELAMARES DROP  ELLEN
SEAGATE  PILUS  AIRGAPS
EYING LCIS  TURNSGRAY
GORGON RAFAEL OLEG RIPE
OVERRATES TRYOUTS LEAPS
OUSE SEETHE  MRS  POESY
PLIED SNEAD PAS  LUNN
SENNET GRD MUN BERG PRI
LIMA JACKINTHEGREEN
CREDITORS BCE OSA RILLE
PEREGRINEPICKLE REENTER
APACHE EMIT AIL  REGENT
SPLATS TINE STS  SNORT
```

10

```
AMPLE SILK HEEPS  RIPSAW
KORAN PLAN ONTAP EMOTER
HOOTCHIECOOTCHIE MALADE
HEAD ETAT  DEROGATES
RAHS SEA HEPTA  EVEREST
ENE HURLYBURLY  SPAS
DELLAS POR APPEAL  CHEM
SATIRE HOITYTOITY HOERS
REDUST NEE  NAS  UVEAS
ROM HODGEPODGE  GREB
BOSNS OWE SRO  VERTIGO
OAK COUNTER BELLAMY EON
TREPANS  ROT IAN  SOJAS
LURE HANKYPANKY  CUE
MATSU TOR  PIR  ABUSES
ABEAM HOCUSPOCUS EREBUS
TERN LETSGO HRH  ARLINE
HEMS HOWDYDOODY  EUR
OCARINA ASTHE ELI  ASPS
CAROLINAS  IMET  ENOL
ADESTE HIGGLEDYPIGGLEDY
LESSON ADORE IRAN RINSE
ATTENT HEROD TOWS ENACT
```

11

```
POSTOFFICE  ALB  INAPOT
HEARNOEVIL HOLESINONE
LAUNDERMATS TOUCHANDGO
DELFT ADONAIS TEL GASES
EMA ALT ROTGUT  SETA
FONDAS DAVINCIS CORDOBA
INGENUES OOHED  TRAILER
CAIRA ACTON ARABIA ODRA
IDUN MUSES SNAKECHARMER
TEM FIX LLOYDC RISE ATA
LON OFOURSKINS  ODIST
YANGTZE TIU  SAMPLED
TWEED CARSONCITY  AUG
OAS LAHR AFGHAN SYS MAW
PHIBETAKAPPA LOCHS FAVI
PICA BISTRO ISTOO AUDEN
ONANOAK TICKS  TOWNSEND
SENSATO UNKNOWNS OTSEGO
RSVP SEISHU  UGH  YEW
SHAMS SHE TSCALES OMERS
KISSMEKATE HELLISHNESS
YESTERYEAR ELEEMOSYNA
ERNANI OLE SENDINGSET
```

12

```
MASS PALM  CAPH  RALSTON
ANIL EQUI SAMOA ELEMENT
EDDO RUNSACROSS FINITES
DEVILANDDANIELWEBSTER
TOWATER IMRE  EERIE
AWAKE INDIA OUTRE SHAWL
RNS SPUR TBARS ENC AREA
ASHE SMOLT FANS COSTING
LET LOOKIT  OVERHEATS
OPALS FLU ENE  RIFTED
CALYPSO BEE DEERE  SOI
UPINYOURFUNKANDWAGNALLS
LAT ORION EWA  MEANIES
OUTLAY STE COE  PUDGY
CLAMSHELL ATESTS  GAR
LEVERET EARL CRIME ADDA
AMEN STU FRESH EELS IAN
PASSU ENCRE NEARS OPART
PORTA CARL  STOOGES
CROSSWORDPUZZLEMAKERS
GUANACO HORIZONTAL SANS
ANNULAR OTARY ECTO IMOU
MANSARD POMS  WHEN ESTE
```

13

```
A N I S E   P A S H A   K I L N   W A S P
M E G I L P   T I N E A R   U S I A   I X I A
M O N D A Y M O R N I N G   K I B I T Z E R S
    S T R A I N S   D U E L S   N E A
M A W   E A R L S   A S A M A   S T R A T A
I N E S   M A S   S L O B S   B L O O D R E D
S T E P O U T   G H O U L   A R O O N   M E D
H I K E R S   Q U A R T E R B A C K   A C T E
A G E N T   T U A N S   O I N K   O T H E R
P U N T   S H I R T   B A T E D   S P E A R S
S A D   I T O L D Y O U S O   T H E T I S
    W I S E N T S   T R I   S T A I N E R
  S A V I N G   C R I T I C I S M S   G A S
M E R I N O   C O H A N   D R E S S   R E V E
I R R E G   M A N U   S L A N E   M A N E T
R A I D   P O S T M O R T E M S   R E V E R T
A P O   M O L T O   B E A R S   S E V E R A L
G E R B I L L E   R E S T S   S O V   S A G E
E S S E N E   B E L I E   S A B E R   L E D
    A I M   C U P I D   M A R I N E R
H I N D S I G H T   S E C O N D G U E S S E S
O R A L   C O A T   K N I V E S   E L V E R S
S K Y E   S A P S   S T E E R   S P A R S
```

14

```
P E S T   S C A M P   T B A R   S P U D
A S H E   C A N O E   E E R Y   O H A R E
S P O N S O R S M E S S A G E   S A N D E
T Y E   T R E E   L A S S O   O I L S U P
    E R N S   B I N E T   C U R T
A P P L E S   K O N E R   A R T I S T R Y
C R A M P   P R O G R A M M E R S   R A E
R I M S   S O I E   O I S E   D A N A
A M P   N E W S R E P O R T S   L I N E R
B E H O O V E S   R U N N Y   R I N S E S
    L A T E R   C O N E S   S E M E L
S E E K E R   N O S I R   S C A N D A L S
K A T E S   T E L E C A S T E R S   T O P
A T E N   I O D O   P O N S   L O C I
T E E   I N P A N T O M I M E   C O R A L
E R R O R H A S   O N E T O   T U S S L E
    B R E R   S T E M S   S U R E
L A B O U R   T O T U P   A M B I   S O U
E Q U I P   T E L E P H O N E B O O T H S
W U R S T   I T E R   I S T L E   N I N E
D I R T   M E S S   S C A L D   T R O D
```

15

```
T H E M A N   S A D S A C K   A L S A C E
T H E V I E W   A R E O L A E   D E N I A L S
R E M A T C H   L A P L A T A   J O U R N A L
I C A N   I O W E   T O L A   G O N G   D I A
P A T   R A C I S T   U N T R U E   P I N T
O V I N E   A N M A K E   D I O R   T I D E S
D E C A M P   S A R A H S   C O N S O L E S
    V E E P   N O T A T E   M E T R O
S O L I T A R Y   C A R E E N   D I S T A L
A P I E   R I O T S   D E L O S   N O E S I S
L E T S   L O G E   S T R E W I N G   D A M P
T N T   R U N S T H E R I S K   W E A
U S E D   F I R S T A I D   S T O A   M E A D
S E R E N E   T E A I N   R E E L S   O L D E
A S S E S S   S I N G L E   R E C A L L E D
    P E T E S   R E S O L E   S U S A
T R I D E N T S   D E B A T E   S C R I M P
C H E S S   T I E R   A S Y I S T   O S C A R
R E V E   B I L L E T   S O T H A T   O R A
I L E   M I M E   A R A B   L E E S   S M I T
M A L T E S E   S M E T A N A   E P I C E N E
E M E R S O N   L E V E R E T   D I L A T E D
B R Y A N T   O R I E N T E   U C A T O R
```

16

```
R A D A R S   G A R A G E S   C E S U R A
A C E T I C   U N A L E R T   L I E N O R
N E C T A R   N A T A T O R   E G R E S S
O D E   N I B B L E S   D I N A H   A T E
F I R S T B L O O D   S E V E N T H S O N
F A N E   B U R G   T O N E R   B E E V E
    P E L E E   C H A T   O M E I
S U T L E R   T H I R S T   O L D A G E
I M P E L S   N E A R S   R A T L I N E S
M A R T S   S I P I D   P A C E S   A N T
P R O S   S E C O N D S I G H T   A G U A
U T A   F E W E R   E P P I E   M E R I T
T E R R A I N S   U G R I C   T I R A N E
E R S A T Z   T E R R E T   B E C A M E
    S H E P   A G E E   R E L E T
A B U S E   A G R E E   B E T E   E S S E
P A P E R M I L L S   L A S T G O S P E L
T I R   T E R A I   P O N I E R S   R I D
E L I C I T   M E D I C A L   A T T U N E
S E S A M E   I S O L A T E   P I E C E R
T E E T E R   S T E E L E D   H A T E R S
```

17

```
A B O M A   C U T U P   R S T A R   P O O N A
I O N I C   A L O M A   A E R I E   A L L O T
D U T C H U N C L E S   F R E N C H L E A V E
A T O E   N O E L   T A F F Y   T E L A M O N
    T I E R   T O P I S   B O R S
P L A N E T S   P A R I S   H A R D   H A H A
H E R E S Y   C U B A N H E E L S   A R R E T
R A G E S   C A N A L   I L L   P E A R L
A G E D   O N I C   P O R P O I S E   B O A
S U N   A S C O T   S U M   O V E R L I E S
Y E T   S P A N I S H B A Y O N E T   E A S T
    I T E R   V I R   N E F   O B A N
S A N E   A B I E S I R I S H R O S E   N O G
C R E A T I O N   K A S   E A R E D   I R E
R O B   I N S T A T E S   C A N T   A G I N
I L E D E   E R A   E R R I S   I C H O R
P L E A D   B R A Z I L N U T S   D O T T L E
T A F T   T R I M   N U D E S   T R U S S E S
    P R A M   I S N O T   R E I S
S E A B E E S   B L U E R   P O P E   A L E E
E N G L I S H P E E R   S I A M E S E C A T S
C O R I N   L I A N E   E M C E E   G R O U T
S W I P E   Y O K E D   S P E O S   G E N I E
```

18

```
B L A S   S C R U B   S L E E P   H A M S
R A G A   P H O N O   C U R S E   A L O T
I G O R   R A S O U M O V S K Y   B E N E
T O N A L I T Y   T I N   T E T R A G O N
    B A N S   M I N C E   R O A N
G E S A N G   S E Q U E N T   N I E L L O
A P I N G   V I R U S   G A P   D R I E D
M E E D   P A D R E   A L S O P   A E R O
B E G   A L L E Y   B R I T T E N   B O N
A S M O D E U S   P A R S E   S O B E I T
    E R O S E   T O R A H   F A R E S
F R I A R S   S E P O Y   C A N T A T A S
L O S   N I E L S E N   M O U T H   R I P
A C T E   S M U T S   C A R S E   C A S E
S C E N T   E R A   M O N E T   T H U L E
H A R R I S   S T R A U S S   C H I M E D
    A T T S   E A G R E   S E A N
T R A V I A T A   M O A   S P A R R I N G
H O N I   T R I O S O N A T A S   E C O N
E T A S   E A G L E   T R I T E   S E T A
M E T H   S P U D S   E R R E D   T R E T
```

19

```
GEMINI SPEC LAMAR COSMO
LEONID KINO ABABE OSCAR
ERODES INTRAVENUS SMART
NINER SPURNS TESTAMENTS
NEON SAPPY PATTE MINTY
    TEMPLES HEXES DECA
CRO YEAR BORED LEER TSE
HUNDRED SORAS SABREJETS
ABOARD GILA POST LUNIK
FLUSH RENDEZVOUS CITOLE
FESS DANK OILS CHEERER
    OOZE SMOCK CHEF
COSTUME SEAM BOAZ ECHO
OPIATE SPLASHDOWN ETHER
SERIF DUAL OURS ASCEND
BRELOQUES HERON NOTHERE
YEN RUST HANDS BENE SIR
    ALIT FALSE CELESTE
CANAL ALIBI MALLS AQUA
CALCULATOR GOODLY GLUTS
ALTON MOONINDIGO BREATH
BLANC ANDES DREW YANKEE
SARAH TESTA SERS ASTERN
```

20

```
COPAL ISTLE OHARA AHALF
ABODE BORIS DORIC RUBAL
NECESSARYFORONEPEOPLETO
ESKS TRUST ORONO VALLEY
SEETHE SQUAM RASSE SEND
    TEARS UPLAY STORM
ENV VIOLA INES EMMA PAY
THEDECLARATION SEASTOBE
RETIA ABED AMUR SKULLS
EBOATS OSIS GAMUT LIES
    LIPAR EELS CIRE ESSE
THATTOSECURETHESERIGHTS
REDO RIRE AERO STENO
ANON TASTE DASH DVORAK
UNSEWS EGAD RHAP ASANE
MASSACRE OFINDEPENDENCE
ASE RAIN STLO LEDGE TEL
    NSTAR SEGAL EARTO
STAG TAMES MOPED ISREAL
TAGORE ONIUM ODETO AARE
OURFORTUNESANDOURSACRED
AREAS BREVE SAUCE GETTO
TIERS ASSES ALTES ASHEN
```

21

```
RACER BLAB BARAS ABAS
AMOLE AIDA EDILE PONT
JOURNEYTOTHEMOON ORDO
    ROOST SEEP FROGMEN
EASY THE REGET WEARE
ODE THEGUMDROP TEENSY
MASSE MONAS MURAS
    TOPCHOICE APRIL DRAT
IFI BOSS GREENCHEESE
    THANT COARSE ELATE
CAPTOR BOOTS DRAMAS
ALLIN OTIOSE CAROL
PLANETPROBE TORE UTE
TANG RIATA SECTIONED
    PEELE CANOF RESIN
LANDIS ASTRONAUTS TNT
OLEAN ASTHE SLY LEAS
VITREUM EERO DRIED
ECHE PUTASPIDERONMOON
LIER OSAGE NERO DOURA
LARS NEWTS DRIP ONTOP
```

22

```
SNUB PIER CATO CHIMES
ATHENE ANNOTATOR LENORE
BROTHERCANYOUSPAREADIME
BARTERS EARL SCOOP LIP
ADELE MEDALS SALON BENE
    EDH MUDS CHIEF PARED
ETCS ADITS HEIL SCAR
THO GLORY CARES ARAMIS
ARI REIS ARLES HANK ARA
TENSEST CLEFS AORTA KID
SETAE MATED ALONG LESE
PENNYWISEPOUNDFOOLISH
PESO AIRER LINES ADDLE
ANT LURES ULNAR BONSOIR
ICE APES FRATS HOVE UNA
DERIVE CLARA SOLES GET
    DARK AILS RUMOR OHNO
STIES OGLES DELE TEN
ERNS BRIAR SUTURE SABAL
RID PEART PERI RISSOLE
AFOOLANDHISMONEYARESOON
PLOVER LENTICULA ANITRA
HERATS EADS SEAM NESS
```

23

```
ICEAGE    TRAIT  PADUA
THEBES TOESTHE TURNSA
METROS ARCHAEOLOGISTS
ORIAL ERST LOSES LORS
STO ONATOOT PIT PLUIE
SNUGASA RISEN ROALDS
    VIXENS NAR OUST
    PESOS PICKANDSHOVEL
MARATS SERAI EDS OILA
ULO SIMPLON DREE TRAP
SARG OREN NOES HUTS
IBAR OLIO CANITBE SEE
NOTA LIT GAZED EXCESS
GRAVELDEPOSIT ATHOS
    EVAS HAT SILTUP
DOONES SATUP FOEMANS
ORRIS PAS PENNERA OTT
REAM MELEE LIES TERRA
EXCAVATIONSITE MINOAN
NILGAI CUSTARD LOCATE
SEELS TENSE ANYDAY
```

24

```
CREPT DECAP DAMPS WHATA
ROBER ORIBI ASNAP HADUP
AGORA WIDEN MAORI OPINE
SUNKMONK CHOPPERHOPPER
HEYS STS TUAN QUEASY
    UPTO EARLET ADIPOSE
SIMPLEWIMPLE ARA ASANOX
INE MONTI STABAT PERI
DESIGN ELF ICESIN APODS
IZAR EVER FARCRY BYBIT
AGILE YBARRA TIA ONE
PERKYTURKEY PALLIDSALAD
OLE RES ORGEAT OMAHA
TASSE IMABUM ERLE AMAH
STOPS VOLUME ROI CESARE
HILL BELAYS STOOD LIL
ONEIDA ESE VENIALMENIAL
TESTERS ROOMIE DELA
    STEEPS STEP AMU PROB
KIPPERSHIPPER MOPYHOPI
ADARS TOTER GAROU ATTAR
RECIT ETUDE EWELL WHORL
LETTS TOPSY SKYED PARTS
```

25

```
ACCOSTS  PACAS  PIASTER
SHOUTAT  IRANI  IMMERGE
SANTAFE  TRENTONPERIOD
ORC  STEPHENAUSTIN  PIR
BLOCH  PLOT  PATES  SOSO
EIRE  ALUM  COTES  MALTS
REDROVER  AHLEN  VALISE
GEOID  BRAID  PAGE
SCRAPS  BEERS  COLUMBUS
COALS  CANAL  POLES  ONE
RAPS  LITTLEROCKS  ASIA
UTE  LORIS  SAMOS  ATTAR
BISMARCK  STIPA  PILOTS
AINE  CHOSE  MORAN
LAMINA  PHONE  LAMENTED
ABELE  VIEWS  BATE  TENO
TASS  TOEYE  RICH  CARTS
ELA  WALTERRALEIGH  REA
ROBERTLANSING  LOAFING
ANIMARE  NUDGE  DEPLETE
LESSPAY  EPEES  ASSURES
```

26

```
GROG  JOCKO  POCUS  CAJOLE
REMO  USHAK  IRANI  PRUNED
AGNI  THEYALEBULLDOGSONG
SLINKS  PER  DIKE  ATREE
SEATO  TIBIA  FIT  NOLA
OHHELL  DARN  PADISHAH
LITTLEMISSBLUEBIRD  HULA
ARAH  FPA  HAIG  ICY  GAMOW
MEMENTO  MACC  IDO  DIDOES
INAWAY  MONKEYS  TWOFERS
AERIE  JAR  BOLA  AUTO
SEAL  BONNYBLUEFLAG  NATO
DIRE  SEAU  OAF  LTCOL
RUBBISH  ATECROW  BOHEME
BALLET  UGH  GOAT  ROBERTA
ADEUX  TRA  POLK  AER  BROS
NAME  WHOBLEWOUTTHEFLAME
GRAYDAWN  ERNS  AMADOU
OONA  VIM  SAXON  XEBEC
PAINT  CHAS  MUD  MYSORE
ANDDARKBLUEISHEREE  IRON
STEERA  AURIC  OVERT  DAST
SHARDS  REESE  CADIZ  EXES
```

27

```
GOPAST  TOLA  MOST
MATADOR  ABACUS  CIPHER
ELIZADOOLITTLE  ORIOLE
SOO  HOVEL  HUNT  LAUREL
ASST  MERCY  PATIO  MTGE
SHEEN  SHUN  SENSE  WAT
LEAK  IMAS  ROSINA
ATLARGE  EARTH  NATIVE
RHO  ALEAF  ROIL  LEVEES
CEN  LONG  LOCKED  LARRY
ORGS  WEEHAWKENNJ  LAIC
LEILA  DROPSY  TEEN  DEE
ASSERT  SLAB  HOSEA  ISE
ELEGIT  TRUDI  TRICOTS
ATONER  OREG  RSVP
TIN  SILIC  GAHN  ELATE
INDO  NEGRI  FLORA  SCOT
ACCUSE  HENS  IRENE  EKA
RAISES  TAKEAGIANTSTEP
ASTERS  SKETCH  TAURINE
HYLA  DIET  ASIANS
```

28

```
ABRASE  BELA  POET  APTS
CUEMAN  HURON  BURRO  WART
ESSOIN  ERICA  ASTROLOGER
THEICEMANCOMETH  ELEME
WED  AIDES  THEPACE  BOA
OSAR  CORONAE  SOSO  DORM
NEHRU  NEWSPAPERBOYS
TOOSMOOTH  ILIA  PAROL
AWN  MTN  ENT  ALLY  ESCARP
JESTER  POH  NEA  ASSEGAI
ATO  RAGES  SOUPY  ORE
BONG  DOCTORZHIVAGO  AGED
UNI  ADLAI  IOLES  NOB
LESACRE  CPO  VEG  DUETTO
GRIGRI  FAIN  EDA  BET  OUR
LIVRE  LEAR  STANDERBY
THEDEERSLAYER  HITON
TROT  RENO  CARAMEL  ATTS
RIM  ASKSFOR  NICEA  HIC
IBEAM  THEBEGGARSOPERA
NURSERYMEN  ARENT  FLORAL
ANUT  ADANO  SIREE  AIDEDE
LENO  PSTS  TEST  TOSSER
```

29

```
IDAS  MOPSA  REDBEAR
NOME  ARRETE  IDEAMEN
EDWIN  GROWINGUPABSURD
LUNGING  SENNAS  MIS
SCHOLA  OID  EVAN  TOUTS
ATI  ERASTUS  EGAL  SNEE
SELS  IFS  PHILEMON  DSC
ELEVATED  ETE  EXEGETE
SADE  ETA  SIDED  DORAD
LUNAR  NATO  SRI  ETTE
FALLOFTHEHOUSEOFUSHER
UNTO  THM  MOST  PARSE
NAHUA  ESTOP  LAP  ALBS
CRESTOF  ESS  OVERLOOK
HEW  TRAPNETS  IRE  WAIF
ATAT  ALEE  OPPOSER  RTE
LAYOF  LABS  EON  VENDRE
PUP  CROTAL  RENEWAL
HIGHERTHANAKITE  AVAIS
UNOARED  TOUCHE  TELL
BIGTOPS  SPEED  ARKS
```

30

```
AMORET  COMO  SAGA  PORES
LAMINA  AVERS  EVIL  ASANA
TRIALBALANCE  DOLLARSIGN
OCT  ABILL  ARTICLES  AMID
NOSTRILS  VALE  EPI  ENE
AGEE  CABINETS  IRONED
UNCLES  TONAL  PARENTS
ROUES  SIMOLEON  IDEST
SETS  SELENE  TONNER  APIS
ALA  SENT  TRIES  CREDO
MOLASSES  CEDES  RAINED
ELEVATE  CALORIC  BANANAS
RELETS  BORED  CEREMONY
ODORS  COLON  OLPE  WHF
SANS  TALENT  STEALS  BIOL
TOAST  GOLCONDA  FOSSA
STELLAE  AULIS  PALEST
CARPAL  DECANTED  ARLO
AMA  SES  MING  CLASSPIN
LAVO  SERENADE  BELIE  IRI
CREDITCARD  ONEASYSTREET
AIRED  CAGE  NORIA  ETERNE
RASSE  ODER  SEER  DOSSER
```

31

```
HABLA   ATAVISM   LAPOF
VALUES  RETINUE   IMINO
BARBRASTREISAND   MINER
UNDERFIRE  PASSAGE  SSE
RYUN  SASS   EELY   SALS
GAP  PETITPOINT  PAWNEE
     DOYEN  RUNS   LEDGE
  SLAKED  RUNNER  PEAN
SCARED  WINCE  ICECREAM
TUNER  DAGGERLOOKS  EVE
ARCS  BOBO   ATEE   ADIT
IVE  SPEARHEADED  FILAR
RECOLORS  ANTED  TORERO
  OTOE   HOTELS  HERESY
PARTA    FERO    EASTS
IMPEND  ARROWSMITH  RAH
AMOR  ACLE   STER   RILE
NOR  SHELVER  ANYONEFOR
INANE  SWORDOFDAMOCLES
SILEX  TELLOFF   PITIES
TASTY  ATTESTS   ETATS
```

32

```
TOADS    BRO  IRANIC  ASAD
OMNIUM  HOED  SENORA  RODE
PAYDAYWAYLAYNAYSAY   EMAN
OHMY   OAT   SOCS  ISOGENS
PAODE  REGALE  HUBS  DAFOE
SHROP   ADIREFIREWIRE
HAE  TEEVEES  ROTA  ANDWOE
OHM  SOCIAL  BAR  VBS  WIN
PAIR  NOT  AMI  SEAT  MILT
  NEW  NAE  AGT  PWR  HALSE
WHITECOLLARDOLLARHOLLER
HEMIDEMISEMIQUAVERSAVER
ALONGSIDETOGUIDETHERIDE
TODAY  CON  TRE  SST  SIE
HIES  PALE  ISA  ASB  AWNS
ASS  ELI  SAG  DEVOTE  WOE
SEISMO  DREW  MAKEFUN  HRE
MAINPLANELANE     AGOOD
LIMNS  EENS  ERASED  MOLEY
ANOTHER  AIMS   EEE   ALAD
PURA  ACOBBLEJOBLLWOBBLE
USAF  THRILL  IDES  ARIOSE
PELE  SETTEE  GET   STOOD
```

33

```
JUTS  RACED   EBOND   SMEW
ANAK  ETHAN   VINCE   OUZO
URBI  THEVANITYOF   FEIN
NUL  THOSE   ILEX  LLANOS
THEWORST  ACES   PAIRS
  TARO  EAGER  ARTISTIC
CHAIRWARMER  FLOE   OENO
HELLS  STER   BLOB  AGRON
ARKS  DUOS   CLOSERTO
SEE  HORN  RHEAS  ATOLLS
SORBILE  FOIST  DIEDOUT
ENSURE  RIANT  BONN  UGO
  RESPONSE   DEWY   SNAP
CASED  HUNT  SIDE  LIGNI
ALMA  LAGS  STOOLPIGEON
PLEURISY  SCARF   ROIL
  ACUTE  COUP  RUINLIKE
GARRET  SOLD  VOLES  ZEP
AMIA  LAMPOONISTS  MANO
ZINC  EROSE  ALERT  ORYX
EDGY  RAGED  MESAS  DDAY
```

34

```
SAGES  SAMBA  RESAW  CACTI
CURLY  TRAIL  OSELA  ARLES
ADAMSNEEDLE  JACKSONCENT
LIN  TONSIL  EAU  AHSO  VOL
POTIONS  SEMIS  ALIS  MERE
  IDLE  LOTUS  CLINICAL
ANNEE  FIN  REDOING  ALAMO
MOAN  VARAN  NUGGET  RENEW
INITIATIVE  HRON  OPPIDAN
RADICLE  EOZOON  ENSEMBLE
  CHI  INLAW  SWEDE  PAIR
CST  SAJOU  GEM  INCUR  YES
ATRI  NONES  REPLY   DAB
SOUTACHE  MAJLIS  MORELLO
ALMADEN  LIRA  MOTIVATION
BEALE  STERIC  ANITA  TNUT
ANNIE  OATCAKE  SLY  RECTO
  CAMENIGH  ETAPE  CERO
ARAN  IGLO  STALE  TUSSLED
SOP  HERS  PES  STUART  NMU
HOOVERAPRON  HARRISONRED
ESTER  SINUS  OCEAN  REESE
STEED  SNARE  CELLO  EDDAS
```

35

```
REPASTE  LIEDER   DACHA
ELECTED  ANGRIER  AGUES
CAPTIVEAUDIENCE   TARAS
LITANY  TRUSS  EYRE  TRI
ANA  GESTES  SAD  ERSATZ
MELD  SEAL  ACCESS  WISE
ESKER  TRELLIS   OATEN
  MILS  DIOR  INTHERED
SPIGOTS  PACING   ITALY
VIE  ASHEN  FLORA  OLIVE
IMAS  TELEG  ELAND  YSER
LINER  SAURY  ARDOR  ERS
MAUVE  THREES  EDUCERS
ANTENNAS   ALOP   ARTY
  GRIEG  ASPIRIN  SACCO
ALAE  HEAVES  ORCA  SLOP
FOLDER  SAP  FRIERS  ELP
FUL  BURT  AGUAS  MAGALO
ODETO  BEHINDTHESCENES
RERUN  IRONAGE  CORTEGE
DRYAD   NETTED  AFEARED
```

36

```
AVOIDS  RAINS  OFFA  FIRMS
CATNIP  INTOW  NAIL  ASHOT
MARSEILLAISE  SUNBONNETS
ELA  STULMS  EMEND  UBOAT
  FREE  STETS  BTES
DAV  BIAS  TOILS  BILLYJOE
INEVERY  BURSE  SEEIT  UPA
AGNATE  EARTHENWARE  SPIT
DEULS  ANNES  AONE  WHINE
ELSE  PRATE  AEROS  WHITEN
MAS  NEPTUNESCUP  THERES
  FLORAE  TAR  BOILER
ALLIED  MERCURYLAMP  SCS
MAYORS  TEREK  HEADS  EBON
ARTYS  ARAG  PENNY  SCENE
NORD  PLUTOCRATIC  LECAMA
SNA  FROES  ROTOS  MITERED
ESPALIER  GAMER  DASH  DNS
  TOSS  ALTAR  LENT
METOO  PREEN  LISTED  MAT
SATURNALIA  THEMOONSTONE
PRUNE  REAM  ICANT  TCARTS
TINED  MASS  CANSO  OSAGES
```

37

```
CRESS   MESH    BESTS
SHUTUP  DACHA   WALKING
PENCILPUSHER    ARMINARM
URN  TARS  OLDTIMES  PEA
DRIP  TOTS  FRATER  BRAT
SYNOD  PENS  OPEN  WROTE
GNAT  RUMPLED  CHILLS
SAWDUST  BILLS  FREELY
ALA  BAIT  LOS  GRIEF
ROTC  REUSED  DOUBLINGS
AHEAD  PRAY  ROTI  SNARE
HARROWING  YACHTS  GROW
RAINS  DEN  SELF  RAE
SWILLS  COAST  DIAMOND
UPHOLD  FOGHORN  PLOW
POOLS  BLUE  MEOW  LAMBS
BILE  FRYPAN  SWIG  NILE
OLE  PHIBETES  ISNT  NUN
WELLTODO  DRESSPARADES
ROYALLY  OVATE  SURETE
TEHEE  GARY  HEADS
```

38

```
ANGLE  RIATA  HADES  ADAGE
FORAY  ONRED  ADULT  DIVAN
ALICEISLAND  NELLANDVOID
RATE  TAEL  SADLY  RELENTS
DART  PURSE  ASWE
NASTILY  CAPRA  AVIS  UMBO
INAWAY  PATTYWAGON  CAIRN
CORAL  TANTO  HIC  ARNIE
ERAS  ONCE  FLANAGAN  NAG
NAH  AMUSE  PIE  DARTLING
EKE  BERYLLINGALONG  CESS
NEAR  EEL  ALI  OILS
MADS  CLARAFICATIONS  KIM
ERITREAN  ELY  ABUSE  INE
DAP  ARCATURE  GNAT  ERST
ABIES  EOS  HAIRS  ACTII
LITUP  EMMAGRATES  SECEDE
SAYS  DAIS  LUNES  SCOLDER
ORRA  BONDS  ETON
STAPLES  MUSTY  AVER  POSH
HELENWHEELS  MARIANHASTE
ALONE  OSAGE  ALACK  ARSON
NATTY  TOTED  NESTS  DROPS
```

39

```
TASS  AKALA  STATE  EQUI
AMAH  TAPES  LANES  NULL
MINI  THESAVANNAH  TEAL
SETPOINT  ANTE  CURERS
APARS  TASTE  POSEN
GAMETE  HOST  BELDAMES
ADARS  CUTTYSARK  ATANY
PERS  FAMER  IDIOT  SROS
EPI  OLDIRONSIDES  YST
STANDARD  OSTE  ARA
NAVE  LADYS  OTIC
ELI  SAGE  BALATRON
IAN  UNITEDSTATES  UNE
BLOC  SIREE  OHSEE  TBAR
EARLE  PERSONALS  ARBIT
TIMESPAN  CANE  PLIERS
ARSIS  SHARE  SHIRR
GUNMEN  ETON  BARTERER
ENDO  ANDREADORIA  MANE
MAIN  ROGER  ORALS  EFTS
SUET  DREWS  PASSE  STET
```

40

```
APPT  ESSE  FLAMS  SIMBA
PULES  ONEIN  AUTOS  KNEAD
PLASTICTABLECLOTH  ISTLE
OSU  INHALE  NEURO  SETSIN
SEDANS  DARED  RHODA
ERISTIC  BISCUITMIX  NOTI
THEDAY  ACUITIES  STRUT
RENE  ETNEAN  CAPERS
TAD  RNWYS  AMS  BOLOGNA
DEFENSE  EASELS  AUDIT
GROFE  DOLLAR  CRAVATS
SNORT  PAPERNAPKIN  ATRIA
STOGIES  EGOIST  TOADY
SALAT  BASALT  BREEDER
LENTILS  LEM  OSTEO  SED
AMIENS  SOLIDS  RAMA
MINDS  SPEEDERS  ANALOG
PLOT  SNOWMOBILE  SNIPING
UNHAT  ASURE  TERROR
ROBROY  FIDOS  ROMAIN  ASE
AWAKE  FREEZEDRIEDCOFFEE
REBEL  DERMO  DECEM  REFIT
ADAYS  RESIN  EDAR  DENS
```

41

```
MUSHER  RANCOR  COASTS
ORIOLE  SOMEONE  AMULET
DALLAS  ALETTES  BIKINI
INKY  OFTEN  THIBET  DON
SIE  GLUES  FEODOR  BERG
TANTRUMS  TARRED  FUSSY
RATE  HELPS  YARD
DERIVE  PALSIES  DOGMA
ENEMY  SULLEN  EMOTIONS
CADS  SHRIMP  PROPHETIC
AMS  PLASTERSAINTS  OLE
MONOLOGUE  ECLATS  GRIN
PROLAPSE  SMOOTH  TREND
SWINE  DEMILLE  PRUDES
VEDA  MISDO  PLAN
CADET  GUILES  BOOMTOWN
OMER  TENNIS  SALTS  BOE
ROB  MADDEN  UPSET  ALOW
ARABIC  INGENUE  INSIDE
LATENT  ECLAIRS  NEIGES
SLEEKS  SEYTON  GERENT
```

42

```
COEDS  ASPEN  SWATSAT  FTS
ONTAP  SNIDE  HASHISH  AHA
ZENDA  CONES  ASTENSE  CIR
DADDYIWANTADIAMONDRING
YEO  PRI  NELL  SIENNA
SOLIDGOLDCADILLAC  EDGES
AMA  ARO  URN  LOP  RUSS
ANITA  AWHALE  ABELE  OPTO
RICHEST  AUSABLEFORKS
ENTERED  AFT  RELEASE
CHIC  ADA  ESTS  EMS  ESSEX
HIGHLY  MINKSTOLE  DEFINE
ALLIA  APT  APEX  ABO  OATS
STUNNED  SAL  ITNEVER
CANDYISDANDY  REDMANS
FISH  ASONE  LEERAT  SETUP
ASTI  SUR  FLU  CHE  ONE
RIALS  PEARLOFGREATPRICE
ANGLER  PAON  AIT  TOO
PLEASESIRIWANTSOMEMORE
AIM  ALAMODE  AHAND  AMISH
RNA  MARINER  MELES  DENSE
TEN  EXETERS  ERASE  EDGAR
```

43

```
MAIDS NAPA ALOP REBAR
INSET IRONCLADS EARLE
SOLER MOONLANDINGSITE
SLADES SHOULD EREBUS
YEN APSE MAG WEE ESE
DEMIT IMP READER
SPUN TERNES AMI TAMPA
TEND SEATS ENCL SPOOL
ADIME PRESENTEES TULE
RAVED SER VICEROY NYC
LENES CREDO PASTE
AIR RACCOON LOA LEASH
LEST CORNSTALKS UNITE
TREES RUTS BERLE SNEW
ASSET ASI NOGOOD ERRS
SULLEN ERE PIEDA
BAM DAS ELA FELT IDS
OREADS NEROLI EARLET
REALESTATEAGENT PEWEE
ACTOR HEARTLINE ENARM
HAYES ORLY ERST STYES
```

44

```
SCAPA QUIT WHILOM SHOE
HAVOC UNTO HECATE HENRY
ILIAC ADEL IRONON EXTRA
FLA OGLE ASCEND TIP HAP
TANTRUM MUCH PITH ETE
ODA DEGUST ELOGE GUS
FORHIMHATHTHINNENOROOME
ORION OVI SALADA EDH
RET GOBIES LESE ASSORTS
AGATTU DROLL AMAT WHEAT
ROSA ROBB IRISH ELL
CHRISTMASEVEISCOMEANDLO
HOI ASIDE ETRE ECTO
OBOLI TERM ORATE THWART
POTENCY VISA MALAYA ZOO
NTH FICKLE BIT VROUW
ONESMALLCHILDFROMHEAVEN
FAR AQUAE SPIRIT AYN
AVE TUNG ELIZ QUETSCH
TAW TEA VETOED GATS ARE
UHHUH TIESUP ADIT ELCID
BOONE ISRAEL YOGA EARED
SNOW CAYUSE STIR NYASA
```

45

```
SLAP OBEYS BAYS FORA
LOLA FUGUE GALOP AMIS
ABOLTFROMTHEBLUE DECK
VAGARIES TINES CHINKS
TENN RINDS TION
PAGING SINGE BRAGGART
AMIND FINGERNAILS SOI
NOVE SAGS URNS SCUP
TRI ONTHESQUARE MORES
SENTRIES LUNGE OATEN
GOADS BOITE ARROW
STOLE CRETE EMBALLED
BAHTS DOESONESBIT ORE
RUES MEED ATIT SOIE
IDA SAWDAYLIGHT BUSED
MIXTURES AIDES DURESS
AVID SNEER ORIG
GOTHAM TACNA STYLISTS
ALUI BURIESTHEHATCHET
MINT ATANY EARED AONE
YOGI SEPT SPARS LEST
```

46

```
CRS ALES JINX AME
QUICKLIME ONEANDONE
PULVERIZED INSTALLING
RAVENS ARGON GINGER
AVERT ARGENTINE BAMRA
HERS RIDE EUROPA RAGS
ART JARS STREWING SYS
ZYME PAWED LOOM
GREENS BOLOS JADEITES
RELAX HELOT PATERNITY
ABEL PERIPHERIES AMUR
DEMOCRATS RAILS CREDO
SLITHERS LERES THESES
SIFT KEELS DIET
SAC CAITIFFS SUEZ DAS
IMAM BEATTO SPED SERT
TAROS RESOURCES CHOSE
AZALEA VRAIC TRADER
REMITTANCE GETHSEMANE
SENTENCER ENRAPTURE
LEO TOSS STEM ESS
```

47

```
FIREI TODAY WEWHO INIGO
ANAGS AMIDO AVION NOSAD
RINGA READY YELLS KAAMA
STANDINGROOMONLY BESHE
ISTOOD AYN AFTS GODHELP
GRIS ANA APO TRAP
THEPEOPLETHEMOBTHECROWD
SONO MOORES AMAH DOA
ABDUL TSIN ONEARM MYNAH
RETRIM SCOWL SLIES SONE
AETAS IRIDS LATA TEA
AHBROKENISTHEGOLDENBOWL
CAL NERO HORAS EMCEE
URET SISAL SANTA STANZA
PASHA NOSEAT DECS SLAYS
EAT NEON SHOTUP AIMS
JOSTLINGANDBEINGJOSTLED
ARTO NUS FUN ISEE
SNOWMAN PERM QUA ITCAME
EPEES MYCUPRUNNETHOVER
EVORA LEROI SATAN IMALL
TENON ADULT VSIGN TEHEE
CRAFT POSES PILES ERIES
```

48

```
PLATINUM SLOB TROUTS
PROVOLONE LAVA HISSAT
REVERENCE IRED INHERE
ISERE MAT DARNING ORE
MAST BASIC DESK ANER
AGE CON NARROWMINDED
LETSON GROANS TIES
HIER PRATE ROC NIE
AMANDA LACE LOVESONG
GRIDS TEACH FUSE PONG
ARNI BLACK TAPER IDEE
BIDE RISE VALET DELED
OVERTAKE WALL TRADED
REX HIE CELLI AERO
PEAN MELLON LINAGE
FASTTHINKING PAN DEV
MANS REST ESSAY FATE
ELD BURNETT HUM RAMON
SLICES ARAM OPERATIVE
TENANT MERE RELEGATED
ANGLES EDEN TRAVELER
```

49

```
CAPES SIRAT SCALE ATIME
OPART INUSE EAGER BONER
HARRYTRUMANCAPOTE LLAMA
ACTS HERON ALERT BALLES
NEY SANER OVERA GAZELLE
   SOLI DOER AUGER
PATRICKHENRYJAMES REC
BOGOTA REGAN ELIS CLARA
ALIA CARA UNITS ROBOT
JESSEJAMESCAGNEY CERISE
ART BUSES ALLYN BLANDER
  LONER HOI BLUME
ANOINTS ASONE CRANE SAM
SARNIA OTTOGRAHAMGREENE
ISLET START LANE ODER
DIODE LALA OPTIC DOSAGE
ESP EARLWARRENHARDING
  BANTU GEAR NOON
CHARLIE BOGGY CLAIR BAH
HAROLD BURRO TRACT MANO
OVENS NORMANTHOMASHARDY
IRATE AIMED RICER ANGEL
RELET GLARE SNERD GEESE
```

50

```
SCOLD PARTED CHAM
STEREO ILOILO HALAS
CLARAANNFOWLER AVERTS
HERON CAFES MITRE IRA
EATS TOILS WESER SEAN
AVE THULE NANDA ONDIT
TERRIERS MANTA DHARNA
EAST ROTE YOUARE
ALLURE TOTARA ARRESTS
RAINA BASIL NITRE SIP
IDLE TULAFINKLEA BLEU
ELY CURER EELER FLEUR
LECTERN YOWLED SLURPS
HOLISM SOLD RHEE
STALIN ALTOS JOUSTING
PAULA BRAID BUNCH TON
ORCS CEIBA CRACK GETA
RAH PIANO CHINA ORRIS
TWOBIT ARCHIBALDLEACH
AISLE DERIDE LEGATE
NAYS EDITED IRATE
```

51

```
CROUP AMPHI WHEE HAWAII
HORSEPLAYER HANDMEDOWNS
INSIDETRACK ODDSANDENDS
DONAS ELKE SAMOA SISS
GLENNS DOW ANIMUS
EYE TUG THAN NAP SRA
NOTBYALONGSHOT AGT CHAR
EMCEE OHIO TOZ ECHOIC
RAU BEAK SADIE REELS
ASST PLAYTHEFIELD IAMB
ITCH TINES VAN INSPAIN
MAR TONGS MEX TOTUP KRA
SKATING WAN SODOM BEDS
ETRE UNDERTHEWIRE URSA
ASCUS AEONS OMEN NOR
TOHEAR SET EBER BREAD
RUED OFT ACROSSTHEBOARD
ITS SUR STHS ION UKE
STEAMY EEL CEDRES
OMOO NANAS ODOR ONALL
TRIPLECROWN DISCJOCKEYS
INTHESADDLE HOMESTRETCH
GOESAT ISSY ANOLD ESTOP
```

52

```
AMASS EARACHES HAREM
LIVEANDLETLIVE TAMARA
PRECIOUSSTONES ONEDAY
ARR LOCO SIGNSUP NITA
COST NERO SETINMOTION
AREAS DAVIT ODOR
RHS NINEMAN VISTAS
FLAGONS DARERS IBERIA
LAMEDUCK SENT SEINERS
ATAS BOOS DEISTS SALS
RED ULUS SETA SAI
EDAM TRINES RUGA JUNE
SAVAGES DRAB DEPLORES
UTAHAN WAFFLE STALEST
PETALS RESEALS SOT
ETAH PEELS SEATS
EARNSAMEDAL CUPS DRAW
ALAI TEARGAS GALL RIA
RENEGE REACHAGREEMENT
TRACES SAVEONESBREATH
OTTER TRESSURE PARSE
```

53

```
ANITA ANNAS PROA ARS
MOLAR MEANT REBS BEV
SATIRE BETSYROSSHOUSE
ATLAS CODA EWE OUSEL
BEACONHILL WALLSTREET
OUT EASE FOCSLE DDE
TREASURE TOOT SCAB
SIR GIRD OREN
MUTT LILTS CONCLUDE
GENRE SALEM RUD LARA
ALISO EMBARCADERO ENID
GOAD NEO HIVES RICES
ENFORCER PERMS USED
EMIL ENES LIL
EVAS PARD PRUNELLA
SCB SMEARY GLEN OAR
THECAPITOL ORANGEBOWL
ALLAH TEL RIND TOKYO
GOLDENTRIANGLE CHASES
ERE AMEN DEALT LOSER
DOS DUNE DANES ESTES
```

54

```
GASPE ISEE ENABLE DAMAS
ADAMS CARBONATION PHONY
BACKTHEWRONGHORSE LEMON
BRODIE GONER METRE REDO
YES MATIN HOMIN GRINNED
BATON COSEC BILLET
MAKETHE BURST GAZES OAS
EMILE DEEPSEATUBE EDUCE
DELISH BARED HIED ESCE
ORLE ADANO ICONS RAIDER
CIT RIANT INURE CUDGEL
SCHOOLROOMS SNAKEDANCES
AERIES WILDS FRIED IRT
ENFOLD ENLAI POOLS ISAR
DEAN TREE SPAWN TANITE
ASTOR HORSECOLLAR SLOES
MET AMESS DOSES ATTENDS
ESTATE NEUTS CARET
ANDTEAR BARRE LABOR ASS
ROCA SABAS ARSEN LOATHE
ARABA CONSIGNTOOBLIVION
ISLAM ESCAPESONES DOMES
LEFTY SCOUTS MESA SWEDE
```

55

```
SHASTA ICTUS ICIEST
ELUVIAL NOOSE MUSTARD
SUGARPLUMTREE BRESLAU
TIGS ESTATE CHORE TIP
ACE PITA GAUDY NONE
REDO RICE PATSY SAFER
ABACA PERCH PANTRY
COTTAGE DEPTH PORCH
OCHERS GRAPH DELAYERS
WAYNE TEASE DELES EEK
ISM GINGERBREAD AVE
SEE ALBIA MAIDS STREW
HYLOZOIC DILLS QUATRE
AMORA HANKY PUNCHER
STEELY FORTH BRAKE
OSAGE PUNTS SOOT TASS
LACA MORES DIRT CWO
ARE TELLY ORDERS ORAL
RIORITA BASILRATHBONE
SNUGGER ELEVE CERISES
ASTERS ESSES TSETSE
```

56

```
5THS AHILL COMM NAIAD
ORAE PODIA 2ADAY ESOPUS
5ANDIOCENT 3MENONAHORSE
OSSIP KAYE SPONGER POEM
HAMITES ROK NARO SENSE
EERY FINIS AMOUR
QUINCY DOSADOS MEDICINE
UNITE SIRE DATA NOTEMAN
EDNA WISER OPENAIR NANO
DEAL HAM OPTIMA ETNAS
ARM REMISED ASTO CRESS
13ER STLO DORR EARP
ALFIE SEEL SNAPOUT ORG
BILIN SERVED HUT CIEL
AMIE DISEASE AGORA ASEA
STOLLEN STOM PLUS STOSS
SONDELIS EMIGRES STONES
SALSA ETAIN THE9
ABOYS TRIS ALL HEARTAS
TANS BEANIES ISIN IAGOS
4LETTERWORDS 5CENTCIGAR
OTTERS ANODE TIRED LINT
SOMAT KENO HOARS SEDA
```

57

```
GUARD ACT STAIRS CANOPY
OSTIA FOR CUTLET ALBINO
NUTTYPINE ANTIQUEDEALER
NAH CORNELL SAUCERS YUK
ELENORE BULB NICLE LAME
BOAC SAMOAN TOY HUMOR
ARMCHAIR PRICES DIRE
URIAH YOKE ODES FEDERAL
KIND RUSTIQUE FIFE ILE
ELK APEX ONUS VASE ICON
EME DICE RESTAURANT
COMMODE PLANTER STRANGE
ADAMSAPPLE MOST EIN
MYNA GOES EIRE MADS TOE
ALT CODA STROLLER BUDS
SELVAGE SEHR LOAN CODES
EASY SENIOR UNICOLOR
LAPSE FHA CREDIT ALAR
EDIT GUESS SIRS CROSSED
SHE JANACEK SESSION EAR
SECRETDRAWERS APPLIEDTO
ORENSE EPERDU YAP ALAIN
NESSUS REDOSE SRI LYNNE
```

58

```
WISTFULLY DRATITS TOM
AVERAGEUP RIGHTEOUSLY
NICECHAPS YPOTENTIALS
LETME PAINLESSLY GRAT
YDS SAY LAY LEN
NAMEDAY OPA ADAPTS
COMO DARN GLOP RUNHIT
ABET TRET UDDER NIDA
VITAM IIIA INFIDELIC
ARA GROUNDLESSLY
SPERO GOLDSMY LOWLY
SAIDIMMANUEL RIO
PRESENTLY DOOM OFWAR
ROME SEOUL VIBE TLRS
ODANTE RUBY ENON LYCO
DENTON ART WRIGGLY
EGO DAD ISA SAG
ITTY OCOMEOCOME DAKUA
MUHAMMADALI SUMMARILY
SAIDMARTIAL ELECTORAL
ONS CROSSLY DANDAILEY
```

59

```
STILE TASSO TIETO QUARE
KEMAL OTTER ENROL UNDUE
ITALIANHERO CHINESEWALL
NEMO RIENS FUOCO HERMES
AGENT GIMPS LANA
MATADORS PHASE FOREPAWS
ELUDES NOOSE BUSED RAP
DORIA SWISSCHEESES RAGA
INKED WISETO WHIR GABOR
ASIT OILER VEAL BONING
SOS ENGLISHHORNS ATEASE
HOMES OUT RUMEN
CITRON ITSGREEKTOME NAM
ABOARD NETS AROSE NIDI
NEWLY PLAY CURARE SIGHS
TRES SIAMESETWINS ETHEL
AIL SWATS HITAT SARTRE
BASELINE SILEX ENCLOSED
AUTO PINER TREES
IATRIC TREND LEARN EZIO
FRENCHLEAVE PERSIANLAMB
ANNEE ORDER ESSEN GENII
TENDS PROSY STERE SCENT
```

60

```
AMOS MESSAGE JASPER
COUTH SETUPSET ULTIMA
ULTRA PROMISER SPINBY
PELISSES DUSE ACHES
OCHOS AVERT SICKED
SPOKEN SHIRE MALAYA
HAKES CHARY TAMES DNA
IRON WRUNG OUTOF SPAR
EMU BEATDOWNBEAT WIRE
SATIRIZE ACER SANDS
CERE PALER MIEN
ICHOR BOCK BALANCES
POON OVERHANGOVER ONA
SOLO CENTS ORNIS SMUG
ELD LENDS LIEUS STERE
UBOATS DOSES CARIES
SPOONS WAVED CUTIN
ETHOS ARNE CARRACES
LOOKER GOTINGOT ATOLL
MOLINE ETONIANS PEMBA
ODDEST DENSELY DEEM
```

61

```
SMA   MAIMS  DIVAS   JOWLED
CINQ  ALDEN  EMILE   ENHALO
ACTU  ILONA  SPACE   WEIMAR
NARA  TENOR  PINON   ERMINE
SHAKERATTLEANDROLL    WADS
      EVER   SWIG   TEETH
CHERI  STH  EREBS   TRIANON
HUMBLE  HEIL   EHEU   OMAHA
AMBO  TREMBLINGASPEN   TAM
SPAN  HUMAN  NAIVEST  PARE
MYRNA  TEN  MAPLES   CURLED
      ETAH  MEWED  AHME
CRETAN  SEATER  JAR  ASTAB
HANS  SKIDDOO  BELOW  ERMA
IDA  QUIVEROFARROWS   NOOK
CAMAU  RAMI  LORN  WATTLE
ORIGINS  ADAZE  YES  ETHER
      ITICS  NIAS  HERE
BITT  SHOULDOFSTOODINBED
ARHATS  ATION  TOPOG  SORE
SEETHE  KIMRI  AWAKE  EXAM
INTERN  ICERS  RECUR  SISI
LEADUS  NASAT  SLAPS   NET
```

62

```
DECOCT   PLUME    BATMEN
ENAMOR  ELOPING  ACHENE
ORRERY  MASSAGE  CREDIT
DOING  SPITE  ITAKE   ISM
ABB  ISAAC  TANIST  TULE
RESH  TINE  TRENCHERMEN
     ASIDE  CINE  HELI
SOLAR  LEONORA  WIPER
LECTURE  RAGS  STREAMED
ORA  DIALECT  OTHO  REDO
BARKINGUPTHEWRONGTREE
APIE  GENT  ENLARGE  GAR
SINECURE  DAVE  SHOVELS
SALOP  TARPOTS  ODIST
     MOTH  ROPY  CURES
TOTALRECALL  ARMS  ACME
ARAN  ORACLE  REPEL  HEX
RIM  BURGH  CORES  APART
SEALAB  ENGAGED  AVENGE
UNROLL  SIERRAS  HANGER
STABLE  DETER   ASTERN
```

63

```
COMES  FEEDS  SALAD  GRAPE
AMATI  RATIO  CHOLO  RAGES
BIZETSIGNAL  HAYDNGOSEEK
STES  ALLA  ICONS  NIPPERS
     AILE  SCOLD  AIDE
AFFABLY  SAIDA  ERSE  AZOF
MERLES  LITTERBACH  SHORE
ELATE  TAXIS  ASA  EARNS
LONE  MITE  SCHEDULE  BAT
INC  SHARI  ARA  ISINLATE
ASK  HANDELWITHCARE  ITER
     EWER  TAI  GOA  RASH
ESNE  BRAHMSBURSTING  EME
RESTROKE  EAT  URGES  GAR
NAT  TROOPERS  KAAN  ERMA
AMERE  LAN  WILLS  BRIES
NAIDS  LITDEFALLA  PRIERE
INNS  NOAH  RUTTY  GRANGER
     FERN  DIMES  BRIT
OFFERED  TENOR  OLIO  AIME
VERDIDSHEGO  RAVELROUSER
IMAGE  IOTAS  AREAL  CRASS
DETER  THESE  TENTS  CARAT
```

64

```
BIOG  WAMP  MEOW   IMATMY
ARRA  ISAR  ALLE  DISHED
MITT  TINE  YEDS  ELPERS
ASH  SHAGS  WEPT  SOIF
HELOT  ASTI  ESTA  SILL
ELFISH  NEATER  ORTHREE
SOLE  ENE  CHAS  LEU  SOW
PRONGLESS  ATI  DONAT
YEW  ROMEO  LHAS  NABOBS
     ROAVE  OSLO  OAT  AFAT
JOYSBEASTHEMONTHOFMAY
ALMS  INA  ATEL  TESTA
SEEING  YODH  DRIFT  YEA
     ASOAK  FRY  SHRIEKING
ARD  IVA  TOFT  AEF  ISTO
DESERET  HELIUM  TINMEN
SOIL  ISME  OMAN  ELGAR
NAIN  EHEU  KALES  YON
TOMTOM  TORR  ALAN  ADZE
ETAETA  RULE  REST  LAOS
MAYDAY  ORES  ISTH  EYAS
```

65

```
ALPACA  ASPEN  ANVIL  RAMA
LIANAS  MAINE  SEATO  ILES
LADYSSLIPPER  PALACECARS
SRS  PAYSAS  MITE  KAHILI
JAMESJ  AMIRS  ASSE
CIDER  OENONE  SILENCER
ONUS  PUTUPONESDUKES  RMA
PACT  ANH  INKY  EASY  LOCH
ASHE  SHINTOS  GAV  POWER
LEER  ANE  PANE  CORNEA
SCS  KINGFISHERS  FURNISH
     STANDS  NOONE  MORGAN
AHEARTY  QUEENSBERRY  GSA
LAPRES  BUSS  ARE  RGTS
CROON  REE  THETIME  ELAN
APIS  FOES  FOAL  NAN  CONE
PIN  COURTBOUILLONS  ORCA
PATRIOTS  ENTREE  BUYER
     ANTS  BETSY  TRIPUP
SPINEL  OARS  TIEBAR  CPA
CASTLEWALK  KNIGHTSSTARS
OTHE  TAHOE  HENRI  TARPOT
TSAR  STUNG  ASSET  ARISTA
```

66

```
LOEB   DISCO  FOAM  BLEB
IRAE  SUNTAN  ANNI  RAIL
DERM  ADUANA  TENS  INDI
     TOONERVILLE  USANCES
SCHARF  EENIE  SLINGERS
ENSNARE  EMILY  STO
TOT  TALC  BLOC  SINFUL
UTA  ENLACE  ANEMIC  OVI
PERM  CAROMS  DEEP  URUK
     ACI  ONETWO  SPANGLE
TRANSSIBERIANRAILROAD
REDLACS  SIERRA  REI
ABLY  OAST  RIENZI  GASP
IBI  SCROOP  IDGIVE  BLA
NEBULA  AGAR  AMEN  DEI
     NAB  RATES  BREVIER
ENTITLES  CLASP  BRACTS
GOATEED  CHATTANOOGA
ARIA  CERO  PEORIA  ATOP
DING  AMID  SELECT  REDE
SATE  RAGE  ENARE  YSER
```

67

```
SEARCH   CAPA   AGA   AMES
ANDAHUG CABAL LRS CROCE
MOUNTRUSHMORE FASTONTHE
ELBA RELIEVE MANWAY HOS
     DYSON ENTO DEN ABIE
FASTESTGUN THEGREATRACE
APERCU PURSE RAT NIL
DELIAN ESNE RAMPART LEG
 SLENDER CHEAM ISA AFAR
  STOLID EXPEND HAILTO
SAJ WINESAP RISS TREES
TWOPINS RATRACE CHASERS
ANNAS AJAR ELECTRA TYE
TEATRO ATTEST EYESOF
URTH PFC RESET RETRIED
ESH SPIKIER RARE YELLOW
 ABI SBS ISSUE PLEURA
RUNOFTHEMILL THEHUSTLER
URSA ESQ AYUB ARIDE
FAW ANNUAL REBUILD ARUI
FLIGHTAID APOLLOLIFTOFF
LIFES RCD RENAS SNOWSOF
ECTO EKA ADES GLOSSY
```

68

```
PASS MUCHOF POILUS
ENABLES ENROLL ARTIST
FORLOVEORMONEY ROSTER
FRT BERNE PEOPLE TSE
AMIS REED OATES LUI
CANNES TIS TIPS ADEPT
ENGIN MOTHHOLE CLUB
FORE HOES RARERIPE
BAFFLERS VAST LIMOGES
ANIL SCENEV RIIS HDS
RISE HELLENIZE CODA
BTH SANA NOMANS ORLY
EROSION TATS RATLINES
RAREBITS BOTH TEEN
CASE LICORICE NAMES
SOUSE FINS AGR BEGONE
AMT NORMS HETO ESSE
ROB MANTIS CAIRN EIN
TRANCE EASYCOMEEASYGO
REININ STONES SAPIENT
ESTERS SUNSET LEND
```

69

```
NAWAB TSARS SALPA ASFAR
ALIBI ROSIE CROON BOOLA
GIRLSCOUTSCOOKIES ARUIS
SMEE AURAE STINT STERNE
TRIPPER STIES CLEATED
SHA COED COLA HARSH OSE
MOPPETS WOMENSCLUBS OSE
ASPIRE SHOER CLOTS AFOX
REEKS CHAPS PAUSE ANJOU
TARA TOILE DONEE GROUND
SUMMERSALTS TIRALEE
RAF IRIS HUE AONE YRS
ELASTIC STANDINGPAT
BACKIN FLIRT MONAS ACIS
ALEUT CRUDE GOMEZ PRONE
TATA CHIME SAGES HOTWAR
OSH CHEAPSKATES MANACLE
EMAIL IRUN BEST ALT
CAMETOA FANON CONSENT
AZURES DEIGN TIROL ACTI
NOSIR FIRSTGRADETEACHER
ELITE ARALU ONEAT FREAK
DECOR SKEET TARSI TERMS
```

70

```
RES LBS TREACLE SARGS
ENTAILS RANGOON SHEET
SHADROE ENDEMIC SUNNY
TARMAC OPT BROB GEOM
ANTIS APA STEERAGEWAY
ICER TRENCHER ITAL
NEDA ERN LEE ANELACES
LANA PELTING ENAMI
AGEOFDISCOVERY LADDER
CRAFT GAINERS SISLER
TART ANT DIP INGE
ETHICS CRASHED MEZEN
ACHENE THEINDIESTRADE
MILOT AGENDAS MANE
PAYCALLS AER SEI VEST
ECOL SIDEREAL EACH
GREATCIRCLE ART MASER
ROAN KNAR AMS FELINE
AMUSE ANIMALS DETENTE
SADES LEMORTE PLEDGER
SNEAK LESSEES STR SDS
```

71

```
LIFEIS CRADLE ARENOT
CAMPION LENIENT NERINES
LEPANTO OSCEOLA DARLENE
OTO EATSUP DRABBED SER
VASE SAUTES ARLES HEIDI
IRENE SPECTA GETSWINDOF
SESAME ARTICLES AIRLESS
MILA SELLER TYPEE
SCOTERS DEED ROSE AIDS
BEAR VITA TOGOUT DEGREE
APR REDUCE REMIT SUAVE
STOPIN MARGARINE STENOG
SILAS BRIEF TERRAE ITE
OMELET LISTED DEEM PAER
SERI USED SAID DESTINE
STRAD SISLER FOOL
SAVARIN CONTUSED NOISED
CREDENTIAL ITISAP KNAVE
AGRLE ABBOT ENTIRE GLIB
LAD DYNAMIC EASELS ADA
ALAMEDA NOTHING DELUDES
RINGMEN ENHANCE INALINE
STRESA SENSES CAMENT
```

72

```
BKS SAAL BBC SPAR
ORE ACCESS SOLA TALE
SAILFLEETOFSPAIN ARIA
SANDEEL APRIL SNORKEL
LESS ERR ERICSON ANS
SOB SECRETS
AMBER SOOTH EIS NOSE
LOADER MAEWEST FEELER
FURSEAL REACT TRIEDTO
ANNE NEED TEHERAN SSS
TALESOFTHESEVENSEAS
LAC CONTOUR MEEK LIAS
ILLFAME PISIA SEDILIA
STEEDS BOTANIC RETOLD
POSE NER INNER TERSE
FRONTAL BRA
APE LETITGO RAM ORBS
SEXTANT UNRRA PENALTY
TRIO TOURISTCLASSFARE
RILE EBAN SEANCE MAT
ALES DER STET EPI
```

73

```
SALS   COLON  OBAN   TAIPEH
TRAIT  ALIVE  FARE   UNMADE
OMINO  NINES  FLAP   STASIS
PACKUPYOURTROUBLES   USES
   ARLO  STEER  SUNLAMP
TRA  IONS  RATS  STEPSOUT
HERESY ALP MUTE ODA RNR
ADEPT  AXIOM  NASA  SATTE
ROASTED  TWOWEEKSWITHPAY
   ORCA  HERE  LETIN  AHN
PRIMAL DORRIT RESH  SONG
AES PIKE SIGHT REAP TEE
PALE PEAL SHARON LAMODE
LAB SARAH ESER DECA
INNOCENTSABROAD ESKIMOS
FIDEL  HERR  STEIN  ARENT
ICH EPI REIN YRS AGENCY
LEOTARDS STAN MAME SEX
  PATELLA APORT TADS
CAPN SEENONESEENTHEMALL
ALINES EVEN ANNUL AERIE
DANITE VIII LEONE LANDS
SIGNED ELLA TERSE ROOT
```

74

```
TRADE  TIMOR  RANCHED
PREMAN INURE  FIREHOSE
RECANT NOSED  OPERETTA
OVERGROW HOUSEPAINTER
SODA ERASE CAMEL EEL
ERE SNARED TOAD WORMY
  DECREE FINN DIP
BLITHE DRIVE DILEMMA
SAINTE STORE COMENEAR
ATONED LIME WAVE HAIR
LANE HAMPSHIRE ANSA
OVER BONE TIDE LANDON
MISTRJST HONEY INDENT
EASIEST CANTO OTTERS
   MSS FIDE PATTED
ASSET PISA MEDALS DEA
MAT PARCH ANOTE SEAL
BLABBERMOUTH RECREATE
LITERATE NOLAN HURLER
ENAMELED CREME ADVERT
RELATED HEROD PEARY
```

75

```
ASHES ROSA TAMALE PLATA
SLASH AVES AGORAS EAVES
FIREEATERS PUTINTHEDARK
AGR APER TEPEE HOLDSNO
TOYERS TESLA SOLEA ETES
HASIDIM ENS PURRER
LAOS SOMITE ELEM SLOOPS
ADUEL PERU STEN WELFARE
SOD AMES RIPON THRASHER
TRIMMED REDAN HOI WEPT
SENIOR SEEER SANREMO
INDIANSNAKECHARMERS
DESPOTS LORAL BADLOT
HANO ROS GENES SENSATE
ELEVATED HORSE CORE TAN
REVERES PONS CLAW RHETT
SCARES RIDE CHORES OMES
MATSUS RAH PEDICLE
NALA ITEAS BEAST GROSSE
OMITTER EVENS ARNE SYN
MYSTERYSNAIL TAKESACARD
ALLEN PEELEE EDEN MAGIE
DOERS EGESTS RARE SNEAD
```

76

```
PORCH BASE PARRS TRE
ADIEU ALUM EBOAT ROES
RONDS KELP ABOMA EDEN
INCITIESFOULEDBYSMOKE
STELLAR URNS LETO
LEM ARIA NEEDAREST
BARBAROUSDISSONANCE
BALS DRUM ECTON DON
EMU GILAS ASHEN FAURE
EARTHDAY TRIES SILENT
HALI GEARS MELT
REFUTE CRAKE COMMONER
ACIDS PRETE SAVES ETA
ILO CHEER APSE PEON
DARKBROWNISTHERIVER
STEARINES OTES OEN
NEMO STER ONSTAGE
CONGREGATIONOFVAPOURS
AREA ARIES DIRE ISLAS
NEAR NANAS EDER NAIVE
ALT SMOKY DSTS ENCES
```

77

```
FLIPSIDE USSERY SCATTED
RIPSAWED NOTATE LOVEHER
ETIOLATE RUHREN EVILEYE
ETNAS ENTETE SPEE LWOW
LESION EPHLAL APR TIRR
DEF FUTUREPERFECT LACEY
AMI YSER NANISM ITALK
MIRO TSANTSAS BIGWHEEL
PSYCHE NOES TEACHIN DOM
SEEAROUND DORRITS WVA
IMWAS PSS BETAG TALIEN
GUANASE EQUALTO ASFATAS
OFNOTE QUITE API UNCLE
RFD ANOUILH SCHLEMIHL
SEB FLUTIST PUTA MENOTS
TABLEMAT FERNSEED AFRO
LUIGI USOPEN DDAY TUI
HASNT SORORITYHOUSE HST
OSAN LMU 12THST CHALET
ATMY EARP RAISEA SEEAS
GOTHURT ACROWD ITSASAFE
IOOOTOI COUPEE GOTITSET
EPOPTIC TWEEDS GRADETWO
```

78

```
STEAM ADMI SCAR SWISH
LODGE ERAS ALBO TITHE
ARDOR CURL MAIA STEEL
GEAR SIE SUDSY CARP
ACACIA DETACH
PAR ARAL SPISSKA ORB
AMUSICAL EHEU TAHOE
CAMPUSMARTIUS POORASA
ENBAS ITER CAPTURED
STANG APSES PARTHIANS
RUBLES TIPTOE
VESPASIAN PELES CAIRO
INNOCENT CLEO ERROR
SCONCED QUINTUSENNIUS
BRUSH UTES LESSONTO
YET UNTRIED PESO GEN
USURER CIDERS
ALOP TONIC TAA AMPS
HARPY JENA ANNA EXALT
ANNEE AGAR LOUD DORIA
BAERS NELL LESE ENTER
```

79

```
HASTO LEMUR ABBAS AMBLE
OLEAN INANE BLUNT CARON
PADRE MINIM CERVI TIERS
IMETALADYCOLDASIC STARK
SORELY STERE TALKTURKEY
     SORB OFAGE JAPE
SKS NEIN ARENEAR AHA
TUQUE EIWOULDNOTWANTTOM
ABUT UNTORN AGRO OOOOO
CLAIMS ARHAT RAIL TIMER
CARLOTS SOMA LAMA SYN
EETHERTWICESHEWASAM
HAM HERE IFHE DOODADS
AMICE EGOS TRANS RUMSON
VALOR RUHR ERNANI AHME
ODELOFDECORUMIAIN SNEER
COS LATHERS DEFT RID
ABOU STERS SIRE
WILDERNESS ELIAS LALALA
ALOHA TNOLADYBUTIMWARUM
GAPES IDLER SATON HIERA
EVERT NOVEM ELENA ANNES
RAZES GRETA EDDYS TEARS
```

80

```
NOEL SLEPT STAR ASTO
AURA HOARY EARL THEME
GRAYMATTER THESCARLET
UINTA OOO ILIONE
PURPLEANDFINELINEN
ARU DORS EON KEEL
INSPACE RESAW DAVINCI
RATATAT MEUSE MANGOS
LITRES REST SONG
EDEN DREI AMAIN VIVE
SORT INANE MONET IMAM
PSST NASTY PESO OPTS
HEAL IRIS STABLE
ASPELL MENTO ASSERTS
HOTTIPS ESTOP STATIUS
SOSO OAR HOAD ANT
WHITEELEPHANTSALES
DOWNON SMU MAYAS
IVORYTOWER BLACKMAGIC
BEVEL SANE EAGRE NATO
REDE STDS TREES AMOY
```

81

```
PATTI PSI PLOT AGR
ARTHURWOOLF IONICFRIEZE
GATECRASHER CREPEHANGER
SHACK TIO AFAR PIA GALL
TARA HET CIA YELL CHIDE
SAAR CADIZ LEE LANA
CASEIN OAR RUSK DEEM
OXFORDANDBALLIOL MODISH
OLAF BNAI VAUD AMP ONTO
NEXT IGN HOW ELIAS GRAY
HILL TACNA ANT DWELL
TWEEDLEDUMANDTWEEDLEDEE
IHAVE BAG TEREK LION
RITE SAYSO WON FOG TACO
ENOL ORA FUJI COTE BLEW
DENVER KENNETHROSSTOOLE
ELEM COIR OUT TOWELS
HITS ISH ESSEX MEOW
PONCE STOA EHS BID OMAN
OPAL BTU VAYA LIL TWICE
REPANDERSON DRILLTOWERS
THEWILDDUCK SERGIOPOLIS
TSP YEAH MAE MOWED
```

82

```
ALL ILED THY AMP
OSEE MANO HOE CARTS
ETNA ABCS ETA RESORT
RETRY OLEUM REACTION
RANN ROOTA EOS EBON
CONTENDSFOR RETROCEDE
LIDO GIE PVTS FELT
IDOL ASS IER ORBITAL
APIG ALE VOUCHFOR
GIBE RID STEAMS ETIO
LABOURANDDOALLTHYWORK
ATAR ACTSOF ISH AONE
STRAPPER IMP EVER
ISNOTSO NAO TIE KEPT
DOON CANO ERR INRE
CUTTHROAT SPELLBINDER
OTHO MRS LEILA AGED
THEWOMAN ADLIB NGAIO
ETAMIN FIB ETON IRAN
RAINS ADO ETRE RELS
TIT TOR NOSE LDS
```

83

```
DESIGN LESAGE CAPP BACH
AREOLA IMOGEN AMAH ICHO
INQUISITORIAL SOLILOQUY
LEU STRETTO ATAS MATURE
EAT KREIS CAB RUDYARD
FENNEL ARE BINATE EPI
LATINIST PEND ODD ENAM
EGIL QUINQUAGESIMAL TEE
ALA KUN AUNT MILANO AND
SELENO SWOOSH REPIN NEA
PIR EAR OOP LOGICAL
SALIC ALBUQUERQUE TRESS
TRICKED MAT OUR SOI
URN EPACT TABBED ANDMRS
ROC REMORA BREE AMS OOO
DYO SESQUIQUADRATE AZUL
YOLK SAU RUNT TIDEGAGE
NUM LEGSIT GTT ICEMEN
THEMAKE OAR TARED DEB
RISQUE ASCI ALIMONY ITS
INQUILINE NOLLEPROSEQUI
AGUA SLOE ANOINT VISUAL
LEET OINK LANCES ASSENT
```

84

```
AMBITS ENTREATY BATHS
CARNIE LOWERTHE ADHOC
THESONALSORISES OMEGA
HARI ILA SINES ICAN
GULL NYACK BRUNT
TIGHTEST CGS ARTIER
EMOTE WHIRS GREAT LAC
NAN STEELE CELIA TOGA
EGGS ELOGE ONES SAFER
TOWNHALL DENOTE OTTER
IOUS DOMICAL AMAH
MITRE IMPOSE INTEREST
ACHES BAER DETER SWEE
METS BENNE INTUIT ITE
ASH SORAS UNDER ALLAN
EATSIN ENG ROULADES
TAWNY ADELE SNIP
AVID TREAT LIB OLES
MINOR THEGRIPESOFROTH
ENDUE RECITERS LATONA
RESTS ACTTHREE TREPAN
```

85

```
CIVIC DELED   ECCE STETS
OTARY OVATE OGHAM TERRA
MADAMIMADAM TRITE ONION
BLE ASIDES STEPONNOPETS
      ONES CHESS DIDI
APR SLID SOOTS  CANONLY
BRIGADE MANET LATEN IES
LESAGE TAT ROTATOR AVOW
ELEVE PATIO ACER  CREME
SATE PALINDROMES MOONED
TWO EATEN DENES HORMONE
   VANCES AFTER CAVEAT
SNORTER BHERA SLIES ORT
TUTORS DRAWOCOWARD KNEW
ADELE SOUL TRESS  REESE
MISE POLITIC DAS TEEVEE
PSI LICET NADER DEIFIED
TRIACID CABER TERN  LDS
    STOE CODON DIET
TOOHOTTOHOOT TIPPIT IAM
ANCON IDOLO EREISAWELBA
ITAMI EASER LEONE AMEER
LOSEA SLED  MENSA SEXES
```

86

```
ACTUP ITHAD ESTE  AIMSAT
BRAKE DIALA ETAL ROOKIE
BEPERFECTLYFRANK OUTING
OPES ISIT SOIL SAM EPEE
TED ALONE REL VAS   TEA
   ARTFORARTSSAKE PAH
DECIDE  LAST TAR ADELE
RUHR RIFELY  BART ROWER
ALIEN FIREATWILL EPHOR
CAPRI IRAN ROLL  GATTO
ULO PASTS PARK SUCH LTD
LIN INTHENICKOFTIME ERE
AET NAHS OCKS LEDER TAA
   HATTE ALOE HOPI OPHIR
ALEPH STANDPATON DRIPS
ROSSE PEON OBANGS ANSI
SAHIB ATL FINI   TINGER
OSU BALLINGTHEJACK
ABU DEL ANT ADORE  MAC
BOLT MOO DARE RICO POLO
ORDEAL SELLABILLOFGOODS
UNEASY AGEE BRAES ASSET
TERMEN RODS SENSE BEERS
```

87

```
 POLARIS DELTA  SHAME
MILITANT ADUWA PARENT
EMINENCE MANOR ORANGE
ROVE DIPLOMAT BOMBARD
GLEN DOIN IRAN  ECAD
EAR BLEND TAMAR CLEVE
   SAINT SALEM HOLDER
 ARENATHEATER SERA
SLACKS ELATE HAN  SER
TENOR AGILE SPARETIME
AMINO WATERMAIN RIGOR
LENDLEASE SABLE TANTA
ENE LAR PAROL DARIEN
  PISE MILITARYBAND
TENANT CALLA REELS
AMONG RAILS STARE DSC
RUNA EARL BOOS  LATH
ALAMODE COMEUPON AREA
WAGING PARIA ONELINER
ATONCE ELAND SEVERELY
 ENTER ALLEY TREADLE
```

88

```
AUBER ODETS ATILT METRO
SNORE FRAIL SARAH OARIN
ACOATOFARMS HARNESSRACE
ILK ARABLE FER DOIT IER
REJECTS YOYOS DAUS OLDS
 ARKS BRER SECTIONB
INCAS HAL TWOACTS PELAT
NAKS DIEOF ATRISK HAN
CHEEREDFOR ROAN IONIZES
ATRACE MOLDED ORNAMENT
 SIE TEMPI AGATE ERDE
DST DICER SNA ITSSO SAD
ACHT VISSI GRAVY  SML
PARAPETS BRAISE SHEETS
PLENARY BEAD STEPINTOMY
LEEKS SPURND THORP SPEE
ESSES LEOTARD ENS SEDER
 URANIANS EVES WEAR
IBIS OCRA ISILL LACTASE
NOT OAKS COS PISANO WAM
TIESTHEKNOT CAPEKENNEDY
ERROR RIATA ASTRE ACRID
RESTE SNEES BOOTS LOSES
```

89

```
ITO4AM THE10TH JUNE17TH
PATINA HISDUE ISEEYOU
IMINES ANCONA TODREAM
EAT WHANG WORSTS   ATE
CRIS SKEIN DOE  ARRET
EAST40TH RIN PROPOSES
  AWAY PONES SITU
 SPRIT SANGOUT LETSUP
TALENT CROSSBAR REUNE
HRUSKA HART SOAS 66CAR
ROM STROVE STIFLE TIL
IYAR SALA 76ERS ENTIRE
PAGE80 MANATBAT ECHOES
SNEADS REGRETS POUND
   MARS SHONE EERY
ALLEYOOP AMI  BREAKS100
FOURS NO103 BATOR SIAM
TAP LASTTO ASONE  TRI
EDITION ERNANI AMATOL
RUNSOUT MUETTE NICENE
125POUNDS PESTER STINGS
```

90

```
SUNDIAL ASTACK GIN LAW
ONEACRE PARLOI ONESIDE
EIGHTEENTWELVEOVERTURE
STS EASE INTERN ROE IHS
ARS ACTCOY ENT  AWEOF
BAHN OCTO HOSTSA MENUS
SHOTINA MUM AHEAD SNR
ASUIT POPSOFFTO BASTES
RDS PROCURE TTUBES
HUGE MACU TEA AHT LIBRA
ALLPRO ONTHEROPES ADREM
STARED MDI GPU  CREOLE
ARSEN GIFTHORSES TUSKER
TASSE ANR ECO AUGS TETS
SWINGA SAMURAI  NOR
CHASED CASTAPALL FRATS
LAN RANTS NAN DELIGHT
NESTS RUSTIC CESA EERY
DANSE WAR ITOVER RBS
UNO CLI EBERLE IOTA AMB
SUCCESSSPOILROCKHUNTER
USEOVER ONEAND ILMETRO
PES IRA ESDRAS EYEFULS
```

91

```
AMATIS  FACES   TABOOS
STAMINA AROSE   AVENUES
WELTERWEIGHTS   GELATIN
EADS  OBERON  TOURS  ODA
ASE  OLES  EILAT  AFER
TENS ONER  OMNIS  ABALL
   LAMED  SNEAD  CLUMSY
CABALAS  ACTUS  GALLO
HELTER  PRAHS  METALLIC
ARIES BERLE EATEN  ENE
RISS  MARIACALLAS  CHAN
GAT  FATES  OMITS  CHIPS
ELEMENTS  FRATS  PURLIE
  RANGY  SENSE  PERILED
ALBINO   ATLES   SRTAS
SEEDY  STAIR  SNEE  TUMP
HIES  PEENS  STAT  NOR
OST  AIRED  LOAFER  AUTO
RULABLE  PAULBUNYANSOX
EREGION  ANNUL  DODGERY
ESTATE  TEASE  STEEDS
```

92

```
MOC  OBTD  BAALS  GUBGUB
RIFLE HAHA AGRIN ONEATA
AMBOY ITER SAMOA BALLET
HOUSEOFTHESEVENGOBBLES
 GEST  LOTH  EDS  MLLE
GOBBLEDEGOOK  DONEE  ISA
ANEYELID  ISTEPID  ENOL
FAA  FLT  GOBELINTAPESTRY
FIRST  THELEVEE  INSETS
ERSE  TOAMAN  DRAGNET GOO
RAE  IMMAD  LOO  RERUN
GIGGLEGABBLEGOBBLEGIT
CUNEO  AHT  SAUNA  SEG
ATI  WATTEAU  SIGNET AGOG
THEINN  FRIEDEGG  DROLL
MRSHEDDAGOBBLER  GME  BLO
AITS  MRMORSE  ROAMABIT
NEA  BOISE  GOLDENGOBLET
 SORN  BAP  SOUP  OTOE
ANTHEGOBBLEUNSLLGITYOU
SPIREA REBEL ETUI OHOHS
BEDAMN CLANK RUMS NEUME
STEWED ASSES SPET  RRS
```

93

```
ATHOME  ANODE  PETULA
ETHANOL DARER ERASERS
THETYPEWRITER  BIRETTA
HELIX  CEILS  ORB  OUTER
INAN STIFF ORALS  PERK
CAS STS TIFF MEAN  RYS
SITTER  LIFE  SNOOP
 ACES  AERIAL  TORERO
BOSSTWEED  ECRU  ANDRED
REEK  STAD  DELTAS  OFME
INC  OLIC  RIOT  EAN
NORM ANITAS  ESTS ACIS
KNEELS  NIRA  SEATURTLE
SETTOS  GOBUST  RAVE
 ASTER  NOVA  BESSES
BAR STEP NEMO NAA  ALP
ANYA SCUMS ABBOT ALLA
LIBRA UBI INLET ASTIR
STIRRER  DICTATORSHIPS
ARRAYAL  AMAHS  NOSENSE
ADULTS  SPLAT  ENTREE
```

94

```
CABANA  ISLES  BRAT ERST
ORATED ACUATE IOTA NOPE
PICTUREWINDOW  DUTCHDOOR
YAK RILL PINSK TATA  MON
 SCOFF ROES EGER MOANS
BATH TIMERS  PROS  SERT
AWAIT NUNC LENO SPLITUP
RAINED REHEAT FANLIGHTS
ERRATIC WELTER SEAN ETS
DES HASHA SIC ACHAT STET
 GERARD CHARTED BOORS
DAIRY BANISTERS  HARPS
ABCS TOTES ROI FOAL RAJ
RAH SADE TRIUNE PROFUSE
GRILLWORK INTHAT TROMPE
OSTEINS IBEG ASIS SUPER
 ESPY CLAN ABELES NUNS
FACTS GAOL CEIL LEEDS
ALT UCUT MOUNT ILEX RDS
BLUEPRINT BREAKFASTNOOK
LORN OLIO DIANAS AREOLE
EYES WEPT TASTY WARMED
```

95

```
SWELL  BAJA  CASK  SERIO
LEXIA  OLAF  OUTOFWHACK
GETONESELFINTOALATHER
DENTS  FOIST  PLOT  SRA
VERSUS  UXOR  PARCS
EDN  MARES  NIDE  HADAT
NOAH YETIS VARS  ENERO
DULAT CHEAPEN POSTERS
STEMWARE LORGNON  APES
 VAIN RAMI LURE  RAI
POINTTHEFINGEROFSCORN
ARD  LEAF  TEST  OTHO
SIES ENLACES UPROOTED
CONCERT BADTURN PLENE
ALCAN YOLK SNEER EDDA
LEERS  MEED  FRAUS  BUN
 FLOWN  EIER  SERERS
GBO AMOI ASTEP STELA
ALLOVERBUTTHESHOUTING
GOLDENRULE EZIO PIECE
ACADS  YSER  REST. SAFER
```

96

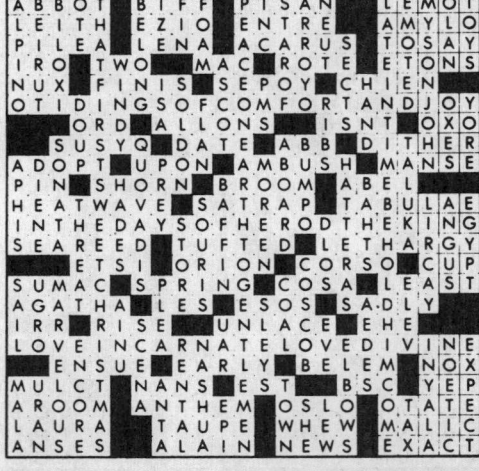

```
ABBOT  BIFF  PISAN  LEMOT
LEITH  EZIO  ENTRE  AMYLO
PILEA  LENA  ACARUS TOSAY
IRO TWO MAC ROTE  ETONS
NUX FINIS SEPOY CHIEN
OTIDINGSOFCOMFORTANDJOY
 ORD ALLONS ISNT  OXO
SUSYQ DATE ABB DITHER
ADOPT UPON AMBUSH MANSE
PIN SHORN BROOM  ABEL
HEATWAVE SATRAP TABULAE
INTHEDAYSOFHERODTHEKING
SEAREED TUFTED LETHARGY
 ETSI ORION CORSO  CUP
SUMAC SPRING COSA LEAST
AGATHA LES ESOS SADLY
IRR RISE UNLACE  EHE
LOVEINCARNATELOVEDIVINE
ENSUE EARLY BELEM  NOX
MULCT NANS EST BSC  YEP
AROOM ANTHEM OSLO OTATE
LAURA TAUPE WHEW MALIC
ANSES ALAIN NEWS EXACT
```

```
G P U . T I E T O . S T O L E . L S T S
S O A P . U N L I T . U R G E S . O T O E
U R N S . S H I F T S G E A R S . N O R A
P E T T I C O A T . H A E M . A N G R Y
. Y A C H T . P E R . Y A J E . . .
B O W T I E . S E L E C T E D S H O R T S
I N A E . B E T E N O I R E . S H O R N
K E I R . P A E A N . A R I C A . N O I O
I T S . N E C K T I E T A C K L E . M O B
N E T W O R K S . R E D S . E V E .
I N S I T U . A M I D E . W E L L E D
. G A S . B R A E . T H I R D A V E
S O P . L A W Y E R S B R I E F S . T E N
T R I M . L E R O I . A I M E E . C E N T
A L L E N . D O N T S L E E P . A B S I
Y E L L O W S N E A K E R S . D I L L O N
. B A N I . L E D . H E L L O .
D O N O T . T I T I . S L A C K S O F F
T A X I . H M S P I N A F O R E . O M O O
I N E E . A B A S E . T A K E N . F E R N
M E S S . L A R E S . E X I S T . F R A
```

```
L A L A . O A S T . S H E K . T R A I L E R
I C E B E R G L E T T U C E . G R I L L A D E
S H O O T T H E B R E E Z E . R U T L E D G E
P E N N A . A D E E M . E N T I C E S . Y A K
E R I E . A S S T S . E M E R G E S . A W R Y
D O N . E S T . A R A R A . A L I S
N E S T S . O S T I A . S N A G . D O N N E
. C H I L L W I L L S . C L A R E N D O N
A R R A S . O P A L S . K E E P M E . S E W S
L E E R . T R A I T . C O L D H A R B O R
I N B E T W E E N . F O A L . A L E E . M T G
S E E S E E . T R A L A . A D H E R E
T E C . L E U D . O I L S . C O L D S O R E S
C O L D T U R K E Y . C A V E S . L E N T
O W A R . L I V E O N . C A F E S . C I S T S
K I D D I E C A R . D E E P F R E E Z E
S N E E S . A L A D . G R E A T . B A R B S
T W A S . T E N E T . L A R . U T A
T E I L . C U R E F O R . B A D I N . A T A R
E R N . D O S A D O S . D I E O F . A U T R E
E S T E E M E D . R O B E R T L E E F R O S T
N E E D L E R S . C A L V I N C O O L I D G E
S T R E E T S . E P E E . A I R S . C O O S
```

```
. R A C E R . C A N O E D . O L A F
. P A R O L E . U S U R P E D . B O R A
D A Y C A M P . P H I L H A R M O N I C
A G O A L . L O O . T E A T I M E . Z I F
R E F S . B A A L S . H B S . L O N E
E S S . J A C K A N A P E S . C H A N G E
. U N I T E S . E R A T . A V A S T
C A N I N E S . T E R R O R . H U I
E S S E X . O O Z E S . E S O T E R I C
A C H T . F O R P E T E S S A K E . A N O
S O I E . A L L O . I A L U . T B S P
E O N . S W E E T W I L L I A M . O B I T
S P E W I N G S . A N O L D . P R I D E
. E D S . S T Y L U S . R O O S T E R
T O T A L . O N E G . S O R R O W
S C O R E S . T O E T H E M A R K . A V A
A T M S . E A U . S L E D S . B R O S
R O T . T E R R I E R . A E S . E A R T H
B O B U P A N D D O W N . T E S S E R A
E M E R . B E L A T E D . E R M I N E
R S V P . R E M A T S . R E E L S
```

```
A G G . A W S . G A L A H A D . S E S A M E S
P A R A S O L . A B A L O N E . A L A B A M A
S T I C K T O O N E S G U N S . L E B A N O N
E S T R E A T S . L E A R . C R O C E . S T D
E R N . T I E R . O R A N T . W H E Y
A S T A S . T E N S . G A M I N S . M O O D S
L A H M . B A N K . C U R B E D . T O O T
A B E . B O N D . P O N I E S . C A L L F O R
T O T T E R S . P U R S E R . S A U T E R N E
E T H A N E . P A N D A S . P E R T . N O S E
R O D . C A R T O N . L A M E . M E L
F E E S . A R M S A N D T H E M A N . H A T S
A V E . G A P E . B E A T E N . A E C
R A M S . A P A R . S U L L E N . A T L A S T
E D U C A T E S . T I T L E S . A N T O N I O
R E S A L E S . M I N T E D . P I S A . N E A
. K R I S . D A N C E R . H E R A . E O N S
S K E E T . C O N G E R . P O S Y . A N N A T
P I T S . D A N T E . C O P E . E T C
A L E . M E U S E . J O H N . T E A H O U S E
S T E L I A S . L O O K E D D A G G E R S A T
M I R A C L E . E N T E R E D . G E N E S I S
S E S T E T S . T A S T E R S . S R S . C L I
```

```
S A M I T E . O C H E R . E B B . B B S
I M I D E S . O R A L E . I R A . B A L I
C A T O T E N T A I L S . G A R P I K E S
. H E L E N A . W R A I T H S . I D E A S
. S I T E . N O T I . P E R K Y
R E D O . N O S E D . S A H L S . E S S
A M O R E . E X I T . H I S . D O M
S I X A N D E L E V E N C E N T S T O R E
. L A N D E D . R E M O R A . E L I Z A S
. C H E T . P R I V . A U G E R S
R A T . O A S I . E L A . E L L E . N E Y
I N W O R N . G A L A . S N I T
A V O C E T . H U S T L E . S H E B A T
T I C K L E S T H E E I G H T Y N I N E S
A L E . D O N . S A N A . G L I N T
N S F . L O I R . R O N D O . K L E E
S I T K A . E T N A . D O R P
A N S E R . M R N I X O N . S C O R I A
C A F E M E N U . S E V E N T H S E N S E
K N O T . E L M . E N A T E . I S O G O N
S E R . G Y P . S O L I D . D E S E R T
```

```
R A J A . S L E E P . L A P S E . C A R T
A M U R . O U T R E . A G I R L . O R E O
T O P G A L L A N T . T O P S Y T U R V Y
E R O . S O U L . A M I N E . S A N
D E N O T E S . P L I N Y . B I S T R O S
. D I O . T R O D S . B R A S S I C A
A C T O R . A R O I D . R U N E . G E N
L A H R . M I D D L E M A N . S H A G
I T E . A M B O S . E D I C T . A E T N A
S C L E R O I D . M O D S . C R A M
T H E C E N T E R O F A T T R A C T I O N
. F L A T . A I T S . H O L D O N T O
A S T A R . S W I S H . L I S L E . D E N
N E W T . C E N T E R I C E . H E R E
A T I . S P A T . R E C K S . G O D O T
C O N C E R N S . P O L I S . A L L
E N G A G E S . T R A I T . B L E M I S H
. N N E . L E A D A . A U L A . D E E
B O T T O M M O S T . B O T T O M L E S S
A W O L . P A S T E . L A I T Y . O A T S
M E R E . T R E Y S . E S T E S . S L O E
```

103

```
AMBER STEAD RIVAL OFFAL
RILLE CARVE ABODE RIATA
GLASSHOUSES CINDERELLAS
ULM TART RIDES RELADLE
EYESORE PARIS STAG MEER
ARM SAGES MIXTURE
COPSE DIVERSIONS LANCET
AMAH CEDES ODDS TATTLER
MAP MACES FLEE AARE OLE
PTEROPOD MAVERICKS STEW
SERENER MUSE NOME TAHRS
TEARAPART KINESCOPE
CHILD TURK LIZA CANASTA
HAGS MILLIPEDE MOMENTAL
IKE GONE NUTS COVES RUT
VERGING VENT CAPEL RENO
ESSENE PASSEDOVER DUETS
RAYLESS RIVES LAI
KALE METE PERES REMNANT
IRONMAN WADER DIVA BOA
WOODENSHOES CLAYPIGEONS
ISSUS EARLS TEPEE EVICT
SEEMS SLATE STERN DALEY
```

104

```
LAM ASPO HIP CAKE
ANY SWAN ACE OPINE
PTAH PENE REP HORNER
REPEL ERRED LETSDRAW
ISHAM TOUGH PEA HOTE
SHORTCHANGE CARRIESON
MORT AES EATS TEDA
SWAB RAT RRS ALBERTO
EDER STA TAUNTERS
PILE TRA ERGONS SAAR
ARROWSCUPIDSANDHEARTS
LIEN POLISH GEO ANSE
LONGLINE LAR FORD
RESORTS ANE STP CPLS
TBAR OMNI THE ORAE
SCHOOLAGE ANCIENTROME
IRED CID HERLS COMBS
PARASITE FRITO UNIAT
MODELS MAR MOUE ESSO
PEDAL ORO ENTS TET
SYNE DAM ASHE SEE
```

105

```
SANTA ATLAST ELBA NODE
SPREES CHIMER LILT EBAN
PATACHOUENLAI OMAR FIDO
ARE HAG LEI DIANA ETES
CELT BAYOU STEN CMDR
ESSEN MANPOWER PETARD
MET TESSELATES AIMEE
RAMPART HELLESPONTIFF
USE RAREES TITANIC INEE
RID MELPOMENEMENE CORR
ADAMS KAIFENG SARA
LELAND SCAT ODDS NECTAR
CYAN REFRAIN CARRY
LAMA BOHEMIAFARROW APA
OBER OVERACT TEEMED IAL
CORTINALOUISE ERRANDS
HIGHS EMERSONIAN TAT
SLEUTH REUTTERS GOLFS
ROAD FAST URALS MALE
AREA TILLS SRI ELY TOA
GELS PROA ALIBABAAURHUM
RASH IGOR REVILE SLEETS
ALEE NENE GRASSY HEEDS
```

106

```
IMAGI CHRONIST ACRES
ARISEN RAISETHE MAUVE
MARINA EINSTEIN ARSON
ANA STRAND SMEETH TKO
NICK IOTAS ELMO BRER
DALI OMEN DODDERSEED
ANEMONES FEN SNEERS
OLIO DECEM TARRIES
SANDS SEDATES TEESUP
GOBO MATH MOTEL TRA
RIBS OREIMPORTAN BAER
ORR MRSAM IMET INKS
WEEDER SCIENCE TESTA
SEVERER ESNES SHAH
INSTEP ITE TEAROOMS
MASTICATES TENN PRAU
PATE ROSO PINSK SANA
ALL BEATUP ALDENS TAV
PAOLO SOCIABLE OOLITE
AGNEW TRAMPLER WIENER
LASTS SENATORS LEDGE
```

107

```
QUAQUA TASKS ACCA BLURB
UNTUNE HUTIA MOAB RASED
ATLAST ETATS BURL EMULS
ROAR MOLES UPGO ABRA
TONTO MOME YELLOW KAPPA
OTTER AVAST MAES OBSESS
SHATTERITTOBITS FIRTREE
VIN SOLE COLE
ABRASING ACU STYX APSE
TRAMPLE FLAGS ICI KAHNS
RIVALS ELI HOOPLE BLORE
AMATI BLOCKBUSTER RETAN
ISLET APPEAR LOS LETSGO
LULUS NAP TEPEE GOATIER
PIRO ASYM AAR BOOKENDS
NINO ELKS IRK
ZETAETA SMASHINGMACHINE
ELOISE COSI ARUBA HAMUS
DOERS MONACO OMEN ABIBS
CILI AYAH SANER ITBE
LURID ROTI APORT OBTAIN
ATONE STAB KORAH TOATEE
BENES HESS ADELA TATERS
```

108

```
CAPE CBD GASTON GISH
HOAX MAUI UMPIRE INTO
ABIE ARTS MOUNTAINEAR
WARMFRONT SUM ARN PIN
PLYMOUTHROCK DSTNS
HALLOS TRIO TENET
AVOIR CABLECAR EPIGON
NEC IAS RRS VEERTO
GRANDBALLROOM PENSEES
BLEAR MCIC ARD ASE
CAPITALPUNISHMENT
NCO ADD LANE ENOLS
OOLONGS WHIPSTHECRACK
CLOTHE BOY UTE KAI
TARTAR LOOPHOLE HIERS
ENSUE LONE PATSYS
HEARD NIAGARAFALLS
OPS LAI GUY STEELPIER
SUNSETSTRIP 1001 ARCH
EROS TOHIDE DUNN RACE
SETT ANOPEN ETS TELA
```

109

```
SEDGE  PSHAW  SHOWS  PATHS
ECRIT  ATONE  TOLET  ETHIC
THEGOLDENTRIANGLE  THERE
SOSO  ADIGE  SNEAK  DEEPEN
  STAMINA  LADYS  BERNESE
BBC  MENS  LULU  ALEAN
ROILING  GIZAPYRAMID  TIM
UNREST  BELOW  SERBS  EASE
INCAS  SLAIN  FARCI  ARGOT
NELS  APART  MAYAS  ORIOLE
STEEPLES  HEAVEN  EXTENTS
  LIRE  ASO  ALII
REQUIEM  ASSORT  RIDERSTO
ICUMEN  ASHEN  OBESE  EQUI
FLAPS  SISAL  AXONE  SCULL
FADS  CEDAR  AVILA  NATALE
STR  CONEYISLAND  COLORER
  ACHES  ASIS  BARS  ESS
CONRADE  METAL  HERMAID
EGGERS  SALIC  BEREA  DAIL
ALLAT  SPHEREOFINFLUENCE
REESE  PEACE  RADIO  TACET
ASSER  TENTS  OSIER  ALERT
```

110

```
 CLAIM  STEAD  BEAST
SHASTAS  HILLER  CANCER
COMMECICOMMECA  ARCADE
ORB  ELOPE  FLIERS  DAS
ODAS  SLAP  ASIT  GINS
TASTE  STEM  ARISE  EASE
ETTES  IRONMEN  BLT
RASAS  SNEAD  ALASKA
 MAMBA  TAP  HAN  IRK
MAGI  ILLS  RAISONDETRE
INRE  SUTE  PARC  REAR
TOURDEFORCE  MUSH  ASSN
TIM  REF  LAC  DEEPS
 APRONS  TORAH  FERRO
 UPS  BRANDED  GREER
FADS  CROOK  SARA  SALSE
AMIE  ETAL  DUMA  TOPS
VOL  SNARLS  ASPEN  AIT
ORACLE  DOUBLEENTENDRE
RATIOS  SPROUT  SEABEE'S
SLEET  EDAMS  STADS
```

111

```
TOR  ESP  SECEDER  PAD  AFT
ANA  ETO  PROVISO  OSE  LIE
FEDERAL  SADISTS  SLIDERS
TOIL  NIP  SELL  ESSE  ARTS
FOURCORNERSOFTHEEARTH
DUE  AIRS  CORE  PIT
FACES  ATES  CARED  MECCA
AMOS  SHER  BOTTE  THEROOT
GER  SPAS  LURES  BEAD  ROI
ORNATUS  MORNS  GOAT  NRS
TIEROD  CEASE  EROSE  CUD
CREW  CORNERSTORE  LOCI
ASS  COALS  BETAS  MELONS
ENT  OUTS  PREEN  DEADPAN
AMO  LIPS  CLOPS  MILK  ITO
RANCORS  CHAOS  CAST  BAER
SNEER  BRINK  SORT  PASSE
DAB  AUNT  SPIT  EAT
CORNISHCOASTOFENGLAND
SARI  TITI  TIER  NOR  AERO
TRICKED  ALINETO  VERNIER
AVE  ORE  NOODLES  ETE  GAT
BEL  SSS  SENSERS  LST  HRS
```

112

```
SWAM  IRISH  ABC  BESTOW
HOPI  MEDEA  PIO  ENTIRE
ERRS  PALET  PSI  ATAMAN
 KICKOVERTHETRACES
 LOIRE  REAR  SHRIVEL
DESILT  FREELOADS  SANO
ETHNO  CREEDS  MIE  PEA
RHO  MELON  EARTHWORM
UAWS  WANDERLUST  EEROS
SNEERERS  DEARS  PRS
TERRORS  GENIE  SHEKELS
 VBS  TAMAR  PHYSIQUE
ATSEA  RODANDREEL  TUMP
DAYDREAMS  OREAD  IBO
RUR  SMA  SWATAT  HONEY
EROS  TARPAULIN  DONORS
MISLAID  HURL  REBEC
 ENVIRONMENTALISTS
MANANA  ANT  GORSE  TIES
CRAVAT  FEE  ELIOT  EARL
STEELE  TYR  DOONE  PLAY
```

113

```
ALORS  SUETS  SOCKO  PEBA
DIVER  INTHE  AFRIT  DANES
HEADINGTHEMOFFATTHEPASS
OGLE  ONION  REEKS  ECARTE
CES  TWEES  MITRE  SLOWEST
 CHITS  JOEYS  SKED
TROAS  SORN  TINE  CLE
THEYWENTTHATAWAYMARSHAL
ARGOS  IRONY  LOLLS  PALO
BIAS  SMEWS  OLDIE  GOESON
ALL  BABA  POEM  AARE
CLEAROUTOFTOWNBYSUNDOWN
LENS  REAL  ESSE  PRO
BEGONE  TRIPE  NAMES  NEAT
ACRO  SHINE  BOXER  HANSA
THEFASTESTDRAWINTHEWEST
HOW  NEER  OLAS  AWARE
DRAM  TUMMY  CALEB
MISTRAL  ARRAY  LURID  DUO
ASLEEP  ALIBI  REACT  MINT
MEANWHILEBACKATTHERANCH
ARMES  SARAN  ADIRE  ANGLE
NEST  TITLE  BATOR  FOYER
```

114

```
HATH  ROWENA  ROSO  ALAS
OCHO  ACORES  ALEF  TOBE
WHEELBARROW  MIAFARROW
BIGDEALS  NARROWBRIDGE
AEROSTAT  NEO  AYE  SAD
DREW  DDAY  EIDO
ENAMOR  MASU  WONTON
SUNSHINE  PAN  RIANT
ENA  ONESTAR  WONDERFUL
APR  YES  EAR  ARK  LEONA
MURA  SPARROWHAWK  EXIT
EROSE  ARR  WOO  ENT  ETE
NEWSMEDIA  SKOALER  SOO
 EYRES  IKE  SLEEPOFF
CROSSE  TINY  ISDEAF
OENS  CANT  SHIP
RTE  LEO  VON  LEVITATE
DAVEGARROWAY  UNIVERSE
AROOSTOOK  POINTBARROW
GETA  ENCE  PURGEE  NOME
EDEN  NAKS  ESTERS  SWEE
```

115

```
PRETEST  BESIDE  EDITORS
LUCERNE  RELINED TOTALUP
ANOMIES ELIZABETHGOUDGE
ISLANDSINTHESTREAM  TAPE
NOO  SIDE  USEE  SNA  DAD
TUGOF  NOWS  NEMOS  BADS
STYLED  LACROSSE  CHUMS
   TEAL  LAINE  HASLET
TAS  SNOB  TAI  RICHARDNEY
OBAN  AVAS  SCOUTCAR  OISE
FORGE  ETH  ENLARGED  GSA
FUTURESHOCK  ALBERTSPEER
LTR  ASTEROID  EDE  CORNS
ETES  COSTUMED  LIES  DIET
ROSEMARIES  PER  TNTS  ASO
   LARYNX  REVES  SOUL
SALEP  ALEWIVES  TROPIC
STDS  GAMES  SETA  FORNO
TEA  GAB  AETA  SALA  EVA
OWNA  URISREICHANDFRASER
MACLAINEANDSHAW  ELOPERS
PRELUDE  GEEZERS  NOSENSE
STRIKER  ARRANT  SWATTER
```

116

```
ROWAN  DOSE  BOBBIE
REBATE  SOTHIS  ALLINA
EDESSA  THRIFT  NEATASA
FIXHERBREAKFAST  CONES
HATTER  SEPTA  KNELT
ESSE  OUTIN  LLAMAS
SPERM  CRI  ENSUE  BOM
THEWAY  HOSSES  RACINE
ASPIRES  NAIL  ABA  LOTS
NOSE  INFIDEL  PEGAS
PRADO  TEN  ORE  RASPY
AARON  HOGGISH  ETON
STEW  ASS  ENCE  DISHOUT
SETSBY  STARRY  PIERRE
ESE  RESIT  AWE  TREAT
ANITAS  PALAU  COLE
ECADS  LENTA  SPINAL
ALTOS  VACUUMHERFLOORS
TERRACE  ENLAIR  RESNAP
FAIRER  STAINS  ERECTS
SPADES  SERG  ETTES
```

117

```
SAFES  SATES  DUPED  SCRIP
TRACE  TREAT  INONE  PHASE
ARCHDIOCESE  ARMOFTHESEA
NATO  SLANT  SPIES  REAPER
WHINY  SOAPS  MART
BESTRIDE  REUSE  DIVESTED
ELOHIM  NOTSO  AEDES  RAE
FIFES  TOOTHANDNAIL  SERF
OCTET  ORCAS  IERS  LEANT
RISS  GREAT  AMENT  MORSEL
ETH  BLABBERMOUTH  AUGURY
OBEAH  OER  ANGER
OCULAR  THUMBTHROUGH  ERR
DELETE  HOSEA  AUNTY  DCII
ENDAS  SERI  ALICE  BEHAN
STET  SKINANDBONES  ABELS
SER  SPURS  ORLES  TRISTE
ARSENALS  TWEED  STRETTOS
PARK  CHOIR  PURUS
SABOTS  VEINS  MANIC  WASP
LIONHEARTED  BOTTLENECKS
ANEYE  FAUVE  AURAL  LIMIT
GERMS  RISER  REINS  FRETS
```

118

```
TONTO  TIDIED  SENATE
AROAR  HAROLDE  RELATED
FIRMA  ONASSIS  AVEDONS
TOMENTOSE  TIPPECANOE
TUR  ORIENT  ENL
HOSS  FACEISRED  TOSS
ABUT  THEPOPS  EYRE
REBALE  RENI  OBL  ATMO
PRUNED  TEARSHAIR  THAN
RCA  OUTTHE  UNL
HUBERTHORATIOHUMPHREY
ANI  CORONA  AAM
LIAR  UNTANGLES  GULOSE
OSSE  USN  NITH  ALINES
ANDS  REPAIRS  DDES
DREE  SEAWOLVES  ESME
WEE  ATLAST  SET
EFFETESNOB  NATTERING
BRAVEST  PIEFACE  REFER
BEMISTS  UTTERED  MAFIA
SMELTS  SEAWAY  SLYLY
```

119

```
LILACS  GILT  PIUS  HEAP
ONOMATOMANIA  MUMBOJUMBO
GOBBLEDYGOOK  HYPOCORISM
ONES  RITA  NEMO  LAKE  LEM
SUS  COSH  PERE  COTS  BINE
BAIT  GOSSAMERS  FIATS
REPAND  BROS  SALE  SIL
INERT  ZEAL  CULL  MALAGAS
BARBARISM  TORA  FIREBALL
ERS  BENTS  ALERTING  ILIA
SMILING  BEL  KINK  LAITY
FOLD  BALLOTERS  CALM
BELGE  GALA  GAY  PULSATE
OMAO  SILLABUB  ATOLL  TAA
MIGRAINE  BLEU  RHOTACISM
ALERCES  PLUS  SOAP  TEASE
HOG  TIAS  SOON  HISSES
CRIER  WHEATGERM  SOOT
RENA  BRED  ERAT  ECON  TEG
ACH  ALEF  DRIP  SDAK  SHOR
DOUBLETALK  TELEGRAPHESE
LAMBDACISM  TACHYPHRASIA
ETES  THRU  YSER  SEDENT
```

120

```
PEG  DECEM  BES  MID
AHNE  DEMERIT  ALTO  IDA
NICELYNICELY  BLOWBLOW
ANA  PATTI  ERG  ROLLIN
REMASK  LASERS  READDS
TAPS  ATILT  EAT  BAO
SEC  ABSALOMABSALOM
DUNDEE  AGAS  ETON
TOUT  WROTE  TOG  PEP
CHANEL  AHAB  USN  ALGA
MILESTOGOBEFOREISLEEP
DRAY  ENE  FIRN  CITARA
RED  PRE  TIOGA  PISH
HEEP  RARA  RATIOS
MERRILYMERRILY  RTE
SAR  NAT  10000  NAVA
MORONS  GROSSA  YESYES
ANCIEN  YUL  DRIED  UNO
JOHNJOHN  TEMPERTEMPER
ORE  DODO  SERENES  CORE
RAS  PSI  PUNTS  INS
```

121

```
STATIC ASCOT ALAS SEMIS
TAMALE SPIER ROLL PROSE
ETAOINSHRDLU ASSOCIATED
LET OTIC LISP AVON ERE
ARIA REAP ASTA BALUSTER
JOURNAL MOIL KALE
BECALM LEO MMES SERUMS
ADORE SPORTSPAGE SINAI
NIM SOTS OPES CUP FIND
ALPS RAINWEAR SULLA TIE
LEONIDS OASTS PROOFREAD
SIRE PIN ARE TEED
EDITORIAL OMAHA STEPPES
LOT NEARS PICAYUNE TRAP
ATOE DOT ITSA RARA EVA
TERRA COMICSTRIP LASER
ERSATZ HYPO TAE BAISSE
SHOD EONS ASTOUND
REDEEMED SAPS TRUG EAST
ACE IBAR ELAN USES NNE
CLASSIFIED SOCIETYPAGES
KARAT TELO MOIST EAGLET
STYES ORAN SPORO DETERS
```

122

```
LAMS OPCIT PATHE BIDS
ATOP NEATH OPIUM ADAK
PAPAYATREE POPGUNNERY
CAPTS MOLDS LEGATE
CAPEMAY PAPAS SAVE
ISOMER SITAR BETIDED
RIPEN PAPALSTATES LAS
CAIN SLUE HEAD PENT
ANN OPANDPOPART SEGUE
SPINA ONAN SCRIBE
OLDTIRE MOIRE SHOOTER
MARINO ECCE ACORN
EDILE FATHERBROWN PAS
GIVE BIDE ECUS FAMA
ADE PATERNOSTER BATON
ALSORAN ANTED BATTLE
APES OTOES CASHIER
RADIUS AFIRE SHIRE
IVANPAVLOV POPULARIZE
MORT REINE LIETO LOIN
AWNS KNEES ELDER YOGA
```

123

```
GALLI CHANC LAOS FROSH
ARIAN MAJOR ATLAS IONIA
SNARK INOVO CHELA SMELT
PORGYANDBASS LOANSHARKS
ESSE POL BITE DLO
APRETTYKETTLEOFFISH
OWLAND EHS BIRLED INNO
FIORE BCDE RECOAL FSTAR
FLOUNDERABOUT UNS OHRID
ILK TULU YAH STO ORIOLE
SHEA NUMB KRAAL ARME
HERRINGBONE BLESSMYSOLE
AREA NANCY TOPO TROD
CAVIAR TEY LST UELE LUI
AMIND SOL FISHORCUTBAIT
NIOBE EYECUP EAST HESSE
OSLO CAESAR RGT PENTAD
THEWORLDSMINEOYSTER
BUY POEM IER LAGS
CATFISHROE HOLYMACKEREL
ADULT AITCH RAMPS NAOMI
REVUE MOTHY AGILE ESSEN
POWER TOES SOREL WHELK
```

124

```
RETAILS WAVERED LIARS
AXILLAE AGITATO INLET
GODSLITTLEACHER SAMBA
BRIO DIONNE SRITA SAT
ADE ROUT NEA NATO
GIST TOLTEC PASS ONER
SATYRINE OBOL KIND
PUNS TAMES LETS
REPENT CALMEST ESTHER
ARADO MALMO EARL SERA
FRI FRANKANDSTEIN MEM
TART IDEA CASAS ADANO
STOWED STEELER TRINES
ADEN HONED REIN
INST COST DESCANTS
TACT ASAN STRESS HEIL
UREY LEI HOSP ARA
GIL SCARP CRONES GRAS
GOOSE WEIGHOFALLFLESH
ESSEN ANTOINE LARUSSE
DOTED YEARNER SWATTER
```

125

```
QUINQUE MASSE SEAFOAM
ERBIUMS PALATAL ENDURED
DENTATE ANIMATE ADORERS
SYSTS DUNGAREE POUR
1IFBYLANDAND2IFBYSEA
PCT OVERSEA SPLIT AYR
AHOP ETRE DMUS HOT CLEM
RERAMS SVT STABAT BOULE
SEPTI EHS IVYS DONDER
ETERNAL REEF ETE ASCOTS
RADIUMA EYELASH ECTO
SHOOTUP SOLUBLE CHORALE
TESS RUSTIER HANDBAG
KISSME NIN ESAU OUTMIME
ERODED EDGE SSD EAGER
YENAN TWEEDS TEC BASALT
STAY SHH ROUT BRAE SILO
TON SPEAR GOTRIPE LAN
ONTHE18THOFAPRILIN75
VERB OVERSIDE SOFTA
ANTIGUA DENTING BEETRED
WBEDELL ARCADIE ANAHEIM
LATERAL SEXES TASSELS
```

126

```
LIRPA LOOF XAOH
ESOOG LLIF ARES
EILLA EOGI MADA
SNR LEHCAR IROB
ALABAC SLARA
NEPOMA IRPAC
RENO SPAEH TEA
ERUTCIP EPAHSER
DTS NAMUH CELA
NIGID ECALAP
SENOZ NEDIEL
TLAS SRELIO ESA
ETET MOTA REURT
TILA ODNE ETROA
STOR NOEP HACIM
```

127

```
CASPAR PAJAMAS CANADA
ASHORE ALAMODE APELET
STOLID DIVORCE ROMERO
CIVILSERVANT PARDONME
ARETE REES     MOAS
    EDAM DESPOT    AWE
LIEN MANNERSMAKYTHMAN
ADVERB CRISPER  RIANT
WEASEL OAS ILES INTER
DOSSIER  MALTA  TIDY
     DREADFULSORRY
SCAR  SMEAR   DEEPENS
WORST TITI JAB PALLET
ABOVE  GERMANY AHEAPO
PROPERBOSTONIANS ANSA
SAM  EASTON    ATTS
   POLL   DIOR AEDES
EXCUSEME THANKYOUMAAM
BEARIN CAROLER PRONTO
UNMEET CHIMERA PISTOL
ROPERS LAMENTS OCTANT
```

128

```
CARIBE  AIDED  OSSIE
ALATED IGNORES VIENNA
TAKEAS BOSTONTEAPARTY
CRIMP DINA STEAL RUER
HIS ANODYNE ULT SCIRE
CHARADE EXTRA ETHNOS
STIGMA  PIE  FLOP
BEYLE GRANDOLDPARTY
BERATE KOINE RYE ROUE
URI ORDERED DIOR TARA
ROMP ARAN JESU  YSER
LIMA PENS BUSSTOP TEN
ACER UME SONIA RAVENS
PARTYPOLITICS  TIRED
YEAN MAL  TAROTS
STAPLE UMBER LILYPAD
ERROL ARE RELABEL VIM
COMO INERT SIRE ILOVE
TWOPARTYSYSTEM KNOWIT
SERENE SERMONS RECEDE
LYRES  DEANS  ASIDES
```

129

```
STPS EBB BISAYAS TCE
AHEY NEA ENAMELS HOS
PENNAMES GAMEWARDENS
OWN GIRT GLOM  NICER
ISBUT IMALABAMYBOUND
ASTRAY LAR EMIL ORCS
REAIR FLO BARBEDWIRE
VITG ORE EAT INSE ELL
ONEA PADDYWAGON ARNIE
DSC ARENTI ELLECKS
ISITI YEL HST ATREE
ALTERTO EOLITH WHO
GLORE CONVERSION TSPS
TIO EATA END RUS AERO
BLUNDERBUS TDS STRIP
REPP ENOL GAD STEVES
PRISONEROFLOVE POSES
MAGOR TUES GNAR TTS
LEAVENWORTH ROCKPILE
LOR REGURGE EVE AMEN
YNS RESTSON EAR DEYS
```

130

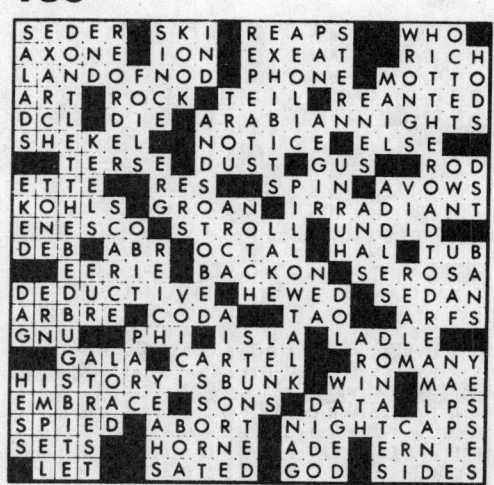

```
SEDER SKI REAPS WHO
AXONE ION EXEAT RICH
LANDOFNOD PHONE MOTTO
ART ROCK TEIL REANTED
DCL DIE ARABIANNIGHTS
SHEKEL NOTICE ELSE
TERSE DUST GUS ROD
ETTE RES SPIN AVOWS
KOHLS GROAN IRRADIANT
ENESCO STROLL UNDID
DEB ABR OCTAL HAL TUB
EERIE BACKON SEROSA
DEDUCTIVE HEWED SEDAN
ARBRE CODA TAO ARFS
GNU PHI ISLA LADLE
GALA CARTEL ROMANY
HISTORYISBUNK WIN MAE
EMBRACE SONS DATA LPS
SPIED ABORT NIGHTCAPS
SETS HORNE ADE ERNIE
LET SATED GOD SIDES
```

131

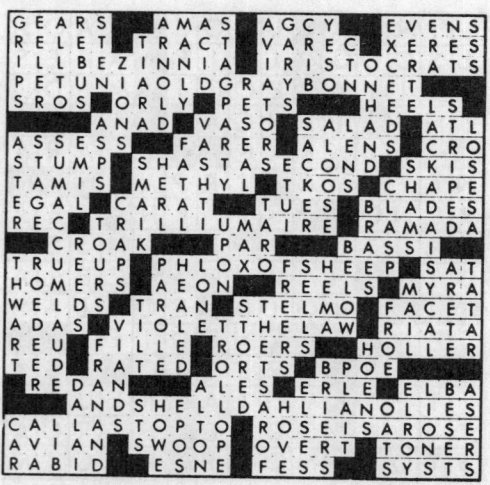

```
GEARS  AMAS AGCY  EVENS
RELET TRACT VAREC XERES
ILLBEZINNIA IRISTOCRATS
PETUNIAOLDGRAY BONNET
SROS ORLY PETS  HEELS
ANAD VASO SALAD ATL
ASSESS FARER ALENS CRO
STUMP SHASTASECOND SKIS
TAMIS METHYL TKOS CHAPE
EGAL CARAT TUES BLADES
REC TRILLIUMAIRE RAMADA
CROAK PAR BASSI
TRUEUP PHLOXOFSHEEP SAT
HOMERS AEON REELS MYRA
WELDS TRAN STELMO FACET
ADAS VIOLETTHELAW RIATA
REU FILLE ROERS HOLLER
TED RATED ORTS BPOE
REDAN ALES ERLE ELBA
ANDSHELLDAHLIANOLIES
CALLASTOPTO ROSEISAROSE
AVIAN SWOOP OVERT TONER
RABID ESNE FESS SYSTS
```

132

```
ALEP SLED MATCH SPADS
BEMA TILE EMILE TRACT
UTES AMRA SALEM AERIE
THEHAPPINESSOFPURSUIT
SERAGLIO VIS  SPTS
RED SENECA TETHER
ALIBI PARADED ORIOLE
RASA STATS LST SMALT
CULM TALI ACTORS EXES
ARABIAN RUBE RITE
AMIMYKEEPERSBROTHER
PEEL OTOE ENCORES
AFAR DRAINS ESME LISA
SAMOA SIR BATED LATS
TRIUNE NACELLE DYNES
AMENDS ENAMEL SIA
DRAG SPA TORRANCE
THEHOUSETHATJACKBUILT
HARES TRAIL ONCE TOOT
ILLAE ANNEE EGER OBOE
SEEDS REARS YARS SETS
```

133

```
SILTS  PAST  SPIRE  PST
GOCART ROMEO EARNER OUR
AMELIA APAIL TWOFER UFO
WEBOMBEDINNEWHAVEN IFFY
KOA BANNEDINBOSTON
ANGI FORTE OLIO TENDING
TESTBAN ORR SCUD RAIDER
SARDS ENO TOA SAIGA
DABBLE LATTENS RIO NORM
OWEA NOSHOW OVERMIAMI
CONCHAE EERY CEM ASP
LIKEGRANTTOOKRICHMOND
TRE ISE RHES PAYLOAD
PHOENIXES KAYOED ILLE
TRAP TEL THEREST ASSAIL
WISER REO IRA ATNO5
ONTOUR SUMP SAF ASTOPTO
STORIES TOPS DIANA OLAF
INSANFRANCISCO ALA
YUMA PHILADELPHIALAWYER
ARE PIANOS LEONE UTHANT
PSI ARROWS LASER COACTS
SAN MEANS STET KITTS
```

134

```
SAMP  PACT  NLAT  SNOW
IGOR HULLE EASES PEDI
RELOCATION IVORYTOWER
RHETTBUTLERSPANTRY
DISARMS BIAS HUGO
AMATI BETTI ABE ENTE
NAMES GARY MANOR BEL
EMUS LOBE OLGAS CARL
SSE COWARD NOIR LAKME
LAINE ENSUE CAREER
PLANTER ILIAD SOSORRY
LODGER ARABY EVENS
ETALS CLAM SPADER DBA
ATMO RIATA ARAS SOUS
SIS ENTER RUIN BIZET
EENS SEE EWELL ADENO
EAST SASS ALIENOR
SHELLEYWINTERSBARK
BADTOWORSE WILLYNILLY
ILLE SWABS EDIES CUTE
COED SPAT DEPR KISS
```

135

```
BRAIN THAI AGLEY SPARTA
MARNE ISSO SEENO LUSHED
THISWONTHURTMUCH ESTILO
ETAS YSER LOVEHONOR
BAIT KEA EARNS OPEROSE
UMT ILLCALLYOU RIIS
LOCATE TKO IMPACT STOA
BRASSY HEWONTBITE LEHAR
ENCASE ORE LES AVERT
OAF SUNNYSKIES GWEN
LINPU TAN SOI BEARERS
ISL NEAREST LINCOLN XES
DRYICES ARA IOS DITCH
GRIN LOWERTAXES OWI
GLOAT BAD TOW ACROSS
POUTY ENDPAYOFFS ADROIT
SUPE QUASAR ULT TEENSY
SURE YOULLGOFAR MAP
SLASHER ASONE MAL DELE
HAPPINESS BEAN CASE
ORIENT THEHORSECANTLOSE
AVANTI OUTER PROD ETAIN
LANDON PREEN SONE MATES
```

136

```
HAVOC FASTAS HIST
CINEMA ASTARTE OLEO
BACKLOT KILLERDILLER
INKED CHE OLDADAM REE
DOOR CHARS WAN DERM
EER HOITYTOITY KUDOS
YVONNE RUNE AIR
PUDDING SUNSET GLOWER
ARIAS MINCE OENOCHOE
RACY HODGEPODGE ELD
ELKS DOMO BIAS REIN
TIO EVENSTEVEN ALTO
TARLATAN CHRIS OKEHS
ANYONE TERREO ASPERSE
SIR CION DIETED
HOTEL MUMBOJUMBO EAR
APAR IDA WORSE RABI
PIC ABARREL NAH TALON
NOLENSVOLENS ICEBERG
EMIR HELLENO GOCART
SANO LESSEN HOSTS
```

137

```
DORAD PILOT REBAR BEADY
ENERO OSOLE ERASE RATIO
ACIER PLAIN GUSTS ASTOR
RENAISSANCEARCHITECTURE
AHINT TRET ALT
ADDS ENDOW ITSA BAS ABS
BROOMS HIC LAIT SLAW
EARLYAMERICANPEWTERWARE
AMIDS OXIME ERNE MADRE
MACAO NIBS ERIC STANDIT
TRAIL ESTE OATY INA
ANCIENTEGYPTIANCARVINGS
NEO SOSO ALDS EMEER
DOTTIER OLDE ANTI NOVEM
ACERS ABIE ABRIN INANE
MEDIEVALEUROPEANARRASES
ANON ICER POE AEGEAN
NER ACT SPOT TOAST ESSE
RHO ANIM SMOTE
TWENTYFIRSTCENTURYABODE
REDYE GNASH SALLE SAMAR
ORDER OFTEA STEEL EDITS
PEATY DOEST YORTY SETAE
```

138

```
UTURN MIXER SCALD ASSET
NIPPY ANILE PANAY MILNE
CRIME OFPASSINGINTEREST
LION TUREEN HEARD ENSETE
ELAS LIE HILLY SAD PAD
SERPENS PEINE OHM MIRE
ASMARA LIPSERVICE CAN
MESNE PILOTS ACTI ARGOT
LEAD CREEK LIBRA
IHS STUFFEDSHIRT DEEDS
MAT CARES RHEES PAW AIM
PIO REAR PEENS FARE UNA
ARC ELL COALS CAROL TEN
INKLE GOLDFISHBOWL YES
RESIN URALS COLD
STATE HATE MOUSEY PASTA
NED LYINGINBED BATHER
SADR BAS ALCAN HECTARE
ELB TAN BASLE POD AMMA
ATOSSA GASPE PHARES RIC
MENTALINSTITUTION OZONO
ENDOR CUTUP PARLE DECAD
WASPS ISERE SHEAR ANKLE
```

139

```
GALORE   SCARAB   BRAZIL
OVERACT  ORMOLU   EUGENE
SINATRA  COMPEL   ADAPTS
SAT CURLICUE  WINE    HAS
IRISH  LIEUT  MANY   DYKE
PYLE  WATTS  DARK   LOREN
    APATHY  MURK   FEZ
OCARINAS  CATS   FACETS
CHICKEN  PARCHMENT   RAM
TITHES  HATCHLING  DEMI
EMEER  WATCHBAND   LAMPS
TESS  RANCHHAND   BAUBLE
SRI  NORTHWARD   MINGLER
ASHERY  ICY  WORN  FINCHERY
  ICY   PORE   FORGET
QUIRK  CARD  MORTE  ERGS
URGE  HARK  BIRCH  CREEP
OSO  BABA  VENGEFUL  VEE
TUREEN  PRAGUE  UTILIZE
ELOPED  EASIER  LEVELED
SATINY  TWENTY  SEVERS
```

140

```
ESTATE  EMBER  RIDE  TAMPA
GIMLET  MOIRE  ONUS  AREAN
GRASSHOPPERS  BLOODYMARY
SEN  SELLER  ETRES  UGANDA
   LEOS  ITHOT  SNED
ADO  TROY  ISTRY  CONTACTS
SORTIES  ANOLE  PLEA  LAT
SOARED  COFFEETEAOR  SEBI
ANNAS  OHROT  USSS  STALL
YEGG  ARAT  PRS  CLARET
SSE  OLDFASHIONED  AIRWAY
  BALLOF  TOWNE  ADITYA
ALLUDE  SCREWDRIVERS  TES
ROONEY  LAD  NINO  MESH
ASSER  HEAP  STUDY  HARTE
BESS  MOONSHINERS  SURFER
IRO  BURN  ASONE  CHILLER
ASMILDAS  PLEBS  RIOT  AMY
  GADS  HIVES  TIER
ASSIZE  RENEW  EAGLES  WED
BUTTERMILK  HOTCHOCOLATE
AMOUR  ALLE  AWAIT  ODDSON
SPARS  PLOD  TESTS  DARINS
```

141

```
ISLET  ETHOS  SCS  NOME
IMPUTE  NHANG  HAM  ICER
TRITON  CIRCS  RSO  NERA
SEVEN-THREE  FIAT  ELIS
   STOATS  ELEVEN+ONE
ATTU  WINE  OSAKA  OTTO
CHARLOTTE  ASPS  ETH
CONGO  NOSES  EMERGES
  EIGHT+SIX  RRS  EACH
SKI  TOOHOT  NES  PERLE
PON  ENGINE  PILATE  EAR
RACER  GEE  ANATID  STE
ALAI  REF  FIVEXZERO
TANGLED  CIVET  OVERT
HAT  ELLE  EASTSIDER
TATS  ANILS  ENOW  DESI
SIX÷TWELVE  UNTROD
LEIF  IRAE  SIXTY÷EIGHT
OSLO  SIR  HONOR  OFPOOR
TULU  PEG  INANE  NOISES
SPAR  SSE  MELEE  EELER
```

142

```
CATT  SCANT  RESTED  PARIS
ULAR  PALER  ERMINE  ABODE
ILLUMINATI  FLAMETHROWER
CUCKOLDS  ALLES  OAKLEAF
APS  ULL  IDEE  HETUP  ILLS
  FREEON  ACE  MARIS
INCANDESCENTLAMPS  ALLAN
POOLS  NIAS  DEY  CREASE
ARRA  ADS  CORES  SARDINES
STU  BUS  HOMER  PITY  STAT
SESTOS  POLIS  KENT  STE
SCINTILLATIONCOUNTERS
  ANN  TIER  SPOON  EARNED
SATS  BEES  STEWS  MAR  FEY
SPIELERS  POSSE  SOT  LION
TOOLED  LIL  TRIO  RESUE
SENSA  THENORTHERNLIGHTS
  DORIS  NER  ASSETS
ACTO  LASSO  CULL  HAH  ELS
CLOCHES  VIREO  FINESPUN
TAKEASHINETO  FLINTSTONE
URIAL  ELATES  TELEO  EDGE
PEONS  SENAMS  SEERS  PEER
```

143

```
STARK  EASTWARDS  HASPS
HEMEN  URIAHHEEP  ONEUP
ANISE  LAGNIAPPE  UTICA
HENIE  OCHER  ARA  SONAR
STOPLIGHTS  AVERSENESS
   SKINS  KNESSET
PARODIZE  CUIRS  ROSTRA
ISAROSE  CHATS  AFLOWER
THRAWS  CHELA  UNDECENT
STERN  FLORA  AMNOT  LEI
CAGE  FLORILEGIUM  AVGS
ABA  SLOYD  UREAL  CLEAT
LUSCIOUS  SMIRK  FLOODS
ELEANOR  NOPES  TRAINEE
SASSER  SORUS  BEESNEST
   QUITTER  HEARS
GALLUPPOLL  TENCENTERS
OMAHA  ERA  BRAZA  OWLET
ROMAN  CATHEADED  TIOGA
ARESO  AGEOFGOLD  EXPAL
SEDAN  CERTAINLY  STELE
```

144

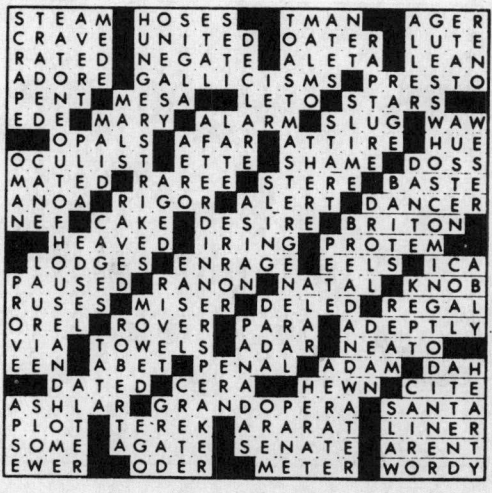

```
STEAM  HOSES  TMAN  AGER
CRAVE  UNITED  OATER  LUTE
RATED  NEGATE  ALETA  LEAN
ADORE  GALLICISMS  PRESTO
PENT  MESA  LETO  STARS
EDE  MARY  ALARM  SLUG  WAW
OPALS  AFAR  ATTIRE  HUE
OCULIST  ETTE  SHAME  DOSS
MATED  RAREE  STERE  BASTE
ANOA  RIGOR  ALERT  DANCER
NEF  CAKE  DESIRE  BRITON
  HEAVED  IRING  PROTEM
LODGES  ENRAGE  EELS  ICA
PAUSED  RANON  NATAL  KNOB
RUSES  MISER  DELED  REGAL
OREL  ROVER  PARA  ADEPTLY
VIA  TOWELS  ADAR  NEATO
EEN  ABET  PENAL  ADAM  DAH
  DATED  CERA  HEWN  CITE
ASHLAR  GRANDPOPA  SANTA
PLOT  TEREK  ARARAT  LINER
SOME  AGATE  SENATE  ARENT
EWER  ODER  METER  WORDY
```

145

```
N A S H E   S C U F F   T R E N D
B O N T O N   H O R A L   H O T T E A
T I S N O W T H E V E R Y W I T C H I N G
A M T   R E R O B E   R A C E S   F O O
C I R C   S A B A N A   I L K S   R I D E
I N U R E   I B N   B O G L E   S E E I T
T I M E O F N I G H T W H E N C H U R C H
E S O   T S E   L T D   Y E N
R E S P I R E   L P S   F R E I G H T
E L A   N A T U R A L   A I L   T O R A H
C I L I   Y A R D S Y A W N A N   N I L E
A H E M S   I D S   E L A S T I C   E L I
P U M P K I N   A R I   S C O F F E R
A A F   A P R   M O W   H C L
D H E L L I T S E L F B R E A T H E S O U
R O V E D   A S T O R   I A M   E A T U P
A R E S   A N I S   O D E L E T   S I R E
F A N   A G A S P   I N T R O S   R O N
T C O N T A G I O N T O T H I S W O R L D
E U R O P E   O U I D A   N E A R E D
T A P E R   K N E E L   D E T E R
```

146

```
T A R T S   L O S E S   B L A S T   S U M B A
A M O R E   A B A N K   W I N C H   O N E U P
R E L I C   S I X C Y L I N D E R E N G I N E
O N E A C A T   E A S E   N E P E R   A N T S
N O T I P   S A N S   S T A L A G
J O N G   O M E R   I D E A   E D E N   C A P
E M E U   P A R A L L E L B A R S   T S A N A
S A U L T   R I D E   R E N T S   D I P P E R
U N S A I D   L O T I   N E E   S A C H E M S
S I E R R A S   N U R E   R A N T S   E L I E
B A S A L   P A T H   S A O   A R I A S
M A D I S O N S Q U A R E G A R D E N
A T O N E   S L O   I D L E   S T E N O
S H O D   P E L T S   E A D S   S T A F F E D
C A R A F E S   A P C   S E L F   S T I L L E
O N A G E R   S T E A R   E I R E   E N A M I
T E G E L   I C E C R E A M C O N E   F R A S
S S E   L A N I   S O T S   E N G R   L E N T
P A S C A L   M I S S   D O N A U
E S T E   A L T O S   N E A T   R E V E R S E
T H R E E P O I N T L A N D I N G   A N I O N
R E E V E   S C E A T   T H R O E   S C O R N
E A M E S   E A R N S   S E E D S   T E T E S
```

147

```
A B A T I S       F L E A   C L O D S
L A B O R E R   S L E D S   A S H E N
D R A W K C A B G N I K O O L   R U M B A
E D S   S T I R R E R S   C A M E   Y A R
N O E L   L I E A T   S I M P   M A R L
S T R I K E B A C K   F L A S H B A C K S
D O M I N O   R O I L   A T H
B A T   B I R D   T O U P   M O H A I R S
I N A W O R D   F A L L S H O R T   N E T
B I K E L S   C A L L S B A C K   E G G S
M E L D   W A L K S B A C K   B A B U
B A S K   P U L L S B A C K   R E S A L E
A T A   H A R K S B A C K   D U S T C A P
H O B O I S M   B A C K   D E R E   K R I
A A R   L A C K   M A R A T S
B A C K T O B A C K   C A M E L S B A C K
A R K S   T U R K   C O R A L   W E R E
C B S   B E R G   G O O D S I D E   R E E
K E E N E   R E G N A N I K C A B K O O L
O L A N D   S E A T S   T R O U B L E
F A T E S   S E T S   I N N E E D
```

148

```
B A R E F O O T   A S H I P   C A M P U S E S
O V E R R I D E   S H A R I   A M O U N T T O
D E G R A D E S   T E P E E   B E R T L A H R
A R I E S   S T R I P   D E A R E   A N E T
O D E T S   H O K E   P A L I R   C D R S
B R N   R H O D E S   N A I R   C E D E S
R O A D   E L A M   D I S P L E A S E   F A D
E G L I   M A R E   O N C E   A S P S   A V E
S E L F B O R N   E N G I R D S   E S P I A L
T R Y F O R   S P L A T   A T I C   A R L O
E D E R   A E T O   S M O L T   I T O N
E V E R Y T H I N G I S F U N N Y A S L O N G
D E M E   H O W D Y   O R S E   A B E L
I N A N   I S A R   M E A D S   L E A F E D
L E N T A N   N O T S E E N   T H E S S A L Y
E E C   A G S T   H O B O   A Y A H   S I L L
S R I   A S H A M E D O F   S L U E   E R I A
P I L A U   A R A D   A S I T I S   T E N
C H A C   M N E M E   Y O R E   E S T A R
H A T I   A P S E S   E D I T S   O S A G E
A N I C O N I C   T O L D O   O B T R U D E S
F O O L L I K E   H O S E S   C O H E R E N T
F I N E S S E S   E N E R O   O N E S I D E D
```

149

```
E F F   S C O R N   P O K E D   A L A I N
C L U E   H A C H E   E N O L A   N A U S E T
H I L T   E S T A R   A T O M Y   D U B L I N
E X C E R P T   P O R C   D O T   T R U A N T
A I R   A H A B   L U E G O   O T H E R
P R A I S E W E S I N G Y O U N O E L N O E L
M U R A N O   T O P   T A T A   G R I
P I C A R D Y   T R O O P E R   E N L A R G E
E T A G E S   M O A   D O V E R   G A M E O F
K A L E   W Y O   J A W   A C E   E X I S T
E L I   C H E R   A V I D   H A M L I N
S O F T L Y T O T H E L I T T L E S T A B L E
H A T I N H   C L E O   T R A Y   L A C
T R A S H   I R A   S U N   O V I   A U N T
S H E N S I   C I N C H   T A R   D O D E C A
O R G I A S T   V I R A G O S   T U T O R E D
R U E   J A P E   O L A   T U R N I P
E M M A N U E L S H A L L C O M E T O T H E E
N O B L E   A T R E E   T A O S   I L L
D O R E M I   B O N   E N D S   S T E N C I L
A N I M A L   I S S E I   U H H U H   E C C E
D I V I D E   A L O N G   L O I R E   R U I N
T E A S E   N O M E N   A D E E M   O P T
```

150

```
H O O P   C O W E D   J O S H   L A B E L
A B L E   A R A R A   U E L E   A B O D E
W I D E A N D F A R   D R Y A N D H I G H
S E R R A T E D   N A Y   P I L O S E
E A S E R   B E G A T   E M E R
S T A G E R   A L L E N A N D B U R N S
W A D E   S E A S E D G E   P E A C E
A R Y   S T O R K   P E E P S   D R I P
P T A   T H R O E   D U N D E E   C O E
U N D O E R S   D A N D Y A N D F I N E
D A R T E   E N C   C H A O S
C A R R Y A N D C A S H   C H O R I S T
L E O   S T E E L E   F L I R T   U R I
A T U B   K O R D A   L O E S S   S U N
M A G O O   M E N S W E A R   H A C K
S H O V E L A N D P I C K   S T O N E S
T E T E   T W I N K   C O U L D
K I L R O Y   H N D   H A R R I E R S
S O D A A N D R Y E   G O W N A N D C A P
E R E C T   E I N E   O N A I R   A H M E
T O S E E   N O E L   D E N S E   Y O S T
```

151

152

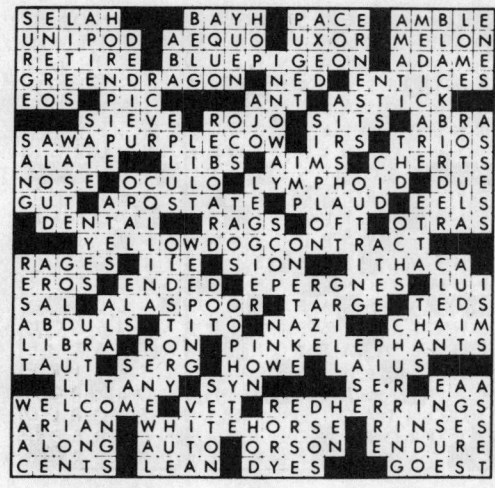

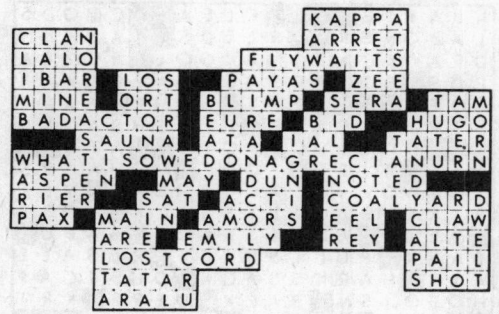

153

154

155

156

157

```
POILU   MAR   MEAD     ASS
ERROR  ICED  ABLY  PAREE
SEEMS  DIVISIBLEBYFOUR
   BIFID  SUDSY  ELISSA
AGEAND     OPE     GORES
FEBRUARYTWENTYNINE
FOLDS  EARNS  RUINS  THE
IDIO   SKI    AGT    RON
XES  THOUSANDWARSOFOLD
  SHORT  FOOLS  ABELES
WELOST  DUTYS  AVIDLY
MORALE  SERIO  ECOTS
CENTENNIALNUMBERS  SMA
MIS    ODD    ART   OPEN
IST  CADET  MARIA  SLATE
LUNISOLARCALENDARS
FRANZ    ARC    TISKET
BAABAA  KEITH  ABAFT
INTERCALARYYEAR  TYROS
SCOLD  MUSE  SORE  ELIDE
SYN    AXED   NEW  REBEC
```

158

```
MALAY  SPLIT  STAFF  STEMS
AMOLE  PRADO  MYLAI  ORLON
RANGA  ROVES  UPTON  HELIO
IHEARDOFASEAGOINGROVERW
ENNUI   TEX    SEA   ISAY
HAM   ATTU  DIANA   RTD
AHEMS  ENE  OREY  MAI  OSF
HOSAILEDFROMMANHATTANTO
STAGGER  INK   ONACLEAR
INAN  TEACARTS  THAMIN
ARO  OSIS  ABORTS  TONE
DOVERHELEFTNEWYEARSEVEW
DUEL  SABLES  DRAW  EDS
STRIES  NOONTIME  TMEN
GETSLOST  CAD  REREDOS
ITHAFLASKUPHISSLEEVEAND
NOE  IFI  OMOO  TEE  ERICA
NED   SPRIG  LAHR   LEK
APOS  GGS   SOI   TAUNT
GOTTHEREALITTLEHUNGOVER
ARTIE  ADIOS  HAVEN  ARALU
ITOLD  CAROM  AVERT  IAMBS
NASTY  ENEMY  MARYS  OLPAE
```

159

```
RATRACE  DEBARS  SWIRLER
TREECATS  ELAINE  PETIOLE
DISTANCE  LENDSA  ELANCED
STACKEDDECK   SHELLGAME
PIET  OCTROI  ADS   PLOY
TIMEARE  STOOPBALL  LISLE
ACE  NERA  ARLENE  IRAN
MOLT  DAT  BALL  REMISSLY
ENDALL  TALL  OLOGIST  EAR
PAYSAGE   CUTLETS   SPA
ASTIR  ORA  MASHIE  OUTSET
CLANGED  TWOPART  VAMOOSE
RINSES  LEAVES  ICE  PARES
ADA   CLOGGED   SCHISTS
LEN  SHOALED  PESO  PYTHON
SANTAANA  UNAN  LGE  SELA
GIRD  SAPOTA  ORCA   REV
MALAR  EASTONITE  ATTABOY
IMIN  RDM  INANES  NATO
SANDWEDGE   MARKEDCARDS
ANTOECI  INSITU  SPLITUPS
IDENTIC  DARNEL  PRENARES
MARGATE  OTIOSE  ESSENCE
```

160

```
PLEDGE   SOFTS    SWARMS
LINEAL  SPIRITS  EOLIAN
UNCAGE  LILIPUT  TRIPLE
MEAN  PLEASE  CAVIL  PIA
BUS  SHAWL  NECKANDNECK
SPECIALS  EDDOES  LADES
ARNO   SNIDE   TWIT
RELET  TERNAR  ENATIC
DELLS  CANONS  OLDENEMY
ECUS  MISTLE  DRAGSTRIP
SOS  MORTALENEMIES  MTR
EVIDENCES  DOTERS  BEAU
REVENGED  CIDERS  WORTS
TRENTE  BISONS  MORSE
TART   AVAST   MIMI
APPAL  RECIFE  SAGACITY
SOULBROTHER  SPURN  COO
SUR  LITHE  IBERIA  HEWN
ALAMOS  ALGERIA  TOOBAD
MENACE  NOONING  ENRAGE
STACKS   RIDGE   DANGER
```

161

```
LACED  ALES  RAADS  REARCH
ITALIANATE  ASLAP  ORCURE
MYFUNNYVALENTINE  DEEDER
BATLET  OWEN  REDDOG  TOPE
OLA  SOI  ANTHONY  REGULUS
SENVANCEHARTKE  SCRIMPS
ETITE  AGE  ALIST   HCL
GGS  OILCUPS  ILONA  AVUS
CROPS  CELL  FLAT  NOSALT
LIVETH  DEARHEART  DROLES
APERIES  FREED  METHANE
TER  LAST  TAO  DEAR  NRA
NOTREAD  OTROS  TRIATIC
IDONOT  BRETHARTE  TANIST
SERINS  OINS  BALK  NONES
ADJT  OARED  ALSTONS  IONA
RIO  AFTER  CRU  REWON
CHARCOT  JIMMYVALENTINE
MANDREL  BUSYBEE  TEA  DUA
ATLE  LEPONT  ONNO  PSALMS
DIONNE  SWEETSTOTHESWEET
ENVIER  STIRS  ASTORIAORE
AGENCY  TONNE  SESS  SYNOD
```

162

```
SEANCE  ELOPES  DEJAVUS
ELOGES  MENACE  OPULENT
ATROPA  MATRON  COGENER
BOT  EUGES  ALECKS   TVA
ARIZ  ATEAM  XII  SWEET
GOCARTS  PNS  ANAPURNA
PERP   PRETE   GIRR
BRAVA  TRISECT  MESMER
SEATON  RELISTED  ETYMA
ALTAIC  ASIA  ORES  SSES
NAA  REBUTS  SPRITE  TRP
ESTA  SUMO  LOLA  ALLEGE
SCATS  BERGERAC  TOURED
TOTTER  NERVOSE  IDLED
UNUM   SEISM   JOEL
HYPNOSES  ETE  ANAEMIA
OILER  TAR  ASANA  DORS
UPA  AFLOAT  MALTA  ROT
SPISULA  SPIRIT  OCTANE
EIDOLON  EROICA  SCALER
SESTETS  SANDAL  SABERS
```

163

```
CASTE  ACRO   OPPOSE  OPAL
AFOOT  SAAR   HEADER  DARIC
MICRO  ANNEBOWLING  ALINE
ARCING TELL   TESS  ALMOND
SEEN  OBOE  ACE  TENNISSEE
ROLLERS  THRU  INS  ETS
PEA  EFTS  CHESSAPEAKE
OCTAVOS  PREC  ALEC  SELLS
SHERIF CLERK  NOTES  REAL
HOST  MEAOW  EMCEE  APIECE
SPEEDY  PRIES  SNEERED
SEC  AXLE  HOSES  MOTE  SSS
CLASSIS  JELLS  COLONY
RUSTIC  CURIO  FLOOD  APSE
IDEE  OCHRE  VALOR  OILIER
PEDAL  RIOT  AMID  AMOUNTS
DAVYCRICKET  FEIN  GAT
ATT  REP  COIR  TORNADO
BRIDGETTE  VAI  EROO  EPOS
RATHER  RIVE  GUNS  SITOUT
ALTOS  POKERHONTAS  RENTE
MEETS  APOGEE  DELE  ANGER
ERIE  DENARY  ODER  STORE
```

164

```
LAMB  STEALA  MOTOS  SPA
ALOE  TINSEL  AIRLETTER
ROTA  ARCHAE  BLUECHIPS
SHORTSALES  ESS  APSE
ARMY  DONEGAL  TERRAIN
PARSES  LIL  ENE  SSE
IGOROT  ELGIN  EDNAS
BOOKLET  AUBURN  USABLE
MOLE  ROSSI  ADMISSION
THELITTLEGUY  ISTRA
ASK  ISALWAYSWRONG  SEM
CHILL  STOREKEEPING
MADEASTIR  EERIE  REMO
ENSURE  EDWARD  ACCEPTS
CITER  RUSSE  ELAINE
SOH  TUX  NAB  ASSETS
PROTYPE  EYESORE  ACTH
ASTO  CHI  WALLSTREET
HOTISSUES  PAROLE  AMMO
INITIATES  PLEBES  SEAM
SSP  STELE  SEDERS  HSTS
```

165

```
ENARE  SPOKE  OPTED  MEAL
XENIA  TABOO  PROVE  SALTY
PETITJURORS  IOWEAFARMER
ODES  OASES  MACES  OTIOSE
WIRES  MITER  ORRA
APPOINTS  DONEE  SKUA  BOP
PROMPTS  AIDESDECAMP  ONE
PEWEES  BLEED  WAYS  FUSE
EMEND  TILTS  STEPS  CANAL
AIRS  ARNO  HARE  MOTTLE
LES  BREDWINNERS  DELAYED
TRAIN  RITES  IRISH
STRAYED  FIGHTINGMEN  USS
PRUNES  DADE  ILES  ANET
RAGED  TENOR  DOSES  ALTAR
EDGE  MARE  SEISE  AMOEBA
EEL  LAMBSGAMBLE  SNEERED
SSE  ESPY  OMITS  FINESSES
AGHA  GNATS  RADAR
ADONAI  FLESH  BETEL  UNAU
BESTCELLARS  COMICSTRIPS
ALLAY  AERIE  ANIMA  AGGIE
SLOE  GAELS  TATAR  LEHAR
```

166

```
HAIL  DOUR  SLUR  MELD
DORSIGRADE  TAKENOTEOF
DRUMSOUTOF  SOUSAPHONE
ANN  TAMS  LINE  PIT
YEAS  DUETS  BREDA  RAZE
DROP  PERE  ROLE  BORE
ATONIC  DIABASE  LEADTO
DOUGLAS  GRACE  CORNETS
DAN  ERAS  OST  CAIN  SIT
ADD  DOMINOS  MONTE  SSE
MLLEMODISTE
AFF  ABELE  BESTARS  RSI
ROI  RATS  POA  ATIE  UEL
CUDGELS  LEERS  ANDANTE
ORDEAL  MISSENT  GRISTS
ILLS  TANK  SEAS  ADAH
ANES  HANDY  TEMIN  AGED
CHA  RITA  IDEE  ATA
TAWNYEAGLE  SCALEARMOR
SNAREDRUMS  ELMERSTUNE
DYAS  SANS  RIIS  TETE
```

167

```
TASS  FITS  BRONC  GURUS
MUFTI  OGEE  RIDEA  ALANT
AFRAMEHOME  ADOWN  BASSOS
STOGIES  PDBS  TALON  TNT
HEAL  DOMES  TOPER  CREE
LEARN  BARON  LAWES  TRUST
ANIS  LUKAN  BARNS  BRIC
SDR  EAN  ELIDES  GRANTEE
ODALIKS  YOGIS  DROPOUTS
FOLKROCK  NOD  REAMS  RUT
DES  ARN  TAKESTO  REDE
HAMES  GRIEG  SAPPA  CEDES
IRUN  COPSOUT  SUI  ARD
GIL  PATES  LIB  BAILOUTS
HOTPANTS  CANAL  UPTIGHT
STILLTO  HAGGAI  AUX  IRA
VEES  BANES  GRASS  MNOP
SMEAR  BORER  CHOWS  MOKPO
WORT  SARDS  PATON  PART
ALS  ATHOL  SYST  SOUTANE
NEISSE  DIARY  HAPPENINGS
STATE  INLOC  OGPU  ASKOS
TYROL  NEATH  WELD  SESS
```

168

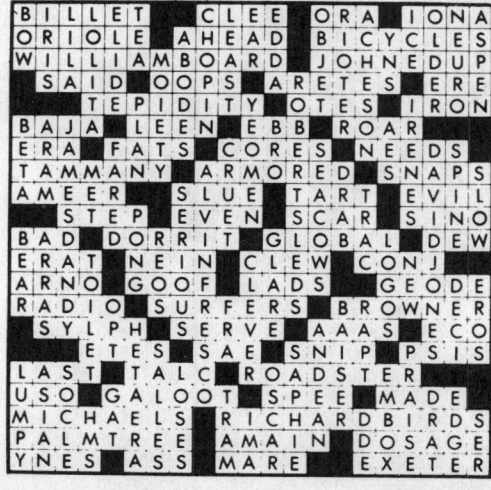

```
BILLET  CLEE  ORA  IONA
ORIOLE  AHEAD  BICYCLES
WILLIAMBOARD  JOHNEDUP
SAID  OOPS  ARETES  ERE
TEPIDITY  OTES  IRON
BAJA  LEEN  EBB  ROAR
ERA  FATS  CORES  NEEDS
TAMMANY  ARMORED  SNAPS
AMEER  SLUE  TART  EVIL
STEP  EVEN  SCAR  SINO
BAD  DORRIT  GLOBAL  DEW
ERAT  NEIN  CLEW  CONJ
ARNO  GOOF  LADS  GEODE
RADIO  SURFERS  BROWNER
SYLPH  SERVE  AAAS  ECO
ETES  SAE  SNIP  PSIS
LAST  TALC  ROADSTER
USO  GALOOT  SPEE  MADE
MICHAELS  RICHARDBIRDS
PALMTREE  AMAIN  DOSAGE
YNES  ASS  MARE  EXETER
```

169

```
EROTIC  STRAP  QED  SCRAPE
RIVERA  AROMA  UNI  PLATER
GRANTS  MONEYBACK  TOTTER
SELF  TOED  STARLET  SEALE
OPEN  SHIR  SHOE  RED
STARE  CADE  ELEM  EURE
HINTS  ILES  ISLANDS  EGGS
RATIO  TIMPANO  TOUT  ENYO
ERIE  MYMY  ACU  REEK  ORD
WASSAIL  TROT  IMPRESSED
SMA  AHOM  BLAA  RHINE
THETHINGGENERALLYRAISED
RAVER  DOOM  TINY  MIL
AGITATION  RACK  EVADERS
IGN  MASS  EXE  CONE  ETAT
LACE  ITEM  MARKOUT  EDUCE
SIER  LAYOPEN  ADIM  RUDER
ALEX  REDD  TASU  ICERS
MET  IDES  SIBS  SPAT
ICONS  SALTARA  PETS  IPSO
TONITE  COLLECTOR  AROUND
ELIDES  RUE  ACORN  LONGED
RECENT  ADS  KOOKS  MISSES
```

170

```
DORMS  SPCA  RICH  8BALL
EXEAT  ILLS  AGHA  OLLIE
BIGLEAGUES  FLATFOOTED
ADA  VIN  AIRFORCE  SODA
RENTED  INSO  OTHERS
INSENSATE  BUOYED
MIMES  SCENICS  CLIMATE
ATI  FAHR  REMAIN  RAN
GOLFCLUB  SAUCERS  IDLY
OFELIA  YAUP  UTAHANS
OFSIN  WISEACRES  GOTAT
TREPANS  SHER  EROICA
SCOT  RICOTTA  MONARCHS
PAN  JETHRO  CANDY  KIT
USELESS  TREFOIL  ESPY
RESEAU  PARODYING
INMOST  TENS  DOGDOM
SHOT  ENTHUSES  SIR  ONE
HOTRODDERS  FATHOMLESS
EATIN  IVES  OGRE  AIRES
AROMA  TEER  READ  LUSTY
```

171

```
THEREIS  ACROBAT  SPRAGS
HEROISM  CHORINE  ELEGANT
ATEINTO  TITANIA  PATERAE
TAP  EIRE  LANES  CANE  MPS
WEST  CELLI  TENURE  SEPT
ARIOT  PLEASU  SOBAT  UNIE
SANGER  ASSERT  RETREATER
APER  STEERS  BEER  SRS
PASTORATES  1000  DEEM
LITERATOR  ENURED  SCARFS
AROD  THS  FALTERED  TEEUP
TWO  ZEES  ATOLL  NESS  CLE
EAGLE  RELIEVES  ACE  TILE
DYEING  DORRIT  TRANSITED
PINT  WEIN  PHYLACTERY
RAM  TOHO  REGALE  STAB
ABASHMENT  STREAK  EDITED
MARE  OLDER  HANINB  STERE
ALGA  LAICAL  TRIES  SLIP
DOR  BOTT  TEASE  TINE  AGO
ANAGOGE  STATION  NATIVOS
NEVERIS  REVENUE  GRADINE
SETSAT  ARENOSE  BELOVED
```

172

```
ALE  SOD  SPLAT  MASCOTS
DEVOTEE  ALATE  ALLURES
INEVERMETAMAN  STABILE
TONER  TENET  SONS
RESCUE  TESTCASE
ABBE  TWINCITIES  OSTE
MARXBROS  ONEND  SAUTES
STEPPES  NDAK  CENTRA
SWOOP  STIRS  HANSOMS
ESE  LARA  PARE  LIT
ACRE  STRANGERS  AONE
IHS  CHAD  OENO  ENG
DAYROOM  ACCTS  HAGIO
PEOPLE  LEES  SIRECHO
CLAYEY  AURAE  SUPPLANT
PISA  AGIANTSTEP  SLOT
ANTLIONS  LADYOF
BRAG  STEEN  LORIS
DEFLATE  CARDINALPOINT
STOUTER  ALONG  BLEDDRY
CAREERS  DINAH  ADS  SEX
```

173

```
WAVED  PAWNS  TALUS  HABIT
ANEMO  ISYOURHEART  ELUDE
STREW  THEHEARTISA  ATLAS
MRBUNCHE  THO  ALLRIGHT
YES  HAY  STY  BSJ  KUT  EOS
TER  RAW  WOO  CHI
BEMOAN  AMOK  CECH  ESOPUS
AVOTRE  JOHN  EEKS  RIDESA
SINATRA  SEEMSTO  INDITER
SAILEAST  ALLAH  SNEEZING
INEED  HEARTBREAKS  SETTO
AMNT  ATRI
LAVAL  MANSHEARTIS  HAITI
EPICEDES  BEAST  MTVERNON
WELLFED  HEATERS  SEASAND
ISLETS  SEAR  LOIS  TRINGA
STEAMS  MATT  ESNE  ETNEAN
RYE  ARI  EEL  ROE
ANA  HRS  TNT  WSW  TAF  ASP
COMPETED  ROI  TANGIBLY
AMARA  TOHEARTTALK  OCCUR
RAZOR  GOESMYHEART  LEDGE
IDEST  ORLOP  AMASS  DRESS
```

174

```
AKINGS  SPECTRA  TALE
NATILLA  HUNCHES  HALOS
ELATION  ENAMELS  OLENT
SILENTS  DIM  WAN  MERGE
FORTHEHOLIDAYS  ENTER
LOGY  OYS  MOT
HEADHOME  HST  SENSORS
UPROOTS  WHO  OCTET  DOT
GONUMB  SHEM  GARTH  DUO
OSAGE  POEME  OBESE  SEW
HOMEFROMTHEWARS
ALB  FETTE  AHORN  ALDAS
ROE  TREAT  KIMS  SNOOPY
CPL  HARSH  ENE  PAGODAS
HEAVENS  EAR  HOMEPORT
IBO  EHS  DEUS
ARMOR  INAPRIVATEHOME
PAULA  CIR  AVE  ELEVONS
INDIV  ISTAKEN  RICARDO
SEINE  ELITIST  NATTIER
HENS  RESISTS  SOENDA
```

175

```
ARCS MUTE SCALP CLOSETO
DIATRIBES LOGIA LANKIER
JANUARIUS EMEER AUDITED
ULT MEET FEBRUARYDAPHNE
STOLA TOMATO LEES ESA
TONI SYNODS PULPY BERYL
NAP ITE SUPER SLY
MEGMARCH APRILINPARIS
SINUATE SATEEN MAYBERRY
INCITES JUNE LANES RAE
PTOSIS GIANT SONAR CEST
UTS DROVE STUDS DAG
OURS ARENA FACTS MATURE
FLA EPEES JULY GENTLER
AUGUSTAN EELERS EMULATE
SEPTEMBERELM OCTOBERS
DER RASPY SAO REC
LOCOS FISTS DEPUTY AMER
AZO ALEE FRESNO BRAVO
NOVEMBERMETEOR TUNA DEO
ANEMONE EDITS DECEMBERS
DERIDER NINES DRAMATIST
OSTLERS TEASY ESNE UNOS
```

176

```
THEME SABINE URSA
THAMAR OPUSONE SOOT
THEFULL NOCTURNESINB
SAUTS KRA HONORER GAS
ANNS LOOTS SYR LSTS
RAF CANTATRICE TEMSE
ITALIA RENA SAGY
PINELOG PASADO PREMED
EMITS PATER SKIPROPE
RASE NACHTMUSIK TEN
UGHS LOGE NILE THRO
SIE ANAMERICAN REGT
ANDERSON MANON MARNE
LESSEE SEEMLY UNACTED
YSER PEPO SPIREA
CAMEL STRAVINSKY UPA
AMPS CSU EMOTE AGAS
RAH SPINOZA PBA LEHRS
MOLTOALLEGRO GHOSTED
ANYA MIDDIES ESTIME
NYET TESTEE STARE
```

177

```
GHOST DISC GAFF TOTAL
REVOIR PONTI ABEL ADAME
ANEDGE RUDYVALLEE MAKES
DINAHSHORE SAY EYELESS
YES TEA OKS ACADIA
TENTS MAIM STEW SNAG
TWOONTHEAISLE ELD SKOAL
ROBES WASH USMA SISTRA
ORES DREAD SPRINTED IHS
YMA FEARSOME ONTAP VOUS
SHARED EADS AIX PANSY
SEMICIRCULARCANAL
SMOTE CEN ECOL BAREST
TALI MALAN EPIBOLIC TAN
ANY HELICOID BABEL SERE
TIMBER BARN JANE SHIRT
ALPES DAS THEBEYOFTUNIS
LAIC BITT ETTA SKEET
CHROME HMS RIA EBB
REPAIRE POP OLMANRIVER
ICONS THEHOLYSEE TAVOLA
CHOCK ERGO AILED STAKED
HOLES RHOS ENOS ENEMY
```

178

```
BBS GAL RESHOWS CHEAP
REALITE ATTACHE HELGA
ATTABOY VAUGHAN ANDES
MAIDEN AET ETTA PENT
BRAID OWN GARDENPARTY
LATE COSTAR ONAIR
EYES ISM ORO ECLATANT
DIN ANNAMESE PISAN
SCLAFF NIAGARA DOESNT
TRAYS RILLE SWEETSUE
YAR PAS OTB MTS
CABOCHON CLAMS USETO
SKIERS NESHOBA CLOSET
SENTA SLOWOVEN REB
PRETTILY IRE WOO SUVA
EOLIA RASCAL INAS
STIRREDWELL AND PSALM
PENH SHOD ANT DOTIME
UNDAM OMICRON JANEDOE
NOILS MACHONE PRERENT
KRAFT ENTICES SES DTS
```

179

```
HEADWAITERS BAGATELLE
ADRIATICSEA ULULATION
DOTTHEISANDCROSSTHETS
ASSAI UTHANT AIDA
SNAGS SERE PERO
BAD ELLER SIDLES PUSS
OVERSTATES DUETS INCA
TELO ECOLE SPATE AGAL
CRIB RENIGS VINTNERS
HAVOC ESNES ESCA TEE
GETTHESHOWONTHEROAD
BER SENT SELAH ALTYN
ADAMSALE DETECT LACO
SONE DIETS ARDOR IBAR
SUCR ISTHE ROOSEVELTS
ITER ETHANS NOTAE ESE
IERS TAUT ROTAS
TANG OCTROI LUCCA
OBSERVETHEFORMALITIES
RAISESTHE ENCASSEROLE
CRESTWOOD RESTAURANTS
```

180

```
AGUA ASTRA CULP HASSLE
IRONCURTAIN ALAE IMPAIR
GREATLEAPFORWARD RIALTO
BASSET KEENED DEMES MTS
OST ITER NOD SOD SOL
ISME ASTRICTS BONED
WILDCATBANKS SOAS ENCRE
OBELUS ANDI SCALERS HOL
RAVED XYZAFFAIR RETRACT
SRI SAMOA TURPS YAMASKA
ESS BANCA RELET DACE
LIANE RANEE RAINY
COCT TARGA SPADE VOL
EBONITE SOUCI RIODE IDO
ARMENIA TWEEDRING RADIO
GAM ESTHERS 1000 RIDEUP
RIOTS CERO FOURFREEDOMS
ENNIS RESONATE OSSA
TSE MOD TOT ALII SHE
PRE COWLE DOABLE DRAPER
SUNTAN ERAOFGOODFEELING
ISSUED SINS ROUGHRIDERS
STERNE SKYE ATSEA NOSY
```

181

```
GROUTS ASFAT REACT CUSP
AUNTIE BOUGH ALTAI ARIA
THEROCKETSREDGLARE RUNS
ERSE ROTOS FIE BRIDGET
CHER PRIX PRISM UDO
ORTHAT SCOUR FUAD ADAIR
SEETHEWHITESOFTHEIREYES
SAL SHIV TOYS DIN
ATEF IRE LIZ AIRY VAST
AGAINSTTHINEOWNBLUESKY
IRAK ADD IASI PREEN
FAEROE MISERLY FACADE
OGDEN COOL POE BONO
WHENYOUAREREADYGRIDLEY
LALO URFE ANN ORA OVAL
USS OVID DISH ELA
DWIGHTDAVIDEISENHOWERII
ROCHE EXEC NOELS SIFTER
AME BOWER SCUT BETA
BALLARD JOE BIDED TAPA
BNAI ARMYANDNAVYFOREVER
LINE LOOEY ACCRA FUSION
ENDS SPOTS YOKED FRESNO
```

182

```
RAPIDS MADCAP LABELS
OPENSUP OTELLO ILOVEA
TORTONI DENIAL SAYING
ESTES CHESS LITIGATE
SEHR BOISTEROUS ENOS
AVERTS ASTOLAT
ASMARA MOBILE ALSTON
TABLOID ORONO COLGATE
ATO SASHAYS MISSILES
NEY CEREALS DID TRESS
BOS DISCARD PAL
ALTAR AGR ONESTAR BAS
FOURSOME PUNSTER OIL
IDREAMT ARTES ASTRIDE
TIFFIN PRISSY LEASED
ORIOLES FLENSE
PESO BEAMISHBOY HILT
ANATOLIA STAIR INDIA
MUMBLE DALLAS DEMEANS
BROODS EXPERT SLASHES
YESYES DESTRY MYSORE
```

183

```
AMICI AHS SHEA PROP KHA
SONOF LEI MAUSOLEUM HUG
LOLLS TAX ANNAPOLIS UNE
AREO REVE GONEY EFTS
PETSTORES PIMAN POILU
SOLEN MANY COLLAPSE
MATURED BELG ORELSE YES
OBIS BEDOG FOR SPRAT
PILO PHOTOMA LIEGE HAL
SELF HALICARNASSUS AMAT
REINED DOM TSARINA
CASHED SEPTEMBER ERODED
ASTORIA OWN LEANAS
SHAD ARTEMISTEMPLE LISP
ATE SMOTE OUTEATS INCA
AMUSE MAL FLARY GRAN
TEE TOMATO BAGS ISTHERE
ADOPTION AARE AMOOT
FOULS BOMBE SNOWWHITE
SIZE SOPPY EDGE ONES
EDE THOUSHALT IRE HULAS
PEU SEVENIRON ZEN OSAKA
TAS PEAR ROND EWE NEWSY
```

184

```
MAJA TSADE LOSES EJBY
ARAB APPAL ASIDE PERO
INCS BOOBYPRIZES IRAN
MAKEGOOD AGEE TASKED
ANION ODDER SEROW
BASTES RUER AUTODAFE
EBSEN DUNCECAPS WETAR
YORE TOSCA ARRAS SETS
ORI DONKEYENGINE REE
UNGUARDS SOUL CAB
LITI RATES PURE
OSU ROBO AIRMEDAL
STD GOOSEPIMPLES OLE
LAUD ARTEL NOPES SPIN
ACMES FOOLSGOLD PHENO
TOBACCOS HONE CRISES
BRAHE SPOTS ALEPH
AGENDA SEAR GLASSEEL
DALE SIMPLESIMON BETE
ELLS ELITE ORANG OTRA
NESS RETIA CANES YSER
```

185

```
ONEPM IKE SAIL SAE HST
RESUE ITEM ANNA ALABAMA
YOUTHSCOMPANION DECRIES
NOAH BLED STNICHOLAS
CHARM PLOT PIECES MERE
SLAMS PREY METRO RID
CAUSERIES BYRON DAN
AMS UPS CAROLE COLETTE
TUSSORE FAVOR WHIPSOUT
SPECTATORS NAISMITH EMU
AIL RIT TRAINS GRID
DAMNS HADES EATNO HORDE
ILES MULATO TEG TUT
ABE BALLYHOO EVERYBODYS
LETMESAY TITLE ALSORAN
SESAMES ASHLEY ORE EWE
GAR LOSEL AMERICANA
GAS ULNAR ALIE TODAD
OFOZ KILROY GIFT BLAST
VANITYFAIR KAMA FOOL
AKENIAL GODEYSLADYSBOOK
TERENCE HUIR AFAR EISEN
EDS EKE TSAR TAR SNORT
```

186

```
DADA ALS CORP PACKS
APOS SOAP AWAIT CROAK
HIGHHORSE PICTURETUBE
LAS HOTTEST ETRE SNOW
TFR ALDA RENE TBS
ORAL SEEMS DEFACE
LYRIC GROUPS REWARMS
DESERTS SABRAS REDSEA
RURAL MILES TRIAL
TWI MOTO INLAID EGGS
HAR BORNYESTERDAY NEE
OTIS PAGANS ELLA SRS
MUSIC PUCCI DEARS
ASHRAF SHROUD SIDEBAR
SIBERIA TENSED STUMP
REARMS SUTES ALIM
MAO EIEI ARNE DEL
ARGS OCAT PLATANO STA
ROUNDNUMBER CUBANHEEL
SMEAR SEALE TREY AYES
HASPS DDAY SEE NEMO
```

187

```
EDGAR  MASON  HARDUP  HAT
SORRY  ADARE  AROUSE  ABSI
CRIMEANDDETECTIONNOVELS
EMPS  DIALS  SKILS  FELON
SSE  FOAMY  TIES  HAMMETT
PARCS  ETHER  OGEE
MARIN  OSEE  MANEATERS
MARYROBERTSRINEHART  LAW
ELKE  ELLES  MONON  LIMA
COIR  STIES  ITSY  QUEASY
URE  JETS  ATUA  UND
MYSTERYANDSUSPENSETALES
EER  AROS  OLEO  EXT
ELLERY  EMEU  GETIN  EPHA
NOON  BREST  BEBOP  BAAL
OCT  SIRARTHURCONANDOYLE
WHODUNITS  NIKE  ABASE
RIEN  TABOO  DEPOT
CREASEY  PARA  ORCAS  EDS
HALTS  TAXES  AGIRL  OMIT
MYSTERYWRITERSOFAMERICA
SOIE  TEEVEE  GIRTS  BALKY
NED  SNEADS  TASSE  BLESS
```

188

```
TEMPI  SMARTS  CODA
LAGOON  TESTAE  AMEND
PILGRIMFATHERS  PENTUP
INLET  EERIE  GALEN  IRE
ENID  IDLES  BEMAS  CHIT
TES  ALIOS  SETON  PRIOR
ATHENIAN  BASSI  FRESNO
ATAS  SOLE  DRIEST
SCARED  SPRITS  INSTARS
TALES  SPORE  CANES  MAE
ARID  SPOKENWORDS  BIRL
GEM  SPITE  TORTS  PANEL
ETERNAL  SHINNY  RENEES
NEATLY  EATS  EAST
SUTURE  EARNS  ASTOUNDS
ERASE  TAPES  APSES  OOP
DATE  FORTS  PRIED  STAR
ANI  PAYNE  PAGAN  KNABE
NIOBIC  IRRECONCILABLE
ANISE  NACRES  ENABLE
STAT  GLAIRY  SENSE
```

189

```
FTS  BABEL  MIA  SCRAM
PASTA  ARENA  ASTIR  ORALE
ALARM  LURID  AMATI  ROBIN
ISRAELINEGYPT  LAFRICANA
DESIRE  AMOY  CELLO  STET
TIAS  AFACE  IES
HAP  CHAC  SLAPDASH  IMBE
ERICA  RANUP  REIN  AGREED
ALCAN  GRENADE  PIS  REDAN
RETRIM  NATIVES  NAPE  INA
TNS  NEVIL  NINE  ALIA  ASS
PROVED  ASLANT
ALI  ALLA  ATIP  AGING  IMA
DUN  REEL  DAVINCI  YAWNED
ACTII  SOT  TENURES  TONTO
PRENSA  FRET  ENERO  EWERS
TERN  DIVIDERS  SILO  ROE
OSE  IDIOT  LOFT
STUB  RINSE  MFRS  AKIMBO
FINLANDIA  HAROLDINITALY
OTTER  ACRES  OVOID  ELSIE
RHINE  EERIE  METRE  VESTS
ZELDA  ANS  ESSES  SEE
```

190

```
TASS  ESAS  PORE  YES
ANEAR  AMULE  ABEL  ATL
INTRO  GIPPER  SIPS  ROY
LOSANGELESRAMS  LEND
HARDER  PIETA  ESNE
HASSLE  BOB  DRAY  SPOT
UTE  DAYTONA  ESK  TARA
BEAR  TROWEL  ESPOSAS
TASSEL  TEAMSTERS
JOSEPH  MISMATER  ILE
EWE  HALFTIMESHOWS  NOR
TLC  AKIHITOS  AIRGUN
ORSENATOR  HURRAY
GENOESE  ENURED  ENDS
EDDY  UBA  MANNISH  AID
ANSA  OPES  DEC  HERMES
NATL  ISNOW  HEGIRA
REAL  GREENBAYPACKER
AMI  LEDA  DECAMP  LOOSE
DON  ORAL  RACES  DOLTS
DOG  PSIS  OAKS  NAST
```

191

```
SANA  ACTED  MIAMI  CHIEF
TMAN  ELAINE  ALCAN  ZENDA
PITY  JAMESFARLEYGRANGER
ASK  PETE  CALX  PEAR  OME
THINICE  ROME  GLORY  STAR
NEXT  ANNEX  LIL  CPA
FOGGY  BOSC  ABASE  HAUSAS
ARCS  SON  ERNEST  CALCULI
TIO  CARET  ODES  PARMESAN
SOLARIA  WOMEN  JOLLY  AME
ONETON  DOWER  DORSE  SNOW
PICT  ORLOPDECK  SNOB
ATOP  JANUS  OHBOY  LEMANS
LAR  DAMON  SPOTS  SARANAC
INTERMIT  PEEL  ELEMI  TIA
ATELIER  SOAPED  ORB  CHAR
SERIES  PALMA  APSE  WOODY
DSO  ENA  USNOT  DAMN
ESTE  TUTOR  LOVE  SAROYAN
QUO  AINU  MVII  THIN  EGO
UPTONSINCLAIRLEWIS  ODER
ERATO  TIDES  ELLERY  NENG
SALON  SARIS  EELER  ANTE
```

192

```
FRETS  ACLASS  NECTAR
AUTHOR  REHATCH  ONRUSH
SCHEME  ARISTAE  ADOBES
THELASTPICTURESHOW
SERA  OHS  OWNERS  FERAL
SURE  SHE  WET  EDO
LASTSTRAW  OSIS  SHABAN
SNOWS  AURAL  SPACETIME
TIRO  THETERMINALMAN
SMERSH  AREO  TIPI
ANDTOE  KEATS  MENTOR
OONA  URAL  DEHAIR
KRAPPSLASTTAPE  ESAU
HEARTLESS  HEMAN  FLING
BERTHA  OTIC  SHOELASTS
ANE  ESP  MAH  UNAS
RERUM  INCITE  IGN  THAI
PULLOUTALLTHESTOPS
TSETSE  TRALEES  APICAL
PATOIS  ESTONIA  DEMURE
STANCE  SIEGES  WESTS
```

193

```
LAPAZ  CRAPES  ABBE   SECT
INAWE  REPORT  REAP   PIXIE
COLLEGECHEER  INTIMIDATE
IDES  AWAIT  OASES  YELLED
TED  AMENS  SPRIT  ARMETS
    SPELT  LAPIN  ELIAS
DEFEATS  HIREDGUNMAN  WHO
APIECE  SOLID  PIED  THAW
TERRE  PANTS  CLANS  HAILE
TESS  LOBO  RUNS  CENTER
OST  RESERVEFUND  GAITERS
  QUIVER  EDEMA  SORROW
BOUNCER  CELEBRITIES  AMP
EVADER  FARE  RUNT  ASEA
BIKES  PANSY  THONG  OCHER
ONER  PANE  ARENT  SURETE
PER  EATGREEDILY  MATISSE
    APSES  MADAM  BOLED
DAVITS  APRIL  DEBAR  JAB
AURORE  AMISS  BEDIM  HAVE
SPECULATOR  ONEPOLICEMAN
TINES  DORE  NOTONE  OBESE
ANAT  OPTS  STATES  BESTS
```

194

```
WABASH  VIOLATE  KNOTTS
ADAGIO  ACROBAT  NOSHOW
TELEPHONEBOOTH  EPHEBE
ELKE  OFDAY  DANGLE  BLL
RIA  FAG  REMINT  PEAT
ENNA  DELETE  ICA  HULME
DESPAIRS  ACT  STROLLER
    ELMS  STOAS  SAYSO
ACADIA  SKIRRET  STAFFS
RUR  AGATE  DRAWUP  TALE
ALTER  WILLPOWER  BETEL
DEEM  LENTIL  ARETE  REL
OTSEGO  TENABLE  HABITS
  IRANI  ROYAL  CARL
COAGMENT  SEB  PANDORAS
OLNEY  SOM  REMOVE  CARP
NEWS  DEBARS  ALE  IRE
FIE  AYEAYE  ASOLA  CLAN
UNLACE  CHURCHILLDOWNS
TELLER  CANALES  SAVAGE
ESSAYS  OPENEST  OBEYER
```

195

```
SCARF    LST  RESAT   BROS
ALBEE  ABACO  EXTRA  BREVI
CONVERSATIONPIECE  LEGIT
HUES  OSTE  OLLAS  BANANA
STR  METE  TOED  TATTLER
  HEMSANDHAWS   BOSH
READE   ROI   OISE   MTS
MULTILINGUAL  CALLORWIRE
INLET  FAUNS  PARLE  SANER
NNE  LISTS  FARE  KLIEG
OER  TAHA  LIEN  GRID
TRYTOTALKYOURWAYOUTOFIT
OWED  NAME   OUSE   RNA
CONTE  ERIS  CAUSE  EAT
ANEAR  SPLAT  MOLLS  SCAPA
PILLOWTALK  DOUBLETALKER
ELL  FIAT  RIP  EXIST
  BLLS  ORALSURGEON
CHARADE  PRAG  SEAT  GAP
AEROBE  SINCE  ESTH  POLO
SATIE  SPEAKEROFTHEHOUSE
TRILL  SECTE  SOUSA  ARGOT
ADES  SWEET  VOL  STEPS
```

196

```
BREWS  HOST  IRAE    OAF
BASIE  ALOE  NOCK  SACCO
CHANT  EDWARDTHEEIGHTH
DEUCE  SAUCE  STORES
PRISMS  ESC  TINED
RENOUNCEDTHETHRONE
USURP  HAE  REAPS  LPS
DIRS  IRBMS  ITT  ILE
ENE  NINETEENTHIRTYSIX
  AGOOD  SPEE  EYELET
STRAWS  STS  BIRLED
SARCIA  BOOT  ARGOL
THEHOUSEOFCOMMONS  DDS
LIS  ETO  TRAMS  GEOL
OBS  CANAL  LAC  BELLE
FORTHEWOMANHELOVED
PAEDO  IDA  DURESS
WALLIS  ARNES  ASONG
ACTOFABDICATION  DEFOE
STONY  RETE  ERNE  EVERT
PSS  ONES  REED  RIDGE
```

197

```
ABATIS  ASP  LIFAR  ACLE
CLEANED  LOA  ANITO  OPHIR
CORPSDEBALI  VERATSARINA
TWOSTEPPE  SEALS  ATT  LES
TARTS  BALLETPTOMAINE
AGLETS  LANK  GATEMEN
BLARE  SPIRO  DAIS  PANAMA
BOYS  BWANA  KIND  RELINES
ABS  CLANG  MINT  TARS  IRK
SOYBEAN  ELIDE  THIS  MTGS
SLOANE  ROND  KEEN  WIRE
PASDEDEUX  MELODRAMA
OHRE  LORD  SERE  AORIST
ANIS  FAGS  SHARP  NONSTOP
TID  COKE  FIAT  HACKS  ETA
TOESHOE  DANG  BOXES  ANAL
UNSEAT  SALE  HONES  LISLE
EMBALMS  CODE  RAREST
SLIPPINGBEAUTY  CRUEL
AIN  ITO  ONERS  PAINTINGS
BARPOSITION  PILLOWAFIRE
ONEON  NOSTO  OVI  MARTLET
TAME  TWEEN  TEE  YESSES
```

198

```
CASTOR   PROP   ADOBE
PONTINE  CREME  REMAND
ENGAGED  REBEL  AVERTED
EDEN  SINECURE  MINERVA
VOL  HIDEOUT  MIL  FAIT
ERODED  ENT  APIS  DANSE
  FAME    ARAL  SOCCER
RIMMED  APOSTLESCREED
ODEON  PLEASE  TOAD
BERN  ALATE  SCOTT  MEG
LACET  LOCH  STAR  ITALO
ELY  EMOTE  SOUSE  AKIN
  TRAM  ATONED  CRETE
SPECIALAGENTS  PATTER
SEATED  ATOM  ARAH
ARRET  FLAG  PAW  SERENE
UVEA  MIA  TALENTS  GEM
CANTEEN  DEARDEAR  DRAB
ENTENTE  ANISE  SATIATE
TATTER  INNER  AMENDED
LEERY  LATE  LINGER
```

199

```
CACHE FOAM CAPP VISITS
ETHAN ELDORADOS ONESHOE
IWANDEREDLONELYASACLOUD
LORD BROSES LICK TEMPI
GLEBE SWISHERS ALT
EPEES TENSION ENCASES
GOODQUEENS REASONWITH
OAF ARRESTS PEAT REAPS
THUR REUTER FRAN
THON TIEPINS SIRS DSO
GEESE OSMO SERA READYTO
ALLEVIATION DISCOMPOSED
GLIDERS THEO FERN FOWLS
GIG NETS ARTEMUS UNES
LEHR ULSTER ALES
ESTOP ACER SALAAMS SOY
BLUETHROAT ANTISELENE
CORETTA HEARTED VIXEN
IMI STILLEST MEANT
NAGAS DEER SAILOR EASE
CHAUCERSCANTERBURYTALES
HADNONE OVERAGAIN AGENT
SETTEE NESS ARKS GESTE
```

200

```
SPASM AWASH ODETS
SHARPY MARIA RISEUP
PISCES BLEAR MOSELLE
PINTHETAILONTHEDONKEY
ANG DICTA ARE IVE
RULES CAIRO TRS GREET
APERCU NOONDAY FRESNO
GURU NOHIT DIOR
CAROLINAS OXTAILSOUPS
ACE LADD RIODE SUPRA
REBA HOUNDSTOOTH TSIN
IRENA INURE BAAL ENT
BACKFINCRAB SERVIETTE
LING SMART YELP
SUPERS PEACOAL STEPPE
AMIDE FLS KORAN SEALS
LIN TEE TRIAD RAT
TAKETHEBULLBYTHEHORNS
SKIRRED SOIES ACACIA
SEDATE APEEK NOSTER
SAMAR KERRY TYPOS
```

201

```
FLIP RHUMB RADAR TACT
OONA IONIA ELEVE ECHO
GRANDFORKS HOMEPLATES
GOTHA VRAI EPOS APARS
AUREA NRA STENO
AGANDER USETO ANITRAS
TARDES ANTLERS CEDARY
QUILT CAL IRATE ROWAN
UNDE SALINE SARA MELO
ETERNAL KOFF DISHEDUP
SILVERPLATTER
CUPOFTEA DIOR RESPECT
ODOR ORLE TWINED OCHO
MALAN SERAC SIA STRIP
ELINOR TOPHATS TUBULE
SLOGGED OPERA MITOSIS
EGGED ERA PATTI
RABBI VIDA LOON ELATH
SPOONRIVER SAUCEREYES
VIEW ANACE ETCHU RANI
PARL MENAD ASHUR SHEA
```

202

```
SPARKS JIBBA BALM ASTRA
CANINE AROOF ABOU CERAM
AGNAIL MOUNT NARD CROCE
BEING SINGH ECCE DROPIN
THREESHEETSINTHEWIND
RAH TOW TUNC HOT CES
OGEE MEASURE FLOATIN
BOLSTERSUP QUILTINGBEE
BROKE SIP REUNED GARBS
EATINA ASSUME SEEM NERO
DESMOND LIP FASCIA DOP
ONCEUPONAMATTRESS
LAC SONNET TAI UNMORAL
ARES NEST THYMES SALADE
IGLUS ARROYO DEA RANIN
COLDCOMFORT WETBLANKET
SAMUELS ARALSEA SLUT
THI TEN AVER LVI ESO
HASSTRANGEBEDFELLOWS
EVOKES ARNS DENIS ALAMO
TABER EVAS MEATS SNORED
INANE MENU INSET STONED
CARED ESTE ASTRO TAPERS
```

203

```
FEAST HALOS SNAP
DILUTE EPOCH OUTLET
SUGARANDSPICE UNEASE
WEB ALDOSE ULAR SIKES
ANAS LOGIA PLEBS DIDO
MARTS NEARBY RAIN MUD
ISSUES ANSA LOLLIPOPS
FACERS NOA LOCI
OLDFORTS MAORIS HEMAL
MOREFUN SENDIN TECALI
LIED BAKEDALASKA ECTO
ARADAS ILLSET ORTOLAN
HEMAN CREEPS SPOOFERS
TAAR CYL RUSTIC
SWEETMEAT IDOL SLAPAT
ORL HEAL STOUTS SKATE
DOIN SMOOT GLACE ENOL
ANJAN PERE CANADA ELL
GATEAU BREADANDJELLY
SHARIF INURE TIARAS
LOAF TARTS SEXES
```

204

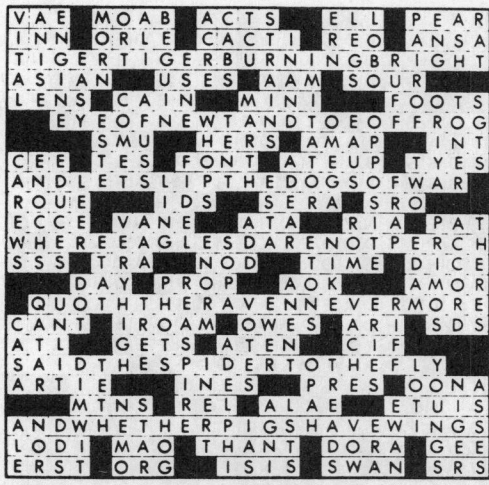

```
VAE MOAB ACTS ELL PEAR
INN ORLE CACTI REO ANSA
TIGERTIGERBURNINGBRIGHT
ASIAN USES AAM SOUR
LENS CAIN MINI FOOTS
EYEOFNEWTANDTOEOFFROG
SMU HERS AMAP INT
CEE TES FONT ATEUP TYES
ANDLETSLIPTHEDOGSOFWAR
ROUE IDS SERA SRO
ECCE VANE ATA RIA PAT
WHEREEAGLESDARENOTPERCH
SSS TRA NOD TIME DICE
DAY PROP AOK AMOR
QUOTHTHERAVENNEVERMORE
CANT IROAM OWES ARI SDS
ATL GETS ATEN CIF
SAIDTHESPIDERTOTHEFLY
ARTIE INES PRES OONA
MTNS REL ALAE ETUIS
ANDWHETHERPIGSHAVEWINGS
LODI MAO THANT DORA GEE
ERST ORG ISIS SWAN SRS
```

205

```
SARAH  DELTAS  FLOUR  BAKE
PLUTO  ELAINE  LORRE  EBER
AUGHT  BUYPARTISANS  TOES
RIA  PRADO  PREEN  TRIUNE
    PLATEN  PEARS  DYED
TWEAKED  TUNS  CULDESAC
SHORTER  BERTHPLACES  OVA
MAULED  MORES  RENTS  AWES
ALLES  BOOT  AINOS  STINT
LIDS  COOKIE  VADE  SPONGE
TAA  PERSIANLAMS  PLUNGES
    NOIRE  GAT  HAREM
SKIRLED  HEIRAPARENT  AMA
PANDAS  MORN  REPEAT  SCOT
ARDOR  MEROE  TALL  LEHAR
DAIS  TARES  GLARY  MARINE
ETA  TAILBEARERS  MATINEE
SENSIBLE  MEND  PARTNER
    ILLS  SLOES  ARRIES
SVELTE  BAIRN  LASER  EDO
COAT  LAIOFTHELAND  DAZUR
ACRE  EVENT  ALERCE  AGREE
TEND  GENES  TAXMEN  YEATS
```

206

```
HOH  CAPE  EVES  ROBE
ELA  LAURA  TITI  COMETH
REDOUBLES  ASHESTOASHE
OLDLADYINTENNISSHOES
ELL  SEAS  INE  ATL
PLANS  TORT  CASSIS
AIDS  DAN  TAP  TIS  NRA
CAVEMEN  WITHINANACEOF
ERA  EUA  RELINE  GROTTO
NYACK  ORELSE  LIMPER
LETA  EAST  TREE  ERSE
INARMS  MEETSA  ASTRO
MCGRAW  OUTRAN  RBI  FAT
BREAKINGPOINT  TAMPICO
YES  ELU  NOD  IHR  ATAN
SADDEN  LIVY  SYSTS
GAP  IDO  GENA  FOO
NOFAULTINSURANCEPLAN
COURTLYLOVE  FOREHANDS
OUSTED  ENES  OVALS  TAT
TEAS  SONS  GOYA  SKY
```

207

```
CAMP  ALUMNI  SAVE  WASP
OREL  POTION  AMEN  ECTO
MERE  SHARIF  MIND  GRIN
BARABOO  LAMA  IMAGERY
ISA  WAS  NONSTOP
COMELEADMETOTHESTABLE
EYE  STRAUSS  HEAT  PIES
LEND  COS  TOWARD  DOORS
AZTEC  STPETE  DOME  TOE
MATERA  ELD  ROUBAIX
INHEAVENLYPEACE
NURTURE  ODD  ELMTEA
ARI  TURP  DESSAU  YUCCA
VINCE  BRIARY  CST  SHAG
IAGO  ALAN  ACTEDAS  RIO
GLORYTOTHENEWBORNKING
OROTUND  OOM  IRS
STARDOM  MEMO  INPETTO
HAZY  PISA  ILLINI  SMUT
ECUA  INON  LEADUS  GABS
MORN  AGUE  DOREMI  ESAU
```

208

```
SCREW  TRAMP  ABASH  BBGUN
MAUVE  IONIA  HOCHI  ELOPE
ORBIT  TWILL  SITON  QUITS
TELLMETELLMEISITTRUENOT
EYE  OXEN  ORNE  SUET
APPR  ALFA  HEADS  AIM
HINGSLEFTOFSEVENTYTWOTI
ADAR  ODETO  EXALT  SARAN
RETARD  BUKH  ANDEAN  STLO
LAY  EER  DORM  NORHAIR
ETATS  ARIOSO  AVAILED
MESATHIEFWEOUGHTTOBANWO
MOUSEIN  KNIFER  AYEAR
IMPINGE  WHIT  APT  GLD
NORA  ODDITY  TASK  RETAKE
PLUMS  INEED  THERE  ATUA
ULDITSPOILSSOMEAWESOMEPL
TYE  APART  TIDY  TUNE
ABET  VATS  AIME  ACE
ANIFIWROTEMYCONGRESSMAN
BANAL  IDOLO  AKORI  TAINT
CRETE  CORER  SERIN  EAGER
DAZES  KRAZY  THING  PROSY
```

209

```
ECTO  SWAMI  IALS  CHE
ALARME  AHEAD  NCAA  AIR
REPAIR  GIRLS  CARVINGS
PFENNIG  LOT  PERSONTHE
STS  UNUSE  TENTERS
STANTHEPERSON  TPKS
APPLE  PIEPERSON  AUER
PEEPPEEP  ERROR  LLDS
POR  ENROL  EAN  LILL
OPS  ROSSI  LCF  CAS  PTA
SLO  SRO  NEPER  OWL  ERS
EEN  OMN  EME  ERNIE  ROS
ORNE  PER  DIPSO  SUE
HOWE  VERSE  SEAFOODS
ORAD  PERSONGER  PANES
PERT  PERSONCHESTER
ASERMON  ASOUR  WDT
BATPERSON  GAS  NASTIER
PRIEDIEU  SORTS  NOODLE
OIL  ARUT  EAGLE  SNOOTS
EAT  NESH  CLOYS  TWAS
```

210

```
GOTHA  DRAW  PLUG  SCIO
ONEUP  REUSE  CEASE  SPEND
BOTTOMOFTHEBARREL  PINTO
IRES  ALATE  RUCKS  PRETER
FILMY  CASAS  MAILER
FAT  ALEE  TONAL  UTTER
ASHAMED  MIDDLEOFTHEROAD
THERED  JANES  ULES  FIR
HOMED  AUNTS  SITUS  SPARE
ERIS  ONNO  SPRIT  SLATED
RED  ENDOFTHELINE  POSTS
DOMES  AURAS  FLOOR
GLAIR  TOPOFTHEHEAP  ADA
CRESTS  WRENS  MANY  SCOT
ROOTS  LOADS  AVERS  PITCH
OFF  TION  AFORE  POLITE
CENTEROFGRAVITY  BALLOON
ORLON  ACARE  BELL  NRS
SWEEPS  STOLE  DARES
BEHAVE  NITRO  SIRES  SHEA
ATETE  BEGINNINGOFTHEEND
BUREN  OMNES  QUINT  ARROZ
APED  BOOR  SGTS  STALE
```

211

```
PECOS ADMI PATIO ESME
EXALTATION INABSENTIA
STREAMOFCONSCIOUSNESS
ORI PELF SAHL SUETY
SACO SEEFIT OCRE IRR
NANAS RAND ROAST LUA
DETER CEDE ASTR ASP
FOURCORNERSOFTHEEARTH
DUR CROC THROE SERGEI
TSE OBOES ACID SNEDS
ASSN HAMAL SPUE
AORTE PELA SPHER IFS
GREECE RAISE LANG NAP
OLDLADYOFTHREADNEEDLE
HES NESS ORNE ODIST
OAK TREES ASIE ONICE
NEB ARCT RECTOR TAFT
AILUR URGE ADAK TRI
MATHEMATICALPRECISION
INONESHEAD NEITHERONE
ESNE CASES GRAS VINTS
```

212

```
PAGED CAAM SASH BETTE
ORATED BALLO UPTO ASHER
TAMALE RESENTMENT STENS
THESULTANOFSWAT LUTRINE
SSS SAE TIC LINEAR
MINEO AGER TYPE GOTA
THEOOMPHGIRL IRS BONER
MOURN RIAS ESTE PANDAS
INRO IDYLL ODEA MAB USO
OTO PRESLEYS SNEER SKEN
ONEEAR GATE IRA SKEDS
THEALLAMERICANBOY
PATRO LOA SNIT ERNEST
ASHE ATTIC DESPISES IWA
MME PIE GRES TINTS STAR
PARSED ALIN RIMU SKINK
ERECT CRO THEMARCHKING
RADA OLIN EAVE ELOIN
BRIDAL ARN ARP VAT
LEAFLET THEGREATPROFILE
ARRAS TREADMILLS OVIBOS
CROCE EARN ALICE RELENT
KANES REND NEMO ROSES
```

213

```
ABELE ZODIACS CEASE
NAVAL UNIFLOW OLLAVE
THEOLDFARMERSALMANAC
HEN EON YEN EDEN PLS
ERI GILD EAGER POOT
RANINTO DEARSIR LARGO
GRAY SONLESS DEPAUW
RESET PROVIDE LEGATEE
ORT WOODIN SLIME ESS
ONADIET LEE UPEND
FORECASTER FROSTDATES
LETHE PRO LESSHOT
ADO FHOLE EASTER EAD
MINARET RAINSIT JOHNS
ISSUER DRUNKEN JUDO
CHENE POETESS CODDLED
AMAT FORDO SORE ILO
LOS POLI LAE TAU DEN
POORRICHARDSALMANACK
SNOOKS SWADDLE LEYTE
STASH ESTATED BOSSY
```

214

```
FRANK PARAS APTTO ASIS
LEROI DINERO LEHAR GINO
ADAPT ENTERS IDEAS ONTO
POLITICALFOOTBALL MIGHT
CESARE HILO HENLEY
SUNDAYDRIVER SCOURGE
ALBI SLATER KEIR FRA
COACHDOG LINEUP STYMIED
AWN OOPOD LAMMAS GALBE
PEG MENTIS ESSES OCEAN
PRISES ARDEN SAHARA
STRIKESOUTONONESOWN
RINGUP KONEV BUSONI
CUBIC SLOPE BEMOAN TEN
OPENS EREMIC RABID MAU
SAGGING ARABIA ALLSTARS
ASI MOOS SNAILS IDEE
NOISOME TRIPLESPACED
MANTLE OSSE ULTIMO
ARISE JOCKEYFORPOSITION
NINE LETHE SORREL DITTO
YEGG TEHEE ENDERS ACERB
ALSO DRAWS ROADS HORAS
```

215

```
SPIED ECARTES HOTBED
SEANCE TOLUENE AVERSE
WARMUP AMMETER RECEPT
AMOY RIMMER RADAR ARE
MEL HELIO SAVIOR SKIR
PRIMADONNA GALL SUITS
ALATESTHIT LATIN
GOBLETS COOLER TONGS
APULSE MONTE OPERATIC
BERET TULIP ABASE HEL
ORNE COLDCOMFORT PERI
RAS MOLES TUFTS LOIRE
STUPIDLY SALES OILCAN
EPODE SEPTIC PUNIEST
TRADE FROSTBITES
ASHES SOFA HIRESAHALL
COED STRUTS OATER FEE
COR FLEAS HANGAR SLAV
ETOILE TIMELAG TULANE
SHADOW OVERATE ENAMEL
SEDERS REMISED DOWER
```

216

```
ANZAC POMES CUBS TOILE
GOUDA ALERT ISLAM ALTAR
ARLEN VIOLA AMARA LETNO
CAULIFLOWER CHILILOOKS
ESSE IOS TAS ARE
ADV FOURTEENCARROTS
CERATE PEPPERBACK AMAH
ASAIL SRAS ARENA ONICE
SPINACHESTNUT RDS CANOE
BED SHAD EAT CHI ARREST
AREA ORAD TESLA PLEA
HARVARDBEET TURNIPACARD
ELIS MAYBE TINA ELEE
CEDRIC MER ALB ONCE IDA
ALAMO WON GREENBEANTOWN
RIVES OUTDO REED TITAN
ODIN ARTICHOKES PELOTA
LETTUCEHAVEPEAS GER
NEA RAY SAL JAMS
CELERYCUTS LEEKYFAUCET
ABODE AGREE ELGIN SITAR
IRONS PLIES SEATO SCENA
NOTAT YOST SANER TEDDY
```

217

```
SPAR  SALOP  IMBAT  SWAM
ORNE  AMEER  NOONE  PYRE
PIKS  LONDONDOWNS  INCA
SMATTERS  VOUS  ETERNAL
AHORSE  LENTE  EVIL
DORE  SIRECHO  RETAIL
ROLES  BOMB  HULA  REUNE
ENDS  PURIST  NEIN  DRAY
ENE  CARAT  UPTAKES  ENT
LANTERNS  GREENEVALLEE
ODES  WANER  NILE
COTTENWEAVER  CHLOASMA
EKE  STOUTER  SHALL  AAR
LAMB  SORT  SATIRE  MIRE
APPLE  DUST  MOLT  BANCA
LILACS  SURREAL  URTH
ENCE  PAINE  FARRAR
REDCLAY  DINA  MARGINAL
IDOL  WARINGBLACK  AGIO
MERE  ALIKE  LACTI  GENS
ANSE  NUDER  EROSE  ELSE
```

218

```
BASRA  SARDE  BISON  CHIP
OCCUR  ASHEN  OBESE  SOANE
WHATISTHEFLOWEROFALASKA
EEL  STILTY  NERIS  NITTER
DRAT  ANAT  SCRIN  PAPIERS
OILER  LHASA  DODOS
SNARE  MAUL  HOSEN  STU
WHATARELITTLEBOYSMADEOF
HIRES  SIRE  NORE  OTTO
INRE  ESTER  LORAN  ARNIES
CTO  ESAU  ALEC  OLEA
HOWMANYPINTSAREINAQUART
AVES  SOIT  SETS  YEA
MOINES  CORDS  HITME  SEAN
ECCO  ALMA  ANOA  ENACT
WHEREISITALONGLONGWAYTO
SOS  USERS  ROEY  RAKES
AGAIN  SCION  HEINE
DEADENS  SALON  MORN  SARD
ATLONG  MACON  SOLACE  DUO
WHEREARETHESPANISHSTEPS
NIMES  ASYET  LADLE  TEPEE
SCAD  HARTE  UREYS  ANTES
```

219

```
STREW  CUFF  ACME  NASA
PHONEY  AFRO  NOEL  EVAN
ROUGEETNOIR  TUSK  WILE
ISTO  TOD  ETHERS  BYLAW
GEER  ITEMS  INTHELEAD
GISELE  HEN  AGUA
BADEN  MASCARAALGERIA
UNESCO  ARIA  PLEB  NRA
MTG  HARI  ORTHO  ROOTER
SIAM  TOSS  PIELS  OTROS
PSYCHOLOGICALMAKEUP
COPRA  KATYN  TOUR  ADAR
IDEALS  MORTS  STAD  EGO
DAR  LEVI  AURA  BAYRUM
LIPSTICKTRACES  HESSE
LOON  EIN  EXTOLL
AMOUNTSTO  ASTRO  LASS
ABOUT  ATONAL  RIM  ODIO
GLUG  EGAN  TAKEAPOWDER
RESH  METE  LIAM  HUELGA
ARES  USES  ESSE  IDEES
```

220

```
ASCREW  HAHA  ADOPT  CHID
NEROLI  FARAD  SENOR  HEMI
GLOBETROTTER  AVISO  IAMA
EMS  CHON  COMPACTMIRROR
LASH  DIDUP  POI  EBO  FBI
UBISUPRA  ANNEXED  RIS
WETTEST  SELL  ENC  ACOLT
VEE  APE  SIGNOFTHETIMES
ALLSTAR  TUBSOF  ADEN
EAST  BAMA  SATANS  ETRE
ANGLIC  AMEBA  ENG  RAG
HARKTHEHERALDANGELSSING
ONA  XIS  COINS  ALIBIS
TAMP  SPATES  GRIT  YALU
IGOR  REPASS  NOBONES
MORSETELEGRAPH  EBB  ETO
AREAR  SIR  NEON  TSETSES
RAS  ENSLAVE  SWATTERS
ITO  NOT  INO  STAIR  EVEN
MONITORLIZARD  LEVI  INA
BRAN  SAIDA  TRACKRECORDS
AINT  EIDER  HAPPY  ROTGUT
SOTO  SNOOD  OTTO  SNOOPY
```

221

```
FOES  CAPET  CRABS  SCAT
RUSH  AGORA  REBEC  OHIO
ISSO  BASESTEALER  YELP
ETERNITY  SEAMY  ERASES
DENTINE  PEAT  MAESTRI
DESTE  WALKEDHOME  POD
TOT  OPS  AIRS  ERNE
SAVON  AMA  WAIVE  PRO
CLIP  DRAWPASSES  ROTES
RAS  MIEN  LITER  RODENT
ARIZONA  LUTES  REBECCA
PITONS  SANER  AIDE  TOG
SCORE  WETGROUNDS  FORE
RAY  ARIES  NNE  DORES
MASH  PSIS  OIE  RAW
AND  COACHESBOX  ALLAH
LAUGHIN  VEIN  STABLES
AGGIES  APARS  SOCIABLE
BOOB  INSIDEPITCH  WEED
AGUE  NOIRE  ODILE  LINE
RETS  GRAND  SERET  STAR
```

222

```
VBYV  SPARTA  SAMOA  RAMAS
ARUI  AENEAS  WHELP  ELOPE
MARI  BAGELS  EATER  ATSEA
PETITIVS  LIFEBEGINSATXL
BINET  IGOR  LEO
CHANEY  ETNA  HOC  ENOCHS
SHALES  ETHEL  EROS  EPHAH
COULD  STAID  CRONE  READA
OILS  CHAIM  JOB  DIX  RPM
TRS  BOAST  MUM  MARL  AQUA
ARUM  IITIMED  INFULL
CAESARSALAD  CATOIXTAILS
ALLOTS  SUNDIAL  SEHR
BAER  EAUX  ELL  STERS  TAP
ABC  DEN  ONE  SLURS  HOPE
RATER  ODETS  REINE  TEXAS
EMOTE  NEXT  MECCA  ARTIST
TAROTS  REO  ISLE  SCIENT
ICH  ATTU  ETHER
SAILTHEVIISEAS  XIIDOZEN
TRIAL  WARNS  TITTLE  DOPE
AMINE  ELIDE  EVERTS  OLIN
BEDES  RESET  DEMAST  XACE
```

223

```
VAMPS   OPAL   TLS    BARON
INURE   SARA   IOLE   AGAVE
MANIA   ALUM   PROS   SERIF
KINGSGAMBITDECLINED
    COPER   ATOP   HINT
COMEDY   ASSERTED   SHEP
AMISS   SEPTA   ORA   OTO
SONS   MELEE   EVATT   TRUK
HOG   PARERS   LOP   ABRADE
   CORAM   RES   FLEECED
QUEENCITYOFTHELAKES
CURATES   HAM   AVERS
RAISER   LEW   DURESS   YAM
IRAE   SEEKS   AVERT   KANE
ETH   MVI   BRASS   TILED
ROSS   SPINDLES   CANUTE
   PAAR   GOAD   SPANG
PRINCEOFTHEAPOSTLES
JOINT   SKIT   VIOL   AERIE
ALTAI   SASH   IDOL   RANTS
MEALS   SHE   LENS   AREAS
```

224

```
CAT   ODOR   RAPS   UNIT
MEAGRE   RULE   OSRIC   PONE
ASSAULTANDBATTERY   PAGED
POT   EDEN   EAGLES   DOE   ETO
SPENDER   ASTA   REB   CRISES
   CURRENTEVENTS   AVOTRE
SCRAP   ADD   DEN   ARLON
ALEA   MIG   DUE   EALING
WEI   GENERATIONGAP   TAURO
ONION   AMON   DOUR   ANNES
   ENDS   PARK   NOT   DES
CHARGEOFTHELIGHTBRIGADE
LAR   DDE   ELEA   EIRE
OMEGA   ALAN   SOAK   LATER
DENIM   POWERSTRUGGLE   ZIP
SAPPHO   LOO   YES   TRES
   PEEPS   TSP   ARO   MIAMI
CAMERA   SHOCKABSORBER
HEARST   HAS   ALES   GENERAL
ERG   ASE   VISTAS   MINT   AZO
MANON   THEELECTRICCIRCUS
TEND   HENRI   EONS   HOTELS
ETES   ASST   SWAT   NED
```

225

```
ACME   FLAT   MARC   GALA
CHOMP   RENO   ALIA   EATEN
HAVEALITTLETALK   SLANT
ERI   SEAT   ENTREE   TILDE
TEASER   BRIE   PAOLO
   MAR   GOAD   FRANCESCA
AGOG   LEST   SIENA   OSAR
SPOKETOTHEWINDS   FLO
CAW   REA   HEEL   SHOOIN
ACIDTEST   MARRY   TEAR
RETURNS   BARRY   HALFWAY
HEED   PASTA   COLDSORE
STOLES   ALTO   ARA   RIA
LIU   SILENCEISGOLDEN
ANTA   TENOR   ORNE   NESS
WESTCOAST   AMIE   SEN
   ALLER   AMIC   ATTEST
BAYOU   CLOVEN   ALAI   PIT
ARION   HAVINGABIGMOUTH
TANSY   EVIL   TILE   EARLE
EDGE   RADA   OMEN   KNEE
```

226

```
STABS   CHAD   ERECT   SPHINX
PALEO   AULO   MINER   TAIPEI
ARICH   SNOW   ITISA   ARRAYS
ROCKOFAGESCLEFTFORME
SKEY   ABUSER   LAV   ADAPT
   #CLAP   IAL   ALEC   ATEO
SAW   RLS   RIMMED   GRU   bTER
AMITEb   RECEIVESA#REBUKE
LIGHTO   ODA   NINER   STUNS
UNSEEN   COMPOSER   IUSE
TOO#   ORO   ERR   BETONIT
ERNS   NOCT   ESQ   HANG   EBRO
HOEDOWN   GUA   REA   DIEM
SOHS   EARRINGS   TOGGLE
SPOOF   BETTI   EAU   ALAMAN
#ERTHANASERPENTS   bPLATE
ADUE   CAR   SEEMTO   STA   NED
SACR   EDNA   VSB   STIED
ANEST   IDS   LECTOR   EXAM
OPERATEONALARGESCALE
JUMPON   NONNY   MIII   TAXED
AFIELD   CRAZE   ARNE   ONINE
BORNEO   EMMET   NOGS   ATSEA
```

227

```
TASTE   IDLES   DWARF
SIFTER   REEVE   RIVALS
COTTONBLOSSOM   ADENOID
ALA   ATION   SKIPPER   ADO
BANE   SUMIE   ENTER   STIP
ICING   MACAW   AAR   RHINE
NECTAR   XAVIERS   DOINGS
   RUBI   LENAS   ARUNG
DATELINE   DDT   FLAGSHIP
ASHES   TED   JEREMIE   ODE
NOES   MERCHANTMAN   ITES
TUG   MINIMUM   SUN   STEAK
ELONGATE   MMS   RASCALLY
   LOESS   SIENA   COAL
GODOTS   MADRIDS   SNIPED
ARENA   LOU   SPUTS   SCENE
VANE   FITCH   SLANG   STIR
ETH   LINSEED   TIEUP   RAE
LEISURE   PROMENADEDECK
SNARER   AMEER   DECALS
DRESS   NASTY   SAKIS
```

228

```
SPOOR   LATETAPE   READER
CUENCA   IRONICAL   ELSENE
ALTERN   BUTTONSANDBOWES
ULE   AIRE   ESSE   TOLER   RTS
DIRE   SALEM   SETA   VAT
AVANT   BENSON   TRET   IMAGO
TANNERIES   VILE   STATUTES
ENDURE   ICECAP   IRELESS
   DINE   BLARED   JACKAL
ERE   SWEETANDLOWE   IBAR
LEW   BETA   ALE   ETA   COATI
STOPE   STALL   BASRA   INERT
AILED   SRO   BEN   EAST   ZEE
SAFE   JUDGEANDJORY   AES
   RECAPS   TIDEOF   NEUN
COMETIC   POLERS   OXIDES
OVERTAKE   ONER   HAPPENSTO
CENSE   SILO   ESKERS   STEAL
ORD   TSAR   ARRIS   ALME
SAW   EARED   OLEO   ASPS   LID
WILDEANDWOOLLEY   ALPENA
ERENOW   EONIMINE   HAIRED
SEDANS   REASONED   IPASS
```

229

```
LAUGHS ■ PULASKI ■ SCUBA
APPLIES ONEUPON ROPES
NOTUPTOSTANDARD ONTAP
ALOT UPAT DIRER STOKE
ILO SPUMONE TAIT WEN
ONSHIP ORCAN UPENDS
ETON FBS ONS REC
URSAE CRO ARS INARUSH
PEERS HOLDUP GOTUPTO
AMAT CINDERS GOVS RAS
NORS RND REM ORE SORT
DRS IOUS ELEANOR LATE
USINGUP LINNET TORUS
PENULTS PIA IRS RAIPS
BOO SEC UPS TANO
UNISON ACTED MISSUS
PUN SARA VISIONS SPA
STURM DANTE TALK SNAP
ERROR UPPERSANDLOWERS
TIEUP LEISTER SENUSSI
SADES TSETSES RAMSES
```

230

```
SET TOLE ERRANT MACAW
OLIVEOYL LEOPARD ARENAS
FELIXFRANKFURTER SANDRA
AMENT ALOHAS SMEES ORRS
SIDES GOIT BATES EEK
ASSORT SOLDO HAWN
ROGERBACON JONES CRUMB
INITIATED SOBER AUFEU
SCRANTON APHID THUG LRG
EEL SENDALONG SEEK OLGA
NED POOH EWERS POET
ACMES CHARLESLAMB MUNRO
SLAW SOARS RAMI COS
TART HURT ORSONBEAN CII
OUT MOPE SWISS WARINESS
DYLAN SHINY BAGATELLE
ELATE STING GENEFOWLER
PIPE LIANG CESARE
SEQ SHILL CUTE SAURA
APUS OPALS HELENE ELVER
SPOKEN GIACOMOMEYERBEER
HERETO ENDURES BOBVEALE
RIDER GERENT OTOE LST
```

231

```
ABACA BAFF BLURB
ATABAL ETUI SAILERS
FACELIFTINGS KNEEHOLE
ILK FARO OUTLANDS WIA
RABI SAIC FATE ABCS
ENROL SLAW ITER GREET
ENID SLEIGHS BABARS
TRAINOF MACHE DEMITS
AIK ENOS SAT RELET
UDIC TROWEL PULLTEETH
PENAL ABEL POLE ERASE
EAGLEEYED MONETS SRAS
LAVER TIS DEEM SRS
CHASED PESTS RELAPSE
THEBES CANTATA DILL
RIALS MAIL LOPE ILIAD
UNDE ANNA PAWS ATLI
FOL ACROSSTO REMO TIN
FOOTNOTE HEARTRENDING
KNOTTED ERSE ATONES
GREEN SPTS RONGS
```

232

```
DARTS ASTA CASH TWICE
BOREHAMWOOD OVERBEARING
PANDEMONIUM MOTHERGOOSE
OLE WEAL RIPEN ARG NUN
ELEMI NEON LISBON INSET
ADS THEBAN ETERNO
WHEREHASMYLITTLEDOGGONE
HAUTBOY INOIL STORES
INC EWE KANA MODISH SAP
FOLIA STAMINA WAC EBONY
FIANCE RYE DEF RELIANT
THELIONOFFLANDERS
SARANAC TVA ICI STEEPS
SADAT MOB INJECTS ARISE
ILA KEATON CART LOI EAU
LIMPID LADYS ILLWILL
KISSTILLTHECOWCOMESHOME
STEELE LANAIS ABE
PATTY ARRANT RAPT ENACT
ANA HID COSER RASH RHO
PICKANUMBER TIGERLILIES
AGNEWSPIROT TOAYOUNGASS
HANKO SAFE ERGS EDENS
```

233

```
TRAIL TEARS CLIMBS
SHORTY TRALEE HONORED
WESTERNEUROPE INSPIRE
AVE MIENS PARAPET TIN
MITT CATTY SEGAR FIAT
PETES TEEUP DAW HASTE
SWEETS DEMOS RAVISHED
SAIL SALOP YENTE
SESTINAS KOLM TERMED
EMU DECLARATION SEPIA
RIGS SEATO HERES DILL
FLAPS SMELLEDARAT RAE
SYRUPY SULI NOTELETS
AREAL PULER LULU
DANGERIS PARED PARRED
ENDED FIR CASES REINE
MESS REBEL LICIT DOFF
IMP HALIBUT DANOS TAU
SOILAGE UNITEDNATIONS
ENCAVES KALINE SALUTE
EELERS ERECT TRESS
```

234

```
WARILY BSA ADD NEP CPAS
ASADOE EIN HUE ANA AETO
INTERNALLY ELF UNDERRAN
IAN MAE WAYS GUILTILY
MOLL ETNOIR AHILL OLA
WANLY RETENT PAT LAUD
ISAY DLOS HAIFA SING
SCL AMPLY OLDYALE DECOR
POLITELY AMIES YAPS ARI
STYRENE ABEAMIS RRS LOM
NOTAGIRL CIELO LOL
WHEE ASTRAY WALLET MYMY
IOU LADOS ILLUSORY
SOP PLN FINALLY SCOOTER
EDH MYTH VEALY BLOWSILY
LOOTS LORELEI FEYLY MAD
YORE LYSOL NORS PETE
ILSE TOY EGRETS TILER
ADC ECRIT ALBEIT HOES
PRAIRIAL ROSY RAE RUS
TALMADGE ALI HELPLESSLY
LCLS EEL MEL AIL TELLER
YOYO ARY SOY SNY SAYYES
```

235

```
TRAP  KOREA  GRIPS   GAS
HEBR  INURN  RANUP  BARE
ASLOWBERNE  ANDSOTIBET
WHYDOI   RAVI   SKILLET
  INTR  TRUE    ANGELO
YANGTZEDOODLEDANDY
ALIAS  SOUR   ROME   BRA
KIEL   ITT   SIMA   PRAM
USC  IMGHANAWASH  CREDO
THEMAINE  OREN   TAIWAN
OIL    SOYAS    INS
RACINE   OSAR  BONNMOTS
INERT  WOMENSLIBYA  VAT
GONE  ENES   OKS   JOLI
ANT   AGIO  SLEE  COLOR
  AMMANFORALLSEASONS
PUTNAM   RIPS   SADE
ARROYOS  AIDA   TIPTOP
DAYTONGAME  JUAREZHELL
ALTE  ITSIN  OSCAR  OLEO
SOO   ASSET  UNITY  FEST
```

236

```
TABLE  ANGINA  OLES   SPIT
ISLES  CORNER  NOVA  ETUDE
TWENTYTWENTY  EVAPORATED
HAND  ARIES  ACRES  NORIAS
END  CREST  SNOOD  EDICTS
  DANSE   CAIRO   CZECH
DOWRIES  MISSAMERICA  GAG
AGRAND  BEDIM  TOOK  GULL
CLOGS  GALEN  SPEWS  PANDA
HENS  CATO   TARN  FARCES
ERG  NOTONERERUN  CARBONS
NEATEN  RENAL   CARSON
STUMPED  ONETWOTHREE  TDS
ARMEES  DRED  RIDS  CROP
LOBES  CROSS  WAITS  BOONE
EVER  CHAN  ARIAS  WILLET
PER  PROFOOTBALL  VALISES
  HEART  NEAPS  REIGN
STARVE  DEANS  CENSE  AMO
SPARSE  BOARD  POSIT  ABEL
COMMONCOLD  ONEHORSETOWN
ARPEN  AREA  NOSALE  LEVEE
READ  LADY  STANDS  SEEDY
```

237

```
DUAD  GETA   TALL   EARL
ESCA  ARAN  THROE  OSTEO
RECU  MARYQUEENOFSCOTS
EGRESS  ULTS   ELAPSE
GBSHAW   CASA    HOOP
LOSTHERROYALHEAD  EVES
ARIES  EON  KILLS   IDE
IGOR  GAUD   TEL  SAVIN
RAN  DOCTOR  ACNE  CRABS
  FOTHERINGHAYCASTLE
TEETH    NTA    AROSE
FIFTEENEIGHTYSEVEN
OFFER  ILLS  EELIER  ETC
SLEDS  TLO   LUNT  FLUO
SIC   ARENA  LFS  HEIDI
ESTA  FORACTSOFTREASON
LSTS    THAW   ALTARS
SOPPER   SUIT   BEDAUB
THEHEADSMANSHAND  REEL
ANSAR  DUELS  OREL  ETTA
TOTS   SEWS   CASE  DHOW
```

238

```
ASSAM  AIDAS  SOU  LAMMAS
TIARO  SENILE  TEN  ASSORT
CLIFFSOFDOVERORWITHFURY
ALL  FOO  ETANIM  IDEE  NIL
ROSEOFTEXASORPAGES  ITSO
ENID  TYNE   ESS  STUKA
SNIPE  ADAMS  PUT  NOISE
  TSAR  REPOSED  WINNER
ATHOS  MAGICORKNIGHT  BEE
TRENT  ILLS  ONES  ROSSO
TIS  ALLY  ANEW  PAT  AYES
ACUS  ILOCKSORSMITH  OSLO
RENT  RIT  ATRY  ASIE  OSU
SATIN  SKIS  ARCA  STRIP
ANE  ELEPHANTORGIN  LACES
BOTANY  BOSKAGE   SOLA
CHOPS  LAW   ROAST  TWERP
REESE  UAR  TALI   SNEE
LOBS  PEOPLEEATERORHEART
AVA  PICS  ENTRAP  RUE  TSU
BIRDOFHAPPINESSORPERIOD
ANODOF  GAP  ANTONY  DOONE
SENTRY  EGO  STENS  SINAS
```

239

```
CASHEW  ACTOR    ISMS
ALCOVE  SHOWER  ADMEN
LOOTED  SIMILE  SEATO
KNOWN  VAC  NEIGH  LOWS
SETA  HAIL  GAGE  CLOUTS
  TOUSLE   SNOWY   NOW
PIERRE  THEODICY   DNA
FERRER  CIA  FELLAHEEN
IRA  SIP  LETIT  DOZERS
BATH  CATE  CLEM   NOA
KEEPAWEATHEREYEOPEN
ALN  DRAW  ROTC   SNOB
CAREEN  IMAGO  SEA  TOE
WINDBLOWN  YAR  LIPASE
ESE  SAVAGISM  ALLUDE
INC   MATHS   REPAST
REDCAP  COOL  ONER  OAST
SOHO  THULE  ACR  ANELE
TERSE  SAMARA   BRIDES
EATER  ETUDES  ACCEPT
SPAT   ERODE   CHESTS
```

240

```
DAMON  PROBATE  ADE   CUP
AMINO  LINEMEN  LAX  COMER
LOSERSELYSEES  LITTLEBEN
ERTS  CALMS  NUDES  RIVERS
SAY  CASEY  BARON  FINALS
  SORES   LAGER   RAVEL
RAGWEED  SOBERPRUNES  GDS
AVOIDS  PETER  ABET  OREL
CIONS  GLASS  TOVES  SIENA
ENDE  HOOT   ORES  ATLAST
DEB  NEWYORKREBS  ARRETES
YEARNS  HAORI   ESCARP
SEDATES  ROBERTLTHAW  EMA
ABORTS  BONE  ATEE  CPAS
BALLY  LIBEL  ATPAR  SUPTS
ONLY  POGO  ECRUS  JAVERT
TOY  RIGHTSIDEUP  GENERIS
  PETIT  UNITE  PASTE
IRONIC  SETTO  AORTA  GAS
ECARTE  ACTII  ADIGE  TENT
CHLOESOUR  MOSBULLRUSSIA
SOLUS  UTE  ANDBLUE  BATTY
RYS   TOW  ESTATES  AREAS
```

241

```
BALI  CMS  ETCH  GRACE
OBOL  SHOT  BRAUT  DUCAT
COOKSTOUR  BARBERSITCH
AUK  TRITONS  LENE  NOTA
OBS  COMA  ORTS  RIN
ROUE  ENACT  TETRAS
ALTER  STRIP  DEALERS
MASTERS  AENEAS  SACQUE
STEPS  KERES  DAUNT
LAW  APRES  ELIDED  NINO
ERR  PRINTERSDEVIL  TEN
TRIP  OTHERS  ERROL  YRS
HITOR  SOLID  SEDAN
EVENED  RECANT  SEMITES
SORTIES  AMORT  ATRIA
SINGTO  NOAHS  RASP
ABC  RAWS  SMEE  DEC
SIRS  ERNE  REPLETE  KRA
TEACHERSPET  LADIESMAN
ARMOR  SUITE  EDEN  KANT
REPTS  PACS  SYR  INGE
```

242

```
OASIS  DREE  SORB  TINSEL
OPTOMETRIST  OREL  INTONE
SATURDAYSCHILDWORKSHARD
PLI  EARS  OATS  AWAIT  NAG
RICE  NOTURNS  TRUSS  EDGE
ENURE  RANTS  NYMPH  EASER
YESOR  OTIS  NOPES  EXGODS
SOGOES  MANED  OBAL
ROI  DETS  LAMPS  UDOMETER
ARMLETS  TAKELESSONS  EVA
TIMONS  CAKEBATTERS  INIT
ANENT  GAMEHUNTERS  GRANT
TORE  PIPEFITTERS  FRANCE
ACS  FIVESISTERS  GLANCER
TOEBONES  STORS  AEON  YDS
OUTS  PHONS  OSTEAL
CEDARS  FAIRS  ARFS  DALIS
OYERS  FERNY  CLARA  AGENT
READ  SOBIG  HOTNESS  OTTO
ISR  BARRE  SUMO  SEED  CER
NOSUBSTITUTEFORHARDWORK
TRILLS  LATE  INHALATIONS
HERESY  ELAM  TAOS  ISTLE
```

243

```
SLUER  RAHS  DADS  SISAL
LINNE  ASEA  DUEL  INTRA
AMIRS  SPAT  ESCALATORS
VELOCIPEDE  SANE  EROS
ABICYCLEBUILTFORTWO
PATENT  TENURE  TAU
ABE  DURA  RISER  TRIPS
PORK  SENSATE  MOTHBALL
AVAIL  STEP  LABIA  AGUA
WELDER  MAP  BUNK  NOSY
ROLLERCOASTER
TEAM  TAEL  TAT  RUSTIC
HERO  OBOES  REBA  MAUDE
INUNISON  PASSAGE  GRIN
SYNOD  RECIT  NEAT  NOT
PEA  AROUND  ROASTS
CABLECARSONPOWELLST
AGRA  TREE  TRAVELTIME
SHANKSMARE  ARGO  BALER
HAVEN  EDNA  KOOK  AREAR
ANEST  DYER  EYNE  RESTS
```

244

```
BASTE  IRK  AYESHA  COBBLE
ASWAN  ROE  NONOON  OBEYIS
CHIPSHOTS  SUNDAYDRIVERS
CEN  IONESCO  AIRPORT  BIE
ARGYLES  EINE  ODORS  LYON
BEAR  FLAILS  ERS  GEESE
GANGSTER  ALPERT  COMB
PACTE  URIS  SEAS  CHASING
ILKA  MANPOWER  ROAD  ROO
GAS  AHS  GABOR  DEVI  IDUN
ELA  TER  OVERDOING
SIGNALS  FERTILE  SLYNESS
PRIVILEGE  HOI  ENS
LEVY  MUIR  ABLER  AGE  APT
INE  VASE  BLUETICK  TROD
TETHERS  HAIN  ODER  FOOLS
HAIK  TOASKA  INAPIQUE
SHELL  DEW  TENACE  ARUN
TULE  GUESS  RIMU  SPEEDER
ARI  GENTLES  SYLVIAS  HRE
GREENSKEEPERS  EAGLEWOOD
EATSAT  RETENU  RIM  TILDA
SHOERS  SPARSE  SNA  STEEN
```

245

```
ORG  AGED  TABAC  FROH
SUPER  DADE  ALIDA  AIDA
OPERAHOUSE  PORER  STEW
BARENESS  OPERAMETERS
ANDE  SENTAS  LIM
MATTED  SET  RENIFORM
CLOSET  STA  OPERATIVES
CAR  SOAPOPERAS  VEST
CESS  REP  STYTHE  ERIA
UNTIL  PEU  ONA  ISR
COOPERATIVEAPARTMENTS
OFS  TAN  TEC  GASPS
SHAS  MARIEE  LAC  TOFF
MOGI  HORSEOPERA  PIL
OPERATIONS  ARE  ETHENE
SESSIONS  PSA  DHARNA
DUC  CLIENT  SISA
COOPERATION  OPENSHOP
LOLA  ASIDO  OPERAGLASS
ONES  CERES  PERI  TETES
TASS  ODORE  TARE  OSS
```

246

```
MODISH  STRIDER  NOODLES
ONATEAR  IRONORE  APRIORI
RUBSTHEWRONGWAY  WEIRDOS
OSSA  ACHED  ASE  GEESE
ION  SAGES  CHIC
DUC  HATS  LAGER  POINTSUP
APHRASE  REVERSEARMS  CNO
BRAUNS  TENOR  ANDS  ARTS
BONED  FUNDY  WAVES  STARE
LOGS  SORES  AXEL  ANIMUS
ETE  BACKWARDNESS  BOMBE
OBELI  HIE  LIBEL
AFLAT  MIXEDDOUBLES  EDS
SPHERY  EDIT  GRIDS  ADIT
ANEND  WAIST  SIGNS  CLEAR
LOAD  VINO  FIVES  WAGGLE
OER  CAPITALIZED  SAVAGES
PATENTEE  NENES  MERE  SRS
MOSS  RAVES  GAR
PACES  IGY  TUNAS  ABET
AROUSAL  GOINTHEOPPOSITE
PASTURE  IGNORES  HABITUE
ATTESTS  DEGREES  SETSIN
```

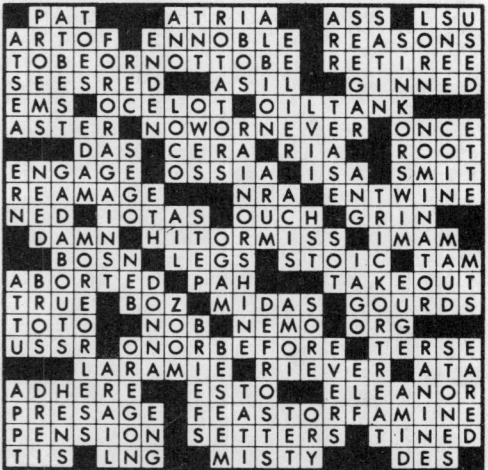
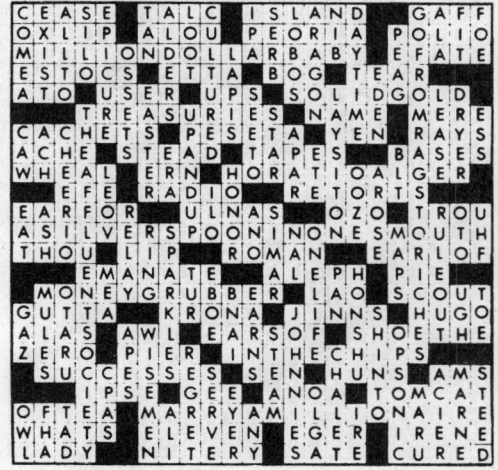

253

```
CHISELS  METHOD  THOMAS
HONOREE  AROUSE  RAREFY
ENSLAVE  JOYTOTHEWORLD
REP SET ODES  RANK RAN
ISIT ROARED FORD  LYME
STRAPS GIS  SLIP DOGEY
HYENA ROT  SPAT  HERO
  GREENY  LAG  REFORMS
SMIRCHY  BARRIERS  OAT
BOOBOO  REPTANTS  MUSE
ADULT GLADHANDS DANCE
NINE FLIPPANT  CONDOR
TUT TREETOPS  BAPTIST
UMPTEEN USP  TABLET
 LEST ARTY RMS LORDS
SCENT AGES FAB ALBERT
TOAD HEAD SOVIET ASEA
IOS TORI ACRE AHS TAG
GLADSTONEBAGS TEATIME
MENIAL SUBLET UNCOVER
ARTERY TREATY PASTERS
```

254

```
 CLEO  SUSAN   JANES
ASHIER SETARIA PILEUP
STALLS HEAVENSTOBETSY
MARY ODEA EGALITE STO
SILL ILLS   ANT  MEIN
ROI BELLADONNA  CATS
TVSETS TACIT  CHM
MOTELS RUNTS LAIQUE
AVERY  SERTA CLOSEUPS
PERE NICENELLYISM EOS
RUD OLAF  ECCE  MEN
ASS MOLLYCODDLES ANTE
DESTINED ORAGE DRAHS
ATEASE  IMAGE  SIGNET
 PTS ALISA POPGUN
ABES BLACKMARIA EEE
REED HEM  AMIL  RSVP
ERR SENORAS EMYS ILES
CATHERINEWHEEL ASTART
ATHENE DONTCRY ERECTS
PEART  SSGTS  ROSE
```

255

```
 HOD HATED SCOFF ELATH
ARARA ORATE HOURI NORIA
MONEYTOBURN EGRET DWARF
OLD TOKO EVER SETAT GET
SETTOWORK EMIT SOTOBED
 ORDER ARRIDES ALERT
RAMEAL DYE LATENT NEONS
IRONY PROVO NERO ADELIE
FEUD SUE IBOS BILL DICE
TNT GETSOVER  SEED VER
SAHARA SLAYER SEASIDERS
 BAHT ELEGANT STAR
RIDETOHOG RATION ALIGNS
OMO ARID NITPICKS OUT
YAWP SNIP DOOR TOE WERE
AGNATE SISI SABOT TASSE
LOTTO UTTERS TUN WELTER
 ONTOP SWELTER GANDO
BEATSTO SCAR GOESTOPOT
BAA ETONS TWIT RENO RPI
ERROR PIANO BRINGTOBEAR
TITLE ACTOR AERIE NASHE
ACHED REEDY LEASE ERS
```

256

```
CABOT  MOAS  HAT POILU
ADANO PANSY SORE LIRAS
DANCESONAIR DANCEPALACE
SMEE PURGE DANES INLETS
 CANOE SANDY PETE
SAD ACCORDANCE CARESSED
CLAWFEET ECCE CARR SOLO
RANEES PARISDANCES FUL
ESSES SHARON ORES TOTAL
EKED SHASI GODEY YEASTY
DAD AHOY ESCROW SEETHES
 UGLIEST AHA SOANDSO
SAVAGES ANDALL GRIS EBB
ANELES CROON OLLAS EDER
INNER AETO CAUSES CLARA
NET SUNDANCEKID RAINES
TARD NEER OLES REENACTS
SLEEPERS CALLADANCE ESE
 ROYS HALOA INCAS
ETOILE GOMER AEGIS TEAM
GANDYDANCER STREETDANCE
APEEP MAKO EMIRS AROMA
LARDS ITS  TOSS WOWED
```

257

```
 UPSET  REDIG  STOAE
NANNA SOLANO HOLDSUP
STACK POLLOI ONEDIME
OTTS ETON INNATE ALBS
GRE POROS  GLASS LOO
PASSOVER ASSOON TASS
UPTAKES OUTPUT  PAN
 KER PUTOUT ERITREA
LYES WITHIN OVERCOAT
DEE BELLOC CLEM OCTO
INRE ELLER SHINE WOOL
AVES ETAT STAVED CUL
COATOVER TEENER SCOT
TIPOVER OUTACT ONA
 PES LUNULE OVERTIP
CAST LETUPS OVERPASS
SON AHANG BAIRD KAI
OUCH ASTONE ERST JETS
UPHOLDS IODIDE AROSE
LEONINE NAILED KUDUS
 RENTS GHEES EGYPT
```

258

```
SHEA SOPH JAMMU MILKY
HARE ALOE ORION ORALE
OMER GALA LEMOT RIGEL
VAMOSAVERALNINOMANUEL
EDILES SAYA  OLGA
DACIA ASTRO ARGO RBI
 TEDDY LAGAN LADEN
ANDHEAVNANDNATURESING
MEASLY TRESTLE ANSATE
ISH SAMBA  ESTA
ETLAPAIXSOITAUXHOMMES
 LAMP NIXIE  OAT
DESIRE FLATTEN MIMOSA
EINKINDLEINISTGEBOREN
FROES HAITI AUDIT
YEW CUPS CROSS DOBBS
 DAVY PHIL PERRON
DORMIDORMIOBELBAMBINO
ELIAN SEOUL FAIN IDIO
FIFTY ANITA IDES KATZ
TOTAL ROLES NYNY ELOY
```

259

```
CASCA  MUMU   ASSIN  STYX
OSCAR  ASONG  BUTNO  POUR
RUBENS HOURI  ISLAM  ALMA
ISOLDE    LUV   YOHO  DDAY
FILLINGINTHE SQUARES
ENDED  OVO  HEI   ITEM  UKE
       CARTRIDGES   PAPER
OF  EBAN  RAMONA   SWINGER
SECULAR  ICHU  MACAROONS
TOHEART   RAKIT    POLE
EDELS   AUNES  SPOOLS  DIB
ROCE  ENDORSEMENTS   ORNA
ORK  EVELYN  ELEGY  BRAWN
    VERO   SCATS   PERIWIG
ESOTERICA  TUNA   OREGANO
REMORSE  BARREN  FIND   ER
DROWSE   MADEITA   ONE
ABO  TWOA  ZAT  EXT  BOOST
    FORGIVEMY  ETY  PUZZLE
JADA   ILLA    LY    ETAOIN
ARUN  TAMPA  EOSIN  TANNED
ZINC  ELAIS  TOEDA  ANNES
ZANY  RANDS   KLAN  LEAST
```

260

```
   SAME   TREES    UPPER
OBERON  RELET  ONESPOT
SECONDFIDDLE  TWOTIMER
CROSS  EPEE  MATINS  ANE
ANNE  TELAR  BESS  INCA
RED  MODEL  THERE  CRIED
NEATED   RHEES   ROMANY
SPARRER  POINT  CONANT
PITONS  FOURS    HOLA
ACUTE  MIRED  SEVENTON
DARI  SEVENCITIES  ANIS
SECONDED   OVERT   STENO
VEER   SUITS   WITHER
TATARS  MOSES  GETLOST
SHIELD  SESIS  BALKER
ARRAS  FEDON  PASTA  SIS
MESS  SUVA  PERCY  TEST
BET  EASELS  LETO  GETSA
ARRANGER  ELEVENTHHOUR
SIXTEEN  LITER  PEEWEE
   PEERS   LEEDS   SEEN
```

261

```
ATTA  AWL  COULD    RIOTS
KIWI  POI  AWNER   INDIES
AMONTHOFSUNDAYS  PRATTLE
ETTE   TIS  ENCLAVE  LOOT
OBI  RELUME   LYRA   ENTO
MOM  CLEPSYDRAE   ENDED
OME  EAT  SOUSA  SWAT  RAW
OBRA  OCT  SEANS  INA  ENE
MATURE   ADE   MINUTEMAN
SLEEPYTIMEGAL  OCK  TACT
PENNON  SPIES  SKILL  ANOA
RAT  DES  ENS  NEE  EON  NNW
INRO  SEARS  SEEDS  POSEDA
NDAK   CHA  THELONGESTDAY
TENANDOUT  OID   MARSHY
ERT  URN  ESENS  EGO  RAGA
DSS  MEDI  TINTA  WAL  LRS
ABETS   ANYOLDTIME   LES
ORBS  OLAN  CORNER   HGT
MOAT  ONESHOE  ARI  OOOO
OTHELLO  HOURGLASSFIGURE
STRAIN   PRIED  TIP  ERYX
SNIDE   ENATE   ERA  ESSE
```

262

```
RAPS  ANNAM  BFAS  ICTUS
ALOT  LIANE  LINN  NAILS
POLITICSIS  ASTI  DROME
TWOLANE   NINH   FROE
THESCIENCEOFHOWWHO
ACH  ASTRO  PARRIER  ION
PHIL   IDAE  GET  ASSE
POLITICSISTHEART  GEES
ROLLWAY  NOTION   SCI
ISM  INCH  PORNOS  ROPED
SEA  CALIF   SNARE   ERR
ERNIE  EGRETS  STAS  ENE
LAP  HALEYS   UMPIRES
SLUE  OFHUMANHAPPINESS
LYNX  REE  CEES   ESTE
URI  SCRATCH  BOAST  SSD
GETSWHATWHENANDWHY
HAEC  EASE   DEISTIC
HORAL  ITAL  APPLESAUCE
ABODE  TAKE  TWEET  YEAR
LIMES  YOST  HANDS  ESNE
```

263

```
DEMDOSE  ETC  ESSO  ROTAS
ENGIRTS  PEI  SKIPTHETALE
WORDBOTCHER  TIPTHESCALE
BIRDWATCHER   ARUT   NUM
ASFATE  THELASTONE  FAIRE
MEETSUP  RES  EXTENUATED
ACCT  PAVO  SPRY   BALM
SOUL  PIN  POE  PAIL  CBS
NNE  RANTER  RSVPS  YOUUP
ADD  EIGHTOFSPADES  ESSE
LFS  SPATEOFAIDES  TROTTY
III  HAS  AGA  LEE  EEE
AGGIES  WINNINGSPIEL  RRR
SHHS  SPINNINGWHEEL  BKS
ETTES  REAWN  OARAGE  PEE
SSS  HSIN  GAD  ESE  RAAB
LOOM  USSR  DESH  OTTO
MARIONETTA  ALI  TITLEON
ERECT  SWISSWATCH  GRANNY
STH  IATE  SNAPTHEWHIP
SHUNSTHEROE  WHAPTHESNIP
RUNSTHESHOW  AIR  RADIALS
SRTAS   EONS  SST  STASHES
```

264

```
ROGUES  DECAL   PAWS  SPEW
EARNSA  ELATER  ELON  ARCH
PRISONERSBASE  ELMOSFIRE
LYME  CAMEL  APARTE  HENIE
MELTS   EGGAR  ONTO   TEL
EDS  OUTOF  REICH  SUTTERS
BALAAM  RIME  RHUS   LAHR
ADAMS  EINEN  SART  STASH
NOWI  VEDDA  TIRATA  NDAK
DEVILSADVOCATE   STETI
SPHERED  ALII  HEATH  VAN
CLOSETED  SNOWS  SCRAPING
RAB  CANEA  LOIS  HAROLDS
ITSAT  CASHIERSCHECKS
MOON  PELTON  MAHAR  IFAT
SNAPE  ERST  SLUDS  STORE
SION  RATE  ESSA  BOSOMS
UPCLOSE  LEROY  STERN  LYS
NAH  LOTS  SCLER  AEONS
AROSE  HORSES  UMBRA  OGGI
BLINDMANS  DEADMANSFLOAT
LACE  ANNO  ENGELS  TELLME
EYED  NEYS  SERIS  SEEDER
```

265

```
TRAM   HANNAH   BLOOM
PHENO  EMERGE   OUTLET
THEODOREBEARS   GRIDLEY
RIOS  REDID  SOIE  HIDE
EAR  BENETS  FINED  ANDA
SLYER  TRI  CLANS  ORDER
LEA  SOPRANO  BROADS
MILANO  NEARS  COAL
BENEDICT  ACE  SOUNDEST
ONERS  TRICK  TWANG  LAO
NARY  RAISEEDWARD  SAIN
ECT  RIVET  RIOTS  APING
RESTYLED  SJD  SEXTANTS
HALS  NEONS  NITRES
APRONS  SIGHTED  SET
REAMS  SAGAN  QUA  NAVEL
RAMA  STAHL  EUCLID  EYE
ALPS  PART  REHAN  TROT
SEABOAT  CHARLESROASTS
DROITE  ARGOTS  ESTES
TYLER  PHAROS  MEAD
```

266

```
SPAS    MAROC    TOMB
SPURTS  AMINES   OHARA
INAFLAP  RIDENT  POKING
MANFORALLSEASONS  EDGE
ARKS  GREET  NOWAY  OGEE
GEE  BARON  DREG  EVERS
ORR  OZONE  GOES  TRESSE
SLEWS  BON  SHIRT
COALER  VOTES  EIN  HTS
ARRAYS  OILS  ODIN  MEOW
STEIN  TELLTALES  BOGIE
SHIN  BURL  OLAM  FINALE
EON  GOB  ASNER  INAPET
TRUSS  TEC  STRAD
ATHENS  SHAD  BURST  PFS
PREPS  SWAN  ORATE  ARU
PICA  WEIRD  GOGIN  PLOD
LAHR  HAVEFROZENASSETS
EDITIO  ELAINE  EMPATHY
SPERM  LISTER  REALTY
SEEP  PTERS  SEME
```

267

```
COSMIC  RAKED  CPAS  RENAL
ATEASE  ISERE  LETS  EXERT
GORILLACHIEF  OTTERCHAOS
EEE  EITHER  IPRAY  ELOPE
BOER  SNAIL  BLUR
SUM  PANS  PAINS  FEASTING
PRIMATE  BRUTE  SANTE  REA
ACCEDE  PROCELOTIZE  CRAM
RHEAS  PRATE  AERO  PRETE
KITT  MAUVE  AGHAS  REELER
YNE  PANDAMONIUM  SHAPER
RELINE  FDR  FEELUP
ASSUME  CAMELFLAGES  HIM
IRITIS  GLUES  IOTAS  RANA
RANEE  MOOT  ATTAR  CENTI
INGE  PORPOISEFUL  SUNTAN
SEE  DINES  DIDOS  ATTACKS
HARDENED  ALTER  LTRS  YET
ABIT  PRESS  TIRO
LAYTO  HINDU  RAMAPO  SAD
GIBBONTAKE  PROHIPPOTORY
AMBER  ALES  OIROT  ENSATE
DEEDS  BORS  NOYES  DAPPER
```

268

```
ACACIA   FRET   PEARL
OROTUND  CLERK  ANNUIT
COMEDIA  RADIO  CRABBES
HUES  MISERIES  HOTBATH
ESS  PIRATED  BAL  ETRE
RETALC  TED  CURS  TRIAD
ONEA  MYNA  OWOODS
SIGNAL  ACRESANDPAINS
MARES  BEHEST  REND
EMIA  OGEES  ABANG  ISM
ABELS  LIAM  SMEW  SENTA
REF  CREST  STILL  YSER
AHIR  PIANOS  ERUPT
TIMEFORSORROW  CLIFTS
NIMBLE  AONE  LIEF
APPEL  PINE  ROC  ASSESS
ATOR  EON  BAGPIPE  RET
COTTONS  FLAGRANT  GALE
PEERAGE  EXILE  TREMBLE
SNERDS  LIZAS  RAVELED
TESSA  LIEN  OPINER
```

269

```
ALANS   MANIC  ACTS  CES
ROGUES  ANODE  ROOT  DAVE
CORNETS  GETAT  ANTI  OSER
NICKELPINCHER  FARFLUNG
ASTER  THOREAU  RELATE
PER  EON  ITIS  ETAL
ELENA  TWERP  SESI  DER
TORERO  VEES  LOS  HAST
PUTINONESTENCENTSWORTH
ENSLAVE  TONES  AWARDER
EROS  TATA  LISSOME
ADAD  PROD  KIT  CALM  ERSE
NEMESIS  DRUM  SELF
OLIVINE  IDEAL  BEGSOFF
AHEARTASSOUNDASADOLLAR
SILL  SPY  TAKE  DIESEL
UGH  ARTE  MECCA  POTSY
SALE  GIAN  TIL  SHE
BEATER  HARDEST  NONOS
ORDINATE  PUMPERQUARTER
DODO  LATH  RIATA  DIDEROT
EDEN  DATA  ELIOT  LEVIES
SEN  SLIT  SENNA  REESE
```

270

```
CICADA  TSAR  AVAL  MARES
ROTATED  ITNO  TAXI  AGONY
OPUNTIA  FUNERALINBERLIN
BAPTISMOFFIRE  SKY  ALSO
ARM  KIEV  DAM  UPA  ELD
STATE  MAN  EASTERPARADES
TODADDY  MRS  TRESTLE
ARA  IRE  ASARULE  HORSDE
FINNEGANSWAKE  LOSS  HER
FLOATA  PARR  TOASK  NOLO
PEPTIC  YAUPS  ASTARIS
APRILSHOWERSMAYCOME
MAGENTA  ETAIN  URSULA
AGED  CAMEL  ESCA  RETEST
SIN  FLOG  TENTHBIRTHDAY
TOTELL  GONZAGA  SKI  GYP
SEASIDE  RAG  ELEVATE
GOLDENWEDDING  DAS  TIROS
ARE  TEA  SSR  EPIC  SHA
SIGN  RRS  ARMISTICEDAYS
HOMECOMINGQUEEN  TENURES
ELATE  ELIA  ENTE  ONECOAT
SENSE  DOXY  STAY  NESTOR
```

271

```
PAPA  SWAMI  CLAN   POSER
ERIN  CAPON  HIRT   ABELE
BEETHOVENSFIFTH     RECAP
ANTEATER  TAMES  BARONS
STARVES  HATER   HADON
   IER  COLOR  DEFENDS
AFTON    HALFALOAF   IKE
LAHR  FAIR   AWLS    SNAP
ACE   OFTENTIMES   RECTO
REFLUXES  EATER  DODOES
  OUTER  PACAS   DATUM
EDUCED  PERIL  DILEMMAS
BERKS  FIRSTOFALL   AWE
BITS  ERAS    OILY   GNAW
SSH   SEVENSEAS   LADYS
  MODISTE  EARLY   CAL
  FINES  TUBAS  RIPOSTE
RAJAHS  TOTOS  REGISTRY
ELUDE  QUARTEROFANHOUR
ALLER  UNDO  RUMER  ELSA
LAYME  ASSN  SEERS  SETS
```

272

```
BUDAPEST  ABRA  PRIS  POLL
IRIDESCE  SLID  REKI  EPEE
LICENSES  HANDSOVER  RECS
ESE  TENTLESS  ICE  IDENTS
   SANE  UNTENDER  CULLEN
PATTE  MADE  ALES  ADMIRE
BURROS  ANEM  VEDAS  SANNS
ELMAN  COGNATE  LUM  NESS
ELSPETH     HECK   BAG
   HUA  ONE  RAB  LESAGE
GREATERMETROPOLITANAREA
ALINEDRIVETHROUGHCENTER
SEMIPROFESSIONALACTRESS
HEINIE  FRC   OPS   YMA
   DAR  YUMA   ESHARPS
ACCA  MAC  ENRAGES  ODIUM
SHANT  FACTS  ENOL  SMILES
BENDER  TORO  COOL  PETER
ESTATE  CHINCHIN  DEYS
SHINES  HEE  HENEQUEN  UTE
TINT  OVERREACT  UNDERPAR
ORAE  DIRE  COKE  ICESHOWS
SESS  SASS  ASSD  PERSONAE
```

273

```
SAUNAS  EMIT   KEATS
GOBRAGH  DANES  MICHAEL
RAINIER  MARCH  ALTERNI
AREAL  EPURE  ERIK  MATA
CIS  SEWAN  ELOPER  TIM
ENID  WILDBILLDONOVAN
GRAVES  ANDES  NOI
  IRISHSETTER  SYNACME
ASSIS  USHER  ICESHED
STHN  EASTERSUNDAY  ALI
SARG  TRIO  NIET  BRAT
ITO  SHEEPHERDERS  ALDO
SOSWEET  EMAIL  AREAR
TREACLE  BREADSTICKS
  DEK  BEARD  INCEPT
SLIDEKELLYSLIDE  RARA
SEA  ENNEAD  ADEEP  RAG
OTRO  NEST  ELSAS  RANIN
DEVOTEE  EMMET  MIOCENE
SEANADS  DEERE  ENSILES
SEAMY   TROD  NEEDLE
```

274

```
ALPS  CAP  PEG  TASS  SOUPS
NARA  ANATOLE  SLUE  ISSUE
THEFIDDLERINTHEBASEMENT
HOSED  CATCHERINTHEVODKA
ERI  SMOTE  UTA   LENES
MEDE  ANEST  DOZEN  IRON
  ENBAS  ESSENE  MONACO
RANGE  WINTERSETMAUGHAM
ANT  REMEMBER  OURS
LTD  GLEAM  INACTIVE  GEM
LEER  LAKEINFERIOR  LEAVE
INWAR  RCA  MAR  STRIA
ENEMY  EIGHTNOTRUMP  ODDS
DAY  ESPRESSO  ARARA  EEL
  MAIA  RESTATES  NNE
LAWRENCEOFISRAEL  TOOTS
ATHENS  BONERS  THIEF
GAOL  CAJUN  SABRA  RAZE
  ALTOS  ELI  GAUGE  TEX
FRATERNITYSISTERS  NOTAT
THEHAIRDRESSEROFSEVILLE
HIRES  AEON  TRIFLED  NEON
SNORT  DSTS  SEX  YDS  KETT
```

275

```
ABASED  CAMPUS  BOAR  SIFT
LAWYER  AVIATE  USIA  AXLE
MYANGELMOTHER  MAMMALIAN
SHY  SAIDIT  ROPY  PLIANT
  DEED  HEAVY  PAON
DAM  SIGN  PACTE  CORRECTS
IMAGINE  MOTHERWORTS  HRH
MATING  FOLIO  AWES  TREE
PLEBE  LATIN  FIXED  LAYME
LIRE  JADES  SURER  JONSON
YEN  MUMSTHEWORD  HUNGARY
  INANE   LAC   ARGON
ATTACKS  MUMBOJUMBOS  TRA
THYMES  PEKES  ONAIR  THIS
HOWES  OILER  FLINT  SIEPI
ERAS  LUTE  CATTY  JAMMED
NOR  MOTHERLODES  MAKEUSE
ANDROIDS  HAZED  NAPE  MTS
  ASTO  FUMED  TUNA
SCATHE  JAMB  IODINE  IAL
MOTHERWIT  EGYPTIANMUMMY
ENTE  EAVE  TEASES  EELIER
WEAR  DYED  HONEST  DUENNA
```

276

```
EMBUS  ALCAN  ASTRA  ASTRO
TOUGH  HARPO  SPOOL  STRAD
HURLS  OVERS  HARTE  TRITE
ITSY  EYEWITNESSACCOUNTS
CHECKS  DECRY  MOT  ARMEES
  UNTO  EILDS  OAR  PODA
CESSIONS  OLGA  CRINGE
RAITT  TOWN  HICE  MARTINI
ACRO  POLIO  ALORS  GASSET
THEMET  ENNUI  UNEVEN  OTE
  EXAMS  ENSENADA  USLTA
SACRIST  SSD  STN  SALUTES
AMASS  HOTHOUSE  RECAP
MOL  TESTAE  NORIA  IRENIC
ARISEN  STAND  OCTAD  RIVA
REFUNDS  IDEE  FEET  ACLES
  ATOMIC  GRAF  ROUGHEST
GALV  RAN  BOMBE  PROA
ETAINS  FOE  AUNTS  INROAD
WHITEELEPHANTSALES  GAGE
GENIE  ORPEN  TIPIN  METAL
ANEED  ANELE  EVENT  ARETE
WASSY  FORDS  DESKS  ESSES
```

277

```
INFLOW  EST  SAAR  SPITE
SALAMI  COO  PULE  HUSHA
AVATAR  CRUSADES  ALAIS
THEELECTRICCOMPANY
PEATS  SHAKO  OLEIC
NAIR ATH EMP FUL TWAS
AVA APSIS PLEURAE ABA
BIGHTS GAD ULT STATIC
OLEOS THRU GOUT ASTRO
BATTERYPARK DREI LSDS
LASSO OWL ENLAI
ASCI VOWS HOUSELIGHTS
UPONA NEAT ACHT LHASA
TUNEIN RUE FLO TETRAD
ORD REVELRY ACTUS PRE
SNUG WAD MEL KER BESS
CUBIC BIGOT ANGER
ALTERNATINGCURRENT
MOORE TREASURE DOTAGE
BARRS EARL SIS OMELET
ONSET DYES TNT NESTLE
```

278

```
ASIDES ABASED THEWS
SERENA PASTEUP COOLIE
PRACTICETHEGOLDENRULE
SONAR ALOES ARRESTED
LESSENS RATIO TESS
OAS ATT FESTE
SHUTTLE BROTHERLYLOVE
EMPOWER EERIE YEOMAN
RESTIR ATTA CLEANEST
ANN STEM SHA NEE
MILKOFHUMANKINDNESS
SAT RIP DIAN ROM
TRACTION TINT ANIMAL
ALLOUT TOSEE CIELITO
GOODNEIGHBORS ENTERON
TRAIN PRE OPE
CHAD PAINT SPEEDER
LOVECALL SULLA RAJAH
ONEFORALLANDALLFORONE
VARESE SERIATE IDEATE
ENTRY MAGNET TERNED
```

279

```
TOUSLE PEDRO SMALLTIME
INNUIT ENROLS TOTALEDUP
MEREBAGATELLE IRONBALLS
EBER MAVIS AMAPOLA KETO
OAT DISEASE IRENE BEDIM
FRUMENTY LAPIN SAT
ROBERS COMRADE TITHER
MINNUSA RUGAE SWEETLOVE
ATEST PRESENCE EBA EPEN
LODI ACH AIDAROLE INT
TREES LIT ABOIL ATLANTA
MUCHADOABOUTNOTHING
TAPROOM REBUS ADS STAMP
ALT POORSORT AGO EGOS
LOIR VUE NETTLERS INAPT
CHEESETUB VOWER HINNIES
SASSER PERIWIG DAMIAN
PAS LEANS IMPASSES
MAKIN GLINT TRIVIAL TRI
ILOT PROTEIN AMINS CHAD
STRIKEOUT NOTHINGTOLOSE
SEENOEVIL GREENE ELOPER
ARAGONESE MEDES DETERS
```

280

```
JAW CHAR MUTTS XMAS
ABES AERO ONAIR GAILY
REAP WATT RIMES ANCON
DRIPDRY POSER BLARES
TOOT ONO FOLD
NOTADRYEYEINTHEHOUSE
ANON ROTC RAVEN TRI
REDD CORGI ITEM MOOR
DROPPER ACCENT ISOLDE
OASTS ALAI ATREE
SLY SPRINKLES ANN
SAINE AARE SEPTI
RINSES TRAMPS RAINBOW
INCH TRUE ALLAN GAME
PET DEALS TRAY STAR
WATERWATEREVERYWHERE
EWES GOV 1000
ENTAIL AMBLE TEDEWEY
TOAST AREEL GENL EVEN
TOLET NITRE RAZE RETE
UKES TASTY AMIR RIB
```

281

```
ARARAT PROFESS BORGE
LAREDO LASALLE LIFEIS
OMELET AKERMAN OFFSET
NOTE TUNE NITS SOAP
GREATESTSTORYEVERTOLD
SORE ERA ARMENIA
MERE BEST LBS SAY
THEDARKESTHOUR OFFERS
EER IDES BRA REO
CRESSET SICK SARGE
HOSTESSWITHTHEMOSTEST
STARK ACRE ENTENTE
IVE RIO BAIT DEN
GARNER NEWYORKSFINEST
REE ISR ANTE ODER
ARAISIN ALE CREW
MOSTUNKINDESTCUTOFALL
SABU LIEB HAIR OBOE
ADULTS INSOFAR EQUINE
KURILE ANTWERP SUNDER
CRECY DYELESS SEDERS
```

282

```
BOGS THEDA FASTS UNCLE
ORRIS OATEN RIPROARIOUS
OCEAN BLACKBERRYWINTERS
THEMED VIOLET ITEMS DEE
HEN LAVENDER AGORA ASSN
SMALTO EDGAR STAG
ETON ALBS SNAGS GAGES
CRUSH ALIFT ELLIS ELOPE
LANAI NULLIFY OLLIE LST
ATT ROSEVILLE AVON SDOT
TEASER NANDI STEPS HEMO
INDIGO TENCH REININ
AONE SORRY GOADS DONATE
CUBE SATE REDLETTER NRA
ATO BATHS AREOLAS MANES
ROYAL SETAT SMOTE SWIPE
ENSUE RELIC SETS OVID
NUBS LOOKS SEALED
SALE REPLY PINKTEAS RAF
ARI TOILE FELONY SHASTA
YELLOWDOGCONTRACT EMAIL
INTERNECINE ITCHY SAROS
TASSE LETOS ESKER TYNE
```

283

```
AMO   SPARSE   WIPES
IGNIS  PINION  NATURAL
MATSU  MANSPREROGATIVE
ILOT  FATTEST  ASE  COX
TONE  APE   IFFY  AFAR
SPIRITS  GIVEA   FRA
 SOOTH  ARNE  THEARTS
  LEE  DAVE  HANT  HAL
TOFEAR  ONER  ESTH  EVAS
RELASH  DRY  RARE  RATE
INAR  UNAPT  ENTER  OGEE
AERY  BOLA  OXA  OFFEND
DUES  BRIM  NITA  FEISTY
SUB  ATNO  ELUL  PIN
 PUGREES  TERP  ENVOY
 LAD  ERODE  LATERAL
OWLS  SOSO   PAR  NOME
ACH  EUR  OLEOOIL  TIME
WHISTLERSFATHER  RIDER
EELIEST  HERONS  BOERS
RENTE  ORKNEY   INS
```

284

```
RAKED  SPEND  AGILE  CREDO
ALICE  CELIA  MAMAN  RIGOR
MATHEMATICS  ALPHABETIZE
AREO  ORATE  STAIR  REESES
  ADELE  POETS  KISS
SWAGGER  ARGUE  CREE  LPS
TABLES  CACOGRAPHERS  ERA
ASCENT  EBONY  LOBS  STOL
BIDEA  PANNE  RIALS  MOTTO
ATE  OISE  AALTO  BALEEN
TAF  INTERSECTION  ALARMS
 GIRDS  MARIA  BLANC
ATHOME  STEREOCHROMY  ADE
TAITAS  TELLS  OARS  RAY
BIJAS  DENTS  AMICE  SARRE
ELKS  SIRS  ARISE  SPLITS
SOL  PHONETICISTS  PAMELA
TRM  LIDS  ANTES  MINARET
 PANE  UNTIL  CLANG
TULANE  ANTON  ALINE  ASKS
ABECEDARIAN  MNEMOTECHNY
MINER  AMORE  ADAIR  BROOD
PIERS  LENAS  BENTS  BOTTS
```

285

```
TICK  URVA  EXO  TAHOE
EBERT  BOIL  PIUS  INEPT
LANAI  OSSA  IOTA  CANTO
GRANDFATHERSCLOCK  RON
 BATON  HOLI  ITTY
 BASIL  CUPIDON  GOAWAY
TICKTOCK  UNICEF  CROCE
ARTISTE  TOCK  LOKEREN
LISP  EQPT  MUG  SKYS
ONOMA  ULES  EASES
NINETYYEARSONTHEFLOOR
 LEARN  WXYZ  TERSE
MOTO  SWY  SOOT  GAMS
BROWNIE  TICK  ROSALIA
MAGNI  DMITRI  TICKTOCK
SLOUCH  ACHANCE  RIOTS
 APER  IKES  ADMEN
WAG  WHENTHEOLDMANDIED
ITALO  ITOO  LAIC  ENATE
SLIER  RECU  LIED  REGIS
PINSK  SKR  ASSI  TOCK
```

286

```
 PATON  TRUDEAU  AIRGAS
PAHLAVI  PONIARDS  SLEEVE
AMITIES  SELASSIE  WARIER
LIL  RAF  ANE  TRA  ASNO
MEIRTANAKACASTROANDCHOU
 PAIN  COKES  HONG  REARS
SCAMP  UELE  JUT  AIS
CONSTANTINEANDOLAVV  POP
UND  OSE  EDIES  FREEPORT
DAR  ELSAS  HRH  PSI  LADES
ONAS  OCREA  PROA  BERG
 TITOPOMPIDOUANDMARCOS
 NOPE  IDIC  STOAT  ARES
VOILE  ANA  AKA  SERES  NRA
EMEERATE  ALECS  YAP  YEG
TOR  ELIZABETHANDJULIANA
 ETE  BED  TARO  INNES
AMENT  ICON  AMINO  STAD
GUSTAVBAUDOUINANDHASSAN
ESTE  EAR  VBS  EEE  ANO
NEARER  RELEASES  BRANDTS
DUTIES  STARDUST  APPEASE
AMENRA  ATTESTS  RABAT
```

287

```
CLING  DIVAN  HAP  EERO
ROMEO  AMINO  ELOGE  CAAM
ODIST  DIVDS  TRAILS  ATTA
CENSOR  TAJ  SITINACORNER
 TIO  VIRILE  TIEDTO
FETCHAPAILOFWATER  DELOS
ROCHE  POLLSTERS  ASSENT
ASPIC  YUL  SELON  ATI
PUP  LAMPS  AVEC  NOR
SLOPPY  OUIS  AGANA
CASABA  PUTTHEKETTLEON
IMAGO  CURES  ORARE  LAVAS
 BREAKONESCROWN  OFTIME
 RYALS  HATI  PONDER
RET  DOTE  ESNES  SRO
OLE  TITUS  XIS  OFALL
NUNCIO  RETAINING  NAPOO
ALOUD  RUNTHROUGHTHETOWN
 CREDOS  TOUSLE  SIS
PULLOUTAPLUM  TNT  SPILLS
ALOE  DOGIES  WOTAN  IDIOT
INCR  SNEER  ARLEN  PENNY
NAKS   STS  STYLE  ESSEX
```

288

```
SCATHE  PASS  USC  ELD
MARRON  TIRAH  SIR  LAUD
URGERS  INANE  ANY  MUNI
DRYAD  SNUGGER  ASS  TKO
GOLDENOPPORTUNITY  RID
ETE  IDA  NESTS  AMPERE
 ISLAND  TAILBACKS
CRAVE  SARDINE  SCOP
REDOX  LEANED  ELLES
ADORES  LANKY  IRE  ROSA
MANYSIDED  CREAMCUPS
SNIT  LEY  GOTOO  RAHRAH
 SOLVE  LUCERN  MALTO
 WEEP  AMTRACS  ASYET
UPPERRAMP  LUPINE
MOTRIL  IDEAL  RAN  DAS
LIB  DIAMONDINTHEROUGH
ANO  ANN  GRECIAN  EVERE
UTAH  ICE  ALANI  SHINER
TATA  NOM  PITON  MANNER
 TSP  GNU  TEAS  UNEASY
```

289

```
LOEWE   ORAS   BOAT   PSTS
ALLEN ARENA SALMI   SACRE
MASTERSANDJOHNSON   CRYIN
AMAS ALLEY TODES CHOLON
     SCALE ROWAN HULLS
SAG  TINY  HOEN  AREA
TRIDENT   GOLDANDFIZDALE
ARLENE  MOINE   ERAN  NEE
RIBES  MADGE CAGEY PEDAL
IVES HARI SOARS  SLACKS
NER GONCOURTBROS  MUSHY
     TAROS NEURO MANTA
LACED MORANANDMACK   RBS
CANNES ALIMS  HANK  PYAT
AUDEN CHAPS AMATI HABLA
RRS SPAN ADANA LARDER
LAURELANDHARDY   CURRIER
   LONE  ELBE  RASP  SNY
SLATE  BALER  TETHS
SPIRIT TOTAL MECCA  TAKE
WAVER ARCHYANDMEHITABEL
ACARE VICES TIPSY BURNS
PENS  EGAN  HIES  STATE
```

290

```
BAR   CARP  WAKA    GBS
EGO ROGER ONUS  APRON
DRAINPIPE LACT BEATER
  STAYOUTOFTHEKITCHEN
BATES  TENE  ERN SEERS
ARE  SERE    NEB  SRS
BARBARA  MAES  LAS
ABSALOM LORDKITCHENER
  DALI  ERUDIT  KIVERS
   LARIN ADS BREAST
TAGLINES    DAGUERRE
CORDON CUE  ALTER
OOLONG ARCOSE  ONES
STOVEPIPEHATS RELIANT
   RIN DORA GRINDER
APA  NIL  TATE    MIO
BRATS NAS SILE  BRINY
ATTHEKKKKITCHENDOOR
SHRINE EERO INUREMENT
UINTA REAM RECUR  RAH
RAG   STEP  TRIG  SEE
```

291

```
BEBOP SEMIS RIAL DAMAGE
OVETA TRADE ENNA IMARET
METER EATER SLIM VOTENO
BREAKFASTOFCHAMPIONS
  AIMEE OONA ORT  TOW
DAME RED NAKEDLUNCH EVA
OLIVIER SOLES MIES AER
OLDER  SHOO  SPACE CARD
DINNERATANTOINES  TENSE
LEI EDILE UNITS BIDDER
ERG SNORT STATE DETESTS
  HALERS DAWNS MILADY
WATTAGE RANEE BATIN MRS
ALCOVE SANTA TRITE POE
STONE AFTERNOONOFAFAUN
HOWE HARTE URIS  PATTI
MOB CASA PENAL SATCHEL
ANO ONTHEBEACH SPP EYRE
NAY ODA MUGS   SLEET
  ALLSWELLTHATENDSWELL
STANCE ERLE ACRES AERIE
TARTAR AGER GLOVE DIANA
UPSETS LETS SUPER ELLEN
```

292

```
YAKKED   BAR  PMS MAKEA
ORNATES ALII KIEL IRREG
KNIFEANDFORK ACKACKFIRE
SACK LAIRS KANKAKEE SIN
KAN KIOSK SEPTEM   USED
AUK EKE GOEST OED AKKRA
SINEWY  METRIC   PIER
KNAPSACK FRANKKNOX IFI
ETCH KLEPT ALTERED KNIT
WAKAS ABOARD STUD ANGLE
   WINORLOSE    STALER
TALKINGBACK BOOKKEEPERS
ARIOSE    STOPKNOBS
SIKHS LISP ONERAP TOQUE
KEEL TINHORN SAGES TUNA
SSH KEUKALAKE SKEPTICS
  OPEN  KABINS  RESCUE
SITIN BLE INEPT HEN KTS
HOCK GRILLE SLATE  TSK
ADA LEAKIEST ICAME PISA
RIKKITIKKI PICKUPSTICKS
KNEAD SEES KAES STICKIT
SESTO ERA  SND  SAYSSO
```

293

```
  NAPS  SCALD  ANGEL
CABOT TOPEE SPARROW
CATCHESACRAB CHOIRBOY
ORAS LANKA SHRIMP SRO
POL ERDA  BIDI  STEW
EMILY AITS GABS SHEAS
NETHER NOTSURE  SPAR
DYADIC ORCAS COURTED
SOFAS EAT BRUNDAGE
ARCA FLORAL OREL SIRE
MEL COCKLEHAT   LEM
BIOS MITT OASEAN SSTS
INSANITY MPS SNOOP
TEENAGE PIETA SCRIMP
ADOS GENDERS TOTALS
MOSES VRAI RIAS SERAI
ADAR RIAL ETTA  TIX
REC MUSSEL ITEAS LINE
LOLLIPOP OYSTERPLANTS
NAILERS SETAN EAVES
METES  STOSS  NEAT
```

294

```
ELMO TWOCAR CASAS  MIA
VIAL PHRASE ULTRA  UND
AVID HEARTANDSOUL  STA
DENSE ENTIRE MONARCHY
ERA LEDGER GAIL  DELE
WRESTLED BARTS    DEF
BUTS HES BOTCH FUTILE
WRECKED DUDES BARONET
ISRAEL MARYS SIDEPOST
TYPE SUCRE SARD   NHU
   ELECTRONICBRAIN
ESK VOTE GNARS  DUBS
SKIBOOTS CLONE BEDOTS
SIDEBET FAINT CASINOS
ANNALS DANSE VON SEME
FED COUTH  VENDETTA
LYLE AGNI LENNON  OCT
SIDELONG NEARTO TOPHI
ACE BLOODANDGUTS LIFE
GKS OLENT SEERED ECUS
ASK WADES ESSEDS OKLA
```

295

```
GWTW  ROWAN  RUERS  HBOMB
RASAS IHADA  ENLAI  ALDER
ONERO ADLAI  SPIKE  LEORA
UNTILBLEEPFREEZESOVER
SESSOR ART  EDNA  TRAP
EREB UAR SUDAN SAD YIPS
  LOIS STNS EST OPAQUE
BLEEPTHETORPEDOES ANURA
LATER AAR EOS SLITSKIRT
UPUP IMMOLATES LEO ETES
RED USE LIDS AVA SHE
BLEEPODOLLY BLEEPEDSPOT
LIL FSA DOUR EEL ORR
ETTE DAR COURTYARD CINE
TRYGVELIE ORA HIS ALLIN
HORRAE BLEEPATIONOFFAUST
EVONNE ENC TENT NORM
LEST PAY TWIST SAN SHER
  LOEB SOHO ELA DABLEE
MYDEARIDONTGIVEABLEEP
OKAPI CAMEL ARLEN LEAVEN
ANNUL AGIRL MALMO YEMEN
STATE SEAMY PLIES PSST
```

296

```
AMBER STEAD RIVAL OFFAL
RILLE CARVE ABODE RIATA
GLASSHOUSES CINDERELLAS
ULM TART RIDES RELADLE
EYESORE PARIS STAG MEER
  ARM SAGES MIXTURE
COPSE DIVERSIONS LANCET
AMAH CEDES ODDS TATTLER
MAP MACES FLEE AARE OLE
PTEROPOD MAVERICKS STEW
SERENER MUSE NOME TAHRS
  TEARAPART KINESCOPE
CHILD TURK LIZA CANASTA
HAGS MILLIPEDE MOMENTAL
IKE GONE NUTS COVES RUT
VERGING VENT CAPEL RENO
ESSENE PASSEDOVER DUETS
  RAYLESS RIVES LAI
KALE METE PERES REMNANT
IRONMAN WADER DIVA BOA
WOODENSHOES CLAYPIGEONS
ISSUS EARLS TEPEE EVICT
SEEMS SLATE STERN DALEY
```

297

```
SWELL BAJA CASK SERIO
LEXIA OLAF OUTOFWHACK
GETONESELFINTOALATHER
DENTS FOIST PLOT SRA
VERSUS UXOR PARCS
EDN MARES NIDE HADAT
NOAH YETIS VARS ENERO
DULAT CHEAPEN POSTERS
STEMWARE LORGNON APES
VAIN RAMI LURE RAI
POINTTHEFINGEROFSCORN
ARD LEAF TEST OTHO
SIES ENLACES UPROOTED
CONCERT BADTURN PLENE
ALCAN YOLK SNEER EDDA
LEERS MEED FRAUS BUN
FLOWN EIER SERERS
GBO AMOI ASTEP STELA
ALLOVERBUTTHESHOUTING
GOLDENRULE EZIO PIECE
ACADS YSER REST SAFER
```

298

```
REPASTE LIEDER DACHA
ELECTED ANGRIER AGUES
CAPTIVEAUDIENCE TARAS
LITANY TRUSS EYRE TRI
ANA GESTES SAD ERSATZ
MELD SEAL ACCESS WISE
ESKER TRELLIS OATEN
MILS DIOR INTHERED
SPIGOTS PACING ITALY
VIE ASHEN FLORA OLIVE
IMAS TELEG ELAND YSER
LINER SAURY ARDOR ERS
MAUVE THREES EDUCERS
ANTENNAS ALOP ARTY
GRIEG ASPIRIN SACCO
ALAE HEAVES ORCA SLOP
FOLDER SAP FRIERS ELP
FUL BURT AGUAS MAGALO
ODETO BEHINDTHESCENES
RERUN IRONAGE CORTEGE
DRYAD NETTED AFEARED
```

299

```
PILAR MCCV SCUM IDLE
ARISE ALLA SAONE MEAN
WAGONTRAIN ENDEARMENT
ETH DATUM ARTE LAIRD
DET DESERTFOX INNS
HOTEL SEE EAGLET
ANONYM SNARER LALO
TORERA RETRACE EYES
TASSE LIONOFJUDAH EVE
HEP ROAST FIGTREE
ORIOLES LAVISTA
CONTACT ELISE DSO
AMA THEKINGFISH SPORT
RAPT RETORTS SPOUSE
OHOH STADIA TALBOT
BALEEN LRG APTER
ETTE BULLMOOSE IVA
MOIRE EROS SPITE OED
GINGERSNAP WHITEMOUSE
ERIE DOONE RENI PIETA
MEIR OTTO YNES SETAL
```

300

```
HOOP COWED JOSH LABEL
ABLE ARARA UELE ABODE
WIDEANDFAR DRYANDHIGH
SERRATED NAY PILOSE
EASER BEGAT EMER
STAGER ALLENANDBURNS
WADE SEASEDGE PEACE
ARY STORK PEEPS DRIP
PTA THROE DUNDEE COE
UNDOERS DANDYANDFINE
DARTE ENC CHAOS
CARRYANDCASH CHORIST
LEO STEELE FLIRT URI
ATUB KORDA LOESS SUN
MAGOO MENSWEAR HACK
SHOVELANDPICK STONES
TETE TWINK COULD
KILROY HND HARRIERS
SODAANDRYE GOWNANDCAP
ERECT EINE ONAIR AHME
TOSEE NOEL DENSE YOST
```

301

```
NEPOS WHICH    LAP   TDS
EPISC HARROW IAMA  DIETS
WHATAREYOUTHINKINGABOUT
TAN LOREN ENCE   ANERVE
 HOWDOESYOURGARDENGROW
    ASK   TSE   EEL
AWL SBS COFFEENOW   AWNS
ACHEW OOM OER TIE   SHOO
TRA WHOSYOURFRIEND  TERN
LATRIAS OGREISM   STANDS
ASWE ITA PEA  AES  AID
WHATAREYOUTRYINGTOPROVE
SRI  DRU  TOD  GIG  EWES
POTATO SASTRES LESSENS
LEHI WHATSTHEMATTER  EEE
ONAN SAC OAO  THE  SEATS
DOTS ETTUBRUTE  ADS  STO
    TOR   ROY   TAA
 DRLIVINGSTONEIPRESUME
LAHORE ETYM  SAARE  AVA
WHOSBEENSLEEPINGINMYBED
MADAM TOTO OFNEED  IRENE
KER  AGO   DOWDS  ASSTS
```

302

```
LEARNS OPTS   RACE   PLIE
INDEEP NORIA ENATE  IOTA
SIDEWHISKERS TIMEPIECES
TDS TIDIES TRITE  INROME
    NODS ARARA  TSAR
ERN AXLE BRINE SHOWERED
DEITIES HANDGRENADE AXI
UTTERS CANOE  LOWE  ADAR
CORES DATES HAIRS  SMILE
EROS EINE  TENSE  SABOTS
DEG AVOTRESANTE GETLOST
   LOVERS COBRA BOPEEP
STYLERS DOGBISCUITS ETD
PACERS BULGY ORAS  CREE
AMENT CONEY BARNS  SHANT
CART TOLE CODAS  STATUE
ELI TEXASSCHOOL STATORS
DENTINES PLATS GARY RET
   EDDY DEALS DATA
ONAPAR CREPE PATINA OWE
LIVELIHOOD THELONGGREEN
ALOE LEAVE SURER  LEANED
FENS  PLED  BUSS  ESTOPS
```

303

```
TENSPOT MORAL  CHASES
AMATEUR ANOMIE ROBERT
DIVERTISSEMENT INSANE
STEER MESTA DESMOINES
   DIA LEWIS STERN
PASSEUL ONOR EASTMAN
ARA SCOFF SHAMAN HILO
REVE OREL OPAL BESOM
ICON UNLESS PLUTO END
SAILER TUPELO PROTEGE
   RARA RUMOR ORIN
DEFIANT DRIFTS USESUP
OLA STATE STEEPS UCLA
MAIRE GOLF URUS PETE
ETRE PARIAH RAMEE NRA
THEVEIL SNUB PANDEAN
   ERROR GRAPH UNA
BADINAGES DROIT OLDAS
OMELET NOBLESSEOBLIGE
ORELSE DIREST RELATOR
MANETS TARTE PRESENT
```

304

```
BORETO  PUPILS  ACARI
UNEVEN  IRELAND SIMON
STREAMOFCONSCIOUSNESS
THUR EBON EDWIN  NET
SENDS ERICS LENT  ITTO
   OHMS COEXIST ILIAC
HOTWATER WALKTHEPLANK
BRINKS OPPOSE  ELS
MARAT TIPOF  IDEOLOGY
REWASH PKTS ARG  AREA
SIDE WEB ERA LAI  DINO
TOOL ALA SOCK  ITSYOU
UNFLORID URIAN  HOLIA
   CTF HABITS DEFEND
OVERTHEFALLS ALLATSEA
CELIA BALLETS  ESTH
TRAP GOLF SYNGE HEMIC
ODS DEALT  OUCH  LORA
BUTDONTGONEARTHEWATER
ERIES SUNRISE  MEKONG
RECIT YEASTS  STEREO
```

305

```
OCALA BASTILLE  PURISMS
ROGERBANNISTER SINISTRO
STAIRCASECURVE INAFLASH
OER EOS LAP MODEL  IAO
   RAM ELL EIDER  ERST
INTERPLAY ETTES  NEWT
SOHO LOT ISHES  CANAAN
OTE SEX SICES LOP  YIN
MATRIX SHOAL BOOP  TRE
ETHIC STOOL TORPEDOES
REIN SCORIA  BANNERET
SDRS STEPTOTHEREAR SHED
TESTONES OATERS  PENE
CRYSTALED RITAS  COSTA
HON UKES IDLES  DOTTED
API PEN SHOER SEQ  ARE
PENROD VIEWS DON  FRAY
LEAR ORGAN  GOODTASTE
HASP BRAND  ERG  RON
EDT REDIP ANA NIP  PCT
ADELAIDE ONESTEPATATIME
REPORTER STAIRCASESHELL
ARSINES THREEONA  SYRIA
```

306

```
ROACH UTAH    ATMOST
INROAD NERITA GAITER
DERIDE HEAVEN INTONE
GETALONGONNEXTTOO BDS
AHOY TSARS AIRS  PROS
GEO OILS  INCA  DIANE
ARN ISTLE HOSS CONGAS
DEFRAYS CAN  TONGA
LOY CADET HOC  BOG
SPOON FORO REEK  DODO
KIVA HAVEOTODO  AUER
APET DUDE NOPE  ENTRY
TEN TON YAHOO  ILS
THONG LIT  ARTLESS
STUART BLUM BLESS ETA
AWRIT SEAM ALSO  AES
NOEL THAT GRETA  SGAW
DSO THEREISOINITFORME
BOWTIE SEALAB  VALLEE
AMIENS ANGELA ELUDER
RENEGE  OWLS   LEONS
```

307

```
AMAH  AREA   CES  SPIEL
RARA  SNAFU  ALAS HASTO
PLAINTIFFS  CARTOUCHES
ALTRUIST  TRUMP   RTE
  LIRE  SEEMS  ABIDING
ADMITS  THREE  ASIN NEE
LEANS   WEEKNIGHTS  CAN
ORNE  HEEL   DEES  SART
PMS  MALEFACTORS  SANER
ALSORAN  MAILS  SHODDY
 ACORN  BITTS  SHANE
SLURRY  CANEA  ANAPEST
CAGES  ALTERNATIVE  CAT
ACHE  ALUI  LATE  TENO
RUT  STOCKSTILL  PUNTO
ANE OINK  PANEL  BARTOK
BARRAGE  SERVE  BURN
  ENE  ETAPE  MOLASSES
PILEDRIVER  SPOILSPORT
IDYLS  VIPS  TELLY  ISEE
TASSO  ELS  SUDS  TOSS
```

308

```
LANAI  THAIS  ROWED  BRAC
AGENT  WARTY  ENATE LOCHS
MRONEMOSTEL FIVEFLUSHER
PANE ASTER  RICES  ESTERS
   SNEER  OUTER  LATE
IRT  OIL  YACHT  SEVENTH
NEWDRAFT  THREETIMER WEE
SHOOT  ROWE  DAYTON  SEAT
TIFTS  TAPIRS  GLEN TENTH
EROS  NASAL  TILES  SIXTHS
PER  LUSH  LOOKER  RATTIS
 THIRTY   PRE   DEFUSE
CHOOSE  GNEISS  UNES  TAS
AHERNE  TAINE  PAVES SHRI
TARNS  SHIN  SLAVES LAHRS
TROY  SCOUTS  ERSE  ABOIL
STA FOURSHEETS  NYTWELVE
ADDEDTO  RATED  EIN  EER
  REDS  EMITS  WOADS
STRODE  ARIAS  LITRA BATH
THENINEBALL  EIGHTLEAGUE
RIVEN  METAL  ASHOW LIANA
SERG  STONY  RATIO STREP
```

309

```
MIS  REELS  TOED  SCOFF
ELUL  APRIL  OPRY PAROLEE
RITE WHENITPAINSITROARS
VARESE  EERO  EARS  TRIM
CARTSANDRAFTS  LOUR  ESE
  ALTMAR   RIPA    PEG
BORN  UNIAT  OBEAH JOULE
APODA  REVWILLIAMSPOONER
HUMBUG  ENROLLS  TOI WOW
SPIRITS  ONEA  ECHINI
 CAPAPE  GYNAEO  EOSIN
ROK PRUDENTSTINTS  LED
VANED  PREWAR  TIRADE
ANTRES  IMAS  DAMOSEL
NCO ISM ONEIROS  STALAG
YOURSHIPISSLOWING SNIDE
ARRET  VILLA  SELIM DEEM
  PIP  ASOK   KNEADS
CAS  CONN  WEEDEMANDREAP
ASTA IOTA  LALO  OSAGES
THEMARTOFTHEHATTER LARA
TEREDOS  AVIV  THEME STOW
ENDTO  RATE  ESTES  ENS
```

310

```
BAGEL  FALL   SETAT SPCA
OTHOI  ODAY   ITISA HAAS
GHOSTWRITE  GHOSTTOWNS
IOS  HITME  PIES  TOCSIN
ESTH  THESPELL  TONK
 DEUCE  TET  GHOSTOFA
WRAITH  ERASMUS  RUES
HANNAHS  SKIPPED  LOTTO
ETC  SUNUP  FEIN  POORER
WEE  NANO  IER  SOPPED
  GETGOOSEPIMPLES
 FORBES  KED  TAUT  USA
NOFEAR  PELF  OGRES  PPD
ORGAN  KARLOFF  TREATED
IGOT  HALYARD  GASHES
REDSCARE  EIR  GENIE
 PAUL  MASCAGNI  AGES
REKILN  MORT  THOSE  HEL
SPIRITUALS  GHOSTSTORY
VENI  ERATO  SESI  SUSIE
PEST  DEMON  ARTS  ENTER
```

311

```
TOEHOLD  PRIMOS  FRISES
ENDURER  RESINA  ROMANO
NIGHTMAREALLEY  IMPUGN
OCAS  MIASMA  BEIGE  COL
NER  TANTE  MYRRH  FIRE
 AZO  SENATE  SITTINGS
 FLORA   CRAWL  SWINGES
FOLIES  FEEBLE  HIRE
ORACULAR  SLING  GOSHES
IGN  POMOS  ENSUE  STASH
LIP  POLTERGEIST  UTE
EVOKE  SIENA  STAID  NAK
DEEPEN  CARPS  AUTOETTE
 DREG  MOPIER  UNREEL
LAJUIVE  SUETY  SKIDS
EYETEETH  TREEOF  ECH
OATY  RUEDE  GNOMY  OAF
TNT  AMPLE  BOLERO  TUNA
AKIMBO  LITERARYGHOSTS
RENOIR  ECOLES  OUTSERT
DEGREE  REPAYS  ULYSSES
```

312

```
MAJOR  BALAC  ACME  TABAC
ARENO  ALAPA  POILU ITALO
NESTS  RENEE  ROSIN VIRAL
ONTHESQUIDS  SCALLOPINE
RASE  AUT  USS    IAL
  DYE  BROTHERSKIPPER
METERS  SEALATROTH  ELLA
ONEGA  EACH  YSAYE  SEEIT
PORGYANDBASS  SAD  UKASE
IRS  SMEE  NEP  CAL ENATES
SMEW  ARLO  NABOB  DAUB
HERRINGAIDS  ALLPORPOISE
 INDY  LEEDS  EARL  ONES
TOGGLE  MSS  ORE  LEAS MAS
OMEGA  CAT  SALMONPCHASE
TALLY  AGORA  EASE  OUTON
UNIE  FRONTPERCH  EUGENE
MIDDLEAGESPRAT   SGT
 AEC   SRI    INA   IRAE
PIANOTUNAS  MUSSELBOUND
ARGOT  LUNAR  EXILE UNION
SARIS  STOKE  NOTER LINDA
SNARE  SNIP  TRESS  BASES
```

313

```
ASHES SILO IBAS TRADE
MOOSE WOOF NITA HOMEY
THETRAILOFTHELONESOME
SORE UTE HERE ERASED
      INC ACER APE
UNDERTHEGREENWOODTREE
PAINE NEE ERNS REND
AMES LINDENTREE EDDA
SAM LACE ERIN HAREM
  SEPIA STAN TEASERS
 THEWINDINTHEWILLOWS
WHITING NILS EBSEN
HARTS NAPE WEIR KAT
ELSE FORESTFIRE BOLA
LIER SULU ALL TULIP
PALMSPRINGSCALIFORNIA
   ARY OAKY ORT
SLEAVE SONG ADA SALT
CUTDOWNTHEOLDPINETREE
OTTER NOIR IRAN LOANS
WEENY EPOS PURE MARAT
```

314

```
UTTER SIE BASRA DINERS
NOEXIT ANN ASTAS USEDTO
SOUPTONUTS CHURN MAIDEN
ETTE PUTONTHEFEEDBAG
NOONS DEWAR FRAY CHIME
TONSURES ROPES TET BOOR
  ECU LETTS HASHHOUSE
BREAKBREAD OTHOS OUR
OUNCE OFT MIEN PUSHOFF
PROCREATED AMPERE HOURI
  ROSA NUBIA ORA OTOE
EMU CANTEENTRUCKS DDE
ATON HIE TEENS POGO
LOUTS DEPART SHOESTRING
ENSLAVE AGAR ERR HENNA
UNE PLAYA BRONZEAGED
BEANERIES APLUS ELS
ALEC ARC ELSAS MANLYART
YACHT KANT IDEAL OSTIA
  EATSNGASONEMILE PROP
MIMOSA PAPER POLARROUTE
EVENTS INERT ORE GROCER
TEASES EASES TYR SNEDS
```

315

```
MIMIC INAS SSTS TIME
ARENA SNORE SLEEP TISON
BANGTHEDRUMSLOWLY HEALY
  SHAVIAN HOVEL MEGALO
CST EZRAS LIVED SERACS
ACH TEEN DIVAN ALAMB
SERVERS BREAKSINTOTEARS
SPEERS WEANS DEAN SOT
ITERS LILTS TOLAN TAHOE
NEBO PESO SOWER DIVEST
ORA BUSHWHACKERS OGIVE
 LARGE ONAIR FERMI
ALGAE BLASTOSPHERE SFT
ABSENT RUNES OILS YSER
BONES DONGS EASEL BOISE
EMO LAIC ENNIS GRUNTS
DASHIELLHAMMETT GEORGIS
TANTE LOOMS TALK EVE
TRUSTS PANTY MAUDE RED
POILUS HORDE TABLEOF
ANKER HAMMARSKJOLDPLAZA
STERE ABBEY MOORE EOSIN
TOSS MEAD SSRS NEIGE
```

316

```
SLAKE COMO ZEBU SWOB
TEPID ORYX MARAT WISE
OBANG DOBE OMNIA ETTA
UKR EVENUNTOBETHLEHEM
TUTT EXOD HRE ATHOS
CREWS DUE ZOO VIE
WHICHTHEYSAWINTHEEAST
WED YEUX ANO ASI LOI
INGE DIPS GUS URANIUM
EXO LEA ELKS ALONSO
ALITTLECHILDINAMANGER
DENOTE TITO MOD ICI
ANALOGY BEF SOIF ENCE
NIP EMP APE POUT HOG
ONEVERCEASETHYSHINING
AIM ARK ACU ROOST
PARTI VAC SOLE TWIT
ASTARYESAGESHOARY INE
CARL OLIVE HAZE ANNEX
KIEL ROSIE ABET REGNA
SLEY KNIT HYDE NESTS
```

317

```
AMARA ADMIS SHOAT ARCAS
SALAS DEATH TONDO SOAPY
SHIFT ANJOU EMEER HONAN
ADEFIANTOLDMAIDPRAYFORG
MINI MOOR DONC TEM JETE
  SRO TENNIS NABO
IVEHERREMARKEDWITHABITO
CEN DABDAB AEN ESSEN
HADJ LIONAT LASCAR RAF
SLOES ASWAN RILLS ASI
SCALP CILI APAP PEER
FAQUIVERTONIGHTISHALLSM
IRUS IOOO ECHO DHAVA
GAI HORSE SETSA AZURE
AWN ONAIRS STAIRS ALOG
RACER ERI INNATE NAA
OKEANDDRINKTILICHOKEAND
 SEAR SEEONE REX
SCOT DUB CENA SIAM CELT
NUTSTOMYLUNGSANDMYLIVER
ARTIE MOORE PHILO ATIME
PIEDA ENCES IMPER METON
SOREL DEIST NEEDY BRAND
```

318

```
GETSBY MASH AMAT IDEA
UTOPIA ONTO PUSHCARTS
SHORTHANDED AFTERMATH
TOTE SPANISH FUME MUY
SHAH PRON ASIT WPA
DECOCT CRANED ETUI
CAT RUSH MALLS EGOIST
ATHLETES ASEM SCONCES
CHEESES CHEMISTRY REA
TOKAY NOAH AYEAYE
ISIS SPELLINGBEE OATH
NEUTRO SOYA AUDIO
ALG FRENCHTIP BARRIER
LASSOED ROOS PUNGENTS
ATEASE NITRE ARTE GOT
SENT TWEEDY URBANE
GEO IPSO ATTA TESO
SOL TINT GERMANY LAME
WRITINGUP BOOKKEEPING
INSISTENT OSSE ATONIA
MOHO ODES NETS RATTAN
```

325

```
BEARS ALIAS WAIST ACRID
ALLONECANDO AGREEABLETO
NICKELODEON STEELGUITAR
DSO LILY NAIAS SLAT ELM
    PLAY BIRR STORMS
BBLS TAOS OPTION EELS
ORRA SENO GNARL UNREAL
MEANIE IRONCROSS STEALA
BASEMENT SALAD TDES DEC
RKS ANOA TWAS TERR APSE
ESKIMOS DEED FORES DIMS
TNTS IRONRATIONS PAPA
SHUT HEARD GIRL STAMENS
TECO ESTE FREE SERS CAT
UNK PATE PEERS PRESTIGE
BELTED SILVERAGE KERNEL
SWEARS HAEMA NESS ACRE
SSTS MAITRE SURE OCHS
     SEPALS NOWS ABLE
IMA VASE NITRO SLED LOU
SILVERSPOON COPPERHEADS
INTERCEPTOR ASSIGNATION
SKATE DOONE SHINS TERRA
```

326

```
ITO IFORANI ISHADOW TAW
NOW RESOLES REALITE ABA
RUNSANIOVER APPLEOFHISI
ETUIS EMIR SNAPS ETAPES
DEPT WREN EMILY SCENT
     BOER FLEAS AVE KITS
SHIPAND ALIEN FRIES
HAWING TOSS TOOLRESTS
AWING TALCS AARON TEHEE
MKTS HOOKANDI MATINEES
SIN TARO OAKS ANDPIE
SER HITSTHEBULLSI SUN
OTSEGO ERIA AGON BGS
PASTEURS IDROPPER BLIP
STERN AMAZE LAPSE MAIDU
ESOTERICA LIVE RANCOR
     STELE DIVER CONDIGN
ALOGA ARE PIMAS GRUS
MUSIC AEGIS ILET BERG
EPILOG SLEET ARAS AURAL
BIRDSIVIEWS ILESSINGAZA
ANI TRIPPET CONSENT TOD
ESS ILASHES SEEITOI ORI
```

327

```
NTH SIZE TRASS TOPER
ORA ITEM BEARIT ULNAE
LINOTYPEMACHINE BEERS
PROP PRAY SLIDERULE
REVS HEARSE TENS MET
OME LOLLS LEAS CARATS
SERRANID BEETS MOTS
   AMEN MACLE STYLI
SPOKES MINTY ANALECTS
TALER VOLAR ALAMO TOL
ENES KINETOSCOPE RITA
EDO PARTS MORES MARAT
LAMELLAE JADES RUDELY
   AVAIL DEGAS LEMA
TRET MIENS AIRBRAKE
ZAGREB AARE ADNUO URN
ILA AGIL TOLDON ARAD
PARACHUTE HEEL ROTO
PRICE ARCHIMEDESSCREW
EINER VETOES OUSE ARE
RAEDA ASSYR NMEX LSD
```

328

```
SIN DUM ARI RRS
ATTA INGA ZINC BEEP
CRAM SWORDOFDAMOCLES
SHALE CORGI ELOQUENT
TIP MARKONS ELD NCO
ALLSTARNINES DAUGHTER
FLEERED ART LOO
FESSO RUS GOVERNORS
SSS JACKET ROBE DOPEY
   ALOOF BALER IRATE
PHOENIXRISENFROMASHES
EARTH EBLIS BONIN
IDAHO YULS LANARK DEB
SATIRISTS FIG NERVE
   CST ARN UTOPIAN
FURSEALS AUGEANSTABLE
ANO LIU STUARTS BUT
ROSALIND TIRRA SILAS
OPENPANDORASBOX ABET
ERNS SERA TOBE FIRE
NYE NEW BAD EDS
```

329

```
CENT COATS CASER BLAME
AMAH TOPHAT PROVE ROBIN
ROPE AMASKEDLUCILLEBALL
OTO OREL EROS NEED TEA
BELABOR PHEN RECTO PERI
EMIT CROON EVE NIL
DROIT GAEL ASSES ORADEA
ROND HID DIETER ORATORS
AMT BASIC SMUT ASADAYIN
PAYMENT HALOS SLICE LEO
ENNEAD CELEB AMISH MYST
ERNE LETTINGIN AMIC
NOPE LIARS LOTTE RETAPE
EAR SWANS TERSE ALTERED
DRIPPING BAAS SPREE TRI
DECEITS HARLEM ITS LEST
ADEATH AORTA OAKS RUBES
REC RUN BARGE CALL
EPOS AMIRS AVER ARCUATE
LEN AREA AMIS BLUE NOR
GWENVERDONPASQUALE ECTO
AERIE INDUE OUTLET SHAD
RESTS TEENS SEEDY TELE
```

330

```
ADAGE POLO OTIC WAMBA
PAREN ALOU RUDO INOUR
EVANGELIST PROMONTORY
RESOLVED BAH LENDERS
VIED SUGAR LAUD
DYES SERENE INPARIS
FRESH BLISS SON STENT
RELEE AUNT CAPES EDDO
IAL MONTE PILESUP DIN
TROUBLES MOVERSDEVICE
WELD BOLES ARES
ANGLERSFLOAT WINESHOP
TER METOOER SATIN BYA
HEER DRYAD PARE NILES
ODEUR OST MITER INURE
LANTERN EVELYN ATES
     HAIG DONOR TELE
HOEDOWN COT HIGHROAD
TOWNINIOWA SLAPGENTLY
ANNIE NOEL OILS RATON
CESAR DRYS KATY BLORE
```

331

```
ALEC BATS ABLED    SLAB
BANA ITEA CROPUP   TORA
BNAI GLUT FIRECARACAS
ACCRABATIC TEE  REGIME
SETONES  NODI  SIDE
    PONT  MISFITS  SLAG
CAIRN   DELHICACY   ADO
ALBA DAVIT  TITHE   POW
HAEC UTENSIL   UMPIRE
NEXT BORG NOD STERNER
   OSLOBOATTOCHINA
STARLIT STE NAES  GARB
HOBSON   TRANSIT   UBER
IRE EDGES   REEKS  ERNE
ETA SEOULDIER    ORION
DEMI MURORAN   ASSE
   DINT ALOP  DESSERT
ILLINI TSP TIRANASAUR
BLOOD TAIPEI LOGS ITSY
MENT YOGURT ALEE  VETS
SUES   KENYA FESS  ERST
```

332

```
AHEMS CAPER   BLEW ADAMS
RABAT LEAVE  MEADE RELEE
ISERE ARLES ERVIN TIGER
SPRINGSALREADYATTHEGATE
ESTA OPTS  WILLSTO  NESS
   MISE LAIC   OVA
TUSCAN FERN ARM  ENTREE
SPRINGUNLOCKSTHEFLOWERS
ASUN SLEEVE  CASTE AIMAT
RETEE MMX SAAL ERA TATE
STILES AID BROO MRASTOR
     RUSTLESOFSPRING
COARSEN ESAU SEE ORLOPS
ONTO SOO PUTS NEG AARON
STRAY BROOD TEASER URIA
THEREISNOTIMELIKESPRING
SEESAW EOS ALAR  TOASTS
    RAG ABES  ABAT
ASSE SAVABLE  BLUR  ALEE
THUSCAMETHELOVELYSPRING
LOTSA BRIAR RETIE ALLTO
ARRET IDONT CITER PEARL
SEANS TING  SLEDS ANCES
```

333

```
 CHRIS   PARSEE   STELE
GROOVE KINETIC SHADOW
MURDERSINTHERUEMORGUE
ESSE MAL HIA  MARNERS
NEE MOLL ERD  TARE
 THEN WARE FENT  ROME
ASHEN SITS BALA  SERIN
STIMULATE SAULT ELAND
TOES  ECHO ERNIE DANCE
OAF MARK CARAT RATTED
  SARAI ALE  TRITE
COBURN NEPAL OUSE  TOT
AVANT ADDON  ATLE THRU
MISSY UNITE  THESCREEN
ENTER RENE COED  LAKME
LEET  ROSA MUNJ  RAMI
  SERS SAN UPON  LAM
INERTIA IRE DUB  ALGA
COMEONLIKEGANGBUSTERS
ENISLE DEVOTEE SHARES
DELTA  ORATED  TERSE
```

334

```
SETTS  DAMAS OBLS  MISFIT
ELIOT ITALY IRAN ARCILA
WEEPNOMOREMYLADY LAIRED
AGRA BENI  SECY LATESTS
LIONET ENAMOR STUDENT
LADYBUG ABEL MANY  CLAN
SCS USIA LADYBIRD PEACE
  PREFAB TEMPTRESS DRU
ACTI LURES ASH  LILYOF
SHINNY  RABI  AVISO
TINKS THELADY ENID LVII
OLDLADYOFTHREADNEEDLEST
ROSA OKET TIGRESS RINSE
   DRIES  AGIN SEPTUM
RUNYON  IAM BIJOU  OSES
INA AGNESSEVE  CATSUP
DAKAR ARABLADY GOAL OST
SUER FORM  REEL SNUFFLE
  DREAMSO MUSSEL NAUSEA
PULASKI TWIN  NORA ETES
AVANTI THELADYOFTHELAKE
LEDGER REEK CARTE AEGIR
LAYERS ARKS  CHESS TRETS
```

335

```
BANFF BUCK  FLOP ASPIRED
ECOLE OREO  ROAR SURNAME
THEORANGEBLOSSOMSPECIAL
HELD VIE LUM SOUPY  SIA
  DIET KENT MICRO  LELY
WHENCOMINTHROTHERYE
LIONS ADZ EUR ASTERIAL
ULT TILL VIOL  ROLLO
SLEW MAMMYGINNYSJUBILEE
HALIFAX EARN ASHERY ITS
 ZUG ALOES ALB  ANTS
THELITTLESCOTCHLASSIE
SIEN NOR  SABRA  NIP
ARN RAPIDS MEER YESICAN
LORDALEXANDERSREEL COLE
ASYET MOAT  GWYN  NIX
LIVEITUP OSH GOA  EPACT
DOWNONTHEBRANDYWINE
SPES OMNIS GEAR  ROTC
HOT SPATE REP BOK ABIE
ILOVEANOLDFASHIONEDSONG
PINTAIL LEAP IDLE USING
SOSORRY ONDE CATS BOSSY
```

336

```
SCANS  CARACO  SEBERG
ALLOW  OREGON  ORATOR
TOOLATETHEPHALAROPE
ETH RIDE  ALE   ENAM
SHASTA  ASONE ISOTOPE
  WHOKILLEDCOCKROBIN
SPLAY ALTAR RIIS  LAO
PAIR GROAN SWANN  BENT
OWEDTOANIGHTINGALE
NEG ROTA  AUNT  YEAST
GRENADE WORDY DRIFTER
ESSEN OISE  ARAN  TAA
  TOKILLAMOCKINGBIRD
BACH LOSER TREVI ERLE
IRR CUTE STALE  BREED
THECATANDTHECANARY
TAMALES RUARK  VULCAN
STAT  WAC  MIES  OCA
THEFEATHERMERCHANTS
EATING UNIATE  ERGOT
DYABLE NAPPED  SCARY
```

337

```
STAEL TSPS  GLORY  CASPAR
HOMME EIRE  ROSIE  ALCOVE
ADMIRALBENBOWINN   ROOKED
HOOTOWL  SALTBED  PRUNER
   TIES  STATOR  LIEDER
AMBI  DOTHEBOYSHALL   FDA
STONG  NRA    ARE   AULIC
TARGET  IRKS APIA TISANE
IRO  BROBDINGNAG SONATAS
ADO  ONE  TEENS    HART
PRIMATE  MELT  HUM  RATEL
CANOT  MIDDLEEARTH  EBONY
STOOL  ADS  VALE  ICEBAGS
    ARNO  CHERI  FLU  EDO
REMANDS  DOONEVALLEY  HRS
EXACTS  JOLT  DECO DAMAGE
PINTA  PAN    CWT   MELEE
STD  NEWGATEPRISON   LLDS
   EDGARS  NOLEAD  RIMA
  PRIEST  LAPLACE CLANGED
DULLES  WUTHERINGHEIGHTS
ORELSE  ALTAR  ATEE  REARM
GEYSER  SLOTS  LSTS  ESTES
```

338

```
πLOT  πSTOL     πBALD
OCANA  NOIRE  AMATORY
ASAMERICANAS  VENETIAN
PITA  ASHπT  TRENTE  PRO
PEI  ESTHS    ARTS   SπNS
ARNEL  SIFE  RISO  MANSE
LENDSA   TOLUENE   TONG
DYNAST  RAπDS  DEADSEA
ASORS  NNE  PRUNEπTS
SEES  NOTYET  SEAT  RGTS
ADM   πINTHESKY    OLE
LUπN  ACNE  EπTOME  ATES
SCRAPBAG  TAL   EARED
ETERNAL  PRIAM  NOTERS
SRAS  SHORTED  SWEETS
AUTOS  AHOY  ENOS  ARSON
SLAW  SPAN  STOAS   TOE
πTT  PEPPED  ICTIC  SAGE
CREDIBLE  EπTHETCALLER
ARECUED  STEER  AGALS
SCAMπ   KHANS   SAPS
```

339

```
ALIAS  OTARY  HADES  SWEEP
LINGO  GELEE  ERODE  PANDA
ADDER  PRODS  DIODE  ELGIN
MOUNTRUSHMORESDAK  AKITE
ONETOO  EAA  TATA  CRANED
FULLSPEEDAHEAD   LED
REAM  GAY  LLS   RIETI
EXHALED  AEI  TENT  OTOES
SPEKE  EBB  HBEAMS  SATRAP
TOMES  DOAQUICKSTEP  LARA
ASI  STU  THE  HAPENNY
THERACEISTOTHESWIFT
SARANAC  COE  HAD   NEA
URIS  QUICKFREEZES  TSARS
BALTEI  DELAND  ELY  ATRIA
JULYS  PLAY  ILL  ROSETTA
PEWEE  ANY  TIN   REAR
FLU  HURRYUPANDWAIT
FRIDAY  HABA  CRO  CORAJI
LANDI  IDONOTCHOOSETORUN
UNDID  VODKA  AMOUR  AMILE
SCENE  ABEET  SOPTO  SADIE
HONGS  RUSES  ABYSS  KNEAD
```

340

```
FACT   ISAWA  APART   ALI
AROOM  SONIC  SAVOR   ROM
RINGAROUNDTHEROSY   MOP
MONAMOUR  TIO  SIS  RATE
ESE  EAT  AHOUSEDIVIDED
ROCK  NORN  NRA   ENARE
STAR  FETE   PETERS
TUMBLING   ISOLDE
CARIBOU  TAKETIMEOUT
ONE  OSAR  PENAL  TUMOR
MIRA  INES  ACTI   TIRE
BLURB  NEPER  EENS   AME
ONCEREMOVED  TRACKED
ELISIR  PLETHORA
LANSAT   SPEE   CURT
EBOLI   EBB  INFO  LERP
SEPARATEROOMS  ISL  SIR
CAPS  SOC  DNA  SELECTEE
ADO  APOCKETFULLOFPOSY
PES  CELLO  OILED  TARTE
EDE  UNSER  KATES  SEED
```

341

```
RADIOS  ADEPT  FLEA  FOMOR
ARISTA  PILAR  LOOM  ENERO
WITHOUTACLUE  UNNUMBERED
ECARTE  MAKES  ORIOLE
COWS  ETTU  ROVER    TIL
OBITER  ULE   SPILLWAY
SEDER  UNINFORMATIVE  ITE
TREES  POROUS  ELATE  ATRA
ALONE  ROAMS  CLARA  CHIS
TIPS  BONNE  CHOCK  SCOUT
ENE  MISSINGLINK  JORUMS
NOISE  HAL   RABAT
CASTLE  MEANINGLESS  MAP
OLPES  BAITS  ARABS  PESO
SCAR  CROSS  ATETE  BOATS
TOCO  WHERE  STATIC  ORNOT
EVE  DRAWINGABLANK  STILE
DESPAIRS  AVA   THENAR
ANT  SPLAT  TAHR   SGTS
HAIRDO  SHEEN  SAMOAN
ILLDEFINED  NOTHINGATALL
COLOR  CEBA  AVION  UTOPIA
KEENS  HEAL  HARED  SORTED
```

342

```
BEARD  ROADHOG  CLUTCH
RANCOR  ARMOIRE  HONORE
HIGHWAYROBBERY  OBEYER
OTIS  GAINS  RISERS  CAM
MEN  FRITO  TOSEED  CASE
BREVIARY  RIGORS  WARES
TALCS  MOERIS   TAB
PRIME  VASSAL  FARAWAY
TOOLS  TEDEUM  MAINLINE
ULUS  BOREUP  SERGEANTS
REB  BURNUPTHEROAD  NOM
FALSESTEP  RIDGES  LINE
EXECUTES  RANGES  RUNIN
DESIRES  WEFTED  FARGO
ERR  LEAFED   CIVET
STONE  PALLID  PUNISHES
CURT  CYCLIC  ALBAN  ELL
ANN  CAROBS  GRAIL  AREA
REASON  MOTORCYCLEGANG
FUTURE  BRIGADE  ARECAS
SPEEDS  ENCODED  PARES
```

343

```
PHOCAL  HUME   NHU   FAST
IRONORE ANERA  CENA  OLLA
NOTIMEFORSERGEANTS   ETON
THECAPTAINKANGAROOSHOW
RILE  AIS  ALTER  ILLINOIS
ABC  SNIPPY  SER  DDT  NNE
DIALS  ASI    TOA   SWAGE
ATRICE  REDAS    TREMOR
THEKENTUCKYCOLONELS
ACHENES  COOEE  AIL  SOCK
KLM  MYNAS   GENERALSTORE
ICAME   ASP   TSE   ESTOP
MAJORLEAGUER  LEMMA  EDT
SPOT  EAR  NEEDS  GOUGERS
PRIVATEINVESTIGATOR
VERSED   ESTAB    EDICTS
RAVER   LEO   AQS   SCARE
PSI  NBA  ASK  SPRUER  ROC
MONGOOSE  TASTE  ISO  NAPA
FRENCHLIEUTENANTSWOMAN
ANON  CORPORALPUNISHMENT
MOST  EROS  ILLAT  NEEDLES
OWES  EYE   LALO   ARNESS
```

344

```
ADAM  SPA  OMITS  MISHAP
MALARKEY  FOLIO  OTIOSE
BISCAYNE  FRANCISSCOTT
USO  WET  OKAY  IDEA  KIT
SIRS  YESMEN  MALS  DEME
HEATS  CLAY  GALE  TOYED
SNAP  OAR  JASS  DUN
LEAST   BELT   TABASCO
KEYWEST  HARLEMITE  HOR
INVADE  PASSERINE  TREK
STORY  MONKEYING  CHURN
MINT  DONKEYMEN  QUINCE
ERN  VENDETTAS  TURNKEY
TEEPEES  REEN  GROAN
RED  TIEA  MAO  RICH
LALOS  SENR  BATU  ASHES
AULD  SHAG  DURESS  HEAP
CRO  MIAS  DINE  STU  EVA
KEYTOTHECITY  KEYNOTER
ENDIVE  THETA  BALDPATE
YESSES  SITON  SUE  THOS
```

345

```
SIGH  PARA   ABBOT   ASHY
MAORI  ALIBI  FLARE  ACTOR
EXTINCTBIRD  TABLESCRAPS
LEANDER  SALT  BYE  ICERS
UNIT   HEAT   STER
DORP  RCA  PARC  ANEARS
FUROR  WORM  EXCLAMATIONS
ORIBI  IDEST  ETANA  ELMAN
PREENED  SNEES  VALE  SAKI
SAN  CEE  SELF  TILER  NIP
TAELS   PET  REO  IMAGES
SASS  TECH   ORGS   IGOR
SPLASH  RYE  AMP  TINED
ION  STRAW  MAIM  ADE  OCA
NOUS  TRON  LORCA  GOESFAR
ELROD  ERASE  MANSE  NEWLY
WESTERNSTATE  LIED  TRALA
DESPOT  EMIR  FAN  RARA
UTES   NAZI   DADA
ERATO  TSE  TUBS  GONDOLA
BITTERVETCH  NEEDLECASES
AREAS  ALICE  IRENE  EVENS
REST  CERES  SPAT  SYST
```

346

```
MULCT  ADLER  RAGA  ATTA
ARARU  LEONE  EWES  QUAR
RETURNENGAGEMENT  URNS
EYE  NINE  BACILLI  ANGE
AEC  BALLAST   MAROON
LETTRES  MEERS  DERIV
IPUT  NATO  STIPE  TAELS
TARHEELERS  EVINCE  RAP
ACNES  KRAIT  ELAL  JAIR
TETES  INOS  EROMANCY
TURNBACKWARDOTIME
OCHREOUS  SIDE  SLEWS
KLAN  ORAL  TATTI  ISLES
RAW  SPINED  TURNSADEAF
ADANO  NATAL  RANT  EATA
YEARS  TREEN  SETAFOX
ROWENA  RERINSE  LON
HARD  SPAREST  LLEW  EVE
ERAL  GOODTURNDESERVES
METE  AKUA  RAYES  LOONS
EDHS  RELY  EPURE  SWEDE
```

347

```
FOCH  SERA  PAWL  WASHER
EPHA  CHAIR  CLAIM  ASHORE
LEADAHORSE  TALKINGHORSE
IRR  LATTENS  STELES  SEL
SALEM  HEAT  SALT  ODE
ESSENE  SAGO  BES  DEWS
PAYS  LENA  TINHAT  EPOCH
OCH  ILE  TWOFEET  CAROMED
SCOUTED  MARTHA  VOL  SANS
TURNS  MOD  HORSEMARINE
ESSE  FSU  HORSEEMMET
DEE  BLACKHORSETROOP  CRS
COACHHORSE  ENS  PLOP
SHORTCOURSE  ORD  TIOGA
OLOR  OUS  SENILE  SANCTUS
PARDONS  SECONDS  ANT  HEM
ANSER  REDANS  TARO  HESS
GERA  DOM  ROUT  RINSES
HOD  HUIT  LAHR  ASHUR
AGE  MAGNET  TRAINED  ONE
QUARTERHORSE  RIVERHORSE
UNDOES  SLAIN  ETAIN  USED
ASSESS  ESNE  DILL  RETS
```

348

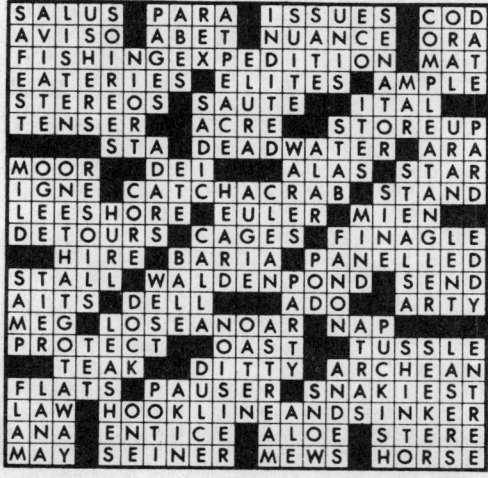

```
SALUS  PARA  ISSUES  COD
AVISO  ABET  NUANCE  ORA
FISHINGEXPEDITION  MAT
EATERIES  ELITES  AMPLE
STEREOS  SAUTE  ITAL
TENSER  ACRE  STOREUP
STA  DEADWATER  ARA
MOOR  DEI  ALAS  STAR
IGNE  CATCHACRAB  STAND
LEESHORE  EULER  MIEN
DETOURS  CAGES  FINAGLE
HIRE  BARIA  PANELLED
STALL  WALDENPOND  SEND
AITS  DELL  ADO  ARTY
MEG  LOSEANOAR  NAP
PROTECT  OAST  TUSSLE
TEAK  DITTY  ARCHEAN
FLATS  PAUSER  SNAKIEST
LAW  HOOKLINEANDSINKER
ANA  ENTICE  ALOE  STERE
MAY  SEINER  MEWS  HORSE
```

349

```
HIGHTEA  MAGICA  WISHES
ENLISTS  AMADOR  RHEIMS
SCAREUP  TALENT  HESTER
TADS  DST  HEAVYSEAS
   ULE  HASSLE  MARINES
ERATO  CAN  NCAR  LOMA
RENEW  LIGHTMEALS  EDEN
ANT  CRO  EIRE  PLT  DET
STE  OAST  CATNIP  STERE
   IMPERO  DIETO  HORSE
  GREATEXPECTATIONS
FARAD  ONEAT  STARRY
IRONY  STARED  ETAT  DIN
NEW  ETO  TSAR  OSS  ADO
GOLF  LONGSTRIDE  TILER
ELEA  ERSE  MUS  ONION
REDRICE  LEGGED  OPT
   FATSKATER  SIC  OLAF
ALERTS  ATONAL  THINICE
RESORT  LINING  ORDERED
MOOMOO  ONSIDE  SEEDERS
```

350

```
SALS  TSARS  GAES  TSELIOT
ASEA  ITHOT  ASIP  HHMUNRO
ICAL  LEOTOLSTOY  ROSTAND
CHRISTIE  DUMAURIER  ESAU
   NOUN  EDNA  IMA  ODETS
REDGAP  DRAGNET  PTAH  TET
YPRES  PAIRS  TOI  SPAS
OSAR  BLUED  EARNS  PRISMS
TOG  BEANS  EDGARALLANPOE
SMOLLETT  WODEHOUSE  COTA
   AERO  DANA  ALT  PLUTO
BADWAY  COGS  GADS  COATOF
AMORT  JOG  FIDS  BALI
NOTE  CORNEILLE  REMARQUE
JOHNDOSPASSOS  JANUS  UPS
ONECUP  SIKES  FONTS  MATT
   ETTU  LER  YEATS  FICHE
AMI  CENS  REWARDS  WICKER
NINTH  THO  ALMS  MINH
ISSU  BRETHARTE  VONNEGUT
THOREAU  HERMANWOUK  NIKE
AAMILNE  ERAT  TETRA  EDEN
SPENSER  ROTH  STENT  REST
```

351

```
ICINGS  SEES  ANOX  SAIL
NOMORE  ORLOP  DORIC  ALDA
RIPVANWINKLE  JULIACHILD
ELS  BARGES  LEONE  MOATED
   TINS  BOLUS  KERR
TAJ  DOTE  PETER  SALAAMED
ORATORS  ISAACNEWTON  ANA
TAMERS  STIRS  BAIT  EDAM
EDENS  LOESS  AGATE  DRAMA
MAST  FILM  ARANS  SEAMEN
SSW  VENUSDEMILO  DAMSELS
HOOVES  RAISE  CANOED
SMITTEN  WARDENLAWES  ERE
LISTER  SHINE  USER  AFAR
ALTOS  SPANS  TARES  STAIN
NILS  SHIN  DINAR  STERNE
TEE  GEORGEMEANY  SPONGES
SURPLICE  NOTRE  STAB  EDT
   RANK  AGORA  EPIC
SNOOZE  ANITA  GARLIC  THO
CULBERTSON  CARRIENATION
ALEE  SUEDE  TWEET  GREENE
BLAS  NAES  NEDS  STARES
```

352

```
ALLTHATW  SABADO  PETE
SELASSIE  PLOWERS  ODOR
STARTERS  ULALUME  AGON
ESNE  SIERRAS  CAAN  AKA
ROE  NEATH  PERMATRON
TURN  AGOGE  MESA  IRANI
STOOPS  REDWARE  ELUL
   SAKIS  IDITOL  ELA
MEAL  BETIDE  SOLI  AMA
MOLLE  NEWNESS  MASONIC
ARMET  MISBUTA  ROPER
AGISTER  TIERODS  ALONE
RUR  ELOI  DREARY  FIES
EAT  SONNET  EMMET
   RENE  FORHESA  SLEEPS
SPORE  HOGS  SIMPS  STAT
HAYMAKERS  STOWE  INA
ILS  PALM  TAENIAS  HEAT
RATA  TEABALL  THECENCI
ACED  ANNABEL  HEROINES
ZERO  STRUMA  INADREAM
```

353

```
OFABAD  CBT  QPL  AMAPA
RICAMA  ALE  ULA  TFELOG
REVERSE  MONDAYS  GORIGHT
EGER  THEPOUND  TARROS
RAF  BEDLAM  ARABIAN  TSAR
UNO  ALLO  ESPIRITU  SEESA
MOURN  APERCU  DTS  BURYIT
  RAD  BID  UELE  PUB  EAT
GOTHA  UNDERMAN  AUTOGENY
ACH  GROGAN  OUTSIT  RANS
PARTETH  TUCREPPU  NUI
SEA  STLO  VUE  SIBS  GMT
EHS  PENSIONS  NOSEPEG
STOA  UNTIDY  IMAWAY  UNA
TOWELROD  ALTEREGO  NUTTY
ERO  MEG  LYNN  RND  OFF
TROCOS  APO  ONEYOU  NAILS
RONAN  BELINDAS  MODY  LAC
AWED  FLOYDOY  PREHEM  LTR
  EALING  THERENTS  ELIA
STANDUP  ANDWAIT  TOOTING
PUKCAB  IOU  STR  OTTAWA
AMEER  NNE  ESO  NOTHIS
```

354

```
PILEUP  FACADES  PHOCIS
ORACLE  ONAWALL  ARRANT
DISHONORABLEDISCHARGE
ESTO  DWC  GET  ERLE
   MILERS  BEHEST  IER
ALIMONYPAYMENTS  OLE
CONING  SENORES  NOODLE
CATCALL  SODAS  CATBOAT
PTER  AER  DET  DOGHOUSE
THRO  WHATS  EYING  STES
   SANE  NASI
FOHS  UVEAL  MELON  KEPT
FLATTIRE  ALA  SLG  AMER
VARIETE  OMENS  EBBTIDE
SNARLS  WREATHE  AORTES
   NSO  WILDGOOSECHASES
ALG  SHADES  STALKS
ROUT  USO  LEA  TASA
OVERDRAWNBANKACCOUNTS
MEREST  ENAMOUR  HARTES
ASSETS  RETIREE  EFFETE
```

355

```
CLARK  NOPAR  QUASI    WHOA
HOMER  OCALA  ENDOR    SHORT
ERICA  VAULT  DOONE    AERIE
RESTIVE  AAR  BYNOMEANS
ISHOTAN↑INTOTHEAIR  LEST
  STABS  ASOU  COME
ZAPS  ISAIDTHESP→  EDGED
EXOTIC  CSO  SHET  MRHYDE
DEERPARK  GMC  IDO  ICEMEN
  MESNE  IDOL  HOWFAIR
TOSEE  DECORUM  NEF  WRAP
UNIT  WITHMYBOWAND→  HELL
BESS  ENL  SCHERZO  SETBY
  BROKEN→  AAAA  RAWER
ROWROW  DES  RRR  BANALITY
ATHOME  OLMS  SOO  EMBAYS
STOAE  SLINGSAND→S  →LET
  DOMO  TELA  ZESTS
ADDA  ARETHEYH→EDTOTHEM→
TURNSTILE  CAR  OFREACH
ERODE  SIXES  RODIN  ARRIE
AEONS  OZARK  AOEDE  DELIA
MRD→  NANNY  STOSS  SAYID
```

356

```
LOAF  PAR  PAM  APT    POP
AMMO  AGA  FABA  PAY  CODA
TABU  REPEATER  RIP  SALES
SHARES  TWENTYNINEACROSS
ASTRO  ERA  JOLT  MAT
SHIN  ALI  CAG  EMBRACES
HADE  TULE  LNG  DEL  OXA
DODO  HESS  HUES  CUE  MOTS
SHOWBOAT  CEES  HOSS  ALES
CORNERS  TAIL  ROLE  AFIRE
  ADELAIDE  EMU  SINN
THEMEDIUMISTHEMESSAGE
RAPE  KRA  SOURNOTE
CORED  NEUN  ERNS  LORELEI
RUDE  BAAS  SNAG  DIRTIEST
INTS  ASS  BATH  TEAK  GATS
ECO  THO  AYR  FERN  PHDS
REPENTER  COY  ARM  ALTA
  NOL  ETON  ORE  SAYSO
HUNDREDTENACROSS  ANDTHE
ANDES  OHM  REPEALER  ORAL
HEAD  SUP  ADES  ULU  WARM
ASK  EMS  SEN  RIM  NYES
```

357

```
PUTSUP  SPACE  TIME  USSS
ATHENS  AGROS  IMET  MUTAS
STEADYSTATETHEORY  SPUNK
HEM  ECCE  IDEES  IMP  EDDA
ARIL  HOLMES  LIED  AERIAL
LEVELLER  BONDIANDGOLD
ASKME  LIL  NIT  SANSEI
RAYAS  ATLONG  ZEND  NAMBY
KIWI  DYE  REBAIL  MINGLE
SNATHE  SCI  ASP  ELECTRON
TYRES  EBENS  STAR  STS
EXPANDINGUNIVERSE
ORA  ALOE  STRUT  IRISH
REDSHIFT  HUH  ROC  TINPAN
UNMOOR  STEERS  OPT  SETA
POILU  MSTS  ODESSA  ITCHY
ADESTE  ERS  AMS  BETAS
SPIRALGALAXY  ALISTAIR
CLOWNS  RENT  SPECIO  NOTT
RODI  AED  IRANO  DONA  GAR
EWING  PULSATINGUNIVERSE
WENDY  OSTE  ADIOS  CARATS
RESP  STDS  REAPT  SLIMES
```

358

```
SUM  KAT  SALEM    CART
ADO  FISH  CLINE  ARNEE
CONCRETE  OLEOS  CATTLE
THEVICAROFWAKEFIELD
KRAIT  OBEY  ART  SON
IAN  TRUE  BASI  ETNA
THATPRINTEROFUDELLS
ELIOT  RELAP  DAB
RUSTUM  RESTORE  ARAMIS
OLIOS  MYNAS  RAMS  ONE
ANON  HIDER  GIVES  COCA
DAU  POLO  ARRAS  HARUM
SEXTON  CRANIAL  METERS
END  TIRON  UBOAT
MAYOROFCASTERBRIDGE
OCAS  OREO  ONAS  EON
POT  PUT  INFO  LIMAS
THEMERCHANTOFVENICE
SORITE  UNIAT  EREMITES
RILEY  SIDLE  LISP  EVA
TADS  SLEYS  SAT  REY
```

359

```
REAM  PEAL  WATCH  HAIL
ALMA  SOCLE  AVARO  ORDO
PYTHAGORAS  GALIMATIAS
ARTHURIANLEGENDS
ANGLES  MODE  ROOTS
PORIA  MINOR  ARU  GOTH
PLEASURES  ITSON  TAO
LAG  PERTH  ARIES  PENN
ENO  PLISSE  NODS  MALTA
RERAN  RHONE  MARION
SITINS  SCAPE  BARMAN
TEAAND  SHUTE  ORGAN
RUNTS  ETAL  ROMANO  LET
ARCS  FRERE  AVISE  OVI
MAA  LEADA  ESTRANGED
STLO  ORD  NEARS  LUIRE
SENTA  TILT  PERCYS
NEWTONIANPHYSICS
OLDMASTERS  HEARTSEASE
AAAA  BREAK  ARRAS  RHEE
TORN  YARNS  SEES  YAWL
```

360

```
PAPA  STRAPS    STOAS
WEIRD  PROSIT  CHOLLA
HELLODOROTHEA  REDLIPS
ANTS  ELITE  TIER  ITIC
IDE  PRINTS  PUREE  SHEA
LYDIA  OTI  FATED  EJECT
MSS  SNAILED  STARES
SLATER  GENES  BLOC
PEAGREEN  RES  LEANOVER
ANNOY  DACIA  LOAM  BONE
ROD  POTHERBERTS  TAG
CRES  LUTE  TOTAL  SPITE
HADABABY  CHI  NEWHAVEN
RUNT  ROUSE  SHORES
INSANE  TORRENT  OTO
LATHS  DRUMS  TIC  ALLAY
ENIF  SOULS  LARIAT  ELA
ATRO  IDEA  LIENS  AMEN
CERRADO  DONALDCOSSACK
SETTLE  ENAMEL  NEONS
RHEES  STEADY  EARS
```

361

```
ELDEST  SCREW  DEEPS  BASS
TAILOR  AHOLE  EERIE  ACTI
COCKLESHELLS  FRIENDSHIP
HST  ESTATE  TAROK  TRIERS
     TAR  OSELA  ASIAN
SKI  ALIAS  TREYS  TENSPOT
HANDLER  CHINESEJUNK  URU
ESTOPS  SHUNS  RUNT  GNAT
ASHES  ALONG  THINS  SETTO
PEER  SPOOK  BOONE  CONFER
ELS  PORTLY  ARMS  PERIODS
  ALINES  DANTE  CAREER
HAMITES  VOID  CRANES  MEC
ERECTS  BIRDS  RENTS  MAUL
BEBES  RORYS  KATES  TETRA
ROOT  MAME  CAFES  CURIOS
ELA  BAMBOORAFTS  LOLLOPS
WATEREE  STORK  THOLE  NEA
   NOWEL  RARAE  END
PALACE  ETANA  SUREST  ADE
SMACKSDOWN  CUTTERNUMBER
SMUT  TANIT  KNEES  ABOLLA
TODS  STENO  SASSY  PEWEES
```

362

```
HTS  APAR  WAVERS  URSA
ARAS  DINE  OLIVET  BOAR
WORKISLOVEMADEVISIBLE
STAID  ANITA  EPI  BAM
  NESS  ERN  SPIED  EME
ANDFAITHWESHALLNEEDIT
NEIL  LEA  WANE  DDT
DEMI  ORTS  OLEA  ALAS
EDEN  PAIR  DAMAGING
SYSTS  MINSK  MISEDIT
  IDONTLIKEWORK
CHARGED  SEDER  SINGE
REDONNED  NANA  MORA
IRED  ASSE  AVIS  IMAT
  ETC  DCIV  ENT  TAPE
LABORANDAREHEAVYLADEN
ERA  ANEAR  RAX  EXIT
EER  STL  DREAR  AISLE
WORKHELPSTOPRESERVEUS
ALOE  EILEEN  TREK  EARS
YAWN  NESTLE  SODA  TEE
```

363

```
SRO  CARIB  ETTE  HATS
AOK  ARIDE  NEED  BATHE
NAIL  SENOR  GLAD  ALIEN
GREETINGLIBRARYCREDIT
  GENOA  BRA  SPRYER
TENSPOT  SEEFIT  LAP
IRITIS  SCRATCH  GAFFS
FILED  DORIC  AEC  ELIOT
FEEL  PINO  HANDON  ATEE
  LIED  LEOS  AREONTHE
FACTORYOLDFIRSTSECOND
AHEARTOF  IPSE  ETRE
TELL  HUGGER  PIGS  COLA
HALER  ROA  OPINE  LOBED
ADOBE  DIAMOND  RELOAD
  ODA  STRIKE  DEALERS
  DIONNE  ISE  NOTRE
RICKENBACKERBOYINGTON
IPASS  OBRA  OATEN  EASY
PARAS  NOIR  OLONA  BEE
STEM  YUBA  TENSE  SET
```

364

```
LAPAZ  GINAS  RIDGE  MAAS
AGATE  AROSE  UNION  TOSCA
BEGINSWITHTANDENDSWITHS
ONES  TASTY  BOITE  PONIES
RAS  TRIES  BLUES  SABERS
  MIENS  SOOTS  PARAS
SATIRE  MOO  ANTS  ROD
TFELOTTHGIRMORFSDAERENO
RILES  HAILS  FEATS  ALOT
URIS  AISLE  PALLY  SAVINE
TEC  ABET  FIRES  PIECES
  ISAFOURLETTERWORD
BARNET  PEERS  HITS  DEC
AVERSE  SPINS  FLOPS  SURE
TOLU  SAENS  LEONE  TAMAR
TWENTYTHREELETTERPHRASE
SSE  REAL  AVE  ARISES
  BOSNS  NAZIS  SATES
SCRIMS  SOLUS  SATIE  AAR
MORALE  ATOLL  SITON  ALSO
ONEHUNDREDFIFTEENACROSS
ADAMS  ITALO  LEVEE  AGREE
SEMS  TYLER  AMEND  POSTS
```

365

```
WABBLE  FIRMA  FATE  COPSE
OBERON  ICIAN  AGAL  ACRID
RADIOSERIALS  CONCERTIZE
STRAP  VENTA  BUDGING  MEN
TOON  REHEARSALS  DOODADS
SRO  HARASS  LITER  WEED
MAOISTS  AL  SPEEDIER  SCORE
OFFERS  GASES  KNOT
HOARDER  SALT  DARE  ERATE
ARRIERE  ARAMAIC  CRIMETS
RACE  RIVET
AYE  MUSICALCOMEDIES  PFC
LESSOR  SKEETED  HULA
PARACHUTE  CREE  ESCAPE
AMASSER  CLOCK  STRIPED
RODS  RESTHOME  OATPIT
TRIOS  STROVE  COALSLIP  ERE
OETA  RICED  FORGES
MADDER  POLYGAMIES  LEERA
AUR  ANOMALY  ALPEN  CIRCA
GRANDOPERA  SILENTMOVIES
MAMIE  ANAT  ALERT  AMENDE
ALAND  RUSE  DYNES  RANGER
```

366

```
SPOUSES  RUB  SIR  SPAN
CASSATT  ARU  JADE  TARA
ATTACHE  JILLOLANTERNS
LEIF  ILIA  LOST  DORSET
DNA  JOANBARLEYCORN
  MOPED  GULP  AVOWS
BAHAI  ICON  HORA  AWAY
AXILS  KAHN  LINT  IRENE
REGATTA  ASLANT  ADDEND
ASHY  USSR  IDEALLY  TOO
  JACQUELINESPILLOW
ALI  AUREOLE  CERO  MIST
MOLINE  STUDIO  OTHELLO
MILNE  GATS  MATT  ALMON
ONES  HOWE  BATS  BEATS
  RUNIN  HAIR  AMBIT
  LETGEORGIADOIT  APT
STRAIT  DREG  CESS  MERE
CHARLENESAUNT  ATTIRES
ARAL  RENE  NEO  IRONIST
RUBY  SES  STR  COYNESS
```

367

```
SHAG  KITH  OFEASE  OSAS
AERO  LARA  SIRUPS  NULL
LIVY  ANAK  TRAGIC  ELMO
ADIEUX  GILA  CREWCUT
DINGDONGMERRILYONHIGH
  OONA  AMORY  WYO
MOAT  SAGS  YEAR  SOCKET
ERROL  CLAUS  NIP  OUSE
SCUBA  POMPOM  CALUMETS
HAMETZ  VALUES  NEMESES
  THEHERALDANGELS
MACHETE  ANDINE  KAFFIR
ACELDAMA  DENDAD  URANO
IDLE  ISM  LARGE  TOTEM
SCAMPI  TONI  OHIO  MAZE
  YOM  ROUGH  GUSH
NOROOMFORTHEMINTHEINN
ARUNDEL  TWAS  MEANIE
MEAD  RANCHI  TODO  VINE
PANE  SIOUAN  CLOD  EGAD
ADAR  ERRING  HATE  NOSY
```

368

```
CRASS  QUASH  ALAPA  SPRAG
RELIC  UNITE  VINES  CLARE
EVADE  ODDER  OBIES  OAKIE
WEWENTTOAPARTYONNEWYEAR
  LICE  ORAN  PLI
ZURICH  SALOME  ANI  TSGT
EBAN  SALAAM  ABLEST  QUA
SEVEATQUARTERTOTWOYOUSU
TRI  PAULS  LEORA  DERE
HAHA  SAP  VIZ  TESTATE
MACARONI  TITI  OOH  KIP
GGESTEDWELEAVEIREFUSEDI
RAM  EOS  COAL  IRONORES
SLENDER  POI  LIL  ILLY
  NEON  FRONS  AGGIE  BOB
DETESTBEINGTOLDWHATTODO
OWE  ERRATA  AMULET  USED
ZEDS  AAR  ELEVEN  WARCRY
  AJI  LUXE  JAVA
APOXONTHEPARTYAPOXONYOU
JASON  HOVEL  RALLY  IDOLS
ARENA  ANENT  ELIOT  DORPS
XRAYS  WELDS  SETTO  STEER
```

369

```
CHEKHOV  MECCA  TROUSER
IONESCO  ATHOS  RAPTURE
CLAYMEN  CHECKOUTTIMES
AIMS  ANTS  CHECKS  LACT
DEO  NEO  SKIRT  SECTS
ARRA  GAWAIN  OTEA
BEAU  ERN  BELT  OLA
CHECKSTONE  CHECKSUPON
HANSEL  STEALER  USAGE
ETC  AREA  LAA  SOMALI
  CHECKERBOARDSQUARES
HAMLET  ORS  CAST  STD
RENEE  AUCTION  SPECIE
ACTUALISTS  BLANKCHECK
PKS  RUFF  HAD  OISE
  EGER  SENSUM  HATH
EGGAR  ETTAS  VIA  BRO
DERM  DASHER  GASP  BRIT
DOUBLECHECKER  TIDIEST
ADELINE  THEME  ISOLATE
SELECTS  ASNEW  CHEKKER
```

370

```
OPA  ERSATZ  TSAR  SET
DAS  BREATHE  RAVE  APE
ESS  DERAILED  ETON  RID
STEPIN  SLAB  NEWDEAL
SORRENTO  SAMITE  ATOM
ARTESIAN  TICONDEROGA
  SENT  COTTON  ONEGUN
PAPS  GEFALLEN  SUNDAES
OCT  STRANDER  HORA
STEREO  CATO  RAW  ABBE
SURRENDEROFCORNWALLIS
EPOS  ERY  BOUE  ARDENT
  SPAS  SUNGMASS  AGO
LEOPARD  WINDISCH  ATOP
AVIATE  CANKER  TIAS
VALLEYFORGE  MONMOUTH
ANTE  INTERN  ARGENTIA
SARANAC  HARD  TEETER
CTN  LOCO  CITEDFOR  ERA
ROK  TERR  PLATOON  RCS
INS  SLED  ALLEGE  SES
```

371

```
BELIE  RATS  LESE  SADIES
IWILL  AGIO  ANTI  INITIAL
JEKYLLSANDHYDES  ANSONIA
OREA  EPIC  ASONE  MAC  ENG
USN  COUNTSOFMONTECRISTO
OPT  ALOES  ASHER
FATTYOIL  LER  THEREUPON
ISHALLNOT  BRIO  ITSELF
SPEWED  BENE  ROMEOS  REL
KIS  LOLALOLAS  STOPROD
ESQ  CALIBAN  TILTY
  HUNCHBACKSOFNOTREDAME
ATEAR  TOETOES  AVS
ISWHERE  CLEOPATRA  SIP
MOM  LAPAIX  STEP  RAMONA
PRESTE  ALTO  ROPEDANCE
SENTRYBOX  ULE  REDROSES
EISEL  MANOR  MEA
SVENGALISANDTRILBYS  NET
WIN  OUF  ONDAS  SOIE  LAVE
ANTENNA  TARZANSANDJANES
PERMITS  OGEE  LUNA  AVANT
REPAST  LEWD  BEDS  NASTY
```

372

```
CADRE  ABATES  AHAB  FIT
ARIEL  HOPETO  PEALE  UNO
SERVICEWOMAN  GATHERINGS
ANT  SHALL  LIAISONPLANES
SAYS  ADELE  CULT  ICY
DEBS  ROAM  SLAPSON  NAP
BEETLE  RIG  YON  KOLA
ALATE  GALLOP  ALOE  OTIC
BULLDOZERS  OREGON  MAINE
ATEE  SINO  DIXON  SOLOED
SER  LINEA  ATNO  DIVANS
  ELECTRONICDEVICES
ARMORY  FUME  MASKS  SMU
ABABYS  SNORE  ONCE  OMEN
LACED  ZIGZAG  FRYINGPANS
ACID  SINS  NAGOYA  NOLLE
RUNS  HOG  LEN  PARLOR
MSG  RENEGER  ROTC  PATTA
BAA  ELBA  SOAKS  HEIST  OMIT
SPORTSMANLIKE  TEXASLEAGUER
FLATTERERS  ORA
AIT  AMERE  ERIVAN  HENNA
XES  TIDY  NOSERS  ROTES
```

373

```
DDS   ARABISTS  SCS  ADA
ROPE  DEPORTEE  AAL  SOL
ALONEALONEALLALLALONE
MONODY   ESNE   BILKERS
ARGUE  OAF    THEMES
SEG  SATAN  PHONED  FIB
HEARTTOHEART    NUDE
BORING   HARTS   STELLA
AMESS  PRIORI   YOWLED
GIDE  BOYSWILLBEBOYS
STUN  EGAL  YOGI  OPAL
COMEONECOMEALL   RENE
AUTUMN   REUSSI   SKENE
STAGES  CLASS   CONDOR
SASH   AROSEISAROSE
THE  ASSESS  CABOT  WAN
TSETSE    NET   AYRES
VERITAS  TROD   ALOCAL
MARYMARYQUITECONTRARY
ARI  ONT  ENSHROUD  KNEE
DYE  VAE  DEPOSERS  ERR
```

374

```
HACKERY  SPRAWL  RESTHOME
ARUNDEL  PREPAY  UNWOODED
LATEDISCLOSURE  PLANNERS
OBTAIN   LIVERY   TANGO
RIDE  RACINE  TRUCK  RAFF
TUNS  SEREST  DEARE  CALLA
ALG  ITERO  GESTE  GOBLIN
LERP  LIT  ORATE  HEMLINE
CREASER  GENERALCOMMENT
MILNE   ABIES   IROAM
PLANET  ILOOK  SPRAT  EROS
EARED  CLEANSPEECH  KNUTE
ACKD  POINT  TERCE  CITRON
EARNA   PARMA   SONIA
TAXDECLARATION  LADOLCE
WARPATH  GAVEL  HAT  NDAK
EMERGE  RAVES  SMOKE  ERE
RENEE  TOPER  STONER  SLDS
ERAS  CRUEL  BLADED  FEIS
SALES   CLONES   SLAVER
RETICENT  BROADSTATEMENT
ETIOLATE  GARNET  RECURSE
MANNERED  SNEERY  INKDYES
```

375

```
GABBER  PLATA  BSA  ENCASE
ARRIVE  EASER  IAN  REAMED
STONES  ATTEN  RVA  SALPAS
WARPSTHEMINDALITTLE
DEBTS  AMER  CANNOT  SARDS
AGEE  IVORS  AVENGE  FLEET
LOA  GOOSE  SAU  POISED
ISTHEWISDOMOFTHEFOOL
OMAR   LAPIS   ASTYLAR
BANI  UNITER  BBL  IZE
ELENA  LIVEN  ROLE  SNOB
ABRIGHTPARTICULARSTAR
ADOS  EARP  ONICE  GORGE
DLI  NAY  LASSES  LEES
ZENANAS   WALES   SAVA
BUTAFRAILTYOFTHEMIND
BESAME  REL  BLEED  NOR
ERASE  DEALER  STORM  STLO
TALER  FEDORA  CRAN  STRAP
AMALADYWITHOUTACURE
CAMETO  OWE  TARDE  SCIPIO
AMINOS  MIR  AMEER  ORPINE
LUSTRE  STS  NARDS  SEEDER
```

376

```
MAIM   HUMID   SHAHS
CANVAS  ERASES  CERATE
PARTAKE  STRATA  OLIVER
ISGONEWITHTHEWIND  EER
THEN  SEGO  ONTHE  ACRO
APRON   GOTHS   MILER
FASTEST  AFEE  SYNODS
MARITA   SIE   HURTS
ACETIC  CONTRA  ABA  ELA
DEFACE  ERIK  POIS  ASAS
ASOR  ISAPENPAL  LHBS
MURS  ASSN  EELS  ABLATE
SPG  CIT  TIPPET  LOUVER
ERATO   SEA   OLDEST
ACTINS  AJAR  CONTEST
DAMES  BLOCS  SLUES
OPEN  CELIA  TESS  TRPS
RUN  AREONTOPOFTHEHEAP
ELOISE  NEKTON  EAGERLY
SETTEE  ARIOSE  DRAMAS
TSARS   SNEAD   KLAN
```

377

```
SALEM  CMS  BAS  MESAS
ANGOLA  HAL  EFTS  ELOGE
BARREN  IDA  DIEWALKURE
BRIDEOFLAMMERMOOR  TED
YENS  FILM  AWE  ONO  HEY
ALREADY   APES
AMELIA  RBI  APT  EPACT
PALERMO  UNFURLS  AMOR
PLACEABET  URI  EMULATE
TINT  NEXT  MIS  NYMPHET
SCREEN   COBOLA
GROUCHO  REL  NARA  BAWL
LATVIAN  FEE  ELASTIQUE
ARIA  SOLDIER  STATURE
DECEM  LYS  NOS  DREAMT
ISEE   LEFTOUT
DOT  SLO  DOE  ZOIC  SLUE
ERI  LASTOFTHEMOHICANS
LATRAVIATA  ENA  ELEMIS
ENLAI  NOEL  ADC  SONATA
STEED  SDL  PAH  STERE
```

378

```
REFER  CASO  ADOS  MOAB
REGULAR  OLAFS  SEVERANCE
ANIMOSE  MARTHASVINEYARD
JOSEPHSBRETHREN  ATONES
DEEPAS  REEF  MITE
CIMARRON  HEED  FINE  SMEW
ERAT  NEMO  AINT  SOAVE
BOR  REDSAILSINTHESUNSET
UNVEIL  ASOLDAS  NEMAT
INDIRA  TROUBLEDWATERS
ETNAS  ATT  DEBAIN  ECARTE
WIG  CHLOE  SKALD  SEG
ELAPSE  AFLOAT  ECO  ANDSO
STRAUSSWALTZES  TIPTOE
DREST  TITANIA  REDGAP
THEFRENCHCONNECTION  RMA
ARNOS  IOEE  NEED  DEAN
USSR  ACER  PACA  NESCIENT
ARKS  OREL  JONAHS
ADVISE  SHORESOFTRIPOLI
BEETHOVENSFIFTH  IGNORED
BARCELONA  SATAN  COUSINS
ADAH  ALEP  LSTS  SPENT
```

379

```
POMADES_CABAL_FUSSED
TRIPOLI_ADELA_ANTARES
ASTOLAT_SATED_TOOLATE
HEED_NAGA_RULE_RISER
_IDRANKATEVERYVINE
MASON_STONY_SILO_ANTS
ATTICA_EVIAN_DISH_GET
THELASTWASLIKETHE
LEY_TRASH_LANE_CHARY
EEL_PREY_PENT_TUNES
STEREOS_FIRST_SKITTLE
SERAC_CANY_CINC_IER
ASSET_LAMP_CIANO_SHA
ICAMEUPONNOWINESO
FTD_NAPE_TRUCE_SNARES
AREO_ROOF_INAPT_SPODE
WONDERFULASTHIRST
NOTES_TORT_ONEA_BACH
EPISTLE_AMIGO_ADROITE
DENSEST_TENET_THEOREM
DEARTH_STEMS_YEOMANS
```

380

```
AHABS_LAKME_BOCA_ABELE
REPEL_INION_SHORT_NADER
UNRRA_PENDS_ANWAR_CEDES
BROOMHANDEL_ESKIMOZART
AINE_IST_AMA_PEN
PTE_RAVELLDSLEAVEOF
EVADES_OVERDIETED_ALVA
NIGER_IAMA_EILAT_UMIAK
CHOPINGCENTER_IRS_SPATE
AAU_LION_TAR_ALE_GUISED
SRTA_GREW_CESTA_CARR
HAYDNGOSEEK_MAHLERPICON
DOLT_YASHI_SINN_CORO
SATIRE_SMU_ITS_STES_ATT
ENATE_STO_SCHUBERTALLEY
CERIN_TOUGH_MAZE_LIEGE
CLIV_BRITTENIAS_SEURAT
OFFENBACHTOBACH_DOM
ELI_LAM_SOD_MARK
DOHOLSTILL_BIZETASABEE
ACADS_ELIOT_IMAGE_AXONE
YAZOO_NYMPH_CANAL_VIDAL
STERN_APSE_SMELL_OMENS
```

381

```
ADAM_NARE_SRO_LACS
STORE_OVERSHOT_ADATS
COLOSSUSOFROADS_BELOW
ONAN_TRENT_SHEEPS_ANI
MAN_HADJ_KGS_AMER
ETTIE_SOME_SARONGGIRL
SAINTS_BAMBINO_AITS
SCHELL_SILTY_SOILY
ARTEL_LAS_SABREJET
SAHL_CERIC_DATA_AVA
ALAE_CHEROKEEKID_ANIL
LAP_HERS_JOKER_UELE
TIPSTERS_BAL_SISIS
YEATS_LUCID_CISSIE
SWAN_BALKANS_STINGE
DIAMONDLIL_NATO_LEGGY
ENRY_NAE_RARE_ENE
EER_REPAVE_SPATE_ANOR
MAINE_PRINCEOFHUMBUGS
SNOOP_LEBANESE_SALES
DROP_EDS_SPED_EXES
```

382

```
CRAMP_GAFFS_ASCAP_FARAD
HANOI_ORRIN_ICANA_ALOUD
AFOOT_LIANA_MORNS_STOLA
STARTOFSCOPESTRIALTODAY
IGETA_SLAT_DUES
MAAM_ERASE_ETYM_END_ACT
ATRIUM_COM_IONA_ADAI
THESPANISHCIVILWAROPENS
ROACH_OTOES_ERLE_DELTA
ISSUE_SOUL_ANTI_SHARPEN
ELLEN_OAST_OSTE_HEE
POTSDAMCONFERENCEBEGINS
IRA_DEEP_TEEN_ENERO
GAMELYN_TEED_TENN_RIVER
SLAVE_CIRR_NISEI_SNIPE
KOREANARMISTICEISSIGNED
IGAL_ALYA_OPE_UNICED
NYC_BOS_LUST_SAFER_NOSY
SUMO_PTAS_TINAS
AMANFIRSTWALKSONTHEMOON
SERIF_AHAIR_INNER_LODGE
IRADE_NORTE_REESE_LOOPS
SOLED_SOPHS_TESTE_STRUT
```

383

```
CHRIST_LIBRAE_SERIALS
HEEDER_ARROWS_INASNIT
ASHEDIEDTOMAKEMENHOLY
STAS_FND_NAK_YORK_ILL
MEN_GODSACRE_ENG_UNIE
SRS_ALP_CHESS_PILATES
GLIA_COS_HEEZES
CAIAPHAS_FATTED_RCD
SHELTERS_BANTER_CARA
AHI_EERS_LOUDER_PATER
GILEAD_BUNNY_PARADE
ELLEN_SALMIS_ONES_TIS
NOEL_RANEES_AMENSEAT
THR_BONNET_GROWSOUT
TAUHID_SLO_SIVA
FABERGE_SALOM_IVE_OBE
AMER_HDS_DISASTER_PAL
UPA_IERS_RMS_WEN_SOLD
LETUSDIETOMAKEMENFREE
TRADEIN_PIERED_SEATER
SESTETS_STRYPE_SAXONS
```

384

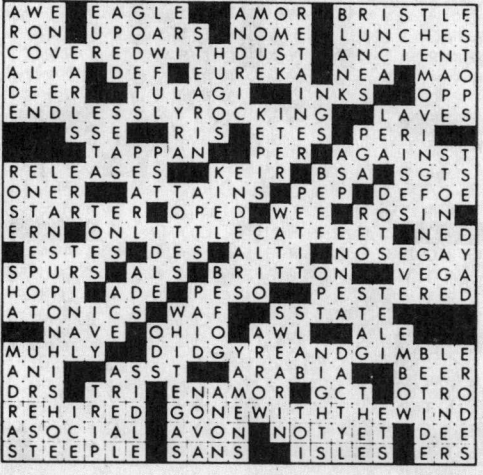

```
AWE_EAGLE_AMOR_BRISTLE
RON_UPOARS_NOME_LUNCHES
COVEREDWITHDUST_ANCIENT
ALIA_DEF_EUREKA_NEA_MAO
DEER_TULAGI_INKS_OPP
ENDLESSLYROCKING_LAVES
SSE_RIS_ETES_PERI
TAPPAN_PER_AGAINST
RELEASES_KEIR_BSA_SGTS
ONER_ATTAINS_PEP_DEFOE
STARTER_OPED_WEE_ROSIN
ERN_ONLITTLECATFEET_NED
ESTES_DES_ALTI_NOSEGAY
SPURS_ALS_BRITTON_VEGA
HOPI_ADE_PESO_PESTERED
ATONICS_WAF_SSTATE
NAVE_OHIO_AWL_ALE
MUHLY_DIDGYREANDGIMBLE
ANI_ASST_ARABIA_BEER
DRS_TRI_ENAMOR_GCT_OTRO
REHIRED_GONEWITHTHEWIND
ASOCIAL_AVON_NOTYET_DEE
STEEPLE_SANS_ISLES_ERS
```

385

```
ADAM  TENOR  SCALES  MOT
MELI  ALIBI  POMADE  ABA
PEEN  FACETHEMUSIC   NOB
SPUN  TIES   OLES  ETUDES
 STER  NNE  ELDER  SRO
     SAREE    IDA  BLAT
  SHIRE  VASTE  MALAISE
MOONED  CAPERS   BONNET
ADIGE  TULIPS  TEOR  SAR
BASE  ARREST   LITRES
  STRIKESTHERIGHTNOTE
  SCENES  METRES   NAPA
ASS  ENTS  ABATER  AGREE
DEPONE  TREVES   STATES
ATAVISM  RARER   TUNES
RIRE  IBO      BLAND
 ERS  TEMPO  TOE  EDAM
CAPTOR  ABOR  AGEE  ARID
AGA  TOOTONESHORN  NINA
PER  IMPEND  TOTED  CAEN
EST  KEENES  READS  ESSE
```

386

```
CARTS  CAPRA  SALTS  FOALS
ANART  ADEEM  AMORE  INNER
NOPAR  SHALE  LUNEL  GENOA
AMINISTERINGANGELTHOU
LIESAT  RLS  ODDS  OUTFLOW
SARG  ATE  HADES  WIN  TAXI
 RONE  ETH  EYE  ASHTON
ASDEADASADOORNAIL  HEINK
LEAST  TAU  MOUSERS  ABOIL
ANNS  ARISTIDES  DTS  ONCE
NAT  ADO  THES  HUI  PAY
STELLA  PRES  FINE  ESSAYS
AIM  OOF  BAPT  BEE  ROW
PHDS  SMU  OPENSIDED  SAKI
LOOTS  ACCURST  DAG  GALEN
ARUBA  SECRETARYOFNATURE
INBENT  RAH  RIE  OILY
DELS  RUS  UTILS  CRO  ACCT
STETSON  ANOD  TOO  BOGORE
 THECHILDRENOFTHEBRAIN
IDIOT  APART  ORATE  EATNO
TAMPA  SIREE  SEGOS  SHIER
SWEET  PLODS  EDENS  EASTS
```

387

```
SHAVER  MORSEL  THANE  E
THOREAU  OTIOSE  HOWARD
HARPERS  ROCOCO  INEVER
ELA  RESET  ATANEND  AMA
ALTA  DEVIL  SPAR  ATRIP
COINS  EME  ETIC  ARTE
TWOGENTLEMEN  OVERSEER
   ELIA  ROLES  ADIT
REALIGNS  NIRA  NERISSA
ELK  GETUP  SARD  ENTER
ELIS  LADYMACDUFF  GAME E
SENAT  DRAB  ILIAD  GIA
ENGLISH  EREB  LATENESS
  ECHO  SATIE  TAMO
SPARKING  THOMASLOVELL
PANI  PERU  TAK  NESIA
INTOW  SENT  ANILE  LEAR
ENO  HETAERA  ANEAR  RID
LINGER  SAIDIT  PREMISE
SEINES  ESTATE  ELEANOR
ROUSE  DEEMED  REDDEN
```

388

```
TULAGI  ROREM  BADE  LAUD
OLERON  APARAS  AVIV  APRA
STARTSAPPHIRE  COMETOPAZ
  HERPES  JASON  NETTLE
SAC  ACIER  WOMAN  STAS
AROA  UEL  SIREN  WISEDUP
DINNERS  ORANGEJADE  ITA
NESTLE  SALEM  DORE  DAMN
ETTES  TOWED  ASSAM  LEMON
STAD  SILO  HEWED  SETOSE
SAN  THEOLDCORAL  AGENT
 TOWERS  RISEN  PETARD
RIVER  MILTONBERYL  TRE
DENIED  HIFIS  ACOR  CHIN
ETONS  DELTA  RANKS  SLEPT
PIPE  PELL  BENDS  TREMOR
TRA  DRAMETHYST  TEAROSE
HELLION  HARES  PEL  KOTA
 EGGS  BRUIT  TOLLS  DET
SPRAIN  SOONG  CRUISE
HAIRTONYX  THEZIRCONGIRL
ANDY  SANE  STRAKE  FORGET
DIES  EYES  SORER  FRONDS
```

389

```
MATRON  SALAD    SHEERS
IGUANA  EMERALD  WARDEN
TORTURECHAMBER  ORGIVE
RUN  SECTARY  GENRE  BOE
ATOP  SHOR  TREADMILLS
LIFER  ORAL  YESNO  SETH
 TRADES  EIRE  AFRO
 SHOVED  MEMOS  DAMP
SCENES  TARPS  ABATERS
LASS  TRACER  CLAMOROUS
ORC  PREMEDITATION  CPO
EARPHONES  SYRIAC  ARID
BELAYED  BORES  LACUNA
WASI  PINAS  REMISE
NENE  ASSN  BASSET
PACO  GREGO  TWIT  TREAD
IRONMAIDEN  EGIS  SAPO
ECU  ONEGA  PILOTED  NOL
CANING  ENFANTTERRIBLE
ENTREE  STOUTER  RAVELS
RESELL  GLORY  ABYDOS
```

390

```
ASST  ACE  TENDS  REO  RET
SHOAL  SRS  ORARE  EMU  ELA
HELLESPONTBYLEANDER  DES
SLAP  SERA  ASTAR  MESAS
EPICS  ICC  SORE  ARETE
LASTROW  ACHES  USBYRAIL
PITT  OOO  LOATHE  SOO  BCS
STL  IRAS  NAIVE  ORGY
SHARPENDS  ENTREPOT  RIGA
TENTING  PILE  TROP  MASON
TEEN  FINAL  DETOURED
MAI  RUBICONBYCAESAR  ARS
ESCORIAL  YEARS  RARE
LIBRE  BLOW  ANTE  RESALES
DAYS  EYEBALLS  CROSSFILE
COST  SISAL  SAID  TIN
ATO  ANT  THRICE  DEA  SETS
DELAWARE  ISERE  ENCLOSE
DRUGS  ORAN  SOW  OTTOI
EMMET  LINGS  WHEN  EBRO
NEB  ATLANTICBYLINDBERGH
DRU  ROE  IONIA  SCI  YETIS
ASS  SED  ENDER  EEL  SENT
```

391

```
IMPART  MOD   PSA        POI
NAUSEA  ALIMENTAL       HANN
ANTHONYFAVORABLE        ARAT
BAS  SKEIN   SEPALS     POTE
INOS   SADO    PTAH     PLEA
TANTRUM  SLAVE    NEWYEAR
RENAL   IGORS     UNSERS
GOODKNIEVEL      CORSA
CARLOS  KNEE  GORE   CLUB
EDILE  KERRS  URDU    KEPI
AGE  STENO   LEOXI      AWL
SENS  HEIL  BRACS    TONAL
ETTU  APOS  ROSA    OCHERS
NOTAB   RICHRICHARD
MAGNUM   EPOCH     DOTER
OILYRAG  RAKES   NOSALES
MRED   DRAY   THAI    SANA
ERNE  EARNED  ORAON   PDL
NADA  IVANTHEWONDERFUL
TIAL  TELECASTS   ASSURE
SDS      USH   SOE  STOLES
```

392

```
LAMB    CANI   ISTOO   CASH
AREA   IRGUN   DRILL   OLEO
FLOW   SOULSHEALED     WILL
FOWLPLAY   IES   TIMEBALM
REEK     ADIOS    CAVE
EGON    TIERFUL    PELHAM
AARON  DONOT  BIT   SLATE
BRIM   SITEFORSORE    ERRS
BEN  ALLE   HAINANS    EIN
ADAMBALM  SEIDS   THORPE
NERVY   WHINE    ARARA
CADDIE  SHERE   SLAYRIDE
ORB  STATISM  ACIS    SAY
ARAG  OFASAILSMAN   LENE
LEROI  RFK  SATAN   LORDS
STELLA   FELSPAR    EASY
FILS    RIALS     BEAN
BARBELLE  FLA   SOARSPOT
OTEA  HORSESCENTS   OESE
ANEW  ESSES  EDICT   MALE
ROLL   THETA   SETH   EROS
```

393

```
REDO   SERAPE   DROME   GAP
OLAV   CRAMIN   RIVAL   OPA
BAREFOOTINTHEPARK       COY
EMERALD    CRAW       PAGE
UNDERTHEYUMYUMTREE
BASSO    URIA     UPSTATE
SPLENDORINTHEGRASS
TIA   AVAL   EAGER     DOG
ALP  SMELL  TAMIS    SCRAP
RESWEAR   RADON    STOUTS
THEGATHERINGSTORM
AVIATE   RATAN    PANAMAS
LACTO  MENUS  MARRY    ELL
INK   LAMAR   ODIC     DEA
THESOUNDANDTHEFURY
SNOOPON   ELEE     DEPTS
AWALKONTHEWILDSIDE
BATE    ERIE    EDITOUT
OLA  PANICINNEEDLEPARK
MEL  ELATH  DEGAGE   ERGO
ASE   TENET  TESTER  RYES
```

394

```
LOBAR   INCA   LAB    SDAK
AKABA   TALC   ICE    HERO
TREAT  SOBAT  GRAB    ISIS
HARSHLY   SMITHEREENS
HEIST   UNIT    DOPIEST
MOYERSTHEPITY   SNEERER
EPOS  TERN  CEES   TESTEE
LED  BEMOAN  RANCH   TSPS
NEMAN    EBON     RARE
ATLAST  LIEU  IASI    ABO
THEBROTHERSKALBAMAZOV
EER  AROE  ETAL    FAMULI
ELAM    SSTS     EMIRS
BOSS  ALLOY  EATERS   ITE
UNPEGS  SOUS  IOUS   UTES
SCALLOP   SCHORRDINNERS
HELLENE   ECON    MODEL
LONELYHARTZ    REWORDS
BLEU  ROUE  TIARA   MOIRE
PERT   TEA   EMMA   ASSET
SASS    AND   NEAP  NEEDS
```

395

```
TODD   ABEL   AGRA  REDUCE
ALEE  QUITO  STOAS  EVENER
DEEPGUFFAW   TINYCAVALIER
SOMALI  FIBER  GEODES   SSS
REEL    NENAS     STIR
AGITATES  ANNES  SOSO   SMA
VON  MUHAMMADALI   SEDATED
ENCS  SABE  STINT   DECADE
SEALS  ROSEA  STRAP   STRIP
TOPICS  TALCS  EXIT    STAT
ANAGRAM  SEEMTEDIOUS   ENS
COATIS   GROSS    SUNNED
ERI  MIDWAYBOAST  SAINTES
METE  NAIL  TREES   STROVE
OCALA  SMOGS  SNEAD   SOFAR
TETONS  SNOOT  UPON    LILI
EDENITE  GATHERPOMES   SUE
RED  LANE  STIPE   REGUSHES
RULE    ORIBI     SARI
SHE  SCRIPS  SCANT   TENDTO
TAKETHECOUNT  LAWYERFEES
AVENUE  IDEAS  ENIDS   URGE
RESAND   TETE   DENS   LESS
```

396

```
LLAMA  HERA  PALM  SLT  CRO
AURAL  IRIS  ALII  TOO  HEN
ISLET  FILM  RIAL  OAK  ALE
THOSENICEANBARKSOFYORE
TRY   LAOS   SOD    OLGAS
AGREES  ALTI  TOLU    DESI
GOODSHIPLOLLIPOP    HIRES
TAN   ENTE   EMS     AIR
STEAMERS  APSE    CENSOR
PERFORM  SKULKS  AVE  NEAT
RES  DOWNI  IFNI    SAGE
BALI  THEHISPANIOLA   IRAN
ALEC   AWOL   PEKAN   RAD
DADA  AVA  LEERAT  BISECTS
ANSWER   GROG   NOAHSARK
QUE    DIA   RIBS     SOY
ACTUP  MAYFLOWERCOMPACT
NORE  AGES  PEAK   MARLOS
TRUER   NOS   PELT    MIB
NINAPINTAANDSANTAMARIA
TIS  GEL  URGE  HIER  ENACT
HEM  ERA  FEAR  IDLE  RIPER
ERS  STS  FANS  PALE  SASSY
```

397

```
POGO  IMMURE  AMICO
VERBS  NOOSES  BANANA
RIDESTOHOUNDS  IRONERS
UNDO  ICONS  ETRE  ITOL
SYL  MATURE  SNIDE  SIMA
ELEMI  ASI  BACKS  AMMAN
ONT  ESCAPEE  SLIEST
RATION  EARPS  AMAN
DARTMOOR  SKY  SPINOFFS
IVIES  HOPEI  CHAT  RILE
NAS  HOUNDSTOOTH  NIN
AGED  ILES  WHENI  NOIRS
RESOUNDS  POI  ETIOLATE
GRDS  CARES  ENGELS
DRAMAS  CATSUPS  AGA
RURAL  FORTE  LAW  INSET
ABIT  MIDDY  DERAIN  TAM
COSI  ENOS  ANTIC  FATA
OUTSING  HOUNDOFHEAVEN
TATTLE  ORATOR  OATER
ESSOR  POWERS  RUES
```

398

```
TAMALE  CRABS  SHAPED
OBERON  HARRIS  SPUMONE
MARRIAGEFEAST  PITAPAT
ASIAN  NETTY  RAILS  TRE
TENN  RAREE  BAGEL  CHER
ODO  TOWER  WANED  CUE
MOVED  MERGE  PASQUA
SKATED  DODGE  MANHUNT
DIETER  TARDE  SANA  EDO
ADEEM  RINSE  SIGIL  SUN
NEPS  ANTEDATED  ATLE
ILI  BRINE  BWANA  FRIAR
TIN  EASY  CLARA  PILOTS
ENGRAVE  BRISK  HELENE
SECURE  IRISH  MEDES
OLD  CRESS  CARAT  LAB
CAME  FLOAT  PANEL  HAMA
AMP  GIANT  PARMA  ROMAN
SEAMIER  HOLYMATRIMONY
ENNOBLE  EVENED  AGENDA
STYLED  ABELE  TARTAN
```

399

```
SPIT  HATTI  GAMBITS
COATIS  APOSORO  ALIENEE
AFLAME  LOOKSIN  BRUSSELS
PILLOWTALK  LEASE  RUT
PAS  TER  ARES  IDE  SORGO
THREESHEETSTOTHEWIND
SPRAY  AND  SPET  FOE  LAD
LOOP  STANDUP  ARR  INSETS
YEMENI  RIFLE  SAO  DOE
ADIT  MATTRESSSTITCHES
ERN  PAT  CREPES  ETAPE
SOTS  RUB  ASHEN  SAC  STEW
QUILT  FORTEA  RAW  CEN
SECURITYBLANKETS  MASH
MES  CIG  CABIO  EXPERT
MORSEL  OSO  EMBARGO  ERIN
ULA  EAT  SATE  REO  ANYAS
SPREADSTHEWORDAROUND
KEENS  PIU  ADAI  FLA  PCE
CTS  NADIR  COMFORTERS
LABORING  ITERATE  UCHEES
OVERATE  SEATSON  SHERPA
PANELED  ADMIT  YEST
```

400

```
JOWL  SOBS  BOCK  CHOSEN
ACHE  STRIKEITRICHLITTLE
NEON  BUFFALOBILLRUSSELL
ALI  STRATAL  SLOE  PERIL
POSTS  TARES  SPED  CAGES
ATSEA  EYAS  SEED  MONO
YAGER  TEAR  BALI  QUE
HELMET  WEAVE  TRI  COUNT
EAVE  HAILMARYQUANT  NEAR
GRIDS  PESO  EPURE  HASSLE
ETA  HAILE  ADROP  JANET
LOPSIDED  REBEC  MUNITION
OWNED  TORUS  BERET  ORO
MOROSE  REMIT  CATO  ASNIT
ENTR  ROBSPETERNERO  AMER
SLEEP  BIT  OSIER  FATALE
SYR  RIOS  AUNT  SAVOR
FORE  ALAS  BANC  ANKLE
CARVE  AGAR  RADAR  LASER
DONEE  SLED  CORONAE  PAR
UNDERSTANDPATBROWN  SIVA
EGGSBENEDICTARNOLD  STET
TOOTSY  ANTS  ASKS  EZRA
```